ECONOMICS

MICHAEL PARKIN MELANIE POWELL

KENT MATTHEWS

FIFTH EDITION

We work with leading authors to develop the
strongest educational materials in economics,
bringing cutting-edge thinking and best learning
practice to a global market.

Under a range of well-known imprints, including
Addison-Wesley, we craft high quality
print and electronic publications which help
readers to understand and apply their content,
whether studying or at work.

To find out more about the complete range of our
publishing please visit us on the World Wide Web at:
www.pearsoneduc.com

ECONOMICS

MICHAEL PARKIN MELANIE POWELL
KENT MATTHEWS

FIFTH EDITION

Addison-
Wesley

An imprint of **Pearson Education**

Harlow, England · London · New York · Reading, Massachusetts · San Francisco
Toronto · Don Mills, Ontario · Sydney · Tokyo · Singapore · Hong Kong · Seoul
Taipei · Cape Town · Madrid · Mexico City · Amsterdam · Munich · Paris · Milan

Pearson Education Limited
Edinburgh Gate
Harlow
Essex CM20 2JE
England

and Associated Companies throughout the world

Visit us on the World Wide Web at:
www.pearsoneduc.com

———————————

Original fifth edition entitled *Economics* published by Addison-Wesley
Publishing Company, Inc.
A Pearson Education company
Copyright © 2000 Addison-Wesley, Inc.

This edition published by Pearson Education Limited 2003
© Pearson Education Limited 2003
Authorised for sale only in Europe, the Middle East and Africa   .

ISBN 0273 658131

British Library Cataloguing-in-Publication Data
A catalogue record for this book is available from the British Library

10 9 8 7 6 5 4 3 2
07 06 05 04 03

Typeset in 9/12.5pt Stone serif by 35
Printed and bound by Mateu-Cromo Artes Graficas, Madrid, Spain

About the Authors

Michael Parkin received his training as an economist at the Universities of Leicester and Essex in England. Currently in the Department of Economics at the University of Western Ontario, Canada, Professor Parkin has held faculty appointments at Brown University, the University of Manchester, the University of Essex and Bond University. He is a past president of the Canadian Economics Association and has served on the editorial boards of the *American Economic Review* and the *Journal of Monetary Economics* and as managing editor of the *Canadian Journal of Economics*. Professor Parkin's research on macroeconomics, monetary economics and international economics has resulted in over 160 publications in journals and edited volumes, including the *American Economic Review*, the *Journal of Political Economy*, the *Review of Economic Studies*, the *Journal of Monetary Economics* and the *Journal of Money, Credit and Banking*. He became most visible to the public with his work on inflation that discredited the use of wage and price controls. Michael Parkin also spearheaded the movement toward European monetary union. Professor Parkin is an experienced and dedicated teacher of introductory economics.

Melanie Powell took her first degree at Kingston University and her MSc in economics at Birkbeck College, London University. She has been a research fellow in health economics at York University, a principal lecturer in economics at Leeds Metropolitan University, and the director of economic studies and part-time MBAs at the Leeds University Business School. She is now a Reader at Derby University Business School. Her main interests as a microeconomist are in applied welfare economics, and she has many publications in the area of health economics and decision making. Her current research uses the experimental techniques of psychology applied to economic decision making.

Kent Matthews received his training as an economist at the London School of Economics, Birkbeck College University of London and the University of Liverpool. He is currently the Sir Julian Hodge Professor of Banking and Finance and Head of Economics at the Cardiff Business School. He has held research appointments at the London School of Economics, the National Institute of Economic and Social Research, the Bank of England and Lombard Street Research Ltd and faculty positions at the Universities of Liverpool, Western Ontario, Leuven, Liverpool John Moores and Humbolt Berlin. He is the author (co-author) of 6 books and over 50 articles in scholarly journals and edited volumes.

Brief Contents

Contents

Chapter 21 Employment and Unemployment   446

Chapter 22 Aggregate Supply and Aggregate Demand   464

Chapter 23 Expenditure Multipliers   486

Chapter 24 Fiscal Policy

Chapter 25 Money

Reviewers

Pearson Education would like to express appreciation for the invaluable advice and encouragement they have received from many educators in the United Kingdom and elsewhere in Europe for this edition.

Wendy Chapple, Nottingham University Business School

Dr Tony Cleaver, Department of Economics and Finance, University of Durham

Emeritus Professor Peter Stubbs, University of Manchester, School of Economics Studies

Dr Martin A. van Tuijl, Department of Economics, Tilburg University

André Watteyne, Faculty of Economics and Applied Economics, Katholieke Universiteit, Leuven Afdeling Kortrijk

Professor Robert E. Wright, University Chair in Economics, Department of Economics, University of Stirling

Preface

Our aim is to present economics as an interesting, lively and relevant subject. Our goal is to change the way that students see the world by opening their eyes to the 'economic way of thinking'. We want to make economics as accessible as possible. We believe every student can gain great insights into the way the world works through developing the 'economic way of thinking'. ◆ We are conscious that many students find economics hard, so we place the student at the centre of the learning experience. We adopt a style and a language that encourages rather than intimidates, that sounds familiar rather than abstract or distant. We illustrate with examples selected to be of interest to students and designed to grab attention. We maintain rigour without the need for mathematical presentation, through our focus on core models and extensive graphical analysis. ◆ The principles of economics are constantly evolving and where there have been substantial shifts in ideas, we have incorporated these, especially in macroeconomics. The principles of economics spring from today's issues: the slowdown in productivity and output, the information revolution, emerging markets, the Asian recession, and the expansion of global trade and investment. We explain these ideas and issues using our core principles and tools. This book allows students to study ideas such as long run economic growth and market failure, using nothing more than the familiar core principles of competition and demand and supply. ◆ Throughout, we have adopted tools designed to help students learn and to appeal to their interest in information technology. The companion websites provide active learning opportunities, with many tutorials, quizzes and access to relevant source materials, as well as interactive learning tools (see p. xxviii).

The Fifth Edition Approach

This new European edition has maintained its traditional focus on core principles, but has placed a stronger emphasis on European and business issues, together with a tighter focus on core study material. For example, we have cut the size of the microeconomic section, but focused more on the core principle of surplus when discussing efficiency in different chapters. We have also developed new features in the chapters designed to strengthen student learning. There are more references to European country examples in chapter material and problems. New to this edition are:

◆ Revised, updated and more focused microeconomic content

◆ Revised and updated macroeconomic content

◆ Business case studies

◆ Within-chapter review quizzes

◆ A selection of problems with answers available on the Web

Revised Microeconomic Content

The main revisions in the microeconomic chapters are:

1 The decision to reduce content by placing material which is outside the core focus on the website. In particular, the chapter on using graphs has been moved to the *Econ100* website, as has the chapter on labour markets. The mathematics boxes have also been moved to the *Econ100* website. However, an appendix dealing with the mathematical approach to demand and supply analysis has been included as part of the revised focus on core material.

2 An improved explanation of opportunity cost in Chapter 2.

3 A revised focus in Chapter 4 on the predictions of elasticity.

4 The addition of an analysis of the Common Agricultural Policy in Chapter 5, Markets in Action, together with efficiency discussions using the concept of surplus.

5 A more brief and concise discussion of the nature of the firm, its objectives and constraints in Chapter 9, Organizing Production, including an applied analysis of market structures.

6 New explanations of single-price and price discriminating monopolies, with more focus on efficiency and distributional aspects using surplus.

7 A more extensive discussion of the role of effects of selling costs and advertising.

8 The discussion of net present value and investment has been moved to Chapter 14, Demand and Supply in Resource Markets, and related to capital.

9 A tighter focus on redistribution in Chapter 15 on Inequality and Redistribution.

10 A more extensive coverage of tax issues in Chapter 16, Market Failure and Public Choice.

Revised Macroeconomic Content

The main revisions in the macroeconomic chapters are:

1 Updating of macroeconomic data to 2000–2001.

2 Material from Chapter 21 on real wages and unemployment determination is moved to Chapter 29.

3 Mathematical appendices explaining the algebra of the Multiplier.

4 A stronger focus on the supply side and the derivation of the aggregate supply curve and potential output in Chapter 29.

5 Greater emphasis on the world economic slowdown in 2001 and policy options available to central banks and governments.

6 Stronger focus on the European Monetary Union, the policy of the European Central Bank and the implications of the introduction of the euro.

Business Case Studies

To develop our emphasis on business, we have introduced a new feature, the **Business Case Study**. These replace some of the *Reading Between the Lines* in Part 3 on Firms and Markets. The *Business Case Study*, like the *Reading Between the Lines* feature, is designed to show students how they can apply their knowledge and develop skills in analysing real world issues. Each case study is based on a particular firm or firms within a particular market. The contents are brief but highlight the essential elements that relate to the content of a particular chapter. The material is then analysed, using graphs or relevant illustrations, to highlight how an aspect of the chapter content can be used to understand a real business problem. In addition, most of the case studies have a strong European market focus.

In-Text Review Quiz

We have replaced the in-text Review of the previous editions with a **Review Quiz**. These brief quizzes invite students to revisit and reflect on the material they have just studied using a set of questions. The aim is to encourage a more critical and thoughtful rereading of difficult material, rather than offering a simple set of statements for learning without consideration.

Selected Problem Answers on the Web

A number of problems in each chapter have answers available on the Web for students. These problems are identified with a star ●. The problems are paired where possible so that each question has one with an answer provided and one without. Also, the solutions to all problems are available to lecturers on the Instructor Resource CD. This format is designed to help students gain confidence, whilst continuing to allow lecturers the flexibility to use problems as assessment material or directed study material.

Features to Enhance Teaching and Learning

Chapter Opener

A one-page introduction that is student-friendly and attention-grabbing. The openers raise questions to stimulate interest in the the chapter content, but also motivate the student to continue. We provide a list of learning objectives for the students to read at the start of the chapter. This helps students to set their goals and identify achievement. We link these goals to the chapter headings.

In-Text Review Quiz

A Review Quiz is provided at the end of each major section within each chapter. This helps the students to identify whether they have understood the section and to determine which parts to reread before moving on.

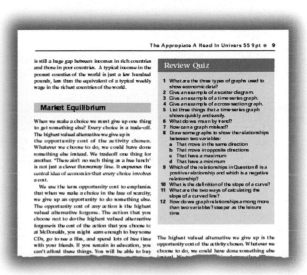

Key Terms

A number of key terms have been highlighted within the text. Each highlighted term appears in the end-of-chapter list with page numbers, in the end-of-book glossary, in the index and in the interactive Economics in Action software. The glossary and interactive software are also available on the Parkin, Powell and Matthews *Econ100* website. This icon ◆ identifies the most important figures and tables. All key figures and tables are listed in the summary at the end of the chapter. PowerPoint slides of selected key figures are available to lecturers (see Lecturer Resources, p. xxvi).

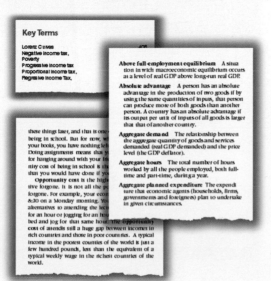

Diagrams To Show Economic Action

Our previous editions have set new standards for the use of diagrams. Our goal has always been to show clearly 'where the economic action is'. The figures and diagrams in this book generate strong positive feedback from students and lecturers, confirming our view that graphical analysis is the most important tool for teaching and learning economics. But students often find graphics difficult to follow. We have developed the whole of the art programme with the student needs in mind.

Our diagrams all feature:

◆ Shifted curves, points of equilibrium and the most important features in red.

◆ Colour-blended arrows to indicate important movements.

◆ Graphs paired with data tables.

◆ Box labels to highlight main features on diagrams.

◆ Extended captions that make each diagram a self-contained object for study and review.

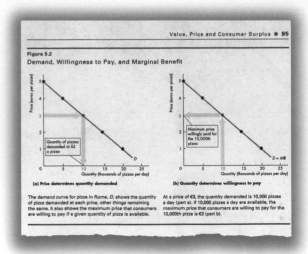

Reading Between the Lines and Business Case Studies

Each chapter contains an economic analysis of real world issues and problems. We use either our tried and tested format of a significant news article or our new business case study feature. The business case studies focus economic analysis on firms and business issues and encourage students to find their own case material. The case studies maintain the format of analysis used in *Reading Between the Lines* for consistency.

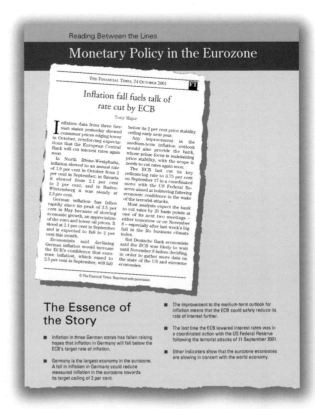

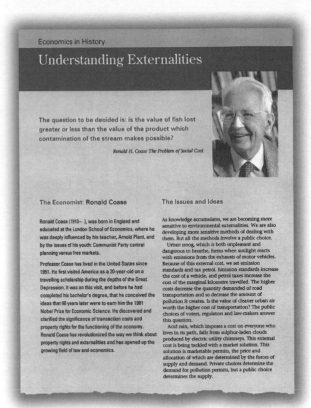

Interviews with Economists and Economics in History

We have continued our feature of substantive interviews with famous economists. These interviews are designed to show how real economists think and work. We include interviews with both academic economists and professional economists. We show how these economists have influenced the development of economics and how they use the ideas that students are studying to develop market analysis for business and institutions and to influence policy development at the national and international level.

The interviews open parts and each interview has been carefully edited to be self-contained. The interviews can be used to introduce the general focus of subsequent chapters or to be reread as part of a study review in conjunction with the *Economics in History* features which have been placed at the end of parts.

End-of-Chapter Study Materials

Each chapter ends with a concise summary organized by major topics, lists of key terms, figures, and tables

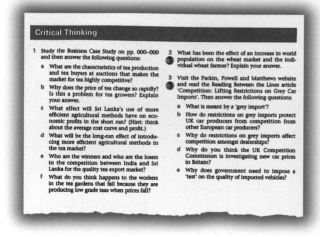

(all with page references), followed by Problems to aid student review and learning of the topic in the chapter. We have introduced new activities in the *Critical Thinking* section to engage students in information search, data analysis and critical thinking. Students are asked to extend the analysis in *Reading Between the Lines* articles or *Business Case Studies* and to analyse information on related or new topics. Questions or activities linked to *Economics in Action* are identified by this icon 🖥. Those linked to the website at http:/www.econ100.com are identified by this icon 🌐.

For the Lecturer

Core Principles, Issues and Controversies

A consistent feature in all our editions is the focus on core principles and the use of these principles throughout both the microeconomic and macroeconomic sections. In addition, we use these principles to explain the important issues of our times such as environmental damage, business regulation and failure, economic slowdown, protectionism, and long-term growth. We further enhance topicality through features such as *Reading Between the Lines* and *Business Case Studies*. These are designed to help lecturers motivate students and highlight the relevance of economics. To ensure rigour and balance in controversies in economic analysis, we have included a *Point-Counterpoint* feature on the website. These can be used to support, focus or or start debate over theoretical controversies.

Designing a Course Structure

We have organized this book as a flexible base for designing courses in economics. To illustrate how different packages for courses can be designed, we provide *Flexibility Guides* and *Alternative Course Guides* on pp. xxxii–xxxv. The *Flexibility Guides* identify Core, Policy and Optional chapters for use in courses. The *Alternative Course Guides* identify four alternative potential courses in both microeconomic and macroeconomics. The Guides show how different chapters can be combined to cover courses such as business economics or microeconomic policy, Keynesian perspectives or late long-term growth.

Lecturer Resources

A fully revised Instructor's Resource Manual with chapter outlines, teaching suggestions and answers to problems, along with a computerized Test Bank and PowerPoint Lecture slides (including enlarged key figures from the text) are available on CD-ROM to lecturers who adopt the text. The Instructor's Manual and PowerPoints are also available to adopters of the text on the lecturer's side of the Pearson resource website for the text at http://www.booksites.net/parkin. Also available to adopters of the text at this location is the *Economics in Action* interactive software, which has been substantially developed to cover all topics. Lecturers can use *Economics in Action* in the lecture room. Its full-screen display option turns many analytical graphs into 'electronic transparencies' for live graph manipulation in lectures. Its real-world data sets and graphing facilities bring animated time-series graphs and scatter diagrams into the lecture room.

Also available to users of the text, existing alongside the Pearson resource website, is the Parkin, Powell and Matthews *Econ100* website at http://www.econ100.com (this can also be directly accessed through the publisher resource website). This regularly updated and maintained site, which is packed with features that can be used for teaching, includes features such as weekly electronic Reading Between the Lines and Quizzes, which can be used for tests, student self-tests and reviews.

For the Student

Text Design

The text contains many features designed to help you study:

◆ Key concepts and Chapter overviews.

◆ Chapter Objectives.

◆ Review Questions to help you find out how much you have absorbed from a section within a chapter.

◆ Problems designed to develop your understanding and test your knowledge. Questions are paired so that you can look at an answer on the website and then try a similar questions without answers.

◆ Critical Thinking problems that use real examples and encourage you to find relevant material on the Web.

◆ Reading Between the Lines features and new Business Case Studies that apply the material you have just studied to real world examples and business problems.

Each chapter helps the student to test their cumulative understanding, to gain experience of answering different types of question, developing critical thinking, and to prepare for assessments and examinations.

Websites

Economics in Action Interactive Software

Buyers of the book can visit the student side of the publisher resource website at www.booksites.net/parkin for direct access to the fantastic *Economics in Action* interactive software. Using this fully updated version of the software, students can work through tutorials with trial and error, get instant explanations, instant feedback and test themselves to monitor learning progress. It's a bit like having a tutor on tap.

The Parkin, Powell and Matthews Website

The authors' exciting website provides online quizzes, study tips, office hours, internet links, electronic Reading Between the Lines, a Point-Counterpoint feature on controversies in economics and much more. For example, to help provide instant feedback, we have provided answers on the website to those Problem questions at the end of each chapter marked with a star ∗. Students can even drop in at the Economics Café and talk to other students from all over the world or ask a tutor for advice on sticky problems. The website is at http://www.econ100.com, or it can be accessed directly through the publisher resource website (see above).

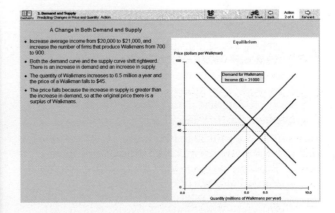

A Companion Website accompanies *Economics*, fifth edition by Michael Parkin, Melanie Powell, and Kent Matthews

Visit the publisher resource Companion Website at www.booksites.net/parkin to find valuable teaching and learning material including:

DOWNLOADS (for lecturers)

PowerPoint slides of key figures and lecture notes
Instructor's Resource Manual

LINKS TO (for students and lecturers):

1. *Economics in Action* interactive software
2. The author-maintained *Econ100* website
   (which can also be accessed directly at www.econ100.com)

There are three basic sections to the *Econ100* website: Learning Tools, Talking Shop and Downloads.

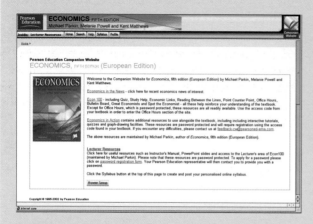

- Study Tips.
- Economic Links, web links to help you with assignments and end-of-chapter problems.

Talking Shop

- Bulletin Board, a place where students and instructors may post messages and create new topics for discussion. Use this facility to share your views and problems with other students around the world.

- Economics Café, an online chat group. Chat with Michael Parkin and other leading economists. Watch for times.

- Office Hours, an opportunity to get your questions answered online instead of by standing in-line outside your professor's office. Ask your question and you will receive a response from Michael Parkin or a member of the *Econ100* teaching team within 48 hours.

- Parkin Internet Exchange, share your views on economics with students around the world by using the Parkin Internet Exchange.

Downloads

- Lecture Notes: PowerPoint, HTML, and Rich-Text format lecture notes. Use these items to organise your own notes on your professor's lectures.

- Textbook, Adobe Acrobat files that contain some chapters from earlier editions of the text as well as interviews with leading economists.

Learning Tools

- Weekly Quiz, a multiple-choice quiz with 40 questions on most chapters organized in four levels. Take a quiz every week to test your progress. New quizzes are posted every week. When you take a quiz, you get instant responses.

- RBL, a "Reading Between the Lines" based on a web news story. This feature is similar to "Reading Between the Lines" in the text but it takes advantage of the Internet and provides links to other relevant sites. Study the weekly RBL to improve your understanding of real events. Your instructor might use the RBL as an assignment.

- Weekly problems, problems to supplement those in your textbook that your instructor might use as an assignment.

- Point-Counterpoint, a periodically updated debate designed to present you with two sides of an argument.

Acknowledgements

One of the problems with writing an introductory text, particularly in a new edition, is that there are so many people who provide help and encouragement, either directly or indirectly, that it becomes impossible to name them all. We would like to extend our gratitude and thanks to the many people who have made a contribution to this new edition, and to all those who made such important contributions to the previous editions on which this edition is based.

In particular, the authors would like to thank their colleagues, past and present, who have helped to shape their understanding of economics and provided information and assistance in the creation of this new edition. We would also like to thank our families for their input and patience.

Melanie Powell and Kent Matthews would like to thank Michael Parkin and Robin Bade for their innovative and continued work on developing ideas, materials and features for the text, the companion website, and on the much expanded interactive learning tool, *Economics in Action*, now available on the website. They would also thank the many colleagues who have helped in the development of this and earlier editions. They extend a particular thanks to the many reviewers who have provided invaluable information for changes to this edition.

The authors would particularly like to acknowledge the innovative work of Robin Bade on new features in the Canadian edition, which have been adopted in this edition. We would also like to acknowledge Richard Parkin for providing the graphics work.

We would like to acknowledge our debt to students past and present who have used previous editions and given us invaluable feedback in the form of comments, criticisms and praise. It would not be possible to write a textbook primarily in the interests of such students without their help and input.

Last, we would like to thank the editorial and production team at Pearson Education Limited. Yet again, this edition was created under very tight schedule, and as a result everyone has had to work at speed to meet the deadlines. It was also created with a largely new team, who have produced outstanding work.

As always, the proof of the pudding is in the eating! The impact and value of this book will be decided by its users and we would like to encourage all instructors and students who use this new edition to feel free to send us comments and suggestions for future developments.

Melanie Powell
Derbyshire Business School
University of Derby
Keddleston Road
Derby, DE22 1GB, United Kingdom
m.j.powell@derby.ac.uk

Kent Matthews
Cardiff Business School
Cardiff University, Colum Drive
Cardiff, CF1 3EU, United Kingdom
MatthewsK@Cardiff.ac.uk

Michael Parkin
Department of Economics
University of Western Ontario
London, Ontario N6A 5C2, Canada
michael.parkin@uwo.ca

Credits

The publisher would like to thank the following for permission to use material in this book:

Chapter 1: Cartoon © John Appleton, News Chronicle; Grape harvesting machinery, George Rose © Gamma Liaison; Harvesting grapes, Owen Franken © gettyimages; Kellog's, Charles Gupton © The Stock Market; McDonald's, David Young-Wolff © PhotoEdit; Cartoon © Chris Riddell, The Independent; Stadium flags (close-up), Scott Foresman/Addison Wesley Longman © Addison Wesley Longman Inc. Reprinted by permission of Pearson Education Inc.; Stadium flags (small), Focus on Sports; Map © PA Weather Centre.

Chapter 2: Adam Smith © Bettmann/Corbis; Pin factory, Culver Pictures; Silicon chip manufacture © Tony Stone/gettyimages.

Chapter 3: Alfred Marshall, Stock Montage; Rail Construction Crew © Hulton-Deutsch Collection/Corbis; Concorde and other craft, Royal Aeronautical Society Library.

Chapter 5: Cartoon © The New Yorker Collection 1985 (Mike Twohy) from cartoonbank.com. All Rights Reserved.

Chapter 8: Jeremy Bentham, Mary Evans Picture Library; Factory workers ice biscuits © Hulton-Deutsch Collection/Corbis; Man and woman in office, Davina Arkell/Addison Wesley Longman.

Chapter 9: Cartoon © David Austin, *Financial Times*.

Chapter 13: John von Neumann © Bettmann/Corbis; Workers on Sugar Plantation © Corbis; Female executive on mobile phone, Robert Harding Picture Library.

Chapter 14: Thomas Robert Malthus © Mary Evans Picture Library; Traffic Jam in Manchester, Manchester Central Library, Local Studies Unit; Cartoon © Robert Hunt, *The Economist*.

Chapter 17: Cartoon © Nick Baker, *Financial Times*.

Chapter 18: Ronald Coase, David Joel Photography; River Pollution © Charles & Josette Lenars/Corbis; Fishing on River Thames, Angling Times.

Chapter 25: Milton Friedman © Marshall Heinrichs/Addison Wesley Longman; Woman Using Paper Money to Light Fire © Bettmann/Corbis; Brazil – Inflation in South America, Carlos Humberto/Colorifics.

Chapter 30: Joseph Schumpeter © Hulton-Deutsch/Corbis; Reaper at Work, Getty Images/Hulton Archive; Fibre Optics, Robert Harding Picture Library.

Chapter 31: Irving Fisher © Bettmann/Corbis; Crowd of People Outside Bank © Bettmann/Corbis; Boarded-up shop, Davina Arkell/Addison Wesley Longman.

Chapter 35: David Ricardo, Mary Evans Picture Library; Clippership © Bettmann/Corbis; Container Ship, Sealand Services.

We are grateful to the following for permission to reproduce copyright material:

Atlantic Syndication Partners for an extract from "Young high-flyers who put college before work" published in the *Evening Standard* 16th July 2001; Guardian News Service Limited for extracts from "Tax rises fail to cut car journeys" by Charlotte Denny published in *The Guardian* 9th September 2000 © The Guardian 2000, "Freezingly low temperatures get cashmere's goat" by Hadley Freeman published in *The Guardian* 17th February 2001 © The Guardian 2001, "Hain plays national champion" by David Gow and Mark Milner published in *The Guardian* 11th May 2001 © The Guardian 2001, and "Precious little platinum drives up price" by Terry McAllister published in *The Guardian* 15th May 2001 © The Guardian 2001; Financial Times Limited for extracts from "EU beef market under pressure to reform" published in the *Financial Times* 12th July 2001, "IMF warns of danger of global recession" published in the *Financial Times* 31st August 2002, "Hidden cost of looking after children put at up to £225 bn" published in the *Financial Times* 16th September 2001, "Claimant figures mask rise in jobless" published in the *Financial Times* 18th October 2001, "Recovery in eurozone not expected until next year" published in the *Financial Times* 9th October 2001, "Tumbling shares cut household wealth by 9.7%" published in the *Financial Times* 26th September 2001, "Fabius to introduce fiscal stimulus" published in the *Financial Times* 16th October, 2001, "Spending spree in Spain heralds end of 'black peseta'" published in the *Financial Times* 20th April 2001, "Inflation fall fuels talk of rate cut by ECB" published in the *Financial Times* 24th October 2001, "Europe's tight corner" published in the *Financial Times* 19th October 2001, "Inflation is key to ECB thinking" published in the *Financial Times* 3rd August 2001, "Brussels in call to free more labour markets" published in the *Financial Times* 30th November 2001, "A miracle revised" published in the *Financial Times* 3rd August 2001, "Argentina appeals for calm as bank withdrawals rise" published in the *Financial Times* 1st December 2001, "Tokyo 'needs to loosen monetary policy'" published in the *Financial Times* 7th December 2001, "Yen mystery unravelled" published in the *Financial Times* 26th November 2001, all © The Financial Times; and Times Newspapers Limited for an extract from "News extra – coffee been and gone" by George Pendle published in *The Times* 2nd March 2001 © George Pendle / Times Newspapers Limited 2001.

In some instances we have been unable to trace the owners of copyright material and we would appreciate any information that would enable us to do so.

Four Alternative Micro Sequences

MICROECONOMIC THEORY

2 The Economic Problem

3 Demand and Supply

4 Elasticity

5 Efficiency and Equity

7 Utility and Demand

8 Possibilities, Preferences and Choices

10 Output and Costs

11 Perfect Competition

12 Monopoly

13 Monopolistic Competition and Oligopoly

14 Demand and Supply in Factor Markets

16 Market Failure and Public Choice

17 Regulation and Privatization

18 Externalities, The Environment and Knowledge

BUSINESS ECONOMICS

2 The Economic Problem

3 Demand and Supply

4 Elasticity

5 Efficiency and Equity

9 Organizing Production

10 Output and Costs

11 Perfect Competition

12 Monopoly

13 Monopolistic Competition and Oligopoly

14 Demand and Supply in Factor Markets

16 Market Failure and Public Choice

17 Regulation and Privatization

18 Externalities, The Environment and Knowledge

33 Trading with the World

MICROECONOMIC POLICY

2 The Economic Problem

3 Demand and Supply

4 Elasticity

5 Efficiency and Equity

6 Markets in Action

7 Utility and Demand

10 Output and Costs

11 Perfect Competition

12 Monopoly

14 Demand and Supply in Factor Markets

15 Inequality, Redistribution and Welfare

16 Market Failure and Public Choice

17 Regulation and Privatization

18 Externalities, The Environment and Knowledge

MANAGEMENT ECONOMICS

2 The Economic Problem

3 Demand and Supply

4 Elasticity

5 Efficiency and Equity

9 Organizing Production

10 Output and Costs

11 Perfect Competition

12 Monopoly

14 Demand and Supply in Factor Markets

16 Market Failure and Public Choice

17 Regulation and Privatization

18 Externalities, The Environment and Knowledge

33 Trading with the World

Four Alternative Macro Sequences

Flexibility Guide: Microeconomic Focus

CORE	POLICY	OPTIONAL
1. What is Economics?		
2. The Economic Problem		
3. Demand and Supply		
4. Elasticity		
5. Efficiency	6. Markets in Action	

A new chapter that unifies the entire coverage of microeconomics.

A unique chapter that gives extensive applications of demand and supply.

7. Utility and Demand		8. Possibilities, Preferences, and Choices

Some teachers like to cover this material before Chapter 3.

Some like to skip it.

Both are possible.

Easy to teach coverage of indifference curves. Strictly optional.

9. Organizing Production

This chapter may be skipped.

10. Output and Cost	
11. Perfect Competition	
12. Monopoly	
13. Monopolistic Competition and Oligopoly	15. Inequality, Redistribution and Welfare
14. Demand and Supply in Factor Markets	16. Market Failure and Public Choice

This chapter gives an overview of all factor markets, labour, capital, and natural resources.

A general introduction to the role of government in the economy and the positive theory of government.

17. Regulation and Privatization

18. Externalities, the Environment and Knowledge

Flexibility Guide: Macroeconomic Focus

CORE

18. A First Look at Macroeconomics

20. Measuring GDP, Inflation and Economic Growth

Chapter 23, Employment, Wages, and Unemployment may be studied immediately following Chapter 22.

22. Aggregate Supply and Aggregate Demand

Chapter 24 may be delayed and studied after Chapter 25.

21. Employment, Wages, and Unemployment

29. Capital, Investment, and Saving

30. Long-term Economic Growth
    This section on growth theory is optional

23. Expenditure Multipliers

25. Money

28. Inflation

POLICY

24. Fiscal Policy

26. The Central Bank and Monetary Policy

32. Macroeconomic Policy Challenges

OPTIONAL

31. The Business Cycle

33. Trading with the World

34. The Balance of Payments, the Pound and the Euro

Part 1

The Scope of Economics

Talking with **Will Hutton**

Will Hutton is Editor-in-Chief of *The Observer* newspaper and Director of Guardian National Newspapers. He joined *The Guardian* as Economics Editor in 1990 after a successful career in television and radio journalism and production. He has been the Editor-in-Chief of the European Business Channel, Economics Editor for BBC2's *Newsnight* programme, and has produced and appeared in many programmes on radio and television. He is a Governor of the London School of Economics and Chairman of the Employment Policy Institute. He is a visiting Professor at both Manchester University Business School and the Institute of Public Policy, University College London, and also a visiting Fellow at Nuffield College, Oxford. As well as writing many articles and reports on the economy, Will Hutton has written three influential books outlining the problems of modern capitalism. He is currently the Chairman of the Commission on NHS Accountability.

Why did you become an economist?

I became an economist because I found it an extraordinarily useful tool kit for explaining the world. From doing 'A' level economics, I found I could explain a lot that a 17-year-old boy wanted to explain, such as why my father wasn't paid as much as he wanted to be paid, my own career choices, and why there was inflation and trade unions. I have found economics as useful all through my life, briefly as a professional economist working in stockbroking in the early 1970s, but also as an investment analyst, and now as a journalist. I always find myself looking for the incentive pattern in any context and I guess I share that with other economists. I believe, like all economists, that economic agents respond to an array of incentives. But of course, I may come to rather different conclusions than many economists.

What do you think are the most important and useful concepts in economics?

There are so many important and interesting concepts such as trading and game theory, equilibrium, disequilibrium and general equilibrium, let alone interest rates and exchange rates, monopoly and market power, and diminishing returns. I could go on. But if I had to single some out, well I think incentives, opportunity costs and trade-offs at the margin are the central concepts. They really define the economic way of thinking. When I think about real-life problems, I am steered by opportunity costs and trade-offs initially. Economics is my compass when writing, but also a compass in my professional and personal life.

As a journalist, you have done a great deal to promote general understanding of economics. Do you think it is important for people to understand basic economics?

Absolutely, yes it is. Let me give you an example. I was writing about Manchester United in the summer of 1999 because I was interested in why the team was becoming the Harlem Globetrotter of football. The answers are not cultural or sociological, but economic. I first started to look at the pattern of incentives for players, the manager, and the board, by being quoted on the stock exchange. The market incentive is profit maximization, but it needn't be if the ownership structure were different. I think a grounding in economics, such as a year of economics at university, is essential if you want to understand such things. You are living in the country of the blind without economics.

Which areas of the economy do you think require most regulation and why?

With regulation we are trying to iron out irregularities in markets. The markets which you can afford to regulate less are those which are nearer the description of a perfect market. These are markets with few barriers to entry, where consumers have a lot of countervailing power and where information is easy to get. The trouble is that there are very few of them and almost every market requires regulation. Banking, for example, needs regulating because entry into the industry is hard and there are huge asymmetries of information. The consumer is largely ignorant and the banker knows far more, hence the misselling of pensions and poor loan deals. Almost all markets in Britain are franchise markets where the companies have control over entry to the market and can extract economic rent. So most markets should be regulated. Capitalism may be the least bad way of producing goods, but it doesn't mean that it should not be regulated.

To what extent should government policy aim to reduce inequality?

It was Plato who said there is no friendship amongst the unequal. Any society which gives up on the value of equality is making a big mistake. If you give up on equality, you give up on equality before the law, on equality of voting, on equality of health, and on friendship. This is a big one for economists. There are some economists who say there is nothing that can be done about the unequal outcomes of market processes and that we should not attempt to regulate them or close the inequality gaps. I believe we have to say that inequality should be reduced for the reasons I said before. But how do we constrain the growth of inequality? Inequality is partly a by-product of excessive private power, monopoly and excessive economic rent. It is also partly a by-product of lack of countervailing power by underprivileged workers, who are weak in relation to capital. In all these areas we have reason to intervene.

What are the most important policy decisions facing Western European governments in the next few years?

The big issue facing the British Government is whether to join the euro or not, and the big issue facing other European Union economies is whether they can sustain membership of the euro. I think the arrangements for international finance are poor. I do not think that floating exchange rates have actually worked as an optimal system for organizing international finance. We have had systematic over and under valuation of exchange rates and huge misallocations of resources as a result. We know that as financial markets get more and more instruments, the effect is to drive up exchange rate volatility. This is one of the reasons why unemployment is so high in Europe and so low in the US. The dollar over the past 25 years has been generally falling, whereas the European exchange rate has been rising. Europe has had low inflation but less growth and slower take-up of new technologies.

If we want a new regime, we can either have an exchange regime like the old exchange rate mechanism, or a single currency. The old regime was not very good at riding shocks. So the single currency is a better option but is it optimal? The institutional systems and the cyclical and structural conjuncture in the European economies are broadly similar, so I think the euro will work. The real argument against the single currency is political. It really comes down to do we want to be part of the European project or be under the control of the Americans. We live in an American empire and we need countervailing power, and that power can be provided by the European Union.

CHAPTER 1

What is Economics?

After studying this chapter you will be able to:

◆ Define economics

◆ Explain the five big questions that economists seek to answer

◆ Explain eight ideas that define the economic way of thinking

◆ Describe how economists go about their work

A Day in Your Life

From the moment you wake up each morning to the moment you fall asleep again each night, your life is filled with choices. When the alarm goes off, will you linger for a few minutes and listen to the radio? What will you wear today? You check the weather forecast and make that decision. Then, what will you have for breakfast? Will you drive to university or take the bus? Which classes will you attend? Which assignments will you complete? What will you do for lunch? Will you play tennis, swim or run today? How will you spend your evening? Will you study, relax at home with a video, or go to see a film? ◆ You face decisions like these every day. But on some days, you face choices that can change the entire direction of your life. What will you study? Will you specialize in economics, business, law or English? ◆ While you are making your own decisions, other people are making theirs. And some of the decisions that other people make will have an impact on your own subsequent decisions. Your university decides what courses it will offer next year. Steven Spielberg decides what his next film will be. A team of eye doctors decides on a new experiment that will lead them to a cure for short sightedness. The government decides to reduce poverty. The European Bank decides to cut interest rates. ◆ All these choices and decisions by you and everyone else are all examples of economics in your life.

◆ ◆ ◆ ◆ This chapter takes a first look at the subject you are about to study. It defines economics. Then it expands on that definition with five big questions that economists try to answer and eight big ideas that define the economic way of thinking. These questions and ideas are the foundation on which your course is built. The chapter concludes with a description of how economists go about their work, the scientific method they use, and the pitfalls they try to avoid. When you have completed your study of this chapter, you will have a good sense of what economics is about and you'll be ready to start learning economics and using it to gain a new view of the world. We are going to answer these questions in this chapter.

A Definition of Economics

All economic questions and problems arise from **scarcity**. They arise because our wants exceed the resources available to satisfy them. We want good health and long life, material comfort, security, physical and mental recreation and knowledge. None of these wants is completely satisfied for everyone, and everyone has some unsatisfied wants. While many people have all the material comfort they want, many others do not. No one feels entirely satisfied with her or his state of health and expected length of life. No one feels entirely secure, even in the post-Cold War era, and no one has enough time for sport, travel, holidays, films, theatre, reading and other leisure pursuits.

The poor and the rich alike, face scarcity. A child in Tanzania is hungry because her parents can't afford food. She certainly faces scarcity. The couple in the cartoon aren't poor, but they are juggling their money to get what they want. They face scarcity. Bill Gates is a millionaire, but if he wants to spend the weekend playing golf and attending a business strategy meeting, he can't do both. He experiences scarcity.

Faced with scarcity, we must choose among the available alternatives. Economics is sometimes called the science of choice because it explains the choices that we make and how those choices change as we cope with scarcity.

'Well dear, if the extra cost of food is offset by the income tax relief and what we save in petrol by not having a car pays the extra on the house, what's become of the money we were going to save by not smoking?'

Drawing by Arthur Horner, 1952 *News Chronicle*.

Big Economic Questions

All economic choices can be summarized in five big questions about the goods and services we produce. These questions are: What? How? When? Where? Who?

1 What?

Goods and services are all the things that we value and are willing to pay for. We produce a dazzling array of goods and services that range from necessities such as houses to leisure items such as sports clothing and equipment. We build more than a million new homes every year. These homes are more spacious and better equipped than they were twenty years ago. We make millions of new items of sports equipment, walking boots, sports shoes, footballs, tennis rackets, mountain bikes and racing bikes, all of which make our sports and leisure time more comfortable and challenging.

What determines whether we build more homes or develop more sporting facilities? How do these choices change over time? And how are they affected by the ongoing changes in technology that make an ever-wider array of goods and services available to us?

2 How?

In a vineyard in France, basket-carrying workers pick the annual grape crop by hand. In a vineyard in California, a huge machine and a few workers do the same job that a hundred French grape harvesters do. Look around you and you will see many examples of

this phenomenon. The same job being done in different ways. In some supermarkets checkout staff key in prices, in others they use a laser scanner. One farmer keeps track of his livestock feeding schedules and inventories by using paper and pencil records, while another uses a personal computer. Volkswagen hires workers to weld auto bodies in some of its plants and uses robots to do the job in others.

Why do we use machines in some cases and people in others? Does mechanization and technological change destroy more jobs than it creates? Do people working with new technology earn more than those working with traditional methods? If so, why? Does introducing new technology make us better off or worse off?

3 When?

On a building site, there is a surge of production activity and people must work overtime to keep production flowing fast enough. A car factory closes for two weeks and temporarily lays off its workers and its production dries up.

Sometimes, economy-wide production slackens off and even shrinks in what is called a recession. At other times, economy-wide production expands rapidly. We call these ebbs and flows of production the business cycle. When production falls, jobs are lost and unemployment climbs. Once, during the Great Depression of the 1930s, production fell so much that one quarter of the workforce was jobless.

During the past few years, production has decreased in Russia and its Central and Eastern Europe neighbours as these countries try to change the way they organize their economies. What makes production rise and fall? When will production rise and when will it fall again in the European Union member states? Can government action prevent production from falling? Would the member governments of the European Union be better able to control recessions individually, or would government action at the European Union level be more effective?

4 Where?

The Kellogg Company, of Battle Creek, Michigan, makes breakfast cereals in 20 countries and sells them in 160 countries. Kellogg's business in Japan is so huge that it has a Japanese language website to promote its products! Honda, the Japanese car producer, makes cars and motor cycles on most continents. 'Globalization through localization' is its slogan. But it produces some cars in one country and ships them for sale in another. In today's global economy, people who are separated by thousands of miles, cooperate to produce many goods and services. For example, software engineers work via the internet with programmers in India. But there is a lot of local concentration of production as well.

A large proportion of UK furniture is made in Wales. There is a strong concentration of telecommunications industries in Finland. Financial services are concentrated in the major capital cities of Europe. A large proportion of Europe's oranges are grown in Spain. Why is this? What determines where goods and services are produced? How do changing patterns of production location change the types of jobs we do and the wages we earn?

Table 1.1	Return from Education		
	Qualification		
	Degree	**A Levels**	**5+ O Levels**
Men	17.5%	13%	21%
Women	35%	11%	26%

The percentage rates of return measure the average increase in your earnings resulting from education.

Source: Blundell, R. *et al.* (1999) Human Capital Investment: the returns from education and training to the individual, the firm and the economy. *Fiscal Studies*, **20**.

5 Who?

Who consumes the goods and services produced depends on the incomes that people earn. Doctors earn much higher incomes than nurses and physiotherapists. So, doctors get more of the goods and services produced than nurses and physiotherapists.

You probably know about many other persistent differences in incomes. From Table 1.1 you can see that university graduates, on average, earn more than school leavers without degrees and school leavers with school certificates earn more than those who leave school without qualifications. In Europe, men on average, still earn more than women, and whites, on average, earn more than ethnic minorities. Europeans, however, earn more on average than Asians and Africans. But there are some significant exceptions. The people of Japan and Hong Kong now earn a similar amount to Europeans. But there is still a huge gap between incomes in rich countries and those in poor countries. A typical income in the poorest counties of the world is just a few hundred pounds, less than the equivalent of a typical weekly wage in the richest countries of the world.

What determines the incomes we earn? Why do doctors earn larger incomes than nurses? Why are average wages higher in Europe than in Africa?

These five big economic questions give you a sense of what economics is about. They tell you about the scope of economics. But they don't tell you what economics is. They don't tell you how economists think about these questions and seek answers to them. Let's find out how economists approach economic questions by looking at some big ideas that define the economic way of thinking.

Review Quiz

◆ How would you define economics?
◆ What is scarcity? Give some examples of rich people and poor people facing scarcity.
◆ Give some examples, different from those in the chapter, of each of the five big economic questions.
◆ Think of some examples of goods which you value highly and some goods on which you place a low value. Why do you care about *what* goods and services are produced?
◆ Think about the cost of goods and then say why you care about *how* goods and services are produced.
◆ Why do you care about *where* or *when* goods and services are produced?
◆ Why do you care about *who* gets the goods and services produced?

The Big Ideas of Economics

The economic way of thinking can be summarized in eight big ideas.

1 Choice, Trade-off and Opportunity Cost

When we make a choice we must give up one thing to get something else – every choice is a trade-off. Whatever we choose to do, we could have done something else instead. **Trade-off** means giving up something to get something else. The old phrase that 'there's no such thing as a free lunch' expresses the central idea in economics – that every choice involves a cost. The highest-valued alternative we give up to get something is the **opportunity cost** of the activity.

We use the term opportunity cost to emphasize that when we make a choice in the face of scarcity, we give up an opportunity to do something else. The opportunity cost of any action is the highest valued alternative forgone. The action that you choose not to do – the highest valued alternative forgone – is the cost of the action that you choose to do. You can quit college or university right now or you can stay in education. If you quit and take a job at McDonald's, you might earn enough to buy some CDs, go to see a film and spend lots of free time with your friends. If you remain in education, you can't afford these things. You will be able to buy these things later and that is

one of the payoffs from being in college. But for now, when you've bought your books, you have nothing left for CDs and films. Doing assignments means that you've got less time for hanging around with your friends. The opportunity cost of being in college is the alternative things that you would have done if you had quit college.

Opportunity cost is the highest valued alternative forgone. It is not all the possible alternatives forgone. For example, your economics lecture is at 8:30 on a Monday morning. You contemplate two alternatives to attending the lecture: staying in bed for an hour or jogging for an hour. You can't stay in bed and jog for that same hour. The opportunity cost of attending the lecture is not the cost of an hour in bed and the cost of jogging for an hour. If these are the only alternatives you contemplate, then you have to decide which one you would do if you did not go to the lecture. The opportunity cost of attending a lecture for a jogger is a forgone hour of exercise; the opportunity cost of attending a lecture for a late sleeper is a forgone hour in bed.

2 Choice at the Margin

We make choices in small steps, or at the margin, and our choices are influenced by incentives. Everything that we do involves a decision to do a little bit more or a little bit less of an activity. You can allocate the next hour between studying and e-mailing your friends. But the choice is not 'all-or-nothing'. You must decide how many minutes to allocate to each activity. To make this decision, you compare **choice at the margin** – you compare the benefit of a little bit more study time with its cost.

A young mother must decide how to allocate her time between being with her child and working for an income. Like your decision about study time, this decision too involves comparing the benefit of a little bit more income with the cost of a little bit less time with her child. The benefit that arises from an increase in an activity is called marginal benefit. For example, suppose that a mother is working 2 days a week and is thinking about increasing her work to 3 days. Her **marginal benefit** is the benefit she will get from the additional day of work. It is not the benefit she gets from all 3 days. The reason is that she already has the benefit from 2 days work, so she doesn't count this benefit as resulting from the decision she is now making.

The cost of an increase in an activity is called **marginal cost**. For the mother, the marginal cost of increasing her work to 3 days a week is the cost of the additional day not spent with her child. It does not include the cost of the two days she is already working. To make her decision, she compares the marginal benefit from an extra day of work with its marginal cost. If the marginal benefit exceeds the marginal cost, she works the extra day. If the marginal cost exceeds the marginal benefit, she does not work the extra day.

By evaluating marginal benefits and marginal costs and choosing only those actions that bring greater benefit than cost, we use our scarce resources in the way that makes us as well off as possible. Our choices respond to incentives. An **incentive** is an inducement to take a particular action. The inducement can be a benefit – a carrot, or a cost – a stick. A change in opportunity cost – in marginal cost – and a change in marginal benefit changes the incentives that we face and leads to changes in our actions.

For example, suppose the daily wage rate rises and nothing else changes. With a higher daily wage rate, the marginal benefit of working increases. For the young mother, the opportunity cost of spending a day with her child has increased. She now has a bigger incentive to work an extra day a week. Whether or not she does so depends on how she evaluates the marginal benefit of the additional income and marginal cost of spending less time with her child.

Similarly, suppose the cost of day care rises and nothing else changes. The higher cost of day care increases the marginal cost of working. For the young mother, the opportunity cost of spending a day with her child has decreased. She now has a smaller incentive to work an extra day a week. Again, whether or not she changes her actions in response to a change in incentives depends on how she evaluates the marginal benefit and marginal cost. A central idea of economics is that by looking for changes in marginal cost and marginal benefit, we can predict the way choices will change in response to changes in incentives.

3 Voluntary Exchange and Efficient Markets

Voluntary exchange makes both buyers and sellers better off, and markets are an efficient way to organize exchange. When you shop for food, you give up some money in exchange for a basket of vegetables. But the food is worth the price you have to pay. You are better off having exchanged some of your money for the vegetables. The food shop receives a payment that makes its operator happy too. Both you and the food shop owner gain from your purchase. Similarly, when you work at a summer job, you receive a wage that you've decided is sufficient to compensate you for the leisure time you must give up. But the value of your work to the firm that hires you is at least as great as the wage it pays you. So again, both you and your employer gain from a **voluntary exchange**.

You are better off when you buy your food. And you are better off when you sell your labour during the summer holidays. Whether you are a buyer or a seller, you gain from voluntary exchange with others.

What is true for you is true for everyone else. Everyone gains from voluntary exchange. In our organized economy, exchanges take place in markets and for money. We sell our labour in exchange for an **income** in the labour market. And we buy the **goods and services** we've chosen to consume in a wide variety of markets, markets for vegetables, coffee, films, videos, pizzas, haircuts, and so on. At the other side of these transactions, firms buy our labour and sell us the hundreds of different consumer goods and services we buy.

Markets are **efficient** in the sense that they send resources to the place where they are valued most highly. For example, a frost kills the orange crop and sends the price of orange juice through the roof. This increase in price, with all other prices remaining unchanged, increases the opportunity cost of drinking orange juice. The people who place the highest value on orange juice are the ones who keep drinking it. People who place a lower value on orange juice now have an incentive to substitute other fruit juices.

Markets and voluntary exchange are not the only way to organize the economy. An alternative is called a **command system**. In a command system, some people give orders (commands) and other people obey those orders. A command system is used in the military and in many firms. A command system was used in the former Soviet Union to organize the entire economy. You can see from the cartoon comparing towns in Russia and the United Kingdom that the allocation method in the old command systems was quite different from the allocation method in market systems.

4 Market Failure

The market does not always work efficiently and sometimes government action is necessary to overcome market problems and lead to a more efficient use of resources. **Market failure** is a state in which the market does not use resources efficiently. If you pay attention to the news media, you might get the impression that the market almost never does a good job. It makes credit card interest rates too high. It makes the wages of fast-food workers too low. From Figure 1.1 you can see it causes the price of coffee to go through the roof every time the crop fails. It increases the world price of oil when political instability threatens the Middle East. These examples are not cases of market failure. They are examples of the market doing its job of helping us to allocate our scarce resources and ensure that they are used in the activities in which they are most highly valued.

Because a high price brings a bigger gain to the seller, there is an incentive for sellers to try to control a market. When a single producer controls an entire market, it can restrict production and raise the price. This action brings market failure. The quantity of the good available is too small. Some people believe that Intel restricts the quantity of computer chips when it introduces a new design in order to get a high price for it. Eventually, the price falls, but at first, Intel sells its new design for a high price and makes a bigger profit.

Market failure can also arise when producers don't take into account the costs they impose on other people. For example, electricity utilities create pollution

MINSK

CROYDON

Drawings by Chris Riddell, 1993, *The Independent*.

Figure 1.1
Coffee Prices

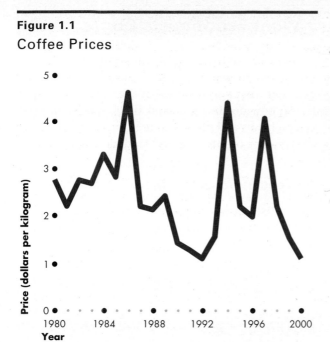

In the coffee market, prices rise sharply when the harvest is bad.

such as acid rain that destroys plants and forests and lowers farm production. If these costs were taken into account, we would produce less electricity. Market failure can also arise because some goods, such as the air traffic control system, must be consumed by everyone equally. None of us has an incentive voluntarily to pay our share of the cost of such a service. Instead, we try to free ride on everyone else. But if everyone tries to free ride, no one gets a ride!

To overcome market failure, governments regulate markets with competition and environmental protection laws. And the government discourages the production and consumption of some goods and services (tobacco and alcohol for example) by taxing them and encourages the production and consumption of some other items (health care and schooling for example) by subsidizing them.

5 Expenditure, Income and the Value of Production

For the economy as a whole, **expenditure** equals **income** equals the **value of production**. When you buy a coffee you spend £2. But what happens to that money? The server gets some of it in wages, the owner of the building gets some of it as rent, and the owner of the café gets some of it as profit. The suppliers of the milk and coffee also get some of your £2. But these suppliers spend part of what they receive on wages and rent. And they keep part of it as profit. Your £2 of expenditure creates exactly £2 of income for all the people who have contributed to making the cup of coffee, going all the way back to the farmer in Brazil who grew the coffee beans. Your expenditure generates incomes of an equal amount. The same is true for everyone else's expenditure. So, for the economy as a whole, total expenditure on goods and services equals total income.

One way to value the things you buy is to use the prices you pay for them. So the value of all the goods and services bought equals total expenditure. Another way to value the items you buy is to use the cost of production. This cost is the total amount paid to the people who produced the items – the total income generated by your expenditure. But we've just seen that total expenditure and total income are equal, so they also equal the value of production.

6 Living Standards and Productivity

Living standards improve when **productivity**, production per person, increases. By automating a car production line, one worker can produce a greater output. But if one worker can produce more cars, then more people can enjoy owning a car. The same is true for all goods and services. By increasing output per person, we enjoy a higher standard of living and buy more goods and services. The **value of production** can increase for any of three reasons: because prices rise, because production per person increases or because the population increases.

But only an increase in productivity brings an improvement in living standards. A rise in prices brings higher incomes, but only in pounds. The extra income is just enough to pay the higher prices, not enough to buy more goods and services. An increase in population brings an increase in total production, but not an increase in production per person.

7 Inflation and Money

We find rising prices when the quantity of money increases faster than production. Prices rise in a process called **inflation** when the quantity of money in circulation increases faster than production. This leads to a situation of 'too much money chasing too few goods'. As people bring more money to market, sellers see that they can raise their prices. But when these sellers go to buy their supplies, they find that the prices they face increase. With too much money around, money starts to lose value.

In some countries, inflation has been rapid. One such country is Poland. Since 1990, prices in Poland have risen more than sevenfold. In most European countries, we have moderate inflation of about 3–5 per cent a year. Some people say that by increasing the quantity of money, we can create jobs. The idea is that if more money is put into the economy, when it is spent, businesses sell more and so hire more labour to produce more goods. Initially, an increase in money might increase production and create jobs. But eventually, it only increases prices and leaves production and jobs unchanged.

8 Unemployment: Efficient or Wasteful?

Unemployment can result from market failure but some unemployment is productive. Unemployment is ever present. Sometimes its rate is low and sometimes it is high. Also, unemployment fluctuates over the business cycle. Some unemployment is normal and efficient. We choose to take our time finding a suitable job rather than rushing to accept the first one that comes along. Similarly, businesses take their time in filling vacancies. The unemployment that results from these careful searches for jobs and workers improves productivity because it helps to assign people to their most productive jobs. Some unemployment results from fluctuations in expenditure and can be wasteful.

Review Quiz

- Give some examples of trade-offs that you have made and the opportunity cost you've incurred today.
- Give some examples of marginal cost and marginal benefit.
- How do markets enable both buyers and sellers to gain from exchange and why do markets sometimes fail?
- For the economy as a whole, why does expenditure equal income and the value of production?
- What makes living standards rise?
- What makes prices rise?
- Is unemployment always a problem?

What Economists Do

Economists use the eight big questions you have just read about to search for the answers to the five big questions that you reviewed at the start of this chapter. So how do they go about their work? What special problems and pitfalls do they encounter? Do they always agree on the answers? Find out below.

Microeconomics and Macroeconomics

Economists answer the big economic questions either from a micro or a macro perspective, and these two perspectives define two major branches of the subject:

- Microeconomics
- Macroeconomics

Microeconomics is the study of the decisions of individual people and businesses and the interaction of those decisions in markets. It seeks to explain the prices and quantities of individual goods and services. Microeconomics also studies the effects of government regulation and taxes on prices and quantities in markets. For example, microeconomics studies the forces that determine the prices of cars and the quantities of cars produced and sold. It also examines the effects of regulations and taxes on the prices and quantities of cars.

Macroeconomics is the study of the national economy and the global economy as a whole. It seeks to explain average prices and the total employment, income and production. It seeks to explain average prices and the total level of employment, income and production. Macroeconomics also studies the effects of taxes, government spending and the government budget deficit on total employment and incomes. It also examines the effects of money and interest rates.

The difference between the micro and the macro perspective is highlighted by the pictures of the Korean sports stadium. You can take a micro view of a single participant and the actions he or she is taking, or you can take a macro view by looking at the whole pattern formed by the joint actions of all the individual participants in the display.

Economic Science

Economics is a social science (along with political science, psychology and sociology). A major task of economists is to discover how the economic world works. In pursuit of this goal, economists (like all scientists) distinguish between two types of statement:

1   What is.
2   What ought to be.

Statements about 'what is' are called positive statements. They say what is currently believed about the way the world operates. A positive statement might be right or wrong, and a positive statement can be tested by checking it against the facts. When a chemist does an experiment in her laboratory, she is attempting to check a positive statement against the facts.

Statements about 'what ought to be' are called normative statements. These statements depend on values and cannot be tested. When the European Parliament debates a motion, it is ultimately trying to decide what ought to be. It is making a normative statement.

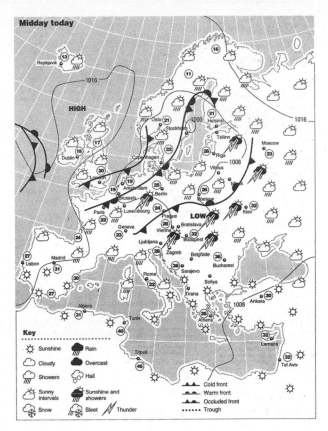

Map supplied by PA Weather

To see the distinction between positive and normative statements, consider the controversy over global warming. Some scientists believe that centuries of the burning of coal and oil are increasing the carbon dioxide content of the earth's atmosphere and leading to higher temperatures that eventually will have devastating consequences for life on this planet. 'Our planet is warming because of an increased carbon dioxide build-up in the atmosphere' is a positive statement. It can (in principle and with sufficient data) be tested. 'We ought to cut back on our use of carbon-based fuels such as coal and oil' is a normative statement. You may agree with or disagree with this statement, but you can't test it. It is based on values.

Health care reform provides an economic example of the distinction. 'Universal health care will cut the amount of work time lost to illness' is a positive statement. 'Every European should have equal access to health care' is a normative statement. The task of economic science is to discover and catalogue positive statements that are consistent with what we observe in the world and that enable us to understand how the economic world works. This task is a large one that can be broken into three steps:

1 Observation and measurement.
2 Model building.
3 Testing models.

Observation and Measurement

First, economists keep track of the amounts and locations of natural and human resources, of wages and work hours, of the prices and quantities of the different goods and services produced, of taxes and government spending, and of the quantities of goods and services bought from and sold to other countries. This list gives a flavour of the array of things that economists can observe and measure.

Model Building

Model building is the second step toward understanding how the economic world works. An **economic model** is a description of some aspect of the economic world that includes only those features of the world that are needed for the purpose at hand. A model is simpler than the reality it describes. What a model includes and what it leaves out result from assumptions about what is essential and what are inessential details.

You can see how ignoring details is useful – even essential – to our understanding by thinking about a model that you see every day, the TV weather map. The weather map shown on page 13 is a model that helps to predict the temperature, wind speed and direction, and precipitation over a future period. The weather map shows lines called isobars – lines of equal barometric pressure. It doesn't show the motorways. The reason is that our theory of the weather tells us that the pattern of air pressure, not the location of the motorways, determines the weather.

An economic model is similar to a weather map. It tells us how a number of variables are determined by a number of other variables. For example, an economic model of inflation would show which variables determined inflation and how a change in each variable affected inflation.

Testing Models

The third step is testing the model. A model's predictions may correspond, or be in conflict, with the facts. By comparing the model's predictions with the facts, we are able to test a model and develop an **economic theory**. An economic theory is a generalization that summarizes what we think we understand about the economic choices that people make and

Figure 1.2

How Economic Theories are Developed

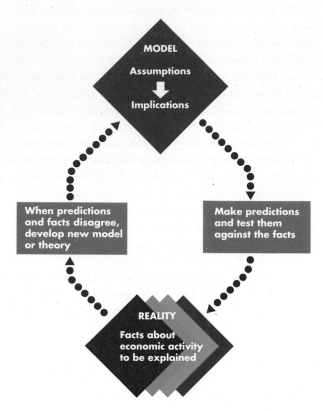

Economists develop economic theories by building and testing economic models. An economic model is based on assumptions about what is essential and what can be ignored and the implications of these assumptions. The implications of a model form the basis of predictions about the world. Economists test those predictions by checking them against the facts. If the predictions are in conflict with the facts, the model-building process begins again with new assumptions. Only when the predictions agree with the facts has a useful theory been developed.

the performance of industries and entire economies. It is a bridge between an economic model and the real economy.

A theory is created by a process of building and testing models. For example, meteorologists have a theory that if the isobars form a particular pattern at a particular time of the year (a model), then it will snow (reality). They have developed this theory by repeated observation and by carefully recording the weather that follows specific pressure patterns.

Figure 1.2 shows the logical structure of the search for new economic knowledge. Economists build a model to create predictions about the way the world works. Theories are developed from generating and testing the model. When the model's predictions conflict with the facts, the theory is discarded or the model modified.

Economics is a young science. It was born in 1776 with the publication of Adam Smith's *The Wealth of Nations* (see pp. 40–41). Over the past 220 years, economics has discovered many useful theories. But in many areas, economists are still looking for answers. The gradual accumulation of economic knowledge gives most economists some faith that their methods will, eventually, provide usable answers to the big economic questions. But progress in economics comes slowly. Let's look at some of the obstacles to progress in economics.

Obstacles and Pitfalls in Economics

Economic experiments are difficult to do. Also, economic behaviour has many simultaneous causes. For these two reasons, it is difficult to unscramble cause and effect in economics.

Scientists try to unscramble cause and effect by changing one factor at a time and holding all the other relevant factors constant. In this way, scientists isolate the factor of interest and are able to investigate its effects in the clearest possible way. This logical device, that all scientists use to identify cause and effect, is called **ceteris paribus**. *Ceteris paribus* is a Latin term that means 'other things being equal' or 'if all other relevant things remain the same'. Ensuring that other things are equal is crucial in many activities, including athletic events, and all successful attempts to make scientific progress use this device.

Economic models (like the models in all other sciences) enable the influence of one factor at a time to be isolated in the imaginary world of the model. When we use a model, we are able to imagine what would happen if only one factor changed. But *ceteris paribus* can be a problem in economics when we try to test a model.

Laboratory scientists, such as chemists and physicists, perform experiments by actually holding all the relevant factors constant except for the one under investigation. This method is called using a 'control'. In the non-experimental sciences such as economics (and astronomy), we usually observe the outcomes of the simultaneous operation of many factors. Consequently, it is difficult to set up a control. It is hard to sort out the effects of each individual factor and to compare the effects with what a model predicts.

To cope with this problem, economists take three complementary approaches.

First, they look for pairs of events in which other things were equal (or similar). An example might be to study the effects of unemployment benefit on the unemployment rate by comparing different European countries on the presumption that the people in the two economies are sufficiently similar. Second, economists use statistical tools called econometrics. And third, when they can, they perform experiments. This relatively new approach puts real subjects (usually students) in a decision-making situation and varies their incentives in some way to discover how they respond to one factor at a time.

Economists try to avoid fallacy – errors of reasoning that lead to a wrong conclusion. But two fallacies are common, and you need to be on your guard to avoid them. They are:

1 The fallacy of composition.
2 The *post hoc* fallacy.

Fallacy of Composition

The fallacy of composition is the (false) statement that what is true of the parts is true of the whole or that what is true of the whole is true of the parts. Think of the true statement, 'Speed kills', and its implication, going more slowly saves lives. If an entire freeway moves at a lower speed, everyone on the highway has a safer ride.

But suppose that one driver only slows down and all the other drivers try to maintain their original speed. In this situation, there will probably be more accidents because more cars will change lanes to overtake the slower vehicle. So, in this example, what is true for the whole is not true for a part.

The fallacy of composition arises mainly in macroeconomics, and it stems from the fact that the parts interact with each other to produce an outcome for the whole that might differ from the intent of the parts. For example, a firm lays off some workers to cut costs and improve its profits. If all firms take similar actions, incomes fall and so does spending. The firm sells less, and its profits don't improve.

Post Hoc Fallacy

Another Latin phrase – *post hoc ergo propter hoc* – means 'after this, therefore because of this'. The *post hoc* fallacy is the error of reasoning that a first event causes a second event because the first occurred before the second. Suppose you are a visitor from a far-off world. You observe lots of people shopping in early December and then you see them opening gifts and partying on Christmas Day. Does the shopping cause Christmas, you wonder. After a deeper study, you discover that Christmas causes the shopping. A later event causes an earlier event.

Unravelling cause and effect is difficult in economics. And just looking at the timing of events often doesn't help. For example, the stock market booms, and some months later the economy expands – jobs and incomes grow. Did the stock market boom cause the economy to expand? Possibly, but perhaps businesses started to plan the expansion of production because a new technology that lowered costs had become available. As knowledge of the plans spread, the stock market reacted to anticipate the economic expansion. To disentangle cause and effect, economists use economic models and data and, to the extent that they can, perform experiments.

Economics is a challenging science. Does the difficulty of getting answers in economics mean that anything goes and that economists disagree on most questions? No, but disagreement and debate are part of the way in which science develops new answers to current problems. Disagreement is a healthy sign in science.

Agreement and Disagreement

Economists have a reputation for not agreeing. Perhaps you've heard the joke: 'If you laid all the economists in the world end to end, they still wouldn't reach agreement'. But actually, while economists like to argue about theory, there is a remarkable amount of agreement. Here is a sample of the degree of consensus on a range of issues.[1] Seventy per cent of economists agree that:

◆ Rent ceilings cut the availability of housing.

◆ Import restrictions have larger costs than benefits.

◆ Wage and price controls do not help slow inflation.

◆ Wage contracts are not a primary cause of unemployment.

Sixty per cent of economists agree that:

◆ Monopoly power of big oil companies was not the cause of a rise in the price of petrol during the Kuwait crisis.

◆ Curtailing the power of environmental agencies would not make the economy more efficient.

◆ If the budget is to be balanced, it should be balanced over a business cycle, not every year.

But economists are divided on these issues:

◆ Anti-monopoly laws should be enforced more vigorously to curtail monopoly power.

◆ Effluent taxes are better than pollution limits.

◆ The government should try to make the distribution of income more equal.

Which are positive and which are normative? Notice that economists are willing to offer their opinions on normative issues as well as their professional views on positive questions. Be on the lookout for normative propositions dressed up as positive propositions.

---

[1] The views of economists are taken from Richard M. Alston, J.R. Kearl and Michael B. Vaughan, Is there a Consensus Among Economists? *American Economic Review*, May 1992, **82**, 203–209.

You are now ready to start doing economics. As you get into the subject, you will see that we rely heavily on graphs. You must be comfortable with this method of reasoning. If you need some help with it, take your time in working carefully through the chapter on Making and Using Graphs available on the Parkin, Powell and Matthews website http://www.econ100.com. If you are comfortable with using graphs, then you can begin to study the fundamental economic problem, scarcity.

Summary

Key Points

A Definition of Economics (p. 5)

- Economics is the *science of choice* – the science that explains the choices that we make to cope with scarcity.

Big Economic Questions (pp. 5–8)

- Economists try to answer five big questions about goods and services:

  1 What?
  2 How?
  3 When?
  4 Where?
  5 Who?

- *What* are the goods and services produced, *how*, *when*, and *where* are they produced, and *who* consumes them?

- These questions interact to determine the standards of living and the distribution of well-being in Europe and around the world.

Big Ideas of Economic (pp. 8–12)

- A choice is a trade-off and the highest-valued alternative forgone is the opportunity cost of what is chosen.

- Choices are made at the margin and are influenced by incentives.

- Markets enable both buyers and sellers to gain from voluntary exchange.

- Sometimes government actions are needed to overcome market failure.

- For the economy as a whole, expenditure equals income and equals the value of production.

- Living standards rise when production per person increases.

- Prices rise when the quantity of money increases faster than production.

Key Terms

Ceteris paribus, **15**
Choice at the margin, **9**
Command system, **10**
Economics, **5**
Economic model, **14**
Economic theory, **14**
Efficient, **9**
Expenditure, **11**
Goods and services, **9**
Incentive, **9**
Income, **9**
Inflation, **11**
Macroeconomics, **13**
Marginal benefit, **9**
Marginal cost, **9**
Market failure, **10**
Microeconomics, **13**
Opportunity cost, **8**
Productivity, **11**
Scarcity, **5**
Trade-off, **8**
Unemployment, **12**
Value of production, **11**
Voluntary exchange, **9**

Problems

•1 You plan to upgrade your computer skills on a training course this summer. If you do, you won't be able to take your usual job that pays €6,000 for the summer and you won't be able to live at home for free. The cost of your tuition will be €2,000, equipment €200, and living expenses €1,400. What is the opportunity cost of your summer training course?

2 You plan a major adventure trip for the summer. You won't be able to take your usual summer job that pays €6,000 and you won't be able to live at home for free. The cost of your travel on the trip will be €3,000, film and video tape will cost you €200, and your food will cost €1,400. What is the opportunity cost of taking this trip?

•3 The local shopping centre has free parking, but the centre is always very busy and it usually takes 30 minutes to find a parking space. Today when you found a vacant spot, Harry also wanted it. Is parking really free at this shopping centre? If not, what did it cost you to park today? When you parked your car today, did you impose any costs on Harry? Explain your answers.

4 A city has built a new high rise car park. There is always a free parking spot but it costs €1 a day. Before the new high rise car park was built, it usually took 15 minutes of cruising to find a parking space. Compare the opportunity cost of parking in the new car park with the old parking system. Which is less costly and by how much?

Critical Thinking

1 Use the link on the Parkin, Powell and Matthews website to visit *Resources for Economists on the Internet*. This site is a good place from which to search for economic information on the internet. Visit the 'general interest' sites and become familiar with the types of information that they contain.

2 Use the link on the Parkin, Powell and Matthews website to get data on European statistics. Use this site to keep informed about the European economy and about the economy of your own region and city.

   a What is the number of people unemployed in your country?

   b Has the percentage of people unemployed risen or fallen recently?

   c What is the average income earned in your country?

3 Imagine a homeless man on the street in your town or city. Use the five big questions and the eight big ideas of economics to organize a short essay about the economic life of this man. Here are some questions to consider in your essay. Does the homeless man face scarcity? Does he make choices? Can you interpret his choices as being in his own best interest? Can either his own choices or the choices of others make this man better off? If so, how?

4 Use the link on the Parkin, Powell and Matthews website to visit the *Financial Times* website.

   a What is the top economic news story today?

   b With which of the five big questions does it deal? (Hint: It must deal with at least one of them and might deal with more than one.)

   c Which of the eight big ideas seem to be relevant to understanding this news item?

   d Write a summary of the news item using as much as possible of the economic vocabulary that you have learned in this chapter and which is in the key terms list on pp. 18–19.

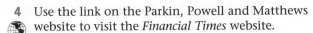

CHAPTER 2

The Economic Problem

After studying this chapter you will be able to:

◆ Explain the fundamental economic problem

◆ Define the production possibility frontier

◆ Define production efficiency

◆ Calculate opportunity cost

◆ Explain how economic growth expands production possibilities

◆ Explain how and why specialization and trade expand production possibilities

Making the Most of It

We live in a style that surprises our grandparents and would have astonished our great grandparents. We live in bigger homes, eat more, grow taller and are even born larger than they were. CDs, mobile phones, genetic engineering, personal computers and microwave ovens did not exist 20 years ago. Economic growth has made us richer than our grandparents, but it has not liberated us from scarcity. Why, despite our immense wealth, must we still make choices and face costs? Why must you choose between working full time and a university education? Why are there no 'free lunches'? ◆ We see an incredible amount of specialization and exchange in the world. Each one of us specializes in a particular job – as a lawyer, a factory worker, a parent. You will have specialized in the university programme you have chosen. We have become so specialized that one farm worker can feed 100 people. Less than one in four of the EU workforce is employed in manufacturing. More than half of the workforce is employed in agriculture, wholesale and retail trade, banking and finance, government and other services. Why do we specialize? How do we benefit from specialization and trade? ◆ Over many centuries, institutions and social arrangements have evolved that we take for granted. One of them is markets. Another is property rights and a political and legal system that protects them. Yet another is money. Why have these arrangements evolved? How do they extend our ability to specialize and increase production?

◆ ◆ ◆ ◆ These are the questions that we tackle in this chapter. We begin with the core economic problem: scarcity and choice and the concept of the production possibility frontier. We use these to learn about the key economic ideas of opportunity cost and production efficiency. We then discover how production is increased by specialization, trade and social institutions in market economies. Finally, we look at the opportunity costs facing school leavers in Reading Between the Lines on pp. 38–39. This chapter covers the fundamental ideas on which all economics is built.

Resources and Wants

Two facts dominate our everyday choices:

1 We have limited resources.

2 We have unlimited wants.

These two facts define **scarcity**, a condition in which the resources available cannot meet all our wants. Scarcity is always present when choices are made. It confronts us individually, it confronts our families, our local communities, our national and international leaders.

Economics is the study of the choices people make to cope with scarcity. It is the study of how we try to get the most out of our own limited resources and of how we interact in the process. The **fundamental economic problem** is how to use our limited resources to produce and consume the things that we value the most. So let's take a closer look at our limited resources and unlimited wants.

Limited Resources

The **limited resources** which are used to produce goods and services are called **factors of production**. There are four types of limited resources:

1 Land.

2 Labour.

3 Capital.

4 Entrepreneurship.

Land is all the gifts of nature. The term includes the air, the water, the land surface, as well as the minerals that lie beneath the surface.

Labour is the time and effort that people devote to producing goods and services. It includes the physical and mental activities of the many thousands of people who make cars and cola, biscuits and glue, wallpaper and watering cans.

Capital is all the resources which have been produced for use in the production of other goods and services. *Physical capital* includes the motorway system, ancient buildings and modern homes, dams and power stations, airports and jumbo jets, car and shirt factories, cinemas and shopping centres. *Human capital* is the skill and knowledge of people, which arise from their education and on-the-job training. *Environmental capital* includes elements of land which are destroyed in the production process, the biodiversity among species and the ability of the environment to absorb waste from production.

Entrepreneurship is the resource that organizes land, labour and capital. Entrepreneurs make business decisions and bear the risks of these decisions, and come up with new ideas about what, how, where, to produce.

Our limited resources are converted into goods and services by using the technologies available. These technologies are limited by our knowledge – our human capital – and by our other resources.

Unlimited Wants

Our wants are limited only by our imagination and are effectively unlimited. We want food and drink, decent clothing and housing, good education and health care. We want some of these so badly that we call them necessities. But let's face it, many of our wants are luxuries even though we think of them as needs. But we also want many other things. We want the latest mobile phone, internet technology or digital television. Perhaps you want the latest Tomb Raider video game or the latest fashion fabric in your clothes.

Some of our wants are less pressing than others, but they are all wants. We cannot even imagine some of the things we will want in the future. We will probably all want to live longer and travel ever faster across ever longer distances.

Our wants will always exceed our limited resource. This scarcity forces us to make choices. We must rank our wants and decide which ones to satisfy first. When we choose to satisfy one want, we leave another unsatisfied.

Review Quiz

◆ What is scarcity?
◆ What is the fundamental economic problem?
◆ Can you give a definition of economics?
◆ What are the resources used to produce goods and services?
◆ How do we cope with the fact that our wants cannot be satisfied with the resources available?

We can now begin our study of the choices people make by looking at production possibilities and the fundamental implication of the economic problem – unsatisfied wants or opportunity cost.

Resources, Production Possibilities and Opportunity Cost

Every day, a huge variety of goods and services are produced by 300 million people across the European Union. *Production* is the process of converting our limited resources into the goods and services we want, using available technologies. These technologies are limited only by our knowledge – our human capital and entrepreneurship – and by our other resources. The limit of our production potential is described by the production possibility frontier.

The **production possibility frontier** (*PPF*) is the boundary between those combinations of goods and services that can be produced and those combinations that cannot be produced. To study the production possibility frontier, we will consider just two goods at a time. In focusing on two goods, we use the *ceteris paribus* assumption. This means we hold the quantities produced of all the other goods constant. We use this assumption to create a *model* in which everything remains the same except the production of the two goods that we are (currently) considering. Let's begin by looking at the production possibility frontier for two goods that you probably buy, magazines and music CDs.

Production Possibility Frontier

The production possibility frontier for magazines and music CDs shows the limits to the production of these two goods, given the total resources available to produce them. Figure 2.1 shows this production possibility curve. It shows the combinations of the quantities of magazines and CDs in units of one million that can be produced given the resources available. The quantity of CDs (millions per year) produced is shown on the *x*-axis and the quantity of magazines (millions per year) produced is shown on the *y*-axis.

Because the *PPF* shows the *limits* to production, our economy cannot produce the combination of points outside the frontier. These are points that describe what we want but cannot have. We can only produce those combinations of magazines and CDs shown *on* or *inside* the *PPF*.

Suppose that in a year, 4 million CDs and 2 million magazines are produced – point *e* in Figure 2.1. The figure shows other production possibilities. For example, if we wanted to read more we might stop producing CDs and put all the creative people who

Figure 2.1

The Production Possibility Frontier for Magazines and CDs

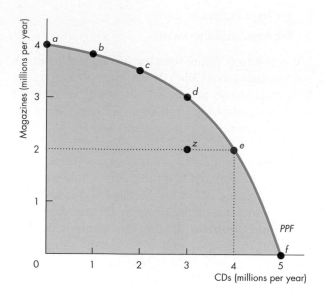

The figure shows six points on the production possibility frontier for magazines and CDs. Point *a* tells us that if we produce no CDs, the maximum quantity of magazines we can produce is four million a year. The line passing through points *a*, *b*, *c*, *d*, *e* and *f* is the production possibility frontier (*PPF*). It separates the attainable from the unattainable. We can produce at any point inside the orange area or on the frontier. Points outside the frontier are unattainable. Points inside the frontier such as point *z* are inefficient because it is possible to use the available resources to produce more of either or both goods.

devise them and all the programmers, production and marketing staff, computers, buildings and other resources used to produce CDs into the publishing industry to produce magazines. This case is shown as point *a* in the figure. The quantity of magazines produced increases to 4 million a year and CD production dries up. Alternatively, we might close down the publishing industry and switch the resources into producing CDs. This case is shown as possibility *f*. The quantity of magazines produced decreases to zero, and the quantity of CDs produced increases to 5 million a year.

Production Efficiency

Production efficiency is achieved when it is not possible to produce more of one good without producing less of some other good. Efficiency occurs only at points on the production possibility frontier. Possible production points *inside* the frontier, such as point *z*, are *inefficient*. They are points at which resources are being either wasted or misallocated.

Resources are wasted when they are idle but could be working. For example, a printing system is wasteful if it is running just 8 hours a day when it could be running for 24 hours a day. Resources are misallocated when they are assigned to inappropriate tasks. For example, a print worker might be assigned to producing CDs, and a musician might be assigned to printing magazines. We could get more magazines and more CDs if we reassigned these same workers to the jobs which most closely match their skills.

If we produce at an inefficient point such as *z*, our resources could be more efficiently used to produce both more magazines and more CDs. But if we are producing at a point like *e* on the *PPF*, we can only produce more of one good if we produce less of the other. We face a trade-off.

Trade-offs

At all points along the *PPF*, there is a trade-off – we must give up something to get something else. On the *PPF* in Figure 2.1, we must give up magazines to get more CDs, or give up CDs to get more magazines.

The lesson we've learned from this example is a fundamental one that applies to every imaginable real-world situation. At any given point in time, the world has a fixed amount of labour, land and capital. By using the available technologies, these resources can be employed to produce goods and services. But there is a limit to what they can produce that defines a boundary between what is attainable and what is not attainable. This boundary is the real-world economy's production possiblity frontier which defines the trade-offs we must make. On the real world *PPF*, producing more of any one good or service requires producing less of some other goods or services.

A prime minister who promises better welfare and better education must at the same time, to be credible, promise either cuts in budget spending or tax increases. Higher taxes mean less money left over for holidays and other consumption goods and services. The trade-off is between better welfare and educational services and less of other goods and services. On a smaller scale but equally important, each time you decide to rent a video you decide not to use your limited income to buy cola, or pizzas, or some other good. The trade-off is renting one more video or having less pizza and cola.

All trade-offs involve a cost – an opportunity cost.

Opportunity Cost

The **opportunity cost** of an action is the best alternative forgone. Of all the things you choose not to do – the alternatives forgone – the best one is the opportunity cost of the action you choose. The concept of opportunity cost can be made more precise by using the production possibility frontier. Along the *PPF* in Figure 2.1, there are only two goods. If we want more of one good there is only one alternative forgone, the other good. Given the current resources and technology, we can produce more magazines and less CDs. Thus the opportunity cost of producing an additional magazine is the quantity of CDs forgone. Similarly, the opportunity cost of producing additional CDs is the quantity of magazines forgone.

For example, at point *c* in Figure 2.1, we produce more magazines and fewer CDs than we do at point *d*. If we choose point *d* over point *c*, the additonal 1 unit of CDs (measured in millions) *costs* 0.5 magazines (measured in millions). The opportunity cost of 1 CD is half a magazine.

We can also work out the opportunity cost of choosing point *e* over point *d* in Figure 2.1. If we move from point *d* to point *e*, the quantity of CDs increases by one unit and the quantity of magazines falls by one unit. The additional 1 unit of CDs costs 1 unit of magazines. The opportunity cost of 1 CD is 1 magazine.

Opportunity Cost is a Ratio

The opportunity cost of producing one additional unit of a good is a ratio. It is the decrease in the quantity produced of one good divided by the increase in the quantity produced of another good as we move along the production possibility frontier.

Because opportunity cost is a ratio, the opportunity cost of producing good *X* (the quantity of units of good *Y* forgone) is always equal to the inverse of the opportunity cost of producing good *Y* (the number of units of good *X* forgone). Let's check this proposition by returning once more to Figure 2.1 and the movement from point *e* to point *f*. To increase the production of CDs from 4 to 5 million an increase of 1 million, the quantity of magazines must decrease from 2 million to zero. The opportunity cost of the extra 1 million CDs is 2 million magazines, or 2 magazines per CD. So, the opportunity cost of 1 magazine is 0.5 CDs and the opportunity cost of 1 CD is 2 magazines ($1/0.5 = 2$).

Increasing Opportunity Cost

The opportunity cost of a CD increases as the quanity of CDs produced increases. Also the opportunity cost of magazines increases as the number of magazines produced increases. This is reflected in the shape of the *PPF* in Figure 2.1, which is bowed outward.

When a large quantity of magazines and a small quantity of CDs are produced – between points *a* and *d* – the *PPF* has a gentle slope. When a large quantity of CDs and a small quantity of magazines are produced – between points *e* and *f* – the *PPF* is steep. So the whole frontier bows outward.

The shape of the *PPF* in Figure 2.1 is a reflection of the fact that we assume that not all resources are equally productive in all activities. Musicians and music technicians can work on magazines, so if they switch from making CDs to producing magazines – moving along the frontier from *f* to *a* – the production of magazines increases. But these people are not as good at producing magazines as the original publishing industry workers. So for a small increase in the quantity of magazines produced, the production of CDs falls a lot.

Similarly, publishing industry workers can produce CDs, but they are not as good at this activity as the people currently making CDs. So when publishing industry workers switch to producing CDs, the quantity of CDs produced increases by only a small amount and the quantity of magazines produced falls a lot. The more we try to produce either good, the less productive are the additional resources we use to produce that good and the larger is the opportunity cost of producing a unit of that good.

Increasing Costs are Everywhere

Most production activities that you could think of will involve increasing opportunity costs. Two examples are the agriculture and health services. We allocate the most skilful farmers and the most fertile land to the production of food, and the best doctors and least fertile land to the production of health care services. If we shift fertile land and farm machinery to hospitals and make farmers do the jobs of health care workers, the production of food drops drastically and the increase in good quality health care services is small. The opportunity cost of a unit of health care services will rise.

While there may be a few occasions when land, labour and capital are equally productive in different uses, it is usually the case that our limited resources must be assigned to tasks for which they are an increasingly poor match. Increasing opportunity costs are a fact of life, they are everywhere.

Review Quiz

◆ How does the production possibility frontier illustrate scarcity?
◆ How does the production possibility frontier illustrate production efficiency?
◆ How does the production possibility frontier show that every choice involves a trade-off?
◆ How does the production possibility frontier illustrate opportunity cost?
◆ Why is opportunity cost a ratio?
◆ Why does the *PPF* for most goods bow outward, so that opportunity cost of a good increases as the quantity produced increases?

We have seen that production possibilities are limited by the production possibility frontier and that production at that point on the *PPF* is efficient. There are lots of efficient combinations of production along the *PPF*, so which one is best? How can we choose between them? We can use our idea of rising opportunity cost to show that there is one point on the *PPF* that is better than all the rest – the one we value most highly.

Efficient Choice

How do we decide whether to spend more on health care and less on building roads? How do we decide whether to expand production of genetically modified crops or invest in alternative energy production? These are very important questions with important consequences.

The best choice – the **efficient choice** – is the one we value most highly. We can see how to make the best choice by studying a much simpler example, like our choice between magazines and CDs. How do we decide how many magazines and how many CDs to produce? We know that all the combinations along the *PPF* are produced efficiently, so which combination along the *PPF* is the best?

We decide by calculating and comparing two numbers:

1 Marginal cost
2 Marginal benefit

Marginal Cost

Marginal cost is the opportunity cost of producing one more unit of a good or service. We already know how to calculate opportunity cost as we move along the production possibility frontier. The marginal cost of an additional unit of CDs is just of the opportunity cost of the foregone magazines. As we move along the *PPF*, the opportunity cost of the additional CD is the quantity of magazines that we must give up to get one more unit of CDs.

Figure 2.2 illustrates the opportunity cost and the marginal cost of CDs. If all the available resources are used to produce magazines, 4 units of magazines (measured in millions) and no CDs are produced each year. If we now produce 1 unit of CDs (measured in millions) we move from *a* to *b* in Figure 2.2(a) and the quantity of magazines decreases by 0.2 units. The opportunity cost of the first unit of CDs is 0.2 units of magazines.

If we now decide to produce another unit of CDs we move from *b* to *c*, and the quantity of magazines decreases by 0.3 units of magazines a year. The second unit of CDs costs 0.3 units of magazines. You can carry on and calculate the opportunity cost of increasing CD production to 3, 4 and finally 5 units. Figure 2.2(a) shows these opportunity costs as a series of steps. The steps – the opportunity costs – get bigger as we produce each additional unit of CDs each year.

In Figure 2.2(b), the line labelled *MC* shows the marginal cost of producing CDs in terms of the number of magazines forgone. The marginal cost of each unit of CDs (in millions) is just the opportunity cost of producing that unit. So we plot the marginal cost of each unit of CDs in Figure 2.2(b) from the height of the steps in Figure 2.2(a). The marginal cost of each unit of CDs increases so the marginal cost of CDs slopes upward.

To work out our most efficient choice, we need to compare the marginal cost with the marginal benefit of producing CDs. Let's look at marginal benefit.

Marginal Benefit

The **marginal benefit** is the benefit that people receive from consuming one more unit of a good or service. The marginal benefit from a good or service is measured by the maximum amount that a person is willing to pay for that extra unit. In general, the more we get of any good or service, the smaller is the marginal benefit that we get from it – so marginal benefit decreases.

Figure 2.2

Opportunity Cost and Marginal Cost

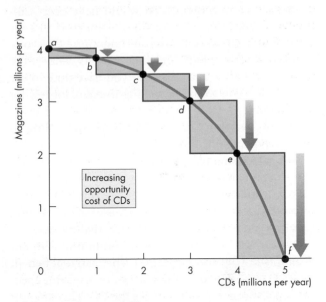

(a) Opportunity cost of CDs

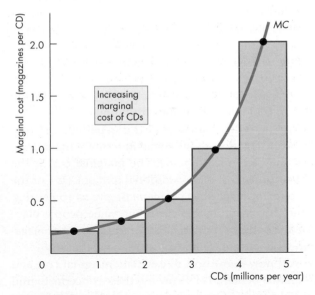

(b) Marginal cost

Opportunity cost is measured along the *PPF* in part (a). If the production of CDs increases from zero to one million, the opportunity cost of the first one million CDs is 0.2 million magazines. If the production of CDs increases from one million to two million, the opportunity cost of the second one million CDs is 0.3 million magazines. The opportunity cost of CDs increases as the production of CDs increases. Marginal cost is the opportunity cost of producing one more unit. Part (b) shows the marginal cost of CDs as the MC curve.

To understand why marginal benefit decreases think about your own consumption of CDs. When CDs were first available, they were hard to come by and everyone wanted them. You would have been willing to pay a high price for one to show off to your friends. As CDs became more common, everyone began collecting them and their novelty value wore off. If you have more CDs than you have time to use them, then you would be willing to pay a lot less for another one.

Usually we think of how much we are willing to pay in terms of prices. But you have just been learning about cost as an opportunity cost – an alternative forgone. You can also think about prices or willingness to pay in this way. The price you are willing to pay is not measured as money but in terms of the goods and services you could have bought with that money.

We can see how this works by continuing with our example of CDs and magazines. The marginal benefit of a CD is measured by the number of magazines people are willing to give up to get the CD. This amount decreases as the quantity of CDs that is available increases. The line labelled *MB* in Figure 2.3 shows the marginal benefit of CDs. People are willing to pay 2 units of magazines for the first unit of CDs, but only 1 unit of magazines for the second unit of CDs. As the quantity of CDs increases, the amount people are willing to pay falls. People are only willing to pay 0.2 units of magazines for the fifth unit of CDs.

The marginal benefit and the marginal cost of a unit of CDs are both measured in terms of magazines, but they are not the same. The marginal cost is the opportunity cost of an additional unit of CDs – or the amount of magazines people *must give up* to get that unit. The marginal benefit is the value people place on an additional unit of CDs – or the amount of magazines people are *willing to give* up to get that unit.

You now know how to calculate marginal cost and marginal benefit. Let's now use these concepts to find out how many CDs to produce, and the most efficient choice of CDs and magazines.

Efficient Choice

Efficient choice is when we produce the goods and services that we value most highly – when we are using our resources efficiently. We use our resources most efficiently when we cannot produce more of anything without giving up something that we value even more highly. It's easy to see where the most efficient choice is if we choose at the *margin*. Choosing at

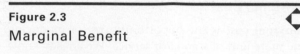

Figure 2.3

Marginal Benefit

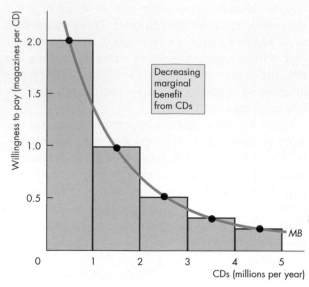

The fewer the number of CDs available, the more magazines people are willing to give up to get an additional CD. If only one unit of CDs (in millions) is available a year, people are willing to pay two units of magazines for an additional unit of CDs. But if four units of CDs are available, people will only pay 0.2 units of magazines for an additional game. Marginal benefit decreases as the quantity available increases.

the margin means comparing marginal cost and marginal benefit for each unit we produce.

There is a simple set of rules to help us find the most efficient choice when we choose at the margin. At any level of production, if the marginal benefit is higher than the marginal cost, we increase production of that good or service. If the marginal benefit is lower than the marginal cost, we decrease production of that good or service. If the marginal benefit equals the marginal cost, we stay at the current level of production of that good or service.

You would use the same kind of concept when you are out shopping. Suppose you have £15 to spend on either a CD or a T-shirt. You are choosing at the margin. You will buy the CD if the you think you will get more benefit from having that CD than it costs. The opportunity cost or the marginal cost is the forgone benefit of having the T-shirt. You will always buy something if you can afford it and you think the

Figure 2.4

Efficient Choices

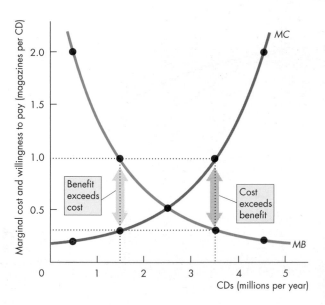

The greater the quantity of CDs produced, the smaller is the marginal benefit (*MB*) from a CD – the fewer magazines people are willing to give up to get an additional CD. But the greater the quantity of CDs produced, the greater is the marginal cost (*MC*) of a CD – the more magazines people must give up to get an additional CD. When marginal benefit equals marginal cost, resources are being used efficiently.

benefit is greater than the cost. Otherwise, you will keep your money or buy something else.

We can illustrate efficient choice using our example of CDs. Figure 2.4 shows the marginal cost and marginal benefit curves for CDs. Should we produce the first unit of CDs? To answer this question, we compare marginal cost and marginal benefit. When production is one unit, marginal cost is 0.2 units of magazines. But the marginal benefit is 2 units of magazines. So people value the first unit of CDs more highly than the cost to produce that unit. This means we can get more out of our resources by switching some resources into producing CDs and out of producing magazines.

Suppose we were producing 4 units of CDs. The marginal cost of the fourth unit of CDs is 1 unit of magazines but the marginal benefit is only 0.3 units of magazines. Because the marginal cost is greater than the marginal benefit, we know that people value the fourth unit of CDs less highly than the cost of

producing it. We can get more from our resources if we switch some resources out of CD production and into magazine production.

Now suppose that we produce the third unit of CDs. Marginal cost and marginal benefit are now equal at 0.5 units of magazines. This choice between CDs and magazines is efficient. Our resources are allocated most efficiently. If more CDs are produced, the forgone magazines are worth more than the additional unit of CDs. If fewer CDs are produced, the forgone magazines are worth less than the additional unit of CDs.

In our example, the most efficient quantity of CDs to produce is 3 units. So what is the most efficient combination of CDs and magazines? Look back at the *PPF* in Figure 2.1 to find out. The efficient combination is at the point on the *PPF* which shows 3 units of CDs and 2 units of magazines.

Review Quiz

◆ What is marginal cost and how is it measured?
◆ What is marginal benefit and how is it measured?
◆ How does the marginal benefit from a good change as the quantity of the good increases? Why?
◆ What is the relationship between marginal cost and the production possibility frontier?
◆ What conditions must be satisfied if resources are used efficiently? Why?

You now understand the limits to production and how to make efficient choices about what to produce. Now we are going to look at how production possibilities can be expanded through economic growth.

Economic Growth

Over the past 30 years, production in the European Union has expanded by 4 per cent per annum. This expansion in production is called **economic growth**. By the year 2010, if the same pace of growth continues, our production possibilities will be even greater. Does growth mean that we can avoid the constraints imposed on us by our limited resources? Can we avoid opportunity costs? The answer is no. As you will see, the faster production grows, the greater is the opportunity cost of economic growth.

The Cost of Economic Growth

The two factors influence economic growth: technological progress and capital accumulation. **Technological progress** is the development of new and better ways of producing goods and services and the development of new goods. **Capital accumulation** is the growth of capital resources.

As a consequence of technological progress and capital accumulation, we have an enormous quantity of cars and aircraft that enable us to transport more than when we had only horses and carriages; we have satellites that make transcontinental communications possible on a scale much larger than that produced by the earlier cable technology. But developing new technologies and accumulating capital involves a new opportunity cost. That opportunity cost is a decrease in the quantity of consumption goods and services because resources are used in research and development as well as to make new machines and other forms of capital. Let's look at this opportunity cost.

Instead of studying the *PPF* for magazines and CDs, we'll hold the quantity of magazines constant and look at the *PPF* for CDs and CD-making machines. Figure 2.5 shows this *PPF* as the blue curve *abc*. If we devote no resources to producing CD-making machines, we can produce 5,000 CDs a year at point *a*. If we devote one-fifth of our capacity to producing machines, we can produce 4 million CDs a year and 1 machine at point *b*. If we produce no CDs, we can produce 2 machines at point *c*.

The amount by which our production possibilities expand depends on how much of our resources we devote to technological change and capital accumulation. If we devote no resources to this activity, the *PPF* remains at *abc* – the original blue curve. If we cut current production of CDs and produce 1 CD making machine (point *b*), then the *PPF* moves out in the future to the position shown by the red curve in Figure 2.5. The fewer resources we devote to current production and the more resources we devote to producing machines, the greater is the expansion of our production possibilities.

But economic growth is not free. There are no free lunches. To achieve growth, we must devote more resources to producing new machines and less to current production. Economic growth is no magic formula for abolishing scarcity. Also, on the new production possibility frontier, we continue to face opportunity costs.

Figure 2.5
Economic Growth in a CD Factory

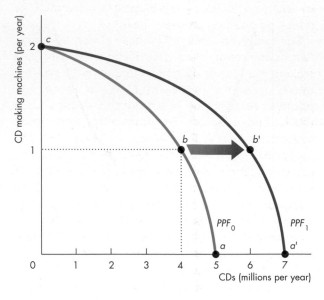

PPF_0 shows the limits to the production of CDs and CD-making machines, with the production of all other goods and services remaining constant. If we devote no resources to producing CD-making machines and produce 5,000 CDs a year, we remain stuck at point *a*. But if we decrease CD production to 4 million a year and produce 1 CD-making machine a year, at point *b*, our production possibilities will expand. After a year, the production possibility frontier shifts outward to PPF_1 and we can produce at point *b'*, a point outside the original *PPF*. We can shift the *PPF* outward, but we cannot avoid opportunity cost. The opportunity cost of producing more CDs in the future is fewer CDs today.

The ideas about economic growth that we have explored in this example also apply to nations. Let's see why.

Economic Growth of the European Union and Hong Kong

If as a nation we devote all our resources to producing food, clothing, housing, vacations and other consumer goods and none to research, development and the accumulation of capital, we will have no more capital and no better technologies in the future than we have at present. Our production possibilities in the future will be the same as today. To expand our production possibilities in the future, we must produce fewer consumption goods today. The resources that we free up today enable us to accumulate capital and to develop better technologies for producing consumption goods in the future. The decrease in the output of consumption goods today is the opportunity cost of economic growth and the attainment of more consumption goods in the future.

The experiences of the European Union and some East Asian economies, such as Hong Kong, provide a striking example of the effects of our choices on the rate of economic growth. In 1970, the production possibilities per person in the European Union (then the European Economic Community) were much larger than those in Hong Kong (see Figure 2.6). The European Union devoted one-fifth of its resources to accumulating capital and the other four-fifths to consumption. It was at point *a* on its *PPF*. But Hong Kong devoted more than one-third of its resources to accumulating capital and less than two-thirds to consumption. Hong Kong was at point *a* on its *PPF*. Both areas experienced economic growth, but growth in Hong Kong was much more rapid than in the European Union because Hong Kong devoted a bigger fraction of its resources to accumulating capital.

By 2000, the *PPF* per person in the European Union and in Hong Kong were similar. If Hong Kong continues to devote a similar proportion of its resources to accumulating capital (point *b* on the 2000 *PPF*), it will continue to grow more rapidly than the economies of the European Union. Its production possibility frontier could move out beyond that of the European Union. If Hong Kong increases its consumption and decreases its capital accumulation (moving to point *c* on its 2000 production possibility frontier), then its rate of economic expansion could slow down to a rate similar to that in Europe.

Hong Kong has been the fastest-growing East Asian economy, but others, such as Singapore, Taiwan, South Korea and recently China, have performed similarly to Hong Kong. These economies were closing the gap on the European Union until the collapse of East Asian currencies in 1998.

Review Quiz

◆ What are the two key factors that generate economic growth?
◆ How does economic growth influence the production possibility frontier?
◆ What is the opportunity cost of economic growth?
◆ Why has Hong Kong experienced faster economic growth than the European Union?

Figure 2.6

Economic Growth in the European Union and Hong Kong

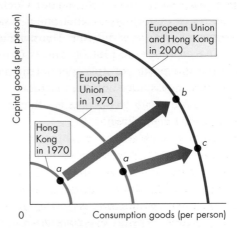

In 1970, the production possibilities per person in the European Union were much larger than those in Hong Kong. But Hong Kong devoted a larger share of its resources to accumulating capital than the European Union, so its production possibility frontier has shifted out more quickly than that of the European Union. By 2000, the two production possibilities per person had become similar.

Now we are going to look at how specialization and trade can help us expand the production possibilities of our economies.

Gains from Trade

People can produce for themselves all the goods that they consume or they can concentrate on producing one good (or perhaps a few goods) and then trade with others – exchange some of their own products for the products of others. Concentrating on the production of only one good or a few goods is called *specialization*. We are going to discover how people gain by specializing in the production of the good in which they have a *comparative advantage* and by trading with each other.

Comparative Advantage

A person has a **comparative advantage** in an activity if that person can perform the activity at a lower opportunity cost than anyone else. Differences in opportunity costs arise from differences in individual abilities and from differences in the characteristics of other resources.

No one excels at everything. One person is an outstanding sales person but a poor investor; another person is a brilliant lawyer but a poor teacher. In almost all human endeavours, what one person does easily, someone else finds difficult. The same applies to land and capital. One plot of land is fertile but has no mineral deposits; another plot of land has outstanding views but is infertile. One machine has great precision but is difficult to operate; another machine is fast but often breaks down.

Although no one excels at everything, some people excel and can outperform others in many activities. But such a person does not have a comparative advantage in every activity. For example, a UK chat show presenter, Clive Anderson, is a better lawyer than most people. But he is an even better humourous chat show host. His comparative advantage is in television. Differences in individual abilities and differences in the quality of other resources mean that there are differences in individual opportunity costs of producing various goods. Such differences give rise to comparative advantage.

We can explore the idea of comparative advantage using a production possibility frontier model of two CD factories, Galactic Sound and Ace CDs. Suppose that both factories can make either music CDs or film DVDs with their technology.

Galactic Sound's Factory

Galactic Sound's *PPF* for CDs and DVDs is shown in Figure 2.7(a). If all the resources are used to make CDs, output will be 5,000 CDs a day. The blue *PPF* curve in Figure 2.7(a) tells us that if all the resources are used to make DVDs, factory production will be 10,000 DVDs a day. But to produce DVDs, production of CDs must decrease. For each 1,000 DVDs, production of CDs must fall by 500.

The opportunity cost of producing 1 DVD at Galactic Sound is 0.5 CDs.

Similarly, if the owner of Galactic Sound wants to increase production of CDs, production of DVDs must fall. For each 1,000 CDs produced, production of DVDs must fall by 2,000.

The opportunity cost of producing 1 CD at Galactic Sound is 2 DVDs.

Ace CDs' Factory

Ace CDs' *PPF* for CDs and DVDs is shown in Figure 2.7(b). If Ace CDs uses all its resources to make DVDs, the factory produces 25,000 DVDs a day. If all the resources are used to make CDs, the factory produces 2,000 CDs a day. To produce CDs, of course, Ace CDs must decrease production of DVDs. For each 1,000 additional CDs produced, Ace CDs must reduce production of DVDs by 12,500.

The opportunity cost of producing 1 CD at Ace CDs is 12.5 DVDs.

Similarly, if Ace CDs want to increase production of DVDs, production of CDs must fall. For each 1,000 additional DVDs produced, production of CDs must fall by 80.

The opportunity cost of producing 1 DVD at Ace CDs is 0.08 CDs.

Comparative Advantage

Suppose that both factories decide to produce the same quantities of CDs and DVDs. That is, they each produce at point *a* on their respective *PPFs*. At this point each produces 1,400 CDs and 7,100 DVDs each day. Their total daily production is 2,800 CDs and 14,200 DVDs.

In which of the two goods does Ace CDs have a comparative advantage? Recall that comparative advantage is a situation in which one person's opportunity cost of producing a good is less than another person's opportunity cost of producing the same good. You can see the comparative advantage by looking at the production possibility frontiers for Ace CDs and Galactic Sound in Figure 2.7. Ace CDs' *PPF* is steeper than Galactic Sound's *PPF*. To produce one more DVD, Ace CDs gives up fewer CDs than Galactic Sound. Hence Ace CDs' opportunity cost of a DVD is less than Galactic Sound's. This means that Ace CDs has a comparative advantage in producing DVDs.

Notice the PPF for Galactic Sound is flatter than Ace CDs'. This means that Galactic Sound gives up fewer DVDs to produce one more CD than Ace CDs does. Galactic Sound's opportunity cost of producing CDs is less than Ace CDs', so Galactic Sound has a comparative advantage in producing CDs.

Achieving the Gains from Trade

If Galactic Sound, who have a comparative advantage in CD production, put all available resources into CD production, the factory can produce 5,000 CDs a day – point *b* on its *PPF*. If Ace CDs, who have a comparative advantage in DVD production, puts all available resources into DVD production, the factory can produce 25,000 DVDs a day – point *b* on its *PPF*. By specializing, Galactic Sound and Ace CDs together can produce a total of 5,000 CDs and 25,000 DVDs a day.

Figure 2.7

The Gains from Specialization and Trade

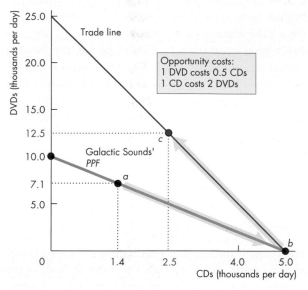

(a) Galactic Sounds' factory

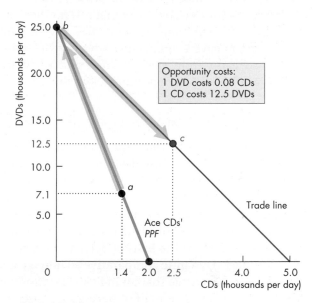

(b) Ace CDs' factory

Galactic Sound (part a) and Ace CDs (part b) each produce at point *a* on their respective *PPF*. For Galactic Sound, the opportunity cost of one CD is two DVDs and the opportunity cost of one DVD is 0.5 CDs. For Ace CDs the opportunity cost of one CD is 12.5 DVDs – higher than Galactic Sound's and the opportunity cost of one DVD is 0.08 CDs – lower than Galactic Sound's. Ace CDs has a comparative advantage in DVDs and Galactic Sound has a comparative advantage in CDs. If Ace CDs specializes in

DVDs and Galactic Sound specializes in CDs, they each produce at point *b* on their respective *PPF*. They then exchange DVDs for CDs along the red 'Trade line'. Ace CDs buys CDs from Galactic Sound for less than its opportunity cost of producing them, and Galactic Sound buys DVDs from Ace CDs for less than its opportunity cost of producing them. They each go to point *c* – a point outside their *PPF* – where a total of 5,000 CDs and 25,000 DVDs are produced per day.

To achieve the gains from specialization, both factories must trade with each other. Suppose they agree to the following deal. Each day, Ace CDs produces 25,000 DVDs and Galactic Sound produces 5,000 CDs. Ace CDs supplies Galactic Sound with 12,500 DVDs in exchange for 2,500 CDs each day. With this deal in place, Galactic Sound and Ace CDs move along the red 'Trade line' to point *c* in Figure 2.7. At this point, each has 12,500 DVDs and 2,500 CDs each day – an additional 1,100 CDs and an additional 5,400 DVDs. These are the gains from specialization and trade.

Both the parties to the trade share the gains. Galactic Sound, who can produce DVDs at an opportunity cost of 0.5 CDs, can buy DVDs more cheaply from Ace CDs at the lower price of 0.2 CDs (2.5 CDs/ 12.5 DVDs at point *c* on the trade line). Ace CDs, who can produce CDs at an opportunity cost of 12.5 DVDs, can buy CDs from Galactic Sound more cheaply at the lower price of 5 DVDs (12.5 DVDs/2.5CDs at point *c* on the trade line). By specialization and trade,

both factories get quantities of CDs and DVDs that are *outside* their individual *PPFs*.

Absolute Advantage

Suppose that Ace CDs invent and patent a production process that makes the factory four times as productive as before. With the new technology, Ace CDs can produce 100,000 DVDs a day (four times the original 25,000), if all available resources go into that activity. Alternatively, the factory can produce 8,000 CDs a day (four times the original 2,000), if all the resources go into that activity. Ace CDs now has an **absolute advantage** in producing both goods – Ace CDs can produce more of both goods than the other factory.

Ace CDs does not have a comparative advantage in both goods. The factory can produce four times as much of both goods as before, but the opportunity cost of producing one CD is still 12.5 DVDs. The opportunity cost of CDs is still higher than Galactic Sound's. So Ace CDs can still get CDs at a lower cost by trading DVDs for CDs with the other factory.

The key point to recognize is that it is not possible for anyone, even someone who has an absolute advantage, to have a comparative advantage in everything. So gains from specialization and trade are always available when opportunity costs differ.

Dynamic Comparative Advantage

At any given point in time, the resources available and the technologies in use determine the comparative advantages that individuals and countries have. But just by repeatedly producing a particular good or service, people can become more productive in that activity, a phenomenon called learning-by-doing. Learning-by-doing is the basis of dynamic comparative advantage. **Dynamic comparative advantage** is a comparative advantage that an individual (factory or country) possesses as a result of having specialized in a particular activity and, through learning-by-doing, gained the lowest opportunity cost.

Finland is an example of a country that has pursued dynamic comparative advantage vigorously. They have developed high technology telecommunications industries in which initially they might not have had a comparative advantage and, through learning-by-doing, have become low opportunity cost producers of high-technology products. Another recent example is the decision of Singapore to develop a genetic engineering industry. It is not clear that Singapore has a comparative advantage in this activity at present, but it might acquire one as its scientists and production workers become more skilled in this area.

Review Quiz

- What gives a person a comparative advantage in producing a good?
- Why is it not possible for anyone to have a comparative advantage at everything?
- What are the gains from specialization and trade?
- Explain the source of the gains from specialization and trade.
- Distinguish between comparative advantage and absolute advantage.
- What is dynamic comparative advantage and how does it arise?

The Market Economy

Individuals and countries can gain by specializing in the production of those goods and services in which they have a comparative advantage. But to reap the gains from trade from billions of people specializing in millions of different activities, trade must be organized. Buyers and sellers need information and they face opportunity costs for the time taken in the trading activity. Trade could be organized and managed through a central authority as it has been in the past in Russia and China. But most countries have now adopted a market economy for organizing trade. Let's see why.

Transactions Costs

The costs of trading and negotiating are called **transactions costs**. These include the costs of finding the buyers and sellers you want to trade with, finding information about the quantity and quality of goods and services for trade, organizing production and distribution, and negotiating prices, amongst many other things. Organizing trade through social institutions is the main way of reducing transactions costs. The most important of these social institutions are:

- Markets.
- Property rights.

Markets

A *market* is any arrangement that enables buyers and sellers to get information and to do business with each other. **Markets** can be physical locations, such as a wholesale meat or fish market. But most markets are networks in which people trade by telephone, fax or computer link. For example, modern stock exchanges are computerized markets for company shares. All markets share a common feature. They bring producers and consumers of goods and services together, helping to reduce the transactions costs of buying and selling.

In our earlier example, the two CD factories agreed to exchange goods in a barter system of exchange. This exchange method can be low cost when there are very few buyers and sellers and very few goods. But with many goods and many traders, the transactions costs of finding and agreeing exchanges are high. In a market economy, the two factories in our example would buy and sell their CDs and DVDs to

Figure 2.8

Circular Flows in the Market Economy

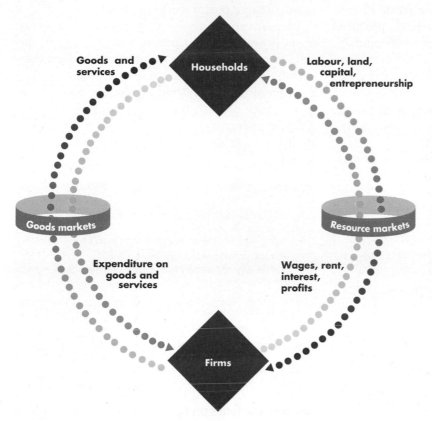

Households and firms make economic choices. Households choose the quantities of labour, land, capital and entrepreneurship to sell or rent to firms in exchange for wages, rent, interest and profits. Households also choose how to spend their incomes on the various types of goods and services available. Firms choose the quantities of resources to hire and the quantities of the various goods and services to produce. Goods markets and resource markets coordinate these choices of households and firms. Resources and goods flow clockwise (red), and money payments flow counterclockwise (green).

each other through dealers. They might not even be aware that the other factory exists.

Property Rights

Property rights are social arrangements that govern the ownership, use and disposal of property – our resources, goods and services. Property rights are protected by laws. *Real property* includes land and buildings, and durable goods such as plant and equipment. *Financial property* includes stocks and bonds and money in the bank. *Intellectual property* is the intangible product of creative effort. This type of property includes books, music, computer programs and inventions of all kinds, and it is protected by copyright and patent laws.

If property rights are not enforced, the incentive to specialize and produce the goods in which each person has a comparative advantage is weakened. Some of the gains from specialization and trade are lost. If people can easily steal other people's property, then

time and resources which could be used for production will be wasted on protecting property, raising transactions costs.

Establishing property rights is one of the greatest challenges facing Russia and other Central European countries as they seek to develop market economies. Even in European Union countries, where property rights are well established in law, upholding intellectual property rights is still proving a challenge. Modern technologies make it relatively easy to pirate music and video material, computer programs and books.

Circular Flow in the Market Economy

Figure 2.8 identifies two types of markets: goods markets and resource markets. *Goods markets* are those in which goods and services are bought and sold. *Resource markets* are those in which resources for production – factors of production – are bought and sold.

Households decide how much of their labour, land, capital and entrepreneurship to sell in resource markets. They receive incomes in the form of wages, rent, interest and profit. Households also decide how to spend their incomes on goods and services produced by firms. Firms sell their output in goods markets. They decide the quantities of resources to hire, how to use them to produce goods and services, what goods and services to produce, and in what quantities.

Figure 2.8 shows the flows resulting from the decisions by households and firms. The red flows are the factors of production that go from households to firms and the goods and services that go from firms to households. The green flows in the opposite direction are the money payments made in exchange for these items. So how do markets coordinate all these decisions?

Coordinating Decisions

Markets coordinate individual decisions through price adjustments. To see how, think about your local market for fresh baked bread. Suppose that some people who want to buy fresh baked bread are not able to do so. To make the choices of buyers and sellers compatible, buyers must scale down their appetites or more fresh baked bread must be offered for sale (or both must happen). A rise in the price of fresh baked bread produces this outcome. A higher price encourages local bakers to produce more bread for sale. It

also encourages some people to change their eating plans. Fewer people buy fresh baked bread, and more buy packaged bread. More fresh baked bread (and more packaged bread) is offered for sale.

Alternatively, suppose that more fresh baked bread is available than people want to buy. In this case, to make the choices of buyers and sellers compatible, more fresh bread must be bought or less fresh bread must be offered for sale (or both). A fall in the price of fresh bread achieves this outcome. A lower price encourages bakers to produce fewer fresh loaves. It also encourages people to buy more fresh bread.

Review Quiz

◆ Why are social arrangements such as markets and property rights necessary?
◆ What are the main functions of markets?

You have now begun to see how economists go about the job of trying to answer economic questions. Scarcity, choice and opportunity costs explain why we specialize and trade and why markets and property rights have developed. You can see evidence of these fundamental ideas all around you. Reading Between the Lines on pp. 38–39 gives an example. It explores the opportunity costs of the choices facing school leavers.

Summary

Key Points

Resources and Wants (p. 21)

- Economic activity arises from scarcity because of limited resources and unlimited wants.
- Our limited resources are labour, land, capital (including human capital) and entrepreneurship.
- The economic problem is how to use our limited resources to produce the best combination of resources.

Resources, Production Possibilities and Opportunity Cost (pp. 22–24)

- The production possibility frontier, *PPF*, is the boundary between attainable and unattainable production.

- Production is efficiency occurs at points on the *PPF*.
- The opportunity cost of producing more of one good is the amount of the other good that must be given up to produce it.
- The opportunity cost of a good increases along the *PPF* as production of the good increases.

Efficient Choice (pp. 24–27)

- The marginal cost of a good is the opportunity cost of producing one more unit.
- The marginal benefit of a good is the maximum someone is willing to pay to get one more unit, measured in terms of the quantity of another good forgone.
- The marginal cost increases and the marginal benefit decreases as the amount of the good increases.

- Efficent choice occurs when resources are used efficiently, where marginal benefit equals marginal cost.

Economic Growth (pp. 27–29)

- Economic growth is the expansion of production possibilities.

- Economic growth results from capital accumulation and technological change.

- The opportunity cost of economic growth is foregone current consumption.

Gains from Trade (pp. 29–32)

- A person has a comparative advantage in producing a good if that person can produce the good at a lower opportunity cost than everyone else.

- People gain by specializing in the activity at which they have a comparative advantage and by trading with others.

- Comparative advantage changes over time and dynamic comparative advantage arises from learning-by-doing.

The Market Economy (pp. 32–34)

- Property rights, markets and money reduce transactions costs and enable people to gain from specialization and trade.

- Markets coordinate decisions and help to allocate resources efficiently – to their most valued use.

Key Figures ◆

Key Terms

Problems

•1 Use the figure to calculate Peter's opportunity cost of an hour of tennis when he increases the time he plays tennis from:

   a 4 to 6 hours a week.

   b 6 to 8 hours a week.

2 Use the figure to calculate Mary's opportunity cost of an hour of skating when she increases her time spent skating from:

   a 2 to 4 hours a week.

   b 4 to 6 hours a week.

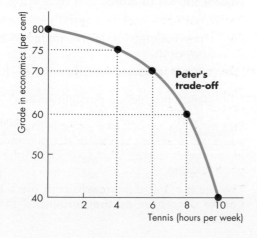

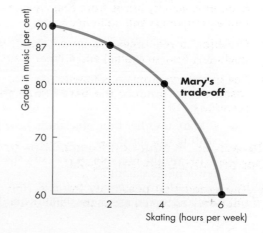

•**3** In problem 1, describe the relationship between the time Peter spends playing tennis and the opportunity cost of an hour of tennis.

4 In problem 2, describe the relationship between the time Mary spends skating and the opportunity cost of an hour of skating.

•**5** Peter, in problem 1, has the following marginal benefit curve:

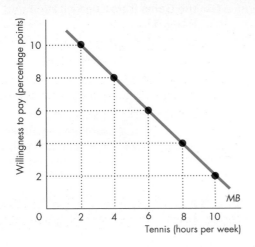

a If Peter uses his time efficiently, what grade will he get?

b Why would Peter be worse off getting a higher grade?

6 Mary, in problem 2, has the following marginal benefit curve:

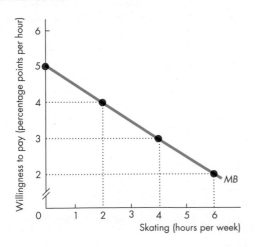

a If Mary uses her time efficiently, how much skating will she do?

b Why would Mary be worse off spending fewer hours skating?

•**7** Leisureland's production possibilities are:

Food (kilograms per month)		Sunscreen (litres per month)
300	and	0
200	and	50
100	and	100
0	and	150

a Draw a graph of Leisureland's production possibility frontier.

b What are Leisureland's opportunity costs of producing food and sunscreen at each output in the table?

8 Jane's Island's production possibilities are:

Corn (kilograms per month)		Cloth (metres per month)
3	and	0
2	and	2
1	and	4
0	and	6

a Draw a graph of the *PPF* on Jane's Island.

b What are Jane's opportunity costs of producing corn and cloth at each output in the table?

•**9** In problem 7, to get a litre of sunscreen people are willing to give up 5 kilograms of food if they have 25 litres of sunscreen; 2 kilograms of food if they have 75 litres of sunscreen; and 1 kilogram of food if they have 125 litres of sunscreen.

a Draw a graph of Leisureland's marginal benefit from sunscreen.

b What is Leisureland's efficient use of sunscreen?

10 In problem 8, to get a metre of cloth Jane is willing to give up 0.75 kilograms of corn if she has 2 metres of cloth; 0.50 kilograms of corn if she has 4 metres of cloth; and 0.25 kilograms of corn if she has 6 metres of cloth.

a Draw a graph of Jane's marginal benefit from cloth.

b What is Jane's efficient quantity of cloth?

•**11** Busyland's production possibilities are:

Food (kilograms per month)		Sunscreen (litres per month)
150	and	0
100	and	100
50	and	200
0	and	300

Calculate Busyland's opportunity costs of food and sunscreen at each output in the table.

12 Joe's production possibilities are:

Corn (kilograms per month)		Cloth (metres per month)
6	and	0
4	and	1
2	and	2
0	and	3

What are Joe's opportunity costs of producing corn and cloth at each output in the table?

•13 In problems 7 and 11, Leisureland and Busyland each produce and consume 100 kilograms of food and 100 litres of sunscreen per month; and they do not trade. Now the countries begin to trade with each other.

a What good does Leisureland sell to Busyland and what good does it buy from Busyland?

b If Leisureland and Busyland divide the total output of food and sunscreen equally, what are the gains from trade?

14 In problems 8 and 12, Jane's Island produces and consumes 1 kilogram of corn and 4 metres of cloth. Joe's Island produces and consumes 4 kilograms of corn and 1 metre of cloth. Now the islands begin to trade.

a What good does Jane sell to Joe and what good does Jane buy from Joe?

b If Jane and Joe divide the total output of corn and cloth equally, what are the gains from trade?

Critical Thinking

1 After you have studied Reading Between the Lines on pp. 38–39, answer the following questions:

a Why is the *PPF* for education goods and services and consumption goods and services bowed outward?

b At what point on the blue *PPF* in Figure 1 on p. 39, is the combination of education goods and services and consumption goods and services efficient?

c Students are facing rising tuition fees. Does this make the opportunity cost of education increase, decrease, or remain unchanged?

2 Use the links on the Parkin, Powell and Matthews website to read about the costs to working mothers and the female poverty trap. Why are the opportunity costs to working mothers falling over time, and why are the opportunity costs lower for highly educated women?

3 Use the links on the Parkin, Powell and Matthews website to visit the European Union's web pages and look up the aims of the Single Market and Enlargement proposals. Why does the European Union want to remove the remaining barriers to trade within the Union? What are the benefits of increased trade to countries like Finland that have specialized production (Finland has specialized in communication technologies)? What kind of trade benefits can be gained from enlarging the European Union to include new member states? Do you think any benefits derived from increased trade will be equally distributed between the member states?

Opportunity Cost: A Student's Choice

THE EVENING STANDARD, 16 JULY 2001

Young high-flyers who put college before work

. . . This year's crop of 16–18 year-old pupils has just finished exams, but a selection of school leavers quizzed at two London comprehensives showed little desire to launch themselves into the workplace . . .

Out of two groups of 15 and 16 year-old pupils polled at Acland Burghley School in Tufnell Park and Mill Hill County High School, all said they would be returning to study A-levels . . .

Going out and earning a living may have been attractive financially, but the consensus was that staying in education would offer a greater chance of finding better-paid and more interesting jobs . . .

Despite mounting levels of debt facing university graduates, school leavers from both Acland Burghley and Mill Hill High all intended to enter higher education . . .

None had considered entering the workplace at 18, considering that another three or four years' study would pay dividends.

'I've got friends who left school at 16 to work, . . .' said Josh Mbaka, 19 from Acland Burghley. 'They're not taking a long-term view of what they want to do. I think you need to get a degree because so many other people have got them – if you haven't, then you'll go to the bottom of the pile.'

Nationally, one in three school leavers goes into higher education by the age of 21. According to the Association of Graduate Recruiters, the median entry-level salary for graduates for the year ending September 2001 was £19,000. But for those who choose to leave school before then, . . . how much can they earn? A snap survey of some of Britain's biggest employers revealed the following: BT, the telecoms multinational recruits applicants from age 16 . . . Typical starting salaries range from £9,000. The M&S Young Manager Training Scheme takes a number of 18 year-olds with A-levels or HNDs each year, . . . Salaries range from £14,650 depending on location. NatWest and Royal Bank of Scotland . . . recruit school-leavers between the ages of 16 and 18 . . . Salaries start between £14,000 and £15,000.

The Essence of the Story

■ A university education offers a greater chance of finding a higher paid and more interesting job.

■ University graduates face mounting levels of debt.

■ A university graduate can expect to earn a higher salary than a 16–18 year-old school leaver.

Economic Analysis

- The opportunity cost of education is forgone consumption. The payoff is an increase in lifetime production possibilities and in future consumption possibilities.

- Figure 1 shows the choices facing a school leaver. This person can consume any combination of educational goods and services on the blue production possibility frontier.

- If the school leaver decides not to attend university, then she could be at point *a* on the blue *PPF* in Figure 1.

- Working full time, the school leaver has an income of £14,000 a year and remains on the blue *PPF* curve in Figure 1.

- By attending university, the student incurs an opportunity cost. She moves from point *a* to point *b* along her *PPF*, forgoes current consumption, and increases the use of educational goods and services to £10,000.

- A graduate with a bachelor degree can earn £19,000 working full time. With a bachelor's degree, the production possibilities expand to the red *PPF* in Figure 1.

- The blue curve in Figure 2 is the same *PPF* as the red in Figure 1. It is the university student's *PPF* following completion of her bachelor's degree.

- After graduation, a university student can quit education with consumption at £19,000 a year, or choose to spend more resources on gaining a Master's degree.

- But to gain a Master's degree, our student must incur another opportunity cost. She must decrease her consumption of goods and services to consume education goods and services, moving around the blue *PPF* from point *c* to point *d*.

- Having completed a master's degree, the student expands her production possibilities further.

- The red *PPF* in Figure 2 shows the expanded possibilities for the student with a master's degree. She can consume at any point on the red *PPF*.

- The greater the resources devoted to education, the greater are future consumption possibilities. By obtaining a degree, the student incurs a cost but she also reaps a large return.

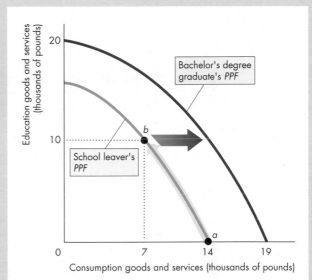

Figure 1 School leaver's choices

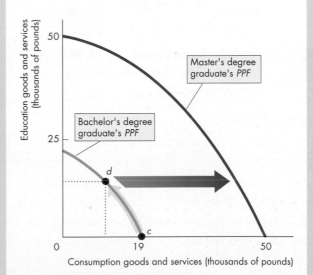

Figure 2 University graduate's choices

Understanding the Sources of Economic Wealth

It is not from the benevolence of the butcher, the brewer, or the baker that we expect our dinner, but from their regard to their own interest.

Adam Smith, The Wealth of Nations

The Father of Economics: Adam Smith

Adam Smith was a giant of a scholar who contributed to ethics and jurisprudence as well as economics. Born in 1723 in Kirkcaldy, a small fishing town near Edinburgh, Scotland, Smith was the only child of the town's customs officer (who died before Adam was born).

His first academic appointment, at age 28, was as Professor of Logic at the University of Glasgow. He subsequently became tutor to a wealthy Scottish duke, whom he accompanied on a two-year grand European tour, following which he received a pension of £300 a year – ten times the average income at that time.

With the financial security of his pension, Smith devoted ten years to writing *An Inquiry into the Nature and Causes of the Wealth of Nations*, which was published in 1776. Many people had written on economic issues before Adam Smith, but he made economics a science. Smith's account was so broad and authoritative that no subsequent writer on economics could advance ideas without tracing their connections to those of Adam Smith.

The Issues and Ideas

Why are some nations wealthy while others are poor? This question lies at the heart of economics. And it leads directly to a second question: what can poor nations do to become wealthy?

Adam Smith, who is regarded by many scholars as the founder of economics, attempted to answer these questions in his book *The Wealth of Nations*, published in 1776. Smith was pondering these questions at the height of the Industrial Revolution. During these years, new technologies were invented and applied to the manufacture of cotton and wool cloth, iron, transportation and agriculture.

Smith wanted to understand the sources of economic wealth and he brought his acute powers of observation and abstraction to bear on the question. His answer was:

- The division of labour.
- Free markets.

The division of labour – breaking work down into simple tasks and becoming skilled in those tasks – is the source of 'the greatest improvement in the productive powers of labour', said Smith. The division of labour became even more productive when it was applied to creating new technologies. Scientists and engineers, trained in extremely narrow fields, became specialists at inventing. Their powerful skills accelerated the advance of technology, so by the 1820s, machines could make consumer goods faster and more accurately than any craftsman could. By the 1850s, machines could make other machines that labour alone could never have made.

But, said Smith, the fruits of the division of labour are limited by the extent of the market. To make the market as large as possible, there must be no impediments to free trade both within a country and among countries. Smith argued that when each person makes the best possible economic choice, that choice leads as if by 'an invisible hand' to the best outcome for society as a whole. The butcher, the brewer and the baker each pursue their own interests but, in doing so, also serve the interests of everyone else.

Then . . .

Adam Smith speculated that one person, working hard, using the hand tools available in the 1770s, might possibly make 20 pins a day. Yet, he observed, by using those same hand tools but breaking the process into a number of individually small operations in which people specialize – by the division of labour – ten people could make a staggering 48,000 pins a day. One draws out the wire, another straightens it, a third cuts it, a fourth points it, a fifth grinds it. Three specialists make the head, and a fourth attaches it. Finally, the pin is polished and packaged. But a large market is needed to support the division of labour: one factory employing ten workers would need to sell more than 15 million pins a year to stay in business.

. . . And Now

If Adam Smith were here today, he would be fascinated by the computer chip. He would see it as an extraordinary example of the productivity of the division of labour and of the use of machines to make machines that make other machines. From a design of a chip's intricate circuits, cameras transfer an image to glass plates that work like stencils. Workers prepare silicon wafers on which the circuits are printed. Some slice the wafers, others polish them, others bake them, and yet others coat them with a light-sensitive chemical. Machines transfer a copy of the circuit onto the wafer. Chemicals then etch the design onto the wafer. Further processes deposit atom-sized transistors and aluminium connectors. Finally, a laser separates the hundreds of chips on the wafer. Every stage in the process of creating a computer chip uses other computer chips. And like the pin of the 1770s, the computer chip of the 1990s benefits from a large market – a global market – to buy chips in the huge quantities in which they are produced efficiently.

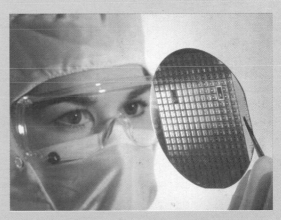

Testing These Ideas Today

Using what you have learned in Chapter 2 about growth and trade, and what you know about Adam Smith's ideas, you should be able to answer the following questions:

■ How does automation and robotics affect the division of labour in a modern car factory?

■ How will the introduction of automation and robotics affect the growth of global car markets today?

Part 2

How Markets Work

Talking with **Sheila Dow**

Sheila Dow holds a Personal Chair in Economics at the University of Stirling, where she has taught since 1979. She previously worked as an economist for the Bank of England and for the Government of Manitoba, Canada, and has had visiting posts with the Universities of Cambridge and Toronto. Her research interests lie in money and banking theory, methodology, history of thought, regional finance and post-Keynesian economics.

Why did you specialize in economics?

Mainly because I found economics interesting. It appealed to me to try to understand how economic systems work, at different times in history and in different types of economies. And it is interesting to try to understand why particular theories emerge and others disappear. It will reveal how long ago I started to learn economics when I say that I found it a nice contrast to my other subject, pure mathematics.

I then worked for several years as a non-academic economist in the public sector. It became obvious that there are many important policy areas to which economists can make important contributions, like the design of the international financial system, or innovations in taxation. Regardless of how economists approach issues, they can contribute important insights which make policy-making more effective. It is amazing how much mileage can be made with basic concepts.

One such concept is opportunity cost, which is useful for government departments, for example, in allocating their budgets between alternative expenditures. But the concept is subject to limitations. Where there are unemployed resources, increasing one economic activity does not necessarily mean having to reduce another. The margin is another useful concept, which allows important distinctions to be drawn, such as between marginal and average tax rates. The concept is a central one for mainstream economic theory, but has limitations in its applicability to policy questions. Changes in a firm's capital stock, for example, are generally discrete (irreversible) shifts from a limited range of possibilities, rather than marginal (reversible) movements along a continuous, infinite array of possibilities.

What are the main principles which distinguish different perspectives on the role of markets and how they work?

In mainstream economics, markets are the centrepiece of economic analysis. They are the vehicle through which individual preferences are satisfied, given factor endowments and technology. In the process they allocate resources and determine the distribution of income. The participants in markets are isolated, rational individuals. The benchmark of analysis is the position of equilibrium in which markets clear. The norm is to assume perfect competition, but there is an expanding area of work in which the implications of imperfect competition are explored.

Other (neo-Austrian) economists share the focus on market activity, but analyse markets as a process, where flux rather than equilibrium is the norm. Others, such as post-Keynesian and Institutionalist economists, prefer to put the emphasis more on production and distribution than exchange, and to see markets in terms of social interaction rather than isolated individuals, with imperfectly competitive markets the norm. One consequence is that supply and demand are seen as interdependent, with production conditions influencing marketing effort and thereby demand, for example. The emphasis then is put more on how supply and demand conditions evolve over time, as a process, rather than on equilibrium outcomes of market clearing.

Within each of these approaches there are different views as to how far markets are socially beneficial, and therefore whether government intervention is required. But as a generalization, it is probably more common for mainstream and neo-Austrian economists to support *laissez-faire* policies, and for post-Keynesian and Institutionalist economists to support intervention.

Are there any basic principles on which most economists agree?

This is a hard question. Whenever I think of a possible shared principle I immediately picture some particular economist raising objections. What precludes shared principles is the absence of a shared theoretical framework.

This is not something to regret; it is inevitable when abstracting from a complex reality that some will choose one form of abstraction and some another. I don't mean just that different economists make different assumptions, but that different groups of economists use terms and concepts quite differently, so that a principle expressed by one economist might convey something quite different to another economist. 'Equilibrium', for example, means something quite different in a model where everything happens at once, compared with a model analysing a process which occurs over time, and which cannot be reversed.

What is the link between microeconomics and macroeconomics?

The link is an obvious one, that the macroeconomy is made up of individual markets, firms and households. There has been an increasing tendency to make sure that theory encapsulates that link by requiring that macroeconomics be built on explicit micro foundations. But economic systems are extraordinarily complex. There is therefore a trade-off between choosing to separate macroeconomics and microeconomics, and accepting the limitations of a theory which extends from assumptions about individuals to the economy as a whole. The main problem to grapple with is that, traditionally, microeconomics dealt with market clearing whereas macroeconomics dealt with markets (particularly the labour market) not clearing. The link is much easier for those whose microeconomics does not require market clearing.

Are there any lessons from the history and development of Western European economies from which Eastern Europe can learn?

The main lesson is that, whether or not market processes are preferable to state planning, institutions and conventions are the glue which holds market economies together in an uncertain world. These are not easy to generate quickly. Nor are there universal truths about which institutions and which conventions will work; so much depends on the economy's prior history.

What do you think are the most important economic problems facing the world today?

The most important problems are undoubtedly distributional, from the problems of the impoverished, unemployed underclass in Western economies to the plight of persistent low-income countries.

CHAPTER 3

Demand and Supply

After studying this chapter you will be able to:

◆ Distinguish between a money price and a real price

◆ Explain the main influences on demand

◆ Explain the main influences on supply

◆ Explain how prices are determined by demand and supply

◆ Explain how quantities bought and sold are determined

◆ Explain why some prices fall, some rise and some fluctuate

◆ Make predictions about price changes using demand and supply

Slide, Rocket and Roller-coaster

Slide, rocket and roller-coaster – are these EuroDisney rides? No. They're commonly used descriptions of the behaviour of prices. CD players have taken a price slide. In 1983, when they first became available, their price tag was around £1,000. Now you can buy one for less than £100, and during the time that CD players have been with us, the quantity bought has increased steadily. Why has there been a slide in the price of CD players? Why hasn't the increase in the quantity bought kept their price high? ◆ The prices of houses rocketed in the 1980s and now the price of platinum is rocketing. Despite rising prices, why do people continue to buy these increasingly expensive goods? ◆ The prices of apples, corn, coffee, wheat and other agricultural commodities are examples of roller-coasters. Why does the price of apples roller-coaster even when people's taste for them hardly changes at all? ◆ The prices of many of the things we buy can remain remarkably steady. The price of cassette tapes is an example. Until recently, despite their steady price, the number of tapes bought increased each year. Why did firms sell more tapes even though they were unable to get higher prices for them, and why did people buy more tapes even though the price of tapes was no lower than it was a decade ago? ◆ The model that explains how markets work is demand and supply. When you have studied demand and supply, you will be able to answer all these questions. You will be able to explain how prices reflect opportunity cost, and how prices help people to cope with scarcity. You will understand how markets determine prices and quantities.

◆ ◆ ◆ ◆ You should study this chapter very carefully. When you understand demand and supply you will see the world through new eyes, and you will be able to make predictions about price rockets, slides and roller-coasters. But first, we must take a closer look at the concept of price. What is a price?

Price and Opportunity Cost

Economic actions arise from scarcity – wants exceed the resources available to satisfy them. Faced with scarcity, people confront opportunity cost and must make choices. Choices are influenced by opportunity costs. If the opportunity cost of a good or service increases, people look for cheaper substitutes and decrease their purchases of the more expensive item.

We are going to build on these fundamental ideas and create a model to help us study both the way people respond to prices and the forces that determine prices. To do this, we need to understand the relationship between opportunity cost and price.

In everyday life, the *price* of a good is the number of euros or pounds that we must give up to buy the good. This is called the *money price*.

The opportunity cost of an action is the best alternative forgone. When you buy a cup of coffee, you forgo something. If the best thing forgone is some biscuits, then the opportunity cost of buying a cup of coffee is a quantity of biscuits forgone. We can calculate this quantity from the money prices of coffee and biscuits.

If the money price of coffee is 50 pence a cup and the money price of biscuits is 25 pence a packet, then the opportunity cost of one cup of coffee is two packets of biscuits. To calculate this opportunity cost, we divide the price of a cup of coffee by the price of a packet of biscuits and find the *ratio* of one price to the other. The ratio of one price to another is called a **relative price** and a relative price is an opportunity cost.

We can express the relative price of coffee in terms of biscuits or any other good. The normal way of expressing a relative price is in terms of a 'basket' of typical goods and services. To calculate this relative price we divide the money price of a good by the price of the 'basket' of goods (called a *price index*). The resulting relative price is called a **real price**. A real price tells us the opportunity cost of an item in terms of how much the 'basket' we must give up to buy it.

Figure 3.1 shows the money price and the real price of wheat. The money price (green) has fluctuated but has tended to rise. The real price (red) shows the price of wheat measured in 1994 pounds, and shows a falling trend.

The theory of demand and supply that we are about to study determines real prices, and the word 'price' means real (relative) price. When we predict

that a price will fall, we do not mean that its money price will fall – although it might. We mean that its real price will fall. That is, its price will fall *relative* to the average price of other goods and services.

Figure 3.1

The Money Price and the Real Price of Wheat

The money price of wheat – the number of pounds that must be given up for a tonne of wheat – has fluctuated between £132 and £95 a tonne. But the real price or opportunity cost of wheat, expressed in 1998 pounds, has fluctuated between £190 and £110. The money price of wheat has tended to rise, but the real price of wheat has tended to fall, a fact obscured by the behaviour of its money price.

Source: Annual Abstract of Statisitcs.

Review Quiz

◆ Explain the distinction between a money price and a real price.
◆ Why is a real price an opportunity cost?
◆ Can you think of an example of a good whose money price and real price have risen?
◆ Can you think of an example of a good whose money price and real price have fallen?

Let's now begin our study of demand and supply, starting with demand.

Demand

To demand something, you must:

◆ Want it.

◆ Be able to afford it.

◆ Have a definite plan to buy it.

Wants are the unlimited desires or wishes that people have for goods and services. How many times have you thought that you would like something 'if only you could afford it' or 'if it weren't so expensive'? When we make choices, scarcity guarantees that many – perhaps most – of our wants will never be satisfied. Demand reflects our plans about which wants to satisfy.

The **quantity demanded** is not necessarily the same amount as the quantity actually bought. Sometimes the quantity demanded is greater than the amount of goods available, so the quantity bought is less than the quantity demanded.

The quantity demanded is measured as an amount per unit of time. For example, suppose a person consumes one cup of coffee a day. The quantity of coffee demanded by that person can be expressed as 1 cup per day or 7 cups per week or 365 cups per year. Without a time dimension, we cannot tell whether a particular quantity demanded is large or small.

What Determines Buying Plans?

The amount of any particular good or service that consumers plan to buy depends on many factors. The main ones are:

◆ The price of the good.

◆ The prices of related goods.

◆ Income.

◆ Expected future prices.

◆ Population.

◆ Preferences.

Let's start by modelling the relationship between the quantity demanded and the price of a good. To study this relationship, we hold constant all other influences on consumers' planned purchases. We can then ask: how does the quantity demanded of the good vary as its price varies?

The Law of Demand

The law of demand states:

Other things remaining the same, the higher the price of a good, the smaller is the quantity demanded.

Why does a higher price reduce the quantity demanded? There are two reasons;

◆ Substitution effect.

◆ Income effect.

Substitution Effect

When the price of a good rises, other things remaining the same, its price rises relative to the prices of all other goods. Equivalently, its opportunity cost increases. Although each good is unique, it has substitutes – other goods that serve almost as well. As the opportunity cost of a good increases, relative to the opportunity costs of its substitutes, people buy less of that good and more of its substitutes.

Income Effect

When the price of a good rises, other things remaining the same, the price rises relative to people's incomes. Faced with a higher price and an unchanged income, the quantities demanded of at least some goods and services must decrease. Normally the good whose price has increased will be one of the goods bought in a smaller quantity.

To see the substitution effect and the income effect at work, think about blank cassette tapes, which we'll refer to as tapes. Many different goods provide a similar service to a tape; for example, a compact disc (CD), a mini disc, a radio or television broadcast and a live concert. Suppose tapes sell for about 90 pence each. If the price of a tape doubles to £1.80 while the prices of all the other goods remain constant, the quantity of tapes demanded decreases. People substitute CDs and prerecorded tapes for blank tapes – the substitution effect. Faced with a tighter budget, people buy fewer tapes as well as less of other goods and services. If the price of a tape falls to 60 pence while the prices of all the other goods remain constant, the quantity of tapes demanded increases. People now substitute blank tapes for CDs and prerecorded tapes – the income effect. With a budget that has some slack from the lower price of tapes, people buy more tapes as well as more of other goods and services.

Demand Curve and Demand Schedule

You are now going to study the demand curve, one of two parts of the most important model in economics.

Figure 3.2

The Demand Curve

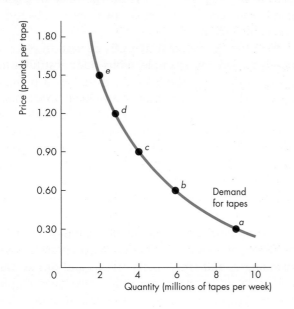

	Price (pounds per tape)	Quantity (millions of tapes per week)
a	0.30	9
b	0.60	6
c	0.90	4
d	1.20	3
e	1.50	2

The table shows a demand schedule listing the quantity of tapes demanded at each price if all other influences on buyers' plans remain the same. At a price of 30 pence a tape, 9 million tapes a week are demanded; at a price of 90 pence a tape, 4 million tapes a week are demanded. The demand curve shows the relationship between quantity demanded and price, everything else remaining the same. The demand curve slopes downward: as price decreases, the quantity demanded increases. The demand curve can be read in two ways. For a given price it tells us the quantity that people plan to buy. For example, at a price of 90 pence a tape, the quantity demanded is 4 million tapes a week. For a given quantity, the demand curve tells us the maximum price that consumers are willing to pay for the last tape bought. For example, the maximum price that consumers will pay for the 6 millionth tape is 60 pence.

Before going any further, you need to understand a critical distinction between *demand* and *quantity demanded*.

The term **demand** refers to the entire relationship between the quantity demanded and the price of a good, illustrated by the demand curve and the demand schedule. The term *quantity demanded* refers to the exact quantity demanded at a particular price, or a particular point on a demand curve.

Figure 3.2 shows the demand curve for music tapes. A **demand curve** shows the relationship between the quantity demanded of a good and its price, when all other influences on consumers' planned purchases remain the same. The table in Figure 3.2 is the demand schedule for tapes. A *demand schedule* lists the *quantities demanded* at each different price, when all the other influences on consumers' planned purchases – such as the prices of related goods, income, expected future prices, population and preferences – remain the same. For example, if the price of a tape is 30 pence, the quantity demanded is 9 million tapes a week. If the price of a tape is £1.50, the quantity demanded is 2 million tapes a week. The other rows of the table show us the quantities demanded at prices between 60 pence and £1.20.

The demand curve is a graph of the demand schedule with quantity demanded on the horizontal axis and price on the vertical axis. The points on the demand curve labelled *a* through to *e* are plotted from the rows of the demand schedule.

Willingness and Ability to Pay

Another way of looking at the demand curve is as a willingness-and-ability-to-pay curve that measures marginal benefit. It tells us the highest price that someone is willing and able to pay for the last unit bought. If a small quantity is available, the highest price that someone is willing and able to pay for one more unit is high. But as the quantity available increases, the marginal benefit of each additional unit falls and the highest price offered falls along the demand curve.

In Figure 3.2, if 9 million tapes are bought each week, the highest price that someone is willing to pay for the 9 millionth tape is 30 pence. But if only 2 million tapes are bought each week, someone is willing to pay £1.50 for the last tape bought.

A Change in Demand

When any factor that influences buying plans changes, other than the price of the good, there is a change in demand. Figure 3.3 illustrates one such change – an increase in demand. When demand increases, the demand curve shifts to the right and the quantity demanded is greater at each price. For example, at a price of £1.50 on the original demand curve (blue), the quantity demanded is 2 million tapes per week.

Figure 3.3

An Increase in Demand

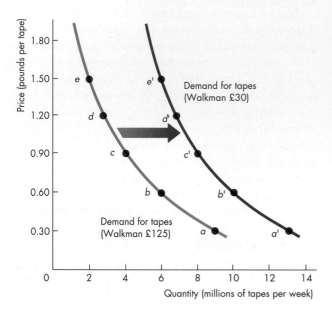

A change in any influence on buyers other than the price of the good itself results in a new demand schedule and a shift of the demand curve. A change in the price of a Walkman changes the demand for tapes. At a price of 90 pence a tape (row *c* of the table), 4 million tapes a week are demanded when a Walkman costs £125 and 8 million tapes a week are demanded when a Walkman costs only £30. A fall in the price of a Walkman increases the demand for tapes because it is a complement of tapes. When demand *increases*, the demand curve shifts rightward, as shown by the shift arrow and the resulting red curve.

Original demand schedule (Walkman £125)			New demand schedule (Walkman £30)		
	Price (pounds per tape)	Quantity (millions of tapes per week)		Price (pounds per tape)	Quantity (millions of tapes per week)
a	0.30	9	*a'*	0.30	13
b	0.60	6	*b'*	0.60	10
c	0.90	4	*c'*	0.90	8
d	1.20	3	*d'*	1.20	7
e	1.50	2	*e'*	1.50	6

On the new (red) demand curve, the quantity demanded is 6 million tapes per week. The quantity demanded is higher at every price.

Let's expand the model of demand to look at how these other factors influence demand.

1 Prices of Related Goods

The quantity of any goods and services that consumers plan to buy depends in part on the price of related goods and services. There are two types: substitutes and complements.

A **substitute** is a good that can be used in place of another good. For example, a bus ride substitutes for a train ride; a hamburger substitutes for a pizza; a pear substitutes for an apple. As we have noted, tapes have many substitutes – mini disks, CDs, radio and television broadcasts and live concerts. If the price of one of these substitutes increases, people economize on its use and buy more tapes. For example, if the price of a CD rises, more tapes are bought and there is more taping of other people's CDs – the demand for tapes increases.

A **complement** is a good used in conjunction with another good. Some examples of complements are hamburgers and chips, party snacks and drinks, cars and petrol, PCs and software. Tapes also have complements: Walkmans, tape recorders and stereo tape decks. If the price of one of these complements increases, people buy fewer tapes. For example, in Figure 3.3 if the price of a Walkman falls, more Walkmans are bought and, as a consequence, more tapes are bought – the demand for tapes increases.

2 Income

Another influence on demand is consumer income. Other things remaining the same, when income increases, consumers buy more of most goods, and when income decreases, they buy less of most goods. Although an increase in income leads to an increase in the demand for most goods, it does not lead to an increase in the demand for all goods. Goods for which demand increases as income increases are called **normal goods**. Goods for which demand decreases when income increases are called **inferior goods**. Examples of inferior goods are cheap cuts of meat and tinned foods. These two goods are a major part of the diet of people with low incomes. As incomes increase, the demand for these goods usually declines as more expensive meat and fresh products are substituted for them.

3 Expected Future Prices

If the price of a good is expected to rise in the future, and if the good can be stored, the opportunity cost of obtaining the good for future use is lower now than it will be when the price has increased. So people substitute over time. They buy more of the good before the expected price rise and the demand for the good increases. Similarly, if the price of a good is expected to fall in the future, the opportunity cost of the good in the present is high relative to what is expected. So again, people substitute over time. They buy less of the good before its price is expected to fall, so the demand for the good now decreases.

4 Population
Demand also depends on the size and the age structure of the population. Other things remaining the same, the larger the population, the greater is the demand for all goods and services, and the smaller the population, the smaller is the demand for all goods and services. Also, other things remaining the same, the larger the proportion of the population in a given age group, the greater is the demand for the types of goods and services used by that age group.

5 Preferences
Finally, demand depends on consumer preferences. *Preferences* are an individual's attitudes towards and tastes for goods and services. For example, a music fanatic has a much greater taste for tapes than a music-hating workaholic. As a consequence, even if they have the same incomes, their demands for tapes will be different. Preferences are shaped by past experience, genetic factors, advertising information, religious beliefs, and other cultural and social factors.

Table 3.1 summarizes the influences on demand and the direction of these influences.

Movement Along Versus a Shift of the Demand Curve

Changes in the factors that influence buyers' plans cause either a movement along the demand curve or a shift of the demand curve.

Movement Along the Demand Curve
If the price of a good changes but everything else remains the same, there is a movement along the demand curve. For example, if the price of a tape changes from 90 pence to £1.50, the result is a movement along the demand curve, from point *c* to point *e* in Figure 3.2. The negative slope of the demand curve reveals that a decrease in the price of a good or service increases the quantity demanded – the law of demand.

Table 3.1   The Demand for Tapes

The law of demand
The quantity of tapes demanded

Decreases if:	*Increases if:*
◆ The price of a tape rises	◆ The price of a tape falls

Changes in demand
The demand for tapes

Decreases if:	*Increases if:*
◆ The price of a substitute falls	◆ The price of a substitute rises
◆ The price of a complement rises	◆ The price of a complement falls
◆ Income falls*	◆ Income rises*
◆ The price of a tape is expected to fall in the future	◆ The price of a tape is expected to rise in the future
◆ The population decreases	◆ The population increases

*A tape is a normal good.

A Shift of the Demand Curve
If the price of a good remains constant but some other influence on buyers' plans changes, there is a change in demand for that good. We illustrate a change in demand as a shift of the demand curve. For example, a fall in the price of a Walkman – a complement of tapes – increases the demand for tapes. We illustrate this increase in demand for tapes with a new demand schedule and a new demand curve. Whether the price of tapes is high or low, if the price of a Walkman falls, consumers buy more tapes. This is what a shift of the demand curve shows. It shows that more tapes are bought at each and every price.

Figure 3.3 illustrates such a shift. The table sets out the original demand schedule when the price of a Walkman is £125 and the new demand schedule when the price of a Walkman is £30. These numbers record the change in demand. The graph in Figure 3.3 illustrates the corresponding shift of the demand curve. When the price of the Walkman falls, the demand curve for tapes shifts rightward.

A Change in Demand Versus a Change in Quantity Demanded
A point on the demand curve shows the quantity demanded at a given price. A movement along the demand curve shows a **change in the quantity demanded**. The entire demand curve shows demand. A shift of the demand curve shows a **change in demand**.

Figure 3.4

A Change in Demand Versus a Change in Quantity Demanded

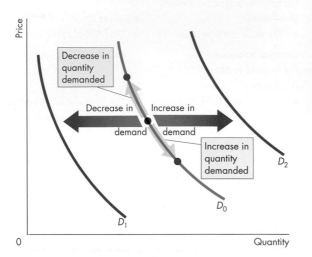

The blue arrow shows a *change in the quantity demanded* when the demand curve is D_0. A rise (fall) in the price of the good leads to a decrease (increase) in the quantity demanded and a movement along the demand curve as shown by the arrow. A change in any factor other than the price of the good, leads to a *change in demand* by shifting the demand curve – to D_2, an increase in demand and D_1, a *decrease in demand*.

Figure 3.4 illustrates and summarizes these distinctions. If the price of a good falls but nothing else changes, then there is an increase in the quantity demanded of that good (a movement down the demand curve D_0). If the price rises, but nothing else changes, then there is a decrease in the quantity demanded (a movement up the demand curve D_0). When any other influence on buyers' planned purchases changes, the demand curve shifts and there is a *change* (an increase or a decrease) *in demand*. A rise in income (for a normal good), in population, in the price of a substitute or in the expected future price of the good, or a fall in the price of a complement, shifts the demand curve rightward (to the red demand curve D_2). This represents an *increase in demand*. A fall in income (for a normal good), in population, in the price of a substitute or in the expected future price of the good, or a rise in the price of a complement, shifts the demand curve leftward (to the red demand curve D_1). This represents a *decrease in demand*. (For an inferior good, the effects of changes in income are in the opposite direction to those described above.)

Review Quiz

◆ Can you define quantity demanded of a good or service?
◆ What is the law of demand and how do we illustrate it?
◆ If a fixed amount of a good is available, what does the demand curve tell us about the price that consumers are willing to pay for that fixed quantity?
◆ Can you list all the influences on buying plans that change demand and for each influence say whether it increases or decreases demand?
◆ What happens to the quantity of CDs demanded and the demand for CDs if the price of a CD falls and all other influences on buying plans remain constant?

Supply

If a firm supplies a good or service, the firm must:

◆ Have the resources and technology to produce it.

◆ Be able to profit from producing it.

◆ Plan to produce and sell it.

Supply is more than just having the resources and technology to produce something. Resources and technology are the constraints that limit what is possible.

Many useful things can be produced, but they are not produced unless it is profitable to do so. Supply reflects a decision about which technologically feasible goods and services to produce.

The **quantity supplied** of a good is the amount that producers plan to sell during a given time period. The quantity supplied is not the amount producers would like to sell but the amount they definitely plan to sell. But the quantity supplied is not necessarily the same as the quantity actually sold. If consumers do not want to buy the quantity producers plan to sell, the sales plans will be frustrated. Like quantity demanded, the quantity supplied is expressed as an amount per unit of time.

What Determines Selling Plans?

The amount that producers plan to sell of any particular good or service depends on many factors. The main ones are:

- The price of the good.
- The prices of factors of production.
- The prices of related goods.
- Expected future prices.
- The number of suppliers.
- Technology.

Let's start to build a model of supply by looking at the relationship between the price of a good and the quantity supplied. In order to study this relationship, we hold constant all the other influences on the quantity supplied. We want to know how the quantity supplied of a good varies as its price varies.

The Law of Supply

The law of supply states:

> Other things remaining the same, the higher the price of a good, the greater is the quantity supplied.

Why does a higher price increase the quantity supplied? It is because of increasing marginal cost. As the quantity produced of any good increases, the marginal cost of producing that good increases. (You can refresh your memory of increasing marginal cost and opportunity cost in Chapter 2, p. 23.)

It would never be worth producing a good if the price you sold it for did not cover the marginal cost of producing it. So producers are only willing to incur the higher marginal cost of increased supply, other things remaining the same, when the price of a good rises. The higher price results in an increase in the quantity supplied.

Let's now illustrate the law of supply with a supply schedule and supply curve.

Supply Schedule and Supply Curve

You are now going study the second part of the most important model in economics, the supply curve. As for demand, you must be able to distinguish between *supply* and *quantity supplied*. The term **supply** refers to the relationship between the quantity supplied of a good and its price, other things constant, and is illustrated by the supply curve and supply schedule. The term quantity supplied refers to a particular point on a supply curve – the quantity supplied at a particular price.

Figure 3.5

The Supply Curve

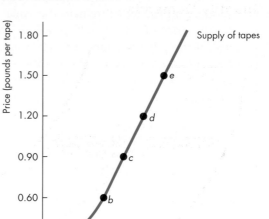

	Price (pounds per tape)	Quantity (millions of tapes per week)
a	0.30	0
b	0.60	3
c	0.90	4
d	1.20	5
e	1.50	6

The table shows the supply schedule of tapes. For example, at 60 pence a tape, 3 million tapes a week are supplied; at £1.50 a tape, 6 million tapes a week are supplied. The supply curve shows the relationship between the quantity supplied and the price, everything else remaining the same. The supply curve usually slopes upward: as the price of a good increases, so does the quantity supplied. A supply curve can be read in two ways. For a given price, it tells us the quantity that producers plan to sell. For example, at a price of 90 pence a tape, producers plan to sell 4 million tapes a week. The supply curve also tells us the minimum acceptable price at which a given quantity will be offered for sale. For example, the minimum acceptable price that will bring forth a supply of 5 million tapes a week is £1.20 a tape.

Figure 3.5 illustrates the supply curve for tapes. A **supply curve** shows the relationship between the quantity supplied and the price of a good, everything else remaining the same. It is a graph of a supply schedule.

The table in Figure 3.5 sets out the supply schedule for tapes. A *supply schedule* lists the quantities supplied at each different price, when all other influences on the amount producers plan to sell remain the same. For example, if the price of a tape is 30 pence, no tapes are supplied. If the price of a tape is £1.20, 5 million tapes are supplied each week. The points on the supply curve labelled *a* to *e* represent the rows of the supply schedule.

Minimum Supply Price

Just as the demand curve has two interpretations, so too does the supply curve. It shows the quantity that producers plan to sell at each possible price. It also shows the minimum price at which the last unit will be supplied. For producers to be willing to supply the 3 millionth tape each week, the price must be at least 60 pence a tape. For producers to be willing to supply the 5 millionth tape each week, they must get at least £1.20 a tape.

A Change in Supply

But we already know that supply changes with other factors like the price of factors of production and related goods, expected future prices and technology. So let's expand the model to look at how these other factors influence supply.

1 Prices of Factors of Production

The prices of the factors of production used to produce a good influence its supply. For example, an increase in the prices of the labour and the capital equipment used to produce tapes increases the cost of producing tapes. So for a given market price, the supplier is willing to supply fewer tapes.

2 Prices of Related Goods

The supply of a good can be influenced by the prices of related goods. For example, if a car assembly line can produce either sports cars or saloons, the quantity of saloons produced will depend on the price of sports cars and the quantity of sports cars produced will depend on the price of saloons. These two goods are *substitutes in production*. An increase in the price of a substitute in production lowers the supply of the good. Goods can also be complements in production. *Complements in production* arise when two things are, of necessity, produced together. For example, extracting chemicals from coal produces coke, coal tar and

nylon. An increase in the price of any one of these by-products of coal increases the supply of the other by-products.

Blank tapes have no obvious complements in production, but they do have substitutes in production: prerecorded tapes. Suppliers of tapes can produce blank tapes and prerecorded tapes. An increase in the price of prerecorded tapes encourages producers to use their equipment to produce more prerecorded tapes and so the supply of blank tapes decreases.

3 Expected Future Prices

If the price of a good is expected to rise in the future, and if the good can be stored, the return from selling the good in the future is higher than it is in the present. So producers substitute over time. They offer a smaller quantity for sale before the expected price rise and the supply of the good decreases. Similarly, if the price of a good is expected to fall in the future, the return from selling it in the present is high relative to what is expected. So again, producers substitute over time. They offer to sell more of the good before its price is expected to fall, so the supply of the good increases.

4 The Number of Suppliers

When new firms enter a market and no firms leave a market, the quantity of the good supplied will increase. Other things remaining the same, the larger the number of firms supplying a good, the larger is the supply of the good.

5 Technology

New technologies that enable producers to use less of each factor of production or cheaper factors of production lower the cost of production and increase supply. For example, the development of a new technology for tape production by BASF, Sony and Minnesota Mining and Manufacturing (3M) has lowered the cost of producing tapes and increased their supply. Over the long term, changes in technology are the most important influence on supply.

Table 3.2 summarizes the influences on supply and the directions of those influences.

Movement Along Versus a Shift of the Supply Curve

Changes in the factors that influence producers' planned sales cause either a movement along the supply curve or a shift of the supply curve.

Table 3.2　The Supply of Tapes

The law of supply

The quantity of tapes supplied

Decreases if:

◆ The price of a tape falls

Increases if:

◆ The price of a tape rises

Changes in supply

The supply of tapes

Decreases if:

◆ The price of a factor of production used to produce tapes increases

◆ The price of a substitute in production rises

◆ The price of a complement in production falls

◆ The price of a tape is expected to rise in the future

◆ The number of firms supplying tapes decreases

Increases if:

◆ The price of a factor of production used to produce tapes decreases

◆ The price of a substitute in production falls

◆ The price of a complement in production rises

◆ The price of a tape is expected to fall in the future

◆ The number of firms supplying tapes increases

◆ More efficient technologies for producing tapes emerge

Movement Along the Supply Curve

If the price of a good changes but everything else influencing suppliers' planned sales remains constant, there is a movement along the supply curve. For example, if the price of tapes increases from 90 pence to £1.50 a tape, there will be a movement along the supply curve from point *c* (4 million tapes a week) to point *e* (6 million tapes a week) in Figure 3.5. The positive slope of the supply curve reveals that an increase in the price of a good or service increases the quantity supplied – the law of supply.

A Shift of the Supply Curve

If the price of a good remains the same but another influence on suppliers' planned sales changes, then there is a change in supply and a shift of the supply curve. For example, as we have already noted, technological advances lower the cost of producing tapes and increase their supply. As a result, the supply schedule changes. The table in Figure 3.6 provides some hypothetical numbers that illustrate such a change. The table contains two supply schedules: the original, based on 'old' technology, and one based on 'new' technology. With the new technology, more tapes are supplied at each price. The graph in Figure

Figure 3.6

An Increase in Supply

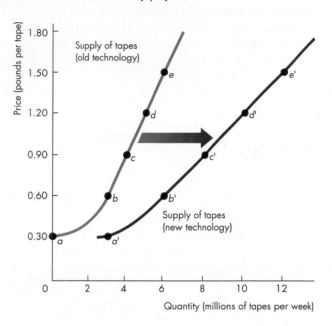

	Original supply schedule (original technology)			New supply schedule (new technology)	
	Price (pounds per tape)	**Quantity (millions of tapes per week)**		**Price (pounds per tape)**	**Quantity (millions of tapes per week)**
a	0.30	0	a′	0.30	3
b	0.60	3	b′	0.60	6
c	0.90	4	c′	0.90	8
d	1.20	5	d′	1.20	10
e	1.50	6	e′	1.50	12

A change in any influence on sellers other than the price of the good itself results in a new supply schedule and a shift of the supply curve. For example, if BASF, Sony and 3M invent a new, cost-saving technology for producing tapes, the supply of tapes changes. At a price of 60 pence a tape (row *b* of the table), 3 million tapes a week are supplied when the producers use the old technology, and 6 million tapes a week are supplied with the new technology. An advance in technology increases the supply of tapes and the supply curve shifts rightward, as shown by the shift arrow and the resulting red curve.

3.6 illustrates the resulting shift of the supply curve. When tape-producing technology improves, the supply curve of tapes shifts rightward, as shown by the shift arrow and the red supply curve.

Figure 3.7

A Change in Supply Versus a Change in the Quantity Supplied

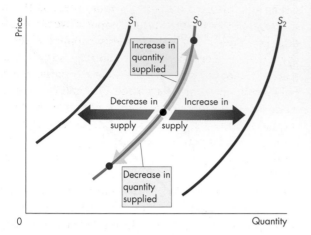

The blue arrow shows a *change in the quantity supplied* when the supply curve is S_0. A rise (fall) in the price of the good leads to a decrease (increase) in the quantity supplied and a movement along the supply curve as shown by the arrow. A change in any factor other than the price of the good, leads to a *change in supply* by shifting the supply curve – to S_2, an *increase in supply* and S_1, a *decrease in supply*.

A Change in Supply Versus a Change in Quantity Supplied

A point on the supply curve shows the quantity supplied at a given price. A movement along the supply curve shows a **change in the quantity supplied**. The entire supply curve shows supply. A shift of the supply curve shows a **change in supply**.

Figure 3.7 illustrates and summarizes these distinctions. If the price of a good falls but nothing else changes, then there is a decrease in the quantity supplied of that good (a movement down the supply curve S_0). If the price of a good rises but nothing else changes, there is an increase in the quantity supplied (a movement up the supply curve S_0). When any other influence on sellers changes, the supply curve shifts and there is a *change in supply*. If the supply curve is S_0 and there is, say, a technological change that reduces the amounts of the factors of production needed to produce the good, then supply increases and the supply curve shifts to the red supply curve S_2. If production costs rise, supply decreases and the supply curve shifts to the red supply curve S_1.

Review Quiz

◆ Can you define the quantity supplied of a good or service?
◆ What is the law of supply and how do we illustrate it?
◆ If consumers are willing to buy only a given quantity, what does the supply curve tell us about the price at which firms will supply that quantity?
◆ Can you list all the influences on selling plans that change supply and for each influence say whether it increases or decreases supply?

We are now going to bring the two concepts of demand and supply together to create the model which will show how prices and quantities are determined.

Market Equilibrium

We have seen that when the price of a good rises, the quantity demanded decreases and the quantity supplied increases. We are now going to see how prices coordinate the choices of buyers and sellers and achieve equilibrium.

An equilibrium is a situation in which opposing forces balance each other, so there is no tendency for change. Market equilibrium occurs when the market price balances the plans of both buyers and sellers. The **equilibrium price** is the price at which the quantity demanded equals the quantity supplied. The **equilibrium quantity** is the quantity bought and sold at the equilibrium price. A market moves towards its equilibrium because:

◆ Price regulates buying and selling plans.
◆ Price adjusts when plans don't match.

Price as a Regulator

The price of a good regulates the quantities demanded and supplied. If the price is too high, the quantity supplied exceeds the quantity demanded. If the price is too low, the quantity demanded exceeds the quantity supplied. There is one price, and only one price, at which the quantity demanded equals the quantity supplied. Let's work out what that price is.

Figure 3.8
Equilibrium

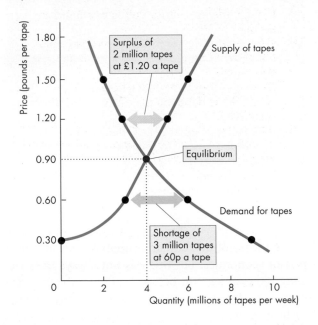

The table lists the quantities demanded and quantities supplied as well as the shortage or surplus of tapes at each price. If the price of a tape is 60 pence, 6 million tapes a week are demanded and 3 million are supplied. There is a shortage of 3 million tapes a week, and the price rises. If the price of a tape is £1.20, 3 million tapes a week are demanded but 5 million are supplied. There is a surplus of 2 million tapes a week, and the price falls. If the price of a tape is 90 pence, 4 million tapes a week are demanded and 4 million are supplied. There is neither a shortage nor a surplus. Neither buyers nor sellers have any incentive to change the price. The price at which the quantity demanded equals the quantity supplied is the equilibrium price.

Price (pounds per tape)	Quantity demanded	Quantity supplied	Shortage (−) or surplus (+)
	(millions of tapes per week)		
0.30	9	0	−9
0.60	6	3	−3
0.90	4	4	0
1.20	3	5	+2
1.50	2	6	+4

Figure 3.8 shows the market for tapes. The table shows the demand schedule (from Figure 3.2) and the supply schedule (from Figure 3.5). If the price of a tape is 30 pence, the quantity demanded is 9 million tapes a week, but no tapes are supplied. The quantity

demanded exceeds the quantity supplied by 9 million tapes a week. In other words, at a price of 30 pence a tape, there is a shortage of 9 million tapes a week. This shortage is shown in the final column of the table. At a price of 60 pence a tape, there is still a shortage but only of 3 million tapes a week. If the price of a tape is £1.20, the quantity supplied exceeds the quantity demanded. The quantity supplied is 5 million tapes a week, but the quantity demanded is only 3 million. There is a surplus of 2 million tapes a week. There is one price and only one price at which there is neither a shortage nor a surplus. The equilibrium price is 90 pence a tape. At that price the equilibrium quantity demanded is equal to the quantity supplied – 4 million tapes a week.

Figure 3.8 shows that the demand curve and the supply curve intersect at the equilibrium price of 90 pence a tape. At that price, the equilibrium quantity demanded and supplied is 4 million tapes a week. At each price *above* 90 pence a tape, the quantity supplied exceeds the quantity demanded. There is a surplus of tapes. For example, at £1.20 a tape the surplus is 2 million tapes a week, as shown by the blue arrow in the figure. At each price *below* 90 pence a tape, the quantity demanded exceeds the quantity supplied. There is a shortage of tapes. For example, at 60 pence a tape, the shortage is 3 million tapes a week, as shown by the red arrow in the figure.

Price Adjustments

You have seen that shortages arise if price is below the equilibrium price, and surpluses arise if price is above the equilibrium price. But why should price change to eliminate a shortage or a surplus? Price will adjust when there is a shortage or a surplus because it is beneficial to both buyers and sellers. Let's see why.

A Shortage Forces the Price Up

Suppose the price of a tape is 60 pence. Consumers plan to buy 6 million tapes a week and producers plan to sell 3 million tapes a week. Consumers can't force producers to sell, so the quantity actually offered for sale is 3 million tapes a week. In this situation, powerful forces operate to increase the price and move it towards the equilibrium price. Some people, unable to find the tapes they planned to buy, offer to pay more. Some producers, noticing lines of unsatisfied consumers, move their prices up. As buyers try to outbid one another, and as producers push their prices up, the price rises towards its equilibrium.

The rising price reduces the shortage because it decreases the quantity demanded and increases the quantity supplied. When the price has increased to the point at which there is no longer a shortage, the forces moving the price stop operating and the price comes to rest at its equilibrium.

A Surplus Forces the Price Down

Suppose the price of a tape is £1.20. Producers plan to sell 5 million tapes a week and consumers plan to buy 3 million tapes a week. Producers cannot force consumers to buy, so the quantity actually bought is 3 million tapes a week. In this situation, powerful forces operate to lower the price and move it towards the equilibrium price. Some producers, unable to sell the quantities of tapes they planned to sell, cut their prices. Some buyers, noticing shelves of unsold tapes, offer to buy for a lower price. As producers try to undercut one another, and as buyers make lower price offers, the price falls towards its equilibrium. The falling price reduces the surplus because it increases the quantity demanded and decreases the quantity supplied. When the price has decreased to the point at which there is no longer a surplus, the forces moving the price stop operating and the price comes to rest at its equilibrium.

The Best Deal Available for Buyers and Sellers

Both shortages and surpluses lead to price changes. In the tape market example, prices were forced up or down until they hit 90 pence a tape. So why don't buyers refuse to pay as price increases? Buyers pay higher prices because they value the good more highly than its current price. So why don't sellers refuse to sell at lower prices? Sellers continue to sell as the price falls because their minimum supply price is below the current price.

At the equilibrium price, the quantity demanded and the quantity supplied are equal and neither buyers nor sellers can do business at a better price. Consumers pay the highest price they are willing to pay for the last unit bought, and producers receive the lowest price at which they are willing to supply the last unit sold.

When people freely make bids and offers and when buyers seek the lowest price and sellers seek the highest price, the price at which trade takes place is the equilibrium price. At this price, the quantity demanded equals the quantity supplied. Price has coordinated the plans of buyers and sellers.

Review Quiz

◆ What is the equilibrium price of a good or service?
◆ Over what range of prices does a shortage arise? What happens to price when there is a shortage?
◆ Over what range of prices does a surplus arise? What happens to price when there is a surplus?
◆ Why is the price at which the quantity demanded equals to quantity supplied called the equilibrium price?
◆ Why is the equilibrium price the best deal available for both buyers and sellers?

The theory of demand and supply is now a central part of economics. But this was not always the case. Only 100 years ago, the best economists of the day were quite confused about matters that today even students in introductory courses can get right (see *Economics in History* on pp. 70–71). You'll discover in the rest of this chapter that the theory of demand and supply helps us to understand and make predictions about changes in prices – including the price slides, rockets and roller-coasters described in the chapter opener.

Predicting Changes in Price and Quantity

The theory we have just studied provides us with a powerful way of analysing influences on prices and the quantities bought and sold. According to the theory, a change in price stems from either a change in demand or a change in supply or a change in both. First, let's use our model to discover the effects of a change in demand.

A Change in Demand

What happens to the price and quantity of tapes if demand for tapes increases? We can answer this question with a specific example. If the price of a Walkman falls from £125 to £30, the demand for tapes increases as is shown in the table in Figure 3.9, as tapes and Walkmans are complements. The original demand schedule and the new one are set out in the first three columns of the table. The table also shows the supply schedule for tapes.

Figure 3.9

The Effects of a Change in Demand

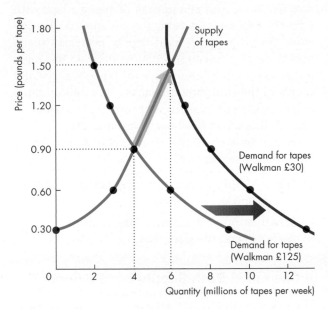

With the price of a Walkman at £125, the demand for tapes is the blue curve. The equilibrium price is 90 pence a tape and the equilibrium quantity is 4 million tapes a week. When the price of a Walkman falls from £125 to £30, there is an increase in the demand for tapes and the demand curve shifts right – the red curve. At 90 pence a tape, there is now a shortage of 4 million tapes a week. The quantities of tapes demanded and supplied are equal at a price of £1.50 a tape. The price rises to this level and the quantity supplied increases. But there is no change in supply. The supply curve does not shift. The increase in demand increases the equilibrium price to £1.50 and increases the equilibrium quantity to 6 million tapes a week.

Price (pounds per tape)	Quantity demanded (millions of tapes per week)		Quantity supplied (millions of tapes per week)
	Walkman £125	Walkman £30	
0.30	9	13	0
0.60	6	10	3
0.90	4	8	4
1.20	3	7	5
1.50	2	6	6

The original equilibrium price is 90 pence a tape. At that price, 4 million tapes a week are demanded and supplied. When demand increases, the price that makes the quantity demanded equal the quantity supplied is £1.50 a tape. At this price, 6 million tapes are bought and sold each week. When demand increases, both the price and the quantity increase.

Figure 3.9 shows these changes. The figure shows the original demand for and supply of tapes. The original equilibrium price is 90 pence a tape and the quantity is 4 million tapes a week. When demand increases, the demand curve shifts rightward. The equilibrium price rises to £1.50 a tape and the quantity supplied increases to 6 million tapes a week, as is highlighted in the figure. There is an increase in the quantity supplied but *no change in supply*. That is, the supply curve does not shift.

The exercise that we've just conducted can easily be reversed. If we start at a price of £1.50 a tape, trading 6 million tapes a week, we can work out what happens if demand decreases to its original level. You can see that the decrease in demand lowers the equilibrium price to 90 pence a tape and decreases the equilibrium quantity to 4 million tapes a week. Such a decrease in demand might arise from a decrease in the price of CDs or of CD players. (CDs and CD players are substitutes for tapes.)

We can now make our two clear market predictions. Holding everything else constant:

1 When demand increases, both the price and the quantity traded in the market increase.

2 When demand decreases, both the price and the quantity traded in the market decrease.

A Change in Supply

Suppose that BASF, Sony and 3M introduce a new cost-saving technology in their tape-production plants. The new technology changes the supply. The new supply schedule (the one that was shown in Figure 3.6) is presented in the table in Figure 3.10. What is the new equilibrium price and quantity? The answer is highlighted in the table: the price falls to 60 pence a tape and the quantity increases to 6 million a week. You can see why by looking at the quantities demanded and supplied at the old price of a tape. The quantity supplied at 90 pence a tape is 8 million tapes a week and there is a surplus of tapes. The price falls. Only when the price is 60 pence a tape does the quantity supplied equal the quantity demanded.

Figure 3.10 illustrates the effect of an increase in supply. It shows the demand curve for tapes and the original and new supply curves. The initial equilibrium price is 90 pence a tape and the original quantity is 4 million tapes a week. When the supply

Figure 3.10

The Effects of a Change in Supply

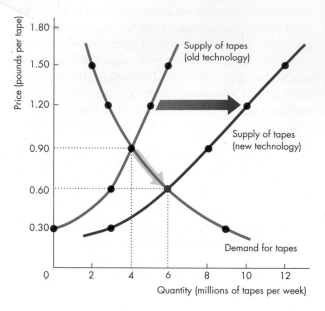

Price (pounds per tape)	Quantity demanded (millions of tapes per week)	Quantity supplied (millions of tapes per week)	
		Original technology	New technology
0.30	9	0	3
0.60	6	3	6
0.90	4	4	8
1.20	3	5	10
1.50	2	6	12

With the original technology, the supply of tapes is shown by the blue curve. The equilibrium price is 90 pence a tape and the equilibrium quantity is 4 million tapes a week. When the new technology is adopted, there is an increase in the supply of tapes. The supply curve shifts right – the red curve. At 90 pence a tape there is now a surplus of 4 million tapes a week. The quantities of tapes demanded and supplied are equal at a price of 60 pence a tape. The price falls to this level and the quantity demanded increases – there is a movement along the demand curve. But there is no change in demand. The demand curve does not shift. The increase in supply lowers the price of tapes to 60p and increases the quantity to 6 million tapes a week.

increases, the supply curve shifts rightward. The equilibrium price falls to 60 pence a tape and the quantity demanded increases to 6 million tapes a week, highlighted in the figure. There is an increase

in the quantity demanded but *no change in demand*. That is, the demand curve does not shift.

The exercise that we've just conducted can be reversed. If we start at a price of 60 pence a tape with 6 million tapes a week being bought and sold, we can work out what happens if supply decreases to its original level. You can see that the decrease in supply increases the equilibrium price to 90 pence a tape and decreases the equilibrium quantity to 4 million tapes a week. Such a decrease in supply might arise from an increase in the cost of labour or raw materials.

We can now make two more predictions. Holding everything else constant:

1 When supply increases, the quantity traded increases and the price falls.

2 When supply decreases, the quantity traded decreases and the price rises.

A Change in Both Supply and Demand

You can now predict the effects of a change in either demand or supply on price and quantity. But what happens if both demand and supply change together? To answer this question, we will look first at the case when demand and supply both change in the same direction – both increase or decrease together. Then we'll look at the case in which they move in opposite directions – demand decreases and supply increases or demand increases and supply decreases.

Demand and Supply Change in the Same Direction

We've seen that an increase in the demand for tapes increases the price of tapes and increases the quantity bought and sold. We've also seen that an increase in the supply of tapes lowers the price of tapes and increases the quantity bought and sold. Let's now examine what happens in our model when both of these changes happen to occur together.

The table in Figure 3.11 brings together the numbers that describe the original quantities demanded and supplied and the new quantities demanded and supplied after the fall in the price of a Walkman and the improved tape production technology. These same numbers are illustrated in the graph. The original (blue) demand and supply curves intersect at a price of 90 pence a tape and a quantity of 4 million tapes a week. The new (red) supply and demand curves also intersect at a price of 90 pence a tape but at a quantity of 8 million tapes a week.

Figure 3.11

The Effects of an Increase in both Demand and Supply

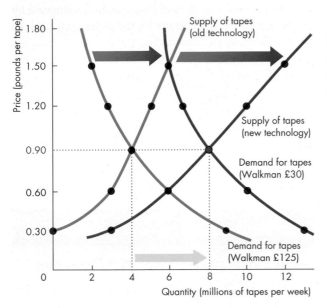

When a Walkman costs £125, and the old technology is used to produce tapes, the price of a tape is 90 pence and the quantity is 4 million tapes a week. A fall in the price of a Walkman increases the demand for tapes, and improved technology increases the supply of tapes. The new technology supply curve intersects the higher demand curve at 90 pence, the same price as before, but the quantity increases to 8 million tapes a week. These increases in demand and supply increase the quantity but leave the price unchanged.

Price (pounds per tape)	Original quantities (millions of tapes per week)		New quantities (millions of tapes per week)	
	Quantity demanded (Walkman £125)	Quantity supplied (original technology)	Quantity demanded (Walkman £30)	Quantity supplied (new technology)
0.30	9	0	13	3
0.60	6	3	10	6
0.90	4	4	8	8
1.20	3	5	7	10
1.50	2	6	6	12

An increase in either demand or supply increases the quantity. Therefore when both demand and supply increase, so does quantity. But an increase in demand increases the price and an increase in supply lowers the price, so we can't say for sure which way

the price will change when demand and supply increase together. In this example, the increases in demand and supply are such that the rise in price brought about by an increase in demand is offset by the fall in price brought about by an increase in supply – so the price does not change. But notice that if demand had increased slightly more than shown in the figure, the price would have risen. If supply had increased by slightly more than shown in the figure, the price would have fallen.

We can now make two more market predictions:

1 When *both* demand and supply increase, the market quantity increases and the price increases, decreases or remains constant.

2 When *both* demand and supply decrease, the market quantity decreases and the price increases, decreases or remains constant.

Demand and Supply Change in Opposite Directions

Let's now see what happens when demand and supply change together but move in *opposite* directions. We'll look yet again at the market for tapes, but this time supply increases and demand decreases. An improved production technology increases the supply of tapes as before. But now the price of CD players falls. A CD player is a *substitute* for tapes. With less costly CD players, more people buy them and switch from buying tapes to buying CDs and the demand for tapes decreases.

The table in Figure 3.12 describes the original and new demand and supply schedules and these schedules are shown as the original (blue) and new (red) demand and supply curves in the graph. The original demand and supply curves intersect at a price of £1.50 a tape and a quantity of 6 million tapes a week. The new supply and demand curves intersect at a price of 60 pence a tape and at the original quantity of 6 million tapes a week. In this example, the decrease in demand and the increase in supply are such that the decrease in the quantity brought about by a decrease in demand is offset by the increase in quantity brought about by an increase in supply – so the quantity does not change.

A decrease in demand or an increase in supply lower the price. Therefore when both a decrease in demand and an increase in supply occur together, the price falls.

A decrease in demand decreases the quantity and an increase in supply increases the quantity, so we can't say for sure which way the quantity will change when

Figure 3.12

The Effects of a Decrease in Demand and an Increase in Supply

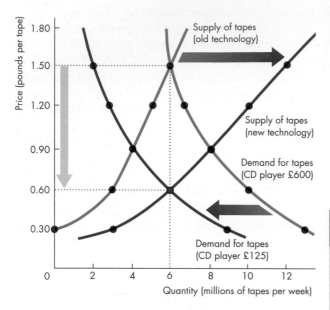

When CD players cost £600 and the old technology is used to produce tapes, the price of a tape is £1.50 and the quantity is 6 million tapes a week. A fall in the price of CD players decreases the demand for tapes, and improved technology increases the supply of tapes. The new technology supply curve intersects the lower demand curve at 60 pence, a lower price, but in this case the quantity remains constant at 6 million tapes a week. The decrease in demand and increase in supply lower the price but leave the quantity unchanged.

Price (pounds per tape)	Original quantities (millions of tapes per week)		New quantities (millions of tapes per week)	
	Quantity demanded (CD player £600)	Quantity supplied (original technology)	Quantity demanded (CD player £125)	Quantity supplied (new technology)
0.30	13	0	9	3
0.60	10	3	6	6
0.90	8	4	4	8
1.20	7	5	3	10
1.50	6	6	2	123

demand decreases and at the same time, supply increases. In this example, the decrease in demand and the increase in supply are such that the increase in quantity brought about by an increase in supply is

offset by the decrease in quantity brought about by a decrease in demand – so the quantity does not change. But notice that if demand had decreased slightly more than shown in the figure, the quantity would have decreased. And if supply had increased by slightly more than shown in the figure, the quantity would have increased.

We can now make two more predictions:

1　When demand decreases and supply increases, the price falls and the quantity increases, decreases, or remains constant.

2　When demand increases and supply decreases, the price rises and the quantity increases, decreases, or remains constant.

Review Quiz

◆　What is the effect on the price of a tape and the quantity of tapes if: (a) the price of a CD rises or (b) the price of a Walkman rises or (c) more firms start to produce tapes or (d) the wages of tape producers rises, or (e) if any pair of these events occur at the same time? (Can you draw the diagrams?)

CD Players, Houses and Apples

At the beginning of this chapter, we looked at some facts about prices and quantities of CD players, house prices and apples. Let's use the theory of demand and supply that we have just studied to explain the movements in the prices and the quantities of these goods.

A Price Slide: CD Players

Figure 3.13(a) shows the market for CD players. In 1984, few firms made CD players and supply was limited. The supply curve was S_0. In 1984, the demand curve was D_0. The quantities supplied and demanded in 1984 were equal at Q_0, and the real price was £730 (1999 pounds). As the technology for making portable CD players improved and as more and more factories began to produce CD players, the supply increased by a large amount and the supply curve shifted rightward from S_0 to S_1. At the same time, increases in incomes and a decrease in the price of CDs increased the demand for CD players. But the increase in demand was much smaller than the increase in supply. The demand curve shifted to the right from

Figure 3.13
Price Slide, Rocket and Roller-coaster

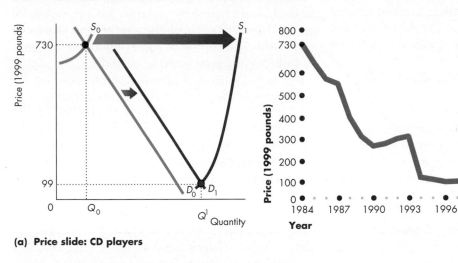

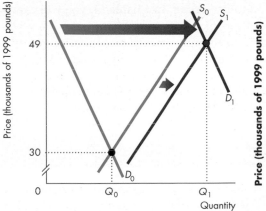

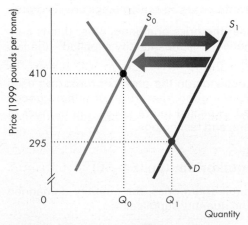

(a) Price slide: CD players

A large increase in the supply of CD players, from S_0 to S_1, between 1984 and 1999, combined with a small increase in demand, from D_0 to D_1, over the same period, resulted in a fall in the average (real) price of CD players from £730 in 1984 to £99 in 1999. The quantity of CD players bought and sold increases from Q_0 to Q_1 (part a). Part (a) shows this price slide.

Source: Author's calculations from retail data.

(b) Price rocket: housing

A large increase in demand for housing, from D_0 to D_1, combined with a smaller increase in the supply, resulted in a rise in the (real) average price of a house from £30,000 in 1984 to £49,000 in 1991 and an increase in the quantity, from Q_0 to Q_1 (part b). Part (b) shows this price rocket.

Source: Department of Environment, *House Price Series*, 1999, London, HMSO.

(c) Price roller-coaster: apples

The demand for apples remains constant at *D*. But supply fluctuates between S_0 and S_1. As a result, the (real) price of apples has fluctuated between £280 per tonne and £410 per tonne – a roller-coaster. Part (c) shows this price roller-coaster.

Source: Central Statistical Office, *Annual Abstract of Statistics*, London, HMSO.

D_0 to D_1. With the new demand curve D_1 and supply curve S_1, the equilibrium price fell to £99 and the quantity increased to Q_1. The large increase in supply combined with a smaller increase in demand resulted in an increase in the quantity of CD players sold and a dramatic fall in the real price. Figure 3.13(a) shows the CD player price slide.

A Price Rocket: Houses

Figure 3.13(b) shows the market for owner-occupied houses. In 1984, the supply curve for housing in the United Kingdom was S_0. The supply of housing increased between 1984 and 1989 to S_1, following new house building and more people wanting to sell existing houses. However, the increase in demand was much higher. Demand increased rapidly because of rising incomes, expectations of rising house prices, expectations of capital gains and more people wanting to set up new households – the growth in demand outstripped the growth in supply. The demand curve shifted from D_0 to D_1 between 1984 and 1991. The combined effect of a large increase in demand and a smaller increase in supply was a rapid rise in average real house prices in that period. Part (b) shows the price rocket. The quantity increased from Q_0 to Q_1.

A Price Roller-coaster: Apples

Figure 3.13(c) shows the market for apples. The demand for apples does not change much over the years. It is described by curve D. But the supply of apples depends mainly on the weather and changes a great deal. The supply of apples fluctuates between S_0 and S_1. With good growing conditions, the supply curve is S_1. With bad growing conditions, supply decreases and the supply curve is S_0. As a consequence of fluctuations in supply, the real price of apples fluctuates between £410 per tonne (1999 prices), the maximum price, and £280 per tonne, the minimum price. The quantity fluctuates between Q_0 and Q_1. Figure 3.13(c) shows the apples price roller-coaster.

By using the theory of demand and supply, you can explain past fluctuations in prices and quantities and also make predictions about future fluctuations. But you will want to do more than predict whether prices are going to rise or fall. In Chapter 4, you will examine a method of predicting *by how much* they will change. In your study of macroeconomics you will learn to explain price fluctuations in the economy as a whole. In fact, the theory of demand and supply can help answer almost every economic question.

Summary

Key Points

Price and Opportunity Cost (p. 45)

- Opportunity cost is a real (relative) price, measured by dividing the price of one good by the price (index) of a basket of all goods.

- Demand and supply determines real (relative) prices.

Demand (pp. 46–50)

- Demand is the relationship between the quantity demanded of a good or service and its price when all other influences on buying plans remain constant.

- The higher the price of a good, other things constant, the smaller is the quantity demanded – the law of demand.

- Demand depends on the prices of substititutes and complements, expected future prices, income, population and preferences.

Supply (pp. 50–54)

- Suppy is the relationship between the quantity supplied of a good or service and its price when all other influences on selling plans are constant.

- The higher the price of a good, other things constant, the larger is the quantity supplied – the law of supply.

- Supply depends on the prices of resources used to produce a good, the prices of related goods produced, expected future prices, the number of producers, and technology.

Market Equilibrium (pp. 54–56)

- At the equilibrium price, the quantity demanded equals the quantity supplied.

- At prices above the equilibrium, there is a surplus and the price falls.

- At prices below the equilibrium, there is a shortage and the price rises.

Predicting Changes in Price and Quantity (pp. 56–62)

- An increase in demand leads to a rise in price and to an increase in the quantity supplied. (A decrease in demand leads to a fall in price and a decrease in the quantity supplied.)

- An increase in supply leads to a fall in price and an increase in the quantity demanded. (A decrease in supply leads to a rise in price and a decrease in the quantity demanded.)

- An increase in both demand and supply, leads to an increase in quantity but the change in price cannot be predicted. An increase in demand and a decrease in supply, brings an increase in price, but the change in quantity cannot be predicted.

Key Figures and Tables ◆

Key Terms

Mathematical Note: Demand, Supply and Equilibrium

Demand Curve

The law of demand states that as the price of a good or service falls, the quantity demanded of it increases. A demand schedule, a demand curve, or a demand equation illustrates the law of demand. When the demand curve is a straight line, a linear equation describes it. A demand equation is

$$P = a - bQ_D,$$

where P is the price and Q_D is the quantity demanded. The a and b are positive constants.

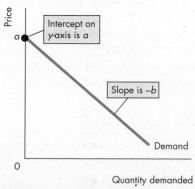

Figure 1 Demand curve

The demand equation tells us three things:

1 The price at which no one is willing to buy the good (Q_D is zero). If the price is a, then the quantity demanded is zero. You can see the price a on the graph. It is the price at which the demand curve hits the y-axis – what we call the demand curve's 'intercept on the y-axis'.

2 As the price falls, the quantity demanded increases. If Q_D is a positive number, then the price P must be less than a. And as Q_D gets larger, the price P becomes smaller. That is, as the quantity increases, the maximum price that buyers are willing to pay of the good falls.

3 The constant b tells us how fast the maximum price that someone is willing to pay for the good falls as the quantity increases. That is, the constant b tells us about the steepness of the demand curve. The equation tells us that the slope of the demand curve is $-b$.

Supply Curve

The law of supply states that as the price of a good or service rises, the quantity supplied of it increases. A supply schedule, a supply curve, or a supply equation illustrates the law of supply. When the supply curve is a straight line, a linear equation describes it. A supply equation is

$$P = c + dQ_S,$$

where P is the price and Q_S the quantity supplied. The c and d are positive constants.

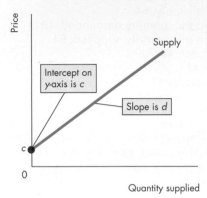

Figure 2 Supply curve

The supply equation tells us three things:

1 The price at which no one is willing to sell the good (Q_S is zero). If the price is c, then the quantity supplied is zero. You can see the price c on the graph. It is the price at which the supply curve hits the y-axis – what we call the supply curve's 'intercept on the y-axis'.

2 As the price rises, the quantity supplied increases. If Q_S is a positive number, then the price P must be greater than c. And Q_S increases, the price P gets larger. That is, as the quantity increases, the minimum price that sellers are willing to accept rises.

3 The constant d tells us how fast the minimum price at which someone is willing to sell the good rises as the quantity increases. That is, the constant d tells us about the steepness of the supply curve. The equation tells us that the slope of the supply is d.

Market Equilibrium

Demand and supply determined the equilibrium price (P^*) and equilibrium quantity (Q^*) at the intersection of the demand curve and the supply curve.

We can use the equations to find the equilibrium price and equilibrium quantity. The price of a good will adjust until the quantity demanded equals the quantity supplied. That is,

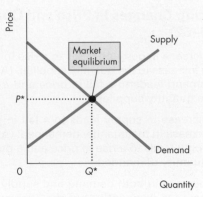

Figure 3 Market equilibrium

$$Q_D = Q_S$$

So at the equilibrium price (P^*) and equilibrium quantity (Q^*),

$$Q_D = Q_S = Q^*$$

To find the equilibrium price and equilibrium quantity: first substitute Q^* for Q_D in the demand equation and Q^* for Q_S in the supply equation. Then the price is the equilibrium price (P^*), which gives

$$P^* = a - bQ^*$$
$$P^* = c + dQ^*$$

Notice that

$$a - bQ^* = c + dQ^*$$

Now solve for Q^*

$$a - c = bQ^* + dQ^*$$
$$a - c = (b + d)Q^*$$
$$Q^* = \frac{a - c}{b + d}$$

To find the equilibrium price (P^*) substitute for Q^* in either the demand equation or the supply equation.

Using the demand equation,

$$P^* = a - b\left(\frac{a - c}{b + d}\right)$$

$$P^* = \frac{a(b + d) - b(a - c)}{b + d}$$

$$P^* = \frac{ad + bc}{b + d}$$

Alternatively, using the supply equation,

$$P^* = a + b\left(\frac{a-c}{b+d}\right)$$

$$P^* = \frac{a(b+d) + b(a-c)}{b+d}$$

$$P^* = \frac{ad + bc}{b+d}$$

An Example

The demand for ice cream cones is

$$P = 800 - 2Q_D$$

The supply of ice cream cones is

$$P = 200 + 1Q_S$$

The price of a cone is expressed in pence and the quantities are expressed in cones per day.

To find the equilibrium price (P^*) and equilibrium quantity (Q^*), substitute Q^* for Q_D and Q_S and P^* for P.

That is,

$$P^* = 800 - 2Q^*$$

$$P^* = 200 + 1Q^*$$

Now solve for Q^*:

$$800 - 2Q^* = 200 + 1Q^*$$

$$600 = 3Q^*$$

$$Q^* = 200$$

And

$$P^* = 800 - 2Q^*$$

$$P^* = 400$$

The equilibrium price is £4 a cone, and the equilibrium quantity is 200 cones per day.

Problems

*1 What is the effect on the price of a tape and the quantity of tapes sold if:

   a The price of a CD rises?

   b The price of a Walkman rises?

   c The supply of CD players increases?

   d Consumers' incomes increase?

   e The workers who make tapes get a pay rise?

   f The price of a Walkman rises and the wages of workers who make tapes rise?

2 What is the effect on the price of hot dogs and the quantity of hot dogs sold if:

   a The price of a hamburger rises?

   b The price of a hot dog bun rises?

   c The supply of hot dog sausages increases?

   d Consumers' incomes decrease?

   e The wage of the hot dog seller increases?

   f The wage of the hot dog seller rises and at the same time prices of ketchup, mustard, and pickles fall?

*3 Suppose that one of the following events occurs:

   i   The price of crude oil rises.

   ii The price of a car rises.

   iii All speed limits on motorways are abolished.

   iv Robot production cuts car production costs.

Which of the above events increases or decreases (state which):

   a The demand for petrol?

   b The supply of petrol?

   c The quantity of petrol demanded?

   d The quantity of petrol supplied?

4 Suppose that one of the following events occurs:

   i   The price of wool rises.

   ii The price of a sweater falls.

   iii A close substitute for wool is invented.

   iv A new high-speed loom is invented.

Which of the above events increases or decreases (state which):

   a The demand for wool?

   b The supply of wool?

   c The quantity of wool demanded?

   d The quantity of wool supplied?

•5   The figure illustrates the market for pizza.

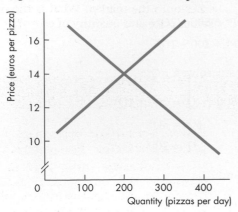

a   Label the curves in the figure.

b   What are the equilibrium price of a pizza and the equilibrium quantity of pizza?

6   The figure illustrates the demand and supply of bread.

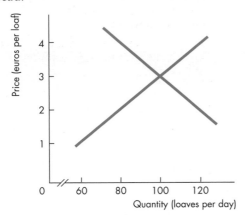

a   Label the curves in the figure.

b   What is the equilibrium price of bread and the equilibrium quantity of bread?

•7   The demand and supply schedules for chewing gum are:

Price (pence per pack)	Quantity demanded (millions of packs a week)	Quantity supplied
20	180	60
30	160	80
40	140	100
50	120	120
60	100	140
70	80	160
80	60	180

a   What are the equilibrium price and quantity of chewing gum?

b   If the price of chewing gum was 70 pence a pack, describe the situation in the chewing gum market and explain what would happen to the price of chewing gum.

8   The demand and supply schedules for potato crisps are:

Price (pence per bag)	Quantity demanded (millions of bags per week)	Quantity supplied
40	170	90
50	160	100
60	150	110
70	140	120
80	130	130
90	120	140
100	110	150
110	100	160

a   What are the equilibrium price and equilibrium quantity of potato crisps?

b   If the price of crisps was 60 pence a bag, describe the situation in the market for potato crisps and explain what would happen to the price of a bag of crisps.

•9   In problem 7, suppose that a fire destroys some chewing gum factories and the supply of chewing gum decreases by 40 million packs a week.

a   Has there been a shift in or a movement along the supply curve of chewing gum?

b   Has there been a shift in or a movement along the demand curve for chewing gum?

c   What is the new equilibrium price and quantity of chewing gum?

10   In problem 8, suppose that a new snack food comes onto the market and as result the demand for potato crisps decreases by 40 million bags a week.

a   Has there been a shift in or a movement along the supply curve of crisps?

b   Has there been a shift in or a movement along the demand curve for crisps?

c   What is the new equilibrium price and quantity of crisps?

•11   In problem 9, suppose an increase in the teenage population increases the demand for chewing gum by 40 million packs per week at the same time as the fire occurs. What is the new equilibrium price and quantity of chewing gum?

12 In problem 10, suppose that a flood destroys several potato farms and as a result supply of potato crisps decreases by 20 million bags a week at the same time as the new snack food comes onto the market. What is the new equilibrium price and quantity of crisps?

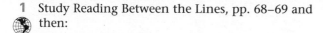

Critical Thinking

1 Study Reading Between the Lines, pp. 68–69 and then:

Use the Parkin, Powell and Matthews website to obtain data on the world price of gold. Draw the demand schedule for gold between 1996 and 2000 and show the effect of falling price on the quantity of gold demanded.

a Decide whether platinum is a complement or a substitute for gold in dental fillings?

b Decide whether gold is a complement or a substitute for palladium in dental fillings?

c Explain why the fall in the price of gold and the rise in the price of palladium led to an increase in the demand for platinum.

2 Use the links on the Parkin, Powell and Matthews website and obtain data on the prices and quantities of wheat.

a Draw a demand and supply diagram to illustrate the market for wheat in 1998.

b Show the changes since 1998 in demand and supply and the changes in the quantity demanded and the quantity supplied that are consistent with the price and quantity data.

3 Turn to pp. 70–71 and read the Economics in History material. Then:

a Explain why there was so much interest in trying to understand the principles of demand and supply during the period of the Industrial Revolution.

b Explain why Alfred Marshall is considered to be the 'father' of modern economics.

Demand and Supply: The Price of Platinum and Palladium

THE GUARDIAN, 15 MAY 2001

Precious little platinum drives up price

Terry Macallister

Precious metals have seen prices soar as demand outstrips supply.... The wholesale price of platinum reached a 13-year high in January.

Stores in Tokyo have seen an increasing number of consumers selling back their rings to have them melted down to take advantage of platinum prices, which rose 50 per cent in 2000 ...

One of the main drivers for platinum demand will be the automobile industry, which has been using platinum on catalytic converters to reduce exhaust emissions.... This need is expected to grow as vehicles come under strict pollution controls.

Dental surgeries are also likely to use more platinum because it is used as a hardening agent alongside gold. Patients are increasingly asking for gold fillings because the price of the yellow metal has fallen while palladium – a good substitute – has soared.

Johnson Matthey, which brings in 70 per cent of its revenues through precious metals, predicts the price of platinum will average between $550 ... and $825 per ounce over the next half year ...

The price of palladium has been even more volatile, with Johnson Matthey predicting a price range of between $550 and $750 an ounce over the next six months.

Much depends on the actions of the Russian government – the dominant supplier of the metal – whose erratic policy of selling off its large reserves has led to wild fluctuations in price. These supply bottlenecks drove the price of palladium up to $1,040 in January after it had spent much of 1990 at $300 and 1996 at $100.

The high price has led to a 5 per cent fall in total demand ...

Non-Russian mines have been trying to increase their outputs to take advantage of prices. Production problems in South Africa undermine their efforts but this year expect to see increases from both Europe and North America ...

The Essence of the Story

- The prices of platinum and palladium (always quoted in dollars) have soared.
- One dealer predicts the price of platinum will range between $550 and $825 an ounce and the price of palladium will range between $550 and $750 an ounce during 2001.
- The demand for platinum is being driven by its use in catalytic converters and by dentists.
- The supply of palladium is dominated by the government of Russia, which holds large reserves and pursues erratic policies.
- Withholding supply drove the price of palladium up to $1,040 an ounce in January 2001. During 1990 it was $300 and in 1996, it fell to $100.
- The high price of palladium led to a 5 per cent fall in demand.
- Mines in South Africa, Europe and North America have tried to increase their output of palladium to take advantage of the higher prices.
- People are selling their platinum rings and having them melted down to take advantage of the high price.

Economic Analysis

- Figure 1 shows the world market for platinum. In January 1999, the supply curve was S and the demand curve was D_{99}. The equilibrium price was $350 an ounce and the quantity was 5.0 million ounces – at point a.

- The world demand for platinum increased and by January 2000, the demand curve for platinum had shifted rightward from D_{99} to D_{00}. The supply of platinum remained constant but the quantity of platinum supplied increased – shown by a movement along the supply curve. The equilibrium price rose to $550 an ounce and the equilibrium quantity increased to 5.6 million ounces – at point b.

- World demand for platinum increased further in 2001 as the need for catalytic converters increased but also because the need for platinum as a hardener in gold fillings increased. The demand curve shifted rightward from D_{00} to D_{01}.

- The supply of platinum remained constant but again the quantity of platinum supplied increased, shown by a further movement up along the supply curve. The equilibrium price rose to $625 an ounce and the equilibrium quantity increased to 6.0 million ounces – at point c. The sale of platinum rings is part of the activity that brings about the increase in the quantity of platinum supplied when the price rises.

- Figure 2 shows the world market for palladium. In 1990, the supply curve was S_{90} and the demand curve was D. The equilibrium price was $300 an ounce and the equilibrium quantity was 5.0 million ounces – at point a.

- When the Russian government sold large reserves between 1990 and 1996, the supply increased and the supply curve shifted righward from S_{90} to S_{96}. The demand for palladium did not change, but the quantity of palladium demanded increased. The equilibrium price fell to $100 an ounce and the equilibrium quantity increased to 5.25 million ounces – shown by a movement down along the demand curve to the new equilibrium at b.

- As Russian stocks of palladium dried up, the world supply of palladium decreased and the supply curve shifted leftward to S_{01}. The equilibrium price rose to $1,040 an ounce and the equilibrium quantity decreased to 4.75 million ounces. The quantity of palladium demanded decreased, shown by a movement upward along the demand curve to point c.

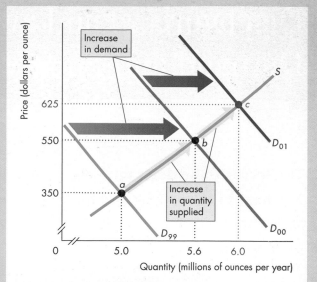

Figure 1 The market for platinum

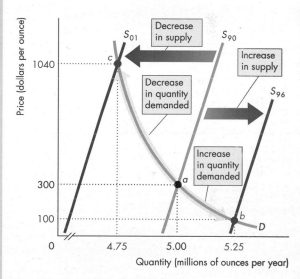

Figure 2 The market for palladium

- The news article confuses demand and quantity demanded. The demand for palladium did not decrease by 5 per cent, as stated in the article. It is the quantity of palladium demanded that decreased by 5 per cent.

- The attempts by South African, European and North American palladium mines to increase their output are movements along the new supply curve as these producers try to take advantage of the new higher price.

Discovering the Laws of Demand and Supply

The forces to be dealt with are . . . so numerous, that it is best to take a few at a time . . . Thus we begin by isolating the primary relations of supply, demand, and price.

Alfred Marshall, The Principles of Economics

The Economist: Alfred Marshall

Alfred Marshall (1842–1924) grew up in an England that was being transformed by the railway and by the expansion of manufacturing. Mary Paley Marshall was one of Marshall's students at Cambridge, and when Alfred and Mary married, in 1877, celibacy rules barred Marshall from continuing to teach at Cambridge. By 1884, with more liberal rules, the Marshalls returned to Cambridge, where Alfred became Professor of Political Economy.

Many others had a hand in refining the theory of demand and supply, but the first thorough and complete statement of the theory as we know it today was set out by Alfred Marshall, with the acknowledged help of Mary. Published in 1890, the monumental treatise *The Principles of Economics*, became the textbook on economics on both sides of the Atlantic for almost half a century. Marshall was an outstanding mathematician, but he kept mathematics and even diagrams in the background. His supply and demand diagram appears only in a footnote.

The Issues and Ideas

The laws of demand and supply that you studied in Chapter 3 were discovered during the 1830s by Antoine-Augustin Cournot (1801–1877), a professor of mathematics at the University of Lyon, France. Although Cournot was the first to use demand and supply, it was the development and expansion of the railways during the 1850s that gave the newly emerging theory its first practical applications. Railways then were at the cutting edge of technology just as airlines are today. And as in the airline industry today, competition among the railways was fierce.

Dionysius Lardner (1793–1859), an Irish professor of philosophy at the University of London, used demand and supply to show railway companies how they could increase their profits by cutting rates on long-distance business on which competition was fiercest and by raising rates on short-haul business on which they had less to fear from other transport suppliers. Today, economists use the principles that Lardner worked out during the 1850s to calculate the freight rates and passenger fares that will give airlines the largest possible profit. The rates calculated have a lot in common with the railway rates of the nineteenth century. On local routes on which there is little competition, fares per kilometre are highest, and on long-distance routes on which the airlines compete fiercely, fares per kilometre are lowest.

Known satirically among scientists of the day as 'Dionysius Diddler', Lardner worked on an amazing range of problems from astronomy to railway engineering to economics. A colourful character, he would have been a regular guest of Clive Anderson if talk shows had been around in the 1850s. Lardner visited the École des Ponts et Chaussées (School of Bridges and Roads) in Paris and must have learned a great deal from Jules Dupuit.

In France, Jules Dupuit (1804–1866), a French engineer/economist, used demand to calculate the benefits from building a bridge and, once the bridge was built, for calculating the toll to charge for its use. His work was the forerunner of what is today called *cost–benefit analysis*. Working with the principles invented by Dupuit, economists today calculate the costs and benefits of motorways and airports, dams and power stations.

Then . . .

Dupuit used the law of demand to determine whether a bridge or canal would be valued enough by its users to justify the cost of building it. Lardner first worked out the relationship between the cost of production and supply and used demand and supply theory to explain the costs, prices and profits of railway operations. He also used the theory to discover ways of increasing revenue by raising rates on short-haul business and lowering them on long-distance freight.

. . . And Now

Today, using the same principles devised by Dupuit, economists calculate whether the benefits of expanding airports and air-traffic control facilities are sufficient to cover their costs, and airline companies use the principles developed by Lardner to set their prices and to decide when to offer 'seat sales'. Like the railways before them, the airlines charge a high price per kilometre on short flights, for which they face little competition, and a low price per kilometre on long flights, for which competition is fierce.

Trying These Ideas Today

Using what you know about demand and supply from Chapter 3, and what you have learned about the ideas of Jules Dupuit, you should be able to answer the following questions:

- What types of transport compete with the big national coach companies for long distance intercity travel?
- Why is it cheaper to travel the 300 kilometres from Leeds to London by coach than it is to travel just 60 kilometres from Leeds to Manchester by coach?

CHAPTER 4

Elasticity

After studying this chapter you will be able to:

◆ Define and calculate the price elasticity of demand

◆ Use a total revenue test and an expenditure test to estimate the price elasticity of demand

◆ Explain the factors that influence the price elasticity of demand

◆ Define and calculate other elasticities of demand

◆ Define and calculate the elasticity of supply

OPEC's Dilemma

The leaders of the Organization of Petroleum Exporting Countries (OPEC) want to increase OPEC's revenue. But they have a dilemma. They know that to increase the price of oil, they must restrict its supply. They also know that to sell more oil, they must lower its price. What should they do: restrict supply or lower the price? Which action will increase OPEC's revenue? ◆ OPEC's leaders need to know a lot about the demand for oil. For example, if the world economy is in recession, how will that slowdown affect the demand for oil? What about substitutes for oil? Will we discover new gas reserves or cheaper technology for using coal? Will nuclear energy become safe and cheap enough to compete with oil? ◆ OPEC is not the only organization with a dilemma. A bumper grape crop is good news for wine consumers. It lowers the price of wine. But is it good news for grape growers? Do they get more revenue? Or does the lower price more than wipe out their gains from larger quantities sold? ◆ Governments also face dilemmas. Wanting greater tax revenue to balance budgets, governments can increase the tax rates on petrol or alcohol. Do the higher tax rates bring in more tax revenue? Will consumers try to find cheaper substitutes, leading to a tax revenue fall? Can raising the price of petrol really cut the number of miles driven as part of an environmental policy?

◆ ◆ ◆ ◆ In this chapter you will learn how to tackle questions such as the ones just posed. You will learn how we can measure in a precise way the responsiveness of the quantities bought and sold to changes in prices and other influences on buyers or sellers. You will examine OPEC's dilemma and you can read about the dilemma facing governments over the use of petrol taxes for environmental policy in Reading Between the Lines on pages 90–91.

The Price Elasticity of Demand

OPEC's economists, like you, know that when supply decreases, the equilibrium price rises and the equilibrium quantity decreases. But does the price of oil rise by a large amount and the quantity decrease by a little? Or does the price barely rise and the quantity decrease by a large amount? The answer depends on the responsiveness of the quantity demanded to a change in the price. You can see why by studying Figure 4.1, which shows two possible scenarios in the world oil market where prices are always quoted in dollars. Figure 4.1(a) shows one scenario and Figure 4.1(b) shows the other.

In both cases, supply is initially S_0. In part (a), the demand for oil is shown by the demand curve D_a. In part (b), the demand for oil is shown by the demand curve D_b. Initially, in both cases, the price is $10 a barrel and the quantity of oil produced and consumed is 40 million barrels per day.

Now suppose OPEC decides to cut production whatever the price. The supply curve shifts leftward to S_1. In case (a), the price of a barrel of oil rises by an enormous $20 to $30 a barrel and the quantity decreases by 17 to 23 million barrels per day. In contrast, in case (b), the price rises by only $5 to $15 a barrel and the quantity decreases by 25 to 15 million barrels per day.

The different outcomes arise from differing degrees of responsiveness of the quantity demanded to a change in the price. But what do we mean by responsiveness? One possible answer is slope. The slope of demand curve D_a is steeper than the slope of demand curve D_b.

In this example, we can compare the slopes of the two demand curves. But we can't always do so. The reason is that the slope of a demand curve depends on the units in which we measure the price and quantity. And we must often compare the demand curves for different goods and services that are measured in unrelated units. For example, an oil producer might want to compare the demand for oil with the demand for natural gas. Which quantity demanded is more responsive to a price change? This question can't be answered by comparing the slopes of two demand curves. The units of measurement of oil and gas are unrelated. The question can be answered with a measure of responsiveness that is independent of units of measurement. Elasticity is such a measure.

Figure 4.1

How a Change in Supply Changes Price and Quantity

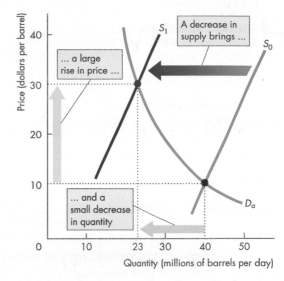

(a) Large price change and small quantity change

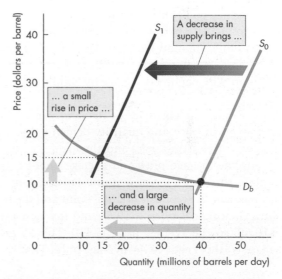

(b) Small price change and large quantity change

Initially the price is $10 a barrel and the quantity sold is 40 million barrels per day. Then supply is decreased from S_0 to S_1. In part (a), the price rises by $20 to $30 a barrel and the quantity decreases by 17 to 23 million barrels a day. In part (b), the price rises by only $5 to $15 a barrel and the quantity decreases by 25 to 15 million barrels a day. This price change is smaller and the quantity change is larger than in case (a). The quantity demanded is more responsive to price in case (b) than in case (a).

The **price elasticity of demand** is a units-free measure of the responsiveness of the quantity demanded of a good to a change in its price when all other influences on buyers' plans remain the same.

Calculating Price Elasticity

We calculate the *price elasticity of demand* by using the formula:

Price elasticity of demand

$$= \frac{\text{Percentage change in quantity demanded}}{\text{Percentage change in price}}$$

To use this formula, we need to know the quantities demanded at different prices when all other influences on buyers' plans remain the same. Suppose we have the data on prices and quantities demanded of oil and calculate the price elasticity of demand for oil.

Figure 4.2 enlarges one section on the demand curve for oil and shows how the quantity demanded responds to a small change in price. Initially the price is $9.50 a barrel and 41 million barrels a day are sold – the original point in the figure. Then the price increases to $10.50 a barrel and the quantity demanded decreases to 39 million barrels a day – the new point in the figure. When the price increases by $1 a barrel, the quantity demanded decreases by 2 million barrels a day.

To calculate the elasticity of demand, we express the changes in price and quantity demanded as percentages of the *average price* and the *average quantity*. By using the average price and average quantity, we calculate the elasticity at a point on the demand curve midway between the original point and the new point. The original price is $9.50 and the new price is $10.50, so the average price is $10. The $1 price increase is 10 per cent of the average price. That is:

$$\Delta P/P_{ave} = (\$1/\$10) \times 100 = 10\%$$

The original quantity demanded is 41 million barrels and the new quantity demanded is 39 million barrels, so the average quantity demanded is 40 million barrels. The 2 million barrel decrease in the quantity demanded is 5 per cent of the average quantity. That is:

$$\Delta Q/Q_{ave} = (2/40) \times 100 = 5\%$$

So the price elasticity of demand, which is the percentage change in the quantity demanded (5 per

Figure 4.2

Calculating Price Elasticity of Demand

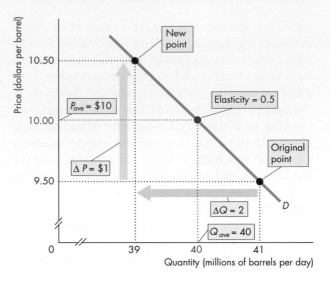

The elasticity of demand is calculated by using the formula:[1]

Price elasticity of demand

$$= \frac{\text{Percentage change in quantity demanded}}{\text{Percentage change in price}}$$

$$= \frac{\%\Delta Q/Q_{ave}}{\%\Delta P/P_{ave}}$$

$$= \frac{2/40}{1/10} = 0.5$$

This calculation measures the elasticity at an average price of $10 a barrel and an average quantity of 40 million barrels.

---

[1] In the formula the Greek letter delta (Δ) stands for 'change in' and % Δ stands for 'percentage change in'.

---

cent) divided by the percentage change in price (10 per cent), is 0.5. That is:

$$\text{Price elasticity of demand} = \frac{\%\Delta Q}{\%\Delta P}$$

$$= \frac{5\%}{10\%} = 0.5$$

Average Price, Average Quantity and Arc Elasticity

We use the average price and average quantity to avoid having two values for the elasticity of demand, depending on whether the price increases or decreases. A price increase of $1 is 10.5 per cent of $9.50, and 2 million barrels is 4.9 per cent of 41 million barrels. If we use these numbers to calculate the elasticity, we get 0.47. A price decrease of $1 is 9.5 per cent of $10.50, and 2 million barrels is 5.1 per cent of 39 million barrels. Using these numbers to calculate the elasticity, we get 0.54. By using average price and average quantity, we get the same value for elasticity regardless of whether price falls or rises. The average price method gives an estimate of the price elasticity of demand between two points on the demand curve – between the prices $9.50 and $10.50 in this case. This is called the **arc elasticity of demand**. You can find examples of how to find the price elasticity value at one specific point – point elasticity – on the Parkin, Powell and Matthews website as well as examples using differential calculus.

A Units-Free Measure

Now that you've calculated a price elasticity of demand, you can see why it is a *units free measure*. Elasticity is the ratio of two percentage change values. When we divide one percentage change by another, the 100s cancel leaving a ratio of proportions without specified units such as barrels or dollars. Elasticity is a units-free measure because the percentage change in each variable is independent of the units in which the variable is measured.

Minus Sign and Elasticity

When the price of a good *rises*, the quantity demanded *decreases* along the demand curve. Because a *positive* change in the price brings a *negative* change in the quantity demanded, the price elasticity of demand is a negative number. But it is the magnitude, or *absolute value*, of the price elasticity of demand that tells us how responsive – how elastic – demand is. To compare elasticities, we use the magnitude of the price elasticity of demand and ignore the minus sign.

Interpreting the Value of Price Elasticity of Demand

Now that you have calculated the value of price elasticity of demand, you need to know what it means. The value of 0.5 for the price elasticity of oil is telling you that a 1 per cent rise in the price of oil will lead to a 0.5 per cent fall in the quantity demanded. Alternatively, a 1 per cent fall in price will lead to a 0.5 per cent rise in quantity demanded.

Inelastic and Elastic Demand

Figure 4.3 shows three demand curves that cover the entire range of possible elasticities of demand. In Figure 4.3(a), the quantity demanded is constant regardless of the price. If the quantity demanded remains constant when the price changes, then the

Figure 4.3

Inelastic and Elastic Demand

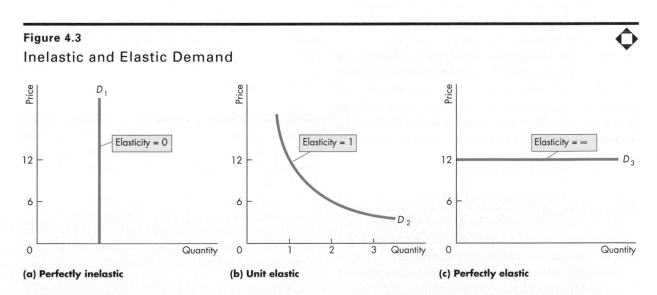

(a) Perfectly inelastic

(b) Unit elastic

(c) Perfectly elastic

Elasticity usually varies along the demand curve, but each demand curve illustrated here has a constant elasticity. The demand curve in part (a) is for a good that has a zero price elasticity of demand. The demand curve in part (b) is for a good with a unit elasticity of demand. The demand curve in part (c) is for a good with an infinite elasticity of demand.

elasticity of demand is zero and demand is said to be **perfectly inelastic**. One good that has a low elasticity of demand is insulin. Insulin is of such importance to some diabetics that they will buy the quantity that keeps them healthy at almost any price.

If the percentage change in the quantity demanded equals the percentage change in price, the elasticity of demand is 1 and demand is said to be **unit elastic**. The demand curve in Figure 4.3(b) is an example of unit elastic demand.

Between the examples shown in parts (a) and (b) of Figure 4.3 are the more general cases when the percentage change in the quantity demanded is less than the percentage change in price. In these cases, the price elasticity of demand lies between zero and one and demand is said to be **inelastic**. Bread and tobacco are examples of goods with inelastic demand.

If the quantity demanded is infinitely responsive to a price change, then price elasticity of demand is infinity and demand is said to be **perfectly elastic**. The demand curve in Figure 4.3(c) is an example of perfectly elastic demand. An example of a good that has a high elasticity of demand (almost infinite) is ballpoint pens from the university bookshop and from the newsagent's shop close by. If the two shops offer pens for the same price, some people buy from one and some from the other. But if the bookshop increases the price of pens, even by a small amount, while the shop close by maintains the lower price, the quantity of pens demanded from the bookshop will fall to zero. Ballpoint pens from the two shops are perfect substitutes for each other.

Between the examples shown in parts (b) and (c) of Figure 4.3 are the general cases when the percentage change in the quantity demanded exceeds the percentage change in price. In these cases, price elasticity of demand is greater than 1 and demand is said to be **elastic**. Wine and fresh meat are examples of goods with elastic demand.

Elasticity Along a Straight-line Demand Curve

Elasticity and slope are not the same but they are related. To understand how they are related, let's look at elasticity along a straight-line demand curve – a demand curve that has a constant slope.

Figure 4.4 illustrates the calculation of elasticity along a hypothetical straight-line demand curve for oil. Let's calculate the price elasticity of demand for oil when the price rises by $20 from $30 to $50 a

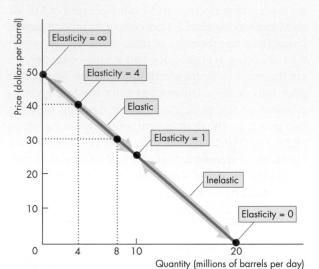

Figure 4.4

Elasticity Along a Straight-line Demand Curve

On a straight-line demand curve, elasticity decreases as the price falls and the quantity demanded increases. Demand is unit elastic at the midpoint of the demand curve (elasticity is 1). Above the midpoint demand is elastic, and below the midpoint demand is inelastic. Demand is perfectly elastic (elasticity = infinity) where quantity demanded is zero, and demand is perfectly inelastic (elasticity = zero) where the price is zero.

barrel. The average price in this case is $40 and so the proportionate change in price is:

$$\Delta P/P_{ave} = \$20/\$40$$

When the price rises from $30 to $50 a barrel, the quantity falls by 8 million barrels per day from 8 to zero and the average quantity demanded is 4 million barrels. So the proportionate change in quantity is:

$$\Delta Q/Q_{ave} = 8/4$$

Now divide the proportionate change in the quantity demanded by the proportionate change in the price to calculate price elasticity of demand:

$$\frac{\Delta Q/Q_{ave}}{\Delta P/P_{ave}} = \frac{8/4}{20/40} = 4$$

You can repeat the calculation that you've just done at any price and quantity along the demand curve. Because the demand curve for oil in this example is a straight line, a $20 price change brings an 8 million barrel quantity change at every average price. So in the elasticity formula, $\Delta Q = 8$ and $\Delta P = 20$ regardless of average quantity and average price. But the lower the average price, the greater is the average quantity demanded. So the lower the average price, the less elastic is demand.

Check this proposition by calculating the elasticity of demand for oil at the midpoint of the demand curve, where the price is $25 a barrel and the quantity demanded is 10 million barrels a day. The proportionate change in price is

$$\Delta P/P_{\text{ave}} = \$20/\$25 = 0.8$$

The proportionate change in the quantity demanded is

$$\Delta Q/Q_{\text{ave}} = 8/10 = 0.8$$

Now divide the proportionate change in quantity demanded by the proportionate change in price to find price elasticity of demand:

$$\frac{\Delta Q/Q_{\text{ave}}}{\Delta P/P_{\text{ave}}} = \frac{8/10}{20/25} = \frac{0.8}{0.8} = 1$$

If the price elasticity of demand is 1, a 1 per cent change in price leads to a 1 per cent change in quantity. On a straight-line demand curve, the price elasticity is always 1 at the midpoint. Above the midpoint demand is elastic, and below the midpoint demand is inelastic. Demand is perfectly elastic (infinity) where the quantity demanded is zero and perfectly inelastic (zero) where the price is zero.

Elasticity and Total Revenue

Total revenue from the sale of a good equals the price of the good multiplied by the quantity sold. So can oil producers like OPEC increase total revenue by cutting supply and raising price? When a price changes, total revenue changes. But a rise in price does not always increase total revenue. The change in total revenue depends on the elasticity of demand.

◆ If demand is elastic, a 1 per cent price rise decreases the quantity sold by more than 1 per cent and total revenue decreases.

◆ If demand is unit elastic, a 1 per cent price rise decreases the quantity sold by 1 per cent and so total revenue does not change.

◆ If demand is inelastic, a 1 per cent price rise decreases the quantity sold by less than 1 per cent and total revenue increases.

Figure 4.5 shows how we can use this relationship between elasticity and total revenue to estimate elasticity using the total revenue test. The total revenue test is a method of estimating the price elasticity of demand by observing the change in total revenue that results from a price change (other things constant).

◆ If a price rise decreases total revenue, demand is elastic.

◆ If a price rise increases total revenue, demand is inelastic.

◆ If a price rise leaves total revenue unchanged, demand is unit elastic.

Figure 4.5 (a) shows the same hypothetical demand curve for oil as in Figure 4.4. Over the price range from $50 to $25, demand is elastic. Over the price range from $25 to zero, demand is inelastic. At a price of $25, demand is unit elastic. In Figure 4.5(b) you can see how total revenue changes. At a price of $50, the quantity sold is zero so total revenue is also zero. At a price of zero, the quantity demanded is 20 million barrels a day, but at a zero price, total revenue is again zero. A price rise in the elastic range brings an decrease in total revenue – the percentage decrease in the quantity demanded is greater than the percentage increase in price. A price rise in the inelastic range brings a increase in total revenue – the percentage decrease in the quantity demanded is less than the percentage increase in price. At the point of unit elasticity, total revenue is at a maximum.

So if when the price of any good rises and you spend less on it, your demand for that good is elastic; if you spend the same amount, your demand is unit elastic; and if you spend more, your demand is inelastic.

The Factors that Influence the Elasticity of Demand

Actual values of elasticities of demand have been estimated and some examples for the United Kingdom are set out in Table 4.1. You can see that these real-world elasticities of demand range from 1.4 for fresh meat, the most elastic in the table, to zero for bread, the least elastic in the table. What makes the demand

Figure 4.5

Elasticity and Total Revenue

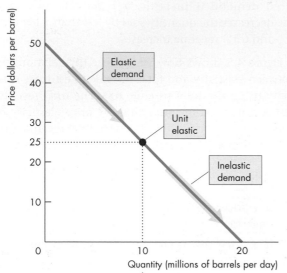

(a) Demand

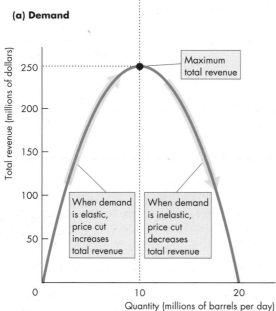

(b) Total revenue

When demand for oil is elastic, in the price range from $50 to $25 (these figures are hypothetical), an increase in price (in part a) brings a decrease in total revenue (in part b). When demand for oil is inelastic, in the price range from $25 to zero, an increase in price (in part a) brings an increase in total revenue (in part b). When demand is unit elastic, at a price of $25 (in part a), total revenue is at a maximum (in part b).

Table 4.1 Some Real-world Price Elasticities of Demand

Good or service	Elasticity
Elastic demand	
Fresh meat	1.4
Spirits	1.3
Wine	1.2
Unit elasticity	
Services	1.0
Cereals	1.0
Inelastic demand	
Durable goods	0.9
Fruit juice	0.8
Green vegetables	0.6
Tobacco	0.5
Beer	0.5
Bread	0.0

Sources: Ministry of Agriculture, Food and Fisheries, *Household Food Consumption and Expenditure*, 1992, London, HMSO. C. Godfrey, Modelling Demand. In *Preventing Alcohol and Tobacco Problems*, Vol. 1, (A. Maynard and P. Tether, eds), Avebury, 1990. J. Muellbauer, 'Testing the Barten Model of Household Composition Effects and the Cost of Children', *Economic Journal*, (September 1977).

for some goods elastic and the demand for others inelastic? Elasticity depends on three main factors:

1 The closeness of substitutes.

2 The proportion of income spent on the good.

3 The time elapsed since a price change.

Closeness of Substitutes

The closer the substitutes for a good or service, the more elastic is the demand for it. For example, tobacco and housing have few real substitutes. As a result, the demand for tobacco and housing is inelastic. In contrast, fresh meat has many substitutes (fish, cheese, vegetables, and prepared meats), as do metals (carbon fibre and plastics), so the demand for these goods tends to be elastic.

In everyday language we call some goods, such as food and housing, *necessities* and other goods, such as exotic vacations, *luxuries*. Necessities are goods that have poor substitutes and that are crucial for our well-being, so generally they have inelastic demands. Luxuries are goods that usually have many substitutes and so have elastic demands.

The degree of substitutability between two goods also depends on how narrowly (or broadly) we define them. For example, even though oil does not have many close substitutes, different types of oil are close substitutes for each other. The elasticity of demand for oil in general is lower than the elasticity of demand for different types of oil.

Proportion of Income Spent on the Good

Other things remaining the same, the higher the proportion of income spent on a good, the more elastic is the demand for it.

Think about your own elasticity of demand for crisps and textbooks. If the price of a packet of crisps doubles, you'll consume nearly as many crisps as you did before. Your demand for crisps is inelastic. But if the price of textbooks doubles, you'll really notice and you'll use the library more and share books with your friends. Your demand for textbooks is more elastic than your demand for crisps. Why the difference? Textbooks take a large proportion of your budget while crisps take only a tiny portion. You don't like either price increase, but you hardly notice the higher price of crisps, but the higher price of textbooks puts your budget under severe strain.

Figure 4.6 shows the proportion of income spent on food and the price elasticity of demand for food in 10 countries. This figure confirms the general tendency we have just described. The larger the proportion of income spent on food, the more price elastic is the demand for food. The general pattern is strong but there are a few exceptions in the figure. For example, in a very poor country like Tanzania, where 62 per cent of income is spent on food, the price elasticity of demand for food is 0.77. In contrast, in a richer country like Germany where 15 per cent of income is spent on food, the elasticity of demand for food is 0.23.

Time Elapsed Since Price Change

The greater the time lapse since a price change, the more elastic is demand. When a price changes, consumers often continue to buy similar quantities of a good for a while. But given enough time, they find acceptable and less costly substitutes. As this process of substitution occurs, the quantity purchased of an item that has become more expensive gradually declines. When a price falls, consumers buy more of the good. But as time passes they too find more creative ways of using less expensive substitutes and demand becomes more elastic.

Figure 4.6

The Price Elasticity of Demand for Food in Ten Countries

As income increases and the proportion of income spent on food decreases, the demand for food becomes less elastic.

Source: Henri Theil, Ching-Fan Chung and James L. Seale Jr, *Advances in Econometrics, Supplement 1*, 1989, *International Evidence on Consumption Patterns*. Greenwich, Connecticut JAI Press Inc.

Review Quiz

◆ Define and calculate the price elasticity of demand.

◆ If the price elasticity of demand for tobacco is 0.5, explain what this means in terms of the impact of a price change on quantity demanded.

◆ Why, when calculating price elasticity of demand, is it useful to express the change in the price as a percentage of the *average* price, and the change in the quantity as a percentage of the *average* quantity?

◆ What is the total revenue test and how does it work?

◆ What are the main influences on the price elasticity of demand that make the demand for some goods elastic and the demand for other goods inelastic at any point in time?

Now you have studied how demand responds to a price change, you are ready to consider two other useful elasticity concepts that tell us how demand responds to other influences.

More Elasticities of Demand

If we discovered huge new reserves of natural gas in European waters, the price of gas would probably fall. OPEC's leaders know that gas is a substitute for oil. If the price of a substitute for oil falls, the demand for oil from Europe will decrease. But by how much? OPEC's leaders know that cars and oil or petroleum products are complements. So if the price of cars falls in Europe, European demand for oil and petroleum products will increase. But by how much? When most of the world is facing a recession and a slump in incomes, OPEC's leaders know the demand for oil tends to decrease. But by how much?

OPEC can answer all these questions if it knows the cross elasticity of demand and the income elasticity of demand for oil. We'll look at these concepts now.

Cross Elasticity of Demand

We measure these influences by using the concept of the cross elasticity of demand. The **cross elasticity of demand** is a measure of the responsiveness of the demand for a good to a change in the price of a substitute or complement, other things remaining the same. It is calculated by using the formula:

$$\text{Cross elasticity of demand} = \frac{\text{Percentage change in quantity demanded}}{\begin{array}{c}\text{Percentage change in the price of}\\\text{a substitute or complement}\end{array}}$$

The cross elasticity of demand is positive for a substitute and negative for a complement.

Figure 4.7 illustrates cross elasticity. When the price of gas – a substitute for oil – falls, the demand for oil decreases and the demand curve for oil shifts leftward from D_0 to D_1. Because a fall in the price of gas brings a decrease in the demand for oil, the cross elasticity of demand for oil with respect to the price of gas is positive (a negative divided by a negative is a positive). When the price of a car – a complement of oil – falls, the demand for oil increases and the demand curve for oil shifts rightward from D_0 to D_2. Because a fall in the price of a car brings an increase in the demand for

Figure 4.7

Cross Elasticity of Demand

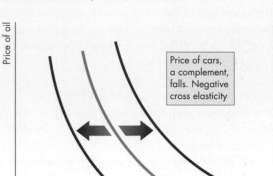

When the price of gas falls, the demand for oil, a *substitute* for gas, decreases and the demand curve for oil shifts leftward from D_0 to D_1. The cross elasticity of the demand for oil with respect to the price of gas is *positive*. When the price of cars falls, the demand for oil, a *complement of cars*, increases and the demand curve for oil shifts rightward from D_0 to D_2. The cross elasticity of the demand for oil with respect to the price of a car is *negative*.

oil, the cross elasticity of demand for oil with respect to the price of a car is negative (a positive divided by a negative is a negative). So positive values identify substitutes and negative values identify complements.

Income Elasticity of Demand

As income falls in a recession, how does the demand for a particular good change? The answer depends on the income elasticity of demand for the good. The **income elasticity of demand** is a measure of the responsiveness of demand to a change in income, other things remaining the same. It is calculated by using the formula:

$$\text{Income elasticity of demand} = \frac{\text{Percentage change in quantity demanded}}{\text{Percentage change in income}}$$

Income elasticities of demand can be positive or negative and fall into three interesting ranges:

Figure 4.8

Income Elasticity of Demand

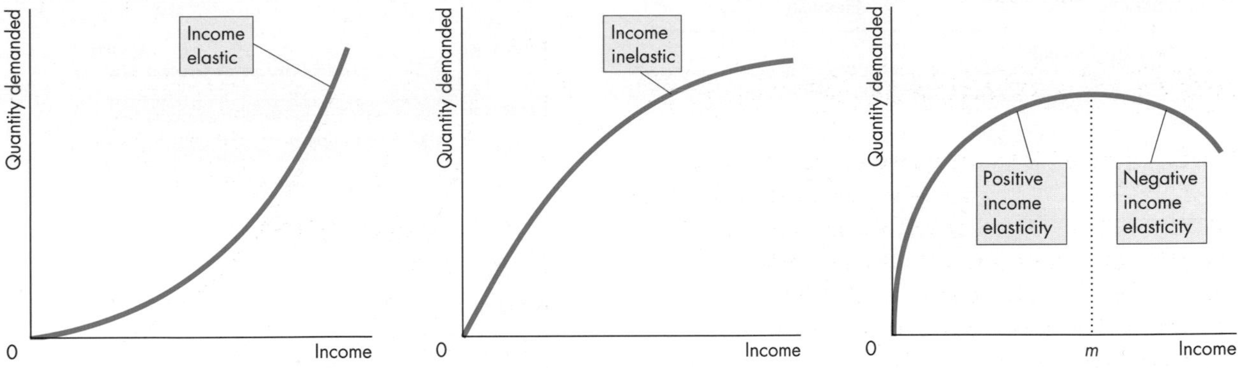

(a) **Elasticity greater than 1**

(b) **Elasticity between zero and 1**

(c) **Elasticity less than 1 and becomes negative**

Income elasticity of demand has three ranges of values. In part (a), income elasticity of demand is greater than 1. In this case, as income increases, the quantity demanded increases but by a bigger percentage than the increase in income. In part (b), income elasticity of demand is between zero and 1. In this case, as income increases, the quantity demanded increases but by a smaller percentage than the increase in income. In part (c), the income elasticity of demand is positive at low incomes but becomes negative as income increases above level m. Maximum consumption of this good occurs at the income m.

1 Greater than 1 (normal good, income elastic).

2 Between zero and 1 (normal good, income inelastic).

3 Less than zero (inferior good).

Figure 4.8(a) shows an income elasticity of demand that is greater than 1. As income increases, the quantity demanded increases, but the quantity demanded increases faster than income. Some examples of income elastic goods are luxuries such as ocean cruises, international travel, jewellery and works of art.

Figure 4.8(b) shows an income elasticity of demand that is between zero and 1. In this case, the quantity demanded increases as income increases, but income increases faster than the quantity demanded. Examples of goods in this category are food, clothing, furniture, newspapers and magazines.

Figure 4.8(c) shows an income elasticity of demand that eventually becomes negative. In this case, the quantity demanded increases as income increases until it reaches a maximum at income m. Beyond that point, as income continues to increase, the quantity demanded declines. The elasticity of demand is positive but less than 1 up to income m. Beyond income m, the income elasticity of demand is negative.

Examples of goods in this category are small motor cycles, potatoes, rice and bread. Low income consumers buy most of these goods. At low income levels, the demand for such goods increases as income increases. But as income increases above point m, consumers replace these goods with superior alternatives. For example, a small car replaces the motor cycle; fruit, vegetables and meat begin to appear in a diet that was heavy in bread, rice or potatoes.

Real-world Income Elasticities of Demand

Table 4.2 shows estimates of some income elasticities of demand in the United Kingdom. Basic necessities such as food and clothing are income inelastic, while luxury goods such as wines and spirits are income elastic. Some goods such as tobacco and bread are inferior goods but their income elasticity values are close to zero.

What is a necessity and what is a luxury depend on the level of income. For people with a low income, food and clothing can be luxuries. So the *level* of income has a big effect on income elasticities of demand. Figure 4.9 shows this effect on the income elasticity of demand for food in 10 countries. In

Table 4.2 Some Real-world Income Elasticities of Demand

Good or service	Elasticity
Normal elastic demand	
Wine	2.6
Services	1.8
Spirits	1.7
Durable goods	1.5
Normal inelastic demand	
Fruit juice	0.9
Beer	0.6
Green vegetables	0.1
Fresh meat	0.0
Cereals	0.0
Inferior	
Tobacco	−0.1
Bread	−0.3

Sources: Ministry of Agriculture, Food and Fisheries, *Household Food Consumption and Expenditure*, 1992, London, HMSO. C. Godfrey, Modelling Demand. In *Preventing Alcohol and Tobacco Problems*, Vol. 1, (A. Maynard and P. Tether, eds), Avebury, 1990. J. Muellbauer 'Testing the Barten Model of Household Composition Effects and the Cost of Children', *Economic Journal*, (September 1977).

Figure 4.9

Income Elasticity of Demand for Food in Ten Countries

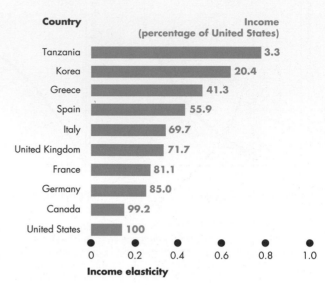

As income increases, the income elasticity of demand for food decreases. For low-income consumers, a larger percentage of any increase in income is spent on food than for high-income consumers.

Source: Henri Theil, Ching-Fan Chung and James L. Seale Jr, *Advances in Econometrics, Supplement 1*, 1989, *International Evidence on Consumption Patterns* 1989, Greenwich, Connecticut JAI Press Inc.

countries with low incomes, such as Tanzania, the income elasticity of demand for food is around 0.75, while in high income countries in Europe and North America, the income elasticity of demand for food is low. These numbers tell us that a 10 per cent increase in income leads to an increase in the demand for food of 7.5 per cent in India and less than 4 per cent in North America and Northern Europe.

Review Quiz

◆ What does cross elasticity of demand measure?
◆ What does the sign (positive or negative) of cross elasticity of demand tell us about the relationship between goods and services?
◆ What does the income elasticity of demand measure?
◆ What does the sign (positive or negative) of income elasticity of demand tell us about a good or service?
◆ Why does the level of income influence the magnitude of the income elasticity of demand?

Now you have studied the different elasticity measures of demand, you are ready to consider the price elasticity of supply.

Elasticity of Supply

You know that when demand decreases, the equilibrium price rises and the equilibrium quantity decreases. But does the price rise by a large amount and the quantity decrease by a little? Or does the price barely rise and the quantity decrease by a large amount?

The answer depends on the responsiveness of the quantity supplied to a change in the price. You can see why by studying Figure 4.10, which shows two possible scenarios in the oil market. Figure 4.10(a) shows one scenario and Figure 4.10(b) shows the other.

Figure 4.10

How a Change in Demand Changes Price and Quantity

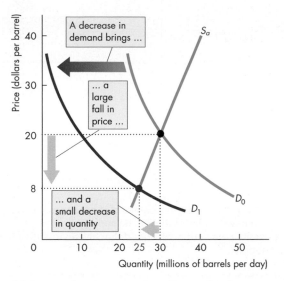

(a) Large price change and small quantity change

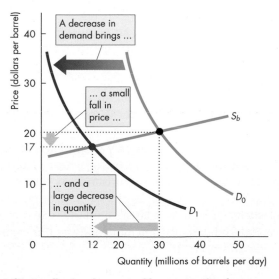

(b) Small price change and large quantity change

Initially, the price is $20 a barrel and the quantity sold is 30 million barrels per day. Then incomes fall in a world recession and demand decreases from D_0 to D_1. In part (a) the price falls by $12 to $8 a barrel and the quantity decreases by just 5 to 25 million barrels per day. In part (b), the price falls by just $3 to $17 a barrel but the quantity decreases by 18 to 12 million barrels per day. The price change is smaller and the quantity change much larger than in case (a). The quantity supplied is more responsive to price in case (b) than in case (a).

In both cases, demand is initially D_0. In part (a), the supply of oil is shown by the supply curve S_a. In part (b), the supply of oil is shown by the supply curve S_b. Initially, in both cases, the price is $20 a barrel and the quantity produced and consumed is 30 million barrels per day.

Now a decrease in income as a result of world recession decreases the demand for oil. The demand curve shifts leftward to D_1. In case (a), the price falls by $12 to $8 a barrel and the quantity decreases by only 5 to 25 million barrels per day. In contrast, in case (b), the price falls by only $3 to $17 a barrel and the quantity decreases by 18 to 12 million barrels per day.

The different outcomes arise from differing degrees of responsiveness of the quantity supplied to a change in the price. We measure the degree of responsiveness by using the concept of the elasticity of supply.

Calculating the Elasticity of Supply

The **elasticity of supply** measures the responsiveness of the quantity supplied of a good to a change in its price. It is calculated by using the formula:

$$\text{Elasticity of supply} = \frac{\text{Percentage change in quantity supplied}}{\text{Percentage change in price}}$$

We use the same method that your learned when you studied the elasticity of demand. Now we can calculate the elasticity of supply for the hypothetical supply curves for oil in Figure 4.10.

In Figure 4.10(a), when the price falls from $20 to $8, the price fall is $12 and the average price is $14, so the price falls by 86 per cent of the average price. The quantity decreases from 30 to 25, so the decrease is 5, the average quantity is 27.5, and the quantity decreases by 18 per cent. The elasticity of supply is equal to 18 per cent divided by 86 per cent, which equals 0.21.

In Figure 4.10(b), when the price falls from $20 to $17, the price fall is $3 and the average price is $18.50, so the price falls by 16 per cent of the average price. The quantity decreases from 30 to 12, so the decrease is 18, the average quantity is 21, and the quantity decreases by 86 per cent. The elasticity of supply is equal to 86 per cent divided by 16 per cent, which equals 5.34.

Figure 4.11 shows the range of supply elasticities. If the quantity supplied is fixed regardless of the price,

Figure 4.11

Inelastic and elastic supply

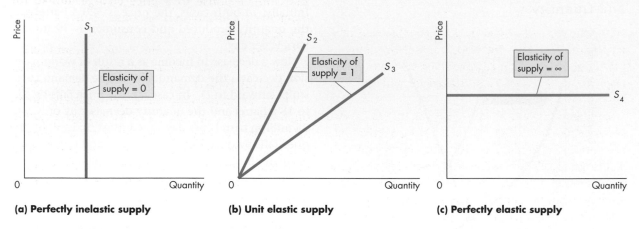

(a) Perfectly inelastic supply   **(b) Unit elastic supply**   **(c) Perfectly elastic supply**

Each supply illustrated here has a constant elasticity. The supply curve in part (a) illustrates the supply of a good that has a zero elasticity of supply. The supply curves in part (b) illustrate the supply of goods that have a unit elasticity of supply. All linear supply curves that pass through the origin have a unit elasticity. The supply curve in part (c) illustrates the supply of a good that has an infinite elasticity of supply.

the supply curve is vertical and the elasticity of supply is zero. Supply is perfectly inelastic. This case is shown in Figure 4.11(a). A special intermediate case is when the percentage change in the price equals the percentage change in quantity. Supply is then unit elastic. This case is shown in Figure 4.11(b). No matter how steep the supply curve is, if it is linear and passes through the origin, supply is unit elastic. If there is a price at which sellers are willing to offer any quantity for sale, the supply curve is horizontal and the elasticity of supply is infinite. Supply is perfectly elastic. This case is shown in Figure 4.11(c).

The Factors that Influence the Elasticity of Supply

The magnitude of the elasticity of supply depends on:

◆ Resource substitution possibilities.

◆ The time-frame for the supply decision.

Resource Substitution Possiblities
Some goods and services are produced by using unique or rare resources of production. These items have a low, and perhaps zero, elasticity of supply. Other goods and services are produced by using more common resources that can be allocated to a wide variety of alternative tasks. Such items have a high elasticity of supply.

A Van Gogh painting is an example of a good with a vertical supply curve and an elasticity of supply equal to zero. At the other extreme, wheat can be grown on land that is almost equally good for growing barley. So it is just as easy to grow wheat or barley, and the opportunity cost of wheat in terms of forgone barley is almost constant. As a result, the supply curve of wheat is almost horizontal and its elasticity of supply is large. Similarly, when a good is produced in many different countries (for example, sugar and beef), the supply of the good is a highly elastic supply.

The supply of most goods and services lies between the two extremes. The quantity produced can be increased but only by incurring higher cost. If a higher price is offered, the quantity supplied increases. Such goods and services have an elasticity of supply between zero and infinity.

Time Frame for Supply Decisions
To study how the length of time elapsing since a price change affects quantity supplied, we distinguish three time frames of supply:

1 Momentary supply.
2 Short-run supply.
3 Long-run supply.

When the price of a good rises or falls, the *momentary supply curve* describes the initial change in the quantity supplied. The momentary supply curve shows the response of the quantity supplied immediately following a price change.

Some goods, such as fruits and vegetables, have a perfectly inelastic momentary supply – a vertical supply curve. The quantities supplied depend on crop planting decisions made earlier. In the case of grapes, for example, planting decisions have to be made many years in advance of the crop being available.

Other goods, such as long-distance phone calls, have an elastic momentary supply. When many people simultaneously make a call, there is a big surge in the demand for cable, computer switching and satellite time and the quantity bought increases (up to the physical limits of the telephone system) but the price remains constant. Long-distance carriers monitor fluctuations in demand and re-route calls to ensure that the quantity supplied equals the quantity demanded without raising the price.

The *long-run supply* curve shows the response of the quantity supplied to a change in price after all the technologically possible ways of adjusting supply have been exploited. In the case of wine, the long run is the time it takes a new vineyard to grow to full maturity – about 15 years. In some cases, the long-run adjustment occurs only after a completely new production plant has been built and workers have been trained to operate it – typically a process that might take several years.

The *short-run supply curve* shows how the quantity supplied responds to a price change when only some of the technologically possible adjustments to production have been made. The first adjustment usually made is in the amount of labour employed. To increase output in the short run, firms make their employees work overtime and perhaps hire additional workers. To decrease their output in the short run, firms lay off workers or reduce their hours of work. With the passage of time, firms can make additional adjustments, perhaps training additional workers or buying additional tools and other equipment. The short-run response to a price change, unlike the momentary and long-run responses, is not a unique response but a sequence of adjustments.

The short-run supply curve slopes upward because producers can take actions quite quickly to change the quantity supplied in response to a price change. For example, in the short run grapes can be left to rot on the vine if the price falls by a large amount. Alternatively, if the price rises, increased use of fertilizers and improved irrigation can increase the yields of existing vines. In the long run, more vines can be planted and increase the quantity supplied even more in response to a given price rise.

Review Quiz

◆ Why do we need a measure of the responsiveness of the quantity supplied of a good or service to a change in its price?
◆ Can you define and calculate the elasticity of supply?
◆ What are the main influences on the elasticity of supply that make the supply of some goods elastic and the supply of other goods inelastic?
◆ Can you provide examples of goods or services whose elasticity of supply are: (a) zero, (b) greater than zero but less than infinity, and (c), infinity?
◆ How does the time frame over which a supply decision is made influence the elasticity of supply?

You have now studied the theory of demand and supply, and you have learned how to measure the elasticities of demand and supply. All the elasticities that you've met in this chapter are summarized in Table 4.3. In the next chapter, we are going to study the efficiency of competitive markets. But before doing that, take a look at Reading Between the Lines, on pp. 90–91 to see elasticity in action.

Table 4.3 A Compact Glossary of Elasticities of Demand ◆

A relationship is described as	When the elasticity value is	Which means that
Price Elasticity of Demand		
Perfectly elastic or infinitely elastic	Infinity	The smallest possible increase in price causes an infinitely large decrease in the quantity demanded*
Elastic	Less than infinity but greater than 1	The percentage decrease in the quantity demanded exceeds the percentage increase in price
Unit elastic	1	The percentage decrease in the quantity demanded equals the percentage increase in price
Inelastic	Greater than zero but less than 1	The percentage decrease in the quantity demanded is less than the percentage increase in price
Perfectly inelastic or completely inelastic	Zero	The quantity demanded is the same at all prices
Cross Elasticity of Demand		
Perfect substitutes	Infinity	The smallest possible increase in the price of one good causes an infinitely large increase in the quantity demanded of the other good
Substitutes	Positive, less than infinity	If the price of one good increases the quantity demanded of the other good also increases
Independent	Zero	The quantity demanded of one good remains constant regardless of the price of the other good
Complements	Less than zero	The quantity demanded of one good decreases when the price of the other good increases
Income Elasticity of Demand		
Income elastic (normal good)	Greater than 1	The percentage increase in the quantity demanded is greater than the percentage increase in income
Income inelastic (normal good)	Less than 1 but greater than zero	The percentage increase in the quantity demanded is less than the percentage increase in income
Negative income elastic (inferior good)	Less than zero	When income increases, quantity demanded decreases
Price Elasticity of Supply		
Perfectly elastic	Infinity	The smallest possible increase in price causes an infinitely large increase in the quantity supplied
Elastic	Less than infinity but greater than 1	The percentage increase in the quantity supplied exceeds the percentage increase in the price
Inelastic	Greater than zero but less than 1	The percentage increase in the quantity supplied is less than the percentage increase in the price
Perfectly inelastic	Zero	The quantity supplied is the same at all prices

* In each description, the directions of change may be reversed. For example in this case: The smallest possible *decrease* in the price causes an infinitely large *increase* in the quantity demanded.

Summary

Key Points

The Price Elasticity of Demand (pp. 73–80)

- Price elasticity of demand is a measure of the responsiveness of the quantity demanded of a good to a change in its price.

- Price elasticity of demand equals the percentage change in the quantity demanded divided by the percentage change in price.

- The larger the magnitude of the elasticity of demand, the greater is the responsiveness of the quantity demanded to a given change in price.

- Price elasticity depends on how easily one good serves as a substitute for another, the proportion of income spent on the good and the length of time that has elapsed since the price change.
- If demand is elastic, a decrease in price leads to an increase in total revenue. If demand is unit elastic, a decrease in price leaves total revenue unchanged. If demand is inelastic, a decrease in price leads to a decrease in total revenue.

More Elasticities of Demand (pp. 80–82)

- Cross elasticity of demand measures the responsiveness of demand for one good to a change in the price of another good (a substitute or a complement).
- The cross elasticity of demand with respect to the price of a substitute is positive. The cross elasticity of demand with respect to the price of a complement is negative.
- Income elasticity of demand measures the responsiveness of demand to a change in income. For normal goods, the income elasticity of demand is positive. For inferior goods, the income elasticity of demand is negative.
- When income elasticity is greater than 1, as income increases, the percentage of income spent on the good increases.
- When income elasticity is less than 1 but greater than zero, as income increases, the percentage of income spent on the good decreases.

Elasticity of Supply (pp. 82–86)

- The elasticity of supply measures the responsiveness of the quantity supplied of a good to a change in its price.
- Supply elasticities are usually positive and range between zero (vertical supply curve) and infinity (horizontal supply curve).

- Supply decisions have three time-frames: momentary, long run and short run.
- Momentary supply refers to the response of suppliers to a price change at the instant that the price changes.
- Long-run supply refers to the response of suppliers to a price change when all the technologically feasible adjustments in production have been made.
- Short-run supply refers to the response of suppliers to a price change after some adjustments in production have been made.

Key Figures and Table

Key Terms

Problems

•1 Rain spoils the Spanish strawberry crop. As a result, the price of strawberries rises from €4 to €6 a box and the quantity demanded decreases from 1,000 to 600 boxes a week. Over this price range,

 a What is the price elasticity of demand?
 b Describe the demand for Spanish strawberries.

2 Good weather brings a bumper French tomato crop. The price of tomatoes falls from €6 to €4 a basket and the quantity demanded increases from 200 to 400 baskets a day. Over this price range,

 a What is the price elasticity of demand?
 b Describe the demand for French tomatoes.

•3 The figure shows the demand for videotape rentals in Germany.

 a Calculate the elasticity of demand for a rise in rental price from €3 to €5.
 b At what price is the elasticity of demand equal to 1?

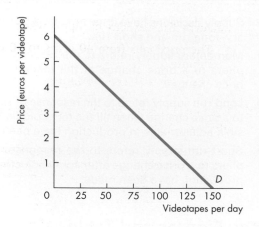

4 The figure shows the demand for pens.

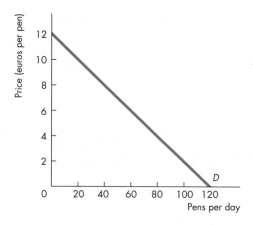

a Calculate the elasticity of demand for a rise in price from €2 to €4.

b At what prices is the elasticity of demand equal to 1, greater than 1, and less than 1?

•5 If the quantity of dental services demanded increases by 10 per cent when the price of dental services falls by 10 per cent, is the demand for dental services inelastic, elastic, or unit elastic?

6 If the quantity of fish demanded decreases by 5 per cent when the price of fish rises by 10 per cent, is the demand for fish elastic, inelastic, or unit elastic?

•7 The demand schedule for computer chips in Europe is:

Price (euros per chip)	Quantity demanded (millions of chips per year)
200	50
250	45
300	40
350	35
400	30

a What will happen to total revenue if the price of a chip falls from €400 to €350?

b What will happen to total revenue if the price of a chip falls from €350 to €230?

c At what price is total revenue maximized?

d What quantity of chips will be sold at the price that answers problem 7(c)?

e At an average price of €350, is the demand for chips elastic or inelastic? Use the total revenue test to answer this question.

8 The demand schedule for coffee in Italy is:

Price (euros per kilogram)	Quantity demanded (millions of kilograms per year)
10	30
15	25
20	20
25	15

a What will happen to total revenue if the price of coffee rises from €10 to €20 per kilogram?

b What will happen to total revenue if the price rises from €15 to €25 per kilogram?

c At what price is total revenue maximized?

d What quantity of coffee will be sold at the price that answers problem 8(c)?

e At an average price of €15 a kilogram, is the demand for coffee elastic or inelastic? Use the total revenue test to answer this question.

•9 In problem 7, at €250 a chip, is the demand for chips elastic or inelastic? Use the total revenue test to answer this question.

10 In problem 8, at €15 a kilogram, is the demand for coffee elastic or inelastic? Use the total revenue test to answer this question.

•11 If a 12 per cent rise in the price of orange juice decreases the quantity of orange juice demanded by 22 per cent and increases the quantity of apple juice demanded by 14 per cent, calculate the cross elasticity of demand between orange juice and apple juice.

12 If a 10 per cent fall in the price of beef increases the quantity of beef demanded by 15 per cent and decreases the quantity of chicken demanded by 20 per cent, calculate the cross elasticity of demand between beef and chicken.

•13 Last year Alex's income increased from €3,000 to €5,000. Alex increased his consumption of bagels from 4 to 8 a month and decreased his consumption of bread rolls from 12 to 6 a month. Calculate Alex's income elasticity of demand for (i) bagels and (ii) bread rolls.

14 Last year Judy's income increased from €10,000 to €12,000. Judy increased her demand for concert tickets by 10 per cent and decreased her demand for bus rides by 5 per cent. Calculate Judy's income elasticity of demand for (i) concert tickets and (ii) bus rides.

•15 The table gives the supply schedule for long-distance phone calls in Greece:

Price (cents per minute)	Quantity supplied (millions of minutes per day)
10	200
20	400
30	600
40	800

Calculate the elasticity of supply when

a The price falls from 40 cents to 30 cents a minute.

b The price is 20 cents a minute.

16 The table gives the supply schedule for designer shoes in Europe.

Price (euros per pair)	Quantity supplied (millions of pairs per year)
120	1,200
125	1,400
130	1,600
135	1,800

Calculate the elasticity of supply when

a The price rises from €125 to €135 a pair.

b The price is €125 a pair.

Critical Thinking

1 Read the article in Reading Between the Lines on pp. 90–91 about the petrol taxes and then:

a Calculate the elasticity value for the demand for petrol when price rises from 82 to 85 pence per litre.

b Calculate the elasticity value for the demand for petrol when price rises from 65 to 70 pence per litre.

c In the March budget after the fuel protests, the Chancellor cut the price of low sulphur petrol and diesel by cutting the fixed tax per litre by at least 2 pence. The result was a revenue loss of £1 bn. Conduct a revenue test using this information.

d If you were the UK chancellor, would you decide to reintroduce the 'escalator tax' next year. Explain your answer.

2 Use the link on the Parkin, Powell and Matthews website to:

a Find information on the price of petrol.

b Use the tools of demand and supply and the concept of elasticity to explain the recent changes in the price of petrol.

c Find the latest price of crude oil.

d Use the tools of demand and supply and the concept of elasticity to explain the recent changes in the price of crude oil.

3 Use the link on the Parkin, Powell and Matthews website to answer the following:

a Find the number of gallons in a barrel.

b What is the cost of the crude oil in one gallon of petrol?

c What are the other costs that make up the total cost of a gallon of petrol?

d If the price of crude oil falls by 10 per cent, by what percentage would you expect the price of petrol to change, other things remaining the same?

e In light of your answer to part (d), do you think the elasticity of demand for crude oil is greater than, less than, or equal to the elasticity of demand for petrol?

Elasticity: Taxes Pump up the Price

THE GUARDIAN, 9 SEPTEMBER 2000

Tax rises fail to cut car journeys

Charlotte Denny

Three years ago, when Gordon Brown announced that he would be hitting motorists with above-inflation increases in fuel duties, he claimed drivers' pain would be the environment's gain.

The theory was that by increasing the costs of filling up at the pump, the Treasury would persuade drivers to leave the wheels at home and take public transport or walk thus decreasing Britain's emissions of greenhouse gases.

In fact, Labour's decision . . . owed more to the gaping government deficit . . . than to environmental considerations.

Revenues from petrol taxes bring a healthy £22 bn a year to the Treasury coffers. When Mr Brown scrapped the escalator last year, opting to increase fuel duties only by inflation, he deprived the Treasury of £2 bn in revenues.

As a result of rapid increases in duties, . . . taxes now account for almost 80 per cent of the cost of a litre of petrol in the UK, the highest proportion in Europe.

Researchers at the Institute of Fiscal Studies estimate that a 10 per cent hike in the cost of driving would reduce the number of miles by less than 5 per cent. 'This is not a very large response, which suggests that any attempt to reduce reliance on the car by increasing the cost of fuel will not have been very successful', the researchers note.

The evidence from the UK certainly bears this out. The annual number of miles driven has risen each year since the introduction of the escalator, despite rising petrol costs. In 1990 British drivers clocked up a total of 253 bn miles . . . Ten years later this had risen by 12 per cent to 284 bn.

The Essence of the Story

- Taxes comprise 80 per cent of the price of petrol in the United Kingdom, the highest proportion in Europe.

- The fuel escalator tax allowed governments to raise the tax on fuel each year by more the rate of inflation.

- When the Chancellor scrapped the fuel escalator tax in 1999, government revenue fell by £2 billion.

- The Government believes that higher petrol prices reduce the number of car journeys and emissions of greenhouse gases.

- Drivers are not very responsive to petrol price increases. Since 1990, the total number of miles driven each year has risen despite petrol price increases.

Economic Analysis

■ The price elasticity of demand equals the percentage change in the quantity demanded divided by the percentage change in price, using the *average* quantity and *average* price.

■ Let's assume a constant relationship between the number of miles driven and the quantity of petrol demanded. Then the percentage change in miles driven is equal to the percentage change in quantity of petrol demanded.

■ The price elasticity of demand for petrol is equal to the percentage change in quantity (5%) divided by the percentage change in price (10%), which is 0.5. The demand for petrol is inelastic.

■ The article was written just after the petrol price protests in September 2000. Farmers and road hauliers in France and the United Kingdom blockaded roads, cities and petrol depots after a sharp rise in petrol price.

■ The news article does not give details of price and quantity changes at the time but these can be found in other sources and are reported in Table 1.

■ Figure 1 illustrates the calculation of the price elasticity of demand for petrol between July and September, 2000.

■ When the price rises from 75 to 82 pence per litre, the quantity demanded decreases from 100 to 95.5 billion litres a year.

■ The price increases by 8.9 per cent of the average price. The quantity demanded decreases by 4.6 per cent of the average quantity. So the price elasticity of demand is 4.6 per cent divided by 8.9 per cent which is 0.52.

■ We can also use the total revenue test to determine whether the price elasticity of demand for petrol is elastic or inelastic. The revenue test says that if a price cut decreases total revenue, demand is inelastic.

Table 1   UK Petrol Price and Quantities

	Price (pence)	Quantity (bn l)
July 2000	75	100
August 2000	82	95.5
Change	7	4.5
Average	78.5	97.75
Change as a % of the Average	8.9	4.6

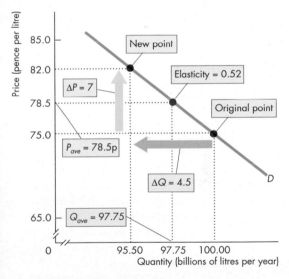

Figure 1

■ When the UK government scrapped the fuel escalator tax in 1999, petrol prices fell with cuts in oil prices. Government revenue decreased by £2 billion confirming that price elasticity of demand for petrol is inelastic.

■ The fact that the number of miles driven each year increases as petrol prices rise can be explained by an annual increase (rightward shift) in the demand for petrol. It does not mean that the demand for petrol is elastic.

CHAPTER 5

Efficiency and Equity

After studying this chapter you will be able to:

◆ Define efficiency

◆ Distinguish between value and price and define consumer surplus

◆ Distinguish between cost and price and define producer surplus

◆ Explain when and why competitive markets move resources to their highest value

◆ Explain the sources of inefficiency in market economies

◆ Explain notions of fairness and assess whether competitive markets result in unfair outcomes

More for Less

People constantly strive to get more for less. As consumers, we love to get a bargain. We enjoy telling our friends about the great deal we got on CDs or some other item we bought at a good price. When we buy something, we express our view about how scarce resources should be used. We try to spend our incomes in ways that get the most out of our scarce resources. For example, we balance the pleasure we get from our expenditure on leisure against the value we get from textbooks and other educational resources. ◆ Is the allocation of our resources between leisure and education, pizza and sandwiches, sports wear and designer jeans, and all the other things we buy the right one? Could we get more out of our resources if we spent more on some goods and less on others? ◆ Scientists and engineers devote enormous effort to find technological innovations that will make more productive use of our scarce land, labour and capital resources. Workers in factories often make suggestions that increase productivity. Is our economy an efficient mechanism for producing goods and services? Do we get the most out of our scarce resources in factories, offices and shops? ◆ Some firms make huge profits year after year. Are they efficient? Are they overcharging for their goods and services. For example, why are DVDs more expensive in Europe than in America? Could this be a sign that the DVD market is not allocating resources in the best possible way and is it fair?

◆ ◆ ◆ ◆ These are the kinds of question that you will explore in this chapter. You will learn some concepts that will help you to think about efficiency more broadly than the everyday use of the word. You will discover that competitive markets can be efficient. You will also discover that markets can be inefficient and that government action can improve market efficiency. Finally, you will learn that firms that make huge profits may be efficient in one sense, but inefficient in a broader sense. You will also learn about different ideas of fairness or equity.

Efficiency: A Refresher

It's hard to talk about efficiency in an ordinary conversation without generating disagreement. To an engineer, an entrepreneur, a politician, a working mother, or an economist, getting more for less seems like a sensible thing to aim for. But some people think that the pursuit of efficiency conflicts with other more worthy goals. Environmentalists worry about contamination from 'efficient' nuclear power plants. Car producers worry about competition from 'efficient' foreign producers.

Economists use the idea of efficiency in a special way that avoids these disagreements. An efficient allocation of resource occurs when we produce the goods and services that people value most highly (see Chapter 2, pp. 24–27). Equivalently, resource use is efficient when we cannot produce more of a good or service without giving up some other good or service that we value more highly.

If people value a nuclear-free environment more highly than they value cheap electric power, it is efficient to use higher-cost, non-nuclear technologies to produce electricity. Efficiency is not a cold, mechanical concept. It is a concept based on value and value is based on people's feelings.

Think about the efficient quantity of pizza. To produce more pizza, we must give up some other goods and services. For example, we might give up some sandwiches. To get more pizzas, we forgo sandwiches. If we have fewer pizzas, we can have more sandwiches. What is the efficient quantity of pizza to produce? The answer depends on marginal benefit and marginal cost.

Marginal Benefit

If we consume one more pizza, we receive a marginal benefit. **Marginal benefit** is the benefit that a person receives from consuming one more unit of a good or service. The marginal benefit from a good or service is measured as the maximum amount that a person is willing to pay for one more unit of it. So the marginal benefit from a pizza is the maximum amount of other goods and services that people are willing to give up in order to get one more pizza. The marginal benefit from pizza decreases as the quantity of pizza consumed increases – the principle of *decreasing marginal benefit*.

We can express the marginal benefit from a pizza as the number of sandwiches that people are willing to

Figure 5.1

The Efficient Quantity of Pizza

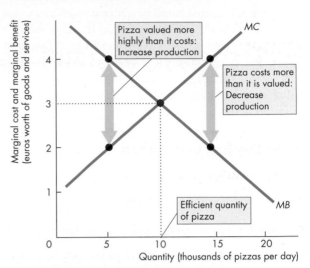

The marginal benefit curve (*MB*) shows what people *are willing to* forgo to get one more pizza. The marginal cost curve (*MC*) shows what people *must* forgo to get one more pizza. If fewer than 10,000 pizzas a day are produced, marginal benefit exceeds marginal cost. Greater value can be obtained by producing more pizzas. If more than 10,000 pizzas a day are produced, marginal cost exceeds marginal benefit. Greater value can be obtained by producing fewer pizzas. If 10,000 pizzas a day are produced, marginal benefit equals marginal cost and the efficient quantity of pizza is available.

forgo to get one more pizza. But we can also express marginal benefit as the money value of other goods and services that people are willing to forgo. Imagine you are visiting Rome. Figure 5.1 shows the marginal benefit in Rome from pizza expressed in this way. As the quantity of pizza increases, the value of other items that people are willing to forgo to get yet one more pizza decreases.

Marginal Cost

If we produce one more pizza, we incur a marginal cost. **Marginal cost** is the opportunity cost of producing *one more unit* of a good or service. The marginal cost of a good or service is measured as the value of the best alternative forgone. So the marginal cost of a pizza is the value of the best alternative forgone to get one more pizza. The marginal cost of a pizza increases as the quantity of pizza produced increases – the principle of *increasing marginal cost*.

We can express marginal cost as the number of sandwiches we must forgo to get one more pizza. But we can also express marginal cost as the euro value of other goods and services we must forgo. Figure 5.1 shows the marginal cost of pizza expressed in this way. As the quantity of pizza produced increases, the value of other items we must forgo to get yet one more pizza increases.

Efficiency and Inefficiency

To determine the efficient quantity of pizza, we compare the marginal cost of a pizza with the marginal benefit from a pizza. There are three possible cases:

1 Marginal benefit exceeds marginal cost.

2 Marginal cost exceeds marginal benefit.

3 Marginal benefit equals marginal cost.

Marginal Benefit Exceeds Marginal Cost

Suppose the quantity of pizza produced is 5,000 a day. Figure 5.1 shows that at this quantity, the marginal benefit of a pizza is €4. That is, when the quantity of pizza available is 5,000 a day, people are willing to pay €4 for the 5,000th pizza.

Figure 5.1 also shows that the marginal cost of the 5,000th pizza is €2. That is, to produce one more pizza, the value of other goods and services that we must forgo is €2. If pizza production increases from 4,999 to 5,000, the value of the additional pizza is €4 and its marginal cost is €2. By producing this pizza, the value of the pizza produced exceeds the value of the goods and services forgone by €2. Resources are used more efficiently – they create more value – if we produce an extra pizza and fewer other goods and services. This same reasoning applies all the way up to the 9,999th pizza. Only when we get to the 10,000th pizza does marginal benefit not exceed marginal cost.

Marginal Cost Exceeds Marginal Benefit

Suppose the quantity of pizza produced in Rome is 15,000 a day. Figure 5.1 shows that at this quantity, the marginal benefit of a pizza is €2. That is, when the quantity of pizza available is 15,000 a day, people are willing to pay €2 for the 15,000th pizza.

Figure 5.1 also shows that the marginal cost of the 15,000th pizza is €4. That is, to produce one more pizza, the value of the other goods and services that we must forgo is €4.

If pizza production decreases from 15,000 to 14,999, the value of the one pizza forgone is €2 and its marginal cost is €4. So by not producing this pizza, the value of the other goods and services produced exceeds the value of the pizza forgone by €2. Resources are used more efficiently – they create more value – if we produce one fewer pizza and more other goods and services. This same reasoning applies all the way down to the 10,001st pizza. Only when we get to the 10,000th pizza does marginal cost not exceed marginal benefit.

Marginal Benefit Equals Marginal Cost

Suppose the quantity of pizza produced is 10,000 a day. Figure 5.1 shows that at this quantity, the marginal benefit of a pizza is €3. That is, when the quantity of pizza available is 10,000 a day, people are willing to pay €3 for the 10,000th pizza.

Figure 5.1 also shows that the marginal cost of the 10,000th pizza is €3. That is, to produce one more pizza, the value of other goods and services that we must forgo is €3.

In this situation, we cannot increase the value of the goods and services produced by either increasing or decreasing the quantity of pizza. If we increase the quantity of pizza, the 10,001st pizza costs more to produce than it is worth. And if we decrease the quantity of pizza produced, the 9,999th pizza is worth more than it costs to produce. So when marginal benefit equals marginal cost, resource use is efficient.

Review Quiz

◆ If the marginal benefit of pizza exceeds the marginal cost of pizza, are we producing too much pizza and too little of other goods, or too little pizza and too much of other goods? Explain.

◆ Explain the relationship between the marginal benefit of pizza and the marginal cost of pizza when we are producing the efficient quanity of pizza.

So does a competitive pizza market produce the efficient quantity of pizza? We'll answer this question now.

Value, Price and Consumer Surplus

To investigate whether a competitive market is efficient, we need to look at the connection between demand and marginal benefit, and supply and marginal cost.

Value, Price and Willingness to Pay

In everyday life we talk about 'getting value for money'. When we use this expression we are distinguishing between *value* and *price*. Value is what we get, and the price is what we pay.

The **value** of one more unit of a good or service is its *marginal benefit*. Marginal benefit can be expressed as the maximum price that people are willing to pay for another unit of the good or service. The willingness to pay for a good or service determines the demand for it.

In Figure 5.2(a) the demand curve shows the quantity demanded in Rome at each price. For example, when the price of a pizza is €3, the quantity demanded is 10,000 pizzas a day. In Figure 5.2(b), the demand curve shows the maximum price that people are willing to pay when there is a given quantity. For example, when 10,000 pizzas a day are available, the most that people are willing to pay for a pizza is €3. This second interpretation of the demand curve means that the marginal benefit from the 10,000th pizza is €3.

When we draw a demand curve, we use a *relative price*, not a *money* price. A relative price is expressed in euro units, but it measures the number of euros-worth of other goods and services forgone to obtain one more unit of the good in question (see Chapter 3, p. 45). So a demand curve tells us the quantity of other goods and services that people are willing forgo to get an additional unit of a good. But this is what a marginal benefit curve tells us too. So, *a demand curve is a marginal benefit curve*.

Figure 5.2

Demand, Willingness to Pay, and Marginal Benefit

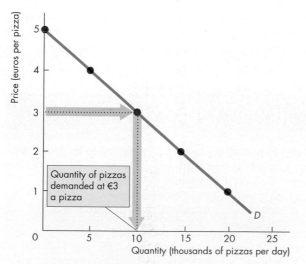

(a) Price determines quantity demanded

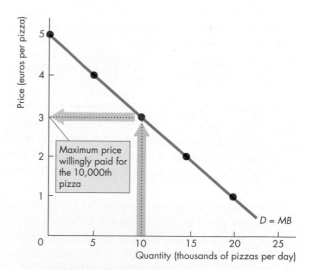

(b) Quantity determines willingness to pay

The demand curve for pizza in Rome, *D*, shows the quantity of pizza demanded at each price, other things remaining the same. It also shows the maximum price that consumers are willing to pay if a given quantity of pizza is available.

At a price of €3, the quantity demanded is 10,000 pizzas a day (part a). If 10,000 pizzas a day are available, the maximum price that consumers are willing to pay for the 10,000th pizza is €3 (part b).

We don't always have to pay the maximum price that we are willing to pay. When we buy something, we often get a bargain. Let's see how.

Consumer Surplus

Figure 5.3

A Consumer's Demand and Consumer Surplus

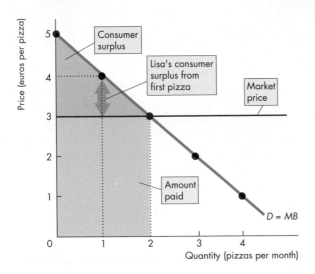

Lisa's demand curve for pizza tells us that at €5 a pizza, she does not buy pizza. At €4 a pizza, she buys one pizza a month; at €3 a pizza, she buys two pizzas a month. Lisa's demand curve also tells us that she is willing to pay €4 for the first pizza and €3 for the second. She actually pays €3 a pizza – the market price – and buys two pizzas a month. Her consumer surplus from pizza is €2 – the area of the green triangle.

When people buy something for less than it is worth to them, they receive a consumer surplus. A **consumer surplus** is the value of a good minus the price paid for it.

To understand consumer surplus, let's look at Lisa's demand for pizza in Rome, which is shown in Figure 5.3. Lisa likes pizza, but the marginal benefit she gets from it decreases quickly as her consumption increases.

If a pizza costs €5, Lisa spends her monthly lunch budget on items that she values more highly than pizza. At €4 a pizza, she buys 1 pizza a month. At €3 a pizza, she buys 2 pizzas a month; at €2 a pizza, she buys 3 pizzas a month, and at €1 a pizza, she buys 4 pizzas a month.

Lisa's demand curve for pizza in Figure 5.3 is also her *willingness-to-pay* or marginal benefit curve. It tells us that if Lisa can have only 1 pizza a month, she is willing to pay €4. Her marginal benefit from the first pizza is €4. If she can have 2 pizzas a month, she is willing to pay €3 for the second pizza. Her marginal benefit from the second pizza is €3.

Figure 5.3 also shows Lisa's consumer surplus from pizza when the price of a pizza is €3. At this price, she buys 2 pizzas a month. A price of €3 a pizza is the most she is willing to pay for the second pizza, so its marginal benefit is exactly the price she pays for it.

But Lisa is willing to pay almost €5 just to get a slice of the first pizza. So the marginal benefit from a slice of this first pizza could be close to €2 more than she pays for it. She receives a *consumer surplus* of almost €2 from just a slice of the first pizza. At a quantity of 1 pizza a month, Lisa's marginal benefit is €4 a pizza. So on this pizza, she receives a consumer surplus of €1. To calculate Lisa's consumer surplus, we must find the consumer surplus on each pizza and add these surpluses together. This sum is the area of the green triangle in Figure 5.3. This area is equal to the base of the triangle (2 pizzas per month) multiplied by the height of the triangle (€2) divided by 2, which is €2 a month.

The blue rectangle in Figure 5.3 is the amount that Lisa pays for pizza, which is €6 a month – 2 pizzas at €3 each. All goods and services are like the pizza example you've just studied. Because of decreasing marginal benefit, people receive more benefit from their consumption than the amount they pay.

Review Quiz

◆ Explain how to measure the value or marginal benefit from a good or service.
◆ Explain the relationship between marginal benefit and the demand curve.
◆ What is consumer surplus and how is it measured?

You've seen how we distinguish between value – marginal benefit – and price. And you've seen that buyers receive a consumer surplus because marginal benefit exceeds price. Next, we're going to study the connection between supply and marginal cost, and learn about producer surplus.

Cost, Price and Producer Surplus

We are now going to look at cost, price and producer surplus in the same way that we looked at the ideas about value, price and consumer surplus in the previous section.

Firms are in business to make a profit. To do so, they must sell their output for a price that exceeds the cost of production. Let's investigate the relationship between cost and price.

Cost, Minimum Supply-price and Supply

When firms earn profit, they receive more (or at least receive no less) for the sale of a good or service than the cost of producing it. Just as consumers distinguish between *value* and *price*, so producers distinguish between *cost* and *price*. Cost is what a producer gives up, and price is what a producer receives.

The cost of producing one more unit of a good or service is its *marginal cost*. And the marginal cost is the minimum price that producers must receive to induce them to produce another unit of the good or service. This minimum acceptable price determines supply.

In Figure 5.4(a), the supply curve shows the quantity supplied at each price. For example, when the price of a pizza is €3, the quantity supplied is 10,000 pizzas a day. In Figure 5.4(b), the supply curve shows the minimum price that producers must be offered to produce a given quantity of pizza. For example, the minimum price that producers must be offered to get them to produce 10,000 pizzas a day is €3 a pizza. This second view of the supply curve means that the marginal cost of the 10,000th pizza is €3.

Because the price is a real price, a supply curve tells us the quantity of other goods and services that *sellers must forgo* to produce one more unit of the good. But a marginal cost curve also tells us the quantity of other goods and services that we must forgo to get one more unit of the good. So, *a supply curve is a marginal cost curve*.

If the price producers receive exceeds the cost they incur, they earn a producer surplus. This producer

Figure 5.4

Supply, Price and Producer Surplus

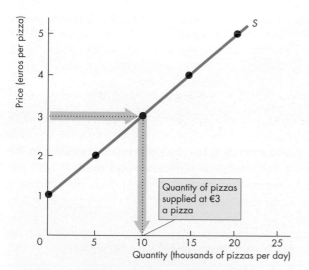

(a) Price determines quantity supplied

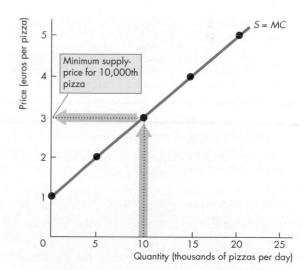

(b) Quantity determines minimum supply-price

The supply curve of pizza, *S*, shows the quantity of pizza supplied at each price, other things remaining the same. It also shows the minimum price that producers must be offered if a given quantity of pizza is to be produced.

At a price of €3, the quantity supplied is 10,000 pizzas a day (part a). If 10,000 pizzas a day are produced, the minimum price that producers must be offered for the 10,000th pizza is €3 (part b).

surplus is the mirror image of the idea of consumer surplus.

Producer Surplus

Figure 5.5

A Producer's Supply and Producer Surplus

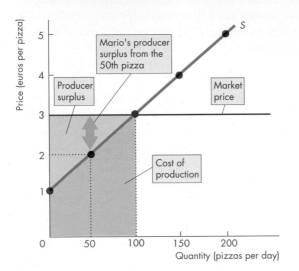

Mario's supply curve of pizza tells us that at a price of €1, Mario plans to sell no pizzas. At a price of €2, he plans to sell 50 pizzas a day; and at a price of €3, he plans to sell 100 pizzas a day. Mario's supply curve also tells us that the minimum he must be offered is €2 for the 50th pizza a day and €3 for the 100th pizza a day. If the market price is €3 a pizza, he sells 100 pizzas a day and receives €300. The red area shows Mario's cost of producing pizza, which is €200 a day, and the blue area shows his producer surplus, which is €100 a day.

When price exceeds marginal costs the firm obtains a producer surplus. A **producer surplus** is the price of a good minus the opportunity cost of producing it. To understand producer surplus, let's look the supply of pizza from Mario's pizza business in Rome in Figure 5.5.

Mario can produce pizza or bake bread that people like a lot. The more pizza he bakes, the less bread he can bake. His opportunity cost of pizza is the value of the bread he must forgo. This opportunity cost increases as Mario increases his production of pizza. If a pizza sells for only €1, Mario produces no pizzas. He uses his kitchen to bake bread. Pizza just isn't worth producing. But at €2 a pizza, Mario produces 50 pizzas a day, and at €3 a pizza, he produces 100 a day.

Mario's supply curve of pizza is also his *minimum supply-price* curve. It tells us that if Mario can sell only one pizza a day, the minimum that he must be paid for it is €1. If he can sell 50 pizzas a day, the minimum that he must be paid for the 50th pizza is €2, and so on.

Figure 5.5 also shows Mario's producer surplus. If the price of a pizza is €3, Mario plans to sell 100 pizzas a day. The minimum that he must be paid for the 100th pizza is €3. So its opportunity cost is exactly the price he receives for it. But his opportunity cost of the first pizza is only €1. So this first pizza costs €2 less to produce than he receives for it. Mario receives a *producer surplus* from his first pizza of €2. He receives a slightly smaller producer surplus on the second pizza, less on the third, and so on until he receives no producer surplus on the 100th pizza.

Figure 5.5 shows Mario's producer surplus as the blue triangle formed by the area above the supply curve and beneath the price line. This area is equal to the base of the triangle (100 pizzas a day) multiplied by the height (€2 a pizza) divided by 2, which equals €100 a day. Figure 5.5 also shows Mario's opportunity costs of production as the red area beneath the supply curve.

Review Quiz

♦ Explain the relationship between the marginal cost or opportunity cost of producing a good or service and the minimum supply price.
♦ Explain the relationship between marginal cost and the supply curve.
♦ What is producer surplus and how is it measured?

Consumer surplus and producer surplus can be used to measure the efficiency of a market. Let's see how we can use these concepts to study the efficiency of a competitive market.

Is the Competitive Market Efficient?

Figure 5.6 shows the market for pizza. The demand for pizza is shown by the demand curve, *D*. The supply of pizza is shown by the supply curve, *S*. The equilibrium price is €3 a pizza, and the equilibrium quantity is 10,000 pizzas a day.

Figure 5.6

An Efficient Market for Pizza

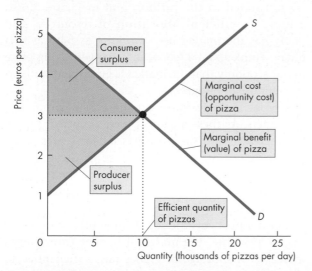

Resources are used efficiently when the sum of consumer surplus and producer suplus is maximized. Consumer surplus is the area below the demand curve and above the market price line – the green triangle. Producer surplus is the area below the price line and above the supply curve – the blue triangle. Here consumer surplus is €10,000, and producer surplus is also €10,000. The total surplus is €20,000. This surplus is maximized when the willingness to pay equals the opportunity cost. The *efficient quantity* of pizza is 10,000 pizzas per day.

The market forces that you studied in Chapter 3, pp. 55–56, will pull the pizza market to this equilibrium. If the price is greater than €3 a pizza, a surplus will force the price down. If the price is less than €3 a pizza, a shortage will force the price up. Only if the price is €3 a pizza is there neither a surplus nor a shortage and no forces operating to change the price.

So the market price and quantity are pulled towards their equilibrium values. But is this competitive equilibrium efficient? Does it produce the efficient quantity of pizza?

Efficiency of a Competitive Market

The equilibrium in Figure 5.6 is efficient. Resources are being used to produce the quantity of pizza that people value most highly. It is not possible to produce more pizza without giving up some other good or service that is valued more highly. And if a smaller quantity of pizza is produced, resources are used to produce some other good that is not valued as highly as the pizza forgone.

To see why the equilibrium in Figure 5.6 is efficient, think about the interpretation of the demand curve as a marginal benefit curve and the supply curve as a marginal cost curve. The demand curve tells us the marginal benefit from pizza. The supply curve tells us the marginal cost of pizza. So where the demand curve and the supply curve intersect, marginal benefit equals marginal cost.

But this condition – marginal benefit equals marginal cost – is the condition that delivers an efficient use of resources. It puts resources to work in the activities that create the greatest possible value. So a competitive equilibrium is efficient.

If production is less than 10,000 pizzas a day, the marginal pizza is valued more highly than its opportunity cost. If production exceeds 10,000 pizzas a day, the marginal pizza costs more to produce than the value that consumers place on it. Only when 10,000 pizzas a day are produced is the marginal pizza worth exactly what it costs. The competitive market pushes the quantity of pizza produced to its efficient level of 10,000 a day. If production is less than 10,000 a day, a shortage raises the price, which stimulates an increase in production. If production exceeds 10,000 a day, a surplus lowers the price, which decreases production.

In a competitive equilibrium, resources are used efficiently to produce the goods and services that people value most highly. And when the competitive market uses resources efficiently, the sum of consumer surplus and producer surplus is maximized.

Buyers and sellers each attempt to do the best they can for themselves and no one plans for an efficient outcome for society as a whole. Buyers seek the lowest possible price and sellers seek the highest possible price.

The Invisible Hand

Writing in his book, *The Wealth of Nations*, in 1776, Adam Smith was the first to suggest that competitive markets send resources to the uses in which they have the highest value. Smith believed that each participant in a competitive market is 'led by an invisible hand to promote an end [the efficient use of resources] which was no part of his intention'.

You can see the invisible hand at work in the cartoon. The cold drinks seller has both cold drinks and shade. He has an opportunity cost of each and a minimum supply-price of each. The park-bench reader has a marginal benefit from a cold drink and from shade. You can see that the marginal benefit from shade exceeds the marginal cost, but the marginal cost of a cold drink exceeds its marginal benefit. The transaction that occurs creates producer surplus and consumer surplus. The seller obtains a producer surplus from selling the shade for more than its opportunity cost and the reader obtains a consumer surplus from buying the shade for less than its marginal benefit. In the third frame of the cartoon both the consumer and the producer are better off than they were in the first frame. The umbrella has moved to its highest value use.

Drawing by M. Twohy; © 1885 The New Yorker Collection.

The Invisible Hand at Work Today

The market economy relentlessly performs the activity illustrated in the cartoon and in Figure 5.6 to achieve an **efficient allocation** of resources. And rarely has the market been working as hard as it is today. Think about a few of the changes taking place in our economy that the market is guiding towards an efficient use of resources.

New technologies have cut the cost of producing computers. As these advances have occurred, supply has increased and the price has fallen. Lower prices that have encouraged an increase in the quantity demanded of this now less costly tool. The marginal benefit from computers is brought into equality with their marginal cost.

An early frost cuts the supply of grapes. With fewer grapes available, the marginal benefit from grapes increases. A shortage of grapes raises their price so that the market allocates the smaller quantity available to the people who value them most highly.

Market forces persistently bring marginal cost and marginal benefit to equality and maximize the sum of consumer surplus and producer surplus.

Obstacles to Efficiency

Although markets generally do a good job at sending resources to where they are most highly valued, they do not always get it right. Sometimes, markets produce too much of a good or service, and sometimes they produce too little. The most significant obstacles to achieving an efficient allocation of resources in a market economy are:

◆ Price ceilings and floors.

◆ Taxes, subsidies and quotas.

◆ Monopoly.

◆ Public goods.

◆ External costs and external benefits.

Price Ceilings and Floors

A **price ceiling** is a regulation that makes it illegal to charge a price higher than a specified level. An example is a price ceiling on housing rents, which some local and regional authorities impose. A price floor is a regulation that makes it illegal to pay a lower price than a specified level. An example is the minimum wage. (We study both of these restrictions on buyers and sellers in Chapter 6.)

The presence of a price ceiling or a price floor blocks the forces of demand and supply and results in a quantity produced that might exceed or fall short of the quantity determined in an unregulated market.

Taxes, Subsidies and Quotas

Taxes increase the prices paid by buyers and lower the prices received by sellers. Taxes decrease the quantity produced (for reasons that are explained in Chapter 6, pp. 120–121). All kinds of goods and services are taxed, but the highest taxes are on petrol, alcohol and tobacco.

Subsidies, which are payments by the government to producers, decrease the prices paid by buyers and increase the prices received by sellers. Subsidies increase the quantity produced.

Quotas, which are limits to the quantity that a firm is permitted to produce, restrict output below the quantity that a competitive market produces. Farms are sometimes subject to quotas.

Monopoly

A **monopoly** is a firm that has sole control of a market. For example, Microsoft has a near monopoly on operating systems for personal computers. Although monopolies earn large profits, they prevent markets from achieving an efficient use of resources. The goal of a monopoly is to maximize profit. To achieve this goal, it restricts production and raises price. (We study monopoly in Chapter 12.)

Public Goods

A **public good** is a good or service where one person's consumption has no effect on the quantity available for everyone else, even if they don't pay for it. Examples are national defence and the enforcement of law and order. Competitive markets would produce too small a quantity of public goods because few people are willing to buy the good. Each person wants to free-ride on the consumption of someone else. It is not in each person's interest to buy her or his share of a public good. So a competitive market produces less than the efficient quantity. (We study public goods in Chapter 16.)

External Costs and Benefits

An **external cost** is a cost not borne by the producer (or consumer) but borne by other people. The cost of pollution is an example of an external cost. When an electric power utility burns coal to generate electricity, it puts sulphur dioxide into the atmosphere. This pollutant falls as acid rain and damages vegetation and crops. The producer does not consider the cost of pollution when it decides what quantity of electric power to supply. Its supply curve is based on its own costs, not on the costs that they inflict on others. As a result, the utility produces more power than the efficient quantity.

An **external benefit** is a benefit that accrues to people other than the buyer of a good. An example is when someone in a neighbourhood paints their home or landscapes their garden. The homeowner does not consider her neighbour's marginal benefit when she decides whether to do this type of work. So the demand curve for house painting and garden improvement does not include all the benefits that accrue. In this case, the quantity falls short of the efficient quantity. (We study externalities in Chapter 18.)

The impediments to efficiency that we've just reviewed and those which you will study in greater detail in later chapters are called market failures. They result in two possible outcomes:

1 Underproduction.

2 Overproduction.

Underproduction

Suppose that one firm owned all the pizza outlets in a city and that it restricted the quantity of pizza produced to 5,000 a day. Figure 5.7(a) shows that at this quantity, consumers are willing to pay €4 for the marginal pizza – marginal benefit is €4. The marginal cost of a pizza is only €2. So there is a gap between what people are willing to pay and what producers must be offered – between marginal benefit and marginal cost.

The sum of consumer surplus and producer surplus is decreased by the amount of the grey triangle in Figure 5.7(a). This triangle is called deadweight loss. **Deadweight loss** is the decrease in consumer surplus and producer surplus that results from an inefficient level of production.

The 5,000th pizza brings a benefit of €4 and costs only €2 to produce. If we don't produce this pizza, we are wasting almost €2. Similar reasoning applies all the way up to the 9,999th pizza. By producing more pizza and less of other goods and services, we get more value from our resources.

Figure 5.7

Underproduction and Overproduction

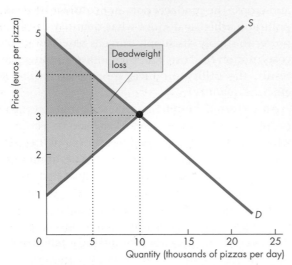

(a) Underproduction

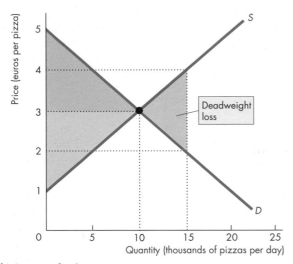

(b) Overproduction

If production is restricted to 5,000 a day, a deadweight loss (the grey triangle) arises. Consumer surplus and producer surplus is reduced to the green area. At 5,000 pizzas, the benefit of one more pizza exceeds its cost. The same is true for all levels of production up to 10,000 pizzas a day. If production increases to 15,000, a deadweight loss arises. At 15,000 pizzas a day, the cost of the 15,000th pizza exceeds its benefit. The cost of each pizza above 10,000 exceeds its benefit. Consumer surplus plus producer surplus equals the green triangle minus the deadweight loss.

The deadweight loss is borne by the entire society. It is not a loss for the consumers and a gain for the producer. It is a *social* loss. You can read about the deadweight loss in the European market for DVDs in Reading Between the Lines on pp. 110–111.

Overproduction

Suppose the pizza lobby gets the government to pay the pizza producers a fat subsidy and that production increases to 15,000 a day. Figure 5.7(b) shows that at this quantity, consumers are willing to pay only €2 for that marginal pizza but the opportunity cost of that pizza is €4. It now costs more to produce the marginal pizza than consumers are willing to pay for it. The gap gets smaller as production approaches 10,000 pizzas a day, but it is present at all quantities greater than 10,000 a day.

Again, deadweight loss is shown by the grey triangle. The sum of consumer surplus and producer surplus is smaller than its maximum by the amount of deadweight loss. The 15,000th pizza brings a benefit of only €2 but costs €4 to produce. If we produce this pizza, we are wasting almost €2. Similar reasoning applies all the way down to the 10,001st pizza. By producing less pizza and more of other goods and services, we get more value from our resources.

Review Quiz

◆ Do competitive markets use resources efficiently? Explain why or why not.
◆ What are the main sources of inefficiency in markets? Explain why each one creates inefficiency.
◆ What is deadweight loss and under what conditions does it arise?

You now know the conditions under which the resource allocation is efficient. You've seen how a competitive market can be efficient and you've seen some impediments to efficiency.

But is an efficient allocation of resources fair? Does the competitive market provide people with fair incomes for their work? And do people always pay a fair price for the things they buy? Don't we need the government to step into some competitive markets to prevent the price from rising too high or falling too low? We'll now study these questions.

Is the Competitive Market Fair?

When a natural disaster strikes, such as a major flood, the price of many essential items jumps. The reason for the price jump is that some people have a greater demand and greater willingness to pay while the items are in limited supply. So the higher prices achieve an efficient allocation of scarce resources. News reports of these price hikes almost never talk about efficiency. Instead, they talk about fairness, or more particularly, unfairness. The claim is that it is unfair for profit-seeking dealers to cheat the victims of natural disaster.

Similarly, when low-skilled people work for a wage that is below what most would regard as a 'living wage', the media and politicians talk of employers taking unfair advantage of their workers.

How do we decide if something is fair or unfair? You know when *you* think something is unfair. But how do you know? What are the *principles* of fairness?

Philosophers have tried for centuries to answer this question. Economists have offered their answers too. But before we look at the proposed answers, you should know that there is no universally agreed answer.

Economists agree about efficiency. That is, they agree that it makes sense to make the economic cake as large as possible and to bake it at the lowest possible cost. But they do not agree about fairness. That is, they do not agree about what are fair shares of the economic cake for all the people who make it. The reason is that ideas about fairness are not exclusively economic ideas. They touch on politics, ethics and religion. Nevertheless, economists have thought about these issues and have a contribution to make. So let's examine the views of economists on this topic.

To think about fairness, think of economic life as a game – a serious game. All ideas about fairness can be divided into two broad groups. They are:

1 It's not fair if the *result* isn't fair.
2 It's not fair if the *rules* aren't fair.

It's not Fair if the *Result* isn't Fair

The earliest efforts to establish a principle of fairness were based on the view that the result is what matters. And the general idea was that it is unfair if people's incomes are too unequal. It is unfair that bank directors earn millions of pounds a year, while bank tellers earn only thousands of pounds a year. It is unfair that a shop owner enjoys a larger profit and her customers pay higher prices in the aftermath of a winter storm.

There was a lot of excitement during the nineteenth century when economists thought they had made the incredible discovery that efficiency requires equality of incomes. To make the economic pie as large as possible, it must be cut into equal pieces, one for each person. This idea turns out to be wrong, but there is a lesson in the reason that it is wrong. So this nineteenth century idea is worth a closer look.

The nineteenth century idea that only equality brings efficiency is called **utilitarianism**. Utilitarianism is a principle that states that we should strive to achieve 'the greatest happiness for the greatest number'. The people who developed this idea were known as utilitarians. They included the most eminent minds such as David Hume, Adam Smith, Jeremy Bentham and John Stuart Mill.

Utilitarianism

Utilitarianism argues that to achieve 'the greatest happiness for the greatest number', income must be transferred from the rich to the poor up to the point of complete equality – to the point that there are no rich and no poor.

They reasoned in the following way: first, everyone has the same basic wants and are similar in their capacity to enjoy life. Second, the greater a person's income, the smaller is the marginal benefit of a pound. The millionth pound spent by a rich person brings a smaller marginal benefit to that person than the marginal benefit of the thousandth pound spent by a poorer person. So by transferring a pound from the millionaire to the poorer person, more is gained than is lost and the two people added together are better off.

Figure 5.8 illustrates this utilitarian idea. Tom and Paul each have the same marginal benefit curve, *MB*. (Marginal benefit is measured on the same scale of 1 to 3 for both Tom and Paul.) Tom is at point *a*. He earns £5,000 a year and his marginal benefit of a pound of income is 3. Paul is at point *b*. He earns £45,000 a year and his marginal benefit of a pound of income is 1. If a pound is transferred from Paul to Tom, Paul loses 1 unit of marginal benefit and Tom gains 3 units. So, adding Tom and Paul together, they are better off. They are sharing the economic pie more efficiently. If a second pound is transferred, the same thing happens: Tom gains more than Paul loses. And the same is true for every pound transferred until

Figure 5.8

Utilitarian Fairness

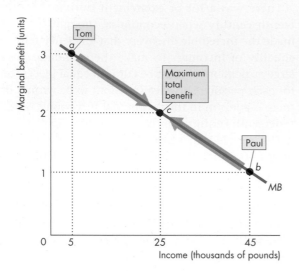

Tom earns £5,000 and has 3 units of marginal benefit of point *a*. Paul earns £45,000 and has 1 unit of marginal benefit of point *b*. If income is transferred from Paul to Tom, Paul's loss is less than Tom's gain. Only when each of them has £25,000 and 2 units of marginal benefit (at point *c*) can the sum of their total benefit increase further.

they each reach point *c*. At point *c*, Tom and Paul each have £25,000 and each have a marginal benefit of 2 units. Now they are sharing the economic pie in the most efficient way. It is bringing the greatest attainable happiness to Tom and Paul.

The big trade-off

One big problem with the utilitarian ideal of complete equality is that it ignores the costs of making income transfers. The economist, Arthur Okun, in his book *Equality and Efficiency: The Big Tradeoff*, described the process of redistributing income as like trying to transfer water from one barrel to another with a leaky bucket. The more we try to increase equity by redistributing income, the more we reduce efficiency. Recognizing the cost of making income transfers leads to what is called 'the big trade-off', – a trade-off between efficiency and fairness.

The big trade-off is based on the following facts. Income can be transferred from people with high incomes to people with low incomes only by taxing incomes. Taxing peoples' income from employment makes them work less. It results in the quantity of labour being less than the efficient quantity. Taxing

peoples' income from capital makes them save less. It results in the quantity of capital being less than the efficient quantity. With smaller quantities of both labour and capital the quantity of goods and services produced is less than the efficient quantity. The economic cake shrinks.

The trade-off is between the size of the economic cake and the degree of equality with which it is shared. The greater the amount of income redistribution through income taxes, the greater is the inefficiency – the smaller is the economic cake.

There is a second source of inefficiency. A pound taken from a rich person does not end up as a pound in the hands of a poorer person. Some of it is spent on administration of the tax and transfer system. The cost of tax-collecting agencies, such as the European Community, and welfare-administering agencies, such as the British Child Benefit Agency, as well as regional government welfare departments, must be paid with some of the taxes collected. Also, taxpayers hire accountants, tax specialists and legal experts to help them ensure that they pay the correct amount of tax. These activities use skilled labour and capital resources that could otherwise be used to produce goods and services that people value.

You can see that when all these costs are taken into account, transferring a pound from a rich person does not give a pound to a poor person. It is even possible that with high taxes, those with low incomes end up being worse off. Suppose, for example, that highly taxed entrepreneurs decide to work less hard and shut down some of their businesses. Low-income workers get fired and must seek other, perhaps even lower-paid work.

Because of the big trade-off, those who say that fairness is equality propose a modified version of utilitarianism.

Rawlsianism

A Harvard philosopher, John Rawls, proposed a modified version of utilitarianism in a classic book entitled *A Theory of Justice*, published in 1971. Rawls says that, taking all the costs of income transfers into account, the fair distribution of the economic pie is the one that makes the poorest person as well off as possible. The incomes of rich people should be taxed and, after paying the costs of administering the tax and transfer system, what is left should be transferred to the poor. But the taxes must not be so high that they make the economic pie shrink to the point that the poorest person ends up with a smaller piece. A bigger share of a smaller cake can be a smaller piece than a smaller share of a bigger cake. The goal is to make the piece enjoyed by the poorest person as big as possible. Most likely this piece will not be an equal share.

The 'fair results' ideas require a change in the results after the game is over. Some economists say these changes are themselves unfair and propose a different way of thinking about fairness.

It's not Fair if the *Rules* aren't Fair

The idea that it's not fair if the rules aren't fair is based on a fundamental principle that seems to be hard wired into the human brain. It is the **symmetry principle**. The symmetry principle is the requirement that people in similar situations be treated similarly. It is the moral principle that lies at the centre of all the big religions. It says, in some form or other, 'behave towards other people in the way you expect them to behave towards you'.

In economic life, this principle translates into *equality of opportunity*. But equality of opportunity to do what? This question is answered by another Harvard philosopher, Robert Nozick, in a book entitled *Anarchy, State, and Utopia*, published in 1974.

Nozick argues that the idea of fairness as an outcome or result cannot work and that fairness must be based on the fairness of the rules. He suggests that fairness obeys two rules. They are:

1   The state must enforce laws that establish and protect private property.

2   Private property may be transferred from one person to another only by voluntary exchange.

The first rule says that everything that is valuable must be owned by individuals and that the state must ensure that theft is prevented. The second rule says that the only legitimate way a person can acquire property is to buy it in exchange for something else that the person owns. If these rules, which are the only fair rules, are followed the result is fair. It doesn't matter how unequally the economic pie is shared provided it is baked by people each one of whom voluntarily provides services in exchange for the share of the pie offered in compensation.

These rules satisfy the symmetry principle. And if these rules are not followed, the symmetry principle is broken. You can see these facts by imagining a world in which the laws are not followed.

First, suppose that some resources or goods are not owned. They are common property. Then everyone is free to participate in a grab to use these resources or goods. The strongest will prevail. But when the strongest prevails, the strongest effectively *owns* the resources or goods in question and prevents others from enjoying them.

Second, suppose that we do not insist on voluntary exchange for transferring ownership of resources from one person to another. The alternative is *involuntary* transfer. In simple language, the alternative is theft.

Both of these situations violate the symmetry principle. Only the strong get to acquire what they want. The weak end up with only the resources and goods that the strong don't want.

In contrast, if the two rules of fairness are followed, everyone, strong and weak, is treated in a similar way. Everyone is free to use their resources and human skills to create things that are valued by themselves and others and to exchange the fruits of their efforts with each other. This is the only set of arrangements that obeys the symmetry principle.

Fairness and Efficiency

Resources will be allocated efficiently if private property rights are enforced and if voluntary exchange takes place in a competitive market, and if there are no sources of inefficiency such as:

◆   Price ceilings and price floors.

◆   Taxes, subsidies, and quotas.

◆   Monopolies.

◆   Public goods.

◆   External costs and external benefits.

According to the Nozick rules, the resulting distribution of income and wealth will be fair. Let's study a concrete example to examine the claim that if resources are allocated efficiently they are also allocated fairly.

A Price Hike in a Natural Disaster

An earthquake has broken the pipes that deliver drinking water to a city. The price of bottled water jumps from £1 to £8 a bottle in the thirty or so shops that have water for sale.

First, let's agree that the water is being used *efficiently*. There is a fixed amount of bottled water in the city and given the quantity available, some people are willing to pay £8 to get a bottle. The water goes to the people who value it most highly. Consumer surplus and producer surplus are maximized.

So, the water resources are being used efficiently. But are they being used fairly? Shouldn't people who can't afford to pay £8 a bottle get some of the available water for a lower price that they can afford? Isn't the fair solution for the shops to sell water for a lower price that people can afford? Or perhaps it might be fairer if the government bought the water and then made it available to people through a government store at a 'reasonable' price. Let's think about these alternative solutions to the water problem of this city.

The first answer that jumps into your mind is that the water should somehow be made available at a more reasonable price. But is this the correct answer?

Shop Offers Water for £4

Suppose that a shop owner, offers water at £4 a bottle. Who will buy it? There are two types of buyer. Jane is an example of one type. She values water at £8 – is willing to pay £8 a bottle. Recall that given the quantity of water available, the equilibrium price is £8 a bottle. If Jane buys the water, she consumes it. Jane ends up with a consumer surplus of £4 on the bottle and the shop owner receives £4 *less* in producer surplus than would have been created at the market price of £8.

Mary is an example of the second type of buyer. Mary would not pay £8 for a bottle. In fact, she wouldn't even pay £4 to consume a bottle of water. However, she buys a bottle for £4. Why? Because she plans to sell the water to someone who is willing to pay £8 to consume it. When Mary buys the water, the shop owner again receives a producer surplus of £4 *less*. Mary now becomes a water dealer. She sells the water for the going price of £8 and earns a producer surplus of £4.

So, by being public spirited and offering water for less than the market price, the shop owner ends up £4 a bottle worse off and the buyers end up £4 a bottle better off. The same people consume the water in both situations. They are the people who value the water at £8 a bottle. But the distribution of consumer surplus and producer surplus is different in the two cases. The shop owner ends up with a smaller producer surplus if the water is sold for £4 and Jane and Mary end up with a larger consumer surplus and producer surplus.

So, which is the fair arrangement? The one that favours the shop owner or the one that favours the buyers? The fair-rules view is that both arrangements are fair. If the shop owner voluntarily sells the water for £4, this will help the community to cope with its water problem. But the choice is for the shop owner who owns the water. It is not fair to compel the shop owner to help. The final distribution will depend on shop owner's attitude towards charitable behaviour and ability of Jane and Mary to pay for water.

Government Buys Water

Now suppose instead that the government buys all the water. The going price is £8 a bottle, so that's what the government pays. Now they offer the water for sale for £1 a bottle, its 'normal' price.

The quantity of water supplied is exactly the same as before. But now, at £1 a bottle, the quantity demanded is much larger than the quantity supplied. There is a shortage of water.

Because there is a large water shortage, the government decides to ration the amount that anyone may buy. Everyone is allocated one bottle. So, everyone lines up to collect his or her bottle. Two of these people are Jane and Mary. Jane, you'll recall, is willing to pay £8 a bottle. Mary is willing to pay less than £4. But they both get a bargain. Jane drinks her £1 bottle and enjoys a £7 consumer surplus. Mary sells her bottle to another person who values the water at £8, and enjoys a £7 producer surplus from her temporary water trading business.

So, the people who value the water most highly consume it. But the consumer and producer surpluses are distributed in a different way than free market outcome. Again, the question arises, which arrangement is fair?

The main difference between the government scheme and shop owner's private charitable contributions lies in the fact that to buy the water for £8 and sell it for £1, the government must tax someone £7 for each bottle sold. So, whether this arrangement is fair depends on whether the taxes are fair.

Taxes are an involuntary transfer of private property so, according to the fair-rules view, they are unfair. But most economists, and most people, think that there is such a thing as a fair tax. In this case a fair tax might redistribute income so that everyone can afford the basic minimum. So it seems that the fair-rules view is too strong. Agreeing that there is such a thing as a fair tax is the easy part. Agreeing on what is a fair tax brings endless disagreement and debate.

Review Quiz

- What are the two big approaches to fairness?
- Explain the utilitarian idea of fairness and what is wrong with it.
- Explain the big trade-off and the idea of fairness developed to deal with it.
- What is the main idea of fairness based on fair-rules? Explain your answer.

You've now studied the two biggest issues that run right through the whole of economics: efficiency and equity, or fairness. In the next chapter, we study some sources of inefficiency and unfairness. And at many points throughout this book – and in your life – you will return to and use the ideas about efficiency and equity that you've learned in this chapter.

Summary

Key Points

Efficiency: A Refresher (pp. 93–94)

- The marginal benefit received from a good or service – the benefit of consuming one additional unit – is the *value* of the good or service to its consumers.

- The marginal cost of a good or service – the cost of producing one additional unit – is the *opportunity cost* of one more unit to its producers.

- Resources allocation is efficient when marginal benefit equals marginal cost.

- If marginal benefit exceeds marginal cost, an increase in production increases the value of production.

- If marginal cost exceeds marginal benefit, a decrease in production increases the value of production.

Value, Price and Consumer Surplus (pp. 95–96)

- Marginal benefit is measured by the maximum price that consumers are willing to pay for a good or service.

- Marginal benefit determines demand, and a demand curve is a marginal benefit curve.

- Value is what people are *willing to* pay; price is what people *must* pay.

- Consumer surplus equals value minus price, summed over the quantity consumed.

Cost, Price and Producer Surplus (pp. 97–98)

- Marginal cost is measured by the minimum price producers must be offered to increase production by one unit.

- Marginal cost determines supply, and a supply curve is a marginal cost curve.

- Opportunity cost is what producers pay; price is what producers receive.

- Producer surplus equals price minus opportunity cost, summed over the quantity produced.

Is the Competitive Market Efficient? (pp. 98–102)

- In a competitive equilibrium, marginal benefit equals marginal cost and resource allocation is efficient.

- Monopoly restricts production and creates deadweight loss.

- A competitive market provides too small a quantity of public goods because of the free-rider problem.

- A competitive market provides too large a quantity of goods and services that have external costs and too small a quantity of goods and services that have external benefits.

Is the Competitive Market Fair? (pp. 103–107)

- Ideas about fairness divide into two groups: those based on the notion that the *results* are not fair, and those based on the notion that the *rules* are not fair.

- Fair-results ideas require income transfers from the rich to the poor.

- Fair-rules ideas require property rights and voluntary exchange.

Key Figures ◆

Key Terms

Problems

*1 The figure shows the demand for and supply of floppy disks.

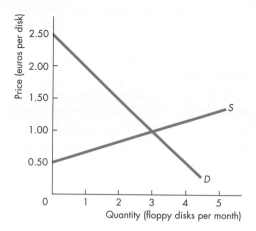

a What are the equilibrium price and equilibrium quantity of floppy disks?

b What is the consumer surplus?

c What is the producer surplus?

d What is the efficient quantity of floppy disks?

2 The figure shows the demand for and supply of tins of beans.

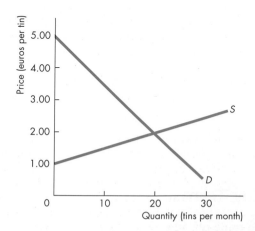

a What are the equilibrium price and equilibrium quantity of tins of beans?

b What is the consumer surplus?

c What is the producer surplus?

d What is the efficient quantity of beans?

*3 The table gives the demand and supply schedules for sandwiches.

Price (pounds per sandwich)	Quantity demanded	Quantity supplied
	(sandwiches per hour)	
0	400	0
1	350	50
2	300	100
3	250	150
4	200	200
5	150	250
6	100	300
7	50	350
8	0	400

a What is the maximum price that consumers are willing to pay for the 250th sandwich?

b What is the minimum price that producers are willing to accept for the 250th sandwich?

c Are 250 sandwiches a day less than or greater than the efficient quantity?

d What is the consumer surplus if the efficient quantity of sandwiches is produced?

e What is the producer surplus if the efficient quantity of sandwiches is produced?

f What is the deadweight loss if 250 sandwiches are produced?

4 The table gives the demand and supply schedules for spring water.

Price (pounds per bottle)	Quantity demanded	Quantity supplied
	(bottles per day)	
0	80	0
0.50	70	10
1.00	60	20
1.50	50	30
2.00	40	40
2.50	30	50
3.00	20	60
3.50	10	70
4.00	0	80

a What is the maximum price that consumers are willing to pay for the 30th bottle?

b What is the minimum price that producers are willing to accept for the 30th bottle?

c Are 30 bottles a day less than or greater than the efficient quantity?

d What is the consumer surplus if the efficient quantity of spring water is produced?

e What is the producer surplus if the efficient quantity of spring water is produced?

f What is the deadweight loss if 30 bottles are produced?

•5 The table gives the demand and supply schedules for train travel for Ben, Beth, and Bill.

Price (pence per passenger kilometre)	Quantity demanded (passenger kilometres)		
	Ben	Beth	Bill
10	500	300	60
20	450	250	50
30	400	200	40
40	350	150	30
50	300	100	20
60	250	50	10
70	200	0	0

a If the price of train travel is 40 pence a passenger kilometre, what is the consumer surplus of each traveller?

b Which traveller has the largest consumer surplus? Explain why.

c If the price of train travel rises to 50 pence a passenger kilometre, what is the change in consumer surplus of each traveller?

6 The table gives the demand and supply schedules for bus travel for Joe, Jean, and Joy.

Price (pence per passenger kilometre)	Quantity demanded (passenger kilometres)		
	Joe	Jean	Joy
10	50	600	300
20	45	500	250
30	40	400	200
40	35	300	150
50	30	200	100
60	25	100	50
70	20	0	0

a If the price of train travel is 50 pence a passenger kilometre, what is the consumer surplus of each passenger?

b Which passenger has the largest consumer surplus? Explain why.

c If the price of train travel falls to 30 pence a passenger kilometre, what is the change in consumer surplus of each passenger?

Critical Thinking

1 Study Reading Between the Lines on pp. 110–111. And then answer the following questions:

a Does the regional tagging system used on DVDs lead to underproduction or overproduction of DVDs? Explain your answer using the concepts of marginal benefit, marginal cost, price, consumer surplus and producer surplus.

b What if anything, do you think the European Commission can do if it finds that DVD prices have been held artificially high?

c As DVD rewriting technology becomes more common, there will be more pirate copies of DVDs made, and these sell at very low prices. Does piracy increase or decrease consumer surplus? Does it increase or decrease the producer surplus of legitimate EU DVD producers? Does it bring the quantity of DVDs closer to the efficient quantity? Explain your answer using the concepts of marginal benefit, marginal cost, price, consumer surplus and producer surplus.

d If the European producers are correct when they say that the tagging system raises their cost above the American market costs, what would be the impact of removing the tagging system on producer surplus in Europe?

2 Write a short description of how you would calculate your own consumer surplus on some item that you buy regularly.

3 Write a short description of how you would determine whether the allocation of your time between studying different subjects is efficient? In what units would you measure marginal benefit and marginal cost? Explain your answer by using the concepts of marginal benefit, marginal cost, price, consumer surplus, and producer surplus.

http://www.econ100.com

Inefficiency: DVD Pricing in Europe

BBC NEWS ONLINE, 11 JUNE 2001

EU to probe DVD pricing

The European Commision is to launch an investigation into the high price paid for DVDs by European consumers. Mario Monti, the EU's competition commissioner has written to Hollywood film companies asking about DVD pricing policy.

DVDs bought in America are cheaper than those available on this side of the Atlantic. But because of a regional disc tagging system, which can make US discs unreadable on foreign players, European customers cannot take advantage of the lower American prices.

'EU consumers are artificially prevented from purchasing DVDs from overseas' Mr Monti said . . .

. . . The Commission reportedly wants to investigate why the companies divide the world into regions which restrict where a DVD can be played.

DVDs cost between £13–£20 in the UK, while US consumers pay just $14–$25 (£11–£18).

'We sent letters on Friday to the seven major distributors to find out whether the US system of regional coding is used to artificially charge a higher price' said EU spokesman, Michael Tscherny.

Film companies have traditionally argued that they use the regional system to facilitate the collection of royalties and prevent piracy. But European electronics makers say they would prefer the codes system was dropped.

The EU investigation follows complaints filed by consumer groups about high prices and the difficulty of ordering DVDs from the US.

The Essence of the Story

- DVDs purchased in America are cheaper than DVDs purchased in Europe.

- The price of a DVD ranges between £13 and £20 in the UK and between £11 and £18 in America.

- The European Commission is investigating the reason for the price difference.

- DVDs are coded with a tagging system which makes American DVDs unreadable on European DVD players.

- The tagging system stops most European customers from buying cheaper American DVDs.

Economic Analysis

■ Figure 1 shows the EU demand curve for DVDs, labelled D. The demand curve is also the marginal benefit curve and is also labelled MB. It tells us the value to EU consumers of one more DVD.

■ Figure 1 also shows the marginal cost of producing DVDs, MC. The curve has a gentle slope, which reflects the assumption that the marginal cost of producing more DVDs does not increase as much as the quantity produced increases.

■ Without the tagging system, European DVDs would be manufactured and sold in competitive world markets. The marginal cost curve would also be the supply curve and the market equilibrium would occur at point a, where the demand and supply curves intersect.

■ European DVDs would sell at the lower price available to American consumers, £14.50 (using the average American price), and the market quantity is Q_a DVDs.

■ Production is efficient at point a – marginal benefit equals marginal cost. The consumer surplus created by DVDs in Europe is the green area and the producer surplus is the blue area in Figure 1.

■ But the European DVD market is not at point a.

■ The tagging system means that the market is at point b in Figure 2. The price is set at £16.50 (using the average UK price) per DVD and the market quantity falls to Q_b DVDs.

■ Point b is inefficient because marginal benefit exceeds marginal cost, creating a deadweight loss shown by the grey area

■ With the higher price and smaller quantity at point b, the producer surplus is greater than at point a. But consumer surplus is smaller. And the decrease in consumer surplus is larger than the increase in producer surplus by the size of the deadweight loss.

■ The American manufacturers argue that the tagging system is needed to avoid piracy and helps with the collection of royalties, but the tagging system is creating an inefficient market.

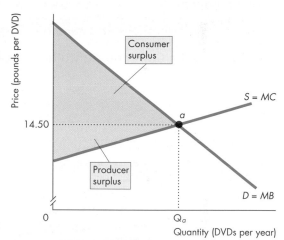

Figure 1 Efficient quantity

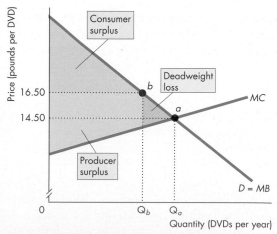

Figure 2 Inefficient quantity

CHAPTER 6

Markets in Action

After studying this chapter you will be able to:

◆ Explain how housing markets work and how house price ceilings affect housing markets

◆ Explain how labour markets work and how minimum wage laws affect labour markets

◆ Explain how sales taxes affect markets

◆ Explain how markets for illegal goods work

◆ Explain why farm prices and revenues fluctuate

◆ Explain how the Common Agricultural Policy affects agricultural markets

Turbulent Times

In January 1995, the Netherlands suffered a devastating flood that destroyed many homes but killed few people. How did the housing market cope with this enormous shock? What happened to rents and to the quantity of housing services available in the flooded regions? Would rent controls have helped to keep housing affordable? ◆ Almost every day, new machines are invented that save labour and increase productivity. How do labour markets react to labour-saving technology? Will the fall in the demand for labour drive wages lower and lower? Can minimum wage laws stop wages from falling and help us to use labour more efficiently? ◆ Almost everything we buy is taxed. How do taxes affect the prices and quantities of the things we buy? Is it the buyers or the sellers who have to bear the tax? ◆ Trading in items such as automatic firearms, certain drugs and enriched uranium is illegal. Does prohibiting trade in these goods actually restrict the amount of these goods consumed? And how does it affect the prices paid by those who trade illegally? ◆ In 1996, droughts reduced grain yields everywhere. How do farm prices and revenues react to such output fluctuations? How does the European Union's Common Agricultural Policy influence prices and farm revenues?

◆ ◆ ◆ ◆ In this chapter, we use the theory of demand and supply (from Chapter 3), the concept of elasticity (from Chapter 4), and the concept of efficiency (from Chapter 5) to answer the questions we have just asked. We start by looking at how a housing market responds to a severe and sudden supply shock. We end by looking at the impact of the CAP on beef markets.

Housing Markets and Rent Ceilings

To see how unregulated markets cope with supply shocks, let's consider the consequences of the flood in the Gelderland province of the Netherlands in January 1995. How did the region cope with such a vast reduction in the supply of housing? Almost overnight, 70,000 people left the area and their devastated homes behind them. The floods wrecked homes and businesses causing more than €450 million worth of damage.

The Market Response to a Decrease in Supply

The market for housing in the worst affected area in the Gelderland province is shown in Figure 6.1. The demand curve for housing before the flood is *D* in part (a). There are two supply curves: the short-run supply curve, labelled *SS*, and the long-run supply curve, labelled *LS*. The short-run supply curve shows how the quantity of housing supplied varies as the price (rent) varies, while the number of houses and blocks of flats remains constant. Supply varies with the intensity with which existing buildings are used. The quantity of housing supplied increases if families decide to rent out rooms that they previously used themselves, and decreases if families decide to use rooms they previously rented out to others.

The *long-run* supply curve shows how the quantity supplied varies over the period of renovation and rebuilding. We will assume that the long-run supply curve is perfectly elastic, as shown. This is reasonable as the cost of building is much the same regardless of whether there are 5,000 or 15,000 flats and houses in existence.

The equilibrium price (rent) and quantity are determined at the point of intersection of the *short-run* supply curve and the demand curve. Before the flood, the equilibrium rent is €1,000 a month and the quantity is 10,000 units of housing. In addition (for simplicity), the housing market is assumed to be on its long-run supply curve, *LS*. Let's now look at the situation immediately after the flood.

Figure 6.1(a) shows the new situation. The damage to buildings decreases the supply of housing and shifts the short-run supply curve *SS* leftward to *SS*_A. If people use the remaining housing units with the same intensity as before the flood and if the rent

Figure 6.1

The Gelderland Housing Market in 1995

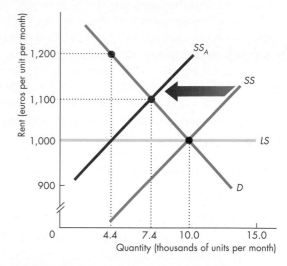

(a) After flood

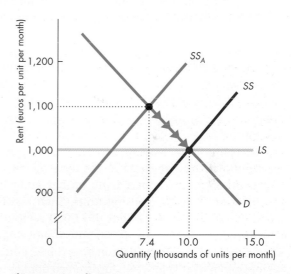

(b) Long-run adjustment

Before the flood, the local housing market in the worst affected area is in equilibrium with 10,000 housing units being rented each month at €1,000 a month (part a). After the flood, the short-run supply curve shifts from *SS* to *SS*_A. The rent rises to €1,100 a month, and the quantity of housing falls to 7,400 units. With rents at €1,100 a month, it is profitable to renovate or rebuild flats and houses quickly. As the renovation and rebuilding programme proceeds, the short-run supply curve shifts rightward (part b). Rents gradually fall to €1,000 a month and the quantity of housing gradually increases to 10,000 units.

remains at €1,000 a month, only 4,400 units of housing are available. But rents do not remain at €1,000 a month. With only 4,400 units of housing available, the maximum rent that someone is willing to pay for the last available apartment is €1,200 a month. So, to get a flat, a higher rent than €1,000 is offered. Rents rise as people try to outbid each other for the available housing. In Figure 6.1(a), they rise to €1,100 a month. At this rent, the quantity of housing supplied is 7,400 units. People economize on their use of space and make spare rooms, attics and basements available to others.

The response we've just seen takes place in the short run. What happens in the long run?

Long-run Adjustments

With sufficient time for renovation and building, supply will increase. The long-run supply curve tells us that in the long run, housing will be supplied at a rent of €1,000 a month. Because the current rent of €1,100 a month is higher than the long-run supply price of housing, there will be a rush to supply new housing. As time passes, more housing is renovated or rebuilt, and the short-run supply curve gradually shifts rightward.

Figure 6.1(b) illustrates the long-run adjustment. As more housing is available, the short-run supply curve shifts rightward and intersects the demand curve at lower rents and higher quantities. The market equilibrium follows the arrows down the demand curve. The process ends when there is no further profit in renovating or building housing units. Such a situation occurs at the original rent of €1,000 a month and the original quantity of 10,000 units of housing.

The analysis of the short-run and long-run response of a housing market that we've just studied applies to a wide range of other markets. It applies regardless of whether the initial shock is to supply (as it is here) or demand.

A Regulated Housing Market

We've just seen how a housing market responds to a decrease in supply. We've also seen that a key part of the adjustment process is a rise in rents. Suppose the government passes a law to stop rents from rising – it imposes a price ceiling. A **price ceiling** is a regulation making it illegal to charge a price higher than a specified level. When a price ceiling is applied to rents in housing markets it is called a **rent ceiling**. How

does a rent ceiling affect the way the housing market works?

The effect of a price (rent) ceiling depends on whether it is imposed at a level that is above or below the equilibrium price (rent). A price ceiling set above the equilibrium price has no effect. The reason is that the market forces are not constrained by the price ceiling. The force of the law and the market forces are not in conflict. But a price ceiling below the equilibrium price has powerful effects on a market. The reason is that it prevents the price from acting as the regulator of the quantities demanded and supplied. The force of the law and the market forces are in conflict, and one (or both) of these forces must yield to some degree. Let's study the effects of a price ceiling set below the equilibrium price by returning to the flood region.

What would have happened after the flood if a rent ceiling of €1,000 a month – the rent before the flood – had been imposed by the government? This question and some answers are illustrated in Figure 6.2. If a rent ceiling holds the rent at €1,000 a month, then the

Figure 6.2

A Rent Ceiling

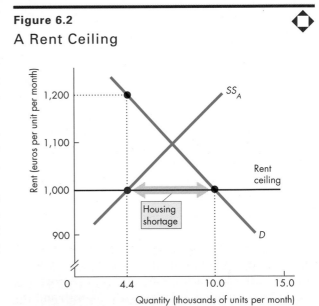

If there had been a rent ceiling of €1,000 a month after the flood, the quantity of housing supplied would have been stuck at 4,400 units. People would willingly have paid €1,200 a month for the 4.4 thousandth unit. Because the last unit of housing available is worth more than the regulated rent, frustrated buyers will spend time searching for housing and frustrated buyers and sellers will make deals in a black market.

quantity of housing supplied is 4,400 units and the quantity demanded is 10,000 units. So there is a shortage of 5,600 units of housing – the quantity demanded exceeds the quantity supplied by 5,600 units.

When the quantity demanded exceeds the quantity supplied, the smaller quantity – the quantity supplied – determines the actual quantity bought and sold. The reason is that suppliers cannot be forced to offer housing for rent, and at a monthly rent of €1,000, they are willing to offer only 4,400 units.

So the immediate effect of a rent ceiling of €1,000 a month is that only 4,400 units of housing are available and a demand for a further 5,600 units is unsatisfied. But the story does not end here. Somehow the 4,400 units of available housing must be allocated among the people demanding 10,000 units. How is this allocation achieved?

In an unregulated market, the shortage would drive the rent up (as shown in Figure 6.1(a)) and the price mechanism would regulate the quantities demanded and supplied and allocate the scarce housing resources. As long as one person was willing to pay a higher price than another person's minimum supply price, the price would rise and the quantity of housing available would increase. When a rent ceiling blocks the market mechanism by making rent increases illegal, two developments occur. They are:

1 Search activity.
2 Black markets.

Search Activity

When the quantity demanded exceeds the quantity supplied, many suppliers have nothing to sell and many demanders have nothing to buy. So unsatisfied demanders devote time and other resources to searching for a supplier. The time spent looking for someone with whom to do business is called **search activity**. Of course, without full information, some search activity occurs in markets even if prices adjust freely, but search activity increases when markets are regulated.

Search activity is costly. It uses time and other resources – telephones, cars, petrol – that could be used in other productive ways. People look for any kind of information about newly available housing to try to avoid the queues. The *total cost* of housing is equal to the rent – the regulated price, plus the cost of search activity – an unregulated price. So rent ceilings

might control the rent portion of the cost of housing, but they do not control the total cost. The total cost may well be *higher* than the unregulated market price.

Black Markets

A **black market** is an illegal trading arrangement in which buyers and sellers do business at a price higher or lower than the legally imposed price. There are many markets that are regulated or taxed and in which economic forces result in black market trading. In countries like Italy and the United Kingdom, the black market is estimated to be worth more than 10 per cent of national output.

In regulated housing markets, a black market usually takes the form of a buyer and a seller colluding to avoid the rent ceiling. They have a written agreement that uses the regulated rent, but agree informally to raise the actual rent. The level of the black market rent depends mainly on how tightly the government polices its rent ceiling regulations, the chances of being caught violating them and the scale of the penalties imposed for violations.

At one extreme, the chance of being caught violating a rent ceiling is small. In this case, the black market will function similarly to an unregulated market, and the black market rent and quantity traded will be close to the unregulated equilibrium. At the other extreme, where policing is highly effective and where large penalties are imposed on violators, the rent ceiling will restrict the quantity traded. In the flood example, strict enforcement of the rent ceiling would restrict the quantity of housing available to 4,400 units. A small number of people would offer housing for sale at €1,200 a month – the highest price that a buyer is willing to pay – and the government would detect and punish some of the black market traders.

Rent Ceilings and Inefficiency

In an efficient housing market, rents are determined by the interaction of demand and supply. The scarce housing resources are allocated efficiently and the sum of producer and consumer surplus is maximized (see Chapter 5).

Figure 6.3 shows how a rent ceiling can cause inefficiency. If the Gelderland government sets the maximum rent at €1,000 a month, then only 4,400 units are supplied. The producer surplus is shown by the blue triangle above the supply curve and below the rent ceiling line. There is a deadweight loss

Figure 6.3

The Inefficiency of a Rent Ceiling

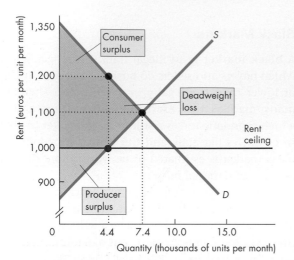

A rent ceiling of €1,000 a month decreases the quantity of housing supplied to 44,000 units. People are willing to pay €1,200 a month for 44,000th unit, so there is a large consumer surplus. Producer surplus shrinks to the blue triangle. A deadweight loss (the grey triangle) arises. If people use no resources in search activity, consumer surplus is shown by the green triangle plus the pink rectangle. But people might use resources in search activity equal to the amount they are willing to pay for the available housing, the pink rectangle.

because the quantity of housing supplied is below the competitive quantity. This loss is borne by consumers and producers. Some consumers would have found housing at the higher rent of €1,100 but now face a housing shortage. Some suppliers, who would have supplied housing when rents were €1,100 a month, now find they can't cover their costs. If there are no search costs, consumers who find housing at the regulated rent will gain more consumer surplus, the area shaded green and pink. But search costs might eat up part of that gain, possibly by as much as the entire amount that consumers are willing to pay – the pink rectangle. So rent ceilings can prevent resources from flowing to their highest-valued use. They can generate inefficiency shown as the deadweight loss.

But you might think that removing rent ceilings would be unfair, in terms of the ideas explored in Chapter 5? When rent ceilings are in force, factors other than rent must allocate the scarce housing. For example, landlords often increase the effective rent

by charging new tenants a high price to replace locks and keys – a device called 'key money', or they simply discriminate on the basis of race, age, family size, or sex. So there is unfairness even with rent ceilings in place.

The effects of rent ceilings in cities such as London, Paris and New York have led Assar Lindbeck, chairman of the economic science Nobel Prize, to suggest that rent ceilings are the most effective means yet invented for destroying cities, even more effective than the hydrogen bomb!

Review Quiz

◆ How does a decrease in the supply of housing change equilibrium rents in the short run? Who gets to consume the scarce resources?
◆ What are the long-run effects of higher rents following a decrease in supply of housing?
◆ What is a rent ceiling and what are the effects of a rent ceiling set below the equilibrium rent?
◆ How do scarce housing resources get allocated when a rent ceiling is in place. Is the allocation fair? Explain.

We've studied the effects of a change in supply in the housing market, so we'll now look at the effects of a change in demand in the labour market.

The Labour Market and Minimum Wages

For most of us, the labour market is the most important market in which we participate. It is the interaction of demand and supply in the labour market that influences the jobs we get and the wages we earn. Firms make decisions about the quantity of labour to demand and households make decisions about the quantity of labour to supply. The wage rate balances the quantities demanded and the quantities supplied and determines the level of employment. But the labour market is constantly being bombarded by shocks, particularly from technological advances. This means that wages and employment prospects are constantly changing.

Labour-saving technology is constantly being invented. As a result, the demand for certain types of labour, usually the least skilled types, is constantly decreasing. How does the labour market cope with this continuous decrease in the demand for unskilled labour? Does it mean that the wages of unskilled workers are constantly falling? We are now going to find out.

Figure 6.4 represents the market for unskilled labour in France. Labour is demanded by firms and, other things remaining the same, the lower the wage rate, the greater is the quantity of labour demanded. The demand curve for labour, D in part (a), shows this relationship between the wage rate and the quantity of labour demanded. Labour is supplied by households and, other things remaining the same, the higher the wage rate, the greater is the quantity of labour supplied. But the longer the period of adjustment, the greater is the elasticity of supply of labour. Thus there are two supply curves, a short-run supply curve SS and a long-run supply curve LS.

The short-run supply curve shows how the hours of labour supplied by a given number of workers changes as the wage rate changes. To get employees to work longer hours, firms must offer higher wages, so the short-run supply curve is upward sloping.

The long-run supply curve shows the relationship between the quantity of labour supplied and the wage rate after enough time has passed for people to acquire new skills and move to new locations and new types of job. The number of people in the unskilled labour market depends on the opportunity cost – the unskilled wage rate compared with skilled wages and the value of leisure time. If the wage rate is high enough, people will enter this market. When it is too low, people leave the labour market – to seek training to enter the skilled labour market, to retire, or to work at home.

Because people are free to enter and leave the unskilled labour market, the long-run supply curve is highly elastic. In Figure 6.4, for simplicity, the long-run supply curve is assumed to be perfectly elastic (horizontal). The unskilled labour market is in equilibrium at a wage rate of €7 an hour and 22 million hours of labour are employed.

What happens if a labour-saving technology decreases the demand for unskilled labour? Figure 6.4(a) shows the short-run effects of such a change. The demand curve before the new technology is introduced is D. After the introduction of the new technology, the demand curve shifts leftward, to D_A. The wage rate falls to €5 an hour, and the quantity of labour employed decreases to 21 million hours. But this is not the end of the story.

Figure 6.4

A Market for Unskilled Labour

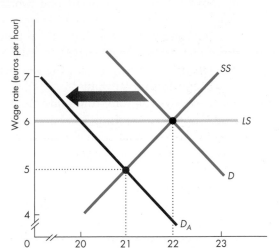

(a) After invention

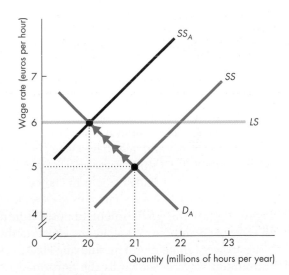

(b) Long-run adjustment

A market for unskilled labour is in equilibrium (part a) at a wage rate of €6 an hour with 22 million hours of labour a year being employed. A labour-saving invention shifts the demand curve from D to D_A. The wage rate falls to €5 an hour and employment decreases to 21 million hours a year. With the lower wage, some workers leave this market and the short-run supply curve starts to shift to SS_A (part b). The wage rate gradually increases, and the employment level decreases. Ultimately, wages return to €7 an hour and employment falls to 20 million hours a year.

People who are now earning only €5 an hour look around for other opportunities. They see that there are many other jobs for workers with more skills that pay wages above €5 an hour. One by one, workers decide to quit the market for unskilled labour. Some may retire, but many go to college to get new qualifications, or take jobs that pay less initially but offer on-the-job training. As a result, the short-run supply curve begins to shift leftward.

Figure 6.4(b) shows the long-run adjustment. As the short-run supply curve shifts leftward, it intersects the demand curve D_A at higher wage rates and lower levels of employment. In the long run, the short-run supply curve must shift all the way to SS_A. At this point, the wage has returned to €7 an hour, and employment has decreased to 20 million hours a year.

If the adjustment process we've just described is long and drawn out, wages remain low for a long period. In such a situation, the government is tempted to intervene in the labour market by legislating a minimum wage to protect the lowest-paid workers.

The Minimum Wage

A **minimum wage law** is a **price floor** regulation that makes hiring labour below a specified wage illegal. If the minimum wage is set *below* the equilibrium wage, it has no effect. The law and the market forces are not in conflict. But if a minimum wage is set *above* the equilibrium wage, the minimum wage is in conflict with the market forces and does have some effects on the labour market. Let's study these effects by returning to the market for unskilled labour in France.

Suppose that when the wage rate falls to €4 an hour (in Figure 6.4(a)) the government imposes a minimum wage of €6 an hour. What are the effects of this law? The answer can be found by studying Figure 6.5. The minimum wage is shown as the horizontal red line labelled 'Minimum wage'. At the minimum wage, only 20 million hours of labour are demanded (point *a*) but 22 million hours of labour are supplied (point *b*). Because the number of hours demanded is less than the number of hours supplied, 2 million hours of available labour are unemployed.

Inefficiency and the Minimum Wage

A labour market without a minimum wage can allocate scarce labour resources to the jobs in which they are valued most highly. The minimum wage

Figure 6.5

Minimum Wages and Unemployment

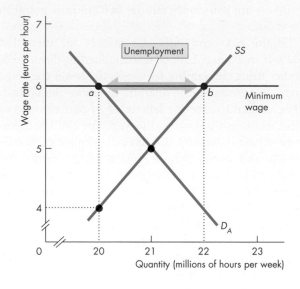

The demand curve for labour is D_A and the supply curve is *SS*. In an unregulated market, the wage rate is €5 an hour and 21 million hours of labour a year are employed. If a minimum wage of €6 an hour is imposed, only 20 million hours are hired but 22 million hours are available. This results in unemployment – *ab* – of two million hours a year. With only 20 million hours being demanded, some workers will willingly supply that 20 millionth hour for €6. These frustrated unemployed workers will spend time and other resources looking for a job.

blocks the market mechanism and results in unemployment – wasted labour – and an inefficient amount of job search.

Look again at Figure 6.5. When only 20 million hours of work are available, you can read off from the supply curve that the lowest wage at which workers are willing to supply that 20 millionth hour is €4. Someone who manages to find a job will earn €6 an hour – €2 an hour more than the lowest wage rate at which someone is willing to work. Therefore it pays the unemployed workers to engage in search activity. Even though only 20 million hours of labour actually get employed, each person spends time and effort searching for one of the scarce jobs.

The Minimum Wage in Reality

Minimum wage laws are used by most governments in Europe and North America. Many European countries have a statutory national minimum wage across all industries, adjusted at regular intervals for changes in the price level or average earnings. In Belgium and Greece, the national minimum wage is set by a process of collective bargaining with trade unions, and a similar process determines industry minimum wages in Denmark, Germany and Italy. A minimum wage law was not introduced in the UK until April 1999.

There is now a hot debate about whether to introduce a Europe-wide minimum wage as part of the European Union's new labour market strategy. Some economists believe that bringing down the barriers to trade in the new single European market will increase competition and create an increasingly low-wage workforce – a process called *social dumping*. Firms will be attracted to low-wage countries and governments will start to compete for this investment by cutting back welfare provision, training and employer costs. Growth will be limited to the low-skill, low-wage sector. Minimum wages are needed to halt the downward pressure on wages.

Other economists believe that minimum wages will fuel inflation as higher paid workers try to raise their wages to keep the same differentials with the lowest paid workers. Minimum wages also stop the market reaching equilibrium and low paid workers only gain higher wages at the opportunity cost of fewer jobs. As low wages are more common among young people, existing minimum wage laws may explain why the highest rates of unemployment in Europe are among such people.

Under some circumstances minimum wages do not lead to unemployment. You can read about this and other labour issues in our chapter on labour markets available on the Parkin, Powell and Matthews website.

Review Quiz

◆ How does a decrease in the demand for unskilled labour affect the equilibrium wage in the short-run.

◆ What are the long-run effects of a lower wage rate for low-skilled workers?

◆ What is a minumum wage regulation and what is the effect of a minimum wage that is set above the equilibrium wage?

◆ What is the effect of a minimum wage that is set below the equilibrium wage?

Now we'll look at the effects of another set of government actions on markets – taxes.

Taxes

In 2000, the UK government raised more than £113.5 billion – an average of nearly £2,400 per person – from indirect tax, that is taxes on the goods and services. These taxes include Value Added Tax (VAT), sales taxes on goods and services like insurance, local government taxes, and excise taxes on petrol, alcoholic beverages and tobacco. VAT is an *ad valorem* tax – a tax set as a percentage of the selling price on all transactions. All countries in the European Union levy this tax, but different countries impose different rates. Excise taxes are usually specific taxes – a specific amount of tax per unit, say 5 pence per cigarette levied on the manufacturer. Sales taxes may be *ad valorem* or specific taxes but are levied at the final point of sale.

If a good or service is taxed, you pay the retail price *plus* an additional amount, the *tax*. What are the effects of taxes on the prices and quantities of goods bought and sold? Do the prices of the goods and services you buy increase by the full amount of the tax? Isn't it always you – the consumer – who pays the entire tax? It can be, but usually it isn't. It is even possible that you actually pay none of the tax, forcing the seller to pay it for you. Let's see how we can make sense of these apparently absurd statements.

Who Pays a Sales Tax?

To study the effect of a tax, we start by looking at a market in which there is no tax. We'll then introduce a tax – a specific sales tax – and see what changes arise. The results for other forms of tax are not examined here but they are similar.

Figure 6.6 shows the UK market for CD players. The demand curve is *D* and the supply curve is *S*. The equilibrium price of a CD player is £100, and the quantity traded is 5,000 players a week.

Suppose the government puts a £10 sales tax on CD players. What are the effects of this tax on the price and quantity in the market for CD players? To answer this question, we need to work out what happens to demand and supply in this market.

When a good is taxed it has two prices – a price that excludes the tax and a price that includes it. Consumers respond only to the price that includes the

Figure 6.6

The Sales Tax

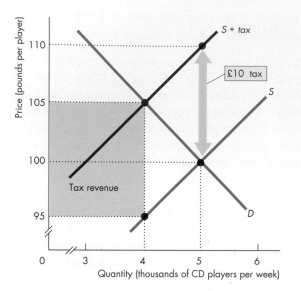

The demand curve for CD players is *D* and the supply curve is *S*. With no tax, the price is £100 a player and 5,000 players a week are bought and sold. Then a sales tax of £10 a player is imposed. The price on the vertical axis is the price *including* the tax. The demand curve does not change, but supply decreases and the supply curve shifts leftward. The curve *S + tax* shows the terms on which sellers will make CD players available. The vertical distance between the supply curve *S* and the new supply curve *S + tax* equals the tax – £10 a player.

The new equilibrium is at a price of £105 with 4,000 CD players a week bought and sold. The tax increases the price by less than the tax, decreases the price received by the supplier, and decreases the quantity bought and sold. It brings in revenue to the government equal to the blue shaded area.

tax. Producers respond only to the price they receive – the price that excludes the tax. The tax is like a wedge between these two prices.

Let's think of the price on the vertical axis of Figure 6.6 as the price paid by the consumer that includes the tax. When a tax is imposed, there is no shift in demand. The demand curve shows quantities demanded at different levels of the total price, with or without a tax.

But the supply curve *does* shift. When a sales tax is imposed on a good, it is offered for sale at a higher price than in a no-tax situation. The supply curve shifts leftward to *S + tax*. The new supply curve is

found by adding the tax to the minimum price that suppliers are willing to accept for each quantity sold. For example, with no tax, suppliers are willing to sell 4,000 players a week for £95 a player. So with a £10 tax, they will supply 4,000 players a week for £105 – a price that includes the tax. The new supply curve *S + tax* lies to the left of the original curve – supply has decreased – and the vertical distance between the original supply curve *S* and the new supply curve *S + tax* equals the tax. The curve *S + tax* describes the price at which the good is available to buyers.

A new equilibrium is determined where the new supply curve intersects the demand curve – at a price of £105 and a quantity of 4,000 CD players a week. The £10 sales tax has increased the price paid by the consumer by only £5 (£105 versus £100), which is less than the £10 tax. And it has decreased the price received by the supplier by £5 (£95 versus £100). The £10 tax paid is made up of the higher price to the buyer and the lower price to the seller.

The tax brings in tax revenue to the government equal to the tax per item multiplied by the items sold. It is illustrated by the blue area in Figure 6.6. The £10 tax on CD players brings in a tax revenue of £40,000 a week.

In this example, the buyer and the seller split the tax equally; the buyer pays £5 a player and so does the seller. The proportion of the tax paid by the buyer and the seller is determined by the elasticity of demand and supply. In extreme cases, the buyer or the seller might have to pay the entire tax. Let's look at these cases.

Tax Division and Elasticity of Demand

The division of the total tax between buyers and sellers also depends on the elasticity of demand. Again, there are two extreme cases:

1 Perfectly inelastic demand – buyer pays.

2 Perfectly elastic demand – seller pays.

Perfectly Inelastic Demand

Figure 6.7(a) shows the UK market for insulin, a life-saving daily medication for diabetics. The quantity demanded is 100,000 bottles a day, regardless of the price. Each one of the 100,000 diabetics in the population would sacrifice all other goods and services for their daily insulin dose. In the absence of a national health service, demand for insulin would reflect this

Figure 6.7

Sales Tax and the Elasticity of Demand

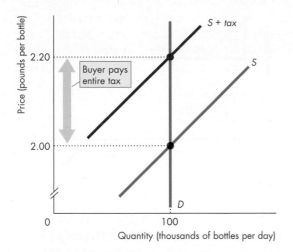

(a) Inelastic demand

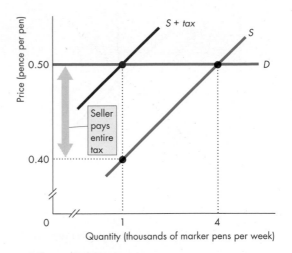

(b) Elastic demand

Part (a) shows the market for insulin. The demand for insulin is perfectly inelastic, as shown by the curve *D*. The supply curve of insulin is *S*. With no tax the price is £2 a bottle and 100,000 bottles a day are bought. A sales tax of 20 pence a bottle increases the price at which sellers are willing to make insulin available, and shifts the supply curve to *S + tax*. The price rises to £2.20 a bottle, but the quantity bought does not change and buyers pay the entire tax.

Part (b) shows the market for pink marker pens. The demand for pink marker pens is perfectly elastic at the price of other coloured marker pens – 50 pence a pen. The demand curve is *D*, the supply curve is *S*, and with no tax the price of a pink marker pen is 50 pence and 4,000 a week are bought. A sales tax of 10 pence a pink pen decreases the supply of pink marker pens, shifting the supply curve to *S + tax*. The price remains at 50 pence a pen, and the quantity of pink markers sold decreases to 1,000 a week. Suppliers pay the entire tax.

fact and would be perfectly inelastic. It is shown by the vertical curve *D*. The supply curve of insulin is *S*. With no tax, the price is £2 a bottle, and the quantity is 100,000 bottles a day.

If insulin is taxed at 20 pence a bottle, we must add the tax to the minimum price at which the drug companies are willing to sell insulin to determine the post-tax supply to consumers. The result is a new supply curve *S + tax*. The price rises to £2.20 a bottle, but the quantity does not change. The buyer pays the entire sales tax of 20 pence a bottle.

Perfectly Elastic Demand

Figure 6.7(b) shows the UK market for pink marker pens. Demand is perfectly elastic at 50 pence a pen as shown by the horizontal curve *D*. If pink markers are less expensive than the others, everyone will use pink. If pink markers are more expensive than the others, no one will use them. The supply curve is *S*.

With no tax, the price of a pink marker is 50 pence and 4,000 a week are bought at that price.

If the sales tax of 10 pence a pen is levied on pink, and only pink, marker pens, we must add the tax to the minimum price at which suppliers are willing to sell them. The new supply curve is *S + tax*. The price remains at 50 pence a pen, and the quantity of pink markers decreases to 1,000 a week. The 10 pence tax has left the price paid by the consumer unchanged, but decreased the amount received by the supplier by the full amount of the tax – 10 pence a pen. As a result, sellers decrease the quantity offered for sale.

In most markets, demand is neither perfectly inelastic nor perfectly elastic, so the tax is split between the buyer and the seller. But the division depends on the elasticity of demand and will rarely be equal. The more inelastic the demand and the more elastic the supply, the larger is the portion of the tax paid by the buyer.

Figure 6.8

Sales Tax and the Elasticity of Supply

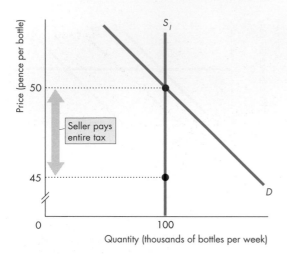

(a) Inelastic supply

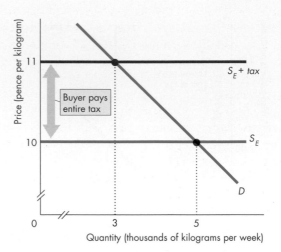

(b) Elastic supply

Part (a) shows the market for water from a mineral spring. Supply is perfectly inelastic and the supply curve is S_I. The demand curve is D, and with no tax the price is 50 pence a bottle. A sales tax of five pence decreases the price received by sellers, but the price remains at 50 pence a bottle and the number of bottles bought remains the same. Suppliers pay the entire tax.

Part (b) shows the market for sand from which silicon is extracted. Supply is perfectly elastic at a price of 10 pence a kilogram. The supply curve is S_E, the demand curve is D, and with no tax the price is 10 pence a kilogram and 5,000 kilograms a week are bought. A sales tax of one penny a kilogram increases the minimum price at which sellers are willing to supply to 11 pence a kilogram. The supply curve shifts to $S_E + tax$. The price increases to 11 pence a kilogram, the quantity bought decreases to 3,000 kilograms a week, and buyers pay the entire tax.

Tax Division and Elasticity of Supply

The division of the total tax between buyers and sellers depends, in part, on the elasticity of supply. There are two extreme cases:

1 Perfectly inelastic supply – seller pays.
2 Perfectly elastic supply – buyer pays.

Perfectly Inelastic Supply

Figure 6.8(a) shows the market for water from a UK mineral spring which flows at a constant rate that can't be controlled. The quantity supplied is 100,000 bottles a week, regardless of the price. The supply is perfectly inelastic and the supply curve is S_I. The demand curve for the water from this spring is D. With no tax, the price is 50 pence a bottle and the 100,000 bottles that flow from the spring are bought at that price.

If the spring water is taxed at 5 pence a bottle. The supply curve does not change because the spring

owners still produce 100,000 bottles a week – even though the price has fallen. Consumers, on the other hand, are willing to buy the 100,000 bottles available each week only if the price is 50 pence a bottle. So the price remains at 50 pence a bottle, and the suppliers pay the entire tax. The tax of 5 pence a bottle reduces the price received by suppliers to 45 pence a bottle.

Perfectly Elastic Supply

Figure 6.8(b) shows the UK market for sand from which computer-chip makers extract silicon. There is a virtually unlimited quantity of sand available, and its owners are willing to supply any quantity at a price of 10 pence a kilogram. So supply is perfectly elastic – the supply curve S_E. The demand curve for sand is D. With no tax, the price is 10 pence a kilogram, and 5,000 kilograms a week are bought at that price.

If sand is taxed at 1 penny a kilogram, we add the tax to the minimum supply price. Suppliers are willing to supply any quantity at 11 pence a kilogram along the curve $S_E + tax$. A new equilibrium is determined where the new supply curve intersects the demand curve – at a price of 11 pence a kilogram and a quantity of 3,000 kilograms a week. The sales tax has increased the price paid by consumers by the full amount of the tax – 1 penny a kilogram – and has decreased the quantity sold.

We've seen that when supply is perfectly inelastic, the seller pays the entire tax and when supply is perfectly elastic, the buyer pays it. In the usual case, where supply is neither perfectly inelastic nor perfectly elastic, the tax is split between the seller and the buyer. But the division depends on the elasticity of supply. The more elastic the supply, the larger is the portion of the tax paid by the buyer.

Indirect Taxes in Practice

We've looked at the range of possible effects of a sales tax by studying extreme cases. In practice, supply and demand are rarely perfectly elastic or inelastic. So does our model of tax help us to understand government tax policy? Let's see. We know that governments tend to choose goods such as alcohol, tobacco and petrol for excise taxes. Why? Because they have a low elasticity of demand. Although the tax raises the price and the quantity bought falls, it does not fall by much. Tax revenue will rise even if the tax is increased. Of course, governments must raise the specific tax on goods every year to keep the real value of the tax constant. Otherwise revenue will start to fall, other things remaining the same. Alternative reasons for taxing these goods are examined in Chapter 18, and in the next section.

Taxes and Efficiency

We've seen that a tax can place a wedge between the price paid by buyers and the price received by sellers. The price paid by buyers is also the buyers' willingness to pay or marginal benefit. The price received by sellers is the sellers' minimum supply price or marginal cost. If a tax puts a wedge between the buyers' price and the sellers' price, it also puts a wedge between marginal benefit and marginal cost. This creates inefficiency.

Figure 6.9 shows the inefficiency of a UK sales tax on CD players. The tax results in a shift of the supply curve to $S + tax$. Price increases to 105 pence and

Figure 6.9
Taxes and Efficiency

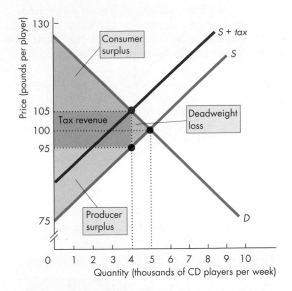

With no sales tax, 5,000 players a week are bought and sold at £100 each. With a sales tax of £10 a player, the buyers' price rises to £105 a player, the sellers' price falls to £95, and the quantity decreases to 4,000 CD players a week. Consumer surplus shrinks to the green area, and producer surplus shrinks to the blue area. Part of the loss of consumer surplus and producer surplus goes to the government as tax revenue, which is shown as the purple area. A deadweight loss also arises, which is shown by the grey area.

quantity falls to four thousand players a week. But both consumer and producer surplus shrink. Part of consumer and producer surplus is transferred to government as tax revenue (the purple area) and so is not lost. But the grey area of consumer and producer surplus becomes a deadweight loss.

The size of the deadweight loss depends on elasticity of demand and supply. In the extreme cases where demand and supply are perfectly inelastic, there will be no deadweight loss as quantity does not change with a price change. The more inelastic either demand or supply, the smaller is the deadweight loss. Most indirect excise duties are put on goods which are inelastic in demand and these taxes may not create much inefficiency. There are also other cases when a tax may create an increase in efficiency and we will look at these in Chapter 18.

Taxes are one way of influencing markets, another is when governments make trade in a good illegal. Let's look at how such a market works.

Markets for Prohibited Goods

The markets for many goods and services are regulated, and buying and selling some goods is prohibited – the goods and services are illegal. The best known examples are drugs. Alcohol and tobacco are currently legally available drugs, but their supply and consumption is regulated in most European countries. Other drugs such as cannabis, ecstasy, cocaine and heroin are more commonly illegal. .

Despite the fact that some drugs are illegal, trade in them is a multi-billion pound global business. This trade can be understood by using the same economic models and principles that explain trade in legal goods and services. There are also occasions when legal drugs are prohibited and illegal drugs are legalized. We can use our models to look at the economic impact of different regulation and control systems.

To study the market for prohibited goods, we're first going to examine the prices and quantities that would prevail if these goods were not prohibited. Next, we'll see how prohibition works. Then we'll see how a tax might be used to limit the consumption of these goods.

A Free Market for Drugs

Figure 6.10 shows a market for a drug. The demand curve, D, shows that, other things remaining the same, the lower the price of the drug, the larger is the quantity demanded. The supply curve, S, shows that, other things remaining the same, the lower the price

Figure 6.10

The Market for a Prohibited Good

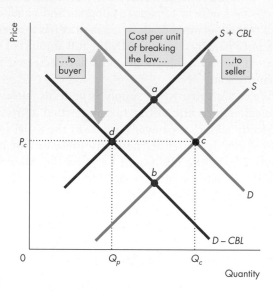

The demand curve for the drug is D and the supply curve is S. With no prohibition or regulation, the quantity consumed is Q_c at a price of P_c – point c. If selling the drug is illegal, the cost of breaking the law (CBL) is added to the other costs and supply decreases to $S + CBL$. The price rises and the quantity consumed decreases – point a. If buying the drug is illegal, the cost of breaking the law is subtracted from the maximum price that buyers are willing to pay, and demand decreases to $D - CBL$. The price falls and the quantity consumed decreases – point b.

If both buying and selling are illegal both the supply curve and the demand curve shift – the quantity consumed decreases even more, but (in this example) the price remains at its unregulated level – point d.

of the drug, the smaller is the quantity supplied. If the drug were not prohibited or regulated, the quantity bought and sold would be Q_c and the price would be P_c.

Prohibiting a Drug

When a good is prohibited, the cost of trading in the good increases. By how much the cost increases and on whom the cost falls depend on the penalties for breaking the law and the effectiveness with which the law is enforced. The larger the penalties and the more effective the policing, the higher are the costs to traders. Fines impose a direct cost but prison sentences involve the opportunity cost of lost earnings and discomfort. Penalties may be imposed on sellers, buyers, or both.

Penalties on Sellers

Drug dealers in all European countries face fines and prison sentences if their activities are detected. For example, a cannabis dealer in most countries would probably serve a 1 year prison term, whereas a heroin dealer would serve a 3 year prison term on average. In the Netherlands, the supply of these drugs is illegal but decriminalized in some circumstances. Penalties for dealing are part of the cost of supplying illegal drugs and they lead to a decrease in supply – a leftward shift in the supply curve. To determine the new supply curve, we add the cost of breaking the law to the minimum price that drug dealers are willing to accept. In Figure 6.10, the cost of breaking the law by selling drugs (*CBL*) is added to the minimum price that dealers will accept and the supply curve shifts leftward to *S* + *CBL*. If penalties are imposed only on sellers, the market moves from point *c* to point *a*. The price increases and the quantity bought decreases.

Penalties on Buyers

In all European countries it is illegal to possess drugs such as cannabis, cocaine and heroin for personal consumption. The penalty for illegal possession of cannabis is usually a fine and prison sentences are rarely more than three months, whereas the penalty for illegal possession of heroin is usually a nine-month prison sentence. In the Netherlands, the possession of these drugs is also illegal but decriminalized under certain circumstances. When penalties for possession apply, they fall on buyers and the cost of breaking the law must be subtracted from the value of the good to determine the maximum price buyers are willing to pay. Demand decreases and the demand curve shifts leftward. In Figure 6.10, the demand curve shifts to *D* – *CBL*. If penalties are imposed only on buyers, the market moves from point *c* to point *b*. The price and the quantity bought decrease.

Penalties on Both Sellers and Buyers

If penalties are imposed on sellers *and* buyers, both supply and demand decrease. In Figure 6.10, the costs of breaking the law are the same for both buyers and sellers, so both curves shift leftward by the same amounts. The market moves to point *d*. The price remains at the competitive market price but the quantity bought decreases to Q_p.

The larger the penalty and the greater the degree of law enforcement, the larger is the decrease in demand and/or supply and the greater is the shift of the demand and/or supply curve. If the penalties are heavier on sellers, the price will rise above P_c, and if the penalties are heavier on buyers, the price will fall below P_c. In many European countries, the penalties on sellers are larger than those on buyers. As a result, the decrease in supply is much larger than the decrease in demand. The quantity of drugs traded decreases and the price increases, compared with an unregulated market.

With high enough penalties and effective law enforcement, it is possible to decrease demand and/or supply to the point at which the quantity bought is zero. But this does not happen in the case of illegal drugs because of the high cost of law enforcement. Because of this, some people suggest that drugs (and other illegal goods) should be legalized and taxed at a high rate in the same way that legal drugs such as alcohol are taxed.

Legalizing and Taxing Drugs

From your study of the effects of taxes, it should now be clear that governments could also reduce the quantity of drugs bought and sold if drugs were legalized and taxed. A high tax rate would probably be needed to keep drug consumption at the level in the market before legalization. High taxes would lead many drug dealers and consumers to evade the tax. This problem can be reduced by requiring sellers to have a licence, as in the case of alcohol and tobacco. Tax evaders would also face the cost of breaking the tax law. If the penalty for tax law violation is severe and the law is as effectively policed as drug dealing laws, then a regulated market could achieve a similar result to prohibition.

Some Pros and Cons of Taxes versus Prohibition

So which works more effectively, prohibition or taxing? The comparison we've just made suggests that the two methods can be made to be equivalent if the taxes and penalties are set at the appropriate levels. But there are some other differences.

In favour of taxes and against prohibition is the fact that the tax revenue can be used to make law enforcement more effective. Some economists argue that a great deal of inner city crime is caused by the prohibition of drugs – burglaries, muggings, shootings and money laundering. Legalization would reduce the social and policing costs associated with this crime. Tax revenue can also be used to run a more effective education campaign against drugs. In favour of prohibition and against taxes is the fact that prohibition sends a strong signal that may influence preferences, decreasing the demand for drugs. Also, some people intensely dislike the idea of the government profiting from trade in harmful substances.

Stabilizing Farm Revenue

Freak gale force storms in 1993 wiped out many crops across Europe. Farm output fluctuates a great deal because of fluctuations in the weather. How do changes in farm output affect farm prices and farm revenues? And how might farm revenues be stabilized? The answers to these questions depend on how the markets for agricultural goods are organized. We'll begin by looking at an unregulated agricultural market.

An Unregulated Agricultural Market

Figure 6.11 illustrates an unregulated European market for wheat. In both parts the demand curve for wheat is D. Once farmers have harvested their crop, they have no control over the quantity supplied and supply is inelastic along a *momentary supply curve*. In normal climate conditions, the momentary supply curve is MS_0 (in both parts of the figure) – the price is €160 a tonne, the quantity produced is four million tonnes, and farm revenue is €640 million (dark blue and red areas).

Suppose the opportunity cost to farmers of producing wheat is also £640 million. Then in normal conditions, farmers just cover their opportunity cost.

Poor Harvest

What happens to the price of wheat and the revenue of farmers when there is a poor harvest? These

---

Figure 6.11

Harvests, Farm Prices and Farm Revenue

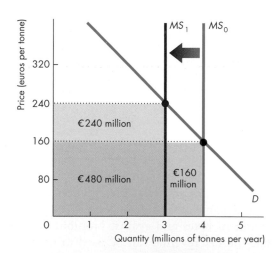

(a) Poor harvest: revenue increases

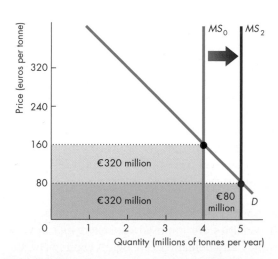

(b) Bumper harvest: revenue decreases

In both parts, the demand curve for wheat is D. In normal times, the momentary supply curve is MS_0, and four million tonnes are sold for €160 a tonne. In part (a), a poor growing season decreases supply, shifting the momentary supply curve to MS_1. The price increases to €240 a tonne and farm revenue *increases* from €640 million to €720 million – the increase in revenue from the higher price (€240 million, light blue area) exceeds the decrease in revenue from

the smaller quantity (€160 million, red area). In part (b), a bumper harvest increases supply, shifting the momentary supply curve to MS_2. The price decreases to €80 a tonne and farm revenue *decreases* to €400 million – the decrease in revenue from the lower price (€320 million, light blue area) exceeds the increase in revenue from the increase in the quantity sold (€80 million, red area).

questions are answered in Figure 6.11(a). Supply decreases and the momentary supply curve shifts leftward to MS_1 where three million tonnes of wheat are produced. With a decrease in supply, the price increases to €240 a tonne. But notice farm revenue *increases* to €720 million (light and dark blue areas). On average, farmers are now making a profit in excess of their opportunity cost.

A decrease in supply will increase the price and farm revenues because the demand for wheat is *inelastic*. The percentage decrease in the quantity demanded is less than the percentage increase in price. You can verify this fact by noticing in Figure 6.11(a) that the increase in revenue from the higher price (€240 million, light blue area) exceeds the decrease in revenue from the smaller quantity (€160 million, red area).

Although total farm revenue increases when there is a poor harvest, some farmers, whose entire crop is wiped out, suffer a fall in revenue. Others, whose crop is unaffected, make an enormous gain.

Bumper harvest

Figure 6.11(b) shows what happens when there is a bumper harvest. Now, supply increases to five million tonnes and the momentary supply curve shifts rightward to MS_2. With the increased quantity supplied, the price falls to €80 a tonne. Farm revenues also decline – to €400 million because the demand for wheat is inelastic. To see this, notice that the decrease in revenue from the lower price (€320 million, light blue area) exceeds the increase in revenue from the increase in the quantity sold (€80 million, red area).

Elasticity of Demand

What happens if the demand for wheat is elastic? The price fluctuations go in the same directions as when demand is inelastic, but revenues fluctuate in the opposite directions. Bumper harvests increase revenue and poor harvests decrease it. In fact, the demand for most agricultural goods is inelastic, and our inelastic example is the relevant one.

Because farm prices fluctuate, the European Union, like most countries, has applied a price support policy to maintain farm revenues. This policy has been in place for 45 years, but at a high cost. It is now being radically revised. Let's see how price support works.

The Common Agricultural Policy

The **Common Agricultural Policy** (CAP) of the European Union is the world's most extensive price

support system. The CAP was set up in 1957 to make sure the bad experiences of wartime shortages and low farm incomes would not be repeated.

The CAP takes the form of price floors set above the equilibrium price – similar to the minimum wage that we studied earlier – and above the production cost of efficient farms. Each year the European Union sets the price floor, called the target price, for each agricultural product. The target price for each product is set above the equilibrium price which would have occurred in the European Union and the world markets. A tariff is charged on all imported agricultural products to make sure their price is the same as the target price. Without the tariff, there would be a flood of cheap imports into the European Union from other parts of the world.

Figure 6.12 illustrates how the CAP works in the European market for wheat. The European demand curve for wheat is D and the supply curve for wheat

Figure 6.12 ◆

The European Union's Agricultural Price Support System

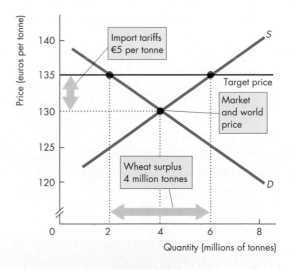

The European Union demand curve for wheat is D and the supply curve is S. In an unregulated European wheat market, the equilibrium price is €130 and the equilibrium quantity is 4 million tonnes per year. If the equilibrium price will not support farm revenues, the European Union sets a target price above the equilibrium price, for example at €135. It also sets a tariff on imported wheat of €5 to stop cheap imports flooding the European market. At the target price of €135, there is an excess supply of wheat which must be bought up and stored.

is S. Initially, the market equilibrium price of wheat is €130 a tonne and the market equilibrium quantity is 4 million tonnes per year. If the European Union decides that the market price of €130 per tonne is too low, it must decide what price is adequate to maintain farm revenues. But what price will it set?

The European Union must set a target price for wheat higher than the current European equilibrium price of €130 per tonne. Suppose the European Union chooses to set the target price at €135 as shown in Figure 6.12. Suppose also that non-EU producers are as efficient as EU producers, so that the world price of wheat is also €130 per tonne. The world price is now less than the European price and cheap imports will flood in. If cheap imports flood the European market, farm revenues will fall. To avoid this, the European Union must set a tariff on all imported wheat equal to the difference between the target price and the world price. The import tariff is €5 per tonne (€135 − €130).

Figure 6.12 shows that at the target price of €135 per tonne, consumers demand only 2 million tonnes of wheat but farmers produce 6 million tonnes. There is an excess supply of 4 million tonnes in the European market. In an unregulated market, an excess supply would cause the price to fall, but the price is fixed at the target price. To avoid black market operations, the European Union must buy up all the excess supply of wheat and store it.

So what happens to the stores of grain? In times of shortage, the European Union can sell off **stocks**. But if the target price is consistently higher than the equilibrium price, the European Union will always buy more than it sells. This has been the case for most agricultural products. We now have the familiar mountains of grain, beef and butter. The cost of storing excess supply falls on the European citizens, while the gains are reaped by a few large efficient farms. The CAP currently costs its citizens about €40bn (£24bn) each year.

But this isn't the end of the story. The European Union is about to expand, letting new countries such as Hungary and Poland join. These countries have large inefficient agricultural sectors which will escalate the cost of maintaining the CAP. As a result, The European Union has begun to reform the CAP – reducing target prices and tariffs, and introducing direct income support payments to farmers. EU agricultural markets are becoming more open to world competition and some of the mountains of butter and lakes of wine are getting smaller.

Review Quiz

◆ Why is the demand for most farm goods inelastic?
◆ Can you explain how poor harvests and bumper harvests influence agricultural prices and farm revenues?
◆ Explain how a price support system can be used to maintain farm revenues using the concepts of excess supply, price floors and tariffs.
◆ Why is the Common Agricultural Policy so expensive to maintain?

You now know how to use the demand and supply model to make predictions about prices, to study government interventions in markets, and to study the problems of inefficiency in markets. To learn more about how the CAP affects European beef markets, turn to Reading Between the Lines on pp. 132–133.

Summary

Key Points

Housing Markets and Rent Ceilings (pp. 113–116)

● A decrease in the supply of housing decreases short-run supply and increases equilibrium rents.

● Higher rents increase the quantity of housing supplied in the short run and stimulate building activity, which increases supply in the long run. Rents decrease and the quantity of housing increases.

● If a rent ceiling prevents rents from increasing, the quantity supplied remains constant and there is a housing shortage, which creates wasteful search and black markets.

The Labour Market and Minimum Wages (pp. 116–119)

- A decrease in the demand for unskilled labour lowers the wage and reduces employment.

- The lower wage encourages people to quit the unskilled market and to acquire skills, decreasing the supply of unskilled labour. The wage rises gradually to its original level and employment decreases.

- Imposing a minimum wage above the equilibrium wage, decreases the demand for labour, creates unemployment and increases the amount of time spent searching for a job.

- Minimum wages bite hardest on people having the fewest skills.

Taxes (pp. 119–124)

- When a good or service is taxed, it is usually offered for sale at a higher price than if it is not taxed. Usually, the quantity bought decreases and the price increases but by less than the amount of the tax. The tax is paid partly by the buyer and partly by the seller.

- The portion of the tax paid by the buyer and by the seller depends on the elasticity of supply and the elasticity of demand.

- The more elastic the supply and the less elastic the demand, the greater is the price increase, the smaller is the quantity decrease, and the larger is the portion of the tax paid by the buyer.

- If supply is perfectly inelastic or demand is perfectly elastic, the seller pays the entire tax. If supply is perfectly elastic or demand is perfectly inelastic, the buyer pays the entire tax.

Markets for Prohibited Goods (pp. 124–126)

- Penalties on sellers of an illegal good increase the cost of selling the good and decrease its supply. Penalties on buyers decrease their willingness to pay and decrease demand for the good.

- The higher the penalties and the more effective the law enforcement, the smaller is the quantity bought. The price is higher or lower than the unregulated price, depending on whether penalties on sellers or buyers are higher.

- A tax set at a sufficiently high rate will also decrease the quantity of a drug consumed, but there will be a tendency for the tax to be evaded.

Stabilizing Farm Revenue (pp. 126–128)

- Farm revenues fluctuate because supply fluctuates.

- The demand for most farm goods is inelastic, so a decrease in supply increases the price and increases farm revenue while an increase in supply decreases the price and decreases farm revenue.

- Governments often try to stabilize farm prices and revenues by using price intervention policies like the Common Agricultural Policy.

Key Figures ◈

Key Terms

Problems

•1 The figure below shows the demand for and supply of rental housing in Village:

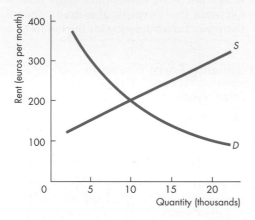

a What is the equilibrium rent and equilibrium quantity of rented housing?

If a rent ceiling is set at €150 a month, what is:

b The quantity of housing rented?

c The shortage of housing?

d The maximum price that someone is willing to pay for the last unit of housing available?

2 The figure below shows the demand for and supply of rental housing in Township:

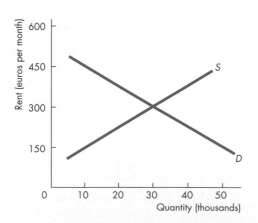

a What is the equilibrium rent and equilibrium quantity of rented housing?

If a rent ceiling is set at €150 a month, what is:

b The quantity of housing rented?

c The shortage of housing?

d The maximum price that someone is willing to pay for the last unit available?

•3 The table gives the demand for and supply of teenage labour in a UK town.

Wage rate (pounds per hour)	Quantity demanded	Quantity supplied
	(hours per month)	
2	3,000	1,000
3	2,500	1,500
4	2,000	2,000
5	1,500	2,500
6	1,000	3,000

a What are the equilibrium wage rate and level of employment?

b What is the quantity of unemployment?

c If a minimum wage of £3 an hour is set for teenagers, how many hours do they work?

d If a minimum wage of £3 an hour is set for teenagers, how many hours of their labour are unemployed?

e If a minimum wage is set at £5 an hour for teenagers, how many hours of their labour are employed and unemployed?

f If a minimum wage is set at £5 an hour and demand increases by 500 hours a month, what is the wage rate paid to teenagers and how many hours of their labour are unemployed?

4 The table gives the demand for and supply of secondary school leavers in a UK town.

Wage rate (pounds per hour)	Quantity demanded	Quantity supplied
	(hours per month)	
6	9,000	4,000
7	8,000	5,000
8	7,000	6,000
9	6,000	7,000
10	5,000	8,000

a What are the equilibrium wage rate and level of employment?

b What is the level of unemployment?

c If a minimum wage is set at £7 an hour, how many hours do secondary school leavers work?

d If a minimum wage is set at £7 an hour, how many hours of labour are unemployed?

e If a minimum wage is set at £9 an hour, how many hours of their labour are employed and unemployed?

f If the minimum wage is £9 an hour and demand increases by 500 hours a month, what is the wage rate paid to secondary school leavers and how many hours of their labour are unemployed?

•5 The table gives the demand and supply schedules for chocolate brownies in the UK.

Price (pence per brownie)	Quantity demanded	Quantity supplied
	(millions per day)	
50	5	3
60	4	4
70	3	5
80	2	6
90	1	7

a If brownies are not taxed, what is the price of a brownie and how many are consumed?

b If brownies are taxed at 20 pence each, what is the price and how many brownies are consumed? Who pays the tax?

6 The table gives the demand and supply schedules for coffee in a UK town.

Price (pounds per cup)	Quantity demanded	Quantity supplied
	(cups per hour)	
1.50	90	30
1.75	70	40
2.00	50	50
2.25	30	60
2.75	10	70

a If there is no tax on coffee, what is the price and how much coffee is consumed?

b If a tax of 75 pence a cup is introduced, what is the price, how much coffee is consumed, and who pays the tax?

Critical Thinking

1 Read the article in Reading Between the Lines on pp. 132–133 again. Use the links on the Parkin, Powell and Matthews website to read about the CAP and the beef market before answering the following questions:

a Explain how the target price for beef is used to maintain farm incomes under the CAP.

b Explain why an import tariff on beef is needed under the CAP.

c Draw a diagram similar to the Figure in Reading Between the Lines on pp. 132–133 to show the import tariff on beef.

d Draw a diagram that illustrates the impact on beef surpluses of a fall in the demand for beef as a result of the BSE crisis between 1998 and 2000.

e Would you expect the import tariff to rise or fall when the demand for beef falls?

f Suppose consumers forget about the BSE and foot-and-mouth crises and demand for beef increases by 2008:

  i What would be the likely effect on beef surpluses?

  ii How might it affect the pressure for reform of the Common Agricultural Policy in the beef market?

g If the CAP reforms result in a fall in the target price of beef, would you expect farmers to be better off or worse off. Explain your answer.

2 Use the links on the Parkin, Powell and Matthews website to obtain information about cigarette smuggling in the European Union. Then answer the following questions.

a What is the main cause of cigarette smuggling in the European Union?

b Who benefits and who loses as a result of cigarette smuggling?

c What do the authorities do to try to stop cigarette smuggling at present?

d What else could be done to reduce the extent of cigarette smuggling?

3 Use the European links on the Parkin, Powell and Matthews website to find out about Agenda 2000 and proposals to reform the CAP. Then answer the following:

a What are the main disadvantages of the CAP at present?

b Why does the prospect of new members put pressure on the EU to reform the CAP?

c How might the EU reform the CAP?

4 Use the links on the Parkin, Powell and Matthews website to find out about the debate on legalization and decriminalization of cannabis. Identify the economic issues in the debate and then argue a case for or against decriminalization in your country.

Price Controls: Mad Cows and Beef Mountains

THE FINANCIAL TIMES, 12 JULY 2001

EU beef market under pressure for reform

Michael Mann

The fallout from the 'mad cow disease' crisis will continue to weigh on the European Union's beef market until well beyond 2008, making reform of the industry an absolute priority, according to forecasts released yesterday by the European Commission.

The report predicts a peak in the 'beef mountain' of around 730,000 tonnes in 2003 and remaining surpluses of 240,000 tonnes five years later. This will give Franz Fischler, EU agriculture commissioner, vital ammunition as he prepares his so called 'mid-term review' of the €40bn (£24bn) Common Agricultural Policy next year.

Following the recent BSE scare and foot-and-mouth disease epidemic, pressure has grown in the EU for root-and-branch changes to the CAP, which still accounts for the lion's share of the EU budget and attracts stinging criticism from its trading partners.

But officials in Brussels believe a wholesale shift in approach is unlikely at this stage . . . A more realistic approach would be emergency surgery on those markets such as beef which need short-term attention, coupled with an attempt to cap the level of subsidies any single farmer may receive.

The Essence of the Story

- The mad cow disease (BSE) and foot-and-mouth outbreaks are making the European Union's beef mountain grow.

- The European Commission predicts that its annual beef surplus will reach a peak of 730,000 tonnes in 2003, and it will still be as high as 240,000 tonnes in 2008.

- Mounting surpluses are putting the EU under increasing pressure to reform the Common Agricultural Policy.

- Reforms are likely to be limited to lowering subsidies.

Economic Analysis

■ The EU Common Agricultural Policy sets a minimum target price for beef farmers above the market equilibrium price.

■ The newspaper article does not provide prices but this information is available from EU sources.

■ The figure shows the European beef market in 2000. The demand curve for beef is D_{00}, and the supply curve for beef is S_{00}.

■ With no EU intervention in the European beef market, the price would be €3,250 per tonne and the quantity produced and consumed (including exports) would be 6.6 million tonnes.

■ The EU sets the target price so that the farmer receives €3,750 per tonne.

■ At this price, the quantity of beef supplied (beef production) increases to 7 million tonnes.

■ However, at the target price, the quantity of beef demanded decreases to 6.3 million tonnes.

■ There is now a beef surplus of 0.7 million tonnes.

■ The EU Commission buys this surplus at €3,750 per tonne and spends a total of €2.65 billion – a considerable proportion of its total €40 billion budget for the Common Agricultural Policy.

■ BSE and foot-and-mouth disease will continue to depress the demand for beef for several years and the beef mountain will remain large unless the target price is brought closer to the market equilibrium price.

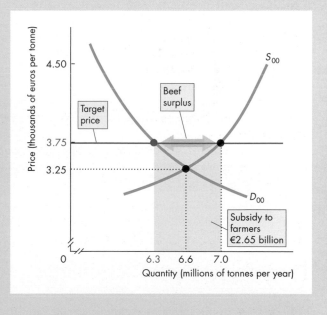

CHAPTER 7

Utility and Demand

After studying this chapter you will be able to:

◆ Explain the connection between individual demand and market demand

◆ Define total utility and marginal utility

◆ Explain the marginal utility theory of consumer choice

◆ Use the marginal utility theory to predict the effects of changing prices and incomes

◆ Explain the paradox of value

Water, Water, Everywhere

We need water to live, but we use diamonds mainly for decoration. If the benefits of water far outweigh the benefits of diamonds, why, then, does water cost practically nothing while diamonds are very expensive? ◆ When OPEC restricted its sale of oil in 1973, it created a dramatic rise in price, but people continued to use almost as much oil as they had before. Our demand for oil was price inelastic. But why? ◆ When the CD player was introduced in 1983, it was sold at a relatively high price and consumers didn't buy many. Since then the price has decreased dramatically, and many households have bought one. Our demand for CD players is price elastic. What makes the demand for some things price elastic while the demand for others is price inelastic? ◆ Over the past 40 years, the real value of European incomes has risen. Over the same period, expenditure on cars has increased from less than 1 per cent of total spending to 14 per cent, while expenditure on food has fallen from 25 per cent of total expenditure to just less than 15 per cent on average today. Thus the proportion of income spent on cars has increased and the proportion spent on food has decreased. Why, as incomes rise, does the proportion of income spent on some goods rise and on others fall?

◆ ◆ ◆ ◆ In the last four chapters, we've seen that demand in any market has an important effect on the price of a good. But what shapes market demand? This chapter starts with market demand by looking at individual behaviour and its influence on demand. It then explains why demand is elastic for some goods and inelastic for others. It also explains why the prices of some things, such as diamonds and water, are so out of proportion to their total benefits. It ends by explaining in Reading Between the Lines on pp. 150–151, why the coffee craze in Britain might be over as people switch from coffee bars to the new soup and juice bars.

Individual Demand and Market Demand

The relationship between the total quantity demanded in a market and the price of a good is called **market demand**. And the relationship between the quantity demanded of a good by an individual and its price is called **individual demand**. The market demand is simply the sum of all the individual demands.

The table in Figure 7.1 illustrates the relationship between individual demand and market demand. In this example we will assume that Lisa and John are the only people. The market demand is the total demand of Lisa and John. At £3 a cinema ticket, Lisa demands 5 films a month and John demands 2 films, so that the total quantity demanded in the market is 7 films a month. Figure 7.1 illustrates the relationship between individual and market demand curves. Lisa's and John's demand curves for films, shown in parts (a) and (b), sum horizontally to give the market demand curve in part (c).

> The market demand curve is the horizontal sum of the individual demand curves formed by adding the quantities demanded by each individual at each price.

We're going to investigate what shapes market demand by looking at what shapes individual demand. We will do this by studying how an individual makes consumption choices.

Individual Consumption Choices

An individual's consumption choices are determined by many factors, and we can model the impact of these factors using two new concepts:

Figure 7.1

Individual Demand and Market Demand Curves

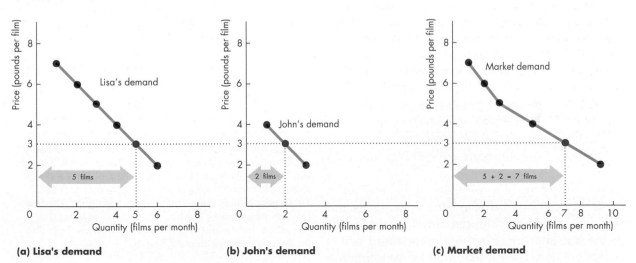

(a) Lisa's demand   **(b) John's demand**   **(c) Market demand**

Price of a cinema ticket (pounds)	Quantity of films demanded		
	Lisa	John	Market
7	1	0	1
6	2	0	2
5	3	0	3
4	4	1	5
3	5	2	7
2	6	3	9

The table and the figure illustrate how the quantity of films demanded varies as the price of a cinema ticket varies. In the table, the market demand in the final column is the sum of the individual demands. For example, at a price of 3, Lisa demands 5 films and John demands 2 films, so the total quantity demanded in the market is 7 films per month. In the figure, the market demand curve is the horizontal sum of the individual demand curves. Thus when the price is 3, the market demand curve shows the quantity demanded as the sum of Lisa and John's demands for 7 films.

1 Budget line.

2 Preferences.

Budget Line

In this model of individual consumption, choices are constrained by income and by the prices of goods and services. We will assume that each individual has a given amount of income to spend, that everyone consumes all the goods they purchase within the relevant time period, and that individuals cannot influence the prices of the goods and services they buy.

The limits to individual consumption choices are described by a *budget line*. To make the concept of the individual's budget line as clear as possible, we'll consider a simplified example of one individual – Lisa – and her choice. Lisa has an income of £30 a month to spend. She spends her income on two goods – cinema films and cola. Cinema tickets cost £6 each; cola costs £3 for a six-pack. If Lisa spends all of her income, she will reach the limits to her consumption of films and cola.

In Figure 7.2, each row of the table shows affordable ways for Lisa to see cinema films and buy cola packs. Row *a* indicates that she can buy 10 six-packs of cola and see no films. You can see that this combination exhausts her monthly income of £30. Row *f* says that Lisa can see 5 films and drink no cola – another combination that exhausts the £30 available. Each of the other rows in the table also exhausts Lisa's income. (Check that each of the other rows costs exactly £30.) The numbers in the table define Lisa's maximum consumption possibilities of films and cola. These consumption possibilities are graphed as points *a* to *f* in Figure 7.2.

Lisa's budget line is a constraint on her choices. It marks the boundary between what is affordable and what is unaffordable. She can afford all the points on the line and inside it. She cannot afford points outside the line. The constraint on her consumption depends on prices and on her income, and the constraint changes when prices and her income change.

Preferences and Utility

How does Lisa divide her £30 between these two goods? The answer depends on her likes and dislikes – or her **preferences**. Economists use the concept of utility to describe preferences. The benefit or satisfaction that a person gets from the consumption of a good or service is called **utility**. But what exactly is utility and in what units can we measure it? Utility is

Figure 7.2

Consumption Possibilities

an abstract concept and its units are arbitrary. The concept of utility helps us make predictions about consumption choices in much the same way that the concept of temperature helps us make predictions about physical phenomena. It has to be admitted, though, that the marginal utility theory is not as precise as the theory that enables us to predict when water will turn to ice or steam.

Let's now see how we can use the concept of utility to describe preferences.

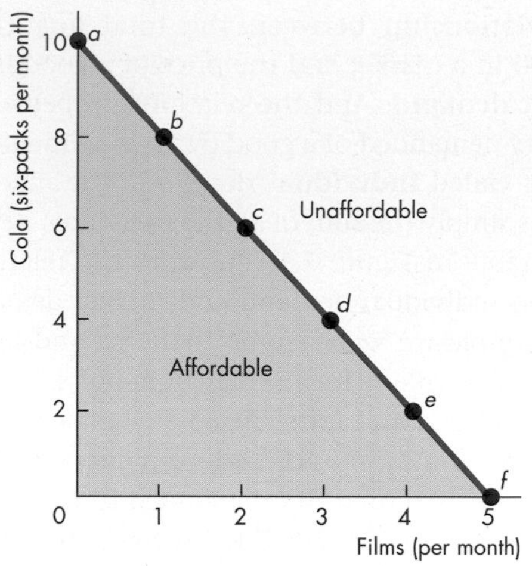

Possibility	Expenditure			
	Films		Cola	
	Quantity	Expenditure (pounds)	Quantity (six-packs)	Expenditure (pounds)
a	0	0	10	30
b	1	6	8	24
c	2	12	6	18
d	3	18	4	12
e	4	24	2	6
f	5	30	0	0

Six possible ways of allocating £30 to films and cola are shown as the rows *a* to *f* in the table. For example, Lisa can see 2 cinema films and buy 6 six-packs (row *c*). Each row shows the combinations of film and cola that cost £30. These possibilities are points *a* to *f* in the figure. The line through those points is a boundary between what Lisa can afford and cannot afford. Her choices must lie inside the orange area or along the line *af*.

Table 7.1   Lisa's Total Utility from Films and Cola

Films		Cola	
Quantity per month	Total utility	Quantity (six packs per month)	Total utility
0	0	0	0
1	50	1	75
2	88	2	117
3	121	3	153
4	150	4	181
5	175	5	206
6	196	6	225
7	214	7	243
8	229	8	260
9	241	9	276
10	250	10	291
11	256	11	305
12	259	12	318
13	261	13	330
14	262	14	341

Total Utility

Total utility is the total benefit or satisfaction that a person gets from the consumption of goods and services. Total utility depends on the person's level of consumption – more consumption generally gives more total utility. Table 7.1 shows Lisa's total utility from consuming different quantities of cinema films and cola. If she does not go to the cinema, she gets no utility from seeing films. If she goes once a month, she gets 50 units of utility. As the number of visits in a month increases, her total utility increases so that if she sees 10 films a month, she gets 250 units of total utility. The other part of the table shows Lisa's total utility from cola. If she drinks no cola, she gets no utility from cola. As the amount of cola she drinks rises, her total utility increases.

Marginal Utility

Marginal utility is the change in total utility resulting from a one-unit increase in the quantity of a good consumed. The table in Figure 7.3 shows the calculation of Lisa's marginal utility from seeing films. When her consumption of films increases from 4 to 5 a month, her total utility from films increases from 150 units to 175 units. Thus for Lisa, the marginal

utility of seeing a fifth film each month is 25 units. Notice that marginal utility appears midway between the quantities of consumption. It does so because it is the *change* in consumption from 4 to 5 films that produces the marginal utility of 25 units. The table displays calculations of marginal utility for each level of film consumption.

Figure 7.3(a) illustrates the total utility that Lisa gets from seeing films. As you can see, the more films Lisa sees in a month, the more total utility she gets. Part (b) illustrates her marginal utility. This graph tells us that as Lisa sees more films, the marginal utility that Lisa gets from seeing films decreases. For example, her marginal utility from the first film is 50 units, from the second 38 units, and from the third 33 units. We call this decrease in marginal utility as the consumption of a good increases the principle of **diminishing marginal utility**.

Marginal utility is positive but diminishes as the consumption of a good increases. Why does marginal utility have these two features? In Lisa's case, she likes films, and the more she sees the better. That's why marginal utility is positive. The benefit that Lisa gets from the last film seen is its marginal utility. To see why marginal utility diminishes, think about how you'd feel in the following two situations. In one, you've just been studying for 15 evenings in a row. An opportunity arises to see a new film. The utility you get from that film is the marginal utility from seeing one film in a month. In the second situation, you've been on a cinema binge. For the past 15 nights, you have not even seen an assignment or test. You are up to your eyeballs in films. You are happy enough to go to a film on yet one more night. But the thrill that you get out of that sixteenth film in 16 days is not very large. It is the marginal utility of the sixteenth film in a month.

Review Quiz

- Explain how a consumer's income and the prices of goods limit consumption possibilities.
- What is utility and how do we use the concepts of utility to describe a consumer's preferences.
- What is the distinction between total utility and marginal utility.
- What is the key assumption about marginal utility?

Figure 7.3

Total Utility and Marginal Utility

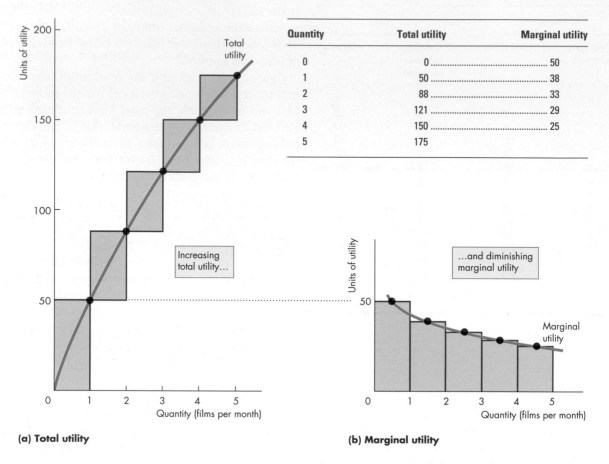

Quantity	Total utility	Marginal utility
0	0	50
1	50	38
2	88	33
3	121	29
4	150	25
5	175	

(a) Total utility

(b) Marginal utility

The table shows that as Lisa's consumption of films increases, so does the total utility she derives from films. The table also shows her marginal utility – the change in utility resulting from the last film seen. Marginal utility declines as consumption increases. The figure graphs Lisa's total utility and marginal utility from films. Part (a) shows her total utility. It also shows the extra utility she gains from each additional film – her marginal utility. Part (b) shows how Lisa's marginal utility from films diminishes by placing the bars shown in part (a) side by side as a series of declining steps.

Maximizing Utility

Individual income and prices limit the utility an individual can obtain from consumption. The key assumption of marginal utility theory is that, taking into consideration the income available for spending and the prices people face, individuals consume the quantities of goods and services that maximize total utility. The assumption of **utility maximization** is a way of expressing the fundamental economic problem. People's wants exceed the resources available to satisfy these wants, so they must make hard choices.

In making choices, they try to get the maximum attainable benefit – they try to maximize total utility.

Let's model Lisa's choice to see how she allocates her spending between cinema films and cola to maximize her total utility. Lisa makes her choice knowing cinema tickets cost £6 each, cola costs £3 a six-pack, and she has £30 a month to spend.

The Utility-maximizing Choice

The most direct way of calculating how Lisa spends her money if she maximizes her total utility is by

Table 7.2 Lisa's Utility-maximizing Combinations of Films and Cola

Films		Total utility from films and cola	Cola	
Quantity	Total utility		Total utility	Quantity
0	0	291	291	10
1	50	310	260	8
2	88	313	225	6
3	121	302	181	4
4	150	267	117	2
5	175	175	0	0

making a table like the one shown in Table 7.2. This table shows the same affordable combinations of films and cola that you can find on her budget line in Figure 7.2. The table records three things: first, the number of cinema films seen and the total utility derived from them (the left side of the table); second, the number of six-packs of cola consumed and the total utility derived from them (the right side of the table); and third, the total utility derived from both films and cola (the centre column of the table).

The first row of Table 7.2 records the situation if Lisa does not go to the cinema but buys 10 six-packs. In this case, she gets no utility from films and 291 units of total utility from cola. Her total utility from films and cola (the centre column) is 291 units. The rest of the table is constructed in the same way.

The consumption of films and cola that maximizes Lisa's total utility is highlighted in the table. When Lisa consumes 2 films and 6 six-packs of cola, she gets 313 units of total utility. This is the best Lisa can do given that she has only £30 to spend and given the prices of cinema tickets and six-packs. If she buys 8 six-packs of cola, she can see only 1 film and gets 310 units of total utility, 3 fewer than the maximum attainable. If she sees 3 films and drinks only 4 six-packs, she gets 302 units of total utility, 11 fewer than the maximum attainable.

We've just described a consumer equilibrium. A **consumer equilibrium** is a situation in which a consumer has allocated his or her income in the way that maximizes total utility.

In finding Lisa's consumer equilibrium, we measured her *total* utility from the consumption of films and cola. There is a better way of determining a consumer equilibrium, which does not involve measuring total utility at all. Let's look at this alternative.

Equalizing Marginal Utility per Pound Spent

Another way to find out the allocation that maximizes a consumer's total utility is to make the marginal utility per pound spent on each good equal for all goods. The **marginal utility per pound spent** is the marginal utility obtained from the last unit of a good consumed divided by the price of the good. For example, Lisa's marginal utility from consuming the first film is 50 units of utility. The price of a cinema ticket is £6, which means that the marginal utility per pound spent on films is 50 units divided by £6, or 7.33 units of utility per pound.

> Total utility is maximized when all the consumer's income is spent and when the marginal utility per dollar spent is equal for all goods.

Lisa maximizes total utility when she spends all her income and consumes films and cola such that

$$\frac{\text{Marginal utility}}{\text{Price of a}} = \frac{\text{Marginal utility of}}{\text{Price of a}}$$
$$\frac{\text{of seeing a film}}{\text{cinema ticket}} = \frac{\text{a six-pack of cola}}{\text{six-pack of cola}}$$

Call the marginal utility from films MU_f, the marginal utility from cola MU_c, the price of a cinema ticket P_f, and the price of cola P_c. Then Lisa's utility is maximized when she spends all her income and when

$$\frac{MU_f}{P_f} = \frac{MU_c}{P_c}$$

Let's use this formula to find Lisa's utility-maximizing allocation of her income.

Table 7.3 sets out Lisa's marginal utilities per pound spent for both films and cola. For example, in row *b* Lisa's marginal utility from films is 50 units and, since cinema tickets cost £6 each, her marginal utility per pound spent on films is 7.33 units per pound (50 units divided by £6). Each row contains an allocation of Lisa's income that uses up her £30. You can see that Lisa's marginal utility per pound spent on each good, like marginal utility itself, decreases as consumption of the good increases.

Total utility is maximized when the marginal utility per pound spent on films is equal to the marginal utility per pound spent on cola, possibility *c*, where

Table 7.3 Maximizing Utility by Equalizing Marginal Utilities per Pound Spent

	Films (£6 per ticket)			Cola (£3 per six-pack)		
	Quantity	Marginal utility	Marginal utility per pound spent	Quantity (six-packs)	Marginal utility	Marginal utility per pound spent
a	0	0		10	15	5.00
b	1	50	8.33	8	17	5.67
c	2	38	6.33	6	19	6.33
d	3	33	5.50	4	28	9.33
e	4	29	4.83	2	42	14.00
f	5	25	4.17	0	0	

Lisa consumes 2 films and 6 six-packs – the same allocation as we calculated in Table 7.2.

Figure 7.4 shows why the rule 'equalize marginal utility per pound spent on all goods' works. Suppose that instead of consuming 2 films and 6 six-packs (possibility *c*), Lisa consumes 1 film and 8 six-packs (possibility *b*). She then gets 8.33 units of utility from the last pound spent on films and 5.67 units from the last pound spent on cola. In this situation Lisa can increase her total utility by spending less on cola and more on films. If she spends a pound less on cola and a pound more on films, her total utility from cola decreases by 5.67 units and her total utility from films increases by 8.33 units. Lisa's total utility increases by 2.66 units (a gain of 8.33 minus a loss of 5.67) if she spends less on cola and more on films.

Or, suppose that Lisa consumes 3 films and 4 six-packs (possibility *d*). In this situation, her marginal utility from the last pound spent on films is less than her marginal utility from the last pound spent on cola. Lisa can now increase her total utility by spending less on films and more on cola.

The Power of Marginal Analysis

The method we've just used to maximize Lisa's utility is an example of the power of *marginal analysis*. By comparing the marginal gain from having more of one good with the marginal loss from having less of another good, Lisa is able to ensure that she gets the maximum attainable utility.

In the example, Lisa consumes at the point at which the marginal utility per pound spent on films

Figure 7.4

Equalizing Marginal Utility per Pound Spent

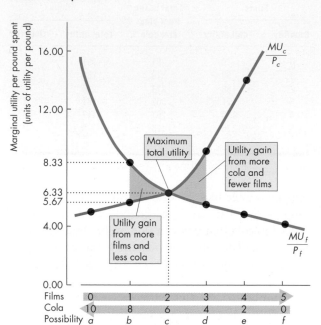

If Lisa consumes 1 cinema film and 8 six-packs of cola (possibility *b*) she gets 8.33 units of utility from the last pound spent on films and 5.67 units of utility from the last pound spent on cola. She can get more total utility if she sees one more film. If she consumes 4 six-packs and sees 3 films (possibility *d*) she gets 5.50 units of utility from the last pound spent on films and 9.33 units of utility from the last pound spent on cola. She can get more total utility by seeing one film fewer. When Lisa's marginal utility per pound spent on both goods is equal, her total utility is maximized.

and cola are equal. Because we buy goods and services in indivisible lumps, the numbers don't always work out so precisely. But the basic approach always applies. The rule to follow is simple: if the marginal utility per pound spent on films exceeds the marginal utility per pound spent on cola, see more films and drink less cola; if the marginal utility per pound spent on cola exceeds the marginal utility per pound spent on films, drink more cola and see fewer films.

More generally, our model of behaviour says that if the marginal gain from an action exceeds the marginal loss, take the action. You will meet this principle time and again in your study of economics. And you will find yourself applying this model every time you make your own economic choices.

Units of Utility

In calculating the utility-maximizing allocation of income in Table 7.3 and Figure 7.4 we have not used the concept of total utility at all. All the calculations have used marginal utility and price. By making the marginal utility per pound spent equal for both goods, we know that Lisa has maximized her total utility.

This way of viewing maximum utility is important; it means that the units in which utility is measured do not matter. We could double or halve all the numbers measuring utility, or multiply or divide them by any other positive number. None of these transformations of the units used to measure utility makes any difference to the outcome. It is in this respect that utility is analogous to temperature. Our prediction about the freezing of water depends on the model or concept of temperature, not on the temperature scale; our prediction about maximizing utility depends on our model of choice, not on the units of utility.

Review Quiz

◆ What is Lisa's goal when choosing the quantities of films she sees or cola she drinks?
◆ What are the two conditions that are met if a consumer like Lisa is maximizing utility?
◆ Explain why equalizing the marginal utility of each good does *not* maximize utility.
◆ Explain why equalizing the marginal utility per pound spent on each good *does* maximize utility?

Predictions of Marginal Utility Theory

Let's now use marginal utility theory and our model of choice to make some predictions. What happens to Lisa's consumption of films and cola when their prices change and when her income changes?

A Fall in the Price of Cinema Tickets

To determine the effect of a change in price on consumption requires three steps. First, determine the combinations of films and cola that can be bought at the new prices. Second, calculate the new marginal

Table 7.4 How a Change in Price of Films Affects Lisa's Choices

Films (£3 per ticket)		Cola (£3 per six-pack)	
Quantity	Marginal utility per pound spent	Quantity (six-packs)	Marginal utility per pound spent
0		10	5.00
1	16.67	9	5.33
2	12.67	8	5.67
3	11.00	7	6.00
4	9.67	6	6.33
5	8.33	5	8.33
6	7.00	4	9.33
7	6.00	3	12.00
8	5.00	2	14.00
9	4.00	1	25.00
10	3.00	0	

utilities per pound spent. Third, determine the consumption of each good that makes the marginal utility per pound spent on each good equal and that just exhausts the money available for spending.

Table 7.4 shows the combinations of films and cola that exactly exhaust Lisa's £30 of income when cinema tickets cost £3 each and cola costs £3 a six-pack. Her preferences do not change when prices change, so her marginal utility schedule remains the same as that in Table 7.3. But now we divide her marginal utility from films by £3, the new price of a cinema ticket, to get the marginal utility per pound spent on films.

What is the effect of the fall in the price of a cinema ticket on Lisa's consumption? You can find the answer by comparing her new utility-maximizing allocation (Table 7.4) with her original allocation (Table 7.3). Lisa responds to a fall in the price of a cinema ticket by seeing more films (up from 2 to 5 a month) and drinking less cola (down from 6 to 5 six-packs a month). That is, Lisa substitutes films for cola when the price of a cinema ticket falls. Figure 7.5 illustrates these effects. In part (a) a fall in the price of cinema tickets produces a movement along Lisa's demand curve for films and in part (b) it shifts her demand curve for cola.

A Rise in the Price of Cola

Table 7.5 shows the combinations of films and cola that exactly exhaust Lisa's £30 of income when cinema tickets cost £3 each and cola costs £6 a six-pack. Now we divide her marginal utility from cola by £6,

Figure 7.5

A Fall in the Price of Cinema Tickets

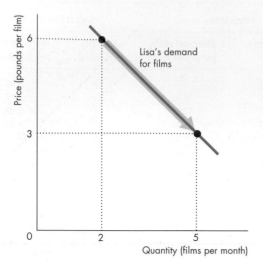

(a) Films

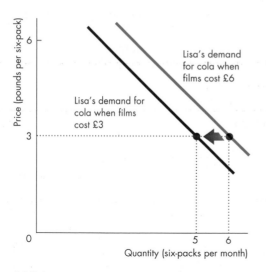

(b) Cola

When the price of cinema tickets falls and the price of cola remains constant, the quantity of films demanded by Lisa increases and in part (a), Lisa moves along her demand curve for films. Also, Lisa's demand for cola decreases and in part (b), her demand curve for cola shifts leftward.

the new price of a six-pack, to get the marginal utility per pound spent on cola.

The effect of the rise in the price of cola on Lisa's consumption is seen by comparing her new utility-maximizing allocation (Table 7.5) with her previous

Table 7.5 How a Change in the Price of Cola Affects Lisa's Choices

Films (£3 per ticket)		Cola (£6 per six-pack)	
Quantity	**Marginal utility per pound spent**	**Quantity (six-packs)**	**Marginal utility per pound spent**
0		5	4.17
2	12.67	4	4.67
4	9.67	3	6.00
6	7.00	2	7.00
8	5.00	1	12.50
10	3.00	0	

allocation (Table 7.4). Lisa responds to a rise in the price of cola by drinking less cola (down from 5 to 2 six-packs a month) and seeing more films (up from 5 to 6 a month). That is, Lisa substitutes films for cola when the price of cola rises. Figure 7.6 illustrates these effects. In part (a) a rise in the price of cola produces a movement along Lisa's demand curve for cola and in part (b) it shifts her demand curve for films.

Marginal utility theory predicts these two results: when the price of a good rises, the quantity demanded of that good decreases; if the price of one good rises, the demand for another good that can serve as a substitute increases. Does this sound familiar? It should. These predictions of marginal utility theory correspond to the assumptions that we made about consumer demand in Chapter 4. There we *assumed* that the demand curve for a good sloped downward, and we *assumed* that a rise in the price of a substitute increased demand.

We have now seen that marginal utility theory predicts how the quantities of goods and services that people demand respond to price changes. The theory helps us to understand both the shape and the position of the demand curve. It also helps us to understand how the demand curve for one good shifts when the price of another good changes. Marginal utility theory also helps us to understand one further thing about demand – how it changes when income changes.

Let's study the effects of a change in income on consumption.

A Rise in Income

Let's suppose that Lisa's income increases to £42 a month and that cinema tickets cost £3 each and a

Figure 7.6

A Rise in the Price of Cola

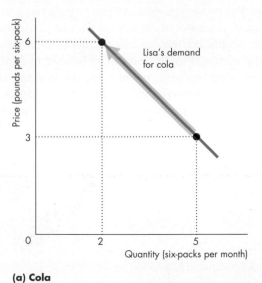

(a) Cola

(b) Films

When the price of cola rises and the price of cinema tickets remains constant, the quantity of cola demanded by Lisa decreases and in part (a), Lisa moves along her demand curve for films. Also, Lisa's demand for films increases and in part (b), her demand curve for films shifts to the right.

six-pack costs £3 (as in Table 7.4). In Table 7.4, we saw that with these prices and with an income of £30 a month, Lisa sees 5 films and consumes 5 six-packs a month. We want to compare this consumption of films and cola with Lisa's consumption at an income of £42. The calculations for the comparison are shown in Table 7.6. With £42, Lisa can see 14 films a month and drink no cola or drink 14 six-packs a month and see no films or any combination of the two goods as shown in the rows of the table. We calculate the marginal utility per pound spent in exactly the same way as we did before and find the quantities at which the marginal utilities per pound spent on films and on cola are equal. With an income of £42, the marginal utility per pound spent on each good is equal when Lisa sees 7 films and drinks 7 six-packs of cola a month.

By comparing this situation with that in Table 7.4, we see that with an additional £12 a month, Lisa drinks 2 more six-packs and sees 2 more films. This response arises from Lisa's preferences, as described by her marginal utilities. Different preferences produce different quantitative responses. But for normal goods, a higher income always brings a larger

Table 7.6   Lisa's Choices with an Income of £42 a Month

Films (£3 per ticket)		Cola (£3 per six-pack)	
Quantity	**Marginal utility per pound spent**	**Quantity (six-packs)**	**Marginal utility per pound spent**
0		14	3.67
1	16.67	13	4.00
2	12.67	12	4.33
3	11.00	11	4.67
4	9.67	10	5.00
5	8.33	9	5.33
6	7.00	8	5.67
7	6.00	7	6.00
8	5.00	6	6.33
9	4.00	5	8.33
10	3.00	4	9.33
11	2.00	3	12.00
12	1.00	2	14.00
13	0.67	1	25.00
14	0.33	0	

Table 7.7 Marginal Utility Theory

Assumptions

◆ A consumer derives utility from the goods consumed.

◆ Each additional unit of consumption yields additional utility; marginal utility is positive.

◆ As the quantity of a good consumed increases, marginal utility decreases.

◆ A consumer's aim is to maximize total utility.

Implication

Utility is maximized when all the available income is spent and when the marginal utility per pound spent is equal for all goods.

Predictions

◆ Other things remaining the same, the higher the price of a good, the lower is the quantity bought (the law of demand).

◆ The higher the price of a good, the higher is the consumption of substitutes for that good.

◆ The higher the consumer's income, the greater is the quantity demanded of normal goods.

---

consumption of all goods. For Lisa, cola and films are normal goods. When her income increases, Lisa buys more of both goods.

You have now completed your study of marginal utility theory and Table 7.7 summarizes the key assumptions, implications and predictions of the theory.

Marginal Utility and the Real World

Marginal utility theory can be used to answer a wide range of questions about the real world. The theory can also be used to interpret some of the facts set out at the beginning of this chapter – for example, why the demand for CD players is price elastic. Elasticities of demand are determined by preferences – by how rapidly marginal utility diminishes.

If marginal utility diminishes rapidly, a small change in the quantity bought brings a big change in the marginal utility per pound spent. So it takes a big price change to bring a small quantity change – demand is inelastic. Conversely, if marginal utility diminishes slowly, even a large change in the quantity bought brings a small change in the marginal utility per pound spent. So it takes only a small price change to bring a large quantity change – demand is elastic.

The marginal utility of CD players diminishes rapidly for individuals. One CD player yields much more marginal utility than a second CD player. But

the demand for CD players is elastic. This is because most people want only the first CD player. They ignore the rapid fall in marginal utility of the second player. For those who demand just one player, a small change in price would cause a big change in the number of people buying, and hence demand is elastic. But the marginal utility theory can be used to explain *all* individual choices. One of these choices, the allocation of time between work in the home, office, or factory and leisure is the theme of Economics in History on pp. 170–171.

Review Quiz

◆ When the price of a good falls and the prices of other goods remain the same, explain what happens to the consumption of the good whose price has fallen and to the consumption of other goods.

◆ Elaborate your answer to the previous question by using demand curves. For which good is there a change in demand and for which is there a change in quantity demanded?

◆ If a consumer's income increases, and if all goods are normal goods, how does the quantity bought of each good change?

Efficiency, Price and Value

Marginal utility theory helps us to deepen our understanding of the concept of efficiency that we developed in Chapter 5. It helps us to see more clearly the distinction between value and price. Let's see how.

Consumer Efficiency and Consumer Surplus

When Lisa allocates her limited budget to maximize utility, he is using her resources efficiently. Any other allocation of her budget would waste some resources.

We know that if Lisa allocates her limited budget to maximize utility, she will be on her demand curve for each good. A demand curve is a description of the planned quantity demanded at each price when utility is maximized. We also know from Chapter 5, that the demand curve shows Lisa's willingness to pay. It tells us her marginal benefit – the benefit from consuming an extra unit of a good. You can now see a deeper meaning in the concept of marginal benefit.

Marginal benefit is the maximum price that a consumer is willing to pay for an extra unit of a good or service when utility is maximized.

The Paradox of Value

More than 200 years ago, Adam Smith posed a paradox that we also raised at the start of this chapter. Water, which is essential to life itself, costs little, but diamonds, which are useless compared with water, are expensive. Why? Adam Smith could not solve the paradox. Not until the theory of marginal utility had been developed could anyone give a satisfactory answer.

You can solve Adam Smith's puzzle by distinguishing between *total* utility and *marginal* utility. The total utility that we get from water is enormous. But remember, the more we consume of something, the smaller is its marginal utility. We use so much water that the marginal utility – the benefit we get from one more glass of water – diminishes to a tiny value. Diamonds, on the other hand, have a small total utility relative to water, but because we buy few diamonds, they have a high marginal utility.

When an individual has maximized total utility, he or she has allocated his or her budget in the way that makes the marginal utility per pound spent equal for all goods. That is, the marginal utility from a good divided by the price of the good is equal for all goods. This equality of marginal utilities per pound spent holds true for diamonds and water. Diamonds have a high price and a high marginal utility. Water has a low price and a low marginal utility. When the high marginal utility of diamonds is divided by the high price of diamonds, the result is a number that equals the low marginal utility of water divided by the low price of water. The marginal utility per pound spent is the same for diamonds as for water.

Another way to think about the paradox of value is through the concept of *consumer surplus*. Figure 7.7 explains the paradox of value using this concept. The supply of water (part a) is perfectly elastic at price P_W, so the quantity of water consumed is Q_W and the consumer surplus from water is the green area. The supply of diamonds (part b) is perfectly inelastic at price Q_D, so the price of diamonds is P_D and consumer surplus is the smaller green area. Water is cheap but brings a large consumer surplus, while diamonds are expensive but bring only a small consumer surplus.

Figure 7.7

The Paradox of Value

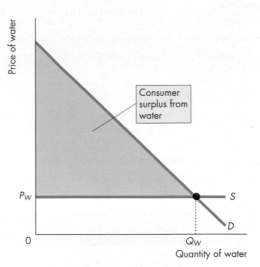

(a) Water

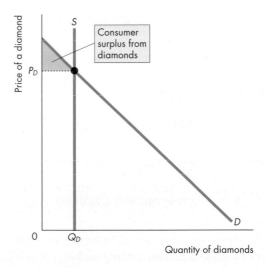

(b) Diamonds

Part (a) shows the demand for water, *D*, and the supply of water, *S*. The supply is (assumed to be) perfectly elastic at the price P_W. At this price, the quantity of water consumed is Q_W and the consumer surplus from water is the large green triangle. Part (b) shows the demand for diamonds, *D*, and the supply of diamonds, *S*. The supply is (assumed to be) perfectly inelastic at the quantity Q_D. At this quantity, the price of a diamond is P_D and the consumer surplus from diamonds is the small green triangle. Water is valuable – has a large consumer surplus – but is cheap. Diamonds are less valuable than water – have a smaller consumer surplus – but are expensive.

Review Quiz

◆ Explain why, along a demand curve, consumer choices are efficient?
◆ Explain the paradox of value and provide an example which is different from diamonds and water.
◆ Does water or diamonds have:
(a) Greater marginal utility, (b) greater total utility, (c) greater consumer surplus?

We've now completed our study of the marginal utility theory of consumption. We've used that theory to examine how one individual – Lisa – allocates her income between the two goods that she consumes – films and cola. We've also seen how the theory can be used to resolve the paradox of value. Furthermore, we've seen how the theory can be used to explain our real-world consumption choices. In the next chapter, we're going to study an alternative theory of individual behaviour. To help you see the connection between the marginal utility theory of this chapter and the more modern theory of consumer behaviour of the next chapter, we'll continue with the same example. We'll meet Lisa again and discover another way of understanding how she gets the most out of her £30 a month.

Summary

Key Points

Individual Demand and Market Demand (p. 135)

• Individual demand is the relationship between the price of a good and the quantity demanded by a single individual.

• Market demand is the sum of all individual demands and the market demand curve is found by summing horizontally all the individual demand curves.

Individual Consumption Choices (pp. 135–137)

• Consumer choices are determined by consumption possibilities and preferences.

• Consumer consumption possibilities are constrained by income and prices. Some combinations of goods are affordable, and some are not affordable.

• Consumer preferences can be described by marginal utility.

• The key assumption of the marginal utility model is that the marginal utility of a good decreases as consumption of it increases.

Maximizing Utility (pp. 138–141)

• Total utility is maximized when all the available income is spent and when the marginal utility per pound spent on each good is equal.

• If the marginal utility per pound spent on good A exceeds that on good B, the consumer can increase total utility by buying more of good A and less of good B.

Predictions of Marginal Utility Theory (pp. 141–144)

• Marginal utility theory predicts how prices and income affect the amounts of each good consumed. First, it predicts the law of demand. That is, other things remaining the same, the higher the price of a good, the lower is the quantity demanded of that good.

• Marginal utility theory predicts that, other things remaining the same, the higher the consumer's income, the greater is the consumption of all normal goods.

Efficiency, Price and Value (pp. 144–146)

• When a consumer maximizes utility, they use resources efficiently.

• Marginal utility theory resolves the paradox of value.

• In common speech, we are thinking about *total* utility or consumer surplus when we speak about value. But price is related to *marginal* utility.

• Water, which we consume in large amounts, has a high total utility and a large consumer surplus, but a low price and low marginal utility.

• Diamonds, which we consume in small amounts, has a low total utility and a low consumer surplus, but a high price and high marginal utility.

Key Figures and Table ◆

Key Terms

Problems

•**1** Jason enjoys rock CDs and spy novels and spends €60 a month on them. The following table shows the utility he gets from each good:

Quantity per month	Utility from rock CDs	Utility from spy novels
1	60	20
2	110	38
3	150	53
4	180	64
5	200	70
6	206	75

a Draw graphs showing Jason's utility from rock CDs and from spy novels.

b Compare the two utility graphs. Can you say anything about Jason's preferences?

c Draw graphs that show Jason's marginal utility from rock CDs and from spy novels.

d What do the two marginal utility graphs tell you about Jason's preferences?

e If rock CDs and spy novels both cost €10 each, how does Jason spend the €60?

2 Mary enjoys classical CDs and travel books and spends €50 a month on them. The following table shows the utility she gets from each good:

Quantity per month	Utility from classical CDs	Utility from travel books
1	30	30
2	40	38
3	48	44
4	54	46
5	58	47

a Draw graphs showing Mary's utility from classical CDs and from travel books.

b Compare the two utility graphs. Can you say anything about Mary's preferences?

c Draw graphs that show Mary's marginal utility from classical CDs and from travel books.

d What do the two marginal utility graphs tell you about Mary's preferences?

e If a classical CD and a travel book cost €10 each, how does Mary spend the €50 a month?

•**3** Max enjoys windsurfing and snorkelling. He obtains the following utility from each of these sports:

Hours per day	Utility from windsurfing	Utility from snorkelling
1	120	40
2	220	76
3	300	106
4	360	128
5	400	140
6	412	150
7	422	158

Max has €35 to spend and he can spend as much time as he likes on his leisure pursuits. Windsurfing equipment rents for €10 an hour, and snorkelling equipment rents for €5 an hour.

a Draw a graph that shows Max's budget line.

b How long does he spend windsurfing and how long does he spend snorkelling?

4 Rob enjoys rock concerts and the opera. The table shows the utility he gets from each activity:

Concerts per month	Utility from rock concerts	Utility from operas
1	100	60
2	180	110
3	240	150
4	280	180
5	300	200
6	310	210

Rob has €100 a month to spend on concerts. A rock concert ticket is €20, and an opera ticket is €10.

a Draw a graph that shows Rob's budget line.

b How many rock concerts and how many operas does he attend?

•5 In problem 3, Max's sister gives him €20 to spend on his leisure pursuits, so he now has €55. Draw a graph that shows Max's budget line. How many hours does Max choose to windsurf and how many hours does he choose to snorkel now that he has €55 to spend?

6 In problem 4, if Rob's uncle gives him €30 to spend on concert tickets, so he now has €130.

a Draw a graph that shows Rob's budget line.

b How many rock concerts and how many operas does he attend now that he has €130 to spend?

•7 In problem 5, if the rent on windsurfing equipment decreases to €5 an hour, how many hours does Max now windsurf and how many hours does he snorkel?

8 In problem 4, if the price of a rock concert decreases to €10, how many rock concerts and operas will Rob attend?

•9 Max takes a Club Med vacation, the cost of which includes unlimited sports activities. There is no extra charge for equipment. If Max windsurfs and snorkels for 6 hours a day, how many hours does he windsurf and how many hours does he snorkel?

10 Rob wins a lottery and has more than enough money to satisfy his desires for rock concerts and opera. He decides that he would like to see 5 concerts each month. How many rock concerts and how many operas does he now attend?

•11 Shirley's and Dan's demand schedules for popcorn are:

Price (cents per carton)	Quantity demanded by	
	Shirley	Dan
	(cartons per week)	
10	12	6
30	9	5
50	6	4
70	3	3
90	1	2

If Shirley and Dan are the only two individuals, what is the market demand for popcorn?

12 Ben's and Jerry's demand schedules for ice cream cones are:

Price (euros per cone)	Quantity demanded by	
	Ben	Jerry
	(cones per week)	
1.00	8	10
1.30	7	8
1.50	6	6
1.70	5	4
1.90	4	2

If Ben and Jerry are the only two individuals, what is the market demand for ice cream cones?

Critical Thinking

1 Read the article in Reading Between the Lines on pp. 150–151 and then:

a Draw Lisa's budget line given that her income for lunchtime drinks is £17.00, and a cappuccino costs £1.70 and soup costs £3.40 a pot.

b Draw Lisa's marginal utility curves for both soup and cappuccino coffee from the table. In what ways are the two marginal utility curves different? Is the demand for soup or cappuccino likely to be more elastic?

c Using a drawing similar to Figure 7.4, show the impact on the demand for coffee and the demand for soup of a fall in price of coffee to £1.13 a cup. Explain how the relationship between utility and price has changed for coffee.

d Using a drawing similar to Figure 7.6, show the impact on the demand for coffee and the demand for soup of a fall in the price of soup, assuming the price of a cappuccino stays at £1.70. Explain how the relationship between utility and price has change for soup.

e If the new breed of soup and juice bars are attracting customers away from coffee bars, what do you think will happen to the price of coffee? Explain your answer.

2 In recent years, bottle water, fruit drinks and sports drinks have become very popular. Use the marginal utility theory you have learned in this chapter to explain the rise in popularity of these 'new age' drinks.

3 Use the links on the Parkin, Powell and Matthews website and read what Henry Schimberg, CEO of Coca-Cola Enterprises, says about the market for bottled water. Use the marginal utility theory you have learned in this chapter to interpret and explain Mr Schimberg's remarks about the bottled-water market.

4 Why do you think the percentage of income spent on food has decreased while the percentage of income spent on cars has increased during the past 50 years? Use the marginal utility theory to explain these trends.

5 Smoking is banned on all airline flights in the European Community and on most international flights. Use marginal utility theory to explain your answers to the following questions:

a What effect does this ban have on the utility of (i) smokers and (ii) non-smokers?

b How do you expect the ban to influence the decisions of (i) smokers and (ii) non-smokers?

In your answer to this question, consider decisions about smoking, flying, and the willingness to pay for a flight.

Utility Theory: Coffee Has-been?

THE TIMES, 2 MARCH 2001

Coffee been and gone?

George Pendle

Is the sweet success of the coffee shop craze beginning to turn a little bitter? Double tall, half-and-half skinny decafs just don't seem to offer the same pizzazz anymore. At least that is the message in a report by Mintel, which found that one in four people feel the drinks served in coffee shops are too expensive . . .

The branded coffee shop was a defining product of the 1990s . . . A recent study by property consultant Healey and Baker found that the British now spend more time in coffee bars than the Italians and the French . . . A report by Allegra says that the number of branded coffee shops in the UK is forecast to grow from 850 to 1700 by 2004.

The supposed public dissatisfaction with coffee bars has not yet affected sales, although there is growing competition in the shape of juice and soup bars. Companies such as Soup and New Covent Garden Soup Company are starting to make their presence felt, although there has yet to be a chain with a comparably strong brand presence.

Lorrie Morgan, director of marketing at Costa Coffee, is not worried by the Mintel report: 'If only 15 per cent of adults used branded coffee shops in the last 12 months there is still so much room to grow.' . . . As for the high prices for a latte, especially with the recent slump in coffee bean prices, this is put down to increasing rent and wage costs. '£1.70 to treat yourself for five or ten minutes isn't all that much. That's not to say it's cheap, nor that we want to keep our prices up forever, but 74 per cent of people disagree that it is expensive.'

The Essence of the Story

- The British craze for the coffee shop may be ending.

- One in four people surveyed thought that drinks in coffee shops were too expensive.

- Consumers can now choose between coffee shops and the new range of juice and soup bars opening in many towns.

- Although the price of coffee beans has fallen, the price of a coffee in a coffee shop is still about £1.70.

- Despite the fact that some coffee drinkers are switching to alternatives, the high price has not cut coffee-shop sales or the potential for growth as yet.

Economic Analysis

- British consumers love the coffee shop but they also like the new soup bars. Lisa is a typical consumer with £17.00 a week to spend on coffee or soup at lunchtimes.

- If there is no soup bar in town and a coffee costs £1.70 per cup, Lisa could buy 10 cappuccino coffees a week. But if a soup bar opens, Lisa faces a new choice.

- The table shows the possible combinations of coffee and soup that Lisa can buy if a cappuccino costs £1.70 and a pot of fresh soup costs £3.40.

- The table also shows Lisa's marginal utility of soup and coffee. The first pot of soup gives her more additional utility that the first two cappuccinos, but soup is more expensive than coffee.

- To maximise her utility, Lisa compares the marginal utility per pound spent on coffee to the marginal utility per pound spent on soup when making a choice of what to drink at lunchtime.

- Figure 1 shows that Lisa maximizes her utility by choosing four cappuccinos and three pots of soup a week, at combination c.

- If Lisa drinks 8 cups of coffee and one pot of soup per week, at point e in Figure 1, she can gain more utility by having fewer cups of coffee and more soup. If Lisa is at combination b, she can gain more utility by increasing coffee consumption and cutting soup consumption.

- Figure 2 shows Lisa's demand curve for cappuccinos, D_0, before the soup bar opens. The price of a cappuccino does not change when the soup bar opens, but Lisa plans to buy fewer cappuccinos. Her demand curve for cappuccinos shifts to the left to D_1.

- The total market for coffee bar drinks can still grow providing the increase in demand from new customers outstrips the decrease in demand from existing customers like Lisa.

Lisa's Weekly Choice of Lunchtime Drinks

	Soup (£3.40 per pot)			Cappuccino Coffee (£1.70 per cup)		
	Quantity (pots)	Marginal utility	Marginal utility per pound	Quantity (cups)	Marginal utility	Marginal utility per pound
a	5	35	14	0	–	–
b	4	50	20	2	56	33
c	3	65	26	4	44	26
d	2	80	32	6	41	24
e	1	100	40	8	35	21
f	0	–	–	10	30	18

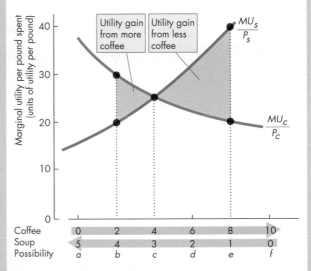

Figure 1 **Maximizing utility**

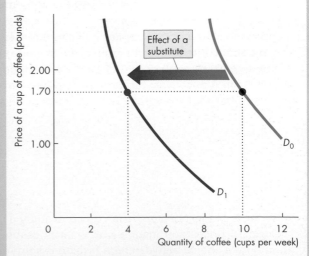

Figure 2 **Lisa's demand for coffee**

CHAPTER 8

Possibilities, Preferences and Choices

After studying this chapter you will be able to:

◆ Calculate and graph a household's budget line

◆ Work out how the budget line changes when prices or income change

◆ Make a map of preferences by using indifference curves

◆ Explain the choices that households make

◆ Predict the effects of price and income changes on consumption choices

◆ Predict the effect of wage changes on work–leisure choices

Subterranean Movements

Like the continents floating on the earth's mantle, our spending patterns change steadily over time. Goods such as home videos and microwave chips now appear on our shopping lists while 78 rpm gramophone records and horse-drawn carriages have disappeared. ◆ But these surface disruptions obscure deeper and slower changes in our spending. We spend a smaller percentage of our income today on food and clothing than we did in 1950. At the same time, the percentage of our income spent on fuel, housing and cars has grown steadily. Why does consumer spending change over the years? What drives a fashion craze for cashmere rather than woollen jumpers? How do people react to changes in income and changes in the prices of the things they buy? ◆ Similar subterranean movements govern the way we spend our time. For example, the average working week has fallen steadily from 70 hours a week in the nineteenth century to 38 hours a week today. Although the average working week is now much shorter than it once was, far more people now have jobs. This change has been especially dramatic for women. Why has the average working week declined? And why do more women work?

◆ ◆ ◆ ◆ In this chapter we are going to study a model of household choice that predicts the effects of changes in prices and incomes on what households buy and how much work they do. You can read about Lisa's choice between high fashion cashmere and cheaper wool mix jumpers in Reading Between the Lines on pp. 168–169.

Consumption Possibilities

Consumption choices are limited by income and by prices. A household has a given amount of income to spend and cannot influence the prices of the goods and services it buys. It takes prices as given. The limits to a household's consumption choices are described by its **budget line**.

Let's look at Lisa's[1] budget line. Lisa is the only person in her household and she has an income of £30 a month to spend. She consumes two goods – cinema films and cola. Cinema tickets cost £6 each; cola costs £3 for a six-pack. If Lisa spends all of her income, she will reach the limit of her consumption of films and cola.

Figure 8.1 shows the affordable ways for Lisa to consume films and cola. Each row shows an affordable way to consume films and cola which just use up Lisa's monthly income of £30. The numbers in the table define Lisa's household consumption possibilities. We can graph these consumption possibilities as points *a* to *f* in Figure 8.1.

Divisible and Indivisible Goods

Some goods – called divisible goods – can be bought in any quantity desired. Examples are petrol and electricity. We can best understand the model of household choice we're about to study if we assume that all goods and services are divisible. For example, Lisa can consume half a film a month *on average* by seeing one film every two months. When we think of goods as being divisible, the consumption possibilities are not just the points *a* to *f* shown in Figure 8.1, but these points plus all the intermediate points that form the line running from *a* to *f*. Such a line is a budget line.

Lisa's budget line is a constraint on her choices. She can afford all the points on the line and inside it. She cannot afford points outside the line. The constraint on her consumption depends on prices and her income, and the constraint changes when prices or her income change. Let's see how by studying an equation that describes her consumption possibilities.

[1] If you have read the preceding chapter on marginal utility theory, you have already met Lisa. This tale of her thirst for cola and zeal for films will sound familiar to you – up to a point. But in this chapter we're going to use a different method for representing preferences – one that does not require us to resort to the idea of utility.

Figure 8.1

The Budget Line

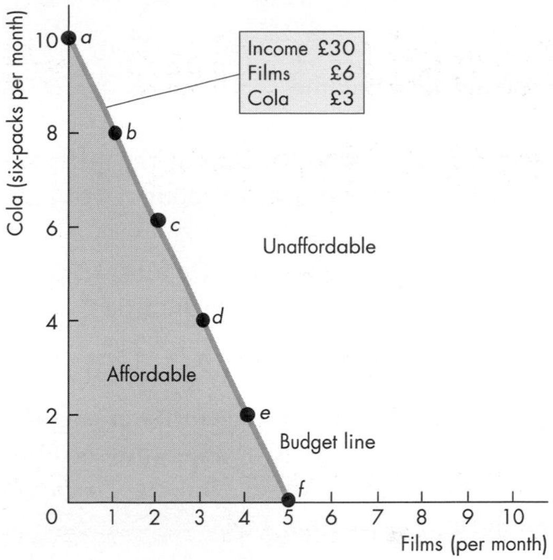

Cola (six-packs per month) vs Films (per month)

Income £30
Films £6
Cola £3

Unaffordable
Affordable
Budget line

Consumption possibility	Films (per month)	Cola (six-packs per month)
a	0	10
b	1	8
c	2	6
d	3	4
e	4	2
f	5	0

Lisa's budget line shows the boundary between what she can and cannot afford. Each row of the table lists Lisa's affordable combinations of cinema tickets and cola when her income is £30, the price of cola is £3 a six-pack, and the price of a ticket is £6. For example, row *a* tells us that Lisa exhausts her £30 income when she buys 10 six-packs and sees no films. The figure graphs Lisa's budget line. Points *a* to *f* on the graph represent the rows of the table. For divisible goods, the budget line is the continuous line *af*. To calculate the equation for Lisa's budget line, start from the fact that expenditure equals income. That is:

$$(£3 \times Q_c + £6 \times Q_f) = £30$$

Divide by £3 to obtain:

$$Q_c + 2Q_f = 10$$

Subtract $2Q_f$ from both sides to obtain:

$$Q_c = 10 - 2Q_f$$

The Budget Equation

We can describe the budget line by using a *budget equation*. The budget equation starts with the fact that:

Expenditure = Income

Expenditure is equal to the sum of the price of each good multiplied by the quantity bought. For Lisa:

Expenditure = Price of cola × Quantity of cola
+ Price of a cinema ticket
× Quantity of films

Call the price of cola P_c, the quantity of cola Q_c, the price of a cinema ticket P_f, the quantity of films Q_f, and income Y. Using these symbols, Lisa's budget equation is:

$$P_cQ_c + P_fQ_f = Y$$

Using the prices Lisa faces, £3 for a six-pack and £6 for a cinema ticket, and Lisa's income, £30, we get:

$$£3Q_c + £6Q_f = £30$$

Lisa can choose any quantities of cola (Q_c) and films (Q_f) that satisfy this equation. To find the relationship between these quantities, we rearrange the equation so that it describes Lisa's budget line. To do so, divide both sides of the equation by the price of cola (P_c) to get:

$$Q_c + \frac{P_f \times Q_f}{P_c} = \frac{Y}{P_c}$$

Now subtract the term $P_f/P_c \times Q_f$ from both sides of this equation to give:

$$Q_c = \frac{Y}{P_c} - \frac{P_f}{P_c} \times Q_f$$

For Lisa, income (Y) is £30, the price of a cinema ticket (P_f) is £6 and the price of a six-pack (P_c) is £3. So Lisa must choose the quantities of films and cola to satisfy the equation:

$$Q_c = \frac{£30}{£3} - \frac{£6}{£3} \times Q_f$$

or

$$Q_c = 10 - 2 \times Q_f$$

To interpret the equation, go back to the budget line of Figure 8.1 and check that the equation you've just derived gives you the results of that budget line. First set Q_f, equal to zero. In this case, the budget equation tells us that Q_c, the quantity of cola, is Y/P_c, which is £30/£3, or 10 six-packs. This combination of Q_f and Q_c is the same as that shown in row *a* of the table in Figure 8.1. Next, set Q_f equal to 5. Q_c is now equal to 0 (row *f* of the table in Figure 8.1). Check that you can derive the other rows.

The budget equation contains two variables chosen by the household (Q_f and Q_c) and two variables (Y/P_c and P_f/P_c) that the household takes as given. Let's look more closely at these variables.

Real Income

A household's **real income** is the maximum quantity of a good that the household can afford to buy. In the budget equation, real income is Y/P_c. This quantity is the maximum number of six-packs that Lisa can buy and is Lisa's real income in terms of cola. It is equal to her money income divided by the price of cola. Lisa's income is £30 and the price of cola is £3 a six-pack, so her real income in terms of cola is 10 six-packs. In Figure 8.1, real income is the point at which the budget line intersects the *y*-axis.

Relative Price

A **relative price** is the price of one good divided by the price of another good. In Lisa's budget equation, the variable (P_f/P_c) is the relative price of a film in terms of cola. For Lisa, P_f is £6 a film and P_c is £3 a six-pack, so P_f/P_c is equal to 2 six-packs per film. That is, to see one more film, Lisa must give up 2 six-packs.

You've just calculated Lisa's opportunity cost of a film. Recall that the opportunity cost of an action is the best alternative forgone. For Lisa to see 1 more film a month, she must forgo 2 six-packs. You've also calculated Lisa's opportunity cost of cola. For Lisa to consume 2 more six-packs a month, she must give up seeing 1 film. So her opportunity cost of 2 six-packs is 1 film.

The relative price of a film in terms of cola is the magnitude of the slope of Lisa's budget line. To calculate the slope of the budget line, recall the formula for slope (introduced in Chapter 2): slope equals the change in the variable measured on the *y*-axis divided by the change in the variable measured on the *x*-axis as we move along the line. In Lisa's case (Figure 8.1), the variable measured on the *y*-axis is the quantity of cola and the variable measured on the *x*-axis is the quantity of films. Along Lisa's budget line, as cola decreases from 10 to 0 six-packs, films increase from 0 to 5. Therefore the slope of the budget line is 10 six-packs divided by 5 films, or 2 six-packs per film. The magnitude of this slope is exactly the same as the relative price we've just calculated. It is also the opportunity cost of a film.

A Change in Prices

When prices change, so does the budget line. The lower the price of the good measured on the horizontal axis, other things remaining the same, the flatter is the budget line. For example, if the price of a cinema ticket falls to £3, real income in terms of cola does not change but the relative price of seeing a film falls. The budget line rotates outward and becomes flatter as shown in Figure 8.2(a). The higher the price of the good measured on the horizontal axis, other things remaining the same, the steeper is the budget line. For example, if the price of a cinema ticket rises to £12, the relative price of seeing a film increases. The budget line rotates inward and becomes steeper as shown in Figure 8.2(a).

A Change in Income

A change in *money* income changes real income but does not change relative prices. The budget line shifts, but its slope does not change. The bigger a consumer's money income, the bigger is real income and the farther to the right is the budget line. The smaller a consumer's money income, the smaller is real income and the farther to the left is the budget line. The effect of a change in income on Lisa's budget line is shown in Figure 8.2(b). The initial budget line is the same one that we began with in Figure 8.1 when Lisa's income is £30. A new budget line shows how much Lisa can consume if her income falls to £15 a month. The new budget line is parallel to the old one but closer to the origin. The two budget lines are parallel – have the same slope – because the relative price is the same in both cases. The new budget line is closer to the origin than the initial one because Lisa's real income has decreased.

Figure 8.2

Changes in Prices and Income

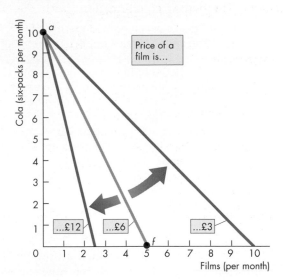

(a) A change in price

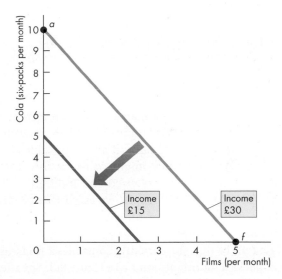

(b) A change in income

In part (a), the price of a cinema ticket changes. A fall in the price from £6 to £3 rotates the budget line outward and makes it flatter. A rise in the price from £6 to £12 rotates the budget line inward and makes it steeper. In part (b), income falls from £30 to £15 while prices remain constant. The budget line shifts leftward but its slope does not change.

Review Quiz

◆ What does Lisa's budget line show?
◆ What is (a) Lisa's real income in terms of cinema films and (b) Lisa's opportunity cost of cola?
◆ If a European household has an income of €40 and consumes only bus rides at €4 each and magazines at €2 each, what is the equation that describes its budget line?
◆ If the price of one good changes, what happens to the relative price and to the slope of the budget line?
◆ If a household's money income changes, but prices don't change, what happens to the household's real income and its budget line?

We've studied the limits to which a household's consumption can go. Let's now see how we can describe the household's preferences.

Preferences and Indifference Curves

Preferences are your likes and dislikes. As you'll see, you can actually make a map a person's preferences. A preference map is based on the intuitively appealing assumption that people can sort all the possible combinations of goods they might consume into three groups: preferred, not preferred and indifferent. To make this idea more concrete, we asked Lisa to rank various combinations of films and cola. Figure 8.3 illustrates her choice.

Lisa tells us that she currently consumes 2 films and 6 six-packs a month at point *c* in Figure 8.3. She then lists all the combinations of films and cola that she thinks is just as good as her current consumption. When we plot the combinations of films and cola that Lisa tells us she likes just as much as the combination at point *c*, we get the green curve shown in Figure 8.3. This curve is the key element in a map of preferences and is called an indifference curve.

An **indifference curve** is a line that shows combinations of goods among which a consumer is indifferent. The indifference curve in Figure 8.3(a) tells us that Lisa is just as happy to consume 2 films and 6 six-packs a month at point *c* as to consume the combination of films and cola at point *g* or at any other point along the curve.

Figure 8.3
A Preference Map

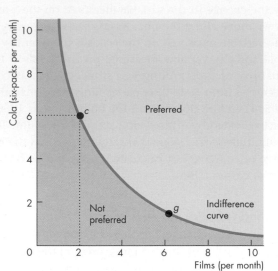

(a) An indifference curve

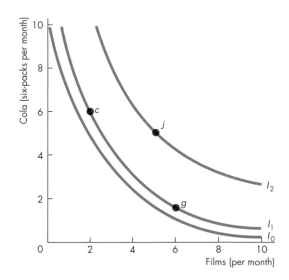

(b) Lisa's preference map

In part (a), Lisa consumes 6 six-packs of cola and 2 films a month at point *c*. She is indifferent between all the points on the green indifference curve such as *c* and *g*. She prefers any point above the indifference curve (yellow area) to any point on it, and she prefers any point on the indifference curve to any point below it (grey area). A preference map is a number of indifference curves. Part (b) shows three – I_0, I_1, and I_2 – that are part of Lisa's preference map. She prefers point *j* to point *c* or *g*, so she prefers any point on I_2 to any point on I_1.

Lisa also says she prefers any combination in the yellow area above the indifference curve to any combination along the indifference curve. And she prefers any combination on the indifference curve to any combination in the grey area below the indifference curve.

The indifference curve shown in Figure 8.3(a) is just one of a whole family of such curves. This indifference curve appears again in Figure 8.3(b). It is labelled I_1 and passes through points c and g. Two other indifference curves are I_0 and I_2. Lisa prefers any point on indifference curve I_2 to any point on indifference curve I_1, and she prefers any point on I_1 to any point on I_0. We refer to I_2 as being a higher indifference curve than I_1 and I_1 as being higher than I_0.

A preference map is a series of indifference curves that look like contour lines on a map. Like looking at a map, we can draw some conclusions about people's preferences by looking at the shape of the contours. In the next two sections, you'll learn how to 'read' a preference map.

Marginal Rate of Substitution

The **marginal rate of substitution** (or *MRS*) is the rate at which a person will give up good y (the good measured on the y-axis) in order to get more of good x (the good measured on the x-axis) and at the same time remain indifferent. The marginal rate of substitution is measured from the slope of an indifference curve.

◆ If the indifference curve is steep, the marginal rate of substitution is high. The person is willing to give up a large quantity of good y in exchange for a small quantity of good x while remaining indifferent.

◆ If the indifference curve is flat, the marginal rate of substitution is low. The person is willing to give up only a small amount of good y in exchange for a large amount of good x to remain indifferent.

Figure 8.4 shows you how to calculate the marginal rate of substitution. The curve labelled I_1 is one of Lisa's indifference curves. Suppose that Lisa drinks 6 six-packs and watches 2 films at point c in the figure. Her marginal rate of substitution is calculated by measuring the absolute magnitude of the slope of the indifference curve at point c. To measure this magnitude, place a straight line against, or tangent to, the indifference curve at point c. The slope of that

Figure 8.4

The Marginal Rate of Substitution

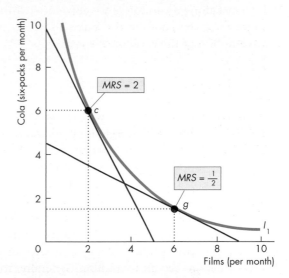

The magnitude of the slope of an indifference curve is called the marginal rate of substitution, *MRS*. The marginal rate of substitution tells us how much of one good a person is willing to give up to gain more of another good, while remaining indifferent. The marginal rate of substitution at point c is 2; at point g it is $^1/_2$.

line is the change in the quantity of cola divided by the change in the quantity of films as we move along the line. As cola consumption decreases by 10 six-packs, film consumption increases by 5. So at point c Lisa is willing to give up cola for films at the rate of 2 six-packs per film. Her marginal rate of substitution is 2.

Now, suppose that Lisa consumes 6 films and 1.5 six-packs at point g in Figure 8.4. Her marginal rate of substitution at this point is found by calculating the absolute magnitude of the slope of the indifference curve at point g. That slope is the same as the slope of the tangent to the indifference curve at point g. Here, as cola consumption decreases by 4.5 six-packs, film consumption increases by 8. So at point g Lisa is willing to give up cola for films at the rate of 0.5 a six-pack per film. Her marginal rate of substitution is 0.5.

As Lisa's consumption of films increases and her consumption of cola decreases, her marginal rate of substitution diminishes. Diminishing marginal rate of substitution is the key assumption of consumer theory. The assumption of **diminishing marginal rate of substitution** is a general tendency for the marginal rate of substitution to diminish as the consumer moves along an indifference curve, increasing consumption of the good on the *x*-axis and decreasing consumption of the good on the *y*-axis.

Your Own Diminishing Marginal Rate of Substitution

You might be able to appreciate why we assume the principle of a diminishing marginal rate of substitution by thinking about your own preferences for films and cola. Suppose in one month you consumed 10 six-packs of cola but you didn't see any films. You would probably be happy to give up lots of cans of cola just to see one film. On the other hand, suppose you saw 6 films this month and consumed only 1 six-pack of cola. You would probably only give up a few cans of cola to see an extra film. Generally, the greater the number of films you see, the smaller is the quantity of cola you will give up to see an extra film.

The shape of the indifference curves incorporates the principle of the diminishing marginal rate of substitution because the curves are bowed towards the origin. The tightness of the bend of an indifference curve tells us how willing a person is to substitute one good for another while remaining indifferent. The examples that follow will make this clear.

Degree of Substitutability

Most of us would not regard films and cola as being close substitutes for each other. We probably have some fairly clear ideas about how many films we want to see each month and how many cans of cola we want to drink. Nevertheless, to some degree, we are willing to substitute between these two goods. No matter how enthusiastic you are for cola, there is surely some increase in the number of films you can see that will compensate you for being deprived of a can of cola. Similarly, no matter how addicted you are to films, surely some number of cans of cola will compensate you for being deprived of seeing one film. A person's indifference curves for films and cola might look something like those shown in Figure 8.5(a).

Close Substitutes

Some goods substitute so easily for each other that most of us do not even notice which we are consuming. A good example concerns different brands of personal computers. Dell, Compaq and Elonex are all clones of the IBM PC – but most of us can't tell the difference between the clones and the IBM. The same holds true for marker pens. Most of us don't care whether we use a marker pen from the university bookshop or the local supermarket. When two goods are perfect substitutes for each other, their indifference curves are straight lines that slope downward, as Figure 8.5(b) illustrates. The marginal rate of substitution between perfect substitutes is constant.

Complements

Some goods cannot substitute for each other at all. Instead they are complements. The complements in Figure 8.5(c) are left and right running shoes. Indifference curves of perfect complements are L-shaped. For most of us, one left running shoe and one right running shoe are as good as one left shoe and two right ones. Two of each is preferred to one of each, but two of one and one of the other is no better than one of each.

The extreme cases of perfect substitutes and perfect complements shown here don't often happen in reality. They do, however, illustrate that the shape of the indifference curve shows the degree of substitutability between two goods. The more any pair of goods become close substitutes, the less bowed the indifference curves and the more the indifference curves look like straight lines. A high degree of substitutability means that the marginal rate of substitution falls less quickly. The more any pair of goods become poor substitutes for each other, or become complementary, the more the indifference curves become bowed and tightly curved. At the extreme, the indifference curves become 'L' shaped like those shown in Figure 8.5(c). A low degree of sustitutability, or a high degree of complementarity, means that the marginal rate of substitution falls more quickly.

Review Quiz

♦ What is an indifference curve and how does an indifference map show preferences?
♦ Why does an indifference curve slope downward, and why is it bowed toward the origin?
♦ What do we call the magnitude of the slope of an indifference curve?
♦ What is the key assumption about a consumer's marginal rate of substitution?

Figure 8.5

The Degree of Substitutability

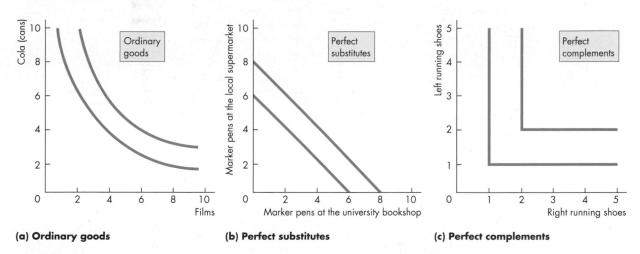

(a) Ordinary goods   **(b) Perfect substitutes**   **(c) Perfect complements**

The shape of the indifference curves reveals the degree of substitutability between two goods. Part (a) shows the indifference curves for two ordinary goods: films and cola. To consume less cola and remain indifferent, one must see more films. The number of films that compensates for a reduction in cola increases as less cola is consumed. Part (b) shows the indifference curves for two perfect substitutes. For the consumer to remain indifferent, one fewer marker pen from the local supermarket must be replaced by one extra marker pen from the university bookshop. Part (c) shows two perfect complements – goods that cannot be substituted for each other at all. Two left running shoes with one right running shoe is no better than one of each. But two of each is preferred to one of each.

The two components of the model of household choice are now in place: the budget line and the preference map. We will use these components to work out the consumer's choice.

Predicting Consumer Behaviour

We are now going to develop a model to predict the quantities of films and cola that Lisa *chooses* to buy? Figure 8.6 shows Lisa's budget line from Figure 8.1 and her indifference curves from Figure 8.3(b). We assume that Lisa consumes at her best affordable point, which is 2 films and 6 six-packs of cola – point *c*. Here Lisa:

◆ Is on her budget line.

◆ Is on the highest attainable indifference curve.

◆ Has a marginal rate of substitution between films and cola equal to the relative price of films and cola.

For every point inside the budget line, such as point *i*, there are points on the budget line that Lisa

prefers. For example, she prefers all the points on the budget line between *f* and *h* to point *i*. So she chooses a point on the budget line.

Every point on the budget line lies on an indifference curve. For example, point *h* lies on the indifference curve I_0. At point *h*, Lisa's marginal rate of substitution is less than the relative price. Lisa is willing to give up more films in exchange for cola than the budget line says she must give up. So Lisa moves along her budget line towards point *c*. As Lisa moves, she passes through a number of indifference curves (not shown in the figure) located between I_0 and I_1. All of these indifference curves are higher than I_0 and therefore Lisa prefers any point on them to point *h*. But when Lisa gets to point *c*, she is on the highest attainable indifference curve. If she keeps moving along the budget line, she starts to encounter indifference curves that are lower than I_1. So Lisa chooses point *c*.

At the best attainable point, the marginal rate of substitution (the magnitude of the slope of the indifference curve) equals the the relative price (the magnitude of the slope of the budget line).

Figure 8.6

The Best Affordable Point

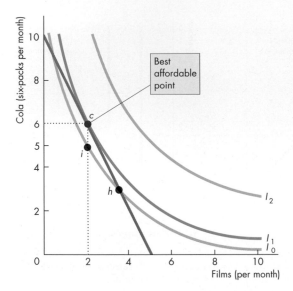

Lisa's best affordable point is *c*. At that point, she is on her budget line and also on the highest attainable indifference curve. At a point such as *h*, Lisa is willing to give up more films in exchange for cola than she has to. She can move to point *i*, which is just as good as point *h* and have some unspent income. She can spend that income and move to *c*, a point that she prefers to point *i*.

You can now use this model of household choice to predict the effects on consumption of changes in prices and income. We'll begin by studying the effects of a price change.

A Change in Price

The effect of a change in price on the quantity of a good consumed is called the **price effect**. We will use Figure 8.7(a) to work out the price effect of a fall in the price of a cinema ticket. We start with tickets costing £6 each, cola costing £3 a six-pack, and with Lisa's income at £30 a month. In this situation, she consumes at point *c*, where her budget line is tangent to her highest attainable indifference curve, I_1. She consumes 6 six-packs and 2 films a month.

Now suppose that the price of a cinema ticket falls to £3. With a lower price of a ticket, the budget line rotates outward and becomes flatter. (Check back with Figure 8.2(a) for a reminder on how a price change affects the budget line.) The new budget line is the darker orange line in Figure 8.7(a). Lisa's best

Figure 8.7

Price Effect and Demand Curve

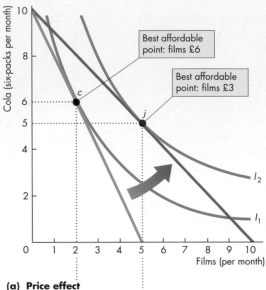

(a) Price effect

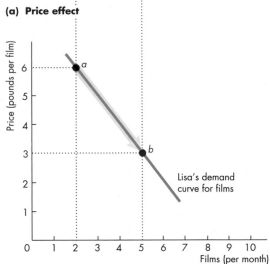

(b) Demand curve

Initially, Lisa consumes at point *c* (part a). If the price of a cinema ticket falls from £6 to £3, she consumes at point *j*. The increase in films from 2 to 5 per month and the decrease in cola from 6 to 5 six-packs is the price effect. When the price of a cinema ticket falls, Lisa sees more films. She also consumes less cola. Part (b) shows Lisa's demand curve for films. When the price of a ticket is £6, she sees 2 a month, at point *a*. When the price of a ticket falls to £3, she sees 5 a month, at point *b*. Lisa's demand curve traces out her best affordable quantity of films as the price of a cinema ticket varies.

affordable point is *j*, where she consumes 5 films and 5 six-packs of cola. She cuts her cola consumption from 6 to 5 six-packs, and increases the number of films she sees from 2 to 5 a month. Lisa substitutes films for cola when the price of a cinema ticket falls, and the price of cola and her income remain constant.

The Demand Curve

In Chapter 3, we asserted that the demand curve slopes downward and that it shifts when the consumer's income changes, or when the price of another good changes. We can now derive a demand curve from a consumer's budget line and indifference curves. By doing so, we can see that the law of demand and the downward-sloping demand curve are consequences of the consumer choosing his or her best affordable combination of goods.

To derive Lisa's demand curve for films, we lower the price of a cinema ticket and finding her best affordable point at different prices, holding all other things constant. We just did this for two ticket prices in Figure 8.7(a). Figure 8.7(b) highlights these two prices and two points that lie on Lisa's demand curve for films. When the price of a cinema ticket is £6, Lisa sees 2 films a month at point *a*. When the price falls to £3, she increases the number of films she sees to 5 a month at point *b*. The demand curve is made up of these two points plus all the other points that tell us Lisa's best affordable consumption of films at each ticket price – more than £6, between £6 and £3, and less than £3 – given the price of cola and Lisa's income. As you can see, Lisa's demand curve for films slopes downward – the lower the price of a cinema ticket, the more films she watches each month. This is the law of demand.

Next, let's examine how Lisa adjusts her consumption when her income changes.

A Change in Income

The effect of a change in income on consumption is called the **income effect**. Let's work out the income effect by examining how consumption changes when income changes and prices remain constant. Figure 8.8(a) shows the income effect when Lisa's income falls. With an income of £30 and with a cinema ticket costing £3 and cola £3 a six-pack, she consumes at point *j* – 5 films and 5 six-packs. If her income falls to £21, she consumes at point *k* – 4 films and 3 six-packs. Thus when Lisa's income falls, she consumes less of both goods.[2]

Figure 8.8

Income Effect and Change in Demand

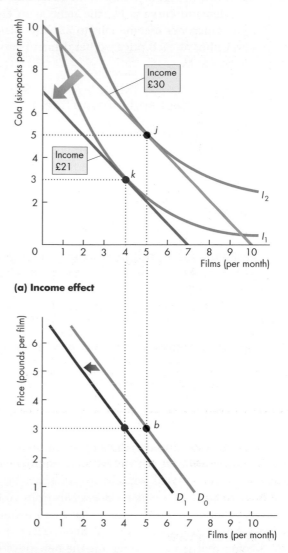

(a) Income effect

(b) Demand curve

A change in income shifts the budget line and changes consumption. In part (a), when Lisa's income decreases, she consumes fewer films and cans of cola. In part (b), when Lisa's income decreases, her demand curve for films shifts leftward. Lisa's demand for films decreases because she will now see fewer films at each price.

---

[2] For Lisa, films and cola are *normal* goods. When her income falls, she consumes less of both goods and when her income rises, she consumes more of both goods. Some goods are *inferior* goods. When income rises, the consumption of an *inferior* good decreases. Try to draw some indifference curves that illustrate an inferior good.

The Demand Curve and the Income Effect

A change in income leads to a shift in the demand curve, as shown in Figure 8.8(b). With an income of £30, Lisa's demand curve is D_0, the same as in Figure 8.8. But when her income falls to £21, she plans to see fewer films at each price, so her demand curve shifts leftward to D_1.

Substitution Effect and Income Effect

Films and cola are *normal goods*. For normal goods, a fall in price always increases the quantity bought. We can prove this assertion by dividing the price effect into two parts:

1   The substitution effect.
2   The income effect.

Figure 8.9(a) shows the price effect and Figure 8.9(b) separates the price effect into the substitution effect and the income effect.

Substitution Effect

The **substitution effect** is the effect of a change in price on the quantities consumed when the consumer (hypothetically) remains indifferent between the original and the new combinations of goods consumed. To work out Lisa's substitution effect, we have to imagine that when the price of a cinema ticket falls, Lisa's income also decreases by an amount that is just enough to leave her on the same indifference curve.

When the price of a cinema ticket falls from £6 to £3, let's suppose (hypothetically) that Lisa's income decreases to £21. What's special about £21? It is the income that is just enough, at the new price of a ticket, to keep Lisa's best affordable point on the same indifference curve as her original consumption point c. Lisa's budget line in this situation is the light orange line shown in Figure 8.9(b). With the new price of a cinema ticket and the new lower income, Lisa's best affordable point is k on indifference curve I_1. The move from c to k isolates the substitution effect of the price change. The substitution effect of the fall in the price of a cinema ticket is an increase in the consumption of films from 2 to 4 and a decrease in the consumption of cola. The direction of the substitution effect never varies; when the relative price of a good falls, the

Figure 8.9

Substitution Effect and Income Effect

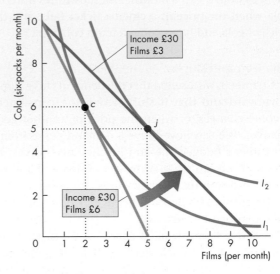

(a) Price effect

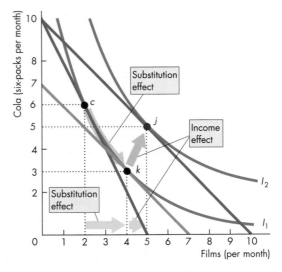

(b) Substitution effect and income effect

The price effect in part (a) can be separated into a substitution effect and an income effect in part (b). To isolate the substitution effect, we confront Lisa with the new price but keep her on her original indifference curve, I_1. The substitution effect is the move from c to k. To isolate the income effect, we confront Lisa with the new price of films but increase her income so that she can move from the original indifference curve, I_1, to the new one, I_2. The income effect is the move from k to j.

consumer substitutes more of that good for the other good.

Income Effect

To calculate the substitution effect, we gave Lisa a £9 pay cut. Now let's give Lisa her £9 back. The £9 increase in income shifts Lisa's budget line outward, as shown in Figure 8.9(b). The slope of the budget line does not change because both prices remain constant. This change in Lisa's budget line is similar to the one illustrated in Figure 8.8, where we study the effect of income on consumption. As Lisa's budget line shifts outward, her consumption possibilities expand and her best affordable point becomes j on indifference curve I_2. The move from k to j isolates the income effect of the price change. In this example, as Lisa's income increases, she increases her consumption of both films and cola. For Lisa, films and cola are normal goods. The income effect always reinforces the substitution effect for normal goods.

Inferior Goods

The example that we have just studied is that of a change in the price of a normal good. The effect of a change in the price of an inferior good is different. Recall that an inferior good is one whose consumption decreases as income increases. For an inferior good, the income effect is negative. Thus for an inferior good a lower price does not always lead to an increase in the quantity demanded. The lower price has a substitution effect that increases the quantity demanded. But the lower price also has a negative income effect, which reduces the demand for the inferior good. Thus the negative income effect offsets the substitution effect to some degree. If the negative income effect exceeded the positive substitution effect, the demand curve would slope upward. The substitution effect usually dominates – confirming the law of demand.

Back to the Facts

We started this chapter by observing how consumer spending has changed over the years. The indifference curve model explains these changes. Spending patterns are determined by best affordable choices and these choices change over time as incomes and prices change.

Work–Leisure Choices

Households make many choices other than those about how to spend their income on the various goods and services available. We can use the model of consumer choice to explain a wide range of other household choices such as how much labour to supply and how much time to spend on leisure rather than work. Some of these are discussed in Economics in History on pp. 170–171. Here we'll study household choices about work and leisure.

Labour Supply

Every week, we allocate our 168 hours between working – called *labour* – and all other activities – called *leisure*. How do we decide how to allocate our time between labour and leisure? We can answer this question by using the theory of household choice.

The more hours we spend on leisure, the smaller is our income. The relationship between leisure and income is described by an *income–time budget line*. The orange lines in Figure 8.10(a) show Lisa's income–time budget lines. If Lisa devotes the entire week to leisure – 168 hours – she has no income and is at point z. By supplying labour in exchange for a wage, she can convert hours into income along the time–budget line. The slope of that line is determined by the hourly wage rate. If the wage rate is £2 an hour,

Figure 8.10

The Supply of Labour

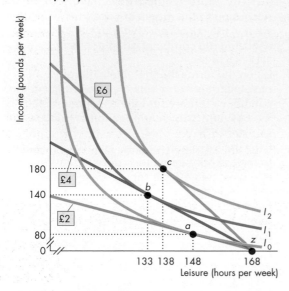

(a) Time allocation decision

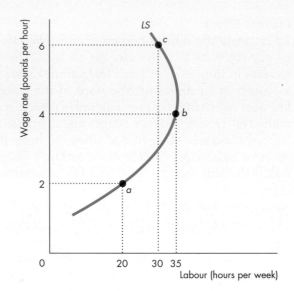

(b) Labour supply curve

In part (a), at a wage rate of £2 an hour, Lisa takes 148 hours of leisure (works 20 hours) a week at point *a*. If the wage rate increases from £2 to £4, she decreases her leisure to 133 hours (increases her work to 35 hours) a week at point *b*. But if the wage rate increases from £4 to

£6, Lisa *increases* her leisure to 138 hours (*decreases* her work to 30 hours) a week at point *c*.

Part (b) shows Lisa's labour supply curve. Points *a*, *b* and *c* on the supply curve correspond to Lisa's choices on her income–time budget line in part (a).

Lisa faces the lowest budget line. If she worked for 68 hours a week, she would make an income of £136 a week. If the wage rate is £4 an hour, she faces the middle budget line. If the wage rate is £6 an hour, she faces the highest budget line. Lisa buys time by not supplying labour and by forgoing income. The opportunity cost of an hour of leisure is the hourly wage rate forgone.

Figure 8.10(a) also shows Lisa's indifference curves for income and leisure. Lisa chooses her best attainable point. This choice of income and time allocation is just like her choice of films and cola. She gets onto the highest possible indifference curve by making her marginal rate of substitution between income and leisure equal to her wage rate. The choice depends on the wage rate Lisa can earn. At a wage rate of £2 an hour, Lisa chooses point *a* and works 20 hours a week (168–148) for an income of £40 a week. At a wage rate of £4 an hour, she chooses point *b* and works 35 hours a week (168–133) for an income of £140 a week. At a wage rate of £6 an hour, she chooses point *c* and works 30 hours a week (168–138) for an income of £180 a week.

The Labour Supply Curve

Figure 8.10(b) shows Lisa's labour supply curve. This curve shows that as the wage rate increases from £2 an hour to £4 an hour, Lisa increases the quantity of labour supplied from 20 hours a week to 35 hours a week. But when the wage rate increases to £6 an hour, she decreases her quantity of labour supplied to 30 hours a week.

Lisa's supply of labour is similar to that described for the economy as a whole at the beginning of this chapter. As wage rates have increased, work hours have decreased. At first, this pattern seems puzzling. We've seen that the hourly wage rate is the opportunity cost of leisure. So a higher wage rate means a higher opportunity cost of leisure. This fact on its own leads to a decrease in leisure and an increase in work hours. But instead, we've cut our work hours. Why? Because our incomes have increased. As the real wage rate increases, real incomes increase, so people demand more of all normal goods. Leisure is a normal good, so as incomes increase, people demand more leisure.

The higher wage rate has both a *substitution effect* and an *income effect*. The higher wage rate increases the opportunity cost of leisure and so leads to a substitution effect away from leisure. The higher wage rate increases income and so leads to an income effect towards more leisure.

This theory of household choice can explain the facts about work patterns described at the beginning of this chapter. First, it can explain why the average working week has fallen steadily from 70 hours a week in the nineteenth century to 35 hours a week today. The reason is that as wage rates have increased, although people have substituted work for leisure, they have also decided to use their higher incomes in part to consume more leisure. Second, the theory can explain why more women now have jobs in the labour market. The reason is that increases in their wage rates and improvements in their job opportunities have led to a substitution effect away from working at home and towards working in the labour market.

In the chapters that follow, you are going to study the choices made by firms. You'll see how, in the pursuit of profit, firms make choices about the supply of goods and services and the demand for resources (factors of production).

Summary

Key Points

Consumption Possibilities (pp. 153–156)

- The budget line shows the limits to a household's consumption given its income and the prices of goods. The budget line is the boundary between what the household can and cannot afford.

- The point at which the budget line intersects the y-axis is the household's real income in terms of the good measured on that axis.

- The magnitude of the slope of the budget line is the relative price of the good measured on the x-axis in terms of the good measured on the y-axis.

- A change in price changes the slope of the budget line. The lower the price of the good measured on the x-axis, the flatter is the budget line. A change in income shifts the budget line (rightward for an increase and leftward for a decrease) but does not change its slope.

Preferences and Indifference Curves (pp. 156–159)

- A consumer's preferences can be represented by indifference curves. An indifference curve joins all the combinations of goods between which the consumer is indifferent.

- A consumer prefers any point above an indifference curve to any point on it and any point on an indifference curve to any point below it. Indifference curves bow towards the origin.

- The magnitude of the slope of an indifference curve is called the marginal rate of substitution.

- The marginal rate of substitution diminishes as consumption of the good measured on the y-axis decreases and consumption of the good measured on the x-axis increases.

Predicting Consumer Behaviour (pp. 159–163)

- A household consumes at its best affordable point. This point is on the budget line and on the highest attainable indifference curve and has a marginal rate of substitution equal to the relative price.

- The price effect can be divided into a substitution effect and an income effect.

- The substitution effect is the effect of a change in price on consumption when the consumer (hypothetically) remains indifferent between the original situation and the new situation.

- The substitution always results in an increase in consumption of the good whose relative price has decreased.

- The income effect is the effect of change in income on consumption.

- For a normal good, the income effect reinforces the substitution effect. For an inferior good, the income effect offsets the substitution effect.

Work–Leisure Choices (pp. 163–165)

- The indifference curve model of household choice enables us to understand how a household allocates its time between leisure and work.

- Work hours have increased and leisure hours have increased because the income effect on the demand for leisure has been greater than the substitution effect.

Key Figures ◆

Key Terms

Problems

●**1** Sara has an income of €12 a week. Popcorn costs €3 a bag, and cola costs €3 a can.

a What is Sara's real income in terms of cola?

b What is her real income in terms of popcorn?

c What is the relative price of cola in terms of popcorn?

d What is the opportunity cost of a can of cola?

e Calculate the equation for Sara's budget line (placing bags of popcorn on the left side).

f Draw a graph of Sara's budget line with cola on the x-axis.

g In part (f), what is the slope of Sara's budget line? What does it represent?

2 Marc has an income of €20 per week. CDs cost €10 each and beer costs €5 a can.

a What is Marc's real income in terms of beer?

b What is his real income in terms of CDs?

c What is the relative price of beer in terms of CDs?

d What is the opportunity cost of a can of beer?

e Calculate the equation for Marc's budget line (placing cans of beer on the left side).

f Draw a graph of Marc's budget line with CDs on the x-axis.

g In part (f), what is the slope of Marc's budget line? What does it represent?

●**3** Sara's income and the prices she faces are the same as in problem 1. The figure illustrates Sara's preferences.

a What are the quantities of popcorn and cola that Sara buys?

b What is Sara's marginal rate of substitution of popcorn for cola at the point at which she consumes?

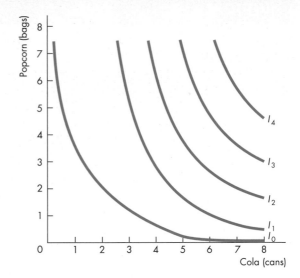

4 Marc's income and the prices he faces are the same as in problem 2. The figure illustrates his preferences.

a What are the quantities of beer and CDs that Marc buys?

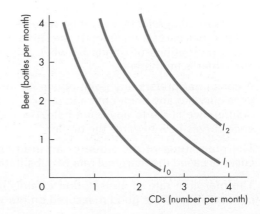

b What is Marc's marginal rate of substitution of CDs for beer at the point at which he consumes?

•**5** Now suppose that in the situation described in problem 3, the price of cola falls to €1.50 per can and the price of popcorn and Sara's income remain constant.

   a Find the new quantities of cola and popcorn that Sara buys.

   b Find two points on Sara's demand curve for cola.

   c Find the substitution effect of the price change.

   d Find the income effect of the price change.

   e Is cola a normal good or an inferior good for Sara?

f Is popcorn a normal good or an inferior good for Sara?

6 Now suppose that in problem 4, the price of a CD falls to €5 and the price of beer and income remain constant.

   a Find the new quantities of beer and CDs that Marc buys.

   b Find two points on Marc's demand curve for CDs.

   c Find the substitution effect of the price change.

   d Find the income effect of the price change.

   e Are CDs a normal good or an inferior good for Marc?

   f Is beer a normal good or an inferior good for Marc?

Critical Thinking

1 Turn back to pp. 170–171 and read the material in Economics in History. Then answer the following questions:

   a What is the role of technology in explaining women's increased participation in the workforce over the past 100 years?

   b Use a diagram similar to Figure 8.11 to illustrate your answer to part (a) of this question.

   c On the basis of your experience and the economics you have studied, do you think that family decisions are in any part economic decisions? Explain your answer.

2 Read the article in Reading Between the Lines on pp. 168–169 and then answer the following questions:

   a Suppose that the price of cashmere jumpers halved while Lisa is still a student.

      i What happens to the slope of the her budget line?

      ii Does Lisa buy more or fewer quality cashmere jumpers? Use an indifference curve drawing to explain your answer.

   b Suppose quality cashmere goes out of fashion when Lisa gets her first job and that wool-mix jumpers are very fashionable.

      i What will happen to the shape of her indifference curves between quality cashmere and wool-mix jumpers?

      ii Use an indifference curve diagram to explain whether she will buy more or less quality cashmere jumpers if the price of cashmere jumpers does not change.

      iii Will quality cashmere jumpers be a luxury good or an inferior good for Lisa now?

3 Value Added Tax (VAT) is a tax on all goods and services in Europe. Until recently there was no VAT on newspapers and magazines in the UK. The European Union has made the UK impose the tax on newspapers and magazines. When this change occurred:

   a What happened to the the relative price of magazines and coffee?

   b What happened to the budget line showing the quantitites of magazines and coffee you can afford to buy?

   c How would your purchases of magazines and coffee change?

   d Why would the European Union want to impose the tax on all goods and services and not allow some to be tax free?

Indifference Curves: Cashmere or Wool?

THE GUARDIAN, 17 FEBRUARY 2001

Freezingly low temperatures get cashmere's goat

Hadley Freeman

Cashmere, that most luxurious of fabrics, and one currently wrapping up the bodies of the most fashionable of folk, is under serious threat . . .

The majority of cashmere comes from northern China and Mongolia . . . The region suffered from terrible drought in 1999 and this winter has been the coldest on record, killing many of the goats and greatly reducing this year's predicted stocks. Louise Hammond, PR manager for cashmere companies Tse and CXD, said consumers would see an increase in price 'of up to one third' by next winter.

Five years ago this news would not have had such a dramatic impact, but cashmere has been enjoying a fashion renaissance of late, thanks to the current popularity of luxury goods . . . the increase in demand has helped to increase price. Three years ago, cashmere fibre cost £35 per kilo. Today it is triple that price.

Cashmere tops began to creep their way onto the high street a few years ago, at a fraction of the normal price. A jumper from The Gap, for example, will set you back £98 . . . Mr Sugden (managing director of Johnstons of Elgin) is scornful of such newcomers to the market: 'Some of the cheaper cashmere is not all it is said to be. Let's just say they are probably not 100 per cent pure'.

He said that to sell their goods this summer at such low prices they will have to be using cashmere blended with angora and silk. 'They probably will be able to continue selling "cashmere" because they can have it manufactured in China . . . , and their cashmere is not necessarily of such high quality'.

The Essence of the Story

- Cashmere is a luxury fabric and currently very fashionable.

- A number of cheaper alternatives have appeared in high street shops. The alternative to pure cashmere is a cheaper mix of poorer quality cashmere and wool or silk.

- A recent drought in China and Mongolia combined with the heavy fashion demand have forced up the price of cashmere fashion clothing.

- The price of cashmere is likely to increase by at least a third this year.

Economic Analysis

- Lisa is a fashion-conscious graduate in her first year of work. She can choose between this season's expensive cashmere jumpers, the cheaper cashmere and wool-mix alternatives.

- Figure 1 shows Lisa's indifference curves, I_0, I_1 and I_2 for best quality cashmere jumpers and cheaper cashmere and wool-mix jumpers.

- The magnitude of the slope of an indifference curve is the marginal rate of substitution (*MRS*). The *MRS* tells how many units of quality cashmere jumpers Lisa is willing to give up to gain more wool-mix jumpers while remaining on the same indifference curve.

- If Lisa consumes on indifference curve I_0, at point *a*, she is willing to give up one quality cashmere jumper to get one extra wool-mix jumper – the move from *a* to *b*.

- On indifference curve I_2, at point *c*, she is willing to give up less than one quality cashmere jumper to get one extra wool-mix jumper – the move from *c* to *d*.

- Figure 2 shows Lisa's choices for jumpers.

- When Lisa was a student, the highest indifference curve she could reach was I_0. Her best affordable point is 4 wool-mix jumpers and no cashmere jumpers.

- With her new job, the highest indifference curve Lisa can reach is I_2. Her best affordable point is now 2 wool-mix jumpers and 3 cashmere jumpers.

- If the price of quality cashmere jumpers increases by a third this year, Lisa's current budget line will change to the dark orange budget line. Her best affordable point on indifference curve I_1 is now 2 wool-mix jumpers and 2 cashmere jumpers.

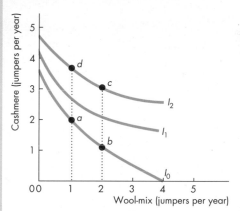

Figure 1 Preferences for jumpers

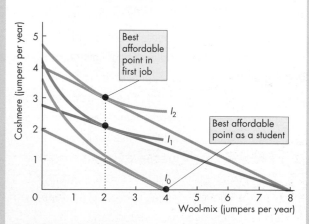

Figure 2 Lisa's choices

Understanding Human Behaviour

. . . it is the greatest happiness of the greatest number that is the measure of right and wrong.

Jeremy Bentham, Fragment on Government

The Economist: Jeremy Bentham

Jeremy Bentham (1748–1832), who lived in London, was the son and grandson of a lawyer and was himself trained as a barrister. But he rejected the opportunity to maintain the family tradition and instead spent his life as a writer, activist and Member of Parliament, in the pursuit of rational laws that would bring the greatest happiness to the greatest number.

Bentham, whose body is partially preserved to this day in a glass cabinet at the University of London, was the first person to use the concept of utility to explain human choices. But in Bentham's day, the distinction between explaining and prescribing was not a sharp one, and Bentham was ready to use his ideas to tell people how they ought to behave. He was one of the first to propose pensions for the retired, guaranteed employment, minimum wages and social benefits such as free education and free medical care.

The Issues and Ideas

The economic analysis of human behaviour in the family, the workplace, the markets for goods and services, the markets for labour services and financial markets is based on the idea that our behaviour can be understood as a response to scarcity. Everything we do can be understood as a choice that maximizes total benefit subject to the constraints imposed by our limited resources and technology. If people's preferences are stable in the face of changing constraints, then we have a chance of predicting how they will respond to an evolving environment.

The economic approach explains the incredible change that has occurred during the past 100 years in the way women allocate their time as the consequence of changing constraints, not of changing attitudes. Technological advances have equipped the nation's farms and factories with machines that have increased the productivity of both women and men, thereby raising the wages they can earn. The increasingly technological world has increased the return to education for both women and men and has led to a large increase in the number of both sexes staying in full-time school and college education. Equipped with an ever widening array of gadgets and appliances that cut the time taken to do household jobs, an increasing proportion of women have joined the workforce.

The economic explanation might not be correct, but it is a powerful one. If it is correct, the changing attitudes are a consequence, not a cause, of the economic advancement of women.

Then . . .

Economists now explain people's actions as the consequences of choices that maximize total utility subject to constraints. Professor Gary Becker of the University of Chicago has transformed the way we think about human choices. In the 1890s, fewer than 20 per cent of women chose paid employment, and most of those who did had low-

paying and unattractive jobs. The other 80 per cent of women chose unpaid work in the home. Professor Becker would explain this as the rational result of women's choices, given the constraints at the time.

. . . And Now

By 1997, more than 60 per cent of women were in the workforce, and, although many had low-paying jobs, women were increasingly found in the professions and in executive positions. What brought about this dramatic change compared with 100 years earlier? Was it a change in preferences or a change in the constraints that women face?

Trying These Ideas Today

Using what you have learned about utility and choice in Chapter 8, and what you know about the participation of women in the workforce, you should be able to answer the following questions:

■ Professor Gary Becker would argue that the decision to have a baby, like the decision to join the workforce, can be modelled as utility maximizing behaviour. Using this model, what costs and benefits do you think parents would take into account in the decision to start a family?

■ Use the utility maximizing behaviour model to explain the falling birth rate in industrialized countries.

Part 3

Firms and Markets

Talking with **David Gowland**

David Gowland is Professor of Financial Economics at the European Business School and Visiting Senior Research Fellow in the Department of Economics, University of Birmingham. He studied at the University of Oxford. He has worked in the Bank of England, The Policy Unit 10 Downing Street and the Universities of York and Derby. He has been appointed as advisor to governments and political parties in 8 post-communist countries and in the People's Republic of China. He is the author of 11 books and numerous articles.

What first attracted you to study economics and in particular, to specialize in the economics of financial markets?

I became interested in economics as a teenager because it seemed to be useful in explaining many issues in politics and history which were then my main interests. My great uncle was a stock market afficianado who interested me in the stock exchange in the same way he did in football and cricket.

I was originally a macroeconomist specializing in monetary policy but came to believe that understanding the workings of financial markets was vital to monetary policy.

In what sense are financial markets similar to or different from most goods and service markets?

The great advantage of financial economics is that many of the assumptions necessary to analyse any market are easier to specify, for example homogeneous products, objectives of market agents, cost and nature of information, etc.

In many ways financial markets are purer and simpler markets than others. Hence many topics can only be studied in financial markets such as the nature of expectation formation, and how prices are actually formed. We all draw supply and demand curves but it is fascinating to see what processes underlie them and to analyse the attainment or non-attainment of equilibrium and how different institutional structures affect this.

To what extent are national and international financial markets competitive?

Financial markets were uncompetitive in 1970. Their history over the last 30 years has largely been the growth of competition due both to deregulation and changes within the financial sector. Competition is almost perfect in wholesale markets (those serving large companies and the very rich). There are still significant monopolies and oligopolies in retail markets, those serving small business and the general public.

The absence of competition is a much bigger problem in emerging markets, the third world and post-communist countries. This is because of lack of information and market infrastructure.

All markets especially financial ones are dependent on a lot of other institutions and signals from other markets. When some are absent or embryonic, then it is much harder for other markets to operate.

Can economic market theory satisfactorily explain the extreme reactions we sometimes see in financial markets?

There are two broad approaches to explaining financial markets. The neo-classical one (sometimes called the efficient market hypothesis (EMH)) is sometimes inadequate in explaining what you call extreme reactions. In particular the EMH implies that prices respond only to news and it is difficult to reconcile this with observed behaviour.

However, the alternative approach is very useful. This is based on two strands of economics. The first is the analysis of interactions that arise because economic agents seek to estimate what others think. Hence an agent may think a share is overvalued but not sell it because he or she believes others believe it undervalued. If everyone thinks in this fashion, share prices may remain at a level which everyone believes to be too high. The second is the implications of asymmetric and imperfect information. Stiglitz in particular has contributed enormously to our understanding. In financial markets it is common for one party to a transaction to have information the other lacks. Both may be aware of this and behave accordingly. Many features of banking can be explained in this way, for example why banks respond to excess demand for loans by rationing rather than by raising interest rates.

Do you think there is a case for more stringent control of financial institutions at the national or international level?

It is difficult to control financial markets because evasion is so profitable and often simple. However, the problems of control are often overstated and the pendulum has swung too far from the excessive controls of the past.

Do you think the European Central Bank has appropriate control over Europe's financial markets?

The ECB is criticized far too often in comparison to other central banks. The eurozone is the closest to a closed economy in the world today and the ECB does a good job in achieving its objectives for this area and has adequate instruments. It would probably not be well-equipped to do such a good job if the UK joined with its trade with the rest of the world and role as an international financial centre. The ECB has to set a single interest rate for the whole of the eurozone. All the present members are oil importers whereas the UK is an oil exporter. Thus the optimal response to a rise in oil prices caused by a war in the Middle East would be different for the UK from the present eurozone.

CHAPTER 9

Organizing Production

After studying this chapter you will be able to:

◆ Explain what a firm is and describe the economic problems that all firms face

◆ Distinguish between technological efficiency and economic efficiency

◆ Define and explain the principal–agent problem

◆ Describe and distinguish between different forms of business organization

◆ Describe and distinguish between the different markets in which firms operate

◆ Explain why firms coordinate some economic activities and markets coordinate others

An Apple a Day

In the autumn of 1990, a British scientist named Tim Berners-Lee invented the World Wide Web. This remarkable idea paved the way for the creation and growth of thousands of profitable businesses. One of these is the German firm, SAP – Europe's biggest software company. ◆ How does SAP and the other 20 million firms that operate in Europe make their business decisions? How do they operate efficiently? ◆ Businesses range from multinational giants, such as Microsoft, to small family restaurants and local internet service providers. Three-quarters of all firms are operated by their owners. But corporations like SAP and Microsoft account for 90 per cent of all business sales. What are the different types of firm? Why do some remain small while others become giants? Why are most firms owner-operated? ◆ Many businesses operate in a highly competitive environment and struggle to earn their profits. Others, like Microsoft, seem to have cornered the market on their products and earn large profits. What are the different types of market in which firms operate and why is it harder to make a profit in some markets than in others? ◆ Most of the components of a Dell personal computer are made by other firms. Microsoft created its Windows operating system and Intel makes its processor chip. Other firms make hard drives and modems, and yet others make DVD drives, sound cards, and so on. Why doesn't Dell make all its own computer components? Why does it leave these activities to other firms and buy from them in markets? How do firms decide what to make themselves and what to buy in the marketplace from other firms?

◆ ◆ ◆ ◆ In this chapter, we are going to learn about firms and the choices they make to cope with scarcity. We begin by studying the economic problems and choices that all firms face. We end by taking a close look at how SAP, Europe's biggest software company, has bucked the trend for falling profits in the technology sector in our first business case study.

The Firm and its Economic Problem

The 20 million firms in the European Union differ in their size and in the scope of what they do. But they all perform the same basic economic functions. Each **firm** is an institution that hires productive resources and that organizes those resources to produce and sell goods and services.

Our goal is to predict firm behaviour. To do so, we need to know a firm's goals and the constraints it faces. We begin with the goals.

The Firm's Goal

Some would talk about making a quality product, others about business growth, others about market share, and others about the job satisfaction of their workforce. All of these goals might be pursued, but they are not the fundamental goal. They are means to a deeper goal.

A firm's goal is to maximize profit. A firm that does not seek to maximize profit is either eliminated or bought out by firms that do seek to maximize profit.

What exactly is the profit that a firm seeks to maximize? To answer this question, let's look at an example of a small airport restaurant called Bites run by Sue.

Measuring a Firm's Profit

Sue runs a successful restaurant business called Bites. The restaurant earns a revenue of €400,000 a year. Its expenses are €80,000 a year for foods, €20,000 for energy, water and other utilities bills, €120,000 for labour, and €10,000 in interest on a bank loan. With receipts of €400,000 and expenses of €230,000, Bites annual surplus is €170,000.

Sue's accountant lowers this number by €20,000, which she says is the depreciation (fall in value) of the firm's buildings and equipment during the year. (Accountants use European Union rules based on standards established by the accounting profession to calculate the depreciation.) So the accountant reports that the profit of Bites is €150,000 a year.

Sue's accountant measures cost and profit to ensure that the firm pays the correct amount of income tax and to show the bank how its loan has been used. But we want to predict the decisions that a firm makes. These decisions respond to *opportunity cost* and *economic profit*.

Opportunity Cost

The **opportunity cost** of any action is the highest-valued alternative forgone. The action that you choose not to do – the highest-valued alternative forgone – is the cost of the action that you choose to do. For a firm, the opportunity cost of production is the value of the firm's best alternative use of its resources.

Opportunity cost is a real alternative forgone. But so that we can compare the cost of one action with that of another action, we express opportunity cost in money units. A firm's opportunity costs are:

◆ Explicit costs.
◆ Implicit costs.

Explicit costs

Explicit costs are paid in money. The amount paid for a resource that could have been spent on something else, so it is the opportunity cost of using the resource. For Sue, her expenditures on foods, utilities, wages, and bank interest are explicit costs.

Implicit costs

A firm incurs implicit costs when it forgoes an alternative action but does not make a payment. A firm incurs implicit costs when it:

1 Uses it's own capital.

2 Uses its owner's time or financial resources.

The cost of using its own capital is an implicit cost – and an opportunity cost – because the firm could rent the capital to another firm. The rental income forgone is the firm's opportunity cost of using its own capital. This opportunity cost is called the **implicit rental rate** of capital.

People rent houses, apartments, cars, telephones, and videotapes. And firms rent photocopiers, earth-moving equipment, satellite launching services, and so on. If a firm rents capital, it incurs an *explicit* cost. If a firm buys the capital it uses, it incurs an *implicit* cost. The implicit rental rate of capital is made up of:

1 Economic depreciation.

2 Interest forgone.

Economic depreciation is change in the *market* value of capital over a given period. It is calculated as the market price of the capital at the beginning of the period minus its market price at the end of the period. For example, suppose that Sue could have sold her restaurant buildings and equipment on December 31, 2000, for €400,000. If she can sell the same capital on December 31, 2001, for €375,000, her economic depreciation during 2000 is €25,000 – the fall in the market value of the equipment. This €25,000 is an implicit cost of using the capital during 2000.

The funds used to buy capital could have been used for some other purpose. And in their next best use, they would have yielded a return – an interest income. This forgone interest is part of the opportunity cost of using the capital. For example, Sue could have bought government bonds instead of a restaurant. The interest forgone on the government bonds is an implicit cost of operating a restaurant.

Cost of Owner's Resources

A firm's owner often supplies *entrepreneurial ability* – the productive resource that organizes the business, makes business decisions, innovates, and bears the risk of running the business. The return to entrepreneurship is profit and the *average* return for supplying entrepreneurial ability is called normal profit. **Normal profit** is part of a firm's opportunity cost, because it is the cost of a forgone alternative – running another firm. If normal profit in the small restaurant business is €50,000 a year, this amount must be added to Sue's costs to determine her opportunity cost.

The owner of a firm also can supply labour (in addition to entrepreneurship). The return to labour is a wage. And the opportunity cost of the owner's time spent working for the firm is the wage income forgone by not working in the best alternative job. Suppose that Sue could take another job that pays €40,000 a year. By working for her restaurant business and forgoing this income, Sue incurs an opportunity cost of €40,000 a year.

Economic Profit

What is the bottom line – the profit or loss of the firm? A firm's **economic profit** is equal to its total revenue minus its opportunity cost. The firm's opportunity cost is the sum of its explicit costs and implicit costs. And the implicit costs, remember, include *normal profit*. The return to entrepreneurial ability is greater than normal in a firm that makes a positive economic profit. And the return to entrepreneurial ability is less than normal in a firm that makes a negative economic profit – a firm that incurs an economic loss.

Table 9.1 Economic Accounting

Item		Amount
Total revenue		400,000
Opportunity costs		
Foods	80,000	
Utilities	20,000	
Wages paid	120,000	
Bank interest paid	10,000	
Total explicit costs		230,000
Sue's wages forgone	40,000	
Sue's interest forgone	20,000	
Economic depreciation	25,000	
Normal profit	50,000	
Total implicit costs		135,000
Total cost		365,000
Economic profit		35,000

Economic Accounting: A Summary

Table 9.1 summarizes the economic accounting concepts that you've just studied. Sue's restaurant, Bites, earns a total revenue of €400,000. Its opportunity cost (explicit costs plus its implicit costs) is €365,000. So its economic profit is €35,000.

To achieve the objective of maximum profit – maximum economic profit – a firm must make five basic decisions:

1 What goods and services to produce and in what quantities.

2 How to produce – the techniques of production to use.

3 How to organize and compensate its managers and workers.

4 How to market and price its products.

5 What to produce itself and what to buy from other firms.

In all these decisions, a firm's actions are limited by the constraints that it faces. Our next task is to learn about these constraints.

The Firm's Constraints

Three features of its environment limit the maximum profit a firm can make. They are:

◆ Technology.

◆ Information.

◆ Market.

Technology Constraints

Economists define technology broadly. A **technology** is any method of producing a good or service. Technology includes the detailed designs of machines. It also includes the layout of the workplace. And it includes the organization of the firm. For example, the shopping centre is a technology for producing retail services. It is a different technology from catalogue shopping, which in turn is different from the high street stores.

It might seem surprising that a firm's profits are limited by technology. For it seems that technological advances are constantly increasing profit opportunities. Almost every day, we learn about some new technological advance that amazes us. With computers that speak and recognise our own speech and cars that can find the address we need in a city we've never visited before, we are able to accomplish ever more.

Technology is advancing. But at each point in time, to produce more output and gain more revenue, a firm must hire more resources and incur greater costs. The increase in profit that the firm can achieve is limited by the technology available for transforming resources into output. For example, using its current plant and workforce, BMW can produce some maximum number of cars per day. To produce more cars per day, BMW must hire more resources and incur greater costs, which limits the increase in profit that BMW can make by selling the additional cars.

Information Constraints

We never possess all the information we would like to make decisions. We lack information about both the future and the present. For example, suppose you plan to buy a new computer. When should you buy it? The answer depends on how the price is going to change in the future. Where should you buy it? The answer depends on the prices at hundreds of different computer shops. To get the best deal, you must compare the quality and prices in every shop. But the opportunity cost of this comparison exceeds the cost of the computer!

Similarly, a firm is constrained by limited information about the quality and effort of its workforce, the current and future buying plans of its customers, and

the plans of its competitors. Workers slacken off when managers believe they are working hard. Customers switch to competing suppliers. Firms must compete against competition from a new firm.

Firms try to create incentive systems for workers to ensure they work hard even when no one is monitoring their efforts. And firms spend millions of euros on market research. But none of these efforts and expenditures eliminates the problems of incomplete information and uncertainty. And the cost of coping with limited information itself limits profit.

Market Constraints

What each firm can sell and the price it can obtain is constrained by the willingness to pay of its customers and by the prices and marketing efforts of other firms. Similarly, the resources that each firm can buy and the prices it must pay are limited by the willingness of people to work for and invest in the firm. Firms spend billions of euros a year marketing and selling their products. Some of the most creative minds strive to find the right message that will produce a knockout television advertisement. Market constraints and the expenditures firms make to overcome them limit the profit a firm can make.

Review Quiz

◆ Why do firms seek to maximize profit? What happens to firms that don't pursue this goal?
◆ Why do accountants and economists calculate a firm's cost and profit in different ways?
◆ What are the items that make opportunity cost depart from the accountants' measure of cost?
◆ Why is normal profit an opportunity cost?
◆ What are the three types of constraint that firms face? How does each constraint limit the profit that a firm can make?

In the rest of this chapter and in Chapters 10 to 13, we study the decisions that firms make. We're going to learn how we can predict a firm's behaviour as the response to the constraints that it faces and to changes in those constraints. We begin by taking a closer look at the technology constraints, information constraints, and market constraints that firms face.

Technology and Economic Efficiency

Microsoft workers possess a large amount of human capital. But the firm uses a small amount of physical capital. In contrast, a coal mining company employs a huge amount of mining equipment (physical capital) and almost no labour. Why? The answer lies in the concept of efficiency. There are two concepts of production efficiency: technological efficiency and economic efficiency. **Technological efficiency** occurs when the firm produces a given output by using the least inputs. **Economic efficiency** occurs when the firm produces a given output at least cost. Let's explore the two concepts of efficiency by studying an example.

Suppose that there are four alternative techniques for making TV sets:

a *Robot production.* One person monitors the entire computer-driven process.

b *Production line.* Workers specialize in a small part of the job as the emerging TV set passes them on a production line.

c *Bench production.* Workers specialize in a small part of the job but walk from bench to bench to perform their tasks.

d *Hand-tool production.* A single worker uses a few hand tools to make a TV set.

Table 9.2 sets out the amounts of labour and capital required by each of these four methods to make 10 TV sets a day in the United Kingdom.

Which of these alternative methods are technologically efficient?

Table 9.2 Four Ways of Making 10 TV Sets a Day

Method	Quantities of inputs	
	Labour	Capital
a Robot production	1	1,000
b Production line	10	10
c Bench production	100	10
d Hand-tool production	1,000	1

Technological Efficiency

Recall that technological efficiency occurs when the firm produces a given output by using the least inputs. Inspect the numbers in the table and notice that method *a* uses the most capital but the least labour. Method *d* uses the most labour but the least capital. Methods *b* and *c* lie between the two extremes. They use less capital but more labour than method *a* and less labour but more capital than method *d*. Compare methods *b* and *c*. Method *c* requires 100 workers and 10 units of capital to produce 10 TV sets. Those same 10 TV sets can be produced by method *b* with 10 workers and the same 10 units of capital. Because method *c* uses the same amount of capital and more labour than method *b*, method *c* is not technologically efficient.

Are any of the other methods not technologically efficient? The answer is no. Each of the other three methods is technologically efficient. Method *a* uses more capital but less labour than method *b*, and method *d* uses more labour but less capital than method *b*.

Which of the methods are economically efficient?

Economic Efficiency

Recall that economic efficiency occurs when the firm produces a given output at least cost. Suppose that labour costs £75 per person-day and that capital costs £250 per machine-day. Table 9.3(a) calculates the costs of using the different methods. By inspecting the table, you can see that method *b* has the lowest cost. Although method *a* uses less labour, it uses too much expensive capital. And although method *d* uses less capital, it uses too much expensive labour.

Method *c*, which is technologically inefficient, is also economically inefficient. It uses the same amount of capital as method *b* but 10 times as much labour, so it costs more. A technologically inefficient method is never economically efficient.

Although *b* is the economically efficient method in this example, method *a* or *d* could be economically efficient with different input prices.

First, suppose that labour costs £150 a person-day and capital costs only £1 a machine-day. Table 9.3(b) now shows the costs of making a TV set. In this case, method *a* is economically efficient. Capital is now so cheap relative to labour that the method that uses the most capital is the economically efficient method.

Table 9.3 The Costs of Different Ways of Making 10 TV Sets a Day

(a) Four ways of making TVs

Method	Labour cost (£75 per day)		Capital cost (£250 per day)		Total cost	Cost per TV set
a	£75	+	£250,000	=	£250,075	£25,007.50
b	750	+	2,500	=	3,250	325.00
c	7,500	+	2,500	=	10,000	1,000.00
d	75,000	+	250	=	75,250	7,525.00

(b) Three ways of making TVs: high labour costs

Method	Labour cost (150 per day)		Capital cost (£1 per day)		Total cost	Cost per TV set
a	£150	+	£1,000	=	£1,150	£115.00
b	1,500	+	10	=	1,510	151.00
d	150,000	+	1	=	150,001	15,000.10

(c) Three ways of making TVs: high capital costs

Method	Labour cost (£1 per day)		Capital cost (£1,000 per day)		Total cost	Cost per TV set
a	£1	+	£1,000,000	=	£1,000,001	£100,000.10
b	10	+	10,000	=	10,010	1,001.00
d	1,000	+	1,000	=	2,000	200.00

Second, suppose that labour costs only £1 a person-day while capital costs £1,000 a machine-day. Table 9.3(c) shows the costs in this case. Method *d*, which uses a lot of labour and little capital, is now the least-cost method and economically efficient method.

From these examples, you can see that while technological efficiency depends only on what is feasible, economic efficiency depends on the relative costs of resources. The economically efficient method is the one that uses the smaller amount of a more expensive resource and a larger amount of a less expensive resource.

A firm that is not economically efficient does not maximize profit. Natural selection favours efficient firms and opposes inefficient firms. Inefficient firms go out of business or are taken over by firms with lower costs. Profit-maximizing firms are stronger and better able to survive temporary adversity than inefficient ones.

Review Quiz

◆ How do we define technological efficiency? Is a firm technologically efficient if it uses the latest technology? Why?
◆ How do we define economic efficiency? Is a firm economically inefficient if it can cut costs by producing less? Why?
◆ Explain the key distinction between technological efficiency and economic efficiency.
◆ Why are some firms capital intensive and others labour intensive?

You have now seen how the technology constraints on a firm influence the amounts of capital and labour that it employs. Next we will study the impact of information constraints and the diversity of organizational structures they generate.

Information and Organizations

Each firm organizes the production of goods and services by combining and coordinating the productive resources it hires. But there is variety across firms in how they organize production. Firms use a mixture of two systems:

1 Command systems.
2 Incentive systems.

Command Systems

A **command system** is a method of organizing production that uses a managerial hierarchy. Commands pass downward through the managerial hierarchy and information passes upward. Managers spend most of their time collecting and processing information about the performance of the people under their control and making decisions about commands to issue and how best to get those commands implemented.

The military uses the purest form of command system. A commander-in-chief makes the big decisions about strategic objectives. Beneath this highest level, generals organize their military resources. Beneath the generals, successively lower ranks organize smaller and smaller units but pay attention to ever increasing degrees of detail. At the bottom of the managerial hierarchy are the people who operate weapons systems.

Command systems in firms are not as rigid as they are in the military. But they share some similar features. A chief executive officer (CEO) sits at the top of a firm's command system. Senior executives who report to and receive commands from the CEO specialize in managing production, marketing, finance, personnel, and perhaps other aspects of the firm's operations. Beneath these senior managers might be several tiers of middle management ranks that stretch downward to the managers that supervise the day-to-day operations of the business. Beneath these managers are the people who operate the firm's machines and who make and sell goods and services.

Small firms have one or two layers of managers while large firms have several layers. As production processes have become ever more complex, management ranks have swollen. Today, more people have management jobs than ever before. But the information revolution of the 1990s slowed the growth of management and, in some industries, it decreased the number of layers of managers and brought a shake-out of middle managers.

Managers make enormous efforts to be well informed. And they try hard to make good decisions and issue commands that end up using resources efficiently. But managers always have incomplete information about what is happening in the divisions of the firm for which they are responsible. It is for this reason that firms use incentive systems as well as command systems to organize production.

Incentive Systems

An **incentive system** is a method of organizing production that uses a market-like mechanism inside the firm. Instead of issuing commands, senior managers create compensation schemes that will induce workers to perform in ways that maximize the firm's profit.

Selling organizations use incentive systems most extensively. Sales representatives who spend most of their working time alone and unsupervised are induced to work hard by being paid a small salary and a large performance-related bonus.

But incentive systems operate at all levels in a firm. A CEO's compensation plan includes a share in the firm's profit, and factory floor workers sometimes receive compensation based on the quantity they produce.

Mixed Systems

Firms will use both commands and incentives in a mixed system if it will help to maximize profit. They use commands when it is easy to monitor performance or when a small deviation from an ideal performance is very costly. They use incentives when monitoring performance is either not possible or too costly to be worth doing.

For example, it is easy and not very costly to monitor the performance of workers on a production line. And if one person works too slowly, the entire line slows. So a production line is organized with a command system.

In contrast, it is costly to monitor a CEO. What, for example, did Jan Leschly (a former CEO of the pharmaceutical giant, SmithKline Beecham) really contribute to the success of the company? Did his actions really warrant his £90 million salary in 1999? This question cannot be answered with certainty, yet big firms must put someone in charge of operations and provide this person with the *incentive* to be efficient. Incentives and the contracts that create them are an attempt to cope with a general problem called the principal–agent problem.

The Principal–Agent Problem

The **principal–agent problem** is the problem of devising compensation rules that induce an *agent* to act in the best interest of a *principal*. For example, the shareholders of the HSBC are *principals* and the bank's managers are *agents*. The shareholders (the principals) must induce the managers (agents) to act in the shareholders' best interest. Similarly, Bill Gates, (a principal) must induce the programmers working on Windows 2000 (agents) to work efficiently.

Agents, whether they are managers or workers, pursue their own goals and often impose costs on a principal. For example, the goal of a shareholder of the HSBC Bank (a principal) is to maximize the bank's profit. But the bank's profit depends on the actions of its managers (agents) who have their own goals. Perhaps a manager takes a customer to a football game on the pretence that she is building customer loyalty, when in fact she is simply taking on-the-job leisure. This same manager is also a principal and her tellers are agents. The manager wants the tellers to work hard and attract new customers so she can meet her operating targets. But the tellers enjoy conversations with each other and keep customers waiting in line. Nonetheless, the bank constantly strives to find ways of improving performance and increasing profits.

Coping with the Principal–Agent Problem

Issuing commands does not address the principal–agent problem. In most firms, the shareholders can't monitor the managers and often the managers can't monitor the workers. Each principal must create incentives that induce each agent to work in the interests of the principal. Three ways of attempting to cope with the principal–agent problem are:

1 Ownership.
2 Incentive pay.
3 Long-term contracts.

Ownership

By assigning to a manager or worker ownership (or part-ownership) of a business, the principal can sometimes induce a job performance that increases a firm's profits. Part-ownership schemes for senior managers are quite common, and they are less common but not unknown for workers. For example, the two largest UK employee share ownership schemes are run by two firms: Baxi Partnership Ltd, a heating system maker, and the Tullis Russell Group, a paper maker. Both companies belonged to the same family firm that decided to distribute over 50 per cent of the shares to employees to raise motivation and profitability. However, this system has its problems as shown in the cartoon.

Incentive pay

Incentive pay schemes – pay related to performance – are very common. They are based on a variety of performance criteria such as profits or production or sales targets. Promoting an employee for good performance is another example of an incentive pay scheme.

Long-term contracts

Long-term contracts tie the long-term fortunes of managers and workers (agents) to the success of the principal(s) – the owner(s) of the firm. For example, a multi-year employment contract for a CEO encourages that person to take a long-term view and devise strategies that achieve maximum profit over a sustained period.

These three ways of coping with the principal–agent problem give rise to different types of business organization. Each type of business organization is a different response to the principal–agent problem. It uses ownership, incentives, and long-term contracts in different ways. Let's look at the main types of business organization.

Types of Business Organization

The three main types of business organization are:

1 Proprietorship.
2 Partnership.
3 Corporation.

Sole Proprietorship

A *proprietorship* is a firm with a single owner – a proprietor – who has unlimited liability. *Unlimited liability* is the legal responsibility for all the debts of a firm up to an amount equal to the entire wealth of the owner. If a sole proprietorship cannot pay its debts, those to whom the firm owes money can claim the personal property of the owner. Corner shops, computer programmers, and artists are all examples of proprietorships.

The proprietor makes management decisions, receives the firm's profits, and is responsible for its

Table 9.4 The Pros and Cons of Different Types of Firms ◆

Type of firm	Pros	Cons
Proprietorship	◆ Easy to set up ◆ Simple decision making ◆ Profits taxed only once as owner's income	◆ Bad decisions not checked by need for consensus ◆ Owner's entire wealth at risk ◆ Firm dies with owner ◆ Capital is expensive ◆ Labour is expensive
Partnership	◆ Easy to set up ◆ Diversified decision making ◆ Can survive withdrawal of partner ◆ Profits taxed only once as owners' incomes	◆ Achieving consensus may be slow and expensive ◆ Owners' entire wealth at risk ◆ Withdrawal of partner may create capital shortage ◆ Capital is expensive
Corporation	◆ Owners have limited liability ◆ Large-scale, low-cost capital available ◆ Professional management not restricted by ability of owners ◆ Perpetual life ◆ Long-term labour contracts cut labour costs	◆ Complex management structure can make decisions slow and expensive ◆ Profits taxed twice as company profit and as shareholders' income

---

losses. Profits from a proprietorship are taxed at the same rate as other sources of the proprietor's personal income.

Partnership

A *partnership* is a firm with two or more owners who have unlimited liability. Partners must agree on an appropriate management structure and on how to divide the firm's profits among themselves. The profits of a partnership are taxed as the personal income of the owners. But each partner is legally liable for all the debts of the partnership (limited only by the wealth of an individual partner). Liability for the full debts of the partnership is called *joint unlimited liability*. Most law firms are partnerships.

Company

A **company** is a firm owned by one or more limited liability shareholders. *Limited liability* means that the owners have legal liability only for the value of their initial investment. This limitation of liability means that if the corporation becomes bankrupt, its owners are not required to use their personal wealth to pay the company's debts.

Company profits are taxed independently of shareholders' incomes. Because shareholders pay taxes on the income they receive as dividends on shares, corporate profits are taxed twice. The shareholders also pay capital gains tax on the profit they earn by selling a share for a higher price than they paid for it.

Company shares generate capital gains when a company retains some of its profit and reinvests it in profitable activities. So even retained earnings are taxed twice because the capital gains they generate are taxed.

Pros and Cons of Different Types of Firms

The different types of business organization arise as different ways of trying to cope with the principal–agent problem. Each type has advantages in particular situations as shown in Table 9.4. Because of this, each type continues to exist throughout Europe and the rest of the world. Each type also has its disadvantages. Companies dominate where businesses use a large amount of capital, and proprietorships and partnerships operate where flexibility in decision making is critical.

The Relative Importance of Different Sizes of Firm

The total number of businesses in the United Kingdom increased from 1.9 million to 2.8 million between 1979 and 1997. This was largely owing to an increase in the number of one-person and two-person businesses – many of them family businesses. Over 26 per cent of employees in the private sector are employed in small businesses with fewer than 10 employees. The majority of single proprietorships and partnerships are small firms of this type.

Figure 9.1
Relative Importance of Firms by Size

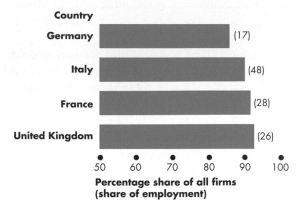

(a) Importance of small firms

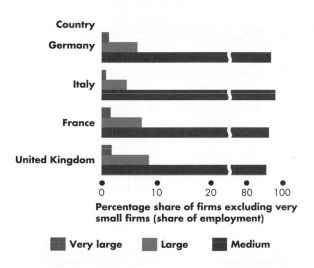

Very large | Large | Medium

(b) Importance of medium, large and very large firms

Very small firms employing fewer than 10 employees account for over 90 per cent of all firms in most western European countries, but usually account for less than 30 per cent of employment. Of the remainder, medium-sized firms are the most important. Very large firms employing more than 500 employees account for less than 2 per cent of medium and large-scale firms, but account for about 40 per cent of all employment.

Source: Enterprises in Europe, Commission of the European Communities, Office for Official Publications of the European Communities, Luxembourg, 1996.

Figure 9.1(a) shows the importance of very small firms in a selection of Western European countries. Firms employing fewer than 10 employees account for fewer than 90 per cent of all firms in most European countries. These firms can account for as little as 17 per cent of employment in Germany or as much as 48 per cent of employment in Italy. The majority of employment in very small firms is in the services, construction and agriculture sectors. Part (b) shows the importance of the remaining medium and larger firms in the same European countries. The pattern is similar across most European countries. Medium-sized firms constitute the largest proportion of this group. While very large corporations employing more than 500 employees only account for just over 1 per cent of firms in most European countries, they account for about 40 per cent of employment.

Review Quiz

◆ Explain the distinction between a command system and an incentive system in business organizations.
◆ What is the principal–agent problem and what are the ways in which firms try to cope with it?
◆ What are the three types of firm? Explain their advantages and disadvantages.
◆ Why do all three types of firm survive and in which sectors are each type most prominent?

You've now seen how technology constraints influence a firm's use of capital and labour and how information constraints influence a firm's organization. We'll now look at market constraints and see how they influence the environment in which firms compete for business.

Markets and the Competitive Environment

The markets in which firms operate vary a great deal. Some are highly competitive and profits are hard to come by. Some appear to be almost free from competition and firms earn large profits. Some markets are dominated by fierce advertising campaigns and some markets display a war-like character.

Economists identify five market types:

1 Perfect competition.

2 Monopolistic competition.

3 Contestable.

4 Oligopoly.

5 Monopoly.

Perfect competition arises when there are many firms each selling an identical product, many buyers, and no restrictions on the entry of new firms into the industry. The many firms and buyers are all well informed about the prices of the products of each firm in the industry. The worldwide markets for corn, rice, and other grain crops are examples of perfect competition.

Monopolistic competition is a market structure in which a large number of firms compete by making similar but slightly different products. Making a product slightly different from the product of a competing firm is called product differentiation. **Product differentiation** gives a monopolistically competitive firm an element of monopoly power. The firm is the sole producer of the particular version of the good in question. For example, in the market for running shoes, Nike, Reebok, Fila, and Asics all make their own version of the perfect shoe. Each of these firms has a monopoly on a particular brand of shoe. Differentiated products are not necessarily different products. What matters is that consumers perceive them to be different. For example, different brands of aspirin are chemically identical (salicylic acid) and differ only in their packaging.

In some markets, there are few firms but entry and exit is so easy that competition from *potential* new firms is fierce. A market in which potential entry is free is called a **contestable market**. Even if there are some small costs to entry and exit, a market can still be highly contestable. An example of a virtually contestable market is that of local private bus routes. Firms can easily switch their buses from one route to another with virtually no entry and exit costs. Contestable markets can also be studied using the model of monopolistic competition.

Oligopoly is a market structure in which a small number of firms compete. Computer software, aeroplane manufacture, and international air transportation are examples of oligopolistic industries. Oligopolies might produce almost identical products, such as the colas produced by Coke and Pepsi. Or they might produce differentiated products such as the Volkswagen Golf and the Peugeot 205.

A **monopoly** is an industry that produces a good or service for which no close substitute exists and in which there is one supplier that is protected from competition by a barrier preventing the entry of new firms. In some places, the phone, gas, electricity, and water suppliers are local monopolies – monopolies restricted to a given location. Microsoft, the software developer that created Windows, the operating system used by PCs, is an example of a global monopoly.

Perfect competition is the most extreme form of competition. Monopoly is the most extreme absence of competition. The other two market types fall between these extremes.

Many factors must be taken into account to determine which market structure describes a particular real-world market. One of these factors is the extent to which the market is dominated by a small number of firms. To measure this feature of markets, economists use indexes called measures of concentration. Let's look at these measures.

Measures of Concentration

The most common measure of concentration is the **five-firm concentration ratio**. The five-firm concentration ratio is the percentage of the value of sales accounted for by the five largest firms in an industry. The range of the concentration ratio is from almost zero for perfect competition to 100 per cent for monopoly. This ratio is the main measure used to assess market structure. The ratio can also be calculated for the percentage of employees rather than the value of sales accounted for by the five largest firms.

Table 9.5 shows two hypothetical calculations of the five-firm concentration ratio, one for shoe manufacturing and one for egg farming. In this example, there are 15 firms in the shoe manufacturing

---

Table 9.5 Concentration Ratio Calculations

Shoemakers		Egg farmers	
Firm	**Sales (million)**	**Firm**	**Sales (million)**
Lace-up plc	250	Bills's	0.9
Finefoot plc	200	Sue's	0.7
Easyfit plc	180	Jane's	0.5
Comfy plc	120	Tom's	0.4
Loafers plc	70	Jill's	0.2
Top 5 sales	820	Top 5 sales	2.8
Other 10 firms	190	Other 1,000 firms	349.2
Industry sales	1,010	Industry sales	352.0

Five-firm concentration ratios:

Shoemakers: $\dfrac{820}{1,010} = 81\%$ Egg farmers: $\dfrac{2.80}{352} = 0.8\%$

Figure 9.2

Some Concentration Measures in the United Kingdom

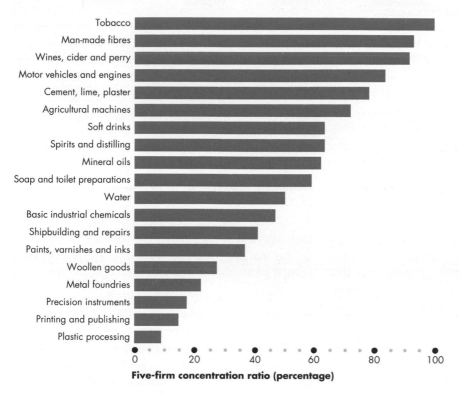

Using the five-firm concentration ratio, tobacco, man-made fibres, wines, ciders and perry are all highly concentrated. Water, chemicals and shipbuilding and repairs have medium concentration. Industries producing woollen goods, precision instruments, plastics and printed products are highly competitive.

Source: Central Statistical Office, *Report of the Census of Production, Business Monitor*, London, HMSO, 2000.

industry. The largest five have 81 per cent of the sales, so the five-firm concentration ratio for that industry is 81 per cent. In the egg industry, with 1,005 firms, the top five firms account for only 0.8 per cent of total industry sales. In this case, the five-firm concentration ratio is 0.8 per cent.

The idea behind calculating five-firm concentration ratios is to get information about the degree of competitiveness of a market. A low concentration ratio indicates a high degree of competition, and a high concentration ratio indicates an absence of competition. In the extreme case of monopoly, the concentration ratio is 100 per cent as the largest (and only) firm makes the entire industry sales. Between these extremes, the five-firm concentration ratio is regarded as being a useful indicator of the likelihood of collusion among firms in an oligopoly. If the ratio exceeds 60 per cent, it is likely that firms in that industry will have a high degree of market power. They are likely to collude and behave like a monopolist. If the ratio is less than 40 per cent, it is likely that the firms

will compete effectively. Between the ratios of 40 and 60 per cent, the industries have oligopolistic and monopolistic competitive structures. But the degree of market power for firms in these industries is likely to be limited by some form of competition.

Concentration in the UK Economy

Concentration ratios for the United Kingdom can be derived from the regular census of manufacturing companies known as the Census of Production. The census is undertaken every year and provides information on the sales, employment and structure of every manufacturing firm in the United Kingdom. Figure 9.2 shows a selection of the five-firm concentration ratio calculations using sales data. As you can see, some industries such as plastics, printing, metal foundries and wool have low concentration ratios – implying firms in these industries are competitive. At the other extreme are industries with high concentration ratios such as tobacco, man-made fibres, wines and

Table 9.6 Market Structure

Characteristics	Perfect competition	Monopolistic competition	Contestable	Oligopoly	Monopoly
Number of firms in industry	Many	Many	Few	Few	One
Product	Identical	Differentiated	Differentiated	Either identical or differentiated	No close substitutes
Barriers to entry	None	None	None	Scale and scope Economies	Scale and scope or legal barriers
Firm's control over price	None	Some	Some	Considerable	Considerable or regulated
Concentration ratio (0–100)	0	Low	Low	High	100
Examples	Agricultural goods	Corner shops, bread, car mechanics	Local restaurants, buses	Washing powders, disposable nappies	Local water utility, postal letter service

ciders, and motor vehicles. These industries appear to have a high degree of monopoly power. Medium concentration ratios are found in industries like mineral oils, water supply and basic chemicals. Firms in these industries have a limited amount of market power.

Limitations of Concentration Measures

Although concentration ratios are useful, they have some limitations. They must be supplemented by other information to determine the structure of an industry and the degree of market power of firms in that industry. The three key problems are:

1 The geographical scope of the market.

2 Barriers to entry and firm turnover.

3 The correspondence between a market and an industry.

Geographical Scope of Market

Concentration ratio data are based on a national view of the market. Many goods are sold on a national market, but some are sold on a regional market and some on a global one. The brewing industry is a good example of one in which the local market is more relevant than the national market. Thus although the national concentration ratio for brewers is in the middle range, there is nevertheless a high degree of concentration in the brewing industry in most regions. The automobile industry is an example of one for which there is a global market. Thus although the largest five car producers in the United Kingdom account for 80 per cent of all cars sold by UK producers,

they account for a smaller percentage of the total UK car market, which includes imports, and an even smaller percentage of the global market for cars.

Barriers to Entry and Turnover

Measures of concentration do not indicate the severity of any barriers to entry in a market. Some industries, for example, are highly concentrated but their markets have virtually free entry and a high turnover of firms. A good example is the market for local restaurants. Many small towns have few restaurants, but there are few restrictions on entering the restaurant industry. So firms enter and exit with great regularity.

Even if the turnover of new firms in a market is limited, an industry might be competitive because of potential entry. This will be the case if the market is *highly contestable*. Table 9.6 summarizes the characteristics of different market structures and their concentration ratios.

Market and Industry

The classifications used to calculate UK concentration ratios allocate every firm in the economy to a particular industry. But markets for particular goods do not usually correspond to these industries.

The main problem is that markets are often narrower than industries. For example, the basic industrial chemicals industry, which has a medium concentration ratio, operates in many separate markets for individual products (for instance tobacco and cement), each one of which has few substitutes. So this industry, which looks relatively competitive, operates in some monopolistic markets.

Another problem arises from the fact that firms make many products. For example, the tobacco firms also operate in insurance. The privatized water companies operate hotels and printing works. The value of sales for each firm can overestimate their contribution to the industry to which they have been assigned.

If concentration ratios are combined with information about the geographical scope, barriers to entry and the extent to which large, multi-product firms straddle a variety of markets, they can provide a basis for classifying industries. The less concentrated an industry and the lower its barriers to entry, the more closely it approximates the perfect competition case. The more concentrated an industry and the higher the barriers to entry, the more it approximates the monopoly case.

Market Structures

The majority of markets for goods and services in Europe are highly competitive and only a few markets are monopolized. For example, more than 70 per cent by value of UK goods and services are traded in highly competitive markets. Where pure monopoly does arise it is usually in the public services although this has declined with privatization. But monopoly power can still be strong in markets like telecommunications when privatization attracts few new entrants. Less than 6 per cent of the value of goods and services traded in the UK are in highly monopolized markets. Oligopoly is more common in manufacturing than in the services sector, but more than 55 per cent of UK manufacturing industries have a concentration ratio of less than 40 per cent.

The overall level of concentration across an economy can be measured by the proportion of total output accounted for by the largest 100 firms. Figure 9.3 shows the UK aggregate concentration ratio in manufacturing since 1949. Aggregate concentration increased in the post-war period indicating an increase in market power, but it levelled off in the 1970s and 1980s and has fallen in recent years. The increase in concentration resulted from several waves of merger activity and the growth of transnational corporations serving new global markets. This is not surprising given the growth in world trade, and advances in telecommunications and low-cost transport. So although the United Kingdom's national aggregate concentration has increased, many of its markets are now globalized and highly competitive.

Figure 9.3

Aggregate Concentration Ratios

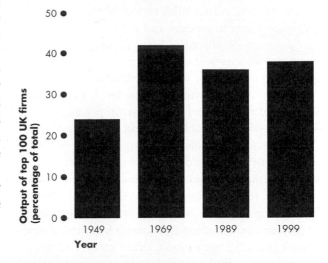

The output of the top 100 manufacturing firms as a percentage of total UK output in manufacturing is a measure of concentration in the manufacturing sector. The concentration ratio as a percentage increased from 22 per cent in 1949 to 43 per cent in 1969, indicating an increase in market power in manufacturing. Concentration has declined since then. The ratio fell to 35 per cent in 1989 and increased slightly in 1999.

Source: Central Statistical Office, *Report of the Census of Production, Business Monitor*, London, HMSO, 2000.

Review Quiz

◆ What are the four market types? Explain the distinguishing characteristics of each.
◆ Describe and explain the main measures of market concentration.
◆ Under what conditions do measures of concentration give a good indication of the degree of competition in the market?
◆ Is our economy competitive? Is it becoming more competitive or less competitive?

You now know the variety of market types and the way we classify firms and industries into the different market types. Our final question in this chapter is what determines the items that firms decide to buy from other firms rather than produce for themselves?

Firms and Markets

At the beginning of this chapter, we defined a firm as an institution that hires factors of production and organizes them to produce and sell goods and services. To organize production, firms coordinate the economic decisions and activities of many individuals. But firms are not the only coordinators of economic decisions. As we learned in Chapter 3, markets also coordinate decisions. By adjusting prices, markets make the decisions of buyers and sellers consistent – make the quantities demanded equal to the quantities supplied of the many different goods and services.

An example of market coordination is the production of a rock concert. A promoter hires a stadium, some stage equipment, audio and video recording engineers and technicians, some rock groups, a superstar, a publicity agent and a ticket agent – all market transactions – and sells tickets to thousands of rock fans, audio rights to a recording company and video and broadcasting rights to a television network – another set of market transactions. If rock concerts were produced like cornflakes, the firm producing them would own all the capital used (stadiums, stage, sound and video equipment) and would employ all the labour needed (singers, engineers, sales persons, and so on).

What determines whether a firm or markets coordinate a particular set of activities? Why is the production of cornflakes coordinated by a firm and the production of a rock concert coordinated by markets? The answer is cost. Taking account of the opportunity cost of time as well as the costs of the other inputs, people use the method that costs least. In other words, they use the economically efficient method.

Firms coordinate economic activity when they can perform a task more efficiently than markets. In such a situation, it is profitable to set up a firm. If markets can perform a task more efficiently than a firm, people will use markets, and any attempt to set up a firm to replace such market coordination will be doomed to failure.

Why Firms?

There are four key reasons why, in many instances, firms are more efficient than markets as coordinators of economic activity. Firms achieve:

1 Lower transactions costs.

2 Economies of scale.

3 Economies of scope.

4 Economies of team production.

Transactions Costs

The idea that firms exist because there are activities in which they are more efficient than markets was first suggested by a University of Chicago economist and Nobel Laureate, Ronald Coase.[1] Coase focused on the firm's ability to reduce or eliminate transactions costs. **Transactions costs** are the costs arising from finding someone with whom to do business, of reaching an agreement about the price and other aspects of the exchange, and of ensuring that the terms of the agreement are fulfilled. *Market* transactions require buyers and sellers to get together and to negotiate the terms and conditions of their trading. Sometimes lawyers have to be hired to draw up contracts. A broken contract leads to still more expenses. A *firm* can lower such transactions costs by reducing the number of individual transactions undertaken.

Consider, for example, two ways of getting your creaking car fixed.

1 *Firm coordination.* You take the car to the garage. Parts and tools as well as the mechanic's time are coordinated by the garage owner and your car gets fixed. You pay one bill for the entire job.

2 *Market coordination.* You hire a mechanic who diagnoses the problems and makes a list of the parts and tools needed to fix them. You buy the parts from the local breaker's yard and rent the tools from ABC Rentals. You hire the mechanic again to fix the problems. You return the tools and pay your bills – wages to the mechanic, rental to ABC and the cost of the parts used to the breaker.

What determines the method that you use? The answer is cost. Taking account of the opportunity cost of your own time as well as the costs of the other inputs that you'd have to buy, you will use the method that costs least. In other words, you will use the economically efficient method.

The first method requires that you undertake only one transaction with one firm. It's true that the firm has to undertake several transactions – hiring the labour and buying the parts and tools required to do the job. But the firm doesn't have to undertake those transactions simply to fix your car. One set of

---

[1] Ronald H. Coase 'The Nature of the Firm', *Economica*, (November 1937) 386–405.

such transactions enables the firm to fix hundreds of cars. Thus there is an enormous reduction in the number of individual transactions that take place if people get their cars fixed at the garage rather than going through an elaborate sequence of market transactions.

Economies of Scale

When the cost of producing a unit of a good falls as its output rate increases, **economies of scale** exist. Many industries experience economies of scale; car manufacturing is an example. One firm can produce 4 million cars a year at a lower cost per car than 200 firms each producing 20,000 cars a year. Economies of scale arise from specialization and the division of labour that can be reaped more effectively by firm coordination rather than market coordination.

Economies of Scope

Economies which are derived from the size of the firm rather than the amount of plant or machinery available are called **economies of scope**. Today's large companies face high costs when developing, financing and marketing a new good – costs which must be recouped from sales of the new product. The bigger a firm's potential volume of sales, the less each unit sold of a new good must contribute to its development costs. So the price of a new good produced by a large firm, which already has a large-scale sales-force and retail outlets, will be less than a similar product launched by a smaller firm.

Economies of Team Production

A production process in which a group of individuals each specializes in mutually supportive tasks is *team production*. Sport provides the best example of team activity. Some team members specialize in striking and some in defending, some in speed and some in strength. The production of goods and services offers many examples of team activity. For example, production lines in car plants and TV manufacturing plants work most efficiently when individual activity is organized in teams, each specializing in a small task. You can also think of an entire firm as being a team. The team has buyers of raw materials and other inputs, production workers and sales persons. There are even specialists within these various groups. Each individual member of the team specializes, but the value of the output of the team and the profit that it earns depend on the coordinated activities of all the team's members. The idea that firms arise as a consequence of the economies of team production was first suggested by Armen Alchian and Harold Demsetz of the University of California at Los Angeles.[2]

Because firms can economize on transactions costs, reap economies of scale and scope, and organize efficient team production, it is firms rather than markets that coordinate most of our economic activity. Reductions in transactions costs explain why Ford, which started hand-building cars in the early 1900s, developed into a company with functional divisions based on production line technology in the 1940s. But there are limits to the economic efficiency of firms. If a firm becomes too big or too diversified in the things that it seeks to do, the cost of management and monitoring per unit of output begins to rise and, at some point, the market becomes more efficient at coordinating the use of resources. This explains why Ford restructured into a global transnational company, effectively creating a set of smaller, more independent national companies. It also explains why companies such as Hanson Trust target segments of large, ailing transnationals to run as separate, more profitable companies.

Sometimes firms enter into long-term relationships with each other that effectively cut out ordinary market transactions and make it difficult to see where one firm ends and another begins. For example, when Rover became part of BMW, it had a long-term relationship with Honda as a supplier of gearboxes. These long-term relationships are also common between supermarkets and manufacturers. Famous cereal manufacturers produce supermarket own-label brands as well as their own more established brands.

Review Quiz

- ◆ Describe the main ways in which economic activity can be coordinated.
- ◆ What determines whether a firm or markets coordinate production?
- ◆ What are the main reasons why firms can often coordinate production at lower cost than markets?

---

[2] Armen Alchian and Harold Demsetz, 'Production, Information Costs, and Economic Organization', *American Economic Review* (December 1972) 57, 5, 777–795.

In this chapter you have begun your study of the economic analysis of firms and markets. You can read about the success of Europe's biggest software company in the Business Case Study on pp. 194–195. You will continue your study of firms and their decisions in the next four chapters. Chapter 10 focuses on the relationship between cost and output that arises in all firms. Chapters 11 to 13 examine the problems that are particular to firms operating in the four main types of market structure – perfect competition, monopoly, monopolistic competition and oligopoly.

Summary

Key Points

The Firm and its Economic Problem (pp. 175–177)

- Firms hire and organize factors of production to produce and sell goods and services.
- Firms seek to maximize economic profit, which is total revenue minus opportunity cost.
- Technology, information and markets limit a firm's profit.

Technology and Economic Efficiency (pp. 178–179)

- A method of production is technologically efficient when to produce a given output, it is not possible to increase output without using more inputs.
- A method of production is economically efficient when the cost of producing a given output is as low as possible.

Information and Organizations (pp. 179–183)

- Firms use a combination of command systems and incentive systems to organize production.
- Faced with incomplete information and uncertainty, firms induce employees to work towards the firm's goals.
- Proprietorships, partnerships and corporations use ownership, incentives and long-term contracts to cope with the principal–agent problem.

Markets and the Competitive Environment (pp. 183–187)

- Perfect competition occurs when there are many buyers and sellers of an identical product and when new firms can easily enter a market.

- Monopolistic competition occurs when a large number of firms compete with each other by making slightly different products.
- Oligopoly is a situation in which a small number of producers compete with each other.
- Monopoly is a firm that produces a good or service for which there are no close substitutes and can protect its market from the entry of competitors by a barrier to entry.

Firms and Markets (pp. 188–190)

- Firms coordinate economic activities when they can achieve lower costs than coordination through markets.
- Firms economize on transactions costs and achieve the benefits of economies of scale, economies of scope and of team production.

Key Figure and Tables

Key Terms

Problems

•1 One year ago, Jack and Jill set up a vinegar bottling firm (called JJVB). Use the following information to calculate JJVB's explicit costs and implicit costs during its first year of operation:

  a Jack and Jill put €50,000 of their own money into the firm.

  b They bought equipment for €30,000.

  c They hired one employee to help them for an annual wage of €20,000.

  d Jack gave up his previous job, at which he earned €30,000, and spent all his time working for JJVB.

  e Jill kept her old job, which paid €30 an hour, but gave up 10 hours of leisure each week (for 50 weeks) to work for JJVB.

  f JJVB bought €10,000 of goods and services from other firms.

  g The market value of the equipment at the end of the year was €28,000.

2 One year ago, Ms Moffat and Mr Spieder opened a cheese firm (called MSCF). Use the following information to calculate MSCF's explicit costs and implicit costs during its first year of operation:

  a Moffat and Spieder put €70,000 of their own money into the firm.

  b They bought equipment for €40,000.

  c They hired one employee to help them for an annual wage of €18,000.

  d Moffat gave up her previous job, at which she earned €22,000, and spent all her time working for MSCF.

  e Spieder kept his old job, which paid €20 an hour, but gave up 20 hours of leisure each week (for 50 weeks) to work for MSCF.

  f MSCF bought €5,000 of goods from other firms.

  g The market value of the equipment at the end of the year was €37,000.

•3 Four ways of completing a tax return are: a personal computer (PC), a pocket calculator, a pocket calculator with pencil and paper, a pencil and paper. With a PC, the job takes an hour; with a pocket calculator, it takes 12 hours; with a pocket calculator and pencil and paper, it takes 12 hours; and with a pencil and paper, it takes 16 hours. The PC and its software cost €1,000, the pocket calculator costs €10, and the pencil and paper cost €1.

  a Which, if any, of the methods is technologically efficient?

  b Which method is economically efficient if the wage rate is

    i €5 an hour?

    ii €50 an hour?

    iii €500 an hour?

4 Sue can do her accounting assignment using a personal computer (PC); a pocket calculator; a pocket calculator and a pencil and paper; or a pencil and paper. With a PC, Sue completes the job in half an hour; with a pocket calculator, it takes 4 hours; with a pocket calculator and with a pencil and paper, it takes 5 hours; and with a pencil and paper, it takes 14 hours. The PC and its software cost €2,000, the pocket calculator costs €15, and the pencil and paper cost €3.

  a Which, if any, of the methods is technologically efficient?

  b Which method is economically efficient if Sue's wage rate is

    i €10 an hour?

    ii €20 an hour?

    iii €50 an hour?

◦5 Alternative ways of laundering 100 shirts are:

Method	Labour (hours)	Capital (machines)
a	1	10
b	5	8
c	20	4
d	50	1

a Which methods are technologically efficient?

b Which method is economically efficient if:

   i The wage rate is €1 an hour and the rental cost of a machine is €100 an hour?

   ii The wage rate is €5 an hour and the rental cost of a machine is €50 an hour?

   iii The wage rate is €50 an hour and the rental cost of a machine is €5 an hour?

6 Alternative ways of making 100 shirts a day are:

Method	Labour (hours)	Capital (machines)
a	10	50
b	20	40
c	50	20
d	100	10

a Which methods are technologically efficient?

b Which method is economically efficient if the hourly wage rate and rental rate are:

   i Wage rate €1, rental rate €100?

   ii Wage rate €5, rental rate €50?

   iii Wage rate €50, rental rate €5?

◦7 Sales of the firms in the tattoo industry are:

Firm	Sales (euros)
Bright Spots	450
Freckles	325
Love Galore	250
Native Birds	200
Tiny Tattoo	200
Other 15 firms	800

a Calculate the four-firm concentration ratio.

b What is the structure of the tattoo industry?

8 Sales of the firms in the pet food industry are:

Firm	Sales (thousands of euros)
Small Collar Co.	50
Big Collar Co.	50
Shiny Coat Co.	75
Friendly Pet Co.	60
Nature's Way Co.	65
Other 7 firms	350

a Calculate the five-firm concentration ratio.

b What is the structure of the industry?

Critical Thinking

1 Study the business case study about the European software company, SAP on pp. 194–195 and then:

  a Describe the economic problem that the firm faced in 1998 and 1999.

  b Use the links on the Parkin, Powell and Matthews website to find information about SAP and its main competitors. What do you think the economic problems of these competitors are?

  c Use the links on the Parkin, Powell and Matthews website to find information about SAP's performance in the third quarter of 2001. Why is SAP suggesting that it must cut labour costs in the USA? What does it hope to achieve by doing this?

  d Compare and contrast how SAP achieves technological efficiency and economic efficiency.

  e SAP and its competitors provide software services which help other companies to reduce their costs and become more efficient. Why might the demand for SAP's services buck the trend when the economy slows down?

2 Use the links on the Parkin, Powell and Matthews website to obtain information about the car industry.

  a What are the main economic problems faced by car producers?

  b Why are car producers merging?

3 Use the links on the Parkin, Powell and Matthews website to obtain information about the steel industry.

  a What are the main economic problems faced by steel producers?

  b Is the number of steel producers likely to increase or decrease during the next few years? Why?

Constraints on Profit

Europe's biggest software company: SAP

The Company

SAP, a German company, is Europe's software giant. It became a public traded company in 1988 and now employs over 27,000 people in more than 50 countries. It runs 36,000 installations of its software serving 10 million users in 13,500 organizations across 120 organizations. Its customers include other corporate giants such as Sony and Microsoft.

The Products

SAP specializes in writing and installing business software, particularly collaborative e-business systems for firms in all types of industries and markets. These systems help companies to run their back-office functions such as distribution, accounting and manufacturing. Much of the companies growth in the late 1990s was due to its provision of millennium bug products and services.

Competition and Market Constraints

SAP's main rivals are US companies like Siebel Systems, Oracle, and PeopleSoft. Companies in this sector have experienced a slowdown in sales and profits in 2001 because of the economic slowdown in the US and limited growth potential in computer hardware.

Information Constraints

SAP was founded in 1972 by five former IBM systems engineers. As it has grown it has adopted a standard corporate structure. Its CEO is Mr Hasso Platne, but three of its original founders still control 40 per cent of the shares.

Technology Constraints

In the late 1990s, SAP realized that its profit was limited by traditional software delivery systems. In 1999, the company launched a new website called mySAP.com. The site supports all types of business software and allows employees, customers and business partners to work together more efficiently, by increasing information flows, raising supply chain efficiency and improving customer-to-business relationships. SAP is also developing internet partnerships with related organizations. In June 2001, SAP linked up with IBM and Compaq to gain access to new customers like Shell Oil.

Economic Analysis

- SAP is in business to maximize profit. It faces all the economic problems described in this chapter.

- SAP operates in a global oligopoly market where a few large firms compete world-wide for customers and where products and technologies change quickly. Its profits are constrained by technology, information and market constraints.

- The table shows how SAP performed relative to its competitors between 1999 and 2000. SAP is the middle-sized organization in terms of number of employees.

- The profit and sales growth figures show SAP failed to keep pace with its competitors which had begun to develop internet services. SAP was constrained by its existing technology. It responded by launching its internet services in 1999 as part of its strategy to raise efficiency by capturing economies of scale and scope.

- Business software can be provided at the lowest possible cost if some firms like Microsoft specialize in design and others, like SAP, specialize in software management. SAP's internet strategy will help it to specialize in management. Its new partnerships will cut transactions costs and capture economies of team production.

- Because SAP's customers are other businesses, sales are constrained by market conditions. The slowdown in the US economy in 2001 decreased demand for hardware and related software. However, in the first three months of 2001, SAP doubled its profits and its sales rose by 29 per cent while its competitors declared warnings of a fall in profits due to poor market conditions. Its new strategy appears to be working.

- The figure shows the difference in the control of the main company founders by 2000. The original founders have maintained greater control in SAP than its competitors which might reduce principal–agent problems in senior management, creating stronger incentives.

Company performance 1999–2000

	SAP	Siebel	Oracle
Employment	24,480	7,389	42,927
(1-year growth)	13%	131%	4%
Profit ($ millions)	596	222	2,561
(1-year growth)	2%	82%	59%
Sales ($ millions)	5,881	1,795	10,860
(1-year growth)	14%	127%	7%

Source: http://cobrands.hoovers.com/

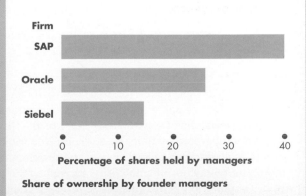

Share of ownership by founder managers

CHAPTER 10

Output and Costs

After studying this chapter you will be able to:

♦ Distinguish between the short run and the long run

♦ Explain the relationship between a firm's output and its costs in the short run

♦ Derive and explain a firm's short-run cost curves

♦ Explain the relationship between a firm's output and costs in the long run

♦ Derive and explain a firm's long-run average cost curve

Survival of the Fittest

Large size does not guarantee survival in business. While some of Europe's large firms – such as Shell and BMW – have been operating for many years, most of their contemporaries from 30 years ago have disappeared. But remaining small does not guarantee survival either. Every year, millions of small businesses close down. Phone a random selection of restaurants and plumbers from last year's Yellow Pages and see how many have vanished. So what does a firm have to do to be one of the survivors? ♦ Firms differ in lots of ways – from the local corner shop to multinational giants producing high-tech goods. But regardless of their size or what they produce, all firms must decide how much to produce and how to produce it. How do firms make these decisions? ♦ Most European car makers can produce far more cars than they can sell. Europe's Airlines have hangers full of mothballed planes. Why do these firms have expensive equipment lying around that isn't fully used? Many electrical suppliers in the United Kingdom don't have enough production equipment on hand to meet demand on the coldest and hottest days and have to buy power from the central pool. Why don't such firms have a bigger production plant so that they can supply the market themselves?

♦ ♦ ♦ ♦ We are going to answer these questions in this chapter. To do so, we are going to model the economic decisions of a small, imaginary firm – Neat Knits Ltd, a producer of knitted jumpers. The firm is owned and operated by Sam. By studying Neat Knits' economic problems and the way Sam solves them, we will be able to get a clear view of the problems that face all firms. We will be able to understand and predict the behaviour of small firms as well as the giants. But you'll also study the problems of Europe's Airline industry in the Business Case Study on page pp. 214–215.

Time Frames for Decisions

People who operate firms make many decisions. All of these decisions are aimed at one overriding objective: maximum attainable profit. But the decisions are not all equally critical. Some of the decisions are big ones. Once made, they are costly (or impossible) to reverse. If such a decision turns out to be incorrect, it might lead to the failure of the firm. Some of the decisions are small ones. They are easily changed. If one of these decisions turns out to be incorrect, the firm can change its actions and survive.

The biggest decision that any firm makes is what industry to enter. For most entrepreneurs, their background knowledge and interests drive this decision. But the decision also depends on profit prospects. No one sets up a firm without believing it will be profitable. And profit depends on total revenue and opportunity cost (see Chapter 9, pp. 183–186).

The firm that we'll study has already chosen the industry in which to operate. It has also chosen its most effective method of organization. But it has not decided the quantity to produce, the quantities of resources to hire, or the price at which to sell its output.

Decisions about the quantity to produce and the price to charge depend on the type of market in which the firm operates. Perfect competition, monopolistic competition, oligopoly and monopoly all confront the firm with their own special problems.

But decisions about how to produce a given output do not depend on the type of market in which the firm operates. These decisions are similar for *all* types of firms in *all* types of markets.

The actions that a firm can take to influence the relationship between output and cost depend on how soon the firm wants to act. A firm that plans to change its output rate tomorrow has fewer options than one that plans to change its output rate six months from now.

To study the relationship between a firm's output decision and its costs, we distinguish two decision time frames:

◆ The short run.
◆ The long run.

The Short Run

The **short run** is a time frame in which the quantities of some resources are fixed. For most firms, the fixed resources are the firm's technology, buildings and capital. The management organization is also fixed in the short run. We call the collection of fixed resources the firm's *plant*. So in the short run, a firm's plant is fixed.

For our firm, Neat Knits, the fixed plant is its factory building and its knitting machines. For an electric power utility, the fixed plant is its buildings, generators, computers and control systems. For an airport, the fixed plant is the runways, terminal buildings and traffic control facilities.

To increase output in the short run, a firm must increase the quantity of variable inputs it uses. Labour is usually the variable input. So to produce more output, the owner of Neat Knits, Sam, must hire more labour and operate its knitting machines for more hours per day. Similarly, an electric power utility must hire more labour and operate its generators for more hours per day. An airport must hire more labour and operate its runways, terminals and traffic control facilities for more hours per day.

Short-run decisions are easily reversed. The firm can increase or decrease output in the short run by increasing or decreasing the labour hours it hires.

The Long Run

The **long run** is a time frame in which the quantities of *all* resources can be varied. That is, the long run is a period in which the firm can change its *plant*.

To increase output in the long run, a firm is able to choose whether to change its plant as well as whether to increase the quantity of labour it hires. The owner of Neat Knits can decide whether to install some additional knitting machines, use a new type of machine, reorganize its management, or hire more labour. An electric power utility can decide whether to install more generators. And an airport can decide whether to build more runways, terminals, and traffic-control facilities.

Long-run decisions are *not* easily reversed. Once a plant decision is made, the firm must live with it for some time. To emphasize this fact, we call the *past* cost of buying a new plant a **sunk cost**. A sunk cost is irrelevant to the firm's decisions. The only costs that influence its decisions are the short-run cost of changing its labour inputs and the long-run cost of changing its plant.

We're going to study costs in the short run and the long run. We begin with the short run and describe the technology constraint the firm faces.

Short-run Technology Constraint

To increase output in the short run, a firm must increase the quantity of a variable input. For Neat Knits the variable input is labour. We describe the relationship between output and the quantity of labour employed by using three related concepts:

1 Total product.

2 Marginal product.

3 Average product.

These product concepts can be illustrated either by product schedules or by product curves. We'll look first at the product schedules.

Product Schedules

Table 10.1 shows some data that describe Neat Knits' total product, marginal product and average product. The numbers tell us how Neat Knits' production

Table 10.1 Total Product, Marginal Product and Average Product

	Labour (workers per day)	Total product (jumpers per day)	Marginal product (jumpers per day)	Average product (jumpers per worker)
a	0	0		
			4	
b	1	4		4.00
			6	
c	2	10		5.00
			3	
d	3	13		4.33
			2	
e	4	15		3.75
			1	
f	5	16		3.20

Total product is the total amount produced. Marginal product is the change in total product resulting from a 1-unit increase in labour. For example, when labour increases from 2 to 3 workers a day (row *c* to row *d*), total product increases from 10 to 13 jumpers a day. (Marginal product is shown between the rows because it is the result of a change in the quantity of labour.) The marginal product of going from 2 to 3 workers is 3 jumpers. Average product of an input is total product divided by the quantity of an input employed. For example, 3 workers produce 13 jumpers a day, so the average product of 3 workers is 4.33 jumpers per worker.

changes as more workers are employed, for a fixed level of plant and machines. They also tell us about the productivity of Neat Knits' labour force.

Look first at the columns headed 'Labour' and 'Total Product'. **Total product** is the total output produced with a given quantity of labour. The table shows how total product increases as Neat Knits employs more labour. For example, when Sam employs 1 worker, total product is 4 jumpers a day and when he employs 2 workers, total product is 10 jumpers a day. Each increase in employment brings an increase in total product.

Marginal product tells us how much total product increases when employment increases by one unit. The **marginal product** of labour is the change in total product resulting from a one-unit increase in the quantity of labour employed. It is calculated by dividing the change in total product by the change in labour. For example, when the quantity of labour increases from 2 to 3 workers, total product increases from 10 to 13 jumpers. The change in total product – 3 jumpers – is divided by the change in labour – 1 worker – so the marginal product of the third worker is 3 jumpers.

The average product shows how productive workers are on the average. The **average product** of labour is equal to total product divided by the quantity of labour employed. For example, in Table 10.1, 3 workers can knit 13 jumpers a day, so the average product of labour is 13 divided by 3, which is 4.33 jumpers per worker.

If you look closely at the numbers in Table 10.1, you can see some patterns. For example, as employment increases, marginal product at first increases and then begins to decrease. For example, marginal product increases from 4 jumpers a day for the first worker to 6 jumpers a day for the second worker and then decreases to 3 jumpers a day for the third worker. Average product also at first increases and then decreases. The relationships between these concepts of product and the number of workers employed can be seen more clearly by looking at the product curves.

Product Curves

The product curves are graphs of the relationships between employment and the three product concepts you've just studied. They show how total product, marginal product, and average product change as employment changes. They also show the relationships among the three concepts. Let's look at the product curves.

Figure 10.1

Total Product Curve

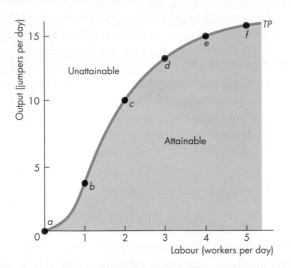

The total product curve (*TP*), based on the data in Table 10.1, shows how many jumpers Neat Knits can produce when it uses 1 knitting machine and different amounts of labour. For example, using 1 knitting machine, 2 workers can produce 10 jumpers a day (row *c*). Points *a* to *f* on the curve correspond to the rows of Table 10.1. The total product curve separates the attainable output from the unattainable output.

Total Product Curve

Figure 10.1 shows Neat Knits' total product curve, *TP*. As employment increases, so does the number of jumpers knitted. Points *a* to *f* on the curve correspond to the same rows in Table 10.1.

The total product curve is similar to the *production possibility frontier* (explained in Chapter 2, p. 22). It separates the attainable output levels from those that are unattainable. All the points that lie above the curve are unattainable. Points that lie below the curve, in the orange area, are attainable. But they are inefficient – they use more labour than is necessary to produce a given output. Only the points *on* the total product curve are technologically efficient.

Look carefully at the shape of the total product curve. As employment increases from zero to 1 worker per day, the curve becomes steeper. Then, as employment continues to increase to 3, 4, and 5 workers per day, the curve becomes less steep. The steeper the slope of the total product curve, the greater is marginal product, as you are about to see.

Marginal Product Curve

Figure 10.2 shows Neat Knits' marginal product of labour with 1 machine. Part (a) reproduces the total product curve from Figure 10.1. Part (b) shows the marginal product curve, *MP*.

In part (a), the height of the orange bars illustrate the marginal product of labour. Marginal product is also measured by the slope of the total product curve. Recall that the slope of a curve is the change in the value of the variable measured on the *y*-axis – output – divided by the change in the variable measured on the *x*-axis – labour input – as we move along the curve. A 1-unit increase in labour input, from 2 to 3 workers, increases output from 10 to 13 jumpers, so the slope from point *c* to point *d* is 3, the same as the marginal product that we've just calculated.

We've calculated the marginal product of labour for a series of unit increases in the amount of labour. But labour is divisible into smaller units than one person. It is divisible into hours and even minutes. By varying the amount of labour in the smallest imaginable units, we can draw the marginal product curve shown in Figure 10.2(b). The *height* of this curve measures the *slope* of the total product curve at a point. The total product curve in part (a) shows that an increase in employment from 2 to 3 workers increases output from 10 to 13 jumpers (an increase of 3). The increase in output of 3 jumpers appears on the vertical axis of part (b) as the marginal product of going from 2 to 3 workers. We plot that marginal product at the midpoint between 2 and 3 workers. Notice that marginal product shown in Figure 10.2(b) reaches a peak at 1 unit of labour and at that point marginal product is more than 6. The peak occurs at 1 unit of labour because the total product curve is steepest at 1 unit of labour.

The total, marginal and average product curves are different for different firms and different types of goods. BMW's product curves are different from those of your local supermarket, which in turn are different from those of Sam's jumper factory. But the shapes of the product curves are similar, because almost every production process incorporates two features:

1 Increasing marginal returns initially.

2 Diminishing marginal returns eventually.

Increasing Marginal Returns

Increasing marginal returns occur when the marginal product of an additional worker exceeds the marginal product of the previous worker.

Figure 10.2

Marginal Product

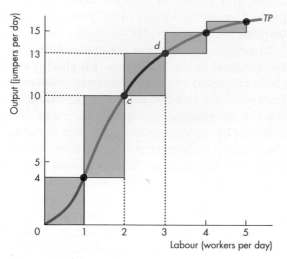

(a) Total product

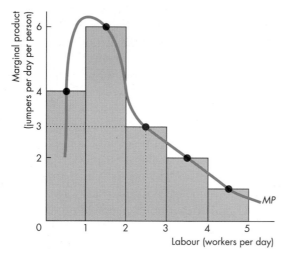

(b) Marginal product

Marginal product is illustrated in both parts of the figure by the orange bars. The height of each bar indicates the size of the marginal product. For example, when labour increases from 2 to 3, marginal product is the orange bar whose height is 3 jumpers. (Marginal product is shown midway between the labour inputs to emphasize that it is the result of *changing* inputs – moving from one level to the next.) The steeper the slope of the total product curve (*TP*) in part (a), the larger is marginal product (*MP*) in part (b). Marginal product increases to a maximum (when 1 worker is employed in this example) and then declines – diminishing marginal product.

If Sam employs just one worker at Neat Knits, that person has to learn all the different aspects of jumper production, running the knitting machines, fixing breakdowns, packaging and mailing jumpers, buying and checking the type and colour of the wool. All of these tasks have to be done by that one person.

If Sam employs a second person, the two workers can specialize in different parts of the production process. As a result, two workers produce more than twice as much as one. The marginal product of the second worker is greater than the marginal product of the first worker. Marginal returns are increasing.

Diminishing Marginal Returns

Most product processes experience increasing marginal returns initially. But all production processes eventually reach a point of diminishing marginal returns. **Diminishing marginal returns** occur when the marginal product of an additional worker is less than the marginal product of the previous worker.

Diminishing marginal returns arise from the fact that more and more workers are using the same machinery in the same plant. As more workers are added, there is less and less for the additional workers to do that is productive. For example, if Sam employs a third worker, output increases but not by as much as it did when he added the second worker. In this case, after two workers are employed, all the gains from specialization and the division of labour have been exhausted. By employing a third worker, the factory produces more jumpers, but the equipment is being operated closer to its limits. There are even times when the third worker has nothing to do because the plant is running without the need for further attention. Adding yet more and more workers continues to increase output but by successively smaller amounts. Marginal returns are diminishing. This phenomenon is such a pervasive one that it is called 'the law of diminishing returns'. The **law of diminishing returns** states that:

> As a firm uses more of a variable input, with a given quantity of fixed inputs, the marginal product of the variable input eventually diminishes.

You will be using the concept of diminishing marginal returns again when you study a firm's costs. Before we do that, we need to look at average product of labour and average product curve.

Figure 10.3

Average Product

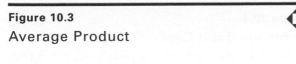
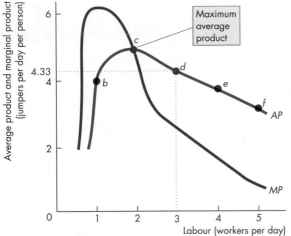

The figure shows the average product of labour, *AP*, and the marginal product of labour, *MP*, and the relationship between the shape of the two curves. With 1 worker per day, marginal product exceeds average product, so average product is increasing. With 2 workers per day, marginal product equals average product, so average product is at its maximum. With more than 2 workers per day, marginal product is less than average product, so average product is decreasing.

Average Product Curve

Figure 10.3 illustrates Neat Knits' average product of labour, *AP*. It also shows the relationship between the average product and marginal product. Points *b* to *f* on the average product curve are plotted from the same rows in Table 10.1. Average product increases from 1 to 2 workers (its maximum value is at point *c*) but then decreases as yet more workers are employed. Notice that average product is largest when average product and marginal product are equal. That is, the marginal product curve cuts the average product curve at the point of maximum average product. For employment levels at which the marginal product exceeds average product, average product is increasing. For employment levels at which marginal product is less than average product, average product is decreasing.

The relationships between the average and marginal product curves that you've just seen are a general feature of the relationship between the average and marginal values of any variable. Let's look at a familiar example.

Marginal Marks and Average Marks

Assume Sam is also a part-time business student who takes one course per semester. Think about the relationship between Sam's average mark and his marginal marks over 5 semesters. In the first semester, Sam gains a mark of 50 per cent in his statistics exam. This mark is his marginal mark. It is also his average mark as it is the first exam taken. Sam takes French in the second semester and gets 60 per cent in the exam. The French exam mark is now his marginal mark, but his average mark rises to 55 per cent, the average of 50 and 60. His average mark rises because his marginal mark is greater than his previous average mark – it pulls his average up. In the third semester, Sam takes economics, his best subject. His marginal mark is 70 per cent, which is higher than his previous average. His marginal mark pulls his average up, this time to 60 per cent, the average of 50, 60 and 70. In the fourth semester, Sam takes accounting. Unfortunately, he achieves only 60 per cent in the exam. This time, his marginal mark is equal to his previous average – so his average does not change. In the fifth semester, Sam takes management but achieves only 50 per cent in the exam. This time his marginal mark is below his previous average, and drags his average down to 55 per cent, the average of 50, 60, 70, 60, and 50 per cent.

This example of an everyday relationship between marginal and average values agrees with the relationship between marginal and average product that we have just discovered. Sam's average mark increases when the mark on the last course taken, the marginal mark, exceeds his previous average. The average mark falls when the mark on the marginal course is below his previous average. His average mark is constant (it neither increases nor decreases) when the mark for the marginal course equals his previous average.

Review Quiz

◆ Explain how the marginal product of labour and the average product of labour change as the quantity of labour employed increases (a) initially and (b) eventually.

◆ What is the law of diminishing marginal returns? Why does marginal product eventually diminish?

◆ Explain the relationship between marginal product and average product. How does average product change when (a) marginal product exceeds average product and (b) when average product exceeds marginal product.

Why should Sam care about Neat Knits' product curves? He cares because they influence costs. Let's look at Neat Knit's costs.

Short-run Cost

To produce more output in the short run, a firm must employ more labour, which means it must increase its costs. We describe the relationship between output and costs by using three concepts:

1 Total Cost.
2 Marginal Cost.
3 Average Cost.

Total Cost

A firm's **total cost** *(TC)* is the cost of the productive resources it uses. Total cost includes the cost of land, capital and labour. It also includes the cost of entrepreurship, which is normal profit (see Chapter 9 p. 176). Total cost is divided into two categories: total fixed cost and total variable cost.

Total fixed cost *(TFC)* is the cost of the firm's fixed inputs. The quantity of a fixed cost like site rent does not change as output changes, and so total fixed costs do not change with output.

Total variable cost *(TVC)* is the cost of the firm's variable inputs. To change its output, a firm must vary its variable inputs, like labour, and so total variable costs do change with output.

Total cost is the sum of total fixed costs and total variable cost. That is:

$$TC = TFC + TVC$$

The table in Figure 10.4 shows Neat Knits' total costs in the short run. Neat Knit's one knitting machine, TFC, costs £25 per day. To produce more jumpers Sam must employ more labour, which costs £25 per day, so TVC is equal to the total wage bill. For example, if Neat Knits employs 3 workers, its total variable cost is (3 × £25), which equals £75. Total cost is the sum of total fixed cost and total variable cost. For example, when Neat Knits employs 3 workers, its total cost is £100 – total fixed cost of £25 plus total variable cost of £75.

Figure 10.4 graphs Neat Knits' short-run total cost curves. These curves graph total cost against total product. The green total fixed cost curve (TFC) is hor-

Figure 10.4

Short-run Total Cost

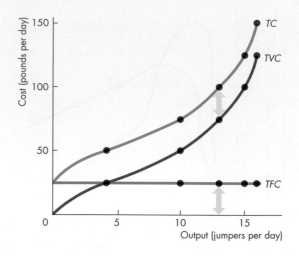

Labour (workers per day)	Output (jumpers per day)	Total fixed cost (*TFC*)	Total variable cost (*TVC*)	Total cost (*TC*)
		(pounds per day)		
0	0	25	0	25
1	4	25	25	50
2	10	25	50	75
3	13	25	75	100
4	15	25	100	125
5	16	25	125	150

Sam rents a knitting machine for £25 a day. This amount is Neat Knits' total fixed cost. Sam hires workers at a wage rate of £25 a day, and this cost is Neat Knits' total variable cost. For example, if Sam employs 3 workers, its total variable cost is (3 × £25), which equals £75. Total cost is the sum of total fixed cost and total variable cost. For example, when Sam employs 3 workers, its total cost is £100 – total fixed cost of £25 plus total variable cost of £75. The graph shows Neat Knits' total cost curves. Total fixed cost (*TFC*) is constant – it graphs as a horizontal line – and total variable cost (*TVC*) increases as output increases. Total cost (*TC*) also increases as output increases. The vertical distance between the total cost curve and the total variable cost curve is total fixed cost, as illustrated by the two arrows' points.

izontal because total fixed cost does not change with output. It is horizontal at £25. The purple total variable cost and the blue total cost curve both increase with output. The vertical distance between TVC and TC curve is shown by the arrows and is a constant £25.

Now we can look at Neat Knits' marginal cost.

Marginal Cost

In Figure 10.4, total variable cost and total cost increase at a decreasing rate at small levels of output and begin to increase at an increasing rate as output increases. To understand these patterns in the changes in total cost, we need to use the concept of *marginal cost*.

A firm's **marginal cost** is the change in total cost resulting from a one-unit increase in output. Marginal cost (MC) is calculated as the change in total cost (ΔTC) divided by the change in output (ΔQ). That is:

$$MC = \frac{\Delta TC}{\Delta Q}$$

The table in Figure 10.5 shows this calculation. When, for example, output increases from 10 jumpers to 13 jumpers, total cost increases from £75 to £100. The change in output is 3 jumpers, and the change in total cost is £25. The marginal cost of one of those 3 jumpers is (£25 ÷ 3), which equals £8.33.

Figure 10.5 graphs the marginal cost data in the table as the red marginal cost curve, *MC*. This curve is U-shaped because, when Sam hires a second worker, marginal cost decreases, but when he hires a third, a fourth, and a fifth worker, marginal cost successively increases.

Marginal cost decreases at low outputs because of economies from greater specialization. It eventually increases because of *the law of diminishing returns*. The law of diminishing returns means that each additional worker produces a successively smaller addition to output. So to get an additional unit of output, ever more workers are required. Because more workers are required to produce one additional unit of output, the cost of the additional output – marginal cost – must eventually increase.

Marginal cost tells us how total cost changes as output changes. The final cost concept tells us what it costs, on the average, to produce a unit of output. Let's now look at Neat Knits' average costs.

Average Cost

Average cost is the cost per unit of output. There are three average costs:

1 Average fixed cost.

2 Average variable cost.

3 Average total cost.

Figure 10.5

Short-run Marginal Cost and Average Cost

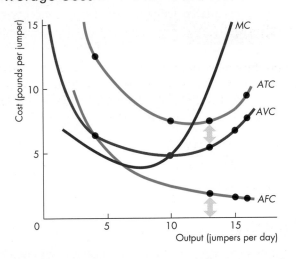

Labour (workers per day)	Output (jumpers per day)	Total cost (*TC*)	Marginal cost (*MC*)	Average fixed cost (*AFC*)	Average variable cost (*AVC*)	Average total cost (*ATC*)
				(pounds per day)		
0	0	25				
			6.25			
1	4	50		6.25	6.25	12.50
			4.17			
2	10	75		2.50	5.00	7.50
			8.33			
3	13	100		1.92	5.77	7.69
			12.50			
4	15	125		1.67	6.00	8.33
			25.00			
5	16	150		1.56	7.81	9.38

Marginal cost is calculated as the change in total cost divided by the change in output. When output increases from 4 to 10, an increase of 6, total cost increases by £25 and marginal cost is £25 ÷ 6, which equals £4.17. Each average cost concept is calculated by dividing the related total cost by output. When 10 jumpers are produced, *AFC* is £2.50 (£25 ÷ 10), *AVC* is £5 (£50 ÷ 10), and *ATC* is £7.50 (£75 ÷ 10).

The figure shows the marginal cost curve and the average cost curves. The marginal cost curve (*MC*) is U-shaped and intersects the average variable cost curve and the average total cost curve at their minimum points. Average fixed cost (*AFC*) decreases as output increases. The average total cost curve (*ATC*) and average variable cost curve (*AVC*) are U-shaped. The vertical distance between these two curves is equal to average fixed cost, as illustrated by the two arrows.

Average fixed cost (*AFC*) is total fixed cost per unit of output. **Average variable cost** (*AVC*) is total variable cost per unit of output. **Average total cost** (*ATC*) is total cost per unit of output. The average cost concepts are calculated from the total cost concepts as follows:

$$TC = TFC + TVC$$

Divide each total cost term by the quantity produced, *Q*, to give

$$\frac{TC}{Q} = \frac{TFC}{Q} + \frac{TVC}{Q}$$

or

$$ATC = AFC + AVC$$

The table in Figure 10.5 shows the calculation of average total costs. For example, when output is 10 jumpers, average fixed cost is (£25 ÷ 10), which equals £2.50, average variable cost is (£50 ÷ 10), which equals £5.00, and average total cost is (£75 ÷ 10), which equals £7.50. Note average total cost is equal to average fixed cost (£2.50) plus average variable cost (£5.00).

Figure 10.5 shows the average cost curves. The green average fixed cost curve (*AFC*) slopes downward. As output increases, the same constant fixed cost is spread over a larger output. The blue average total cost curve (*ATC*) and the purple average variable cost curve (*AVC*) are U-shaped. The vertical distance between the average total cost and average variable cost curves is equal to average fixed cost – as indicated by the arrows. That distance shrinks as output increases because average fixed cost declines with increasing output.

The red marginal cost curve (*MC*) intersects the average variable and average total cost curve at their minimum point. That is, when marginal cost is less than average cost, average cost is decreasing, and when marginal cost exceeds average cost, average cost is increasing. This relationship holds for both the *ATC* and the *AVC* curves and is just another example of the relationship you saw in Figure 10.3.

Why the Average Total Cost Curve is U-shaped

Average total cost, *ATC*, is the sum of average fixed cost, *AFC*, and average variable cost, *AVC*. So the shape of the *ATC* curve combines the shapes of the *AFC* and *AVC* curves. The U-shape of the average total cost curve arises from the influence of two opposing forces:

1 Spreading fixed cost over a larger output.

2 Eventually diminishing returns.

When output increases, the firm spreads its fixed costs over a larger output and its average fixed cost decreases – its average fixed cost curve slopes downward.

Diminishing returns means that as output increases, ever-larger amounts of labour are needed to produce an additional unit of output. So average variable cost eventually increases and the firm's *AVC* curve eventually slopes upward.

The shape of the average total cost curve combines these two effects. Initially, as output increases, both average fixed cost and average variable cost decrease, so average total cost decreases and the *ATC* curve slopes downward. But as output increases further and diminishing returns set in, average variable cost begins to increase. Eventually, average variable cost increases more quickly than average fixed cost decreases, so average total cost increases and the *ATC* curve slopes upward.

Cost Curves and Product Curves

A firm's cost curves are determined by its technology, described by the product curves. Figure 10.6 shows the links between the product curves and the cost curves. The upper part of the figure shows the average product curve and the marginal product curve – like those in Figure 10.3. The lower part of the figure shows the average variable cost curve and the marginal cost curve – like those in Figure 10.5.

Notice that at over the output range in which marginal product and average product are rising, marginal cost and average variable cost are falling. Then, at the point of maximum marginal product, marginal cost is a minimum. At output levels above this point, marginal product diminishes and marginal cost increases. But there is an intermediate range of output over which average product is still rising and average variable cost is falling. Then an output is reached at which average product is a maximum and average variable cost is a minimum. At outputs above this level, average product diminishes and average variable cost increases.

Figure 10.6

Product Curves and Cost Curves

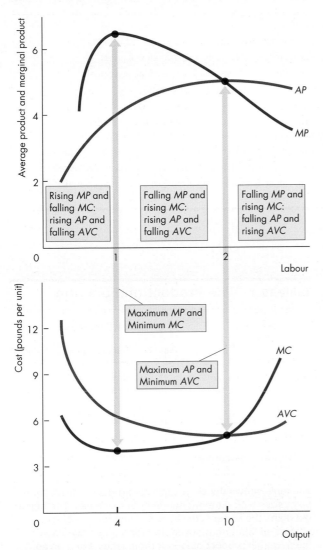

A firm's cost curves are linked to its product curves. Over the range of rising marginal product, marginal cost is falling. When marginal product is a maximum, marginal cost is a minimum. Over the range of rising average product, average variable cost is falling. When average product is a maximum, average variable cost is a minimum. Over the range of diminishing marginal product, marginal cost is rising. And over the range of diminishing average product, average variable cost is rising.

Shifts in the Cost Curves

The position of a firm's short-run cost curves depends on two factors:

1 Technology.

2 Prices of factors of production.

Technology

A technological change that increases productivity shifts the total product curve upward. It also shifts the marginal product curve and the average product curve upward. With better technology, the same inputs can produce more output, and so technological change lowers cost and shifts the cost curves downward.

For example, advances in robotic production techniques have increased productivity in the car industry. As a result, the product curves of BMW, Renault and Volvo have shifted upward and their cost curves have shifted downward. But the relationships between their product curves and cost curves have not changed. The curves are still linked in the way shown in Figure 10.6.

Price of Factors of Production

An increase in factor prices increases costs and shifts the cost curves. But the way the curves shift depends on which factor prices change. A change in rent or some other component of *fixed* cost shifts the fixed cost curves (TFC and AFC) and the total cost curve (TC) upward, but leaves the variable cost curves (AVC and TVC) and the marginal cost curve (MC) unchanged. A change in wages or some other component of *variable* cost shifts the variable curves (TVC and AVC), the total cost curve (TC) and the marginal cost curve (MC) upward, but leaves the fixed cost curves (AFC and TFC) unchanged.

You have now completed your study of short run costs. All the concepts that you've met are summarized in a compact glossary in Table 10.2.

Review Quiz

◆ Describe the relationship between a firm's short-run cost curves.
◆ How does marginal cost change as output increases (a) initially, and (b) eventually?
◆ What does the law of diminishing returns imply for the shape of the marginal cost curve?
◆ What is the shape of the average total cost curve and why?
◆ What are the shapes of the average variable cost curve and average total cost curve and why?

Table 10.2 A Compact Glossary of Costs

Term	Symbol	Equation	Definition
Fixed cost			Cost that is independent of the output level
Variable cost			Cost that varies with the output level
Total fixed cost	TFC		Cost of the fixed inputs (equals their number times their unit price)
Total variable cost	TVC		Cost of the variable inputs (equals their number times their unit price)
Total cost	TC	$TC = TFC + TVC$	Cost of all inputs (equals fixed costs plus variable costs)
Total product (output)	TP		Total quantity produced (Q)
Marginal cost	MC	$MC = \Delta TC \div \Delta Q$	Change in total cost resulting from a one-unit increase in total product (equals the change in total cost divided by the change in total product)
Average fixed cost	AFC	$AFC = TFC \div Q$	Total fixed cost per unit of output (equals total fixed cost divided by total product)
Average variable cost	AVC	$AVC = TVC \div Q$	Total variable cost per unit of output (equals total variable cost divided by total product)
Average total cost	ATC	$ATC = AFC + AVC$	Total cost per unit of output (equals average fixed cost plus average variable cost)

Long-run Cost

In the short run, a firm can vary the quantity of a variable factor like labour but the quantity of capital is fixed. In the long run, a firm can vary both the quantity of labour and the quantity of capital. We are now going to see how costs vary when the quantities of labour and capital vary. That is, we are going to study a firm's long-run costs. *Long-run cost* is the cost of production when a firm uses the economically efficient quantities of labour and capital.

The behaviour of long-run cost depends on the firm's *production function*, which is the relationship between the maximum output attainable and the quantities of both labour and capital.

The Production Function

Table 10.3 shows Neat Knits' production function. The table lists the total product for four different quantities of capital. The quantity of capital is defined as the plant size. Plant 1 represents a factory with one knitting machine, the short-run example we studied before. The other three plants have 2, 3 and 4 machines. If Sam doubles the plant size to 2 knitting machines, the various amounts of output that labour can produce are shown in the third column of the table. The other two columns show the outputs of yet larger plants. Each column in the table could be graphed as a total product curve for each plant size.

Table 10.3 The Production Function

Labour (workers per day)	Output (jumpers per day)			
	Plant 1	Plant 2	Plant 3	Plant 4
1	4	10	13	15
2	10	15	18	21
3	13	18	22	24
4	15	20	24	26
5	16	21	25	27
Knitting machines (number)	1	2	3	4

The table shows the short-run total product data for four plant sizes with different numbers of machines. The bigger the plant, the larger is the total product for any given amount of labour employed. But for a given plant size, the marginal product of labour diminishes. For a given quantity of labour, the marginal product of capital also diminishes.

Diminishing Returns

Diminishing returns occur in all four plants as the labour input increases. You can check that fact by doing similar calculations for the larger plants to those you've already done for a plant with one machine. Regardless of the plant size, as the labour input increases, its marginal product (eventually) decreases.

Figure 10.7

Short-run Costs of Four Different Plants

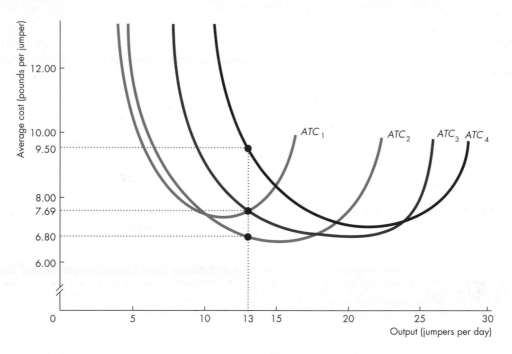

The figure shows short-run average total cost curves for four different quantities of capital. Neat Knits can produce 13 jumpers a day with 1 knitting machine on ATC_1 or with 3 knitting machines on ATC_3 for an average cost of £7.69 per jumper. It can produce the same number of jumpers by using 2 knitting machines on ATC_2 for £6.80 per jumper or with 4 machines on ATC_4 for £9.50 per jumper. If Neat Knits produces 13 jumpers a day, the least-cost method of production – the long-run method – is with 2 machines on ATC_2.

Diminishing Marginal Product of Capital

Just as we can calculate the marginal product of labour for each plant size, we can also calculate the marginal product of capital for each quantity of labour. The *marginal product of capital* is the change in total product divided by the change in capital employed when the amount of labour employed is constant. Equivalently, it is the change in output resulting from a one-unit increase in the quantity of capital employed. For example, if Neat Knits employs 3 workers and increases the number of machines from 1 to 2, output increases from 13 to 18 jumpers a day. The marginal product of capital is 5 jumpers a day. The marginal product of capital diminishes, just like the marginal product of labour. For example, if with 3 workers Neat Knits increases the number of machines from 2 to 3, output increases from 18 to 22 jumpers a day. The marginal product of the third machine is 4 jumpers a day, down from 5 jumpers a day for the second machine.

We can now see what the production function implies for long run costs.

Short-run Cost and Long-run Cost

Continue to assume that labour costs £25 per worker per day and capital costs £25 per machine per day. Using these input prices and the data in Table 10.3, we can calculate and graph the average total cost curves for factories with different plant sizes. We've already studied the costs of a factory with 1 machine in Figures 10.5 and 10.6. The average total cost curve for that case is shown in Figure 10.7 at ATC_1. Figure 10.7 also shows the average total cost curve for a factory with 2 machines, ATC_2, with 3 machines, ATC_3, and with 4 machines, ATC_4.

You can see, in Figure 10.7, that plant size has a big effect on the firm's average total cost. Two things stand out:

1   Each short-run average total cost curve is U-shaped.

2   For each short-run average total cost curve, the larger the plant, the greater is the output at which average total cost is a minimum.

Each short-run average total cost curves is U-shaped because, as the quantity of labour increases, its marginal product at first increases and then diminishes. These patterns in the marginal product of labour, which we examined in some detail for the plant with 1 knitting machine on pp. 199–200, occur at all plant sizes.

The minimum average total cost for a larger plant occurs at a greater output than it does for a smaller plant because the larger plant has a higher fixed cost and therefore, for any given output level, a higher average fixed cost.

Which one of the short-run average cost curves Neat Knits' operates on depends on its plant size. In the long run, plant size is determined by the owner, Sam. His choice of plant size depends on the output he plans to produce. The reason is that the average total cost of producing a given output depends on the plant size.

To see why, suppose that Sam plans to produce 13 jumpers a day. With 1 machine, the average total cost curve is ATC_1 (in Figure 10.7) and the average total cost of 13 jumpers a day is £7.69 per jumper. With 2 machines, on ATC_2, average total cost is £6.80 per jumper. With 3 machines on ATC_3, average total cost is £7.69 per jumper, the same as with 1 machine. Finally, with 4 machines, on ATC_4, average total cost is £9.50 per jumper.

The economically efficient plant size for producing a given output is the one that has the lowest average total cost. For Sam, the economically efficient plant to use to produce 13 jumpers a day is the one with 2 machines.

In the long run, Sam chooses the plant size that minimizes average total cost. When a firm is producing a given output at the least possible cost, it is operating on its *long-run average cost curve*.

The **long-run average cost curve** is the relationship between the lowest attainable average total cost and output when both the plant size and labour are varied. The long-run average cost curve is a planning curve. It tells the firm the plant size and the quantity of labour to use at each output to minimize cost. Once the plant size is chosen, the firm operates on the short-run cost curves that apply to that plant size.

The Long-run Average Cost Curve

Figure 10.8 shows the long-run average cost curve (*LRAC*) for Neat Knits. This long-run average cost curve is derived from the short-run average total cost curves in Figure 10.7. Figure 10.8 shows, ATC_1 has the lowest average total cost for all output rates up to 10 jumpers a day. ATC_2 has the lowest average total cost for output rates between 10 and 18 jumpers a day. ATC_3 has the lowest average total cost for output rates between 18 and 24 jumpers a day. And ATC_4 has the lowest average total cost for output rates in excess of 24 jumpers a day. The segment of each of the four average total cost curves for which that plant has the lowest average total cost is shown as dark blue. The scallop-shaped curve made up of these four segments is the long-run average cost curve.

Economies and Diseconomies of Scale

Economies of Scale

Economies of scale are features of a firm's technology that lead to falling long-run average cost as output increases. When economies of scale are present, the *LRAC* curve slopes downward. The *LRAC* in Figure 10.8 shows that Neat Knits experiences economies of scale for outputs up to 15 jumpers per day.

With given input prices, economies of scale occur when the percentage increase in output exceeds the percentage increase in inputs. If economies of scale are present, when a firm doubles all inputs, its output will more than double, and so average costs fall.

The main source of economies of scale are the specialization of labour and capital. For example, if BMW produces only 100 cars a week, each worker and each machine must be capable of performing many different tasks. But if it produces 10,000 cars a week, each worker and each piece of equipment can be highly specialized. Workers specialize in a small number of tasks at which they become highly proficient. Capital can also be specialized and more productive.

Constant Returns to Scale

Constant returns to scale are features of a firm's technology that leads to constant long-run average costs as output increases. With constant returns, the *LRAC* is horizontal.

With given input prices, constant returns to scale occur if the percentage increase in output equals the percentage increase in inputs. If constant returns are

Figure 10.8

The Long-run Average Cost Curve

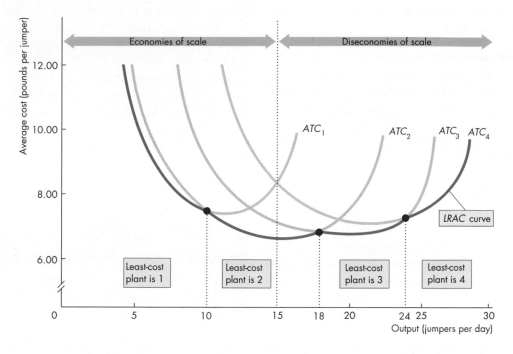

The figure shows the construction of the long-run average cost curve. The curve traces the lowest attainable costs of production at each output when both capital and labour inputs can be varied. On the long-run average cost curve, Neat Knits uses 1 machine to produce up to 10 jumpers a day, 2 machines to produce between 11 and 18 jumpers a day, 3 machines to produce between 19 and 24 jumpers a day, and 4 machines to produce more than 24 jumpers a day. Within any one range, factory output can only be varied by changing labour input

---

present, when a firm doubles its inputs, its output will double and so average costs remain the same. For example, BMW can double its production of its 5-series by doubling its production facility for those cars. It can build an identical production line and hire an identical number of workers. With the two identical production lines, BMW produces exactly twice as many cars.

Diseconomies of Scale

Diseconomies of scale are features of a firm's technology that leads to rising long-run average costs as output increases. When diseconomies of scale are present, the LRAC curve slopes upward. In Figure 10.8, Neat Knits experiences diseconomies of scale at ouputs greater than 15 jumpers.

With given input prices, diseconomies of scale occur if the percentage increase in output is less than the percentage increase in inputs. If diseconomies of scale are present, a firm doubles all its inputs and its output less than doubles, so average costs rise.

Decreasing returns to scale occur in all production processes at some output rate, but may not appear until a very large output rate is achieved. The most common source of decreasing returns to scale is the increasingly complex management and organizational structure required to control a large international firm. The larger the organization, the larger are the number of layers in the management pyramid and the greater are the costs of monitoring and maintaining control of the production and marketing process.

Minimum Efficient Scale

A firm experiences economies of scale up to some output level. Beyond that level, it moves into constant returns to scale or diseconomies of scale. A firm's **minimum efficient scale** is the smallest quantity of output at which long-run average cost reaches its lowest level. The minimum efficient scale plays a role in determining market structure, as you will learn in the next three chapters. The minimum efficient scale also helps to answer some questions about real businesses.

Economies of Scale at Neat Knits

Neat Knits' production technology, shown in Table 10.3, illustrates economies of scale and diseconomies of scale. If Sam decides to double the labour and capital input from one of each to 2 of each, output more than doubles, rising from 4 jumpers to 15 jumpers per day. Neat Knits is experiencing economies of scale and the long-run average cost decreases. But if Sam decides to increase inputs from 2 workers and 2 machines to 3 of each, inputs increase by 50 per cent but output increases by less than 50 per cent, rising from 15 jumpers to 22 jumpers per day. Now Neat Knits experiences diseconomies of scale and its long-run average costs increases. Neat Knits experiences minimum efficient scale at 15 jumpers per day.

Producing Cars and Generating Electric Power

At the beginning of this chapter, we noted that most car makers can produce far more cars than they can sell. We posed the question: why do car makers have expensive equipment lying around that isn't fully used? You can now answer this question. Car producers experience economies of scale. The minimum cost of production occurs on a short-run average total cost curve that looks like ATC_1 in Figure 10.8.

We also noted that many electrical suppliers don't have enough production equipment on hand to meet demand on the coldest and hottest days and have to buy power from other producers. You can now see why this occurs and why they don't build a bigger plant. Power producers use the plant size that minimizes average total cost for the level of output on a typical day. It produces above minimum efficient scale and experience diseconomies of scale. They have short-run average total cost curves like ATC_3. If they had larger plants, their average total costs of producing their normal output would increase.

An alternative analysis of the issues in this chapter, using isoquant and isocost models, can be found on the Parkin, Powell and Matthews website.

Review Quiz

◆ What does a firm's production function show and how is it related to a total product curve?

◆ Does the law of diminishing returns apply to capital as well as labour? Explain.

◆ What does a firm's long-run average cost curve show? How is it related to the firm's short-run average cost curve?

◆ What are economies and diseconomies of scale? How do they arise? What do they imply for the shape of the long-run average cost curve?

◆ How is a firm's minimum efficient scale determined?

Summary

Key Points

Time Frames for Decisions (p. 197)

● In the short run, the quantity of one input in production is fixed and the quantities of another can be varied.

● In the long run, the quantities of all inputs can be varied.

Short-run Technology Constraint (pp. 198–202)

● A total product curve shows how much output a firm can produce using a given quantity of capital and different quantities of labour.

● Initially, marginal product increases as the quantity of labour increases. But eventually, marginal product diminishes – the law of diminishing marginal returns.

● Average product increases initially and eventually diminishes.

Short-run Cost (pp. 202–206)

● As output increases, total fixed cost is constant, and total variable cost and total cost increase.

● As output increases, average variable cost, average total cost, and marginal cost decrease at small outputs and increase at large outputs. These costs curves are U-shaped.

Long-run Cost (pp. 206–210)

- Long-run cost is the cost of production when all inputs – labour as well as plant and equipment – have been adjusted to their economically efficient levels.

- There is a set of short-run cost curves for each different plant size. There is one least-cost plant for each output. The larger the output, the larger is the plant that will minimize average total cost.

- The long-run average cost curve traces the relationship between the lowest attainable average total cost and output when both capital and labour inputs can be varied.

- With economies of scale, the long-run average cost curve slopes downward. With diseconomies of scale, the long-run average cost curve slopes upward.

Key Figures and Table ◇

Key Terms

Problems

•1 Rubber Toys' total product schedule is:

Labour (workers per week)	Output (rubber boats per week)
1	1
2	3
3	6
4	10
5	15
6	21
7	26
8	30
9	33
10	35

a Draw the total product curve.

b Calculate the average product of labour and draw the average product curve.

c Calculate the marginal product of labour and draw the marginal product curve.

d What is the relationship between average product and marginal product when Rubber Toys' produces (i) fewer than 30 boats a week and (ii) more than 30 boats a week?

2 Charlie's Chocolates' total product schedule is:

Labour (workers per day)	Output (boxes per day)
1	12
2	24
3	48
4	84
5	132
6	192
7	240
8	276
9	300
10	312

a Draw the total product curve.

b Calculate the average product of labour and draw the average product curve.

c Calculate the marginal product of labour and draw the marginal product curve.

d What is the relationship between the average product and marginal product when Charlie's Chocolates produces (i) less than 276 boxes a day and (ii) more than 276 boxes a day?

●3 In problem 1, the price of labour is €400 a week, total fixed cost is €1,000 a week.

a Calculate total cost, total variable cost, and total fixed cost for each output and draw the short-run total cost curves.

b Calculate average total cost, average fixed cost, average variable cost, and marginal cost at each output and draw the short-run average and marginal cost curves.

4 In problem 2, the price of labour is €50 per day, total fixed costs are €50 per day.

a Calculate total cost, total variable cost, and total fixed costs for each level of output and draw the short-run total cost curves.

b Calculate average total cost, average fixed cost, average variable cost, and marginal cost at each level of output and draw the short-run average and marginal cost curves.

●5 In problem 3, suppose that Rubber Toys' total fixed cost increases to €1,100 a week. Explain what changes occur to the short-run average and marginal cost curves.

6 In problem 4, suppose that the price of labour increases to €70 per day. Explain what changes occur to the short-run average and marginal cost curves.

●7 In problem 3, Rubber Toys buys a second plant and now the total product of each quantity of labour doubles. The total fixed cost of operating each plant is €1,000 a week. The wage rate is €400 a week.

a Set out the average total cost schedule when Rubber Toys operates two plants.

b Draw the long-run average cost curve.

c Over what output range is it efficient to operate one plant and two plants?

8 In problem 4, Charlie's Chocolates buys a second plant and now the total product of each quantity of labour doubles. The total fixed cost of operating each plant is €50 a day. The wage rate is €50 a day.

a Set out the average total cost curve when Charlie's operates two plants.

b Draw the long-run average cost curve.

c Over what output range is it efficient to operate one plant and two plants?

Critical Thinking

1 Read the Business Case Study about the European airline industry on pp. 214–215 about the problems of the European airlines, and use the links on the Parkin, Powell, and Matthews website to read the original articles and gain more information about the problems of the European airlines. Then answer the following questions:

a What is the main difference between the structure of the US airlines and the European airlines?

b Why can't the European airlines cut costs sufficiently to maintain profits when demand decreases?

c If an airline like Sabena is insolvent, why might it be the target for a takeover by another airline?

d Why have the European airlines been unable to merge or take each other over?

e What would be the effect of mergers in the European airline industry?

f Why does Robert Ayling, former BA CEO, say that the European airlines need a much more flexible method of providing aeroplanes?

g What does Robert Ayling recommend, and what effect would it have on airline cost structures?

2 Use the links on the Parkin, Powell and Matthews website to read about teleworking and then answer the following questions:

a What is the short-run impact of introducing teleworking on company costs?

b Why does teleworking involve investing in new technology?

c What is the long-run impact of introducing teleworking on company costs?

d What do you think are the advantages and disadvantages for employees of teleworking?

e Why do you think companies thought that employees would take more time off when working?

f Why might employees tend to work harder as a result of teleworking from home as opposed to working from an office or depot?

3 A telecommunication company is considering replacing human telephone operators with computers. This change will increase total fixed cost and decrease total variable cost. Either use the spreadsheet on the Parkin, Powell and Matthews website or create your own example and sketch:

a The total cost curves for the original technology that uses human operators.

b The average cost curves for the original technology that uses human operators.

c The marginal cost curves for the original technology that uses human operators.

d The total cost curves for the new technology that uses computers.

e The average cost curves for the new technology that uses computers.

f The marginal cost curves for the new technology that uses computers.

Short- and Long-run Costs

The Airline Consolidation Crisis

The Industry

The European airline industry in 2000 comprised over 40 flagcarrier airlines plus some large scheduled airlines. There were about 15 main international carriers, with the remainder concentrating on European routes. In 2000, there were 1.6 bn passengers worldwide and passenger numbers increased by 5 per cent annually between 1995 and 2000. Despite rising demand, airlines profit margins rarely exceeded 3 per cent.[1] Europe's 7 largest airlines carry 47 per cent of passenger traffic compared with the USA, where the 7 largest airlines carry over 80 per cent of passenger traffic.[2]

The Crisis

After the events of September 11, 2001, demand for international and European flights fell by up to 30 per cent within a week. Several European Airlines announced insolvency, most announced massive cuts in staff, many announced wage freezes, wage cuts and cuts in service provision as shown in the table.[3] Share prices plunged and airlines failed to pay dividends. Losses of up to £7 bn worldwide were expected.[1]

The Way Ahead

Rigas Dognais, former chairman and CEO of Olympic Airways said 'Unless European airlines can consolidate around a handful of the larger and more successful players they have little hope of long-term survival . . . .[2] He said that cross-border mergers and acquisitions between carriers, currently disallowed by European Commission rules, would be needed. Rod Eddington, BA's current CEO, confirmed that the likely survivers would be British Airways, Air France and Lufthansa.[4] Robert Ayling, a former BA CEO said 'There needs to be a new model that allows airlines to shed costs as quickly as they shed revenues. We need a much more flexible method of providing aeroplanes . . . Someone else should take on the risky business of owning aircraft.'[1]

European Airlines in Crisis

Airline	Staff cuts in 2000	Employees in 2000	Capacity/ operating cuts in 2001	Passengers in 2000	Wage cuts in 2001
Aer Lingus	2,500	6,600	25%	7 mn	
Alitalia	2,500	23,500		25 mn	
British Airways	7,000	56,000	10%	48 mn	✓15%
Iberia	3,000	29,000	11%	30 mn	✓10%
KLM	2,500	33,700	15%	16 mn	✓
Lufthansa		69,500	3 routes	40 mn	
Sabena		11,000	Insolvency	11 mn	
SAS	9,000	30,000	(shut down)		
Swiss Air	2,600	71,000	(shut down)		

Source: Airline web pages and[3]

[1] Financial Times (9 October 2001), Brussels unwilling to offer airlines aid, http://news.ft.com/ft.gx..../ftc?pagename=View&c=Article&cid=FT3Q68X1MSC&live=tru
[2] R. Doganis (15 October 2001), Opinion: Saving Europe's airlines, http://news.ft.com/ft/gx..../ftc?pagename=View&c=Article&cid=FT3JGM9EUSC&live=tru
[3] BBC (19 October 2001), Round-up: Aviation in crisis, http://news.bbc.co.uk/hi/english/business/newsid_1578000/1578795.stm
[4] BBC (21 October 2001), Euro airlines must merge to survive, http://news.bbc.co.uk/hi/english/business/newsid_1611000/1611841.stm

Economic Analysis

■ Aer Lingus, KLM and British Airways (BA) are all large firms offering passenger and freight air transport services throughout Europe and worldwide. These firms are large because there are economies of scale in many of their service activities.

■ Figure 1 shows the technology these firms face in the form of the total product curve for passenger services in 2000. Aer Lingus, KLM and BA operate on total product curve TP_0.

■ Aer Lingus employs 6,250 people and carries 7 million passengers a year. KLM employs 33,700 people and carries 16 million passengers a year. BA employs 65,000 people and carries 35 million passengers a year.

■ The crisis has led to short run cuts in staff and wages. Airlines move back along the existing total product curve, TP_0, as shown by the arrows in Figure 1. To increase productivity in the long run, industry experts recommend consolidation through merger to save on sales organization and route management, and new methods of capital management to save on aeroplane storage.

■ If BA, KLM and Aer Lingus successfully merged into a single airline, they could operate on the new total product curve TP_1 in Figure 1.

■ Figure 2 shows the potential effect of merger on average total costs.

■ The three airlines are operating on ATC_0 before the merger. This curve uses an average of fixed costs for the three separate airlines.

■ After the merger, the new airline operates on ATC_1. The merged airline has greater fixed costs than the three separate airlines, so for low passenger numbers, ATC_1 is higher than ATC_0.

■ For high passenger numbers, ATC_1 is lower than ATC_0 and the merged airline has benefited from economies of scale.

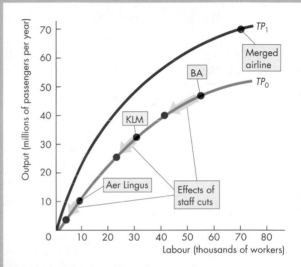

Figure 1 Total product

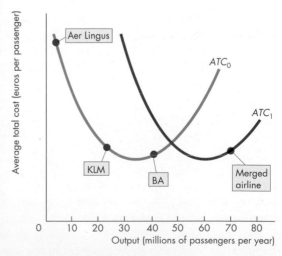

Figure 2 Average total cost

CHAPTER 11

Perfect Competition

After studying this chapter you will be able to:

◆ Define perfect competition

◆ Explain how price and output are determined in a competitive industry

◆ Explain why firms sometimes shut down temporarily and lay off workers

◆ Explain why firms enter and leave an industry

◆ Predict the effects of a change in demand and of a technological advance

◆ Explain why perfect competition is efficient

Rivalry in Personal Computers

Personal computers are big business in Europe. Millions of PCs are bought and sold each year in a multi-billion pound market. Competition in supply is strong. National names such as Elonex and Gateway compete with international contenders such as Dell and IBM. New firms enter and try their luck while other firms are squeezed out of the industry. How does competition affect prices and profits? What causes some firms to enter an industry and others to leave it? What are the effects on profits and prices of new firms entering and old firms leaving an industry? ◆ In 2000, 17 million people were unemployed in the European Union. Of these, many were unemployed because they had been laid off by firms seeking to trim their costs and avoid bankruptcy. By 2001, Europe's economies were slowing down and firms in almost every sector of the economy laid off workers. Why do firms lay off workers? When will a firm temporarily shut down, laying off its workers? ◆ Over the past few years, there has been a dramatic fall in the prices of PCs. For example, a slow Pentium 1 computer cost almost £2,000 a few years ago and a much faster Pentium III costs only £1,000 today. What goes on in an industry when the price of its output decreases sharply? What happens to the profits of the firms producing such goods and the number of people they employ?

◆ ◆ ◆ ◆ Computers, like most other goods, are produced and supplied by more than one firm and these firms compete with each other. In order to study competitive markets, we are going to build a model of a market in which competition is as fierce and extreme as possible. We call this case perfect competition. You can see an example of the impact on profits when we apply the model to the world's tea markets in the Business Case Study on pp. 238–239.

Perfect Competition

The firms that you study in this chapter face the force of raw competition. This type of extreme competition is called perfect competition. Perfect competition is an industry in which:

◆ Many firms sell identical products to many buyers.

◆ There are no restrictions on entry into the industry.

◆ Established firms have no advantage over new ones.

◆ Sellers and buyers are well informed about prices.

How Perfect Competition Arises

First, perfect competition arises if the minimum efficient scale of a single producer is small relative to the demand for a good or service (see Chapter 10, p. 184). The **minimum efficient scale** is the smallest quantity of output at which long-run average costs reaches its lowest level. Where the minimum efficient scale of a firm is small relative to the demand, there is room for many firms in the industry.

Second, perfect competition arises when consumers don't care which firm they buy from. This usually happens when the goods and services produced by any one firm has no distinctive characteristics which differentiate it from the output of other firms in the industry.

Price Takers

Firms in perfect competition make many decisions, but the one decision they never make is the price at which to sell their output. Firms in perfect competition are said to be price takers. A **price taker** is a firm that cannot influence the price of a good or service.

The reason why a perfectly competitive firm is a price taker is that it produces a tiny fraction of the total output of a particular good or service and buyers are well informed about the prices of other firms.

Imagine for a moment that you are an apple farmer in Brittany in France. You have a thousand acres under cultivation – which sounds like a lot. But when you take a drive around Brittany you see thousands more acres like yours full of apples. Your thousand acres is just a drop in an ocean of apples.

Nothing makes your fruit any better than any other farmer's, and all the buyers of apples know the price at which they can do business. If everybody else sells their apples for €0.5 a kilogram, and you want €0.6, why would people buy from you? They can simply go to the next farmer, and the one after that, and the next, and buy all they need for €0.5 a kilogram. You are a price taker. A price-taking firm faces a demand curve that is perfectly elastic.

The market demand for apples is not perfectly elastic. The market demand curve is downward-sloping, and its elasticity depends on the substitutability of apples for other fruits such as pears, bananas and oranges. The demand for apples from farm A is perfectly elastic because apples from farm A are a *perfect substitute* for apples from farm B. A price taker faces a perfectly elastic demand curve.

Economic Profit and Revenue

The goal of a firm is to maximize **economic profit**, which is equal to total revenue minus total cost. Total cost is the opportunity cost of production, which includes the firm's **normal profit**, the return that the firm's entrepreneur can obtain in the best alternative business.

A firm's **total revenue** equals the price of its output multiplied by the number of units of output sold (price × quanitty). **Marginal revenue** is the change in total revenue divided by the change in quantity. Marginal revenue is calculated by dividing the change in total revenue by the change in the quantity sold.

Figure 11.1 illustrates these concepts. Neat Knits is one of a thousand similar small firms. In Figure 11.1(a), demand and supply in the jumper market determine the price at £25 a jumper. The owner, Sam, cannot influence price by changing the quantity of jumpers he produces.

The table shows three different quantities of jumpers sold. As the quantity sold varies, the price stays constant – in this example at £25. Total revenue is equal to price multiplied by quantity. For example, if Neat Knits sells 8 jumpers, total revenue is 8 times £25, which equals £200. Average revenue is total revenue divided by quantity. Again, if Neat Knits sells 8 jumpers, average revenue is total revenue (£200) divided by quantity (8), which equals £25. Marginal revenue is the change in total revenue resulting from a 1-unit change in quantity. For example, when the quantity sold increases from 8 to 9, total revenue increases from £200 to £225, so marginal revenue is £25. (Notice that in the table, marginal revenue appears *between* the lines for the quantities sold. This arrangement presents a visual reminder that

Figure 11.1

Demand, Price and Revenue in Perfect Competition

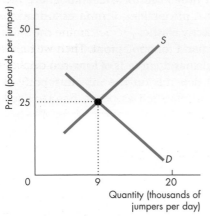

(a) Jumper industry

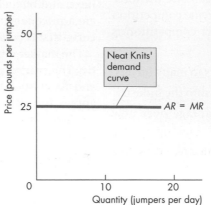

(b) Neat Knits' demand, average revenue and marginal revenue

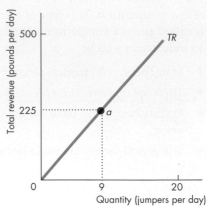

(c) Neat Knits' total revenue

Quantity sold (Q) (jumpers per day)	Price (P) (pounds per jumper)	Total revenue (TR = P × Q) (pounds)	Average revenue (AR = TR/Q) (pounds per jumper)	Marginal revenue (MR = ΔTR/ΔQ) (pounds per jumper)
8	25	200	25	
				25
9	25	225	25	
				25
10	25	250	25	

Market demand and supply determine the market price. In part (a), the market price is £25 and 9,000 jumpers are bought and sold. Neat Knits faces a perfectly elastic demand at the market price of £25 per jumper. The table calculates Neat Knits' total revenue, average revenue and marginal revenue. Part (b) of the figure shows Neat Knits' demand curve, which is also its marginal revenue curve (MR) and average revenue curve (AR). Part (c) shows Neat Knits' total revenue curve (TR). Point *a* corresponds to the second row of the table.

marginal revenue results from the *change* in the quantity sold.)

Figure 11.1(b) shows Neat Knits' marginal revenue curve (*MR*). This curve tells us the change in total revenue that results from selling one more jumper. Because the price remains constant when the quantity sold changes, the change in total revenue resulting from a one-unit increase in the quantity sold equals price. So, in perfect competition, marginal revenue equals price.

The marginal revenue curve is also the firm's demand curve in perfect competition. Neat Knits is a price taker and so it can sell any quantity it chooses at the current market price of £25. The firm faces a perfectly elastic demand for its output.

The total revenue curve (*TC*), shown in part (c), shows total revenue at each quantity sold. For example, when Neat Knits sells 9 jumpers, total revenue

is £225 (point *a*). Because each additional jumper sold brings in a constant amount – in this case £25 – the total revenue curve is an upward-sloping straight line.

Review Quiz

◆ Explain why a firm in perfect competition is a price taker.
◆ Explain the relationship between a firm's demand curve and the market demand curve in perfect competition.
◆ Why is a firm's demand curve also its marginal revenue curve in perfect competition?
◆ Why is the total revenue curve in perfect competition an upward-sloping straight line?

The Firm's Decisions in Perfect Competition

Firms in a perfectly competitive industry face a given market price and have the revenue curves that you've just studied. These revenue curves summarize the market constraint faced by a perfectly competitive firm.

Firms also have a technology constraint, which is described by the product curves (total product, average product and marginal product) that you studied in Chapter 10. The technology available to the firm determines its costs, which are described by the cost curves (total cost, average cost and marginal cost) that you also studied in Chapter 10.

The task of the competitive firm is to make the maximum profit possible, given the constraints it faces. To achieve this objective, a firm must make four key decisions, two in the short run and two in the long run.

Short-run Decisions

The short run is a time frame in which each firm has a given plant and the number of firms in the industry is fixed. But many things can change in the short run and the firm must react to these changes. For example, the price for which the firm can sell its output might have a seasonal fluctuation, or it might be affected by general business fluctuations.

The firm must react to such short-run price fluctuations and decide:

1 Whether to produce or to temporarily shut down.

2 If the decision is to produce, what quantity to produce.

Long-run Decisions

The long run is a time frame in which each firm can change the size of its plant and can decide whether to enter or leave an industry. So in the long run, both the plant size of each firm and the number of firms in the industry can change. Many additional things can change in the long run to which the firm must react. For example, the demand for a good can permanently fall. Or a technological advance can change an industry's costs.

The firm must react to such long-run changes and decide:

1 Whether to increase or decrease its plant size.

2 Whether to stay in the industry or leave it.

The Firm and the Industry in the Short Run and the Long Run

To study a competitive industry, we begin by looking at an individual firm's short-run decisions. We then see how the short-run decisions of all the firms in a competitive industry combine to determine the industry price, output and economic profit. Then we turn to the long run and study the effects of long-run decisions on the industry price, output and economic profit.

All the decisions we study are driven by the single objective: to maximize profit.

Profit-maximizing Output

A perfectly competitive firm cannot influence profit by choosing a price. But it can maximize profit in the short run by choosing its output level. One way of finding the profit-maximizing output is to study a firm's total revenue and total cost curves and to find the output level at which total revenue exceeds total cost by the largest amount. Figure 11.2 shows you how to do this for Neat Knits. The table lists Neat Knits' revenue and total cost at different outputs, and part (a) of the figure shows Neat Knits' total revenue and total cost curves. These curves are graphs of the numbers shown in the first three columns of the table. The total revenue curve (*TR*) is the same as that in Figure 11.1(c). The total cost curve (*TC*) is similar to the one that you met in Chapter 10. As output increases, so does total cost.

Economic profit equals total revenue minus total cost. The fourth column of the table in Figure 11.2 shows Neat Knits' economic profit and part (b) of the figure illustrates these numbers as Neat Knits' profit curve. This curve shows that Neat Knits makes an economic profit at outputs greater than 4 and fewer than 12 jumpers a day. At outputs of fewer than 4 jumpers a day, Neat Knits incurs a loss. It also incurs a loss if output exceeds 12 jumpers a day. At outputs of 4 jumpers and 12 jumpers a day, total cost equals total revenue and Neat Knits' economic profit is zero. An output at which total cost equals total revenue is called a *break-even point*. Because normal profit is part of total cost, a firm makes normal profit at a break-even point. That is, at the break-even point, the entrepreneur makes an income equal to the best alternative return forgone.

Notice the relationship between the total revenue, total cost and profit curves. Economic profit is measured by the vertical distance between the total revenue and total cost curves. When the total revenue

Figure 11.2

Total Revenue, Total Cost and Economic Profit

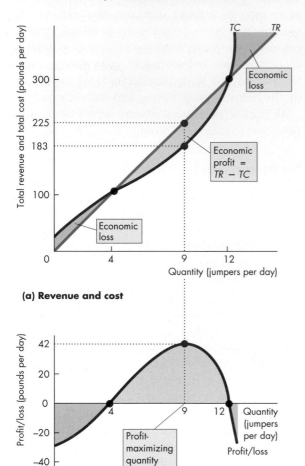

(a) Revenue and cost

(b) Economic profit and loss

Quantity (Q) (jumpers per day)	Total revenue (TR) (pounds)	Total cost (TC) (pounds)	Economic profit (TR − TC) (pounds)
0	0	22	−22
1	25	45	−20
2	50	66	−16
3	75	85	−10
4	100	100	0
5	125	114	11
6	150	126	24
7	175	141	34
8	200	160	40
9	225	183	42
10	250	210	40
11	275	245	30
12	300	300	0
13	325	360	−35

The table lists Neat Knits' total revenue, total cost and economic profit. Part (a) graphs the total revenue and total cost curves. Economic profit is seen in part (a) as the blue area between the total cost and total revenue curves. The maximum economic profit, £42 a day, occurs when 9 jumpers are produced – where the vertical distance between the total revenue and total cost curves is at its largest. At outputs of 4 jumpers a day and 12 jumpers a day, Neat Knits makes zero economic profit – these are break-even points. At outputs fewer than 4 and greater than 12 jumpers a day, Neat Knits incurs a loss. Part (b) of the figure shows Neat Knits' profit curve. The profit curve is at its highest when profit is at a maximum and cuts the horizontal axis at the break-even points.

curve in part (a) is above the total cost curve, between 4 and 12 jumpers, the firm is making an economic profit and the profit curve in part (b) is above the horizontal axis. At the break-even point, where the total cost and total revenue curves intersect, the profit curve intersects the horizontal axis. The profit curve is at its highest when the distance between *TR* and *TC* is greatest. In this example, profit maximization occurs at an output of 9 jumpers a day. At this output, Neat Knits' economic profit is £42 a day.

Marginal Analysis

Another way of finding the profit-maximizing output is to use *marginal analysis*, by comparing marginal cost, *MC*, with marginal revenue, *MR*. As you have seen, marginal revenue in perfect competition is constant and marginal cost changes as output increases.

If marginal revenue exceeds marginal cost (if *MR* > *MC*), then the extra revenue from selling one more unit exceeds the extra cost incurred to produce it. The

Figure 11.3

Profit-maximizing Output

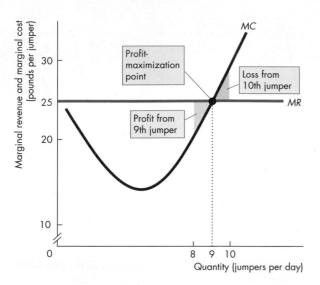

Quantity (Q) (jumpers per day)	Total revenue (TR) (pounds) per jumper)	Marginal revenue (MR) (pounds	Total cost (TC) (pounds) per jumper)	Marginal cost (MC) (pounds	Economic profit (TR – TC) (pounds)
7	175		141		34
		 25		 19	
8	200		160		40
		 25		 23	
9	225		183		42
		 25		 27	
10	250		210		40
		 25		 35	
11	275		245		30

Another way of finding the profit-maximizing output is to determine the output at which marginal revenue equals marginal cost. The table shows that if output increases from 8 to 9 jumpers, marginal cost is £23, which is less than the marginal revenue of £25. If output increases from 9 to 10 jumpers, marginal cost is £27, which exceeds the marginal revenue of £25. The figure shows that marginal cost and marginal revenue are equal when Neat Knits produces 9 jumpers a day. If marginal revenue exceeds marginal cost, an increase in output increases profit. If marginal revenue is less than marginal cost, an increase in output decreases profit. If marginal revenue equals marginal cost, economic profit is maximized.

firm makes an economic profit on the marginal unit, so economic profit increases if output increases.

If marginal revenue is less than marginal cost (if $MR < MC$), then the extra revenue from selling one more unit is less than the extra cost incurred to produce it. The firm makes an economic loss on the marginal unit, so its economic profit decreases if output rises, and its economic profit increases if output *decreases*.

Economic profit is maximized when the firm produces the quanitity at which marginal revenue equals marginal cost ($MR = MC$).

The rule $MR = MC$ is a prime example of marginal analysis. To check the rule works look at Figure 11.3. The table records Neat Knits' marginal revenue and marginal cost and the figure shows the marginal revenue and marginal costs curves. Marginal revenue is constant at £25 per jumper and marginal cost increases over the output range shown in the table.

Focus on the highlighted rows of the table. If output increases from 8 jumpers to 9 jumpers, marginal revenue is £25 and marginal cost is £23. Because marginal revenue exceeds marginal cost, economic profit increases. The last column of the table shows that economic profit increases from £40 to £42, an increase of £2. This profit from the ninth jumper is shown as the blue area in the figure.

If output increases from 9 jumpers to 10 jumpers, marginal revenue is still £25, but marginal cost is £27. Because marginal revenue is less than marginal cost, economic profit decreases. The last column of the table shows that economic profit decreases from £42 to £40. This loss from the tenth jumper is shown as the red area in the figure.

Neat Knits maximizes economic profit by producing 9 jumpers a day, the quantity at which marginal revenue equals marginal cost.

Profit and Losses in the Short Run

In the short run, when a firm has set its marginal cost equal to its marginal revenue and maximized profit, it might make an economic profit, break even (making normal profit), or incur an economic loss. To determine which of these three possible outcomes occurs, we compare the firm's total revenue and total cost, or we can compare price with average total cost. If price exceeds average total cost, a firm makes an economic profit. If price equals average total cost, a firm breaks even – makes a normal profit. If price is less than

Figure 11.4

Three Possible Profit Outcomes in the Short-run

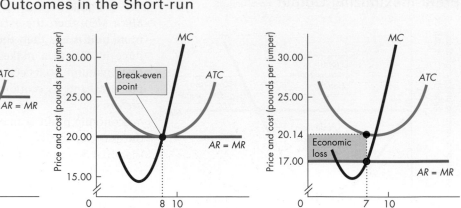

(a) Economic profit   **(b) Normal profit**   **(c) Economic loss**

In the short run, firms might make an economic profit, break even (making a normal profit), or incur a loss. If the market price is higher than the average total cost of producing the profit-maximizing output, the firm makes an economic profit (part a). If price equals minimum average total cost, the firm breaks even and makes a normal profit (part b). If the price is below minimum average total cost, the firm incurs an economic loss (part c). The firm's economic profit is shown as the blue rectangle and the firm's economic loss is the red rectangle.

average total cost, a firm incurs an economic loss. Figure 11.4 shows these three possible short-run profit outcomes.

Three Possible Profit Outcomes

In part (a), price exceeds average total cost and Neat Knits makes an economic profit. Price and marginal revenue are £25 a jumper and the profit-maximizing output is 9 jumpers a day. Neat Knits' total revenue is £225 a day (9 × £25). Average total cost is £20.33 a jumper and total cost is £183 a day (9 × £20.33). Neat Knits' economic profit is £42 a day. Economic profit equals total revenue minus total cost, which is £225 – £183 or £42 a day. Economic profit also equals economic profit per jumper, which is £4.67 (£25.00 – £20.33), multiplied by the number of jumpers (£4.67 × 9 = £42). The blue rectangle in the figure shows this economic profit. The height of the rectangle is profit per jumper, £4.67, and the length is the quantity of jumpers produced, 9 a day, so the area of the rectangle measures Neat Knits' economic profit of £42 a day.

In part (b), price equals average total cost and Neat Knits breaks even – makes normal profit and zero economic profit. Price and marginal revenue are £20 a jumper and the profit-maximizing output is

8 jumpers a day. At this output, average total cost is at its minimum.

In part (c), price is less than average total cost and Neat Knits incurs an economic loss. Price and marginal revenue are £17 a jumper and the profit-maximizing (loss-minimizing) output is 7 jumpers a day. Neat Knits' total revenue is £119 a day (7 × £17). Average total cost is £20.14 a jumper and total cost is £141 a day (7 × £20.14). Neat Knits' economic loss is £22 a day. Economic loss equals total revenue minus total cost, which is £119 – £141 = –£22 a day. The economic loss, £22, also equals economic loss per jumper, £3.14 (£20.14 – £17.00), multiplied by the number of jumpers (£3.14 × 7 = £22). The pink rectangle in the figure shows this economic loss. The height of the rectangle is the economic loss per jumper, £3.14, and the length is the quantity of jumpers produced, 7 a day, so the area of the rectangle measures Neat Knits' economic loss of £22 a day.

The Firm's Short-run Supply Curve

A perfectly competitive firm's supply curve shows how the firm's profit-maximizing output varies as the market price varies, other things remaining the same. Figure 11.5 shows you how to derive Neat

Figure 11.5

A Firm's Supply Curve

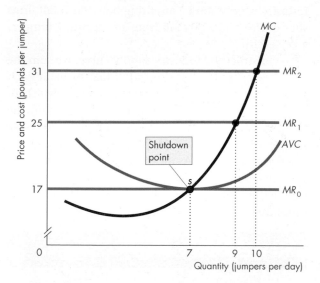

(a) Marginal cost and average variable cost

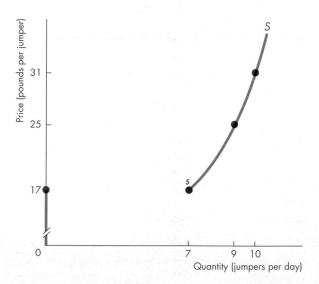

(b) Neat Knits' supply curve

Part (a) shows Neat Knits' profit-maximizing output at each market price. At £25 a jumper, Neat Knits produces 9 jumpers. At £17 a jumper, Neat Knits produces 7 jumpers. At any price below £17 a jumper, Neat Knits produces nothing as Neat Knits' shutdown point is *s*. Part (b) shows Neat Knits' supply curve – the number of jumpers Neat Knits will produce at each price. Neat Knits' supply curve is made up of its marginal cost curve (part a) at all points above the average variable cost curve, and the vertical axis at all prices below minimum average variable cost.

Knits' entire supply curve. Part (a) shows Neat Knits' marginal cost and average variable cost curves and part (b) shows its supply curve. Let's look at the link between the marginal cost and average variable cost curves and the supply curve.

Temporary Plant Shutdown

In the short run, a firm cannot avoid its fixed costs. It can only avoid variable costs by temporarily laying off workers or shutting down. If a firm shuts down and produces no output, it incurs a maximum loss equal to its total fixed cost. A firm shuts down if price falls below the minimum of average variable cost. A firm's **shutdown point** is the level of output and price where the firm is just covering its total *variable* costs, point *s* in Figure 11.5(a). If the price is £17, the marginal revenue curve is MR_0, and the profit max-imizing output is 7 jumpers a day at point *s*. But both price and average variable cost equal £17, so the firm's revenue equals its total variable cost. The owner, Sam, incurs an economic loss equal to total fixed cost. If the price falls below £17, no matter what quantity Sam produces, average variable cost exceeds price and Neat Knits loss exceeds total fixed cost. So Sam will shut down the factory.

The Short-run Supply Curve

If the price is above minimum average variable cost, Sam maximizes profit by producing the output at which marginal cost equals price. We can determine the quantity produced at each price from the mar-ginal cost curve. At a price of £25, the marginal rev-enue curve is MR_1 and Neat Knits maximizes profit by producing 9 jumpers. At a price of £31, the marginal revenue curve is MR_2 and Neat Knits produces 10 jumpers.

Neat Knit's supply curve is shown in Figure 11.5(b). It has two parts. In the range of prices that exceed minimum average variable cost, the supply curve is the same as the marginal cost curve above the shut-down point (*s*). At prices below minimum average variable cost, Neat Knits shuts down and produces nothing. Its supply curve runs along the vertical axis. At a price of £17, Neat Knits is indifferent between shutting down and producing 7 jumpers a day. Either way, Sam incurs a loss of £25 a day.

Short-run Industry Supply Curve

The **short-run industry supply curve** shows how the quantity supplied by the industry varies as the market

Figure 11.6

Industry Supply Curve

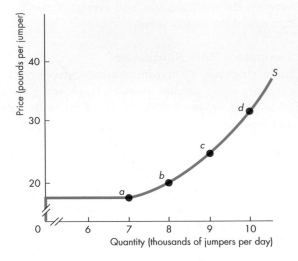

The industry supply schedule is the sum of the supply schedules of all individual firms. An industry that consists of 1,000 identical firms will supply a quantity 1,000 times as large as that of the individual firm (see table). The industry supply curve is *S*. Points *a*, *b*, *c* and *d* correspond to the rows of the table. At the shutdown price of £17, each firm produces either 0 or 7 jumpers per day. The industry supply curve is perfectly elastic at the shutdown price.

	Price (pounds per jumper)	Quantity supplied by Neat Knits (jumpers per day)	Quantity supplied by industry (jumpers per day)
a	17	0 or 7	0 to 7,000
b	20	8	8,000
c	25	9	9,000
d	31	10	10,000

supplies nothing. At £17, each firm is indifferent between shutting down and producing 7 jumpers. Some firms will produce and others will shut down. Industry supply can be anything between 0 (all firms shut down) and 7,000 (all firms producing 7 jumpers a day each).

To construct the industry supply curve, we sum the quantities supplied by the individual firms at each price. Every firm in the industry has a supply schedule exactly like Neat Knits. At prices below £17, the industry supply curve runs along the price axis. At a price of £17, the industry supply curve is horizontal – it is perfectly elastic. As the price rises above £17, each firm increases its quantity supplied and the quantity supplied by the industry also increases, but by 1,000 times that of each individual firm.

So far, we have seen that the firm's profit-maximizing actions depend on the market price. But how is the market price determined? Let's find out.

Output, Price and Profit in Perfect Competition

To determine the market price and the quantity bought and sold in a perfectly competitive market, we need to study how market demand and market supply interact. We begin this process by studying a perfectly competitive market in the short run when the number of firms is fixed and each firm has a given plant size.

Short-run Equilibrium

Industry demand and supply determine market price and industry output. Figure 11.7(a) shows three

price varies when the plant size of each firm and the number of firms in the industry remain the same. The quantity supplied by the industry at a given price is the sum of the quantities supplied by all firms in the industry at that price.

Figure 11.6 shows the supply curve for the competitive jumper industry. In this industry there are 1,000 firms exactly like Neat Knits. At each price, the quantity supplied by the industry is 1,000 times the quantity supplied by a single firm.

The table in Figure 11.6 shows the firms and the industry's supply schedule and how the industry supply curve is constructed. At prices below £17, every firm in the industry shuts down so that the industry

Figure 11.7

Short-run Equilibrium

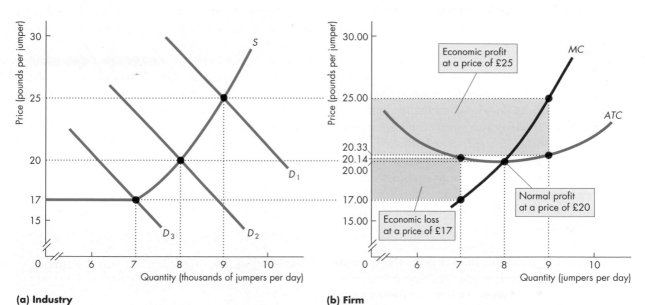

(a) Industry

In part (a), the competitive jumper industry's supply curve is *S*. If demand is D_1, the price is £25 and the industry produces 9,000 jumpers. If demand is D_2, the price is £20 and industry output is 8,000 jumpers. If demand is D_3, the price is £17 and industry output is 7,000 jumpers.

(b) Firm

In part (b), when the price is £25, an individual firm is making an economic profit; when the price is £20, it is breaking even (making normal profit), and when the price is £17 it is incurring an economic loss.

---

possible short-run equilibrium positions. The industry supply curve, *S*, is the same supply curve as in Figure 11.6. If the industry demand curve is D_1, the equilibrium price is £25. Each firm takes this price as given and produces its profit maximizing output. Because the industry has 1,000 firms, industry output is 9,000 jumpers a day. If the demand curve is D_2, the price is £20 and industry output is 8,000 jumpers a day. If the demand curve is D_3, the price is £17 and industry output is 7,000 jumpers a day.

Figure 11.7(b) shows the situation facing each of the 1,000 individual firms. With demand curve D_1, the price is £25 a jumper, so each firm produces 9 jumpers a day and makes an economic profit (the blue rectangle); if the demand curve is D_2, the price is £20 a jumper, so each firm produces 8 jumpers a day and makes zero economic profit (normal profit); and if the demand curve is D_3, the price is £17 a jumper, so each firm produces 7 jumpers a day and incurs a loss (the red rectangle).

If the demand curve shifts farther leftward than D_3, the price remains constant at £17 because the

industry supply curve is horizontal at that price. Some firms continue to produce 7 jumpers a day and others shut down. Firms are indifferent between these two activities and, whichever they choose, they incur a loss equal to total fixed cost. The number of firms continuing to produce is just enough to satisfy the market demand at a price of £17.

In the short-run, the number of firms and plant size of each firm is fixed. In the long run, each of these features of an industry can change. Let's now look at the forces that operate in the long run.

Long-run Adjustments

In short-run equilibrium, a firm might make an economic profit, incur an economic loss, or break even (make normal profit). Although each of these three situations is a short-run equilibrium, only one of them is a long-run equilibrium. To see why, we need to examine the forces at work in a competitive industry in the long run.

In the long run, an industry adjusts in two ways:

1 Entry and exit.

2 Changes in plant size.

We'll look at entry and exit first.

Entry and Exit

In the long run, firms respond to economic profit and economic loss by either entering or exiting an industry. Entrepreneurs looking for good returns will set up firms and enter industries in which firms are making an economic profit. Entrepreneurs will close down firms and exit an industry when they incur economic losses. Temporary economic profit and loss are random events and do not trigger entry and exit. But the prospect of persistent economic profit and loss do. So persistent economic profit and economic loss are the signals which prompt entry and exit decisions.

Entry and exit influence market price, the quantity produced and economic profit. The immediate effect of entry and exit is to shift the industry supply curve. If more firms enter an industry, the industry supply curve shifts rightward: supply increases. If firms exit an industry, the industry supply curve shifts leftward: supply falls. Let's see what happens when new firms enter an industry.

The Effects of Entry

Figure 11.8 shows the effects of entry. Suppose that the demand curve for jumpers is *D* and the industry supply curve is S_A, so jumpers sell for £23 and 7,000 jumpers are being produced. Firms in the industry are making an economic profit. Some new firms enter the industry. As they do so, the industry supply curve shifts rightward to S_0. With the greater supply and unchanged demand, the market price falls from £23 to £20 a jumper and the quantity produced increases from 7,000 to 8,000 jumpers a day.

As the price falls, Neat Knits and every other firm in the industry moves down along its supply curve and decreases output. That is, for each existing firm in the industry, the profit-maximizing output decreases. Because the price falls and each firm sells less, economic profit decreases. When the price falls to £20, economic profit disappears and each firm makes a normal profit.

You have just discovered a key proposition:

As new firms enter an industry, the price falls and the economic profit of each existing firm decreases.

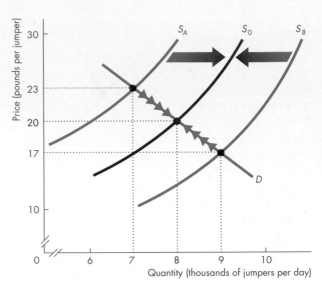

Figure 11.8

Entry and Exit

When new firms enter the jumper industry, the industry supply curve shifts rightward, from S_A to S_0. The equilibrium price falls from £23 to £20, and the quantity produced increases from 7,000 to 8,000 jumpers. When firms exit the jumper industry, the industry supply curve shifts leftward, from S_B to S_0. The equilibrium price rises from £17 to £20, and the quantity produced decreases from 9,000 to 8,000 jumpers.

A good example of this process has occurred in the last few years in the personal computer industry. When IBM introduced its first personal computer in the early 1980s, there was little competition and the price of PCs gave IBM a big profit. But new firms such as Amstrad, Dell, Elonex and a host of others soon entered the industry with machines technologically identical to the IBM PC. In fact, they were so similar that they came to be called 'clones'. The massive wave of entry into the personal computer industry shifted the supply curve rightward and lowered the price and the economic profit for all firms.

Let's now see what happens when firms leave an industry.

The Effects of Exit

Figure 11.8 shows the effects of exit. Suppose that the demand curve is *D* and the supply curve is S_B, so the market price is £17 and 9,000 jumpers are being produced. Firms in the industry are incurring an economic loss. As firms leave the industry, the supply curve shifts leftward to S_0. With the decrease in supply, industry output decreases from 9,000 to 8,000 jumpers and the price rises from £17 to £20.

As the price rises, Neat Knits and every other firm in the industry moves up along its supply curve and increases output. That is, for each existing firm in the industry, the profit-maximizing output increases. Because the price rises and each firm sells more, economic loss decreases. When the price rises to £20, economic loss disappears and each firm makes a normal profit.

You have just discovered a second key proposition:

As firms leave an industry, the price rises and so do the economic profits of the remaining firms.

An example of a firm leaving an industry is Escom UK – the United Kingdom's largest high street specialist computer chain in 1996. Escom's German parent company, Escom AG, also went bankrupt after making losses of £76 million in 1995. Escom entered the UK market in 1993, and expanded in 1995 when it took over 231 Rumbelows shops. Its agressive price-cutting strategy did not generate sufficient revenue as other retailers also reduced their prices. Profit margins in the industry were squeezed. Escom eventually exited the industry because it made persistent economic losses. When it exited the industry, it had already closed down many of its outlets. This decrease allowed the remaining retailers to break even or regain some economic profit.

Changes in Plant Size

A firm changes its plant size if, by doing so, its profit increases. Figure 11.9 shows a situation in which Neat Knits can increase its profit by increasing its plant size. With its current plant, Neat Knits' marginal cost curve is MC_0 and its short-run average total cost curve is $SRAC_0$. The market price is £25 a jumper, so Neat Knits' marginal revenue curve is MR_0 and Neat Knits maximizes profit by producing 6 jumpers a day.

Neat Knits' long-run average cost curve is $LRAC$. By increasing its plant size – installing more knitting machines – Neat Knits can move along its long-run average cost curve. As Neat Knits increases its plant size, its short-run marginal cost curve shifts rightward.

Recall that a firm's short-run supply curve is linked to its marginal cost curve. As Neat Knits' marginal

Figure 11.9

Plant Size and Long-run Equilibrium

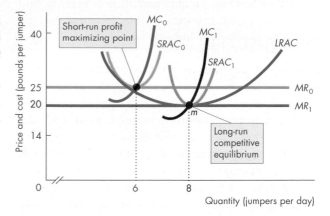

Initially, Neat Knits' plant has marginal cost curve MC_0 and short-run average total cost curve $SRAC_0$. The market price is £25 a jumper and Neat Knits' marginal revenue is MR_0. The short-run profit-maximizing quantity is 6 jumpers a day. Neat Knits can increase its profit by increasing its plant size. If all firms in the jumper industry increase their plant sizes, the short-run industry supply increases and the market price falls.

In long-run equilibrium, a firm operates with the plant that minimizes its average cost. Here, Neat Knits operates the plant with short-run marginal cost MC_1 and short-run average total cost $SRAC_1$. Neat Knits is also on its long-run average cost curve $LRAC$ and produces at point m. Output is 8 jumpers a day and average total cost equals the price of a jumper at £20.

cost curve shifts rightward, so does its supply curve. If Neat Knits and the other firms in the industry increase their plant size, the short-run industry supply curve shifts rightward and the market price falls. The fall in the market price limits the extent to which Neat Knits can profit from increasing its plant size.

Figure 11.9 also shows Neat Knits in a long-run competitive equilibrium. This situation arises when the market price has fallen to £20 a jumper. Marginal revenue is MR_1, and Neat Knits maximizes profit by producing 8 jumpers a day. In this situation, Neat Knits cannot increase its profit by changing its plant size. It is producing at minimum long-run average cost (point m on $LRAC$).

Because Neat Knits is producing at minimum long-run average cost, it has no incentive to change its plant size. Either a bigger plant or a smaller plant has a higher long-run average cost.

If all firms in the jumper industry are in the situation described in Figure 11.9, the industry is in long-run equilibrium. No firm has an incentive to change its plant size. Also, because each firm is making zero economic profit (normal profit), no firm has an incentive to enter the industry or to leave it.

Long-run Equilibrium

Long-run equilibrium occurs in a competitive industry when firms are earning normal profit and economic profit is zero. If the firms in a competitive industry make an economic profit, new firms enter the industry and the supply curve shifts rightward. As a result, the market price falls and so does economic profit. Firms continue to enter and economic profit continues to decrease as long as the industry is earning positive economic profits. Only when the economic profit has been eliminated and normal profit is being made do firms stop entering.

If the firms in a competitive industry incur an economic loss, some of the firms exit the industry and the supply curve shifts leftward. As a result, the market price rises and the industry's economic loss shrinks.

Firms continue to leave and economic loss continues to decrease as long as the industry is incurring an economic loss. Only when the economic loss has been eliminated and normal profit is being made do firms stop exiting. Also, when firms are operating with the least-cost plant size, they stop downsizing.

So, in long-run equilibrium in a competitive industry, firms neither enter nor exit the industry.

Review Quiz

◆ What is the relationship between the firm's marginal cost, marginal revenue and price for a firm that maximizes profit in perfect competition?
◆ If the firms in a competitive industry earn an economic profit, what happens to supply, price, output and economic profit?
◆ If the firms in a competitive industry incur an economic loss, what happens to supply, price, output and economic profit?

We've seen how economic loss triggers exit, which eventually eliminates the loss, and we've seen how economic profit triggers entry, which eventually eliminates the profit. In the long run, normal profit is earned. But a competitive industry is rarely in a long-run equilibrium. It is restlessly evolving towards such an equilibrium and the conditions the industry faces are constantly changing. The two most persistent sources of change are in tastes and technology. Let's see how a competitive industry reacts to such changes.

Changing Tastes and Advancing Technology

Increased awareness of the health hazard of smoking has caused a decrease in the demand for tobacco and cigarettes. The development of cheap cars and air travel has caused a huge decrease in the demand for long-distance trains and buses. Solid-state electronics have caused a large decrease in the demand for TV and radio repair. The development of good quality budget clothing has decreased the demand for sewing machines. What happens in a competitive industry when there is a permanent decrease in the demand for its products?

The development of the microwave oven has produced an enormous increase in demand for paper, glass and plastic cooking utensils, and for plastic wrap. The demand for almost all products is steadily increasing as a result of increasing population and increasing incomes. What happens in a competitive industry when the demand for its product increases?

Advances in technology are constantly lowering the costs of production. New biotechnologies have dramatically lowered the costs of many food and pharmaceutical products. New electronic technologies have lowered the cost of producing just about every good and service. What happens in a competitive industry when technological change lowers its production costs?

Let's use the theory of perfect competition to answer these questions.

A Permanent Change in Demand

Figure 11.10(a) shows an industry that initially is in long-run competitive equilibrium. The demand curve is D_0, the supply curve is S_0, the market price is P_0 and industry output is Q_0. Figure 11.10(b) shows a single firm in this initial long-run equilibrium. The firm produces q_0 and makes a normal profit and zero economic profit.

Figure 11.10

A Decrease in Demand

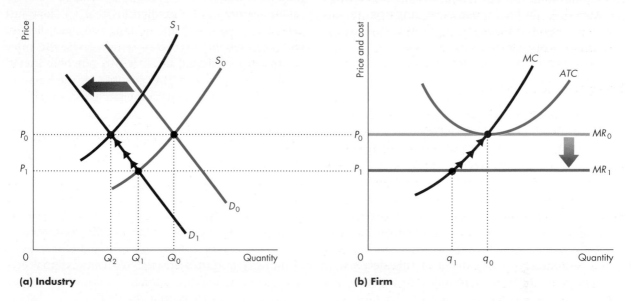

(a) Industry

(b) Firm

An industry starts out in long-run competitive equilibrium. Part (a) shows the industry demand curve D_0 and the industry supply curve S_0, the equilibrium quantity Q_0 and the market price P_0. Each firm sells at price P_0, so its marginal revenue curve is MR_0 in part (b). Each firm produces q_0 and makes a normal profit. Demand decreases from D_0 to D_1 (part a). The equilibrium price falls to P_1, each firm decreases its output to q_1 (part b) and industry output decreases to Q_1 (part a). In this new situation, firms are incurring losses and some firms leave the industry. As they do so, the industry supply curve gradually shifts leftward, from S_0 to S_1. This shift gradually raises the industry price from P_1 back to P_0. While the price is below P_0, firms are incurring losses and some leave the industry. Once the price has returned to P_0, each firm makes a normal profit. Firms have no further incentive to leave the industry. Each firm produces q_0 and industry output is Q_2.

Now suppose that demand decreases and the demand curve shifts leftward to D_1, as shown in part (a). The price falls to P_1 and the quantity supplied by the industry decreases from Q_0 to Q_1 as the industry slides down its short-run supply curve S_0. Part (b) shows the situation facing a firm. Price is now below minimum average total cost so the firm incurs an economic loss. But to keep its loss to a minimum, the firm adjusts its output to keep price equal to marginal cost. At a price of P_1 each firm produces an output of q_1.

The industry is now in short-run equilibrium but not long-run equilibrium. It is in short-run equilibrium because each firm is maximizing profit. But it is not in long-run equilibrium because each firm is incurring an economic loss – its average total cost exceeds the price.

The economic loss is a signal for some firms to leave the industry. As they do so, short-run industry supply decreases and the supply curve shifts leftward.

As supply decreases, the price rises. At each higher price a firm's profit-maximizing output is greater, so those remaining in the industry increase their output as the price rises. Each slides up its marginal cost or supply curve (part b). That is, as firms exit the industry, industry output decreases but the output of the firms that remain in the industry increases. Eventually, enough firms leave the industry for the supply curve to have shifted to S_1 (part a). At this time, the price has returned to its original level, P_0. At this price, the firms remaining in the industry produce q_0, the same quantity as they produced before the decrease in demand. Because firms are now making normal profits and zero economic profit, no firm wants to enter or exit the industry. The industry supply curve remains at S_1 and industry output is Q_2. The industry is again in long-run equilibrium.

The difference between the initial long-run equilibrium and the final long-run equilibrium is the number of firms in the industry. A permanent decrease in demand has decreased the number of firms. Each remaining firm produces the same output in the new long-run equilibrium as it did initially and earns a normal profit. In the process of moving from the initial equilibrium to the new one, firms that remain in the industry incur losses.

We've just worked out how a competitive industry responds to a permanent *decrease* in demand. A permanent increase in demand triggers a similar response, except in the opposite direction. The increase in demand brings a higher price, profit and entry. Entry increases supply and eventually lowers the price to its original level.

The market for mainframe computers is one that has experienced a decrease in demand in recent years. As personal computers have become faster and cheaper, more and more data processing has been done on people's desktops rather than in big computer laboratories. The effects of this decrease in demand have been similar to those we have just studied.

We've now studied the effects of a permanent change in taste that brings a permanent change in demand for a good. We began and ended in a long-run equilibrium and examined the *process* that gets a

market from one equilibrium to another. It is this process that describes the real world, not the equilibrium points.

One feature of the predictions that we have just generated seems odd: in the long run, regardless of whether demand increases or decreases, the price returns to its original level. Is this outcome inevitable? In fact, it is not. It is possible for the long-run equilibrium price to remain the same, rise, or fall.

External Economies and Diseconomies

The change in the long-run equilibrium price depends on external economies and external diseconomies. **External economies** are factors beyond the control of an individual firm that lower its costs as *industry* output increases. **External diseconomies** are factors outside the control of a firm that raise its costs as industry output increases. With no external economies or external diseconomies, a firm's costs remain constant as industry output changes.

Figure 11.11 illustrates these three cases and introduces a new supply concept, the long-run industry supply curve. A **long-run industry supply curve** shows how the quantity supplied by an industry

Figure 11.11

Long-run Changes in Price and Quantity

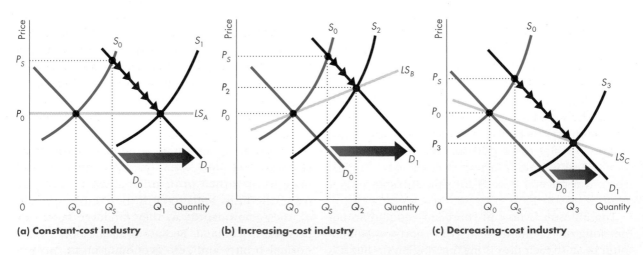

(a) Constant-cost industry **(b) Increasing-cost industry** **(c) Decreasing-cost industry**

Three possible long-run changes in price and quantity are illustrated. When demand increases from D_0 to D_1, entry occurs and the industry supply curve shifts from S_0 to S_1. In part (a), the long-run supply curve LS_A is horizontal. The quantity increases from Q_0 to Q_1 and the price remains constant at P_0. In part (b), the long-run supply curve is LS_B;

the price increases to P_2 and the quantity increases to Q_2. This case occurs in industries with external diseconomies. In part (c), the long-run supply curve is LS_C; the price decreases to P_3 and the quantity increases to Q_3. This case occurs in an industry with external economies.

varies as the market price varies after all the possible adjustments have been made, including changes in plant size and changes in the number of firms in the industry.

Part (a) shows the case we have just studied – no external economies or diseconomies. The long-run industry supply curve (LS_A) is perfectly elastic. In this case, a permanent increase in demand from D_0 to D_1 has no effect on the price in the long run. The increase in demand brings a temporary increase in price to P_S, and a short-run quantity increase from Q_0 to Q_S. Entry increases short-run supply from S_0 to S_1, which lowers the price to its original level, P_0, and increases the quantity to Q_1.

Part (b) shows the case of external diseconomies. In this case, the long-run supply industry curve (LS_B) slopes upward. A permanent increase in demand from D_0 to D_1 increases the price in both the short run and the long run. As in the previous case, the increase in demand brings a temporary increase in price to P_S, and a short-run quantity increase from Q_0 to Q_S. Entry increases short-run supply from S_0 to S_1, which lowers the price to P_2 and increases the quantity to Q_2.

One source of external diseconomies is congestion. The airline industry provides a good illustration. With bigger airline industry output, there is more congestion of both airports and airspace, which results in longer delays and extra waiting time for passengers and aircraft. These external diseconomies mean that as the output of air travel services increases (in the absence of technological advances), average cost increases. As a result, the long-run supply curve is upward-sloping. So a permanent increase in demand brings an increase in quantity and a rise in the price. Technological advances decrease costs and *shift* the long-run supply curve downward. So even an industry that experiences external diseconomies might have falling prices over the long run.

Part (c) shows the case of external economies. In this case, the long-run industry supply curve (LS_C) slopes downward. A permanent increase in demand from D_0 to D_1, increases the price in the short run and lowers it in the long run. Again, the increase in demand brings a temporary increase in price to P_S, and a short-run quantity increase from Q_0 to Q_S. Entry increases short-run supply from S_0 to S_3, which lowers the price to P_3 and increases the quantity to Q_3.

One of the best examples of external economies is the growth of specialist support services for an industry as it expands. As farm output increased in the nineteenth and early twentieth centuries, the services available to farmers expanded and their costs fell. For example, markets developed in farm machinery and fertilizers that lowered farm costs. Farms enjoyed the benefits of external economies. As a consequence, as the demand for farm products increased, the quantity produced increased but the price fell.

Over the long term, the prices of many goods and services have fallen, not because of external economies but because of technological change. Let's now study this influence on a competitive market.

Technological Change

Industries are constantly discovering lower-cost techniques of production. Most cost-saving production techniques cannot be implemented, however, without investing in new plant and equipment. As a consequence, it takes time for a technological advance to spread through an industry. Some firms whose plants are on the verge of being replaced will be quick to adopt the new technology, while other firms whose plants have recently been replaced will continue to operate with an old technology until they can no longer cover their average variable cost. Once average variable cost cannot be covered, a firm will scrap even a relatively new plant (embodying an old technology) in favour of a plant with a new technology.

New technology allows firms to produce at a lower cost and to make a larger profit than the existing technology. As a result, as firms adopt a new technology, their cost curves shift downward. With lower costs, firms are willing to supply a given quantity at a lower price or, equivalently, they are willing to supply a larger quantity at a given price. In other words, supply increases and the supply curve shifts rightward. With a given demand, the quantity produced increases and the price falls.

Two forces are at work in an industry undergoing technological change. Firms that adopt the new technology make an economic profit. So there is entry by new-technology firms. Firms that stick with the old technology incur economic losses. They either exit the industry or switch to the new technology.

As old-technology firms disappear and new-technology firms enter, the price falls and the quantity produced increases. Eventually, the industry arrives at a long-run equilibrium in which all the firms use the new technology, produce at minimum long-run average cost and make zero economic profit (a normal profit). Because in the long run competition eliminates economic profit, technological change brings only temporary gains to producers. But the lower prices and better products that technological advances bring are permanent gains for consumers.

The process that we've just described is one in which some firms experience economic profits and others experience economic losses. It is a period of dynamic change for an industry. Some firms do well and others do badly. Often the process has a geographical dimension – the expanding new-technology firms bring prosperity to the 'rust-belt' regions where traditional industries have gone into decline. Sometimes the new-technology firms are in a foreign country, while the old-technology firms are in the domestic economy. Scotland's 'silicon glen' is an example of a high-tech industry which has located in a traditionally agricultural area. The information revolution of the 1990s has produced many examples of changes like these. Technological advances are not confined to the information industry. Even milk production is undergoing a major technological change, which arises from the use of hormones in cattle.

Review Quiz

◆ Outline the events that follow a decrease in demand in a competitive industry in the short and long run. Explain how the presence of external economies or diseconomies influences the outcome.

◆ Outline the events that follow an increase in demand in a competitive industry in the short and long run. Explain how the presence of external economies or diseconomies influences the outcome.

◆ Outline the events that follow the adoption of new technology in a competitive industry in the short and long run.

Competition and Efficiency

A competitive industry can achieve an efficient use of resources. You studied efficiency in Chapter 5 using only the concepts of demand, supply and consumer surplus. But with your knowledge of what lies behind demand and supply curves in a competitive market, you can now gain a deeper understanding of how a competitive market achieves efficiency.

Efficient Use of Resources

Recall that resource use is efficient when we produce the goods and services that people value most highly (see Chapter 5, pp. 98–100). If someone can become better off without anyone else becoming worse off, resources are *not* being used efficiently. For example, suppose we produce a computer that no one uses and that no one will ever use. Suppose also that many people want and demand more video games. If we produce one less computer and reallocate the unused resources to produce more video games, some people will become better off and no one will be worse off. So the initial resource allocation was inefficient.

So, resource use is efficient when marginal benefit equals marginal cost. In the CD and magazines example in Chapter 2, the marginal benefit of magazines exceeds the marginal cost. And the marginal cost of a CD exceeds its marginal benefit. So by producing fewer CDs and more magazines, we move resources towards a higher-value use.

You can use what you have learned about the decisions made by consumers and competitive firms and market equilibrium to describe an efficient use of resources.

Value, Equilibrium and Efficiency

Maximum Value

Consumers allocate their budgets to get the most value possible out of them. Consumer demand is derived by finding how the best budget allocation changes as the price of a good changes. So consumers get the most value out of their resources at all points along their demand curves, which are also their marginal benefit curves.

Competitive firms produce the quantity that maximizes profit, and the firm's supply curve is derived by finding the profit-maximizing quantities at each price. So firms get the most value out of their resources at all points along their supply curves, which are also their marginal cost curves. Remember, when firms are on their supply curves they are *technologically efficient* – they get the maximum possible output from given inputs, and are also *economically efficient* – they combine resources to minimize cost (see Chapter 9, pp. 178–179).

Equilibrium

In competitive equilibrium, the quantity demanded equals the quantity supplied. So the price equals the consumers' marginal benefit and the producers' marginal cost. In this situation, the gains from trade between consumers and producers are maximized. These gains from trade are the consumer surplus plus the producer surplus. The gains from trade for consumers are measured by *consumer surplus*, which is the area between the demand curve and the price paid (see Chapter 5, p. 96). The gains from trade for producers are measured by *producer surplus*, which is the area between the marginal cost curve and the price received. The total gains from trade are the sum of consumer surplus and producer surplus.

Allocative Efficiency

If the people who consume and produce a good or service are the only ones affected by it, and if the market for the good or service is in equilibrium, then resources have been allocated to their most efficient use. **Allocative efficiency** occurs when no resources in the economy are wasted – resources cannot be reallocated to increase their value.

In such a situation, there are no *external benefits* or *external costs*. **External benefits** are benefits that accrue to people other than the buyer of a good. For example, you might get a benefit from your neighbour's expenditure on her garden. Your neighbour buys the quantities of garden plants that make her as well off as possible, not her plus you. In the absence of external benefits, the market demand curve measures **marginal social benefit** – the value that *everyone* places on one more unit of a good or service.

External costs are costs not borne by the producer of a good or service but by someone else. For example, a firm might lower its costs by polluting. The cost of pollution is an external cost. Firms produce the output level that maximizes their own profit and they do not count the cost of pollution as a charge against their profit.

In the absence of external costs, the market supply curve measures **marginal social cost** – the entire marginal cost that *anyone* bears to produce one more unit of a good or service.

An efficient allocation of resources also maximizes the value to both producers and consumers, measured by surplus. The total sum of consumer and producer surplus is called total social welfare (*TSW*).

An Efficient Allocation

Figure 11.12(a) illustrates how a competitive market equilibrium is an efficient allocation. Consumers are

Figure 11.12

Efficiency of Competition

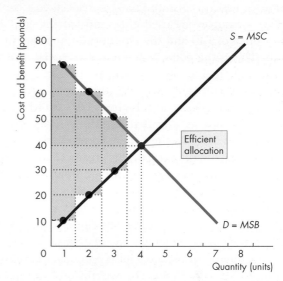

(a) Allocative efficiency

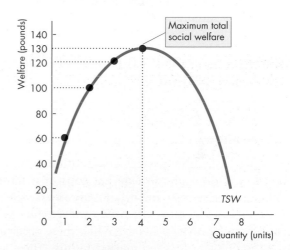

(b) Maximizing welfare

If there are no external costs or benefits, an efficient allocation occurs when consumers are on their demand curves and producers are on their supply curves, and the market is in equilibrium. Resources are efficiently used when 4 units are produced, as demand, *D*, equals marginal social benefit (*MSB*) and supply, *S*, equals marginal social cost (*MSC*) as shown in part (a). Total social welfare (*TSW*) shown in part (b) is the sum of consumer and producer surplus. If the first unit is produced, *MSB* is greater than *MSC* and the sum of consumer and producer surplus generated is positive. Total social welfare (*TSW*) increases. At the efficient allocation *D* = *S*, *MSB* = *MSC*, no resources are wasted and total social welfare is maximized at £130.

efficient at all points on the demand curve *D*, (which is also the marginal social benefit curve (*MSB*). Producers are efficient at all points on the supply curve, *S* (which is also the marginal social cost curve (*MSC*). Resources are used effficiently at the equilibrium price of £40 and the equilibrium quantity of 4 units. This is the point where marginal social benefit equals marginal social cost, and total social welfare, the sum of consumer surplus (green area) and producer surplus (blue area) is highest. Let's see why.

When output is 1 unit in Figure 11.12a, *MSB* is greater than *MSC*. As the benefit to everyone in society of producing the extra unit is greater than the cost to everyone, there will be a positive surplus from producing the first unit. A positive surplus means that total social welfare must increase. Total social welfare, *TSW*, at each unit of output is shown in part (b). The first unit of output generates £60 of extra surplus (£30 of consumer surplus and £30 of producer surplus), making *TSW* equal £60. The second unit of output generates £40 of extra surplus (£20 of consumer surplus and £20 of producer surplus), making *TSW* equal £100 (£60 for the first and £40 for the second unit). *TSW* is maximized at £130 when 4 units are produced.

If output goes beyond 4 units to 5 units, *MSB* is less than *MSC*. The surplus will be negative and total social welfare will decrease.

Obstacles to Efficiency in Perfect Competition

You have seen how perfect competition achieves efficiency if there are no external costs or external benefits. External costs and benefits are an example of obstacles to efficiency which can prevent markets achieving allocative efficiency. When these obstacles arise the problem is called **market failure**. There are three main types of market failure.

1 Monopoly.

2 Public goods.

3 External costs and external benefits.

Monopoly (Chapter 12) arises when a firm can stop new firms from entering the industry and bidding down the market price. As a result, a monopoly firm can restrict output below its competitive level and raise price to increase profit. Government policies (Chapter 17) can help to achieve a more efficient allocation of resources when monopoly arises.

Public goods are the type of goods and services that the market sector is reluctant to supply because the marginal cost of providing an extra unit is close to zero. Market supply is unprofitable and so too little of the good is produced. Examples are national defence and law enforcement. However, Government policies (Chapter 16) can help to overcome the inefficient allocation of public goods.

External costs and external benefits are characteristics of many markets. The production of agricultural products and chemicals can generate air and water pollution and perfect competition might produce too large a quantity of these goods. Government policies (Chapter 18) can help to achieve an efficient allocation of resources in these markets.

You have now completed our study of the model of perfect competition. It has given us an insight into the way that firms make choices when competition is strong and firms have little influence over price. However, perfect competition is not an appropriate model for every market and our next task is to study markets where there is a significant amount of market failure. We'll start by studying a model where firms have the power to influence prices by restricting output. We study the simplest case, monopoly, in the next chapter and other cases, monopolistic competition and oligopoly, in Chapter 13.

Summary

Key Points

Perfect Competition (pp. 217–218)

- Perfectly competitive competition arises when demand is large relative to the efficient scale of production and when firms produce identical products.

- A competitive firm is a price taker.

The Firm's Decision in Perfect Competition (pp. 219–224)

- The firm produces the output at which marginal revenue (price) equals marginal cost.

- In short-run equilibrium, a firm can make an economic profit, incur an economic loss, or break even.

- If price is less than minimum average variable cost, the firm temporarily shuts down.

- A firm's supply curve is the upward-sloping part of its marginal cost curve above minimum average variable cost.

- An industry supply curve shows the sum of the quantities supplied by each firm at each price.

Output, Price and Profit in Perfect Competition (pp. 224–228)

- Market demand and supply determine price.

- The firm produces the output at which price equals marginal cost.

- Economic profit induces entry. Economic loss induces exit.

- Entry and plant expansion increase supply and lower price and profit. Exit and plant contraction decrease supply and raise price and profit.

- In the long-run equilibrium, economic profit is zero. There is no entry, exit, or change in plant size.

Changing Tastes and Advancing Technology (pp. 228–232)

- A permanent decrease in demand leads to a smaller industry output and a smaller number of firms.

- A permanent increase in demand leads to a larger industry output and a larger number of firms.

- The long-run effect of a change in demand on price depends on whether there are external economies (price falls), external diseconomies, (price rises) or neither (price remains constant).

Competition and Efficiency (pp. 232–234)

- Resources are used efficiently when we produce goods and services in the quantities that everyone values most highly.

- When there are no external benefits or external costs, perfect competition achieves an efficient allocation. Marginal benefit equals marginal cost and total welfare, the sum of consumer and producer surplus, is maximized.

- The main obstacles to achieving allocative efficiency are monopoly, public goods and external costs and benefits.

Key Figures ◈

Key Terms

Problems

•1 Quick Copy is one of the many copy shops in London. The figure shows Quick Copy's cost curves.

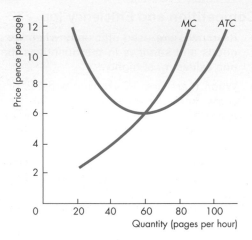

a If the market price of copying one page is 10 pence, what is Quick Copy's profit-maximizing output?

b Calculate Quick Copy's profit.

c With no change in demand or technology, how will the price change in the long run?

2 Bob's is one of many burger stands at Leeds United football stadium. The figure shows Bob's cost curves.

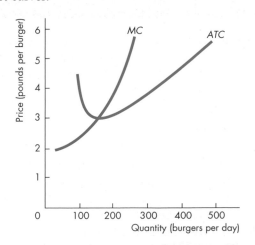

a If the market price of a burger is £4, what is Bob's profit-maximizing output?

b Calculate the profit that Bob's makes.

c With no change in demand or technology, how will the price change in the long run?

•3 Pat's Pizza Kitchen is a price taker in Rome. Pat's cost of producing pizza is:

Output (pizzas per hour)	Total cost (euros per hour)
0	10
1	21
2	30
3	41
4	54
5	69

a If a pizza sells for €14, what is Pat's profit-maximizing output per hour? How much economic profit does Pat make?

b What is Pat's shutdown point?

c Derive Pat's supply curve.

d Over what price range will Pat leave the pizza industry?

e Over what price range will other firms with costs identical to Pat's enter the industry?

f What is the price of a pizza in the long run?

4 Lucy's Lasagne is a price taker in Rome. Lucy's cost of producing lasagne is:

Output (plates per hour)	Total cost (euros per hour)
0	5
1	20
2	26
3	35
4	46
5	59

a If lasagne sells for €7.50 a plate, what is Lucy's profit-maximizing output?

b What is Lucy's shutdown point?

c Over what price range will Lucy leave the lasagne industry?

d Over what price range will other firms with costs identical to Lucy's enter the industry?

e What is the price of lasagne in the long run?

•5 The market demand schedule for cassettes in Rotterdam is:

Price (euros per cassettes)	Quantity demanded (thousands of cassettes per week)
3.65	500
5.20	450
6.80	400
10.00	300
11.60	250
13.20	200
14.80	150

The market is perfectly competitive, and each firm has the following cost structure:

Output (cassettes per week)	Marginal cost (euros per additional cassette)	Average variable cost (euros per cassette)	Average total cost
150	6.00	8.80	15.47
200	6.40	7.80	12.80
250	7.00	7.00	11.00
300	7.65	7.10	10.43
350	8.40	7.20	10.06
400	10.00	7.50	10.00
450	12.40	8.00	10.22
500	12.70	9.00	11.00

There are 1,000 firms in the industry.

a What is the market price?

b What is the industry's output?

c What is the output produced by each firm?

d What is the economic profit made by each firm?

e Do firms enter or exit the industry?

f What is the number of firms in the long run?

6 The same demand conditions as those in problem 5 prevail, and there are 1,000 firms in the industry, but fixed costs increase by €980. What now are your answers to the questions in problem 5?

●7 In problem 5, the price of a compact disc decreases the demand for cassettes and the demand schedule becomes:

Price (euros per cassette)	Quantity demanded (thousands of cassettes per week)
2.95	500
4.13	450
5.30	400
6.48	350
7.65	300
8.83	250
10.00	200
11.18	150

What now are your answers to the questions in problem 5?

8 In problem 6, the price of a compact disc decreases the demand for cassettes and the demand schedule becomes that given in the table in problem 7. What now are your answers to the questions in problem 6?

Critical Thinking

1 Study the Business Case Study on pp. 238–239 and then answer the following questions:

a What are the characteristics of tea production and tea buyers at auctions that makes the market for tea highly competitive?

b Why does the price of tea change so rapidly? Is this a problem for tea growers? Explain your answer.

c What effect will Sri Lanka's use of more efficient agricultural methods have on economic profits in the short run? (Hint: think about the average cost curve and profit.)

d What will be the long-run effect of introducing more efficient agricultural methods in the tea market?

e Who are the winners and who are the losers in the competition between India and Sri Lanka for the quality tea export market?

f What do you think happens to the workers in the tea gardens that fail because they are producing low grade teas when prices fall?

2 What has been the effect of an increase in world population on the wheat market and the individual wheat farmer? Explain your answer.

3 Visit the Parkin, Powell and Matthews website and read the Reading Between the Lines article 'Competition: Lifting Restrictions on Grey Car Imports'. Then answer the following questions:

a What is meant by a 'grey import'?

b How do restrictions on grey imports protect UK car producers from competition from other European car producers?

c Why do restrictions on grey imports affect competition amongst dealerships?

d Why do you think the UK Competition Commission is investigating new car prices in Britain?

e Why does government need to impose a 'test' on the quality of imported vehicles?

 http://www.econ100.com

Perfect Competition

Indian and Sri Lankan Tea Gardens

The Market

Tea is grown and produced by millions of small scale tea farmers in tea gardens across eight countries producing about 2.5 million tonnes a year. Production and prices for tea from the worlds largest producer, India, and the world's largest exporter, Sri Lanka are shown in the table.

Supply and Demand

The world's supply of tea is affected by agricultural methods. Sri Lanka has expanded production using more efficient agricultural methods to produce higher quality tea, compared to India. Demand for high quality teas has increased but demand for Indian tea fell in 2000.

The Price

Price is determined at the major tea auction centres in Jakarta, Colombo and Mombasa. Average prices, shown in the table, slumped for Indian tea in 2000 but increased elsewhere.

The Effect on Indian Tea Farmers

According to the world's largest tea broker, J. Thomas, most of the tea gardens in India were forced to sell tea below the cost of production in 2000. Gardens that neglected quality went out of business. India's tea producers are trying to move towards growing higher quality teas.

Country	Production (tonnes)		Average Price (rupees)	
	1999	2000	1999	2000
India	805,612	823,421	72.80	61.71
Sri Lanka	283,761	305,844	114.96	135.06

*Source: K. Bose, Sri Lankan tea gains at expense of India, *Financial Times*, 27 March 2001, p. 38. J. Thomas (2001), The Tea Market Annual Report, 2000.

Economic Analysis

- Figure 1 shows the market in 1999 for Indian teas as perfectly competitive. The market in part (a) determines the price at 72.80 rupees per kilogram. This is also the demand curve and marginal revenue curve (MR_0) for every tea garden shown in part (b). Each tea garden produces the quantity of tea at which marginal revenue equals marginal cost (MC_0) and makes an economic profit shown by the blue rectangle.

- Figure 2 part (a) shows supply shifting to the right in 2000 in response to economic profits earned in 1999, but world demand for Indian tea decreases. The combined effect is a price fall to 61.71 rupees per kilogram.

- Figure 2 part (b) shows that Indian tea growers make economic losses at the lower price. Some growers leave the industry, others cut costs with more efficient agriculture. Eventually supply will decrease and prices rise, returning the market to long-run equilibrium with no economic profit.

- Figure 3 part (a) shows price in the market for Sri Lankan high quality tea. Economic profit in 1999 means supply shifts to the right in 2000. But price rises because of a big increase in world demand for quality tea, increasing economic profits in 2000.

- Eventually, India's move towards higher quality teas and further increases in Sri Lankan production will increase world supply and tend to bid down the price of high quality teas. This will squeeze out the economic profits being made and return the Sri Lankan tea market to long-run equilibrium.

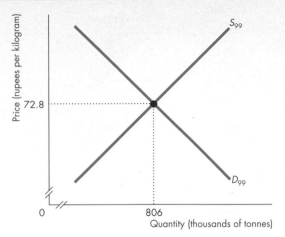

(a) Tea market

Figure 1 Indian tea, 1999

(b) Tea garden

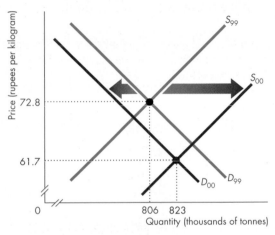

(a) Tea market

Figure 2 Indian tea, 2000

(b) Tea garden

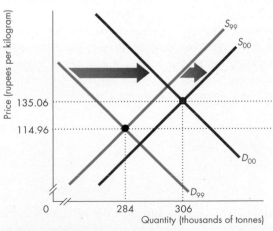

(a) Tea market

Figure 3 Sri Lankan tea, 2000

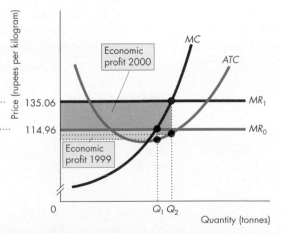

(b) Tea garden

CHAPTER 12

Monopoly

After studying this chapter you will be able to:

◆ Explain how monopolies arise and distinguish between a single price monopoly and a price-discriminating monopoly

◆ Explain how a monopoly determines its price and output

◆ Compare the performance and efficiency of single price monopoly and competition

◆ Define rent seeking and explain why it arises

◆ Explain how price discrimination increases profit

◆ Explain how monopoly regulation influences output, price, economic profit and efficiency

The Profits of Generosity

We've talked a lot about firms that want to maximize profit. But are all firms really so intent on maximizing profit? After all, you have probably been offered a student's discount at some bookshops, theatres and record shops. Airlines often give a discount for buying a ticket in advance and rail companies offer discounts for student travel. Are all these firms simply being generous? Are they throwing money away? Or perhaps the perfectly competitive model does not apply in all cases. ◆ When you buy water, you don't shop around. You buy from your water utility, which is your only available supplier. If you live in the UK in Yorkshire and you want a water supply, you only have one option: buy from Yorkshire Water. These are examples of a single producer of a good or service controlling its supply. Such firms are obviously not like firms in perfectly competitive industries. They don't face a market-determined price. They can choose the price they charge. How do such firms behave? How do they choose the quantity to produce and the price at which to sell it? How does their behaviour compare with firms in perfectly competitive industries? Do such firms charge prices that are too high and that damage the interests of consumers? Do such firms bring any benefits? How and why are monopolies regulated?

◆ ◆ ◆ ◆ In this chapter we are going to build a model of a monopoly supplier. We will use this model to study markets in which an individual firm can influence quantity supplied and also determine price. We also examine whether monopoly is as efficient as competition. Finally, in our Business Case Study (see pp. 260–261), we look at why Europe's major producers of vitamins colluded illegally to act like a monopoly.

Market Power

Market power and competition are the two forces that operate in most markets. Market power is the ability to influence the market, and in particular the market price, by influencing the total quantity offered for sale.

The firms in perfect competition that you studied in Chapter 11 have no market power. They face the force of raw competition and are price takers. The firms that we study in this chapter operate at the opposite extreme. They face no competition and exercise raw market power. We call this extreme *monopoly*.

Monopolies can be local, national or international. Examples include the distribution of water, natural gas distribution, as well as DeBeers, the South African diamond producer, and Microsoft, the software developer that created your computer's operating system.

A monopoly is an industry that produces a good or service for which no close substitute exists and in which there is one supplier that is protected from competition by a barrier preventing the entry of new firms. The lack of close substitutes and the barriers to entry are the reasons why monopoly is a form of market failure.

How Monopoly Arises

Monopoly has two key features:

1 No close substitutes.
2 Barriers to entry.

No Close Substitutes

If a good does have a close substitute, even though only one firm produces it, that firm effectively faces competition from the producers of substitutes. Electricity supplied by a local public utility is an example of a good that does not have close substitutes. While mains gas and oil are substitutes for domestic heating, there is no realistic substitute for domestic electrical appliances.

Monopolies are constantly under attack from new products and ideas that substitute for products produced by monopolies. For example, the spread of international courier services such as DHL, the development of the fax machine and e-mail finally broke down the monopoly in the UK postal service in 2001. Advances in telecommunications technology have also weakened the monopoly of telecommunications firms in most European countries. In particular, cell-phones have begun to undermine the monopoly in local calls.

So monopolies are constantly looking for new products. The development of the computer has created monopolies, the most obvious of which is Microsoft's PC operating system – DOS. Similarly, research in the pharmaceuticals industry is constantly creating new monopolies in drugs.

Barriers to entry

Legal or natural constraints that protect a firm from competition from potential new entrants are called **barriers to entry**. Firms can sometimes create barriers to entry by owning a unique and natural resource such as diamonds, but most monopolies arise because of legal and natural barriers.

Legal Barriers to Entry

Legal barriers to entry create legal monopoly. A **legal monopoly** is a market in which competition and entry are restricted by the granting of a franchise, licence, patent or copyright, or in which a firm has acquired ownership of a significant proportion of a key resource.

A *monopoly franchise* is an exclusive right granted to a firm to supply a good or service. An example of a monopoly franchise is the UK Post Office, which has been granted the exclusive right to provide some letter-carrying services.

A *government licence* controls entry into particular occupations, professions and industries. Government licensing in the professions is the most common example of this type of barrier to entry. For example, a licence is required to practise medicine, law and dentistry among many other professional services. Licensing need not create monopoly, but it does restrict competition. When a new TV channel is offered for franchise, the successful bidder gains a licence to broadcast for a limited period. In this case, it confers a monopoly on the channel broadcaster. Where the number of channels is restricted, competition in broadcasting will be limited.

A **patent** is an exclusive right granted to the inventor of a product or service. A **copyright** is an exclusive right granted to the author or composer of a literary, musical, dramatic or artistic work. Patents and copyrights are valid for a limited time period that varies from country to country. In the United Kingdom, a patent is valid for 16 years. Patents protect inventors by creating a property right and thereby encourage invention by preventing others from copying an invention until sufficient time has elapsed for the inventor to have reaped some benefits. They also stimulate *innovation* – the use of new inventions – by increasing the incentives for inventors to publicize their discoveries and offer them for use under licence.

Natural Barriers to Entry Natural barriers to entry create **natural monopoly**, which is an industry in which one firm can supply the entire market at a lower price than two or more firms can.

Figure 12.1 shows a UK natural monopoly in the distribution of electric power. The demand for electric power is *D* and the average total cost curve is *ATC*. Because average total cost decreases as output increases, economies of scale prevail over the entire length of the

ATC curve. One firm can produce 4 million kilowatt-hours at 5 pence a kilowatt-hour. At this price, the quantity demanded is 4 million kilowatt-hours. So if the price was 5 pence, one firm could supply the entire market. If two firms shared the market, it would cost each of them 10 pence a kilowatt-hour to produce a total of 4 million kilowatt-hours. If four firms shared the market, it would cost each of them 15 pence a kilowatt-hour to produce a total of 4 million kilowatt-hours. So in conditions like those shown in Figure 12.1, one firm can supply the entire market at a lower cost than two or more firms can. Electricity generating utilities are an example of natural monopoly. Another example is natural gas distribution.

Most monopolies in the real world, whether legal or natural, are regulated in some way by government or by government agencies. We will study such regulation in Chapter 17. Here we will study unregulated monopoly for two reasons. First, we can better understand why governments regulate monopolies and the effects of regulation if we also know how an unregulated monopoly behaves. Second, even in industries with more than one producer, firms often have a strong degree of monopoly power, arising from locational advantages or from differences in product quality protected by patents. The theory of monopoly sheds light on the behaviour of many of these firms and industries.

A major difference between monopoly and competition is that a monopoly sets its own price. But in doing so, it faces a market constraint. Let's see how the market limits a monopoly's pricing choices.

Monopoly Price-setting Strategies

All monopolies face a trade-off between price and the quantity sold. To sell a larger quantity, the monopolist must charge a lower price. But there are two broad monopoly situations that create different trade-offs. They are:

1 Single price.

2 Price discrimination.

Single Price

DeBeers sells diamonds (of a given size and quality) for the same price to all its customers. If it tried to sell at a low price to some customers and at a higher price to others, only the low-price customers would buy from DeBeers. Others would buy from DeBeers' low-price

Figure 12.1
Natural Monopoly

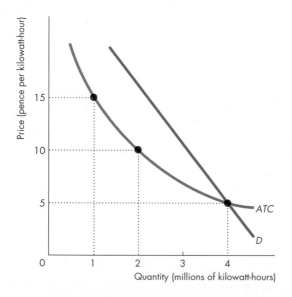

The demand curve for electric power is *D* and the average total cost curve is *ATC*. Economies of scale exist over the entire *ATC* curve. One firm can produce a total output of 4 million kilowatt-hours at a cost of 5 pence a kilowatt-hour. This same total output costs 10 pence a kilowatt-hour with two firms and 15 pence a kilowatt-hour with four firms. So one firm can meet the demand in this market at a lower cost than two or more firms can and the market is a natural monopoly.

customers. DeBeers is a *single-price* monopoly. A **single-price monopoly** is a firm that must sell each unit of its output for the same price to all its customers.

Price Discrimination

Many firms price discriminate, and most are *not* monopolies. Airlines offer a dizzying array of different prices for the same trip. Pizza producers charge one price for a single pizza and almost give away a second pizza. These are examples of *price discrimination*. **Price discrimination** is the practice of selling different units of a good or service for different prices. Different customers might pay different prices (like airline passengers) or one customer might pay different prices for different quantities bought (like the bargain price for a second pizza).

The starting point for understanding how a single-price monopoly chooses its price and output is to work out the relationship between the demand for the good produced by the monopoly and the monopoly's revenue.

When a firm price discriminates, it looks as if it is doing its customers a favour. In fact, it is charging the highest possible price for each unit sold and making the largest possible profit.

Not all monopolies can price discriminate. The main obstacle to price discrimination is resale by customers who buy for a low price. Because of resale possibilities, price discrimination is limited to monopolies that sell services that cannot be resold.

We'll look first at single-price monopoly.

A Single-price Monopoly's Output and Price Decision

To understand how a single-price monopoly makes its output and price decision, we must first study the link between price and marginal revenue.

Price and Marginal Revenue

Because in a monopoly there is only one firm, the demand curve facing that firm is the industry demand curve. Let's look at an example of a local monopoly: Cut and Dry, the only hairdressing salon in a 15-mile radius in a small town in North Yorkshire. The table in Figure 12.2 shows the market demand schedule for Cut and Dry. At a price of £20, the salon sells no

Figure 12.2

Demand and Marginal Revenue

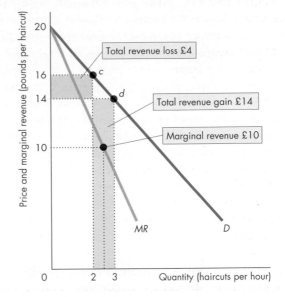

	Price P (pounds per haircut)	Quantity demanded Q (haircuts per hour)	Total revenue TR = P × Q (pounds)	Marginal revenue MR = ΔTR/ΔQ (pounds per haircut)
a	20	0	0	
				18
b	18	1	18	
				14
c	16	2	32	
				10
d	14	3	42	
				6
e	12	4	48	
				2
f	10	5	50	

The table shows the demand schedule for haircuts. Total revenue (*TR*) is price multiplied by quantity sold. For example, row *c* shows that when the price is £16 a haircut, two haircuts are sold for a total revenue of £32. Marginal revenue (*MR*) is the change in total revenue resulting from a 1-unit increase in the quantity sold. For example, when the price falls from £16 to £14 a haircut, the quantity sold increases from 2 to 3 haircuts and total revenue increases by £10. The marginal revenue of the third haircut is £10. The demand curve, *D*, and the marginal revenue curve, *MR*, are based on the numbers in the table and illustrate the calculation of marginal revenue when price falls from £16 to £14.

haircuts. The lower the price, the more haircuts per hour it can sell. For example, at a price of £12, consumers demand 4 haircuts per hour (row *e*).

Total revenue (*TR*) is the price (*P*) multiplied by the quantity sold (*Q*). For example, in row *d*, Cut and Dry sells 3 haircuts at £14 each, so total revenue is £42. *Marginal revenue* (*MR*) is the change in total revenue (Δ*TR*) resulting from a 1-unit increase in the quantity sold. For example, if the price falls from £18 (row *b*) to £16 (row *c*), the quantity sold increases from 1 to 2 haircuts. Total revenue rises from £18 to £32, so the change in total revenue is £14. Because the quantity sold increases by 1 haircut, marginal revenue equals the change in total revenue and is £14. When recording marginal revenue, it is written between the two rows to emphasize that marginal revenue relates to the *change* in the quantity sold.

Figure 12.2 shows the demand curve (*D*) and the marginal revenue curve (*MR*). It also illustrates the calculation you have just read about. Notice that the marginal revenue curve is less than price at each level of output. Why is marginal revenue less than price? It is because when the price is lowered to sell one more unit, there are two opposing effects on total revenue. The lower price results in a revenue loss and the increased quantity sold results in a revenue gain. For example, at a price of £16, the salon sells 2 haircuts (point *c*). If the price is reduced to £14, it sells 3 haircuts and revenue increases by £14 on the third haircut. But if all haircuts are sold at the same price, the salon receives only £14 on the first two as well – £2 less than before. As a result, the salon loses £4 of revenue on the first 2 haircuts. This is deducted from the revenue gain of £14. Marginal revenue – the difference between the revenue gain and the revenue loss – is £10.

Marginal Revenue and Elasticity

A single-price monopoly's marginal revenue is related to the *elasticity of demand* for its good. The demand for a good can be *elastic* (the elasticity of demand is greater than 1), *inelastic* (the elasticity of demand is less than 1), or *unit elastic* (the elasticity of demand is equal to 1). You know that a monopoly produces a good or service for which there is no close substitute. And you perhaps recall (see Chapter 4, p. 78 for a refresher) that the *closer* the substitutes for a good or service, the *more* elastic is the demand for it. So you might expect that the demand for what a monopoly produces is inelastic. It turns out that this conclusion is incorrect. A monopoly always operates where

demand is elastic! To see why, you need to recall the relationship between elasticity and revenue (see Chapter 4, p. 78).

If demand is elastic total revenue increases when the price decreases. The reason is that the positive effect on revenue from an increase in the quantity sold outweighs the negative effect from a lower price. If demand is inelastic total revenue decreases when the price decreases. In this case, the positive effect on revenue from an increase in the quantity sold is outweighed by the negative effect from a lower price. If demand is unit elastic total revenue does not change when the price changes. In this case, the positive effect on revenue from an increase in the quantity sold is offset by an equal negative effect from a lower price.

Figure 12.3 illustrates the relationship between marginal revenue, total revenue and elasticity. As the price of a haircut gradually falls from £20 to £10, the quantity of haircuts demanded increases from 0 to 5 an hour. Over this output range, marginal revenue is positive (part a), total revenue increases (part b), and the demand for haircuts is elastic. As the price falls from £10 to £0 a haircut, the quantity of haircuts demanded increases from 5 to 10 an hour. Over this output range marginal revenue is negative (part a), total revenue decreases (part b), and the demand for haircuts inelastic. When the price is £10 a haircut, marginal revenue is zero, total revenue is at a maximum, and the demand for haircuts is unit elastic.

Monopoly Demand is Always Elastic

The relationship that you have just discovered implies that a profit-maximizing monopoly never produces an output in the inelastic range of its demand curve. If it did so, it could charge a higher price, produce a smaller quantity, and increase its profit. Let's now look more closely at a monopoly's output and price decision.

Output and Price Decision

To determine the output level and price that maximize a monopoly's profit, we need to study the behaviour of both revenue and costs as output varies. A monopoly faces the same types of technology and cost constraints as a competitive firm. But it faces a different market constraint. The competitive firm is a price taker, whereas the monopoly's production decision influences the price it receives. Let's see how.

The revenue for the Cut and Dry salon is shown again in Table 12.1. The table also contains information on the salon's costs and economic profit. Total cost (*TC*)

Figure 12.3

A Single-price Monopoly's Revenue Curves

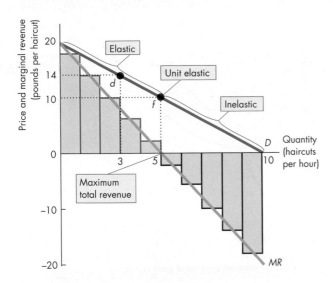

(a) Demand and marginal revenue curves

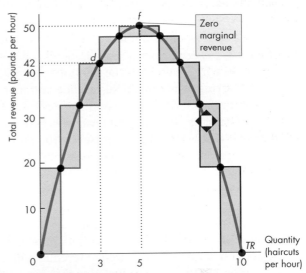

(b) Total revenue curve

In part (a), the demand curve is *D* and marginal revenue curve is *MR*. In part (b) the total revenue curve is *TR*. Over the range 0–5 haircuts an hour, total revenue is increasing and marginal revenue is positive, as shown by the blue bars. Demand is elastic. Over the range

5–10 haircuts an hour, total revenue declines, so marginal revenue is negative, as shown by the red bars. Demand is inelastic. At 5 haircuts an hour, total revenue is maximized and marginal revenue is zero. Demand is unit elastic.

Table 12.1   A Monopoly's Output and Price Decision

Price (*P*) (pounds per haircut)	Quantity demanded (*Q*) (haircuts per hour)	Total revenue (*TR* = *P* × *Q*) (pounds)	Marginal revenue (*MR* = $\Delta TR/\Delta Q$) (pounds per haircut)	Total cost (*TC*) (pounds)	Marginal cost (*MC* = $\Delta TC/\Delta Q$) (pounds per haircut)	Profit (*TR* − *TC*) (pounds)
20	0	0		20		20
			18		1	
18	1	18		21		3
			14		3	
16	2	32		24		+8
			10		6	
14	3	42		30		+12
			6		10	
12	4	48		40		+8
			2		15	
10	5	50		55		5

This table gives the information needed to find the profit maximizing output and price. Total revenue (*TR*) equals price multiplied by the quantity sold. Profit equals total revenue minus total cost (*TC*). Profit is maximized when

the price is £14 and 3 haircuts are sold. Total revenue is £42 and hour, total cost is £30 an hour, and economic profit is £12 an hour (£42 − £30).

rises as output increases and so does total revenue (*TR*). Economic profit equals total revenue minus total cost. As you can see in the table, the maximum profit (£12) occurs when the salon sells 3 haircuts for £14 each. Selling 2 haircuts for £16 each or 4 haircuts for £12 each would mean less economic profit at only £8.

You can see why 3 haircuts is the profit-maximizing output by looking at the marginal revenue and marginal cost columns. When the salon increases output from 2 to 3 haircuts, the marginal revenue is £10 and the marginal cost is £6. Profit increases by the difference – £4 an hour. If the salon increases output yet further, from 3 to 4 haircuts, marginal revenue is £6 and marginal cost is £10. In this case, marginal cost exceeds marginal revenue by £4, so profit decreases by £4 an hour. When marginal revenue exceeds marginal cost, profit increases if output increases. When marginal cost exceeds marginal revenue, profit increases if output decreases. When marginal cost and marginal revenue are equal, profit is maximized.

The information set out in Table 12.1 is shown graphically in Figure 12.4. Part (a) shows the Cut and Dry salon's total revenue curve (*TR*) and total cost curve (*TC*). Economic profit is the vertical distance between *TR* and *TC*. Profit is maximized at 3 haircuts an hour – economic profit is £42 minus £30, or £12.

Figure 12.4(b) shows the salon's demand curve (*D*) and the marginal revenue curve (*MR*) along with the marginal cost curve (*MC*) and average total cost curve (*ATC*). To maximize profit, a monopolist, like a competitive firm, sets marginal cost equal to marginal revenue. For this salon, marginal cost equals marginal revenue when output is 3 haircuts a day. But what price is charged in the salon? To set the price, the monopolist uses the demand curve to find the highest price at which the profit maximizing output can be sold. For the Cut and Dry salon, they sell 3 haircuts an hour at a price of £14.

All firms maximize profit by producing the output at which marginal cost equals marginal revenue. For a competitive firm, price equals marginal revenue, so price also equals marginal cost. For a monopoly, price is higher than marginal revenue at all output levels, so price also exceeds marginal cost.

A monopoly charges a price that exceeds marginal cost, but does it always make an economic profit? It depends on average costs. When the Cut and Dry salon produces 3 haircuts an hour, the average total cost is £10 (read from the *ATC* curve) and the price is £14 (read from the *D* curve). The profit per haircut is

Figure 12.4

A Monopoly's Output and Price

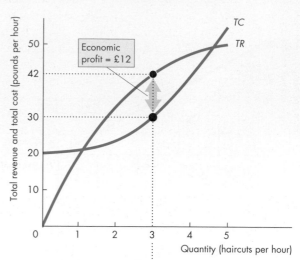

(a) Total revenue and total cost curves

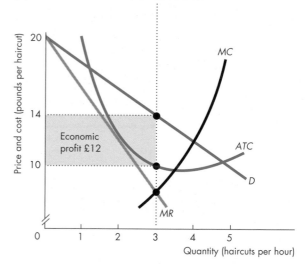

(b) Demand and marginal revenue and cost curves

In part (a), economic profit is the vertical distance between total revenue (*TR*) and total cost (*TC*), and it is maximized at 3 haircuts an hour. In part (b), economic profit is maximized where marginal cost (*MC*) equals (*MR*). The price is determined by the demand curve (*D*) and is £14. Economic profit, the blue rectangle, is £12 – the profit per haircut (£4) multiplied by 3 haircuts.

£4 (£14 minus £10). The economic profit is indicated by the blue rectangle, which equals the profit per haircut (£4) multiplied by the number of haircuts (3), making a total of £12.

The salon makes a positive economic profit. But suppose that the owner of the salon rents the premises. If the rent is increased by £12 an hour, the fixed cost increases by £12 an hour. The marginal cost and marginal revenue don't change, so the profit-maximizing output remains at 3 haircuts an hour. However, profit has fallen by £12 an hour to zero. If the salon owner pays more than an additional £12 an hour for the shop lease, the salon makes an economic loss. If this situation was permanent, the owner would go out of business. But entrepreneurs are a hardy lot, and it might pay to find another shop where the rent is lower.

Review Quiz

◆ What is the relationship between marginal cost and marginal revenue when a single-price monopolist maximizes profit?
◆ How does a single-price monopoly determine the price it will charge its customers?
◆ What is the relationship between marginal revenue and marginal cost when a single-price monopoly is maximizing profit?
◆ Why can a monopoly make a positive economic profit even in the long run?

Figure 12.5

Monopoly and Competition Compared

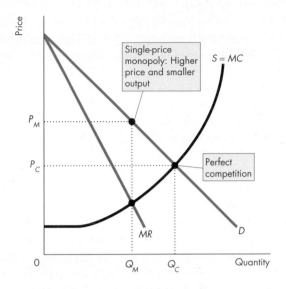

A competitive industry produces the quantity Q_C and price P_C. A single-price monopoly produces the output Q_M at which marginal revenue equals marginal cost and sells that quantity at the price P_M. Compared to perfect competition, a single-price monopoly restricts output and raises the price.

Single-price Monopoly and Competition Compared

Imagine an industry that is made up of many small firms operating in perfect competition. Then imagine that a single firm buys out all these small firms and creates a monopoly. What will happen in this industry? Will the price rise or fall? Will the quantity produced increase or decrease? Will economic profit increase or decrease? Will either the original competitive situation or the new monopoly situation be efficient?

These are the questions we're now going to answer. First, we look at the effects of monopoly on the price and quantity produced. Then we turn to the questions about efficiency.

Comparing Output and Price

Figure 12.5 shows the market we are studying. The market demand curve is D and is the same whether it is a monopoly or competitive. However, the market

supply is different under competition and monopoly. We'll look at the case of perfect competition first.

Perfect Competition

Initially, with many small perfectly competitive firms in the market, the market supply is S. This supply curve is obtained by summing the supply curves of all the individual firms in the market.

In perfect competition, equilibrium occurs where the supply curve and the demand curve intersect. The quantity produced is Q_C and the price is P_C. Each firm takes the price P_C and maximizes its profit by producing the output at which its own marginal cost equals the price. Because each firm is a small part of the total industry, there is no incentive for any firm to try to manipulate the price by varying its output.

Single-price Monopoly

Now suppose that this industry is taken over by a single firm. Consumers do not change so the market demand curve remains the same as in perfect competition. But now, the monopoly recognizes this demand curve as a constraint on its sales. The monopoly is confronted with the marginal revenue curve, *MR*, in Figure 12.5.

The monopoly maximized profit by producing the quantity at which marginal revenue equals marginal cost. To find the monopoly's marginal cost curve, first recall that in perfect competition, the industry supply curve is the sum of the supply curves of the firms in the market. Also recall that each firm's supply curve is its marginal cost curve (see Chapter 11, p. 223). No changes in production techniques occur, so the monopolist has identical costs to the original industry. So when the industry is taken over by a single firm, the monopolist's marginal cost curve is the competitive industry's supply curve, labelled *MC* in Figure 12.5.

The monopolist produces Q_M, where marginal revenue equals marginal cost. This output is smaller than the competitive output, Q_C. The monopoly charges the highest price for which output Q_M can be sold, and that price is P_M. We have just established that:

> Compared with a perfectly competitive industry, a single-price monopoly restricts its output and charges a higher price.

We've seen how the output and price of a monopoly compare with those in a competitive industry. Let's now compare the efficiency of the two types of market.

Efficiency Comparison

When we studied efficiency in perfect competition, (see Chapter 11, pp. 232–234), we discovered that if there are no external costs and benefits, perfect competition results in an efficient use of resources. Along the demand curve, consumers are efficient. Along the supply curve, producers are efficient. Where the curves intersect – the competitive equilibrium – both consumers and producers are efficient. Price equals marginal cost and the sum of consumer surplus and producer surplus is maximized.

Monopoly restricts output below the competitive level and is inefficient. If a monopoly's output was increased, marginal benefit would exceed marginal cost and resources would be used more efficiently.

Figure 12.6 illustrates the inefficiency of monopoly and shows the loss of consumer and producer surpluses in a monopoly. In perfect competition (part a),

Figure 12.6

Allocative Efficiency of Monopoly

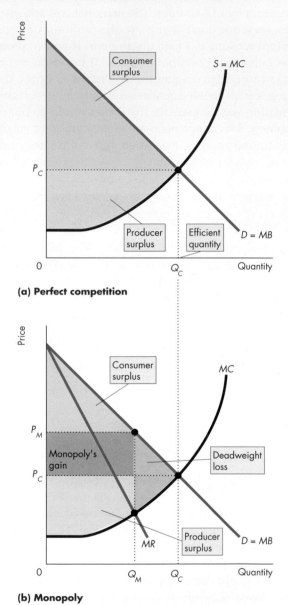

(a) Perfect competition

(b) Monopoly

In perfect competition (part a), quantity is Q_C, price is P_C and consumer surplus is the green triangle. With free entry, firms' economic profits in long-run equilibrium are zero. Consumer surplus is maximized. Under a single-price monopoly (part b), output is restricted to Q_M and the price increases to P_M. Consumer surplus is reduced to the smaller green triangle. The monopoly takes the blue rectangle for itself, but the grey triangle is a deadweight loss. Part of the deadweight loss (above P_C) is a loss of consumer surplus, and part (below P_C) is a loss of producer surplus.

consumers pay P_C for each unit bought and obtain a consumer surplus represented by the green triangle.

The marginal cost of production (opportunity cost) in perfect competition is shown by the supply curve ($S = MC$). The amount received by the producer in excess of this marginal cost is **producer surplus**. This is the blue area in Figure 12.6(a).

In a competitive equilibrium, the sum of consumer surplus and producer surplus is maximized and resources are used efficiently.

In Figure 12.6(b), a monopoly restricts output to Q_M and sells that output for P_M. Consumer surplus is decreased to the smaller green triangle. Consumers lose partly by having to pay more for what is available and partly by getting less of the good. Part of the original producer surplus is also lost. The total loss resulting from the smaller monopoly output (Q_M) is the grey triangle and is called the deadweight loss. **Deadweight loss** is also a measure of the loss of allocative efficiency resulting from a restriction of output below its efficient level. Part of the grey triangle, above P_C, is the loss of consumer surplus created because some consumers can no longer afford the monopolist's output. The part below P_C is the loss of producer surplus caused by the loss of output under monopoly.

Redistribution of Surpluses

You can see that monopoly is inefficient. The sum of consumer surplus and producer surplus is smaller with monopoly than with competition. There is a social loss measured by the size of the deadweight loss. But monopoly also brings a redistribution of surpluses. Some of the loss in consumer surplus goes to the monopoly. In Figure 12.6, the monopoly gets the difference between the higher price, P_M, and the competitive price, P_C, on the quantity sold, Q_M. So the monopoly takes the part of the consumer surplus shown by the blue rectangle. This portion of the loss of consumer surplus is not a loss to society. It is redistribution from consumers to the monopoly producer.

Rent Seeking

As you know, monopoly creates a deadweight loss and is inefficient. But the social cost of monopoly exceeds the deadweight loss because of an activity called rent seeking. **Rent seeking** is the attempt to capture consumer surplus, producer surplus, or economic profit. The activity is not confined to monopolists. But the attempt to make an economic profit is a major form of rent seeking.

A monopoly makes its economic profit by diverting part of consumer surplus to itself. Thus the pursuit of an economic profit by a monopolist is rent seeking. It is the attempt to capture consumer surplus.

Rent seekers pursue their goals in two main ways. They can:

1 Buy a monopoly.

2 Create a monopoly.

Buy a Monopoly

This type of rent seeking is the searching out of existing monopoly rights that can be bought for a lower price than the monopoly's economic profit – that is, seeking to acquire existing monopoly rights. An example is the purchase of taxi licences. In most cities, taxis are regulated. The city restricts both the fares and the number of taxis that are permitted to operate. Operating a taxi results in economic profit or rent. A person who wants to operate a taxi must buy the right to do so from someone who already has that right.

But buying an existing monopoly does not assure an economic profit. The reason is that there is freedom of entry into the activity of rent seeking. Rent seeking is like perfect competition. If an economic profit is available, a new entrant will try to get some of it. Competition among rent seekers pushes the price that must be paid for a monopoly right up to the point at which only a normal profit can be made by operating the monopoly. The economic profit – the rent – goes to the person who created the monopoly in the first place. For example, competition for the right to operate a taxi in UK cities leads to a price of more than £10,000, which is sufficiently high to eliminate long-run economic profit for the taxi operator. But the person who acquired the right in the first place collects the economic rent. This type of rent seeking transfers wealth from the buyer to the seller of the monopoly.

Create a Monopoly

This type of rent seeking activity takes the form of lobbying and seeking to influence the political process. Such influence is sometimes sought by making political contributions in exchange for legislative support or by indirectly seeking to influence political outcomes through publicity in the media or more direct contacts with politicians and bureaucrats. An example would be the donations to political parties that the alcohol and tobacco companies make in an attempt to avoid a tightening of legislation on activities such as advertising and licensing, which might affect their profits.

This type of rent seeking is a costly activity that uses up scarce resources. In aggregate, firms spend millions of pounds lobbying Parliament in the pursuit of licences and laws that create barriers to entry and establish a monopoly right. Everyone has an incentive to rent seek, and because there are no barriers to entry into the rent-seeking activity, there is a great deal of competition for new monopoly rights.

Rent Seeking Equilibrium

How much will a person be willing to give up to obtain a monopoly right? The answer is the entire value of a monopoly's economic profit. Barriers to entry create monopoly, but rent seeking activity is like perfect competition. There is no barrier to rent seeking. As long as the value of the resources used to create a monopoly falls short of the monopoly's economic profit, there is an economic profit to be earned. There is an incentive to rent seek. Rent seeking continues until all the potential for economic profit through monopoly is exhausted.

Figure 12.7 shows a rent seeking equilibrium. The cost of rent seeking is a fixed cost that must be added to a monopoly's other costs. Rent seeking and rent-seeking costs increase to the point at which no economic profit is made. The average total cost curve, which includes the fixed cost of rent seeking, shifts upward until it just touches the demand curve. Economic profit (and producer surplus) are zero. They have been lost in rent seeking. Consumer surplus is unaffected. But the deadweight loss of monopoly now includes the original deadweight loss triangle plus the lost producer surplus, shown by the enlarged darker grey area in the figure.

Review Quiz

♦ Why does a single-price monopoly produce a smaller output and charge a higher price than would prevail if the industry were perfectly competitive?
♦ Why is single-price monopoly inefficient?
♦ What is rent seeking and how does it influence the inefficiency of monopoly?

Figure 12.7
Rent Seeking Equilibrium

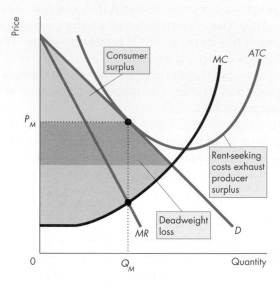

With competitive rent-seeking, a monopoly uses all its economic profit to prevent another firm taking its economic rent. The firm's rent seeking costs are fixed costs. They are equivalent to total fixed cost and average total cost. The *ATC* curve shifts upward until, at the profit maximizing price, the firm breaks even.

So far we have only studied monopolies that set a single price. But many monopolies price discriminate. We'll look at how this works now.

Price Discrimination

Price discrimination – selling a good or service at a number of different prices – is widespread. You can see it when you travel, go to the cinema, go shopping, or go out to eat. Most price discriminators are not monopolies, but monopolies use price discrimination when they can. To be able to price discriminate, a monopoly must:

1 Identify and separate different buyer types.
2 Sell a product that cannot be resold.

Price discrimination is charging different prices for a single good or service because differences exist in buyers' willingness to pay, and not because of differences in production costs. So not all price *differences* imply price discrimination. For example, the marginal cost of producing electricity depends on the time of day. If an electric power company charges a higher price for consumption between 7.00 and 9.00 in the morning and between 4.00 and 7.00 in the evening than it does at other times of the day, this practice is not called price discrimination. However, the price differences you see between business and economy class tickets on small planes are not related to differences in the cost of service. The main costs of the aeroplane, the insurance, the fuel and the staff are the same for all passengers.

At first sight, it appears that price discrimination contradicts the assumption of profit maximization. Why would a railway company give a student discount? Why would a hairdresser charge students and senior citizens less? Aren't these producers losing profit by being so generous?

Deeper investigation shows that far from losing profit, price discriminators actually make a bigger profit than they would otherwise. So a monopoly has an incentive to find ways of price discriminating and charging each buyer the highest price possible. Some people pay less with price discrimination, but others pay more.

Price Discrimination and Consumer Surplus

Demand curves slope down because the value that an individual places on a good falls as the quantity consumed of that good increases. When all the units consumed can be bought for a single price, the consumers gain a benefit. We call this benefit *consumer surplus*. (You can refresh your memory on consumer surplus by rereading Chapter 5, pp. 96–97). Price discrimination can be seen as an attempt by a monopoly to capture the consumer surplus (or as much of the surplus as possible) for itself.

To extract all the consumer surplus from every buyer, the monopoly would have to offer each individual customer a separate price schedule based on that customer's own willingness to pay. Clearly, such price discrimination cannot be carried out in practice because a firm does not have enough information about each consumer's demand curve.

But firms try to extract as much consumer surplus as possible and, to do so, they discriminate in two broad ways:

1 Among units of a good.

2 Among groups of buyers.

Discriminating Among Units of a Good

One form of price discrimination charges each single buyer a different price on each unit of a good bought. An example of this type of discrimination is a discount for bulk buying. The larger the order, the larger is the discount – and the lower is the price. This type of price discrimination works because each individual's demand curve slopes downward. Some discounts for bulk arise from lower costs of production for greater bulk. In these cases, such discounts are not price discrimination.

Discriminating Between Groups

Price discrimination often takes the form of discriminating between different groups of consumers on the basis of age, employment status or some other easily distinguished characteristic. This type of price discrimination works only if each group has a different average willingness to pay for the good or service.

For example, a face-to-face sales meeting with a customer might bring a large and profitable order. So for business travellers, the marginal benefit from a trip is large and the price that such a traveller will pay for a trip is high. In contrast, for a holiday traveller, any of several different trips or even no holiday trip are options. So for holiday travellers, the marginal benefit of a trip is small and the price that such a traveller will pay for a trip is low. Because business travellers are willing to pay more than vacation travellers are it is possible for an airline to profit by price discriminating between these two groups. Similarly, because students have a lower willingness to pay for a haircut than a working person does it is possible for a hairdresser to profit by price discriminating between these two groups.

Let's see how an airline exploits the differences in demand by business and holiday travellers and increases its profit by price discriminating.

Profiting by Price Discrimination

Global Air is a European Airline with a monopoly on an exotic route. Figure 12.8 shows the demand curve (*D*) and the marginal revenue curve (*MR*) for travel on this route. It also shows Global Air's marginal cost curve (*MC*) and average total cost curve (*ATC*).

Initially, Global is a single-price monopoly and maximizes its profit by producing 8,000 trips a year (the quantity at which *MR* equals *MC*). The price is €1,200 per trip. The average total cost of a trip is €600,

Figure 12.8
A Single Price for Air Travel

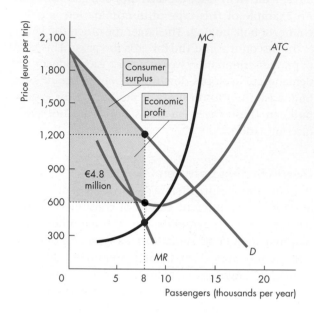

Figure 12.9
Price Discrimination

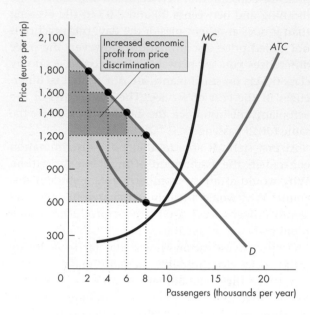

Global Air has a monopoly on an air route. The market demand is *D* and the marginal revenue is *MR*. Global Air's marginal cost curve is *MC* and its average total cost curve is *ATC*. As a single price monopoly, Global maximizes profit by selling 8,000 trips a year at €1,200 a trip. Its profit is €4.8 million a year (the blue rectangle). Global's customers enjoy a consumer surplus (the green area).

Global revises its fare structure. No restrictions at €1,800; 7-days advance purchase at €1,600; 14-days advance purchase at €1,400; and must stay over weekend at €1,200. Global sells 2,000 tickets at each of its four new fares. Its economic profit increases by €2.4 million a year to €7.2 million a year (the blue rectangle plus the blue steps). The consumer surplus of Global's customers shrinks.

so economic profit is €600 a trip. On 8,000 trips, Global's economic profit is €4.8 million a year, shown by the blue rectangle. Global's customers enjoy a consumer surplus shown by the green triangle.

Global is struck by the fact that many of its customers are business travellers and Global suspects they are willing to pay more than €1,200 a trip. So Global does some market research, which tells Global that some business travellers are willing to pay as much as €1,800 a trip. Also, these customers almost always change their travel plans at the last moment. Another group of business travellers is willing to pay €1,600. These customers know a week ahead when they will travel and they never want to stay over a weekend. Yet another group would pay up to €1,400 and these travellers know two weeks ahead when they will travel, and they don't want to stay over a weekend.

So Global announces a new fare schedule. No restrictions, €1,800; 7-days advance purchase, no cancellation, €1,600; 14 days advance purchase,

no cancellation, €1,400; 14 days advance purchase and must stay over a weekend, €1,200.

Figure 12.9 shows the outcome with this new fare structure and also shows why Global is pleased with its new fares. It sells 2,000 seats at each of its four prices. Global's economic profit increases by the blue steps in Figure 12.9. Its economic profit is now its original €4.8 million a year plus an additional €2.4 million from its new higher fares. Consumer surplus has shrunk to the smaller green area.

Perfect Price Discrimination

Global can do even better. It plans to achieve perfect price discrimination, which extracts the entire consumer surplus. To do so, Global must come up with a host of additional fares ranging between €1,200 and €2,000 each one of which appeals to a small market segment of the business market and that extracts the entire consumer surplus from the business travellers.

With perfect price discrimination, something special happens to marginal revenue. For the perfect price discriminator, the demand curve becomes the marginal revenue curve. The reason is that when the price is cut to sell a larger quantity, the firm sells only the marginal unit at the lower price. All the other units continue to be sold for the highest price the buyers are willing to pay.

With marginal cost equal to price, Global can obtain yet greater profit by increasing output up to the point at which price (and marginal revenue) is equal to marginal cost.

So, Global now seeks additional travellers who will not pay as much as $1,200 a trip but who will pay more than marginal cost. More creative pricing comes up with vacation specials and other fares that have combinations of advance reservation, minimum-stay, and other restrictions that make these fares unattractive to its existing customers but attractive to a further group of travellers. With all these fares and specials, Global increases sales, extracts the entire consumer surplus, and maximizes economic profit.

Figure 12.10 shows the outcome with perfect price discrimination. The dozens of fares paid by the original travellers who are willing to pay between €1,200 and €2,000 has extracted the entire consumer surplus from this group and converted it into economic profit for Global.

The new fares between €900 and €1,200 have attracted 3,000 additional travellers but taken their entire consumer surplus also. Global is earning an economic profit of more than €9 million.

Efficiency and Rent Seeking with Price Discrimination

With perfect price discrimination, output increases to the point at which price equals marginal cost – where the marginal cost curve intersects the demand curve. This output is identical to that of perfect competition. Perfect price discrimination pushes consumer surplus to zero but increases producer surplus to equal the sum of consumer surplus and producer surplus in perfect competition. Deadweight loss with perfect price discrimination is zero. So perfect price discrimination achieves efficiency.

The more perfectly the monopoly can price discriminate, the closer its output gets to the competitive output and the more efficient is the outcome.

Figure 12.10

Perfect Price Discrimination

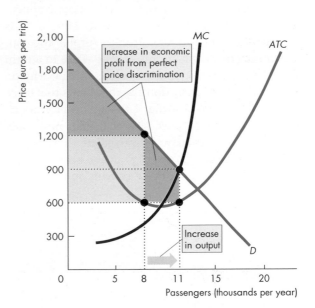

Dozens of fares discriminate among different types of business traveller and many new low fares with restrictions appeal to holiday travellers. With perfect price discrimination, the demand curve becomes Global's marginal revenue curve. Economic profit is maximized when the lowest price equals marginal cost. Global sells 11,000 tickets between €2,000 and €900 each and makes an economic profit of €9.35 million each year.

But there are two differences between perfect competition and perfect price discrimination. First, the distribution of the surplus is different. It is shared by consumers and producers in perfect competition while the producer gets it all with perfect price discrimination. Second, because the producer grabs the surplus, rent seeking becomes profitable.

Review Quiz

◆ What is price discrimination and how is it used to increase a monopoly's profit?
◆ What happens to consumer surplus when a monopoly price discriminates?
◆ What happens to consumer surplus, economic profit, and output if a monopoly perfectly price discriminates?
◆ What are some of the ways that the real-world airlines use to price discriminate?

Monopoly Policy Issues

The comparison of monopoly with perfect competition can make monopoly look bad. Monopoly is inefficient and it captures consumer surplus and converts it into producer surplus or pure waste in a form of rent-seeking costs. If monopoly is so bad, why do we put up with it? Why don't we have laws that crack down on monopoly so hard that it never rears its head? We do indeed have laws that limit monopoly power. We also have laws that regulate those monopolies that exist. But monopoly can also bring benefits. We are going to look at these benefits and then look at monopoly regulation.

The main reasons why monopoly might have some advantages are:

◆ Economies of scale and economies of scope.

◆ Incentives to innovate.

Economies of Scale and Scope

A firm experiences *economies of scale* when an increase in its production of a good or service brings a decrease in the average total cost of producing it – see Chapter 10, p. 208. **Economies of scope** arise when an increase in the *range of goods produced* brings a decrease in average total cost. Economies of scope occur when highly specialized (and usually expensive) technical inputs can be shared by different goods. For example, McDonald's can produce both hamburgers and chips at an average total cost that is lower than what it would cost two separate firms to produce the same goods because hamburgers and chips share the use of specialized food storage and preparation facilities. Firms producing a wide range of products can hire specialist computer programmers, designers and marketing experts whose skills can be used across the product range, thereby spreading their costs and lowering the average total cost of production of each of the goods.

Economies of scale and scope can lead to natural monopoly, where a single firm in the industry can produce at a lower average cost than a larger number of firms can achieve.

Large-scale firms that have control over supply and can influence price – and that therefore behave like the monopoly firm that we've been studying in this chapter – can reap these economies of scale and scope; small, competitive firms cannot. As a con-

sequence, there are situations in which the comparison of monopoly and competition that we made earlier in this chapter is not a valid one. Recall that we imagined the takeover of a large number of competitive firms by a single monopoly firm. But we also assumed that the monopoly would use exactly the same technology as the small firms and have the same costs. But if one large firm can reap economies of scale and scope, its marginal cost curve will lie below the supply curve of a competitive industry made up of thousands of small firms. It is possible for such economies of scale and scope to be so large as to result in a higher output and lower price under monopoly than a competitive industry would achieve.

Examples of industries in which economies of scale are so significant that they lead to natural monopolies are becoming more rare. Public utilities such as gas and electric power were once natural monopolies, but customers can now buy their gas and electricity from a number of different suppliers. Water distribution, however, remains a local natural monopoly. There are many examples where a combination of economies of scale and economies of scope arise. These include the brewing of beer, the manufacture of refrigerators, other household appliances and pharmaceuticals, and the refining of petroleum.

Incentives to Innovate

Innovation is the first-time application of new knowledge in the production process. Innovation may take the form of developing a new product or a lower-cost way of making an existing product. Controversy has raged among economists over whether large firms with monopoly power or small competitive firms lacking such monopoly power are the more innovative. It is clear that some temporary monopoly power arises from innovation. A firm that develops a new product or process and patents it obtains an exclusive right to that product or process for the term of the patent.

But does the granting of a monopoly, even a temporary one, to an innovator increase the pace of innovation? One line of reasoning suggests that it does. With no protection, an innovator is not able to enjoy the profits from innovation for long. Thus the incentive to innovate is weakened. A contrary argument is that monopolies can afford to be lazy while competitive firms cannot. Competitive firms must strive to innovate and cut costs even though they know that they cannot hang on to the benefits of their innovation for long. But that knowledge spurs them on to greater and faster innovation.

The evidence on whether monopoly leads to greater innovation than competition is mixed. It shows that large firms do much more research and development than small firms. But measuring research and development is measuring the volume of inputs into the process of innovation. What matters is not input but output. Two measures of the output of research and development are the number of patents and the rate of productivity growth. On these measures, there is no clear evidence that big is better. But there is a clear pattern in the process of diffusion of technological knowledge. After innovation, a new process or product spreads gradually through the industry. Whether an innovator is a small firm or a large firm, large firms jump on the bandwagon more quickly than do the remaining small firms. Thus large firms speed the process of diffusion of technological advances.

Regulating Natural Monopoly

Where demand and cost conditions create a natural monopoly, a government agency usually regulates the prices of the monopoly. By regulating a monopoly, some of the worst aspects of monopoly can be avoided, or at least made more moderate. One such natural monopoly is in the distribution of natural gas in European economies. Let's look at the regulation of this activity.

Figure 12.11 shows the market demand curve D and the marginal revenue curve, MR, the average total cost curve ATC, and the marginal cost curve MC for a gas distribution company that is a natural monopoly.

The firm's marginal cost is constant at 10 cents per cubic metre. But average total cost decreases as output increases. The reason is that the natural gas company has a large investment in pipelines and so has high fixed costs. These fixed costs are part of the company's average total cost and so appear in the ATC curve. The average total cost curve slopes downward because as the number of cubic metres sold increases, the fixed cost is spread over a larger number of units. (To refresh your memory on how the average total cost curve is calculated, take a quick look back at Chapter 10, pp. 203–204.)

This one firm can supply the entire market at a lower cost than two firms can because average total cost is falling even when the entire market is supplied. (Refer back to p. 242 if you need a quick refresher on natural monopoly.)

Figure 12.11

Regulating a Natural Monopoly

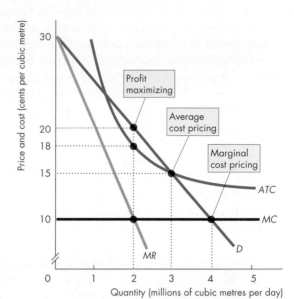

A natural monopoly is an industry in which average total cost is falling even when the entire market demand is satisfied. A natural gas producer faces the market demand curve D. The firm's marginal cost is constant at 10 cents per cubic metre, as shown by the curve labelled MC. Fixed costs are large, and the average total cost curve, which includes average fixed cost, is shown as ATC. A marginal cost pricing rule sets the price at 10 cents per cubic metre. The monopoly produces 8 million cubic metres per day and incurs an economic loss. An average cost pricing rule sets the price at 15 cents per cubic metre. The monopoly produces 3 million cubic metres a day and makes normal profit.

Profit Maximization

First, suppose the natural gas company is not regulated and instead maximizes profit. Figure 12.11 shows the outcome in this case. The company produces 2 million cubic metres a day, the quantity at which marginal cost equals marginal revenue. It prices this gas at 20 cents a cubic metre and makes an economic profit of 2 cents a cubic metre, or €40,000 a day.

This outcome is fine for the gas company, but it is inefficient. Price or marginal benefit is 20 cents a cubic metre when marginal cost is 10 cents a cubic metre. Also, the gas company is making a big profit. What can regulation do to improve this outcome?

The Efficient Regulation

If the European monopoly regulator wants to achieve an efficient use of resources, it must require the gas monopoly to produce the quantity of gas that brings marginal benefit into equality with marginal cost. Marginal benefit is what the consumer is willing to pay and is shown by the market demand curve. Marginal cost is shown by the firm's marginal cost curve. You can see in Figure 12.11 that this outcome occurs if the price is regulated at 10 cents per cubic metre and if 4 million cubic metres per day are produced. The regulation that produces this outcome is called a **marginal cost pricing** rule. A marginal cost pricing rule sets price equal to marginal cost. It maximizes total surplus in the regulated industry. In this example, that surplus is all consumer surplus and is the area of the triangle under the demand curve and above the marginal cost curve.

The marginal cost pricing rule is efficient. But it leaves the natural monopoly incurring an economic loss. Because average total cost is falling as output increases, marginal cost is below average total cost. And because price equals marginal cost, price is below average total cost. Average total cost minus price is the loss per unit produced. It's pretty obvious that a natural gas company that is required to use a marginal cost pricing rule will not stay in business for long. How can a company cover its costs and, at the same time, obey a marginal cost pricing rule?

One possibility is price discrimination. The company might charge a higher price to some customers but marginal cost to the customers who pay least. Another possibility is to use a two-part price (called a two-part tariff). For example, the gas company might charge a monthly fixed fee that covers its fixed cost and then charge for gas consumed at marginal cost.

But a natural monopoly cannot always cover its costs in these ways. If a natural monopoly cannot cover its total cost from its customers, and if the government wants it to follow a marginal cost pricing rule, the government must give the firm a subsidy. In such a case, the government raises the revenue for the subsidy by taxing some other activity. But as we saw in Chapter 6, taxes themselves generate deadweight loss. Thus the deadweight loss resulting from additional taxes must be subtracted from the efficiency gained by forcing the natural monopoly to adopt a marginal cost pricing rule.

Average Cost Pricing

Regulators almost never impose efficient pricing because of its consequences for the firm's profit. Instead, they compromise by permitting the firm to cover all its costs and to earn a normal profit. Normal profit, recall, is a cost of production and we include it along with the firm's other fixed costs in the average total cost curve. So pricing to cover cost and normal profit means setting price equal to average total cost – called an **average cost pricing** rule.

Figure 12.11 shows the average cost pricing outcome. The natural gas company charges 15 cents a cubic metre and sells 3 million cubic metres per day. This outcome is better for consumers than the unregulated profit-maximizing outcome. The price is 5 cents a cubic metre lower and the quantity consumed is 1 million cubic metres per day more. And the outcome is better for the producer than the marginal cost pricing rule outcome. The firm earns normal profit. The outcome is inefficient, but less so than the unregulated profit-maximizing outcome.

Review Quiz

- ◆ What are the two main reasons why monopoly is worth tolerating?
- ◆ Think up some examples of economies of scale and economies of scope?
- ◆ Why might a monopoly have a greater incentive to innovate than a small competitive firm?
- ◆ What is the price that achieves an efficient outcome for a regulated monopoly? What is the problem with this price?
- ◆ Compare the consumer surplus, producer surplus, and deadweight loss that arise from average cost pricing with those of profit-maximization pricing and marginal cost pricing.

You've now studied two market structures: perfect competition and monopoly. In the next chapter, you will study the actions of firms that lie between these two extreme structures.

Summary

Key Points

Market Power (pp. 241–243)

- A monopoly is an industry in which there is a single supplier of a good, service or resource. Monopoly arises because of barriers to entry that prevent competition.

- Barriers to the entry of new firms may be legal or natural and can arise when a firm owns control of a resource.

- A monopoly might be able to price discriminate when there is no resale possibility.

- Where there is resale possibility, a monopoly charges one price.

A Single-price Monopoly's Output and Price Decision (pp. 243–247)

- The demand for a monopoly's output is the market demand curve and a single-price monopoly's marginal revenue is less than price.

- A monopoly maximizes profit by producing the output at which marginal revenue equals marginal cost and by charging the highest price that consumers are willing to pay for that output.

Single-price Monopoly and Competition Compared (pp. 247–250)

- A single-price monopoly charges a higher price and produces a smaller quantity than a perfectly competitive industry.

- A single-price monopoly restricts output and creates a deadweight loss.

- Monopoly imposes costs that equal its deadweight loss plus the cost of resources devoted to rent seeking.

Price Discrimination (pp. 250–253)

- Price discrimination is an attempt by a monopoly to convert consumer surplus into economic profit.

- Perfect price discrimination extracts all the consumer surplus. Such a monopoly charges a different price for each unit sold and obtains the maximum price that each consumer is willing to pay for each unit bought.

- With perfect price discrimination, the monopoly produces the same output as would a perfectly competitive industry.

- Rent seeking with perfect price discrimination might eliminate the entire consumer surplus and producer surplus.

Monopoly Policy Issues (pp. 254–256)

- Monopolies with large economies of scale and scope can produce a larger quantity at a lower price than a competitive industry can achieve and monopoly might be more innovative than competition.

- Efficient regulation requires a monopoly to charge a price equal to marginal cost, but for a natural monopoly such a price is less than average total cost.

- Average cost pricing is a compromise pricing rule that covers a firm's costs and provides a normal profit but is not efficient. It is more efficient than unregulated profit maximization.

Key Figures

Key Terms

Problems

◦1 Minnie's European Mineral Springs, a single-price monopoly, faces the market demand schedule:

Price (euros per bottle)	Quantity demanded (bottles)
10	0
8	1
6	2
4	3
2	4
0	5

a Calculate the total revenue schedule for Minnie's company.

b Calculate the marginal revenue schedule.

2 Danny's European Diamond Mines, a single-price monopoly, faces the market demand schedule:

Price (euros per kilogram)	Quantity demanded (kilograms per day)
2,200	5
2,000	6
1,800	7
1,600	8
1,400	9
1,200	10

a Calculate the total revenue schedule for Danny's mine.

b Calculate the marginal revenue schedule.

◦3 Minnie's European Mineral Springs in problem 1 has the following total cost:

Quantity produced (bottles)	Total cost (euros)
0	1
1	3
2	7
3	13
4	21
5	31

Use a graph to calculate the profit-maximizing

a Output.

b Price.

c Marginal cost.

d Marginal revenue.

e Economic profit.

f Does Minnie's use resources efficiently? Explain your answer.

4 Danny's European Diamond Mines in problem 2 has the following total cost:

Quantity produced (kilograms per day)	Total cost (euros)
5	8,000
6	9,000
7	10,200
8	11,600
9	13,200
10	15,000

Use a graph to calculate the profit-maximizing

a Output.

b Price.

c Marginal cost.

d Marginal revenue.

e Economic profit.

f Does Danny's Mines use resources efficiently? Explain your answer.

◦5 The figure illustrates the situation facing the publisher of the only newspaper containing local news in an isolated UK community.

a What quantity of newspapers will maximize the publisher's profit?

b What price will the publisher charge?

c What is the publisher's daily total revenue?

d At the price charged for a newspaper, is the demand elastic or inelastic? Why?

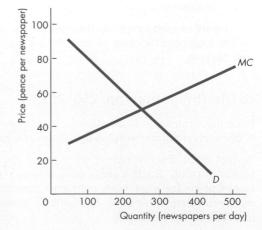

6 In problem 5, the publisher installs a new print-ing press that makes the marginal cost constant at 20 cents per copy.

   a What quantity of newspapers will maximize the publisher's profit?

   b What price will the publisher charge?

   c What is the publisher's daily total revenue?

   d At the price charged for a newspaper, is the demand elastic or inelastic? Why?

●7 In problem 5, what is:

   a The efficient quantity of newspapers to print each day? Explain your answer.

   b Consumer surplus?

   c Deadweight loss created by the publisher?

8 In problem 6, what is:

   a The efficient quantity of newspapers to print each day? Explain your answer.

   b Consumer surplus?

   c Deadweight loss created by the publisher?

●9 In problem 3, what is the maximum value of resources that will be used in rent seeking to acquire Minnie's monopoly? Considering this loss, what is the total social cost of Minnie's monopoly?

10 In problem 4, what is the maximum value of resources that will be used in rent seeking to

acquire Danny's monopoly? Considering this loss, what is the total social cost of Danny's monopoly?

11 The figure illustrates the situation facing a UK natural monopoly.

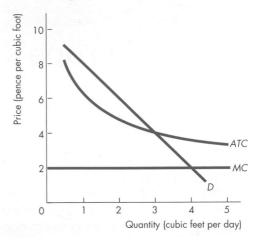

What quantity will be produced and what will be the deadweight loss if the firm is:

   a An unregulated profit-maximizer?

   b Regulated to earn only normal profit?

   c Regulated to be efficient?

12 What are the answers to the three questions in problem 11, if marginal cost falls by 50 per cent?

Critical Thinking

1 Read the Business Case Study on pp. 260–261 and then answer the following:

   a How did the major producers of vitamins create their cartel?

   b What does Mario Monti mean when he says the cartel is 'damaging' to consumers?

   c Is a cartel likely to produce any of the benefits associated with some monopolies? Explain your answer.

   d Why was the cartel so successful and so damaging?

   e What is the purpose of the European Union's fines on the colluding companies?

2 Use the links on the Parkin, Powell and Matthews website to study the market for computer chips.

   a Is it correct to call Intel a monopoly? Explain why or why not?

   b How does Intel try to raise barriers to entry in this market?

3 Use the links on the Parkin, Powell and Matthews website to obtain information on Microsoft. Then answer the following questions.

   a Is it correct to call Microsoft a monopoly? Explain why or why not.

   b How do you think that Microsoft set the price of Windows 98 and decided how many copies of the program to produce?

   c How would the arrival of a viable altern-ative operating system to Windows affect Microsoft?

   d How would you regulate the software industry to ensure that resources are used efficiently?

   e 'Anyone is free to buy shares in Microsoft, so everyone is free to share in Microsoft's economic profit, and the bigger that eco-nomic profit, the better for all.' Evaluate this statement.

http://www.econ100.com

Monopoly

Europe's Vitamin Cartel

The Companies

In November, 2001, the European Commission announced that it was imposing record fines of €855 million on 5 European and 3 Japanese vitamin producing companies. These companies, shown in the table below, are competitors in the bulk vitamin market. At the time they avoided competition by forming a cartel to set vitamin prices.

Company	Country base	Fine (mn)
Roche	Switzerland	462
BASF	Germany	296
Takeda	Japan	37
Daiichi	Japan	23
Eisai	Japan	13
Solvay	Belgium	9
Merck	Germany/USA	9
Aventis	France	5

Source: (1) http://news.bbc.co.uk www.ft.com/healthcare

The Cartel

Within the cartel, sales staff in the various companies agreed to fix prices for bulk vitamins bought by other companies for use in a vast range of products including cereals, biscuits, drinks, animal feeds, pharmaceuticals and cosmetics. Roche and BASF were found to be the main instigators and the severity of their fines reflect this. Their early cooperation with the Commission saved them from fines twice as large. Both Roche and BASF were also fined by the US Antitrust Authorities in 1999 for the same offence.

The Impact

EU Competition Commissioner, Mario Monti said 'The companies' collusive behaviour enabled them to charge higher prices than if the full forces of competition had been at play, damaging consumers and allowing the companies to pocket illicit profits'.[1] The fines will be added to the budget of the European Union and send a strong signal to companies that price fixing cartel agreements will not be accepted in Europe.

Economic Analysis

- The companies involved created a cartel to set price as if they were the single monopoly supplier in the market.

- Figure 1 shows how the cartel, acting as a monopolist, faces the downward sloping market demand curve. Average total cost across all the firms in the cartel is ATC, marginal cost is MC and marginal revenue is MR.

- To maximize profits, the cartel produces the quantity, Q_M, where $MR = MC$, and charges the highest price for bulk vitamins that the market will bear, P_M.

- The cartel earns an economic profit equal to the blue area in Figure 1 and distributes this profit between its members according to an agreed split.

- Figure 2 shows in a competitive market, the price of bulk vitamins would be set where market demand, D, equals market supply, MC. The monopoly price, P_M is higher than the competitive price, P_C, allowing the cartel to take the dark blue area of consumer surplus as profit in addition to the light blue area of producer surplus.

- The EU Competition Commission regulates against monopoly because it is inefficient. Figure 2 shows the inefficiency as the deadweight loss (the grey area).

- Consumer surplus (grey area above P_C) is lost because some consumers cannot afford the higher price of those products produced using the cartels high price vitamins. Producer surplus is also lost (grey area below P_C) as the cartel's output at Q_M is less than the competitive output at Q_C.

- By breaking up the cartel, the US and EU competition authorities lower the price of bulk vitamins and quantity increases towards the competitive equilibrium level, Q_C. The deadweight loss is reduced, increasing efficiency, and the offending firms forfeit some of their additional profits as fines.

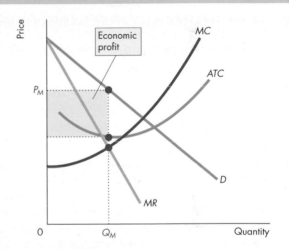

Figure 1 Vitamin cartel's monopoly profit

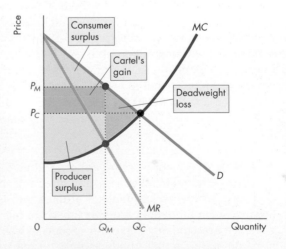

Figure 2 Inefficiency of the vitamin cartel

CHAPTER 13

Monopolistic Competition and Oligopoly

After studying this chapter you will be able to:

- Explain how price and output are determined in a monopolistically competitive industry

- Explain why advertising costs are high in a monopolistically competitive industry

- Explain why the price might be sticky in an oligopoly industry

- Explain how price and output are determined when there is one dominant firm and several small firms in an industry

- Use game theory to make predictions about price wars and competition among small numbers of firms

Fliers and War Games

Every week, all over Europe we receive a newspaper stuffed with supermarket fliers describing this week's 'specials', providing coupons and other enticements. They are all designed to persuade us that Tesco, Carrefour, Metro, Macro and Delhaize have the best deals in town. One claims the lowest price, another the best brands, yet another the best value for money even if its prices are not the lowest. How do firms locked in such fierce competition set their prices, pick their goods and services and choose the quantities to produce? How are the profits of such firms affected by the actions of other firms? ◆ Until 1994, only one firm made the chips that drive IBM and compatible PCs – Intel Corporation. Then prices of powerful personal computers based on Intel's fast 486 and Pentium chips collapsed. The reason: Intel suddenly faced competition from new chip producers. The price of Intel's Pentium processor, set at more than £1,500 when it was launched in 1993, fell to less than £150 by spring 1998, and the price of Pentium II-based computers fell to less than £900. How did competition among a small number of chip makers bring such a rapid fall in the price of chips and computers? ◆ Why do firms spend millions developing and marketing new brands only to see their market share competed away?

◆ ◆ ◆ ◆ The theories of monopoly and perfect competition do not predict the kind of behaviour just described. There are no adverts and discounts, best brands or price wars in perfect competition because each firm produces an identical product and is a price taker. Similarly, there are none in monopoly because each monopoly firm has the entire market to itself. To understand discounts, adverts and price wars, we need the more complex models explained in this chapter. We start by looking at markets where firms differentiate their products through marketing. We end with a case study explaining the ongoing battle for market share between Europe's biggest firms in the household detergent market.

Monopolistic Competition

We have studied two types of market structure – perfect competition and monopoly. In perfect competition, a large number of firms produce identical goods and there are no barriers to the entry of new firms into the industry. In this situation, each firm is a price taker and, in the long run, there is no economic profit. In monopoly, there is just one firm in the industry which is protected by barriers, preventing the entry of new firms. The firm sets its price to maximize profit and might enjoy economic profit even in the long run.

Many real-world markets are competitive, but not as competitive as perfect competition. Firms in these markets possess some power to set their prices like monopolies do. We call this type of market monopolistic competition.

Monopolistic competition is a market structure in which:

◆ A large number of firms compete.

◆ Each firm produces a differentiated product.

◆ Firms compete on quality, price and marketing.

◆ Firms are free to enter and exit the industry.

Large Number of Firms

In monopolistic competition, as in perfect competition, the industry consists of a large number of firms. The presence of a large number of firms has three implications for the firms in the industry:

Small Market Share
In monopolistic competition, each firm supplies only a small part of the total industry output. As a result, each firm has only limited power to influence the price of its product. For any one firm, the price it sets can only deviate a small amount from the average price in the industry.

Ignoring Other Firms
In monopolistic competition, firms are sensitive to the average market price, but they are not sensitive to individual competitors. Because each firm has a small market share, no one firm can dictate market conditions and so no one firm can directly affect the actions of other firms.

Collusion is Impossible
In monopolistic competition, firms would like to collude together to fix a higher price. But the large number of firms in the industry makes such collusion impossible.

Product Differentiation

Product differentiation occurs when firms try to make their product slightly different from similar products being made by competing firms in their market. A differentiated product is one that is a close substitute but not a perfect substitute for the products of other firms. Some people will pay more for one variety of the product, so when its price rises, the quantity demanded falls but it does not (necessarily) fall to zero. For example, Adidas, Asics, New Balance, Nike, Puma and Reebok all make differentiated running shoes, as do many other firms. Other things remaining the same, if the price of Adidas running shoes rises and the prices of the other shoes remain constant, Adidas sells fewer shoes and the other producers sell more. But Adidas shoes don't disappear from the market unless the price rises by a large amount.

Competing on Quality, Price and Marketing

Product differentiation enables a firm to compete with other firms in three ways: through product quality, through price and through marketing activities.

Quality
The quality of a product is the physical attributes that make it different from the products of other firms. Quality includes design, reliability, the service provided to the buyer, and the buyer's ease of access to the product. Quality lies on a spectrum that runs from high to low. Some firms – Dell Computers is an example – offer high-quality products. They are well designed and reliable and the customer receives quick and efficient service. Other firms offer lower-quality products. These are less well designed, might not work perfectly, and the buyer might have to travel some distance to obtain them.

Price
Because of product differentiation, a firm in monopolistic competition faces a downward-sloping demand

curve. So, like a monopoly, the firm can set both its price and its output. But there is a trade-off between the product's quality and price. A firm that makes a high-quality product can charge a higher price than a firm that makes a low-quality product.

Marketing

Because of product differentiation, a firm in monopolistic competition must market its product. Marketing takes two main forms: advertising and packaging. A firm that produces a high-quality product wants to sell it for a suitably high price. To be able to do so, it must advertise and package its product in a way that convinces buyers that they are getting the higher quality for which they are paying a higher price. For example, drug companies advertise and package their brand-name drugs to persuade buyers that these items are superior to the lower-priced generic alternatives. Similarly, a low-quality producer uses advertising and packaging to persuade buyers that although the quality is low, the low price more than compensates for this fact.

Entry and Exit

In monopolistic competition, there are no barriers to entering and exiting the market. Firms are free to enter and exit. Consequently, a firm cannot make an economic profit in the long run. When firms make an economic profit, new firms enter the industry. This entry lowers prices and eventually eliminates economic profit. When economic losses are incurred, some firms leave the industry. This exit increases prices and profits and eventually eliminates the economic loss. In long-run equilibrium, firms neither enter nor leave the industry and the firms in the industry make zero economic profit.

Monopolistic Competition and Branding

Monopolistic competition is visible just about everywhere you look. Firms in monopolistic competition can be very small or very large firms. They can be competing against other firms at the local level, like family restaurants and food retailers; at the national level, such as clothing stores, furniture makers and wholesalers; or in global markets, such as sports shoe makers, food producers and soft drink makers. In each case, the firms face stiff competition but each one tries to differentiate its product from the rest through promotions, advertising and branding.

Differentiation in national and global markets usually results in 'branding' – the process of creating a name and image of quality in customers' mind to create allegiance to the brand. A few companies have created incredibly successful and very long lasting brands. Just think of Coca-Cola, created in 1868; Heinz Tomato Ketchup, created in 1875; and Kellogg's Corn Flakes, created in 1906. But most brands come and go within a few months or years. To find out why, we'll look at the output and price decisions of firms in monopolistic competition and then examine their marketing strategies.

Review Quiz

◆ What are the distinguishing characteristics of monopolistic competition?
◆ How do firms in monopolistic competition compete?
◆ Provide some examples of industries located near you that operate in monopolistic competition (other than the examples provided).

Output and Price in Monopolistic Competition

In this section, we look at a model of how output and price are determined in monopolistic competition. First, we'll assume that the firm has already decided on the quality of its product and on its marketing programme. For a given product and a given amount of marketing activity, the firm faces given costs and market conditions.

Figure 13.1 shows how a firm in monopolistic competition determines its price and output. Part (a) deals with the short run, and part (b) deals with the long run. We'll concentrate first on the short run.

Short Run: Economic Profit

The demand curve D shows the demand for product of a specific UK clothing firm, Batex. It is the demand curve for Batex jackets not jackets in general. The curve labelled MR is the marginal revenue curve associated with the demand curve. It is derived just like the marginal revenue curve of a single-price

Figure 13.1

Output and Price in Monopolistic Competition

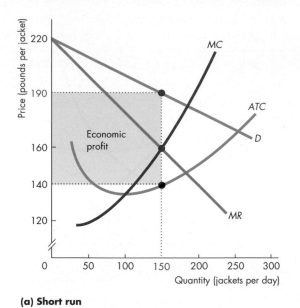

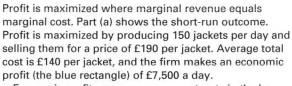

(a) Short run

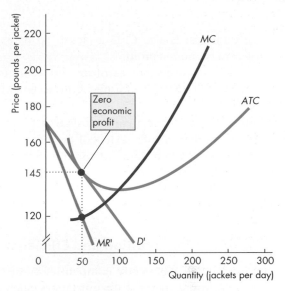

(b) Long run

Profit is maximized where marginal revenue equals marginal cost. Part (a) shows the short-run outcome. Profit is maximized by producing 150 jackets per day and selling them for a price of £190 per jacket. Average total cost is £140 per jacket, and the firm makes an economic profit (the blue rectangle) of £7,500 a day.

Economic profit encourages new entrants in the long run and part (b) shows the long-run outcome. The entry of new

firms decreases each firm's demand and shifts the demand curve and marginal revenue curve leftward. When the demand curve has shifted to *D'*, the marginal revenue curve is *MR'* and the firm is in long-run equilibrium. The output that maximizes profit is 50 jackets a day and the price is £145 per jacket. Average total cost is also £145 per jacket, so economic profit is zero.

monopoly that you studied in Chapter 12. The figure also shows the firm's average total cost (*ATC*) and marginal cost (*MC*). These curves are similar to the cost curves that you first encountered in Chapter 10.

Batex maximizes profit by producing the output at which marginal revenue equals marginal cost. In Figure 13.1, this output is 150 jackets a day. Batex charges the maximum price that buyers are willing to pay for this quantity, which is determined by the demand curve. This price is £190 a jacket. When Batex produces 150 jackets a day, the firm's average total cost is £140 a jacket, so it makes a short-run economic profit of £7,500 a day (£50 a jacket multiplied by 150 jackets a day). The blue rectangle shows this economic profit.

So far, the firm in monopolistic competition looks just like a single-price monopoly. It produces the quantity at which marginal revenue equals marginal

cost and then charges the highest price that buyers are willing to pay for that quantity, determined by the demand curve. The key difference between monopoly and monopolistic competition lies in what happens in the long run.

Long Run: Zero Economic Profit

There is no restriction on entry in monopolistic competition, so economic profit attracts new entrants. As new firms enter the industry, the firm's demand curve and marginal revenue curve start to shift leftward. At each point in time, the firm maximizes its short-run profit by producing the quantity at which marginal revenue equals marginal cost and by charging the highest price that buyers are willing to pay for this quantity. But as the demand curve shifts leftward, the profit-maximizing quantity and price fall.

Figure 13.1(b) shows the long-run equilibrium. Batex's demand curve has shifted leftward to *D'*, and its marginal revenue curve has shifted leftward to *MR'*. Batex produces 50 jackets a day and sells them at a price of £145 each. At this output level, the firm's average total cost is also £145 a jacket. So Batex is making zero economic profit.

When all the firms are earning zero economic profit, there is no incentive for new firms to enter the industry.

If demand is so low relative to costs that firms are incurring economic losses, exit will occur. As firms leave an industry, the demand for the remaining firm's products increases and their demand curves shift rightward. The exit process ends when all the firms are making zero economic profit.

Monopolistic Competition and Efficiency

When we studied a perfectly competitive industry, we discovered that in some circumstances, such an industry allocates resources efficiently. A key feature of efficiency is that marginal benefit equals marginal cost. Price measures marginal benefit, so efficiency requires price to equal marginal cost. When we studied monopoly, we discovered that such a firm creates an inefficient use of resources because it restricts output to a level at which price exceeds marginal cost. In such a situation, the marginal benefit exceeds marginal cost and production is less than its efficient level.

Monopolistic competition shares this feature of monopoly. Even though there is zero economic profit in long-run equilibrium, the monopolistically competitive industry produces an output at which price equals average total cost but exceeds marginal cost. This outcome means that firms in monopolistic competition always have excess capacity in long-run equilibrium.

Excess Capacity

A firm's **capacity output** is the output produced when average total cost is at its minimum point – the output at the minimum of the U-shaped *ATC* curve. This output is 100 jackets a day in Figure 13.2. In monopolistic competition, in the long run, firms always have excess capacity. In Figure 13.2, Batex produces 50 jackets a day and has excess capacity of 50 jackets a day. That is, Batex produces a smaller output than that which minimizes average total cost. As a consequence, the consumer pays more than the minimum average total cost. This result arises from

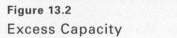

Figure 13.2
Excess Capacity

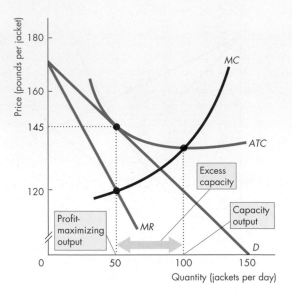

In long-run equilibrium, entry decreases demand to the point at which the firm makes zero economic profit. Batex produces 50 jackets a day. The firm's capacity is the output at which average total cost is at a minimum. Here, capacity output is 100 jackets a day. Because the demand curve in monopolistic competition slopes downward, the output that maximizes profit is always less than capacity output in long-run equilibrium. The firm operates with excess capacity in long-run equilibrium.

the fact that the firm faces a downward-sloping demand curve. The demand curve slopes down because of product differentiation – because one firm's product is not a perfect substitute for another firm's product. Thus it is product differentiation that produces excess capacity.

You can see the excess capacity in monopolistic competition all around you. Family restaurants (except for the truly outstanding ones) almost always have a few empty tables. You can always get a pizza delivered in less than 30 minutes and many local service garages will offer an exhaust emission test on the spot without an appointment. It is rare for the bakery to have no leftover bread and cakes at the end of the day.

These industries are all examples of monopolistic competition. The firms have excess capacity. They could sell more by cutting their prices. But they would then incur economic losses.

Because in monopolistic competition, price exceeds marginal cost, this market structure, like monopoly, is inefficient. The marginal cost of producing one more unit of output is less than the marginal benefit to the consumer, determined by the price the consumer is willing to pay. But the inefficiency of monopolistic competition arises from product differentiation – from product variety. Consumers value variety, but it is achievable only if firms make differentiated products. So the loss in efficiency that occurs in monopolistic competition must be weighed against the gain of greater product variety.

Review Quiz

◆ How does a firm in monopolistic competition decide how much to produce and at what price to offer its product for sale?
◆ Why can a firm in monopolistic competition earn an economic profit only in the short run?
◆ Is monopolistic competition efficient?
◆ Why do firms in monopolistic competition operate with excess capacity?

You've seen how the firm in monopolistic competition determines its output and price in the short run and the long run when it produces a given product and undertakes a *given* marketing effort. But how does the firm choose its product quality and marketing effort? We'll now study these decisions.

Product Development and Marketing

In the model of monopolistic competition we just looked at, we assumed that the firm had already made its product and marketing decisions. But how did they make these decisions? We can look at these decisions and the impact they have on firm's output, price and economic profit.

Innovation and Product Development

To enjoy economic profits, firms in monopolistic competition must be in a state of continuous product development. Its easy to see why. Wherever economic profits are earned, imitators emerge and enter the industry. So to maintain an economic profit, a firm must seek out new products that will provide it with a competitive edge, even if the advantage is only temporary. A firm that manages to introduce a new and differentiated variety can increase the demand for its product temporarily. If it succeeds, it can temporarily increase its price to make an economic profit. Eventually, new firms that make close substitutes for the new product will enter and compete away the economic profit arising from this initial advantage. So to restore economic profit, the firm must again innovate.

The decision to innovate is based on the same type of profit maximizing calculation that you've already studied. Innovation and product development are costly activities but they also bring in additional revenues. The firm must balance the cost and benefit at the margin. At a low level of product development, the marginal revenue from a better product exceeds the marginal cost. When the marginal dollar spent on product development brings in a dollar of revenue, the firm is spending the profit maximizing amount on product development.

For example, when Eidos Interactive released Tomb Raider III, it was probably not the best game that Eidos could have created. Rather, it was the game that balanced the marginal benefit and willingness of the consumer to pay for further game enhancements against the marginal cost of these enhancements.

Efficiency and Product Innovation

Is product innovation an efficient activity? Does it benefit the consumer? There are two views about these questions. One view is that monopolistic competition generates many improved products in the market that bring great benefits to the consumer. Clothing, kitchen and other household appliances, computers, computer programs, cars, and many other products keep getting better every year and the consumer benefits from these improved products.

The other view is that many so-called improvements amount to little more than changing the appearance of a product. The improvement may be nothing more than a change in the packaging or definition of ingredients. In these cases, there is little objective benefit to the consumer.

But regardless of whether a product improvement is real or imagined, its value to the consumer is its marginal benefit, which equals the amount the consumer is willing to pay. In other words, the value of product improvements is the increase in price that the consumer is willing to pay. The marginal benefit to the producer is marginal revenue, which equals marginal cost. Because price exceeds marginal cost in monopolistic competition, product development is not pushed to its efficient level.

Marketing

Some product differentiation is achieved by designing and developing products that are actually different from those of the other firms. But firms also attempt to create a consumer perception of product differentiation even when actual differences are small. Advertising and packaging are the principal means used by firms to achieve this end. A Platinum credit card is a different product from a Gold or standard credit card. But the actual differences are not the main ones that credit card companies emphasize in their marketing. The deeper message is that if you use a Platinum card, people will think you are a high flyer or celebrity.

Marketing Expenditures

Firms in monopolistic competition incur huge costs in order to persuade buyers to appreciate and value the differences between their own products and those of their competitors. So a large proportion of the prices that we pay cover the cost of selling a good. And this proportion is rising dramatically. Advertising expenditure in the United Kingdom topped £17,000 million in 2000, a 35 per cent rise in real terms since 1995, and a 56 per cent rise in real terms since 1990.

Advertising in newspapers and magazines and on radio and television is the main selling cost, but not the only one. Selling costs include the cost of rentals in splendid new shopping centres; the cost of glossy catalogues, direct mail advertising; promotions, exhibitions and the salaries, airfares, and hotel bills of sales staff.

Selling costs might represent 15 per cent of the price of many goods, subject to standard VAT tax rates. Costs will vary depending on the type of advertising used. Figure 13.3 shows UK advertising expenditure for a range of industries in 2000. The highest expenditures are in those sectors that rely on expensive television and national newspaper advertising.

Advertising expenditures and other selling costs affect the profits of firms in two ways. They increase costs and they change demand. Let's look at these effects.

Figure 13.3
Advertising Expenditure

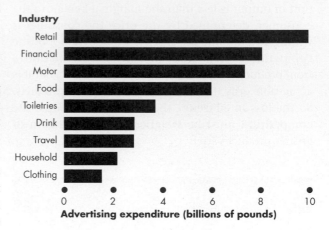

Advertising expenditures are highest for retailers and the finance, motor and food sectors, who rely on television and newspaper advertisements. Advertising expenditure is low by comparison on clothing.

Selling Costs and Total Costs

Selling costs such as advertising expenditures increase the costs of a monopolistically competitive firm above those of a competitive firm or a monopoly. Advertising costs and other selling costs are fixed costs. They do not vary as total output varies. So, just like fixed production costs, advertising costs per unit decrease as production increases.

Figure 13.4 shows how selling costs and advertising expenditures change a firm's average total cost. The blue curve shows the average total cost of production. The red curve shows the firm's average total cost of production plus advertising. The height of the red area between the two curves shows the average fixed cost of advertising. The *total* cost of advertising is fixed. But the *average* cost of advertising decreases as output increases.

The figure shows that if advertising increases the quantity sold sufficiently, it can lower average total cost. For example, if the quantity sold increases from 25 jackets a day with no advertising to 130 jackets a day with advertising, average total cost falls from £170 a jacket to £160 a jacket. The reason is that although the total fixed cost has increased, the greater fixed cost is spread over a greater output, so average total cost decreases.

Figure 13.4

Selling Costs and Total Costs

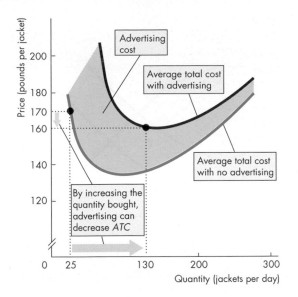

Selling costs such as the cost of advertising are fixed costs. When added to the average total cost of production, these costs increase average total cost (*ATC*) by a greater amount at small outputs than at large outputs. If advertising enables the quantity sold to increase from 25 jackets to 130 jackets a day, it *lowers* average total cost from £170 to £160 a jacket.

Selling Costs and Demand

How do advertising and other selling activities change the demand for a firm's product. Does demand increase or decrease as a result? The most natural answer is that advertising increases demand. By informing people about the quality of its products or by persuading people to switch from the products of other firms, a firm might expect to increase the demand for its own products.

But all firms in monopolistic competition advertise. And all seek to persuade customers that they have the best deal around. If advertising enables a firm to survive, it might increase the number of firms. And to the extent that it increases the number of firms, it decreases the demand faced by any one firm.

Efficiency: The Bottom Line

To the extent that selling costs provide consumers with services that they value and with information about the precise nature of the differentiation of products, they serve a useful purpose to the consumer and enable a better product choice to be made. But the opportunity cost of the additional services and information must be weighed against the gain to the consumer.

The bottom line on the question of efficiency of monopolistic competition is ambiguous. In some cases, the gains from extra product variety unquestionably offset the selling costs and the extra cost arising from excess capacity. The tremendous varieties of books and magazines, clothing, food and drinks are examples of such gains. It is less easy to see the gains from being able to buy brand-name drugs that have a chemical composition identical to that of a generic alternative. But some people do willingly pay more for the brand-name alternative.

Review Quiz

◆ What are the two main ways other than by adjusting price, in which a firm in monopolistic competition competes with other firms?
◆ Why might product innovation and development be efficient and why might it be inefficient?
◆ How do advertising expenditures influence a firm's cost curves? Do they increase or decrease average total costs?
◆ How do advertising expenditures influence a firm's demand curve? Do they increase or decrease demand?
◆ Why is it difficult to determine whether monopolistic competition is efficient or inefficient? What is your opinion about the bottom line and why?

Oligopoly

Another type of market that stands between the extremes of perfect competition and monopoly is oligopoly. **Oligopoly** is a market structure in which a small number of firm compete with each other.

In oligopoly, the quantity sold by any one producer depends on that producer's price and the prices and quantities sold by the other producers. The main feature of oligopoly is that each firm must take into account the effects of its own actions on the actions of other firms.

To see the interplay between prices and sales, suppose you run one of the three service garages in a small town. If you lower the price you charge for an hour's work and your two competitors don't lower theirs, you will get more hours of work, but the other two firms will get less work. In such a situation, the other firms are likely to lower their prices too. If they do cut their prices, hours of work and profits will fall again. So before deciding to cut your price, you try to predict how the other firms will react and you attempt to calculate the effects of those reactions on your own profit.

Several models have been developed to explain the determination of price and quantity in oligopoly markets. No one theory has been found that can explain all the different types of behaviour that we observe in such markets. The models fall into two broad groups: traditional models and game theory models. We'll look at examples of both types, starting with two traditional models.

The Kinked Demand Curve Model

The kinked demand curve model is based on assumptions about the reaction of other firms. Each firm believes that:

1   If it raises its price, other firms will not.

2   If it cuts its price, so will all other firms.

Figure 13.5 shows a demand curve, D, that reflects these beliefs. The demand curve has a kink occurring at the current price, P. A small price rise above P, leads to a big fall in quantity demanded as the firm loses its market share to other firms that do not raise price. So the demand curve is relatively elastic above P. Even a large price cut below P only leads to a small increase in quantity. In this case, other firms match the price cut, so the firm gets very little price advantage over its competitors. So demand is relatively inelastic below P.

The kink in demand curve D creates a break in the marginal revenue curve (MR). To maximize profit, the firm produces the quantity that makes marginal cost and marginal revenue equal. But that output, Q, is where the marginal cost curve passes through the discontinuity in the marginal revenue curve – the gap ab. If marginal cost fluctuates between a and b, like the marginal costs curves MC_0 and MC_1, the firm does not change price or output. Only if marginal cost fluctuates outside the range ab will the firm change its price and output levels. So, the kinked demand curve model predicts that price and quantity are insensitive to small changes in cost. Prices and quan-

Figure 13.5
The Kinked Demand Curve

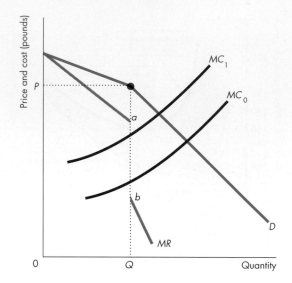

The price in an oligopoly market is P. Each firm believes it faces the demand curve D. At prices above P, demand is highly elastic because the firm believes that its price increases will not be matched by other firms. At prices below P, demand is less elastic because the firm believes its price cuts will be matched. Because the demand curve is kinked, the marginal revenue curve, MR, has a break ab. Profit is maximized by producing Q. Marginal cost changes inside the range ab leave the price and quantity unchanged.

tities will fluctuate less as a result of small changes in costs in oligopoly markets.

One problem with the kinked demand curve model is that it does not tell us how price is set. Another problem is that the firm's beliefs about how competitors will react are not always correct, and firms will work this out for themselves. If marginal cost increases by enough to cause the firm to increase its price, and all other firms experience the same cost rise, all firms will increase prices together. Each firm will quickly realize that its previous belief that other firms will not follow a price rise, is false. Any firm that bases its actions on beliefs that are wrong will not maximize profit and may even make economic losses.

Dominant Firm Oligopoly

The second traditional model deals with the case in which firms differ in size and one firm dominates the

Figure 13.6

A Dominant Firm Oligopoly

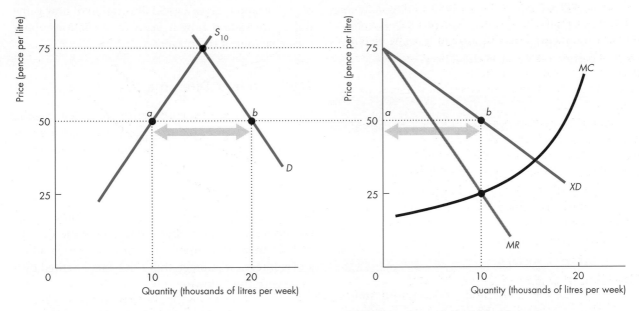

(a) Ten small firms and market demand

(b) Big-G's price and output decision

The demand curve for petrol in a city is *D* in part (a). There are 10 small competitive firms which together have a supply curve of S_{10}. In addition, there is one large firm, Big-G, shown in part (b). Big-G faces the demand curve, *XD*, determined as market demand *D* minus the supply of the other firms S_{10} – the demand that is not satisfied by the

small firms. Big-G's marginal revenue is *MR* and marginal cost is *MC*. Big-G sets its output to maximize profit by equating marginal cost, *MC*, and marginal revenue, *MR*. This output is 10,000 litres. The price at which Big-G can sell this quantity is 50 pence a litre. The other 10 firms take this price and each firm sells 1,000 litres.

industry. A dominant firm oligopoly arises when one firm – the dominant firm – has a substantial cost advantage over the other firms and produces a large part of the industry output. The dominant firm sets the market price and the other firms are price takers. An example of a dominant firm oligopoly is a large petrol retailer or a big video rental company that dominates its local market.

To see how a dominant firm oligopoly works, suppose that 11 firms operate petrol stations in a UK city. Big-G is the dominant firm. It sells 50 per cent of the city's petrol. The other firms are small and each sells 5 per cent of the city's petrol.

Figure 13.6 shows the market for petrol in this city. In part (a), the demand curve *D* tells us how the total quantity of petrol demanded in the city is influenced by its price. The supply curve S_{10} is the supply curve of the 10 small suppliers. These firms are price takers.

Part (b) shows the situation facing Big-G. Its marginal cost curve is *MC*, its demand curve is *XD*, and its marginal revenue curve is *MR*. Big-G's demand curve shows the excess demand not met by the 10 other small firms. For example, at a price of 50 pence a litre, the market quantity demanded is 20,000 litres per week. The 10 small firms supply 10,000 litres, and the excess quantity demanded is 10,000 litres, measured by the distance *ab* in part (a). The distance *ab* determines Big-G's demand at the price 50 pence a litre as shown in part (b).

To maximize its profit, Big-G operates like a monopoly. It sells 10,000 litres of petrol for 50 pence a litre. This price and quantity of sales gives Big-G the biggest possible profit. The 10 small firms take the price of 50 pence a litre and behave like firms in perfect competition. The quantity of petrol demanded in the entire city at 50 pence a litre is 20,000 litres, as shown in part (a). Of this amount, 10,000 litres are sold by Big-G and 10,000 litres are sold by the 10 small firms which sell 1,000 litres each.

The traditional theories of oligopoly are limited and do not enable us to understand all oligopoly markets. In recent years, economists have developed some interesting new oligopoly models based on game theory. Let's look at these now.

Review Quiz

◆ What are the main predictions of the kinked demand curve and the dominant firm models?
◆ In what ways do the two models differ?

Game Theory

Game theory is a method of analysing *strategic behaviour* – behaviour that takes into account the expected behaviour of others and the mutual recognition of interdependence. Game theory was invented by John von Neumann in 1937 and extended by von Neumann and Oskar Morgenstern in 1944. Today it is a major research field in economics. You can read about John von Neumann in Economics in History on pp. 290–291.

Game theory seeks to understand oligopoly as well as political and social rivalries by using a method of decision analysis specifically designed to understand games of all types, including the familiar games of everyday life. We will begin our study of game theory, and its application to the behaviour of firms, by considering those familiar games.

What is a game?

What is a game? At first thought, the question seems silly. After all, there are many different games. There are ball games and board games, games of chance and games of skill. What do games of such diversity and variety have in common? In answering this question, we will focus on those features of games that are relevant for game theory and for analysing oligopoly as a game. All games have three things in common:

1 Rules.
2 Strategies.
3 Payoffs.

Let's see how these common features of games apply to a game called 'the prisoners' dilemma'. This game, it turns out, captures some of the essential features of oligopoly and it gives a good illustration of how game theory works and how it leads to predictions about the behaviour of the players.

The Prisoners' Dilemma

John and Bob have been caught red-handed stealing a car. Facing watertight cases, they will receive a sentence of 2 years each for their crime. During her interviews with the prisoners, the arresting police officer begins to suspect the two men were responsible for a multimillion-pound bank robbery some months earlier. But, the police officer knows she cannot charge the suspects of the greater crime unless she can get each of them to confess to it. She decides to adopt a new interview strategy that can be represented by a game with the following rules.

Rules

Each prisoner (player) is placed in a separate room and there is no communication between them. Each is told that he is suspected of having carried out the bank robbery and that if both he and his accomplice confess to the larger crime, each will receive sentences of 3 years; if he alone confesses and his accomplice does not, he will receive an even shorter sentence of 1 year while his accomplice will receive a 10-year sentence.

Strategies

In game theory, as in ordinary games, **strategies** are all the possible actions of each player. The strategies in the prisoners' dilemma game are very simple. Each prisoner (player) can do only one of two things:

1 Confess to the bank robbery.
2 Deny having committed the bank robbery.

Payoffs

Because there are two players, each with two strategies, there are four possible outcomes.

1 Neither player confesses.
2 Both players confess.
3 John confesses but Bob does not.
4 Bob confesses but John does not.

Table 13.1   Prisoners' Dilemma Payoff Matrix

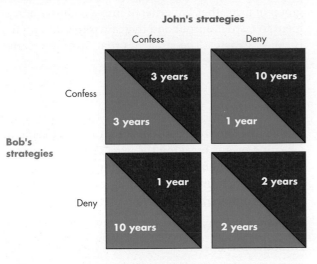

John's strategies

	Confess	Deny
Confess	John: 3 years / Bob: 3 years	John: 10 years / Bob: 1 year
Deny	John: 1 year / Bob: 10 years	John: 2 years / Bob: 2 years

Bob's strategies

Each square shows the payoffs for the two players, John and Bob, for each possible pair of actions. In each square, John's payoff is shown in the pink triangle and Bob's in the blue triangle. For example, if both confess, the payoffs are in the top-left square. John reasons as follows: if Bob confesses, I should confess because then I get 3 years rather than 10. If Bob denies, I should confess because then I get 1 year rather than 2. Regardless of what Bob does, I should confess. John's dominant strategy is to confess. Bob reasons similarly. Since each player's dominant strategy is to confess, the equilibrium of the game is for both players to confess and each to get 3 years.

Each prisoner can work out exactly what will happen to him – his *payoff* – in each of these four situations. We can tabulate the four possible payoffs for each of the prisoners in what is called a payoff matrix for the game. A **payoff matrix** is a table that shows the payoffs for every possible action by each player for every possible action by each other player.

Table 13.1 shows a payoff matrix for John and Bob. The squares show the payoffs for each prisoner – the pink triangle in each square shows John's and the blue triangle Bob's. If both prisoners confess (top-left), they each get a prison term of 3 years. If Bob confesses but John denies (top-right), John gets a 10-year sentence and Bob gets a 1-year sentence. If John confesses and Bob denies (bottom-left), John gets a 1-year sentence and Bob gets a 10-year sentence. Finally, if both of them deny (bottom-right), neither can be convicted of the bank robbery charge but both are sentenced for the car theft – a 2-year sentence.

The Dilemma

The dilemma arises as each prisoner contemplates the consequences of denying. Each prisoner knows that if both of them deny, they will only be sentenced to 2 years. But neither prisoner has any way of knowing that his accomplice will deny. Each prisoner asks himself the following question: should I deny and rely on my accomplice to deny in the hope that we both get 2 years? Or should I confess in the hope that if my accomplice denies, I will only get 1 year, but knowing that if he confesses as well, we will both get 3 years in prison. The dilemma is resolved by finding the equilibrium for the game.

Equilibrium

The equilibrium of a game is when player *A* takes the best possible action given the action of player *B*, and player *B* takes the best possible action given the action of player *A*. In the prisoners' dilemma, the equilibrium occurs when John makes his best choice, given Bob's choice, and Bob makes his best choice, given John's choice. Let's find the equilibrium of the prisoners' dilemma game.

Look at the situation in Table 13.1 from John's point of view. John realizes that his outcome depends on the action Bob takes. If Bob confesses, it pays John to confess also, for in that case, he will be sentenced to 3 years rather than 10 years. But if Bob does not confess, it still pays John to confess for in that case he will receive 1 year rather than 2 years. John reasons that regardless of Bob's action, his own best action is to confess.

Now look at the dilemma from Bob's point of view. Bob knows that if John confesses, he will receive 10 years if he does not confess or 3 years if he does. Therefore if John confesses, it pays Bob to confess. Similarly, if John does not confess, Bob will receive 2 years for not confessing and 1 year if he confesses. Again, it pays Bob to confess. Bob's best action, regardless of John's action, is to confess.

Each prisoner's best action is to confess. The equilibrium of the game is that both prisoners confess. The crime is solved and both prisoners get a 3-year sentence.

Nash Equilibrium

An equilibrium when each player takes the best possible action, given the action of the other player, is called a **Nash equilibrium**. It is named after Nobel Prize winner, John Nash, who proposed the equilibrium for this game. The prisoners' dilemma has a special kind of Nash equilibrium called a dominant strategy equilibrium. A *dominant strategy* is a strategy that is the same regardless of the action taken by the other player. In other words, there is a unique best action regardless of what the other player does. A **dominant strategy equilibrium** occurs when there is a dominant strategy for each player.

A Bad Outcome

For the prisoners, the equilibrium of the game, with each confessing, is not the best outcome. If neither of them confesses, each will get only 2 years for the lesser crime. Isn't there some way in which this better outcome can be achieved? It seems that there is not, because the players cannot communicate with each other since they are interviewed separately. Each player can put himself in the other player's place, and so each player can figure out that there is a dominant strategy for each of them. The prisoners are indeed in a dilemma. Each knows that he can serve 2 years only if he can trust the other not to confess. But each prisoner also knows that it is not in the best interest of the other not to confess. Thus each prisoner knows that he has to confess, thereby delivering a bad outcome for both.

Let's now see how we can use the ideas we've just developed to understand price fixing, price wars and the behaviour of firms in oligopoly.

An Oligopoly Price Fixing Game

To understand how oligopolies fix price, we are going to study a special case of oligopoly, called duopoly. **Duopoly** is a market structure in which there are two producers of a commodity competing with each other. There are few cases of duopoly on a national and international scale but many cases of local duopolies, such as, two car rental firms or two university bookshops. But the main reason for studying duopoly is not its 'realism'. It is the fact that it captures all the essential features of oligopoly, but remains simple.

We want to be able to predict prices charged and quantities produced by two firms in a duopoly. We'll do this by building a model of a duopoly industry and then creating a duopoly game.

Suppose that only two UK firms, Trick and Gear, make a particular kind of electric switchgear. Both firms enter into a collusive agreement. A **collusive agreement** is an agreement between two (or more)

producers to restrict output to raise prices and profits. Such an agreement is illegal in the United Kingdom and under EU rules and is undertaken in secret. A group of firms that has entered into a collusive agreement to restrict output and increase prices and profits is called a **cartel**. The strategies that firms in a cartel can pursue are to:

◆ Comply.
◆ Cheat.

Complying simply means sticking to the agreement. Cheating means breaking the agreement in a manner designed to benefit the cheating firm.

Because each firm has two strategies, there are four possible combinations of actions for the two firms:

1 Both firms comply.
2 Both firms cheat.
3 Trick complies and Gear cheats.
4 Gear complies and Trick cheats.

We begin by describing the cost and demand conditions in a duopoly industry.

Cost and Demand Conditions

Trick and Gear face identical costs and Figure 13.7(a) shows their average total cost curve (*ATC*) and the marginal cost curve (*MC*). The market demand curve for switchgears (*D*) is shown in Figure 13.7(b). Each firm produces an identical switchgear product, so one firm's switchgear is a perfect substitute for the other's. The market price of each firm's product, therefore, is identical. The quantity demanded depends on that price – the higher the price, the lower is the quantity demanded.

In our example, there is room for only two firms in the industry. For each firm the *minimum efficient scale* of production is 3,000 switchgears a week. When the price equals the average total cost of production at the minimum efficient scale, total industry demand is 6,000 switchgears a week.

Colluding to Maximize Profits

We can now work out the payoffs to the two firms. Let's start by looking at the payoff if they both collude to make the maximum industry profit by acting like a monopoly. The calculations that the two firms will perform are exactly the same calculations that a monopoly performs. (You studied these calculations

Figure 13.7

Costs and Demand

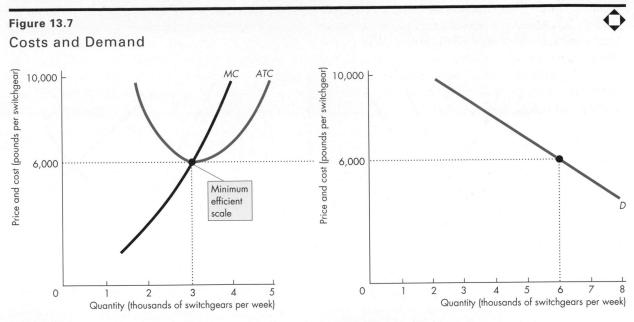

(a) Individual firm

(b) Industry

Part (a) shows the costs facing Trick and Gear, two duopolists which make switchgears. Each firm faces identical costs. The average total cost curve for each firm is *ATC* and the marginal cost curve is *MC*. For each firm the minimum efficient scale of production is 3,000

switchgears a week and the average total cost of producing that output is £6,000 a unit. Part (b) shows the industry demand curve. At a price of £6,000, the quantity demanded is 6,000 switchgears per week. There is room for only two firms in this industry.

in Chapter 12, pp. 245–248.) The only additional thing that the duopolists have to do is to agree on how much of the total output each of them will produce.

Figure 13.8 shows the price and quantity that maximizes industry profit for the duopolists. Part (a) shows the situation for each firm and part (b) for the industry as a whole. The curve labelled *MR* is the industry marginal revenue curve. The curve labelled MC_I is the industry marginal cost curve if each firm produces the same level of output. That curve is constructed by adding together the outputs of the two firms at each level of marginal cost. That is, at each level of marginal cost, industry output is twice as much as the output of each individual firm. Thus the curve MC_I in part (b) is twice as far to the right as the curve *MC* in part (a).

To maximize industry profit, the duopolists agree to restrict output to the rate that makes the industry marginal cost and marginal revenue equal. That output rate, as shown in part (b), is 4,000 switchgears a week. The highest price for which the 4,000 switchgears can be sold is £9,000 each. Let's suppose that Trick and Gear agree to split the market equally

so that each firm produces 2,000 switchgears a week. The average total cost (*ATC*) of producing 2,000 switchgears a week is £8,000, so the profit per unit is £1,000 and economic profit is £2 million (2,000 switchgears × £1,000 per unit). The economic profit of each firm is represented by the blue rectangle in Figure 13.8(a).

We have just described one possible outcome for the duopoly game: the two firms collude to produce the monopoly profit-maximizing output and divide that output equally between themselves. From the industry point of view, this solution is identical to a monopoly. A duopoly that operates in this way is indistinguishable from a monopoly. The economic profit that is made by a monopoly is the maximum total profit that can be made by colluding duopolists.

One Firm Cheats on a Collusive Agreement

In any a collusive agreement, there is often an incentive to cheat. For example, if one firm can cut its price when the other firm does not, more will be added to

Figure 13.8

Colluding to Make Monopoly Profits

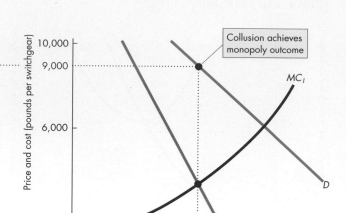

(a) Individual firm

(b) Industry

If Trick and Gear come to a collusive agreement, they can act as a single monopolist and maximize profit. To maximize profit, the firms first calculate the industry marginal cost curve, MC_i (part b), which is the horizontal sum of the two firms' marginal cost curves, MC (part a). Next they calculate the industry marginal revenue, MR. They then choose the output rate that makes marginal revenue equal to marginal cost (4,000 switchgears per

week). They agree to sell that output for a price of £9,000, the price at which 4,000 switchgears are demanded. Each firm has the same costs, so each produces half the total output – 2,000 switchgears per week. Average total cost is £8,000 per unit, so each firm makes an economic profit of £2 million (blue rectangle) – 2,000 switchgears multiplied by £1,000 profit per unit.

revenue than to costs, so profit for the cheating firm will increase. Let's look at how this might happen.

Suppose Trick convinces Gear that industry demand has fallen and that it cannot sell its share of the output at the agreed price. It tells Gear that it plans to cut its price in order to sell the agreed 2,000 switchgears each week. Because the two firms produce a virtually identical product, Gear matches Trick's price cut, but still produces just 2,000 units a week.

In fact, there has been no fall in demand. Trick plans to increase output, which it knows will lower the price, and Trick wants to ensure that Gear's output remains at the agreed level of 2,000 units.

Figure 13.9 illustrates the consequences of Trick cheating in this way. Suppose that Trick decides to cheat. Trick raises output from 2,000 to 3,000 switchgears a week – the output at which average total cost is minimized. If Gear sticks to the agreement and produces only 2,000 switchgears a week, total output will be 5,000 a week. Given the industry

demand shown in part (c), the price will have to be cut to £7,500 a unit.

Gear continues to produce 2,000 switchgears a week at a cost of £8,000 a unit, and incurs a loss of £500 a unit or £1 million a week. This loss is shown as the red rectangle in part (a). Trick produces 3,000 switchgears a week at an average total cost of £6,000 each. With a price of £7,500, Trick makes a profit of £1,500 a unit and an economic profit of £4.5 million. This economic profit is shown as the blue rectangle in part (b).

We've now described a second possible outcome for the duopoly game – one of the firms cheats on the collusive agreement. In this case, the industry output is larger than the monopoly output and the industry price is lower than the monopoly price. The total economic profit made by the industry is also smaller than the monopoly's economic profit. Trick (the cheat) makes an economic profit of £4.5 million and Gear (the complier) incurs a loss of £1 million. The

Figure 13.9

One Firm Cheats

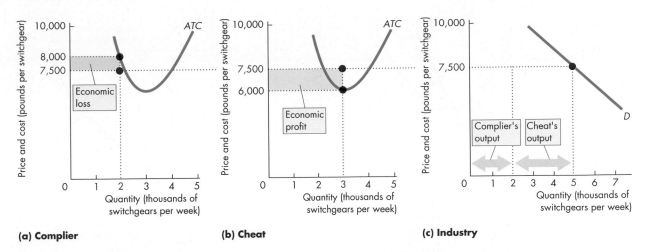

(a) Complier   **(b) Cheat**   **(c) Industry**

One firm, shown in part (a), complies with the agreement and produces 2,000 switchgears. The other firm, shown in part (b), cheats on the agreement and increases production to 3,000 switchgears. Given the market demand curve, shown in part (c), and with a total production of 5,000 switchgears a week, the market price falls to £7,500.

At this price, the complier in part (a) incurs an economic loss of £1 million (£500 × 2,000 units) shown as the red rectangle. In part (b), the cheat makes an economic profit of £4.5 million (£1,500 × 3,000 units), shown as the blue rectangle.

industry makes an economic profit of £3.5 million, which is £0.5 million less than the economic profit a monopoly would make. But that profit is distributed unevenly. Trick makes an even bigger profit than it would under the collusive agreement, while Gear incurs a loss.

A similar outcome that would arise if Gear cheated and Trick complied with the agreement. The industry profit and price would be the same but in this case Gear (the cheat) would make an economic profit of £4.5 million and Trick (the complier) would incur a loss of £1 million.

Both Firms Cheat on a Collusive Agreement

Suppose that instead of just one firm cheating on the collusive agreement, both firms cheat. In particular, suppose that each firm behaves in exactly the same way as the cheating firm that we have just analysed. Each tells the other that it is unable to sell its output at the going price and that it plans to cut its price. But because both firms cheat, each will propose a successively lower price. So long as price exceeds marginal

cost, each firm has an incentive to increase its production – to cheat. Only when price equals marginal cost is there no further incentive to cheat. This situation arises when the price has reached £6,000. At this price, marginal cost equals price. Also price equals minimum average cost. At a price of less than £6,000, each firm incurs a loss. At a price of £6,000, each firm covers all its costs and makes zero economic profit – makes normal profit. Also at a price of £6,000, each firm wants to produce 3,000 switchgears a week, so that the industry output is 6,000 switchgears a week. Given the demand conditions, 6,000 switchgears can be sold at a price of £6,000 each.

Figure 13.10 shows the situation just described. Each firm, shown in part (a), is producing 3,000 switchgears a week, and this output level occurs at the point of minimum average total cost (£6,000 per unit). The market as a whole, shown in part (b), operates at the point at which the demand curve (D) intersects the industry marginal cost curve. This marginal cost curve is constructed as the horizontal sum of the marginal cost curves of the two firms. Each firm has lowered its price and increased its output in order to try to gain an advantage over the other firm. They

Figure 13.10

Both Firms Cheat

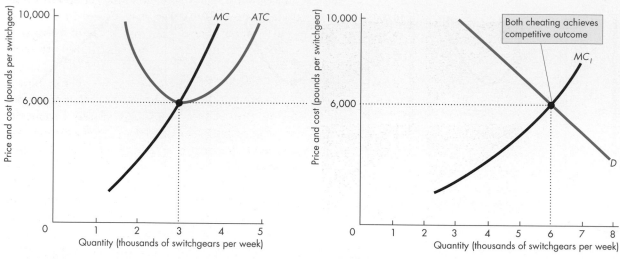

(a) Individual firm

(b) Industry

If both firms cheat by raising their output and lowering the price, the collusive agreement completely breaks down. The limit to the breakdown of the agreement is the competitive equilibrium. Neither firm will want to cut the price below £6,000 (minimum average total cost), for to do so will result in losses. Part (a) shows the situation facing each firm. At a price of £6,000, the firm's profit-maximizing output is 3,000 switchgears per week. At that output rate,

price equals marginal cost, and it also equals average total cost. Economic profit is zero. Part (b) describes the situation in the industry as a whole. The industry marginal cost curve (MC_1) – the horizontal sum of the individual firms' marginal cost curves (MC) – intersects the demand curve at 6,000 switchgears per week and at a price of £6,000. This output and price is the one that would prevail in a competitive industry.

have each pushed this process as far as they can without incurring an economic loss.

We have now described a third possible outcome of this duopoly game – both firms cheat. If both firms cheat on the collusive agreement, the output of each firm is 3,000 switchgears a week and the price is £6,000. Each firm makes zero economic profit.

The Payoff Matrix

Now that we have described the strategies and payoffs in the duopoly game, let's summarize the strategies and the payoffs in the form of the game's payoff matrix and then calculate the equilibrium.

Table 13.2 sets out the payoff matrix for this game. It is constructed in exactly the same way as the payoff matrix for the prisoners' dilemma in Table 13.1. The squares show the payoffs for the two firms – Gear and Trick. In this case, the payoffs are profits. (In the case of the prisoners' dilemma, the payoffs were losses.)

The table shows that if both firms cheat (top-left), they achieve the perfectly competitive outcome – each firm makes zero economic profit. If both firms comply (bottom-right), the industry makes the monopoly profit and each firm earns an economic profit of £2 million. The top-right and bottom-left squares show what happens if one firm cheats while the other complies. The firm that cheats collects an economic profit of £4.5 million and the one that complies incurs a loss of £1 million.

This duopoly game is just like the prisoners' dilemma that we examined earlier in this chapter; it is a duopolist's dilemma.

Equilibrium of the Duopolists Dilemma

So will our firms comply or cheat? To find the equilibrium, look at things from the point of view of Gear. Gear reasons as follows. Suppose that Trick cheats. If we comply with the agreement, we incur a loss of

Table 13.2   Duopoly Payoff Matrix   ◆

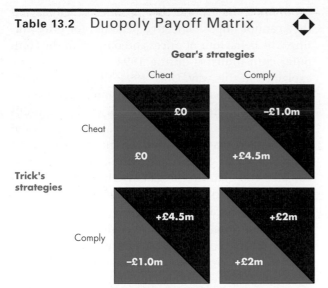

Each square shows the payoffs from a pair of actions. For example, if both firms comply with the collusive agreement, the payoffs are recorded in the square at the bottom-right corner of the table. The pink triangle shows Gear's payoff and the blue triangle shows Trick's. The equilibrium is a Nash equilibrium in which both firms cheat.

£1 million. If we also cheat, we make zero economic profit. Zero economic profit is better than a £1 million loss, so it will pay us to cheat. But suppose Trick complies with the agreement. If we cheat, we will make a profit of £4.5 million, and if we comply, we will make a profit of £2 million. A £4.5 million profit is better than a £2 million profit so it would again pay us to cheat. Thus regardless of whether Trick cheats or complies, it pays us to cheat. Gear's dominant strategy is to cheat.

Trick comes to the same conclusion as Gear. Therefore both firms will cheat. The equilibrium of this game is that both firms cheat on the agreement. Although there are only two firms in the industry, the price and quantity are the same as in a competitive industry. Each firm makes zero economic profit.

Although we have done this analysis for only two firms, it would not make any difference (other than to increase the amount of arithmetic) if we were to play the game with three, four, or more firms. In other words, although we have analysed duopoly, the game theory approach can also be used to analyse oligopoly. The analysis of oligopoly is much harder, but the essential ideas that we have learned also apply to oligopoly.

Repeated Games

The games we've studied were just played once. By contrast, most real-world duopolists get opportunities to play repeatedly against each other. In fact, real-world duopolists might find some way of learning to cooperate so that their efforts to collude are more effective.

If a game is played repeatedly, one player always has the opportunity to penalize the other player for previous 'bad' behaviour. If Trick refuses to cooperate this week, then Gear can refuse to cooperate next week (and vice versa). If Gear cheats this week, perhaps Trick will cheat next week. Before Gear cheats this week, shouldn't it take account of the possibility of Trick cheating next week? What is the equilibrium of this more complicated prisoners' dilemma game when it is repeated indefinitely?

Actually there is more than one possibility. One is the Nash equilibrium that we have just analysed. Both players cheat with each making zero economic profit forever. In such a situation, it will never pay one of the players to start complying unilaterally, for to do so would result in a loss for that player and a profit for the other. The price and quantity will remain at the competitive levels forever. But another equilibrium, called a cooperative equilibrium, is possible. A **cooperative equilibrium** is one in which the players make and share the monopoly profit. How might this equilibrium come about? The key to answering this question is the fact that when a prisoners' dilemma game is played repeatedly, the players have an increased array of strategies. Each player can punish the other player for previous actions.

There are two extremes of punishment. The smallest penalty that one player can impose on the other is what is called 'tit-for-tat'. A *tit-for-tat strategy* is one in which a player cooperates in the current period if the other player cooperated in the previous period, but cheats in the current period if the other player cheated in the previous period. The most severe form of punishment that one player can impose on the other arises in what is called a trigger strategy. A *trigger strategy* is one in which a player cooperates if the other player cooperates, but plays the Nash equilibrium strategy forever thereafter if the other player cheats.

In the duopoly game between Trick and Gear, a tit-for-tat strategy keeps both players cooperating and earning monopoly profits. Let's see why.

If both firms stick to the collusive agreement in period 1, they make an economic profit of £2 million each. Suppose that Trick contemplates cheating in period 2. The cheating produces a quick £4.5 million profit and inflicts a £1 million loss on Gear. Adding up the profits over two periods of play, Trick comes out ahead by cheating (£6.5 million compared with £4 million if it did not cheat). In the next period Gear will hit Trick with its tit-for-tat response and cheat. Both will make zero economic profit in period 3. If Trick reverts to cooperating, to induce Gear to cooperate in period 4, Gear now makes a profit of £4.5 million and Trick incurs a loss of £1 million. Adding up the profits over four periods of play, Trick would have made more profit by cooperating. In that case, its profit would have been £8 million compared with £5.5 million from cheating and generating Gear's tit-for-tat response.

What is true for Trick is also true for Gear. Because each firm makes a larger profit by sticking with the collusive agreement, both firms do so and the monopoly price, quantity and profit prevail in a cooperative equilibrium. This equilibrium is called a *cooperative equilibrium*.

In reality, whether a cartel works like a one-play game or a repeated game, depends on the number of players and the ease of detecting and punishing cheating. The larger the number of players, the easier it is to cheat, and the harder it is to maintain a cartel.

Games and Price Wars

The theory of price and output determination under duopoly can help us understand real-world behaviour and, in particular, price wars. Some price wars can be interpreted as the implementation of a tit-for-tat strategy. We've seen that with a tit-for-tat strategy in place, firms have an incentive to stick to the monopoly price. But fluctuations in market demand lead to fluctuations in the monopoly price and a firm might mistakenly believe this price change is a sign of another firm cheating. So a price war breaks out. The price war ends only when each firm has satisfied itself that the other is ready to cooperate again. The price war is not damaging to the collusive agreement because it maintains the credibility of the tit-for-tat threat. We often see cycles of price wars and the restoration of collusive agreements. Fluctuations in the world price of oil can be interpreted in this way.

Some price wars arise from the entry of a small number of firms into an industry that had been a monopoly. Although the industry has a small num-

ber of firms, the firms are in a prisoners' dilemma and they cannot impose effective penalties for price cutting. The behaviour of prices and outputs in the computer chip industry during 1994 and 1995 can be explained in this way. Until 1994, the market for PC chips was dominated by one firm, Intel Corporation, which was able to make maximum economic profit by producing the quantity of chips at which marginal cost equalled marginal revenue. The price of Intel's chips was set to ensure that the quantity demanded equalled the quantity produced. Then, in 1994 and 1995, with the entry of a small number of new firms, the industry became an oligopoly. If the firms had maintained Intel's price and shared the market, together they could have made economic profits equal to Intel's profit. But the firms were in a prisoners' dilemma. So prices tumbled to competitive levels.

Review Quiz

◆ Why does a collusive agreement to restrict output and raise price create a game like the prisoners' dilemma?

◆ What creates an incentive for firms in a collusive agreement to cheat and increase production?

◆ What is the equilibrium strategy for each firm in a prisoners' dilemma and why do the firms not collude?

◆ If a prisoners' dilemma game is played repeatedly, what punishment strategies might the players employ and how does playing the game repeatedly change the equilibrium?

The game theory model can be extended to deal with a much wider choice of strategies for firms in oligopoly or duopoly industries. Let's look at some examples of these other games.

Other Oligopoly Games

Firms have to decide whether to mount expensive advertising campaigns; whether to modify products; whether to improve product reliability; whether to price discriminate and, if so, among which groups of customers and to what degree; whether to undertake a large research and development (R&D) effort aimed at lowering production costs; or whether to enter or leave an industry. All of these choices can be analysed by using game theory. All of these strategic choices can be modelled using game theory. The basic method you have studied can be applied to these problems by working out the payoff for each of the alternative strategies and then finding the equilibrium of the game.

We'll look at two examples: an R&D game and an entry-deterrence game.

An R&D Game

There are two big players in the European disposable nappy market – Procter & Gamble (the maker of Pampers) and Kimberly-Clark (the maker of Huggies). Procter & Gamble has the largest share, but both firms have about one third of the market. The disposable nappy industry is fiercely competitive. When Procter & Gamble launched the product, it was a pathbreaking brand. The high cost of research and development resulted in new machines that could make disposable nappies at a low enough cost to achieve the initial competitive edge against low cost, traditional laundered nappies. But as the industry has matured, a large number of firms entered in a bid to take Procter & Gamble's market share. Now the two industry leaders battle to maintain or increase their reduced market share through innovations.

During the 1990s, Kimberly-Clark was the first to introduce Velcro fasteners. Later on, Procter & Gamble introduced 'breathable' nappies. The key to success is to innovate products that parents value highly relative to the cost of producing them. The firm that develops and uses the least-cost technology gains a competitive edge, undercutting the rest of the market, increasing its market share and increasing its profit. But the research and development effort that has to be undertaken to achieve even small cost reductions is itself very costly. The cost of R&D has to be deducted from the profit resulting from the increased market share that lower costs achieve. If no firm conducts R&D, every firm can be better off, but if one firm initiates the R&D activity, all must.

Each firm is in a research and development dilemma that is similar to the game played by John and Bob. Although the two firms play an ongoing game against each other, it has more in common with the one-play game than a repeated game. The

Table 13.3 Pampers versus Huggies: An R&D Game

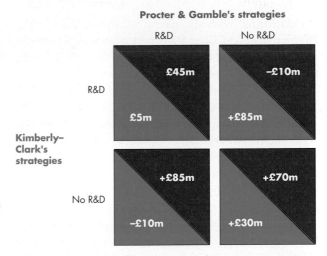

If both firms undertake R&D, their payoffs are those shown in the top-left square. If neither firm undertakes R&D, their payoffs are in the bottom-right square. When one firm undertakes R&D and the other one does not, their payoffs are in the top-right and bottom-left squares. The pink triangle shows Procter & Gamble's payoff and the blue triangle shows Kimberly-Clark's. The dominant strategy equilibrium for this game is for both firms to undertake R&D. The structure of this game is the same as that of the prisoners' dilemma.

reason is that R&D is a long-term process. Effort is repeated, but payoffs occur only infrequently and uncertainly.

Table 13.3 illustrates the dilemma (with hypothetical numbers) for the R&D game that Kimberly-Clark and Procter & Gamble are playing. Each firm has two strategies: to spend £25 million a year on R&D or to spend nothing on R&D. If neither firm spends on R&D, they make a joint profit of £100 million, £30 million for Kimberly-Clark and £70 million for Procter & Gamble (bottom-right square of payoff matrix). If each firm conducts R&D, market shares are maintained but each firm's profit is lower, by the amount spent on R&D (top-left square of payoff matrix). If Kimberly-Clark pays for R&D but Procter & Gamble does not, Kimberly-Clark gains a large part of Procter & Gamble's market. Kimberly-Clark profits and Procter & Gamble loses (top-right square of payoff matrix). Finally, if Procter & Gamble invests in

R&D and Kimberly-Clark does not, Procter & Gamble gains market share from Kimberly-Clark, increasing its profit, while Kimberly-Clark incurs a loss (bottom-left square).

Confronted with the payoff matrix in Table 13.3, the two firms calculate their best strategies. Kimberly-Clark reasons as follows: if Procter & Gamble does not undertake R&D, we make £85 million if we do and £30 million if we do not; therefore it pays to conduct R&D. If Procter & Gamble conducts R&D, we lose £10 million if we don't and make £5 million if we do. Again, R&D pays off. Thus conducting R&D is a dominant strategy for Kimberly-Clark. Doing it pays regardless of Procter & Gamble's decision.

Procter & Gamble reasons similarly. So R&D is the dominant strategy for both companies.

Because R&D is a dominant strategy for both players, it is the Nash equilibrium. The outcome of this game is that both firms conduct R&D. They make lower profits than they would if they could collude to achieve the cooperative outcome of no R&D.

The real-world situation has more players than Kimberly-Clark and Procter & Gamble. There are a large number of other firms sharing a small portion of the market, all of them ready to eat into the market share of Procter & Gamble and Kimberly-Clark. So the R&D effort by these two firms not only serves the purpose of maintaining shares in their own battle, but also helps to keep barriers to entry high enough to preserve their joint market share.

Let's now study an entry-deterrence game in which a firm tries to prevent other firms from entering an industry. Such a game is played in a type of market called a contestable market.

Contestable Markets

A **contestable market** is a market in which one firm (or a small number of firms) operates but in which both entry and exit are free so that the firm (or firms) in the market faces perfect competition from *potential* entrants. Examples of contestable markets are routes served by airlines and by private bus companies. These markets are contestable because even though only one or a few firms actually operate on a particular air or bus route, other firms could enter those markets if an opportunity for economic profit arose and could exit those markets if the opportunity for economic profit disappeared. The potential entrance prevents the single firm (or small number of firms) from making an economic profit.

If the five-firm concentration ratio is used to determine the degree of competition, a contestable market appears to be uncompetitive. It looks like an oligopoly or monopoly. But a contestable market behaves as if it were perfectly competitive. You can see why by thinking about a game that we'll call an entry-deterrence game.

Entry-deterrence game

In the entry-deterrence game we'll study, there are two players. One player is Better Bus, the only firm operating on a particular route. The other player is Wanabe Co., a potential entrant. The strategies for Better Bus are to set its price at the monopoly profit-maximizing level or at the competitive (zero economic profit) level. The strategies for Wanabe are to enter and set a price just below that of Better Bus or not to enter.

If Wanabe does not enter, Better Bus earns a normal profit by setting a competitive price and earns maximum monopoly profit (a positive economic profit) by setting the monopoly price. If Wanabe does enter and undercuts Better Bus' price, Better Bus incurs an economic loss regardless of whether it sets its price at the competitive or monopoly level. The reason is that Wanabe takes the market with the lower price, so Better Bus incurs a cost but has zero revenue. If Better Bus sets a competitive price, Wanabe earns a normal profit if it does not enter, but incurs an economic loss if it enters and undercuts Better Bus by setting a price that is less than average total cost. If Better Bus sets the monopoly price, Wanabe earns a positive economic profit by entering and a normal profit by not entering.

The Nash equilibrium for this game is a competitive price at which Better Bus earns a normal profit and Wanabe does not enter. If Better Bus raised the price to the monopoly level, Wanabe would enter and by undercutting Better Bus' price would take all the business, leaving Better Bus with an economic loss equal to total cost. Better Bus avoids this outcome by sticking with the competitive price and deterring Wanabe from entering.

Limit Pricing

Limit pricing is the practice of charging a price below the monopoly profit-maximizing price and producing a quantity greater than that at which marginal revenue equals marginal cost in order to deter entry. The game that we've just studied is an

Table 13.4 Comparison of Market Structures

Characteristics	Perfect competition	Monopolistic competition	Oligopoly	Monopoly
Number of firms in industry	Many	Many	Few	One
Product	Identical	Differentiated	Either identical or differentiated	No close substitutes
Barriers to entry	None	None	Scale and scope economies	Scale and scope or legal barriers
Firm's control over price	None	Some	Considerable	Considerable or regulated
Concentration ratio (0–100)	0	Low	High	100
Examples	Agricultural goods	Corner shops, foods, sports shoes	Washing powders, Disposable nappies	Local water utility, postal letter service

example of limit pricing, but the practice is more general. For example, a firm can use limit pricing to try to convince potential entrants that its own costs are so low that new entrants will incur an economic loss if they enter the industry.

We have now studied the four main market structures – perfect competition, monopolistic competition, oligopoly and monopoly – and discovered how prices and output, revenue, cost and economic profit are determined in these industries. Table 13.4 summarizes the difference between these models studied so far in Chapters 11–13.

A key element in our analysis of these different markets is the behaviour of costs. Costs are determined partly by technology and partly by the prices of factors of production. We have treated those factor prices as given. In the next chapter you will see how factor prices are determined in factor markets and how they interact with goods markets. Firms decide *how* to produce and the interactions of households and firms in goods markets decide *what* will be produced. But factor prices determine *for whom* the various goods and services are produced. We'll study these important interactions in the next chapter.

Summary

Key Points

Monopolistic Competition (pp. 263–264)

- Monopolistic competition occurs when a large number of firms compete with each other on product quality, price and marketing.

Output and Price in Monopolistic Competition (pp. 264–267)

- Firms in monopolistic competition face a downward-sloping demand curve and produce the quantity at which marginal revenue equals marginal cost.

- Entry and exit result in zero economic profit and excess capacity in the long-run equilibrium.

Product Development and Marketing (pp. 267–269)

- Firms in monopolistic competition innovate and develop new products to maintain economic profit.

- Advertising expenditures increase total cost but they might lower average total cost if they increase the quantity sold by enough.

- Advertising expenditures might increase demand but they might also decrease the demand facing a firm by increasing competition.

- Whether monopolistic competition is inefficient depends on the value we place on product variety.

Oligopoly (pp. 269–272)

- If rival firms match price cuts but do not match price rises, they face a kinked demand curve and change prices only when large cost change occur.

- If one firm dominates a market, it acts like a monopoly and the small firms take its price as given and act like perfectly competitive firms.

Game Theory (pp. 272–274)

- Game theory is a method of analysing strategic behaviour.

- In the prisoners' dilemma game, two prisoners, each adopt the strategy in their own best interest, but end up not acting in their joint best interest.

An Oligopoly Price Fixing Game (pp. 274–280)

- An oligopoly price fixing game is like the prisoners' dilemma game.

- The firms might collude, one firm might cheat, or both firms might cheat.

- In a one-play game, both firms cheat and the industry output and price are the same as in perfect competition.

- In a repeated game, a punishment strategy can produce a cooperative equilibrium in which price and output are the same as in a monopoly.

Other Oligopoly Games (pp. 280–283)

- Firms' decisions about whether to enter or leave an industry, how to market or modify a product, and whether to undertake research and development, can also be modelled using game theory.

Key Figures and Tables

Key Terms

Problems

°1 The figure shows the situation facing Lite and Kool Plc., a European producer of running shoes.

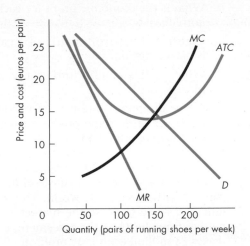

a What quantity does Lite and Kool produce?

b What does it charge?

c How much profit does Lite and Kool make?

2 The figure shows the situation facing Well Done Plc., a European producer of steak sauce.

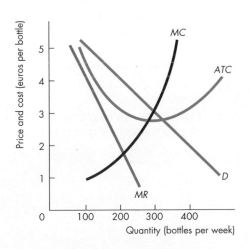

a What quantity does Well Done produce?

b What does it charge?

c How much profit does Well Done make?

°3 A firm in monopolistic competition produces running shoes. If it spends nothing on advertising, it can sell no shoes at €100 a pair and, for each €10 cut in price, the quantity of shoes it can sell increases by 25 pairs a day so that at €20 a pair, it can sell 200 pairs a day. The firm's total fixed cost is €4,000 a day. Its average variable cost and marginal cost is a constant €20 per pair. If the firm spends €3,000 a day on advertising it can double the quantity of shoes sold at each price.

a If the firm doesn't advertise, what is the quantity of shoes produced and what is the price per pair?

b What is the firm's economic profit or economic loss?

c If the firm does advertise, what is the quantity of shoes produced and what is the price per pair?

d What is the firm's economic profit or economic loss?

e Will the firm advertise or not? Why?

4 The firm in problem 3 has the same demand and costs as before if it does not advertise. But it hires a new advertising agency. If the firm spends €3,000 a day on advertising with the new agency, it can double the amount that consumers are willing to pay at each quantity demanded.

a If the firm hires the new agency, what is the quantity of shoes produced and what is the price per pair?

b What is the firm's economic profit or economic loss?

c Will the firm advertise or not? Why?

d What is the firm's economic profit in the long run?

°5 A firm with a kinked demand curve experiences an increase in its fixed costs. Explain the effects on the firm's price, output and economic profit/loss.

6 A firm with a kinked demand curve experiences an increase in its variable cost. Explain the effects on the firm's price, output and economic profit/loss.

°7 An industry with one very large firm and 100 very small firms experiences an increase in the demand for its product. Use the dominant firm model to explain the effects on the price, output and economic profit of:

a The large firm.

b A typical small firm.

8 An industry with one very large firm and 100 very small firms experiences an increase in total variable cost. Use the dominant firm model to explain the effects on the price, output and economic profit of:

a The large firm.

b A typical small firm.

●**9** Consider the following game: the game has two players, and each player is asked a question. The players can answer the question honestly or they can lie. If both answer honestly, each receives a payoff of €100. If one answers honestly and the other lies, the liar gains at the expense of the honest player. In that event, the liar receives a payoff of €500 and the honest player gets nothing. If both lie, then each receives a payoff of €50.

a Describe this game in terms of its players, strategies and payoffs.

b Construct the payoff matrix.

c What is the equilibrium for this game?

10 Describe the game known as the prisoners' dilemma. In describing the game:

a Make up a story that motivates the game.

b Work out a payoff matrix.

c Describe how the equilibrium of the game is arrived at.

●**11** Two firms, Soapy and Suddsies Plc., are the only producers of soap powder. They collude and agree to share the market equally. If neither firm cheats on the agreement, each makes €1 million economic profit. If either firm cheats, the cheater increases its economic profit to €1.5 million while the firm that abides by the agree-ment incurs an economic loss of €0.5 million. Neither firm has any way of policing the other's actions.

a Describe the best strategy for each firm in a game that is played once.

b What is the economic profit for each firm if both cheat?

c Construct the payoff matrix of a game that is played just once.

d What is the equilibrium if the game is played once?

e If this duopoly game can be played many times, describe some of the strategies that each firm might adopt.

12 Two firms, Faster and Quicker, are the only two producers of sports cars on an island that has no contact with the outside world. The firms col-lude and agree to share the market equally. If neither firm cheats on the agreement, each firm makes €3 million economic profit. If either firm cheats, the cheater can increase its economic profit to €4.5 million, while the firm that abides by the agreement incurs an economic loss of €1 million. Neither firm has any way of policing the actions of the other.

a What is the economic profit for each firm if they both cheat?

b What is the payoff matrix of a game that is played just once?

c What is the best strategy for each firm in a game that is played once?

d What is the equilibrium if the game is played once?

e If this game can be played many times, what are two strategies that could be adopted?

Critical Thinking

1 Read the Business Case Study on pp. 288–289, and then explain:

   a Why do Procter & Gamble and Unilever spend huge amounts of money on washing powder products?

   b Do the two companies benefit from advertising and if so in what way?

   c Do consumers benefit from advertising and if so in what way?

   d Would there be an efficiency gain from eliminating this type of advertising? Explain your answer.

   e Would you expect these companies to spend as much on advertising their packaged 'snack' or 'haircare' products. Explain why or why not.

   f One explanation of why some brands have been so long lasting is that they satisfy basic needs. Why do you think Procter & Gamble have not managed to create a blockbuster brand innovation since Pampers were introduced in 1960?

2 Suppose that Netscape and Microsoft each develop their own versions of a great new web browser that allows advertisers to target consumers with great precision. Also, the new browser is easier and more fun to use than existing browsers. Each firm is trying to decide whether to sell the browser or to give it away free. Explain what the benefits from each action are likely to be and which is more likely to occur.

3 Explain the behaviour of the prices of computer chips in 1994 and 1995 by using the prisoners' dilemma game. Describe the types of strategies that individual firms in the industry have adopted.

4 Use the model of oligopoly to explain why producers of pet foods spend so much on advertising.

Duopoly Game

Procter & Gamble vs Unilever

The Companies

Procter & Gamble (P&G) and Unilever (UniL) are long-established players in Europe's household products markets. They are best known for their soap powders and toiletries, but they also produce packaged food like Pringles crisps and Ben and Jerry's ice cream.

P&G has over 300 brands and UniL has over 400. The two firms compete against a handful of firms in the European soap powder market, but are the main players in the UK soap powder market. Both earn revenues of approximately €45,000 million a year.

The Strategies

Both firms engage in constant research and development to create new brands, supported by massive advertising campaigns. P&G spends nearly £2 bn a year on research and development alone.

The two firms have been running a 15 year tit-for-tat innovation war to gain a key market share in Europe's €8.8 bn detergent market. It started with cheap brands, then UniL launched liquids, P&G launched biological agents and powder concentrates, then UniL introduced washing powder tablets and a home cleaning and laundry service called Myhome.

The Payoffs

P&G gained 50 per cent of the UK's €1,440 soap powder market in 1995, after announcing that UniL's Persil Power rotted clothes. UniL's share fell to 38 per cent but bounced back to 52 per cent when Persil soap powder tablets were launched in 1998. P&G's share slumped to 40 per cent.

P&G launched its Ariel tablets a year later, supported by a €28 million advertising campaign, leading to a slow recovery.

P&G have not followed UniL's latest innovation in home services, preferring to raise its brand rices supported by its advertising campaign on higher quality.

Economic Analysis

■ Procter & Gamble (P&G) and Unilever (UniL) are the major players in Europe's detergent markets, operating a virtual duopoly in the UK's soap powder market.

■ The figure shows the UK soap powder market position of the two companies in 1995 after P&G's anti-Persil Power campaign. P&G achieved a 50 per cent share while UniL's share fell to 37 per cent after the product was withdrawn.

■ The figure also shows that launching the new Persil tablets in 1998 boosted UniL's share to 50 per cent and cut P&G's share to 40 per cent.

■ The competition is represented as a strategic game in the table. If neither company introduces tablets, both save on advertising revenue, market shares are equal and profits rise for both companies by 8 per cent (top-left box). Advertising reduces profits, so if both companies successfully introduce tablets, market shares are equal and economic profits are cut to 4 per cent (bottom-right box).

■ When Unilever introduced tablets, Procter & Gamble did not follow and lost market share. Profits increased by 12 per cent for Unilever and fell by 4 per cent for Procter & Gamble (top-right box). This is one stage in a repeated game.

■ P&G have not followed UniL's latest innovation move, preferring to compete on higher quality. If these initiatives fail, both companies will be back to square one with even market shares.

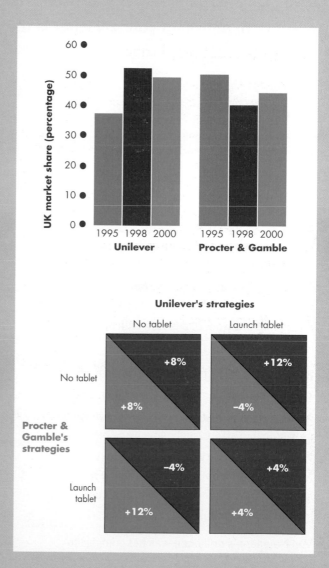

Understanding Market Power

Real life consists of bluffing, of little tactics of deception, of asking yourself what is the other man going to think I mean to do.

*John von Neumann told to Jacob Bronowski
(in a London taxi) and reported in The Ascent of Man*

The Economist: John von Neumann

John von Neumann was one of the great minds of the twentieth century. Born in Budapest, Hungary, in 1903, Johnny, as he was known, showed early mathematical brilliance. His first mathematical publication was an article that grew out of a lesson with his tutor, which he wrote at the age of 18.

By the age of 25, in 1928, von Neumann published the article that began a flood of research on game theory – a flood that has still not receded today. In that article, he proved that in a zero-sum game (like sharing a pie), there exists a best strategy for each player. Von Neumann's work has revolutionized the way that economists model market power by focusing on the interdependent nature of firms' strategies.

Von Neumann's brilliance was not confined to economics. He invented and helped to build the first modern practical computer, the basis for so much of our modern technology.

Von Neumann believed that the social sciences would progress only if they used mathematical tools. But he believed that they needed different tools than those developed from the physical sciences.

The Issues and Ideas

It is not surprising that firms with market power will charge higher prices than those charged by competitive firms. But how much higher?

This question has puzzled generations of economists. Adam Smith said 'The price of a monopoly is upon every occasion the highest which can be got'. But he was wrong. Antoine-Augustin Cournot first worked out the price a monopoly will charge. It is not the 'highest which can be got', but the price that maximizes profit. Cournot's work was not appreciated until almost a century later when Joan Robinson explained how a monopoly sets its price.

Questions about monopoly became urgent and practical during the 1870s, a time when rapid technological change and falling transport costs enabled huge monopolies to emerge all over Europe. Monopolies dominated oil, steel, railways, tobacco and even sugar. Industrial empires grew ever larger.

The success of the nineteenth century monopolies led to the creation of our competition laws – laws that limit the use of monopoly power. Those laws have been used to prevent monopolies from being set up and to break up existing monopolies. These laws have been used to investigate the big monopolies in the oil and tobacco industries, the sugar industry and more recently in the 1990s the pharmaceutical industry. They have formed the basis of regulating the privatized state monopolies such as telecommunications and electricity. Despite these efforts, near monopolies still exist. Among the most prominent today are those in computer chips and operating systems. Like their forerunners, today's near monopolies make huge profits. But unlike the situation in the nineteenth century, the technological change taking place today is strengthening the forces of competition. Today's information technologies are creating substitutes for services that previously had none. Direct satellite TV is competing with cable and new phone companies are competing with the traditional phone monopolies.

Then . . .

Ruthless greed, exploitation of both workers and customers – these are the traditional images of monopolies and the effects of their power. These images appeared to be an accurate description during the 1880s, when monopolies were at their peak of power and influence. The power of some monopolies, like British Sugar, was based on exclusive and protected access to colonial resources within the British Empire at the time. The earlier trade in slaves and control of overseas lands brought power and wealth to the monopolies.

. . . And Now

In spite of competition laws that regulate monopolies, monopoly power still exists. British Sugar still controls the vast majority of sugar beet production, sugar processing and refining. The large pharmaceutical companies may only control a 20 per cent share of the total world market, but they exercise complete monopoly over their patented drugs. National telecommunications companies showed record profits in the late 1990s associated with their virtual monopoly control of access lines to the internet. Internet lines are the fastest growing traffic for telecommunications networks and an easy source of monopoly profit in countries with monopoly suppliers of residential local lines. In 1998, The British Monopolies and Merger Commission ordered Vodaphone, Cellnet and BT to cut their prices for calls from BT phones to mobile phones. The regulator believed that consumers were being cheated out of £200 million by the network operators' price strategy. But already, competition in these markets is increasing. Computer retailers are moving into the telephone line supply market to offer free internet access and free internet calls. This will start to erode BT's monopoly profit. So BT and other large telecommunications companies have anticipated the threat and are now looking for new ways to maintain profits. The last few years have seen a tide of mergers and merger proposals between telecommunications companies across the world, as well as joint inititiatives between telecommunications companies and software giants like Microsoft. These moves can all be seen as part of an ongoing strategic war for monopoly profit.

Trying These Ideas Today

Using what you have learned about monopoly and oligopoly games in Chapters 12 and 13, and what you know about the development of monopoly power, you should be able to answer the following question:

■ In 2001, European Union legislation was introduced to increase competition in the market that provides telecommunications links between local exchanges and homes. The local access markets are dominated by the national telecommunications companies. Why do you think that the European Commission wants to free up the local access markets?

CHAPTER 14

Demand and Supply in Factor Markets

After studying this chapter you will be able to:

◆ Explain how firms choose the quantities of labour, capital and land and natural resources to employ

◆ Explain how people choose the quantities of labour, capital, land and entrepreneurship to supply

◆ Explain how wages, interest, rent and normal profit are determined in competitive factor markets

◆ Explain the concept of economic rent and distinguish between economic rent and opportunity cost

Many Happy Returns

It may not be your birthday, and even if it is chances are you are spending most of it working. But at the end of the week or month (or, if you're devoting all your time to college, when you graduate), you will receive the *returns* from your labour. These returns vary a lot. Julie Adams, who spends her working days as a professional nurse, earns a happy return of £8.20 an hour, about £16,000 a year. Jan Leschly, the chief executive of the pharmaceutical giant, SmithKline Beecham, had a very happy return on an annual pay rise of £20 million, more than £7,500 an hour! England footballer, David Beckham, earns £6.5 million a year, more than £3,500 an hour. Students working at what have been called 'McJobs' – serving fast food, labouring, or cleaning – earn just a few pounds an hour. Why aren't *all* jobs well-paid? ◆ Most of us have little trouble spending our pay. But most of us do manage to save some of what we earn. What determines the amount of saving that people do and the returns they make on that saving? How do the returns on saving influence the allocation of savings across the many industries and activities that use our capital resources? ◆ Some people receive income from supplying land, but the amount earned varies enormously with its location and quality. For example, an acre of farm land in Devon or Brittany rents for about £1,000 a year while a block of offices in London or Paris rents for several million pounds a year. What determines the rent that people are willing to pay for different blocks of land? Why are rents so enormously high in big cities and so relatively low in the great farming regions of the European Union?

◆ ◆ ◆ ◆ In this chapter we study the markets for resources – the factors of production – labour, capital, land and entrepreneurship. We'll learn how their prices are set and how people's incomes are determined. You can see how the salaries of UK premiership footballers are set in Reading Between the Lines on pp. 318–319.

Factor Prices and Incomes

Goods and services are produced by using the four factors of production – *labour, capital, land* and *entrepreneurship*. (These factors of production are defined in Chapter 2, p. 21.) Incomes are determined by the combination of factor prices – the wage rate for labour, the interest rate for capital, the rental rate for land and the rate of normal profit for entrepreneurship – and the quantities of factors used.

In addition to the four factor incomes, a residual income, *economic profit* (or *economic loss*) is paid to (or borne by) firms' owners. A firm's owners might be the suppliers of any of the four factors of production. For a small firm, the owner is usually the entrepreneur. For a large corporation, the owners are the shareholders, who supply the capital.

An Overview of a Competitive Factor Market

We're going to learn how a competitive factor market determines the prices, the quantities used and the incomes of factor suppliers. The tool that we will use is the demand and supply model.

The quantity demanded of a factor depends on its price, and the law of demand applies to factors just as it does to goods and services. The lower the price of a factor, other things remaining the same, the greater is the quantity demanded. Figure 14.1 shows the demand curve for a factor of production as the curve labelled *D*.

The quantity supplied of a factor also depends on its price. With a possible exception that we'll identify later in this chapter, the law of supply applies to factors of production. The higher the price of a factor of production, other things remaining the same, the greater is the quantity supplied of the factor. Figure 14.1 shows the supply curve of a factor as the curve labelled *S*.

The equilibrium factor price is determined at the point of intersection of the factor demand and factor supply curves. In Figure 14.1, *PF* is the factor price and *QF* is the quantity of the factor used.

The income earned by a factor of production is its price multiplied by the quantity used. In Figure 14.1 factor income is the blue rectangle in the figure. This income is the total income received by the factor. Each person supplying a factor receives the resource price multiplied by the quantity supplied. Changes in

Figure 14.1

Demand and Supply in a Factor Market

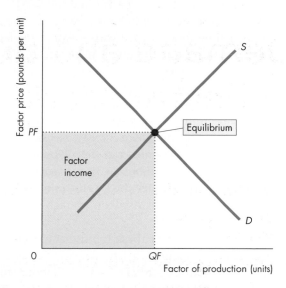

The demand curve for a factor of production (*D*) slopes downward and the supply curve (*S*) slopes upward. Where the demand and supply curves intersect, the factor price (*PF*) and the quantity of a factor used (*QF*) are determined. The factor income is the product of the factor price and the quantity of the factor, as represented by the blue rectangle.

demand and supply change the equilibrium price and quantity, and also change the income received.

An increase in demand for a factor shifts the demand curve rightward, increasing price, quantity and income. An increase in supply shifts the supply curve rightward and decreases price. The quantity used increases and factor income can increase, decrease or remain constant. The change in income that results from an increase in supply depends on the elasticity of demand for the factor. If demand is elastic, income rises; if demand is inelastic, income falls, and if demand is unit elastic, income remains constant (see Chapter 4, p. 78).

The rest of this chapter explores more closely the impact of changes in demand and supply on factors of production. We're also going to study the influences on the elasticities of supply and demand for factors. These elasticities are important because of their effects on factor prices and the incomes earned.

We begin with the market for labour. Most of what we learn about the market for labour will also apply to other factor markets considered later in the chapter.

Labour Markets

For most of us, the labour market and the wage we earn is our main source of income. We expect wages to rise over time to keep pace with inflation. In fact real wages, taking out the effect of inflation, have risen in most European countries over the past 30 years. Table 14.1 shows historical annual growth rates of real wages in different European countries. Wage growth has been mainly positive and real wages have risen over time, but the rate of increase has slowed to almost zero in some countries in the 1990s. In most countries, the total number of hours worked has increased, but in others, like the UK, the total number of hours worked has not risen on average over the period.

Figure 14.2 shows why these trends have occurred in most European countries. The demand for labour has increased from LD_{65} to LD_{94}, and the labour supply increased, but by much less, from LS_{65} to LS_{94}. The combined effect is that the real wage rises over time, but the number of hours worked increased by a smaller proportion.

Of course, there is a lot of diversity behind these average wage rates. Not all labour markets have rising real wages. Real wages have fallen for some types of worker. To understand the trends in labour markets, we must investigate the forces that influence the demand and supply of labour. This chapter studies these forces. Let's begin with the demand for labour.

Figure 14.2
Labour Market Trends in Europe

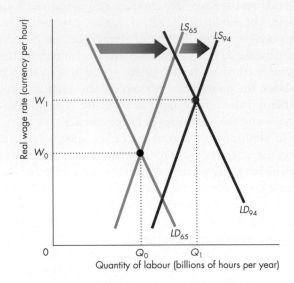

Between 1965 and 1994, the real wage rate has risen in most Western European countries. The quantity of labour employed has also risen. This is the result of an increase in labour demanded and a smaller increase in labour supplied.

Table 14.1 Real Wage Rate Growth in Europe (%)

Year	France	Italy	Spain	Sweden	UK
1965	3	4	6		3
1970	5	7	3	7	6
1975	5	2	5	−4	4
1980	3	1	3	−4	0
1985	1	1	−1	1	3
1990	2	1	1	−2	2
1994	0	0	0	1	0

Real wage growth rates have been positive in most years in most countries. Real wages have risen but the rate of increase has slowed to almost zero.

Source: Adapted from G. Bertola and A. Ichino (1995), Economic Policy, Vol. 21, October, 1995.

The Demand for Labour

The demand for labour is a derived demand. A **derived demand** is a demand for an item not for its own sake but in order to use it in the production of goods and services. A firm's demand for labour (and its demand for all other factor inputs) stems from its desire to maximize profits.

You learned in Chapters 11, 12, and 13 that a profit-maximizing firm produces the output at which marginal cost equals marginal revenue. This principle holds true whether the firm is in a perfectly competitive industry, in monopolistic competition, in oligopoly or a monopoly.

A firm that maximizes profit hires the quantity of labour that can produce the profit maximizing output. What is that quantity of labour and how does it change as the wage rate changes? We can answer these questions by comparing the marginal revenue earned by hiring an extra worker with the marginal

Table 14.2 Marginal Revenue Product at Max's Wash 'n' Wax

	Quantity of labour (L) (workers)	Total product (TP) (cars washed per hour)	Marginal product (MP = ΔTP/ΔL) (washes per worker)	Marginal revenue product (MRP = MR × MP) (pounds per workers)	Total revenue TR = P × Q (pounds)	Marginal revenue product (MRP = ΔTR/ΔL) (pounds per worker)
a	0	0			0	
			5	20		20
b	1	5			20	
			4	16		16
c	2	9			36	
			3	12		12
d	3	12			48	
			2	8		8
e	4	14			56	
			1	4		4
f	5	15			60	

The car wash market is perfectly competitive and the price is £4 a wash. Marginal revenue is also £4 a wash. Marginal revenue product equals marginal product (column 3) multiplied by marginal revenue. For example, the marginal product of the second worker is 4 washes and marginal revenue is £4 a wash. So the marginal revenue product of the second worker (in column 4) is £16. Alternatively, if Max hires 1 worker (row b), total product is 5 washes an hour and total revenue is £20 (column 5). If he hires 2 workers (row c), total product is 9 washes an hour and total revenue is £36. By hiring the second worker, total revenue rises by £16 – the marginal revenue product of labour is £16.

cost of hiring that worker. Let's look first at the marginal revenue side of this comparison.

Marginal Revenue Product

The change in total revenue resulting from employing one worker, holding the quantity of all other factors constant, is called **marginal revenue product**. Table 14.2 shows you how to calculate marginal revenue product for a perfectly competitive firm.

The first two columns show the total product schedule for Max's Wash 'n' Wax car wash business. (Look back to p. 199 to refresh your memory on total product.) The total product schedule tells us how the number of car washes per hour varies as the quantity of labour increases. The third column shows the marginal product of labour. This is the change in output that results when an extra unit of labour is employed. (Look back at p. 200 to refresh your memory on marginal product.)

The car wash market is perfectly competitive, and if we assume the market price is £4, Max can sell as many washes as he chooses at that price. So Max's marginal revenue is £4 a wash.

Given this information, we can calculate Max's marginal revenue product (fourth column). It equals marginal product multiplied by marginal revenue. For example, the marginal product of hiring a second worker is 4 car washes an hour and because marginal revenue is £4 a wash, the marginal revenue product of the second worker is £16 (4 washes at £4 each).

The last two columns of Table 14.2 show an alternative way to calculate the marginal revenue product of labour. Total revenue is equal to total product multiplied by price. For example, two workers produce 9 washes per hour and generate a total revenue of £36 (9 washes at £4 each). One worker produces 5 washes per hour and generates a total revenue of £20 (5 washes at £4 each). Marginal revenue product, in the sixth column, is the change in the total revenue from hiring one more worker. When the second worker is hired, total revenue increase from £20 to £36, an increase of £16. So the marginal revenue product of the second worker is £16, which agrees with the previous calculation.

Diminishing Marginal Revenue Product

As the quantity of labour rises, the marginal revenue product of labour falls. For a firm in perfect competition, marginal revenue product diminishes because marginal product diminishes. In monopoly (or monopolistic competition) marginal revenue product diminishes for a second reason. When more labour is hired and total product increases, the firm must cut its price to sell the extra product. So marginal product and marginal revenue decrease, both of which bring decreasing marginal revenue product.

The Labour Demand Curve

Figure 14.3 shows how the labour demand curve is derived from the marginal revenue product curve. The *marginal revenue product curve* graphs the marginal revenue product of a factor at each quantity of the factor hired. Figure 14.3(a) illustrates the marginal revenue product curve for workers employed by Max. The horizontal axis measures the number of workers that Max hires and the vertical axis measures the marginal revenue product of labour. The blue bars show the marginal revenue product of labour as Max employs more workers. These bars correspond to the numbers in Table 14.2. The curve *MRP* is Max's marginal revenue product curve.

A firm's demand for labour curve is based on its marginal revenue product curve. Figure 14.3(b) shows Max's demand for labour curve (*D*). The horizontal axis measures the number of workers hired – the same as part (a). The vertical axis measures the wage rate in pounds per hour. The demand for labour curve is exactly the same as the firm's marginal revenue product curve. For example, when Max employs 3 workers an hour, his marginal revenue product is £10 an hour, as in Figure 14.3(a); and at a wage rate of £10 an hour, Max hires 3 workers an hour, as in Figure 14.3(b).

The demand for labour curve identical to the marginal revenue product curve because the firm hires the profit-maximizing quantity of labour. If the cost of hiring one more worker – the wage rate – is less than the additional revenue that the worker brings in – the marginal revenue product of labour – then the firm can increase its profit by employing one more worker. If the cost of hiring one more worker is greater than the additional revenue that the worker brings in – the wage rate exceeds the marginal revenue product – then the firm can increase its profit by employing one fewer worker. But if the cost of hiring one more worker is equal to the additional revenue that the worker brings in – the wage rate equals the marginal revenue product – then the firm cannot increase its profit by changing the number of workers it employs. The firm is making the maximum possible profit. This situation occurs when the wage rate equals the marginal revenue product of labour. Thus the quantity of labour demanded by the firm is such that the wage rate equals the marginal revenue product of labour.

Figure 14.3

The Demand for Labour at Max's Wash 'n' Wax

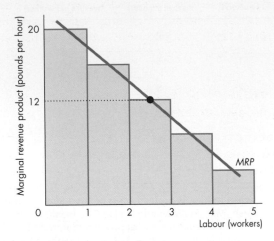

(a) Marginal revenue product

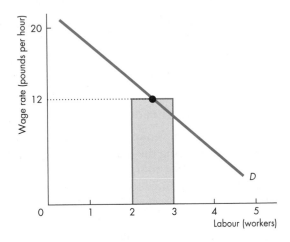

(b) Demand for labour

Max's Wash 'n' Wax operates in a perfectly competitive car wash market and can sell any quantity of washes at £4 a wash. The blue bars in part (a) represent the firm's marginal revenue product of labour. They are based on the numbers in Table 14.1. The orange line is the firm's marginal revenue product of labour curve. (Each point is plotted midway between the quantity of labour used in its calculation.) Part (b) shows Max's demand for labour curve. This curve is identical to Max's marginal revenue product curve. Max demands the quantity of labour that makes the wage rate, which is the marginal cost of labour, equal to the marginal revenue product of labour.

You already know one condition for maximizing profit-producing the output level where marginal revenue equals marginal cost. You've now discovered another condition for maximizing profit, where marginal revenue product of labour equals the wage. This condition holds for all other factor inputs into the firm. Let's now study the connection between these two conditions.

Equivalence of Two Conditions for Profit Maximization

Profit is maximized when at the quantity of labour hired, *marginal revenue product* equals the wage rate and when, at the quantity produced, *marginal revenue* equals *marginal cost*. These two conditions for maximum profit are equivalent. The quantity of labour that maximizes profit produces the output that maximizes profit. To see the equivalence of the two conditions for maximum profit, first recall that

Marginal revenue product
= Marginal revenue × Marginal product

If we call marginal revenue product *MRP*, marginal revenue *MR*, and marginal product *MP*,

$$MRP = MR \times MP$$

If we call the wage rate *W*, the first condition for maximum profit is

$$MRP = W$$

But *MRP* = *MR* × *MP*, so

$$MR \times MP = W$$

This equation tells us that when profit is maximized, marginal revenue multiplied by marginal product equals the wage rate.

Divide the last equation by marginal product, *MP*, to obtain

$$MR = W \div MP$$

This equation states that when profit is maximized, marginal revenue equals the wage rate divided by the marginal product of labour. The wage rate divided by the marginal product of labour equals marginal cost. It costs the firm *W* to hire one more hour of labour.

Table 14.3 Two Conditions for Maximum Profit

Symbols

Marginal product	*MP*
Marginal revenue	*MR*
Marginal cost	*MC*
Marginal revenue product	*MRP*
Factor price	*PF*

Two conditions for maximum profit

1. *MR* = *MC*   2. *MRP* = *PF*

Equivalence of conditions

1. *MRP*/*MP* = *MR* = *MC* = *PF*//*MP*
    Multiply by *MP* to give   Multiply by *MP* to give
    MRP = *MR* × *MP*   *MC* × *MP* = *PF*
    Flipping the equation over   Flipping the equation over
2. *MR* × *MP* = *MRP* = *PF* = *MC* × *MP*

Marginal revenue product (*MR*) equals marginal cost (*MC*), and marginal revenue product (*MRP*) equals the price of the factor (*PF*). The two conditions for maximum profit are equivalent because marginal revenue product (*MRP*) equals marginal revenue (*MR*) multiplied by marginal product (*MP*), and the factor price (*PF*) equals marginal cost (*MC*) multiplied by marginal product (*MP*).

But the labour produces *MP* units of output. So the cost of producing one of those units of output, which is marginal cost, is *W* divided by *MP*. If we call marginal cost *MC*, then

$$MR = MC$$

which is the second condition for maximum profit.

Because the first condition for maximum profit implies the second condition, these two conditions are equivalent. Table 14.3 summarizes the reasoning and calculations that show the equivalence between the two conditions for maximum profit.

We've just derived the law of demand as it applies to the labour market. We've discovered that the same principles that apply to the demand for goods and services apply here as well. The demand for labour curve slopes downward. Other things remaining the same, the lower the wage rate (the price of labour), the greater is the quantity of labour demanded. Let's now study the influences that change in the demand for labour and shift in the demand for labour curve.

Changes in the Demand for Labour

The position of a firm's demand for labour curve depends on three factors:

1 The price of the firm's output.
2 The prices of other factors of production.
3 Technology.

The higher the price of a firm's output, the greater is the quantity of labour demanded by the firm, other things remaining the same. The price of output affects the demand for labour through its influence on marginal revenue product. A higher price for the firm's output increases marginal revenue which, in turn, increases the marginal revenue product of labour. A change in the price of a firm's output leads to a shift in the firm's demand for labour curve. If the output price increases, the demand for labour curve shifts to the right.

The other two influences on the demand for labour have their main effects not in the short run but in the long run. The short-run demand for labour is the relationship between the wage rate and the quantity of labour demanded when the firm's capital is fixed and labour is the only variable factor. The long-run demand for labour is the relationship between the wage rate and the quantity of labour demanded when all factors can be varied. A change in the relative price of factors of production – such as the relative price of labour and capital – leads to a substitution away from the factor whose relative price has increased and towards the factor whose relative price has decreased. Thus if the price of using capital decreases relative to that of using labour, the firm substitutes capital for labour, increasing the quantity of capital demanded and decreasing its demand for labour.

Finally, a new technology that influences the marginal product of labour also affects the demand for labour. For example, the development of electronic telephones with memories and a host of clever features decreased the marginal product of telephone operators and so decreased the demand for telephone operators. This same technological change increased the marginal product of telephone engineers and so increased the demand for telephone engineers. Again, these effects are felt in the long run when the firm adjusts all its factors and incorporates new technologies into its production process.

As we saw earlier, in Figure 14.2, the demand for labour curve has increased over time, shifting rightward. We can now give some reasons for the demand

curve shifting rightward over time. The main factors are advances in technology and investment in new capital that increases the marginal product of labour. Both of these factors have increased the demand for labour.

Table 14.4 summarizes the influences on a firm's demand for labour.

Market Demand

So far we've studied only the demand for labour by an individual firm. The market demand for labour is the total demand by all firms. The market demand curve for labour is found by adding together the quantities demanded by all firms at each wage rate. Because each firm's demand for labour slopes downward, so does the market demand for labour.

Elasticity of Demand for Labour

The elasticity of demand for labour measures the responsiveness of the quantity of labour demanded to the wage rate. We calculate this elasticity in the same way that we calculate a price elasticity. The elasticity of demand for labour equals the magnitude of the percentage change in the quantity of labour demanded divided by the percentage change in the wage rate.

The demand for labour is less elastic in the short run, when only labour can be varied, than in the long run, when labour and other factors can be varied. The elasticity of demand for labour depends on:

Table 14.4   A Firm's Demand for Labour

The law of demand

The quantity of labour demanded by a firm

Decreases if:	*Increases if:*
◆ The wage rate increases	◆ The wage rate decreases

Changes in demand

A firm's demand for labour

Decreases if:	*Increases if:*
◆ The firm's output price decreases	◆ The firm's output price increases
◆ The prices of other factors decrease	◆ The prices of other factors increase
◆ A technological change decreases the marginal product of labour	◆ A technological change increases the marginal product of labour

- The labour intensity of the production process.
- The elasticity of demand for the product.
- The substitutability of capital for labour.

Labour Intensity

A labour-intensive production process is one that uses a lot of labour and little capital – a process that has a high ratio of labour to capital. Home building is an example. The larger the labour–capital ratio, the more elastic is the demand for labour, other things remaining the same. To see why, suppose wages are 90 per cent of total cost. A 10 per cent increase in the wage rate increases total cost by 9 per cent. Firms will be extremely sensitive to such a large change in total cost. If the wage rate increases, firms will decrease the quantity of labour demanded by a large amount. If wages are 10 per cent of total cost, a 10 per cent increase in the wage rate increases total cost by 1 per cent. Firms will be less sensitive to this increase in cost. If wage rates increase in this case, firms will decrease the quantity of labour demanded by a small amount.

The Elasticity of Demand for the Product

The greater the elasticity of demand for the good, the larger is the elasticity of demand for the factors of production used to produce it. To see why, think about what happens when the wage rate increases. An increase in the wage rate increases marginal cost and decreases the supply of the good. The decrease in the supply of the good increases the price of the good and decreases the quantity demanded of the good and the factors that produce it. The greater the elasticity of demand for the good, the larger is the decrease in the quantity demanded of the good and so the larger is the decrease in the quantities of the factors of production used to produce it.

The Substitutability of Capital for Labour

The substitutability of capital for labour influences the long-run elasticity of demand for labour but not the short-run elasticity. In the short run, capital is fixed. In the long run, capital can be varied, and the more easily capital can be substituted for labour in production, the more elastic is the long-run demand for labour. For example, it is fairly easy to substitute robots for assembly-line workers in car factories and automatic picking machines for labour in vineyards and orchards. At the other extreme, it is difficult (though not impossible) to substitute robots for newspaper reporters, bank loan officers and teachers. The more readily capital can be substituted for labour, the more elastic is the firm's demand for labour in the long run.

Now you have examined the demand side of the labour market, we can turn to the supply side and look at the decisions people make about how to allocate their time between working and other activities.

Supply of Labour

People can allocate their time to two broad activities – labour supply and leisure. (Leisure is a catch-all. It includes all activities other than supplying labour.) For most people, leisure is more enjoyable than supplying labour. To consider an example, we'll look at the labour supply decision of Amy. Like most people, Amy enjoys her leisure time, and she'd prefer not to have to spend her weekends working on a supermarket checkout. But Amy has chosen to work weekends. The reason is that she is offered a wage rate that exceeds her *reservation wage*. Amy's reservation wage is the lowest wage at which she is willing to supply labour. If the wage rate exceeds her reservation wage, she supplies some labour. But how much labour does she supply? The quantity of labour that Amy is willing to supply depends on the wage rate.

Substitution Effect

Other things remaining the same, the higher the wage rate Amy is offered, at least over a range, the greater is the quantity of labour that she supplies. The reason is that Amy's wage rate is her *opportunity cost of leisure*. If she quits work an hour early to catch a movie, the cost of that extra hour of leisure is the wage rate that Amy forgoes. The higher the wage rate, the less willing is Amy to forgo the income and take the extra leisure time. This tendency for a higher wage rate to induce Amy to work longer hours is a *substitution effect*.

But there is also an *income effect* that works in the opposite direction to the substitution effect.

Income Effect

The higher Amy's wage rate, the higher is her income. A higher income, other things remaining the same, induces Amy to increase her demand for most goods. Leisure is one of those goods. Because an increase in income creates an increase in the demand for leisure, it also creates a decrease in the quantity of labour supplied.

Backward-Bending Supply of Labour Curve

As the wage rate rises, the substitution effect brings an increase in the quantity of labour supplied, while the income effect brings a decrease in the quantity of labour supplied. At low wage rates, the substitution effect is larger than the income effect, so as the wage rate rises, people supply more labour. But as the wage rate continues to rise, the income effect eventually becomes larger than the substitution effect and the quantity of labour supplied decreases. The labour supply curve is *backward bending*.

Figure 14.4(a) shows the labour supply curves, for Amy, and two friends, Jack and Lisa. Each labour supply curve is backward bending but the three people have different reservation wage rates.

Market Supply

The market supply of labour curve is the sum of the individual supply curves. Figure 14.4(b) shows the market supply curve (S_M) derived from the supply curves of Amy, Jack, and Lisa (S_A, S_B, S_C) in Figure 14.4(a). At wage rates of less than €1 an hour, no one supplies any labour. At a wage rate of €1 an hour, Amy works but Jack and Lisa don't. As the wage rate increases and reaches €7 an hour, all three of them work. The market supply curve S_M eventually bends backward but it has a long upward-sloping section.

Changes in the Supply of Labour

The supply of labour changes when influences other than the wage rate change. The key factors that change the supply of labour and that over the years have increased it are:

1 Adult population.

2 Technological change and capital accumulation.

An increase in the adult population increases the supply of labour. Also, an increase in capital in home production (of meals, laundry services and cleaning services) increases the supply of labour. These factors that have increased the supply of labour have shifted the labour supply curve rightward.

Let's now build on what we've learned about the demand for labour and the supply of labour and

---

Figure 14.4

The Supply of Labour

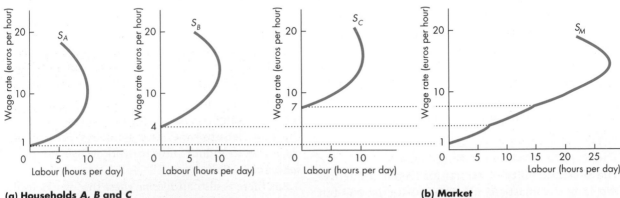

(a) Households A, B and C

(b) Market

Part (a) shows the labour supply curves of (Amy, S_A, Jack, S_B, and Lisa, S_C). Each person has a reservation wage below which it will supply no labour. As the wage rises above the reservation wage, the quantity of labour supplied rises to a maximum. If the wage continues to rise, the quantity of labour supplied begins to decline. Each household's supply curve eventually bends backward.

Part (b) shows how, by adding together the quantities of labour supplied by each person at each wage rate, we derive the market supply curve of labour (S_M). The market supply curve also eventually bends backward, but has a long upward-sloping region before it bends backward.

study labour market equilibrium and the trends in wage rates and employment.

Labour Market Equilibrium

Wages and employment are determined by equilibrium in the labour markets. You saw, in Figure 14.2, that the wage rate has risen and that total hours of employment in most European countries have also risen. But this picture hides some important differences between different types of labour market. Now you can see why.

Trends in Labour Demand

The demand for labour had increased in most European countries because of technological change. As a result, the demand for labour in the UK has shifted to the right.

Some people think that technological improvements destroy jobs rather than increase labour demand. Of course, some technology changes destroy some types of job. For example, banks are cutting the number of tellers and middle managers because telephone and internet banking are lower cost ways of providing banking services. However, technology also creates jobs. Thousands of jobs have been created in telephone centres by the introduction of telephone banking. Technology tends to create more jobs than it destroys, and on average, the new jobs pay more than the old ones did. So, on average, the demand for labour will shift to the right if more jobs are created than destroyed by telephone banking. The demand for labour in high-skilled technology-based jobs has definitely increased with the invention of the computer 'chip', but most of the new jobs, have been for less skilled work in the service sector.

Trends in Labour Supply

The supply of labour increased in the 1970s and 1980s but has started to decrease with the falling birthrate. Changes in attitudes to women working and the provision of child care outside the home, have increased the supply of labour by women over time, but mainly in the market for less skilled part-time labour. Changing attitudes to men doing housework and child care have also reduced the full-time male labour supply. So as with the demand for labour, trends in the supply of labour are different in different types of labour market. The main types of labour market are for skilled and unskilled work and for part-time and full-time work.

Trends in Labour Market Equilibrium

To understand the underlying causes of the changes shown in Figure 14.2, we need to understand the different trends in different labour markets, particularly in the UK. The overall effect on full-time, high-skilled jobs is for the demand for labour to increase with new technology and the supply of labour to remain constant. This has the effect of raising the real wage for labour in these markets and increasing the quantity of hours worked. However, more people are working fewer hours in these labour markets, which reduces the hours worked per week on average. In the UK, the average hours worked per week has fallen from 42 to 40 hours over the 30-year period illustrated in the figure.

However, a different picture emerges if we look at the market for less skilled part-time work. The demand for labour has also increased with new technology, but the supply of labour has also increased substantially as more women enter the labour market. This has the effect of shifting both the demand and the supply of labour rightwards. The overall impact is a smaller rise in real wages in these markets but an increase in the number of part-time hours worked. Overall, the total number of hours worked in the UK has fluctuated around a constant level of 48 billion hours per year. You will study this in more detail again in Chapter 21.

Review Quiz

◆ Describe and explain the trends in wage rates and employment for your economy.

◆ Why is the demand for labour called a derived demand? From what is it derived?

◆ What is the distinction between marginal revenue product and marginal revenue? Provide an example that illustrates the distinction.

◆ When a firm's marginal revenue product equals the wage rate, marginal revenue also equals marginal cost. Why? Provide a numerical example different from the one in the text.

◆ What determines the amount of labour that households plan to supply?

Capital Markets

Capital markets are the channels through which firms obtain *financial* resources to buy *physical* capital. These financial resources come from household saving.

For most people, capital markets are where we make our biggest transactions. We borrow in a capital market to get a mortgage to buy a home. We lend in capital markets to build up a pension fund for income in retirement. Do rates of return in capital markets follow a similar pattern to the return to labour, the wage rate?

Table 14.5 shows you a selection of real interest rates for various European countries. Our measure of real interest rates means we have subtracted the loss of the value of money caused by inflation. You can see that interest rates fluctuate and that they can even be negative in years when inflation has been very high. Over the past 30 years, there has been a tendency for the value of real interest rates to fluctuate widely in most European countries around a rising trend.

Figure 14.5 shows why the rising trend in real interest rates has occurred. Demand for financial capital has increased from KD_{65} to KD_{94} and similarly, supply of financial capital has also increased from KS_{65} to KS_{94}. The result is an increase in the price of capital, the real interest rate, and an increase in the quantity of financial capital supplied.

To understand the trends in capital markets, we must examine the forces of demand and supply in

Figure 14.5
Capital Market Trends

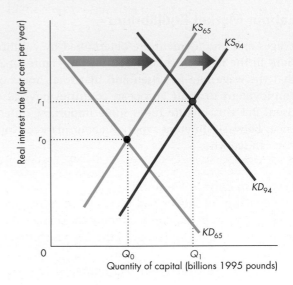

Between 1965 and 1994, the real interest rate has risen in most western European countries. The quantity of capital employed has also risen. This is the result of an increase in the demand for financial capital and a smaller increase in the supply of financial capital.

more detail. Many of the ideas you have already met in your study of demand and supply in labour markets apply to the capital markets as well. But there are some special features of capital markets. Its main feature is that people compare *present* costs with *future* benefits when making decisions in capital markets. Let's discover how these comparisons are made by studying the demand for capital.

The Demand for Capital

A firm's demand for *financial* capital stems from its demand for *physical* capital, and the amount that a firm plans to *borrow* in a given time period is determined by its planned investment – purchases of new capital. Decisions about the quantity of financial capital needed are driven by profit maximization. As a firm increases the quantity of physical capital employed, other things remaining the same, the marginal revenue product of physical capital eventually diminishes. To maximize profit, a firm will increase the quantity of physical capital, usually in the form of plant and machinery, only if the marginal

Table 14.5 Trends in Real Interest Rates in Europe (%)

Year	France	Germany	Portugal	UK
1965	2.5	3.6	−1	1.1
1970	3.6	1	0.8	2.2
1975	−4.5	−1.2	−10.0	−12.4
1980	−1.5	3.6	5.3	0.4
1985	−1.9	3.3	1.6	6.9
1990	7.1	5.7	4.3	7.0
1994	4.7	5.5	9.5	5.0

Real short-term interest rates have been positive in most years in most countries and have tended to rise over time.

Source: Adapted from Eurostat figures.

revenue product of the capital exceeds the cost of capital. But the marginal revenue product comes in the *future*, and the capital cost must be paid for in the *present*. So the firm must convert what it expects will be the marginal revenue product in the future, into a present value, so that it can be compared with the present price of new equipment.

To make this conversion, we use the technique of discounting.

Discounting and Present Value

Discounting is converting a future amount of money to its present value. The **present value** of a future amount of money is the amount that, if invested today, will grow to be as large as that future amount, taking into account the interest it will earn.

Discounting is converting a future amount of money to a present value. And the present value of a future amount of money is the amount that, if invested today, will grow to be as large as that future amount when the interest that it will earn is taken into account.

The easiest way to understand discounting and present value is to begin with the relationship between an amount invested today, the interest that it earns, and the amount that it will grow to in the future. The future amount is equal to the present amount (present value) plus the interest it will accumulate in the future. That is:

Future amount = Present value + Interest income

The interest income is equal to the present value multiplied by the interest rate, r, so

Future amount = Present value + ($r \times$ Present value)

or

Future amount = Present value $\times (1 + r)$.

If you have €100 today and the interest rate is 10 per cent a year ($r = 0.1$), one year from today you will have €110 – the original €100 plus €10 interest. Check that the above formula delivers that answer: €100 $\times$ 1.1 = €110.

The formula that we have just used calculates a future amount one year from today from the present value and an interest rate. To calculate the present value, we just work backward. Instead of multiplying

the present value by $(1 + r)$, we divide the future amount by $(1 + r)$. That is,

$$\text{Present value} = \frac{\text{Future amount}}{(1 + r)}.$$

You can use this formula to calculate present value. This calculation of present value is called discounting. Let's check that we can use the present value formula by calculating the present value of €110 one year from now when the interest rate is 10 per cent a year. You'll be able to guess that the answer is €100 because we just calculated that €100 invested today at 10 per cent a year becomes €110 in one year. Thus it follows immediately that the present value of €110 in one year's time is €100. But let's use the formula. Putting the numbers into the above formula, we have

$$\text{Present value} = \frac{€110}{(1 + 0.1)}$$
$$= \frac{€110}{1.1} = €100$$

Calculating the present value of an amount of money one year from now is the easiest case. But we can also calculate the present value of an amount any number of years in the future. As an example, let's see how we calculate the present value of an amount of money that will be available two years from now.

Suppose that you invest €100 today for two years at an interest rate of 10 per cent a year. The money will earn €10 in the first year, which means that by the end of the first year, you will have €110. If the interest of €10 is invested, then the interest earned in the second year will be a further €10 on the original €100 plus €1 on the €10 interest. Thus the total interest earned in the second year will be €11. The total interest earned overall will be €21 (€10 in the first year and €11 in the second year). After two years, you will have €121. From the definition of present value, you can see that the present value of €121 two years hence is €100. That is, €100 is the present amount that, if invested at an interest rate of 10 per cent a year, will grow to €121 two years from now.

To calculate the present value of an amount of money two years in the future, we use the formula

Present value
$$= \frac{\text{Amount of money two years in future}}{(1 + r)^2}$$

Use this formula to calculate the present value of €121 two years from now at an interest rate of 10 per cent a year. With these numbers the formula gives

$$\text{Present value} = \frac{\text{€}121}{(1 + 0.1)^2}$$

$$= \frac{\text{€}121}{(1.1)^2}$$

$$= \frac{\text{€}121}{1.21} = \$100$$

We can calculate the present value of an amount of money any number of years in the future by using a formula based on the two that we've already used. The general formula is

$$\text{Present value}$$
$$= \frac{\text{Amount of money } n \text{ years in future}}{(1 + r)^n}$$

For example, if the interest rate is 10 per cent a year, €100 to be received 10 years from now has a present value of €38.55. That is, if €38.55 is invested today at an interest rate of 10 per cent, it will accumulate to €100 in 10 years. (You might check that calculation on your pocket calculator.)

You've seen how to calculate the present value of an amount of money one year in the future, two years in the future, and n years in the future. Most practical applications of present value calculate the present value of a sequence of future amounts of money that spread over several years. To calculate the present value of a sequence of amounts over several years, we use the formula you have learned and apply it to each year. We then sum the present values for each year to find the present value of the sequence of amounts.

For example, suppose that a firm expects to receive €100 a year for each of the next five years. And suppose that the interest rate is 10 per cent per year (0.1 per year). The present value of these five payments of €100 each is calculated by using the following formula:

$$PV = \frac{\text{€}100}{1.1} + \frac{\text{€}100}{1.1^2} + \frac{\text{€}100}{1.1^3} + \frac{\text{€}100}{1.1^4} + \frac{\text{€}100}{1.1^5}$$

which equals:

$$PV = \text{€}100.00 + \text{€}90.91 + \text{€}82.64 + \text{€}75.13 + \text{€}68.30$$

$$= \text{€}416.98$$

You can see that the firm receives €500 over five years. But because the money arrives in the future, it is not worth €500 today. Its present value is only €416.98. And the farther in the future it arrives, the smaller is its present value. The €100 received one year in the future is worth €90.91 today. And the €100 received five years in the future is worth only €68.30 today.

Let's now see how a firm uses the concept of present value to achieve an efficient use of capital.

The Present Value of a Computer

Tina runs Taxfile plc, a UK firm that sells advice to taxpayers. Tina is considering buying a new high-power computer workstation that costs £10,000 in total. The workstation has a life of two years, after which it will be worthless. If Tina buys the workstation, she will pay out £10,000 now and she expects to generate business that will bring in an additional £5,900 at the end of each of the next two years.

To calculate the present value, PV, of the marginal revenue product of a new computer, Tina uses the formula:

$$PV = \frac{MRP_1}{(1 + r)} + \frac{MRP_1}{(1 + r)^2}$$

Here, MRP_1 is the marginal revenue product received by Tina at the end of the first year. It is converted to a present value by dividing it by $(1 + r)$. The term MRP_2 is the marginal revenue product received at the end of the second year. It is converted to a present value by dividing it by $(1 + r)^2$. Table 14.6 summarizes the data. Part (b) puts Tina's numbers into the present value formula and calculates the present value of the marginal revenue product of a workstation.

The first calculation in Table 14.6 is for the case in which Tina can borrow or lend at an interest rate of 4 per cent a year. The present value (PV) of £5,900 one year in the future is £5,900 divided by 1.04 (4 per cent as a proportion is 0.04). The present value of £5,900 two years in the future is £5,900 divided by $(1.04)^2$. Working out these two present values and then adding them gives Tina the present value of the future stream of marginal revenue products, which is £11,128.

Tina's Decision to Buy

Tina decides whether to buy the workstation by comparing the present value of its stream of marginal

Table 14.6 Net Present Value of an Investment Taxfile plc

(a) Data

Price of workstation	10,000
Life of workstation	2 years
Marginal revenue product	5,900 at end of each year
Interest rate	4% a year

(b) Present value of the flow of marginal revenue product:

$$P = \frac{MRP_1}{(1+r)} + \frac{MRP_2}{(1+r)^2}$$

$$= \frac{5,900}{1.04} + \frac{5,900}{(1.04)^2}$$

$$= 5,673 + 5,455$$

$$= 11,128$$

(c) Net present value of investment:

$NPV = PV$ of marginal revenue product – Cost of workstation

$$= 11,128 - 10,000$$

$$= 1,128$$

Table 14.7 Taxfile's Investment Decision

(a) Data

Price of workstation	£10,000
Life of workstation	2 years
Marginal revenue product:	
Using 1 workstation	£ 5,900 a year
Using 2 workstations	£ 5,600 a year
Using 3 workstations	£ 5,300 a year

(b) Present value of the stream of marginal revenue product

If r = 0.04 (4% a year):

Using 1 workstation: $\quad PV = \dfrac{5,900}{1.04} + \dfrac{5,900}{(1.04)^2} = 11,128$

Using 2 workstations: $\quad PV = \dfrac{5,600}{1.04} + \dfrac{5,600}{(1.04)^2} = 10,562$

Using 3 workstations: $\quad PV = \dfrac{5,300}{1.04} + \dfrac{5,300}{(1.04)^2} = 9,996$

If r = 0.08 (8% a year):

Using 1 workstation: $\quad PV = \dfrac{5,900}{1.08} + \dfrac{5,900}{(1.08)^2} = 10,521$

Using 2 workstations: $\quad PV = \dfrac{5,600}{1.08} + \dfrac{5,600}{(1.08)^2} = 9,986$

If r = 0.12 (12% a year):

Using 1 workstation: $\quad PV = \dfrac{5,900}{1.12} + \dfrac{5,900}{(1.12)^2} = 9,971$

revenue product with its purchase price. She makes this comparison by calculating the net present value (*NPV*) of the computer. **Net present value** is the present value of the future return – the future stream of marginal revenue product generated by the capital minus the cost of buying the capital. If net present value is positive, the firm should buy additional capital. If net present value is negative, the firm should not buy additional capital. Table 14.6(c) shows the calculation of Tina's net present value of a workstation. The net present value is £1,128 – greater than zero – so Tina buys the workstation.

Tina can buy any number of workstations that cost £10,000 and have a life of two years. But like all other factors of production, capital is subject to diminishing marginal returns. The greater the amount of capital employed, the smaller is its marginal revenue product. So if Tina buys a second workstation or a third one, she gets successively smaller marginal revenue products from the additional workstations.

Table 14.7(a) sets out Tina's marginal revenue products for one, two and three workstations. The marginal revenue product of one computer workstation (the case just reviewed) is £5,900 a year. The marginal revenue product of a second workstation is £5,600 a year, and the marginal revenue product of a third computer is £5,300 a year. Table 14.7(b) shows the calculations of the present values of the marginal

revenue products of the first, second and third computer workstations.

You've seen that with an interest rate of 4 per cent a year, the net present value of one workstation is positive. At an interest rate of 4 per cent a year, the present value of the marginal revenue product of a second workstation is £10,562, which exceeds its price by £562. So Tina buys a second computer workstation. But at an interest rate of 4 per cent a year, the present value of the marginal revenue product of a third workstation is £9,996, which is £4 less than the price of the computer. So Tina does not buy a third workstation.

A Change in the Interest Rate

We've seen that at an interest rate of 4 per cent a year, Tina buys two computer workstations but not three. Suppose that the interest rate is 8 per cent a year. In this case, the present value of the first computer is £10,521 (see Table 14.7(b)), so Tina still buys one workstation because it has a positive net present value. At an interest rate of 8 per cent a year, the net present value of the second workstation is £9,986, which is less than £10,000, its price. So, at an interest rate of 8 per cent a year, Tina buys only one computer workstation.

Suppose that the interest rate is even higher at 12 per cent a year. In this case, the present value of the marginal revenue product of one workstation is £9,971 (see Table 14.7(b)). At this interest rate, Tina buys no computer workstations.

These calculations trace Taxfile's demand schedule for capital. They show the number of computer workstations demanded – and the value of funds – at each interest rate. Other things remaining the same, the higher the interest rate, the smaller is the quantity of *physical* capital demanded. But to finance the purchase of physical capital, firms demand financial capital. So the higher the interest rate, the smaller is the quantity of *financial* capital demanded.

Demand Curve for Capital

A firm's demand curve for capital shows the relationship between the quantity of physical capital demanded by the firm and the interest rate, other things remaining the same. The quantity of capital demanded by a firm depends on the marginal revenue product of capital and the interest rate. The market demand curve for capital (as shown in Figure 14.5) shows the relationship beween the total quantity of capital demanded and the interest rate, other things remaining the same.

Changes in the Demand for Capital

Figure 14.5 showed that the demand for capital has increased over the past 30 years in European countries. The demand for capital changes when expectations about the future marginal revenue production of capital change. The two main factors affecting the marginal revenue product of capital, and hence demand, are:

1 Population growth.
2 Technological change.

An increase in population size increases the demand for goods and services, and so increases the demand for capital to produce them. Technological change leads to fluctuations in the demand for capital. Technological advances increase the demand for some types of physical capital and decrease the demand for other types. For example, the development of diesel engines for railway transport decreased the demand for steam engines and increased the demand for diesel engines. In this case, the railway industry's overall demand for capital did not change much. In contrast, the development of desktop computers increased the demand for office computing equipment, decreased the demand for electric typewriters and increased the overall demand for capital in the office.

Let's now look at the supply side of the capital market.

The Supply of Capital

The quantity of capital supplied results from people's saving decisions. The main factors that determine household savings are:

◆ Current income.

◆ Expected future income.

◆ The interest rate.

Current Income

Saving is the act of converting current income into future consumption. Typically, the higher your income, the more you plan to consume both in the present and in the future. If you want to increase your future income, you must save. So, other things remaining the same, the higher your income, the more you save. The relationship between saving and income is remarkably stable. Most people save a constant proportion of any extra income earned.

Expected Future Income

Because a major reason for saving is to increase future consumption, the amount you save depends on your current income, but also on your expected future income. A person with a low current income compared with expected future income, saves little and might even have negative saving. A person with high current income compared with expected future income saves a great deal in the present in order to be able to consume more in the future.

Young people typically have a low current income compared with their expected future income, while older working people have a high current income relative to their expected future income. The consequence of this pattern in income over the life cycle is that young people have negative saving and older working people have positive saving. Thus the young incur debts (such as consumer credit) to acquire durable goods and to consume more than their income, while older working people save and accumulate assets (often in the form of pension and life insurance arrangements) to provide for their retirement years.

The Interest Rate

The interest rate measures the opportunity cost of consuming this year rather than next year. The higher the interest rate, the greater is the amount that a pound saved today becomes in the future. So the higher the interest rate, the greater is the opportunity cost of current consumption. With a higher opportunity cost of current consumption, people cut their consumption and increase their saving.

The Supply Curve of Capital

The supply curve of capital, as shown in Figure 14.5, shows the relationship between the quantity of capital supplied and the interest rate, other things remaining the same. It is worth remembering that capital is the total value of accumulated saving. For an economy, that capital is measured as the sum of all its physical and natural capital. An increase in the interest rate leads to an increase in the quantity of capital supplied and a movement along the supply curve. The supply curve of capital is inelastic in the short run and more elastic in the long run. The reason is that in any one year, the total amount of savings is small relative to the size of the capital stock. So even a large change in the amount of saving, in response to a change in the interest rate, will only bring a small change in the quantity of capital supplied.

Changes in the Supply of Capital

The main influences on the supply of capital are the level of income and the size and age distribution of the population.

Other things remaining the same, an increase in income or an increase in the population bring an increase in the supply of capital. Also, other things remaining the same, the more unequally income is distributed, the higher is the saving rate. The reason is that low-income and middle-income families have low saving rates, while high-income families have high saving rates. So the larger the proportion of total income earned by the highest-income families, the greater is the amount of saving. Finally, and again other things remaining the same, the larger the

proportion of middle-aged people, the higher is the saving rate. The reason is that middle-aged people do most of the saving as they build up a pension fund to provide an income in their retirement.

Let's use what we have learned about the demand and supply of capital to see how the interest rate is determined.

The Interest Rate

Saving plans and investment plans are coordinated through capital markets and interest rates adjust to make these plans compatible.

Figure 14.6 shows the UK capital market. Initially, the demand for capital is KD_0 and the supply of capital is KS_0. The equilibrium real interest rate is 6 per cent and the quantity of capital is £10 bn at 1992 prices. The market forces that bring about this equilibrium are the same as those that we studied in the markets for goods and services. If the interest rate exceeds 6 per cent a year, the quantity of financial capital demanded is less than the quantity supplied. There is a surplus of funds in the capital market. In such a

Figure 14.6

Capital Market Equilibrium

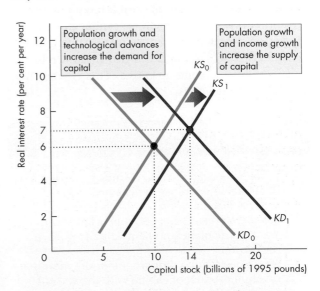

Initially, the demand for capital is KD_0 and the supply of capital is KS_0. The equilibrium interest rate is 6 per cent a year, and the capital stock is £10 bn. Over time, demand and supply increase, to KD_1 and KS_1. The capital stock and the real interest rate increase. Demand and supply increase because they are influenced by common factors.

situation, as lenders compete to make loans, interest rates fall. The quantity of financial capital demanded increases as firms increase their borrowing and buy more capital goods. The interest rate continues to fall until lenders are able to lend all the funds they wish at that interest rate.

Similarly, if the interest rate is below 6 per cent a year, the quantity of financial capital supplied is less than the quantity demanded. There is a shortage of funds in the capital market. Borrowers are unable to borrow all the funds they wish so they offer a higher interest rate. Interest rates increase until there are no unsatisfied borrowers. In either case, the interest rate converges on 6 per cent a year, the equilibrium interest rate.

Over the past 30 years, both the demand for capital and the supply of capital have increased in European countries. The demand curve shifts rightwards to KD_1, and the supply curve also shifts rightward to KS_1. Both curves shift because technological advances increase both demand and supply, leading to a rising trend in real interest rates. The reason why real interest rates fluctuate over time is because the demand and supply of capital do not change uniformly. Sometimes rapid technological change leads to an increase in demand for capital before it brings rising incomes that will increase the supply of capital. When this happens, as in the 1990s, the real interest rate rises.

At other times, the demand for capital grows slowly or even decreases temporarily. In this situation, supply outstrips demand and the real interest rate falls and may even become negative. This is what happened in the mid-1970s.

Review Quiz

- What have been the main trends in the quantity of capital and interest rates since 1965?
- What is discounting and how is it used to calculate present value? When might you want to calculate a present value to make a decision?
- How does a firm compare the future marginal revenue product of capital with the current cost of capital?
- What are the main influences on a firm's demand for capital?
- What are the main influences on the supply of capital?
- How can we explain the trends in the capital stock and interest rates?

We can now use what we have learned about capital markets to understand how the prices of natural resources change over time. Let's see how.

Land and Exhaustible Natural Resource Markets

Land is the stock or quantity of natural resources. All natural resources are called *land*, and they fall into two categories:

1 Non-exhaustible.
2 Exhaustible.

Non-exhaustible natural resources are natural resources that can be used repeatedly without depleting the potential stock available for future use. Examples of non-exhaustible natural resources are land (in the everyday sense of the word), seas, rivers, lakes, rain and sunshine.

Exhaustible natural resources are natural resources that can be used only once and that cannot be replaced once used. Examples of exhaustible natural resources are coal, natural gas and oil – the so-called hydrocarbon fuels.

The demand for natural resources as inputs into production is based on exactly the same principles of marginal revenue product as for labour and capital. But the supply of natural resources is quite different. Let's look first at the supply of non-exhaustible natural resources.

The Supply of Land (Non-exhaustible Natural Resources)

The quantity of land and other non-exhaustible natural resources is fixed. The quantity supplied cannot be changed by individual decisions. People can vary the amount of land they own, but when one person sells land, another person buys it. People cannot vary the total quantity available. The total quantity of land supplied of any particular type and in any particular location is fixed, regardless of the decisions of any one individual. The rare exception is when new land is reclaimed from the sea or from old lakes. So the supply of any particular piece of land is perfectly inelastic. Figure 14.7 illustrates this case. Regardless of the rent available, that quantity of land supplied in the centre of Paris, London or Bonn is a fixed number of square metres.

Figure 14.7

The Supply of Land

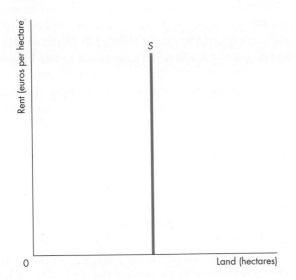

The supply of a given piece of land is perfectly inelastic. No matter what the rent, no more land than exists can be supplied.

As the supply of any piece of land is fixed, regardless of its price, price is determined by demand. The greater the demand for a particular piece of land, the higher is its price.

Expensive land can be, and is, used more intensively than inexpensive land. For example, high-rise buildings enable land to be used more intensively. However, to use land more intensively, it has to be combined with another factor of production – capital. Increasing the amount of capital per block of land does not change the supply of land itself. But it does enable land to become more productive. A rising price of land strengthens the incentive to find ways of increasing its productivity. These issues are explored more fully in Economics in History on pp. 320–321.

Although the supply of each type of land is fixed and its supply is perfectly inelastic, each individual firm, operating in competitive land markets, faces an elastic supply of land. For example, Oxford Street in London has a fixed amount of land, but Waterstones, a bookshop, could rent some space from John Lewis, a department store. Each firm can rent the quantity of land that it demands at the going rent, which is determined in the marketplace. So provided land markets are highly competitive, firms are price takers in these markets, just as they are in the markets for other factors of production.

The Supply of Exhaustible Natural Resources

To understand the supply of an exhaustible natural resource, we must distinguish between three supply concepts:

1 The stock supply.

2 The known stock supply.

3 The flow supply.

The *stock supply* of a natural resource is the quantity in existence at any given time. This supply is *perfectly inelastic*, just like land. No matter what its price, the quantity cannot be changed at that time.

The *known stock supply* is the quantity of a natural resource that has been discovered. This supply is *elastic*. If the price of a natural resource rises, other things remaining the same, the known quantity increases. This is because an increase in the price of the resource, increases the potential profit from selling the resource, and raises the incentive to search for additional resources. The known supply also increases over time at any given price – the supply curve shifts rightward. This is because advances in technology enable the more inaccessible resources to be discovered.

The *flow supply* is the quantity of a natural resource that is offered for use during a given time period. This supply is *perfectly elastic* at a price that equals the present value of the next period's expected price. The flow supply of an exhaustible natural resource is perfectly elastic at the price that equals the present value of the next period's expected price. This is because not supplying the resource means holding it and selling it later. If next year's expected price exceeds this year's price by a percentage that exceeds the interest rate, then it pays to hold onto the resource. It pays to sell it next year rather than this year. The reason is that the rate of return from holding the resource exceeds the interest rate. Equivalently, if this year's price is less than the present value of next year's expected price, it pays to hold onto the resource and sell it next year. This year's price is too low relative to next year's expected price.

Similarly, if this year's price exceeds the present value of next year's expected price, it pays to sell the resource now rather than wait until next year. This year's price is too high relative to next year's expected price.

Figure 14.8

An Exhaustible Natural Resource

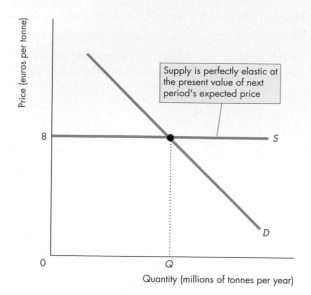

The supply of an exhaustible natural resource is perfectly elastic at the *present value* of next period's expected price. The demand for an exhaustible natural resource is determined by its marginal revenue product. The price is determined by supply and equals the *present value* of next period's expected price.

What happens if this year's price equals the present value of next year's expected price? In this case, it makes no difference whether the owner of the resource sells it now or sells it next year. A euro today is worth the same value as the present value of a euro plus the interest on a euro, a year from today. Because the two amounts are equal, a resource owner is indifferent between supplying and not supplying. Supply is perfectly elastic at the present value of the next period's expected price.

As supply is perfectly elastic at the present value of the next period's expected price, the actual price of the natural resource also equals the present value of the next period's expected price. Figure 14.8 shows the equilibrium in the European market for metals. Any change in the present value of the next period's expected metal price will lead to a shift in the supply curve, and a change in the actual price of metals.

Price and the Hotelling Principle

The idea that the price of an exhaustible natural resource is expected to rise at a rate equal to the inter-est rate is called the **Hotelling Principle**. It was first proposed by Harold Hotelling, a mathematician and economist at Columbia University.

The price of a natural resource is expected to grow at a rate equal to the interest rate on similarly risky financial capital because it makes the expected inter-est rate on the natural resource equal to the interest rate on similarly risky financial capital. Firms look for the highest returns they can find, holding risk con-stant. So if the expected interest rate on a stock of a natural resource exceeds that on similarly risky finan-cial capital, firms buy the stocks of natural resources and sell financial capital. Conversely, if the expected interest rate on a natural resource is less than that on similarly risky financial capital, firms buy financial capital and sell stocks of natural resources.

Equilibrium occurs in the market for the stock of a natural resource when prices and expectations about future prices for the stock have adjusted to make the *expected* interest rate earned on the natural resource equal to the interest rate on similarly risky financial capital. Figure 14.9 shows that the prices of exhaust-ible natural resources do not follow the Hotelling Principle. The real price of metals has fallen over time. So how can we explain this?

The answer lies in the fact that the future is unpre-dictable. Expected technological change is reflected in the price of a natural resource. But what hap-pens when an unexpected technological change leads to the discovery of new stocks or allows firms and households to use known stocks more efficiently? Unexpected technological change leads to a fall in the price of an exhaustible natural resource. This is the explanation for falling world oil prices and falling world metal prices.

Review Quiz

- ◆ Why is the supply of a non-exhaustible natural resource such as land perfectly inelastic?
- ◆ At what price is the flow supply of an exhaustible natural resource perfectly elastic and why?
- ◆ Why is the price of an exhaustible natural resource expected to rise at a rate equal to the interest rate?
- ◆ Why do the prices of exhaustible resources not follow the path predicted by the Hotelling Principle?

Figure 14.9

Falling Metal Prices

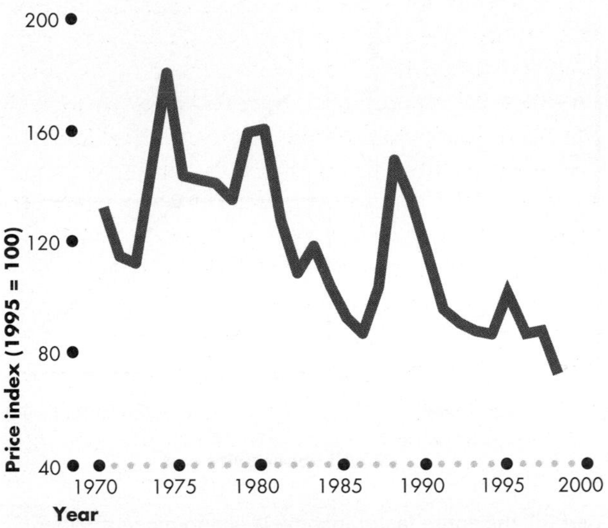

The prices of metals (here an average of the prices of aluminium, copper, iron ore, lead, manganese, nickel, silver, tin and zinc) have tended to fall over time, not rise as predicted by the Hotelling Principle. The reason is that unanticipated advances in technology have decreased the cost of extracting metals and greatly increased the exploitable known reserves.

Source: *International Financial Statistics*, International Monetary Fund, Washington, DC (various issues).

People supply resources to earn income. But some people earn enormous incomes while other people earn tiny incomes. How does income affect people's desire to work and supply other resources? Let's now answer this question.

Income, Economic Rent and Opportunity Cost

We've seen how the price of factors such as labour, capital and land are determined by the interaction of demand and supply. We've seen that demand is determined by marginal productivity and supply is determined by the resources available and by people's choices about their use. The interaction of demand and supply in factor markets determines who receives a large income and who receives a small income.

Large and Small Incomes

Why does the director of a large corporation earn a large income? It must be because such a person has a high marginal revenue product. This is reflected in the demand curve for his or her services. The supply of people with the combination of talents needed for this kind of job is also small and this is reflected in the supply curve. Equilibrium occurs at a high wage rate and a small quantity employed.

Why do 'McJobs' pay low wages? It is because they have a low marginal revenue product – reflected in the demand curve – and there are many households able and willing to supply their labour for these jobs. Equilibrium occurs at a low wage rate and large quantity employed.

If the demand for news readers increases, their incomes increase by a large amount and the number of news readers barely changes. If the demand for workers in 'McJobs' increases, the number of people doing these jobs increases by a large amount and the wage rate barely changes.

You can get a further insight into people's incomes by learning about the distinction between economic rent and opportunity cost.

Economic Rent and Opportunity Cost

The total income of a factor of production is made up of its economic rent and its opportunity cost. **Economic rent** is an income received by the owner of a factor over and above the amount required to induce that owner to offer the factor for use. Any factor of production can receive an economic rent. The income required to induce the supply of a factor of production is the opportunity cost of using a factor of production – the value of the factor in its next best use.

Figure 14.10 illustrates the concepts of economic rent and opportunity cost. Figure 14.10(a) shows the market for rock singers. It could be *any* factor of production – labour, capital, land or entrepreneurship. The demand curve for the factor of production is D and its supply curve is S. The factor price in this case is the wage, W, and the quantity of the factor used is C. The income of the factor is the sum of the yellow and blue areas. The yellow area below the supply curve measures opportunity cost and the green area below the factor price but above the supply curve measures economic rent.

To see why the area below the supply curve measures opportunity cost, recall that a supply curve can be

Figure 14.10

Economic Rent and Opportunity Cost

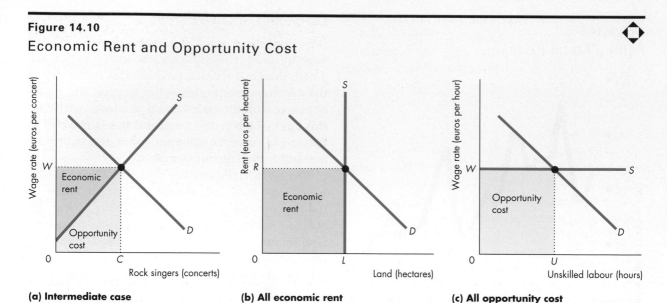

(a) Intermediate case **(b) All economic rent** **(c) All opportunity cost**

When a factor supply curve slopes upward – the general case – as in part (a), part of the factor income is rent (green) and part is opportunity cost (yellow). When the supply of a factor is perfectly inelastic (vertical), as in part (b), the entire factor income is economic rent. When the supply of a factor is perfectly elastic (horizontal), as in part (c), the entire factor income is opportunity cost.

---

interpreted in two different ways. One interpretation is that a supply curve indicates the quantity supplied at a given price. But the alternative interpretation of a supply curve is that it shows the minimum price at which a given quantity is willingly supplied. If suppliers receive only the minimum amount required to induce them to supply each unit of the factor of production, they will be paid a different price for each unit. The prices will trace the supply curve and the income received is entirely opportunity cost – the yellow area in Figure 14.10(a).

The concept of economic rent is similar to the concept of consumer surplus that you met in Chapter 5. Remember that consumer surplus is the difference between the price the household pays for a good and the maximum price it would be willing to pay, as indicated by the demand curve. In a parallel sense, economic rent is the difference between the factor price a household actually receives and the minimum factor price at which it would be willing to supply a given amount of a factor of production.

Economic rent is not the same thing as *rent*. Rent is the price paid for the services of land. Economic rent is a component of the income received by any factor of production.

The portion of the income of a factor of production that consists of economic rent depends on the elasticity of the supply of the factor of production. When the supply of a factor of production is perfectly inelastic, its entire income is economic rent. Most of Madonna's income is economic rent. Also, a large part of the income of an international football player is economic rent. When the supply of a factor of production is perfectly elastic, none of its income is economic rent. Most of the income of a babysitter is opportunity cost. In general, when the supply curve is neither perfectly elastic nor perfectly inelastic (like that illustrated in Figure 14.10(a)), some part of the factor income is economic rent and the other part opportunity cost.

Part (b) of Figure 14.10 shows the market for a particular block of land in London. The land is fixed in size at *L* hectares. Therefore the supply curve of the land is vertical – perfectly inelastic. No matter what the rent on the land is, there is no way of increasing the quantity that can be supplied.

The demand for that block of land is determined by its marginal revenue product. The marginal revenue product in turn depends on the uses to which the land can be put. In a central business district such as

Canary Wharf, the marginal revenue product is high because a large number of people are concentrated in that area, making it a prime place for conducting business. Suppose that the marginal revenue product of this block of land is shown by the demand curve in Figure 14.10(b). The entire income accruing to the owner of the land is the green area in the figure. This income is economic rent. The rent charged for this piece of land depends entirely on its marginal revenue product – on the demand curve. If the demand curve shifts rightward, the rent rises. If the demand curve shifts leftward, the rent falls. The quantity of land supplied remains constant at L.

Figure 14.9(c) shows the market for a factor of production that is in perfectly elastic supply. An example of such a market might be that for unskilled labour in a poor country such as India or China. In these countries, large amounts of labour flock to the cities and are available for work at the going wage rate (in this case, W). Thus in these situations, the supply of labour is almost perfectly elastic. The entire income earned by this labour is opportunity cost. They receive no economic rent.

Review Quiz

- Why do football players earn larger incomes than shop workers?
- What is the distinction between an economic rent and an opportunity cost?
- Is the income that England's National Team pays to David Beckham an economic rent or compensation for opportunity cost?
- Is a McDonald's hamburger more expensive in Paris than Vannes in Brittany because rents are higher in Paris, or are rents higher in Paris because people in Paris are willing to pay more for a McDonald's hamburger?

Reading Between the Lines on pp. 318–319 looks at the market for football players. You now understand how factor incomes are determined in resource markets. In the next chapter, we will look at how the income from wages and capital are distributed, and how governments try to redistribute them and modify the outcomes of resource markets.

Summary

Key Points

Factor Prices and Incomes (p. 293)

- An increase in the demand for a factor of production increases its price and total income; a decrease in the demand for a factor of production decreases its price and total income.

- An increase in the supply of a factor of production increases the quantity used but decreases its price and might increase or decrease its total income, depending on whether demand is elastic or inelastic.

Labour Markets (pp. 294–301)

- The marginal revenue product of labour determines the demand for labour.

- The demand for labour increases if the price of the firm's output rises or if technological change and capital accumulation increase marginal product.

- The elasticity of demand for labour depends on labour intensity in production, the elasticity of demand for the product, and the ease with which labour can be substituted for capital.

- The quantity of labour supplied increases as the real wage rate increases, but at high wage rates, the supply curve may bend backwards.

- An increase in population or an advance in home production technology can increase the supply of labour.

Capital Markets (pp. 302–308)

- To make an investment decision, firms compare the present value of the expected marginal revenue product of capital with the current price of capital.

- Population growth and technological change increase the demand for capital.

- The higher the interest rate, the greater are the amount of saving and the quantity of capital supplied.

- The supply of capital increases as incomes increase.

- Capital market equilibrium determines interest rates.

Land and Exhaustible Natural Resource Markets (pp. 308–311)

- The demand for natural resources is determined by its marginal revenue product.

- The supply of land is inelastic.

- The supply of exhaustible natural resources is perfectly elastic at a price equal to the present value of the expected future price.

- The price of exhaustible natural resources is expected to rise at a rate equal to the interest rate but fluctuates and sometimes falls because of unexpected changes in technology.

Income, Economic Rent and Opportunity Cost (pp. 311–313)

- Economic rent is the income received by a factor over and above the amount needed to induce the factor owner to supply the resource for use.

- The rest of a resource's income is opportunity cost.

- When the supply of a factor is perfectly inelastic, its entire income is made up of economic rent. When the supply of a factor is perfectly elastic, its entire income is made up of opportunity cost.

Key Figures and Tables

Key Terms

Problems

°1 The figure illustrates a European market for strawberry pickers:

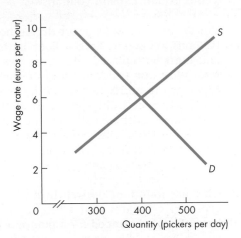

a What is the wage rate paid to strawberry pickers?

b How many strawberry pickers get hired?

c What is the income received by strawberry pickers?

2 In problem 1, if the demand for strawberry pickers increases by 100 a day,

a What is the new wage rate paid to the pickers?

b How many additional pickers get hired?

c What is the total income paid to pickers?

°3 The European fish packing industry is competitive and Wanda owns a fish shop. She employs students to sort and pack the fish. Students can pack the following amounts of fish in an hour:

Number of students	Quantity of fish (kilograms)
1	20
2	50
3	90
4	120
5	145
6	165
7	180
8	190

The market price of fish is 50 cents a kilogram and the wage rate of packers is €7.50 an hour.

a Calculate the marginal product of the students and draw the marginal product curve.

b Calculate the marginal revenue product of the students and draw the marginal revenue product curve.

c Find Wanda's demand for labour curve.

d How many students does Wanda employ?

4 The European ice market is competitive and Barry makes bags of ice. He employs workers to bag the ice who can produce the following quantities in an hour:

Number of workers	Quantity of ice (bags)
1	40
2	100
3	180
4	240
5	290
6	330
7	360
8	380

The market price of ice is 25 cents a bag and the wage rate of a bagger is €5.00 an hour.

a Calculate the marginal product of the workers and draw the marginal product curve.

b Calculate the marginal revenue product of the workers and draw the marginal revenue produce curve.

c Find Barry's demand for labour curve.

d How much ice does Barry sell?

°5 Back at Wanda's fish shop described in problem 3, the price of fish falls to €33.33 a kilogram but fish packers' wages remain at €7.50 an hour, what happens to:

a Wanda's marginal product?

b Wanda's marginal revenue product?

c Wanda's demand for labour curve?

d Number of students Wanda employs?

6 Back at Barry's ice making plant described in problem 4, the price of ice falls to 10 cents a bag but baggers' wages remain at €5.00 an hour, what happens to:

a Barry's marginal product?

b Barry's marginal revenue product?

c Barry's demand for labour curve?

d Number of students Barry employs?

•7 Back at Wanda's fish shop described in problem 3, packers' wages increase to €10 an hour, but the price of fish remains at 50 cents a kilogram.

a What happens to marginal revenue product?

b What happens to Wanda's demand for labour curve?

c How many students does Wanda employ?

8 Back at Barry's ice shop described in problem 4, baggers' wages increase to €10 an hour, but the price of ice remains at 25 cents a bag.

a What happens to marginal revenue product?

b What happens to Barry's demand for labour curve?

c How many baggers does Barry employ?

•9 Using the information in problem 3, calculate Wanda's marginal revenue, marginal cost, and marginal revenue product. Show that when Wanda is making maximum profit, marginal cost equals marginal revenue and marginal revenue product equals the wage rate.

10 Using the information in problem 4, calculate Barry's marginal revenue, marginal cost, and marginal revenue product. Show that when Barry is making maximum profit, marginal cost equals marginal revenue and marginal revenue product equals the wage rate.

•11 Venus makes Firecrackers, which she sells in December each year for New Year's celebrations. She must decide how many firecracker production lines to install. Each production line costs €1 million and operates for only two years, after which it must be replaced. With one production line, Venus expects to sell €590,000 worth

of firecrackers a year. With two production lines, she expects to sell €1,150,000 worth of firecrackers each year. And with three production lines, she expects to sell €1,680,000 worth of firecrackers a year. The interest rate is 5 per cent a year. How many production lines does Venus install? Explain your answer.

12 Vulcan Balloon Rides must decide how many balloons to operate. Each balloon costs €10,000 and must be replaced after three years of service. With one balloon, Vulcan expects to sell €5,900 worth of rides a year. With two balloons, it expects to sell €11,500 worth of rides each year. And with three balloons, it expects to sell €16,800 worth of rides a year. The interest rate is 8 per cent a year. How many balloons does Vulcan operate? Explain your answer.

•13 Greg has found an oil well in his backyard. A geologist estimates that a total of 10 million barrels can be pumped for a pumping cost of a euro a barrel. The price of oil is €20 a barrel. How much oil does Greg sell each year? If you can't predict how much he will sell, what extra information would you need to be able to do so?

14 Orley has a wine cellar in which he keeps choice wines from around the world. What does Orley expect to happen to the prices of the wines he keeps in his cellar? Explain your answer. How does Orley decide which wine to drink and when to drink it?

•15 Use the figure in problem 1, and show on the figure the strawberry pickers' economic rent and opportunity cost.

16 In the situation described in problem 2, show on the figure the strawberry pickers' economic rent and opportunity cost.

Critical Thinking

1 Study Reading Between the Lines on pp. 318–319 and answer the following questions:

a What determines the demand for football players?

b What determines the supply of football players?

c What do you think top players like David Beckham would do if they didn't play football?

d What does your answer to (c) tell you about the opportunity cost of these players?

e What does your answer to (c) tell you about the economic rent received by these players ?

f Why don't footballers have contracts that give them their entire marginal revenue product?

g Why is the economic rent of most premiership players less than the top-performing players?

h Would a trainee player gain as much economic rent as established players? Explain your answer?

2 'We are running out of natural resources and must take urgent action to conserve our precious reserves.' 'There is no shortage of resources that the market cannot cope with.' Identify the pros and cons for each view, and discuss each in turn. What is your view and why?

3 Why do we keep finding new reserves of oil? Why don't we do a big once-and-for-all survey to catalogue the earth's entire inventory of natural resources?

Wage Income: What's a Footballer Worth?

THE BBC, 18 APRIL 2000

Premiership players cash in

England's top footballers net £4,000,000 a year on average, a survey revealed. The basic salary for Premiership players aged over 20 is £409,000 a year, or nearly £8,000 a week, reports the *Independent*. More than one in three – 36 per cent – of players in the same age group earn more than £500,000 a year. And 9 per cent – about 100 players – earn more than £1 million a year.

The survey – the largest done of professional footballers in England – was based on the answers of nearly 600 players, who responded on a confidential basis. . . . The survey was carried out by the *Independent* and the players' union the PFA.

The results also revealed how, at the other end of the pay scale, young players and trainees aged between 17 and 20 earn between 19,000 and £45,000 a year on average . . .

And the high pay levels among top footballers are not matched by their counterparts in the three divisions of the Nationwide League. Senior First Division players earn £128,000 a year on average, while their colleagues in the Second and Third Divisions earn £42,000 and £37,000 a year respectively. The youngest players in each division earn as little as £3,000 a year.

The Essence of the Story

- The incomes of top clubs in the premier football league have soared since breaking from the Football League in 1992.

- Premier club footballers earn £400,000 a year on average.

- About 100 players in the first division earn more than £1 million a year.

- Trainee footballers earn much lower salaries, between £19,000 and £45,000 a year on average.

- Senior players in the second and third divisions earn less than their first division counterparts.

Economic Analysis

- The marginal revenue product of top footballers in the premier league is enormous because they generate huge incomes for their teams.

- The supply of top players is limited. No one would be willing to train to be a top player at a wage below the industrial average. But a large number of people are willing to train to play competitive football at wage rates above the industrial average.

- Very few footballers have the talent to perform at the top level. No matter how much footballers' wage rate rises above the average industrial wage, the quantity of top-performing players does not increase. The supply is inelastic.

- In Figure 1, the supply of top-performing footballers is the curve labelled S. The average industrial wage rate is at a. As players' wages rise above a, the quantity of premier league players supplied increases. The maximum quantity, Q_0, is determined by the limited pool of talent.

- The demand for the best 100 players is determined by their marginal revenue product, shown by the curve D_0 in Figure 1.

- Equilibrium in the market for these star players occurs at an average wage rate of about £3 million. They earn at least £1 million and as much as David Beckham's £6.5 million a year.

- Most of the income of these players is economic rent, the green area in Figure 1, and only a small proportion is opportunity cost, the yellow area.

- The marginal revenue product of the majority of premiership players, D_1 is not as high as that of the star players. The equilibrium wage for this group on average is about £700,000 and they gain less economic rent than star players.

- Figure 2 shows the situation facing an individual premiership team. The team faces a perfectly elastic supply of star players, S_i, at the equilibrium wage. Given the team's demand curve, D_i, it hires Q_i star players. Competition between teams for star players means that teams must pay the going wage.

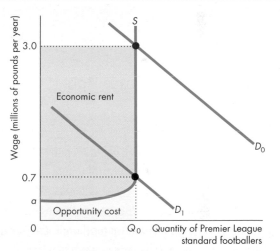

Figure 1 The market for Premier League footballers

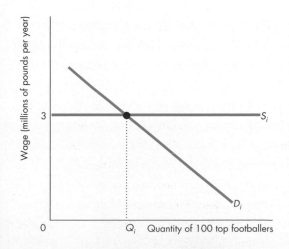

Figure 2 The individual Premiership team

Running Out?

The passion between the sexes has appeared in every age to be so nearly the same, that it may always be considered, in algebraic language as a given quantity.

Thomas Robert Malthus An Essay on the Principle of Population

The Economist: Thomas Robert Malthus

Thomas Robert Malthus (1766–1834), an English parson and economist, was an extremely influential social scientist. In his best-selling *An Essay on the Principle of Population*, published in 1798, he predicted that population growth would outstrip food production and said that wars, famine and disease were inevitable unless population growth was held in check by what he called 'moral restraint'. By 'moral restraint' he meant marrying at a late age and living a celibate life. At the age of 38 he married a wife of 27, marriage ages that he recommended for others. Malthus's ideas were regarded as too radical in their day. But they had a profound influence on Charles Darwin, who got the key idea that led him to the theory of natural selection from reading the *Essay on Population*. Also, David Ricardo and the classical economists were strongly influenced by Malthus's ideas. Modern-day Malthusians believe that his basic idea was right and that it applies not only to food but also to every natural resource.

The Issues and Ideas

Is there a limit to economic growth, or can we expand production and population without effective limit? Thomas Malthus gave one of the most influential answers to these questions in 1798. He reasoned that population, unchecked, would grow at a geometric rate – 1, 2, 4, 8, 16, . . . , while the food supply would grow at an arithmetic rate – 1, 2, 3, 4, 5, . . . To prevent the population from outstripping the available food supply, there would be periodic wars, famines and plagues. In Malthus's view, only what he called moral restraint could prevent such periodic disasters.

As industrialization proceeded through the nineteenth century, Malthus's idea came to be applied to all natural resources, especially those that are exhaustible. A modern-day Malthusian, ecologist Paul Ehrlich, believes that we are sitting on a 'population bomb' and that the government must limit both population growth and the resources that may be used each year.

In 1931, Harold Hotelling developed a theory of natural resources with different predictions from those of Malthus. The Hotelling Principle is that the relative price of an exhaustible natural resource will steadily rise, bringing a decline in the quantity used and an increase in the use of substitute resources.

Julian Simon, a contemporary economist, has challenged both the Malthusian gloom and the Hotelling Principle. He believes that people are the 'ultimate resource' and predicts that a rising population lessens the pressure on natural resources. A bigger population provides a larger number of resourceful people who can work out more efficient ways of using scarce resources. As these solutions are found, the prices of exhaustible resources actually fall. To demonstrate his point, in 1980, Simon bet Ehrlich that the prices of five metals – copper, chrome, nickel, tin and tungsten – would fall during the 1980s. Simon won the bet!

Then . . .

No matter whether it is agricultural land, an exhaustible natural resource, or the space in the centre of Manchester, and no matter whether it is 1998 or, as shown opposite, 1914, there is a limit to what is available, and we persistently push against that limit. Economists see urban congestion as a consequence of the value of doing business in the city centre relative to the cost. They see the price mechanism, bringing ever-higher rents and prices of raw materials, as the means of allocating and rationing scarce natural resources. Malthusians, in contrast, explain congestion as the consequence of population pressure, and they see population control as the solution.

. . . And Now

In Tokyo, the pressure on space is so great that in some residential neighbourhoods, a parking space costs £1,000 a month. To economize on this expensive space – and to lower the cost of car ownership and hence boost the sale of cars – Honda, Nissan and Toyota, three of Japan's big car producers, have developed a parking machine that enables two cars to occupy the space of one. The most basic of these machines costs a mere £7,500, less than 6 months' worth of parking fees.

Trying These Ideas Today

Using what you have learned about factor markets in Chapter 14 and what you have read about Malthus and the challenge to Malthusian ideas, you should be able to answer the following questions:

- London's roads, like those of most modern cities, are highly congested. The average speed is just 3 miles an hour! We don't yet pay for road use directly, so what is the price that motorists have to pay for ever more congested roads, and is it rising or falling over time?
- In what ways do you think that technology could resolve this 'overcrowding' problem?

Part 4

Government Policy and Regulation

Talking with **David Smith**

David Smith studied economics at Trinity College Cambridge and the University of Essex in the middle and late 1960s. He has since been employed at the Bank of England, Royal Bank of Scotland, National Westminster Bank, Cambridge Econometrics and the London Business School's Centre for Economic Forecasting. He joined London stockbrokers Williams de Broe plc as its Chief Economist in 1982. David Smith is currently a member of the 'Shadow Monetary Policy Committee' run by the Institute for Economic Affairs and was a member of the Economics Board of the Council for National Academic Awards in the late 1970s and early 1980s. He is also a visiting lecturer at the Cardiff University Business School and the University of Derby. David Smith is involved with several independent think tanks, most notably the Institute of Economic Affairs and Politeia, for whom he has recently written a pamphlet about the effects of government expenditure on economic performance. David is married and has two grown-up sons, neither of whom are economists.

What first attracted you to study economics and why did you become a professional economist?

I started studying economics at 'A' level at the age of fifteen in 1961. The reason was that my main interest was history, and I was short of an arts 'A' level to go with it.

I did not become 'hooked' on economics until I was working at the Bank of England in the late 1960s. It was at the Bank that I picked up all my statistical and computer programming knowledge, and my enthusiasm for the practical application of monetary economics.

What is the role of professional economists working in financial markets?

Economists have three main functions in the securities industry. One is the public relations aspect of trying to generate favourable publicity through the printed and electronic media. The second role is in a marketing function, trying to attract new clients. Finally, there is the economics itself.

The economic function can be divided into three main categories. The first of these involves forecasting the various monthly economic indicators and advising your sales desks about what the figures mean when they flash across dealing room screens. The second is macroeconomic forecasting over a longer time horizon. Finally, City economists produce a lot of one-off analyses covering topical market-sensitive issues. Because of the global nature of world financial markets, it is essential to have a view on US monetary policy and the likely actions of the European Central Bank. However, financial markets can also melt down unexpectedly or react to unforeseen events.

To what extent is the size and growth rate of government expenditure an important economic issue?

The expansion in the role and functions of the state was the most striking economic development of the twentieth century. Thus, if one looks at the industrialized countries, the share of public spending in national output typically rose from around one-tenth before the 1914–18 War to between one-fifth and one-quarter in the interwar period and around one-quarter to one-third by 1960 or so. There was then a rapid expansion in the size of government through the next two decades or so, although this slowed somewhat thereafter. Today, government spending still absorbs only one-fifth to one-quarter of national output in the South East Asian 'Tiger' economies and well under one-third in the US and Ireland. However, and at the other extreme, this rises to over one-half in France, and almost 57 per cent in Sweden. Total general government expenditure, including transfers, now accounts for $42^3/_4$ per cent of the basic price measure of national output in Britain – which is more than twice the size of manufacturing industry, for example.

There are several reasons why the magnitude and continued expansion of the state sector makes it an overriding issue in contemporary economics. Firstly, economists have only limited understanding of what determines the growth, size and behaviour of public spending. Secondly, government spending has to be financed either through higher taxes, increased borrowing, or the potentially hyper-inflationary route of borrowing from the central bank. There is widespread evidence from simulations on econometric models that high taxes slow economic growth and destroy private sector jobs, and that Budget deficits crowd out private sector activity, for Ricardian equivalence and other reasons.

Finally, and arguably most importantly, there are the consequences of large public sectors for personal liberty, especially when allowance is made for the additional effects of regulation in curtailing freedom.

Can economists explain why government spending in most European economies is rising as a proportion of output?

There are several explanations for the increasing share of public spending in national output. One is that societies which have known a long period of peace and political stability gradually become more rigid because vested interest groups gradually turn the power of the state to their own advantage. Another is that bureaucrats are always trying to expand their empires and that state-funded bureaucrats can do so in a way that private managers cannot, because the latter would bankrupt their companies.

A third explanation is the breakdown of the link between taxation and representation in many western welfare states. This breakdown occurs when a majority of the electorate take more out of the state than it puts in, so the tax burden is concentrated on a smaller number of high income individuals and disenfranchised bodies, such as businesses. Also, the scope for politicians and bureaucrats to extort bribes and kickbacks rises with the degree of government intervention, and this is a massive problem in many developing countries. However, one of the main reasons why public spending has expanded so much seems to be that the point at which government revenue is maximized is beyond the point at which the public sector makes its optimal contribution to economic and social welfare.

What is your opinion on the need to control government spending?

The evidence from international studies is that the optimal size of state from the viewpoint of social welfare is somewhere around 30 per cent of national output, whereas the revenue maximizing point may be around 45 per cent. Back of the envelope calculations, based on international cross-section studies, suggest that the expansion in the size of the public sector over the past forty years has slowed the yearly growth rate in the typical developed country by roughly $2^1/_4$ percentage points, an amount that accumulates up to some 135 per cent of current national output. The resulting loss of economic well-being probably means that even the poorest members of society would have been better off in a more prosperous low-spending and high-growth society than they are in today's welfare states.

CHAPTER 15

Inequality and Redistribution

After studying this chapter you will be able to:

◆ Describe inequality in income and wealth

◆ Explain why wealth inequality is greater than income inequality

◆ Explain how economic inequality arises

◆ Explain the effects of taxes and cash benefits on economic inequality

Riches and Rags

Bernie Ecclestone, the British Formula One owner, earned more than £600 million (€960 million) in 2000 when he sold his capital stake in SLEC. Former Beatles stars, Paul McCartney, Ringo Starr and George Harrison, each earned approximately £50 million (€80 million) in 2000. They are at the top of the top richest entertainers in Europe. The annual earnings of Europe's top footballers at about £7 million (€11.2 million) seem small in comparison. At the same time, 10 per cent of Europe's citizens have incomes so low that they are defined as living in poverty. Some are so poor that they have no income and own nothing more than the clothes they stand up in. ◆ Why are some people exceedingly rich, owning a great deal of wealth, while others are very poor and own almost nothing? ◆ Will this level of inequality persist? Are the rich getting richer and the poor poorer? Does the information we have about the inequality of income and wealth paint an accurate picture or a misleading one? ◆ Surely government policy reduces poverty? How do taxes and social security benefits influence economic inequality? What is an equitable distribution of economic well-being? Can government spending on services like education and health care affect the distribution of resources?

◆ ◆ ◆ ◆ In this chapter, we study economic inequality – its extent, its sources and its potential remedies. We look at taxes and government policies designed to redistribute the incomes in a market economy and study their effects on economic inequality. You studied the problem of defining inequality in Chapter 5. Here, we focus on how much inequality arises, why it arises and how government policy can reduce it. Let's begin by looking at some facts about economic inequality. We'll end by examining the impact of health care systems on inequality in a Policy Case Study on pp. 338–339.

Economic Inequality in the United Kingdom

We can study inequality by looking at the distribution of income or wealth. A family's income is the amount that it receives in a given period of time. A family's wealth is the value of the things it owns at a point in time.

We measure annual income as the wages, interest, rent and profit earned by a family in a year. In 1999/2000, the average income in the United Kingdom was £480 a week. But there was considerable inequality around that average. The poorest 20 per cent received only 4 per cent of total income. Their incomes were just one-fifth of the average. The next poorest 20 per cent received just 8 per cent of total income. But the richest 20 per cent received just less than 50 per cent of total income, their incomes being more than twice the average.

We measure wealth as the value of holdings of property and financial assets minus any debts. Average individual wealth (family data are not available) in 1999/2000 was £55,500. But the variation around this value was enormous. The wealthiest 10 per cent of the population owned 24 per cent of the nation's wealth and the wealthiest 25 per cent owned a staggering 75 per cent of the nation's wealth. The poorest half of the population owned just 6 per cent of the nation's wealth.

Lorenz Curves

Income and wealth distributions are shown in Figure 15.1. Part (a) of the table divides households into five income groups, called *quintiles*, ranging from the income of the lowest 20 per cent (row *a*) to the income of the top 20 per cent (row *e*). It shows the percentage share of total income taken by each of

Figure 15.1

Lorenz Curves for Income and Wealth

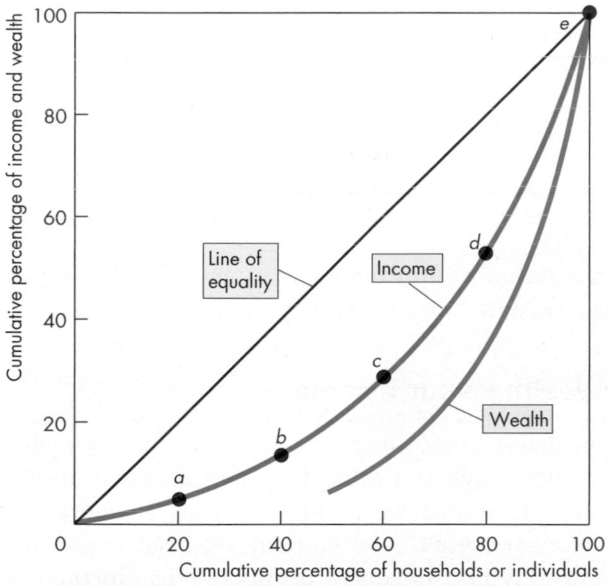

Part (a)	Households		Income	
	Percentage	Cumulative percentage	Percentage	Cumulative percentage
a	Lowest 20	20	4	4
b	Second 20	40	8	12
c	Third 20	60	16	28
d	Fourth 20	80	24	52
e	Highest 20	100	48	100

Part (b)	Individuals		Wealth	
	Percentage	Cumulative percentage	Percentage	Cumulative percentage
a'	Lowest 50	50	6	6
b'	Next 25	75	19	25
c'	Next 10	85	19	44
d'	Next 5	90	12	56
e'	Next 9	98	20	76
f'	Highest 1	100	24	100

The cumulative percentages of income are graphed against the cumulative percentage of households. If income were distributed equally, each 20 per cent of households would have 20 per cent of the income – the line of equality. Points *a* to *e* on the Lorenz curve for income correspond to the rows in part (a) of the table. The Lorenz curve for wealth plots the cumulative percentage of wealth against the cumulative percentage of adults from part (b) of the table. The distribution of wealth is more unequal than the distribution of income.

Sources: *Social Trends, 2000*, Office for National Statistics, The Stationery Office, London Table 5.26, 2001.

these income groups. For example, row *a* tells us that the lowest quintile of households received 4 per cent of total income. The table also shows the *cumulative* percentages of households and original income. Original income is income before any taxes are deducted and before any government benefits are received. For example, row *b* tells us that the lowest two quintiles (lowest 40 per cent) received 12 per cent of total income (4 per cent for the lowest quintile and 8 per cent for the next lowest). The data on cumulative income shares are illustrated by a Lorenz curve. A **Lorenz curve** graphs the cumulative percentage of income against the cumulative percentage of households.

If income was distributed equally to every household, the cumulative percentages of income received by the cumulative percentages of households would fall along the straight line labelled 'Line of equality' in Figure 15.1. The actual distribution of income is shown by the Lorenz curve labelled 'Income'. The closer the Lorenz curve is to the line of equality, the more equal is the distribution.

Figure 15.1 also shows a Lorenz curve for individual wealth, based on the distribution in part (b) of the table. As you can see from the two Lorenz curves, the Lorenz curve for wealth is much farther away from the line of equality than the Lorenz curve for income. Athough the two curves are not directly comparable, they show a common pattern.

The distribution of wealth is much more unequal than the distribution of income.

Income Inequality Over Time

Figure 15.2 shows changes in inequality over time using the Gini Coefficient. The Gini coefficient is calculated by dividing the value of the area under the Lorenz curve (the area under the green line in Figure 15.1), by the value of the area under the line of total equality (the area under the black diagonal line) and multiplying by 100. A Gini coefficient of 0 implies total equality and a Gini coefficient of 100 implies total inequality.

The Gini coefficient for original income, wages and investments before tax, and gross income, original income plus benefits, has risen over time. Inequality of income is rising, despite government policy. The rich may be getting richer because rapid technological change has increased the return to education. The poor may be getting poorer because wages for low-skilled workers have been kept low by increased interna-

Figure 15.2

UK Income Inequality: 1978–1998

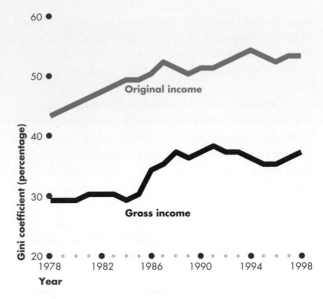

Changes in the distribution of income can be measured using the Gini coefficient. The Gini coefficient is a numerical measure of the Lorenz curve for each year. The distribution of income in the United Kingdom became more equal in the late 1980s and early 1990s. Inequality in income has been steadily increasing since 1978.

Source: *Economic Trends*, May 1998. Office for National Statistics, The Stationery Office, London.

tional competition and mobility, and by technological advances that decrease the demand for their labour.

Wealth versus Income

Inequality in income has risen, but income inequality is not as high as wealth inequality as shown in Figure 15.1. So when we measure inequality, should we use income or wealth? To find out, we need to see why wealth is more unequally distributed than income.

Wealth is a stock of assets and income is just the flow of earnings resulting from that stock of wealth. So wealth and income are simply different ways of looking at the same thing. The reason why the distribution of wealth in Figure 15.1 is more unequal than the distribution of income is due to measurement issues.

Wealth data measure only tangible assets and exclude the value of human capital as an asset. Income data measure income from both tangible assets and human capital. If wealth data included human capital, there would be no difference in inequality between two distributions for the same household. For these reasons, the income distribution is a more accurate measure of economic inequality.

Poverty

Households at the low end of the income distribution are so poor that they are considered to be living in poverty. **Poverty** is a state in which a household's income is too low for it to be able to buy the quantities of food, shelter and clothing that are deemed necessary. Because poverty is a relative concept, poverty is defined by a *poverty line* – an imaginary benchmark which determines when people become poor. One such definition is the number of people living at or below 60 per cent of typical (median) income. According to UK government figures, 18 per cent of households in the United Kingdom had an income at or below 60 per cent of typical income in 1998. Using this measure, poverty rates were at their highest in 1991, when 21 per cent were living in poverty, and at their lowest in 1977, when just 10 per cent were

living in poverty. Poverty rates vary over time, but also among countries – even within the European Union. Using the same definition of the poverty line, the highest rates of EU poverty in 1996 were over 20 per cent in Portugal and Greece, and 17–18 per cent in the UK, Italy, Eire and Spain. The lowest rates of between 12 and 13 per cent were found in the Netherlands, Sweden, Denmark, Luxembourg, Belgium and Austria.

Who are the Poor and the Rich?

What are the characteristics of poorer and richer households? The lowest-income household in the United Kingdom today is likely to comprise a retired person over 75 years of age, living alone in low-cost rented accommodation, somewhere in Northern Ireland. The highest-income household in the United Kingdom today is likely to comprise two adults aged between 30 and 50, both graduates with professional or managerial jobs, living together with two children somewhere in the south east of England.

These snapshot profiles are the extremes in Figure 15.3. The figure illustrates the importance of household size, age, education and economic status of the

---

Figure 15.3

The Distribution of Income by Selected Household Characteristics in 1999/2000

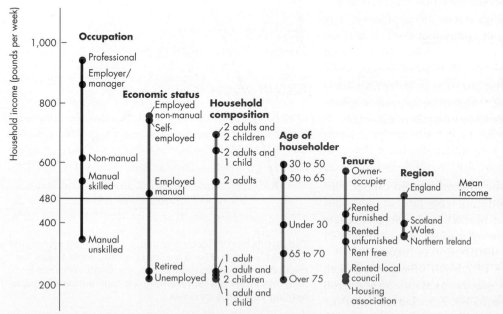

The figure shows that being a single adult household or one parent family, being unemployed or aged over 75 are common characteristics of poor households in the United Kingdom. You are also likely to be poor if you are employed as a manual worker, if you are living in local council accommodation, or if you live in Wales.

Source: Office for National Statistics, *Family Spending: A Report on the 1999/2000 Family Expenditure Survey, 2000*, London, The Stationery Office.

householder, and the region of residence, in influencing the likelihood that a household is poor, living on an income well below average.

The information in Figure 15.3 also shows that a major factor affecting poverty is limited access to high-paid employment. We'll look at the influence of factor prices and endowments on income inequality in the next section.

Review Quiz

◆ What does a Lorenz curve measure and how is it related to the Gini coefficient?
◆ Describe one measure of the poverty line and explain why a poverty line is needed.
◆ What are the main characteristics of low income households?

Factor Prices, Endowments and Choices

A household's income depends on three things:

1 Factor prices.

2 Factor endowments.

3 Choices.

The distribution of income depends on the distribution of these three things across the population. The first two are outside our individual control and are determined by market forces and by history. From the viewpoint of each one of us, they appear to be determined by luck. The last item is under individual control. We make choices that influence our incomes. Let's look at these three determinants of incomes.

Factor Prices

Everyone faces the same interest rates in capital markets, but people face differing wage rates in the labour market. As the labour market is the biggest single source of income for most people, wage differences are likely to affect the distribution of income.

Changes in the rate of growth of wages between occupational groups partly explains the overall changes in income inequality. For example, over the past 20 years in the United Kingdom, wages of non-manual workers have risen faster than those of less well paid manual workers. When the wages of higher-paid groups rise faster than those of the lower-paid groups, income inequality tends to rise.

Factor Endowments

There is a large amount of variety in a household's endowments of capital and of human abilities. Differences in capital and ability are also important contributions to differences in incomes.

The distribution of individual ability across individuals is a major source of inequality in income and wealth. But it is not the only source. If it were, the distributions of income and wealth would look like the bell-shaped curve that describes the distribution of most physical and mental abilities. In fact, the distributions of income and wealth are positively skewed and look like the curve in Figure 15.4. This figure shows income on the horizontal axis and the percentage of households receiving each income on the vertical axis. The median income is £400 per week. The

Figure 15.4

The Distribution of Income

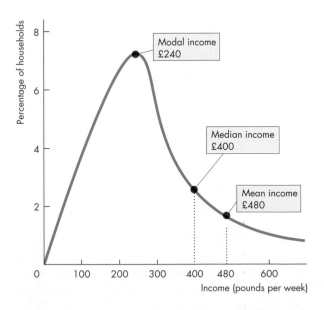

The distribution of income is unequal and is not symmetric around the mean. There are many more people below the mean than above the mean. Also, the distribution has a long thin upper tail representing a small number of people earning very large incomes.

most common income – called the modal income – is less than the median income and is £240. The mean income – also called the average income – is greater than the median income and is £480. A positively skewed distribution like the one shown in Figure 15.4 is one in which many more people have incomes below the average than above it, a large number of people have very low incomes, and a small number of people have very high incomes. The distribution of (non-human) wealth has a similar shape to the distribution of income but is even more skewed.

The skewed shape of the distribution of income cannot be explained by the bell-shaped distribution of individual abilities. It results from the choices that people make.

Choices

A household's income and wealth depend partly on the choices that its members make. People choose how much to supply of each of the factors of production they own. They also choose whether to baby-sit or look for a job in a bank, whether to put their savings in the bank or in shares. You will see that the choices people make exaggerate the differences among them. Their choices make the distribution of income more unequal than the distribution of abilities and explain the skewed shape of the distribution of income.

Wages and the Supply of Labour

Other things remaining the same, the quantity of labour that a person supplies increases as that person's wage rate increases. A person who has a low wage rate chooses to work fewer hours than a person who has a high wage rate.

Because the quantity of labour supplied increases as the wage rate increases, the distribution of income is more unequal than the distribution of hourly wages. It is also positively skewed. People whose wage rates are below the average tend to work fewer hours than the average, and their incomes bunch together much below the average. People whose wage rates are above the average tend to work more hours than the average, and their incomes stretch out above the average.

Saving and Bequests

Another choice that results in unequal distributions in income and wealth is the decision to save and make bequests. A *bequest* is a gift from one generation to the next. The higher a family's income, the more that family tends to save and accumulate wealth across different generations.

Saving and bequests are not inevitably a source of increased inequality. If a family saves to redistribute an uneven income over the life cycle and enable consumption to be constant, the act of saving decreases the degree of inequality. If a lucky generation that has a high income saves a large amount and makes a bequest to a generation that is unlucky, this act of saving also decreases the degree of inequality. But two features of bequests make intergenerational transfers of wealth a source of increased inequality:

1 Debts cannot be bequeathed.

2 Mating is assortative.

Debts Cannot be Bequeathed Although a person may die with debts that exceed assets – with negative wealth – debts cannot be forced on to other family members. Because a zero inheritance is the smallest inheritance that anyone can receive, bequests can only add to future generations' wealth and income potential.

Most people inherit nothing or a very small amount. A few people inherit enormous fortunes. As a result, bequests make the distribution of income and wealth not only more unequal than the distribution of ability and job skills but also more persistent. A family that is poor in one generation is more likely to be poor in the next. A family that is wealthy in one generation is likely to be wealthy in the next. Even so, there is also a tendency for income and wealth to converge, across generations, to the average. One feature of human behaviour that slows down convergence and makes inequalities persist is assortative mating.

Assortative Mating *Assortative mating* is the tendency for people to marry within their own socioeconomic class – like attracts like. Although there is a good deal of folklore that 'opposites attract', perhaps such Cinderella tales appeal to us because they are so rare in reality. Marriage partners tend to have similar socioeconomic characteristics. Wealthy individuals seek wealthy partners. The consequence of assortative mating is that inherited wealth becomes more unequally distributed.

Review Quiz

◆ What role do wage rates, endowments, and choices play in creating income inequality?

◆ What is the main reason that wage rates are unequal?

◆ If the distribution of endowments is bell shaped, what makes the distribution of income skewed?

◆ Which of the choices that people make generate a skewed distribution of income?

◆ How do bequests and assortive mating make the distribution of wealth more unequal and skewed?

We've now examined why inequality exists. Next we'll see how government policies redistribute income and wealth.

Income Redistribution

European governments use three main types of policies to redistribute income and alleviate poverty in addition to direct intervention in the labour market through the minimum wage. They are:

1 Income taxes.
2 Benefit payments.
3 Subsidized welfare services.

Income Taxes

Income taxes may be progressive, regressive or proportional. A **progressive income tax** is one that taxes income at a marginal rate which increases with the level of income. The term 'marginal', applied to income tax rates, refers to the fraction of the last pound earned that is paid in taxes. A **regressive income tax** is one that taxes income at a marginal rate which decreases with the level of income. A **proportional income tax** (also called a *flat-rate income tax*) is one that taxes income at a constant rate regardless of the level of income.

Income taxes have a progressive component in all EU member states. For example, in 2001 in the United Kingdom, the poorest households paid no income tax as everyone can earn £4,535 tax free before tax payments start. After this point in the first

tax band, poor households pay 10 per cent tax on the next £1,880 earned over £4,535. Middle-income households in the second tax band pay 22 per cent tax on the next £29,400 earned. Finally, richer households pay 40 per cent on all additional income earned beyond the second tax band. Only Germany has a higher top band income tax rate at 51 per cent.

The importance of income tax in the redistribution policies of European governments also varies. For example, income taxes constitute just 14 per cent of all taxes in the United Kingdom and Ireland, 19 per cent in Spain and Portugal, 25 per cent in Finland and the Netherlands, and over 30 per cent in Sweden and Denmark.

Benefit Payments

Benefit payments redistribute income by making direct payments to people in the lower part of the income distribution. In 2000, the UK government paid out £109 billion in benefit payments, 28 per cent of total government expenditure. The main types of benefit payments are:

◆ Income support payments.

◆ Tax credits.

◆ State pensions.

Income Support Payments

Governments can use a wide range of income support payments to raise household incomes and reduce poverty. These include unemployment benefits, disability payments and child support payments. For example, in the United Kingdom, the Job Seekers Allowance is paid to individuals who have lost their jobs involuntarily and have no other main source of income. It is available for six months and is awarded on the condition that individuals register as unemployed and are actively seeking work. They may also be required to attend training courses and attend for interviews for suitable jobs. This allowance was £52.20 for those aged over 25 in 2001, the same as the basic income support allowance. A child allowance was also paid at £15.50 a week for each child, whatever the level of family income.

Tax Credits

Tax credits are a method of helping individuals and families in employment, when family income falls below a given amount. A tax credit raises income by reducing the annual tax bill to individuals or families based on eligibility criteria. For example, in the United Kingdom, the Working Families Tax Credit helps families where at least one person is in work, but the family wage is below a given level. The basic credit was worth up to £58.15 a week in 2001. For families with children, there is an additional children's tax credit, worth £10 a week. The Working Families Tax Credit also includes a child care tax credit which repays 70 per cent of eligible child care costs and is worth up to £94.50 a week.

State Pensions

State pensions are the main component of all benefit payment systems. All European economies operate a system whereby the current taxpayers pay for the pensions of the current elderly people. In the United Kingdom state pensions are a contributory benefit – you must have made sufficient National Insurance tax contributions to be eligible. The full basic pension was £72.50 a week in 2001 and was paid to 7 million people, 70 per cent of people of pensionable age. Many women do not get a full state pension because they have not been employed or because part-time work generates insufficient contributions. At retirement age, their incomes will be based on income support payments.

Benefit payments reduce inequality. This is clear in Figure 15.2 because the Gini coefficient on gross income line is always below the Gini coefficient on original income. Benefit payments also alleviate poverty but do not remove it. Comparing expenditure on benefit payments across EU countries, spending is higher in northern countries, with the exception of Northern Ireland. Denmark spends the most on transfer payments, three times more than the amount spent by Portugal.

Subsidized Welfare Services

A great deal of redistribution takes place in most European countries through the subsidized provision of welfare goods and services. These are the goods and services provided by the government at prices below marginal cost. The taxpayers who consume these goods and services receive a transfer in kind from taxpayers who do not consume them. The two most important areas in which this form of redistribution takes place are education – from nursery care through to university – and health care.

In the United Kingdom, 50 per cent of government expenditure is on benefits in kind – 24 per cent on the National Health Service (NHS), 21 per cent on education, the remainder on other services. The NHS provides almost all health care free at the point of demand. Primary and secondary education are provided free for all children in the United Kingdom. Vouchers are available to help parents pay for the cost of nursery care and government subsidizes the cost of university education by paying tuition fees for most undergraduate students.

The extent and method of subsidizing education and health care services varies greatly between EU member states. In addition to free provision, Governments also reimburse health care costs provided by the private sector, or enforce compulsory insurance systems. Whatever the method, where subsidies ensure that everyone gains access to good-quality health care and education, they reduce inequality in health status and basic human capital. This helps to reduce inequality in income.

The Scale of Income Redistribution

The combined effect of taxes and benefit payments is a reduction in poverty and income inequality. Let's look at the impact of taxes and benefits on income distribution in the UK in more detail.

Figure 15.5 shows the impact of taxes and benefits for the five quintile income groups, from bottom fifth (the poorest) to top fifth (the richest). You can see that the value of cash benefits received by the poorest group is much higher than the value of cash benefits received by the richest group. On average, the poorest fifth received £4,800 of cash benefits each year, while the richest fifth received only £1,120. The richest group receives a small amount of benefit because some are universally available. The effect of cash benefits and tax credits is limited by low take-up rates. Means testing on income and form filling bureaucracy put some people off claiming.

The impact on income of benefits in kind – the NHS and education – is more evenly distributed across all income groups, but the poorest groups still receive more in total. These benefits are strongly progressive as they are worth over 70 per cent of post-tax income to the poorest fifth, but just 7 per cent for the richest fifth. Clearly take-up rates will be very high.

Direct taxes also have a strong effect on the distribution of income. Figure 15.5 shows that the richest

Figure 15.5

The Effect of Taxes and Benefits on the Distribution of Income

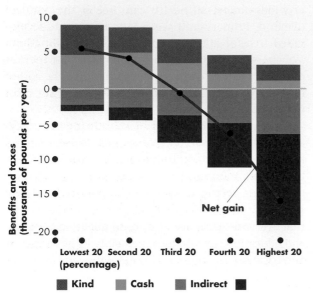

The impact of taxes and benefits in 1999 was to redistribute income from the richest (top) 40 per cent to the poorest (bottom) 40 per cent. The poorest groups receive more income as cash benefits and benefits in kind than the richest groups and the poorest groups pay less tax than the richest groups. Cash benefits and direct taxes on income have the strongest redistributive effects on income.

Source: Office of National Statistics, *Social Trends, 2000*, London, The Stationery Office, Table 5.19, 2001

fifth pay £12,660 in direct taxes on income each year and the poorest fifth pay just £910 each year. Indirect taxes on expenditure have a less dramatic redistributive effect because the poorest groups spend proportionately more of their total income on goods. Overall, the net impact on income distribution is to redistribute income from the top 40 per cent to the bottom 40 per cent, with a small net loss to the middle 20 per cent.

The Big Trade-off

You learned about the Big Trade-off between equity and efficiency in Chapter 5, p. 104. Any redistribution policy requires the use of skilled labour and

other scarce resources. The bigger the redistributive policy, the greater is the opportunity cost of running it and the greater is the efficiency trade-off. Government can only introduce redistributive policies by taxing richer people to pay for benefits to poorer people. This reduces the income of richer people so they work and save less, resulting in less output and consumption for everybody – rich and poor. The taxes also create inefficiency through their deadweight loss. A final source of inefficiency in most benefit systems is the benefit trap. This has been the main reason for reforming the benefits system in Australia, the United Kingdom and the United States. Let's look at benefit traps in more detail.

The Benefit Trap

The benefit system has been criticized for creating disincentives to work by catching people in the *benefit trap*. Benefit traps arise when people who are receiving benefits do not think it is worthwhile taking up employment or working longer hours. If people lose £1 of benefit for every extra £1 that they earn – a *withdrawal rate* of 100 per cent – they will be no better off. They are facing a marginal tax rate of 100 per cent, much higher than all other taxpayers! This problem is unavoidable if benefits are withdrawn as people earn additional income.

There are two main types of benefit trap – the unemployment trap and the poverty trap. In the unemployment trap, people make decisions based on the replacement ratio – the ratio of the expected wage to the benefits received. If the expected wage is only marginally higher than the level of unemployment benefit, the rational choice for most people is to remain unemployed. In the poverty trap, people are already in low-paid work but still receiving benefit. They may want to work longer hours to earn an extra £10, but they will pay tax on the extra £10 and lose up to £10 of benefit. As a result, they are facing a marginal tax rate in excess of 100 per cent! The rational choice is not to work more hours.

UK Reforms

For practical reasons, most political reforms are piecemeal. They are a response to the most pressing problems of the day. The UK benefit reforms began when the 1986 Social Security Act removed the worst aspect of the poverty trap by calculating benefit on income after tax was implemented. At the time, some people faced marginal tax rates of up to 120 per cent. This reform eliminated marginal tax rates in excess of 100 per cent. But many more people now face extremely high marginal tax rates of between 60 and 90 per cent.

In 1998, the UK Government raised benefit levels, cut the rate at which benefit was withdrawn as extra income is earned, and introduced a system of paying benefit as tax credits. The lower withdrawal rate and higher levels of benefit reduce the poverty trap and the tax credit system increases uptake. These reforms are a movement towards the more radical reform of a negative income tax system. Let's look at this in more detail.

Negative Income Tax

Negative income tax has been proposed by some economists as the best method of removing poverty traps. A **negative income tax** gives every household a *guaranteed annual income* and decreases the household's benefit at a specified *withdrawal rate* as the household's original income increases. For example, suppose the guaranteed annual income is £10,000 and the withdrawal rate and the income tax rate are set at 25 per cent. A household with no earnings receives the £10,000 guaranteed income. A household with earnings of £8,000 loses 25 per cent of that amount – £2,000 – and receives a total income of £16,000 (£8,000 earnings plus £10,000 guaranteed income minus £2,000 benefit loss). A household earning £40,000 receives an income of £40,000 (£40,000 earnings plus £10,000 guaranteed income minus £10,000 benefit loss). Such a household is at the break-even income level. Households with earnings exceeding £40,000 pay more in taxes than they receive in benefits.

A negative income tax is illustrated and compared with our current arrangements in Figure 15.6. In both parts of the figure, the horizontal axis measures

Figure 15.6

Comparing the Current Benefit System and a Negative Income Tax

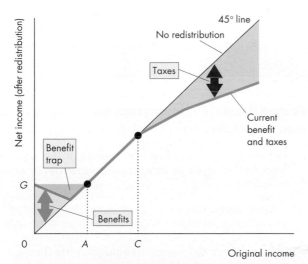

(a) Current redistribution arrangements

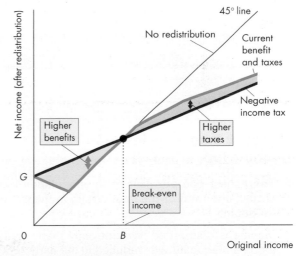

(b) A negative income tax

Part (a) shows the current redistribution arrangements – the blue line. Benefits of *G* are paid to those with no income. As incomes increase from zero to *A*, benefits are withdrawn, *lowering* income after redistribution below *G* and creating a welfare trap – the grey triangle. As incomes increase from *A* to *C*, there is no redistribution. As incomes increase above *C*, income taxes are paid at successively higher rates.

In part (b), a negative income tax gives a guaranteed annual income of *G* and decreases benefits at the same rate as the tax rate on incomes. The red line shows how market incomes translate into income after redistribution. Households with market incomes below *B*, the break-even income, receive net benefits. Those with market incomes above *B* pay net taxes.

original income – that is, income *before* taxes are paid and benefits received – and the vertical axis measures net income *after* taxes are paid and benefits received. The 45° line shows the hypothetical case of 'no redistribution'.

Part (a) shows the current redistribution arrangements – the blue line. Benefits of *G* are paid to those with no income. As original incomes increase from zero to *A*, benefits are withdrawn, *lowering* net income below *G*. This arrangement creates a *benefit trap* shown as the grey triangle. Over the income range *A* to *C*, each additional pound of original income increases net income by a pound. At incomes greater than *C*, income taxes are paid at successively higher rates, and net income is smaller than original income.

Part (b) shows the negative income tax. The guaranteed annual income is *G* and the break-even income is *B*. Households with original incomes below *B* receive a net benefit (blue area) and those with incomes above *B* pay taxes (red area). You can see why such a scheme is called a negative income tax. Every household receives a guaranteed minimum income and every household pays a tax on its earnings – losing benefits is like paying a tax – but households with incomes below the break-even income

receive more than they pay and so, in total, pay a negative amount of tax.

A negative income tax removes the benefit trap (the grey triangle) and gives greater encouragement to low-income households to seek additional employment, even at a low wage. But it has a high cost. Basic tax rates would have to rise above 50 per cent to achieve a guaranteed income of just £6,000 a year.

Review Quiz

◆ What are the methods that governments in Europe use to redistribute income?
◆ To what extent does government policy succeed in redistributing income in the United Kingdom?
◆ Why has the UK government introduced a system of tax credits to replace many standard cash payments?
◆ What problem is the negative income tax designed to solve? Why is the UK government unlikely to introduce a full scale negative income tax?

Summary

Key Points

Economic Inequality in the United Kingdom (pp. 325–328)

● The richest one per cent of the population own almost one-third of the total wealth in the United Kingdom.

● Income is distributed less unevenly than wealth. Income inequality was reduced in the early 1960s and 1970s but increased in all other periods.

● The poorest people in the United Kingdom are likely to be single retired women over the age of 75, with no qualifications, living in Wales. The richest are university-educated couples, aged between 30 and 50, who live in the South East.

● The distribution of income is a more accurate measure of inequality than the distribution of wealth.

Factor Prices, Endowments and Choices (pp. 328–330)

● Differences in income and wealth arise partly from differences in individual endowments and partly from differences in factor prices.

● People who face a high hourly wage rate generally choose to work longer than those who face a low wage rate. As a result, the distribution of income becomes more unequal than the distribution of wage rates.

Income Redistribution (pp. 330–334)

● Governments redistribute income through transfer payments such as income taxes, cash benefits and benefits in kind.

● Income taxes are progressive.

● Redistribution suffers from the big trade-off problem between equity and efficiency. The trade-off arises because the process of redistribution uses resources and weakens incentives to work and save.

- Benefit system reforms try to lessen the severity of the benefit traps. A more radical reform known as negative income tax would strengthen the incentives but increase the tax burden.

Key Figures ◆

Key Terms

Problems

•1 You are provided with the following information about income shares in an economy:

Percentage of families	Income shares (per cent)
Lowest 20%	5
Second 20%	11
Third 20%	17
Fourth 20%	24
Highest 20%	43

a Draw the Lorenz curve for income in this economy.

b Compare the distributions of income in this economy with that in the United Kingdom. Is UK income distributed more equally or less equally than in the economy described in the table?

2 You are provided with the following information about wealth shares in an economy:

Percentage of families	Wealth shares (per cent)
Lowest 20%	0
Second 20%	1
Third 20%	3
Fourth 20%	11
Highest 20%	85

a Draw the Lorenz curve for wealth in this economy.

b Compare the distribution of wealth in this economy with that in the United Kingdom. Is UK wealth distributed more equally or less equally than in the economy described in the table?

c Explain which of the two variables – income in problem 1 or wealth in problem 2 – is more unequally distributed.

•3 Imagine an economy with five people who are identical in all respects. Each lives for 70 years. For the first 14 of those years, they earn no income. For the next 35 years, they work and earn €30,000 a year from their work. For their remaining years, they are retired and have no income from labour. To make the arithmetic easy, let's suppose that the interest rate in this economy is zero; the individuals consume all their income during their lifetime and at a constant annual rate. What are the distributions of income and wealth in this economy if the individuals have the following ages:

a All are 45.

b 25, 35, 45, 55, 65.

Does case (a) have greater inequality than case (b)?

4 In the economy described in problem 3, there is a 'baby boom'. Two people who were born in the same year are now 25. One person is 35, one 45, one 55, and no one is 65. What are the distributions of income and wealth:

a This year?

b 10 years in the future?

c 20 years in the future?

d 30 years in the future?

e 40 years in the future?

f Comment on and explain the changes in the distributions of income and wealth in this economy.

°5 An economy consists of 10 people, each of whom has the following labour supply schedule:

Wage rate (euros per hour)	Hours worked per day
1	1
2	2
3	4
4	6
5	8

The people differ in ability and earn different wage rates. The distribution of *wage rates* is as follows:

Wage rate (euros per hour)	Number of people
1	1
2	2
3	4
4	2
5	1

a Calculate the average wage rate.

b Calculate the ratio of the highest to the lowest wage rate.

c Calculate the average daily income.

d Calculate the ratio of the highest to the lowest daily income.

e Sketch the distribution of hourly wage rates.

f Sketch the distribution of daily incomes.

6 In the economy described in problem 5, the productivity of low-skilled labour falls and that of high-skilled labour rises. Consequently, the distribution of *wage rates* changes to the following:

Wage rate (euros per hour)	Number of people
0	1
1	2
3	4
5	2
6	1

The labour supply schedule is the same as in problem 5. For this changed situation:

a Calculate the average wage rate.

b Calculate the ratio of the highest to the lowest wage rate.

c Calculate the average daily income.

d Calculate the ratio of the highest to the lowest daily income.

e Sketch the distribution of hourly wage rates.

f Sketch the distribution of daily incomes.

g What important lesson is illustrated by comparing the economy in this problem with the one in problem 5?

°7 The table shows the distribution of market income in an economy.

Percentage of families	Income (millions of euros)
Lowest 20%	5
Second 20%	10
Third 20%	18
Fourth 20%	28
Highest 20%	39

The government redistributes income with the taxes and benefits shown in the following table:

Percentage of families	Income taxes (per cent of income)	Benefits (millions of euros)
Lowest 20%	0	10
Second 20%	10	8
Third 20%	15	3
Fourth 20%	20	0
Highest 20%	30	0

a Draw the Lorenz curve for this economy after taxes and benefits.

b Is the scale of redistribution of income in this economy greater or smaller than in Canada?

8 In the economy described in problem 7, the government replaces its existing taxes and benefits with a negative income tax. What changes do you expect to occur in the economy?

Critical Thinking

1   Read the Policy Case Study on pp. 338–339 and the answer the following questions:

   a   How can efficiency be measured in a health care service?

   b   How can equity or fairness be measured in a health care service?

   c   What is meant by the 'big trade-off' in the UK NHS?

   d   Are health care systems in Europe generally progressive, regressive or proportionate in financing?

   e   In your opinion, which European country has the best health care system? Explain your answer.

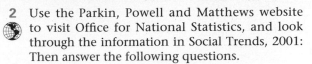

2   Use the Parkin, Powell and Matthews website to visit Office for National Statistics, and look through the information in Social Trends, 2001: Then answer the following questions.

   a   What is the poverty line used in Social Trends?

   b   How has the distribution of income across different income groups changed over time? Which groups are getting richer and which groups poorer?

   c   What other ways are there of measuring poverty?

   d   Do the poorest have access to the same level of goods and services as the richest? Does it matter?

Efficiency and Equity in Health Care

Comparing Health Care Systems

Health Care Provision In Europe

EU health care is provided and financed in different ways, but all States subsidize health care to improve health and to redistribute income. The most common method is majority provision and finance by the public sector. This is the case in 9 of the 15 states and includes the UK's national health service. Austria, Belgium, France, Germany and Luxemburg have a broad mix of public and private supply, but backed by public sector finance. The Netherlands has a broad mix of public and private provision and finance.[1]

Efficiency and Equity

In a recent World Health Organization (WHO) report, the UK health system came twenty-fourth on the global list in terms of efficiency, behind countries like Oman, Italy, France and Spain in the top ten.

Efficiency was measured as the amount of health care provided for resources spent.

In a WHO report including equity as well as efficiency measures, the UK fared slightly better at eighteenth, with France at the top.[2] In the European Union, only Luxemburg spends less on health care spending out of GDP (5.9 per cent) than the UK (6.7 per cent) against the EU average of 9.2 per cent.

The UK Problem

The UK government has pledged to raise health care spending to 8 per cent of GDP by 2006 to improve performance. But the problem is not caused by cuts in spending. The real level of spending on health care in the UK has grown every year since 1979. Even the real level of private spending has increased in all but 3 years over the period.[1]

---

[1] C. Propper (2001), Expenditure on Healthcare in the UK: A Review of the Issues, *Fiscal Studies*, vol. 22, no. 2, pp. 151–183.

[2] S. Bosely, NHS healthcare lags in world efficiency list, *The Guardian*, 10 August 2001, p. 8.

Economic Analysis

- The efficiency of health care systems is usually compared in terms of health outcomes achieved for resources spent. Figure 1 shows a comparison of one widely used measure of health outcome, infant mortality, against health care spending *per capita*.

- Generally, higher spending countries have higher outcome measures than the UK in Europe, but the relationship is not clear. For example, the USA is the biggest spender, but has the worst outcome rates.

- The fairness of different health care systems can be measured by the distribution of access to health care between groups, such as equal treatment for equal need, or by the distribution of payment among different income groups.

- Figure 2 shows the percentage of UK NHS expenditure, standardized for need, received from the poorest 20 per cent to the richest 20 per cent in 1987, and the average expenditure on each group in 1999. The NHS benefits all income groups, but favours the poorest 40 per cent.

- Figure 3 shows measures of progressivity for the financing of health care and the delivery of health care. A value of zero for the financing measure means everyone pays the same proportion of their income for health care. A positive (negative) value indicates progressivity (regressivity), the rich pay proportionately more (less) than the poor.

- Figure 3 shows that the UK and Finland are most progressive in financing but many are inequitable – the poor pay proportionately more. However, the UK system delivers a lower proportion of health care services to the poor than the rich.

- Because the NHS is free at the point of demand, it helps the richest as well as the poorest. It suffers from a 'big trade-off'. It is equitable in finance but redistributing more towards the poor creates more 'leakage' to the rich, reducing efficiency.

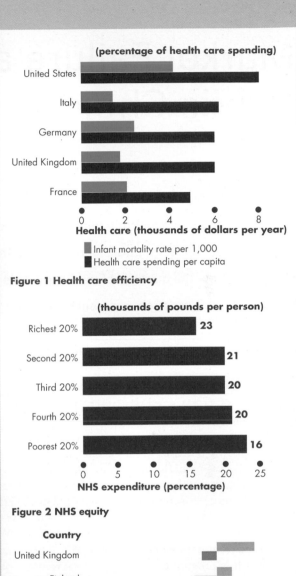

Figure 1 Health care efficiency

Figure 2 NHS equity

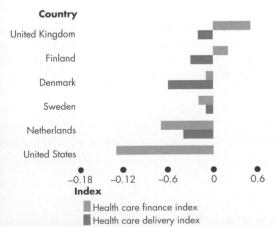

Figure 3 Health care equity

Source: C. Propper (2001), Expenditure on Healthcare in the UK: A Review of the Issues, *Fiscal Studies*, vol. 22, no. 2, pp. 151–183.

CHAPTER 16

Market Failure and Public Choice

After studying this chapter you will be able to:

◆ Explain how the economic role of government arises from market failure and inequality

◆ Distinguish between public goods and private goods and explain the free-rider problem

◆ Explain how the quantity of public goods is determined

◆ Explain why most government's raise the majority of revenue from income taxes, and why these taxes are progressive

◆ Explain why some goods are taxed at a higher rate than others

Government: Solution or Problem?

In 2000, the government in the United Kingdom spent £344 billion – 39 per cent of the value of UK output to achieve its aims. In other countries, governments spend an even higher proportion of their national output. Do we need this much government? Is government too big? Or, despite its enormous size, is government too small to do all the things it must attend to? The European Union spends just 2 per cent of the value of Europe's output on its policies. Is government not contributing enough to economic life? ◆ Government touches many aspects of our lives from birth to death. It supports health care when we're born and our schools, colleges and teachers. It is present throughout our working lives, taxing our incomes and employers, regulating our work environment and paying us benefits when we are unemployed. It is present throughout our retirement, paying us a small income, and when we die, taxing our bequests. Governments also create laws, and provide goods and services such as policing and national defence. ◆ But the government does not make all our choices. We decide what work to do, how much to save and what to spend our income on. Why does the government participate in some aspects of our lives but not in others? Many people think the European Union is overly bureaucratic? Why is the European Commission so unpopular? What determines the scale on which our public services are provided and how government raises money through taxation to pay for them?

◆ ◆ ◆ ◆ In this chapter we describe the government sector and explain how, in the absence of government, the market economy fails to achieve an efficient allocation of resources. We then study how the scale of government is determined and why governments prefer certain types of taxes to pay for its expenditure.

The Economic Theory of Government

The economic theory of government tries to predict the economic actions of government and the consequences of these actions. Governments exist to help people cope with scarcity and to provide non-market mechanisms for allocating scarce resources. If markets fail to achieve an efficient allocation of resources, then government policy can help to reallocate resources, and improve efficiency. Figure 16.1 shows that government policy has three main aims. The first is to help markets to work efficiently through the types of microeconomic policy you'll study in the next few chapters. The second is to help achieve an more equitable distribution of resources as you discovered in Chapter 15. The third is to help stabilize the whole economy. You'll look at these macroeconomic issues in Parts 5 and 6 of this book.

Figure 16.1

The Aims of Government Policy

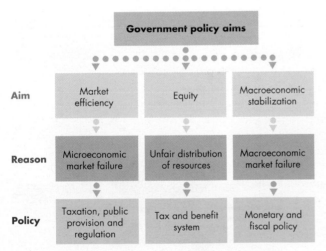

Government policy has three aims. First, governments try to improve efficiency by reducing the impact of microeconomic market failure. They can use a mixture of taxation, public provision and regulation to help individual markets work more efficiently. Second, governments try to improve equity by redistributing incomes and wealth. This can be done by designing an appropriate tax and benefit system which transfers income and wealth, for example, from the rich to the poor. Third, governments try to reduce the impact of uncertainty and limited information on macroeconomic growth by using a mixture of monetary and fiscal policies.

The main types of microeconomic problems that government policies aim to affect are:

◆ Public goods.

◆ Monopoly.

◆ Externalities.

◆ Economic inequality.

Public Goods

Some goods can be consumed simultaneously by everyone. Examples are national defence, law and order, public health and waste disposal services. This means that the provider of national defence cannot isolate individuals and refuse to protect them. Airborne diseases from untreated sewage do not select who they infect. A good or service that can be consumed simultaneously by everyone and from which no individuals can be excluded are called **public goods**.

If the provider of a public good tries to ask people how much they are willing to pay to receive it, consumers say they don't want it. Why? Because the consumers know that once the good is provided they can consume it even if they don't pay for it. This is called the free-rider problem. Every consumer tries to take a free ride on every other consumer. We look at this problem in more detail later in the chapter.

Monopoly

Monopoly and *rent seeking* prevent the allocation of resources from being efficient. Markets fail when monopoly power exists, because it is usually possible to increase profit by restricting output and increasing price. Until a few years ago, for example, most European national telecommunication companies had a monopoly on telephone services and the price of business and domestic telephone services was higher than it is today.

Although some monopolies arise from *legal barriers to entry* – barriers to entry created by governments – a major activity of government is to regulate monopoly and to enforce laws that prevent cartels and other restrictions on competition. We'll study competition and monopoly regulations in Chapter 17.

Externalities

An **externality** is a cost or a benefit arising from an economic transaction that falls on people who do not participate in that transaction. They cannot participate because there is no market for the cost or benefit.

For example, when a chemicals factory (legally) dumps its waste into a river and kills the fish, it imposes an externality – in this case, an external cost – on the fisherman who lives downstream. External costs and benefits are not taken into account by the people whose actions create them if there are no markets – and no prices – for these costs and benefits. For example, the chemicals factory does not take the damaging effects on the fish into account when deciding whether to dump waste into the river because there is no market for waste water. We study externalities and the way governments and markets cope with them in Chapter 18.

The three problems considered above cause an inefficient allocation of resources and are called microeconomic **market failure**. The market either overproduces or underproduces these goods and services. Government policy aims to reallocate these market resources to make some people better off without making anyone worse off – increasing welfare to consumers and producers. Government policy attempts to modify market outcomes and so moderate the effect of market failure.

Economic Inequality

Government economic activity also arises because an unregulated market economy delivers what most people regard as an unfair distribution of income. To lessen the degree of inequality, government can tax some people and pay benefits to others as you discovered in Chapter 15. In this chapter, we'll look further at taxes and try to explain why the income tax is progressive and why some goods are taxed at extremely high rates.

Before we look at government policy, we need to understand the arena in which governments operate. To do this we are going to build a model of the 'political marketplace'.

Public Choice and the Political Marketplace

Government is a complex organization made up of millions of individuals, each with their *own* economic objectives. Government policy choices are the outcome of the choices made by these individuals. To analyse these choices, economists have developed a theory of the political activity called public choice theory. We can use this theory to build a model of the political marketplace similar to our market models.

The actors in the model of the political marketplace are:

◆ Voters.

◆ Politicians.

◆ Bureaucrats.

Figure 16.2 illustrates the choices and interactions of these actors. We'll look at each in turn.

Figure 16.2

The Political Market Place

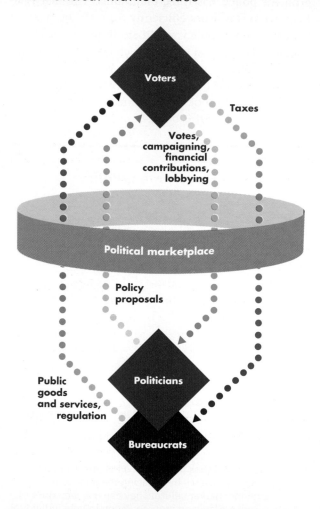

The voters express their demands for policies by voting, election campaigning, making financial contributions to political parties and joining interest groups to lobby government. Politicians propose policies to appeal to a majority of voters. Bureaucrats try to maximize the budgets of their departments or agencies. A political equilibrium emerges in which no group can improve its position by making different choices.

Voters

Voters are the consumers of the political process. In markets for goods and services, people express their demands by their willingness to pay. In the political marketplace, they express their demands by voting, campaigning, lobbying and making financial contributions. Public choice theory assumes that people support policies that they believe will make them better off and oppose policies that they believe will make them worse off. They neither oppose nor support – they are indifferent towards – policies that they believe have no effect on them. Voters' *perceptions* of policy outcomes are what guide their choices.

Politicians

Politicians are the elected administrators and legislators at all levels of government. Economic models of public choice assume that the objective of a politician is to get elected and to remain in office. Votes, to a politician, are like pounds to a firm. To get enough votes, politicians form coalitions – political parties – to develop policy proposals, which they expect will appeal to a majority of voters.

Bureaucrats

Bureaucrats are employed staff who work in government departments at all levels. They are responsible for enacting government policy. The most senior bureaucrats are hired by politicians. Junior bureaucrats are hired by senior bureaucrats. Bureaucrats are assumed to maximize their own utility, and to achieve this objective, they try to maximize the budget of the agency or department in which they work. This is because the bigger the budget, the greater is the prestige of the agency or department boss and the larger is the opportunity for promotion for people further down the bureaucratic ladder. To maximize their budgets, bureaucrats devise programmes that they expect will appeal to politicians and they help politicians to sell programmes to voters.

Political Equilibrium

Voters, politicians and bureaucrats make their economic choices to maximize their own objectives. But each group is constrained by the preferences of the other groups and by what is technologically feasible. The outcome of the choices of voters, politicians and bureaucrats is the **political equilibrium**, which is a situation in which the choices of voters, politicians and bureaucrats are all compatible and in which no group can improve its position by making a different choice.

Let's see how voters, politicians and bureaucrats interact to determine the quantity of public goods.

Public Goods and the Free-rider Problem

Why does the government provide public goods and services such as national defence and health services – goods and services that can be consumed simultaneously by everyone and from which no one can be excluded? Why don't we leave the provision of these goods and services to private firms that sell their output in markets? Why don't we buy environmental protection from a company that competes for our pounds in the marketplace in the same way that McDonald's and Coca-Cola do? The answer to these questions lies in the *free-rider problem* created by public goods. To explore this further we need to know a little more about the characteristics of public goods.

Public Goods

A pure **public good** is a good or service that can be consumed simultaneously by everyone and from which no one can be excluded. One characteristic of public goods is that they are non-rival in consumption because one person's consumption of the good does not affect the quantity available for anyone else. Most goods, by contrast, are rival in consumption. For example, if I eat a pizza, that pizza is no longer available for anyone else. A second characteristic of public goods is that they are non-excludable. A good is non-excludable if it is impossible, or extremely costly, to prevent someone from benefiting from the good who has not paid for it. An example of a non-excludable good is national defence because government cannot refuse to protect people who may not have paid taxes towards paying for defence. Most goods are excludable because the producer can stop non-payers from consuming the good.

Figure 16.3 classifies examples of goods according to these two characteristics. National defence is an example of a pure public good. Most goods, like cars, are both rival and excludable, and these are called private goods. Some goods, however, have public elements but are not pure public or private goods. An example is a motorway. A motorway is non-rival until

Figure 16.3

Public Goods and Private Goods

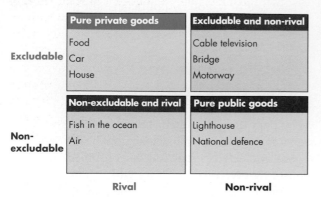

A pure public good (bottom-right) is one for which consumption is non-rival and from which it is impossible to exclude a consumer. Pure public goods pose a free-rider problem. A pure private good (top-left) is one for which consumption is rival and from which consumers can be excluded. Some goods are non-excludable but are rival (bottom-left) and some goods are non-rival but are excludable (top-right).

Source: Adapted from and inspired by E.S. Savas, *Privatizing the Public Sector*, Chatham, NJ, Chatham House Publishers Inc., 1982, p. 34.

it becomes congested. But the use of road tolls and electronic road pricing could exclude non-payers. Ocean fish are rival because a fish taken by one person is not available for anyone else. But ocean fish are non-excludable because it is difficult to stop other people catching them.

The Free-rider Problem

A **free rider** is a person who consumes a good without paying for it. Public goods create a free-rider problem because the quantity of the good that a person is able to consume is not influenced by the amount the person pays for the good. So no one has an incentive to pay enough for a public good. Let's look more closely at the free-rider problem by studying an example.

The Benefit of a Public Good

Suppose that for its effective defence, the EU decides to launch some communication and surveillance satellites. The benefit provided by a satellite is the *value* of its services. The value of a *private* good is the maximum amount that the *person* is willing to pay for one more unit of the good, shown by the demand curve. Similarly, the value to an individual of a *public* good is the maximum amount that the *people* are willing to pay for one more unit of the good.

Total benefit is the total euro value that a person places on a given level of provision of a public good. The greater the quantity of the public good, the larger is a person's total benefit. The increase in total benefit resulting from a one-unit increase in the quantity of a public good is the **marginal benefit**.

Figure 16.4 shows an example of the marginal benefit that arises from the defence satellites for a society of just two people, Lisa and Max. Lisa's and Max's marginal benefits are graphed as MB_L and MB_M, respectively, in parts (a) and (b) of the figure. As you can see, the marginal benefit for a public good, like a private good, decreases as the quantity increases. For Lisa, the marginal benefit from the first satellite is €80. For Max, the marginal utility from the first satellite is €50. By the time the fifth satellite is launched, Lisa perceives no additional benefits and Max perceives only €10 worth of benefit.

Part (c) of the figure shows the economy's marginal benefit curve, MB (where the economy has only two people, Lisa and Max). An individual's marginal benefit curve for a public good is similar to the individual's demand curve for a private good. But the economy's marginal benefit curve for a public good is different from the market demand curve for a private good. To obtain the market demand curve for a private good, we add up the quantities demanded by each individual at each price. In other words, we sum the individual demand curves horizontally.[1] In contrast, to find the economy's marginal benefit curve of a public good, we add the marginal benefit of each individual at each quantity provided, as one person's consumption does not reduce the amount available for another. So we sum the individual marginal benefit curves of Lisa and Max vertically. The resulting marginal benefit curve for the whole economy of two people is graphed in part (c) – the curve MB. Lisa's marginal benefit from the first satellite gets added to Max's marginal benefit from the first satellite because they both enjoy its security value.

---

[1] The derivation of the market demand curve from the individual demand curves is explained in Figure 7.1, p. 135.

Figure 16.4

Benefits of a Public Good

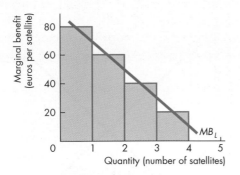

(a) Lisa's marginal benefit

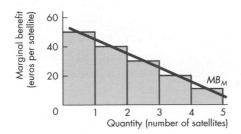

(b) Max's marginal benefit

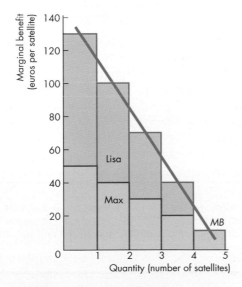

(c) Economy's marginal benefit

The figure shows the marginal benefit for two individuals, Lisa and Max, and for the whole economy (comprising only Lisa and Max) for different quantities of satellites. The marginal benefit curves are MB_L for Lisa, MB_M for Max and MB for the economy. The marginal benefit to the economy at each quantity of the public good is the sum of the marginal benefits to each individual.

The Efficient Quantity of a Public Good

In reality, an economy with two people would not buy any satellites – the total benefit falls far short of the cost. But the European Union of 300 million people might. To determine the efficient quantity, we need to take cost as well as benefit into account.

The cost of a satellite is based on technology and the prices of the factors of production used to produce it. It is an opportunity cost and is derived in the same way as the cost of producing jumpers – explained in Chapter 10. The efficient quantity is the one that maximizes *net benefit* – total benefit minus total cost.

Figure 16.5 illustrates the efficient quantity of satellites. The first three columns of the table show the total and marginal benefits to an economy consisting of 300 million people. The next two columns show the total and marginal cost of producing satellites. The final column shows net benefit. Total benefit, *TB*, and total cost, *TC*, are graphed in part (a) of the figure. Net benefit (total benefit minus total cost) is maximized when the vertical distance between the *TB* and *TC* curves is at its largest, a situation that occurs with two satellites. This is the efficient quantity.

Another way of describing the efficient scale uses marginal benefit and marginal cost. The marginal benefit, *MB*, and marginal cost, *MC*, of satellites are graphed in part (b). When marginal benefit exceeds marginal cost, net benefit increases if the quantity produced increases. When marginal cost exceeds marginal benefit, net benefit increases if the quantity produced decreases. Marginal benefit equals marginal cost at *M* in part (b) with two satellites. So making marginal cost equal to marginal benefit maximizes net benefit and determines the allocatively efficient quantity of the public good.

Private Provision

We have now worked out the quantity of satellites that maximizes net benefit. Would a private firm – Eurozone Protection plc – deliver that quantity? It would not. To do so, it would have to collect €2 billion to cover its costs – or €8 from each of the 250 million people in the economy. But no one would have an incentive to buy his or her 'share' of the satellite system. Each person would reason as follows. The number of satellites provided by Eurozone Protection is not affected by my €8. My consumption of other goods will be greater if I free ride and do

Figure 16.5

The Efficient Quantity of a Public Good

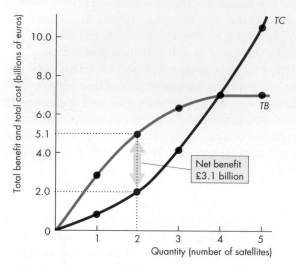

(a) Total benefit and total cost

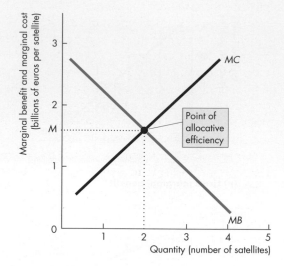

(b) Marginal benefit and marginal cost

Quantity (number of satellites)	Total benefit (billions of euros)	Marginal benefit (billions of euros per satellite)	Total cost (billions of euros)	Marginal cost (billions of euros per satellite)	Net benefit (billions of euros)
0	0		0		0
		3		0.7	
1	3		0.7		2.3
		2.1		1.3	
2	5.1		2		3.1
		1.2		2	
3	6.3		4		2.3
		1.0		3.3	
4	7.3		7.3		0
		0		4	
5	7.3		11		−3.7

Total benefit and total cost are graphed in part (a) as the total benefit curve, *TB*, and the total cost curve, *TC*. Net benefit the vertical distance between the two curves is maximized when two satellites are installed.

Part (b) shows the marginal benefit curve, *MB*, and marginal cost curve, *MC*. When marginal cost equals marginal benefit, net benefit is maximized and allocative efficiency is achieved.

---

not pay my share of the cost of the satellite system. If I do not pay and everyone else does, I enjoy the same level of security and can buy more private goods.

If everyone reasons the same way, Eurozone Protection has no revenue and can't supply any satellites. The market does not provide the efficient level – two satellites – so private provision is inefficient.

Public Provision

Suppose Europe's voters have a chance to vote on the issue of satellite provision through the European Parliament. To simplify the model, assume there are just two political parties in the European Parliament, the Blues and the Greens, and they agree with each other on all issues except satellites. The Blues would like to provide four satellites at a cost of €7.3 billion, with benefits of €7.3 billion and a net benefit of zero, as shown in Figure 16.5. The Greens would like to provide one satellite at a cost of €0.7 billion, a benefit of £3 billion and a net benefit of €2.3 billion.

Before campaigning, the two political parties do a 'what-if' analysis. Each party reasons as follows. If each group offers the satellite programme it wants – Blues four satellites and Greens one satellite – the voters will get a net benefit of €2.3 billion from the Greens, zero net benefit from the Blues, and the Greens will win the election.

Contemplating this outcome, the Blues realize that their party is too Blue to get elected. They figure that they must offer net benefits in excess of €2.3 billion if they are to beat the Greens. So they scale back their proposal to two satellites. At this level of provision, total cost is €2 billion, total benefit is €5.1 billion and net benefit is €3.1 billion. If the Greens stick with one satellite, the Blues will win the election.

But contemplating this outcome, the Greens realize that the best they can do is to match the Blues. They too propose to provide two satellites on exactly the same terms as the Blues. If the two parties offer the same number of satellites, the voters are indifferent between the parties. They toss coins to decide their votes and each party receives around 50 per cent of the vote.

The result of the politicians' 'what-if' analysis is that each party offers two satellites so regardless of who wins the election, this is the quantity of satellites installed. This quantity is efficient because it maximizes the perceived net benefit of the voters. Thus in this example, competition in the political marketplace results in the efficient provision of a public good. But for this outcome to occur, voters must be well-informed and able to evaluate the alternatives. We'll see below that they do not always have an incentive to do so.

In the example we've just studied, both parties eventually propose identical policies. This is called the principle of minimum differentiation. We have analysed the behaviour of politicians but not that of the bureaucrats who translate the choices of the politicians into programmes. Let's now see how the economic choices of bureaucrats influence the political equilibrium.

The Role of Bureaucrats

We've seen in Figure 16.5 that two satellites at a cost of €2 billion maximize net benefit and that com-

Figure 16.6

Bureaucratic Overprovision

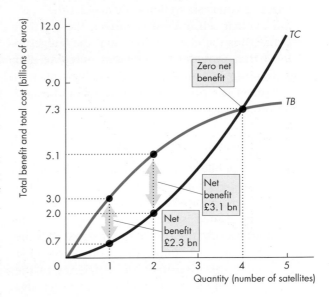

The goal of a bureaucracy is to maximize its budget. A bureau that maximizes its budget will seek to increase cost all the way to the total benefit and to expand output and expenditure as far as possible. Here, the EU's Defence DG tries to get €2 billion to provide two satellites and to increase the quantity of satellites to four with a budget of €7.3 billion.

petition between two political parties delivers this outcome. But will the European Commission's bureaucrats cooperate?

Suppose the EU's Directorate General (DG) for Defence aims to maximize the defence budget. To achieve its objective, the Defence DG will try to persuade Parliament that two satellites cost more than €2 billion. As Figure 16.6 shows, it will argue that they cost €5.1 billion – the entire benefit. Pressing its position even more strongly, the Defence DG will argue for more satellites. It will press for four satellites and a budget of €7.3 billion. In this situation, total benefit and total cost are equal and net benefit is zero.

But won't the politicians always control the bureaucracy and keep spending down to the efficient level – the level that maximizes the perceived net benefits of the voters? We've already seen that when there are two political parties competing for votes, the party that comes closest to maximizing net benefit gets the most votes. Don't these forces of competition for votes dominate the aims of the bureaucrats to ensure that the EU's Defence DG only gets a budget big enough to provide two satellites – to maximize net benefit?

If Europe's voters are well-informed and if their perception of their self-interest is correct, the political party that wins the election does hold the budget to the level that provides the efficient outcome. But there is another possible political equilibrium. It is one based on the principle of voter ignorance and well-informed interest groups.

Rational Ignorance

A principle of public choice theory is that it is rational for a voter to be ignorant about an issue unless that issue has a perceptible effect on the voter's income. **Rational ignorance** is the decision *not* to acquire information because the cost of doing so exceeds the expected benefit. For example, each voter knows that he or she can make virtually no difference to the defence policy of the government. Each voter also knows that it would take an enormous amount of time and effort to become even moderately well-informed about alternative defence technologies. So voters remain relatively uninformed. (Though we are using defence policy as an example, the same applies to all aspects of government economic activity.)

All Europe's voters are consumers of national defence. But only a few voters are producers of national defence. Those voters who own or work for firms that produce satellites or produce inputs into the production of satellites, have a direct personal interest in defence because it affects their incomes. Such voters have an incentive to become well-informed about defence issues and to form or join interest groups to lobby government and further their own interests. In collaboration with the EU's Defence DG bureaucracy, these voters exert a larger influence than the relatively uninformed voters who only consume defence.

When the rationality of the uninformed voter and special interest groups are taken into account, the political equilibrium provides public goods in excess of the efficient quantity. So in the satellite example, three or four satellites might be launched rather than the efficient quantity, which is two satellites.

Two Types of Political Equilibrium

We've seen that two types of political equilibrium are possible: efficient and inefficient. These two types of political equilibrium correspond to two theories of government:

1   Public interest theory.
2   Public choice theory.

Public Interest Theory

Public interest theory predicts that governments make choices about policies to achieve efficiency. This outcome occurs in a perfect political system in which voters are fully informed about the effects of policies and refuse to vote for outcomes that can't be improved upon. The result of government policy is an improvement in efficiency and a reduction in market failure.

Public Choice Theory

Public choice theory predicts that governments make choices that result in inefficiency. This outcome occurs in political markets in which voters are rationally ignorant and base their votes only on issues that they know affect their own net benefit. Voters pay more attention to their interests as producers than their interests as consumers. Public officials also act in their own interest. The result of government policy is government failure that parallels market failure.

Why Government is Large and Grows

Government expenditure as a proportion of the value of output has grown steadily for the past 20 years in all developed economies. Now that we know how the quantity of public goods is determined, we can explain part of the reason for this growth of government. Government grows in part because the demand for some public goods increases at a faster rate than the demand for private goods. There are two possible reasons for this growth:

1   Voter preferences.
2   Inefficient overprovision.

Voter Preferences

The growth of government can be explained by voter preferences in the following way. As voters' incomes increase (as they usually do in most developed economies), the quantity of public goods demanded increases more quickly than income. The *income elasticity of demand* for public goods is greater than one. Many (and the most expensive) public goods are in this category. They include communication systems, such as motorways, airports and air-traffic control, public health, education and defence. If government's did not support increasing expenditure, they would not get elected. So this first reason for government growth seems convincing.

Inefficient Overprovision

Inefficient overprovision might explain the *size* of government but not the *growth* of government. It only explains why government might be *larger* than its efficient scale at any point in time. However, it does explain government attempts to control government spending. These include privatization programmes, budget cuts, the use of contracting and performance indicators in public services, and the introduction of auditing and management practice into public services.

Voters Strike Back

If government expenditure grows too large relative to voters' preferences, there is always the possibility of a voter backlash. Governments have to pay for their spending and policies by raising revenue through taxation or borrowing. Higher taxes reduce voters' incomes – reducing voter utility – so governments must balance the increase in voter utility from spending against the decrease in voter utility from taxation.

If governments borrow too much, they will generate inflation and become equally unpopular. When governments fear they will lose the next election as a result of rising public sector expenditure, taxation or inflation, they'll start to cut expenditure. You can find examples of cuts in welfare spending for this reason all over Europe – particularly in Belgium, France, Germany, Italy, the United Kingdom and Sweden.

Review Quiz

◆ What is the free-rider problem and why does it make the private provision of a public good inefficient?
◆ Under what conditions will competition among politicians for votes result in an efficient quantity of a public good?
◆ How do rationally ignorant voters and budget maximizing bureaucrats prevent competition in the political marketplace from producing the efficient quantity of a public good? Do they result in too much or too little being provided?
◆ Private provision of a public good creates a free-rider problem and provides less than the efficient quantity of the good.

We've now seen how voters, politicians and bureaucrats interact to determine the quantity of public goods and services. But public goods must be paid for with taxes. How does the political marketplace determine the scale and variety of taxes that we pay?

Taxes

Taxes generate the financial resources that governments use to provide voters with public goods and other benefits. Five main groups of taxes are used:

◆ Income taxes.
◆ Property taxes.
◆ Employment social contributions.
◆ Excise taxes.
◆ Value Added Tax (VAT).

Figure 16.7 shows the relative amounts raised by indirect taxes which comprise VAT, property taxes and excise taxes; direct taxes, which are mainly individual

Figure 16.7

Taxes in the European Union

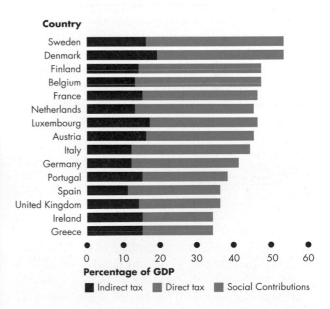

About half of the European Union member states raise the majority of their revenue from income taxes. The remainder rely more heavily on indirect taxes. A few raise the majority of their revenue from social contribution taxes.

Source: European Commission.

income tax with a small proportion of corporation tax; and social contribution taxes. The dependence on different taxes for revenue varies widely throughout the European Union. Some countries like Denmark, Sweden, Finland and Belgium raise the majority of their revenue through income taxes. Most other countries in the European Union, raise most of their revenue through indirect taxes on goods and services. A few EU countries, like France, the Netherlands and Germany and Spain gain the largest proportion of their revenues from social contribution taxes. Let's take a closer look at each type of tax.

Income Taxes

Income taxes are paid on personal incomes and corporate profits. In 2001, the personal income tax raised £104 billion for the UK central government. Corporate profits taxes raised just £38 billion and the business rate raised £17 billion for central government. We'll look first at the effects of personal income taxes and then at corporate profits taxes.

Personal Income Tax

The amount of income tax that a person pays depends on her or his *taxable income*. Taxable income equals total income minus expenses and other adjustments. The *tax rate* (per cent) in the European Union depends on the income level and varies across the European Union. In the United Kingdom, for example, there are four tax effective tax rates. For anyone under 65 with no additional allowances, they are:

Income bands	Marginal tax rate
£0 to £4,535	0 per cent
£4,536 to £6,415	10 per cent
£6,416 to £33,934	22 per cent
£33,935 or more	40 per cent

The percentages in this list are marginal tax rates. A marginal tax rate is the percentage of an additional pound of income that is paid in tax. For example if taxable income increases from £4,535 to £4,536, the additional tax paid is 10 pence and the marginal tax rate is 10 per cent. If income increases from £6,415 to £6,416 the additional tax paid is 22 pence and the marginal tax rate is 22 per cent.

The average tax rate is the percentage of income that is paid in tax. The average tax rate is less than the marginal tax rate. For example, a single person with a taxable income of £25,000 in 2001 pays £4,277 in

income tax. This person's average tax rate is 17.1 per cent. A person whose taxable income is £100,000 a year pays £32,668 in income tax, an average tax rate of 32.7 per cent.

The average tax rate increases as income increases. When the average tax rate increases as income increases, the tax is called a progressive tax. Contrast a **progressive tax** with a **proportional tax**, which has the same average tax rate at all income levels, and a **regressive tax**, which has a decreasing average tax rate as income increases.

The Effect of Income Taxes   Figure 16.8 shows how the income tax affects European labour markets. Part (a) shows the market for low-wage workers and part (b) shows the market for high-wage workers. These labour markets are competitive and with no income taxes, they work just like all the other competitive markets you have studied. The demand curves are *LD* and the supply curves are *LS* (in both parts of the figure). Both groups work 40 hours a week. Low-wage workers earn €9 an hour and high-wage workers earn €170 an hour. What happens when an income tax is introduced?

If low-wage workers are willing to supply 40 hours a week for €9 an hour when there is no tax, then they are willing to supply that same quantity in the face of a 25 per cent tax only if the wage rises to €12 an hour. That is, they want to get the €9 an hour they received before plus the €3 (25 per cent of €12) that they now must pay to the government. So the supply of labour decreases because the amount received from work is lowered by the amount of income tax paid. The acceptable wage rate at each level of employment rises by the amount of the tax that must be paid. For low-wage workers who face a tax rate of 25 per cent, the supply curve shifts to *LS + tax*. The equilibrium wage rate rises to €10 an hour, but the after-tax wage rate falls to €7.50 an hour. Employment falls to 36 hours a week.

For high-wage workers who face a tax rate of 50 per cent, the supply curve shifts to *LS + tax*. The equilibrium wage rate rises to €200 an hour, and the after-tax wage rate falls to €100 an hour. Employment decreases to 32 hours a week. The decrease in employment of high-wage workers is larger than that of low-wage workers because of the differences in the marginal tax rates they each face.

Notice that both the employer and the worker pay the income tax. In the case of low-wage workers, the employer pays an extra €1 an hour and the worker

Figure 16.8

The Effect of Income Taxes

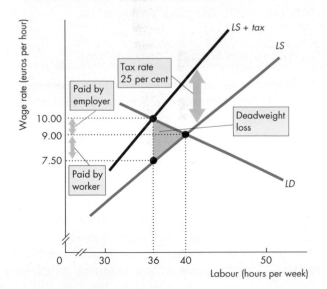

(a) Lowest income tax rate

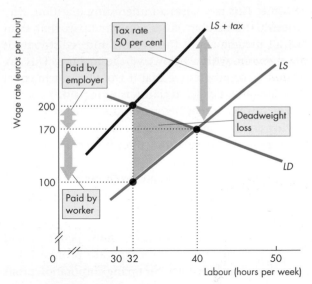

(b) Highest income tax rate

The demand for labour is *LD* and with no income taxes, the supply of labour is *LS* (both parts). In part (a), low-wage workers earn €9 an hour and each works 40 hours a week. In part (b), high-wage workers earn €170 an hour and each works 40 hours a week. An income tax decreases the supply of labour and the labour supply curve shifts leftward. For low-wage workers in part (a), whose marginal

tax rate is 25 per cent, supply decreases to *LS + tax*. Employment falls to 36 hours a week. For high-wage workers in part (b), whose marginal tax rate is 50 per cent, supply decreases to *LS + tax*. Employment falls to 32 hours a week. The deadweight loss from the high marginal tax rate on high-wage workers is much larger than that from the low marginal tax rate on low-wage workers.

pays €1.50 an hour. In the case of high-wage workers, employers pay an extra €30 an hour and workers pay €70 an hour. The split depends on the elasticities of demand and supply.

Notice also the difference in the *deadweight loss* for the two groups. (Check back in Chapter 5 on p. 102 if you need a refresher on the concept of deadweight loss.) The deadweight loss is much larger for the high-wage workers than for the low-wage workers.

Why Do We Have a Progressive Income Tax?

We have a progressive income tax because it is part of the political equilibrium. A majority of voters support it, so politicians who support it get elected.

The economic model that predicts progressive income taxes is called the *median voter* model. The core idea of the median voter model is that political parties pursue policies most likely to attract the support of the median voter. The median voter is the one in the middle – one-half of the population lies on one side

and one-half on the other. Let's see how the median voter model predicts a progressive income tax.

Imagine that government programmes benefit everyone equally and are paid for by a proportional income tax. Everyone pays the same percentage of his or her income. In this situation, there is redistribution from high-income voters to low-income voters. Everyone benefits equally but because they have higher incomes, the high-income voters pay a larger amount of taxes.

Is this situation the best one possible for the median voter? It is not. Suppose that instead of using a proportional tax, the marginal tax rate is lowered for low-income voters and increased for high-income voters – a progressive tax. Low-income voters are now better off and high-income voters are worse off. Low-income voters will support this change and high-income voters will oppose it. But there are many more low-income voters than high-income voters, so the low-income voters win.

The median voter is a low-income voter. In fact, because the distribution of income is skewed, the median voter has a smaller income than the average income. This fact raises an interesting question: why doesn't the median voter support taxes that skim off all income above the average and redistribute it to everyone with a below-average income. This tax would be so progressive that it would result in equal incomes after taxes and transfers were paid.

The answer is that high taxes discourage work and saving and the median voter would be worse off with such radical redistribution than under the arrangements that prevail today.

Let's now look at corporate profit taxes.

Corporate Profits Tax

In popular discussions of taxes, most people would prefer government to tax corporate profits rather than individual income. But taxing corporation profit can be inefficient. Let's see why.

First, the tax is misnamed. It is only partly a tax on economic profit. It is mainly a tax on the income from capital. Taxing the income from capital works like taxing the income from labour except for two critical differences: (a) the supply of capital is highly (perhaps perfectly) elastic, and (b) the quantity of capital influences the productivity of labour and wage income. Because the supply of capital is highly elastic, the tax is fully borne by firms and the quantity of capital decreases. With a smaller capital stock than we would otherwise have, the productivity of labour and incomes are lower than they would otherwise be. Governments use this inefficient tax because it redistributes income in favour of the median voter, just like the income tax.

Property Taxes

Property taxes are collected by local and regional governments in the European Union to provide local public goods. A local public good is a public good that is consumed by all the people who live in a particular area. Examples of local public goods are parks, museums, and local waste disposal. There is a much closer connection between property taxes paid and benefits received than in the case of national taxes. This close connection make property taxes similar to a price for local services. Because of this connection, property taxes change both the demand for and supply of property in a locality. A higher tax lowers supply, but improved local public goods increase

demand. So some localities have high taxes and high-quality local government services and other neighbourhoods have low taxes and low-quality services. Both can exist in the political equilibrium.

Employment Social Contributions

Employment social contributions are the payments made by employers and employees to provide for welfare benefits.

Unions try to get employers to pay a bigger share of these taxes and employers' organizations try to get workers to pay a bigger share of them. But this lobbying effort is not worth much. For who *really* pays these taxes depends in no way on who writes the cheques. It depends on the elasticities of demand and supply for labour. Figure 16.9 shows you why.

In both parts of the figure, the demand curve LD and the supply curve LS are identical. With no employment social contribution, the quantity of labour employed is QL^* and the wage rate is W^*.

An employment social contribution is now introduced. In Figure 16.9(a) the contribution is treated as a tax on the employee's salary; in Figure 16.9(b) the contribution is a charge on employers. When the contribution is a salary deduction, supply decreases and the supply of labour curve shifts leftward to $LS + tax$. The vertical distance between the supply curve LS and the new supply curve $LS + tax$ is the amount of the tax. The wage rate rises to WC, after-tax wage rate falls to WT, and employment decreases to QL_0. When the contribution is a charge on employers (Figure 16.9b), demand decreases and the demand for labour curve shifts leftward to $LD - tax$. The vertical distance between the curve LD and the new demand curve $LD - tax$ is the amount of the tax. The wage rate falls to WT but the cost of labour rises to WC, and employment decreases to QL_0.

So regardless of which side of the market is taxed, the outcome is identical. If the demand for labour is perfectly inelastic or if the supply of labour is perfectly elastic, the employer pays the entire tax. And if the demand for labour is perfectly elastic or if the supply of labour is perfectly inelastic, the employee pays the entire tax. These cases are exactly like those for the sales tax that you studied in Chapter 6.

Excise Taxes

An **excise tax** is a tax on the sale of a particular commodity. We'll now study the effects of an excise tax

Figure 16.9

Employment Social Contributions

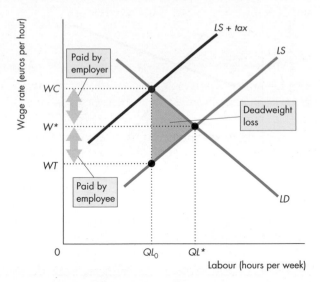

(a) Tax on employees

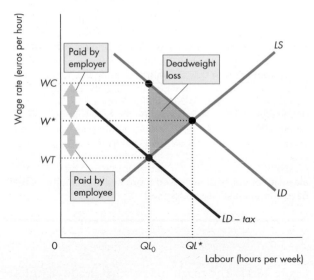

(b) Tax on employers

The labour demand curve is *LD* and the supply curve is *LS*. With no employment contributions, the quantity of labour employed is *QL** and the wage rate is *W** (in both parts). In part (a), the employment social contribution is a tax on employees' salaries. Supply decreases and the supply of labour curve shifts leftward to *LS + tax*. The wage rate rises to *WC*, after-tax wage rate falls to *WT*, and employment decreases to *QL*₀. In part (b), the employment social contribution is a charge on employers. Demand decreases and the demand for labour curve shifts leftward to *LD – tax*. The wage rate falls to *WT* but the cost of labour rises to *WC*, and employment decreases to *QL*₀. The outcome is identical in both cases.

Figure 16.10

An Excise Tax

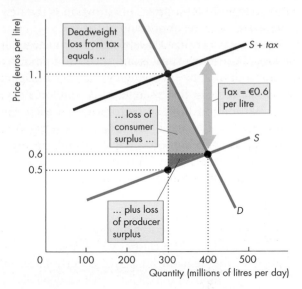

The demand curve for petrol is *D* and the supply curve is *S*. In the absence of any taxes, petrol will sell for €0.6 a litre and 400 million litres a day will be bought and sold. When a tax of €0.6 a litre is imposed, the supply curve shifts upward to become the curve *S + tax*. The new equilibrium price is €1.1 pence a litre and 300 million litres a day are bought and sold. The excise tax creates a deadweight loss represented by the grey triangle. The tax revenue collected is €0.6 pence a litre on 300 million litres, which is €180 million a day. The deadweight loss from the tax is €30 million a day. That is, to raise tax revenue of €180 million a day a deadweight loss of €30 million a day is incurred.

by considering the tax on petrol shown in Figure 16.10. The demand curve for petrol is *D* and the supply curve is *S*. If there is no tax on petrol, its price is €0.6 a litre and 400 million litres of petrol a day are bought and sold.

Now suppose that a tax is imposed on petrol at the rate of €0.6 a litre. If producers are willing to supply 400 million litres a day for €0.6 when there is no tax, then they are willing to supply that same quantity in the face of a €60 tax only if the price increases to €1.2 a litre. That is, they want to get the €0.6 a litre they received before, plus the additional €0.6 that they now have to hand over to the government in the form of a petrol tax. As a result of the tax, the supply of petrol decreases and the supply curve shifts leftward. The magnitude of the shift is such that the vertical distance between the original and the new supply curve is the amount of the tax. The new supply curve is the red curve *S + tax*. The new supply curve intersects the demand curve at 300 million litres a day and €1.1 a litre. This situation is the new equilibrium after the imposition of the tax.

The excise tax creates a deadweight loss made up of the loss of consumer surplus and the loss of producer surplus, indicated by the two grey triangles in Figure 16.10. The value of that triangle is €30 million a day. Since 300 million litres of petrol are sold each day and since the tax is €0.6 a litre, total revenue from the petrol tax is €180 million a day (300 million litres multiplied by €0.6 a litre). Thus to raise tax revenue of €180 million a day using the petrol tax, a deadweight loss of €30 million a day – one-sixth of the tax revenue – is incurred.

One of the main influences on the deadweight loss arising from a tax is the elasticity of demand for the product. As the demand for petrol is fairly inelastic, when a tax is imposed the quantity demanded falls by a smaller percentage than the percentage rise in price.

To see the importance of the elasticity of demand, let's consider a different commodity – orange juice. To help make a direct comparison, let's assume that the orange juice market is exactly as big as the market for petrol. Figure 16.11 illustrates this market. The demand curve for orange juice is *D* and the supply curve is *S*. When orange juice is not taxed, the quantity of orange juice traded is 400 million litres a day and the price of orange juice is €0.6 a litre.

Now suppose that the government contemplates abolishing the petrol tax and taxing orange juice instead. The demand for orange juice is more elastic than the demand for petrol. It has many more good substitutes in the form of other fruit juices. The government wants to raise €180 million a day so that its total revenue is not affected by this tax change. The government's economists, armed with their statistical estimates of the demand and supply curves for orange juice that appear in Figure 16.11, work out that a tax of €0.9 a litre will do the job. This tax will shift the supply curve upward to the curve labelled *S + tax*. This new supply curve intersects the demand curve at a price of €1.3 pence a litre and at a quantity of 200 million litres a day. The price at which suppliers are willing to produce 200 million litres a day is €0.4 a litre. The government collects the required revenue of £180 million pounds a day – €0.9 a litre on 200 million litres a day.

But what is the deadweight loss in this case? The answer can be seen by looking at the grey triangle in

Figure 16.11

Why We Don't Tax Orange Juice

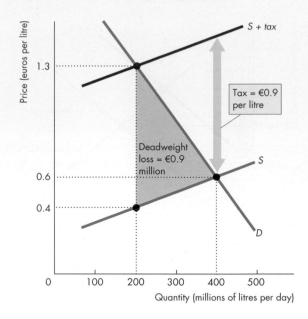

The demand curve for orange juice is *D* and the supply curve is *S*. The equilibrium price is €0.6 a litre and 400 million litres of juice a day are traded. To raise €180 million of tax revenue, a tax of €0.9 a litre will have to be imposed. The introduction of this tax shifts the supply curve to *S + tax*. The price rises to €1.3 a litre and the quantity bought and sold falls to 200 million litres a day. The deadweight loss is represented by the grey triangle and equals €90 million a day. The deadweight loss from taxing orange juice is much larger than that from taxing petrol (Figure 16.10) because the demand for orange juice is more elastic than the demand for petrol. Items that have a low elasticity of demand are taxed more heavily than items that have a high elasticity of demand.

Figure 16.11. The magnitude of that deadweight loss is £90 million. Notice how much bigger the deadweight loss is from taxing orange juice than that from taxing petrol. In the case of orange juice, the deadweight loss is one-half of the revenue raised, while in the case of petrol it is only one-sixth. What accounts for this difference? The supply curves and the initial pre-tax prices and quantities were identical in each case. The only difference is the elasticity of demand. In the case of petrol, the quantity demanded falls by only 25 per cent when the price almost doubles. In the case of orange juice, the quantity demanded falls by 50 per cent when the price only slightly more than doubles.

You can see why taxing orange juice is not on the political agenda of any of the major parties. Vote-seeking politicians seek out taxes that benefit the median voter. Other things remaining the same, this means that they try to minimize the deadweight loss of raising a given amount of revenue. Equivalently, they tax items with poor substitutes more heavily than items with close substitutes.

Value Added Tax

Value Added Tax (VAT) is a tax on goods and services, charged as a percentage of the value added at each stage of production. It is eventually paid by the consumer as a percentage of the final price. The European Union introduced VAT in all member states in 1969 to harmonize purchase taxes. It is levied on most goods and services although some have been granted temporary exemptions in some countries.

Unlike income tax, sales taxes like VAT are *regressive*. The reason they are regressive is that savings increase with income but sales taxes are paid on only the part of income that is spent.

Suppose, for example, that VAT is 15 per cent. A family with an income of €20,000 that spends all its income pays €3,000 VAT. Its average VAT rate is 15 per cent. A family with an income of €100,000 that spends €60,000 and saves €40,000 pays sales taxes of £9,000 (15 per cent of €60,000). So this family's average tax rate is 9 per cent.

We explained that a progressive income tax can be the outcome of a voting system that places a large weight on the views of the median voter. If VAT is regressive, why would a median voter support it?

People usually vote on general policy issues rather than specific issues. So regressive VAT may be voted for as part of an overall progressive tax policy. Governments also use VAT because it can make the whole tax system more efficient. The more goods that are taxed, the broader the tax base, and fewer untaxed goods are available as a substitute for taxed goods. The demand for taxed goods is more inelastic and hence the deadweight loss associated with higher rates of VAT is lower.

Review Quiz

◆ How do income taxes influence employment and efficiency? Why are income taxes progressive?
◆ Can parliament make employers pay a larger share of the social contributions from employment?
◆ Why do some localities have high taxes and high-quality public services and others have low taxes and low-quality public services?
◆ Why does the government impose excise taxes at high rates on goods that have a low elasticity of demand?

We looked at how government policy can help to relieve poverty and inequality in Chapter 15. In this chapter, we have looked at how government policy can reduce market failure by providing public goods. In the next two chapters, we are going to look more closely at government policy to overcome the other forms of market failure – monopoly and externalities.

Summary

Key Points

The Economic Theory of Government (pp. 341–343)

- Government policy is an attempt to cope with problems created by market failure – public goods, monopoly, externalities – and also the problems of economic inequality.

- Public choice theory is a model of the political marketplace in which voters, politicians and bureaucrats interact with each other.

Public Goods and the Free-rider Problem (pp. 343–349)

- A public good is a good or service that is consumed by everyone and that is non-rival and non-excludable.

- A public good creates a free-rider problem where no one has an incentive to pay for their share of the cost of providing the public good.

- The efficient level of provision of a public good maximizes the value of total benefit minus total cost – where marginal benefit equals marginal cost.

- Competition between political parties, each of which tries to appeal to the maximum number of voters, can lead to the efficient scale of provision of a public good and to both parties to proposing the same policies.

- Bureaucrats try to maximize their budgets, and if voters are rationally ignorant, producer interests may result in voting to support taxes that provide public goods in quantities that exceed those that maximize net benefit.

Taxes (pp. 349–355)

- Most government revenue comes from income taxes, property taxes, employment social contributions, excise taxes and VAT.

- Income taxes decrease the level of employment and create a deadweight loss.

- Taxes can be progressive (the average tax rate rises with income), proportional (the average tax rate is constant) or regressive (the average tax rate falls with income).

- Income taxes are progressive because this is in the interest of the median voter.

- Property taxes change both demand and supply and can result in high taxes and high-quality service areas and low tax and low-quality service areas.

- Social contributions from employment are paid by the employer and the employee in amounts that depend on the elasticities of demand and supply.

- Excise taxes at high rates on goods with inelastic demand create a smaller deadweight loss than would taxes on goods with more elastic demand.

Key Figures ◆

Key Terms

Problems

°1 You are provided with the following information about a sewage disposal system that a European city of 1 million people is considering installing:

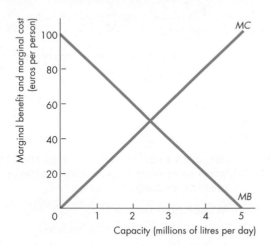

a What is the capacity that achieves maximum net benefit?

b How much will each person have to pay in taxes to pay for the efficient capacity level?

c What is the political equilibrium if voters are well informed?

d What is the political equilibrium if voters are rationally ignorant and bureaucrats achieve the highest attainable budget?

2 You are provided with the following information about a government control policy:

Marginal quantity (km² sprayed per day)	Marginal cost (euros per day)	Marginal benefit (euros per day)
0	0	0
1	1,000	5,000
2	2,000	4,000
3	3,000	3,000
4	4,000	2,000
5	5,000	1,000

a What is the quantity of spraying that achieves maximum net benefit?

b What is the total tax revenue needed to pay for the efficient quantity of spraying?

c What is the political equilibrium if voters are well informed?

d What is the political equilibrium if voters are rationally ignorant and bureaucrats achieve the highest attainable budget?

°3 An economy has two groups of people, A and B. The population consists of 80 per cent A-types and 20 per cent B-types. A-types have a perfectly elastic supply of labour at a wage rate of €10 an hour. B-types have a perfectly inelastic supply of labour and their equilibrium wage rate is €100 an hour.

a What kinds of tax arrangements do you predict this economy will adopt?

b Analyse the labour market in this economy and explain what will happen to the wage rates and employment levels of the two groups when the taxes you predict in your answer to part (a) are introduced.

4 Suppose that in the economy described in problem 3, the proportion of A-types was 20 per cent and the proportion of B-types was 80 per cent. Everything else remains the same.

a Now what kinds of tax arrangements do you predict the economy will adopt?

b Analyse the labour market in this economy and explain what will happen to the wage rates and employment levels of the two groups when the taxes you predict in your answer to part (a) are introduced.

c Compare the economy in problem 3 with the economy in this problem. Which economy more closely resembles our actual economy?

°5 An economy has a competitive labour market, which is described by the following demand schedule and supply schedule:

Wage rate (euros per hour)	Quantity demanded (hours per week)	Quantity supplied (hours per week)
20	0	50
16	15	40
12	30	30
8	45	20
4	60	10
0	75	0

a What are the equilibrium wage rate and hours of work done?

b If an employment contribution of €4 an hour is imposed on employers:

   i What is the new wage rate?

   ii How many hours are worked?

   iii What is the after-tax wage rate?

   iv What is the tax revenue?

   v What is the deadweight loss?

6 In the economy described in problem 5, the employment contribution on employers is eliminated and a new employment contribution of €4 an hour is imposed on employees.

  a What is the new wage rate?

  b How many hours are worked?

  c What is the after-tax wage rate?

  d What is the tax revenue?

  e What is the deadweight loss?

  f Compare the situation in problem 5 with that in this problem and explain the similarities and differences in the two situations.

•7 In a competitive market for biscuits:

Price (euros per kilogram)	Quantity demanded (kilograms per month)	Quantity supplied (kilograms per month)
10	0	28
8	4	24
6	8	20
4	12	16
2	16	12

  a Find the equilibrium price and quantity.

  b If biscuits are taxed €2 a kilogram:

   i What is the new price of biscuits?

   ii What is the new quantity bought?

8 In the competitive market for biscuits in problem 7, the government wants to change the tax on a kilogram of biscuits so that it brings in the greatest possible amount of revenue.

  a What is that tax rate?

  b What is the new price of biscuits?

  c What is the new quantity bought?

  d What is the tax revenue?

  e What is the deadweight loss?

Critical Thinking

1 Read the story in Reading Between the Lines on the Parkin, Powell and Matthews website on 'Bringing Business to the Public Sector' and then answer the following questions:

   a How will targets help to make ministers and bureaucrats more accountable?

   b How will targets help to make the government sector more efficient?

   c Why might targets fail to measure the performance of the government sector? Use the example of setting targets for school grade achievement to answer this question.

2 Use the Parkin, Powell and Matthews website to obtain data on UK government expenditure.

   a Which government department accounts for the majority of expenditure?

   b What proportion of government expenditure is spent on goods and services, rather than transfers such as benefits and transfers?

   c What percentage of government expenditure is spent on each of the following: health, social security and defence?

   d What proportion of government revenue is generated by tax receipts?

3 Use the Parkin, Powell and Matthews website to find out what happened in the last UK budget.

   a By how much did government raise tax on cigarettes, wines and beer?

   b What reasons did government give for raising these excise taxes?

   c What reasons have been given for changes in tax credits?

   d What areas of expenditure have been increased or decreased and what reasons are given for the change?

Excise Tax: European Taxes on Music Tracks

THE BBC NEWS ONLINE, 17 JANUARY 2001

A tax on music tracks

Mark Ward

French musicians and movie makers who lose royalties because of digital piracy are to be compensated for the money they have lost.

Next month, the French Government will impose taxes on blank CDs and other recordable storage media in a bid to recoup some of the losses when people copy rather than pay for music, images or film.

Initially it was considering extending the tax to cover hard disks, set-top boxes and advanced video recorders, but protests have prompted it to scrap them.

The French action follows a similar move by the German Government, which imposed a levy on computers at the beginning of the year. This year Denmark also started imposing taxes on blank CDs.

Many European nations, with the exception of the UK and Luxembourg, impose 'artist taxes' on video and audio tapes. The money generated is used to recompense artists losing royalties because people are copying rather than buying their work.

But the march of new technology is reducing the pot of cash generated by these taxes as people turn to new media . . . So far only France and Germany are tackling the problem by extending the scope of existing taxes . . . France . . . sees a significant decline in tax revenue from tapes. In 1994, this tax produced about 750m FF (£73 million); last year the figure slumped to 450m FF (£43 million) . . .

The government was considering whether to extend the tax to other devices that could be used to record music and movies . . . The plan was condemned by the French electronics industry, which threatened to take its protest to the highest court in the land . . . because it penalised everyone, rather than just those pirating music and movies.

The Essence of the Story

- The French Government is introducing a tax on blank CDs, recordable DVDs and MP3 players in a bid to repay musicians for the income they lose from illegal copying.

- The French action follows similar moves in Germany and Denmark. The UK and Luxembourg are the only EU states that do not impose 'artists taxes' of some form.

- The French action was prompted by a significant fall in the revenue earned from its tax on blank audio tapes.

- The French electronics industry is strongly opposed to the tax because it penalizes everyone, not just the copy pirates.

Economic Analysis

- The market for French audio tapes is shown in Figure 1. The demand for tapes in 1994 is D_{94} and the supply of tapes is S. The price of tapes is P_0 and Q_0 tapes are sold.

- The French tax on audio tapes is an excise tax. A tax of t per tape shifts the supply of tapes to $S + tax$ as shown in Figure 1. The French government gains a revenue of 750 FF shown by the blue area.

- The introduction of new media such as recordable CDs, mini-disks and DVDs, provides substitutes for audio tapes. Increasing the number of substitutes increases the elasticity of demand for audio tapes.

- Figure 2 shows the market for French audio tapes in 2000. Demand in 2000 is D_{00}, which is more elastic than D_{94} as shown by its relatively shallow slope. With the same tax per tape, the quantity of tapes sold decreases from Q_1 to Q_2, and the price falls from P_1 to P_2.

- Revenue from the audio tape tax falls to 450 FF, shown as the blue area in Figure 2, because demand is more elastic.

- The deadweight loss in Figures 1 and 2 is shown as the grey area. The grey area in Figure 1 is smaller than the equivalent area in Figure 2. The efficiency of the audio tape tax is therefore higher in 1994 than in 2000 because the same tax per tape is applied to a more elastic market demand.

- The revenue raised from the new tax on CDs and DVDs will be determined by the elasticity of demand for these goods. The tax will only generate sufficient revenue and remain relatively efficient while demand is inelastic.

- Overall artist taxes will only be efficient if the revenue generated adequately compensates musicians for the value of surplus lost through piracy, without generating high deadweight losses or high compliance and administration costs.

- French producers dislike the tax because they lose producer surplus as a result. They also consider artist taxes to be unfair as they transfer surplus from consumers who don't pirate to consumers who do.

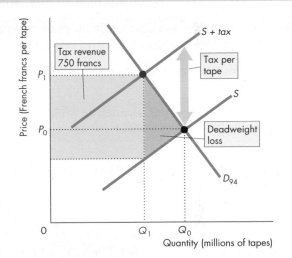

Figure 1 Tape tax in 1994

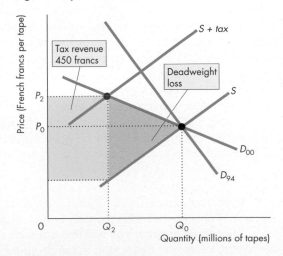

Figure 2 Tape tax in 2000

CHAPTER 17

Regulation and Competition

After studying this chapter you will be able to:

◆ Define regulation, public ownership and laws designed to promote competition

◆ Distinguish between the public interest and capture theories of regulation

◆ Explain how regulation affects prices, outputs, profits and the distribution of the gains from trade between consumers and producers

◆ Explain how monopoly control laws are applied in the European Union and in the United Kingdom

◆ Explain how public ownership affects prices, output and allocative efficiency

Public Interest or Special Interest

When you consume water, electric power, natural gas, or telephone services you buy from a regulated local monopoly. Why and how are the industries that produce these goods and services regulated? Do the regulations work in the public interest – the interest of all consumers and producers – or do they serve special interests – the interests – of particular groups of consumers or producers? ◆ Regulation extends beyond monopoly to oligopoly. For example, until 1987, the price of tickets and the routes that airlines could fly throughout Europe were regulated to create a cartel. EU member states agreed to deregulate airline routes in 1997 to free up access to European routes and promote cut-price tickets. Similarly Europe's electricity industry has been deregulated to promote new competition. Why do we regulate and then deregulate some industries? ◆ Europe's Competition Commissioner, Mario Monti, is regularly cited in the newspapers, as Europe's firms and industries are investigated for anti-competitive practices. European rail monopolies, pharmaceutical markets, and music markets all came under scrutiny in 2001. What are anti-monopoly laws and whose interest do they serve? ◆ After 1945, many monopolies, flagship firms and major industries were bought by governments. Since 1979, many of these have been privatized. Why do governments buy up firms and industries and then sell them off?

◆ ◆ ◆ ◆ This chapter examines government regulation. You will draw on your knowledge of consumer and producer surplus to study how consumers and producers redistribute the gains from trade in the political marketplace. You will find out who stands to gain and who stands to lose from government intervention. We end by looking at the progress of deregulation and privatization in Europe's electricity and gas markets in Reading Between the Lines on pp. 380–381.

Market Intervention

The government intervenes in monopolistic and oligopolistic markets to influence prices, quantities produced and the distribution of the gains from economic activity. It intervenes in three main ways:

1 Regulation.
2 Monopoly control laws.
3 Pubic ownership.

Regulation

Regulation consists of rules administered by a government agency to influence economic activity by determining prices, product standards and types, and the conditions under which new firms may enter an industry. Price and entry condition regulations are typically applied at the industry level to banking and financial services, telecommunications, gas and electricity suppliers, railways, airlines and buses. Regulation is also widely applied at the product level and is constantly developing. The identification of genetically modified food products is a recent area of regulation development at the European Union level. But as more regulation develops at one level, there is a tendency to deregulate at another level.

Deregulation is the process of removing restrictions on prices, product standards and types, and entry conditions. In recent years, the European Union has enforced deregulation to increase competition in Europe's airways, transport systems and telecommunications services. The most important deregulation at the European Union level was the removal of border controls to create the Single European Market and cross-border competition.

Monopoly Control

Monopoly control law regulates and prohibits certain kinds of market behaviour, such as monopoly and monopolistic practices. European firms suspected of gaining monopoly power through creating barriers to entry, colluding over prices, or through merger activity, can be investigated under European Union law or under the laws of particular member states. Individual member states have their own monopoly control laws, but all are subject to European Union law.

To understand why government intervenes to control monopoly and to examine the impact of this intervention, we need to identify the gains and losses that these actions create. These gains and losses are the consumer and producer surpluses associated with different levels of output and prices.

Public Ownership

After the Second World War, many European governments took a wide range of industries and firms into public ownership. Typically, gas, electricity generation, transport, iron, steel and coal industries came into public ownership through compulsory purchase. Governments also bought some firms through direct dealings on the stock market because of their importance to the economy and others because they were struggling under intense international competition. However, most European governments are now in the process of privatizing firms and industries in public ownership. **Privatization**, in this context, means the sale of assets in government ownership to the private sector.

We'll start with the economic theory of regulation.

Economic Theory of Regulation

The economic theory of regulation is part of the broader theory of public choice explained in Chapter 16. Here, we apply the public choice theory to regulation. We'll examine the demand for government actions, the supply of those actions and the political equilibrium that emerges.

Demand for Regulation

The *demand for regulation* is expressed through political activity – voting, lobbying and making campaign contributions. But engaging in political activity is costly and people demand political action only if the benefit that they individually receive from such action exceeds their individual costs in obtaining the action. The four main factors that affect the demand for regulation are:

◆ Consumer surplus per buyer.
◆ Number of buyers.
◆ Producer surplus per firm.
◆ Number of firms.

The larger the consumer surplus per buyer resulting from regulation, the greater is the demand for regulation by buyers. Also, as the number of buyers increases, so does the demand for regulation. But numbers alone do not necessarily translate into an effective political force. The larger the number of buyers, the greater is the cost of organizing them, so the demand for regulation does not increase proportionately with the number of buyers.

The larger the producer surplus per firm arising from a particular regulation, the larger is the demand for that regulation by firms. Also, as the number of firms that might benefit from some regulation increases, so does the demand for that regulation. But again, as in the case of consumers, large numbers do not necessarily mean an effective political force. The larger the number of firms, the greater is the cost of organizing them.

For a given level of consumer or producer surplus, the smaller the number of households or firms which share that surplus, the larger is the demand for the regulation that creates it.

Supply of Regulation

Regulation is supplied by politicians and bureaucrats. According to public choice theory, politicians choose policies that appeal to a majority of voters, thereby enabling themselves to achieve and maintain office. Bureaucrats support policies that maximize their budgets (see Chapter 16, pp. 347–348). Given these objectives, the *supply of regulation* depends on the following factors:

◆ Consumer surplus per buyer.

◆ Producer surplus per firm.

◆ The number of persons affected.

The larger the consumer surplus per buyer or producer surplus per firm generated, and the larger the number of persons affected by a regulation, the greater is the tendency for politicians to supply that regulation. Politicians are most likely to supply regulation that benefits a large number of people by a large amount per person. They are also likely to supply regulation that benefits a small number of people when the benefit per person is large and the cost is spread widely and not easily identified. But they are unlikely to supply a regulation that brings a small benefit per person.

Political Equilibrium

In a political equilibrium, no interest group feels it is worthwhile to use additional resources to press for

changes, and no group of politicians plans to offer different regulations. Being in a *political equilibrium* is not the same thing as everyone being in agreement. Some interest groups devote resources to trying to change regulations that are already in place; others devote resources to maintaining the existing regulations. But no one will feel it is worthwhile to *increase* the resources they are devoting to such activities. Also, political parties might not agree with each other. Some support the existing regulations and others propose different regulations. In equilibrium, no one wants to change the proposals that they are making.

What will a political equilibrium look like? The answer depends on whether the regulation serves the public interest or the interest of the producer. Let's look at these two possibilities.

Public Interest Theory

Public interest theory maintains that regulations are supplied to satisfy the demand of consumers and producers to maximize total surplus – that is, to attain allocative efficiency. Public interest theory implies that the political process relentlessly seeks out deadweight loss and introduces regulations that eliminate it. For example, where monopoly practices exist, the political process will introduce price regulations to ensure that outputs increase and prices fall to their competitive levels.

Capture Theory

Capture theory maintains that regulations are supplied to satisfy the demand of producers to maximize producer surplus – that is, to maximize economic profit. The key idea of capture theory is that the cost of regulation is high and only those regulations that increase the surplus of small, easily identified groups and that have low organization costs are supplied by the political process. Consumers bear the cost of this regulation but the costs are spread so thinly and widely that they go unnoticed and do not affect votes.

The predictions of the capture theory are less clear cut than the predictions of the public interest theory. According to capture theory, regulations benefit cohesive interest groups by large and visible amounts and impose small costs on everyone else. But these costs are so small, in per person terms, that no one feels it is worthwhile to incur the cost of organizing an interest group to avoid them. To make these predictions concrete enough to be useful, the capture theory needs a model of the costs of political organization.

Whichever theory of regulation is correct, according to public choice theory, the political system delivers amounts and types of regulations that best further the electoral success of politicians. Because producer-oriented and consumer-oriented regulation are in conflict with each other, the political process can't satisfy both groups in any particular industry. Only one group can win. This makes the regulatory actions of government a bit like a unique good – for example, a painting by Rembrandt. There is only one original and it will be sold to just one buyer. Normally, a unique commodity is sold through an auction; the highest bidder takes the prize. Equilibrium in the regulatory process can be thought of in much the same way: the suppliers of regulation will satisfy the demands of the higher bidder. If the producer demand offers a bigger return to the politicians, either directly through votes or indirectly through political contributions, then the producers' interests will be served. If the consumer demand translates into a larger number of votes, then the consumers' interests will be served by regulation.

Review Quiz

◆ How do consumers and producers express their demand for regulation? What are their objectives? What are the costs of expressing a demand for regulation?

◆ When politicians and bureaucrats supply regulation, what are they trying to achieve? Do politicians and bureaucrats have the same objectives? Explain your answer.

◆ What is a political equilibrium? When does the political equilibrium achieve economic efficiency. When does the political equilibrium serve the interests of producers? When do the bureaucrats win?

We have now completed our study of the theory of regulation in the marketplace. We now turn our attention to the regulations that exist in our economy today. Which of these regulations are in the public interest and which are in the interests of producers?

Regulation and Deregulation

The past 20 years have seen dramatic changes in the way in which European economies are regulated by government. We're going to examine some of these changes. To begin we'll look at what is regulated and also at the scope of regulation. Then we'll turn to the regulatory process itself and examine how regulators control prices and other aspects of market behaviour. Finally, we'll tackle the more difficult and controversial questions. Why do we regulate some things but not others? Who benefits from this regulation – consumers or producers?

The Scope of Regulation

Table 17.1 shows some of the main regulatory agencies that operate in the United Kingdom. At the top are institutions created by agreement among countries. These institutions regulate firms indirectly by restricting government protection of domestic industry. The World Trade Organization (WTO) oversees and monitors agreements to reduce tariffs and aims to avoid tariff wars among its 124 participating countries. Below this are the Directorates General of the European Commission. The European Commission is responsible for ensuring its member states comply with EU-level regulation of industries and markets, based on its legal Treaties. EU directives control many aspects of business activity both directly and indirectly. For example, EU directives determine standards of production and marketing, the pricing of agricultural products, employment practices, health and safety, industrial pollution, monopoly power, collusive practices and mergers.

Firms are also subject to general and specific regulation by agencies at the national level. Some regulatory agencies cover all industries, for example, the Health and Safety Executive and the Environment Agency. Other agencies regulate specific activities within specific industries, such as in OFGEM and OFWAT. Local and regional governments, may also regulate firms, for example in relation to waste management and building planning regulations. Many firms are also subject to voluntary regulation by professional and industrial organizations, such as the British Medical Association.

The Regulatory Process

Although regulatory agencies vary in size and scope and in the detailed aspects of economic life that they control, there are certain features common to all agencies.

First, the bureaucrats, who are the key decision makers in the main regulatory agencies, are appointed

Table 17.1 Regulatory Agencies

Level	Agency	Activity
Global	World Trade Organization	Monitors and enforces rules on tariff agreements
European Union	European Commission	Monitors and enforces rules on member states
UK National Government	Departments/Ministries	Monitor and control public provision in health, agriculture, industry, education, and so on
◆ General	Monopolies and Mergers Commission	Investigates monopoly and recommends action
	Health and Safety Executive	Investigates breaches of health and safety law
	Environment Agency	Monitors and enforces environmental law
	Finance and Securities Agency	Regulates financial investment firms and other financial agencies
	Bank of England	Regulates banks and building societies and enforces monetary policy
	Civil Aviation Authority	Monitors and regulates airlines, airports and air-traffic control
◆ Specific	OFGEM	Monitors and regulates gas and electricity markets
	Office of Gas and Electricity Markets	
	OFWAT	Monitors and regulates water companies
	Office of Water Services	
Local and Regional Government	Departments	Control and monitor planning, waste management, etc.
Industry	Professional organizations	Control and monitor participating industries

by central and local governments. In addition, all agencies have a permanent bureaucracy made up of experts in the industry being regulated, who are often recruited from the regulated firms. Agencies are allocated financial resources by government to cover the costs of their operations.

Second, each agency adopts a set of practices or operating rules for controlling prices and other aspects of economic or professional performance. We will concentrate on the main agencies and on industry-specific economic regulation. These rules and practices are based on well-defined physical and financial accounting procedures that are quite easy to administer and to monitor.

In a regulated industry, individual firms are usually free to determine the technology that they will use in production. The exceptions are those industries whose production technology is regulated by the Environment Agency. Regulation usually involves limiting the power of firms to determine one or more of the following: the price of output, the quantities sold, the quality of the product, or the markets served. The regulatory agency grants certification to a company to serve a particular market with a particular line of products, and it determines the level and structure of prices that will be charged. In some cases, the

agency also determines the scale and quality of output permitted.

To analyse the way in which industry-specific regulation works, it is convenient to distinguish between the regulation of natural monopoly and the regulation of cartels. Let's begin with natural monopoly.

Natural Monopoly

Natural monopoly was defined in Chapter 12 (p. 242) as an industry in which one firm can supply the entire market at a lower price than can two or more firms. As a consequence, a natural monopoly experiences economies of scale, no matter how high an output rate it achieves. Examples of natural monopolies include telephone and cable companies, local electricity and water companies, and rail infrastructure. It is much more expensive to have two or more competing sets of wires, pipes and railway lines serving every area than it is to have a single set. (What is a natural monopoly changes over time as technology changes. With the introduction of fibre optic cables, both telephone companies and cable television companies can compete with each other in both markets, so what was once a natural monopoly is becoming a more competitive industry.)

Figure 17.1
Natural Monopoly: Marginal Cost Pricing

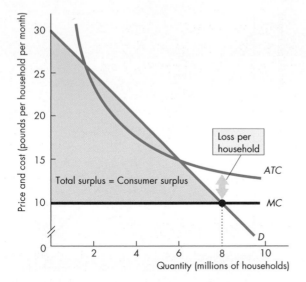

A natural monopoly is an industry in which average total cost is falling even when the entire market demand is satisfied. A cable TV operator faces the demand curve *D*. The firm's marginal cost is constant at £10 per household per month, as shown by the curve *MC*. Fixed costs are large and the average total cost curve, which includes average fixed cost, is shown as *ATC*. A marginal cost pricing rule that maximizes total surplus sets the price at £10 a month, with 8 million households being served. It also maximizes consumer surplus, shown as the green area. The firm incurs a loss on each household, indicated by the red arrow. To remain in business, the cable operator must either price discriminate or receive a subsidy.

Let's consider the example of UK cable TV, which is shown in Figure 17.1. The demand curve for cable TV is *D*. The cable TV company's marginal cost curve is *MC*. That marginal cost curve is (assumed to be) horizontal at £10 per household per month – that is, the cost of providing each additional household with a month of cable programming is £10. The cable company has a heavy investment in satellite receiving dishes, cables and control equipment and so has high fixed costs. These fixed costs are part of the company's average total cost curve, shown as *ATC*. The average total cost curve slopes downward because as the number of households served increases, the fixed cost is spread over a larger number of households. (If you need to refresh your memory on how the average total cost curve is calculated, take a quick look back at Chapter 10, pp. 203–204.)

Regulation in the Public Interest

How will cable TV be regulated according to the public interest theory? It is regulated to maximize total surplus, which occurs if marginal cost equals price. As you can see in Figure 17.1, that outcome occurs if the price is regulated at £10 per household per month and if 8 million households are served. Such a regulation is called a marginal cost pricing rule. A **marginal cost pricing rule** sets price equal to marginal cost. It maximizes total surplus and consumer surplus in the regulated industry.

A natural monopoly that is regulated to set price equal to marginal cost incurs an economic loss. Because its average total cost curve is falling, marginal cost is below average total cost. Because price equals marginal cost, price is below average total cost. Average total cost minus price is the loss per unit produced. It's pretty obvious that a cable TV operator that is required to use a marginal cost pricing rule will not stay in business for long. How can a company cover its costs and, at the same time, obey a marginal cost pricing rule?

One possibility is price discrimination. Some natural monopolies can fairly easily price discriminate using a two-part tariff that gives consumers a bill for connection and a bill for units used. For example, a gas supply company can charge consumers a monthly fee for being connected to the gas supply and then charge a price equal to marginal cost for each unit of gas supplied. A cable TV operator can price discriminate by charging a one-time connection fee that covers its fixed cost and then charging a monthly fee equal to marginal cost.

But a natural monopoly cannot always price discriminate. It is difficult to operate a two-part tariff on a rail network. When a natural monopoly cannot price discriminate, it can cover its total cost and follow a marginal cost pricing rule only if it receives a subsidy from the government. In this case, the government raises the revenue for the subsidy by taxing some other activity. But as we saw in Chapter 16, taxes themselves generate deadweight loss. Thus the deadweight loss resulting from additional taxes must be offset against the allocative efficiency gained by forcing the natural monopoly to adopt a marginal cost pricing rule.

The deadweight loss could be minimized if government allows the natural monopoly to cover its costs rather than using a subsidy from a tax on some other sector of the economy. This form of regulation is called an average cost pricing rule. An **average cost pricing rule** sets price equal to average total cost. Figure 17.2

Figure 17.2 ◆

Natural Monopoly: Average Cost Pricing

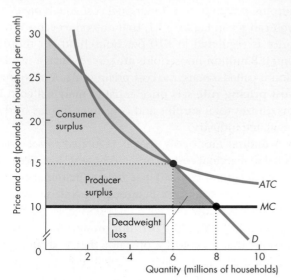

Average cost pricing sets price equal to average total cost. The cable TV operator charges £15 a month and serves 6 million households. In this situation the firm breaks even – average total cost equals price. Deadweight loss, shown by the grey triangle, is generated. Consumer surplus is reduced to the green area.

Figure 17.3 ◆

Natural Monopoly: Profit Maximization

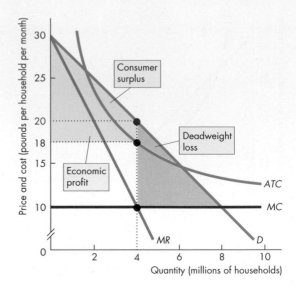

The cable TV operator would like to maximize profit. To do so, marginal revenue (*MR*) is made equal to marginal cost. At a price of £20 a month, 4 million households buy cable services. Consumer surplus is reduced to the green triangle. The deadweight loss increases to the grey triangle. The monopoly makes the profit shown by the blue rectangle. If the producer can capture the regulator, the outcome will be the situation shown here.

shows the average cost pricing solution. The cable TV operator charges £15 a month and serves 6 million households. A deadweight loss arises, which is shown by the grey triangle in the figure, but consumer surplus is less than under marginal cost pricing regulation.

Capturing the Regulator

What does the capture theory predict about the regulation of this industry? According to the capture theory, the producer gets the regulator to set rules that serve the interests of the producer. The producer's interests are served by being allowed to operate at the same output and price as an unregulated monopoly. In Figure 17.3, the monopoly's marginal revenue curve is *MR*. Marginal revenue equals marginal cost when output is 4 million households and the price is £20 a month. At this output, the producer maximizes profit. So regulation in the interest of the producer maintains the unregulated monopoly outcome.

But how does the producer capture the regulator to achieve the monopoly profit-maximizing outcome? To answer this question, we need to look at the way

agencies determine a regulated price. A key method used is called rate of return regulation.

Rate of Return Regulation

Rate of return regulation determines a regulated price by setting the price at a level that enables the regulated firm to earn a specified target percentage return on its capital. The target rate of return is determined with reference to what is normal in competitive industries. This rate of return is part of the opportunity cost of the natural monopolist and is included in the firm's average total cost. By examining the firm's total cost, including the normal rate of return on capital, the regulator attempts to determine the price at which average total cost is covered. Thus rate of return regulation is equivalent to average cost pricing.

In Figure 17.2, average cost pricing results at a regulated price of £15 a month with 6 million households being served. Thus rate of return regulation, based on a correct assessment of the producer's average total cost curve, results in a price and quantity that favour the consumer and do not enable the producer to maximize monopoly profit. The special interest group will have failed to capture the regulator and the outcome will be closer to that predicted by the public interest theory of regulation.

But there is a feature of many real-world situations that the above analysis does not take into account – the ability of the monopoly firm to mislead the regulator about its true costs.

Inflating Costs

The managers of a regulated firm might be able to inflate the firm's costs by spending part of its revenue on inputs that are not strictly required for the production of the good. By this device, the firm's apparent cost curves exceed the true cost curves. This is sometimes called X-inefficiency. On-the-job luxury in the form of sumptuous office suites, expensive company cars, free football match tickets (disguised as public relations expenses), lavish international travel and entertainment are all ways in which managers can inflate costs.

If the managers of the cable firm inflate costs and persuade the regulator that the firm's true cost curve is that shown as *ATC (inflated)* in Figure 17.4, then the regulator, applying the normal rate of return principle, will regulate the price at £20 a month. In this example, the price and quantity will be the same as in an unregulated monopoly. It might be impossible for firms to inflate their costs by as much as that shown in the figure. But to the extent that costs can be inflated, the apparent average total cost curve lies somewhere between the true *ATC* curve and *ATC (inflated)*. The greater the ability of the firm to pad its costs in this way, the closer its profit (measured in economic terms) approaches the maximum possible. The shareholders of this firm don't receive this economic profit because it gets used up in football match tickets, luxury offices and the other actions taken by the firm's managers to inflate the firm's costs.

Public Interest or Capture?

It is not clear whether actual regulation produces prices and quantities that more closely correspond with the predictions of capture theory or public interest theory. One thing is clear, however, price regulation does not require natural monopolies to use the marginal cost pricing rule. If it did, most natural monopolies would make losses and receive hefty

Figure 17.4

Natural Monopoly: Inflating Costs

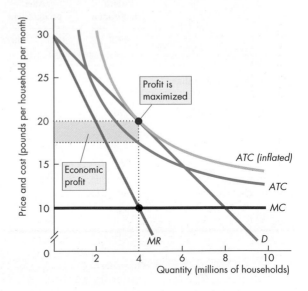

If the cable TV operator is able to inflate its costs to *ATC* (inflated) and persuade the regulator that these are genuine minimum costs of production, rate of return regulation results in a price of £20 a month – the profit-maximizing price. To the extent that the producer can inflate costs above average total cost, the price rises, output falls and deadweight loss increases. The profit is captured by the managers, not the shareholders (owners) of the firm.

government subsidies to enable them to remain in business. But there are even exceptions to this conclusion. For example, many telecommunications companies do not appear to use marginal cost pricing for telephone calls. They cover total cost by charging a flat fee each month for being connected to the telephone system and then charge each call at its marginal cost.

A test of whether natural monopoly regulation is in the public interest or the interest of the producer is to examine the rates of return earned by regulated natural monopolies. If these rates of return are significantly higher than those in the rest of the economy, then, to some degree, the regulator may have been captured by the producer. If the rates of return in the regulated monopoly industries are similar to those in the rest of the economy, then we cannot tell, for sure, whether the regulator has been captured or not for we cannot know the extent to which costs have been inflated by the managers of the regulated firms.

Table 17.2 Rates of Return in Monopolies

	Before privatization	After privatization	
	1979	1990	1992
		(percentage)	
Regulated natural monopolies			
British Gas	5	6	7
British Telecommunications	14	24	21
Other monopolies			
British Steel	3	18	1
British Airways	14	24	12

Source: D. Parker, 'Privatization and Business Restructuring: Change and Continuity in the Privatized Industries', *The Review of Policy Issues*, 1994, 1 (2).

It is difficult to assess regulatory capture in the United Kingdom because all the regulated natural monopolies were under government ownership in the 1970s and 1980s. All were privatized in the 1990s and there is insufficient evidence to make a meaningful comparison. Table 17.2 compares the rates of return on assets before and after privatization. Two of the monopolies are natural monopolies and were subject to regulation after privatization. Rates of return had improved in all the monopolies by 1990. The improvement was small in the case of the regulated natural monopoly, gas, and the improvement was cut back substantially by 1992 in the case of the non-regulated monopoly, steel.

The evidence on capture in Table 17.2 is inconclusive. However, the regulatory agencies of the privatized monopolies have tried to avoid capture by setting annual price caps which make the *real prices* of the monopoly's output fall over time. Price caps force monopolies to cut costs continuously. They are also simple to apply and so reduce regulatory costs. Overall, it seems likely that these regulations have been in the public interest.

After privatizatation, most government monopolies became industries with an oligopoly structure. Oligopoly is also regulated. So now we turn to regulation in oligopolistic industries – the regulation of cartels.

Cartel Regulation

A *cartel* is a collusive agreement among a number of firms designed to restrict output and achieve a higher profit for the cartel's members. Cartels are illegal in the United Kingdom, the European Union and most other countries. But international cartels can sometimes operate legally, such as the international cartel of oil producers known as OPEC (the Organization of Petroleum Exporting Countries).

Illegal cartels can arise in oligopolistic industries. An oligopoly is a market structure in which a small number of firms compete with each other. We studied oligopoly (and duopoly – two firms competing for a market) in Chapter 13. There we saw that if firms manage to collude and behave like a monopoly, they can set the same price and sell the same total quantity as a monopoly firm would. But we also discovered that in such a situation, each firm will be tempted to 'cheat', increasing its own output and profit at the expense of the other firms. The result of such 'cheating' on the collusive agreement is the unravelling of the monopoly equilibrium and the emergence of a competitive outcome with zero economic profit for producers. Such an outcome benefits consumers at the expense of producers.

How is oligopoly regulated? Does regulation prevent monopoly practices or does it encourage those practices?

According to public interest theory, oligopoly is regulated to ensure a competitive outcome. Consider, for example, the market for road haulage of carrots from East Anglia to Yorkshire in the United Kingdom, illustrated in Figure 17.5. The demand curve for trips is *D*. The industry marginal cost curve – and the competitive supply curve – is *MC*. Public interest regulation will regulate the price of a trip at £20 and there will be 300 trips a week.

How would this industry be regulated according to the capture theory? Regulation that is in the producer interest will maximize profit. To find the outcome in this case, we need to determine the price and quantity when marginal cost equals marginal revenue. The marginal revenue curve is *MR*. So marginal cost equals marginal revenue at 200 trips a week. The price of a trip is £30.

One way of achieving this outcome is to place an output limit on each firm in the industry. If there are 10 haulage companies, an output limit of 20 trips per company ensures that the total number of trips in a week is 200. Penalties can be imposed to ensure that no single producer exceeds its output limit.

All the firms in the industry would support this type of regulation because it helps to prevent cheating and to maintain a monopoly outcome. Each firm

Figure 17.5

Collusive Oligopoly

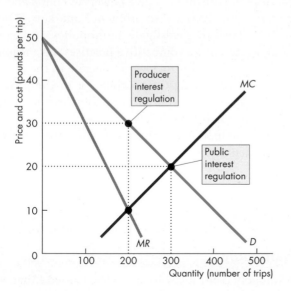

Ten road haulage firms transport carrots from East Anglia to Yorkshire. The demand curve is *D* and the industry marginal cost curve is *MC*. Under competition, the *MC* curve is the industry supply curve. If the industry is competitive, the price of a trip will be £20 and 300 trips will be made each week. Producers will demand regulation that restricts entry and limits output to 200 trips a week. This regulation raises the price to £30 a trip and results in each producer making maximum profit – as if it were a monopoly. Industry marginal revenue is equal to industry marginal cost.

knows that without effectively enforced production quotas every firm has an incentive to increase output. (For each firm, price exceeds marginal cost so a greater output brings a larger profit.) So each firm wants a method of preventing output from rising above the industry profit-maximizing level and the quotas enforced by regulation achieve this end. With this type of cartel regulation, the regulator enables a cartel to operate legally and in its own best interest.

What does cartel regulation do in practice? Although there is disagreement about the matter, the consensus view is that regulation tends to favour the producer. Regulating taxis (by local authorities) and airlines (by the Civil Aviation Authority) are specific examples in which profits of producers increased as a result of regulation.

Making Predictions

Most industries have a few producers and many consumers. In these cases, public choice theory predicts that regulation will protect producer interests because a small number of people stand to gain a large amount and so they will be fairly easy to organize as a cohesive lobby. Under such circumstances, politicians will be rewarded with political contributions rather than votes. But there are situations in which the consumer interest is sufficiently strong and well-organized and thus able to prevail. There are also cases in which the balance switches from producer to consumer, as seen in the deregulation process that began in the late 1970s.

Deregulation raises some hard questions for economists seeking to understand and make predictions about regulation. Why were were so many sectors deregulated across Europe in the 1980 and 1990s? If producers gained from regulation and if the producer lobby was strong enough to achieve regulation, what happened in the 1980s to change the equilibrium to one in which the consumer interest prevailed? We do not have a complete answer to this question at the present time. But regulation had become so costly to consumers, and the potential benefits to them from deregulation so great, that the cost of organizing the consumer voice became a price worth paying.

One factor that increased the cost of regulation borne by consumers in the airline sector, eventually bringing deregulation, was the large increase in energy prices in the 1970s. These price hikes made route regulation extremely costly and changed the balance in favour of consumers in the political equilibrium. Another factor was technological change. This also affected the airline sector, but many other sectors such as finance and telecommunications. Computerized accounts, automatic tellers, satellite communications and mobile phones all made smaller producers able to offer low-cost services, forcing deregulation.

In the case of EU airlines, most member states allowed only two airlines on any one route, and regulated fares and traffic in such a way that airlines could not compete. These restrictions were lifted in 1997 to encourage competition. Now, airlines from one European country can launch domestic services in another. Ryanair and EasyJet operate dramatic cut-price services, making economic profits when the big flag ship carriers face economic losses. How is it done? These airlines use direct telephone sales technology, pick the cheapest airports to run from, cut red tape and can adopt a 'no frills' service approach.

REMEMBER SANDERS
THIS IS ONE OF THE NEW
CUT-PRICE, NO-FRILLS,
MINIMUM SERVICE AIRLINES

© Nick Baker, *Financial Times*, 18 December 1995.

Customers get what they pay for, as you can see in the cartoon, but low quality is accepted on short haul flights. If rapid technological change continues, we could expect to see more consumer-oriented regulation in future.

Review Quiz

◆ Why does a natural monopoly need to be regulated?

◆ What pricing rule enables a natural monopoly to operate in the public interest?

◆ Why is a marginal cost pricing rule difficult to implement?

◆ What pricing rule is typically used to regulate a natural monopoly and what problems does it create?

◆ Why is it necessary to regulate a cartel and how could cartels be regulated in the public interest?

We can now turn to monopoly control laws.

Monopoly Control Law

Monopoly control laws give powers to courts and to government agencies to influence markets. They include laws to investigate monopolies and laws designed to ensure competitive practices. Like regulation, monopoly control law can operate in the public interest, maximizing total surplus, or in the private interest, maximizing the surpluses of particular interest groups such as producers.

European monopoly control laws cover three aspects of firm activity:

1 Monopoly.

2 Mergers.

3 Restrictive practices.

Monopoly

Monopoly control law began in the United Kingdom in 1948 when the Monopolies and Restrictive Practices Act created an agency called the Monopolies and Restrictive Practices Commission (MRPC). Its role was to investigate the activities of reported monopolies to assess whether they act against the public interest. The interpretation of public interest is still a political rather than judicial matter. Several subsequent Acts of Parliament have adapted the law, and monopoly is now defined as a firm with a 25 per cent share of a local or national market. UK monopoly investigations are triggered by the existence of monopoly, defined as a market structure, and the UK government has the power to break up monopolies or impose restrictions on activities of UK firms.

European Union monopoly control laws define monopoly in a different way. Monopoly investigations, under EU law, are triggered by indications of abuse of power by a firm in a dominant position. Monopoly power is illegal if it affects trade among member states by creating unfair trading conditions. Abuse includes imposing unfair price and purchase conditions, limiting production, applying different conditions in different countries and imposing restrictive contracts. The European Commission has wide-ranging powers to enforce its decisions with fines for the offending firms operating in the European Union.

Recent EU Cases

In July 2001, the European Commission told the Italian government-owned rail monopoly, Ferrovie dello Stato, that it must grant other firms access to its railway system. The Italian state railway has repeatedly refused to allow the German rail operator, GVG, the right to run passenger trains from Germany to Milan. The European Commission declared that the refusal constituted an abuse of a dominant position and threatened fines. EU fines can be as high as 10 per cent of a company's turnover. In May, 2001, the Commission fined Europe's biggest car manufacturer, Volkswagen, €30.96 million for preventing car dealers from selling one of its models at a discount price.

Mergers

A **merger** occurs when the assets of two or more firms are combined to form a single new firm. The UK Monopolies Commission became the Monopolies and Mergers Commission (MMC) in 1965, extending powers to investigating any merger likely to create a monopoly or lead to abuse of monopoly power which would be against 'the public interest'. According to the 1973 Fair Trading Act, 'public interest' in this case means any practice that maintains and promotes effective competition – or total surplus. This suggested consumer surplus is given a higher weighting than producer surplus in evaluating merger proposals.

In contrast, the EU Merger Control Regulation of 1990 allows the European Commission to investigate mergers between firms which have dominant positions in European markets. The Commission only accepts proposed mergers if any strengthening of a dominant position does not lead to a reduction in competition. The huge wave of international mergers in 1998 led to a large number of EU investigations, but few mergers are ever blocked.

Recent EU Cases

In November, 1999, the EU agreed to the $80 billion merger between the two biggest US oil companies, Exxon and Mobil, creating the world's largest publicly traded oil group. These companies already had dominant positions in some European countries but the merger was not deemed to affect competition. By contrast the EU blocked the £80 billion merger between MCI Worldcom and Sprint, because the merged company would carry 45 per cent of the world's internet traffic, threatening competition in the European market.

Restrictive Practices

The UK 1973 Fair Trading Act defines **restrictive practices** as agreements between firms on prices, terms and conditions of sale, and market share. Such practices are illegal unless the parties can prove to the Restrictive Practices Court that they are in the public interest. The law sets out eight possible defences. Firms must prove at least one defence and that on balance, the benefits of the agreement to consumers outweigh the costs.

A restrictive practice under EU law is any agreement that affects trade among member states and reduces competition. Firms can, but don't have to register their agreements. Restrictive practices are illegal unless they improve production and distribution or technical progress and do not reduce competition.

EU law is concerned with the *effect* of the agreement, while UK law is focused on its *form*. Focusing on effect reduces the cost of investigation and increases the chance that anti-competitive agreements are identified. The European Commission has much greater powers of enforcement than the UK Restrictive Practices Court – imposing fines of up to 10 per cent of a firm's turnover.

Recent EU Cases

In January, 2001, the European Commission began investigating pricing practices between Europe's main music labels and retailers, suspecting cartel pricing. The investigation followed a similar US investigation which found that the big five firms had been setting minimum retail prices for CDs for several years. In July, 2001, the Commission raided the offices of all UK and German mobile telephone operators, gathering evidence for an investigation into price fixing of calls made outside consumers' home markets. In the past, the Commission has imposed heavy fines on price fixing arrangements. You have already read about the record €855 million fine for the vitamin cartel in Reading Between the Lines on pp. 260–261.

Public or Special Interest?

It appears that monopoly control law has evolved to protect the public interest and to restrain profit-seeking and the anti-competitive actions of producers. Although the interests of the producer can influence the way in which the national law is interpreted and applied, the overall thrust of EU law is towards achieving allocative efficiency and serving the public interest. The European Commission is now more proactive and forceful in its application of monopoly control laws in a drive to increase competition in the European single market.

Review Quiz

◆ What main aspects of firms' activities do monopoly control laws cover?
◆ What are the main differences between the UK and EU monopoly control laws?

Let's now turn to public ownership.

Public Ownership and Privatization

The main type of **public ownership** is in the form of nationalized companies. Nationalization involves the 100 per cent ownership of companies by governments, either through compulsory purchase or share purchase. Most European governments followed a continuous programme of nationalization and purchase after the Second World War. But in the 1980s and 1990s many nationalized companies throughout Europe were privatized. Governments also sold off the part-shares they held in many private companies.

The UK case is an interesting example because it is extreme. The range of UK public companies in 1979 included the main utilities, transport systems, key industries such as coal and steel, and many firms from relatively competitive industries. Among these were Jaguar Cars, Sealink Ferries, Cable and Wireless, Britoil and Unipart. Between 1979 and 1999, nearly all of the publicly owned companies had been sold. So why were so many UK firms brought into public ownership and then sold again? Let's look at an economic model of public ownership to find out.

Efficient Public Ownership

Public ownership is another way in which government can influence the behaviour of a natural monopoly. Suppose that an industry under public ownership is operated in a manner that results in economic efficiency – maximization of total surplus. Let's consider the example of a railway. Figure 17.6(a) illustrates the UK demand for freight service and the railway's costs. The demand curve is *D*. The marginal cost curve, *MC*, is horizontal at £2 a tonne. The railway has large fixed costs that feature in the company's average total cost curve, *ATC*. The average total cost curve slopes downward because as the number of tonnes of freight carried increases, the fixed costs are spread over a larger number of tonnes. To be efficient, a publicly owned railway adopts the rule:

> Produce an output such that price equals marginal cost.

In this example, that output level is moving 8 billion tonnes of freight a year at a price – and marginal cost – of £2 a tonne. To be able to operate in this manner, a publicly owned railway has to be subsidized; the subsidy on each unit of output must equal the difference between average total cost and marginal cost. So the subsidy must be collected through taxation rather than through the price of the good or service. If the government taxes each household a fixed amount, the consumer surplus will shrink to the green triangle shown Figure 17.6(a), but consumer surplus will be at its maximum.

The situation depicted in Figure 17.6(a) achieves an efficient outcome because consumer surplus is maximized. But this outcome might not be in the interests of the managers of a publicly owned railway. The behaviour of managers in companies under public ownership can be predicted using the economic theory of bureaucracy. We'll look at this now.

A Bureaucratic Model of Public Ownership

The basic assumption of the economic theory of bureaucracy is that bureaucrats aim to maximize their departmental budgets. The equivalent assumption for managers in a company under public ownership is that they seek to maximize the company budget. The effect on the company under public ownership depends on the pricing constraints under which the managers operate. We will consider two alternative cases:

◆ Budget maximization with marginal cost pricing.

◆ Budget maximization at a zero price.

Budget Maximization with Marginal Cost Pricing

If managers maximize the budget but follow the marginal cost pricing rule, the outcome is efficient. In our case, the railway moves 8 billion tonnes of freight a year at a cost of £2 a tonne, as Figure 17.6(b) illustrates. But the railway managers do not minimize production costs because the internal control mechanisms, that ensure efficiency in a private company, are weak. So the railway pads its costs and becomes

Figure 17.6

Public Ownership

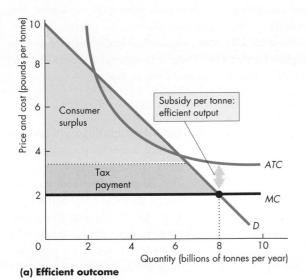

(a) Efficient outcome

(b) Budget maximization

Part (a) shows a railway in public ownership that produces the output at which price equals marginal cost. Its output is 8 billion tonnes a year and the price is £2 a tonne. The railway receives a subsidy that enables it to cover its total cost and that cost is the minimum possible cost of providing the efficient quantity. Part (b) shows what happens if the managers of the railway under public

ownership pursue their own interest and maximize their budget by padding costs. Average total cost now increases to *ATC* (*inflated*). If the railway is required to keep price equal to marginal cost, the quantity produced is efficient, but the managers divert the consumer surplus to themselves.

---

inefficient. The managers hire more workers than required to move the efficient quantity and average total costs rise to *ATC* (*inflated*).

How far can the railway pad its costs? The answer is the maximum that railway freight customers can be made to pay through taxation. That maximum is the total consumer surplus – the area beneath the demand curve and above the marginal cost curve. From Figure 17.6(b) this is £32 billion (1/2 × £8 billion × £8). This will be the upper limit that any government – in a political democracy – can extract from the taxpaying consumers of the output of the publicly owned company. Spread over 8 billion tonnes, £32 billion gives a subsidy of £4 a tonne, the amount shown in the figure.

Budget Maximization at Zero Price

What happens if a government department provides its goods or services free? Of course, it is unlikely that a publicly owned railway would be able to persuade politicians and taxpayers that its activities should be

expanded to the point of providing its services free. But there are many examples in Europe of health and education services that are provided free of charge by government departments. As you saw in Chapter 15, governments provide goods in kind such as health and education, as a method of redistributing income. However, to maintain the comparison in the Figure 17.6, we'll continue with the example of the railway.

If in Figure 17.6(b) the transport department increases output to the point at which the price that consumers are willing to pay for the last unit produced is zero, output rises to 10 billion tonnes a year. A deadweight loss is created because the marginal cost of production, £2 a tonne, is higher than the marginal benefit or willingness to pay, £0 per tonne. The department will also be inefficient and inflate its costs. The subsidy will increase to the highest that the public will be willing to pay. The maximum subsidy will equal the consumer surplus. If the subsidy were higher, people would vote to shut down the publicly owned railway because the subsidy would exceed the consumer surplus.

The UK Health Service

In the UK's National Health Service (NHS), health care is free at the point of demand but costs have been rising faster than the rate of inflation. Rising costs have been due in part to inefficient cost inflation. For example, in 1998, the average cost of a hip replacement in the NHS could be as little as £1,834 or as much as £6,494 depending on the region. To reduce the burden on taxation, Government successfully imposed tight budget controls. In 2001, UK health care spending per head was below the EU average and below that in some of the private health care systems in Europe. However, health outcome measures had also fallen. In 2001, the UK government announced a policy to increase subsidies to the NHS, based on the view that public opinion had changed and now favoured tax increases for this purpose.

Privatization

The reasons for privatization are derived from the predictions of our bureaucracy model. According to this model, firms in public ownership tend to overproduce and to inflate costs, although realistically not to the extent suggested in Figure 17.6(b). As the subsidy level rises, consumer interest shifts towards supporting privatization as a means of increasing efficiency. Many publicly owned companies are not natural monopolies. Privatization exposes these companies to the forces of market competition, forcing down average total costs, reducing prices, and removing the needs for subsidies and taxes.

Some economists have questioned the benefits of privatizing natural monopolies. Natural monopolies must be regulated even in the private sector. As you have seen, regulatory capture means that private regulation may not be more effective than public ownership. However, as privatized monopolies have the extra monitoring of shareholders, they may be less likely to inflate costs. But pressure from shareholders to cut costs may work against other aspects of public interest such as safety and equity. This has been an important issue in debate about provision of rail and health services in the United Kingdom. The UK government took the provision of the rail infrastructure out of the private sector and placed it under the control of a non-profit making organization in 2001, after a series of rail disasters highlighted safety concerns.

Other economists argue that competition after privatization of natural monopolies can also be achieved by separating out the service part of the business from the ownership of physical networks. For example, the retail supply of gas and electricity, telecommunications and rail services are retail activities and can be highly competitive. The real natural monopolies lies in the network of pipes, lines or track.

The UK gas and electricity case

Every week in 2001, 57,000 households switched gas supplier and 139,000 switched electricity supplier in the United Kingdom. Since privatization, British Gas (Centrica), which still has 70 per cent of all gas customers, has seen its average domestic bill fall 23 per cent from £397.69 to £301.67. In the last five years, on average across all suppliers, gas bills have fallen 17 per cent and electricity bills have fallen 22 per cent. The National Audit Office estimates that electricity consumers saved £750 million and gas consumers saved £1bn since privatization in 1997. However, the 35 per cent fall in electricity generation prices have not been passed on to customers and wholesale gas prices have more than doubled. Competition in service has driven down prices, but regulating the natural monopoly of the network and generation has been less successful.

Review Quiz

◆ How might a company under public ownership operate efficiently?
◆ What are the effects of budget maximization by managers in publicly owned companies?
◆ Why might governments want to privatize a publicly owned corportation? When is privatization likely to be most successful and why?

In this chapter, we've seen how governments intervene in markets to affect prices, quantities, consumer surplus and producer surplus. You can read about the problems of deregulation in Europe's gas and electricity markets in Reading Between the Lines on pp. 380–381.

Summary

Key Points

Market Intervention (p. 363)

- Governments intervene to regulate monopolistic and oligopolistic markets in three ways: regulation, (and deregulation), monopoly control laws, and public ownership.

Economic Theory of Regulation (pp. 363–365)

- Consumers and producers express their demand for the regulation by voting, lobbying and making campaign contributions.

- The larger the surplus that can be generated by a particular regulation and the smaller the number of people adversely affected, the larger is the demand for the regulation.

- Regulation is supplied by politicians who pursue their own best interest.

- The larger the surplus per person generated and the larger the number of persons affected by it, the larger is the supply of regulation.

- Public interest theory predicts that total surplus will be maximized; capture theory predicts that producer surplus will be maximized.

Regulation and Deregulation (pp. 365–372)

- Regulation is conducted by agencies controlled by political appointments and staffed by a permanent bureaucracy.

- Regulated firms must comply with agency rules about price, product quality and output levels.

- Although the number of regulatory agencies continues to grow with the creation of special agencies to control privatized monopolies, there has been a tendency to deregulate many areas of the economy.

- Public interest theory predicts that deregulation occurs because the balance of power has shifted to consumers who demand lower prices, but they are also likely to demand more regulation serving their interests.

Monopoly Control Law (pp. 372–374)

- Monopoly control law allows governments to control monopoly and monopolistic practices.

- Monopoly control laws define monopoly in terms of market structure and/or market power.

- The overall thrust of European monopoly control law is directed towards serving the public interest.

Public Ownership and Privatization (pp. 374–376)

- European countries have a long history of public ownership of firms, but many of these firms have now been privatized – sold to private investors.

- Privatization is in the consumer interest if regulatory costs fall and firms are exposed to competition.

- Privatization may not be in the consumer interest if public interest factors like equity and safety are compromised by increased competition.

Key Figures

Figure 17.1 Natural Monopoly: Marginal Cost Pricing, **367**

Figure 17.2 Natural Monopoly: Average Cost Pricing, **368**

Figure 17.3 Natural Monopoly: Profit Maximization, **368**

Figure 17.5 Collusive Oligopoly, **371**

Figure 17.6 Public Ownership, **375**

Key Terms

Average cost pricing rule, **367**
Capture theory, **364**
Deregulation, **363**
Marginal cost pricing rule, **367**
Merger, **373**
Monopoly control law, **363**
Privatization, **363**
Public interest theory, **364**
Public ownership, **374**
Rate of return regulation, **368**
Regulation, **363**
Restrictive practices, **373**

Problems

●1 Elixir Springs, Inc., is an unregulated European natural monopoly that bottles Elixir, a unique health product with no substitutes. The total fixed cost incurred by Elixir Springs is €150,000, and its marginal cost is 10 cents a bottle. The figure illustrates the demand for Elixir.

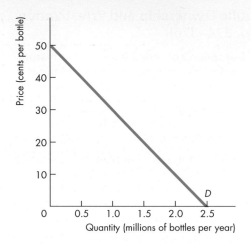

a What is the price of a bottle of Elixir?

b How many bottles does Elixir Springs sell?

c Does Elixir Springs maximize total surplus or producer surplus?

2 Cascade Springs, Inc., is a natural monopoly that bottles water from a spring high in the Alps. The total fixed cost it incurs is €120,000, and its marginal cost is 20 cents a bottle. The figure illustrates the demand for Cascade Springs bottled water.

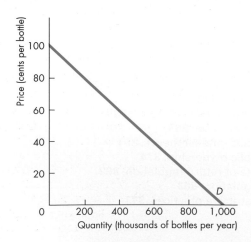

a What is the price of Cascade Springs water?

b How many bottles does Cascade Springs sell?

c Does Cascade Springs maximize total surplus or producer surplus?

●3 The EU Competition Commission regulates Elixir Springs in problem 1 by imposing a marginal cost pricing rule.

a What is the price of a bottle of Elixir?

b How many bottles does Elixir Springs sell?

c What is Elixir Springs' economic profit?

d What is the consumer surplus?

e Is the regulation in the public interest? Explain.

4 The EU Competition Commission regulates Cascade Springs in problem 2 by imposing a marginal cost pricing rule.

a What is the price of Cascade Springs water?

b How many bottles does Cascade Springs sell?

c What is the economic profit?

d What is the consumer surplus?

e Is the regulation in the public interest? Explain.

●5 The EU Competition Commission regulates Elixir Springs in problem 1 by imposing an average cost pricing rule.

a What is the price of a bottle of Elixir?

b How many bottles does Elixir Springs sell?

c What is Elixir Springs' economic profit?

d What is the consumer surplus?

e Is the regulation in the public interest? Explain.

6 The EU Competition Commission regulates Cascade Springs in problem 2 by imposing an average cost pricing rule.

a What is the price of Cascade Springs water?

b How many bottles does Cascade Springs sell?

c What is Cascade Springs' economic profit?

d What is the consumer surplus?

e Is the regulation in the public interest? Explain.

●7 Two airlines share an international route. The figure shows the demand curve for trips on this route and the marginal cost curve that each firm faces. This air route is regulated.

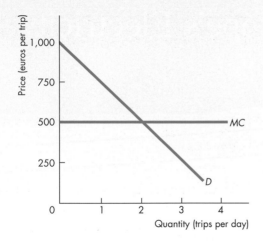

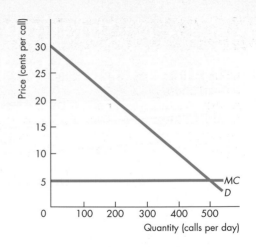

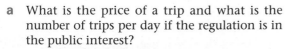

a What is the price of a trip and what is the number of trips per day if the regulation is in the public interest?

b What is the price of a trip and what is the number of trips per day if the airlines capture the regulator?

c What is the deadweight loss in part (b)?

d What do you need to know to predict whether the regulation will be in the public interest or the producer interest?

8 Two telephone companies offer local calls in an area. The figure shows the market demand curve for calls and the marginal cost curves of each firm. These firms are regulated.

a What is the price of a call and what is the number of calls per day if the regulation is in the public interest?

b What is the price of a call and what is the number of calls per day if the telephone companies capture the regulator?

c What is the deadweight loss in part (b)?

d What do you need to know to predict whether the regulation will be in the public interest or the producer's interest?

Critical Thinking

1 After you have studied Reading Between the Lines on pp. 380–381, answer the following questions.

  a Why does the European Union want deregulation and liberalization in the electricity and gas markets?

  b What is the effect of deregulation on new entrants into the UK supply market?

  c Why does the UK want the European Union to take action against France and Germany?

  d Why does the European Union want to convert the 15 national electricity markets into one integrated market?

  e Would a fully integrated European electricity market still need regulation? If so, what type of regulation?

2 Use the Parkin, Powell and Matthews website to visit the *Financial Times* and look up the surveys on the telecoms sector and the issue of British Telecom's local loop monopoly. Then answer the following questions.

  a How can British Telecom generate economic profit from charging for calls to the internet?

  b Why has British Telecom focused on developing its dominance in domestic calls to the internet?

  c What effect would 'local loop unbundling' have on competition and price for local calls.

  d What effect would 'local loop unbundling' have on British Telecom's profits?

  e Is it better to regulate price for calls or open access to new entrants into line supply? Explain your answer.

3 Use the link on the Parkin, Powell and Matthews website to visit the European Union site and find information on cases of mergers, abuse of monopoly power and cartels. In each case, explain why the activities are thought to reduce competition.

http://www.econ100.com

Deregulating Europe's Electricity and Gas Market

THE GUARDIAN, 11 MAY 2001

Hain plays national champion

David Gow and Mark Milner

The European Union cannot be competitive unless it has low gas and electricity prices – and that means 'full scale liberalization', says Peter Hain, the (UK) trade and industry minister . . . Mr Hain, is increasingly exasperated that continental groups can take over UK utilities but British firms are effectively barred from crossing the Channel . . . There is no sign of British utilities following the lead of . . . Electricité de France (London Electricity) and now E.On (agreed £10 bn takeover of PowerGen).

It is not just that they are too small or that Britain has no national champions. Mr Hain insists that they are blocked from reciprocal ventures in Europe, especially by France and Germany, by legislative and regulatory barriers amounting to a serious infringement of the single market.

The process of liberalizing the EU gas and electricity markets – allowing all consumers to choose their supplier but also eventually giving distributors and suppliers universal access to transmission networks via common carriage – has been under way for some years. The directive on the electricity market was launched in 1996: that covering the gas market two years later.

. . . The EC reckons that, about 78 per cent of the gas market is open to choice and 66 per cent for electricity. The picture is far from uniform – Britain and Sweden, for example have opened their markets completely . . . Existing operators have responded to competition with price cuts . . . Others are some way short of total deregulation . . . The Commission . . . is taking legal action against France on the grounds that it is lagging behind.

A second aim is to convert 15 national markets into a single, integrated whole. That will take some doing. Only 8 per cent of EU electricity generation, for example, is traded across borders . . .

The problem is compounded by . . . privatization. Senior sources grumble that the likes of Electricité de France and Gaz de France are able to take a more aggressive approach to acquisitions because they have a much lower cost of capital than private sector rivals . . .

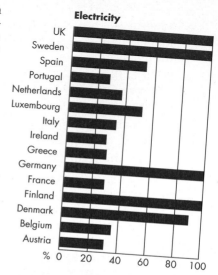

Electricity

	% 0	20	40	60	80	100
UK						
Sweden						
Spain						
Portugal						
Netherlands						
Luxembourg						
Italy						
Ireland						
Greece						
Germany						
France						
Finland						
Denmark						
Belgium						
Austria						

The Essence of the Story

- The European Commission introduced directives to deregulate the electricity markets and gas markets in 1996 and 1998 respectively.

- The first phase is to create national markets where all consumers can choose their supplier.

- Deregulation (liberalization) will increase competition and reduce prices to consumers.

- Progress has been uneven. In 2001, the UK and Sweden had fully open markets, but other countries still had state monopolies or imposed some barriers to new entrants as shown in the chart.

- The UK complained to the European Commission that it could not gain reciprocal access to other EU markets, limiting competition.

Economic Analysis

- Before privatization, the UK gas and electricity markets were dominated by national monopoly suppliers.

- Figure 1 shows the monopoly supplier in the UK electricity domestic supply market, facing a downward sloping demand curve for domestic electricity, *D*, with marginal cost *MC*, and marginal revenue, *MR*.

- The UK monopoly supplier maximizes profit by setting $MR = MC$, supplying Q_M at price P_M. The monopoly profit is the area shaded dark blue and the deadweight loss is the area shaded grey in Figure 1.

- After privatization, the UK domestic electricity supply market is deregulated to remove barriers to entry and new firms, like the French state monopoly, enter the market. Firms are also subject to new price capping regulation to force price cuts.

- Figure 2 shows the combined effect of deregulating market access and reregulating pricing on the UK market. Supply shifts from S_{96} to S_{00}. Price fall from P_M to P_C and quantity rises from Q_M to Q_C.

- The fall in price removes the UK monopoly profit shown in Figure 1 and increases consumer surplus by the area of the deadweight loss.

- Figure 3 shows the impact on the the State owned French monopoly. Demand facing the French monopoly increases from D_{96} to D_{00}, leading to an increase in profit from the dark blue to the light blue area.

- French consumers lose more surplus as new entrants are barred from the French market. The European Commission is taking action against France as efficiency gains from privatization and deregulation in the UK are counterbalanced by efficiency losses from monopoly in the French market.

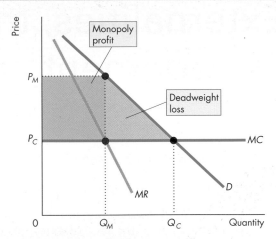

Figure 1 UK national monopoly

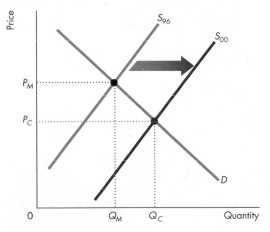

Figure 2 UK privatization and deregulation

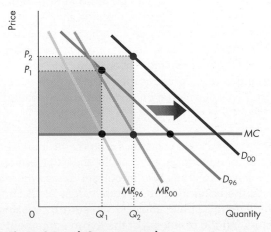

Figure 3 French State monopoly

CHAPTER 18

Externalities, the Environment and Knowledge

After studying this chapter you will be able to:

◆ Explain how property rights can overcome externalities

◆ Explain how emission charges, standards, marketable permits and taxes can be used to achieve efficiency in the face of external costs

◆ Explain the costs and benefits of a carbon-fuel tax, and explain why we do not have such a tax

◆ Explain how grants, subsidies and public provision can make the quantity of education, training and invention more efficient

◆ Explain how patents increase efficiency

Greener and Smarter

We burn huge quantities of fossil fuels – coal, natural gas and oil – that cause acid rain and possibly global warming. The persistent and large-scale use of chlorofluorocarbons (CFCs) may have caused irreparable damage to the earth's ozone layer. The demand for air travel has been rising for the past 10 years but air travel produces more greenhouse gases for every passenger kilometre travelled than any other type of transport. We dump toxic waste into rivers, lakes and oceans. Everyone is put at risk by the continued damage to our environment and yet no one individual can take the necessary action to protect it. What, if anything, can government do to protect our environment? How can government action help us to take account of the damage that we cause others every time we turn on our heating or drive our cars? ◆ Almost every day, we hear about a new discovery. The advance of knowledge seems boundless. And more and more people are learning more and more of what is already known. But is our stock of knowledge advancing fast enough? Are we spending enough on research and development? And do we spend enough on education? Do enough people remain in school for long enough? Would we be better off if we spent more on research and education?

◆ ◆ ◆ ◆ In this chapter we study the inefficiency that arises from externalities – when our actions affect other people, for good or ill, in ways that we do not take into account when we make our own economic choices. We study two important areas where the market fails through externalities – the environment and the accumulation of knowledge. We'll find out if the inefficiency caused by private choices can be reduced by public choices. We start by looking at the underlying problem of externalities and end by studying the problems of the Kyoto agreement in Reading Between the Lines on pp. 398–399.

Economics of the Environment

Environmental problems are not new. Our European cities were polluted with sewage before the nineteenth century and with smog right into the twentieth century. Nor is the desire to find solutions to these problems new. The Romans were keen architects and built aquaducts to provide clean water and drains to flush away sewage. But the gains from public sewage works of the nineteenth century were counterbalanced by the creation of urban smog in the industrial revolution. It seems that no sooner has one environmental problem been resolved than another is created.

Popular discussions of the environment usually pay little attention to economics. They focus on physical aspects of the environment, not costs and benefits. A common assumption is that if people's actions cause *any* environmental degradation, these actions must cease. In contrast, an economic study of the environment emphasizes costs and benefits. An economist talks about the efficient amount of pollution or environmental damage. This emphasis on costs and benefits does not mean that economists, as citizens, do not share the same goals as others and do not value a healthy environment. Nor does it mean that economists have the right answers and everyone else has the wrong ones (or vice versa). Economics provides a set of tools and principles which clarify the issues. It does not provide an agreed list of solutions.

The starting point for an economic analysis of the environment is the demand for a healthy environment.

The Demand for Environmental Quality

The demand for a clean and healthy environment has grown and is higher today than it has ever been. We express our demand for a better environment in a number of ways. We can join 'green' organizations to lobby governments for environmental regulations and policies. We can vote for political parties that reflect our views and implement 'greener' policies. We can buy 'green' products like organic foods and products produced with minimum waste and packaging, even if we pay more to do so.

The demand for a cleaner and healthier environment has grown for two main reasons. First, as our incomes increase, we demand a larger range of goods and services and one of these 'goods' is a high-quality

environment. We value clean air, unspoiled natural scenery and wildlife, and we are willing to pay to protect these valuable resources.

Second, as our knowledge of the effects of our actions on the environment grows, so we are able to take measures that improve the environment. For example, now that we know how sulphur dioxide causes acid rain and how clearing rain forests destroys natural stores of carbon dioxide, we are able, in principle, to design measures that limit these problems.

Let's look at the range of environmental problems that have been identified and the actions that create these problems.

The Sources of Environment Problems

Environmental problems arise from pollution of the air, water and land and these individual sources of pollution interact through the *ecosystem*.

Air Pollution

Figure 18.1(a) shows the five main economic activities that create UK air pollution. It also shows the relative contributions of each activity. More than two-thirds of air pollution comes from road transport and industrial processes. Only one-sixth arises from coal and gas-fired electric power generation.

A common belief is that air pollution is getting worse. On many fronts, as we will see later in this chapter, *global* air pollution is getting worse. But air pollution in the United Kingdom and the European Union is getting less severe for some substances. Figure 18.1(b) shows projected UK trends in the emissions of a major pollutant – carbon dioxide. Carbon dioxide is a 'greenhouse' gas thought to create global warming and increases are mostly created by economic activity. Total emissions fell between 1970 and 1980 but increased after 1980. The projected rise to 2020 is mainly due to increasing use of cars and rising trends in fuel consumption in the production of goods and services.

While the facts about the sources and trends in air pollution are not in doubt, there is considerable disagreement in the scientific community about the *effects* of air pollution. The least controversial problem is *acid rain*, which is caused by sulphur dioxide and nitrogen oxide emissions from coal- and oil-fired power stations. Acid rain begins with air pollution and it leads to water pollution and damages vegetation.

More controversial are airborne substances (suspended particulates) such as lead from leaded petrol

Figure 18.1

Air Pollution

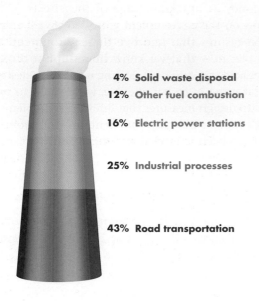

4% **Solid waste disposal**

12% **Other fuel combustion**

16% **Electric power stations**

25% **Industrial processes**

43% **Road transportation**

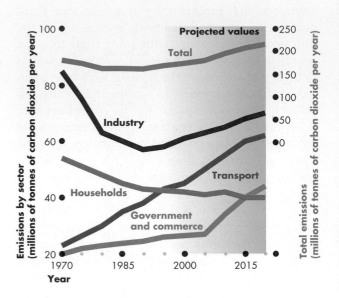

(a) Sources of emission

(b) UK carbon dioxide emissions

Part (a) shows that road transport is the largest source of air pollution, followed by industrial production and power stations. Part (b) shows that carbon dioxide emissions – the most important gas thought to cause global warming – fell after 1970 but have recently begun to rise. Forecasts of future emissions suggest the most important source of increase will be from transport – particularly increased use of cars.

Source: Royal Commission on Environmental Pollution, *18th Report*, London, HMSO, 1994 and UK Department of the Environment, Transport and the Regions, 1998.

and diesel fuel. Some scientists believe that in sufficiently large concentrations, these substances (of which currently 189 have been identified) cause cancer, asthma and other life-threatening conditions.

Even more controversial is *global warming*, which some scientists believe results from the carbon dioxide emissions of road transport and power stations, methane created by cows and other livestock, nitrous oxide emissions from power stations and from fertilizers, and chlorofluorocarbons or CFCs from refrigeration equipment and (in the past) aerosols. The earth's average temperature has increased over the past 100 years, but most of the increase occurred *before* 1940. Determining what causes changes in the earth's temperature and separating out the effect of carbon dioxide and other factors is proving to be difficult.

Equally controversial is the problem of *ozone layer depletion*. There is no doubt that a hole in the ozone layer exists over Antarctica. There is also no doubt

that the ozone layer protects us from cancer-causing ultraviolet rays from the sun. But how the ozone layer is influenced by our industrial activity is simply not understood at this time.

While air pollution from leaded petrol has almost been eliminated in developed economies, sulphur dioxide and the so-called greenhouse gases are a much tougher problem to tackle. The alternatives to road vehicles and power stations are costly or have environmental problems of their own. Road vehicles can be made greener in a variety of ways. One way is to use alternative fuels such as alcohol, natural gas, propane and butane, and hydrogen. Another way is to reduce exhaust emissions by fitting catalytic converters and changing the chemistry of petrol. Similarly, electric power can be generated in cleaner ways by harnessing solar power, tidal power, or geothermal power. Although technically possible, these methods are more costly than conventional carbon-fuelled generators. Another alternative is nuclear power. This method is good for air pollution but bad for land and water pollution because there is no known safe method of disposing of spent nuclear fuel.

Water Pollution

The largest sources of water pollution are the dumping of industrial waste and treated sewage in lakes and rivers and the run-off from agricultural fertilizers. A more dramatic source is the accidental spilling of crude oil into the oceans, such as the *Exxon Valdez* spill in Alaska and an even larger spill in the Russian Arctic in 1994. The most frightening is the dumping of nuclear waste in the ocean. In 1997 there were 200 major substantiated water pollution incidents in the UK, of which the largest share, 30 per cent, were of agricultural origin.

Polluting the waterways and oceans has two main alternatives. One is the chemical processing of waste to render it inert or biodegradable. The other, in wide use for nuclear waste, is to use land sites for storage in secure containers.

Land Pollution

Land pollution arises from dumping toxic waste products. Ordinary household rubbish does not pose a pollution problem unless toxic elements in the rubbish seep into the water supply. This possibility increases as less suitable landfill sites are used. It is estimated that 80 per cent of existing landfills will be full by 2010. Some countries such as Japan and the Netherlands have run out of landfills already. The alternatives to landfill are recycling and incineration. Recycling is an apparently attractive alternative, but it requires an investment in new technologies to be effective. Incineration is a high-cost alternative to landfill and it produces air pollution.

We've seen that the demand for a quality environment has grown and we've described the range of environmental problems. Let's now look at the ways these problems can be handled. We'll begin by looking at property rights and how they relate to environmental externalities.

Property Rights and Environmental Externalities

Externalities arise when there are no markets for a good or service because of an *absence* of property rights. **Property rights** are social arrangements that

govern the ownership, use and disposal of factors of production and goods and services. In modern societies, a property right is a legally established title that is enforceable in the courts.

Property rights are absent when externalities arise. No one owns the air, the rivers and the oceans. So it is no one's private business to ensure that these resources are used in an efficient way. In fact, there is an incentive to use them more than if there were property rights.

Figure 18.2 shows how an environmental externality arises in the absence of property rights. A chemical factory upstream from a fishing club must decide how to dispose of its waste. Dumping waste pollutes the river and kills fish, reducing the membership and revenue of the fishing club.

The factory's marginal benefit curve, *MB*, in part (a) tells us how much an additional tonne of waste dumped into the river is worth to the factory. The *MB* curve is also the firm's demand curve for the use of the river, which is a productive resource. The demand curve for a resource slopes down because of the law of diminishing marginal returns (see Chapter 14, p. 296).

The marginal social cost is the additional cost of dumping an extra tonne of waste in the river, shown by the *MSC* curve in part (a) of Figure 18.2. **Marginal social cost** is the sum of the marginal private cost of waste disposal for the factory plus the marginal cost imposed on others – the marginal external cost on the fishing club. The factory bears no cost of dumping and so all the costs are borne by the fishing club. The *MSC* curve tells us the cost borne by the fishing club for each additional tonne of waste dumped into the river. Marginal social cost rises as the quantity dumped increases.

If no one owns the river, the factory dumps the amount of waste that maximizes its own total benefit. This is the point where marginal benefit of dumping is zero. If the marginal cost of dumping is zero (horizontal along the *x* axis), the factory dumps 8 tonnes a week to maximize total benefit. At this level, the marginal social cost of the waste, all borne by the fishing club, is £200 a tonne. Marginal cost exceeds marginal benefit and so the outcome is inefficient. Let's see why.

The efficient level of dumping waste is 4 tonnes a week, where *MB* equals *MSC*. This amount generates the maximum level of total social welfare – £400 a week – as shown in part (b) of Figure 18.2. Total social welfare is the difference between total benefit – the

Figure 18.2

Externalities and the Coase Theorem

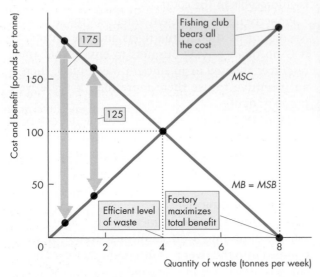

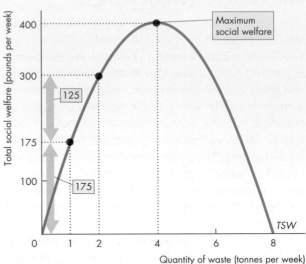

(a) Marginal cost and marginal benefit

(b) Total social welfare

The *MB* curve in part (a) is the factory's marginal benefit curve which equals marginal social benefit, *MSB*. The *MSC* curve measures the marginal social cost to the fishing club of one additional tonne of waste being dumped in the river. If no one owns the river, the factory maximizes total benefit by dumping 8 tonnes a week. This is inefficient. The efficient level of dumping shown in part (b) is 4 tonnes a

week – where *MSB* equals *MSC* and *TSW* is maximized. Using the Coase theorem from part (a), if the polluter owns the river, the victim will pay £400 a week (£100 a tonne × 4 tonnes a week) to the polluter for the assurance that pollution will not exceed 4 tonnes a week. If the victim owns the river, the polluter will pay £400 for pollution rights to dump 4 tonnes a week.

---

area under the *MB* curve, and total cost – the area under the *MSC* curve. The first tonne dumped generates £175 of total social welfare. The second tonne dumped adds £125 pounds raising total social welfare to £300 (£175 + £125). After the fourth tonne, each additional tonne of waste dumped adds more to total cost than to total benefit, so total social welfare falls. When 8 tonnes of waste are dumped each week, total social welfare is zero.

Property Rights and the Coase Theorem

It may be possible to correct an externality by establishing a property right where one does not currently exist. For example, suppose that the chemical factory owns the river. Now, the fishing club must pay the factory for the right to use the river. But the price that the club is willing to pay depends on the number and quality of fish, which in turn depends on how much waste the factory dumps in the river. The greater the

amount of pollution, the smaller is the amount the fishing club is willing to pay for the right to fish. The chemicals factory is now confronted with the cost of its pollution decision. It might still decide to pollute, but if it does, it faces the opportunity cost of its actions – forgone revenue from the fishing club.

Alternatively, suppose that the fishing club owns the river. Now the factory must pay a fee to the fishing club for the right to dump its waste. The more waste it dumps (equivalently, the more fish it kills), the more it must pay. Again, the factory faces an opportunity cost for the pollution it creates.

So does it matter how property rights are assigned? At first thought, the assignment seems crucial, but in 1960, Ronald Coase had a remarkable insight, now known as the Coase theorem. The **Coase theorem** states that if property rights exist and transactions costs are low, the individual choices of people in markets lead to the efficient quantity even when external costs exist. All the costs and benefits are taken into account by the transacting parties. So it doesn't matter how the property rights are assigned.

You can see the Coase theorem at work by looking again at part (a) of Figure 18.2. At the efficient level of waste – 4 tonnes a week – the fishing club bears a cost of £100 for the last tonne dumped in the river, and the factory gets a benefit of £100 a tonne dumped. If waste disposal is restricted below 4 tonnes a week, an increase in waste disposal benefits the factory more than it costs the club. The factory will bribe the club to put up with more waste disposal and both the club and the factory can gain. If waste disposal exceeds 4 tonnes a week, an increase in waste disposal costs the club more than it benefits the factory. The club will now bribe the factory to cut its waste disposal and again, both the club and the factory can gain. Only when the level of waste disposal is 4 tonnes a week – the efficient level – can neither party do any better.

The outcome is the same regardless of who owns the river. If the factory owns it, the club pays £400 for fishing rights and for an agreement that waste disposal will not exceed 4 tonnes a week. If the club owns the river, the factory pays £400 for the right to dump 4 tonnes of waste a week.

Assigning property rights will only result in the efficient quantity if transactions costs are very low. The factory and the fishing club can easily negotiate the deal that produces the efficient outcome. But in many situations transactions costs are high and property rights cannot be enforced. Imagine, for example, the transactions costs of 8 million people who live in Sweden trying to negotiate an agreement with the 5,000 factories in the United Kingdom that emit sulphur dioxide and cause acid rain! In a case such as this, governments resort to alternative methods of coping with externalities. They use a range of policies including:

◆ Emission charges.
◆ Emission standards.
◆ Marketable permits.
◆ Taxes.

Economics in History on pp. 400–401 reviews some examples of the use of these methods and how ideas about how to cope with externalities have changed. In the United Kingdom, the government has established the Environment Agency (EA), to coordinate and administer the country's environment policies. Let's look at the tools the EA could use and see how they work.

Emission Charges

Emission charges are a method of using the market to achieve efficiency, even in the face of externalities. The government (or regulatory agency) sets the emission charges, which are, in effect, a price per unit of pollution. The more pollution a firm creates, the more it pays in emission charges. This method of dealing with environmental externalities is common throughout Europe. For example, in France, Germany and the Netherlands water polluters pay a waste disposal charge.

To work out the emission charge that achieves efficiency, the regulator must determine the marginal social cost and marginal social benefit of pollution. **Marginal social benefit** is the marginal benefit received by the consumer of a good – marginal private benefit – *plus* the marginal benefit to others – the external benefit. To achieve efficiency, the price per unit of pollution must be set to make the marginal social cost of the pollution equal to its marginal social benefit.

Figure 18.3 illustrates an efficient emissions charge for European sulphur dioxide pollution. The marginal benefit of pollution, *MB*, accrues to the polluters alone, and so equals marginal social benefit, *MSB*, as there is no external benefit. The marginal social cost of pollution is *MSC* and is entirely an external cost, falling on other firms and people who live in the affected country. The efficient level of sulphur dioxide emissions is 10 million tonnes a year – where *MSB* = *MSC*. This can be achieved by setting an emission charge of €10 per tonne. Polluters carry on increasing emissions until the marginal benefit just equals the charge per tonne.

In practice, it is hard to determine the marginal benefit of pollution. The people who are best informed about the marginal benefit, the polluters, have an incentive to mislead the regulators about the benefit. As a result, if a pollution charge is used, the most likely outcome is for the price to be set too low. For example, in Figure 18.3, the price might be set at €7 per tonne. At this price, polluters find it worthwhile to pay for 15 million tonnes a year. At this level of pollution, the marginal social cost is €15 a tonne and the amount of pollution exceeds the efficient level.

One way of overcoming excess pollution is to impose general emission standards, which dictate the maximum safe quantity of a pollutant in any output of waste. A more sophisticated method is to issue

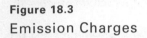

Figure 18.3

Emission Charges

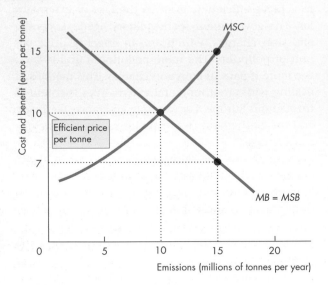

Power stations obtain marginal benefits from sulphur dioxide emissions of *MB* and everyone else bears a marginal social cost of *MSC*. The efficient level of pollution – 10 million tonnes a year in this example – is achieved by imposing an emission charge on power stations of €10 a tonne. If the emission charge is set too low, at €7 a tonne, the resulting amount of pollution is greater than the efficient amount – at 15 million tonnes a year. In this case, the marginal social cost is €15 a tonne, and it exceeds the marginal benefit of €7 a tonne.

quantitative limits that firms can buy and sell – marketable permits. Let's look at these two methods.

Emission Standards

Instead of imposing emission charges on polluters, pollution agencies might set a single emission standard. An **emission standard** is a regulation which limits the quantity of the pollutant in any volume of waste and sets penalties for breaking the regulation. Emission standards for water and air are widely used throughout the European Union. The benefit of using a uniform standard is that it is simple and cheap to apply. The problem is that standards are inefficient. Let's see why.

If firm *H* has a higher marginal benefit than firm *L*, an efficiency gain can be achieved by decreasing the standard for firm *L* and increasing the standard for firm *H*. As it is virtually impossible to determine the

marginal benefits of each firm in practice, quantitative restrictions cannot be allocated to each producer in an efficient way. Uniform emission standards will always be inefficient. Despite their inefficiency, standards are widely used because it is easy for producers to comply with a uniform standard. Also, it is often difficult to value the damage caused by pollutants to establish the marginal external cost. Policies that attempt to set a price for pollution cannot succeed unless the value of the marginal external cost is known.

Marketable Permits

Marketable permits are a clever way of overcoming the need for the regulator to know every firm's marginal benefit schedule. Each firm can be allocated a permit to emit a certain amount of pollution and firms may buy and sell these permits. Firms that have a low marginal benefit from sulphur dioxide emissions will be willing to sell their permits to other firms that have a high marginal benefit. If the market in permits is competitive, the price at which firms trade permits makes the marginal benefit of pollution equal for all firms. If the correct number of permits has been allocated, the outcome can be efficient.

Evidence from the United States suggests that permit trading can be administratively costly if there are a great many polluters. By contrast, if there are only a few polluters, these firms may buy up all available permits and refuse to trade them – leading to a barrier to entry to new firms. Permit trading will only lead to the efficient level of emissions if the efficient level of total emissions is known to start with. The benefit of permit trading is that for any given level of permits allocated, trading will ensure that they are efficiently distributed between different producers.

Taxes and External Costs

Taxes can be used to provide incentives for producers or consumers to cut back on an activity that creates external costs. The European Union wants to introduce this type of tax on carbon fuels in power stations and fuels for vehicles, because they are a major source of pollution. To see how the tax works, let's look at the market for petrol.

The cost of petrol to drivers is not the only cost of using petrol as a vehicle fuel. External costs arise from exhaust emissions, particularly from the carbon dioxide, a greenhouse gas, that cannot be removed by a

Figure 18.4

Taxes and Pollution

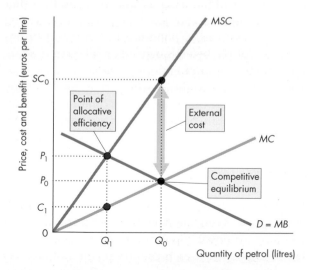

The demand curve for petrol is also the marginal benefit curve ($D = MB$). The marginal cost curve of producing petrol is MC. If the market is competitive, Q_0 litres of petrol are produced and the price is P_0 per litre. The marginal social cost of petrol is shown by the curve MSC. Because of environmental pollution, the marginal social cost of petrol, SC_0, exceeds the marginal private cost, P_0, when the quantity of petrol is Q_0. If the government imposes a tax on petrol supply equal to the external cost, producers face a marginal cost equal to the MSC curve. The price of petrol increases to P_1 per litre and the quantity decreases to Q_1 litres. Allocative efficiency is achieved.

---

catalytic converter. External costs may also arise from the fire risk when road accidents occur. The marginal social cost of petrol use is the sum of the private cost of petrol to petrol users plus all the marginal external costs of petrol use.

Figure 18.4 shows the market for petrol. The demand curve, D, is also the marginal benefit curve, MB. This curve tells us how much consumers value different amounts of petrol. The curve MC measures the marginal *private* cost of using petrol – the costs directly incurred by users of petrol or the marginal cost of producing petrol.

If the petrol market is competitive and unregulated, drivers will balance the marginal cost of petrol, MC, against their own marginal benefit, MB, and buy Q_0 litres of petrol at a price of P_0 per litre. At this level of petrol use, the marginal social cost is SC_0. The marginal social cost minus the marginal private cost,

$SC_0 - P_0$, is the marginal cost imposed on others – the marginal external cost.

Suppose the EU imposes a new 'green' tax on petrol and that it sets the tax equal to the external marginal cost. The tax makes the suppliers of petrol incur a marginal cost equal to the marginal social cost. That is, the marginal private cost plus the tax equals the marginal social cost. The market supply curve is now the same as the MSC curve. The price of petrol rises to P_1 a litre and at this price, the quantity bought falls to Q_1. The marginal cost of the resources used in producing Q_1 litres of petrol is C_1, and the marginal external cost is P_1 minus C_1. That marginal external cost is paid by the consumer through the tax.

The situation at the price P_1 and the quantity Q_1 is efficient. At an output rate above Q_1, marginal social cost exceeds marginal benefit, so net benefit increases by decreasing petrol production. At an output rate below Q_1, marginal benefit exceeds marginal social cost, so net benefit increases by increasing petrol production.

A Carbon-fuel Tax?

The European Union introduced the idea of a tax on carbon emissions as part of its sustainable environmental policy in 1992. The issue is still pressing. Today, annual carbon emissions worldwide are a staggering 6 billion tonnes. By 2050, with current policies, that annual total is predicted to be 24 billion tonnes. If the rich countries used carbon taxes to keep emissions to their 1990 level and the developing countries remove subsidies from coal and oil, total emissions in 2050 might be held at 14 billion tonnes. So why have the European Union and other rich countries worldwide failed to introduce carbon taxes?

Uncertainty About Global Warming

Part of the reason we do not have a high, broad-based, carbon-fuel tax is that the scientific evidence that carbon emissions produce global warming is not accepted by everyone. Climatologists are uncertain about how carbon emissions translate into atmospheric concentrations – about how the *flow* of emissions translates into a *stock* of pollution. The main uncertainty arises because carbon drains from the atmosphere into the oceans and vegetation at a rate that is not well understood. Climatologists are also uncertain about the connection between carbon concentration and temperature. Economists are uncertain about how a temperature increase translates into economic costs and benefits. Some economists believe the costs and benefits are almost zero, while others believe that a temperature increase of 3°C by 2090 will reduce the total output of goods and services by 20 per cent.

Present Cost and Future Benefit

Another factor weighing against a large change in fuel use is that the costs would be borne now while the benefits, if any, would accrue many years in the future. To compare future benefits with current costs, we must use an interest rate. If the interest rate is 5 per cent a year, a pound today becomes more than £17,000 in 200 years. So at an interest rate of 5 per cent a year, it is worth spending £1 million today only if this expenditure avoids £17 billion in environmental damage in 2195.

Because large uncertain future benefits are needed to justify small current costs, a general tax on carbon fuels is not a high priority on the political agenda.

International Factors

A final factor against a large change in fuel use is the international pattern of the use of carbon fuels. At present, carbon pollution comes in even doses from the industrial (OECD)[1] countries and the developing countries. But by 2050, three-quarters of the carbon pollution will come from the developing countries (if the trends persist). One reason for the high pollution rate in some developing countries is that their governments *subsidize* the use of coal or oil. These subsidies lower producers' marginal costs and encourage the use of fuel beyond the efficient quantity – and by a large amount.

These countries argue that it is not fair to ask them to cut back at the same rate as developed economies, as the developed economies have already benefited from using more than the efficient quantity of carbon fuels. So developed countries should pay less developed countries to cut their use. This is clearly an issue of equity which requires international negotiation and may become part of any agreement on the allocation of polluting permits worldwide.

---

[1] The OECD is the Organization for Economic Cooperation and Development, an international agency based in Paris, the member nations of which include the United States, Canada, Japan and the industrial countries of Western Europe and Australasia.

A Global Warming Dilemma

With the high output rate of greenhouse gases in the developing world, the European Union and the other industrial countries are faced with a global warming dilemma. Decreasing pollution is costly and brings benefits. But the benefits depend on all countries taking action to limit pollution. If the European Union acts alone, other countries will gain benefits, but the European Union bears the cost of limiting pollution and gets almost no benefits. So it is worthwhile taking steps to limit global pollution only if all nations act together.

The global warming dilemma faced by the European Union and the developing countries is shown in Table 18.1. The numbers are hypothetical. Each country (we'll call the developing countries a country) has two possible policies: to introduce a carbon tax or to pollute. If each country pollutes, it receives a zero net return (by assumption) shown in the top-left square in the table. If each country introduces a carbon tax, it bears the cost of using more expensive

---

Table 18.1 A Global Warming Dilemma

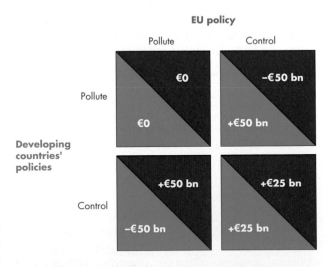

If the European Union and developing countries both pollute, their payoffs are those shown in the top-left square. If neither pollutes, their payoffs are shown in the bottom-right square. When one country pollutes and the other one does not, their payoffs are shown in the top-right and bottom-left squares. The outcome of this game is for both countries to pollute. The structure of this game is the same as that of the prisoners' dilemma (see pp. 272–273).

fuels and gets the benefit of less pollution. Its net return is €25 billion, as shown in the bottom-right square of the table. If the European Union alone introduces a carbon tax, the European Union pays €50 billion more than it benefits and the developing countries benefit by €50 billion more than they pay, as shown in the top-right corner of the table. Finally, if the developing countries alone introduce a carbon tax, they lose €50 billion and the European Union gains €50 billion, as shown in the bottom-left corner of the table.

Confronted with these possible payoffs, the European Union reasons as follows. If the developing countries do not introduce a carbon tax, we break even if we pollute and we lose €50 billion if we introduce a tax. Conclusion, we are better off polluting. If the developing countries introduce a tax, we gain €50 billion if we pollute and €25 billion if we introduce a tax. Again, we are better off polluting. The developing countries reach the same conclusion. So no one introduces a carbon tax and pollution continues unabated.

Treaties and International Agreements

To break the dilemma, many countries attempt to negotiate international agreements – treaties. These treaties must have incentives for countries to comply with the agreements, otherwise, the situation remains as we've described in Table 18.1.

The most important international agreement is the United Nation's Framework Convention on Climate Change which came into effect on 1994. This convention is an agreement among 60 countries to limit their output of greenhouse gases. The agreement was extended with the Kyoto Protocol in 1999 and targets were set for reducing six greenhouse gases in developed economies. But neither the Convention nor the Protocol can be enforced.

To cut emissions, the rich countries need big increases in energy taxes which will be costly. Energy taxes will induce a substitution towards more costly but cleaner alternative fuels. Without energy taxes, only a large technological advance in solar, wind, tidal, or nuclear power that makes these sources less costly than coal can create the incentive needed to give up carbon fuels. But there is still no agreement on the use of energy taxes or carbon emission permits amongst developed countries, and in 2001, the US announced it would not ratify the Kyoto agreement.

You can read about the problems of the Kyoto agreement in Reading Between the Lines on pp. 398–399.

Review Quiz

◆ Why do externalities cause markets to be inefficient?
◆ How can an externality be eliminated by assigning property rights? Under what circumstances does this method of coping with an externality work?
◆ How do emission charges, standards and permits deal with externalities? Is one method better than any other?
◆ How do taxes help to deal with externalities? What is the best level at which to set a pollution tax and why?

Economics of Knowledge

Knowledge, the things people know and understand, has a profound effect on our economies. The economics of knowledge is an attempt to explain that effect. It is also an attempt to understand the process of knowledge accummulation and the incentives people face to learn and transmit knowledge.

Knowledge is both a consumer good and a factor of production. The demand for knowledge – the willingness to pay to acquire knowledge – depends on the marginal benefit it provides to its possessor. As a consumer good, knowledge provides utility and this is one source of its marginal benefit. As a factor of production – part of the stock of capital – knowledge increases productivity and this is another source of its marginal benefit.

Knowledge creates benefits not only for its possessor, but for others as well – external benefits. External benefits arise from education and training – passing on existing knowledge to others. When children learn basic skills at school, they are better able to communicate and interact with each other. Similarly, when people are trained at work, they make better employees for other firms. But when people make decisions about how much schooling to undertake, or when firms decide about how much training to provide, they do not value the external benefits created.

External benefits also arise from research and development activities that lead to the creation of new knowledge. Once someone has worked out how to do something, others can copy the basic idea. They do have to work to copy an idea, so they face an opportunity cost. But (usually) they do not have to pay the person who made the discovery to use it. When Isaac Newton worked out the formulas for calculating the rate of response of one variable to another – calculus – everyone was free to use his method. When a spreadsheet program called VisiCalc was invented, others were free to copy the basic idea. Lotus Corporation developed its 1-2-3 and later Microsoft created Excel and both became highly successful, but they did not pay for the key idea first used in VisiCalc.

When people make decisions about the quantity of education to undertake, or when firms decide on the amount of research and development and training that they provide, they balance the *private* marginal costs against the private marginal benefits. They do not take into account the value of the external benefits. As a result, if we were to leave education, training and research and development to individual market choice we would get too little of these activities. To deliver them in efficient quantities, we make public choices through government policy to modify the market outcome.

Governments can use three policies to achieve an efficient allocation of resources in the presence of the external benefits from education and research and development. They are:

1 Subsidies.

2 Below-cost provision.

3 Patents.

Subsidies

A **subsidy** is a payment made by the government to producers that depends on the level of output. By subsidizing private activities, government can, in principle, encourage private decisions to be taken in the public interest. A government subsidy programme might alternatively enable private producers to capture resources for themselves. Although subsidies cannot be guaranteed to work successfully, we'll study an example in which they do achieve their desired objective.

Figure 18.5 shows how subsidizing education can increase the amount of education undertaken and

Figure 18.5

Efficiency in Education

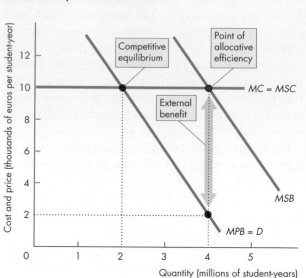

The demand curve for education measures the marginal private benefit of education (*MPB = D*). The curve *MSC* shows the marginal social cost of education – in this example, €10,000 per student-year. If college education is provided in a competitive market with no government intervention, tuition is €10,000 a year and 2 million students are enrolled in college. Education produces an external benefit and adding the external benefit to the marginal private benefit gives marginal social benefit, *MSB*. Allocative efficiency is achieved if the government provides education services on a scale such that marginal social cost equals marginal social benefit. This scale of provision is 4 million students a year, which is achieved if the government either subsidizes private colleges or provides education below cost in public colleges. In this example, people pay an annual tuition fee of €2,000 and the government pays €8,000.

achieve allocative efficiency. Suppose that the marginal cost of producing a student-year of college or university education in Europe is a constant €10,000. This marginal social cost is shown by the *MSC* curve. We'll assume that all these costs are borne by the colleges and there are no external costs. The maximum price that students (or parents) are willing to pay for an additional year of study determines the marginal private benefit curve and the demand curve for education. This curve is *MPB = D*. In this example, a competitive market in private university or college education results in 2 million students being enrolled and tuition fees of €10,000 a year.

Suppose that the external benefit – the benefit derived by people other than those who receive the education – results in external benefits. The marginal social benefit – marginal private benefit plus marginal external benefit – is the curve *MSB*. Allocative efficiency occurs when marginal social cost equals marginal social benefit. In the example in Figure 18.5, this occurs when 4 million students are enrolled. One way of getting 4 million students enrolled is to subsidize private universities or colleges. In our example, a subsidy of €8,000 per student per year paid to the colleges does the job. With a subsidy of €8,000 and marginal cost of €10,000, colleges and universities earn an economic profit on any fee above €2,000. Competition drives the tuition fee down to €2,000 and at this price, the quantity demanded is 4 million. So a subsidy can achieve an efficient outcome.

A subsidy can also be used to increase the stock of knowledge through research and development in industry and through subsidized training. By subsidizing these activities, the government can move the allocation of resources towards a more efficient outcome. Another way to achieve an efficient amount of education and research and development is through public provision sold below cost.

Below-cost Provision

Instead of subsidizing private colleges and universities, the government can establish public sector colleges and universities that provide schooling below cost. Instead of subsidizing research and development in industry and the universities, the government can establish its own research facilities and make discoveries available to others. Let's see how this approach works by returning to the example in Figure 18.5.

By creating public sector universities with places for 4 million students, the government can supply the efficient quantity of higher education directly. To ensure that this number of places is taken up, the public universities charge a tuition fee, in this example, of €2,000 per student per year. The government provides this tuition below its marginal cost of €10,000 per student per year. At this price, the number who attend university is the efficient number where marginal social benefit equals marginal social cost.

We've now looked at two examples of how government action can help market participants take account of the external benefits deriving from education to achieve an outcome different from that of a private unregulated market. In reality, governments use both methods of encouraging an efficient quantity of education. They subsidize private colleges and universities and run their own institutions, selling their services at below cost. But in education, the public sector is by far the larger. In research and development, subsidies to the private sector are far larger and government provides little direct research.

Patents

Knowledge may well be the only factor of production that does not display *diminishing marginal productivity*. More knowledge (about the right things) makes people more productive. And there seems to be no tendency for the additional productivity from additional knowledge to diminish.

For example, in just 15 years, advances in knowledge about microprocessors has given us a sequence of processor chips that has made our personal computers increasingly powerful. Each advance in knowledge about how to design and manufacture a processor chip has brought apparently ever larger increments in performance and productivity. In the space of 80 years, we have moved from a simple one-seater plane to the most modern Boeing 747, which can carry 400 people halfway around the world non-stop. These examples can be repeated again and again in fields as diverse as agriculture, biogenetics, communications, engineering, entertainment, medicine and publishing.

A key reason why the stock of knowledge increases without diminishing returns is the sheer number of different techniques that can in principle be tried. Paul Romer explains this fact with an amazing example. Suppose, says Romer,

> that to make a finished good, 20 different parts have to be attached to a frame, one at a time. A worker could proceed in numerical order, attaching part one first, then part two . . . Or the worker could proceed in some other order, starting with part ten, then adding part seven . . . With 20 parts, a standard (but incredible) calculation shows that there are about 10^{18} different sequences one can use for assembling the final good. This number is larger than the total number of seconds that have elapsed since the big bang created the universe, so we can be confident that in all activities, only a very

small fraction of the possible sequences have ever been tried.[1]

Think about all the processes and all the products and all the different bits and pieces that go into each, and you can see that we have only begun to scratch around the edges of what is possible.

Because knowledge is productive and creates external benefits, it is necessary to use government policy to ensure that markets face sufficient incentives to produce the efficient level of effort in invention and innovation. The main way of creating the right incentives is to provide the creators of knowledge with property rights in their discoveries – called **intellectual property rights**. The legal device for creating intellectual property rights is the patent or copyright. A **patent** or **copyright** is a government-sanctioned exclusive right granted to the inventor of a good, service, or productive process, to produce, use and sell the invention for a given number of years. A patent enables the developer of a new idea to prevent, for a limited number of years, others from benefiting freely from an invention. But to obtain the protection of the law, an inventor must make knowledge of the invention public.

Although patents encourage invention and innovation, they do so at an economic cost. While a patent is in place, its holder has a monopoly – generating more market failure. To maximize profit, a monopoly (patent holder) produces the quantity at which marginal cost equals marginal revenue. The monopoly sets the price above marginal cost and equal to the highest price at which the profit-maximizing quantity can be sold. In this situation, consumers value the good more highly (are willing to pay more for one more unit of it) than its marginal cost. So the quantity of the good available is less than the efficient quantity.

But without a patent, less effort is put into developing new goods, services, or processes and the flow of new inventions is slowed. So the efficient outcome is a compromise that balances the social welfare gain of more inventions against the social welfare loss of temporary monopoly power in newly invented activities.

Review Quiz

- ◆ What is special about knowledge as a consumer good and as a factor of production?
- ◆ What are the external benefits that arise from education and training, and from research and development?
- ◆ How can governments use subsidies, below-cost provision, and patents and copyrights to achieve an efficient allocation of research and development.
- ◆ How might governments use subsidies, below-cost provision and patents to deliver an efficient amount of education?
- ◆ Why might knowledge be special in not displaying diminishing returns?
- ◆ If patents and copyrights stimulate research, why don't we just award unlimited patents and copyrights to inventors and creators of new knowledge?

We've now completed our study of how governments intervene to alter market outcomes to achieve a fairer and a more efficient distribution of resources.

In our study of microeconomics, you have learned how all economic problems arise from scarcity and involve opportunity cost. Prices are opportunity costs and are determined by the interactions of buyers and sellers in markets. Consumers choose what to buy and what resources to sell to maximize their own utility. Firms choose what to produce and sell and what resources to buy to maximize profit. Consumers and producers interact in markets. The resulting equilibrium might be efficient or inefficient, fair or unfair. Government policy can modify the outcome of the market to improve efficiency and equity and raise social welfare. Governments can use tax and benefits, provide public goods, curb monopoly power, and cope with externalities to achieve these ends.

You have completed your study on microeconomics. You can now move on to study macroeconomics and issues in international economics, drawing on the microeconomics you have learned.

---

[1] From Paul Romer 'Ideas and Things', in *The Future Surveyed*, a supplement to *The Economist*, 11 September 1993, pp. 71–72. © 1993 The Economist Newspaper Group, Inc. The 'standard calculation' that Romer refers to is the number of ways of selecting and arranging in order 20 objects from 20 objects – also called the number of permutations of 20 objects 20 at a time. This number is *factorial* 20, or $20! = 20 \times 19 \times 18 \times \ldots 2 \times 1 = 10^{18.4}$.

A standard theory (challenged by observations made by the Hubble space telescope in 1994) is that a big bang started the universe 15 billion years, or $10^{17.7}$ seconds, ago. Although $10^{18.4}$ and $10^{17.7}$ look similar, $10^{18.4}$ is *five* times as large as $10^{17.7}$, so if you started trying alternative sequences at the moment of the big bang and took only one second per trial you would still have tried only one fifth of the possibilities. Amazing?

Summary

Key Points

Economics of the Environment (pp. 383–391)

- Popular discussion of the environment frames the debate in terms of right and wrong, but economists emphasize costs and benefits and a need to find a way to balance the two.

- The demand for environmental policies has grown because incomes have grown and awareness of the connection between actions and the environment has increased.

- Air pollution in the form of urban smog, air toxins, acid rain, global warming, and ozone layer depletion arise from road transport, power stations and industrial processes.

- Externalities (environmental and others) arise when property rights are absent. Sometimes it is possible to overcome an externality by assigning a property right.

- The Coase theorem states that private market transactions are efficient – there are no externalities. In this case, the same efficient outcome is achieved regardless of who has the property right, the polluter or the victim.

- When property rights cannot be assigned, governments might overcome environmental externalities by using emission charges, uniform standards, marketable permits, or taxes.

- Standards are inefficient but widely used because it is difficult to identify the information needed to set efficient charges, permits or taxes.

- Global externalities, such as greenhouse gases and substances that deplete the earth's ozone layer, can be overcome only by international action. Each country acting alone has insufficient incentive to act in the interest of the world as a whole. There is also a great deal of scientific uncertainty and disagreement about the effects of greenhouse gases and ozone depletion, and in the face of this uncertainty, international resolve to act is weak.

- The world is locked in a type of 'prisoners' dilemma' game in which it is in every country's self-interest to let other countries carry the costs of environmental policies.

Economics of Knowledge (pp. 391–394)

- Knowledge is both a consumer good and a factor of production that creates external benefits.

- External benefits from education – passing on existing knowledge to others – arise because the skills and training equip people to interact and communicate more effectively.

- External benefits from research – creating new knowledge – arise because once someone has worked out how to do something, others can copy the basic idea.

- Governments can use policies to encourage the efficient level of education, training and innovation to take place.

- Three devices are available to governments: subsidies, below-cost provision and patents.

- Subsidies and public provision can achieve an efficient provision of education and training.

- Patents and copyrights create intellectual property rights and increase the incentive to innovate. As patents create a temporary monopoly, the cost must be balanced against the benefit of more inventive activity.

Key Figures ◆

Key Terms

Problems

•1 A pesticide maker can dump waste into a lake or truck it to a safe storage place. The marginal cost of trucking is €100 a tonne. A trout farm uses the lake and its profit, shown in the following table, depends on how much waste is dumped.

Quantity of waste (tonnes per week)	Trout farm profit (euros per week)
0	1,000
1	950
2	875
3	775
4	650
5	500
6	325
7	125

a What is the efficient amount of waste to be dumped into the lake?

b If the trout farm owns the lake, how much waste is dumped and how much does the pesticide maker pay to the farmer per tonne?

c If the pesticide maker owns the lake, how much waste is dumped and how much rent does the farmer pay the factory for the use of the lake?

2 A steel smelter is located at the edge of a residential area. The table shows the cost of cutting the pollution of the smelter. It also shows the property taxes that people are willing to pay at different levels of pollution.

Pollution cut (percentage)	Property taxes willingly paid (euros per day)	Total cost of pollution cut (euros per day)
0	0	0
10	150	10
20	285	25
30	405	45
40	510	70
50	600	100
60	675	135
70	735	175
80	780	220
90	810	270
100	825	325

Assume that the increase in property taxes that people are willing to pay measures the change in total benefit of cleaner air that results from a change in the percentage decrease in pollution.

a What is the efficient percentage decrease in pollution?

b With no regulation of pollution, how much pollution will there be?

c If the city owns the smelter, how much pollution will there be?

d If the city is a company town owned by the steel smelter, how much pollution will there be?

•3 Back at the pesticide plant and trout farm described in problem 1, suppose that no one owns the lake and that the government introduces a pollution tax.

a What is the tax per tonne of waste dumped that will achieve an efficient outcome?

b Explain the connection between the answer to part (a) and the answer to problem 1.

4 Back at the steel-smelting city in problem 2, suppose that the city government introduces a pollution tax.

a What is the tax per percentage of waste dumped that will achieve an efficient outcome?

b Explain the connection between the answer to part (a) and the answer to problem 2.

•5 Using the information provided in problem 1, suppose that no one owns the lake and that the government issues marketable pollution permits to both the farmer and the factory. Each may dump the same amount of waste in the lake, and the total that may be dumped is the efficient amount.

a What is the quantity that may be dumped into the lake?

b What is the market price of a permit? Who buys and who sells?

c What is the connection between the answer to parts (a) and (b) and the answers to problems 1 and 2?

6 Using the information given in problem 2, suppose that the city government issues marketable pollution permits to citizens and the smelter. Each may pollute the air by the same percentage, and the total is the efficient amount.

a What is the percentage of pollution?

b What is the market price of a permit? Who buys and who sells?

c What is the connection between the answer to parts (a) and (b) and the answers to problems 2 and 4?

•7 The marginal cost of educating a student is €4,000 a year and is constant. The figure shows the marginal private benefit curve.

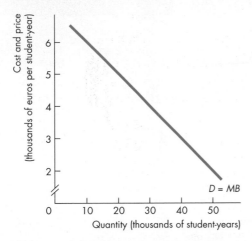

a With no government involvement and if the schools are competitive, how many students are enrolled and what is the tuition?

b The external benefit from education is €2,000 per student-year and is constant. If the government provides the efficient amount of education, how many school places does it offer and what is the tuition?

8 Online learning aids cuts the marginal cost of educating a student to €2,000 a year and is constant. The marginal private benefit is the same as in problem 7. The external benefit from education increases to €4,000 per student-year and is constant.

a With no government involvement and if the schools are competitive, how many students are enrolled and what is the tuition?

b If the government provides the efficient amount of education, how many school places does it offer and what is the tuition?

c Compare the outcomes in problem 8 with those in problem 7. Explain the differences between the two situations.

Critical Thinking

1 After you have studied Reading Between the Lines on pp. 398–399, answer the following questions:

a What are the developed countries required to do under the Kyoto Protocol and why?

b Why does President Bush think that ratifying the Protocol will harm the US economy?

c Why reasons are given in the various reports to suggest that ratifying the Protocol will increase economic growth?

d Do you think economies can grow without damaging the environment? If economies have to trade off environmental quality against growth, do you think there is an efficient level of such a trade-off? Explain your answer.

2 Use the links on the Parkin, Powell and Matthews website to get two viewpoints on global warming. Then answer the following questions:

a What are the benefits and costs of greenhouse gas emissions?

b Do you think the environmentalists are correct in the view that greenhouse gas emissions must be cut or do you think the costs of reducing greenhouse gas emissions exceed the benefits? Explain your answer.

c If greenhouse gas emissions are to be reduced, should reductions be achieved by assigning quotas or by using the price mechanism?

3 Use the Parkin, Powell and Matthews website to visit the UK Environment Agency and then answer the following questions:

a Describe the trend in emissions of carbon dioxide and sulphur dioxide into the atmosphere for all UK sources over the past 20 years.

b Describe the trend in nitrogen oxides and volatile organic compounds into the atmosphere for all UK sources over the past 20 years.

c Do these figures give any indication of the success of environmental policies to control emissions?

4 To decrease the amount of overfishing in their territorial waters, the governments of Iceland and New Zealand have introduced private property rights with an allocation of Individual Transferable Quotas (ITQs). To check out the effects of this system, use the link on the Parkin, Powell and Matthews website to visit the Fraser Institute in Vancouver. Then answer the following questions:

a Would the introduction of ITQs in the United Kingdom help to replenish UK fish stocks?

b Explain why ITQs generate an incentive not to overfish.

c Who would oppose ITQs and why?

 http://www.econ100.com

Externalities in the Kyoto Protocol

BBC NEWS ONLINE, 16 JULY 2001

Climate treaty 'will boost economies'

Alex Kirby

Conservationists say the economies of Europe and Japan will gain if they ratify the Kyoto Protocol, the global climate treaty . . . The European Union supports ratification of the treaty, but Japan's position remains ambiguous. The claim that ratifying the protocol would be economically beneficial comes in two reports commissioned by the World Wide Fund for Nature . . .

Mr Bush has said the US will not ratify Kyoto partly because he believes it would damage the US economy . . . But the report says unilateral implementation of the protocol by the EU could give its industries a head start in developing new technologies to cut emissions . . . The report says the cost of achieving its Kyoto target could be just 0.06 per cent of the EU's gross domestic product (GDP) in 2010. It states: 'Since climate protection policies also reduce other air pollutants, this would lead to financial savings on end-of-pipe technologies that reduce acid rain and local air pollution in Europe. Those savings could substantially cover the small cost to the EU of meeting the Kyoto targets'.

The report on Japan . . . says actively implementing the treaty could mean a 0.9 per cent increase in GDP, of around $47.3 bn . . . The report's authors say ratifying Kyoto could give Japan a springboard out of its long slump, and they foresee spill over benefits for its trading partners . . . Their analysis projects GDP increasing by about $11.5bn in south-east Asia and India, and by $13.9bn in western Europe, as a consequence of Japan's ratification.

By contrast, it believes the GDP of the US could shrink by about $45.5bn – around 0.6 per cent – mainly because of a lack of pressure to innovate. Professor Kornelis Blok, one of the authors of the European report, said that 'in order to reduce greenhouse gas emissions, you have to innovate and come up with new technologies. If the US does not ratify Kyoto and the EU and Japan do, they will gain a competitive advantage'. Dr Ute Collier, of WWF, said that 'by ratifying the protocol, Europe and Japan will be onto an economic winner. It will give them new opportunities in new markets'.

The Essence of the Story

■ Europe has agreed to ratify the Kyoto Protocol, but Japan is still undecided. The US has refused to ratify the agreement believing its economy will suffer.

■ Conservationists argue that the economies of Europe and Japan will gain from the innovation and new technology needed to ratify the Kyoto Protocol.

■ Japan could increase GDP by 0.9 per cent. The cost of ratifying in Europe could be just 0.06 per cent of GDP, which would be more than replaced by savings from new technology.

■ The US economy could shrink by 0.6 per cent if Europe and Japan gain a competitive advantage through ratifying.

■ The improvement in the economies of Europe and Japan will also create spillover benefits for their trading partners.

Economic Analysis

- The Kyoto agreement requires cuts in carbon emissions from burning fuels. A carbon tax on energy production is one method of achieving these cuts.

- Figure 1 shows the effect of imposing a carbon tax in the energy market. The marginal benefit from energy use is *MB,* the marginal production cost of energy is *MPC,* and the marginal social cost of energy is *MSC. MSC* is the sum *MPC* and marginal external costs, *MEC,* from carbon emissions.

- Without a tax, energy use (and the associated level of carbon emissions) is at Q_a where *MPC* equals *MB.* If a tax equal to the marginal external cost is imposed, energy use falls to the efficient level at Q_e, where $MSC = MB,$ and associated carbon emissions fall.

- A reduction in energy use can slow economic growth. Table 1 illustrates President Bush's short-term fears for the US economy as a strategic dilemma. The US decision is 'don't ratify' or 'ratify' along the top of Table 1. The decision for the EU and Japan (shown as one decision group) is the same.

- If both groups ratify they incur costs which slow growth to 0 per cent per annum. If both groups don't ratify, they save costs and their economies continue to grow at 1 per cent per annum. If Europe and Japan ratify but the USA does not, the USA gains a 2 per cent growth rate while Europe and Japan slow down and vice versa.

- If both groups believe in the payoffs in Table 1, the dominant strategy will lead to the collapse of the Kyoto Protocol.

- Table 2 shows the long-term payoffs from the EU perspective. If both groups don't ratify, long-term growth falls by 1 per cent in all countries due to the environmental damage. If both groups ratify, long-term growth will rise to 1.2 per cent through new market opportunities and spillover benefits from trade.

- If the EU and Japan ratify but the US does not, the EU and Japan gain a competitive advantage of 0.9 per cent and the US growth rate falls by 0.6 per cent. The dominant strategy from this perspective is for all to sign.

- Clearly, the result depends on belief in payoffs and the effect of technology and spillovers. President Bush may also take a shorter-term view than the European Commission, due to the political cycle.

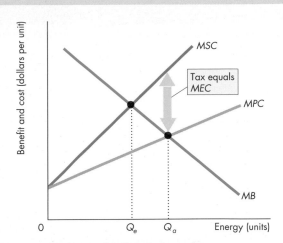

Figure 1 Impact of carbon fuel tax

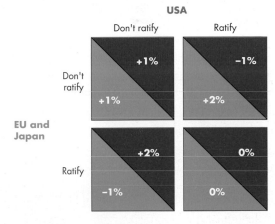

Table 1 USA view

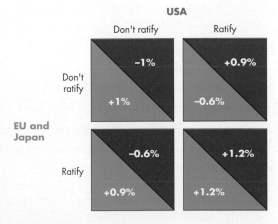

Table 2 EU view

Understanding Externalities

The question to be decided is: is the value of fish lost greater or less than the value of the product which contamination of the stream makes possible?

Ronald H. Coase The Problem of Social Cost

The Economist: Ronald Coase

Ronald Coase (1910–), was born in England and educated at the London School of Economics, where he was deeply influenced by his teacher, Arnold Plant, and by the issues of his youth: Communist Party central planning versus free markets.

Professor Coase has lived in the United States since 1951. He first visited America as a 20-year-old on a travelling scholarship during the depths of the Great Depression. It was on this visit, and before he had completed his bachelor's degree, that he conceived the ideas that 60 years later were to earn him the 1991 Nobel Prize for Economic Science. He discovered and clarified the significance of transaction costs and property rights for the functioning of the economy. Ronald Coase has revolutionized the way we think about property rights and externalities and has opened up the growing field of law and economics.

The Issues and Ideas

As knowledge accumulates, we are becoming more sensitive to environmental externalities. We are also developing more sensitive methods of dealing with them. But all the methods involve a public choice.

Urban smog, which is both unpleasant and dangerous to breathe, forms when sunlight reacts with emissions from the exhausts of motor vehicles. Because of this external cost, we set emission standards and tax petrol. Emission standards increase the cost of a vehicle, and petrol taxes increase the cost of the marginal kilometre travelled. The higher costs decrease the quantity demanded of road transportation and so decrease the amount of pollution it creates. Is the value of cleaner urban air worth the higher cost of transportation? The public choices of voters, regulators and law-makers answer this question.

Acid rain, which imposes a cost on everyone who lives in its path, falls from sulphur-laden clouds produced by electric utility chimneys. This external cost is being tackled with a market solution. This solution is marketable permits, the price and allocation of which are determined by the forces of supply and demand. Private choices determine the demand for pollution permits, but a public choice determines the supply.

As cars stream onto a motorway at morning rush hour, the motorway clogs and becomes an expensive car park. Each rush-hour traveller imposes external costs on all the others. Today, road users bear private congestion costs but do not face a share of the external congestion costs they create. But a market solution to this problem is now technologically feasible. It is a solution that charges road users a fee similar to a toll that varies with the time of day and degree of congestion. Confronted with the social marginal cost of their actions, each road user makes a choice and the market for motorway space is efficient. Here, a public choice to use a market solution leaves the final decision about the degree of congestion to private choices.

Then . . .

The River Thames had a reputation in early Victorian times for sustaining many aspects of commercial trade, including fishing. However, as the nineteenth century progressed, the number of factories sited near the river and using it as a dumping ground for waste products increased greatly. The result was a decline in fish stocks, particularly in salmon, until the 1940s when the Thames became incapable of sustaining a viable fish stock.

. . . And Now

Today, the Thames supports a diverse fish stock including the occasional salmon just as it did many years ago. The river is no longer viewed as a conduit for rubbish, industrial waste and chemicals and the result is a burgeoning ecosystem including many nesting birds. Pollutants are recognized as having potential externalities and the Department for the Environment is enforcing much more stringent laws regarding dumping. The imposition of penalties has shown how the River Thames' externality problem has been reduced by government regulation.

Trying These Ideas Today

Using your knowledge of environmental economics from Chapter 18, and what you have read about the success of environmental policy, you should be able to answer the following questions:

■ Ronald Coase was the first economist clearly to explain the underlying cause of external costs of pollution. Why did the lack of clearly defined property rights to clean water cause the River Thames to become so polluted?

■ How do the pollution fines and environmental standards imposed on modern industry around the River Thames today affect property rights to clean water?

■ The technology now exists to fit cars with electronic tags to charge for the use of roads. How will this technology affect the property rights to accessing roads?

Part 5

Macroeconomics and Fundamentals

Talking with **Roger Bootle**

One of the City of London's most respected economists, Roger Bootle now runs his own consultancy, Capital Economics, having formerly been Group Chief Economist of the HSBC Group, the parent of Midland Bank, where he was also an Executive Director of HSBC Greenwell. Roger Bootle is also a Visiting Professor at Manchester Business School, Economic Adviser to Deloitte & Touche, and a Specialist Adviser to the House of Commons Treasury Committee. Before the change of government he was a member of the former Chancellor's panel of Independent Economic Advisers, the so-called 'Wise Men'.

Roger studied at Oxford University and subsequently became a Lecturer in Economics at St Anne's College, Oxford. Most of his career has been spent in the City of London and he joined the Midland Group, which was subsequently absorbed into HSBC, in 1989.

He has written many articles on monetary economics and is joint author of the book *Theory of Money*, and author of *Index-Linked Gilts*. His latest book, *The Death of Inflation*, was published in 1996 and became a best-seller, subsequently translated into nine languages. Initially dismissed as extreme, this book is now widely recognised as prophetic.

A regular columnist on *The Sunday Telegraph*, Roger also appears frequently on national television and radio.

How did you get into economics?

I studied economics at school. I was at the time very interested in political things and obviously economic subjects cropped up the whole time in political disputes. I started studying economics and quickly came to enjoy it.

What do you do at Capital Economics?

We provide economic analysis, forecasting, commentary, studies, research, and all sorts for a wide variety of clients. We have certain regular services, which we sell on subscription and we do that to pension funds, insurance companies, fund managers, banks, just about anybody who will pay for them, but in practice they tend to be large financial companies with responsibility for managing large amounts of money.

Give me an example of what type of study you do for a client.

We recently had a commission from Logica, the software company, to look into the prospects for electronic money. The conclusion was that the essence of the problem standing between the current system, which is in many ways extremely inefficient, and something much more efficient and heavily electronic was not primarily technological. The technology is already there. The problem is a combination of consumer resistance and vested self-interest by the banks and financial institutions involved in running the current system. Although this is already changing what is so striking is how little the system has changed in the last thirty years given the possibilities.

What do you think are the major dangers facing the world economy today?

I think there are several dangers. The first is deflation, which I think is potentially a serious threat for America and Europe. Obviously Japan is in that position now and my strong belief is that deflation is much more difficult to get out of than the textbooks tell you. Just as inflation was much more difficult to subdue than the textbooks told us. I am seriously worried about the fact that the Japanese experience seems to vindicate that. I am also very concerned about the danger of protectionism and the break up of the international trading system. Clearly one cannot divorce all this from the events of 11 September 2001 and by contrast, I am extremely optimistic about the medium-term potential as a result of the bringing into the world trading system of not only China but also Eastern Europe. But that depends upon a confident open world trading system. I think the consequences of very weak demand with deflationary pressures in some countries and the political fall out from the terrorist attacks, will be, at least in the short term, that the movement will go in the opposite direction.

What is your book *The Death of Inflation* about?

The book argues that the high and volatile inflation that many countries in the West experienced in the 1970s/1980s is now a thing of the past and indeed that the main danger facing the West is deflation rather than high inflation. What I think distinguished the book was the emphasis that it placed on real structural factors rather than straightforward monetary ones. That is not to say that I don't think that monetary forces are important. But the attitude of monetary authorities towards inflation was only part of the story in the collapse of inflation and the downward surprises on inflation that we experienced in the 90s, in particular in Britain and the United States. The downward surprises were accompanied by upward surprises with regard to output and employment. In other words, it looked as though the trade-off between unemployment and inflation has changed in a favourable direction. The way I like to put this in the book, was that a lot of people fell into the trap of thinking that the natural rate of unemployment was fixed or that it was a mechanistic concept. Whereas it is quite clear from Friedman's early writing and others' that it certainly isn't – it's highly variable and depends on institutions and circumstances. Just as the natural rate rose in the 1970s, the book argues that increased competition, the collapse of trade union power, the break down of the old corporatism, combined to create an improvement in the trade-off. I argued that there would follow a period of very low inflation accompanied by low unemployment and strong growth which I think is more or less what we got in both Britain and America.

Who are the economists that have inspired you and why?

I had the great good fortune, as a young graduate student, to be supervised by Professor Sir John Hicks. He was not inspiring in person – he had a terrible stutter and a very diffident manner but I did greatly admire the clarity of his writing and his contribution to economics overall. The greatest inspiration for me was undoubtedly Keynes. The combination of his writing and thinking I found electrifying. That is not to say that I think he wasn't wrong on a number of issues. But what I really admired about Keynes is that he was an economist who lived in the real world, he was plugged into the wider social and political context where I think economics properly belongs. He was no slouch with regard to the technical aspects of the subject. He knew history, literature and had great powers of communication.

What advice would you give to an economics student today?

I think there is a big difference between making your way in the world of academic economics and wanting to be a practical economist. They start off the same but they end up I think very divergent. My advice would be to read widely, not to forget the wider context in which economics exists and from which it draws its justification, the very reason for its existence. We are trying to understand and to explain and to some extent predict the way the world works and behaves, and in order to do that you have to have a certain knowledge of the history, the politics, and culture, of human institutions. Economics is a subject in my view about human beings, not in my view subject to technology or high mathematics. Certainly one needs a good grasp of mathematics, but I would personally place history and economic history alongside mathematics.

CHAPTER 19

A First Look at Macroeconomics

After studying this chapter you will be able to:

◆ Describe the origins of macroeconomics and the problems it deals with

◆ Describe the long-term trends and short-term fluctuations in economic growth, unemployment, inflation and the balance of international payments

◆ Explain why economic growth, unemployment, inflation and the balance of international payments are important

◆ Identify the macroeconomic policy challenges and describe the tools available for meeting them

Boom or Bust?

During the past 100 years, the quantity of goods and services produced in the United Kingdom has increased nearly sixfold. In 2000, production expanded more quickly than the average. This rapid growth raised fears that the economy was overheating. How does an economy overheat? Why was rapid economic growth feared? ◆ One reason overheating was feared is because it was thought that output growth was faster than the economy's capacity to sustain that growth. Another reason was the decrease in unemployment to one million. But how can the economy be overheating when so many people are unemployed? ◆ In contrast, 2001 was a year when production growth was slow raising fears of a slide into recession. What is a recession? How can we move so quickly from overheating (boom) to recession (bust)? Can a slowdown in one country influence the economic performance of another? In Reading Between the Lines (pp. 422–423) we examine how major economies interact so as to have common output growth patterns ◆ Prices have increased slowly in recent years. But with rapid production growth and falling unemployment, it was feared that inflation might break out again. That's what overheating means – an economy growing so quickly that inflation increases. What exactly is inflation, and why does it matter? Will an economic slowdown reduce the fear of inflation? ◆ To prevent the economy from overheating and inflation increasing, the Bank of England in the UK or the European Central Bank in the European Monetary Union may take preventive action. What kinds of action do the Bank of England or ECB take? How do those actions influence production, jobs, inflation and the ability of people to compete in the global marketplace? Can these two central banks overdo things and drive the economy from overheating into recession?

◆ ◆ ◆ ◆ These questions are the subject matter of macroeconomics – the branch of economics that seeks to understand economic growth, unemployment, inflation and the balance of international payments and to design policies to improve macroeconomic performance. The macroeconomic events through which we are now living are tumultuous and exciting. With what you learn in these chapters, you will be able to understand these events, the policy challenges they bring and the political debate they stir. ◆ Let's begin by looking at the origins of macroeconomics and the key issues it deals with.

Origins and Issues of Macroeconomics

Economists began to study long-term economic growth, inflation and international payments as long ago as the 1750s, and this work was the beginning of macroeconomics. But modern macroeconomics emerged much later, as a response to the **Great Depression**, a decade (1929–39) of high unemployment and stagnant production throughout the world economy. In the United Kingdom, the Great Depression came on top of an existing situation of slump and mass unemployment. In the worst year, 1931, total production fell by over 5 per cent and in the following year unemployment reached a record 15 per cent of the workforce. These were years of human misery on a scale that is hard to imagine today. A deep pessimism about the ability of the market economy to work properly was created. Many people believed that the experience of mass unemployment demonstrated that the economic system of private ownership and free markets was a failure. The perceived failure was so extreme that it raised the deeply disturbing question of whether liberal–democratic political institutions could survive.

The economic dogma of the period had no solutions. The major alternative economic system of central planning and the political system of socialism seemed increasingly attractive to many people. It was in this climate of economic depression and political and intellectual turmoil that macroeconomics emerged. Its origin was the publication in 1936 of John Maynard Keynes' *The General Theory of Employment, Interest, and Money*.

Short-term versus Long-term Goals

Keynes' theory was that depression and high unemployment result from insufficient private spending and that to cure these problems, the government must increase its spending. Keynes' focus was primarily the *short term*. He wanted to cure an immediate and serious problem almost regardless of what the *long-term* consequences of the cure might be. 'In the long run', said Keynes, 'we're all dead'.

But Keynes believed that after his cure for depression had restored the economy to a normal condition, the long-term problems of inflation and economic growth would become the central ones. He even suspected that his cure for depression, increased government spending, might trigger inflation and also might lower the long-term growth rate of production. With a lower long-term growth rate, fewer jobs would be created. If this outcome did occur, a policy aimed at lowering unemployment might end up increasing it in the long run.

By the late 1960s and through the 1970s, these long-term concerns became a reality. Inflation increased, economic growth slowed down, and in some countries unemployment became persistently high. The causes of these developments are complex. But they point to an inescapable conclusion: the long-term issues of inflation, slow growth and persistent unemployment and the short-term issues of depression and economic fluctuations intertwine, and are most usefully studied together. So although macroeconomics was reborn during the Great Depression, it has today returned to its older tradition. Nowadays, it is a subject that tries to understand the long-term issues of economic growth and inflation as well as short-term economic fluctuations and the unemployment these fluctuations bring.

The Road Ahead

There is no unique way to study macroeconomics. Because its rebirth was a product of economic depression, it was common for many years to pay most attention to short-term output fluctuations and unemployment. But long-term issues were never completely forgotten. During the late 1960s and 1970s, when a serious inflation emerged, this topic returned to prominence. Rising inflation in this period was coupled with a slowing down in long-term growth and rising unemployment. A new word had come into being to describe this phenomenon – **stagflation**. Economists redirected their energy towards tackling this problem. In the 1990s, when information technologies had shrunk the globe, the international dimension of macroeconomics became more prominent. The result of all these events is that modern macroeconomics is a broad subject that pays attention to all the issues we've just reviewed: long-term economic growth, unemployment, inflation and international economic activity.

Over the past 40 years, economists have developed a clearer understanding of the forces that determine macroeconomic performance and they have devised policies that, while imperfect, stand some chance of preventing the extremes of depression and inflation.

Your main goal is to become familiar with the theories of macroeconomics and the policies they make possible. To set you on your path towards this goal, we're going to take a first look at the macroeconomic issues of economic growth, unemployment, inflation and the balance of international payments and learn why they are problems that merit our attention.

Economic Growth

Your parents are richer than your grandparents were when they were young. But are you going to be richer than your parents? And are your children going to be richer than you? The answers depend on the rate of economic growth.

Economic growth is the expansion of the economy's capacity to produce goods and services. It is an expansion of the economy's production possibilities and can be pictured as an outward shift of the production possibility frontier (*PPF*) (see Chapter 2, p. 22).

We measure economic growth by the increase in real gross domestic product. **Real gross domestic product** (also called **real GDP**) is the value of *aggregate* or *total* production – the output of all the coun-try's farms, factories, shops and offices – measured in the prices of a single year. At the present time, real GDP in the United Kingdom is measured in prices that prevailed in 1995 (1995 prices). We use the prices of a single year so that we can eliminate the influence of *inflation* – the increase in prices – and determine how much production has grown from one year to another. (The concept of real GDP is explained more fully in Chapter 20 on pp. 425–429.)

Real GDP is not a perfect measure of total production. For example, it does not include the things we produce for ourselves such as do-it-yourself jobs (DIY) in the home or other housework. Nor does it include things people produce that are illegal or are legal but unrecorded so as to avoid taxes – known as the underground economy. But despite its shortcomings real GDP is the broadest measure of total production available. What does it tell us about economic growth in the United Kingdom and other countries in Europe?

Economic Growth in the United Kingdom

Figure 19.1 shows real GDP in the United Kingdom since 1960 and it highlights two features of economic growth:

Figure 19.1

Economic Growth in the United Kingdom: 1960–2000

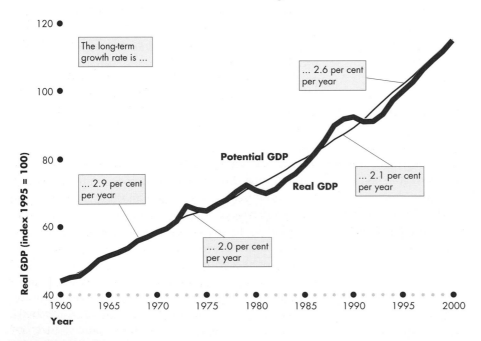

The long-term economic growth rate, measured by the growth of potential GDP, was 2.9 per cent a year during the 1960s but slowed to 2.0 per cent a year during the 1970s, 2.1 in the 1980s and 2.6 per cent in the 1990s. Real GDP fluctuates around potential GDP.

Sources: National Statistics and Lombard Street Research Ltd. Estimates of potential GDP are obtained by applying a Hodrick–Prescott Filter.

1 The growth of potential GDP.

2 Fluctuations of real GDP around potential GDP.

The Growth of Potential GDP

Potential GDP is the real GDP the economy would produce if all its resources – labour, capital, land and entrepreneurial ability – were fully employed. The rate of long-term economic growth is measured by the steepness of the potential GDP line.

Look closely at Figure 19.1. You can see that there are four trends in potential GDP. The potential GDP line is steeper in the 1960s than in the 1970s and steeper again in the 1980s and again in the 1990s. During the 1960s, potential GDP grew at an average annual rate of 2.9 per cent a year. Growth slowed during the 1970s as a result of a **productivity growth slowdown** – a slowdown in the growth rate of output per person. Growth in potential GDP in the 1970s was at an average of only 2.0 per cent. Faster growth in potential GDP returned during the 1980s and 1990s. Growth in potential GDP in the 1980s was 2.1 per cent and in the 1990s was 2.6 per cent.

Why did the productivity growth slowdown occur? This is not an easy question to answer. Many factors were at work in the 1970s, but two were critical: oil price shocks and rapid inflation. The oil price shocks of 1973–74 triggered the development of new energy-saving technologies and a high level of investment in energy efficient equipment. But these innovations and investments did not increase labour productivity. The rapid inflation of the 1970s brought increased uncertainty and made it hard for people to make wise long-term investment decisions. This brief explanation of the productivity slowdown is expanded in Chapter 30.

Was the United Kingdom alone in experiencing a productivity growth slowdown? No. We'll see some other examples later in this chapter when we look at long-term growth around the world. But the consequence is that we have much smaller incomes today than we would have had if productivity growth had not slowed. But let's now look at the second feature of economic growth, namely the fluctuations around trend.

Fluctuations Around Trend

Real GDP fluctuates around potential GDP in a business cycle. A **business cycle** is the periodic but irregular up and down movement in economic activity. It is measured by fluctuations in real GDP around poten-

tial GDP. When real GDP is less than potential GDP, some resources are underused. For example, some labour is unemployed and capital is underutilized. When real GDP is greater than potential GDP, some resources are being overused. For example, many people are working longer hours than they are willing to put up with in the long run and capital is being worked so intensively that there is no time to keep it in prime working order.

Business cycles are not regular, predictable, or repeating cycles like the phases of the moon. Their timing changes unpredictably. But cycles do have some things in common. Every business cycle has two turning points:

1 Peak.

2 Trough.

and two phases:

1 Recession.

2 Expansion.

Figure 19.2 shows these features of the most recent business cycle. A *peak* is the upper turning point of a business cycle where an expansion ends and a recession begins. A peak occurred in the second quarter of 1990. A *trough* is the lower turning point of a business cycle where a recession ends and a recovery begins. A trough occurred in the first quarter of 1992.

A **recession** is a period during which real GDP decreases – the growth rate of real GDP is negative – for at least two successive quarters. In Figure 19.2, a recession began in the second quarter of 1990 and ended in the first quarter of 1992.

An **expansion** is a period during which real GDP increases. It begins at a trough and ends at a peak. In Figure 19.2, an expansion ended at the 1990 peak and another expansion began at the 1992 trough.

The Recent Recession in Historical Perspective

The recession of 1990–92 that is shown in Figure 19.2 seemed pretty severe while we were passing through it, but compared with earlier recessions it was relatively mild. You can see how mild it was by looking at Figure 19.3, which shows a longer history of economic growth. The most precipitous decline in real GDP occurred immediately after the First World War. A large fall in real GDP also occurred in 1931 and immediately following the Second World War. In more recent times, milder decreases in real GDP occurred during the mid-1970s – the time of oil price

Figure 19.2

The Most Recent UK Business Cycle

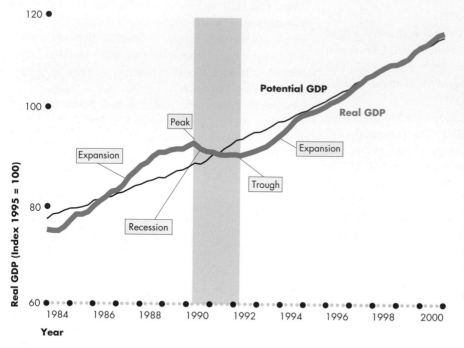

A business cycle has two turning points: a peak and a trough. In the most recent business cycle, the peak occurred in the second quarter of 1990 and the trough occurred in the first quarter of 1992. A business cycle has two phases: recession and expansion. The most recent recession ran from the peak in 1990 to the trough in 1992 as indicated by the pink area on the figure. The most recent expansion began in the second quarter of 1992 and has run through to the end of 2000.

Source: National Statistics.

Figure 19.3

Long-term Economic Growth in the United Kingdom

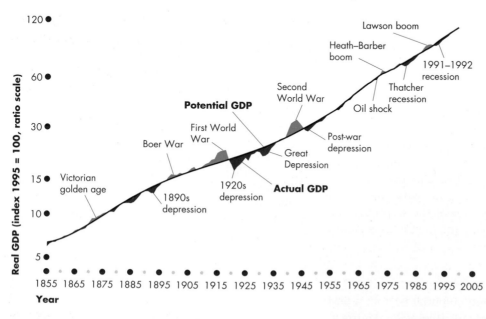

The thin black line shows potential GDP. Along this line, real GDP grew at an average rate of 2.0 per cent a year between 1856 and 2000. The blue areas show when real GDP was above potential GDP and the red areas show when it was below potential GDP. During some periods, such as the Second World War, real GDP expanded quickly. During other periods, such as the Great Depression and more recently in 1974–75, 1980–81 and 1990–92, real GDP declined.

Sources: GDP 1855–1947: C.H. Feinstein, *National Income Expenditure and Output of the United Kingdom, 1855–1965*, 1972, Cambridge, Cambridge University Press; GDP 1948–2000 National Statistics. Potential GDP Lombard Street Research Ltd and author estimates.

Figure 19.4

Economic Growth in Three Major Economies

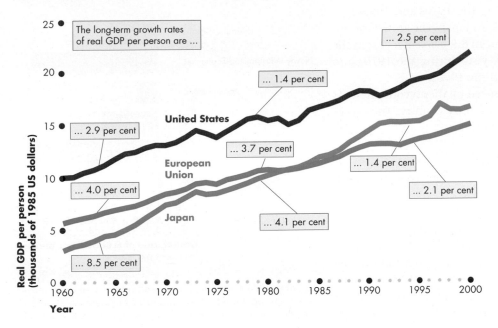

The long-term growth rates of real GDP per person are ...

... 2.5 per cent

... 1.4 per cent

United States

... 2.9 per cent

... 3.7 per cent

... 1.4 per cent

European Union

... 4.0 per cent

... 2.1 per cent

Japan

... 4.1 per cent

... 8.5 per cent

Real GDP per person (thousands of 1985 US dollars)

Year

Economic growth in the three large economies, the United States, Japan and the EU-15 has followed a similar pattern. The growth rate in all three countries slowed during the 1970s and 1980s and each country has similar business cycles. But Japan has grown fastest and the EU-15 too has grown faster than the United States.

Sources: The data for 1960 through 1992 are from 'The Penn World Table', *Quarterly Journal of Economics*, May 1991, pp. 327–368. New computer disk supplement (Mark 5.6a). The data use comparable international relative prices converted to 1985 US dollars. The data for 1993–2000 are calculated from Eurostat sources.

hikes by OPEC – and during the early 1980s and early 1990s.

While each of these economic downturns was considered to be severe at the time, you can see that the downturn that occurred in the interwar period was more severe than anything that followed it. This episode was so extreme that we don't call it a recession. We call it a depression. The term *depression* is used to describe a severe contraction of production that brings extreme and prolonged hardship.

The fact that the last truly great depression occurred before governments started taking policy actions to stabilize the economy (and before the birth of macroeconomics) has led to speculation that perhaps macroeconomics has made a contribution to economic stability. We'll examine this speculation on a number of occasions in this book.

We've seen that real GDP has increased over the long term. We've seen that long-term growth slowed during the 1970s. We've seen that recessions have interrupted the broad upward sweep of real GDP. Is the UK experience typical? Do other countries share this experience? Let's see if they do.

Economic Growth Around the World

A country might have a rapid growth rate of real GDP, but it might also have a rapid population growth rate. To compare growth rates over time and across countries, we use the growth rate of real GDP *per person*. **Real GDP per person** is real GDP divided by the population.

Figure 19.4 shows the growth of real GDP per person between 1960 and 2000 for three major economies: the United States, Japan, and the European Union-15. Three features of the paths of real GDP per person stand out:

1 Similar productivity growth slowdowns.

2 Similar business cycles.

3 Different long-term trends in potential GDP.

Similar Productivity Growth Slowdowns

The countries shown in Figure 19.4 have experienced similar productivity growth slowdowns. Between 1960 and 1973 EU-15 real GDP growth per person was 4.0 per cent a year, but it slowed to 3.7 per cent in the 1970s and 80s and 2.1 per cent in the 1990s. In the United States, growth of real GDP per person was 2.9 per cent a year during the 1960s, but it slowed to 1.4 per cent a year during the 1970s and 1980s and 2.5 per cent in the 1990s. In Japan, the growth of real GDP per person slowed from 8.5 per cent a year in the 1960s to 4.1 per cent a year during the 1970s and 1980s and 1.4 per cent in the 1990s.

The slowdown experienced by these economies was also experienced by almost every country. The exceptions were the major oil producers.

Similar Business Cycles

The major economies have experienced similar business cycles. Each economy had an expansion running from the early or mid-1960s to 1973–74, a recession between 1973 and 1975, an expansion to 1979, another recession in the early 1980s, and a long expansion through the rest of the 1980s followed by recession between 1991 and 1993 and the long recovery to 2000. Like the common productivity growth slowdown, this common business cycle is shared by most economies around the world. In Reading Between the Lines (see pages 422–423) we examine why the major economies share a common business cycle. The predicted slowdown in the US economy in 2001 and the continuing weakness of the Japanese economy have raised fears that the world economy will slide into a global recession in 2001 and 2002.

Different Long-term Trends in Potential GDP

Perhaps the most striking feature of Figure 19.4 is the variation in the long-term growth rates of the big economies. In 1960, real GDP per person was $5,500 in the EU-15, $9,800 in the United States, and $3,000 in Japan. So, in round numbers, in 1960, the United States produced three times as much per person as Japan, and nearly twice as much per person as the whole EU.

But during the 1960s, Japan's output streaked upward like a rocket. When US long-term growth in real GDP per person was 2.9 per cent a year, and the EU-15 achieved a rate of 4.0 per cent a year, real GDP in Japan grew at an astonishing 8.5 per cent a year. These differences in the long-term growth trend survived the productivity growth slowdown. After the slowdown, when Japan's growth rate halved, its growth of real GDP per person still exceeded the US rate before the slowdown.

Because it has achieved such a high growth rate, Japan has narrowed the gap between its own production level and that of the other economies. But a

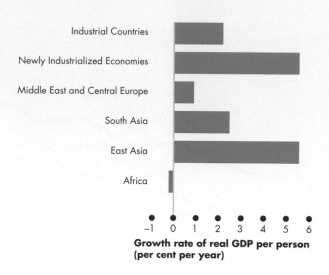

Figure 19.5

Growth Rates Around the World

Between 1970 and 1998, the growth rate of real GDP per person in the industrialized countries has been a modest 2.2 per cent per year. The developing countries of East Asia and the newly industrialized economies have had the most rapid growth rates. Africa has had the slowest growth.

Source: *World Economic Outlook* (Washington DC: International Monetary Fund, May 2000), p. 113.

major banking and financial crisis in Japan resulted in a fall in output in 1997 and 1998. The stagnation in Japan's growth rate will have major consequences for the fast growing economies of East Asia and for the world economy in general.

Figure 19.5 compares the growth rates of the industrial countries and other economies between 1970 and 1998. In this period the industrial countries as a whole grew at a modest rate per year. The fastest growth has been with the East Asian economies (including China) and the newly industrialized economies. The slowest growth has been in Africa where GDP per person has fallen over this period.

Benefits and Costs of Economic Growth

What are the benefits and costs of economic growth? Does it matter if the long-term growth rate slows down as it did during the 1970s?

The main benefit of long-term economic growth is expanded consumption possibilities, including greater welfare and support for the poor, the elderly and the disadvantaged. Other benefits include more expenditure on education and health, better roads, and more and better housing. We can even have a cleaner environment.

When the long-term growth rate slows, the resources that would have been used for these benefits are lost and the loss can be large. However, it must be understood that the proportion of a country's resources devoted to welfare issues and the long-term rate of growth are interrelated. It is certainly the case that the lower the long-term rate of growth the fewer resources are available for welfare. But it is also true that if more resources are spent on welfare there are fewer available for the productive sectors that generate growth. Finding the balance between resources available for current consumption such as welfare spending and resources devoted to future consumption through growth is one of the big issues of macroeconomics.

While economic growth brings enormous benefits, it also has costs. The main cost of economic growth is the current consumption forgone. To sustain a high growth rate over a large number of years, resources must be devoted to advancing technology and accumulating capital rather than to producing goods and services for current consumption.

A second possible cost of faster long-term economic growth is more rapid depletion of exhaustible natural resources such as oil and natural gas. A third possible cost is environmental degradation such as increased pollution of the air, rivers and oceans. But none of these problems are inevitable. The technological advances that bring economic growth often help us to economize on natural resources and to achieve a cleaner environment. For example, more efficient internal combustion engines have decreased the amount of petrol a car uses and cut lead and carbon emissions.

A fourth possible cost of faster long-term economic growth is more frequent changes in the jobs we do and the place we live. Faster long-term growth means that the number of new businesses starting up increases and possibly existing businesses fail at a faster pace. With the birth and death of businesses, jobs are created and destroyed. Faster long-term growth increases the pace of job creation and job destruction. In a fast-growing economy, people must be ready to accept changes in the jobs they do and the places in which they live and to bear the costs of these changes.

The choices that people make, to balance the benefits and costs of economic growth, determine the actual pace of economic growth. We'll study these choices and their consequences in Chapter 30.

Review Quiz

- What is economic growth and how is the long-term economic growth rate measured?
- What is the distinction between real GDP and *potential* GDP?
- What is a business cycle and what are its phases?
- In what phase of the business cycle was the UK economy during 2000?
- What happened to productivity growth in the UK and other countries during the 1970s?
- What are the similarities and differences in growth among the major economies?
- What are the benefits and the costs of long-term economic growth?

We've seen that real GDP grows and that it also fluctuates over the business cycle. Business cycles bring fluctuations in jobs and unemployment. Let's now examine this core macroeconomic problem.

Jobs and Unemployment

What kind of labour market will you enter when you graduate? Your decision to take a university course may have been prompted by your assessment of the chances of securing a good job after taking a degree. Whether there will be plenty of good jobs to choose from, or whether you will be forced to take a low-paying job that doesn't use your education will depend, in part, on the total number of jobs available and on the unemployment rate.

Jobs

Between 1979 and 2000 10.2 million jobs were created in the European Union. This number may appear to be impressive but let's put it in an international perspective. In the United States – a comparably sized economy – 42 million jobs were created over the same period. In the United Kingdom the number of jobs created were 2.4 million. But these figures disguise the considerable changes that have been going on in the jobs market. There has been a general switch from manufacturing jobs to services, from male to female workers and from full-time to part-time. Of course new jobs are created every month, but there are many that are also destroyed. The pace of job creation and destruction fluctuates over the business cycle. More jobs are destroyed than created during a recession, so the number of jobs decreases. But more jobs are created than destroyed during a recovery and expansion, so the number of jobs increases. For example, 1.7 million jobs were lost between 1979 and 1983. In the long recovery to 1989 3.2 million jobs were created, in the recession of 1990–1992 the number of jobs fell by nearly 1.9 million and in the recovery from 1993 to 2000 2.8 million jobs were created.

Unemployment

An internationally recognized definition of unemployment is that a person is defined as being **unemployed** if he or she does not have a job but is available for work, willing to work and has made some effort to find work within the previous four weeks. The sum of the people who are unemployed and the people who are employed is called the workforce. The **unemployment rate** is the percentage of the people in the workforce who are unemployed.

(The concepts of the workforce and unemployment are explained more fully in Chapter 21 on pp. 446–457.)

The unemployment rate is not a perfect measure of the underutilization of labour for two main reasons. First, it excludes discouraged workers. A **discouraged worker** is a person who does not have a job, is available for work and willing to work, but who has given up the effort to find work. Many people switch between the unemployment and discouraged worker categories in both directions every month. Second, the unemployment rate measures unemployed persons rather than unemployed labour hours. It excludes those people who have a part-time job but who want a full-time job.

Despite these two limitations, the unemployment rate is the best available measure of underused labour resources. Let's look at some facts about unemployment.

Unemployment in the United Kingdom

Figure 19.6 shows the unemployment rate in the United Kingdom from 1855 to 2000. Two features

---

Figure 19.6

Unemployment in the United Kingdom: 1855–2000

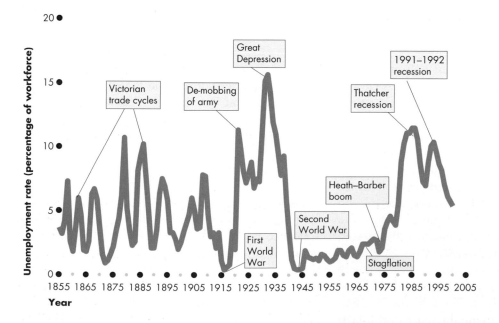

Unemployment is a persistent feature of economic life, but its rate varies. At its worst – during the Great Depression – nearly 16 per cent of the workforce was unemployed. Even in recent recessions, the unemployment rate climbed to 11 per cent. Between 1945 and the late 1960s unemployment remained stable. From the mid-1970s, there has been a general tendency for the unemployment rate to increase.

Sources: C. H. Feinstein, *National Income Expenditure and Output of the United Kingdom, 1855–1965*, 1972, Cambridge, Cambridge University Press; Eurostat.

Figure 19.7

Unemployment in the Industrial Economies

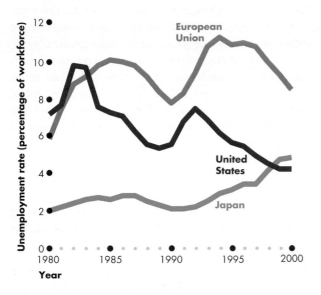

The unemployment rate in the European Union has in general been higher than that in the United States but has been falling in recent years. EU unemployment has a cycle that is out of phase with the United States. Japanese unemployment barely changed in the 1980s but has risen in the 1990s and is now higher than in the United States.

Source: Eurostat.

stand out. First, we have had high unemployment in the past. Unemployment in the depressed interwar years reached a peak of 15.6 per cent. In the period after the Second World War the average unemployment rate remained low until the late 1970s.

Second, although we have not recently experienced anything as high as the mass unemployment of the interwar years, we have seen high unemployment rates during recessions. The figure highlights two recent experiences – the 1980–1981 recession and the 1990–1992 recession.

But how does UK unemployment compare with unemployment in other countries?

Unemployment Around the World

Figure 19.7 shows the unemployment rate in the United States, the European Union, and Japan. Over the period shown in this figure, US unemployment averaged 6.4 per cent, much higher than Japanese

unemployment, which averaged 2.9 per cent, but lower than unemployment in the European Union, which averaged 9.3 per cent.

The figure shows that unemployment fluctuates over the business cycle. It increases during a recession and decreases during an expansion. The cycle in the United States is out of phase with Europe. Japanese unemployment has been remarkably stable but has risen steadily in the 1990s and by 2000 was higher than in the United States.

We've looked at some facts about unemployment in the United Kingdom and in other countries. Let's now look at some of the consequences of unemployment that make it the serious problem that it is.

Why Unemployment is a Problem

Unemployment is a serious economic, social and personal problem for two main reasons:

1   Lost production and incomes.
2   Lost human capital.

Lost Production and Incomes

The loss of a job brings an immediate loss of income. This loss can be devastating for the person who faces it. Jobseeker's allowance creates a short term safety net but does not always provide the same living standard as a job.

Lost Human Capital

Prolonged unemployment can permanently damage a person's job prospects. For example, a middle-aged manager loses his job when his firm downsizes. Short of income, he takes a job as a taxi driver. After a year he discovers that he cannot compete with young MBA graduates. He eventually finds a job as a shop manager and at a lower wage than his previous managerial job. He has lost some of his human capital.

Review Quiz

♦   How many new jobs have been created in the United Kingdom since 1979?
♦   What have been the main trends and cycles in the unemployment rate in the UK since 1933?
♦   How does unemployment in the EU compare with unemployment in the USA and Japan?
♦   What are the main costs of unemployment that make it a serious problem?

Inflation

Inflation is a process of rising prices. We measure the *inflation rate* as the percentage change in the *average* level of prices or **price level**. A common measure of the price level is the *Retail Prices Index* (RPI). The RPI tells us how the average price of all the goods and services bought by a typical household changes from month to month. (The RPI is explained in Chapter 20, pp. 433–436.) Every month the television news and the newspapers report the rate of inflation. How is this calculated?

So that you can see in a concrete way how the inflation rate is measured, let's do a calculation. In July 2000, the RPI was 170.6, and in July 2001, it was 173.3, so the inflation rate in mid 2001 was:

$$\text{Inflation} = \frac{173.3 - 170.6}{170.6} \times 100 = 1.6\%$$

Inflation in the United Kingdom

Figure 19.8 shows the UK inflation rate from 1960 to 2000. You can see from this figure that during the early 1960s the inflation rate was between 2 and 3 per cent a year. Inflation began to increase in the late 1960s, but the largest increases occurred in 1975 and 1980. These were years in which the actions of OPEC resulted in exceptionally large increases in the price of oil, but domestic policies also contributed to the inflation process. Inflation was brought under control in the early 1980s when the government instructed, the Bank of England to push interest rates up in an effort to reduce demand. Today the Monetary Policy Committee of the Bank of England targets a measure of the Retail Price Index excluding the influence of mortgage rates – known as RPIX.

The inflation rate rises and falls over the years, but it rarely becomes negative. If the inflation rate is negative, the price *level* is falling. Since the 1930s, the price level has generally risen – the inflation rate has been positive. Thus even when the inflation rate is low, as it was in 1961 and 1993, the price level is rising.

Inflation Around the World

Figure 19.9 shows inflation in the major industrial economies since 1970. You can see in part (a) that the

---

Figure 19.8

Inflation in the United Kingdom: 1960–2000

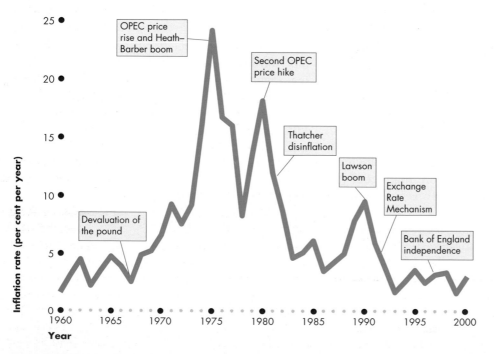

Inflation has been a persistent feature of economic life in the United Kingdom. The inflation rate was low in the first half of the 1960s, but it increased during the second half with the rise in world inflation. It increased further with the OPEC oil price hikes but declined during the Thatcher years of the 1980s as a result of policy actions. The inflation rate rose at the end of the 1980s and has fallen during the 1990s.

Source: National Statistics.

Figure 19.9

Inflation Around the World

(a) Inflation in industrial economies

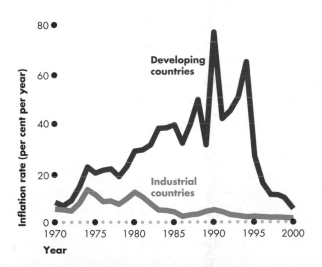

(b) Industrial countries and developing countries

Inflation in the industrial economies follows a similar pattern. They all shared the burst of double digit inflation in the 1970s and low inflation in the 1990s. Compared with the developing countries, inflation in the industrial economies is low.

Source: International Monetary Fund, *International Financial Statistics Yearbook*, 2000, Washington, DC.

inflation rates in the USA, EU and Japan have had a similar pattern. You can see that they all shared the burst of double digit inflation during the 1970s, the fall in inflation during the 1980s and low inflation in

the 1990s. You can see in part (b) that the average inflation rate of the industrial economies have been low compared with that of the developing countries. Among the developing countries, the most extreme inflation has occurred in the former Yugoslavia, where its rate has exceeded 6,000 per cent per year.

Why is Inflation a Problem?

If inflation were predictable, it would not be much of a problem. But inflation is not predictable. Unpredictable inflation makes the economy behave like a giant casino in which some people gain and some lose and no one can accurately predict where the gains and losses will fall. Gains and losses occur because of unpredictable changes in the value of money. Money is used as a measuring rod of value in the transactions that we undertake. Borrowers and lenders, workers and employers all make contracts in terms of money. If the value of money varies unpredictably over time, then the amounts *really* paid and received – the quantity of goods that the money will buy – also fluctuate unpredictably. Measuring value with a measuring rod whose units vary is a bit like trying to measure a piece of cloth with an elastic ruler. The size of the cloth depends on how tightly the ruler is stretched.

In a rapid inflation, resources are diverted from productive activities to forecasting inflation. It becomes more profitable to forecast the inflation rate correctly than to invent a new product. Doctors, lawyers, accountants, farmers – just about everyone – can make themselves better off, not by practising the profession for which they have been trained but by becoming amateur economists and inflation forecasters. From a social perspective, this diversion of talent resulting from inflation is like throwing our scarce resources on to the rubbish heap. This waste of resources is a cost of inflation.

The most serious type of inflation is called *hyperinflation* – an inflation rate that exceeds 50 per cent a month. Hyperinflation is rare, but it occurred in Germany, Poland and Hungary during the 1920s and Hungary and China during the 1940s. At the height of these hyperinflations, workers were paid twice a day because money lost its value so quickly. As soon as they were paid, people rushed off to spend their wages before they lost too much value. But hyperinflation is not just a historical curiosity. In 1994, the African country of Zaire had a hyperinflation that peaked at a *monthly* inflation rate of 76 per cent. Also during 1994, Brazil almost reached the hyperinflation stratosphere with a monthly inflation rate of 40 per cent. A cup of coffee that cost 15 cruzeiros in 1980 cost 22 *billion* cruzeiros in 1994. With numbers this big, Brazil twice changed the name of its currency and twice lopped off three zeros to keep the magnitudes of monetary values manageable.

Inflation imposes costs, but lowering inflation is also costly. Policies that lower the inflation rate increase the unemployment rate. Most economists think that the increase in unemployment that accompanies a fall in inflation is temporary. Others say that higher unemployment is a permanent cost of low inflation. The cost of lowering inflation must be evaluated when an anti-inflation policy is followed.

Review Quiz

◆ What is inflation and how does it influence the value of money?
◆ How is inflation measured?
◆ What has been the UK's inflation record since 1960?
◆ How does inflation in the UK compare with inflation in other industrial countries and in developing countries?
◆ What are some of the costs of inflation that make it a serious economic problem?

We've now looked at economic growth and the business cycle, unemployment and inflation, let's turn to the fourth macroeconomic problem: the balance of international payments. What happens when a country buys more from other countries than it sells to them? Does it face the problem that you and I would face if we spent more than we earned? Does it run out of money? Let's look at these questions.

International Payments

When we import goods and services from the rest of the world, we make payments to foreigners. When we export goods and services to the rest of the world, we receive payments from foreigners. We keep track of the values of our imports and exports in our international current account.

The Current Account

The **current account** records the receipts from exports (sales of goods and services to other countries), the

payments for imports (purchases of goods and services from other countries), income from workers employed abroad, income from investments abroad, and transfers by the government to the European Union (EU). The largest component of the current account in the UK is the trade in goods and services. The current account is made up of credit entries and debit entries. The credit entries are exports of goods and services, incomes received from workers abroad and investments abroad and receipts of transfers from the EU. The debit entries are imports of goods and services, incomes payable on foreign workers employed in the UK and investments by foreigners in the UK, and transfer payments to the EU. If our credits exceed our debits, we have a current account surplus. If our debits exceed our credits, we have a current account deficit.

The Current Account in the United Kingdom

Figure 19.10 shows the history of the UK current account since 1960. It shows that the United Kingdom has always had a problem with the balance of trade. The current account was in deficit in several years in the 1960s. It built up a surplus between 1969 and 1972 and slipped into deficit at the time of the OPEC oil crisis. Large surpluses occurred in the first half of the 1980s and deficits in the second half.

The current account balance fluctuates with the business cycle. In a recession, imports fall and the deficit decreases (or the surplus increases). During an expansion, imports rise and the current account deficit increases. For example, a large deficit emerged during the period of the major expansion of demand engineered by the Conservative Heath administration between 1973 and 1974. During the early 1980s, a huge surplus was generated following the deflationary policies of the Conservative Thatcher government. But after 1986, a persistent current account deficit emerged with the economic boom of the late 1980s. At times the deficit has been large. In 1989, for example, it was £21bn. How can we have a persistent current account deficit? The answer is because we have a capital and financial account surplus.

The Capital and Financial Account

The **capital and financial account** records the receipts from foreign investments in the United Kingdom and UK investments in the rest of the world.

Figure 19.10

The UK Current Account Balance: 1960–2000

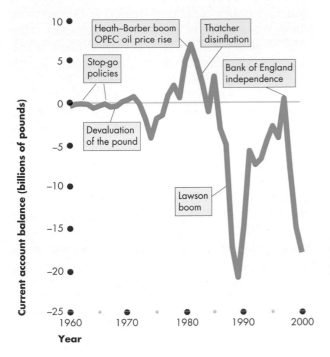

The current account records our exports and imports of goods and services. During the 1960s, our current account was generally in balance. In the mid-1970s, a deficit emerged following the expansionary policies of the Conservative Heath government. Since the 1980s, the current account has swung back and forth from surplus to deficit ending with a deficit by the end of the 1990s.

Source: National Statistics.

When we have a current account deficit, we borrow from foreigners or we sell some UK assets to foreigners to pay for it. When we have a current account surplus, we loan our surplus to the rest of the world or we buy foreign assets.

So a current account surplus is always matched by a capital and financial account deficit, and a current account deficit is always matched by a capital and financial account surplus. We do not, as a nation, run out of cash to pay our bills. But is borrowing from the rest of the world a problem? It might be, but it is not inevitably a problem.

Just as an individual can borrow to consume, so also can a country. Borrowing to consume is usually not a good idea. It builds up a debt that grows as interest is added to the debt, and at some point the debt plus the interest must be paid off. But an individual or a country can also borrow to invest in assets that earn interest. Borrowing to invest in assets that earn interest is potentially profitable. It creates an income stream that can pay off a debt and the interest on the debt. So long as the interest rate earned on the investment exceeds that on the debt, the deficit and the debt do not pose a problem.

You will learn more about the balance of international payments further on in this book.

Review Quiz

◆ What is the current account and how is it measured?
◆ What is a current account deficit? Surplus? Why does it matter for a country to be in surplus or deficit?
◆ What is the relationship between the current account and the business cycle?
◆ What is the capital and financial account?
◆ Why is a current account deficit matched by a capital and financial account surplus?

Let's close this chapter by looking at the macroeconomic policy challenges.

Macroeconomic Policy Challenges and Tools

From the time of Adam Smith's *The Wealth of Nations* until the establishment of macroeconomics in 1936, the general view was that the proper role of government in economic life was to provide the legal framework in which people could freely pursue their own best interests. The macroeconomics of Keynes, published in *The General Theory of Employment, Interest, and Money* in 1936, challenged this view and argued that government could (and should) take policy actions aimed at achieving and maintaining full employment.

The policy goal of full employment became the declared objective of the government following the publication of the White Paper on Employment Policy in 1944.

Policy Challenges

Today, the widely agreed challenges for macroeconomic policy in the UK and the rest of the EU are to:

1 Boost long-term growth.

2 Stabilize the business cycle.

3 Lower unemployment.

4 Keep inflation low.

5 Prevent a large current account deficit.

6 Prevent the government budget deficit from increasing above 3 per cent of GDP.

But how can we do all these things? What are the tools available to pursue the macroeconomic policy challenges?

Macroeconomic policy tools are divided into two broad categories:

1 Fiscal policy.

2 Monetary policy.

Fiscal Policy

Fiscal policy is the government's attempt to influence the economy by setting and changing taxes, government spending, and the government's deficit and debt. This range of policy actions is under the control of the Chancellor of the Exchequer and the Treasury. Fiscal policy can be used to try to change the total amount of spending or to change incentives so that investment and productivity increase. When the economy is in a recession, the government might cut taxes or increase its spending in an attempt to lower the unemployment rate. Conversely, when the economy is expanding and real GDP is above potential, the government might increase taxes or cut its spending in an attempt to prevent the economy from overheating.

Through most of the 1970s and 1980s, the government has spent more than it has raised in taxes. When government spending exceeds tax revenues, the government has a **budget deficit**. The government has stated as a long-term objective the desirability of eliminating the budget deficit. Also the Stability Pact imposes certain constraints on the fiscal deficits of member countries in the European Monetary Union (the eurozone). The constraints include a budget deficit target of 3 per cent of GDP. The existence of a budget deficit target has limited the scope for the use of fiscal policy to stabilize the business cycle.

Monetary Policy

Monetary policy consists of changes in interest rates and in the amount of money in the economy. This range of policy actions is under the control of the Bank of England in the UK and the European Central Bank for the economies of the eurozone. The Bank of England has the task of keeping inflation within a narrow range (currently between 1.5 and 2.5 per cent). A committee of experts (the Monetary Policy Committee – MPC) including academics and senior officials from the Bank of England determine monetary policy by setting the rate of interest. When the economy is in recession and inflation looks like falling below the lower band, the MPC might lower interest rates and inject money into the economy. When the economy is expanding too quickly, it might increase interest rates in an attempt to prevent the economy from overheating. The European Central Bank also has the objective of price stability defined as keeping inflation within the narrow band of 0–2 per cent.

Review Quiz

◆ What are the six macroeconomic policy challenges?

◆ What policy tools are available to the government to meet these challenges?

◆ What is the Stability Pact? How does it constrain fiscal policy for countries that belong to the EMU?

◆ What are the tools of monetary policy?

In your study of macroeconomics, you will find out what is currently known about the causes of long-term economic growth, business cycles, unemployment, inflation and the international balance of payments, and about the policy choices and challenges that the government faces. The next step in your pursuit of these goals is to learn more about macroeconomic measurement – about how we measure real GDP and the price level.

Summary

Key Points

Origins and Issues of Macroeconomics (pp. 405–406)

- Macroeconomics studies both the long-term trends and short-term fluctuations in economic growth, unemployment, inflation and the balance of international payments.

Economic Growth (pp. 406–411)

- Economic growth is the expansion of the economy's capacity to produce goods and services, measured by the increase in real GDP. Real GDP fluctuates around potential GDP in a business cycle. Every business cycle has an expansion, peak, recession, trough, recovery and new expansion.

- When we compare countries, we find similar productivity growth slowdowns and similar business cycles but different long-term trends in potential GDP.

- The main benefit of long-term economic growth is expanded consumption possibilities, and the main costs are reduced current consumption.

Jobs and Unemployment (pp. 411–413)

- The rate at which jobs are created and destroyed in the UK varies with the business cycle. Just over 500,000 jobs a year are created in the expansion phase of a business cycle. But just under 500,000 jobs a year are lost in the contraction phase.

- The UK unemployment rate fluctuates over the business cycle. It rises during a recession and falls during an expansion.

- Unemployment is a serious economic, social and personal problem. It can permanently damage a person's job prospects.

Inflation (pp. 414–416)

- Inflation is a process of rising prices which is measured by the percentage change in a price index such as the RPI.

- Inflation is a problem because it lowers the value of money at an unpredictable rate and makes money less useful as a measuring rod of value.

International Payments (pp. 416–417)

- When imports exceed exports, a nation has a current account deficit. The current account balance is cyclical and fluctuates with the business cycle – the current account deficit decreases in a recession and increases in an expansion.

- A current account deficit is financed by borrowing from abroad or by selling UK assets to foreigners. International borrowing and lending and asset sales and purchases are recorded in the capital account.

Macroeconomic Policy Challenges and Tools (pp. 417–418)

- The challenges for macroeconomic policy are to boost long-term growth, stabilize the business cycle, lower unemployment, maintain low inflation and prevent a large current account deficit.

- The tools available for meeting these challenges are fiscal policy and monetary policy.

Key Figures ◆

Key Terms

Problems

●1 Use Variable Graphing in Chapter 19 of *Economics in Action* to answer the following questions. In which country in 1992 was

a The growth rate of real GDP highest: Canada, France, Japan or the United States?

b The unemployment rate highest: Canada, Japan, the United Kingdom or the United States?

c The inflation rate lowest: Canada, Germany, the United Kingdom or the United States?

d The government budget deficit (as a percentage of GDP) largest: Canada, Japan, the United Kingdom or the United States?

2 Use Variable Graphing in Chapter 19 in *Economics in Action* to answer the following questions. In which country in 1996 was

a The growth rate of real GDP highest: Canada, France, Japan or the United States?

b The unemployment rate lowest: Canada, Japan, the United Kingdom or the United States?

c The inflation rate lowest: Canada, Finland, Ireland or the United States?

d The government budget deficit (as a percentage of GDP) smallest: Canada, Australia, Ireland or the United States?

e Is it possible to say in which country consumption possibilities are growing faster? Why or why not?

●3 The figure shows real GDP growth rate in India and Pakistan from 1989 to 1996.
In which years did economic growth in

a India increase? And in which year was growth the fastest?

b Pakistan decrease? And in which year was growth the slowest?

c Compare the paths of economic growth in India and Pakistan during this period.

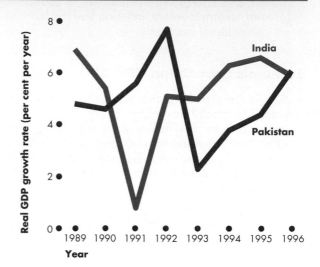

4 The figure shows real GDP per person in Australia and Japan from 1989 to 1996. In which years did economic growth in

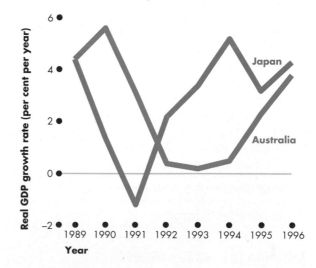

a Australia increase? And in which year was growth the fastest?

b Japan decrease? And in which year was growth the slowest?

c Compare the paths of economic growth in Australia and Japan during this period.

•5 The figure shows real GDP in Germany from the first quarter of 1991 to the second quarter of 1994.

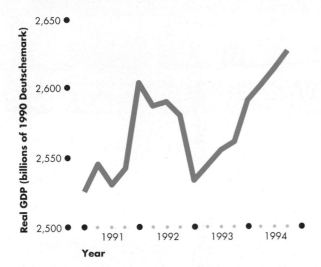

a How many recessions did Germany experience during this period?

b In which quarters, if any, did Germany experience a business cycle peak?

c In which quarters, if any, did Germany experience a business cycle trough?

d In which quarters, if any, did Germany experience an expansion?

6 Use the links on the Parkin, Powell and Matthews website to obtain data on quarterly real GDP for Canada since the fourth quarter of 1998 and update Figure 19.2. Use what you have discovered to answer the following questions:

a Is the Canadian economy now in a recession or an expansion?

b If the economy is still in an expansion, how long has the expansion lasted? If the economy is now in recession, how long has the economy been in recession?

c During the last year, has the growth rate sped up or slowed down?

•7 Use Variable Graphing in Chapter 19 in *Economics in Action* to answer the following questions. Which country, in 1988, had

a The largest budget deficit: Canada, Japan, the United Kingdom or the United States?

b A current account surplus: Canada, Japan, Germany or the United States?

8 Use Variable Graphing in Chapter 19 in *Economics in Action* to answer the following questions. Which country, in 1988, had

a The largest budget surplus: Canada, Japan, the United Kingdom or the United States?

b The largest current account deficit: Canada, Japan, Germany or the United States?

•9 Use Variable Graphing in Chapter 19 in *Economics in Action* to make a scatter diagram of the inflation rate and the unemployment rate in the UK.

a Describe the relationship.

b Do you think that low unemployment brings an increase in the inflation rate?

10 Use Variable Graphing in Chapter 19 in *Economics in Action* to make a scatter diagram of the government budget deficit as a percentage of GDP and the unemployment rate in Canada.

a Describe the relationship.

b Do you think that low unemployment brings a decrease in the budget deficit?

Critical Thinking

1 Study Reading Between the Lines on pp. 422–423 and then answer the following questions:

a What has happened to economic growth in the USA in 1999 and 2000 and what is predicted to happen in 2001 and 2002?

b Why might a downturn in the US economy create a danger of a global recession?

c What danger does a recession in the USA pose for the European economies?

2 Use the links on the Parkin, Powell and Matthews website to obtain the latest data on real GDP, unemployment, and inflation in the Eurozone countries (countries that belong to the European Monetary Union).

a Draw a chart of GDP growth, inflation and unemployment since 1999.

b What dangers does the the Eurozone economy face today?

c What actions, if any, do you think might be needed by the European Central Bank to keep the economy strong?

http://www.econ100.com

Global Recession

THE FINANCIAL TIMES, 31 AUGUST 2001

IMF warns of danger of global recession

Ed Crooks

A leaked draft version of the IMF's *World Economic Outlook*, which has been obtained by *The Financial Times*, predicts that the world economy will grow by 2.8 per cent this year warns there could be 'a much deeper and more protracted global downturn'.

The focus of the concern is the outlook for the US. Although the IMF forecasters have not changed the prediction they made in April, that the US will grow by 1.5 per cent this year and 2.5 per cent next year – roughly in line with the expectations of the US administration – they see a serious risk of a much worse outcome. If US productivity growth is less than

expected then stock markets could fall, triggering sharp declines in business investment and private consumption.

That would cause a global recession and possibly what the economists describe as 'substantial financial market turbulence', including 'a possible abrupt decline in the value of the dollar'.

The impact of that combination of global recession and market turbulence might be particularly severe for developing countries, the IMF economists note.

The global fallout from the US economy would be made worse by the weakness of the Japanese and European economies.

The Essence of the Story

- The International Monetary Fund predicts slow growth for the world economy in 2001 but warns that there could be a deeper and longer recession.

- The main economy that is driving the potential of global recession is the United States.

- The IMF expects the US economy to grow by 1.5 per cent in 2001 and 2.5 per cent in 2002. However, if US

productivity growth is less than expected that could trigger a sharp fall in stock market values.

- The fall in stock prices will lead to a decline in business investment and consumer spending which in turn will have a negative effect on the world economy.

- The impact on the world economy from a downturn in the US economy would be made worse by the weakness of the Japanese and European economies.

Economic Analysis

- Economic growth in the US economy during 1999 and 2000 has been 4.2 per cent and 5.0 per cent raising fears of overheating.

- The tightening of US monetary policy in 1999, a rise in oil prices and a weakening of share prices in the stock market has lead to a decline in investment spending.

- A decline in productivity will signal a further weakening in production and raise fears of falling profits which will result in further falls in share prices.

- Figure 1 shows the recent and forecasted growth performance for the USA, Japan and the EU. All three economies show a marked slowdown in 2001 and 2002.

- The slowdown in the USA will have a global effect on the rest of the world through its effect on international trade. Imports to the USA will decline which results in a fall in demand in the rest of the world. This in turn leads to a fall in imports in the rest of the world which feeds back into the slowdown in the USA. Figure 2 shows the movement in the stock market in the US and UK. The fall in share values in the US would exert a depressing influence on consumer spending and capital spending.

- Figure 3 shows the growth in investment in the three big economies in 1998–2000 and the forecasts for 2001–2002. The growth in investment in the EU is steady and is expected to remain so but forecasts of investment growth in the USA show a slowdown. In Japan investment growth remains weak.

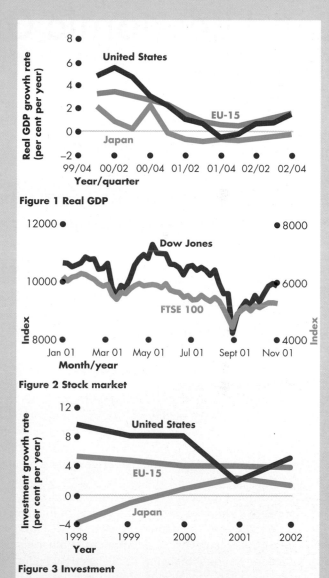

Figure 1 Real GDP

Figure 2 Stock market

Figure 3 Investment

CHAPTER 20

Measuring GDP, Inflation and Economic Growth

After studying this chapter you will be able to:

◆ Explain why aggregate income, expenditure and output are equal

◆ Explain how GDP is measured

◆ Explain how the Retail Prices Index (RPI) and the GDP deflator are measured

◆ Explain the shortcomings of changes in the RPI and the GDP deflator as measures of inflation

◆ Explain how real GDP is measured

◆ Explain the shortcomings of real GDP growth as a measure of improvements in living standards

Economic Barometers

When Mercedes-Benz contemplates opening a car plant in the United States, it pays close attention to long-term forecasts of US real GDP. When British Telecommunications plans to expand its fibre optics network, it uses forecasts of long-term growth in the UK economy. The outcome of many business decisions turns on the quality of forecasts of global and national macroeconomic conditions. ◆ Key inputs for making economic forecasts are the latest estimates of the gross domestic product, or GDP. The GDP data are a barometer of our country's economy. Economists pore over the latest numbers looking at past trends and seeking patterns that might give a glimpse of the future. How do economic statisticians add up all the economic activity of the country to arrive at the number called GDP? What exactly *is* GDP? ◆ Most of the time, our economy grows and sometimes it shrinks. But to reveal the rate of growth (or shrinkage), we must remove the effects of inflation on GDP and assess how *real* GDP is changing. How do we remove the inflation component of GDP to reveal real GDP? ◆ From economists to housewives, all types of people pay close attention to another economic barometer, the Retail Prices Index, or RPI. The Office for National Statistics publishes new figures each month, and analysts in newspapers and on TV quickly leap to conclusions about the causes of recent changes in prices and the prospects for future changes. How does the government determine the RPI? How well does it measure a consumer's living costs and the inflation rate? ◆ Some countries are rich while others are poor and only now are in the process of developing their industries and reaching their productive potential. How do we compare incomes in one country with incomes in another? How can we make international comparisons of GDP?

◆ ◆ ◆ ◆ In this chapter you are going to find out how economic statisticians measure real GDP and the price level. You are also going to learn how they use these measures to assess the economic growth rate and the inflation rate and to compare macroeconomic performance across countries.

Gross Domestic Product

Gross domestic product (GDP) is the value of *aggregate* production of goods and services in a country during a given time period – usually a year. The GDP of the United Kingdom, which measures the value of aggregate output in the United Kingdom during a year, was £934.9 billion in 2000. How was this number calculated? What does it mean? You are going to discover the answers to these questions in this chapter. But first, how is GDP calculated? Two fundamental concepts form the foundation on which GDP measurements are made:

1 The distinction between stocks and flows.
2 The equality of income, expenditure and the value of production.

Stocks and Flows

To keep track of our personal economic transactions and the economic transactions of a country, we distinguish between stocks and flows. A **stock** is a quantity that exists at a point in time. The water in a bath is a stock. So is the number of CDs that you own and the amount of money in your savings deposit. A **flow** is a quantity per unit of time. The water that is running from an open tap into a bath is a flow. So is the number of CDs that you buy in a month and the amount of income that you earn in a month. GDP is another flow. It is the value of production in a country *in a given time period*.

Capital and Investment

The key macroeconomic stock is **capital**, the plant, equipment, buildings and stocks of raw materials and semifinished goods that are used to produce other goods and services. The amount of capital in the economy is a crucial factor that influences GDP. Two macroeconomic *flows* change the *stock* of capital: investment and depreciation. **Investment** is the purchase of new plant, equipment and buildings and the additions to stocks. Investment *increases* the stock of capital. **Depreciation** is the decrease in the stock of capital that results from wear and tear and the passage of time. Another name for depreciation is capital consumption. The total amount spent on adding to the stock of capital and on replacing depreciated capital is called **gross investment**. The amount spent on adding to the stock of capital is called **net invest-**

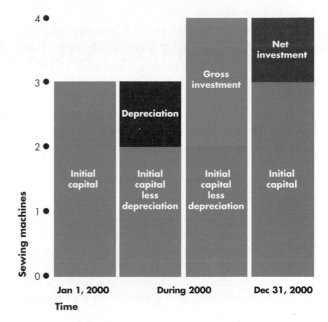

Figure 20.1

Capital and Investment

Tom's Tapes has a capital stock at the end of 2000 that equals its capital stock at the beginning of the year plus its net investment. Net investment is equal to gross investment less depreciation. Tom's Tapes gross investment is the 2 new sewing machines bought during the year, and its depreciation is the 1 sewing machine that it scrapped during the year.

ment. Net investment equals gross investment minus depreciation.

Figure 20.1 illustrates these concepts. On 1 January 2000, Tom's Tapes Inc. had 3 sewing machines. This quantity was its initial capital. During 2000, Tom's scrapped an older machine. This quantity is its depreciation. After depreciation, Tom's stock of capital was down to 2 machines. But also during 2000, Tom's bought 2 new sewing machines. This amount is its gross investment. By 31 December 2000, Tom's Tapes had 4 machines so its capital had increased by 1 machine. This amount is Tom's net investment. Tom's net investment equals its gross investment (the purchase of 2 new machines) minus its depreciation (1 machine scrapped).

The example of Tom's Tapes factory can be applied to the economy as a whole. The nation's capital stock decreases because capital depreciates and increases because of gross investment. The change in the nation's capital stock from one year to the next equals its net investment.

Wealth and Saving

Another macroeconomic stock is **wealth**, which is the value of all the things that people own. What people *own*, a stock, is related to what they *earn*, a flow. People *earn* an *income*, which is the amount they receive during a given time period from supplying the services of factors of production. Income can be either consumed or saved. **Consumption expenditure** is the amount spent on consumption goods and services. **Saving** is the amount of income left over after meeting consumption expenditures. Saving adds to wealth, and dissaving (negative saving) decreases wealth.

For example, at the end of the academic year, you have a £500 overdraft on your bank account and computer equipment worth £1,000. That's all you own. Your wealth is £500. Suppose that over the summer you earn an income of £3,000. You are extremely careful and spend only £500. When Uni starts again you have paid off your overdraft and you have £2,000 in your savings account. Your wealth is now £3,000. Your wealth has increased by £2,500 which equals your saving of £2,500. And your saving of £2,500 equals your income during the summer of £3,000 minus your consumption expenditure of £500.

National wealth and national saving work just like this personal example. The wealth of a nation at the start of a year equals its wealth at the start of the previous year plus its saving during the year. And its saving equals its income minus its consumption.

We'll make the idea of the nation's income and consumption more precise a bit later in this chapter. Before doing so, let's see what the stocks and flows that we've just learned about imply for the recurring theme of macroeconomics: short-term fluctuations and long-term trends in production.

The Short Term Meets the Long Term

You saw in Chapter 19 that potential GDP grows steadily, year after year. You also saw that real GDP grows and fluctuates around potential GDP. Both the long-term growth in potential GDP *and* the short-term fluctuations in real GDP are influenced by the stocks and flows that you've just studied. One of the reasons that potential GDP grows is that the capital stock grows. And one of the reasons that real GDP fluctuates is that investment fluctuates. So capital and

investment as well as wealth and saving are part of the key to understanding the growth and fluctuations of GDP.

The flows of investment and saving together with the flows of income and consumption expenditure interact in a circular flow of income and expenditure. In this circular flow, income equals expenditure, which also equals the value of production. This amazing equality is the foundation on which a nation's economic accounts are built and from which its GDP is measured.

The Equality of Income, Expenditure and the Value of Output

To see that for the economy as a whole, income equals expenditure and also equals the value of output, we study the circular flow of income and expenditure. Figure 20.2 illustrates the circular flow. In the figure, the economy consists of four sectors: households, firms, governments and the rest of the world (the purple diamonds). It has three aggregate markets: factor markets, goods and services markets and financial markets. Let's focus first on households and firms.

Households and Firms

Households sell and firms buy the services of labour, capital, land and entrepreneurship in factor markets. For these factor services, firms pay income to households – wages for labour services, interest for the use of capital, rent for the use of land and profits for entrepreneurship. Firms' retained earnings – profits that are not distributed to households – are also part of the household sector's income. (You can think of retained earnings as being income that households save and lend back to firms.) Figure 20.2 shows the *aggregate income* received by all households in payment for factor services by the blue dots labelled Y.

Firms sell and households buy consumer goods and services – such as beer, and pizzas, microwave ovens and dry cleaning services – in the markets for goods and services. The aggregate payment that households make for these goods and services is *consumption expenditure*. Figure 20.2 shows consumption expenditure by the red dots labelled C.

Firms buy and sell new capital equipment in the goods market. For example, Compaq sells 1,000 PCs to Virgin or BAC sells an aircraft to British Airways. Some of what firms produce might not be sold at all

Figure 20.2

The Circular Flow of Income and Expenditure

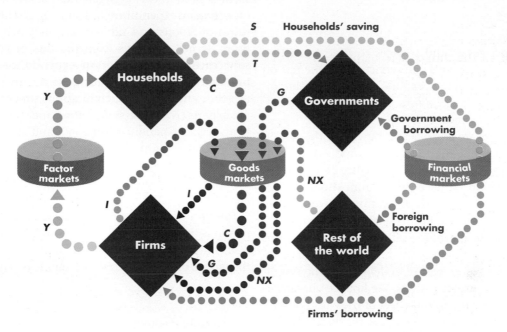

In the circular flow of income and expenditure, households receive incomes (*Y*) from firms (blue flow) and make consumption expenditures (*C*); firms make investment expenditures (*I*); governments purchase goods and services (*G*); the rest of the world purchases net exports (*NX*)(red flows). Aggregate income (blue flow) equals aggregate expenditure (red flows).

Households' saving (*S*) and net taxes (*NT*) leak from the circular flow. Firms borrow to finance their investment expenditures and governments and the rest of the world borrow to finance their deficits or lend their surpluses – (green flows).

and is added to stock. For example, if Ford (UK) produces 1,000 cars and sells 950 of them, the other 50 cars remain unsold and Ford's stock of cars increases by 50. When a firm adds unsold output to stock, we can think of the firm as buying goods from itself. The purchase of new plant, equipment and buildings and the additions to stocks are *investment*. Figure 20.2 shows investment by the red dots labelled *I*. Notice that in the figure investment flows from firms through the goods markets and back to firms. Some firms produce capital goods and other firms buy them (and firms 'buy' stocks from themselves).

Firms finance their investment by borrowing from households in financial markets. Households place their saving and firms do their borrowing in the financial markets. Figure 20.2 shows these flows by the green dots labelled 'Households' saving' or *S* and 'Firms' borrowing'. These flows are neither income

nor expenditure. Income is a payment for the services of a factor of production and expenditure is a payment for goods or services.

Governments

Governments buy goods and services from firms. In Figure 20.2, these **government purchases** are shown as the red flow *G*. Governments pay for their purchases from taxes. Figure 20.2 shows taxes as net taxes by the green dots *T*. **Net taxes** are taxes paid to governments minus transfer payments received from governments and minus interest payments on government debt. *Transfer payments* are cash transfers from governments to households and firms such as social security benefits, unemployment compensation and subsidies.

When government purchases (*G*) exceed net taxes (*T*), the government sector has a budget deficit, which it finances by borrowing in financial markets. This borrowing is shown by the green dots labelled 'Government borrowing'.

Rest of World Sector

Firms export goods and services to the rest of the world and import goods and services from the rest of the world. The value of exports minus the value of imports is called **net exports**. Figure 20.2 shows net exports by the red flow *NX*.

If net exports are positive and flow from the rest of the world to firms, the rest of the world is in deficit with us and we are in surplus. To finance its deficit the rest of the world either borrows from the domestic economy or sells domestic assets that it owns. These transactions take place in financial markets and they are shown by the green flow labelled 'Foreign borrowing'. If net exports are negative and flow from firms to the rest of the world, we are in deficit and the rest of the world is in surplus with us. We finance our deficit by either borrowing from the rest of the world or selling foreign assets that we own. Again, these transactions take place in financial markets. To illustrate this case in the figure, we would reverse the directions of the flows of net exports and foreign borrowing.

To help you keep track of the different types of flows that make up the circular flow of income and expenditure, they are colour-coded. In Figure 20.2, red flows are expenditures on goods and services, blue flows are incomes, and green flows are financial transfers. So the expenditure flows (red flows) are consumption expenditure, investment, government purchases and net exports. The income flow (blue flow) is aggregate income. The financial transfers (green flows) are saving, net taxes, government borrowing, foreign borrowing and firms' borrowing.

Gross Domestic Product

Gross domestic product is the value of *aggregate output* in a country during a year. Output can be valued in two ways:

1   By what buyers pay for it.
2   By what it costs producers to make it.

To buyers, goods are worth the prices paid for them. To producers, goods are worth what it costs to make them. If these two values are equal, we'll have a unique concept of GDP regardless of which one we use.

Fortunately, the two concepts of value do give the same answer. Let's see why.

Expenditure Equals Income

The total amount that buyers pay for the goods and services produced is *aggregate expenditure*. Let's focus on aggregate expenditure in Figure 20.2. The expenditures on goods and services are shown by the red flows. Firms' revenues from the sale of goods and services equal consumption expenditure (*C*) plus investment by firms (*I*) plus government purchases of goods and services including investment (*G*) plus net exports (*NX*). The sum of these four flows is equal to aggregate expenditure on goods and services.

The total amount it costs producers to make goods and services is equal to the incomes paid for factor services. This amount is shown by the blue flow in Figure 20.2.

The sum of the red flows equals the blue flow. The reason is that everything a firm receives from the sale of its output is paid out as incomes to the owners of the factors of production that it employs. That is:

$$Y = C + I + G + NX$$

or aggregate income (*Y*) equals aggregate expenditure (*C + I + G + NX*).

The buyers of aggregate output pay an amount equal to aggregate expenditure, and the sellers of aggregate output pay an amount equal to aggregate income. But because aggregate expenditure equals aggregate income, these two methods of valuing aggregate output give the same answer. So aggregate output, that is GDP, equals aggregate expenditure or aggregate income.

The circular flow of income and expenditure is the foundation on which the national economic accounts are built. It is used to provide the two approaches to measuring GDP and it is used to create other accounts that help us to keep track of the flows of saving and investment, the government's budget, and the balance of our exports and imports.

Let's look next at how the circular flows you've just studied enable us to keep track of how investment is financed.

How Investment is Financed

Investment, which adds to the stock of capital, is one of the determinants of the rate at which aggregate output grows. Investment is financed by national saving and by borrowing from the rest of the world.

National Saving

The sum of household saving and government saving is called **national saving**. Household saving is aggregate income minus net taxes ($Y - T$), which is called *disposable income*, less consumption expenditure. So:

$$S = (Y - T) - C$$

Government saving equals net taxes minus government purchases, ($T - G$). If ($T - G$) is positive, the government has a budget surplus and this surplus is added to household saving as an additional source of finance for investment. But if ($T - G$) is negative, the government has a budget deficit. In this case, part of household saving is used to finance the government deficit. So:

$$\text{National saving} = S + (T - G)$$

Borrowing From the Rest of the World

If foreigners spend more on UK goods and services than we spend on theirs, they must borrow from us to pay the difference. That is, if the value of exports (X) exceeds the value of imports (M), we must lend to the rest of the world an amount equal to $X - M$. In this situation, part of our national saving flows to the rest of the world and is not available to finance investment.

Conversely, if we spend more on foreign goods and services than the rest of the world spends on ours, we must borrow from the rest of the world to pay the difference. That is, we must borrow from the rest of the world an amount equal to $M - X$. In this case, part of the rest of the world's saving flows into the United Kingdom and becomes available to finance investment.

In 2000, investment in the United Kingdom was £167.8 billion. This investment was financed by £148.8 billion of national saving and £19 billion from borrowing from the rest of the world.

Review Quiz

- What is the distinction between a stock and a flow? What are the main macroeconomic stocks? What are the flows that change them?
- What are the components of aggregate expenditure?
- Why does aggregate income equal aggregate expenditure and the value of output (GDP)?
- What is the distinction between government expenditures of goods and services and transfer payments?

Let's now see how the Office for National Statistics (ONS) uses the circular flow of income and expenditure to measure GDP.

Measuring UK GDP

To measure GDP, the Office for National Statistics uses three approaches:

1 Expenditure approach.
2 Factor incomes approach.
3 Output approach.

The Expenditure Approach

The *expenditure approach* measures GDP by collecting data on consumption expenditure (C), investment (I), government purchases of goods and services (G) and net exports (NX). Table 20.1 illustrates this approach. The numbers refer to 2000 and are in millions of pounds. To measure GDP using the expenditure approach, we add together the individual components in Table 20.1.

Personal consumption expenditures are the expenditures by households on goods and services produced in the United Kingdom. They include goods such as

Table 20.1 GDP: The Expenditure Approach

Item	Symbol	Amount in 2000 (billions of pounds)	Percentage of GDP
Personal consumption expenditures	C	612.2	65.5
Gross domestic investment + stockbuilding	I	167.8	17.9
Government purchases of goods and services	G	173.9	18.6
Net exports	NX	−19.0	−2.0
Gross domestic product	Y	934.9	100.0

The expenditure approach measures GDP by adding together personal consumption expenditures (C), gross private domestic investment plus stockbuilding (I), government purchases of goods and services (G), and net exports (NX).

Source: National Statistics, *Economic Trends*, August 2001, London: The Stationery Office.

beer, CDs, books and magazines as well as services such as insurance, banking and legal advice. They do not include the purchase of new residential houses, which is counted as part of investment.

Gross private domestic investment is expenditure on capital equipment and buildings by firms and expenditure on new residential houses by households. It also includes the change in firms' stocks.

Government purchases of goods and services are the purchases of goods and services by all levels of government – from Westminster to the local town hall. This item of expenditure includes the cost of providing national defence, law and order, street lighting, refuse collection, and so on. It does not include *transfer payments*. Such payments do not represent a purchase of goods and services but rather a transfer of funds from government to households.

Net exports of goods and services are the value of exports minus the value of imports. When Rover sells a car to a buyer in the United States, the value of that car is part of UK exports. When your local VW dealer stocks up on the latest model, its expenditure is part of UK imports.

Table 20.1 shows the relative importance of the four items of aggregate expenditure. The largest component is personal consumption expenditure and the smallest is net exports (negative in 2000).

Expenditures not in GDP

Aggregate expenditure, which equals GDP, does not include all the things that people and businesses buy. To distinguish total expenditure on GDP from other items of spending, we call the expenditure included in GDP *final expenditure*. Items that are not part of final expenditure and not part of GDP include the purchase of:

1 Intermediate goods and services.

2 Second-hand goods.

3 Financial securities.

Intermediate goods and services are the goods and services that firms buy from each other and use as inputs in the goods and services that they eventually sell to final users. An example of an intermediate good is a computer chip that Dell buys from Intel. A Dell computer is a final good, but an Intel chip is an intermediate good. To count the expenditure on intermediate goods and services as well as the expenditure on the final good involves counting the same thing twice – known as *double counting*.

Some goods are sometimes intermediate goods and sometimes final goods. For example, the ice cream that you buy on a hot summer day is a final good, but the ice cream that a restaurant buys and uses to make a dessert is an intermediate good. Whether a good is intermediate or final depends on what it is used for, and not on what it is.

Expenditure on *second-hand* goods is not part of GDP because these goods were counted as part of GDP in the period in which they were produced and in which they were new goods. For example, a 1995 car was part of GDP in 1995. If the car is sold in the second-hand car market in 1999, the amount paid for the car is not part of GDP in 1999.

Firms often sell *financial securities* such as bonds and stocks to finance purchases of newly produced capital goods. The expenditure on newly produced capital goods is part of GDP, but the expenditure on financial securities is not. GDP includes the amount spent on new capital, not the amount spent on pieces of paper.

Let's look at the second way of measuring GDP.

The Factor Incomes Approach

The *factor incomes approach* measures GDP by summing all the incomes paid by firms to households for the services of the factors of production they hire – wages for labour, interest for capital, rent for land and profits paid for entrepreneurship. Let's see how the factor incomes approach works.

Factor incomes are divided into four categories:

1 Compensation of employees.

2 Rent.

3 Gross trading profits and surplus.

4 Income from self-employment.

Compensation of employees is the total payments by firms for labour services. This item includes the net wages and salaries (called take-home pay) that workers receive each week or month plus taxes withheld on earnings plus fringe benefits such as social security and pension fund contributions.

Rent is the payment for the use of land and other rented inputs. It includes payments for rented housing and imputed rent for owner-occupied housing. (Imputed rent is an estimate of what homeowners would pay to rent the housing they own and use themselves. By including this item in the national income accounts, we measure the total value of housing services, whether they are owned or rented.)

Gross trading profits and surplus are the total profits made by corporations and the surpluses generated by publicly owned enterprises. Some of these profits are paid to households in the form of dividends, and some are retained by corporations as undistributed profits. The surpluses from public enterprises are either retained by the enterprises or paid to the government as part of its general revenue.

Income from self-employment is a mixture of the elements that we have just reviewed. The proprietor of an owner-operated business supplies labour, capital and perhaps land and buildings to the business. It is difficult to split up the income earned by an owner-operator into its component parts – compensation for labour, payment for the use of capital, rent payments for the use of land or buildings and profit – so the national income accounts lump all these separate incomes into one category – called *mixed income*.

In fact it is difficult to separate out profits from rent. Many corporations own property on which they earn rents and are declared as profits. The Office for National Statistics (ONS) identifies the profits and surpluses of each sector – private, public, financial and non-financial corporations and lumps them together and calls them *Gross Operating Surplus*.

The sum of these components of factor incomes is called *domestic income at factor cost*. It is not GDP. One further adjustment is needed to get to GDP – from factor cost to market prices.

Factor Cost to Market Price

When we add up all the final expenditures on goods and services, we arrive at a total called gross domestic product at *market prices*. These expenditures are valued at the market prices that people pay for the various goods and services. Another way of valuing goods and services is at factor cost. *Factor cost* is the value of a good or service measured by adding together the costs of all the factors of production used to produce it. If the only economic transactions were between households and firms – if there were no government taxes or subsidies – the market price and factor cost values would be the same. But the presence of indirect taxes and subsidies makes these two methods of valuation differ.

An *indirect tax* is a tax paid by consumers when they buy goods and services. (In contrast, a *direct tax* is a tax on income.) Value added tax (VAT) and purchase taxes on alcohol, petrol and tobacco are indirect taxes. Because of indirect taxes, consumers pay more for some goods and services than producers

Table 20.2   GDP: The Factor Incomes Approach

Item	Amount in 2000 (billions of pounds)	Percentage of GDP
Wages and salaries	520.7	55.7
Mixed income	44.9	4.8
Gross Operating Surplus	239.3	25.6
Indirect taxes *less* Subsidies	130.0	13.9
Gross domestic product	934.9	100.0

The sum of all factor incomes equals domestic income at factor cost. GDP equals net domestic income plus taxes less subsidies. In 2000, GDP measured by the factor incomes approach was 934.9 billion. Compensation of Employees was by far the largest part of total factor incomes.

Source: National Statistics, *Economic Trends*, August 2001, London: The Stationery Office.

receive. The market price is greater than the factor cost. For example, at a VAT rate of 17.5 per cent the purchase of a CD at a cost of £12.99 means you will have paid £11.06 as the cost price and £1.93 VAT.

A *subsidy* is a payment by the government to a producer. Payments made to your local Training and Enterprise Council (TEC) are to subsidize training courses. Because of subsidies, consumers pay less for some goods and services than producers receive. The market price is less than the factor cost.

To use the factor incomes approach to measure GDP, we must add indirect taxes to total factor incomes and subtract subsidies. Making this adjustment gets us to GDP.

Table 20.2 summarizes these calculations and shows how the factor incomes approach leads to the same estimate of GDP as the expenditure approach. National Statistics no longer separates out income from self-employment, rental income and profits and surpluses. These are now treated as surpluses to different sectors and added together. The measures of profits and surpluses exclude the gains made from the appreciation of assets and so the factor incomes added together with taxes less subsidies should give us GDP at market prices. Table 20.2 shows the relative magnitudes of the various factor incomes. As you can see, compensation of employees makes up by far the largest factor income.

Figure 20.3

Value Added and Final Expenditure

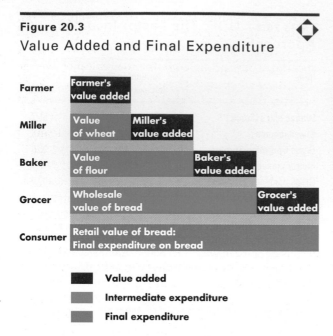

- ■ Value added
- ■ Intermediate expenditure
- ■ Final expenditure

A consumer's expenditure on a loaf of bread is equal to the sum of the value added at each stage in its production. Intermediate expenditure, for example the amount paid for the purchase of flour by the baker from the miller, equals the value added by the farmer and the miller. If intermediate expenditure is included in the total, then parts of value added are counted twice.

The Output Approach

The third method used to measure GDP is the output method. This method measures the contribution that an industry makes to GDP. But to measure the value of production of an individual industry, we must be careful to count only the value added by that industry. **Value added** is the value of a firm's production minus the value of the *intermediate goods* bought from other firms. Equivalently, it is the sum of the incomes (including profits) paid to the factors of production used by the firm to produce its output. Let's illustrate value added by looking at the production of a loaf of bread.

Figure 20.3 takes you through the brief life of a loaf of bread. It starts with the farmer, who grows the wheat. To do so, the farmer hires labour, capital equipment and land. Wages are paid to farm workers and interest and rent are paid. The farmer also earns a profit. The entire value of the wheat produced is the farmer's value added. The miller buys wheat from the farmer and turns it into flour. To do so, the miller

hires labour and capital equipment. Wages are paid to mill workers, interest is paid on the capital and the miller earns a profit. The miller has now added value to the wheat bought from the farmer. The baker buys flour from the miller. The price of the flour includes the value added by the farmer and by the miller. The baker adds more value by turning the flour into bread. Wages are paid to bakery workers, interest is paid on the capital used by the baker and the baker earns a profit. The grocer buys the bread from the baker. The price paid by the grocer includes the value added by the farmer, the miller and the baker. At this stage the value of the loaf is its *wholesale* value. The grocer adds further value by making the loaf available in a convenient place at a convenient time. The consumer buys the bread for a price – its *retail price* – that includes the value added by the farmer, the miller, the baker and the grocer.

Final Goods and Intermediate Goods

To value output, we count only *value added* because the sum of the value added at each stage of production equals expenditure on the *final good*. By using value added, we avoid double counting. In the above example, the only thing that has been produced and consumed is a loaf of bread – shown by the green bar in Figure 20.3. The value added at each stage is shown by the red bars, and the sum of the red bars equals the green bar. The transactions involving intermediate goods, shown by the blue bars, are not part of value added and are not counted as part of the value of output or of GDP.

Aggregate Expenditure, Income and GDP Output

You've seen that aggregate expenditure equals aggregate income. And you've seen that National Statistics uses both aggregate expenditure and aggregate income to measure GDP. Why does it use two approaches when they are supposed to be the same? The answer is that although the two concepts of the value of aggregate output are identical, the actual measurements, which are based on samples of information, give slightly different answers. The expenditure approach uses data from *Family Expenditure Survey*, house building, business investment, the accounts of central and local government, HM Customs and Excise records and many other sources. The factor incomes approach uses data supplied by the Inland Revenue. None of these sources gives a complete coverage of all the items that make up aggregate expenditure and aggregate factor incomes. So by using the two approaches, National Statistics can check one aggregate against the other. The discrepancy (known as the *Initial Residual Difference* – IRD) has at times been large and has been used as an indicator of the underground economy. The discrepancy is used to adjust both income and expenditure to make them equal.

Review Quiz

◆ Why does GDP measured by the expenditure approach equal GDP measured by the income approach?

◆ What is the distinction between expenditure on final goods and expenditure on intermediate goods?

◆ What is value added? How is it calculated?

So far, in our study of GDP and its measurement, we've been concerned with the nominal (or money) value of GDP and its components. But GDP can change either because prices change or because there is a change in the volume of goods and services produced – a change in real GDP. Let's now see how we measure the price level and distinguish between the nominal value and the real value of GDP.

The Price Level and Inflation

The *price level* is the average level of prices measured by a *price index*. To construct a price index, we take a basket of goods and services and calculate its value in the current period and its value in a base period. The price index is the value of the basket in the current period expressed as a percentage of the value of the same basket in the base period.

Two main price indexes are used to measure the price level in the United Kingdom today. They are:

1 The Retail Prices Index.
2 The GDP deflator.

Retail Prices Index

The **Retail Prices Index** (RPI) measures the average level of prices of the goods and services that a typical UK household consumes. The RPI is published every month by National Statistics. To construct the RPI, National Statistics first selects a base period. Currently, it is 13 January 1987. Then it surveys consumer spending patterns to determine the typical or average 'basket' of goods and services that people buy in the base period. Around 500 different goods and services feature in the RPI.

Every month, National Statistics sends a team of observers to more than 180 geographical locations in the United Kingdom and takes some 150,000 price quotations to record the prices for the 500 items. When all the data are in, the RPI is calculated by valuing the basket of goods and services at the current month's prices. That value is expressed as a percentage of the value of the same basket in the base period.

To see more precisely how the RPI is calculated, let's work through a simplified example. Table 20.3 summarizes the calculations. Let's suppose that there are only three goods in the typical consumer's basket: apples, haircuts and bus rides. The table shows the quantities bought and the prices prevailing in the base period. It also shows total expenditure in the base period. The typical consumer buys 200 bus rides at 30 pence each and so spends £60 on bus rides. Expenditure on apples and haircuts is worked out in the same way. Total expenditure is the sum of expenditures on the three goods, which is £98.

To calculate the price index for the current period, we need only to discover the prices of the goods in the current period. We do not need to know the quantities bought. Let's suppose that the prices are those set out in Table 20.3 under 'Current period'. We can now calculate the current period's value of the (base-period) basket of goods by using the current period's prices. For example, the current price of apples is down to 24 pence a kilogram, so the current period's value of the base-period quantity (5 kilograms) is £1.20. The base-period quantities of haircuts and bus rides are valued at this period's prices in a similar way. The total value of the base-period basket in the current period is £107.80.

We can now calculate the RPI – the ratio of this period's value of the basket to the base period's value, multiplied by 100. In this example the RPI for the current period is 110. The RPI for the base period is, by definition, 100.

ONS also publishes a price index that eliminates the mortgage interest component of typical household expenditure on the basket of goods. The main reason for the exclusion of mortgage interest is because the RPI will show a rise in prices when the

Table 20.3 The Retail Price Index: A Simplified Calculation

Base period basket	Base period		Current period	
	Price	Expenditure	Price	Expenditure
5 kilograms of apples	£0.40/kilogram	£2.00	£0.24/kilogram	£1.20
6 haircuts	£6.00 each	£36.00	£6.10 each	£36.60
200 bus rides	£0.30 each	£60.00	£0.35 each	£70.00
Total expenditure		£98.00		£107.80
RPI	$\frac{£98.00}{£98.00} \times 100 = 100$		$\frac{£107.80}{£98.00} \times 100 = 110$	

A fixed basket of goods – 5 kilograms of apples, 6 haircuts and 200 bus rides – is valued in the base period at 98. Prices change, and that same basket is valued at 107.80 in the current period. The RPI is equal to the current-period

Value of the basket divided by the base-period value of the basket multiplied by 100. In the base period the RPI is 100, and in the current period the RPI is 110.

rate of interest is raised to control inflation. The new price index is known as the *RPIX*. It is argued that *RPIX* is a better indicator of underlying inflation. While there is some truth in this argument, it is also true that mortgage interest payment is a valid expenditure by households.

GDP Deflator

The **GDP deflator** measures the average level of prices of all the goods and services that are included in GDP. Currently, the base period for the GDP deflator is 1995.

We are going to learn how to calculate the GDP deflator by studying an imaginary economy that has just three final goods: a consumption good that households buy (apples), a capital good that firms buy (computers) and a good that the government buys (red tape). Net exports are zero in this example. Table 20.4 summarizes the calculations of the GDP deflator in this economy.

To calculate the GDP deflator, we use the formula;

$$\text{GDP deflator} = \frac{\text{Nominal GDP}}{\text{Real GDP}} \times 100$$

To calculate nominal GDP, we use the expenditure approach. The table shows the quantities of the final goods and their prices. To calculate nominal GDP, we work out the expenditure on each good and then total the three expenditures. Consumption expend-

iture (apples) is £2,226, investment (computers) is £5,250 and government purchases (red tape) are £530, so nominal GDP is £8,006.

Now let's calculate real GDP, a measure of the physical volume of output. To do so, we value the current-period quantities at the base-period prices. Because the base year is 1995, we refer to the units in which real GDP is measured as '1995 prices'. The table shows the prices for the base period. Real expenditure on apples for the current period is 4,240 kilograms valued at 50 pence a kilogram, which is £2,120. If we perform the same types of calculations for computers and red tape and add up the real expenditures, we arrive at a real GDP of £7,650.

Let's put the numbers we've found into the formula for the GDP deflator. Nominal GDP is £8,006 and real GDP is £7,650, so the GDP deflator is:

$$\text{GDP deflator} = \frac{£8,006}{£7,650} \times 100 = 104.7$$

Notice that when the current period is also the base period, nominal GDP equals real GDP and the GDP deflator is 100.

You can think of nominal GDP as a balloon that is being blown up by growing production and rising prices. Figure 20.4 illustrates this idea. The GDP deflator lets the inflation air out of the nominal GDP balloon – the contribution of rising prices – so that we can see what has happened to *real* GDP. The red balloon for 1995 shows real GDP in that year. The

Table 20.4 Nominal GDP, Real GDP and the GDP Deflator: Simplified Calculations

Current year output	Base-period values		Current-period values	
	Price	Expenditure	Price	Expenditure
4,240 kilograms of apples	50p/kilogram	£2,120	52.5p/kilogram	£2,226
5 computers	£1,000 each	£5,000	£1,050 each	£5,250
1,060 metres of red tape	50p/metre	£530	50p/metre	£530
	Real GDP	**£7,650**	**Nominal GDP**	**£8,006**

$$\text{GDP deflator} = \frac{£8,006}{£7,650} \times 100 = 104.7$$

An imaginary economy produces only apples, computers and red tape. In the current period, nominal GDP is £8,006. If the current-period quantities are valued at the base-period prices, we obtain a measure of real GDP, which is £7,650. The GDP deflator in the current period – which is calculated by dividing nominal GDP by real GDP in that period and multiplying by 100 – is 104.7.

Figure 20.4
The GDP Balloon

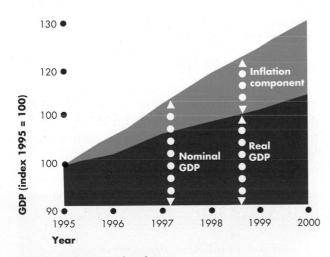

(a) Nominal GDP and real GDP

(b) Deflating nominal GDP

Part of the rise in GDP comes from inflation and part from increased production – an increase in real GDP (part a). The GDP deflator lets some air out of the GDP balloon (part b) so that we can see the extent to which production has grown.

Source: National Statistics, *Economic Trends*, August 2001.

green balloon shows *nominal* GDP in 2000. The red balloon for 2000 shows real GDP for that year. To see real GDP in 2000, we *deflate* nominal GDP using the GDP deflator.

What the Inflation Numbers Mean

A major purpose of the RPI and the GDP deflator is to measure inflation, and the measures are put to practical use. For example, the RPI is used to determine cost of living adjustments to state pensions, job-seekers' allowance, other social security payments and upward adjustment of tax allowances – the income ranges over which different income tax rates apply. How good a measure of inflation does the RPI or the GDP deflator give? Does a 2.7 per cent increase in the RPI mean that the cost of living has increased by 2.7 per cent? And does a 3 per cent increase in the GDP deflator mean that the prices of the goods and services that make up real GDP have increased by 3 per cent? Let's find out.

Measuring the inflation rate accurately is of crucial importance. It tells us how the value of money is changing, and it affects our assessment of changes in real GDP. A 1 per cent upward bias in the estimated inflation rate translates into a 1 per cent downward bias in the estimated growth rate of real GDP and real wage rates. And a 1 per cent a year bias sustained over 10 years throws the estimate of real GDP and real wages off by more than 10 per cent. Despite the importance of getting the numbers right, the RPI and the GDP deflator sometimes give different views of the inflation rate, and neither index is a perfect measure. Worse, *both* measures of inflation probably overstate the inflation rate. The main sources of bias are:

◆ New goods bias.

◆ Quality change bias.

◆ Substitution bias.

New Goods Bias
New goods keep replacing old goods. For example, CDs have replaced LP records and PCs have replaced typewriters. If you want to compare the price level in 1995 with that in 1975, you somehow have to compare the price of a CD and a computer today with that of an LP and typewriter in 1975. Because CDs and PCs are more expensive today than LPs and typewriters, the arrival of these new goods puts an upward bias into the estimate of the price level.

Quality Change Bias
Most goods undergo constant quality improvement. Cars, computers, CD players and even textbooks get better year after year. Improvements in quality often mean increases in price. But such price increases are not inflation. For example, suppose that a 1999 car is 5 per cent better and costs 5 per cent more than a 1995 car. Adjusted for the quality change, the price of

the car has been constant. But in calculating the RPI, the price of the car will be counted as having increased by 5 per cent.

Estimates have been made of the importance of quality change bias, especially for obvious changes such as those in cars and computers. Allowing for quality improvements changes the inflation picture by between 1 and 2 percentage points a year, on the average, according to some economists. That is, correctly measured, the inflation rate might be as much as 2 percentage points a year less than the published numbers.

Substitution Bias
A change in the RPI measures the percentage change in the price of a *fixed* basket of goods and services. But changes in relative prices lead consumers to seek less costly items. For example, by shopping more frequently at discount stores and less frequently at convenience stores, consumers can cut the prices they pay. By using discount fares on airlines, they can cut the cost of travel. This kind of substitution of cheaper items for more costly items is not picked up by the RPI. Because consumers make such substitutions, a price index based on a fixed basket overstates the effects of a given price change on the inflation rate.

To reduce the bias problems, the National Statistics revises the basket used for calculating the RPI about every five years based on the spending patterns of households within a specified income group. Yet despite periodic updating, the RPI is of limited value for making comparisons of the cost of living over long periods of time and even has shortcomings as a measure of year-to-year inflation rates.

Review Quiz

◆ What does the Retail Prices Index measure? What are the main ways in which the RPI is an upward biased measure of the price level?
◆ What does the GDP deflator measure? How does it differ from the RPI?
◆ By how much does the RPI overstate the inflation rate?

You now know how inflation is calculated and what the inflation numbers mean. You also know that by letting the inflationary air out of the GDP balloon, we can reveal real GDP. But what does real GDP really mean? Let's find out.

What Real GDP Means

Estimates of real GDP and the real GDP growth rate are used for many purposes. But the three main uses are:

1 To assess changes in economic welfare over time.

2 To make international comparisons of GDP.

3 For business cycle assessment and forecasting.

Economic Welfare

Economic welfare is a comprehensive measure of the general state of well-being. Improvements in economic welfare depend on the growth of real GDP. But they also depend on many other factors not measured by GDP. Some of these factors are:

◆ Quality improvements.

◆ Household production.

◆ The underground economy.

◆ Health and life expectancy.

◆ Leisure time.

◆ The environment.

◆ Political freedom and social justice.

Quality Improvements

You have seen that the price indices we use to measure inflation give a downward biased estimate of the growth rate of real GDP. When car prices rise because cars have improved (becoming safer, faster, more fuel efficient, more comfortable), the RPI and the GDP deflator count the price increase as inflation. So what is really an increase in production is counted as an increase in price rather than an increase in real GDP. It is deflated away by the wrongly measured higher price level.

Household Production

An enormous amount of production takes place every day in our homes. Changing a light bulb, cutting the grass, washing the car and growing vegetables are all examples of productive activities that do not involve market transactions and are not counted as part of GDP. But should it be counted? How should it be valued? Reading Between the Lines (pp. 444–445) examines attempts by the Office for National Statistics to value the total amount of household production involved in child care.

Household production has become much more capital intensive over the years. As a result, less labour is used in household production than in earlier periods. For example, a microwave meal that takes just a few minutes to prepare uses a great deal of capital and almost no labour. Because we use less labour and more capital in household production, it is not easy to work out whether this type of production has increased or decreased over time. But it is likely that market production counted in GDP has increasingly replaced household production. Two trends point in this direction. One is the trend in female employment, which has increased from 37 per cent of the female population of working age in 1960 to 53 per cent in 2000. The other trend is the marketization of traditionally home-produced goods and services. For example, more and more households now buy takeaways, eat in fast food restaurants and use nursery services. This trend means that increasing proportions of food preparation and child care that used to be part of household production are now measured as part of GDP.

The Underground Economy

The *underground economy* is the part of the economy purposely hidden from view by the people operating in it to avoid taxes and regulations or because the goods and services they are producing are illegal. Because underground economic activity is unreported, it is omitted from GDP.

The underground economy is easy to describe, even if it is hard to measure. It includes the production and distribution of drugs, prostitution, production that uses illegal labour that is paid less than the minimum wage, and jobs done for cash to avoid paying income taxes. This last category might be quite large and includes tips earned by taxi drivers, hairdressers, and hotel and restaurant workers. Estimates of the scale of the underground economy range between 3.5 and 13.5 per cent of GDP (£32 billion to £125 billion) in the United Kingdom and much more in some countries. In Reading Between the Lines (pp. 444–445) we examine the most recent estimates of the underground economy for a number of countries.

Provided the underground economy is a reasonably stable proportion of the total economy, its omission from GDP does not pose a problem. The growth rate of real GDP still gives a useful estimate of the long-term growth rate and of business cycle fluctuations. But sometimes production shifts from the underground to the rest of the economy and sometimes it shifts the other way. The underground economy expands relative to the rest of the economy if taxes become especially high or if regulations become especially restricting. And the underground economy shrinks relative to the rest of the economy if the burden of taxes and regulations are eased. During the 1980s, when tax rates were cut, there was an increase in tax revenues. Some of this may have been due to the existing workforce, particularly high-paid labour, working harder, taking greater risks and being more productive, but some of it could have been due to a switch from what was previously underground activity to recorded activity. So some part (but probably a small part) of the expansion of real GDP during the 1980s represented a shift from the underground economy rather than an increase in production.

Health and Life Expectancy

Good health and a long life – the hopes of everyone – do not show up in real GDP, at least not directly. A higher real GDP does enable us to spend more on medical research, health care, healthy food and exercise equipment. And as real GDP has increased, our life expectancy has lengthened – from 70 years at the end of the Second World War to approaching 80 years today. Infant deaths and death in childbirth, two fearful scourges of the nineteenth century, have almost been eliminated.

But we face new health and life expectancy problems every year. AIDS, drug abuse, suicide and murder are taking young lives at a rate that causes serious concern. And in recent years, the number of households, mostly single parent families, which are living below the official poverty level has increased. When we take these negative influences into account, we see that real GDP growth overstates the improvements in economic welfare.

Leisure Time

Leisure time is an economic good that adds to our economic welfare. Other things remaining the same, the more leisure we have, the better off we are. Our time spent working is valued as part of GDP, but our leisure time is not. Yet from the point of view of economic welfare, that leisure time must be at least as valuable to us as the wage that we earn for the last hour worked. If it was not, we would work instead of taking the leisure. Over the years, leisure time has steadily increased. The working week has become

shorter, and the number and length of holidays have increased.

These improvements in economic well-being are not reflected in GDP.

The Environment

The environment is directly affected by economic activity. The burning of hydrocarbon fuels is the most visible activity that damages our environment. But it is not the only example. The depletion of exhaustible resources, the mass clearing of forests, and the pollution of lakes and rivers are other major environmental consequences of industrial production.

Resources used to protect the environment are valued as part of GDP. For example, the value of catalytic converters that help to protect the atmosphere from carbon emissions are part of GDP. But if we did not use such pieces of equipment and instead polluted the atmosphere, we would not count the deteriorating air that we were breathing as a negative part of GDP.

An industrial society possibly produces more atmospheric pollution than an agricultural society does. But it is not always the case that such pollution increases as we become wealthier. One of the things that wealthy people value is a clean environment, and they devote resources to protecting it. Compare the pollution that was discovered in the former East Germany and the former Soviet Union in the late 1980s with pollution in the western developed countries. East Germany, a relatively poor country, polluted its rivers, lakes and atmosphere in a way that would have been unimaginable in wealthy West Germany.

Political Freedom and Social Justice

Most people value political freedoms such as those provided by the western democracies. They also value social justice or fairness – equality of opportunity and of access to social security safety nets that protect people from the extremes of misfortune.

A country might have a large real GDP per person, but have limited political freedom and equity. For example, a small elite might enjoy political liberty and extreme wealth while the vast majority are effectively enslaved and live in abject poverty. Such an economy would generally be regarded as having less economic welfare than one that had the same amount of real GDP but in which political freedoms were enjoyed by everyone. Today, China has rapid real GDP growth but limited political freedoms, while Russia has a decreasing real GDP and an emerging democratic political system. Economists have no easy way to determine which of these countries is better off.

The Bottom Line

What is the bottom line? Do we get the wrong message about changes (or differences) in economic welfare by looking at changes (or differences) in real GDP? The influences omitted from real GDP are probably important and could be large. Developing countries have a larger underground economy and a larger amount of household production than do developed countries. So as an economy develops and grows, part of the apparent growth might reflect a switch from underground to recorded production and from home production to market production. This measurement error overstates the rate of economic growth and the improvement in economic welfare.

Other influences on living standards include the amount of leisure time available, the quality of the environment, the security of jobs and homes, the safety of city streets, and so on. It is possible to construct broader measures that combine the many influences that contribute to human happiness. Real GDP will be one element in these broader measures, but it will by no means be the whole of them.

International Comparisons of GDP

All the problems we've just reviewed affect the economic welfare of every country, so, in order to make international comparisons of economic welfare, factors additional to real GDP must be used. But real GDP comparisons are a major component of international welfare comparisons and two special problems arise in making these comparisons. First, the real GDP of one country must be converted into the same currency units as the real GDP of the other country. Second, the same prices must be used to value the goods and services in the countries being compared. Let's look at these two problems by using a striking example, a comparison of the United States and China.

In 1992 (the most recent year for which we can make this comparison), real GDP per person in the United States was $24,408. The official Chinese statistics published by the International Monetary Fund (IMF) say that real GDP per person in China in 1992 was 2,028 Yuan (the Yuan is the currency of China). On average, during 1992, $1 US was worth 5.762 Yuan. If we use this exchange rate to convert Chinese Yuan into US dollars, we get a value of $352.

The official comparison of China and the United States makes China look extremely poor. In 1992, real GDP per person in the United States was 69 times that in China.

GDP in the United States is measured by using prices that prevail in the United States. China's GDP is measured by using prices that prevail in China. But the relative prices in the two countries are very different. Some goods that are expensive in the United States cost very little in China. These items get a small weight in China's real GDP. If, instead of using China's prices, all the goods and services produced in China are valued at the prices prevailing in the United States, then a more valid comparison can be made of GDP in the two countries. Such a comparison uses prices called *purchasing power parity prices*.

Robert Summers and Alan Heston, economists in the Center for International Comparisons at the University of Pennsylvania, have used purchasing power parity prices to construct real GDP data for more than one hundred countries. These data, which are published in the Penn World Table (PWT), tell a remarkable story about China. The PWT data use 1985 as the base year, so they are measured in 1985 dollars. According to the Penn World Table, in 1992, real GDP per person in the United States was 12 times that of China, not the 69 times shown in the official data.

Despite large differences in estimates of the level of China's real GDP, there is much less doubt about its growth rate. The economy of China is expanding at an extraordinary rate.

US real GDP is measured quite reliably. But China's is not. The alternative measures of China's real GDP are somewhat unreliable, and the truth about GDP in China is not known.

Business Cycle Assessment and Forecasting

When the Bank of England or the European Central bank decides to raise interest rates and slow an expansion that it believes is too strong, it looks at the latest estimates of inflation and real GDP growth. But don't the measures of inflation used to calculate real GDP overstate the inflation rate? They do, but not in a cyclical way. They are out by a similar amount every year. So while the possible mismeasurement of inflation may lead to wrong estimates of long-term real GDP growth, it probably does not cause a wrong assessment of the phase of the business cycle.

The fluctuations in economic activity measured by real GDP tell a reasonably accurate story about the phase of the business cycle the economy is in. When real GDP grows the economy is in a business cycle expansion phase and when real GDP shrinks (for two quarters) the economy is in a recession. Also, as real GDP fluctuates, so do employment and unemployment.

But real GDP fluctuations probably exaggerate or overstate the fluctuations in total production and economic welfare. The reason is that when business activity slows down in a recession, household production increases and so does leisure time. When business activity speeds up in an expansion phase, household production and leisure time decrease. Because household production and leisure time increase in a recession and decrease in an expansion, they are countercyclical. As a result, real GDP fluctuations tend to overstate the fluctuations in total production and in economic welfare. But the directions of change of real GDP, total output and economic welfare are probably the same.

Review Quiz

◆ Does real GDP measure economic welfare? If not why not?
◆ Does real GDP measure total production of goods and services? If not, what are the main omissions?
◆ How can we make valid international comparisons of real GDP?
◆ Do the fluctuations in real GDP measure the business cycle accurately? If not, why not?

In Chapter 19, pp. 404–423, we studied the macroeconomic performance of the United Kingdom in recent years – the growth and fluctuations in real GDP, unemployment, inflation and the balance of international payments. We've now studied the methods used to measure some of these indicators of macroeconomic performance. We've seen how real GDP and the price level are measured, and we've seen what these measures mean. In Chapter 22, we study aggregate demand and aggregate supply. This aggregate model parallels the demand and supply model of a single market. And it serves as an overview and backdrop against which to place your study of economic growth, unemployment, and inflation. An understanding of this model will help you find your way through what can sometimes seem like a macroeconomic maze.

Summary

Key Points

Gross Domestic Product (pp. 425–429)

● Gross domestic product (GDP) is the value of aggregate output in a country in a given time period (usually a year).

● The concept of GDP is based on the circular flow of expenditure and income.

● Aggregate expenditure on goods and services equals aggregate income.

● The value of aggregate output – GDP – is equal to aggregate expenditure or aggregate income.

Measuring UK GDP (pp. 429–433)

● Because aggregate expenditure, aggregate income and the value of aggregate output are equal, we can measure GDP by either the expenditure approach or the factor incomes approach.

● The expenditure approach adds together consumption expenditure, investment, government purchases of goods and services and net exports to arrive at an estimate of GDP.

● The factor incomes approach adds together the incomes paid to the factors of production – labour, capital, land and profit paid to entrepreneurs.

● To use the factor incomes approach, it is necessary to add indirect taxes and subtract subsidies to arrive at GDP.

The Price Level and Inflation (pp. 433–436)

- The two main indices that measure the price level are the Retail Prices Index and the GDP deflator.

- The RPI measures the average price level of goods and services typically consumed by UK households.

- The GDP deflator measures the average price level of all the goods and services that make up GDP.

- Inflation is measured by the rate of change of the RPI or the GDP deflator.

- The RPI and the GDP deflator give an upward-biased measure of inflation because some goods disappear and new goods become available, the quality of goods and services changes over time.

What Real GDP Means (pp. 437–440)

- Real GDP is not a perfect measure of either aggregate economic activity or economic welfare.

- Real GDP excludes quality improvements, household production, underground production, environmental damage and the contribution to economic welfare of health and life expectancy, leisure time, and political freedom and equity.

Key Figures and Tables

Key Terms

Problems

•1 Martha owns a copy shop that has 5 copiers. One copier wears out each year and is replaced. In addition, this year Martha will expand her business to 7 copiers. Calculate Martha's initial capital stock, depreciation, gross investment, net investment and final capital stock.

2 Wendy operates a weaving shop with 10 looms. One loom wears out each year and is replaced. But this year, Wendy will expand her business to 12 looms. Calculate Wendy's initial capital stock, depreciation, gross investment, net investment and final capital stock.

•3 The figure overleaf shows the flows of income and expenditure on Lotus Island. During 1997: *A* was £10 million; *B* was £30 million; *C* was

£12 million; *D* was £15 million; and *E* was £3 million. Calculate

a Aggregate expenditure.

b Aggregate income.

c GDP.

d Government budget deficit.

e Household saving.

f Government saving.

g Foreign borrowing.

h National saving.

4 In problem 3, during 1998: *A* was £10 million; *B* was £50 million; *C* was £15 million; *D* was £15 million; and *E* was –£5 million. Calculate the quantities in problem 3 during 1998.

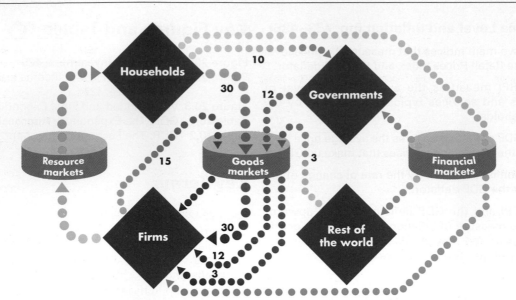

•5 The transactions in Ecoland last year were:

Item	Euros
Wages paid to labour	800,000
Consumption expenditure	600,000
Taxes	250,000
Transfer payments	50,000
Profits	200,000
Investment	250,000
Government expenditures	200,000
Exports	300,000
Saving	300,000
Imports	250,000

a Calculate Ecoland's GDP.

b Did you use the expenditure approach or the income approach to make this calculation?

c Do injections equal leakages?

6 The transactions in Highland last year were:

Item	Euros
Wages paid to labour	800,000
Consumption expenditure	650,000
Net taxes	200,000
Profits	250,000
Investment	300,000
Government expenditures	250,000
Exports	250,000
Saving	300,000
Imports	300,000

a Calculate Highland's GDP.

b What extra information do you need in order to calculate net domestic product?

c Where does Highland get the funds to finance its investment?

•7 A typical family on Sandy Island consumes only juice and cloth. Last year, which was the base year, the family spent £40 on juice and £25 on cloth. In the base year, juice was £4 a bottle and cloth was £5 a length. In the current year, juice is £4 a bottle and cloth is £6 a length. Calculate

a The basket used in the RPI.

b The RPI in the current year.

c The inflation rate in the current year.

8 A typical family on Lizard Island consumes only mangoes and nuts. Last year, which was the base year, the family spent £60 on nuts and £10 on mangoes. In the base year, mangoes were £1 each and nuts were £3 a bag. In the current year, mangoes are £1.50 each and nuts are £4 a bag. Calculate

a The basket used in the RPI.

b The RPI in the current year.

c The inflation rate in the current year.

•9 Bananaland produces only bananas and sunscreen. The base year is 1997 and the tables give the quantities produced and the prices.

Good	Quantity	
	1997	1998
Bananas	1,000 bunches	1,100 bunches
Sunscreen	500 bottles	525 bottles

Good	Price	
	1997	1998
Bananas	£2 a bunch	£3 a bunch
Sunscreen	£10 a bottle	£8 a bottle

Calculate Bananaland's

a   GDP and real GDP in 1997 and 1998.

b   Growth rate of real GDP in 1998.

c   GDP deflator in 1998.

10   Sea Island produces only lobsters and crabs. The base year is 1997 and the tables give the quantities produced and the prices.

Good	Quantity	
	1997	1998
Lobsters	1,000	1,100
Crabs	500	525

Good	Price	
	1997	1998
Lobsters	£20 each	£25 each
Crabs	£10 each	£12 each

Calculate Sea Island's

a   GDP and real GDP in 1997 and 1998.

b   Growth rate of real GDP in 1998.

c   GDP deflator in 1998.

Critical Thinking

1   Study Reading Between the Lines on pp. 444–445 and then answer the following questions:

a   How is child care valued by the ONS statisticians? What is the aggregate value of total household production relative to GDP? What is the aggregate value of child care relative to GDP?

b   What other currently excluded economic activities could be included in the GDP measure?

c   What is meant by the underground economy and why do some countries have a larger underground economy than others?

d   How would the inclusion of household production and the underground economy in our measure of GDP affect economic decision makers such as the Treasury or Bank of England?

2   Use the Parkin, Powell and Matthews website to link on to the National Statistics site. There you can obtain data on real GDP and nominal GDP for the United Kingdom.

a   What is the GDP deflator for the most recent year available?

b   What was the GDP deflator in the previous year?

c   What is the inflation rate as measured by the GDP deflator between these two years?

d   What is real GDP for the most recent year available?

e   What was real GDP in the previous year?

f   What is the real GDP growth rate between these two years?

g   Check from the data you have obtained that the growth in nominal GDP is the growth in real GDP less the rate of inflation as measured by the GDP deflator.

Measuring the Economy

THE FINANCIAL TIMES, 16 SEPTEMBER 2001

FT

Hidden cost of looking after children put at up to £225 bn

David Turner

The 88 bn hours spent looking after children without financial reward in 1999 were worth up to £225 bn, based on market rates for child care, according to the Office for National Statistics.

This would have increased the country's gross domestic product by more than a quarter, the ONS said in its provisional estimate of the economic value of unpaid child care by parents, relatives and friends. Even an uninterrupted night's sleep is, according to the ONS, 'household production' – on the grounds that if you were not asleep in the house you would have to pay someone else to stay there instead.

Sue Holloway, ONS statistician, said: 'If you're looking after children it's quite hard not to be productive'.

In March the ONS will publish 'household satellite accounts' assigning a value to all unpaid work in the UK – including child care, housework and cooking.

Initial ONS calculations last year showed their total value could have more than doubled the size of the economy if added to GDP figures. But the official statisticians insist the figures will remain separate from GDP.

Others have more radical ideas. Ed Mayo, director of the left-leaning New Economics Foundation, said: 'If a single parent leaves full-time child care by entering the labour market, more money changes hands so the economy grows. But there may have been a decline in well-being.'

But a 'sustainable economic welfare' measure that exploited these new calculations would start with GDP but then adjust for falls in the total amount of unpaid work, he said.

The Essence of the Story

- A total of 88 billion hours were spent in looking after children, without any payment in 1999.

- If these hours are valued at the market rates for child care, the total will be worth £225 billion.

- The Office for National Statistics intend to publish national accounts assigning a monetary value to all unpaid work, including child care, housework and cooking.

- Initial estimates of 'household production' by the Office for National Statistics show that their total value would double the size of the economy if added to GDP.

- A measure of 'sustainable economic welfare' would account for household production. So if a single parent gave up full-time child care to do paid work, the monetary economy would grow but there might be a decline in economic welfare.

Economic Analysis

■ The total amount of time spent in child care is estimated to be 88 billion hours a year. These activities are productive but not traded and therefore placing a market value on them is not easy. An appropriate measure of economic welfare would include both GDP and the monetary value of household production.

■ Figure 1 shows the breakdown of a measure of economic welfare between GDP, and components of household production.

■ The ONS statisticians have used the average cost of child care per hour in the private sector to value the total estimated time spent in household child care. This means that if a female lawyer took maternity leave to look after her child, measured economic welfare would decline because GDP would decline by more than than the increase in household production. However, if a female child care worker took maternity leave, measured economic welfare would remain unchanged.

■ Figure 2 shows the value of child care between 1995 and 1999. The ONS provide a range of estimates. The figure shows the highest and lowest estimates.

■ Another part of the economy that is not measured by GDP is the size of the underground economy. The underground economy covers work that could be done in the regular economy but is unrecorded for purposes of tax evasion and work that is illegal such as drug production and distribution and prostitution.

■ Table 1 shows the estimates of the underground economy for the industrialized economies obtained from research conducted by Professors Schneider and Enste.

■ Greece had the largest underground economy relative to GDP in 1996–97 and Switzerland had the smallest.

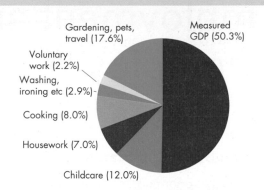

Figure 1 Economic welfare measure

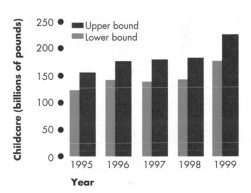

Figure 2 Value of childcare

Country	1994/95	1996/97
	(percentage of GDP)	
Australia	13.8	13.9
Austria	7.0	8.6
Belgium	21.5	22.2
Canada	14.8	14.9
Denmark	17.8	18.2
France	14.5	14.8
Germany	13.5	14.8
Great Britain	12.5	13.0
Greece	29.6	30.1
Ireland	15.4	16.0
Italy	26.0	27.2
Japan	10.6	11.3
Netherlands	13.7	13.8
Norway	18.2	19.4
Portugal	22.1	22.8
Spain	22.4	23.0
Sweden	18.6	19.5
Switzerland	6.7	7.8
United States	9.2	8.8

Table 1 Shadow economies of OECD countries

CHAPTER 21

Employment and Unemployment

After studying this chapter you will be able to:

◆ Define the unemployment rate, the workforce economic activity rate, the economic activity rate and aggregate hours

◆ Describe the trends and fluctuations in the indicators of labour market performance

◆ Describe the sources of unemployment, its duration and the groups most affected by it

◆ Explain how employment and wage rates are determined by demand and supply in the labour market

Vital Signs

Each month, we chart the course of the unemployment rate as a measure of economic health. How do we measure the unemployment rate? What does it tell us? Is it a reliable vital sign for the economy? ◆ December 1992 was a month in which unemployment peaked at almost 3 million. How can this large number of people be unemployed? How do people become unemployed? Do most of them get fired or do most simply quit their jobs to look for better ones? How long do spells of unemployment last for most people? A week or two or several months? And how does the length of unemployment spell vary over the business cycle? ◆ You may know that unemployment is more common among young people than older people. It affects ethnic minorities much more severely than whites. Why isn't unemployment 'shared' more equitably by all age and racial groups? ◆ Another feature of the labour market that we regularly monitor is the number of people working. This number fluctuates as the unemployment rate fluctuates. At the start of 2001, 28 million people in the United Kingdom had a job. What does this information tell us about the health of the economy? Does the number of jobs grow quickly enough to keep pace with the increase in population? ◆ The European Union is an economy that is comparable in size with the United States, but unemployment in the EU is nearly twice as high as in the USA. Why is this? What special factors contribute to unemployment in Europe that do not exist in the USA? ◆ Yet other signs of economic health are the hours people work and the wages they receive. Are work hours growing as quickly as the number of people with jobs? Or are most of the new jobs part time? Also, are most new jobs high-wage or low-wage jobs?

◆ ◆ ◆ ◆ These are the questions we study in this chapter. You will discover that while there are things about the UK labour market that are not healthy there are other aspects that give grounds for optimism. The economy has been creating good jobs that pay good wages and benefits. But you'll also see that the economy has destroyed many jobs. While some people have seen their wages rise, others have seen no change and a few have seen their wages fall. So there have been big changes in the distribution of jobs and big changes in spread between the highest and the lowest wages. We begin by looking at the key labour market indicators and the way they are measured.

Employment and Wages

The quantity of real GDP supplied depends on the quantities of labour and capital and the state of technology. Potential GDP depends on the quantity of capital, labour and technology employed at *full employment*. In this chapter we study the forces that determine the quantity of labour employed and the concept of full employment. We begin by learning how the state of the labour market is observed and measured.

Population Survey

The Office for National Statistics (ONS), periodically publishes a measure of employment in the United Kingdom based on the Labour Force Survey (LFS), which is a survey of households. The LFS conforms to internationally recognized norms and includes demographic information such as age, qualifications and ethnic origin. Because LFS surveys are conducted in all EU and other OECD countries they are also useful for international comparison.

In the UK, unemployment figures are obtained in two different ways: from the LFS and from the claimant count. To be counted as *unemployed* in the LFS, people must be available for work within the two weeks following their interview and must be in one of three categories:

1   Without work, but having made specific efforts to find a job within the previous four weeks.

2   Waiting to be called back to a job from which they have been laid off.

3   Waiting to start a new job within 30 days.

The claimant count measures unemployment as the number of people who are eligible and claim unemployment-related benefits (jobseekers' allowance). This measure differs from the LFS and is sensitive to changes in the regulations for benefit entitlement (jobseekers' allowance). For example, a married woman who wishes to return to work after a period of absence from the labour market is not counted as being unemployed according to the claimant count but is counted in the LFS. Similarly, young people under the age of 18 are excluded from the claimant count but are included in the LFS. Sometimes the two measures provide conflicting information about trends in the labour market as discussed in Reading Between the Lines on pp. 462–463.

The LFS defines the **working-age population** as the total number of people aged between 16 years

Figure 21.1

Population Workforce Categories

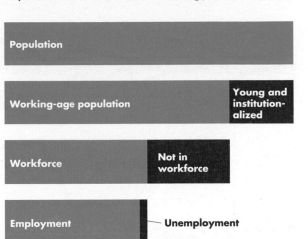

The population is divided into the working-age population and the young and institutionalized. The working-age population is divided into the workforce and those not in the workforce. The workforce is divided into the employed and the unemployed.

Source: *Annual Abstract of Statistics*, 2001.

and retirement who are not in jail, hospital, or some other form of institutional care. The working-age population is divided into two groups: those who are economically active (the **workforce**) and those who are economically inactive. The workforce is also divided into two groups: the employed and the unemployed. So the workforce is the sum of the employed and the unemployed.

To be counted as employed, a person must have either a full-time job or a part-time job. This includes students who do part-time work while at college. People in the working-age population who are neither employed nor unemployed are classified as not in the workforce.

Figure 21.1 shows the population categories used by the LFS.

Three Labour Market Indicators

We can use official data to calculate three indicators of the state of the labour market which are shown in Figure 21.2. They are:

Figure 21.2

Employment, Unemployment and Economic Activity Rate: 1960–2000

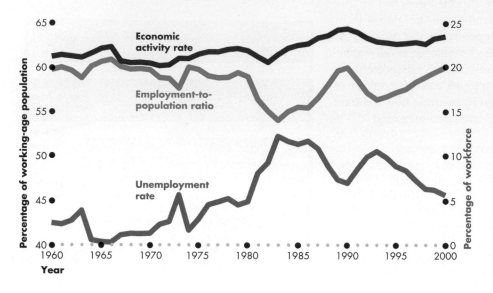

The state of the labour market is indicated by the economic activity rate, the employment-to-population ratio and the unemployment rate. The economic activity rate has increased a little since 1960. The employment-to-population ratio has decreased slightly and fluctuates with the business cycle, but it has fluctuated more in the 1980s and 1990s.

Sources: National Statistics *Labour Force Survey*, 2001.

1 The unemployment rate.

2 The economic activity rate.

3 The employment-to-population ratio.

The Unemployment Rate

The amount of unemployment is an indicator of the extent to which people who want jobs can't find them. The **unemployment rate** is the percentage of the people in the workforce who are unemployed. That is:

$$\text{Unemployment rate} = \frac{\text{Number of people unemployed}}{\text{Workforce}} \times 100$$

and

$$\text{Workforce} = \text{Number of people employed} + \text{Number of people unemployed}$$

In June 2001, the number of people employed in the United Kingdom according to the LFS was 28.1 million and the number unemployed was 1.5 million. By using the above equations, you can verify that the workforce was 29.6 million, and the unemployment rate was 5.1 per cent in the UK. In contrast, the unemployment rate in Euroland (the 11 countries that make up the European Monetary Union) was 8.3 per cent and in the United States, was 4.5 per cent.

The unemployment rate in Figure 21.2 (graphed in orange and plotted on the right scale) shows how labour market conditions have changed. The average unemployment rate in the 1960s and 1970s was 2.5 per cent, but the average rate in the 1980s and 1990s is 9 per cent. Unemployment reached its most recent peak in 1993 following the recession of 1990–92, and a trough in 1990.

The Economic Activity Rate

The number of people who join the workforce is an indicator of the willingness of the people of working age to take jobs. The **economic activity rate** is the percentage of the working-age population who are members of the workforce. That is:

$$\text{Activity rate} = \frac{\text{Workforce}}{\text{Working-age population}} \times 100$$

In June 2001, the workforce was 29.6 million and the working-age population was 46.6 million. By using the above equation, you can calculate the work-force economic activity rate. It was 63.5 per cent.

In Figure 21.2, the economic activity rate (graphed in red and plotted on the left scale) tells us about the growth of the workforce relative to the population. It has increased a little, rising from 61.2 per cent in 1960 to 63.4 per cent in 2000. It peaked in 1990. It has also had some mild fluctuations, resulting from unsuccessful job seekers becoming discouraged workers. **Discouraged workers** are people who during a recession temporarily leave the workforce and who during a recovery and expansion re-enter the workforce and become more active job seekers. The movements of discouraged workers out of and back into the workforce change the economic activity rate. Fluctuations in the workforce economic activity rate give an estimate of the number of discouraged workers.

The Employment-to-population Ratio

The number of people of working age who have jobs is an indicator of the availability of jobs and the degree of match between people's skills and jobs. The **employment-to-population ratio** is the percentage of the people of working age who have jobs. That is:

$$\text{Employment-to-population ratio} = \frac{\text{Number of people employed}}{\text{Working-age population}} \times 100$$

In June 2001, employment in the United Kingdom was 28.1 million and the working-age population was 46.6 million. By using the above equation, you can calculate the employment-to-population ratio. It was 60.3 per cent.

The employment-to-population ratio in Figure 21.2 (graphed in blue and plotted against the left scale) tells us about the growth in the number of people employed relative to the population. This ratio has fallen from 59.7 per cent in 1960 to 54 per cent in 1983 and risen to 60 per cent in 2000. The fact that the employment-to-population ratio has increased since 1983 means that the economy has created jobs at a faster rate than the working-age population has grown. This labour market indicator also fluctuates, and its fluctuations coincide with but are opposite to those in the unemployment rate. The employment-to-population ratio falls during a recession and increases during a recovery and expansion.

Why has the economic activity rate increased but the employment-to-population ratio remained roughly the same as in 1960? The main reason is an increase in the unemployment rate. Between 1960 and 2000,

Figure 21.3

The Changing Face of the Labour Market

The male participation rate and the employment-to-population ratio have decreased. This is because increasing numbers of men are in higher education, some are retiring earlier and some are specializing in the household jobs that were previously done by women. The female participation rate has been rising and many new jobs are part time employing female labour.

Source: National Statistics, *Labour Force Survey* 2001.

the rate of unemployment increased from 2.4 per cent to 5.3 per cent, reaching a peak of 12.2 per cent in 1983. In other words, the total number of jobs has not kept up with the increase in the working-age population. But this statement has to be qualified. Figure 21.3 shows that the female workforce economic activity rate has increased from 38 per cent in 1960 to 55 per cent in 2000. Other things are also changing. Shorter working hours, higher productivity and an increased emphasis on white-collar jobs have expanded the job opportunities and wages available to women. At the same time, technological advances have increased productivity in the home and freed women from some of their more traditional jobs outside the job market.

Figure 21.3 also shows another remarkable fact about the UK workforce: the economic activity rate and the employment-to-population ratio for men have *decreased*. Between 1960 and 2000, the male economic activity rate decreased from 87 per cent to

72 per cent. It has decreased because increasing numbers of men are in higher education, some are retiring earlier and some are specializing in the household jobs that previously were done almost exclusively by women.

Aggregate Hours

The three labour market indicators that we've just examined are useful signs of the health of the economy and directly measure what matters to most people: jobs. But they don't tell us the quantity of labour used to produce GDP, and we can't use them to calculate the productivity of labour. The productivity of labour is significant because it influences the wages people earn.

The reason the number of people employed does not measure the quantity of labour employed is that jobs are not all the same. Some jobs are part time and involve just a few hours of work a week. Others are full time, and some of these involve regular overtime work. For example, one shop might hire six students who each work for three hours a day. Another might hire two full-time workers who each work nine hours a day. The number of people employed in these two shops is eight, but six of the eight do the same total amount of work as the other two. To determine the total amount of labour used to produce GDP, we measure labour in hours rather than in jobs. **Aggregate hours** is the total number of hours worked by all the people employed, both full time and part time, during a year.

Figure 21.4(a) shows aggregate hours in the economy from 1970 to 2000. They fluctuate around a flat trend. Between 1970 and 2000, the number of people employed in the UK economy increased by about 12 per cent. However, during that same period, aggregate hours had not risen by much. Why the difference? Because average weekly hours per worker have fallen over the same period.

Figure 21.4(b) shows average weekly hours per worker. From around 36.2 hours a week in 1970, average hours per worker decreased to 32.8 hours a week in 2000. This shortening of the average workweek has arisen partly because of a decrease in the average hours worked by full-time workers but mainly because the number of part-time jobs has increased faster than the number of full-time jobs.

Fluctuations in aggregate hours and average hours per worker line up with the business cycle. Figure 21.4 highlights the past three recessions during

Figure 21.4

Aggregate Hours: 1970–2000

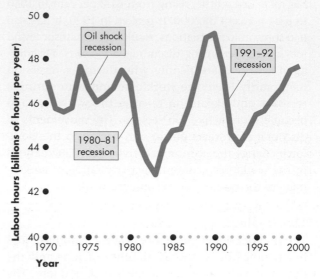

(a) Aggregate hours

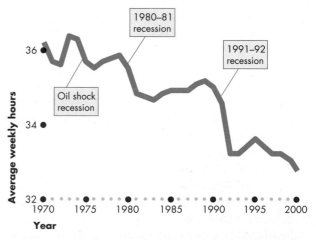

(b) Average weekly hours per person

Aggregate hours (part a) measure the total labour used to produce real GDP more accurately than does the number of people employed because an increasing proportion of jobs are part time. Between 1970 and 2000, aggregate hours fluctuated around a flat trend. Fluctuations in aggregate hours coincide with business cycle fluctuations. Aggregate hours have stayed roughly the same while the number of jobs has increased because the average workweek has shortened (part b).

Sources: National Statistics, *Labour Force Survey* 2001; and author's calculations.

which aggregate hours decreased and average hours per worker decreased more quickly than the trend. While both measures show a fall that corresponds with the downturn of the economy in a recession, aggregate hours fall by more because people lose their jobs.

Wage Rates

The **real wage rate** is the quantity of goods and services that an hour's work can buy. It is equal to the money wage rate (pounds per hour) divided by the price level. If we use the GDP deflator as the price level, the real wage rate is expressed in 1995 pounds because the GDP deflator is 100 in 1995. The real wage rate is a significant economic variable because it measures the reward for labour.

What has happened to the real wage rate in the United Kingdom? Figure 21.5 answers this question. It shows three measures of the average hourly real wage rate in the UK economy between 1970 and 2000.

The first measure of the real wage rate is the New Earnings Survey calculation of the average hourly earnings of adult manual workers measured in 1995 pounds. This measure of the hourly wage rate reached £4.85 in 1976. It fell to £4.70 in 1977 but accelerated in the second half of the 1980s, slowed in the first half of the 1990s and accelerated in the second half.

The second measure of the hourly real wage rate is based on the national income accounts. It is calculated by dividing total wages and salaries by aggregate hours. This measure of the hourly wage rate is broader than the first and includes the incomes of all types of labour, whether their rate of pay is calculated by the hour or not. It includes managers and supervisors and all types of workers. This measure shows a sustained upward trend during the 1970s and 1980s and a flattening in the 1990s.

An increasing proportion of labour cost now takes the form of employer's add-on costs, such as employer's National Insurance contributions, and graduated pension contributions. To take this trend into account, Figure 21.5 shows a third measure of the hourly real wage rate, which equals *real labour compensation* – wages, salaries and supplements – divided by aggregate hours. This measure is the most comprehensive one available, and it shows that the average hourly wage rate has increased. All three measures show that there was a common slowdown coinciding with the productivity slowdown of the 1970s.

Figure 21.5

Real Wage Rates: 1970–2000

- ▬ Real labour compensation
- ▬ Real wage of all workers
- ▬ Real wage adult male workers

The average hourly real wage rate of manual workers kept pace with the other two measures based on national income accounts. It accelerated in the late 1980s but slowed in the 1990s. All three measures of average hourly real wage rates reflect the productivity growth slowdown of the 1970s.

Sources: National Statistics, *New Earnings Survey* 2000.

Review Quiz

◆ What are the trends in the workforce economic activity rate, the employment-to-population ratio and the unemployment rate?
◆ What are the trends in the female workforce economic activity rate and male workforce economic activity rate?
◆ Why have aggregate hours not grown while total employment has?
◆ How have average hourly real wage rates changed since 1970?

We've seen that employment grows and that employment and unemployment fluctuate with the business cycle. Let's now focus more sharply on unemployment.

Unemployment and Full Employment

How do people become unemployed, how long do they remain unemployed and who is at greatest risk of becoming unemployed? Let's answer these questions by looking at the anatomy of unemployment.

The Anatomy of Unemployment

People become unemployed if they:

1 Lose their jobs.

2 Leave their jobs.

3 Enter or re-enter the workforce.

People end a spell of unemployment if they:

1 Are hired or recalled.

2 Withdraw from the workforce.

People who are laid off, either permanently or temporarily, from their jobs are called **job losers**. Some job losers become unemployed but some immediately withdraw from the workforce. People who voluntarily quit their jobs are called **job leavers**. Like job losers, some job leavers become unemployed and search for a better job, while others withdraw from the workforce temporarily or permanently retire from work. People who enter or re-enter the workforce are called **entrants** and **re-entrants**. Entrants are mainly people who have just left school. Some entrants get a job straight away and are never unemployed, but many spend time searching for their first job and during this period they are unemployed. Re-entrants are people who have previously withdrawn from the workforce. Most of these people are formerly discouraged workers or women returning to the labour market after an extended absence while raising a family. But an increasing number of unemployed people have been in this state for a period longer than a year. They are referred to as the **long-term unemployed**. Figure 21.6 shows these labour market categories.

Let's see how much unemployment arises from the three different ways in which people can become unemployed.

The Sources of Unemployment

Table 21.1 shows the proportion of unemployment by reason for becoming unemployed. Job losers are the biggest source of unemployment. These are the

Figure 21.6

Labour Market Flows

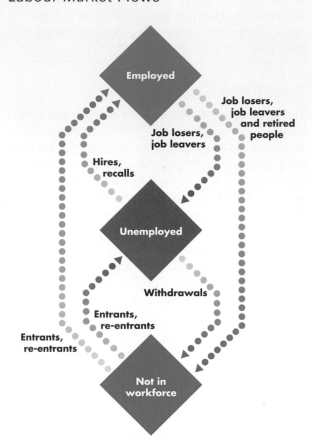

Unemployment results from employed people losing or leaving their jobs (job losers and job leavers) and from people entering the workforce (entrants and re-entrants). Unemployment ends because people get hired or recalled or because they withdraw from the workforce.

Table 21.1 Unemployment by Reasons (per cent)

Decade	Job losers	Entrants and re-entrants	Job leavers
1980s	46	44	10
1990s	58	28	14

Source: *Labour Force Survey*.

people that make up the redundancy statistics we hear so regularly on the television news and read in the newspapers. Their number fluctuates a great deal. In the 1990s, which includes the 1991–92 recession, over half of the unemployment was due to job losses. In contrast, in the business cycle peak year of 1990, fewer than 22 per cent of the unemployed were job losers.

Entrants are also a significant component of the unemployed. They are picked up in the LFS as school leavers. On any given day in the 1990s, over one-quarter of those recently unemployed were entrants to the labour market.

Job leavers are the smallest and most stable source of unemployment. On any given day in 1990s, fewer than 15 per cent of people unemployed were because they were job leavers.

The Duration of Unemployment

Some people are unemployed for a week or two, and others are unemployed for periods of a year or more. Figure 21.7 examines the duration of unemployment at the peak and the trough of the business cycle. We can see that in the peak a higher proportion of the unemployed were jobless for under 13 weeks than in the trough, and a lower proportion of the unemployed were jobless for more than 13 weeks than in the trough. But the most noticeable feature is the proportion of people who have been unemployed for over one year. This is the definition of long-term unemployment, which is a pressing social problem both in the United Kingdom and in the rest of the European Union. In the peak of 1989, 33 per cent of the jobless population were classified as long-term unemployment; in the trough of 1992 that proportion increased to 44 per cent. While most people who are unemployed find work within a year, the proportion of the long-term unemployed has remained stubbornly in the range 35–45 per cent over the business cycle.

The Demographics of Unemployment

Figure 21.8(a) and (b) shows unemployment for different demographic groups. The figure shows that the high unemployment rates occur among young workers, especially young men, and also ethnic minority groups, especially among blacks. In the spring of 2001, the unemployment rate of all ethnic minorities was 11 per cent; for blacks as a whole it was 13 per cent compared with whites for whom it was only 4 per cent. Figure 21.8(b) shows that the gap between

Figure 21.7

Unemployment by Duration

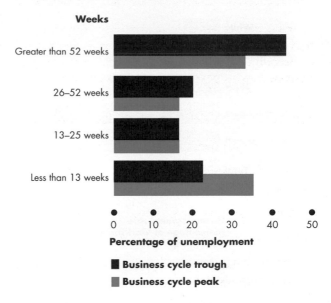

At a business cycle peak when unemployment is at its lowest level, 35 per cent of unemployment lasts for under 13 weeks, 16 per cent lasts for 13–25 weeks, 16 per cent lasts for 26–52 weeks and 33 per cent lasts for one year or more. At a business cycle trough when unemployment is at its highest level, only 20 per cent of unemployment lasts for under 13 weeks, 16 per cent lasts for 13–25 weeks, 20 per cent lasts for 26–52 weeks and 44 per cent lasts for one year or more.

Sources: *Labour Force Survey*; Quantime Ltd.

white and non-white unemployment increases in the trough and decreases in the peak. Teenagers also have a higher than average unemployment rate. In spring 2001, the unemployment rate of all 16–17 year-olds was 18.0 per cent, while that of teenage men was 20 per cent.

Why are teenage unemployment rates so high? There are three reasons. First, young people are still in the process of discovering what they are good at and trying different lines of work. So they leave their jobs more frequently than older workers. Second, firms sometimes hire teenagers on a short-term trial basis. So the rate of job loss is higher for teenagers than for other people. Third, most teenagers are not in the workforce but are at school. This means that the percentage of the teenage population unemployed is much lower than the teenage unemployment rate.

Figure 21.8

Unemployment by Demographic Group

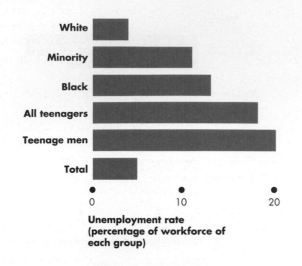

(a) Demographic groups

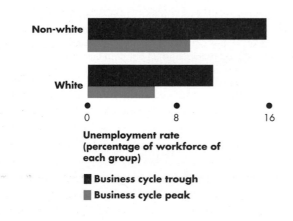

(b) Ethnic groups

Teenagers experience unemployment rates nearly four-and-a-half times higher than the average, and unemployment among blacks is over three-and-a-quarter times the average. Even at a business cycle trough when unemployment is at its highest rate, the ratio of non-white to white unemployment is 1.7.

Sources: *Labour Force Survey*; Spring 2001.

Ethnic minorities' unemployment rates are higher than white unemployment rates. One reason is that ethnic minorities face unequal opportunities and possible discrimination in the labour market. In the peak of the business cycle unemployment among non-

whites is 1.8 times higher than unemployment among whites. Even in the trough of the business cycle when unemployment is higher all round, the ratio of non-white to white unemployment falls to only 1.7.

Types of Unemployment

Unemployment is classified into three types that are based on its causes. They are:

1 Frictional.

2 Structural.

3 Cyclical.

Frictional Unemployment

Frictional unemployment is the unemployment that arises from normal labour turnover. Frictional unemployment is not usually regarded as a problem, but it is a permanent, long-term phenomenon.

Normal labour turnover arises for two reasons. First, people are constantly entering the workforce – young people leave school, mothers return to the workforce and previously discouraged workers try once more to find jobs. At the same time, other people retire and create job vacancies for the new entrants and re-entrants to fill. This constant churning of the individuals in the workforce is the first reason for normal labour turnover.

The second reason is the constant churning of individual businesses. Some businesses fail, close down and lay off their workers. Other new businesses start up and hire workers. The people who lose their jobs in this process are frictionally unemployed and are trying to match their skills to jobs that are opening up.

The unending flow of people into and out of the workforce and of job creation and job destruction creates the need for people to search for jobs and for businesses to search for workers. Always there are businesses with unfilled jobs and people seeking jobs. Look in your local newspaper and you will see that there are always some jobs being advertised. Businesses don't usually hire the first person who applies for a job, and unemployed people don't usually take the first job that comes their way. Instead, both firms and workers spend time searching out what they believe will be the best match available. By this process of search, people can match their own skills and interests with the available jobs and find a satisfying job and income. While these unemployed people are searching, they are frictionally unemployed.

The amount of frictional unemployment depends on the rate at which people enter and re-enter the workforce and on the rate at which jobs are created and destroyed. During the 1960s, the amount of frictional unemployment increased as a consequence of the post-war baby boom that began during the 1940s. By the 1960s, the baby boom created a bulge in the number of school leavers. As these people entered the workforce, the amount of frictional unemployment increased.

The amount of frictional unemployment is also influenced by the level of unemployment benefit. The greater the number of people covered by unemployment benefit (jobseekers' allowance) and the more generous the benefit, the longer is the average time taken in job search and the greater is the amount of frictional unemployment. The LFS indicates that 92 per cent of the unemployed are covered by unemployment benefit. Studies of unemployment in the European Union indicate that a strong statistical correlation exists between the length of time people are able to receive unemployment benefit and the duration of unemployment.

Structural Unemployment

Structural unemployment is the unemployment that arises when changes in technology or international competition destroy jobs that use different skills or are located in different regions from the new jobs that are created. Structural unemployment usually lasts longer than frictional unemployment because it is often necessary to retrain and possibly relocate to find a job. For example, on the day the shipyards in the Upper Clyde announced the loss of 600 jobs, a computer chip company in Gwent announced the creation of 750 new jobs. The unemployed former shipyard workers remain unemployed for several months until they move home, retrain and get one of the new jobs being created in other parts of the country.

Structural unemployment is painful, especially for older workers for whom the best available option might be to retire early, but with a lower income than they had expected. For example, a shipyard worker from Humberside who is made redundant may reluctantly accept to remain unemployed rather than retrain, accept a lower wage for another type of job, or move south where new jobs are being created. Such a person has opted to join the ranks of the long-term unemployed. The decision to accept long-term unemployment is governed by the options available to and the constraints on the structurally unemployed person. A person with different circumstances may make an entirely different decision. A younger person with family commitments may retrain, or take a job as a taxi driver in the short term until a better opportunity turns up, or relocate to take advantage of job opportunities elsewhere. One of the many factors that influence a person's decision is the level of unemployment benefit. The higher the level of benefit, the less incentive there is to accept the alternatives to long-term unemployment.

At certain times structural unemployment can become a serious long-term problem. It began to increase in the 1970s during the period of stagflation, when an increasingly competitive international environment brought a decline in the number of jobs in traditional industries.

Cyclical Unemployment

Cyclical unemployment is the fluctuating unemployment that coincides with the business cycle. It is a repeating short-term problem. The amount of cyclical unemployment increases during a recession and decreases during a recovery and expansion. A worker in a car components factory who is laid off because the economy is in a recession and who gets rehired some months later when the recovery begins has experienced cyclical unemployment.

Figure 21.9 illustrates cyclical unemployment in the United Kingdom between 1980 and 2000. Part (a) shows the fluctuations of real GDP around potential GDP. Part (b) shows fluctuations in the unemployment rate around a line labelled 'Natural rate of unemployment'. The **natural rate of unemployment** is the unemployment rate when there is no cyclical unemployment or, equivalently, when all the unemployment is frictional and structural. The divergence of the unemployment rate from the natural rate is cyclical unemployment.

In Figure 21.9, the unemployment rate fluctuates around the natural rate of unemployment (part b) just as real GDP fluctuates around potential GDP (part a). When the unemployment rate equals the natural rate of unemployment, real GDP equals potential GDP. When the unemployment rate is less than the natural rate of unemployment, real GDP is greater than potential GDP. And when the unemployment rate is greater than the natural rate of unemployment, real GDP is less than potential GDP. However, it is not always the case that when GDP equals potential GDP, unemployment equals the natural rate. While it is true to argue that when unemployment is at its natural rate GDP is at its potential, the reverse is not always the case. This is because, while production of goods and services can be increased by working the

Figure 21.9

Unemployment and Real GDP

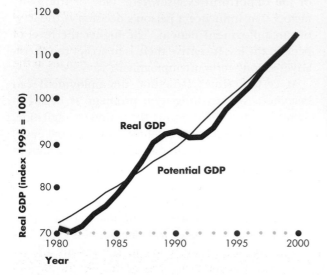

(a) Real GDP and potential GDP

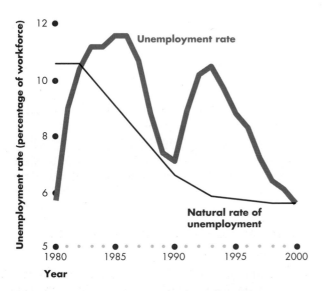

(b) Unemployment and the natural rate of unemployment

As real GDP fluctuates around potential GDP (part a), the unemployment rate fluctuates around the natural rate of unemployment (part b). In the recession of 1991–1992, the unemployment rate peaked at 10 per cent. The labour market reforms of the 1980s helped to reduce the natural rate of unemployment. We don't know how far the natural rate of unemployment has fallen.

Sources: Lombard Street Research Ltd; and author's estimates.

existing employed workforce more intensively through increased overtime, the process of hiring labour takes time. Hence adjustments to the unemployment rate can lag behind the movements in GDP.

Full Employment

There is always *some* unemployment – someone looking for a job or laid off and waiting to be recalled. So what do we mean by full employment? **Full employment** occurs when the unemployment rate equals the natural rate of unemployment. There can be quite a lot of unemployment at full employment, and the term 'full employment' is an example of a technical economic term that does not correspond with everyday ideas. The term 'natural rate of unemployment' is another example of a technical economic term that does not correspond with everyday language. We can think of the natural rate of unemployment as the rate of unemployment when all markets are in equilibrium. Another way of thinking about the natural rate of unemployment is that it is the rate of unemployment that produces a stable (unchanging) rate of inflation.

For most people, there is nothing *natural* about unemployment – especially for the unemployed. These terms remind us that frictions and structural changes are unavoidable features of the economy and that they create unemployment.

In Figure 21.9(b), the natural rate of unemployment was 10.5 per cent in 1980 and it falls continuously to 5.5 per cent in 2000. This view of the natural rate of unemployment in the United Kingdom is an estimate that some, but not all, economists would accept.

There is not much controversy about the existence of a natural rate of unemployment. Nor is there much controversy that it fluctuates. The natural rate of unemployment arises from the existence of frictional and structural unemployment, and it fluctuates because the frictions and the amount of structural change fluctuate. But there is controversy about the magnitude of the natural rate of unemployment and the extent to which it fluctuates. Some economists believe that the natural rate of unemployment fluctuates frequently, and that at times of rapid demographic and technological change, its rate can be high. Others argue that restrictive practices by trade unions and increases in real unemployment benefits will increase the natural rate, and that the labour market reforms of the 1980s led to a reduction in the natural rate to an even lower figure than that shown in Figure 21.9(b).

We've described the trends and fluctuations in employment, wage rates and unemployment. And we've described the labour market flows that bring changes in employment and unemployment. We've also described the anatomy of unemployment and classified it as frictional, structural and cyclical. You are now ready to learn about the forces that make real GDP grow and fluctuate and that bring changes in the price level, wages, employment, and unemployment.

Review Quiz

◆ What are the categories of people who become unemployed?

◆ Define frictional, structural, and cyclical unemployment and provide an example of each type of unemployment?

◆ What is the *natural rate of unemployment*?

Summary

Key Points

Employment and Wages (pp. 447–451)

- The population is divided into four labour market categories: employed, unemployed, not in the workforce, and young and institutionalized people.

- The workforce is the sum of the employed and the unemployed.

- The working-age population is the sum of the workforce and the people not in the workforce.

- The population is the sum of the working-age population and young and institutionalized people.

- These population categories are used to calculate the unemployment rate, the workforce economic activity rate and the employment-to-population ratio.

- The economic activity rate and the employment-to-population ratio fluctuate with the business cycle.

- The female economic activity rate has increased but the male economic activity rate has decreased.

- Aggregate hours, the total number of hours worked by all the people employed during a year, has remained roughly constant, but it also fluctuates in line with the business cycle. While aggregate hours have remained roughly the same in the past 25 years, average hours per worker have decreased.

- The average hourly real wage rate of adult manual workers has kept pace with other measures of real wages. It increased slightly ahead of the average in the second half of the 1980s but slowed down in the 1990s.

- Broader measures of average hourly real wage rates were slightly ahead of the average in the second half of the 1980s but slowed down in the 1990s.

Unemployment and Full Employment (pp. 452–457)

- The unemployment rate rises because people lose their jobs (*job losers*), leave their jobs (*job leavers*) and enter (or re-enter) the workforce (*entrants* or *re-entrants*), and it falls because people get hired or recalled or withdraw from the workforce.

- The duration of unemployment fluctuates over the business cycle but the phase of the business cycle makes little difference to the demographic patterns in unemployment.

- Unemployment can be *frictional* (arising from normal labour market turnover), *structural* (arising when there is a long-lasting decline in the number of jobs available in a region or industry) and *cyclical* (arising from the business cycle).

- When all the unemployment is frictional and structural, unemployment is at its natural rate, and there is *full employment*.

- There can be a substantial amount of unemployment at full employment, and the natural rate of unemployment fluctuates because of fluctuations in frictional and structural unemployment.

Key Figures ◇

Key Terms

Problems

•1 In 1998, the Office for National Statistics measured the UK's labour force at 29,049,000, employment at 27,227,000, and the working-age population at 46,253,000. Calculate for 1998 the

  a Unemployment rate.

  b Labour force participation rate.

  c Employment-to-population ratio.

2 In 2000, the Office for National Statistics measured the UK's labour force at 29,574,000, employment at 27,913,000 and the working-age population at 46,581,000. Calculate for 2000 the

  a Unemployment rate.

  b Labour force participation rate.

  c Employment-to-population ratio.

•3 During 1999, the working-age population increased by 178,000 employment increased by 333,000, and the labour force increased by 307,000. Use the data in problem 1 to calculate the change in unemployment and the change in the number of discouraged workers during 1999.

4 During 2001, the working-age population increased by 251,000, employment increased by 267,000, and the labour force increased by 60,000. Use the data in problem 2 to calculate the change in unemployment and the change in the number of discouraged workers during 2001.

•5 In August 1997, the unemployment rate was 6.8 per cent. In August 1998, the unemployment rate was 6.3 per cent. What do you predict happened between August 1997 and August 1998 to the numbers of

  a Job losers and job leavers?

  b Labour force entrants and re-entrants?

6 In January 2000, the unemployment rate was 5.8 per cent. In January 2001, the unemployment rate was 5.2 per cent. (These are seasonally adjusted rates that exclude the winter seasonal unemployment.) What do you predict happened in 2000 to the numbers of

  a Job losers and job leavers?

  b Labour force entrants and re-entrants?

•7 The figure shows the numbers of working-age people who were employed, unemployed, and not in the labour force in the nation of Labecon in July 2001 and the labour market flows during August 2001.

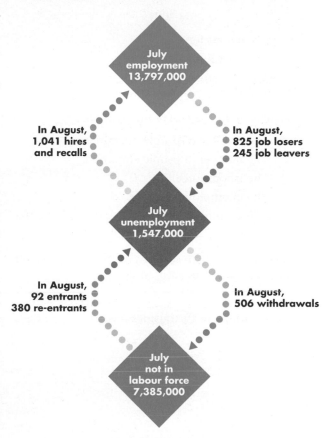

Calculate for July 2001:

  a The labour force.

  b The unemployment rate.

  c The working-age population.

  d The employment-to-population ratio in July 2001.

Calculate for the end of August 2001:

  e The number of people unemployed.

  f The number of people employed.

  g The labour force.

  h The unemployment rate.
  i The employment-to-population ratio if the labour force participation rate is 65.5 per cent.

8 The figure shows the numbers of working-age people who were employed, unemployed, and not in the labour force in the nation of Ecolab in July 2001 and the labour market flows during August 2001.
   Calculate for July 2001:

  a The labour force.
  b The unemployment rate.
  c The working-age population.
  d The employment-to-population ratio.

Calculate for the end of August 1998:

  e The number of people unemployed.
  f The number of people employed.
  g The labour force.
  h The unemployment rate.
  i The employment-to-population ratio if the labour force participation rate is 60 per cent.

●9 Describe the main features of the labour market at the peak of the business cycle.

10 Describe the main features of the labour market at the trough of the business cycle.

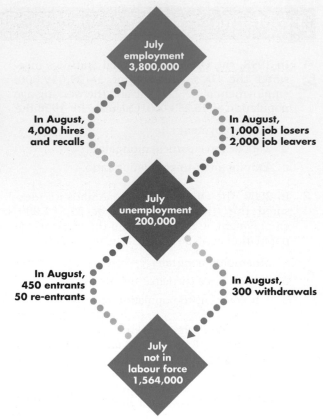

Critical Thinking

1 Study Reading Between the Lines on pp. 462–463 and then answer the following questions:

    a What is the labour market signalling about the trend in unemployment in 2001?

    b Why does the claimant count give a different picture about the trend in unemployment than the LFS measure?

    c What is the reason for the rise in unemployment?

    d Which sectors are particularly hit by job losses and why?

2 Use the links on the Parkin, Powell and Matthews website to obtain data on unemployment in your economic region of the UK.

    a Compare unemployment in your region with that in the United Kingdom as a whole.

    b Why do you think your region might have a higher or a lower unemployment rate than the UK average?

    c Try to identify those industries that have expanded most and those that have shrunk in your region.

    d What are the problems in your region's labour market that you think local government and Development Agencies can do to solve?

    e Use the demand and supply model of the labour market to aid your analysis.

3 The figures below show the rate of unemployment based on the claimant count in the United Kingdom for the 18 months from January 2000 to June 2001.

Month	Rate (%)
January 00	3.9
February 00	3.8
March 00	3.8
April 00	3.7
May 00	3.7
June 00	3.6
July 00	3.6
August 00	3.5
September 00	3.5
October 00	3.5
November 00	3.4
December 00	3.4
January 01	3.3
February 01	3.3
March 01	3.3
April 01	3.2
May 01	3.2
June 01	3.2

    a What has been the trend in UK unemployment in 2000–01?

    b From your knowledge of the state of the UK economy, do you think unemployment is above or below the natural rate?

    c If the unemployment rate is below the natural rate, what is your prediction for the economy in the rest of 2001? Has your prediction been borne out?

    d If the unemployment rate is above the natural rate, explain why the natural rate has fallen?

    e Is the claimant count a good measure of the rate of unemployment in the UK?

Wages and Unemployment

THE FINANCIAL TIMES, 18 OCTOBER 2001

FT

Claimant figures mask rise in jobless

Christopher Adams

A fresh fall in the number of people out of work and claiming benefit has masked a big jump in wider unemployment.

The headline jobless measure, the claimant count, fell 4,900 last month to 942,100, the lowest level since October 1975, the Office for National Statistics said yesterday. But the decline contrasted with separate data showing a sharp rise in the number out of work.

According to the government's preferred measure, the Labour Force Survey, which also records jobless not claiming benefit, unemployment rose 53,000 to 1,507m in the three months to August, the biggest rise for more than eight years.

The increase in Labour Force Survey unemployment follows comparable rises in the US and Germany and may ease the way for interest rate cuts. It suggests that, despite growth in distribution, financial services and the public sector, the labour market is poised for a downturn.

Economists blamed the global economic slowdown, which has hit manufacturing particularly hard, for rising Labour Force Survey unemployment.

Several forecast that the thousands of redundancies announced since the September 11 terrorist attacks on the US would help push the claimant count higher.

Redundancy levels rose over the summer and the percentage of workers re-employed fell, the ONS said.

At the same time, total employment dipped slightly dragged down by steep declines in part-time and temporary work. A rising number of working-age women have opted for 'inactivity' choosing not to look for jobs.

Retailers are among those driving jobs growth. With consumer spending still strong, the high street is enjoying a mini-boom and Safeway and Tesco have unveiled big expansion programmes. Higher government spending on health and education will support public sector growth.

But the trend elsewhere is worsening. Outside manufacturing, jobs have been cut in air travel, business services, media, investment banking and telecommunications.

Over the past year, some 123,000 employee jobs have been lost in manufacturing, many in metals and textiles. With the figures showing slower growth in manufacturing productivity, fresh job cuts are likely as companies struggle to restore margins.

The Essence of the Story

- Unemployment measured by the claimant count fell further in September 2001.

- But the alternative Labour Force Survey measure showed a rise in unemployment which is consistent with a slowdown in the UK economy.

- The rise in the LFS measure of unemployment is consistent with similar rises in the US and Germany.

- The rise in unemployment is consistent with the global economic slowdown.

- Unemployment increased because of job losses and decreased employment.

Economic Analysis

■ A widely predicted slowdown in the world and UK economy will eventually affect the jobs market in the UK. The rise in unemployment measured by the LFS is consistent with a slowdown.

■ However, the claimant count continued to show a drop in unemployment. The claimant count measures unemployment in terms of those in receipt of unemployment benefits (jobseekers' allowance), whereas the LFS measures those who are looking for work.

■ The conflicting picture means that it is too early to say if the trend in the labour market is reflecting an overall slowdown in the economy. The retail sector continues to create jobs while the manufacturing sector continues to shed jobs. Figure 1 shows the movements of both measures.

■ The slowdown in employment is consistent with a weakening global economy. Figure 2 shows the most recent growth rate of real GDP and unemployment in the USA, Germany and the UK. Both the US and Germany show a rise in unemployment.

■ The slowdown in economic growth will lead to an increase in cyclical unemployment as shown in Figure 3. If real GDP falls below potential GDP, unemployment is expected to rise above the natural rate.

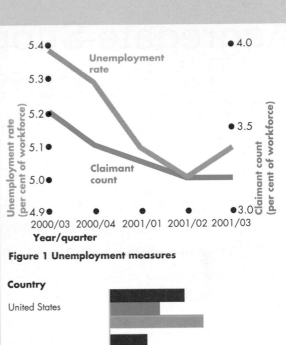

Figure 1 Unemployment measures

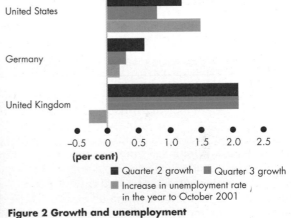

Figure 2 Growth and unemployment

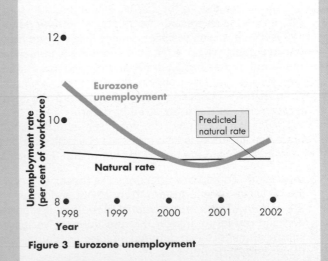

Figure 3 Eurozone unemployment

CHAPTER 22

Aggregate Supply and Aggregate Demand

After studying this chapter you will be able to:

◆ Explain the purpose of the aggregate supply–aggregate demand model

◆ Explain what determines aggregate supply and aggregate demand

◆ Explain macroeconomic equilibrium

◆ Explain the effects of changes in aggregate demand and aggregate supply on economic growth inflation and business cycles

◆ Explain the recent history of economic growth inflation and business cycles in the United Kingdom

Catching the Wave

Our economy is a bit like an ocean. Like the tide, the general direction or long-term trend of the economy is predictable and is governed by fundamental forces that are reasonably well understood. And like individual waves that ebb and flow, the economy rises and falls in a sequence of cycles that seem to repeat but are never quite like anything that went before and that are hard to predict. Like champion surfers, people who study the economy sometimes learn how to catch a wave and get a good economic ride. But the economic waves are hard to read. What makes the economy ebb and flow in waves around its long-term trend? ◆ Sometimes the economic waves rise high and then crash, and sometimes they rise and roll on a high for a long period like they did during the mid-1980s. Sometimes the waves are inflationary like they were during the 1970s. And sometimes they hit a low and remain there for some time like they did during the depression years of the interwar period, and like they did during the early 1980s and early 1990s. What makes the economic waves vary so much, with real GDP growth and inflation fluctuating in unpredictable ways? ◆ The UK economy is influenced by economic and political events in other parts of the world. For example, the economic policies of our partners in the rest of the European Union, particularly the interest rate policy of the European Central Bank have implications for economic policy at home. A short-term concern is the fall-out from the terrorist attack on New York and Washington on 11 September 2001 on an already deteriorating US and world economy. Reading Between the Lines (pp. 484–485) examines the implications of the slowdown in the world economy on growth in the euro area. The economy is also influenced by policy actions taken by the government and the Bank of England. How do events in the rest of the world and domestic policy actions affect production and prices?

◆ ◆ ◆ ◆ To address questions like these, we need a model of macroeconomic fluctuations – of fluctuations around the long-term trends. Our main task in this chapter is to build such a model – the *aggregate supply–aggregate demand model*. Our second task is to use the aggregate supply–aggregate demand model to answer the questions we've just posed. You'll discover that the model of aggregate supply and aggregate demand enables us to understand many important economic events which have a major impact on our lives.

Aggregate Supply

The aggregate supply–aggregate demand model enables us to understand three features of macroeconomic performance:

1 Growth of potential GDP.

2 Inflation.

3 Business cycle fluctuations.

The model uses the concepts of *aggregate* supply and *aggregate* demand to determine real GDP and the price level (the GDP deflator), other things remaining the same. We begin by looking at the fundamental limits to production that influence aggregate supply.

Aggregate Supply Fundamentals

The *quantity of real GDP supplied* (*Y*) depends on three factors:

1 The quantity of labour (*N*).

2 The quantity of capital (*K*).

3 The state of technology (*T*).

These factors are inputs into the production process that determine the quantity of real GDP supplied.

The influence of these three factors on the quantity of real GDP supplied is described by the **aggregate production function**, which is written as the equation:

$$Y = F(N, K, T)$$

Literally, the quantity of real GDP supplied is a function (*F*) of the factors *N*, *K*, and *T*. What this says is, if we want to produce more output, we must employ more inputs. The larger any one of these factors is, the greater is *Y*.

At any given time, the quantity of capital and the state of technology can be viewed as fixed. They depend on decisions made in the past. We can think of changes to capital and technology occurring only in the long run. In the short run, the population can also be viewed as fixed but the quantity of labour is not fixed. It will depend on the total supply and demand for labour.

Firms demand labour only if it is profitable to do so. The lower the wage rate, which is the cost of labour, the greater is the quantity of labour demanded (other things being equal). Similarly, people supply labour only if doing so is the most valuable use of their time. The higher the wage rate, which is the return to labour, the greater is the quantity of labour supplied. The wage rate that makes the quantity of labour demanded equal to the quantity of labour supplied is the equilibrium wage rate. At this wage rate, there is **full employment**.

Even at full employment, there are always people who are looking for jobs and firms looking for people to employ. The reason is that there is a constant turnover in the labour market. Everyday jobs are destroyed as businesses restructure, downsize, or simply go bust. At the same time jobs are created as new businesses start up, or existing ones expand. Some workers, for a number of personal reasons, may leave to look for better positions, while others start looking for work. This continuous churning in the labour market prevents unemployment from ever disappearing even at full employment. The unemployment rate at full employment is called the **natural rate of unemployment**.

The real GDP that is supplied when unemployment is at its natural rate is **potential GDP**. Potential GDP depends on the full employment of labour, capital and the state of technology. We examine the determinants of full employment and potential GDP in greater depth in Chapter 29, pp. 656–670.

To study the economy at full employment and over the business cycle we distinguish two time-frames for aggregate supply:

1 Long-run aggregate supply.

2 Short-run aggregate supply.

Long-run Aggregate Supply

The economy is constantly bombarded by events that move real GDP away from potential GDP and, equivalently, that move the unemployment rate away from equilibrium employment. Following such an event, forces operate to take real GDP back towards potential GDP and restore full employment. The **macroeconomic long run** is a time-frame that is sufficiently long for these forces to have done their work so that real GDP equals potential GDP and full employment prevails.

The **long-run aggregate supply curve** is the relationship between the quantity of real GDP supplied and the price level in the long run when real GDP equals potential GDP. Figure 22.1 illustrates long-run aggregate supply as the vertical line labelled *LAS*.

Figure 22.1

Long-run Aggregate Supply

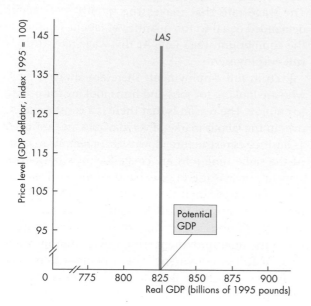

The long-run aggregate supply (*LAS*) curve shows the relationship between the quantity of real GDP supplied and the price level when real GDP equals potential GDP and there is full employment. This level of real GDP is independent of the price level so the *LAS* curve is vertical at potential GDP.

Along the long-run aggregate supply curve, as the price level changes, real GDP remains at potential GDP, which in Figure 22.1 is £825 billion. The long-run aggregate supply curve is always vertical and located at potential GDP.

The long-run aggregate supply curve is vertical because potential GDP is independent of the price level. The reason for this independence is that a movement along the long-run aggregate supply curve is accompanied by changes in *two* sets of prices: the prices of goods and services (the price level) and the prices of factors of production. A 10 per cent increase in the prices of goods and services is matched by a 10 per cent increase in wage rates and in other factor prices. That is, the price level, wage rate and other factor prices all change by the same percentage and *relative prices* and the *real wage rate* remain constant. When the price level changes but relative prices and the real wage rate remain constant, real GDP also remains constant.

Production at a Pepsi Plant

You can see why real GDP remains constant in these circumstances by thinking about production decisions at a Pepsi bottling plant. The plant is producing the quantity of Pepsi that maximizes profit. It could increase production further but to do so it would have to incur a higher *marginal cost* (see Chapter 10). If the price of bottled Pepsi increased and wage rates and other bottling costs did not change, the firm would have an incentive to increase its production. But if the price of bottled Pepsi increases and wage rates and other bottling costs also increase by the same percentage, the firm has no incentive to change its production.

Short-run Aggregate Supply

The **macroeconomic short run** is a period during which GDP is above or below potential GDP. At the same time unemployment is lower or higher than the natural rate.

The **short-run aggregate supply curve** is the relationship between the quantity of real GDP supplied and the price level in the short run when the money wage rate and all other influences on production plans remain constant. For the economy as a whole, with the money wage rate and other factor prices remaining the same. Figure 22.2 illustrates this short-run aggregate supply response as an aggregate supply schedule and as the upward-sloping curve labelled *SAS*. This curve is based on the short-run aggregate supply schedule and each point on the aggregate supply curve corresponds to a row of the aggregate supply schedule. For example, point *a* on the short-run aggregate supply curve and row *a* of the schedule tell us that if the price level is 105, the quantity of real GDP supplied is £775 billion.

Back at the Pepsi Plant

You can see why the short-run aggregate supply curve slopes upward by going back to the Pepsi bottling plant. Recall that the plant is producing at the profit maximizing position. If the price of bottled Pepsi rises and wage rates and other bottling costs don't change, the firm has an incentive to increase its production. The higher price for Pepsi more than covers the *marginal cost* of hiring more labour, and its profit rises. So in this situation, the firm increases its production.

Again, what's true for Pepsi bottlers is true for the producers of all goods and services. So when the price

Figure 22.2

Short-run Aggregate Supply

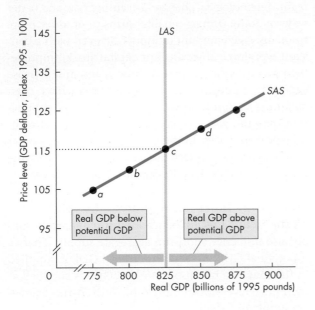

	Price level (GDP deflator)	Real GDP (billions of 1995 pounds)
a	105	775
b	110	800
c	115	825
d	120	850
e	125	875

The short-run aggregate supply (*SAS*) curve shows the relationship between the quantity of real GDP supplied and the price level when the money wage rate, other factor prices and potential GDP are constant. The short-run aggregate supply curve *SAS* is based on the schedule in the table. The *SAS* curve is upward-sloping because firms' costs increase as the rate of output increases so a higher price is needed to bring forth an increase in the quantity produced.

level rises and the money wage rate and other factor prices remain constant, aggregate production and the quantity of real GDP supplied increase.

Movements Along *LAS* and *SAS*

Figure 22.3 summarizes what you've just learned about the *LAS* and *SAS* curves. A rise in the price level and an equal percentage rise in the money wage rate

Figure 22.3

Movements Along the Aggregate Supply Curves

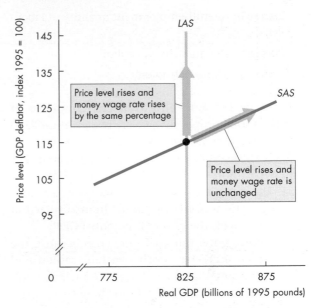

A rise in the price level with the money wage rate unchanged brings an increase in the quantity of real GDP supplied and a movement along the short-run aggregate supply curve. A rise in the price level with an equal percentage rise in the money wage rate keeps the quantity of real GDP supplied constant and brings a movement along the long-run aggregate supply curve.

brings a movement along the *LAS* curve. Real GDP remains constant at potential GDP. A rise in the price level and no change in the money wage rate bring a movement along the *SAS* curve.

You've now learned about the long-run and short-run aggregate supply curves and the factors that make the long-run aggregate supply curve vertical and the short-run aggregate supply curve slope upward. But what makes aggregate supply change? Let's find out.

Changes in Aggregate Supply

You've just seen that a change in the price level, other things remaining the same, brings a movement along the aggregate supply curves but it does not change aggregate supply. Aggregate supply changes when any other influences on production plans change. Let's study these influences beginning with those that affect potential GDP.

Changes in Potential GDP

Long-run aggregate supply changes when potential GDP changes and potential GDP changes for three reasons:

1 Change in the full-employment quantity of labour hours.

2 Change in the quantity of capital.

3 Improvement in technology.

Change in the Full-employment Quantity of Labour Hours

Suppose there are two identical Pepsi bottling plants except that one employs 100 hours of labour and the other employs 10 hours of labour. The plant with more labour produces more bottles of Pepsi. The same is true for the economy as a whole. The larger the number of labour hours utilized at full-employment, the greater is potential GDP.

Over time, potential GDP increases because the labour force increases. With constant capital and technology, potential GDP increases only if the full-employment quantity of labour hours increases. Fluctuations in employment and labour hours over the business cycle bring fluctuations around potential GDP. But they are not changes in potential GDP.

Change in the Quantity of Capital

A Pepsi plant that has two production lines has more capital and produces more output than a Pepsi plant that has one production line. For the economy as a whole, the larger the capital stock, the more productive the workforce is, the greater is the output that it can produce. The capital-rich UK economy produces a vastly greater real GDP per hour of labour than countries that have a small amount of capital, such as the developing countries. But the fast-growing capital stock of the Asian economies is bringing faster real GDP growth than the United Kingdom and other EU countries have achieved.

Capital includes *human capital*. The manager of one Pepsi plant is an economics graduate with an MBA and its workforce has an average of 10 years' experience. The manager of another identical plant has no business training and its workforce is new to bottling. The first plant has a higher stock of human capital than the second and its output is larger. For the economy as a whole, the larger the stock of *human capital* – the skills that people have acquired at school and through on-the-job training – the greater is potential GDP.

Improvement in Technology

One Pepsi plant has a production line that was designed in the 1970s before the computer age. Another uses the latest robot technology. Even with a smaller workforce, the second plant produces more bottles per day than the first plant. Technological change – inventing new and better ways of doing things – enables firms to produce more from any given amount of inputs. So even with a constant workforce and constant capital stock, improvements in technology increase production and increase aggregate supply. Technological advances have been by far the most important source of increased production over the past two centuries. As a result of technological advances, in the UK today, one farm worker produces enough to feed 60 people in a year, and one carworker can produce 12 cars and trucks in a year.

Changes in Short-run Aggregate Supply

All the factors that influence long-run aggregate supply also influence short-run aggregate supply. That is, if potential GDP increases, more real GDP is supplied in the long run but also more real GDP is supplied at each price level in the short run. So short-run aggregate supply increases.

The only influences on short-run aggregate supply that do not also change long-run aggregate supply are the money wage rate and the money price of any other factor of production. Money wages affect short-run aggregate supply through their influence on firms' costs. The higher the money wage rate, the higher are firms' costs and the smaller is the quantity that firms are willing to supply at each price level. Thus an increase in the money wage rate decreases short-run aggregate supply.

Changes in money wages do not affect long-run aggregate supply. The reason is that along the long-run aggregate supply curve real GDP remains constant at potential GDP because when the money wage changes, the price level also changes by the same percentage. So real wages are unchanged and the labour market is back in equilibrium.

Shifts in *LAS* and *SAS*

Figure 22.4 illustrates changes in long-run aggregate supply and short-run aggregate supply as shifts in the aggregate supply curves. Part (a) shows the effects of a change in potential GDP. Initially, the long-run aggregate supply is LAS_0 and short-run aggregate supply is SAS_0. An improvement in technology or increase in capital increases potential GDP to £875 billion. As a result, the long-run aggregate supply increases and the long-run aggregate supply curve shifts rightward to LAS_1. Short-run aggregate supply also increases and

Figure 22.4

Changes in Aggregate Supply

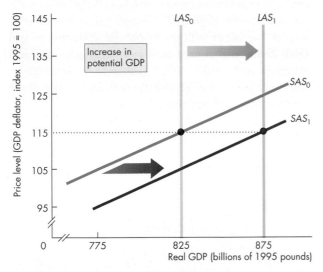

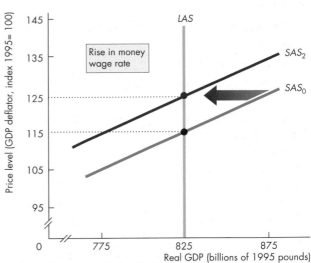

(a) Change in potential GDP shifts LAS and SAS

In part (a), an increase in potential GDP increases both long-run aggregate supply and short-run aggregate supply and shifts both aggregate supply curves rightward from LAS_0 to LAS_1 and from SAS_0 to SAS_1.

(b) Change in the money wage rate shifts SAS

In part (b), a rise in the money wage rate decreases short-run aggregate supply and shifts the short-run aggregate supply curve leftward from SAS_0 to SAS_2. A rise in the money wage rate does not change long-run aggregate supply so the LAS curve does not shift.

the short-run aggregate supply curve shifts rightward to SAS_1.

Figure 22.4(b) shows the effects of an increase in the money wage rate (or other factor price) on aggregate supply. Initially, the short-run aggregate supply curve is SAS_0. A rise in the money wage rate *decreases* short-run aggregate supply and shifts the short-run aggregate supply curve leftward to SAS_2. Long-run aggregate supply does not change when the money wage rate changes, so the LAS curve remains at LAS.

Review Quiz

◆ If the price level rises and if the money wage rate also rises by the same percentage, what happens to the quantity of real GDP supplied? Along which aggregate supply curve does the economy move?

◆ If the price level rises and the money wage rate remains constant, what happens to the quantity of real GDP supplied? Along which aggregate supply curve does the economy move?

◆ If potential GDP increases, what happens to aggregate supply? Is there a shift of or a movement along the LAS curve and the SAS curve?

◆ If the money wage rate rises and potential GDP remains the same, what happens to aggregate supply? Is there a shift of or a movement along the LAS curve and the SAS curve?

Aggregate Demand

Real GDP equals aggregate expenditure which is the sum of consumption expenditure (C), investment (I), government purchases (G) and net exports (X) (see Chapter 20, pp. 424–432). *Aggregate planned expenditure* is the total amount of final goods and services produced in the UK that households, businesses, governments and foreigners plan to buy. What factors determine these spending plans? Spending plans depend on a number of factors but we first focus on the relationship on the quantity of real GDP demanded and the price level.

Figure 22.5

Aggregate Demand

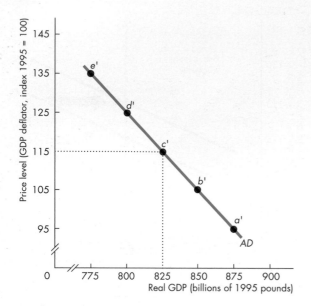

	Price Level (GDP deflator)	Real GDP (billions of 1990 pounds)
a'	95	875
b'	105	850
c'	115	825
d'	125	800
e'	135	775

The aggregate demand curve (*AD*) shows the relationship between the quantity of real GDP demanded and the price level. The aggregate demand curve is based on the schedule in the table. Each point *a'* to *e'* on the curve corresponds to the row in the table identified by the same letter. Thus when the price level is 110, the quantity of real GDP demanded is 750 billion, illustrated by point *c'* in the figure.

Figure 22.5 illustrates **aggregate demand** as an aggregate demand schedule and as the downward-sloping curve labelled *AD*. This aggregate demand curve is based on the aggregate demand schedule and each point on the aggregate demand curve corresponds to a row of the aggregate demand schedule. For example, point *c'* on the aggregate demand curve and row *c'* of the aggregate demand schedule tell us that if the price level is 115, the quantity of real GDP demanded is £825 billion.

In constructing the aggregate demand schedule and aggregate demand curve, we hold constant all the

influences on the quantity of real GDP demanded other than the price level and the interest rate. As the price level changes, the interest rate also changes (for a reason that is explained below) and there is a movement along the aggregate demand curve. A change in any of the other influences on the quantity of real GDP demanded results in a new aggregate demand schedule and a shift in the aggregate demand curve. But why does the aggregate demand curve slope downwards? Let's see why.

Why the Aggregate Demand Curve Slopes Downward

The aggregate demand curve slopes downward for two reasons.

1   Real money balances effect.

2   Substitution effects.

Real Money Balances Effect

Money in the United Kingdom is currency and bank and building society deposits – the things you use to buy goods and services and pay bills. In most other countries of the European Union, money is simply currency and bank deposits. **Real money** is the *purchasing power* of money or the quantity of goods and services that money will buy. It is measured by the quantity of money divided by the price level. The **real money balances effect** is the change in the quantity of real GDP demanded that results from a change in the quantity of real money. The greater the quantity of real money – the greater the purchasing power of money – the greater is the quantity of real GDP demanded. But the quantity of real money increases if the price level falls, so a fall in the price level brings an increase in the quantity of real GDP demanded and a movement along the aggregate demand curve.

To see how the real money balances effect works, think about your own spending plans. You have £5 to spend, and coffee costs £1 a cup. Your money can buy 5 cups of coffee. But if coffee costs 50 pence a cup, your £5 can buy 10 cups. The lower the price, the more you can buy with a given quantity of money so the greater is your purchasing power. And the greater your purchasing power, the more goods you plan to buy.

Substitution Effects

The substitution effect is made up of two components; the **intertemporal substitution effect** and the

international substitution effect. The intertemporal substitution effect involves the substitution of goods in the future for goods in the present. This comes about through a change in the rate of interest. When the price level rises, other things remaining the same, the interest rate rises. The reason is connected to the *real money balances effect* that you've just learned about. With a higher price level, people have less purchasing power, so the amount they want to lend decreases and the amount they want to borrow increases (again, other things remaining the same). A decrease in the supply of loans and an increase in the demand for loans means that interest rates rise. But the higher the interest rate, the less the expenditure by people and firms on capital and consumer durables. Also by not buying today, but by saving, you can earn interest and increase the amount available for spending in the future. The international substitution effect works through international prices. The higher the price level in the United Kingdom, other things remaining the same, the higher are the prices of UK-produced goods and services relative to foreign-produced goods and services people buy. So the higher the price level, other things remaining the same, the smaller is the quantity of real GDP demanded. An example of international substitution is your decision to buy a Honda car that was made in Japan instead of a Ford made in the United Kingdom. Another example is your decision to take a holiday in Spain instead of Cornwall.

For the reasons we've just reviewed, the aggregate demand curve slopes downward. The higher the price level in the United Kingdom, the smaller is the quantity demanded of UK-produced goods and services – UK real GDP. The reverse is the case for a lower price level. Figure 22.6 illustrates changes in the quantity of real GDP demanded. But how do other influences on spending plans affect aggregate demand?

Changes in Aggregate Demand

The aggregate demand schedule and aggregate demand curve describe aggregate demand at a point in time. But aggregate demand frequently changes. As a consequence, the aggregate demand curve frequently shifts. The main influences on aggregate demand that shift the aggregate demand curve are:

◆ Expectations.

◆ International factors.

◆ Fiscal policy and monetary policy.

Figure 22.6

Changes in the Quantity of Real GDP Demanded

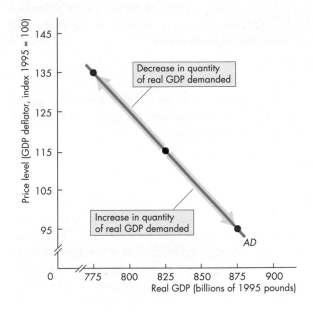

The quantity of real GDP demanded

Decreases if the price level *increases*

Increases if the price level *decreases*

Because of the:

Real money balances effect

◆ An increase in the price level decreases the quantity of real money

◆ A decrease in the price level increases the quantity of real money

Intertemporal substitution effect

◆ An increase in the price level increases interest rates

◆ A decrease in the price level decreases interest rates

International substitution effect

◆ An increase in the price level increases the cost of domestic goods and services relative to foreign goods and services

◆ A decrease in the price level decreases the cost of domestic goods and services relative to foreign goods and services

Expectations

Expectations about future incomes, inflation and profits influence people's decisions about spending today. An increase in expected future income, other things remaining the same, increases the amount that households plan to spend today on consumption goods and consumer durables and increases aggregate demand. The reverse is the case when households expect slow future income growth, or even a decline in income.

An increase in the expected future inflation rate, other things remaining the same, leads to an increase in aggregate demand because people decide to buy more goods and services today before prices rise. An increase in firms' expected future profit increases their demands for new capital equipment and increases aggregate demand.

International Factors

Two main international factors that influence aggregate demand are the foreign exchange rate and foreign income. A change in the UK price level, other things remaining the same, changes the prices of domestically produced goods and services *relative* to the prices of goods and services produced in other countries. Another influence on the price of UK-produced goods and services relative to those produced abroad is the *foreign exchange rate*. The foreign exchange rate is the amount of a foreign currency that you can buy with £1. A rise (appreciation) in the foreign exchange rate decreases aggregate demand. To see how, suppose that £1 is worth 1,800 South Korean won. You can buy a Samsung portable TV (made in South Korea) that costs 180,000 won for £100. If the price of a Ferguson TV (made in the United Kingdom) is the same, you may be willing to buy the Ferguson TV. Now suppose the pound rises to 2,000 won and you now pay only £90 to buy the 180,000 won needed to buy the Samsung TV. You may substitute the Samsung for the Ferguson. The demand for UK-made TVs falls as the foreign exchange value of the pound rises. So as the foreign exchange value of the pound rises, everything else remaining the same, aggregate demand decreases.

The income of foreigners affects the aggregate demand for UK-produced goods and services. For example, an increase in income in the United States, Japan and Germany increases the demand by American, Japanese and German consumers and producers for UK-produced consumption goods and capital goods. The United Kingdom is an open economy, which means that what it exports and imports is a significant part of its GDP (approximately one-third). Thus these sources of change in aggregate demand have always been important in UK history.

Fiscal Policy and Monetary Policy

Fiscal policy is the government's attempt to influence the economy by setting and changing taxes, government spending, and the government's deficit and debt. The scale of government purchases of goods and services has a direct effect on aggregate demand. If taxes are held constant, the more hospitals, motorways, schools, and colleges the government funds, the larger are government purchases of goods and services and so the larger is aggregate demand. A decrease in taxes increases aggregate demand. An increase in transfer payments – unemployment benefits, social security benefits and welfare payments – also increases aggregate demand. Both of these influences operate by increasing households' *disposable* income. The higher the level of disposable income, the greater is the demand for goods and services. Because lower taxes and higher transfer payments increase disposable income, they also increase aggregate demand.

Decisions about the money supply and interest rates are made by the Bank of England in the UK and the European Central Bank in the eurozone countries. These decisions influence aggregate demand. The Bank of England's attempt to influence the economy by varying the money supply and interest rates is called **monetary policy**. The money supply is determined by the Bank of England and the banks and building societies (in a process described in Chapters 25 and 26). The greater the *quantity of money* the greater is the level of aggregate demand. An easy way to see why money affects aggregate demand is to imagine what would happen if the Bank used helicopters to sprinkle millions of pounds worth of new £10 notes across the country. We would all stop whatever we were doing and rush out to pick up our share of the newly available money. But we wouldn't just put the money we picked up in the bank. We would spend some of it, so our demand for goods and services would increase. Although this story is pretty extreme, it does illustrate that an increase in the quantity of money increases aggregate demand.

In practice, changes in the quantity of money are brought about by a change in the interest rate at which the Bank of England is willing to lend to the commercial banks (the bank rate), and so have an additional influence on aggregate demand by changing the amount of investment and the demand for consumer durables. The Bank speeds up the rate at which new money is being injected into the economy by lowering the bank rate, banks have more funds to lend and interest rates fall. The Bank slows down the pace at which it is creating money by raising the bank rate, commercial banks have less funds to lend and interest rates rise. Thus a change in the quantity of

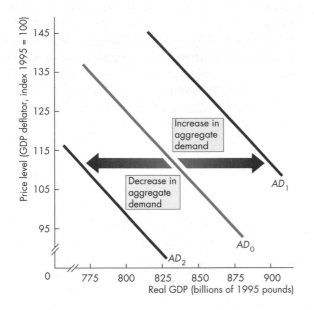

Figure 22.7

Changes in Aggregate Demand

Real GDP (billions of 1995 pounds)

The aggregate demand curve shifts rightward, from AD_0 to AD_1 when expected future profit increases, the expected inflation rate increases, the foreign exchange rate falls, income in the rest of the world increases, government purchases of goods and services increase, taxes are cut, transfer payments increase, or the money supply increases and interest rates fall.

The aggregate demand curve shifts leftward, from AD_0 to AD_2, when expected future profit decreases, the expected inflation rate decreases, the foreign exchange rate rises, income in the rest of the world decreases, government purchases of goods and services decrease, taxes are increased, transfer payments decrease, or the money supply decreases and interest rates rise.

Aggregate demand

Decreases if:

◆ Expected inflation or expected profits decrease

◆ The exchange rate increases or foreign income decreases

◆ Fiscal policy decreases government spending or increases taxes

◆ Monetary policy decreases the money supply and increases interest rates

Increases if:

◆ Expected inflation or expected profits increase

◆ The exchange rate decreases or foreign income increases

◆ Fiscal policy increases government spending or decreases taxes

◆ Monetary policy increases the money supply and decreases interest rates

Review Quiz

◆ What does the aggregate demand curve show, and what factors change and what factors remain the same when there is a movement along the aggregate demand curve?
◆ Why does the aggregate demand curve slope downward?
◆ How do changes in fiscal policy and monetary policy, changes in the world economy, and changes in expectations about the future change aggregate demand and shift the aggregate demand curve?

money has a second effect on aggregate demand, operating through its effects on commercial bank interest rates.

Now that we've reviewed the factors that influence aggregate demand, let's summarize their effects on the aggregate demand curve.

Shifts of the Aggregate Demand Curve

We illustrate a change in aggregate demand as a shift in the aggregate demand curve. Figure 22.7 illustrates two changes in aggregate demand, and summarizes the factors bringing about such changes. Aggregate demand is initially AD_0, the same as in Figure 22.5.

Macroeconomic Equilibrium

The purpose of the aggregate supply–aggregate demand model is to understand and predict changes in real GDP and the price level. To achieve this purpose, we combine aggregate supply and aggregate demand and determine macroeconomic equilibrium. There is a macroeconomic equilibrium for each of the time frames for aggregate supply: a long-run equilibrium and a short-run equilibrium. Long-run equilibrium is the state towards which the economy is heading. Short-run equilibrium describes the state of the economy at each point in time on its path towards long-run macroeconomic equilibrium. We'll begin our study of macroeconomic equilibrium by looking at the short run.

Figure 22.8

Short-run Macroeconomic Equilibrium

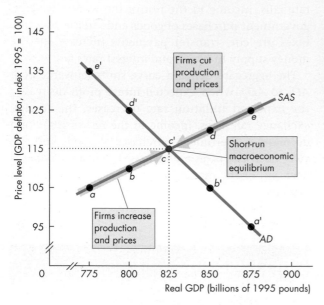

Short-run macroeconomic equilibrium occurs when real GDP demanded equals real GDP supplied at the intersection of the aggregate demand curve (*AD*) and the short-run aggregate supply curve (*SAS*). Here, such an equilibrium occurs at points *c* and *c'* where the price level is 115 and real GDP is £825 billion. If the price level was 125 and real GDP was £875 billion, point *e*, firms would not be able to sell all their output. They would decrease production and cut prices. If the price level was 105 and real GDP was £775 billion, point *a*, people would not be able to buy all the goods they demanded. Firms would increase production and raise their prices. Only when the price level is 115 and real GDP is £825 billion can firms sell all they produce and people buy all they demand. This is the short-run macroeconomic equilibrium.

Short-run Macroeconomic Equilibrium

The aggregate demand curve tells us the quantity of real GDP demanded at each price level, and the short-run aggregate supply curve tells us the quantity of real GDP supplied at each price level. **Short-run macroeconomic equilibrium** occurs when the quantity of real GDP demanded equals the short-run quantity of real GDP supplied at the point of intersection of the *AD* curve and the *SAS* curve. Figure 22.8 illustrates such an equilibrium at a price level of 115 and real GDP of £825 billion (point *c* and *c'*).

To see why this position is an equilibrium, let's work out what happens if the price level is something

other than 115. Suppose, for example, that the price level is 125 and that real GDP is £875 billion (at point *e*) on the *SAS* curve. The quantity of real GDP demanded is less than £875 billion so firms are unable to sell all their output. Unwanted stocks pile up and firms cut both production and prices. Production and prices are cut until firms can sell all their output. This situation occurs only when real GDP is £825 billion and the price level is 115.

Next consider what happens if the price level is 105 and real GDP is £775 billion (at point *a*) on the *SAS* curve. The quantity of real GDP demanded exceeds £775 billion so firms are not able to meet demand. Stocks are running out and customers are clamouring for goods. So firms increase production and raise their prices. Production and prices are increased until firms can meet demand. This situation occurs only when real GDP is £825 billion and the price level is 115.

Short-run Macroeconomic Equilibrium and Business Cycles

Short-run macroeconomic equilibrium does not necessarily occur at full employment. At full employment, the economy is on its *long-run* aggregate supply curve. But short-run macroeconomic equilibrium occurs at the intersection of the *short-run* aggregate supply curve and the aggregate demand curve and can occur at, below, or above potential GDP. We can see this fact by considering the three possible cases shown in Figure 22.9.

In part (a) there is a below full-employment equilibrium. A **below full-employment equilibrium** is a macroeconomic equilibrium in which potential GDP exceeds real GDP. The amount by which potential GDP exceeds real GDP is called a **recessionary gap**. This name reminds us that a gap has opened up between potential GDP and real GDP either because the economy has experienced a recession or because real GDP, while growing, has grown more slowly than the long-term growth rate.

The below full-employment equilibrium illustrated in Figure 22.9(a) occurs where aggregate demand curve AD_0 intersects short-run aggregate supply curve SAS_0 at a real GDP of £775 billion and a price level of 115. The recessionary gap is £50 billion. The UK economy was in a situation similar to that shown in Figure 22.9(a) in 1980–81 and again in 1991–92. In those years, unemployment was high and real GDP was less than potential GDP.

Figure 22.9

Three Types of Macroeconomic Equilibrium

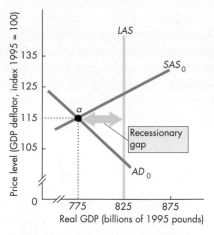

(a) Below full-employment equilibrium

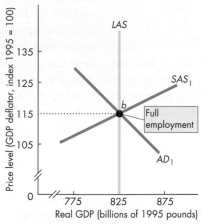

(b) Full-employment equilibrium

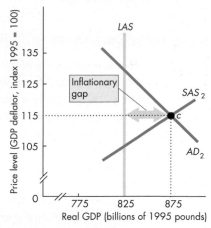

(c) Above full-employment equilibrium

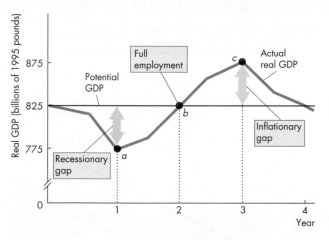

(d) Fluctuations in real GDP

Part (a) shows a below full-employment equilibrium, part (b) shows a full-employment equilibrium, part (c) shows an above full-employment equilibrium and part (d) shows how real GDP fluctuates around potential GDP in a business cycle. In year 1, there is a recessionary gap and the economy is at point *a* (in parts a and d). In year 2, there is full employment and the economy is at point *b* (in parts b and d). In year 3, there is an inflationary gap and the economy is at point *c* (in parts c and d).

Figure 22.9(b) is an example of full-employment equilibrium. **Full-employment equilibrium** is a macroeconomic equilibrium in which real GDP equals potential GDP. In this example, the equilibrium occurs where the aggregate demand curve AD_1 intersects the short-run aggregate supply curve SAS_1 at an actual and potential GDP of £825 billion. The economy was in a situation such as that shown in Figure 22.9(b) in 2000.

Figure 22.9(c) illustrates an above full-employment equilibrium. An **above full-employment equilibrium** is a macroeconomic equilibrium in which real GDP exceeds potential GDP. The amount by which real

GDP exceeds potential GDP is called an **inflationary gap**. This name reminds us that a gap has opened up between real GDP and potential GDP which is placing inflationary pressure on the economy.

The above full-employment equilibrium illustrated in Figure 22.9(c) occurs where the aggregate demand curve AD_2 intersects the short-run aggregate supply curve SAS_2 at a real GDP of £875 billion and a price level of 115. There is an inflationary gap of £50 billion. The economy was in a situation similar to that depicted in part (c) in 1987–89.

The economy moves from one type of equilibrium to another as a result of fluctuations in aggregate demand and in short-run aggregate supply. These fluctuations produce fluctuations in real GDP and the price level. Figure 22.9(d) shows how real GDP fluctuates around potential GDP.

Long-term Growth and Inflation

Long-term economic growth comes about because, over time, the long-run aggregate supply curve shifts rightward. The pace at which it shifts is determined by the growth rate of potential GDP.

Inflation comes about because, over time, the aggregate demand curve shifts rightward at a faster pace than the shift in the long-run aggregate supply curve. The pace at which it shifts is determined mainly by the growth rate of the quantity of money. At times when the quantity of money is increasing rapidly, aggregate demand is increasing quickly and the inflation rate is high. When the growth rate of the quantity of money slows down, other things

remaining the same, the inflation rate eventually slows down.

But the economy does not experience steady real GDP growth and steady inflation. Instead, it fluctuates around its long-term growth path and its long-term inflation rate. When we study these fluctuations, we ignore the long-term trends. We examine how GDP and the price level are determined in a model economy that has no trends. By ignoring the trends, we can see the short-term fluctuations more clearly.

Let's now look at some of the sources of fluctuations around the long-term trends.

Fluctuations in Aggregate Demand

We're going to work out how real GDP and the price level change following an increase in aggregate demand. Let's suppose that the economy starts out at full employment and, as illustrated in Figure 22.10(a), is producing £825 billion worth of goods and services

Figure 22.10

An Increase in Aggregate Demand

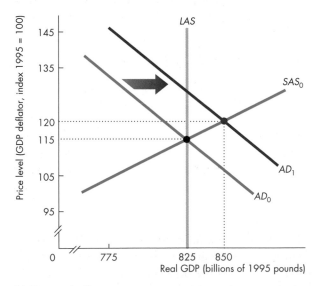

(a) Short-run effect

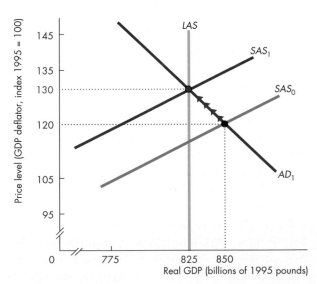

(b) Long-run effect

An increase in aggregate demand shifts the aggregate demand curve from AD_0 to AD_1. Initially (part a), with sticky prices, real GDP increases from £825 billion to £850 billion along the SAS curve. Firms start to raise their prices and cut back production (part b) and the SAS curve shifts upward. In the short-run equilibrium, real GDP is £850 billion and the price level rises to 120. In this situation,

there is an inflationary gap. The money wage rate rises and the short-run aggregate supply curve shifts leftward from SAS_0 to SAS_1 in part (b). As it shifts, it intersects the aggregate demand curve AD_1 at higher price levels and lower real GDP levels. Eventually, the price level rises to 130 and real GDP falls back to £825 billion – potential GDP and full employment.

at a price level of 115. The economy is on the aggregate demand curve AD_0, the short-run aggregate supply curve SAS_0 and the long-run aggregate supply curve LAS.

Now suppose that the world economy grows more quickly and the demand for UK-made goods increases in Japan and the United States. The increase in exports increases aggregate demand and the aggregate demand curve shifts rightward. Suppose that the aggregate demand curve shifts from AD_0 to AD_1 in Figure 22.10(a).

Faced with an increase in demand firms increase production and raise prices. For the economy as a whole, real GDP increases and the price level rises. Real GDP rises to £850 billion and the price level rises to 120. In this short-run macroeconomic equilibrium, firms are producing the quantities they want to produce, given the price level and the money wage rate. But the economy is at an above full-employment equilibrium. Real GDP exceeds potential GDP, and there is an inflationary gap.

The increase in aggregate demand has increased the prices of all goods and services. Faced with higher prices, firms have increased their output rates. At this stage, prices of goods and services have increased but wage rates have not changed. (Recall that as we move along a short-run aggregate supply curve, wage rates are constant.)

The economy cannot produce in excess of potential GDP forever. Why not? What are the forces at work that bring real GDP back to potential GDP and restore full employment?

If the price level has increased and wage rates have remained constant, workers have experienced a fall in the purchasing power of their wages. Furthermore, firms have experienced an increase in revenue and no change in their costs. Firms' profits have increased. In these circumstances, workers demand higher wages, and firms, anxious to maintain their employment and output levels, meet those demands. If firms do not raise wage rates, they either lose workers or have to hire less productive ones.

As wage rates rise, the short-run aggregate supply curve begins to shift leftward. In Figure 22.10(b), the short-run aggregate supply curve moves from SAS_0 towards SAS_1. The rise in wages and the shift in the SAS curve produce a sequence of new equilibrium positions. Along the adjustment path, real GDP falls and the price level rises and the economy moves up along its aggregate demand curve as shown by the arrow heads in the figure. Eventually, wages will have

risen by so much that the SAS curve is SAS_1. At this time, the aggregate demand curve AD_1 intersects SAS_1 at a full-employment equilibrium. The price level has risen to 130, and real GDP is back where it started, at potential GDP. Unemployment is again at its natural rate.

Throughout the adjustment process, higher wage rates raise firms' costs and, with rising costs, firms offer a smaller quantity of goods and services for sale at any given price level. By the time the adjustment is over, firms are producing the same amount as they initially produced, but at higher prices and higher costs.

A decrease in aggregate demand has similar but opposite effects to those that we've just studied. That is, a decrease in aggregate demand decreases real GDP to less than potential GDP and unemployment increases above its natural rate. A recessionary gap emerges. Firms cut prices. The lower price level increases the purchasing power of wages, and increases firms' costs relative to their output prices because wages remain unchanged. Eventually, the slack economy leads to falling wage rates and the short-run aggregate supply curve shifts rightward. Real GDP gradually returns to potential GDP and full employment is restored.

Let's now work out how real GDP and the price level change when aggregate supply changes.

Fluctuations in Aggregate Supply

Fluctuations in short-run aggregate supply can bring fluctuations in real GDP around potential GDP. We'll study a decrease in aggregate supply. Suppose that initially, real GDP equals potential GDP. Then there is a large but temporary rise in the money price of raw materials. (Similar to an increase in the price of oil as in 1973–74 and again in 1979–80 when OPEC used its market muscle.) What happens to real GDP and the price level?

Figure 22.11 answers this question. The aggregate demand curve is AD_0, the short-run aggregate supply curve is SAS_0 and the long-run aggregate supply curve is LAS_0. Equilibrium real GDP is £825 billion, which equals potential GDP, and the price level is 115. Then the price of oil rises. Faced with a higher price of raw materials, firms' costs rise and they decrease production. Short-run aggregate supply decreases, and the short-run aggregate supply curve shifts leftward to SAS_1.

As a result of this decrease in short-run aggregate supply, the economy moves to a new equilibrium where SAS_1 intersects the aggregate demand curve

Figure 22.11

A Decrease in Aggregate Supply

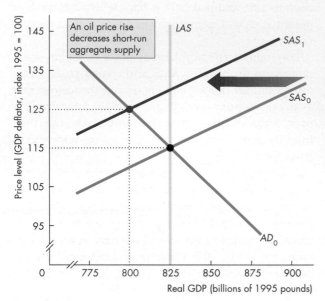

An increase in the price of oil decreases short-run aggregate supply and shifts the short-run aggregate supply curve leftward from SAS_0 to SAS_1. Real GDP falls from £825 billion to £800 billion and the price level increases from 115 to 125. The economy experiences both recession and inflation – stagflation.

AD_0. The price level rises to 125, and real GDP decreases to £800 billion. Because real GDP falls, the economy experiences recession. Because the price level increases, the economy experiences inflation. Such a combination of recession and inflation – called *stagflation* – actually occurred in the mid-1970s.

Review Quiz

♦ Does economic growth result from increases in aggregate demand, short-run aggregate supply, or long-run aggregate supply?
♦ Does inflation result from increases in aggregate demand, short-run aggregate supply, or long-run aggregate supply?
♦ Can you describe three types of short-run macroeconomic equilibrium?

Let's put our new knowledge to work and see how it helps us understand macroeconomic performance.

Long-term Growth, Inflation and Cycles in the UK Economy

The economy is continually changing. If you imagine the economy as a video, then an aggregate supply–aggregate demand figure such as Figure 22.11 is a freeze-frame. We're going to run the video – an instant replay – but keep our finger on the freeze-frame button, looking at some important parts of the previous action. Let's run the video from 1960.

Figure 22.12 shows the state of the economy in 1960 at the point of intersection of its aggregate demand curve AD_{60} and short-run aggregate supply curve SAS_{60}. Real GDP was £230 billion and the GDP deflator was 10 (less than one-tenth of its 2000 level). By 2000, the economy had reached the point marked by the intersection of aggregate demand curve AD_{2000} and short-run aggregate supply curve SAS_{2000}. Real GDP was £820 billion and the GDP deflator was 114.

There are three important features of the economy's path traced by the points:

1   Long-term growth.

2   Inflation.

3   Cycles.

Long-term Growth Over the years, real GDP grows – shown in Figure 22.12 by the rightward movement of the points. The faster the growth rate of real GDP, the larger is the horizontal distance between successive dots in the figure. The force generating long-term growth is an increase in long-run aggregate supply. And long-run aggregate supply increases because of workforce growth, the accumulation of capital – both physical plant and equipment and human capital – the discovery of new resources and technological change.

Inflation The price level rises over the years – shown in Figure 22.12 by the upward movement of the points. The more rapid the inflation rate, the larger is the vertical distance between successive dots in the figure. The main force generating the persistent increase in the price level is a tendency for aggregate demand to increase at a faster pace than the increase in long-run aggregate supply. All of the factors that increase aggregate demand and shift the aggregate demand curve influence the pace of inflation. But one factor – the growth of the quantity of money – is the

Figure 22.12

Aggregate Supply and Aggregate Demand: 1960–2000

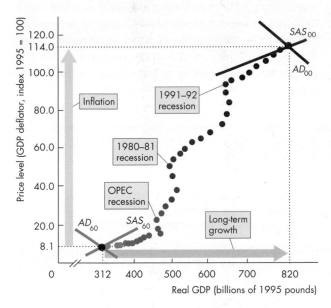

Each point indicates the value of the GDP deflator and real GDP in a given year. In 1960, these variables were determined by the intersection of the aggregate demand curve AD_{60} and the short-run aggregate supply curve SAS_{60}. Each point is generated by the gradual shifting of the AD and SAS curves. By 1998, the curves were AD_{2000} and SAS_{2000}. Real GDP grew and the price level increased. But growth and inflation did not proceed smoothly. Real GDP grew quickly and inflation was moderate in the 1960s; real GDP growth sagged in 1974–75 and again, more strongly, in 1980–81. The 1974–75 slowdown was caused by an unusually sharp increase in oil prices. The 1980–81 recession was caused by a sharp slowdown in the growth of aggregate demand, which resulted mainly from Mrs Thatcher's tough monetary policy. Inflation was rapid during the 1970s but slowed after the 1980–81 recession. The period from 1982 to 1989 was one of strong, persistent recovery. A recession began in 1991 and a recovery took place in 1994.

most important source of *persistent* increases in aggregate demand and persistent inflation.

Cycles Over the years, the economy grows and shrinks in cycles – shown in Figure 22.12 by the wavelike pattern made by the points, with recessions highlighted in pink. The cycles arise because both the expansion of short-run aggregate supply and the growth of aggregate demand do not proceed at a

fixed, steady pace. Recessions are difficult to predict, but since the Second World War they have not been as severe as recessions before the war.

The Evolving Economy: 1960–2000

During the 1960s, real GDP growth was rapid and inflation was low. This was a period of rapid increases in aggregate supply and of moderate increases in aggregate demand.

The mid-1970s were years of rapid inflation and recession – of stagflation. The major sources of these developments were a series of massive oil price increases and domestic supply side factors that produced X-inefficiency in production that shifted the short-run aggregate supply curve leftward, and rapid increases in the quantity of money that shifted the aggregate demand curve rightward. Recession occurred because the aggregate supply curve shifted leftward at a faster pace than the aggregate demand shifted rightward.

The rest of the 1970s saw high inflation – the price level increased quickly – and only moderate growth in real GDP.

In 1979 the government introduced a policy to keep aggregate demand growth in check. In 1980–81 most people expected high inflation to persist, and wages grew at a rate consistent with those expectations. The short-run aggregate supply curve shifted leftward. Aggregate demand increased only a little, but not fast enough to make inflation as high as most people expected. As a consequence, during 1980–81 the leftward shift of the short-run aggregate supply curve was so strong relative to the weak growth of aggregate demand that the economy went into a deep recession.

The main factor in the recovery in long-term growth was the introduction of supply side policies, which weakened the power of trade unions and altered work practices, lower direct taxes and greater competition through deregulation of markets (and privatization) resulted in a sustained rightward shift of the long-run aggregate supply curve. Aggregate demand growth kept pace with the growth of aggregate supply. Sustained-but-steady growth in aggregate supply and aggregate demand kept real GDP growing and inflation steady until 1986–87. The economy moved from a recession with real GDP less than potential GDP in 1980–81 to above full-employment in 1987–90. Inflation began to rise during this period and it was in this condition when a decrease in aggregate demand led to the 1990–92 recession. The economy again embarked on a path of expansion over the rest of the 1990s up until 2000. Fears of a global recession are expected to slowdown the economy in 2001.

The aggregate supply–aggregate demand model can be used to understand long-term growth, inflation and business cycles. The model is a useful one because it enables us to keep our eye on the big pic-

ture – on the broad trends and cycles in inflation and real GDP. But the model lacks detail. It does not tell us as much as we need to know about the components of aggregate demand – consumption, investment, government purchases of goods and services, and exports and imports. It doesn't tell us what determines interest rates or wage rates or even, directly, what determines employment and unemployment. In the following chapters, we're going to start to fill in that detail.

Summary

Key Points

Aggregate Supply (pp. 465–469)

- In the long run, real GDP equals potential GDP and there is full employment. The long-run aggregate supply curve is vertical – long-run aggregate supply is independent of the price level – at potential GDP. Long-run aggregate supply changes only when potential GDP changes.

- In the short run, real GDP deviates from potential GDP. Short-run aggregate supply is the relationship between the quantity of real GDP supplied and the price level when wage rates and other factor prices are constant. The short-run aggregate supply curve is upward-sloping – with factor prices and all other influences on supply held constant.

- A change in potential GDP changes both long-run and short-run aggregate supply. A change in factor prices changes short-run aggregate supply only.

Aggregate Demand (pp. 469–473)

- Other things held constant, the higher the price level, the smaller is the quantity of real GDP demanded – the aggregate demand curve slopes downward.

- The aggregate demand curve slopes downward for two reasons: money and goods are substitutes (*real money balances effect*); goods today and goods in the future or domestic goods and foreign goods are substitutes (*substitution effect*).

- The main factors that change aggregate demand – and shift the aggregate demand curve – are expectations about future inflation and profits, international factors (economic conditions in the rest of the world and the foreign exchange rate),

fiscal policy (government purchases of goods and services and taxes) and monetary policy (the money supply and interest rates).

Macroeconomic Equilibrium (pp. 473–478)

- In a long-run macroeconomic equilibrium, real GDP equals potential GDP and aggregate demand determines the price level.

- In a short-run macroeconomic equilibrium, real GDP and the price level are determined simultaneously by the interaction of aggregate demand and short-run aggregate supply. Short-run macroeconomic equilibrium tells us how real GDP and the price level evolve.

- Below full-employment equilibrium occurs when equilibrium real GDP is less than potential GDP. There is a recessionary gap and unemployment exceeds its natural rate. When equilibrium real GDP exceeds potential GDP, there is an inflationary gap and unemployment is less than its natural rate.

- Long-term growth of real GDP occurs because potential GDP increases. Inflation occurs because aggregate demand grows more quickly than potential GDP.

- Fluctuations in aggregate demand and short-run aggregate supply bring fluctuations in the price level and deviations of real GDP from potential GDP.

Long-term Growth, Inflation and Cycles in the UK Economy (pp. 478–480)

- Long-term growth is the growth of potential GDP.

- Inflation persists in the economy because of steady increases in aggregate demand brought about by increases in the quantity of money.

- The economy experiences cycles because the short-run aggregate supply and aggregate demand curves shift at an uneven pace.

- Large oil price hikes in 1973 and 1974 signalled the beginning of stagflation.

- Restraint in aggregate demand growth in 1980–81 resulted in recession in those years and a lower inflation rate.

- Steady technological advance and capital accumulation resulted in a sustained expansion from 1982 to 1989.

- A slowdown in aggregate demand growth brought recession in 1991.

- Recovery in the domestic and world economies saw a small improvement in the trend rate of growth.

Key Figures ◇

Key Terms

Problems

●1 The following events occur that influence the economy of Toughtimes:

  i   A deep recession hits the world economy.

  ii Oil prices rise sharply.

  iii Businesses expect huge losses in the near future.

  a   Explain the separate effects of each of these events on real GDP and the price level in Toughtimes, starting from a position of long-run equilibrium.

  b   Explain the combined effects of these events on real GDP and the price level in Toughtimes, starting from a position of long-run equilibrium.

  c   Explain what the Toughtimes government and central bank can do to overcome the problems faced by the economy.

2 The following events occur that influence the economy of Coolland:

  i   A strong expansion in the world economy.

  ii Businesses expect huge profits in the near future.

  iii The Coolland government cuts its expenditure.

  a   Explain the separate effects of each of these events on real GDP and the price level in Coolland, starting from a position of long-run equilibrium.

  b   Explain the combined effects of these events on real GDP and the price level in Coolland, starting from a position of long-run equilibrium.

  c   Explain why the Coolland government or central bank might want to take action to influence the Coolland economy.

•3 The economy of Mainland has the following aggregate demand and supply schedules:

Price level	Real GDP demanded	Real GDP supplied in the short run
		(billions of 2000 euros)
90	450	350
100	400	400
110	350	450
120	300	500
130	250	550
140	200	600

a In a figure, plot the aggregate demand curve and short-run aggregate supply curve.

b What are the values of real GDP and the price level in Mainland in a short-run macroeconomic equilibrium?

c Mainland's potential GDP is €500 billion. Plot the long-run aggregate supply curve in the same figure in which you answered part (a).

4 The economy of Miniland has the following aggregate demand and supply schedules:

Price level	Real GDP demanded	Real GDP supplied in the short run
		(billions of 2000 euros)
90	600	150
100	500	200
110	400	250
120	300	300
130	200	350
140	100	400

a In a figure, plot the aggregate demand curve and short-run aggregate supply curve.

b What are the values of real GDP and the price level in Miniland in a short-run macroeconomic equilibrium?

c Miniland's potential GDP is €250 billion. Plot the long-run aggregate supply curve in the same figure in which you answered part (a).

•5 In problem 3, aggregate demand is increased by €100 billion. How do real GDP and the price level change in the short run?

6 In problem 4, aggregate demand is decreased by €150 billion. How do real GDP and the price level change in the short run?

•7 In problem 3, aggregate supply decreases by €100 billion. What now is the short-run macroeconomic equilibrium?

8 In problem 4, aggregate supply increases by €150 billion. What now is the short-run macroeconomic equilibrium?

•9 In the economy shown in the figure, initially the short-run aggregate supply is SAS_0 and aggregate demand is AD_0. Then some events change aggregate demand and the aggregate demand curve shifts rightward to AD_1. Later, some other events change aggregate supply and shift the short-run aggregate supply curve leftward to SAS_1.

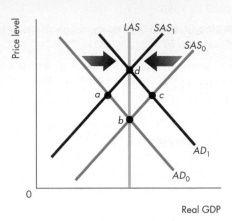

a What is the equilibrium point after the change in aggregate demand?

b What is the equilibrium point after the change in aggregate supply?

c What events could have changed aggregate demand from AD_0 to AD_1?

d What events could have changed aggregate supply from SAS_0 to SAS_1?

10 In the economy shown in the figure, initially long-run aggregate supply is LAS_0, short-run aggregate supply is SAS_0, and aggregate demand is AD. Then some events change aggregate supply and the aggregate supply curves shift rightward to LAS_1 and SAS_1.

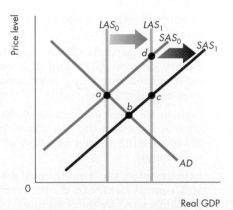

a What is the equilibrium point after the change in aggregate supply?

b What events could have changed long-run aggregate supply from LAS_0 to LAS_1?

c What events could have changed short-run aggregate supply from SAS_0 to SAS_1?

d After the increase in aggregate supply, is the real GDP greater than or less than potential GDP?

e What change in aggregate demand will make real GDP equal to potential GDP?

Will there be a recessionary gap or an inflationary gap? By how much?

Critical Thinking

1 After you have studied Reading Between the Lines on pp. 484–485, answer the following questions.

   a What is the expected growth rate in the euro-zone in 2001 and 2001?

   b What factors are contributing to the downturn in eurozone growth?

   c What is the outlook for inflation in the euro-zone countries?

   d What policy options are available to the European Central Bank to help reduce the impact of the global slowdown?

2 You are the chief economic adviser at HM Treasury and you are trying to work out where the economy is likely to go next year. You have the following forecasts for the *AD*, *SAS* and *LAS* curves:

Price level	Real GDP demanded	Short-run real GDP supplied (billions of 1995 pounds)	Long-run aggregate supply
115	650	350	520
120	600	450	520
125	550	550	520
130	500	650	520

This year, real GDP is £500 billion and the price level is 120. The prime minister wants answers to the following questions:

   a What is your forecast of next year's real GDP?

   b What is your forecast of next year's price level?

   c What is your forecast of the inflation rate?

   d Will unemployment be above or below its natural rate?

   e Will there be a recessionary gap or an inflationary gap? By how much?

3 Use the links on the Parkin, Powell and Matthews website to obtain the 2001 data on real GDP and the price level for the UK. Then:

   a Use the data to update Figure 22.12.

   b What has happened to real GDP and the price level?

   c What has happened to aggregate demand and short-run aggregate supply in 2001?

Aggregate Supply and Aggregate Demand in Action

THE FINANCIAL TIMES, 9 OCTOBER 2001

Recovery in eurozone not expected until next year

Tony Barber

Economic conditions in the eurozone are noticeably deteriorating and a recovery will not happen until at least early next year, according to the latest growth indicator produced for *The Financial Times, FT Deutschland* and *Les Echos.*

The indicator, suggests that year-on-year economic growth will be only 1.2 per cent in the third and fourth quarters of this year.

One month ago, the indicator was predicting growth of 1.6 per cent in both quarters. The consortium attributed the downward revision mainly to a darker outlook for the industrial and retail trade sectors.

'The economic climate in Europe is worsening considerably,' the consortium said in a commentary. 'This is not immediately the outcome of the terrorist attacks on the US but started far earlier with a damping of external demand and subdued internal demand in Europe.'

The prospects of an economic upturn have become uncertain because of the negative economic impact of the September 11 attacks, the consortium said 'European leading indicators, especially in the area of industrial production point strongly downwards, and a recovery cannot be expected in coming quarters.'

The euro's relatively low level against the dollar on foreign exchange markets is still a positive factor for eurozone growth but the effect is markedly less strong now than in the first half of this year, the consortium said.

Conversely, real short-term interest rates are still having a negative impact on the FT indicator but this is diminishing as a result of the European Central Bank's two interest rate cuts on August 30 and September 17.

Wim Duisenberg, the ECB president, indicated last weekend that the eurozone's inflation outlook was benign enough to permit another rate cut.

'We are in a consistency mode,' he said. 'We strongly believe that the current monetary policy stance is consistent with the maintenance of price stability.' He also reaffirmed the ECB's view that the economic slowdown would be short-lived.

The Essence of the Story

- Growth in the eurozone countries is expected to weaken further in 2001.

- The outlook for the retail and industrial sectors in the eurozone economies has worsened significantly.

- The principal cause is the slowdown in demand both by the external sector and the internal sector.

- The inflation outlook for the eurozone economies is good and a further easing of monetary policy is possible.

- The European Central Bank expects the economic slowdown to be short-lived.

Economic Analysis

- The slowdown in world demand has reduced the demand for eurozone countries' exports. Domestic demand has also slowed as expectations of lower income growth have taken root.

- Figure 1 shows the growth of real GDP in the eurozone economies and the recent consensus forecast for growth in 2001 and 2002 obtained from *The Economist* on 6 October 2001. The dotted line shows the consensus forecast in September.

- Figure 2 shows the path of inflation in 1999 and 2000 and consensus forecasts for 2001 and 2002 made in October 2001. The dotted line shows the forecast made in September 2001.

- High real short-term rates of interest have depressed domestic spending. The ECB is able to reduce interest rates further because the outlook for inflation is good. The reduction in interest rates will stimulate domestic demand in the eurozone economies.

- Figure 3 shows an increase in aggregate demand as a shift in the AD curve from AD_{00} to AD_{02}, but the increase in potential GDP is seen as a shift from LAS_{00} to LAS_{02}. The slowdown in external and internal demand means that real GDP increases by less than potential GDP. The recessionary gap will cause the money wage rate to rise very slowly and therefore inflation will be less than expected. Lower interest rates will push the AD curve out further to AD'_{02} and create higher growth.

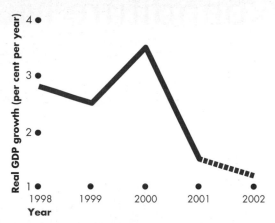

Figure 1 Eurozone growth

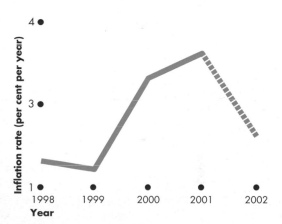

Figure 2 Eurozone inflation

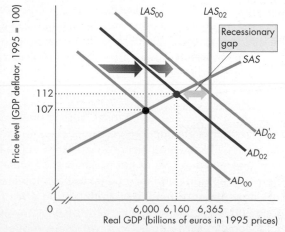

Figure 3 Aggregate demand and potential GDP growth

CHAPTER 23

Expenditure Multipliers

After studying this chapter you will be able to:

◆ Explain how expenditure plans are determined

◆ Explain how real GDP is determined when the price level is fixed

◆ Explain the expenditure multiplier

◆ Explain how imports and taxes influence the multiplier

◆ Explain how recessions and recoveries begin

◆ Explain the relationship between aggregate expenditure and aggregate demand

◆ Explain how the multiplier gets smaller as the price level changes

Economic Amplifier or Shock Absorber?

At the Baths of Caracalla in Rome, Luciano Pavarotti begins his passionate rendition of *Nessun Dorma* in the bel canto style he is famous for. Moving to a louder passage, the volume of his voice increases and, with the aid of electronic amplification, booms across the open-air concert stadium. ◆ Brian Tyrer, an Everton supporter, is driving some of his friends in his BMW to see Everton play Manchester. Some of the roads around Liverpool are badly potholed. The car's wheels are bouncing and vibrating, but Brian and his friends are completely undisturbed, thanks to the car's efficient shock absorbers. ◆ Investment and exports fluctuate like the volume of Pavarotti's voice and the uneven surface of a Liverpool road. How does the economy react to those fluctuations? Does it react like Brian's BMW, absorbing the shocks and providing a smooth ride for the economy's passengers? Or does it behave like Pavarotti's amplifier, blowing up the fluctuations and spreading them out to affect the many millions of participants in an economic opera concert? Is the economic machine built to a design that we simply have to put up with, or does it change over time? Also, can the government modify the design of the economy and change its amplifying and shock-absorbing powers in a way that gives us all a smoother ride?

◆ ◆ ◆ ◆ You will explore these questions in this chapter. You will learn how a recession or a recovery begins when a change in investment or exports triggers a larger change in *aggregate* expenditure and real GDP – like the amplifier. You will learn about how changes in the value of assets less debts influence consumer expenditure as in the Reading Between the Lines (pp. 514–515). You will also learn how, over the years, imports and income taxes have lowered the power of the amplifier. Finally, you will discover that in contrast to the initial amplification effect, the economy's imperfect shock absorbers, which are price and wage changes, pull real GDP back towards the long-term growth path of potential GDP.

To achieve these objectives, we use a model called the *aggregate expenditure model*. This model explains changes in aggregate expenditure in a very short time frame during which prices do not change.

Fixed Prices and Expenditure Plans

Most firms are like your local supermarket. They set their prices, advertise their products and services, and sell the quantities their customers are willing to buy. If they persistently sell a greater quantity than they plan to and are constantly running out of stocks, they eventually raise their prices. And if they persistently sell a smaller quantity than they plan to and have stocks piling up, they eventually cut their prices. But in the very short term their prices are fixed. They hold the prices they have set, and the quantities they sell depend on demand, not supply.

The Aggregate Implications of Fixed Prices

Fixed prices have two immediate implications for the economy as a whole:

1 Because each firm's price is fixed, the *price level* is fixed.
2 Because demand determines the quantities that each firm sells, *aggregate demand* determines the aggregate quantity of goods and services sold, which equals real GDP.

So to understand the fluctuations in real GDP when the price level is fixed, we must understand aggregate demand fluctuations. The aggregate expenditure model explains fluctuations in aggregate demand by identifying the forces that determine expenditure plans.

Expenditure Plans

The components of aggregate expenditure are:

1 Consumption expenditure.
2 Investment.
3 Government purchases of goods and services.
4 Net exports (exports *minus* imports).

These four components of aggregate expenditure sum to real GDP (see Chapter 20, pp. 424–433).

Aggregate planned expenditure is equal to *planned* consumption expenditure plus *planned* investment plus *planned* government purchases plus *planned* exports minus *planned* imports.

In the very short term, *planned* investment, *planned* government purchases and *planned* exports are fixed.

But *planned* consumption expenditure and *planned* imports are not fixed. They depend on the level of real GDP itself.

A Two-way Relationship between Aggregate Expenditure and GDP

Because real GDP influences consumption expenditure and imports, and because consumption expenditure and imports are components of aggregate expenditure, there is a two-way relationship between aggregate expenditure and GDP. Other things remaining the same:

1 An increase in real GDP increases aggregate planned expenditure.
2 An increase in aggregate expenditure increases real GDP.

You are going to learn how this two-way relationship between aggregate expenditure and real GDP determines real GDP when the price level is fixed. The starting point is to consider the first piece of the two-way relationship – the influence of real GDP on planned consumption expenditure and saving.

Consumption Function and Saving Function

Consumption and saving are influenced by several factors and the more important ones are:

◆ Real interest rate.
◆ Disposable income.
◆ Purchasing power of assets minus debts.
◆ Expected future income.

Real Interest Rate
Other things remaining the same, the lower the real interest rate, the greater is the amount of consumption expenditure and the smaller is the amount of saving. The real interest rate is the opportunity cost of consumption. This opportunity cost arises regardless of whether a person is a borrower or a lender. For a borrower, increasing consumption this year means paying more interest next year. For a lender, increasing consumption this year means receiving less interest next year.

The effect of the real interest rate on consumption expenditure is an example of the principle of substitution. If the opportunity cost of an action increases, people substitute other actions in its place. In this case, if the opportunity cost of current consumption increases, people cut current consumption and substitute future consumption in its place.

For example, if the real interest rate on your credit card was 20 per cent, you would probably cut your consumption expenditure (buy cheaper food, find cheaper accommodation) and borrow a smaller amount. Similarly, with a 20 per cent real interest rate, lenders try to cut back on current consumption in order to increase their lending and profit from the high real interest rate. But if the real interest rate on your credit card was 5 per cent a year, you might increase your consumption and borrow a larger amount.

Disposable Income

The higher a household's disposable income, other things remaining the same, the greater is its consumption expenditure and the greater is its saving.

For example, a student works during the summer and earns a disposable income of £2,000. She spends the entire £2,000 on consumption during the year. When she graduates as an economist, her disposable income jumps to £22,000 a year. She now spends £20,000 on consumption and saves £4,000. The increase in disposable income of £20,000 has brought an increase in consumption of £16,000 and an increase in saving of £4,000.

Purchasing Power of Assets minus Debts

A household's assets are what it *owns* and its liabilities are what it *owes*. A household's *net assets* are its assets minus its liabilities. The purchasing power of a household's net assets, the *real* value of its net assets, are the goods and services that its net assets can buy. The higher the purchasing power of a household's net assets, other things remaining the same, the greater is its consumption expenditure. That is, if two households have the same disposable income in the current year, the household with the larger net assets will spend a larger portion of current disposable income on consumption goods and services.

For example, both Cindy and Stuart are department store executives and each earns a disposable income of £20,000 a year. Cindy has £10,000 in the bank and no debts. Stuart has no money in the bank and owes £5,000 on his car loan. Cindy spends most of her £20,000 each year, but Stuart tries to keep his consumption at £19,000 so he can pay off his car loan. (Paying off a loan is not consumption expenditure.

When Stuart bought his car, that was consumption expenditure. When he pays off his loan, he is saving.)

The purchasing power of net assets (assets minus debts) is influenced by the price level. The higher the price level, other things remaining the same, the smaller is the purchasing power of net assets and the smaller is the amount of consumption expenditure. For example, if the price level rises by 10 per cent, everything else remaining the same, a household with £50,000 in a savings deposit experiences a £5,000 decrease in its purchasing power. This household will probably cut its consumption and increase its saving. (A rise in the price level decreases the real value of debts, which works in the opposite direction to the effect on the real value of assets. As the purchasing power that must be given up to repay a household's debts decreases, consumption might increase. But most households have assets that exceed their debts, so an increase in the price level brings a decrease in consumption expenditure.)

Expected Future Income

The higher a household's expected future income, other things remaining the same, the greater is its consumption expenditure. That is, if two households have the same disposable income in the current year, the household with the larger expected future income will spend a larger portion of current disposable income on consumption goods and services.

Look at Cindy and Stuart again. Cindy has just been promoted and will receive a £3,000 pay rise next year. Stuart has just been told that his contract will not be renewed at the end of the year. On receiving this news, Cindy buys a new car – increases her consumption expenditure, and Stuart cancels his summer holiday plans – decreases his consumption expenditure.

Although consumption and saving are influenced by several factors, we focus on the relationship between consumption and disposable income when all other factors (the real interest rate, the purchasing power of assets minus debts and expected future income) are constant. We do this because disposable income and consumption are interrelated. Each helps to determine the other.

Consumption and Saving Plans

The table in Figure 23.1 shows an example of the relationship among planned consumption expenditure, planned saving and disposable income. It lists the consumption expenditure and the saving that people

Figure 23.1

Consumption and Saving Function

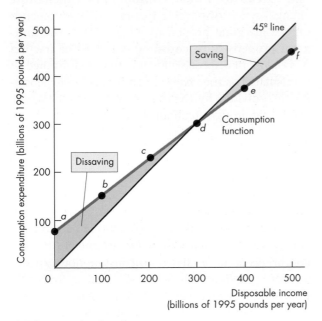

(a) Consumption function

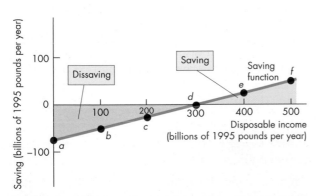

(b) Saving function

	Disposable income	Planned consumption expenditure (billions of 1995 pounds per year)	Planned saving
a	0	75	−75
b	100	150	−50
c	200	225	−25
d	300	300	0
e	400	375	25
f	500	450	50

The table shows consumption expenditure and saving plans at various levels of disposable income. Part (a) of the figure shows the relationship between consumption expenditure and disposable income (the consumption function). Part (b) shows the relationship between saving and disposable income (the saving function). Points *a* to *f* on the consumption and saving functions correspond to the rows in the table. The 45° line in part (a) is the line along which consumption expenditure equals disposable income. Consumption expenditure plus saving equals disposable income. When the consumption function is above the 45° line, saving is negative (dissaving occurs) and the saving function is below the horizontal axis. When the consumption function is below the 45° line, saving is positive and the saving function is above the horizontal axis. At the point where the consumption function intersects the 45° line, all disposable income is consumed, saving is zero and the saving function intersects the horizontal axis.

plan to undertake at each level of disposable income. Notice that at each level of disposable income, consumption expenditure plus saving always equals disposable income. The reason is that households can only consume or save their disposable income. So planned consumption plus planned saving always equals disposable income.

The relationship between consumption expenditure and disposable income, other things remaining the same, is called the **consumption function**. The

relationship between saving and disposable income, other things remaining the same, is called the **saving function**. Let's study the consumption and saving functions, beginning with the consumption function.

Consumption Function Figure 23.1(a) shows a consumption function. The *y*-axis measures consumption expenditure and the *x*-axis measures disposable income. Along the consumption function, the points labelled *a* to *f* correspond to the rows of the table. For example, point *e* shows that when disposable income is £400 billion, consumption expenditure is £375 billion. Along the consumption function, as disposable income increases, consumption expenditure also increases.

At point *a* on the consumption function, consumption expenditure is £75 billion even though disposable income is zero. This consumption expenditure is called *autonomous consumption*. It is the amount of consumption expenditure that would take place in the short run, even if people had no current income. Consumption expenditure in excess of this amount is called *induced consumption*. It is expenditure that is induced by an increase in disposable income.

45° Line   Figure 23.1(a) also contains a line labelled '45° line'. At each point on this line, consumption expenditure (on the *y*-axis) equals disposable income (on the *x*-axis). In the range over which the consumption function lies above the 45° line – between *a* and *d* – consumption expenditure exceeds disposable income; in the range over which the consumption function lies below the 45° line – between *d* and *f* – consumption expenditure is less than disposable income; and at the point at which the consumption function intersects the 45° line – at point *d* – consumption expenditure equals disposable income.

Saving Function   Figure 23.1(b) shows a saving function. The *x*-axis is exactly the same as that in part (a). The *y*-axis measures saving. Again, the points marked *a* to *f* correspond to the rows of the table. For example, point *e* shows that when disposable income is £400 billion, saving is £25 billion. Along the saving function, as disposable income increases, saving also increases. At disposable income levels below point *d*, saving is negative. Negative saving is called *dissaving*. At disposable income levels above point *d*, saving is positive, and at point *d*, saving is zero.

Notice the connection between the two parts of Figure 23.1. When consumption expenditure exceeds disposable income in part (a), saving is negative in part (b). When disposable income exceeds consumption expenditure in part (a), saving is positive in part (b). And when consumption expenditure equals disposable income in part (a), saving is zero in part (b).

When saving is negative (when consumption expenditure exceeds disposable income), past saving is used to pay for current consumption. Such a situation cannot last forever but it can occur if disposable income falls temporarily.

Marginal Propensities to Consume and Save

The extent to which consumption expenditure changes when disposable income changes depends on the marginal propensity to consume. The **marginal propensity to consume** (*MPC*) is the fraction of a *change* in disposable income that is consumed. It is calculated as the *change* in consumption expenditure (ΔC) divided by the *change* in disposable income (ΔYD) that brought it about. That is:

$$MPC = \frac{\Delta C}{\Delta YD}$$

In the table in Figure 23.1, when disposable income increases from £300 billion to £400 billion, consumption expenditure increases from £300 billion to £375 billion. The change in disposable income of £100 billion brings about a change in consumption expenditure of £75 billion. The *MPC* is £75 billion divided by £100 billion, which equals 0.75. In Figure 23.1, the *MPC* is a constant 0.75. For example, an increase in disposable income from £200 billion to £300 billion increases consumption expenditure from £225 billion to £300 billion, so again the *MPC* is 0.75.

The **marginal propensity to save** (*MPS*) is the fraction of a *change* in disposable income that is saved. It is calculated as the *change* in saving (ΔS) divided by the *change* in disposable income (ΔYD) that brought it about. That is:

$$MPS = \frac{\Delta S}{\Delta YD}$$

Again, using the numbers in the table in Figure 23.1, an increase in disposable income from £300 billion to £400 billion increases saving from zero to £25 billion. The change in disposable income of £100 billion brings about a change in saving of £25 billion. The *MPS* is £25 billion divided by £100 billion, which equals 0.25. In Figure 23.1, the *MPS* is a constant 0.25. For example, an increase in disposable income from £200 billion to £300 billion increases saving from –£25 billion to zero, so again the *MPS* is 0.25.

The marginal propensity to consume plus the marginal propensity to save must always equal 1. This is because what is not consumed out of disposable income is always saved. You can see that from the equation:

$$\Delta C + \Delta S = \Delta YD$$

Divide both sides of the equation by the change in disposable income to obtain:

$$\frac{\Delta C}{\Delta YD} + \frac{\Delta S}{\Delta YD} = 1$$

$\Delta C/\Delta YD$, is the *marginal propensity to consume (MPC)* and $\Delta S/\Delta YD$ is the *marginal propensity to save (MPS)*, so:

$$MPC + MPS = 1$$

Marginal Propensities and Slopes

You can think of the marginal propensity to consume as the slope of the consumption function shown in Figure 23.2(a). A £100 billion increase in disposable income from £300 billion to £400 billion is the base of the red triangle. The increase in consumption expenditure that results from this increase in income is £75 billion and is the height of the triangle. The slope of the consumption function is given by the formula 'slope equals rise over run' and is £75 billion divided by £100 billion, which equals 0.75 – the *MPC*.

The marginal propensity to save is the slope of the saving function in Figure 23.2(b). A £100 billion increase in disposable income from £300 billion to £400 billion (the base of the red triangle) increases saving by £25 billion (the height of the triangle). The slope of the saving function is £25 billion divided by £100 billion, which equals 0.25 – the *MPS*.

The marginal propensity to consume plus the marginal propensity to save always equals 1.

Other Influences on Consumption Expenditure and Saving

You've seen that a change in disposable income leads to changes in consumption expenditure and saving. A change in disposable income brings movements along the consumption function and saving function. A change in other influences on consumption expenditure and saving shifts both the consumption function and the saving function. These other factors include the real interest rate, expected future income and the purchasing power of net assets.

When the real interest rate falls or when the purchasing power of net assets (assets minus debts) or expected future income increases, consumption expenditure increases and saving decreases. Figure 23.3 shows the effects of these changes on the consumption function and the saving function. The consumption

Figure 23.2

Marginal Propensities to Consume and Save

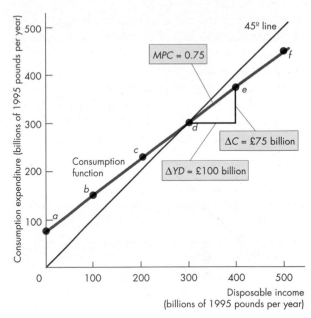

(a) Consumption function

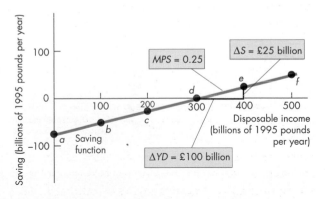

(b) Saving function

The marginal propensity to consume, *MPC*, is equal to the change in consumption expenditure divided by the change in disposable income, other things remaining the same. It is measured by the slope of the consumption function. In part (a), the *MPC* is 0.75. The marginal propensity to save, *MPS*, is equal to the change in saving divided by the change in disposable income, other things remaining the same. It is measured by the slope of the saving function. In part (b), the *MPS* is 0.25.

Figure 23.3

Shifts in the Consumption and Saving Functions

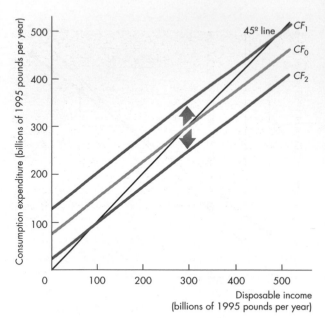

(a) Consumption function

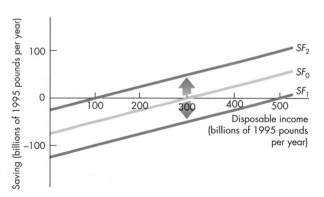

(b) Saving function

A fall in the real interest rate, an increase in the purchasing power of net assets, or an increase in expected future income increases consumption expenditure, shifts the consumption function upward from CF_0 to CF_1 and shifts the saving function downward from SF_0 to SF_1. Similarly, a rise in the real interest rate, a decrease in the purchasing power of net assets, or a decrease in expected future income shifts the consumption function downward from CF_0 to CF_2 and shifts the saving function upward from SF_0 to SF_2.

function shifts upward from CF_0 to CF_1, and the saving function shifts downward from SF_0 to SF_1. Such shifts commonly occur during the expansion phase of the business cycle because, at such times, expected future income increases.

When the real interest rate rises or when the purchasing power of net assets or expected future income decreases, consumption decreases and saving increases. Figure 23.3 also shows the effects of these changes on the consumption function and the saving function. The consumption function shifts downward from CF_0 to CF_2, and the saving function shifts upward from SF_0 to SF_2. Such shifts often occur when a recession begins because at such a time, expected future income decreases.

We've studied the theory of the consumption function. Let's now see how that theory applies to the economy.

The Consumption Function

Figure 23.4 shows the consumption function in the United Kingdom. Each point identified by a blue dot

Figure 23.4

The UK Consumption Function

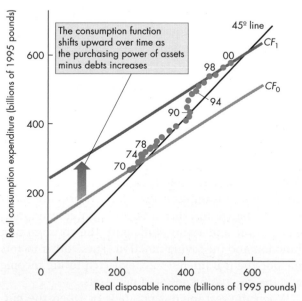

Each blue dot represents consumption expenditure and disposable income for a particular year. The orange lines are an estimate of the UK consumption function in 1970 and 2000.

represents consumption expenditure and disposable income for a particular year. (The dots are for the years 1970–2000.) The orange line shows the average relationship between consumption expenditure and disposable income and is an estimate of the consumption function. The slope of this line is 0.84, which means that a £100 billion increase in disposable income brings a £84 billion increase in consumption expenditure. That is, on the average, over the period 1970–2000, the marginal propensity to consume in the United Kingdom was about 0.84.

The relationship between consumption expenditure and disposable income in any given year does not fall exactly on the orange line. The reason is that the position of the consumption function in each year depends on other factors – such as the real interest rate, expected future income and the purchasing power of net assets – which influence consumption expenditure and shift the consumption function.

Consumption as a Function of Real GDP

You've seen that consumption expenditure changes when disposable income changes. Disposable income changes when either real GDP changes or net taxes change. If tax rates don't change, real GDP is the only influence on disposable income and so when prices are fixed, consumption depends not only on disposable income but also on real GDP. We use this link between consumption and real GDP to determine equilibrium expenditure. But before we do so, we need to look at one further component of aggregate expenditure: imports. Like consumption expenditure, imports are also influenced by real GDP.

Import Function

Imports to the United Kingdom are determined by a number of factors, but in the short run with fixed prices, one factor dominates and that is UK real GDP.

Other things remaining the same, the greater the United Kingdom real GDP, the larger is the quantity of United Kingdom imports. So an increase in real GDP brings an increase in imports, and the magnitude of the increase in imports is determined by the marginal propensity to import. The **marginal propensity to import** is the fraction of an increase in real GDP that is spent on imports. It is calculated as the change in imports divided by the change in real GDP that brought it about, other things remaining the same. So, for example, if real GDP increases by

£100 billion and imports increase by £30 billion, the marginal propensity to import is 0.3. The marginal propensity to import has been increasing in the UK. In 1970 it was 0.2. In 1980 it was 0.33.

Review Quiz

◆ Which components of aggregate planned expenditure are influenced by real GDP?
◆ Define the marginal propensity to consume.
◆ What is your estimate of your own marginal propensity to consume? After you graduate and begin work, will your marginal propensity to consume change? Why or why not?
◆ How do we calculate the effects of real GDP on consumption expenditure and imports?

We've studied the influence of real GDP on consumption expenditure and imports. Next we will see how these components of aggregate expenditure interact with investment, government purchases and exports to determine aggregate expenditure and real GDP.

Real GDP with a Fixed Price Level

We are now going to discover how aggregate expenditure plans interact to determine real GDP when the price level is fixed. The first step in this process is to look at the relationship between aggregate planned expenditure and real GDP.

The relationship between aggregate planned expenditure and real GDP can be described by either an aggregate expenditure schedule or an aggregate expenditure curve. The *aggregate expenditure schedule* lists aggregate planned expenditure generated at each level of real GDP. The *aggregate expenditure curve* is a graph of the aggregate expenditure schedule.

Aggregate Planned Expenditure and Real GDP

The table in Figure 23.5 sets out an aggregate expenditure schedule together with the components of aggregate planned expenditure. To calculate aggregate planned expenditure at a given real GDP, we add the various components together. The first column of

Figure 23.5

Aggregate Expenditure

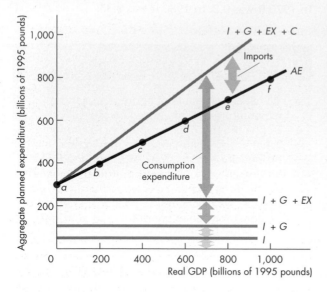

The relationship between aggregate planned expenditure and real GDP is shown by an aggregate expenditure schedule and illustrated by an aggregate expenditure curve. Aggregate planned expenditure is the sum of planned consumption expenditure, investment, government purchases of goods and services, and net exports. For example, in row *b* of the table, when real GDP is £200 billion, planned consumption expenditure is £225 billion, planned investment is £50 billion, planned government purchases of goods and services are £55 billion, planned exports are £120 billion, and planned imports are £50 billion. Thus when real GDP is £200 billion, aggregate planned expenditure is £400 billion (£225 + £50 + £55 + £120 − £50). The schedule shows that aggregate planned expenditure increases as real GDP increases. This relationship is graphed as the aggregate expenditure curve *AE*, the line *af*. The components of aggregate expenditure that increase with real GDP are consumption expenditure and imports. The other components − investment, government purchases and exports − do not vary with real GDP.

	Real GDP (*Y*)	Planned expenditure					Aggregate expenditure (*AE = C + I + G + NX*)
		Consumption expenditure (*C*)	Investment (*I*)	Government purchases (*G*) (billions of 1995 pounds)	Exports (*EX*)	Imports (*IM*)	
a	0	75	50	55	120	0	300
b	200	225	50	55	120	50	400
c	400	375	50	55	120	100	500
d	600	525	50	55	120	150	600
e	800	675	50	55	120	200	700
f	1,000	825	50	55	120	250	800

the table shows real GDP and the second column shows the consumption expenditure generated by each level of real GDP. When real GDP is £200 billion, consumption expenditure is £225 billion. A £200 billion increase in real GDP generates a £150 billion increase in consumption expenditure.

The next two columns show investment and government purchases of goods and services. Investment depends on the real interest rate and the expected rate of profit. At a given point in time these factors generate a level of investment that is independent of real GDP. Suppose this amount of investment is £50 billion. Government purchases of goods and services are also independent of real GDP and their value is £55 billion.

The next two columns show exports and imports. Exports are influenced by events in the rest of the world, prices of foreign-produced goods and services relative to the prices of similar goods and services produced at home, and foreign exchange rates. But they are not directly affected by real GDP in the United Kingdom. In the table, exports appear as a constant £120 billion. In contrast, imports increase as real GDP increases. A £200 billion increase in real GDP generates a £50 billion increase in imports.

The final column of the table shows aggregate planned expenditure. This amount is the sum of planned consumption expenditure, investment, government purchases of goods and services, and exports minus imports.

Figure 23.5 plots an aggregate expenditure curve. Real GDP is shown on the *x*-axis and aggregate planned expenditure on the *y*-axis. The aggregate expenditure curve is the red line *AE*. Points *a* to *f* on this curve correspond to the rows of the table. The *AE* curve is a graph of aggregate planned expenditure (the last column) plotted against real GDP (the first column).

Figure 23.5 also shows the components of aggregate expenditure. The constant components – investment (*I*), government purchases of goods and services (*G*), and exports (*EX*) – are shown by the horizontal lines in the figure. Consumption expenditure (*C*) is the vertical gap between the lines labelled *I + G + EX + C* and *I + G + EX*.

To construct the *AE* curve, subtract imports (*IM*) from the *I + G + EX + C* line. Aggregate expenditure is expenditure on UK-produced goods and services. But the components of aggregate expenditure, *C*, *I* and *G*, include expenditure on imported goods and services. For example, a student's purchase of a new motorbike is part of consumption expenditure, but if that motorbike is a Honda made in Japan, expenditure on it must be subtracted from consumption expenditure to find out how much is spent on goods and services produced in the United Kingdom – on UK real GDP. Money paid to Honda for car imports from Japan does not add to aggregate expenditure in the United Kingdom.

Figure 23.5 shows that aggregate planned expenditure increases as real GDP increases. But as real GDP increases only some of the components of aggregate planned expenditure increase. These components are consumption expenditure and imports. The sum of the components of aggregate expenditure that vary with real GDP is called **induced expenditure**. The sum of the components of aggregate expenditure that are not influenced by real GDP is called **autonomous expenditure**. The components of autonomous expenditure are investment, government purchases, exports and the part of consumption expenditure that does not vary with real GDP. That is, autonomous expenditure is equal to the level of aggregate planned expenditure when real GDP is zero. In Figure 23.5, autonomous expenditure is £300 billion. As real GDP increases from zero to £200 billion, aggregate expenditure increases from £300 billion to £400 billion. Induced expenditure is £100 billion – £400 billion minus £300 billion.

The aggregate expenditure curve summarizes the relationship between aggregate planned expenditure

and real GDP. But what determines the point on the aggregate expenditure curve at which the economy operates? What determines real GDP?

Actual Expenditure, Planned Expenditure and Real GDP

Actual aggregate expenditure is always equal to real GDP, as we saw in Chapter 20, pp. 424–433. But aggregate *planned* expenditure is not necessarily equal to actual aggregate expenditure and, therefore, is not necessarily equal to real GDP. How can actual expenditure and planned expenditure differ from each other? Why don't expenditure plans get implemented? The main reason is that firms might end up with more stocks than planned or with less stocks than planned. People carry out their consumption expenditure plans, the government implements its planned purchases of goods and services, and net exports are as planned. Firms carry out their plans to purchase new buildings, plant and equipment. One component of investment, however, is the increase in firms' stocks of goods. When aggregate planned expenditure differs from real GDP, firms end up with more or less stocks than they had planned. If aggregate planned expenditure is less than real GDP, stocks increase, and if aggregate planned expenditure exceeds real GDP, stocks decrease.

Equilibrium Expenditure

Equilibrium expenditure is the level of aggregate expenditure that occurs when aggregate *planned* expenditure equals real GDP. It is a level of aggregate expenditure and real GDP at which everyone's spending plans are fulfilled. When the price level is fixed, equilibrium expenditure determines real GDP. When aggregate planned expenditure and actual aggregate expenditure are unequal, a process of convergence towards equilibrium expenditure occurs. And throughout this convergence process real GDP adjusts. Let's examine equilibrium expenditure and the process that brings it about.

Figure 23.6(a) illustrates equilibrium expenditure. The table sets out aggregate planned expenditure at various levels of real GDP. These values are plotted as points *a* to *f* along the *AE* curve. The 45° line shows all the points at which aggregate planned expenditure equals actual aggregate expenditure (and equals real GDP). Thus where the aggregate expenditure curve intersects the 45° line, point *d*, aggregate

Figure 23.6
Equilibrium Expenditure

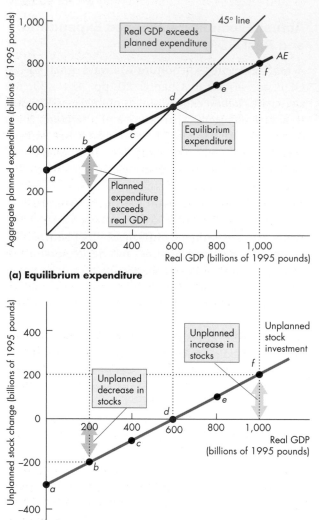

(a) Equilibrium expenditure

(b) Unplanned stock changes

	Real GDP (Y)	Aggregate planned expenditure (AE) (billions of 1995 pounds)	Unplanned stock change (Y − AE)
a	0	300	−300
b	200	400	−200
c	400	500	−100
d	600	600	0
e	800	700	100
f	1,000	800	200

The table shows expenditure plans at different levels of real GDP. When real GDP is £600 billion, aggregate planned expenditure equals real GDP. Part (a) of the figure illustrates equilibrium expenditure, which occurs when aggregate planned expenditure equals real GDP at the intersection of the 45° line and the *AE* curve. Part (b) of the figure shows the forces that bring about equilibrium expenditure. When aggregate planned expenditure exceeds real GDP stocks decrease – for example, point *b* in both parts of the figure. Firms increase production and real GDP increases. When aggregate planned expenditure is less than real GDP stocks increase – for example, point *d* in both parts of the figure. Firms decrease production and real GDP decreases. When aggregate planned expenditure equals real GDP there are no unplanned stock changes and real GDP remains constant at equilibrium expenditure.

---

planned expenditure equals actual aggregate expenditure. Point *d* illustrates equilibrium expenditure and determines real GDP. At this point, real GDP is £600 billion.

Convergence to Equilibrium

What are the forces that move aggregate expenditure towards its equilibrium level? To answer this question, we must look at a situation in which aggregate expenditure is away from its equilibrium level. Suppose that in Figure 23.6, real GDP is £200 billion. With real

GDP at £200 billion, aggregate expenditure is also £200 billion. But aggregate *planned* expenditure is £400 billion (point *b* in Figure 23.6(a)). Aggregate planned expenditure exceeds *actual* expenditure. When people spend £400 billion, and firms produce goods and services worth £200 billion, firms' stocks fall by £200 billion (point *b* in Figure 23.6(b)). Because the change in stocks is part of investment, *actual* investment is £200 billion less than *planned* investment.

Real GDP doesn't remain at £200 billion for long. Firms have stock targets based on their sales. When the ratio of stocks to sales falls below target, firms increase production to restore stocks to the target level. To increase stocks, firms hire additional labour and increase production. Suppose that they increase production in the next period by £200 billion. Real GDP increases by £200 billion to £400 billion. But again, aggregate planned expenditure exceeds real GDP. When real GDP is £400 billion, aggregate planned expenditure is £500 billion (point c in Figure 23.6(a)). Again, stocks decrease but this time by less than before. With real GDP of £400 billion and aggregate planned expenditure of £500 billion, stocks decrease by £100 billion (point c in Figure 23.6(b)). Again, firms hire additional labour and production increases; real GDP increases yet further.

The process that we have just described – planned expenditure exceeds real GDP, stocks decrease and production increases to restore the level of stocks – ends when real GDP has reached £600 billion. At this real GDP, there is an equilibrium. There are no unplanned stock changes and firms do not change their production.

You can do a similar experiment to the one we've just done, but starting with a level of real GDP greater than equilibrium expenditure. In this case, planned expenditure is less than actual expenditure, stocks pile up and firms cut production. As before, real GDP keeps on changing (decreasing this time) until it reaches its equilibrium level of £600 billion.

Review Quiz

◆ Explain the relationship between aggregate planned expenditure and real GDP.
◆ What is the relationship between aggregate planned expenditure and real GDP at equilibrium expenditure?
◆ What adjustments occur to bring aggregate planned expenditure to equality with actual expenditure?
◆ If real GDP and aggregate expenditure are less than their equilibrium levels, what happens to unplanned inventories, production, and real GDP?
◆ If real GDP and aggregate expenditure exceed their equilibrium levels, what happens to unplanned inventories, production, and real GDP?

We've learned that when the price level is fixed, real GDP is determined by equilibrium expenditure.

And we have seen how unplanned changes in stocks and the production response they generate bring a convergence towards equilibrium. We're now going to study *changes* in equilibrium, and we are going to discover an economic amplifier called the multiplier.

The Multiplier

Investment and exports can change for many reasons. A fall in the real interest rate might induce firms to increase their planned investment. A major wave of innovation, such as occurred with the spread of IT in the 1980s, might increase expected future profits and lead firms to increase their planned investment. Stiff competition in the car industry from Japanese or South Korean imports might force Ford, Vauxhall and Rover to increase their investment in robotic assembly lines. An economic boom in developing countries might lead to a large increase in their expenditure on UK-produced goods and services – on UK exports. These are all examples of increases in autonomous expenditure.

When autonomous expenditure increases, aggregate expenditure increases, and so too does equilibrium expenditure. The increase in equilibrium expenditure and real GDP is larger than the change in autonomous expenditure. The **multiplier** is the amount by which a change in autonomous expenditure is magnified or multiplied to determine the change in equilibrium expenditure and real GDP.

It is easiest to get the basic idea of the multiplier if we work with an example economy in which there are no income taxes and no imports. So we'll first assume that these factors are absent. Then, when you understand the basic idea, we'll bring these factors back into play and see what difference they make to the multiplier.

The Basic Idea of the Multiplier

Suppose that investment increases. The additional expenditure by businesses means that aggregate expenditure and real GDP increases. Disposable income also increases, and with no income taxes, real GDP and disposable income increase by the same amount. The increase in disposable income brings an increase in consumption expenditure. And the increased consumption expenditure adds even more to aggregate expenditure. Real GDP and disposable income increase further, and so does consumption

Figure 23.7
The Multiplier

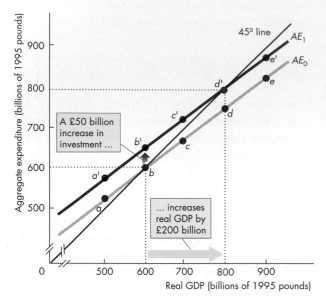

Real GDP (Y)		Aggregate planned expenditure Original (AE₀) (billions of 1995 pounds)		Aggregate planned expenditure New (AE₁)
500	a	525	a′	575
600	b	600	b′	650
700	c	675	c′	725
800	d	750	d′	800
900	e	825	e′	875

A 50 billion increase in autonomous expenditure shifts the
AE curve upward by 50 billion from AE₀ to AE₁. Equilibrium
expenditure increases by 200 billion from 600 billion to
800 billion. The increase in equilibrium expenditure is
four times the increase in autonomous expenditure,
so the multiplier is 4.

expenditure. The initial increase in investment brings
an even bigger increase in aggregate expenditure
because it induces an increase in consumption expenditure. The magnitude of the increase in aggregate
expenditure that results from an increase in autonomous expenditure is determined by the *multiplier*.

The table in Figure 23.7 sets out aggregate planned
expenditure. Initially, when real GDP is £500 billion,
aggregate planned expenditure is £525 billion. For
each £100 billion increase in real GDP, aggregate
planned expenditure increases by £75 billion. This

aggregate expenditure schedule is shown in the figure
as the aggregate expenditure curve AE_0. Initially, equilibrium expenditure is £600 billion. You can see this
equilibrium in row *b* of the table, and in the figure
where the curve AE_0 intersects the 45° line at the
point marked *b*.

Now suppose that autonomous expenditure increases
by £50 billion. What happens to equilibrium expenditure? You can see the answer in Figure 23.7. When
this increase in autonomous expenditure is added to
the original aggregate planned expenditure, aggregate
planned expenditure increases by £50 billion at each
level of real GDP. The new aggregate expenditure
curve is AE_1. The new equilibrium expenditure, highlighted in the table (row *d′*), occurs where AE_1 intersects the 45° line and is £800 billion (point *d′*). At this
point, aggregate planned expenditure equals real
GDP.

The Multiplier Effect

In Figure 23.7, the increase in autonomous expenditure of £50 billion increases equilibrium expenditure
by £200 billion. That is, the change in autonomous
expenditure leads to an amplified change in equilibrium expenditure. This amplified change is the *multiplier effect* – equilibrium expenditure increases by *more
than* the increase in autonomous expenditure.

Initially, when autonomous expenditure increases,
aggregate planned expenditure exceeds real GDP. As a
result, stocks decrease. Firms respond by increasing
production so as to restore their stocks to the target
level. As production increases, so does real GDP. With
a higher level of real GDP, *induced expenditure* increases.
Thus equilibrium expenditure increases by the sum of
the initial increase in autonomous expenditure and
the increase in induced expenditure. In this example,
induced expenditure increases by £150 billion, so
equilibrium expenditure increases by £200 billion.

Although we have just analysed the effects of an
increase in autonomous expenditure, the same analysis applies to a decrease in autonomous expenditure.
If initially the aggregate expenditure curve is AE_1,
equilibrium expenditure and real GDP are £800 billion.
A decrease in autonomous expenditure of £50 billion
shifts the aggregate expenditure curve downward by
£50 billion to AE_0. Equilibrium expenditure decreases
from £800 billion to £600 billion. The decrease in
equilibrium expenditure (£200 billion) is larger than
the decrease in autonomous expenditure that brought
it about. In this example, the multiplier is 4.

Why is the Multiplier Greater than 1?

We've seen that equilibrium expenditure increases by more than the increase in autonomous expenditure. This makes the multiplier greater than 1. How come? Why does equilibrium expenditure increase by more than the increase in autonomous expenditure?

The multiplier is greater than 1 because of induced expenditure – an increase in autonomous expenditure *induces* further increases in expenditure. If BT spends £10 million on a new video communications system, aggregate expenditure and real GDP immediately increase by £10 million. But that is not the end of the story. Electrical engineers and construction workers now have more income, and they spend part of the extra income on cars, microwaves, holidays and a host of other goods and services. Real GDP now rises by the initial £10 million plus the extra consumption expenditure induced by the £10 million increase in income. The producers of cars, microwaves, holidays and other goods now have increased incomes, and they, in turn, spend part of the increase in their incomes on consumption goods and services. Additional income induces additional expenditure, which creates additional income.

We have seen that a change in autonomous expenditure has a multiplier effect on real GDP. But how big is the multiplier effect?

The Size of the Multiplier

Suppose that the economy is in recession. Profit prospects start to look better and firms are making plans for large increases in investment. The world economy is also heading towards recovery, and exports are increasing. The question on everyone's lips is: how strong will the recovery be? This is a hard question to answer. But an important ingredient in the answer is working out the size of the multiplier.

The *multiplier* is the amount by which a change in autonomous expenditure is multiplied to determine the change in equilibrium expenditure that it generates. To calculate the multiplier, we divide the change in equilibrium expenditure by the change in autonomous expenditure. Let's calculate the multiplier for the example in Figure 23.8. Initially, equilibrium expenditure is £600 billion. Then autonomous expenditure increases by £50 billion, and equilibrium expenditure increases by £200 billion to £800 billion.

The multiplier is:

Figure 23.8

The Multiplier Process

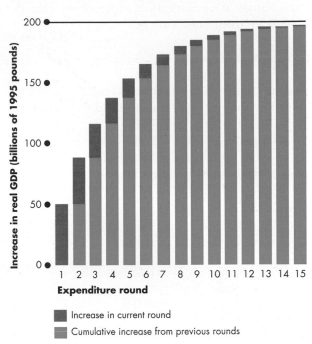

■ Increase in current round
■ Cumulative increase from previous rounds

Autonomous expenditure increases in round 1 by £50 billion. As a result, real GDP increases by the same amount. With a marginal propensity to consume of 0.75, each additional pound of real GDP induces an additional 0.75 of a pound of aggregate expenditure. The round 1 increase in real GDP induces an increase in consumption expenditure of £37.5 billion in round 2. At the end of round 2, real GDP has increased by £87.5 billion. The extra £37.5 billion of real GDP in round 2 induces a further increase in consumption expenditure of £28.1 billion in round 3. Real GDP increases yet further to £115.6 billion. This process continues with real GDP increasing by ever smaller amounts. When the process comes to an end, real GDP has increased by a total of £200 billion.

$$\text{Multiplier} = \frac{\Delta \text{ equilibrium expenditure}}{\Delta \text{ autonomous expenditure}}$$

$$= \frac{£200 \text{ billion}}{£50 \text{ billion}} = 4$$

The Multiplier and the Marginal Propensities to Consume and Save

What determines the magnitude of the multiplier? The answer is the marginal propensity to consume. The larger the marginal propensity to consume, the larger is the multiplier. To see why, let's do a calculation.

Aggregate expenditure and real GDP (Y) change because consumption expenditure (C) changes and investment (I) changes. The change in GDP equals the change in consumption expenditure plus the change in investment. That is:

$$\Delta Y = \Delta C + \Delta I$$

But the change in consumption expenditure is determined by the change in real GDP and the MPC. It is:

$$\Delta C = MPC \times \Delta Y$$

Now combine these two facts to give:

$$\Delta Y = MPC \times \Delta Y + \Delta I$$

Now, solve for the change in Y as:

$$(1 - MPC) \times \Delta Y = \Delta I$$

and rearranging:

$$\Delta Y = \frac{\Delta I}{(1 - MPC)}$$

The multiplier that we want to calculate is:

$$\text{Multiplier} = \frac{\Delta Y}{\Delta I}$$

So divide both sides of the previous equation by the change in I to give:

$$\text{Multiplier} = \frac{\Delta Y}{\Delta I} = \frac{\Delta I}{(1 - MPC)}$$

Using the numbers for Figure 23.8, the MPC is 0.75, so the multiplier is:

$$\text{Multiplier} = \frac{1}{(1 - 0.75)} = \frac{1}{0.25} = 4$$

There is another formula for the multiplier. Because the marginal propensity to consume (MPC) plus the marginal propensity to save (MPS) adds up to 1, the term $(1 - MPC)$ equals MPS. Therefore, another formula for the multiplier is:

$$\text{Multiplier} = \frac{1}{MPS}$$

Again using the numbers in Figure 23.8:

$$\text{Multiplier} = \frac{1}{0.25} = 4$$

Because the marginal propensity to save (MPS) is a fraction – a number lying between 0 and 1 – the multiplier is greater than 1.

Figure 23.8 illustrates the multiplier process. In round 1, autonomous expenditure increases by £50 billion. At this time, induced expenditure does not change, so aggregate expenditure and real GDP increase by £50 billion. In round 2, the larger real GDP induces more consumption expenditure. Induced expenditure increases by 0.75 times the increase in real GDP, so the increase in real GDP of £50 billion induces a further increase in expenditure of £37.5 billion. This change in induced expenditure, when added to the initial change in autonomous expenditure, increases aggregate expenditure and real GDP by £87.5 billion. The round 2 increase in real GDP induces a round 3 increase in expenditure. The process repeats through successive rounds. Each increase in real GDP is 0.75 times the previous increase. The cumulative increase in real GDP gradually approaches £200 billion.

So far, we've ignored imports and income taxes. Let's now see how these two factors influence the multiplier.

Imports and Income Taxes

The multiplier is determined, in general, not only by the marginal propensity to consume but also by the marginal propensity to import and by the marginal tax rate. Imports make the multiplier smaller than it otherwise would be. To see why, think about what happens following an increase in investment. An increase in investment increases real GDP, which in turn increases consumption expenditure. But part of investment and part of the consumption expenditure are expenditure on imported goods and services, not UK-produced goods and services. It is the expenditure on only UK-produced goods and services that increases real GDP in the United Kingdom.

Income taxes also make the multiplier smaller than it otherwise would be. Again, think about what happens following an increase in investment. An increase in investment increases real GDP. Because income taxes increase with income, the increase in real GDP increases income taxes. And the increase in income

Figure 23.9

The Multiplier and the Slope of the *AE* Curve

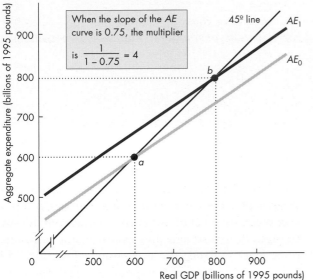

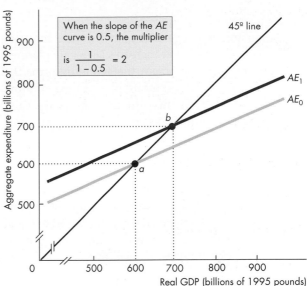

Imports and income taxes make the *AE* curve less steep and reduce the value of the multiplier. In part (a), with no imports and income taxes the slope of the *AE* curve is 0.75 (the marginal propensity to consume) and the multiplier

is 4. But with imports and income taxes, the slope of the *AE* curve is less than the marginal propensity to consume. In part (b), the slope of the *AE* curve is 0.5. In this case, the multiplier is 2.

---

taxes decreases disposable income. Consumption expenditure depends on disposable income, so the greater the increase in income taxes, the smaller is the increase in consumption expenditure, other things remaining the same. It is only the increase in *disposable* income that induces an increase in consumption expenditure.

The marginal propensity to import and the marginal tax rate together with the marginal propensity to consume determine the slope of the *AE* curve and the multiplier. The multiplier is equal to 1 divided by 1 minus the slope of the *AE* curve. Figure 23.9 compares two situations. In Figure 23.9(a) there are no imports and no taxes. The marginal propensity to consume, which also equals the slope of the *AE* curve, is 0.75 and the multiplier is 4. In Figure 23.9(b) imports and income taxes decrease the slope of the *AE* curve to 0.5. In this case the multiplier is 2.

Over time, the value of the multiplier changes as tax rates change and as the marginal propensity to consume and the marginal propensity to import change. These ongoing changes make the multiplier hard to

predict. But they do not change the fundamental fact that an initial change in autonomous expenditure leads to a magnified change in aggregate expenditure and real GDP.

Now that we've studied the multiplier and the factors that influence its magnitude, let's use what we've learned to gain some insights into the most critical points in the life of an economy: business cycle turning points.

Business Cycle Turning Points

At a business cycle trough, the economy moves from recession into recovery and at a peak, it moves from recovery, into recession. Economists understand these turning points like seismologists understand earthquakes. They know quite a lot about the forces that produce them and the mechanisms at work when they occur, but they can't predict them. The forces that bring business cycle turning points are the swings in autonomous expenditure – in investment and exports. The mechanism that gives momentum to the new direction the economy is taking is the multiplier process that we've just studied. Let's use what we've now learned to examine these turning points.

An Expansion Begins

An expansion is triggered by an increase in autonomous expenditure that increases aggregate planned expenditure. At the moment the economy turns the corner into recovery, aggregate planned expenditure exceeds real GDP. In this situation, firms see their stocks taking an unplanned dive. The recovery now begins. To meet their stock targets, firms increase production and real GDP begins to increase. This initial increase in real GDP brings higher incomes that stimulate consumption expenditure. The multiplier process kicks in and the recovery picks up speed. The expansion ends when real GDP has increased to equal aggregate planned expenditure and there are no unplanned stock changes.

A Recession Begins

The process we've just described works in reverse at a business cycle peak. A recession is triggered by a decrease in autonomous expenditure that decreases aggregate planned expenditure. At the moment the economy turns the corner into recession, real GDP exceeds aggregate planned expenditure. In this situation, firms see unplanned stocks piling up. The recession now begins. To lower their stocks, firms cut production and real GDP begins to decrease. This initial decrease in real GDP brings lower incomes that cut consumption expenditure. The multiplier process reinforces the initial cut in autonomous expenditure and the recession takes hold. The recession ends when real GDP has fallen to equal aggregate planned expenditure and there are no unplanned stock changes. Reading Between the Lines on pp. 514–515 examines the multiplier in action in the UK.

The Next UK Recession?

During 2001 investment began to slow and stocks increased in the United Kingdom. If these stock increases were planned, they would *not* trigger a change in production. But if they were unplanned, firms would cut production and real GDP growth could fall in 2001 and 2002. However, a reduction in the rate of growth of GDP is not a reduction in the level of GDP. Many economists are predicting a growth slowdown in 2001–02. It is much harder to predict exactly when the next recession will occur.

We've seen that the economy does not operate like the shock absorbers on Brian Tyrer's car. The economy's potholes and bumps are changes in autonomous expenditure – mainly brought about by changes in investment and exports. And while the price level is fixed, these economic potholes and bumps are not smoothed out. Instead they are amplified. But we've only considered the adjustments in spending that occur in the very short term when the price level is fixed. What happens when the price level changes? And what happens in the long run? Let's answer these questions.

The Multiplier, Real GDP and the Price Level

When firms are having trouble keeping up with sales and their stocks fall below target, they increase production, but at some point they raise their prices. Similarly, when firms find unwanted stocks piling up, they decrease production, but eventually they cut their prices. So far, we've studied the macroeconomic consequences of firms changing their production levels when their sales change, but we've not looked at the effects of price changes. When individual firms change their prices, the economy's price level changes.

To study the simultaneous determination of real GDP and the price level, we use the *aggregate demand–aggregate supply model*, which is explained in Chapter 22, pp. 464–480. There is a connection between the aggregate demand–aggregate supply model and the equilibrium expenditure model that we've used in this chapter. The key to the relationship between these two models is the distinction between the aggregate *expenditure* curve and the aggregate *demand* curve.

Aggregate Expenditure and Aggregate Demand

The aggregate expenditure curve is the relationship between the aggregate planned expenditure and real GDP, all other influences on aggregate planned expenditure remaining the same. The aggregate demand curve is the relationship between the aggregate quantity of goods and services demanded and the price level, all other influences on aggregate demand remaining the same. Let's explore the links between these two relationships.

Aggregate Expenditure and the Price Level

At a given price level, there is a given level of aggregate planned expenditure. But if the price level changes, so does aggregate planned expenditure. Why? There are two main reasons. We examined these reasons in more detail in Chapter 22, pp. 470–473. They are:

1 The real money balances effect.

2 The substitution effect.

Real money is the purchasing power of money, which is measured by the quantity of money divided by the price level. A rise in the price level, other things remaining the same, decreases the quantity of real money and a smaller quantity of real money decreases aggregate planned expenditure – the *real money balances effect*. A rise in the price level, other things remaining the same, makes current goods and services more costly relative to future goods and services, and results in a delay in purchases – the *intertemporal substitution effect*. A rise in the price level, other things remaining the same, makes UK-produced goods more expensive relative to foreign-produced goods and services, and increases imports and decreases exports – the *international substitution effect*.

When the price level rises, each of these effects reduces aggregate planned expenditure at each level of real GDP. As a result, when the price level rises, the aggregate expenditure curve shifts downward. A fall in the price level has the opposite effect. When the price level falls, the aggregate expenditure curve shifts upward.

Figure 23.10(a) illustrates these effects. Here we are going to derive the same AD curve we first encountered as Figure 22.6 in Chapter 22, p. 471. When the price level is 115, the aggregate expenditure curve is AE_0, which intersects the 45° line at point *b*. Equilibrium expenditure and real GDP are £825 billion. If the

Figure 23.10

Aggregate Demand

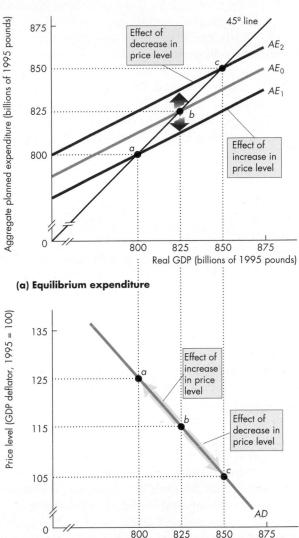

(a) Equilibrium expenditure

(b) Aggregate demand

The position of the *AE* curve depends on the price level. When the price level is 115, the *AE* curve is AE_0. Equilibrium expenditure is at point *b*, and real GDP demanded is £825 billion. When the price level rises to 125, the *AE* curve shifts downward to AE_1, and equilibrium expenditure is at point *a*. Real GDP demanded is £800 billion. When the price level falls to 105, the *AE* curve shifts upward to AE_2, and equilibrium expenditure is at point *c*. Real GDP demanded is £850 billion.

Part (b) shows the *AD* curve. A change in the price level shifts the *AE* curve but results in a *movement along* the *AD* curve. Points *a*, *b* and *c* on the *AD* curve correspond to the equilibrium expenditure points *a*, *b* and *c* in part (a).

price level increases to 125, the aggregate expenditure curve shifts downward to AE_1, which intersects the 45° line at point *a*. Equilibrium expenditure and real GDP are £800 billion. If the price level decreases to 105, the aggregate expenditure curve shifts upward to AE_2, which intersects the 45° line at point *c*. Equilibrium expenditure and real GDP are £850 billion.

We've just seen that when the price level changes, other things remaining the same, the aggregate expenditure curve shifts and equilibrium expenditure changes. And when the price level changes, other things remaining the same, there is a movement along the aggregate demand curve. Figure 23.10(b) illustrates these movements. At a price level of 115, the aggregate quantity of goods and services demanded is £825 billion – point *b* on the aggregate demand curve *AD*. If the price level increases to 125, the aggregate quantity of goods and services demanded decreases to £800 billion. There is a movement along the aggregate demand curve to point *a*. If the price level decreases to 105, the aggregate quantity of goods and services demanded increases to £850 billion. There is a movement along the aggregate demand curve to point *c*.

Each point on the aggregate demand curve corresponds to a point of equilibrium expenditure. The equilibrium expenditure points *a*, *b* and *c* in Figure 23.10(a) correspond to points *a*, *b* and *c* on the aggregate demand curve in Figure 23.10(b).

When the price level changes, other things remaining the same, the aggregate expenditure curve shifts and there is a movement along the aggregate demand curve. When any other influence on aggregate planned expenditure changes, both the aggregate expenditure curve and the aggregate demand curve shift. For example, an increase in investment or in exports increases both aggregate planned expenditure and aggregate demand and shifts both the *AE* curve and the *AD* curve. Figure 23.11 illustrates the effect of such an increase.

Initially, the aggregate expenditure curve is AE_0 in part (a) and the aggregate demand curve is AD_0 in part (b). The price level is 115, real GDP is £825 billion, and the economy is at point *a* in both parts of the figure. Now suppose that investment increases by £25 billion. At a constant price level of 115, the aggregate expenditure curve shifts upward to AE_1. This curve intersects the 45° line at an equilibrium expenditure of £875 billion (point *b*). This equilibrium expenditure of £875 billion is the aggregate quantity of goods and services demanded at a price level of 115, as shown by point *b* in part (b). Point *b* lies on a new

Figure 23.11

A Change in Aggregate Demand

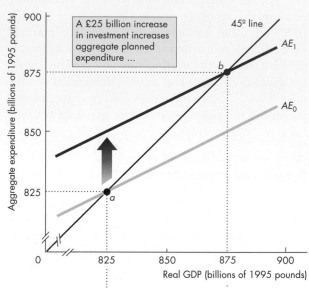

(a) Aggregate expenditure

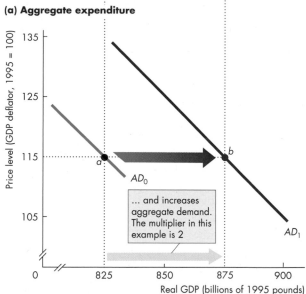

(b) Aggregate demand

The price level is 115. When the aggregate expenditure curve is AE_0 (part a), the aggregate demand curve is AD_0 (part b). An increase in autonomous expenditure shifts the aggregate expenditure curve upward to AE_1. The new equilibrium occurs where AE_1 intersects the 45° line at a real GDP of £875 billion. Because the quantity of real GDP demanded at a price level of 115 increases to £875 billion, the aggregate demand curve shifts rightward to AD_1. The magnitude of the rightward shift of the aggregate demand curve is determined by the change in autonomous expenditure and the size of the multiplier.

aggregate demand curve. The aggregate demand curve has shifted rightward to AD_1.

But how do we know by how much the AD curve shifts? The answer is determined by the multiplier. The larger the multiplier, the larger is the shift in the aggregate demand curve that results from a given change in autonomous expenditure. In this example, the multiplier is 2. A £25 billion increase in investment produces a £50 billion increase in the aggregate quantity of goods and services demanded at each price level. That is, a £25 billion increase in autonomous expenditure shifts the aggregate demand curve rightward by £50 billion.

A decrease in autonomous expenditure shifts the aggregate expenditure curve downward and shifts the aggregate demand curve leftward. You can see these effects by reversing the change that we've just studied. Suppose that the economy is initially at point b on the aggregate expenditure curve AE_1 and the aggregate demand curve AD_1. A decrease in autonomous expenditure shifts the aggregate planned expenditure curve downward to AE_0. The aggregate quantity of goods and services demanded falls from £875 billion to £825 billion and the aggregate demand curve shifts leftward to AD_0.

We can summarize what we have just discovered in the following way. An increase in autonomous expenditure arising from some source other than a change in the price level shifts the AE curve upward and the AD curve rightward. The magnitude of the shift of the AD curve is determined by the change in autonomous expenditure and the multiplier.

Equilibrium GDP and the Price Level

In Chapter 22, we learned that aggregate demand and short-run aggregate supply determine equilibrium real GDP and the price level. We've now put aggregate demand under a more powerful microscope and discovered that a change in investment (or in any component of autonomous expenditure) changes aggregate demand and shifts the aggregate demand curve. The magnitude of the shift depends on the multiplier. But whether a change in autonomous expenditure results ultimately in a change in real GDP, or a change in the price level, or some combination of the two depends on aggregate supply. There are two time frames to consider:

1   The short run.

2   The long run.

First, we'll see what happens in the short run. Then we'll look at the long run.

An Increase in Aggregate Demand in the Short Run

Figure 23.12 describes the economy. In part (a), the aggregate expenditure curve is AE_0, and equilibrium expenditure and real GDP are £825 billion – point a. In part (b), aggregate demand is AD_0 and the short-run aggregate supply curve is SAS. (Look at Chapter 22, pp. 466–469, if you need to refresh your understanding of this curve.) Equilibrium is at point a, where the aggregate demand and short-run aggregate supply curves intersect. The price level is 115 and real GDP is £825 billion.

Now suppose that investment increases by £25 billion. With the price level fixed at 115, the aggregate expenditure curve shifts upward to AE_1. Equilibrium expenditure increases to £875 billion – point b in part (a). In part (b), the aggregate demand curve shifts rightward by £50 billion, from AD_0 to AD_1. How far the aggregate demand curve shifts is determined by the multiplier when the price level is fixed. But with this new aggregate demand curve, the price level does not remain fixed. The price level rises and as it does so, the aggregate expenditure curve shifts downward. The short-run equilibrium occurs when the aggregate expenditure curve has shifted downward to AE_2 and the new aggregate demand curve, AD_1, intersects the short-run aggregate supply curve. Real GDP is £860 billion and the price level is 122 (at point c).

Taking price level effects into account, the increase in investment still has a multiplier effect on real GDP, but the effect is smaller than it would be if the price level was fixed forever. The steeper the slope of the short-run aggregate supply curve, the larger is the increase in the price level and the smaller is the multiplier effect on real GDP.

An Increase in Aggregate Demand in the Long Run

In the long run, the economy is at full-employment equilibrium and on its long-run aggregate supply curve. When the economy is at full employment, an increase in aggregate demand has the same short-run effect as we've just worked out, but its long-run effect is different.

Figure 23.12

The Multiplier in the Short Run

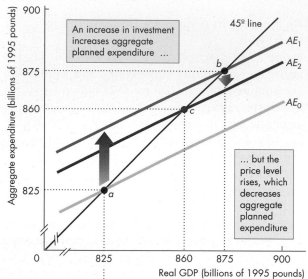

(a) Aggregate expenditure

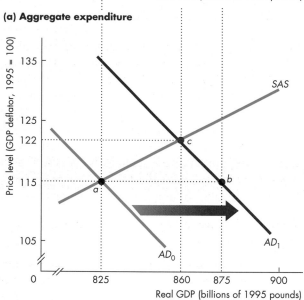

(b) Aggregate demand

Figure 23.13

The Multiplier in the Long Run

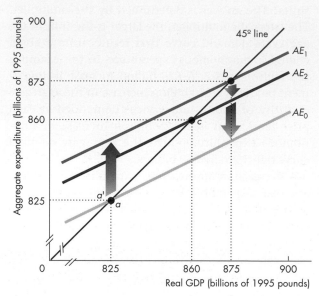

(a) Aggregate expenditure

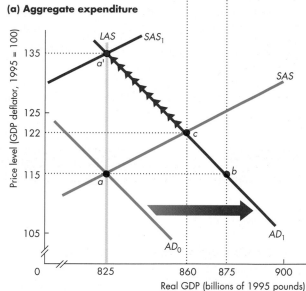

(b) Aggregate demand

An increase in investment shifts the *AE* curve upward from AE_0 to AE_1 (part a). As a result, the *AD* curve shifts from AD_0 to AD_1 (part b). The distance *ab* is determined by the multiplier when the price level is sticky. At the price level 115, there is excess demand. The price level rises, and the higher price level shifts the *AE* curve downward to AE_2. The economy moves to point *c* in both parts. With flexible prices, the multiplier is smaller than when prices are sticky. The steeper the *SAS* curve, the larger is the increase in the price level, the smaller is the increase in real GDP, and the smaller is the multiplier.

Starting from point *a*, an increase in investment shifts the *AE* curve to AE_1 and shifts the *AD* curve to AD_1. In the short run, the economy moves to point *c*. In the long run, the money wage rate rises, the *SAS* curve shifts to SAS_1, the *AE* curve shifts back to AE_0, the price level rises and real GDP falls. The economy moves to point *a′* and the long-run multiplier is zero.

Figure 23.13 illustrates the long-run effect. Potential GDP is £825 billion so long-run aggregate supply is *LAS*. When investment increases by £25 billion, the aggregate expenditure curve shifts upward to AE_1 and the aggregate demand curve shifts rightward to AD_1. The price level rises to a short-run equilibrium with real GDP at £860 billion and the price level at 122. But this situation is an above full-employment equilibrium. The workforce is more than fully employed, and there are shortages of labour. The money wage rate begins to rise. The higher money wage rate increases costs, and short-run aggregate supply decreases. The *SAS* curve begins to shift leftward. As a result, the price level increases further. As the price level rises, aggregate planned expenditure decreases and the *AE* curve shifts downwards toward AE_0. Eventually, when the money wage rate and the price level have increased by the same percentage, real GDP is again at its full-employment level. The multiplier in the long run is zero.

We've now seen how real GDP deviates from its long-term growth path when aggregate demand fluctuates, and we've studied the multiplier effect that amplifies the disturbances to aggregate demand. In the next three chapters we're going to see how macroeconomic policy can be used to smooth economic fluctuations. In Chapter 24, we study fiscal policy and discover what the government can do (and can't do) with taxes and its own spending to smooth economic fluctuations and stimulate production, and in Chapters 25 and 26, we study money and the actions the government, the Bank of England and the European Central Bank can take to smooth fluctuations and to restrain inflation.

Review Quiz

◆ What does a change in the price level do to the *AE* curve and the *AD* curve?
◆ What is the effect of a change in autonomous expenditure not caused by a change in the price level on both the *AE* curve and the *AD* curve?
◆ Why is an increase in real GDP that results from an increase in autonomous expenditure, smaller than the increase in aggregate demand.
◆ What is the effect of an increase in aggregate demand on real GDP and the price level when the economy is at full employment? What is the long-run multiplier?

Summary

Key Points

Fixed Prices and Expenditure Plans (pp. 487–493)

● When the *price level* is fixed, *aggregate* expenditure determines real GDP.

● *Planned* consumption expenditure is determined by disposable income.

● The influence of disposable income on consumption expenditure is determined by the marginal propensity to consume (*MPC*), which is equal to the slope of the consumption function.

● The influence of real GDP on imports is described by the import function. An increase in real GDP brings an increase in imports, and the magnitude of the increase in imports is determined by the marginal propensity to import.

Real GDP with a Fixed Price Level (pp. 493–497)

● The aggregate expenditure curve shows the relationship between aggregate *planned* expenditure and real GDP.

● *Actual* aggregate expenditure is always equal to real GDP. But aggregate *planned* expenditure is not necessarily equal to actual aggregate expenditure and real GDP.

● Equilibrium expenditure occurs when aggregate planned expenditure equals real GDP.

The Multiplier (pp. 497–502)

● The multiplier is the magnified effect of a change in autonomous expenditure on real GDP.

● The multiplier is equal to 1 divided by the marginal propensity to save.

- The larger the marginal propensity to consume, the smaller the marginal propensity to save, the larger is the multiplier.

- The multiplier is also influenced by the marginal propensity to import and by the marginal income tax rate.

The Multiplier, Real GDP and the Price Level (pp. 502–507)

- The aggregate demand curve is the relationship between the quantity of real GDP demanded and the price level, other things remaining the same.

- The aggregate expenditure curve is the relationship between aggregate planned expenditure and real GDP, other things remaining the same.

- At a given price level, there is a given aggregate expenditure curve. A change in the price level changes aggregate planned expenditure and shifts the aggregate expenditure curve. A change in the price level also creates a movement along the aggregate demand curve. Thus a movement along the aggregate demand curve is associated with a shift in the aggregate expenditure curve.

- A change in autonomous expenditure not caused by a change in the price level shifts the aggregate expenditure curve and also shifts the aggregate demand curve.

- The size of the shift in the aggregate demand curve depends on the size of the multiplier and the change in autonomous expenditure.

- The multiplier decreases as the price level changes and in the long run the multiplier is zero.

Key Figures ◆

Key Terms

Problems

●1 You are given the following information about the economy of Heron Island:

Disposable income	Consumption expenditure
(millions of euros per year)	
0	5
10	10
20	15
30	20
40	25

Calculate Heron Island's

a   Marginal propensity to consume.

b   Saving at each level of disposable income.

c   Marginal propensity to save.

2 You are given the following information about the economy of Spendthrift Island:

Disposable income (millions of euros per year)	Saving
0	−100
500	−50
1,000	0
1,500	50
2,000	100
2,500	150
3,000	200

Calculate Spendthrift Island's

a   Marginal propensity to save.

b   Consumption expenditure at each level of disposable income.

c Marginal propensity to consume.

d Why is the island called spendthrift?

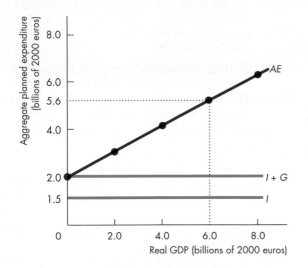

•3 Turtle Island has no imports or exports, the people of Turtle Island pay no income taxes, and the price level is fixed. The figure above illustrates the components of aggregate planned expenditure on Turtle Island.

On Turtle Island, what is:

a Autonomous expenditure?

b The marginal propensity to consume?

c Equilibrium expenditure?

d Happening to inventories if real GDP is €4 billion?

e Happening to inventories if real GDP is €6 billion?

f The multiplier?

4 The spreadsheet figure lists the components of aggregate planned expenditure in Spice Bay. The numbers are in billions of cloves, the currency of the Bay.

	A	B	C	D	E	F	G
		Y	C	I	G	X	M
1							
2	a	100	110	50	60	60	15
3	b	200	170	50	60	60	30
4	c	300	230	50	60	60	45
5	d	400	290	50	60	60	60
6	e	500	350	50	60	60	75
7	f	600	410	50	60	60	90

In Spice Bay, what is:

a Autonomous expenditure?

b The marginal propensity to consume?

c Aggregate planned expenditure when real GDP is 200 billion cloves?

d Happening to inventories if real GDP is 200 billion cloves?

e Happening to inventories if real GDP is 500 billion cloves?

f The multiplier in Spice Bay?

•5 In the economy of Zee, autonomous consumption expenditure is €100 billion and the marginal propensity to consume is 0.9. Investment is €460 billion, government expenditures on goods and services are €400 billion, and net taxes are €400 billion and do not vary with income. Zee has no imports or exports.

a What is the consumption function?

b What is the equation that describes the aggregate expenditure curve?

c Calculate equilibrium expenditure.

d If investment decreases to €360 billion, what is the change in equilibrium expenditure and what is the size of the multiplier?

6 You are given the following information about the economy of Antarctica: autonomous consumption expenditure is €1 billion, and the marginal propensity to consume is 0.95. Investment is €4 billion, government expenditures on goods and services are €4 billion, and net taxes are a constant €4 billion – they do not vary with income.

a What is the consumption function?

b What is the equation that describes the aggregate expenditure curve?

c Calculate equilibrium expenditure.

d If investment decreases to €3 billion, what is the change in equilibrium expenditure and what is the size of the multiplier?

•7 Suppose that in problem 5 the price level is 100 and real GDP equals potential GDP. If investment increases by €100 billion,

a What is the change in the quantity of real GDP demanded?

b In the short run, does equilibrium real GDP increase by more than, less than, or the same amount as the increase in the quantity of real GDP demanded?

c In the long run, does equilibrium real GDP increase by more than, less than, or the same amount as the increase in the quantity of real GDP demanded?

d In the short run, does the price level in Zee rise, fall, or remain unchanged?

e In the long run, does the price level in Zee rise, fall, or remain unchanged?

8 Suppose that in problem 6 the price level is 100 and real GDP equals potential GDP. If investment increases by €50 billion,

a What is the change in the quantity of real GDP demanded?

b In the short run, does equilibrium real GDP increase by more than, less than, or the same amount as the increase in the quantity of real GDP demanded?

c In the long run, does equilibrium real GDP increase by more than, less than, or the same amount as the increase in the quantity of real GDP demanded?

d In the short run, does the price level in Antarctica rise, fall, or remain unchanged?

e In the long run, does the price level in Antarctica rise, fall, or remain unchanged?

Critical Thinking

1 Study Reading Between the Lines on pp. 514–515 and then answer the following questions.

a What has caused the fall in current value of household net wealth?

b What has caused the fall in the real value of household net wealth?

c What is the effect of the fall in the real value of wealth on consumer spending?

d What is the effect of a fall in the rate of interest on consumer spending?

e What is your prediction for real consumer spending in 2001 and 2002?

f Use the links on the Parkin, Powell and Matthews website to obtain quarterly data on real consumer spending in 2001 and 2002 and check your prediction.

2 Visit the Penn World Table website (linked from the Parkin, Powell and Matthews website) and obtain data on real GDP per person and consumption as a percentage of real GDP for the United States, China, South Africa, and Mexico since 1960.

a In a spreadsheet, multiply your real GDP data by the consumption percentage and divide by 100 to obtain data on real consumption expenditure per person.

b Make graphs like Figure 23.4, which show the relationship between consumption and real GDP for these four countries.

c Based on the numbers you've obtained, in which country do you expect the multiplier to be largest (other things being equal)?

d What other data would you need in order to calculate the multipliers for these countries?

e You are an Economic Assistant at HM Treasury. You've been asked to draft a note for the Chancellor that explains the power and limitations of the multiplier. The Chancellor wants only 250 words of crisp, clear, jargon-free explanation together with a lively example by tomorrow morning.

Appendix to Chapter 23
The Algebra of the Multiplier

This note explains the multiplier in greater detail. We begin by defining the symbols we need:

♦ Aggregate planned expenditure, AE

♦ Real GDP, Y

♦ Consumption expenditure, C

♦ Investment, I

♦ Government expenditures, G

♦ Exports, X

♦ Imports, M

♦ Net taxes, NT

♦ Disposable income, YD

♦ Autonomous consumption expenditure, a

♦ Marginal propensity to consume, b

♦ Marginal propensity to import, m

♦ Marginal tax rate, t

♦ Autonomous expenditure, A

Aggregate Expenditure

Aggregate planned expenditure (AE) is the sum of the planned amounts of consumption expenditure (C), investment (I), government expenditures (G), and exports (X) minus the planned amount of imports (M). That is:

$$AE = C + I + G + X - M$$

Consumption Function Consumption expenditure (C) depends on disposable income (YD) and we write the consumption function as:

$$C = a + bYD$$

Disposable income (YD) equals real GDP minus net taxes ($Y - NT$). So replacing YD with ($Y - NT$), the consumption function becomes:

$$C = a + b(Y - NT)$$

Net taxes equal real GDP (Y) multiplied by the marginal tax rate (t). That is:

$$NT = tY$$

Use this equation in the previous one to obtain:

$$C = a + b(1 - t)Y$$

This equation describes consumption expenditure as a function of real GDP.

Import Function Imports depend on real GDP and the import function is:

$$M = mY$$

Aggregate Expenditure Curve Use the consumption function and the import function to replace C and M in the aggregate planned expenditure equation. That is:

$$AE = a + b(1 - t)Y + I + G + X - mY$$

Collect the terms on the right-side of the equation that involve Y to obtain:

$$AE = [a + I + G + X] + [b(1 - t) - m]Y$$

Autonomous expenditure (A) is $[a + I + G + X]$, and the slope of the AE curve is $[b(1 - t) - m]$. So the equation for the AE curve, which is shown in Figure A23.1, is:

$$AE = A + [b(1 - t) - m]Y$$

Equilibrium Expenditure

Equilibrium expenditure occurs when aggregate planned expenditure (AE) equals real GDP (Y). That is:

Figure A23.1

Aggregate Expenditure Curve

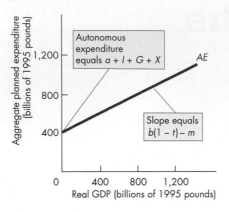

$$AE = A + [b(1 - t) - m]Y$$

$$AE = Y$$

replace AE with Y in the AE equation to obtain:

$$Y = A + [b(1 - t) - m]Y$$

The solution for Y is:

$$Y = \frac{1}{1 - [b(1 - t) - m]}A$$

The Multiplier

The multiplier equals the change in equilibrium expenditure and real GDP (Y) that results from a change in autonomous expenditure (A) divided by the change in autonomous expenditure. A change in autonomous expenditure (ΔA) changes equilibrium expenditure and real GDP (ΔY) by:

$$\Delta Y = \frac{1}{1 - [b(1 - t) - m]}\Delta A$$

$$\text{Multiplier} = \frac{1}{1 - [b(1 - t) - m]}$$

$$AE = Y$$

In Figure A23.2 below, the scales of the x-axis (real GDP) and the y-axis (aggregate planned expenditure) are identical, so the 45° line shows the points at which aggregate planned expenditure equals real GDP. That is, along the 45° line, AE equals Y.

The figure shows the point of equilibrium expenditure at the intersection of the AE curve and the 45° line.

To calculate equilibrium expenditure and real GDP, we solve the equations for the AE curve and the 45° line for the two unknown quantities AE and Y. So, starting with:

The slope of the AE curve is $b(1 - t) - m$, so the

$$\text{Multiplier} = \frac{1}{1 - \text{Slope of the } AE \text{ curve}}$$

Figure A23.2

Aggregate Expenditure Equals Aggregate Income

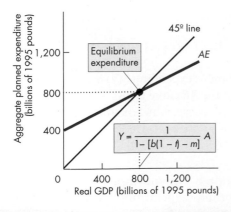

Figure A23.3

Multiplier Effect

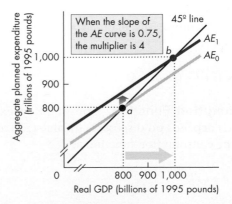

When the slope of the AE function is 0.75, the multiplier is 4.

The size of the multiplier depends on the slope of the AE curve and the larger the slope, the larger is the multiplier. So the multiplier is larger,

◆ The greater the marginal propensity to consume (b)

◆ The smaller the marginal tax rate (t)

◆ The smaller the marginal propensity to import (m)

An economy with no imports and no marginal taxes has $m = 0$ and $t = 0$. In this special case, the multiplier equals $1/(1 - b)$. If b is 0.75, then the multiplier is 4 as shown in the Figure A23.3. In an economy with $b = 0.75$, $t = 0.2$, and $m = 0.1$, the multiplier is 1 divided by 1 minus $0.75(1 - 0.2) - 0.1$, which equals 2. Make up some more examples to show the effects of b, t, and m on the multiplier.

The Multiplier in Action

THE FINANCIAL TIMES, 26 SEPTEMBER 2001 — FT

Tumbling shares cut household wealth by 9.7%

Ed Crooks

Household wealth in Britain has fallen by almost 10 per cent in real terms over the past year as a result of the fall in share prices.

The figures suggest that the British public may soon begin to reduce spending and increase their saving in order to restore their wealth.

A calculation by economists at Citigroup has shown that net household wealth, including shares, bonds, pension funds and houses, has dropped by 7.3 per cent since September 2000 – the steepest drop since official records were first collected in the 1960s.

Allowing for inflation, the real value of household wealth has fallen by 9.7 per cent – the sharpest fall since 1975.

The value of wealth held in houses and land has risen by 11.5 per cent over the year, principally as a result of rising house prices. But over half of all household wealth is now held in financial assets including insurance and pension funds, and the value of that has fallen by 13 per cent. The global fall in share prices has brought the FTSE 100 share index down over 25 per cent in the past 12 months.

Michael Saunders, UK economist at Citigroup, said that the effect of falling wealth would be to an extent offset by rising incomes.

'I would certainly expect the savings rate to rise a bit. But I don't think consumer demand will collapse the way it did on previous occasions when wealth fell in 1974–75 and 1990–92. Today incomes are stronger, and interest rates are lower.'

The Essence of the Story

- Household wealth is the purchasing power of all individuals' assets minus their debts. The value of household wealth fell by 9.7 per cent from September 2000 to September 2001.

- The composition of assets includes shares, bonds, pension funds and the value of houses.

- The total value of assets has fallen by 7.3 per cent in the year. Some components of wealth have increased in value, such as housing which has risen by 11.5 per cent but others, like shares, have fallen by 25 per cent.

- Over half of household assets are in the form of financial assets and in total these have fallen by over 13 per cent.

- Taking into account inflation, the fall in the real value of assets minus liabilities is 9.7 per cent.

Economic Analysis

■ The stock market collapse during 2000–2001 has reduced the current value of household net (assets minus debts) wealth.

■ House prices have risen but more than half of household wealth is made up of financial assets and these have fallen by more in value. Inflation has further eroded the real value of net wealth.

■ The decrease in wealth will reduce consumption expenditure as shown in Figure 1. CF_0 shifts down to CF_1.

■ However, the Bank of England has lowered interest rates but inflation has also fallen and real interest rates have stayed the same at about 4.5 per cent, as shown in Figure 2. This means that the fall in wealth has not been offset by a fall in real interest rates.

■ The overall effect is that unless there is a fall in real interest rates, the downward shift of the consumption function caused by the reduction in wealth will lead to a fall in aggregate expenditure as shown in Figure 3 as AE_0 shifts down to AE_1.

■ The article includes some poor economic thinking. The Citibank economist says that the fall in wealth will be offset by the rise in income, but consumption and income are interrelated. The fall in wealth will reduce consumption which in turn reduces income.

■ The fall in household wealth reinforces the view that there will be a recession in 2001–2002.

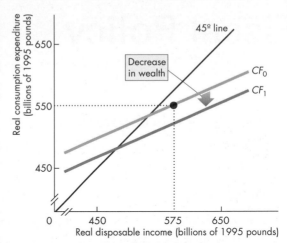

Figure 1 Decrease in wealth

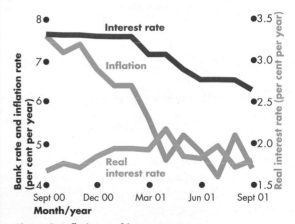

Figure 2 Inflation and interest rates

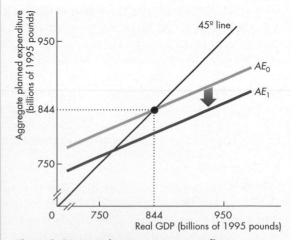

Figure 3 Decrease in aggregate expenditure

CHAPTER 24

Fiscal Policy

After studying this chapter you will be able to:

◆ Describe the recent history of government expenditures, tax revenues, and the budget deficit in the UK

◆ Distinguish between automatic and discretionary fiscal policy

◆ Define and explain the fiscal policy multipliers

◆ Explain the effects of fiscal policy in both the short run and the long run

◆ Distinguish between and explain the demand side and the supply side effects of fiscal policy

Balancing Acts at Westminster

In March 2001, the government planned to spend £394 billion between 2001 and 2002. What are the effects of government spending on the economy? Does it create jobs? Or does it destroy them? Does a pound spent by the government on goods and services have the same effect as a pound spent by someone else? ◆ The government planned to *spend* 42 pence of every pound earned, it also planned to tax us by about the same. Its plans were for tax and social security revenues of £398 billion. What are the effects of taxes on the economy? Do taxes harm employment and economic growth? ◆ The plan to have tax revenues that are greater than expenditures is rare. The United Kingdom had a strong budget surplus in 2000, but usually the government has planned to spend more than it expected to receive. ◆ But the government of the UK is not alone in Europe in spending less than what it received in revenues. Many of the governments of the countries in the European Union, ended up spending less than they received in revenues during 2000. ◆ Government debt as a percentage of GDP fell from 52 per cent in 1996–97 to 44 per cent in 1999–00. What are the effects of an ongoing government surplus and falling debt? Do they improve economic growth? Do they reduce the burden on future generations – on you and your children? Many of the countries that belong to the European Monetary Union have different levels of government deficits and government debt as a proportion of GDP. The stability pact made by countries in the EMU have specified ceilings on their budget deficits. For some countries this will mean reducing government expenditure and possibly imposing higher taxes. What will be the likely effects of such a policy on the individual countries and in Europe generally? In Reading Between the Lines, pp. 540–541, we look at the policy problems the French government face as a result of the stability pact.

◆ ◆ ◆ ◆ These are the questions that you will explore in this chapter. We'll begin by describing the budget and the components that contribute to it. We'll also look at the development of the budget in the United Kingdom and other EU countries. We'll then use the multiplier analysis of Chapter 23 and the aggregate supply–aggregate demand model of Chapter 22 to study the effects of the budget on the economy.

The Government Budget

Every year the Chancellor of the Exchequer makes an annual statement to Parliament of the expenditures and tax revenues of the government. The main purpose of the statement – known as the budget – is:

1 To state the items of expenditure of the government and to lay out the plans to finance its activities.

2 To stabilize the economy.

3 To raise the economy's long-term rate of growth.

The first, and original, purpose of the budget is to ensure that funds are available to finance the business of the government. Until the view that government spending can play a part in generating aggregate demand became generally accepted, the budget had no other purpose. The second purpose is to pursue the government's fiscal policy. **Fiscal policy** is the use of the budget to achieve macroeconomic objectives such as full employment, sustained long-term economic growth and price-level stability. It is this second purpose that we focus on in this chapter.

Highlights of the 2001 Budget

Table 24.1 shows the main items in the **government budget**. The numbers are projected amounts for the fiscal years April 2001 to end-March 2002. Notice first the three main parts of the table: *expenditures* are the government's outlays, *total receipts* are the government's receipts and the *deficit* is the amount by which the government's expenditures exceed its tax revenues. The next item is the public corporations' market and overseas borrowing. This represents the net borrowing of the industries that come under state control. In the United Kingdom this item is small and is expected to decline as more and more public enterprises are privatized. The final item is the Public Sector Net Cash Requirement (PSNCR) which refers to the deficit for the public sector as a whole.

Expenditures

Expenditures are classified in three categories:

1 Expenditure on goods and services.

2 Transfer payments.

3 Debt interest.

The largest item of spending, is government expenditure. *Expenditure on goods and services* are expenditures on final goods and services. These expenditures

Table 24.1 The Public Finances in 2000–2001 and 2001–2002

Item	2000/01	2001/02
	(billions of pounds)	
Expenditure	363.7	393.7
Expenditure on goods and services	197.0	217.0
Transfer payments	139.9	149.7
Debt interest	26.8	27.0
Total receipts	382.1	398.4
Value added taxes and other indirect taxes	131.8	137.5
Taxes on income and wealth	144.3	151.7
Social security contributions	61.6	62.8
Other receipts and royalties	44.4	46.4
Financial surplus (–) deficit(+)	–18.4	–4.7
Financial transactions	–18.6	4.3
PSNCR (surplus –, deficit +)	–37.0	–0.4

Source: HM Treasury, *Budget 2001.*

include those on defence, the National Health Service, computers for schools, construction of new roads and motorways, and urban regeneration. This component of the budget is government purchases of goods and services that appears in the circular flow of expenditure and income and in the national income and product accounts (see Chapter 20, p. 427).

Transfer payments are payments to individuals, businesses, other levels of government and the rest of the world. It includes social security benefits, health care, unemployment benefits, welfare supplements, grants to local authorities and aid to developing countries.

Debt interest is the interest on the government debt minus interest received by the government on its own investments.

Total current receipts

Total current receipts come from four sources:

1 Taxes on income.

2 Social security contributions.

3 Value added taxes (VAT) and other taxes on expenditure.

4 Other receipts and royalties.

The largest source of revenue is taxes on *income and wealth*, which includes taxes on corporate profits. These are the taxes paid by individuals on their incomes, assets and the taxes expected from the

Figure 24.1

The UK Government Spending

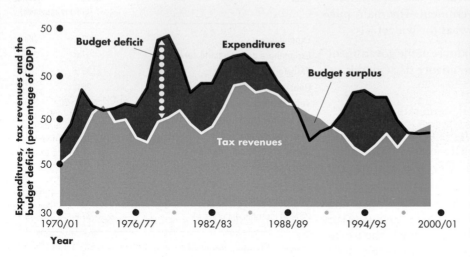

The figure records the UK government's expenditures, tax revenues and budget deficit from 1970/71 to 2000/01. During the 1970s the deficit became large and persisted through to the 1980s. A budget surplus occurred in the late 1980s, but the budget deficit increased again in the 1990s. The increase in the 1990s came about through a combination of a decrease in tax revenues from tax cuts in the 1980s and an increase in expenditures. The budget was in balance in 1997/98 and in surplus in 1998/99 and 1999/00.

Source: HM Treasury, *Budget 2001*.

profits of businesses and the rates businesses pay for government services. The second largest source of revenue is *taxes on expenditure*. These are the taxes paid by consumers on goods that carry VAT (currently 17.5 per cent), and special duties and taxes on gambling, alcoholic drinks, petrol and luxury items and imported goods. Third in size are *social security contributions*. These are taxes paid by workers and employers to fund the welfare and health programmes. Fourth in size are *other receipts and royalties*. These are small items including oil royalties, stamp duties, car taxes, miscellaneous rents, dividends from abroad and profits from nationalized industries.

Deficit

The government's budget balance is equal to its tax revenues minus its expenditures. That is:

Budget balance = Tax revenues − Expenditures

If tax revenues exceed expenditures, the government (the public sector as a whole) has a **budget surplus**. If expenditures exceed tax revenues, the government has a **budget deficit**. If tax revenues equal expenditures, the government has a **balanced budget**. In 2001/02, with projected expenditures of £393.7 billion and tax revenues of £398.4 billion, the government

projected a surplus of £4.7 billion. After allowing for borrowing from public corporations the projected PSNCR was a surplus £0.4 billion.

This is quite a small surplus, but this was not the case in previous years. To get a better sense of the magnitude of taxes, spending and the deficit we often express them as percentages of GDP. Expressing them in this way lets us see how large government is relative to the size of the economy, and it also helps us to study *changes* in the scale of government over time.

How typical is the budget of 2001? Let's look at its recent history.

The Budget in Historical Perspective

Figure 24.1 shows the government's tax revenues, expenditures and budget deficit since 1970/71. Throughout most of this period there was a budget deficit. The deficit rises in recessions and falls in recoveries. The deficit rose to a peak following the recession of the 1970s. Government receipts were actually higher than expenditures in the fiscal years 1987–89. But the deficit increased again during the 1990s and has fallen sharply and has been in surplus in recent years.

Why did the government deficit grow so sharply in the 1990s? The immediate answer is that expenditures

Figure 24.2

UK Government Tax Revenues and Expenditures

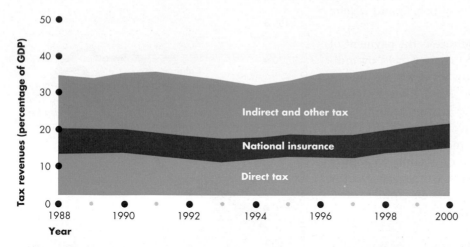

(a) Tax revenues

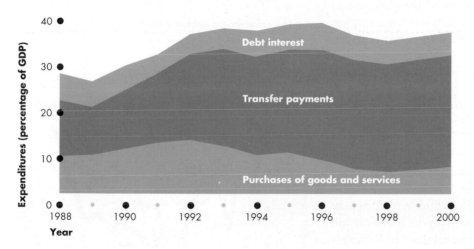

(b) Expenditures

Part (a) shows the three components of government tax revenues: direct income taxes (including corporate income taxes), indirect taxes (including VAT) and national insurance contributions. Revenues from direct income taxes declined in 1993 but rose in 1994. Receipts from direct taxes fell in 1994 and rose consistently through to 2000.

Part (b) shows three components of government expenditures: purchases of goods and services, debt interest and transfer payments. Purchases of goods and services has fallen steadily since 1992. Transfer payments have risen in the 1990s recession. Debt interest has fallen since 1996.

Source: HM Treasury, *Budget 2001.*

increased and tax revenues decreased. But which components of expenditures increased and which sources of tax revenues decreased? Let's look at tax revenues and expenditures in a bit more detail.

Tax Revenues

Figure 24.2(a) shows the components of tax revenues received by the government as a percentage of GDP, between 1988 and 2000. Central government receipts increased as a percentage of GDP to 1991 and then declined in the following three years. The reason for this is that the recession reduced the amount of tax receipts obtained from direct taxes. Firms' profits

declined, reducing the take from corporate taxes, and the increase in unemployment reduced the amount of tax gained from personal taxes. Tax revenues as a percentage of GDP increased from 1994 to 2000 as the economy settled into a long boom.

Expenditures

Figure 24.2(b) shows the components of central government expenditures as percentages of GDP, between 1988 and 2000. Total expenditures increased as a proportion of GDP during the first half of the 1990s. The main reason for this is that transfer payments increased substantially while purchases of goods and services increased only slightly up until 1992. Transfer payments increased because the unemployment and early retirements caused by the recession have led to a higher level of benefit and welfare payments.

Part of government expenditure is the payment of interest on the existing level of debt held by individuals. A high level of debt means that more interest payments have to be made. The United Kingdom does not have a high level of debt in relation to its GDP in comparison with many other countries in the European Union. However, high debt interest payments can make it difficult for a country to control its deficit. To understand why, we need to see the connection between the deficit and government debt.

Deficit and Debt

Government debt is the total amount of borrowing by the government. It is the sum of past deficits minus the sum of past surpluses. If the government has a deficit, its debt increases, and if it has a surplus, its debt decreases. Once a persistent deficit emerges, the deficit begins to feed on itself. The deficit leads to increased borrowing; increased borrowing leads to larger interest payments; and larger interest payments lead to a larger deficit. This is one of the reasons high-debt countries like Italy and Belgium find it difficult to reduce their debt.

Figure 24.3(a) shows the history of government debt in Italy and Belgium since 1970. In the case of Italy, the level of debt as a proportion of GDP doubled in the decade of the 1980s. With Belgium, the level of debt increased sharply in the recession years of the early 1980s but has declined only moderately at the end of the decade. Figure 24.3(b) shows the budget deficits of each country as a percentage of GDP. A negative value in the chart indicates that revenues are less than expenditures. The peak in the deficit occurred in the recession of the early 1980s, but both countries succeeded in controlling their deficit in 1998 to qualify for entry to the European Monetary Union and have reduced their deficits further as part of the stability pact that places restrictions on fiscal policy for the eurozone economies.

Debt and Capital

When individuals and businesses incur debts, they usually do so to buy capital – assets that yield a return. In fact, the main point of debt is to enable people to buy assets that will earn a return that exceeds the interest paid on the debt. The government is similar to individuals and businesses in this

Figure 24.3

The Government Debt of Italy and Belgium

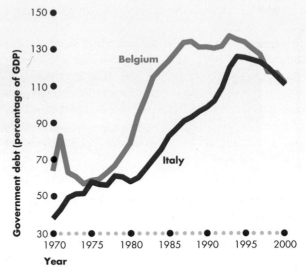

(a) The government debt of Italy and Belgium

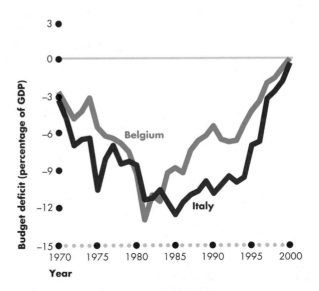

(b) The budget deficit of Italy and Belgium

In part (a) you can see the government debt (the accumulation of past budget deficits less past budget surpluses) of Italy and Belgium. Both countries had debt in excess of 100 per cent of GDP in 2000. Both countries have reduced their debt since 1995. In part (b) you can see the budget deficits of both countries. The peak in the deficit occurred in the recession of the early 1980s. Since the 1980s, both countries have been struggling to get their respective budget deficits below the 3 per cent target set as a condition for European Monetary Union.

Source: *European Economy, Economic Trends*, March/April 2001.

regard. Much government expenditure is on public assets that yield a return. Roads, bridges, schools and universities, public libraries and the stock of national defence capital all yield a social rate of return that probably far exceeds the interest rate the government pays on its debt.

Total government debt in the United Kingdom was around £400 billion in 1999, whereas the capital stock of the general government – that is, central government, local governments and public enterprises – was nearly £450 billion. Therefore the UK public finances are not in bad shape. But how do the deficit and debt compare with deficits and debts in the rest of the European Union?

The Budget Deficit and Debt Levels in a European Perspective

Do other countries in Europe have large budget deficits or do they have budget surpluses? Are their levels of debt comparable with that of the United Kingdom? Figure 24.4 answers these questions. Figure 24.4(a) shows the government budget deficits of all countries in the European Union as a percentage of GDP in 1999. Figure 24.4(b) shows the levels of debt as a percentage of GDP. Portugal, Austria, Italy, France, Spain, Greece, Germany and Belgium had budget deficits in 1999. But the UK, Sweden, Finland, Netherlands, Luxembourg, Ireland and Denmark has budget surpluses. Belgium, Greece and Italy have levels of debt in excess of 100 per cent of GDP. The countries that have joined the EMU have a stabilty pact that places a ceiling of 3 per cent of GDP on their budget deficits. This can be sustained by cuts in government spending or increases in taxes. What will be the likely effects of such cuts in spending? This question will be examined in the next section.

Figure 24.4

Government Deficits and Debt in the European Union

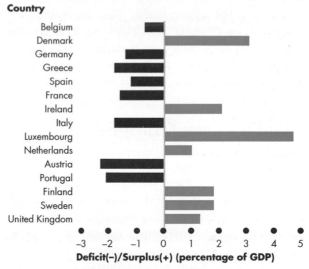

(a) Government deficits in European Union

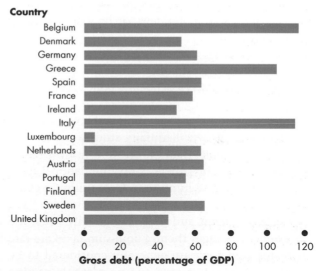

(b) General government gross debt

Part (a) shows that half of the countries in the European Union had budget deficits (negative being a deficit) in 1999. The largest deficits are Portugal, Austria, Greece and Italy. Countries that had a surplus included Denmark, Ireland, Sweden, UK and Finland. Part (b) shows that many countries in the European Union have large levels of debt in relation to GDP. These include Belgium, Greece and Italy. Countries with low relative levels of debt include Luxembourg, Denmark, Ireland, Finland and the United Kingdom.

Source: *European Economy, Economic Trends*, March/April 2001.

Review Quiz

◆ What are the main functions of fiscal policy?
◆ What are the main items of government revenues and expenditures?
◆ Under what circumstances does the government have a budget surplus? Which countries in the EU ran a budget surplus in 1999?
◆ Explain the connection between a government deficit and a government debt.

We have now described the government budget. Your next task is to study the effects of fiscal policy on the economy. We'll begin by learning about its effects on expenditure plans when the price level is sticky. You will see that fiscal policy has multiplier effects like the expenditure multipliers that are explained in Chapter 23. Then we'll study the influences of fiscal policy on both aggregate demand and aggregate supply and look at its short-run and long-run effects on real GDP and the price level.

Fiscal Policy Multipliers

Fiscal policy actions can be either automatic or discretionary. **Automatic fiscal policy** is a change in fiscal policy that is triggered by the state of the economy. For example, an increase in unemployment triggers an *automatic* increase in payments to unemployed workers. A fall in incomes triggers an *automatic* decrease in tax receipts. That is, fiscal policy adjusts automatically. **Discretionary fiscal policy** is a policy action that is initiated by the Chancellor of the Exchequer. It requires a change in tax laws or in some spending programme. For example, a decrease in the standard rate of income tax or an increase in defence spending are discretionary fiscal policy actions. That is, discretionary fiscal policy is a deliberate policy action.

We begin by studying the effects of *discretionary* changes in government spending and taxes. To focus on the essentials, we'll initially study a model economy that is simpler than the one in which we live. In our model economy, there is no international trade and the taxes are all lump sum. **Lump sum taxes** are taxes that do not vary with real GDP. They are fixed by the government and they change only when the government changes them. Lump-sum taxes are rare in reality and they are generally considered to be unfair because rich people and poor people pay the same amount of tax. (It is said that the former prime minister, Margaret Thatcher, lost her job because of the unpopularity of a lump sum tax called the 'poll tax', which was a fixed tax per person to pay for local government services.) We use lump sum taxes in our model economy only because they make the principles we are studying easier to understand. Once we've grasped the principles, we'll explore our real economy with its international trade and income taxes – taxes that *do* vary with real GDP.

Like our real economy, the model economy we study is constantly bombarded by shocks. Exports fluctuate because incomes fluctuate in the rest of the world. Business investment fluctuates because of swings in profit expectations and interest rates. These fluctuations set up multiplier effects that begin a recession or a recovery. If a recession takes hold, unemployment increases and incomes fall. If a recovery becomes too strong, inflationary pressures build up. To minimize the effects of these swings in spending, the government might change either its purchases of goods and services or net taxes (taxes minus transfer payments, see Chapter 23, p. 500). By changing either of these items, the government can influence aggregate expenditure and real GDP. But it also changes its budget deficit or surplus. An alternative fiscal policy action is to change purchases and taxes together so budget balance does not change. We are going to study the initial effects of these discretionary fiscal policy actions in the very short run when the price level is sticky. Each of these actions creates a multiplier effect on real GDP. These multipliers are:

◆ The government purchases multiplier.

◆ The lump-sum tax multiplier.

◆ The balanced budget multiplier.

The Government Purchases Multiplier

The **government purchases multiplier** is the amount by which a change in government purchases of goods and services is multiplied to determine the change in equilibrium expenditure that it generates.

Government purchases are a component of aggregate expenditure. So when government purchases change, aggregate expenditure changes and so does real GDP. The change in real GDP induces a change in consumption expenditure which brings an additional change in aggregate expenditure. A multiplier process ensues. This multiplier process is like the one described in Chapter 23, pp. 497–500. Let's look at an example.

Peace Dividend Multiplier

After the fall of the Berlin Wall and the ending of the Cold War, the NATO countries looked forward to a reduction in expenditure on defence and a scaling back of arms spending. In the United Kingdom, this has led to a rationalization of military installations and restructuring of operations. Part of the restructuring has been the downgrading of the Rosyth naval base in Scotland, and the removal of its main

Table 24.2 The Government Purchases Multiplier

	Real GDP (Y)	Taxes (T)	Disposable income (YT)	Consumption expenditure (C)	Investment (I)	Initial government purchases (G)	Initial aggregate planned expenditure (AE = C + I + G)	New government purchases (G')	New aggregate planned expenditure (AE' = C + I + G')
					(billions of pounds)				
a	500	50	450	375	100	50	525	100	575
b	600	50	550	450	100	50	600	100	650
c	700	50	650	525	100	50	675	100	725
d	800	50	750	600	100	50	750	100	800
e	900	50	850	675	100	50	825	100	875

operations to Portsmouth in the south of England. The downgrading of the Rosyth naval base will badly affect a region that is already blighted by high unemployment. The reduction in military expenditure will have severe effects on the region's GDP and employment in the short term. Because military personnel and workers on the base spend most of their incomes locally, consumption expenditure in the region depends on defence spending in the area. Retail shops and hotels depend on the spending power of people whose incomes are associated or linked with the base. In the long term the Rosyth area will learn to develop other types of industries but in the short term there will be negative multiplier effects for the region.

The Size of the Multiplier

Table 24.2 illustrates the government purchases multiplier with a numerical example. The first column lists various possible levels of real GDP. Our task is to find equilibrium expenditure and the change in real GDP when government purchases change. The second column shows taxes. They are fixed at £50 billion, regardless of the level of real GDP. (This is an assumption that keeps your attention on the key idea and makes the calculations easier to do.) The third column calculates disposable income. Because taxes are lump sum, disposable income equals real GDP minus the £50 billion of taxes. For example, in row b, real GDP is £600 billion and disposable income is £550 billion. The next column shows consumption expenditure. In this example, the *marginal propensity to consume* is 0.75 or 3/4. That is, a £1 increase in disposable income brings a 75 pence increase in consumption expenditure. Check this fact by calculating the increase in consumption expenditure when

disposable income increases by £100 billion from row b to row c. Consumption expenditure increases by £75 billion. The next column shows investment, which is a constant of £100 billion. And the next column shows the initial level of government purchases, which is £50 billion. Aggregate planned expenditure is the sum of consumption expenditure, investment and government purchases.

Equilibrium expenditure and real GDP occur when aggregate planned expenditure equals real GDP. In this example, equilibrium expenditure is £600 billion (highlighted in row b of the table).

The final two columns of the table show what happens when government purchases increase by £50 billion to £100 billion. Aggregate planned expenditure increases by £50 billion at each level of real GDP. For example, at the initial real GDP of £600 billion, aggregate planned expenditure increases to £650 billion. Because aggregate planned expenditure exceeds real GDP, stocks decrease and firms increase production to restore their stocks. Output, incomes and expenditure continue to increase. The increased incomes bring a further increase in aggregate planned expenditure. But aggregate planned expenditure increases by less than income, and eventually a new equilibrium is reached. In this example, the new equilibrium expenditure is at a real GDP of £800 billion.

A £50 billion increase in government purchases has increased equilibrium expenditure and real GDP by £200 billion. Therefore the government purchases multiplier is 4. The size of the multiplier depends on the marginal propensity to consume, which in this example, is 3/4. The following formula shows the connection between the government purchases multiplier and the marginal propensity to consume (*MPC*):

Figure 24.5

The Government Purchases Multiplier

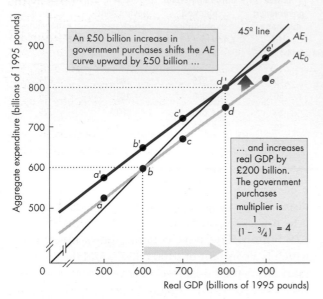

Initially, the aggregate expenditure curve is AE_0 and real GDP is £600 billion (at point *b*). An increase in government purchases of £50 billion increases aggregate planned expenditure at each level of real GDP by £50 billion. The aggregate planned expenditure curve shifts upward from AE_0 to AE_1 – a parallel shift. At the initial real GDP of £600 billion, aggregate planned expenditure is now £650 billion. Because aggregate planned expenditure is greater than real GDP, real GDP increases. The new equilibrium is reached when real GDP is £800 billion – the point at which the AE_1 curve intersects the 45° line (at *d'*). In this example, the government purchases multiplier is 4.

$$\text{Government purchases multiplier} = \frac{1}{(1 - MPC)}$$

Let's check this formula by using the numbers in the above example. The marginal propensity to consume is 3/4, so the government purchases multiplier is 4.

Figure 24.5 illustrates the government purchases multiplier. Initially, aggregate planned expenditure is shown by the curve labelled AE_0. The points on this curve, labelled *a* to *e*, correspond with the rows of Table 24.2. This aggregate expenditure curve intersects the 45° line at the equilibrium level of real GDP, which is £600 billion.

When government purchases increase by £50 billion, the aggregate expenditure curve shifts upward by that amount to AE_1. With this new aggregate expenditure curve, equilibrium real GDP increases to

£800 billion. The increase in real GDP is four times the increase in government purchases. The government purchases multiplier is 4.

You've seen that in the very short term, when the price level is sticky, an increase in government purchases increases real GDP. But to produce more output, more people must be employed, so in the short term an increase in government purchases can create jobs.

Changing its purchases of goods and services is one way in which the government can try to stimulate the economy. A second way in which the government might act to increase real GDP in the very short run is by decreasing lump sum taxes. Let's see how this action works.

The Lump Sum Tax Multiplier

The **lump sum tax multiplier** is the amount by which a change in lump sum taxes is multiplied to determine the change in equilibrium expenditure that it generates. An *increase* in taxes leads to a *decrease* in disposable income and a decrease in aggregate expenditure. The amount by which aggregate expenditure initially decreases is determined by the marginal propensity to consume. In our example, the marginal propensity to consume is 3/4, so a £1 tax cut increases disposable income by £1 and increases aggregate expenditure initially by 75 pence.

This initial change in aggregate expenditure has a multiplier just like the government purchases multiplier. We've seen that the government purchases multiplier is $1/(1 - MPC)$. Because a tax *increase* leads to a *decrease* in expenditure, the lump sum tax multiplier is *negative*. And because a change in lump sum taxes changes aggregate expenditure initially by only the *MPC* multiplied by the tax change, the lump sum tax multiplier is equal to:

$$\text{Lump sum tax multiplier} = \frac{-MPC}{(1 - MPC)}$$

In our example, the marginal propensity to consume is 3/4, so the lump sum multiplier is:

$$\text{Lump sum tax multiplier} = \frac{-3/4}{(1 - 3/4)} = -3$$

Figure 24.6 illustrates the lump sum tax multiplier. Initially, the aggregate expenditure curve is AE_0 and equilibrium expenditure is £800 billion. Taxes increase by £100 billion and disposable income falls by that amount. With a marginal propensity to consume

Figure 24.6

The Lump Sum Tax Multiplier

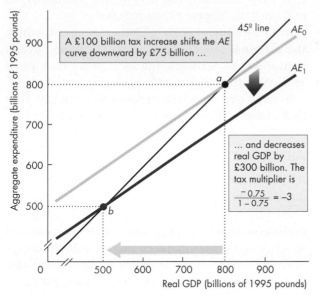

Initially, the aggregate expenditure curve is AE_0, and equilibrium expenditure is £800 billion. The marginal propensity to consume is 0.75. Lump sum taxes increase by £100 billion, so disposable income falls by £100 billion. The decrease in aggregate expenditure is found by multiplying this change in disposable income by the marginal propensity to consume and is £100 billion x 0.75 = £75 billion. The aggregate expenditure curve shifts *downward* by this amount to AE_1. Equilibrium expenditure falls by £300 billion, and the lump-sum tax multiplier is –3.

of 3/4, aggregate expenditure decreases initially by £75 billion and the aggregate expenditure curve shifts downward by that amount to AE_1. Equilibrium expenditure and real GDP fall by £300 billion to £500 billion. The lump sum tax multiplier is –3.

Lump Sum Transfers

The lump sum tax multiplier also tells us the effects of a change in lump sum transfer payments. Transfer payments are like negative taxes, so an increase in transfer payments works like a decrease in taxes. Because the tax multiplier is negative, a decrease in taxes increases expenditure. An increase in transfer payments also increases expenditure. So the lump sum transfer payments multiplier is positive. It is:

$$\text{Lump sum transfer payments multiplier} = \frac{MPC}{(1 - MPC)}$$

The Balanced Budget Multiplier

A balanced budget fiscal policy action is one that changes *both* government purchases and taxes by the same amount so that the government's budget deficit or surplus remains *unchanged*. The **balanced budget multiplier** is the amount by which a simultaneous and equal change in government purchases and taxes is multiplied to determine the change in equilibrium expenditure. What is the multiplier effect of this fiscal policy action?

To find out, we must combine the government purchases multiplier and the lump sum tax multiplier. These two multipliers are:

$$\text{Government purchases multiplier} = \frac{1}{(1 - MPC)}$$

$$\text{Lump sum tax multiplier} = \frac{-MPC}{(1 - MPC)}$$

Adding these two multipliers gives the balanced budget multiplier, which is:

$$\text{Balanced budget multiplier} = \frac{1 - MPC}{1 - MPC} = 1$$

The balanced budget is smaller than the other multipliers but it is not zero. This fact is interesting because it means that in principle, fiscal policy can be used to increase aggregate planned expenditure if a recession is expected without increasing the government deficit. It also means that in the long run, as government grows, even if the growth of taxes keeps pace with the growth of expenditures, government adds to aggregate demand and squeezes out some private consumption expenditure or private investment, or both.

Induced Taxes and Welfare Spending

In the examples we've studied so far, taxes are lump sum taxes. But in reality, net taxes (taxes minus transfer payments) vary with the state of the economy.

On the tax revenues side of the budget, the government passes tax laws that define the tax *rates* to be paid, not the tax *pounds* to be paid. As a consequence, tax *revenues* depend on real GDP. We call those taxes that vary as real GDP varies **induced taxes**. If the economy is in an expansion phase of the business cycle, induced taxes increase because real GDP increases. If the economy is in a recession phase of the business cycle, induced taxes decrease because real GDP decreases.

On the government expenditures side of the budget, the government pays out various benefits, principally to unemployed workers in the form of the job seekers' allowance. But it also subsidizes training programmes and start-up schemes, which result in transfer payments that depend on the economic state of individual citizens and businesses. For example, when the economy is in a recession, unemployment is high and government transfer payments increase. When the economy is in a boom, transfer payments decline.

The existence of induced taxes and benefits decreases the government purchases and lump sum tax multipliers because they loosen the link between real GDP and disposable income and so dampen the effect of a change in real GDP on consumption expenditure. When real GDP increases, induced taxes increase and benefits decrease. So disposable income does not increase by as much as the increase in real GDP. As a result, consumption expenditure does not increase by as much as it otherwise would have done and the multiplier effect is reduced.

The extent to which induced taxes and benefits decrease the multiplier depends on the *marginal tax rate*. The marginal tax rate is the proportion of an additional pound of real GDP that flows to the government in net taxes (taxes minus transfer payments). The higher the marginal tax rate, the larger is the proportion of an additional pound of real GDP that is paid to the government and the smaller is the induced change in consumption expenditure. The smaller the change in consumption expenditure induced by a change in real GDP, the smaller is the multiplier effect of a change in government purchases or lump sum taxes.

International Trade and Fiscal Policy Multipliers

Not all expenditure on final goods and services in the United Kingdom is on domestically produced goods and services. Some of it is on imports – foreign-produced goods and services. The extent to which an additional pound of real GDP is spent on imports is determined by the *marginal propensity to import*. Expenditure on imports does not generate UK real GDP and does not lead to an increase in UK consumption expenditure. The larger the marginal propensity to import, the smaller is the increase in consumption expenditure induced by an increase

in real GDP and the smaller are the government purchases and lump sum tax multipliers. (Imports affect the fiscal policy multipliers in exactly the same way that they influence the investment multiplier, as explained in Chapter 23, see p. 500.)

In today's increasingly global economy in which the marginal propensity to import is much greater than it was 20 years ago, the fiscal policy multipliers are smaller than they used to be.

So far, we've studied *discretionary* fiscal policy. Let's look at automatic stabilizers.

Automatic Stabilizers

Automatic stabilizers are mechanisms that operate without the need for explicit action by the government. Their very name is borrowed from engineering and conjures up images of shock absorbers, thermostats and sophisticated devices that keep aircraft and ships steady in turbulent air and seas. Automatic fiscal stabilizers arise from the fact that income taxes and transfer payments fluctuate with real GDP. If real GDP begins to fall, tax revenues also fall and transfer payments rise. These changes in taxes and transfers affect the economy. Let's study the budget deficit over the business cycle.

Fiscal Policy over the Business Cycle

Figure 24.7 shows the business cycle and fluctuations in the budget deficit since 1980. Part (a) shows the fluctuations of real GDP around potential GDP. Part (b) shows the government budget deficit (the PSNCR). Both parts highlight the most recent recession by shading this period. By comparing the two parts of the figure, you can see the relationship between the business cycle and the budget deficit. As a rule, when the economy is in the expansion phase of a business cycle, the budget deficit declines. (In the figure, a declining deficit means a deficit that is getting closer to zero.) As the expansion slows before the recession begins, the budget deficit increases. It continues to increase during the recession and for a further period after the recession is over. Then, when the expansion is well under way, the budget deficit declines again.

The budget deficit fluctuates with the business cycle because both tax revenues and expenditures fluctuate with real GDP. As real GDP increases during an expansion, tax revenues increase and transfer payments decrease, so the budget deficit automatically decreases. As real GDP decreases during a recession, tax revenues decrease and transfer payments increase, so the budget deficit automatically increases.

Figure 24.7

The Business Cycle and the Budget Deficit

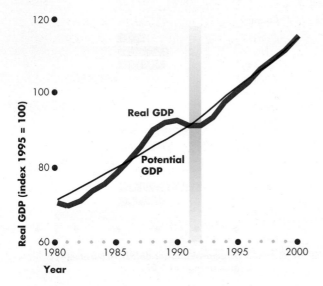

(a) Real GDP and potential GDP

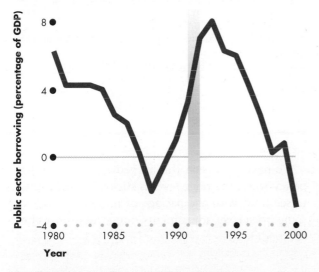

(b) The UK public sector net cash requirement

As real GDP fluctuates around potential GDP (part a), the budget deficit fluctuates (part b). During a recession (shaded areas), tax revenues decrease, transfer payments increase and the budget deficit increases. The deficit also increases *before* a recession as the growth rate of real GDP slows and *after* a recession before the growth rate of real GDP speeds up. When the growth rate of real GDP is high during a recovery, tax revenues increase, transfer payments decrease and the deficit decreases.

Sources: National Statistics.

Fluctuations in investment or exports have a multiplier effect on real GDP. But automatic fluctuations in tax revenues (and the budget deficit) act as an automatic stabilizer. They decrease the swings in disposable income and make the multiplier effect smaller. They dampen both the expansions and recessions.

The Cyclically Adjusted Deficit

The cyclically adjusted deficit is a measure for judging whether the budget deficit is cyclical or structural. A **cyclical deficit** is a budget deficit that is present only because real GDP is less than potential GDP and taxes are temporarily low and transfer payments are temporarily high. A **structural deficit** is a budget that is in deficit even though real GDP equals potential GDP. With a structural deficit, expenditures are too high relative to tax revenues over the entire business cycle.

Figure 24.8 illustrates the concepts of cyclical and structural deficits. The blue curve shows expenditures. When real GDP is less than potential GDP, transfer payments are temporarily high. As real GDP increases, transfer payments fall and expenditures decrease. The green curve shows tax revenues. Because most taxes increase with income, tax revenues increase as real GDP increases. In this example, if real GDP is £750 billion, the government has a *balanced budget*. Expenditures and tax revenues each equal £140 billion. If real GDP is £650 billion, expenditures exceed tax revenues and there is a budget deficit. And if real GDP is £850 billion, expenditures are less than tax revenues and there is a budget surplus.

To determine whether there is a structural deficit, we need to know potential GDP. If, in Figure 24.8, potential GDP is £825 billion, the budget has a structural deficit of zero. As the real GDP fluctuates, the budget fluctuates around zero. If, in Figure 24.8, potential GDP is £725 billion, there is a structural deficit, and if potential GDP is £925 billion, there is a structural surplus.

The EU Commission estimate that the United Kingdom has a structural budget surplus of 1.3 per cent of potential GDP. However, they calculate that there are a number of countries in the EU that have significant structural budget deficits. Figure 24.9 shows a selection of countries' structural budget deficits. Sweden, Netherlands, Ireland, Finland, Denmark and the UK have structural budget surpluses, but Portugal, Austria, Greece and France have large structural budget deficits. This means that unless public expenditure is brought under control, these countries will still have budget deficits even when real GDP equals potential GDP.

Figure 24.8

Cyclical and Structural Deficits

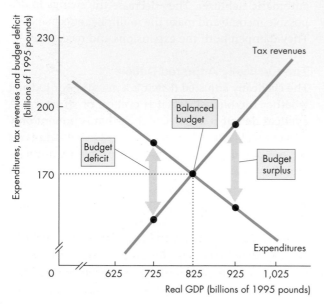

Government expenditures (blue line) decrease as real GDP increases because transfer payments decrease. Tax revenues (green line) increase as real GDP increases because most taxes are linked to income and expenditures. If real GDP is £825 billion, the government has a *balanced budget*. If real GDP is less than £825 billion, expenditures exceed tax revenues and the government has a budget deficit. If real GDP exceeds £825 billion, expenditures are less than tax revenues and the government has a budget surplus. If potential GDP is £825 billion, there is not a structural deficit – the budget deficits and surpluses are cyclical. But if potential GDP is less than £825 billion, there is a structural deficit.

Figure 24.9

Structural Budget Deficits in the European Union

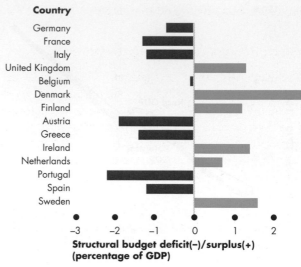

The EU Commission calculates that most of the countries in the European Union will have had a structural budget deficit in 1999. The United Kingdom has an estimated structural budget surplus of 1.3 per cent of potential GDP. Portugal, Austria and Greece have had high structural budget deficits in 1999, while Denmark, Ireland and Sweden have had structural budget surpluses.

Source: *European Economy, Economic Trends*, March/April 2001.

Review Quiz

◆ Explain why, when the price level is fixed, does a change in government expenditures or autonomous taxes have a multiplier effect on real GDP.

◆ Explain why the multiplier effect of a change in government purchases is greater than that of a change in lump sum taxes.

◆ Explain why the balanced budget multiplier is one.

◆ How do the presence of income taxes and imports influence the fiscal policy multipliers?

◆ Why do income taxes and transfer payments work as automatic stabilizers to dampen the business cycle?

We have now seen the immediate effects of fiscal policy when the price level is sticky. The next task is to see how, with the passage of more time and with some price level adjustments, these multiplier effects are modified.

Fiscal Policy Multipliers and the Price Level

We've seen how real GDP responds to changes in fiscal policy when the price level is fixed and all the adjustments that take place are in spending, income and production. Once production starts to change, prices also start to change. The price level and real GDP change together, and the economy moves to a new short-run equilibrium.

To study the simultaneous changes in real GDP and the price level that result from fiscal policy, we use the *AS–AD* model of Chapter 22, pp. 464–480. In the long run, the price level and the money wage rate responds to fiscal policy. As these adjustments occur the economy moves to a new long-run equilibrium.

We begin by looking at the effects of fiscal policy on aggregate demand and the *AD* curve.

Fiscal Policy and Aggregate Demand

The relationship between aggregate demand, aggregate expenditure, and equilibrium expenditure is covered in Chapter 23, pp. 486–507. You are now going to use what you learned there to work out what happens to aggregate demand, the price level, real GDP and jobs when fiscal policy changes. We'll start by looking at the effects of a change in fiscal policy on aggregate demand.

Figure 24.10 shows the effects of an increase in government purchases on aggregate demand. Initially, the aggregate expenditure curve is AE_0 in part (a), and the aggregate demand curve is AD_0 in part (b). The price level is 115, real GDP is £825 billion, and the economy is at point *a* in both parts of the figure. Now suppose that government purchases increase by £50 billion. At a constant price level of 115, the aggregate expenditure curve shifts upward to AE_1. This curve intersects the 45° line at an equilibrium expenditure of £1,025 billion at point *b*. This amount is the aggregate quantity of goods and services demanded at a price level of 115, as shown by point *b* in part (b). Point *b* lies on a new aggregate demand curve. The aggregate demand curve has shifted rightward to AD_1.

The distance by which the aggregate demand curve shifts rightward is determined by the government purchases multiplier. The larger the multiplier, the larger is the shift in the aggregate demand curve resulting from a given change in government purchases. In this example, a £50 billion increase in government purchases produces a £200 billion increase in the aggregate quantity of goods and services demanded at each price level. The multiplier is 4. So the £50 billion increase in government purchases shifts the aggregate demand curve rightward by £200 billion.

Figure 24.10 shows the effects of an increase in government purchases. But a similar effect occurs for *any* expansionary fiscal policy. An **expansionary fiscal policy** is an increase in government expenditures or a decrease in tax revenues.

Figure 24.10 can also be used to illustrate the effects of a contractionary fiscal policy. A **contractionary**

Figure 24.10

Changes in Government Purchases and Aggregate Demand

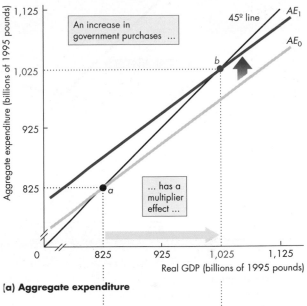

(a) Aggregate expenditure

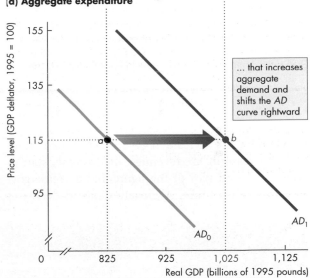

(b) Aggregate demand

The price level is 115. When the aggregate expenditure curve is AE_0 (part a), the aggregate demand curve is AD_0 (part b). An increase in government purchases shifts the aggregate expenditure curve upward to AE_1. The new equilibrium occurs where AE_1 intersects the 45° line at a real GDP of £1,025 billion. Because the quantity of real GDP demanded at a price level of 115 increases to £1,025 billion, the aggregate demand curve shifts rightward to AD_1. The magnitude of the rightward shift of the aggregate demand curve is determined by the change in government purchases and the size of the multiplier.

Figure 24.11

Fiscal Policy, Real GDP and the Price Level

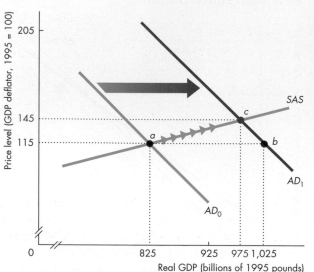

(a) Short-run effect

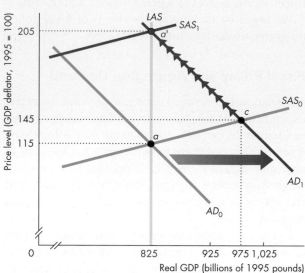

(b) Long-run effect

An increase in government purchases shifts the *AD* curve from AD_0 to AD_1. With a sticky price level, real GDP would have increased from £825 billion to £1,025 billion – to point *b*. But in the short run, the price level is not sticky and the

economy moves along the *SAS* curve to point *c*. The price level increases to 145, and real GDP increases to £975 billion. The steeper the *SAS* curve, the larger is the increase in the price level and the smaller is the increase in real GDP.

---

fiscal policy is a decrease in government expenditures or an increase in tax revenues. In this case, start at point *b* in each part of the figure and decrease government expenditure. Aggregate demand decreases from AD_1 to AD_0.

Equilibrium GDP and the Price Level in the Short Run

We've seen how an increase in government purchases increases aggregate demand. Let's now see how it changes real GDP and the price level. Figure 24.11(a) describes the economy. Aggregate demand is AD_0 and the short-run aggregate supply curve is *SAS*. (Check back to Chapter 22, pp. 464–480, if you need to refresh your understanding of the *SAS* curve.) Equilibrium is at point *a*, where the aggregate demand and short-run aggregate supply curves intersect. The price level is 115, and real GDP is £825 billion.

An increase in government purchases of £50 billion shifts the aggregate demand curve rightward from AD_0 to AD_1. While the price level is fixed at 115,

the economy moves towards point *b* and real GDP increases towards £1025 billion. But during the adjustment process, the price level does not remain constant. It gradually rises and the economy moves along the short-run aggregate supply curve to the point of intersection of the short-run aggregate supply curve and the new aggregate demand curve – point *c*. The price level rises to 145 and real GDP increases to £975 billion.

When we take the price-level effect into account, the increase in government purchases still has a multiplier effect on real GDP, but the effect is smaller than it would be if the price level remained constant. Also, the steeper the slope of the short-run aggregate supply curve, the larger is the increase in the price level, and the smaller is the increase in real GDP, the smaller is the government purchases multiplier. But the multiplier is not zero.

In the long run, real GDP equals potential GDP – the economy is at full-employment equilibrium. When real GDP equals potential GDP, an increase in aggregate demand has the same short-run effect as we have just worked out, but the long-run effect is different. The increase in aggregate demand raises the price level, but in the long-run real GDP remains at potential GDP.

Let's see what happens if the government embarks on an expansionary fiscal policy when real GDP equals potential GDP.

Fiscal Expansion at Potential GDP

When real GDP equals potential GDP, unemployment is equal to the natural rate of unemployment. Suppose that the actual and natural rates of unemployment are high so that the government mistakenly thinks that the unemployment rate exceeds the natural rate. The government tries to lower the unemployment rate by using an expansionary fiscal policy.

Figure 24.11(b) shows the effect of an expansionary fiscal policy when real GDP equals potential GDP. In this example, potential GDP is £825 billion. Aggregate demand increases and the aggregate demand curve shifts rightward from AD_0 to AD_1. The short-run equilibrium, point c, is an above full-employment equilibrium. The workforce is more than fully employed, and there are shortages of labour. Wage rates begin to increase. Higher wage rates increase costs, and short-run aggregate supply decreases. The SAS curve begins to shift leftward from SAS_0 to SAS_1. The economy moves up along the aggregate demand curve AD_1 toward point a'.

Eventually, when all adjustments to wage rates and the price level have been made, the price level is 205 and real GDP is again at potential GDP of £825 billion. The multiplier in the long run is zero. There has been a temporary decrease in the unemployment rate during the process you've just looked at but not a permanent decrease.

Review Quiz

◆ Why is the effect of the fiscal policy multiplier on real GDP less when the price level is not fixed than when it is fixed?

◆ Why is the effect of the fiscal policy multiplier on real GDP greater than zero when real GDP is less than potential GDP?

◆ What is the long-run fiscal multiplier effect on real GDP and the price level?

Fiscal Policy and Aggregate Supply

So far we've considered only the demand-side effects of fiscal policy. But fiscal policy also has supply-side effects. On the expenditures side, the government buys capital goods, which increases the quantity of real GDP supplied. On the tax revenues side, taxes on labour income act as a disincentive to work and decrease the quantity of labour employed and the quantity of real GDP supplied. With fewer people employed, the jobless rate is higher.

Similarly, taxes on interest income weaken the incentive to save and invest and so decrease the quantity of capital and decrease the quantity of real GDP supplied. This effect is an ongoing one that affects not only the current level of real GDP but also the trend growth rate of potential GDP.

The influences of fiscal policy on the quantity of real GDP supplied mean that to assess the impact of an expansionary fiscal policy, especially a tax cut, we must take into account changes in both aggregate demand and aggregate supply.

Figure 24.12 shows the supply-side effects of an expansionary fiscal policy such as a tax cut. Part (a) shows the effects that are most likely to occur. An expansionary fiscal policy has a large effect on aggregate demand and a small effect on aggregate supply. The aggregate demand curve shifts rightward by a larger amount than the rightward shift in the short-run aggregate supply curve. The outcome is a rise in the price level and an increase in real GDP.

During the 1980s, a school of thought known as the *supply-siders* became prominent in the United States. Although their ideas did not catch on as well in the United Kingdom and continental Europe, they did have their supporters. Part of the stated aim of the UK governent's fiscal policy is to stimulate the supply side. Supply-siders believe that tax cuts would strengthen incentives and have a large effect on aggregate supply. Figure 24.12(b) shows the effects that supply-siders believe might occur. An expansionary fiscal policy still has a large effect on aggregate demand but it has a similarly large effect on aggregate supply. The aggregate demand curve and the short-run aggregate supply curve shift rightward by similar amounts. In this particular case, the price level remains constant and real GDP increases. A slightly larger increase in aggregate supply would have

Figure 24.12

Supply-side Effects of Fiscal Policy

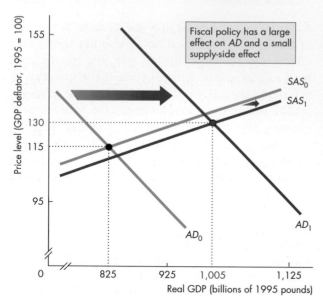

(a) The traditional view

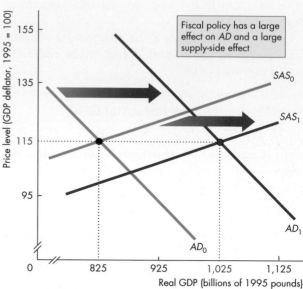

(b) The supply-side view

An expansionary fiscal policy such as a tax cut increases aggregate demand and shifts the *AD* curve rightward from AD_0 to AD_1 (both parts). Such a policy change also has a supply-side effect. If the supply-side effect is small, the *SAS* curve shifts rightward from SAS_0 to SAS_1 in part (a). In this case, the demand-side effect dominates the supply-side effect, real GDP increases and the price level rises.

If the supply-side effect of a tax cut is large, the *SAS* curve shifts rightward from SAS_0 to SAS_1 in part (b). In this case, the supply-side effect is as large as the demand-side effect. Real GDP increases and the price level remains constant. But if the supply-side effect was larger than the demand-side effect, the price level would actually fall.

brought a fall in the price level, a possibility that some supply-siders believe could occur.

The general point that everyone agrees with is that an expansionary fiscal policy that strengthens incentives increases real GDP by more and is less inflationary than one that does not change or that weakens incentives.

You've seen how fiscal policy influences the way real GDP fluctuates around its trend and how it influences the long-term growth rate of real GDP. Your next task is to study the other main arm of macroeconomic policy, monetary policy. We begin in the next chapter by describing the monetary system of a modern economy.

Review Quiz

◆ What is the supply-side argument for cuts in income taxes?
◆ Why is there disagreement about the overall effect of a tax cut on the price level?

Summary

Key Points

The Government Budget (pp. 517–522)

- The government budget finances the activities of the government and is used to stabilize real GDP.

- Tax revenues come from personal income and corporate taxes, social security contributions, and indirect taxes.

- Government expenditures include transfer payments, purchases of goods and services, and debt interest.

- The budget balance is equal to tax revenues minus expenditures.

Fiscal Policy Multipliers (pp. 522–528)

- Fiscal policy actions are either automatic, or discretionary.

- The government purchases multiplier equals $1/(1 - MPC)$. The lump sum tax multiplier equals $-MPC/(1 - MPC)$.

- The balanced budget multiplier equals 1.

- Income taxes and benefits make each of the multipliers smaller than they otherwise would be. They also bring fluctuations in tax revenues and transfer payments over the business cycle and help the shock-absorbing capacities of the economy.

Fiscal Policy Multipliers and the Price Level (pp. 528–531)

- An expansionary fiscal policy increases aggregate demand and shifts the aggregate demand curve rightward. It increases real GDP and raises the price level.

- A contractionary fiscal policy has the opposite effect.

- Price level changes dampen fiscal policy multiplier effects.

- When real GDP equals potential GDP, an expansionary fiscal policy increases the price level but leaves real GDP unchanged.

- The fiscal policy multiplier in the long-run is zero.

Fiscal Policy and Aggregate Supply (pp. 531–532)

- Fiscal policy has supply-side effects because the government buys capital goods that increase aggregate supply and taxes weaken the incentives to work, save and invest.

- These supply-side influences mean that an expansionary fiscal policy increases real GDP and if the supply-side effect is stronger than the demand-side effect, an expansionary fiscal policy might lower the price level.

Key Figures ◈

Key Terms

Problems

●1 In the economy of Zap, the marginal propensity to consume is 0.9. Investment is €50 billion, government expenditures on goods and services are €40 billion, and autonomous taxes are €40 billion. Zap has no exports, no imports, and no income taxes.

a The government cuts its expenditures on goods and services to €30 billion. What is the change in equilibrium expenditure?

b What is the value of the government expenditures multiplier?

c The government continues to buy €40 billion worth of goods and services and cuts autonomous taxes to €30 billion. What is the change in equilibrium expenditure?

d What is the value of the tax multiplier?

e The government simultaneously cuts both its expenditures on goods and services and taxes to €30 billion. What is the change in equilibrium expenditure? Why does equilibrium expenditure decrease?

2 In the economy of Zip, the marginal propensity to consume is 0.8. Investment is €60 billion, government expenditures on goods and services are €50 billion, and autonomous taxes are €60 billion. Zip has no exports, no imports, and no income taxes.

a The government increases its expenditures on goods and services to €60 billion. What is the change in equilibrium expenditure?

b What is the value of the government expenditures multiplier?

c The government continues to purchase €60 billion worth of goods and services and increases autonomous taxes to €70 billion. What is the change in equilibrium expenditure?

d What is the value of the tax multiplier?

e The government simultaneously increases both its expenditures on goods and services and taxes by €10 billion. What is the change in equilibrium expenditure? Why does equilibrium expenditure increase?

●3 Suppose that the price level in the economy of Zap as described in problem 1 is 100. The economy is also at full employment.

a If the government of Zap increases its expenditures on goods and services by €10 billion, what happens to the quantity of real GDP demanded?

b How does Zap's aggregate demand curve change? Draw a two-part diagram that is similar to Figure 24.12 to illustrate the change in both the *AE* curve and the *AD* curve.

c In the short run, does equilibrium real GDP increase by more than, less than, or the same amount as the increase in the quantity of real GDP demanded?

d In the long run, does equilibrium real GDP increase by more than, less than, or the same amount as the increase in the quantity of real GDP demanded?

e In the short run, does the price level in Zap rise, fall, or remain unchanged?

f In the long run, does the price level in Zap rise, fall, or remain unchanged?

4 Suppose that the price level in the economy of Zip as described in problem 2 is 100. The economy is also at full employment.

a If the government of Zip decreases its expenditures on goods and services by €5 billion, what happens to the quantity of real GDP demanded?

b How does Zip's aggregate demand curve change? Draw a two-part diagram that is similar to Figure 24.12 to illustrate the change in both the *AE* curve and the *AD* curve.

c In the short run, does equilibrium real GDP decrease by more than, less than, or the same amount as the decrease in the quantity of real GDP demanded?

d In the short run, does the price level in Zip rise, fall, or remain unchanged?

e Why does real GDP in the short run decrease by a smaller amount than the decrease in aggregate demand?

●5 The figure shows revenues and outlays of the government of Dreamland. Potential GDP is €40 million.

a What is the government's budget balance if real GDP is €40 million?

b Does Dreamland have a structural surplus or deficit if its real GDP is €40 million? What is its size? Explain why.

c What is the government's budget balance if real GDP is €30 million?

d If Dreamland's real GDP is €30 million, does Dreamland have a structural surplus or deficit? What is its size? Explain why.

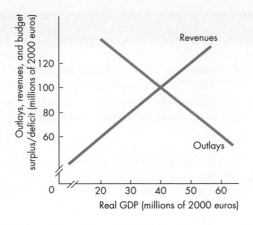

e   If Dreamland's real GDP is €50 million, does Dreamland have a structural surplus or deficit? What is its size? Explain why.

6   In problem 5, if Dreamland's real GDP in €40 million:

a   What is the government's budget balance?

b   If potential GDP is €30 million, does Dreamland have a cyclical surplus or deficit? What is its size? Explain why.

c   If potential GDP is €40 million, does Dreamland have a cyclical surplus or deficit? What is its size? Explain why.

d   If potential GDP is €50 million, does Dreamland have a cyclical surplus or deficit? What is its size? Explain why.

e   How can the Dreamland government eliminate a structural deficit/surplus and avoid a cyclical deficit/surplus if potential GDP is €40 million?

Critical Thinking

1 In the figure, aggregate demand is initially AD_0 and short-run aggregate supply is initially SAS_0. A tax cut increases aggregate demand to AD_1. This same tax cut influences incentives and increases aggregate supply. At first, there is no supply-side effect. Then short-run aggregate supply increases to SAS_1. Eventually, short-run aggregate supply increases to SAS_2.

2 Study Reading Between the Lines on pp. 540–541, and then answer the following questions.

   a Why is the French government preparing a fiscal policy to boost the economy?

   b What is the expected effect on the economy of the fiscal stimulus?

   c What are the implications for the budget deficit if the economy is in decline?

   d Analyse the constraints and options available to the French government in designing a fiscal stimulus.

3 Use the link on the Parkin, Powell and Matthews website to obtain data on the amounts of government expenditure in the main industrial countries. Then use the fiscal policy multiplier analysis that you've learned about in this chapter to predict which countries have strong automatic stabilizers and which have weak ones. Explain the reasons for your predictions.

Appendix to Chapter 24
The Algebra of the Fiscal Policy Multiplier

This note explains the algebra of the fiscal policy multiplier in greater detail. We begin by defining the symbols we need:

- Aggregate planned expenditure, AE
- Real GDP, Y
- Consumption expenditure, C
- Investment, I
- Government expenditures, G
- Exports, X
- Imports, M
- Net taxes, NT
- Autonomous consumption expenditure, a
- Autonomous taxes, T_a
- Autonomous transfer payments, T_r
- Autonomous expenditure, A
- Marginal propensity to consume, b
- Marginal propensity to import, m
- Marginal tax rate, t

Equilibrium Expenditure

Aggregate planned expenditure is:

$$AE = C + I + G + X - M$$

The consumption function is:

$$C = a + b(Y - NT)$$

Net taxes equals autonomous taxes minus autonomous transfer payments plus induced taxes, which is:

$$NT = T_a - T_r + tY$$

Use the last equation in the consumption function to give consumption expenditure as a function of GDP:

$$C = a - bT_a + bT_r + b(1 - t)Y$$

The import function is:

$$M = mY$$

Use the consumption function and the import function to replace C and M in the aggregate planned expenditure equation to obtain:

$$AE = a - bT_a + bT_r + b(1 - t)Y + I + G + X - mY$$

Collect the terms on the right side of the equation that involve Y to obtain:

$$AE = [a - bT_a + bT_r + I + G + X] + [b(1 - t) - m]Y$$

Autonomous expenditure (A) is given by:

$$A = a - bT_a + bT_r + I + G + X$$

so:

$$AE = A + [b(1 - t) - m]Y$$

Equilibrium expenditure occurs when aggregate planned expenditure (AE) equals real GDP (Y). That is:

$$AE = Y$$

To calculate equilibrium expenditure we solve the equation:

$$Y = A + [b(1 - t) - m]Y$$

to obtain:

$$Y = \frac{1}{1 - [b(1 - t) + m]}A$$

Government Expenditures Multiplier

The government expenditures multiplier equals the change in equilibrium expenditure (Y) that results from a change in government expenditures (G) divided by the change in government expenditures. Because autonomous expenditure is:

$$A = a - bT_a + bT_r + I + G + X$$

the change in autonomous expenditure equals the change in government expenditures. That is:

$$\Delta A = \Delta G$$

The government expenditures multiplier is found by working out the change in Y that results from the change in A. You can see from the solution for Y that:

$$\Delta Y = \frac{1}{1 - [b(1 - t) + m]} \Delta G$$

The government expenditures multiplier equals:

$$\frac{1}{1 - [b(1 - t) + m]}$$

In an economy in which $t = 0$ and $m = 0$, the government expenditures multiplier is $1/(1 - b)$. With $b = 0.75$, the government expenditures multiplier equals 4, as part (a) of Figure A24.1 shows. Make up some examples and use the above formula to show how b, m, and t influence the government expenditures multiplier.

Autonomous Tax Multiplier

The autonomous tax multiplier equals the change in equilibrium expenditure (Y) that results from a change in autonomous taxes (T_a) divided by the change in autonomous taxes. Because autonomous expenditure is:

$$A = a - bT_a + bT_r + I + G + X$$

the change in autonomous expenditure equals *minus* b multiplied by the change in autonomous taxes. That is:

$$\Delta A = -b\Delta T_a$$

You can see from the solution for Y that:

$$\Delta Y = \frac{-b}{1 - [b(1 - t) + m]} \Delta T_a$$

The autonomous tax multiplier equals:

$$\frac{-b}{1 - [b(1 - t) + m]}$$

In an economy in which $t = 0$ and $m = 0$, the autonomous tax multiplier is $-b/(1 - b)$. With $b = 0.75$, the autonomous tax multiplier equals -3, as part (b) of Figure A24.1 shows. Make up some examples and use the above formula to show how b, m, and t influence the autonomous tax multiplier.

Figure A24.1

Fiscal Policy Multipliers

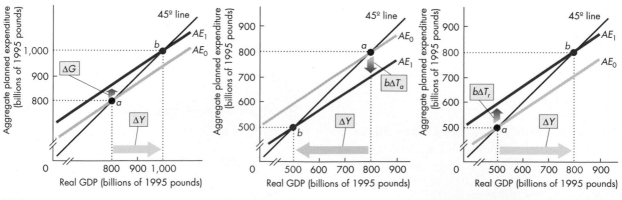

(a) Government expenditures multiplier   **(b) Autonomous tax multiplier**   **(c) Autonomous transfer payments multiplier**

Autonomous Transfer Payments Multiplier

The autonomous transfer payments multiplier equals the change in equilibrium expenditure (Y) that results from a change in autonomous transfer payments (T_r) divided by the change in autonomous transfer payments. Because autonomous expenditure is:

$$A = a - bT_a + bT_r + I + G + X$$

the change in autonomous transfer payments changes autonomous expenditure such that:

$$\Delta A = b\Delta T_r$$

Because transfer payments are like negative taxes, the autonomous transfer payments multiplier equals minus the autonomous tax multiplier. The autonomous transfer payments multiplier equals:

$$\frac{b}{1 - [b(1 - t) + m]}$$

In an economy in which $t = 0$ and $m = 0$, the autonomous transfer payments multiplier is $b/(1 - b)$. With $b = 0.75$, the autonomous transfer payments multiplier equals 3, as part (c) of Figure A24.1 shows. Make up some examples and use the above formula to show how b, m, and t influence the autonomous transfer payments multiplier.

Fiscal Policy in France

THE FINANCIAL TIMES, 16 OCTOBER 2001

FT

Fabius to introduce fiscal stimulus

Robert Graham

Laurent Fabius, French finance minister, will today unveil measures to boost the flagging economy by increasing household incomes.

Mr Fabius is also expected to make some gesture to halt the decline in business confidence, which has accelerated after the September 11 terrorist attacks.

The finance ministry has been under strong conflicting pressures in drawing up a list of measures. Mr Fabius has faced vociferous demands from the government's left-wing supporters to increase public spending and raise household incomes. The prospects of next year's presidential and parliamentary elections being held against the backdrop of an economic slowdown has given added weight to these calls.

Mr Fabius has had to balance these considerations against France's responsibilities under the eurozone's stability pact, which imposes strict budgetary discipline. Indeed, the prospect of France increasing the level of public spending and allowing the budget deficit to rise too sharply has led to talk of Paris pushing for a more flexible interpretation of the pact.

Already, the economic slowdown has seen Treasury receipts slip, leaving the 2001 budget probably short of FFr 25 bn ($3.2 bn). As a result, the steady fall in the deficit since the government took office in 1997 has been halted and will now rise to almost 1.5 per cent of gross domestic product, at least temporarily.

One of the main measures being studied has been some form of extension to the earned income tax credit, which took effect in September and benefited 8 m low-paid households.

The Essence of the Story

- The French finance minister announced a plan to stimulate the weakening French economy.

- Business confidence has weakened even further after the terrorist attack on September 11.

- The French government has been under increasing pressure from its left-wing supporters to increase public spending and raise people's disposable income.

- The French government has had to balance the desire to stimulate the economy with a fiscal boost with the restrictions on fiscal spending placed by the stability pact for eurozone countries.

- The slowdown in the economy has reduced receipts and the budget deficit is expected to rise to 1.5 per cent of GDP.

Economic Analysis

- The slowdown in the French economy has reduced tax revenues and will increase government transfer payments. Look again at fiscal policy over the business cycle in Chapter 24 and Figure 24.7.

- The effect of the downturn is to increase the budget deficit. The automatic reduction in tax revenue and increase in transfer payments act as an automatic stabilizer that dampens the effect of the slowdown.

- Figure 1 shows the fall in the growth of GDP and the forecast for GDP growth. The expected decline in output growth will have included the effect of the automatic stabilizer of increasing the budget deficit.

- Figure 2 shows that the expected budget deficit in the absence of a fiscal stimulus could increase to 2.0 per cent of GDP but the stability pact that eurozone economies have to keep to has a restriction that places a maximum budget deficit of 3 per cent of GDP.

- Figure 3 shows that if a fiscal stimulus is conducted, the economy will move from AD_{01} to AD_{02} and reduce the recessionary gap, but the policy may push the budget deficit over the maximum allowed under the stability pact.

- In 1999, France had a structural budget deficit of over 1 per cent which makes it difficult for the French government to meet the conflicting demand for a fiscal expansion to cushion the downturn in the economy and meet the stability pact.

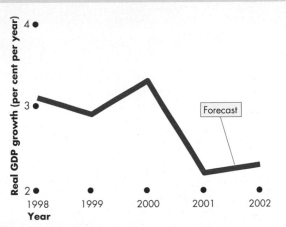

Figure 1 Real GDP growth

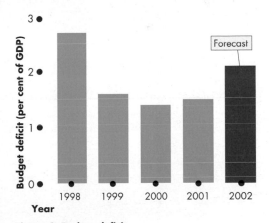

Figure 2 Budget deficit

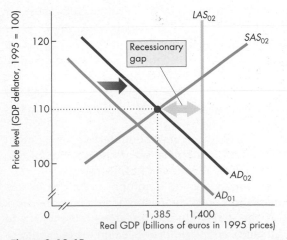

Figure 3 *AS–AD*

Part 6

The Central Bank and Monetary Policy

Talking with **Sushil Wadhwani**

Dr Sushil Wadhwani was appointed a full-time external member of the Monetary Policy Committee on 1 June 1999. The MPC is responsible for setting UK interest rates to meet the government's 2.5 per cent inflation target.

From 1995–1999 Dr Wadhwani was Director of Research at Tudor Proprietary Trading LLC, a fund management company. He was previously Director of Equity Strategy at Goldman Sachs International (1991–95) and before that Reader/ Lecturer in economics at the London School of Economics (1984–91).

Dr Wadhwani was educated at the London School of Economics, where he obtained a BSc (Econ), MSc (Econ) and PhD (Econ).

He has published a number of articles in academic journals. His past research includes work on the determinants of unemployment and inflation, and various articles on the efficiency of financial markets.

What made you interested in economics?

It was almost accidental. I went up to the LSE to study Accounting and Finance. However, I became interested in economics by attending various public lectures and because of a possibly naïve belief that it would enable me, even if only in a small way, to help make the world a better place.

You have worked as an academic economist, a professional and now a policy-maker. Describe the sort of work you have done in each capacity? Which of these have you found the most interesting?

I feel greatly privileged in terms of having had the opportunity to use my knowledge of economics in a variety of different areas. As an academic economist, I greatly enjoyed empirical research, as one was always learning something new about how things work. Then, when I worked in the financial sector, trying to explain and predict moves in the markets was an endless source of fascination to me. Of course, I now have the awesome responsibility of helping to set the 'correct' rate of interest. I am fortunate in that my current job entails, among other things, following the markets and carrying out empirical research.

You have been described as a 'dove' in the MPC which means that you have usually voted for cuts in interest rates when colleagues have not, and stronger cuts when your colleagues have voted for moderate ones. Why is this?

I don't like the term 'dove', as I do not regard myself as being genetically predisposed to vote for lower rates. I have only tended to vote for lower rates since December 2000, but that was primarily because I was more pessimistic about the prospects for the global economy. It was also my view that the MPC's published projection for inflation was understating the supply potential of the British economy, e.g. overstating capacity utilization (on which the MPC has recently revised its view).

Do you believe that the MPC has solved the problem of inflation?

No, it would be a mistake to become complacent about inflation. While we have been fortunate in that inflation has stayed within 1 per cent of the target since the inception of the MPC, one needs to allow for the possibility that there might be larger shocks which might be more difficult to handle. It is important that economists are humble about what they can deliver. One is, for example, struck by the current predicament of the Japanese economy, where an independent Bank of Japan has, so far, found it difficult to prevent deflation.

What do you think are the major problems for the world economy today?

Most commentators are currently preoccupied with whether or not the US will have a 'V'-shaped recovery during 2002. Obviously, a more prolonged downturn in the US will be problematic in the short run. However, even if activity turns up as expected, one is still left with possible imbalances in the US economy, e.g. a stock market that might be overvalued, a savings ratio that might be too low, and the related fact that the current account deficit might be too high. Obviously, the fact that the second largest economy (Japan) is unable to grow at its potential rate and overcome deflation is worrisome. Moving beyond macroeconomic issues, growing global poverty is a major unsolved challenge.

Who are the economists that having inspired you?

By far, reading Keynes has been the most important influence. Many of his insights are relevant to policy today, and many of the cul-de-sacs encountered by academic economists in recent years would have been avoided by a more thorough reading of Keynes.

What advice would you give a student of economics?

My single biggest regret is that I did not take more courses in economic history. While my formal training in economics has been indispensable to everything that I do, I feel that I would have found it easier to understand markets and set policy if my knowledge of the economic history of the last two centuries was deeper.

CHAPTER 25

Money

After studying this chapter you will be able to:

- ◆ Define money and describe its functions
- ◆ Explain the economic functions of banks and other financial institutions
- ◆ Describe the financial innovations of the 1980s
- ◆ Explain how banks create money
- ◆ Explain why the quantity of money is an important economic magnitude
- ◆ Explain the quantity theory of money

Money Makes the World Go Around

Money, like fire and the wheel, has been around for a very long time. An incredible array of items have served as money. Cowrie shells were used in the Pacific Islands, wampum (beads made from shells) were used by North American Indians, whales' teeth were used by Fijians and tobacco was used by early American colonists. In ancient Greece, cattle served as money, indeed the word 'pecuniary' is derived from *pecunia*, the Latin for money, which in turn is derived from *pecus*, meaning cattle. Today, when we want to buy something, we use coins or notes, write a cheque, or present a credit card. Tomorrow, we'll use a 'smart card' that keeps track of spending and that our pocket computer can read. Are all these things money? ◆ When we deposit some coins or notes into a bank or building society, is that still money? What happens when the bank or building society lends the money in our deposit to someone else? How can we get our money back if it's been lent out? Does lending by banks and building societies create money – out of thin air? ◆ In the 1970s, there were two types of account with banks. There were demand deposits (sometimes called sight deposits) that did not pay interest, and there were time deposits, or deposit accounts as they are known in the United Kingdom, that did pay interest. Today, there's a wide variety of accounts that provide the convenience of a cheque facility and the income of a savings deposit. Why were these new kinds of bank deposits introduced? ◆ During the 1970s and periods of the 1980s, the quantity of money in existence in the United Kingdom increased very quickly, but in the 1990s it increased at a much slower pace. In Russia and in some Latin American countries the quantity of money has increased at an extremely rapid pace. In Switzerland and Germany, the quantity of money has increased at a slower pace. Does the rate of increase in the quantity of money matter? What are the effects of an increasing quantity of money on our economy? In Reading Between the Lines (pp. 568–569) we look at the implications of the changeover from pesetas to euros in Spain as people try to spend the pesetas obtained from illegal activity.

◆ ◆ ◆ ◆ In this chapter we'll study that useful invention: money. We'll look at its functions, its different forms, and the way it is defined and measured in the United Kingdom today. We'll also study banks and other financial institutions and explain how they create money. Finally, we'll examine the effects of money growth on the economy.

What Is Money?

What do cowrie shells, wampum, whales' teeth, tobacco, cattle and pennies have in common? Why are they all examples of money? To answer these questions we need a definition of money. **Money** is any commodity or token that is generally acceptable as a means of payment. A **means of payment** is a method of settling a debt. When a payment has been made there is no remaining obligation between the parties to a transaction. So what cowrie shells, wampum, whales' teeth, cattle and pennies have in common is that they have served (or still do serve) as the means of payment. But money has three other functions as:

1 A medium of exchange.

2 A unit of account.

3 A store of value.

Medium of Exchange

A *medium of exchange* is an object that is generally accepted in exchange for goods and services. Money acts as such a medium. Without money, it would be necessary to exchange goods and services directly for other goods and services – an exchange called **barter**. For example, if you want to buy a hamburger, you offer the paperback novel you've just finished reading in exchange for it. Barter requires a *double coincidence of wants*, a situation that occurs when Erika wants to buy what Kazia wants to sell, and Kazia wants to buy what Erika wants to sell. To get your hamburger, you must find someone who's selling hamburgers and who wants your paperback novel. Money guarantees that there is a double coincidence of wants because people with something to sell will always accept money in exchange for it. Money acts as a lubricant that smoothes the mechanism of exchange.

Unit of Account

A *unit of account* is an agreed measure for stating the prices of goods and services. To get the most out of your budget you have to figure out, among other things, whether seeing one more film is worth the price you have to pay, not in pounds and pence, but in terms of the number of ice creams, beers and cups of tea that you have to give up. It's easy to do such calculations when all these goods have prices in terms

Table 25.1 The Unit of Account Function of Money Simplifies Price Comparisons

Good	Price in money units	Price in units of another good
Cinema ticket	£4.00 each	4 pints of beer
Beer	£1.00 per pint	2 ice-cream cones
Ice cream	£0.50 per cone	1 cup of tea
Tea	£0.50 per cup	5 rolls of mints
Mints	£0.10 per roll	1 local phone call

Money as a unit of account. 1 cinema ticket costs £4 and 1 cup of tea costs 50 pence, so a film costs 8 cups of tea $(4.00/0.5 = 8)$.

No unit of account. You go to a cinema and learn that the price of a film is 4 pints of beer. You go to a café and learn that a cup of tea costs 5 rolls of mints. But how many rolls of mints does seeing a film cost you? To answer that question, you go to the Students' Union bar and find that a pint of beer costs 2 ice-cream cones. Now you head for the ice-cream shop, where an ice cream costs one cup of tea. Now you get out your pocket calculator: 1 film costs 4 pints of beer, or 8 ice-cream cones, or 8 cups of tea, or 40 rolls of mints!

of pounds and pence (see Table 25.1). If a cinema ticket costs £4 and a pint of beer in the Students' Union costs £1, you know straight away that seeing one more film costs you 4 pints of beer. If a cup of tea costs 50 pence, one more cinema ticket costs 8 cups of tea. You need only one calculation to figure out the opportunity cost of any pair of goods and services.

But imagine how troublesome it would be if your local cinema posted its price as 4 pints of beer; and if the Students' Union announced that the price of a pint of beer was 2 ice-cream cones; and if the corner shop posted the price of an ice-cream cone as 1 cup of tea; and if the café priced a cup of tea as 5 rolls of mints! Now how much running around and calculating do you have to do to work out how much that film is going to cost you in terms of the beer, ice cream, tea, or mints that you must give up to see it? You get the answer for beer straight away from the sign posted at the cinema, but for all the other goods you're going to have to visit many different stores to establish the price of each commodity in terms of another and then calculate prices in units that are relevant for your own decision. Cover up the column labelled 'price in money units' in Table 25.1 and see how hard it is to figure out the number of local telephone calls it costs to see one film. It is much simpler for everyone to express their prices in terms of pounds and pence.

Store of Value

Any commodity or token that can be held and exchanged later for goods and services is called a *store of value*. Money acts as a store of value. If it did not, it would not be acceptable in exchange for goods and services. The more stable the value of a commodity or token, the better it can act as a store of value, and the more useful it is as money. There are no stores of value that are completely safe. The value of a physical object, such as a house, a car, or a work of art, fluctuates over time. The value of commodities and tokens used as money also fluctuate and, when there is inflation, they persistently fall in value.

Money must satisfy all three functions discussed above. Therefore money must be a medium of exchange, a unit of account and a store of value. But the most important function is the medium of exchange. Something can be a store of value, like a national savings account you can obtain at the post office, but it cannot be used to buy something. Similarly, a unit of account alone is not money unless it is first a medium of exchange. An example of a unit of account that is not money in the strict sense was the euro. The euro became money in the strict sense on 1 January 2002 when euro notes and coin came into circulation with the public. Prior to 1 January 2002, the euro was a unit of account used by banks to settle transactions.

The objects used as money have evolved over many centuries and we can identify four main forms of money:

1   Commodity money.
2   Convertible paper money.
3   Fiat money.
4   Deposit money.

Commodity Money

A physical commodity that is valued in its own right and also used as a means of payment is **commodity money**. An amazing array of items have served as commodity money at different times and places, seven of which were described at the beginning of this chapter. But the most common commodity monies have been coins made from metals such as gold, silver and copper. The first known coins were made in Lydia, a Greek city-state, at the beginning of the seventh century BC.

There are two problems with commodity money. First, there is a constant temptation to cheat on the value of the money. Two methods of cheating have been commonly used – clipping and debasement. *Clipping* is reducing the size of coins by an imperceptible amount, thereby lowering their metallic content. *Debasement* is the creation of a coin that has a lower silver or gold content (the balance being made up of some cheaper metal).

The temptation to lower the value of commodity money led to a phenomenon known as Gresham's Law, after the sixteenth-century British financial expert, Sir Thomas Gresham. **Gresham's Law** is the tendency for bad (debased) money to drive good (not debased) money out of circulation. To see why Gresham's Law works, suppose you are paid with two coins, one debased and the other not. Each coin has the same value if you use it to buy goods. But the good coin is more valuable as a commodity than it is as money. You will not, therefore, use the good coin as money. You will always pay with a debased coin (if you have one). In this way, bad money drives good money out of circulation.

The second problem with commodity money is its opportunity cost. Gold and silver used as money could be used to make jewellery or ornaments instead. This opportunity cost creates incentives to find alternatives to the commodity itself for use in the exchange process. One such alternative is a paper claim to commodity money.

Convertible Paper Money

When a paper claim to a commodity circulates as a means of payment, that claim is called **convertible paper money**. The first known example of paper money occurred in China during the Ming dynasty (AD 1368–99). This form of money was also used extensively throughout Europe in the Middle Ages.

The inventiveness of goldsmiths and their clients led to the widespread use of convertible paper money. Because gold was valuable, goldsmiths had well-guarded safes in which to keep their own gold. They also rented space to artisans and others who wanted to put their gold in safe-keeping and issued a receipt entitling them to reclaim their 'deposits' on demand. (These receipts were similar to the cloakroom ticket that you get at a theatre or museum.) Because the gold receipts entitled the holder of the receipt to reclaim gold, they were 'as good as gold' and circulated as money. When Isabella of Spain bought some land from Henry IV, she simply gave him a gold receipt for the appropriate value. The paper money is *backed* by the gold held by a goldsmith and is *convertible* into commodity money – gold.

Fractional Backing – the Origin of Banking

Once a convertible paper money system is operating and people are using paper claims to gold rather than gold itself as the means of payment, goldsmiths notice that their vaults are storing a lot of gold that is never withdrawn. This gives them a brilliant idea. Why not lend people gold receipts? The goldsmith can charge interest on the loan and the loan is created just by writing on a piece of paper. As long as the number of such receipts created is not too large in relation to the stock of gold in the goldsmith's safe, the goldsmith is in no danger of not being able to honour his promise to convert receipts into gold on demand. The gold in the goldsmith's safe is a *fraction* of the gold receipts in circulation. By this device, *fractionally backed* convertible paper money was invented.

Until the 1880s the United Kingdom was the only country in the world that maintained a **gold standard**. The gold standard was a monetary system with fractionally backed convertible paper in which the pound sterling could be converted into gold at a guaranteed value on demand. The gold value of the pound was fixed by the market price of gold in terms of silver and the silver content of the shilling. The old units of account had 20 shillings to the pound, which gave the convertible value of the pound to gold as the value of the silver content of 20 shillings. Being on the gold standard meant that it was easy to calculate the value of one currency, such as the pound, in terms of another, such as the US dollar. The amount of gold one pound sterling could be exchanged for was just over 486 per cent of the amount of gold one US dollar could buy, and except for a brief period after the First World War, the value of the pound was fixed at $4.86 until 1931.

Even with fractionally backed paper money, valuable commodities that could be used for other productive activities are tied up in the exchange process. There remains an incentive to find a yet more efficient way of facilitating exchange and of freeing up the commodities used to back the paper money. This alternative is fiat money.

Fiat Money

The term *fiat* means 'let it be done' or 'by order of the authority'. **Fiat money** is an intrinsically worthless (or almost worthless) commodity that serves the functions of money. Some of the earliest fiat monies were the continental currency issued during the American War of Independence and the 'greenbacks' issued during the American Civil War, which circulated until 1879. These early experiments with fiat money ended in rapid inflation because the amount of money created was allowed to increase quickly, causing the money to lose value. Provided the quantity of fiat money is not allowed to grow too rapidly, it has a reasonably steady value in terms of the goods and services that it buys.

The notes and coins that we use in the United Kingdom today – collectively known as **currency** – are examples of fiat money. They are money because the government, through the Bank of England, declares them to be so. The Bank of England, has a virtual monopoly in issuing notes in the UK. In Scotland, various banks issue similar notes but they are fully backed by Bank of England notes. Because of the creation of fiat money, people are willing to accept a piece of paper with a special watermark, printed in special ink and worth not more than a few pence as a commodity, in exchange for £20 worth of goods and services. The small metal coin that we call 10 pence is worth almost nothing as a piece of metal, but it pays for a local phone call and many other small commodities. The replacement of commodity money by fiat money enables the commodities themselves to be used productively.

Deposit Money

In the modern world, there is a fourth type of money – deposit money. **Deposit money** consists of deposits at banks and other financial institutions (building societies in the UK). This type of money is an accounting entry in an electronic database in the banks' and other financial institutions' computers. It is money because it is used to settle debts. In fact, it is the main means of settling debts in modern societies. The owner of a deposit transfers ownership to another person simply by writing a cheque – an instruction to a bank – that tells the bank to change its database, debiting the account of one depositor and crediting the account of another.

We'll have more to say about deposit money shortly. But before doing so, let's look at the measure of money

Figure 25.1

The Measure of Money

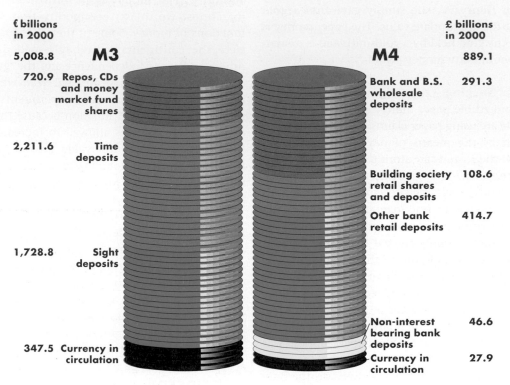

€ billions in 2000

£ billions in 2000

5,008.8	**M3**		**M4**	889.1
720.9	Repos, CDs and money market fund shares		Bank and B.S. wholesale deposits	291.3
2,211.6	Time deposits		Building society retail shares and deposits	108.6
			Other bank retail deposits	414.7
1,728.8	Sight deposits			
			Non-interest bearing bank deposits	46.6
347.5	Currency in circulation		Currency in circulation	27.9

M4 is the measure of broad money in the UK. It includes currency, bank deposits and building society deposits. M3 is the eurozone measure of broad money that is monitored by the European Central Bank. It includes currency, Sight deposits and Time deposits.

Source: Bank of England, ECB.

and its relative magnitude in the United Kingdom today.

The Measure of Money

In most countries, money consists of *currency* (notes and coins) and *deposits* at banks and other financial institutions. There are different types of deposits and, as a result, different measures of money. Deposits are classified as sight deposits and time deposits. A sight deposit is a chequeable deposit. A person holding such a deposit will issue cheques from their sight deposit account. A time deposit is a deposit that has a fixed term to maturity. Although this is not usually a chequeable deposit, technological advances in the banking industry have made it easy to switch funds from time deposits to sight deposits. The cost of

switching funds is the bank charge and the penalty of lost interest. Because of the ease with which time deposits can be switched into sight deposits, they are included in the definition of money. The official measure of money in the United Kingdom is known as **M4**. M4 includes currency held by the public and their holdings of bank and building society deposits, but does *not* include currency held by banks and building societies. In the eurozone economies, the main measure of money is M3. M3 basically consists of currency in circulation plus sight and time deposits. Figure 25.1 shows the components that make up M4 in the UK and M3 in the eurozone.

Is M4 Really Money?

Money is the means of payment. So the test of whether an asset is money is whether it serves as a means of payment. Currency passes the test. What about deposits? Chequeing deposits are money because they can be transferred from one person to another by writing a cheque. Such a transfer of ownership is equivalent to handing over currency. Both banks and building societies issue chequeable deposits.

But what about time deposits? A few time deposits are just as much a means of payment as a sight deposit. You can use the cash dispenser (automated teller machine – ATM) to transfer funds directly from such accounts to pay for your purchase. But most time deposits are not direct means of payments. They are *liquid assets*. **Liquidity** is the property of being instantly convertible into a means of payment with little loss in value. Most time deposits have this property, but there are some deposits that do not. These are large deposits known as *Certificates of Deposits* or *CDs*. CDs have maturities from three months to up to two years. They are not bank deposits in the normal sense as they have to be held for the period of the maturity, but they can be sold in the financial markets quickly and easily. Because time deposits are quickly and easily converted into currency or chequeing deposits, they are operationally similar to sight deposits but technically they are not money.

Currency is only a small part of our money. It accounts for only 3 per cent of M4, while sight deposits total more than 66 per cent.

Deposits are Money but Cheques are Not

In defining money, we included, along with currency, deposits at banks and other financial institutions. But we did not count the cheques that people write as money. Why are deposits money and cheques not?

To see why deposits are money but cheques are not, think about what happens when Colleen buys some roller blades for £100 from Rocky's Rollers. When Colleen goes to Rocky's shop she has £250 in her deposit account at the Co-op Bank. Rocky has £1,000 in his deposit account – at the same bank, as it happens. The total deposits of these two people is £1,250. On June 11, Colleen writes a cheque for £100. Rocky takes the cheque to Co-op Bank straight away and deposits it. Rocky's bank balance rises from £1,000 to £1,100. But when the bank credits Rocky's account with £100, it also debits Colleen's account £100, so that her balance falls from £250 to £150. The total deposits of Colleen and Rocky are still the same as before, £1,250. Rocky now has £100 more and Colleen £100 less than before. These transactions are summarized in Table 25.2.

Table 25.2   Paying by Cheque

Colleen's Chequeing Deposit Account

Date	Item	Debit	Credit	Balance
June 1	Opening balance			£250.00 CR*
June 11	Rocky's Rollers	£100.00		£150.00 CR

Rocky's Rollers Chequeing Deposit Account

Date	Item	Debit	Credit	Balance
June 1	Opening balance			£1,000.00 CR
June 11	Colleen buys roller blades		£100.00	£1,100.00 CR

*CR means 'credit': the bank owes the depositor.

This transaction has transferred money from Colleen to Rocky. The cheque itself was never money. There wasn't an extra £100 worth of money while the cheque was in circulation. The cheque was an instruction to the bank to transfer money from Colleen to Rocky.

In the example, Colleen and Rocky use the same bank. The same story, but with additional steps, describes what happens if Colleen and Rocky use different banks. Rocky's bank credits the cheque to Rocky's account and then takes the cheque to a cheque-clearing centre. Colleen's bank pays Rocky's bank £100 and then debits Colleen's account £100. This process can take a few days, but the principles are the same as when two people use the same bank.

Credit Cards are Not Money

So cheques are not money. But what about credit cards? Isn't having a credit card in your wallet and presenting the card to pay for your roller blades the same thing as using money? Why aren't credit cards somehow valued and counted as part of the quantity of money?

When you pay by cheque you are usually asked to guarantee the cheque with a *cheque guarantee card*. It would never occur to you to think of your *cheque guarantee card* as money. It's just an ID card. But it is an ID card that enables you to guarantee your cheque up to a certain value. A credit card is also an ID card but one that lets you take a loan at the instant you buy something. When you sign a credit card sales slip, you are saying: 'I agree to pay for these goods when the credit card company bills me'. Once you get your statement from the credit card company, you must make the minimum payment due (or clear your balance). To make that payment you need money – you need to have currency or a chequeing deposit to pay the credit card company. So although you use a credit card when you buy something, the credit card is not the *means of payment* and it is not money.

Review Quiz

♦ What is the distinguishing feature of money and what are the functions that money performs?
♦ What are the main forms that money has taken in the past and what serves as money in the UK today?
♦ What are the largest components of money circulating in the UK and the eurozone today?
♦ Why are cheques, debit cards and credit cards not counted as money?

We've seen that the main component of money in the United Kingdom is deposits at banks (and building societies). Let's take a closer look at these institutions.

Financial Intermediaries

We are going to study the banking and financial system by first describing the variety of financial intermediaries that operate in the United Kingdom today. Then we'll examine the operations of banks and of other financial intermediaries. After describing the main features of financial intermediaries, we'll examine their economic functions, describing what they produce and how they make a profit.

A **financial intermediary** is a firm that takes deposits from households and firms and makes loans to other households and firms. There are two types of financial intermediary whose deposits are components of the nation's money:

1 Banks.
2 Building societies.

Let's begin by looking at the banks.

Banks

A **bank** is a private firm, licensed by the Bank of England under the Banking Act of 1987 to take deposits and make loans and operate in the United Kingdom. There are over 400 commercial banks in the United Kingdom today. These banks can be categorized into two main groups: retail banks and wholesale banks. The distinction between retail banks and wholesale banks is based on the size of deposit. In general, the minimum deposit accepted by a wholesale bank is £250,000 while retail banks accept deposits as small as £1. Retail banks operate extensive branch networks, while wholesale banks have few branches and operate mainly in London. Wholesale banks form a varied group, comprising UK merchant banks, other UK banks such as finance houses that specialize in lending to businesses, leasing companies that specialize in financing the leasing of equipment to businesses, other small regional banks and overseas banks.

To understand the operations of commercial banks, it is useful to study their balance sheets. The *balance sheet* of a bank (or of any other business) is a list of assets, liabilities and net worth. *Assets* are what the bank owns, *liabilities* are what the bank owes and *net worth*, which is equal to assets minus liabilities, is the value of the bank to its shareholders – its owners. A bank's balance sheet can be described by the equation:

$$\text{Liabilities} + \text{Net worth} = \text{Assets}$$

Among a bank's liabilities are the deposits that are part of the nation's money. Your deposit at the bank is a liability to your bank (and an asset to you) because the bank must repay your deposit (and sometimes the interest on it too) whenever you decide to take your money out of the bank.

Profit and Prudence: A Balancing Act

The aim of a bank is to maximize its net worth – its value to its stockholders. To achieve this objective, a bank lends the money deposited with it at interest rates higher than the rates it pays for deposits. But a bank must perform a delicate balancing act. Lending is risky, and the more it ties up its deposits in high-risk, high-interest rate loans, the bigger is its chance of not being able to repay its depositors. And if depositors perceive a high risk of not being repaid, they withdraw their funds and create a crisis for the bank. So a bank must be prudent in the way it uses its deposits, balancing security for the depositors against profit for its shareholders.

Reserves and Loans

To achieve security for its depositors, a bank divides its funds into two parts: reserves and loans. **Reserves** are cash in a bank's vault plus its deposits at the Bank of England. The cash in a bank's vaults is a reserve to meet the demands that its customers place on it – it keeps that ATM replenished every time you and your friends need to use it for a midnight pizza. A commercial bank's deposit at the Bank of England is similar to your deposit at your own bank. Commercial banks use these deposits in the same way that you use your bank account. A commercial bank deposits cash into or draws cash out of its account at the Bank of England and writes cheques on that account to settle debts with other banks.

If a bank kept all its assets as cash in its vault or as deposits at the Bank of England, it wouldn't make any profit. In fact it keeps only a small fraction of its funds in reserves and lends the rest. A bank makes three different types of loan, or equivalently, holds three different types of asset. They are:

1   Liquid assets.
2   Investment securities.
3   Loans.

A bank's *liquid assets* are government Treasury bills and commercial bills. These assets can be sold and instantly converted into cash with virtually no risk of loss. Because liquid assets are virtually risk free, they have a low interest rate.

A bank's *investment securities* are longer-term government bonds and other bonds. These assets can be sold quickly and converted into cash but at prices that fluctuate. Because their prices fluctuate, these assets are riskier than liquid assets but they also have a higher interest rate.

A bank's *loans* are lines of credit extended to companies to finance the purchase of capital equipment and stocks, and to households – personal loans – to finance consumer durable goods, such as cars or boats. The outstanding balances on credit card accounts are also bank loans. Loans are the riskiest assets of a bank because they cannot be converted into cash until they are due to be repaid. And some borrowers default and never repay. Because they are the riskiest of a bank's assets, they also carry the highest interest rate.

Commercial bank deposits are only one component of the nation's money. But building societies also take deposits that form part of the nation's money.

Building Societies

A **building society** is a financial intermediary that traditionally obtained its funds from savings deposits (sometimes called share accounts) and that made long-term mortgage loans to home buyers. The first building societies were founded in the late eighteenth century as *mutuals*. A mutual is an organization that belongs to its members. In the case of a building society, its mutual status means that by law it belongs to its depositors and borrowers. Up until the 1980s the societies had concentrated on their traditional function of lending to home buyers. However, the societies had begun to compete with the banks in the late 1970s by offering depositors accounts that gave them instant access to their money but paid a rate of interest for a minimum amount left in the account. The Building Societies Act of 1986 allowed for the progressive deregulation of the societies enabling them to offer financial products that brought them directly into competition with the banks. The act also enabled building societies to give up their mutual status and become banks. The Abbey National, took this route in 1989 and became a bank, similarly the merged Halifax/Leeds building society did the same in 1997. Many other Building Societies have demutualized recently.

The structure and balance sheets of building societies are similar to those of banks. Like banks, they have developed a branch network, and they have liabilities that are deposits and CDs. Like bank deposits, building society deposits are chequeable and are accepted in shops in exchange for goods. Building societies also offer similar services to banks, such as credit cards, personal lending and foreign currency.

The assets of building societies include cash reserves, but unlike the banks they do not have to hold deposits at the Bank of England. However, they do hold deposits and CDs at commercial banks. They also hold liquid assets such as CDs of other building societies and Treasury bills. Like banks, they also hold government bonds, but unlike banks most of building society lending is for house purchase. These assets have a much longer maturity than the normal lending of the commercial banks. Mortgage loans are typically for 25 years and are viewed as very safe assets.

The Economic Functions of Financial Intermediaries

All financial intermediaries make a profit from the spread between the interest rate they pay on deposits and the interest rate at which they lend. Why can financial intermediaries borrow at a low interest rate and lend at a higher one? What services do they perform that makes their depositors willing to put up with a low interest rate and their borrowers willing to pay a higher one?

Financial intermediaries provide four main services that people are willing to pay for:

1   Creating liquidity.
2   Minimizing the cost of obtaining funds.
3   Minimizing the cost of monitoring borrowers.
4   Pooling risk.

Creating Liquidity

Financial intermediaries create liquidity. *Liquid* assets are those that are easily and with certainty convertible into money. Some of the liabilities of financial intermediaries are themselves money; others are highly liquid assets that are easily converted into money.

Financial intermediaries create liquidity by borrowing short and lending long. Borrowing short means taking deposits but standing ready to repay them at short notice (and even at no notice in the case of chequeing deposits). Lending long means making loan commitments for a prearranged, and often quite long, period of time. For example, when a person makes a deposit with a building society, that deposit can be withdrawn at any time. But the building society makes a lending commitment for perhaps up to 25 years to a home buyer.

Minimizing the Cost of Obtaining Funds

Finding someone from whom to borrow can be a costly business. Imagine how troublesome it would be if there were no financial intermediaries. A firm that was looking for £1 million to buy a new production plant would probably have to hunt around for several dozen people from whom to borrow in order to acquire enough funds for its capital project. Financial intermediaries lower such costs. A firm needing £1 million can go to a single financial intermediary to obtain those funds. The financial intermediary has to borrow from a large number of people, but it's not doing that just for this one firm and the £1 million it wants to borrow. The financial intermediary can establish an organization capable of raising funds from a large number of depositors and can spread the cost of this activity over a large number of borrowers.

Borrowing a very large amount may be too much for one financial intermediary. This is because a single financial intermediary may not be willing to take the risk of exposing itself to one large borrower. In such cases a number of financial intermediaries are brought together and each intermediary will lend a proportion of the total loan. This is called a 'syndicated loan' and is typical of the way a large loan, such as the loan to build the Channel Tunnel, is raised in the international financial market.

Minimizing the Cost of Monitoring Borrowers

Lending money is a risky business. There's always a danger that the borrower may not repay. Most of the money lent gets used by firms to invest in projects that they hope will return a profit. But sometimes these hopes are not fulfilled. Checking up on the activities of a borrower and ensuring that the best possible decisions are being made for making a profit and avoiding a loss is a costly and specialized activity. Imagine how costly it would be if each and every household that lent money to a firm had to incur the costs of monitoring that firm directly. By depositing funds with a financial intermediary, households avoid those costs. The financial intermediary performs the monitoring activity by using specialized resources that have a much lower cost than that which each household would incur if it had to undertake the activity individually.

Pooling Risk

As we noted above, lending money is risky. There is always a chance of not being repaid – of default. The risk of default can be reduced by lending to a large number of different individuals. In such a situation, if one person defaults on a loan it is a nuisance but not a disaster. In contrast, if only one person borrows and that person defaults on the loan, the entire loan is a write-off. Financial intermediaries enable people to pool risk in an efficient way. Thousands of people lend money to any one financial intermediary and, in turn, the financial intermediary re-lends the money to hundreds, and perhaps thousands, of individual firms. If any one firm defaults on its loan, that default is spread across all the depositors with the intermediary and no individual depositor is left exposed to a high degree of risk.

Lending a large amount of money to one person or one firm is also a risky business. If that person or firm defaults on the loan, the write-off of the loan could endanger the viability of the financial intermediary.

Financial Regulation, Deregulation and Innovation

Financial intermediaries are highly regulated institutions. But regulation is not static, and in the 1980s some important changes in their regulation as well as deregulation took place. Also, the institutions are not static. In their pursuit of profit, they constantly seek lower-cost ways of obtaining funds, monitoring borrowers, pooling risk and creating liquidity. They are also inventive in seeking ways to avoid the costs imposed on them by financial regulation. Let's take a look at regulation, deregulation and innovation in the financial sector in recent years.

Financial Regulation

Financial intermediaries face two types of regulation:

1   Deposit insurance.
2   Balance sheet rules.

Deposit Insurance

The deposits of financial intermediaries are insured by the Bank of England deposit protection scheme. The scheme is financed by a flat rate contribution by banks in proportion to their deposits. The scheme covers 90 per cent of the first £20,000 per depositor. Therefore small depositors are basically covered for up to 90 per cent of the value of their deposits but large depositors have cover only up to £20,000.

The existence of deposit insurance provides protection for depositors in the event that a financial intermediary fails. But it also limits the incentive for the owner of a financial intermediary to make safe investments and loans. Some economists believe that deposit insurance can create a banking system that is prone to take excessive risks with depositors' money. This is the problem of *moral hazard*. Because depositors are sure that their deposits are insured, they do not keep an eye on what banks are doing with their money. Banks in turn, knowing that depositors are not worried about their funds, will aim to maximize profits by lending to high-risk businesses. It has been argued that this is precisely what happened with Savings & Loans associations (S&Ls) in the United States in the 1980s. Savers, knowing that their deposits were being used to make high-risk loans, did not remove their deposits from S&Ls because they knew they had the security of deposit insurance. The S&L owners making high-risk loans knew they were making a one-way bet. If their loans paid off, they made a high rate of return. If they failed and could not meet their obligations to the depositors, the insurance fund would step in. Bad loans were good business!

Because of this type of problem, all financial intermediaries face regulation of their balance sheets.

Balance Sheet Rules

The most important balance sheet regulations are:

1   Capital requirements.
2   Reserve requirements.

Capital requirements are the minimum amount of an owner's own financial resources that must be put into an intermediary. This amount must be sufficiently large to discourage owners from making loans that are too risky. Banks in the EU and in the developed economies are moving away from a specified capital requirement set at 8 per cent of its assets, to voluntary ratios based on an individual bank's assessment of risk. Different banks will eventually have different capital–asset ratios based on the type of assets they hold on their balance sheets. The riskier the assets, the more capital they will hold.

Reserve requirements are rules setting out the minimum percentages of deposits that must be held in currency or other safe, liquid assets. These minimum percentages vary across the different types of intermediary and deposit. The Bank of England does not specify a reserve requirement, however, banks in other EU countries have reserve requirements and countries in the EMU have a common set of reserve requirements specified by the European Central Bank.

Deregulation in the 1980s

The 1980s was a period of deregulation of the banking and financial system in the United Kingdom. In

1979 exchange controls were abolished. The abolition of these controls meant that banks could borrow and lend overseas unhindered. The most important deregulatory measure in 1980 was the abolition of the *corset*. The corset was a system of regulation that controlled the amount of deposits the banks were allowed to take. With the removal of this and other controls, banks were free to compete with building societies in the market for housing finance. A further deregulatory measure was the removal in 1983 of the arrangement whereby the building societies fixed the interest rate on mortgages. This measure injected further competition into the mortgage market, because now any individual building society could set its interest rate according to the pressures of the market and not wait for all the remaining building societies to change their interest rates together. In 1986 the Building Societies Act allowed the societies to offer similar services to those of banks.

Financial Innovation

The development of new financial products – of new ways of borrowing and lending – is called **financial innovation**. The aim of financial innovation is to lower the cost of borrowing or increase the return from lending or, more simply, to increase the profit from financial intermediation. There are three main influences on financial innovation. They are:

1 Economic environment.

2 Technology.

3 Regulation.

The pace of financial innovation was remarkable in the 1980s, and all three of these forces played a role.

Economic Environment

Some of the innovations that occurred in the 1970s and 1980s were a response to high inflation and high interest rates. An important example is the development of variable interest rate loans for businesses. Traditionally, companies had borrowed long-term funds at fixed interest rates. Rising interest rates brought rising borrowing costs for banks, which led them to develop variable rate lending. Another important innovation in the 1970s was the payment of interest on sight deposits. This had the effect of making the holding of bank deposits as opposed to a savings account more attractive. In the 1980s, depositors who maintained a certain minimum amount in their sight deposit accounts had all bank charges waived, making such accounts even more attractive.

Technology

Other financial innovations resulted from technological change, most notably that associated with the decreased cost of computing and long-distance communication. The use of ATMs and direct debit cards such as Switch cards, which allow stores to debit your bank or building society account directly, is an example of the advance of financial innovation caused by improved technology. The growth in the use of credit cards and the development of international financial markets – for example, the increased importance of Eurodollar[1] – are consequences of technological change. The Mondex card is another example of technological innovation. It is a 'smart card' that has an implication for the payments system. The Mondex card allows a person to carry units of money that can be used electronically as a medium of exchange. It can be credited from their bank account and debited for purchases. It is hoped that one day the Mondex card will replace cash and cheques as the medium of exchange. Experiments with the Mondex card are not conclusive. Many people still like to carry and pay using cash or cheques.

Regulation

A good deal of financial innovation takes place to avoid regulation. For example, when the corset was in operation in the 1970s, banks were not allowed to expand their deposits beyond a certain point. Other financial intermediaries sprang up with different types of deposit to grab the business that banks had to turn away.

Deregulation, Innovation and Money

Deregulation and financial innovation that have led to the development of new types of deposit account have brought important changes in the composition of the nation's money. In the 1960s, M1 consisted of only currency and chequeing sight deposits at commercial banks. In the 1980s, other new types of chequeing deposits expanded while traditional

---

[1] Eurodollars are US dollar bank accounts held in other countries, mainly in Europe. They were 'invented' during the 1960s when the former Soviet Union wanted the security and convenience of holding funds in US dollars but was unwilling to place deposits in US banks.

chequeing sight deposits declined. Similar changes took place in the composition of money. Bank time deposits expanded and building society share accounts began to offer the same services as bank accounts. The result of these changes was that what was measured as the money supply changed and a new measure – M4 – was born.

Review Quiz

◆ What was the effect on the money supply of the deregulatory measures of the 1980s that eliminated the practical distinction between commercial banks and building societies.
◆ What is financial innovation? What are the principal reasons that drove financial innovation in the 1980s and 1990s?
◆ What are the principal rules and regulations commercial banks face and what are the reasons behind these regulations?

Because financial intermediaries are able to create liquidity and to create assets that are a means of payment – money – they occupy a unique place in our economy and exert an important influence on the quantity of money in existence. Let's see how money is created.

How Banks Create Money

Banks create money.[2] But this doesn't mean that they have smoke-filled back rooms in which counterfeiters are busily working. Remember, most money is deposits, not currency. What banks create is deposits and they do so by making loans. But the amount of deposits they can create is limited by their reserves.

Reserves: Actual and Required

We've seen that banks don't have £100 in notes for every £100 that people have deposited with them. In fact, a typical bank today has about 60 pence in currency and another 26 pence on deposit at the Bank of England, a total reserve of less than £1, for every £100 deposited in it. But there is no need for panic. Banks

---

[2] In this section, we'll use the term *banks* to refer to all the depository institutions whose deposits are part of the money supply: commercial banks and building societies.

have learned, from experience, that these reserve levels are adequate for ordinary business needs.

The fraction of a bank's total deposits that are held in reserves is called the **reserve ratio**. The value of the reserve ratio is influenced by the actions of a bank's depositors. If a depositor withdraws currency from a bank, the reserve ratio decreases. If a depositor puts currency into a bank, the reserve ratio increases.

The **required reserve ratio** is the ratio of reserves to deposits that banks are required, by regulation, to hold. A bank's *required reserves* are equal to its deposits multiplied by the required reserve ratio. A bank's **desired reserve ratio** is the ratio of reserves to deposits that banks consider to be prudent to hold in order to meet withdrawals and to carry on their business. A bank's desired reserves are equal to its deposits multiplied by the desired reserve ratio. Actual reserves minus *required* or *desired reserves* are **excess reserves**. Whenever banks have excess reserves, they are able to create money.

To see how banks create money we are going to look at two model banking systems. In the first model there is only one bank. In the second model there are many banks.

Creating Deposits by Making Loans in a One-bank Economy

In the model banking system that we'll study, there is only one bank and its required reserve ratio is 25 per cent. That is, for each £1 deposited, the bank keeps 25 pence in reserves and lends the rest. The balance sheet of One-and-Only Bank is shown in Figure 25.2(a). Its deposits are £400 million and its reserves are 25 per cent of this amount – £100 million. Its loans are equal to deposits minus reserves and are £300 million.

The story begins with Silas Marner, who has decided that it is too dangerous to keep on hiding his fortune under his mattress. Silas has been holding his fortune in currency and has a nest egg of £1 million. He decides to put his £1 million on deposit at the One-and-Only Bank. On the day that Silas makes his deposit, the One-and-Only Bank's balance sheet changes and the new situation is shown in Figure 25.2(b). The bank now has £101 million in reserves and £401 million in deposits. It still has loans of £300 million.

The bank now has *excess reserves*. With reserves of £101 million, the bank would like to have deposits of £404 million and loans of £303 million. And being the One-and-Only Bank, the manager knows the

Figure 25.2

Creating Money at the One-and-Only Bank

(a) Balance sheet on January 1

Assets (millions of pounds)		Liabilities (millions of pounds)	
Reserves	£100	Deposits	£400
Loans	£300		
Total	£400	Total	£400

(b) Balance sheet on January 2

Assets (millions of pounds)		Liabilities (millions of pounds)	
Reserves	£101	Deposits	£401
Loans	£300		
Total	£401	Total	£401

(c) Balance sheet on January 3

Assets (millions of pounds)		Liabilities (millions of pounds)	
Reserves	£101	Deposits	£404
Loans	£303		
Total	£404	Total	£404

In part (a), the One-and-Only Bank has deposits of £400 million, loans of £300 million and reserves of £100 million. The bank's desired reserve ratio is 25 per cent. When the bank receives a deposit of £1 million (part b), it has excess reserves. It lends £3 million and creates a further £3 million of deposits. Deposits increase by £3 million and loans increase by £3 million (in part c).

reserves will remain at £101 million. That is, she knows that when she makes a loan, the amount lent remains on deposit at the One-and-Only Bank. She knows, for example, that all the suppliers of Sky's-the-Limit Construction, her biggest borrower, are also depositors of One-and-Only. So she knows that if she makes the loan that Sky's-the-Limit has just requested, the deposit she lends will never leave One-and-Only. When Sky's-the-Limit uses part of its new loan to pay £100,000 to I-Dig-It Building Company for some excavations, the One-and-Only Bank simply moves the funds from Sky's-the-Limit's chequeing account to I-Dig-It's chequeing account.

So the manager of One-and-Only calls Sky's-the-Limit's accountant and offers to lend the maximum

that she can. How much does she lend? She lends £3 million. By lending £3 million, One-and-Only's balance sheet changes to the one shown in Figure 25.2(c). Loans increase by £3 million to £303 million. The loan shows up in Sky's-the-Limit's deposit initially and total deposits increase to £404 million – £400 million plus Silas Marner's deposit of £1 million plus the newly created deposit of £3 million. The bank now has no excess reserves and has reached the limit of its ability to create money.

The Deposit Multiplier

The **deposit multiplier** is the amount by which an increase in bank reserves is multiplied to calculate the increase in bank deposits. That is:

$$\text{Deposit multiplier} = \frac{\text{Change in deposits}}{\text{Change in reserves}}$$

In the example we've just worked through, the deposit multiplier is 4. The £1 million increase in reserves created a £4 million increase in deposits. The deposit multiplier is linked to the required reserve ratio by the following equation:

$$\text{Deposit multiplier} = \frac{1}{\text{Desired revenue ratio}}$$

In the example, the desired reserve ratio is 25 per cent, or 0.25. That is:

$$\text{Deposit multiplier} = 1/0.25$$

$$= 4$$

Creating Deposits by Making Loans with Many Banks

If you told the student loans officer at your own bank that she creates money, she wouldn't believe you. Bankers see themselves as lending the money they receive from others, not creating money. But in fact, even though each bank only lends what it receives, the banking *system* creates money. To see how, let's look at another example.

Figure 25.3 is going to keep track of what is happening in the process of money creation by a banking system in which each bank has a required reserve ratio of 25 per cent. The process begins when Alan decides to decrease his currency holding and put

Figure 25.3

The Multiple Creation of Bank Deposits

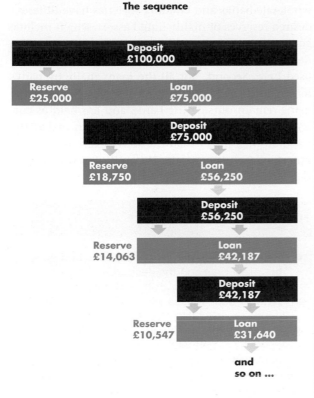

The sequence

	Reserves	Loans	Deposits
Deposit £100,000			
Reserve £25,000 / Loan £75,000	£25,000	£75,000	£100,000
Deposit £75,000			
Reserve £18,750 / Loan £56,250	£43,750	£131,250	£175,000
Deposit £56,250			
Reserve £14,063 / Loan £42,187	£57,813	£173,437	£231,250
Deposit £42,187			
Reserve £10,547 / Loan £31,640	£68,360	£205,077	£273,437
and so on ...	£100,000	£300,000	£400,000

The running tally

When a bank receives deposits, it keeps 25 per cent in reserves and lends 75 per cent. The amount lent becomes a new deposit at another bank. The next bank in the sequence keeps 25 per cent and lends 75 per cent, and the process continues until the banking system has created enough deposits to eliminate its excess reserves. The running tally tells us the amount of deposits and loans created at each stage. At the end of the process, an additional £100,000 of reserves creates an additional £400,000 of deposits.

£100,000 on deposit. Now Alan's bank has £100,000 of new deposits and £100,000 of additional reserves. With a required reserve ratio of 25 per cent, the bank keeps £25,000 on reserve and lends £75,000 to Amy. Amy writes a cheque for £75,000 to buy a photocopy-shop franchise from Barbara. At this point, Alan's Bank has a new deposit of £100,000, new loans of £75,000 and new reserves of £25,000. You can see this situation in Figure 25.3 as the first row of the 'running tally'.

For Alan's bank, that is the end of the story. But it's not the end of the story for the entire banking system. Barbara deposits her cheque for £75,000 in another bank, which has an increase in deposits and reserves of £75,000. This bank puts 25 per cent of its increase in deposits, £18,750 into reserve and lends £56,250 to Bob. And Bob writes a cheque to Carl to pay off a business loan. The current state of play is seen in Figure 25.3. Now, bank reserves have increased by

£43,750 (£25,000 plus £18,750), loans have increased by £131,250 (£75,000 plus £56,250) and deposits have increased by £175,000 (£100,000 plus £75,000).

When Carl takes his cheque to his bank, its deposits and reserves increase by £56,250, £14,060 of which it keeps in reserve and £42,190 of which it lends. This process continues until there are no excess reserves in the banking system. But the process takes a lot of further steps. One additional step is shown in Figure 25.3. The figure also shows the final tallies – reserves increase by £100,000, loans increase by £300,000 and deposits increase by £400,000.

The sequence in Figure 25.3 is the first four stages of the entire process. To figure out the entire process, look closely at the numbers in the figure. At each stage, the loan is 75 per cent (0.75) of the previous loan and the deposit is 0.75 of the previous deposit. Call that proportion L ($L = 0.75$). The complete sequence is:

$1 + L + L^2 + L^3 + \ldots$

Remember, L is a fraction, so at each stage in this sequence the amount of new loans gets smaller. The total number of loans made at the end of the process is the above sum which is:[3]

$$\frac{1}{(1 - L)}$$

Using the numbers from the example, the total increase in deposits is:

£100,000 + 75,000 + 56,250 + 42,190 + . . .

= £100,000 × (1 + 0.75 + 0.5625 + 0.4219 + . . .)

= £100,000 × (1 + 0.75 + 0.75^2 + 0.75^3 + . . .)

= £100,000 × (1 ÷ (1 − 0.75))

= £100,000 × (1 ÷ 0.25)

= £100,000 × 4

= £400,000

By using the same method, you can check that the totals for reserves and loans are the ones shown in Figure 25.3.

So even though each bank only lends the money it receives, the banking system as a whole does create money by making loans. And the amount created is the same in a multibank system as in a one-bank system.

The Deposit Multiplier in the United Kingdom

The deposit multiplier in the United Kingdom works in the same way as the deposit multiplier we've just

---

[3] Both here and in the expenditure multiplier process in Chapter 26, the sequence of values is called a convergent geometric series. To find the sum of such a series, begin by calling the sum S. Then write out the sum as:

$S = 1 + L + L^2 + L^3 + \ldots$

Multiply by L to give:

$LS = L + L^2 + L^3 + \ldots$

and then subtract the second equation from the first to give:

$S(1 - L) = 1$

or:

$S = 1 \div (1 - L)$

worked out for a hypothetical economy. But the actual deposit multiplier differs from the one we've just calculated for two reasons. First, there is no required reserve ratio for UK banks, and retail banks, wholesale banks and building societies have different desired reserves of highly liquid assets, which include government Treasury bills and short-term loans. The desired ratio will be smaller than the one we have used here. Second, not all the loans made by banks return to them in the form of reserves. Some of the loans remain outside the banks and are held as currency. The smaller required reserve ratio makes the UK multiplier larger than the above example. But the other two factors make the UK multiplier smaller.

Review Quiz

◆ Explain how banks create deposits and how their reserves and the desired reserve ratio determine the amount they can lend.
◆ When a bank makes a loan, what happens to deposits and desired reserves at other banks?
◆ Can you explain why, when a bank's desired reserves are equal to its actual reserves, the bank has reached the limit of its ability to create money?
◆ What is the magnitude of the deposit multiplier and how is it related to the desired reserve ratio?

We've now seen what money is and how banks create it. The amount of money created by the banks has a powerful influence on the economy. Our next task is to examine that influence.

Money, Real GDP and the Price Level

You now know that in a modern economy such as that of the United Kingdom today, most of the money is bank deposits. You've seen that banks actually create money by making loans. Does the quantity of money created by the banking and financial system matter? What effect does money have? Does it matter whether the quantity of money increases quickly or slowly? In particular, how does the quantity of money influence real GDP, the price level and the inflation rate?

Figure 25.4

Short-run Effects of a Change in the Quantity of Money

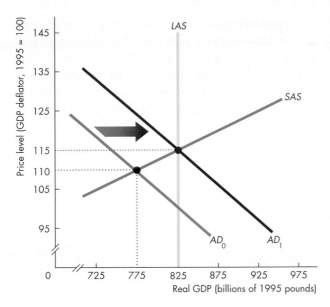

Real GDP is less than potential GDP. An increase in the quantity of money increases aggregate demand and shifts the aggregate demand curve rightward from AD_0 to AD_1. The price level rises to 115 and real GDP expands to £825 billion. The increase in the quantity of money moves real GDP to potential GDP.

We're going to answer these questions first by using the aggregate supply–aggregate demand model, which explains how money affects real GDP and the price level in the short run. Then we're going to study a theory called the quantity theory of money, which explains how money growth influences inflation in the long run. We'll also look at some historical and international evidence on the relationship between money growth and inflation.

The Short-run Effects of a Change in the Quantity of Money

Figure 25.4 illustrates the AS–AD model that explains how real GDP and the price level are determined in the short run. (For a full explanation of the AS–AD model, see Chapter 22, pp. 464–480.) We are going to use this model to study the short-run effect of a change in the quantity of money on real GDP and

the price level. Potential GDP is £825 billion and the long-run aggregate supply curve is LAS. The short-run aggregate supply curve is SAS. Initially, the aggregate demand curve is AD_0. Equilibrium real GDP is £775 billion and the price level is 110 at the intersection of the AD curve and the SAS curve.

Suppose there is now an increase in the quantity of money. This increase results from the process of money creation we've just studied. With more money in their bank accounts, people plan to increase their consumption expenditure and businesses plan to increase their investment. Aggregate demand increases and the aggregate demand curve shifts rightward to AD_1. A new equilibrium emerges at the intersection point of AD_1 and SAS. Real GDP expands to £825 billion and the price level rises to 115. Real GDP now equals potential GDP and there is full employment. This increase in the quantity of money has increased both real GDP and the price level.

Now imagine the reverse situation. Real GDP is initially £825 billion and the price level is 115 at the intersection point of AD_1 and SAS. The quantity of money *decreases*. With *less* money in their bank accounts, people and businesses plan to decrease their expenditures. Aggregate demand decreases and the aggregate demand curve shifts leftward to AD_0. A recession occurs as real GDP shrinks to £775 billion and the price level falls to 110.

These influences of the quantity of money on real GDP and the price level are *short-run* effects. In the long run, a change in the quantity of money, perhaps surprisingly, has no effect on real GDP. All its effects are on the price level. Let's see why this outcome occurs.

The Long-run Effects of a Change in the Quantity of Money

Figure 25.5 explains how real GDP and the price level are determined in both the short run and the long run. Again, potential GDP is £825 billion and the long-run aggregate supply curve is LAS. The short-run aggregate supply curve is SAS_1. Initially, the aggregate demand curve is AD_1. Equilibrium real GDP is £825 billion and the price level is 115. So real GDP equals potential GDP and there is full employment.

Now suppose the quantity of money increases. Aggregate demand increases and the aggregate demand curve shifts rightward to AD_2. The new short-run equilibrium is at the intersection point of AD_2 and SAS_1. The price level rises to 119, and real GDP expands

Figure 25.5

Long-run Effects of a Change in the Quantity of Money

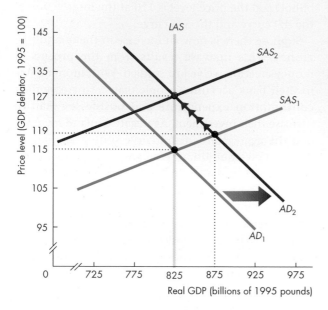

Real GDP equals potential GDP. An increase in the quantity of money shifts the aggregate demand curve from AD_1 to AD_2. The price level rises to 119 and real GDP increases to £875 billion. Real GDP exceeds potential GDP and the money wage rate rises. Short-run aggregate supply decreases and the SAS curve shifts leftward from SAS_1 to SAS_2. Real GDP returns to potential GDP and the price level rises to 127. In the long run, the increase in the quantity of money increases the price level and has no effect on real GDP.

to £875 billion. This short-run adjustment has put real GDP above potential GDP and decreased unemployment below the natural rate. A shortage of labour raises the money wage rate. As the money wage rate rises, short-run aggregate supply decreases and the SAS curve shifts leftward towards SAS_2. As short-run aggregate supply decreases, the price level rises to 127 and real GDP decreases back to potential GDP at £825 billion.

Thus from one full-employment equilibrium to another, an increase in the quantity of money increases the price level and has no effect on real GDP. This relationship between the quantity of money and the price level at full employment is made more precise by the quantity theory of money, which tells us about

the quantitative link between money growth and inflation.

The Quantity Theory of Money

The **quantity theory of money** is the proposition that in the long run, an increase in the quantity of money brings an equal percentage increase in the price level. The original basis of the quantity theory of money is a concept known as the velocity of circulation and an equation called the equation of exchange.

The **velocity of circulation** is the average number of times a unit of money is used annually to buy the goods and services that make up GDP. GDP is equal to the price level (P) multiplied by real GDP (Y). That is:

$$GDP = PY$$

Call the quantity of money M. The velocity of circulation, V, is determined by the equation:

$$V = PY/M$$

For example, if nominal GDP is £950 billion (real GDP multiplied by the price level and divided by 100) and the quantity of money is £475 billion, the velocity of circulation is 2. On the average, each unit of money circulates twice in its use to purchase the final goods and services that make up GDP. That is, each unit of money is used twice in a year to buy GDP.

Figure 25.6 shows the history of the velocity of circulation of M4 in the United Kingdom. You can see that the velocity of circulation has been falling steadily. The reason the velocity of circulation has decreased is because deregulation and financial innovation have created new types of deposit and higher interest rates on those deposits have attracted funds that were normally held as savings. More and more people are having their salaries and wages paid directly into bank accounts and now use cheques and direct debit cards. Direct debit cards enable shops to debit sums of money electronically from your bank account. They are substitutes for cheques.

Banks also have developed better methods of cash management and need to keep fewer stocks in their vaults. Except in the 'hidden' economy where cash is the main medium of exchange, today more people use cheques and cards than use cash. You can see that there was a sharp fall in velocity in the UK during the 1980s. This is because the pace of deregulation and

Figure 25.6

The Velocity of Circulation in the United Kingdom: 1969–2000

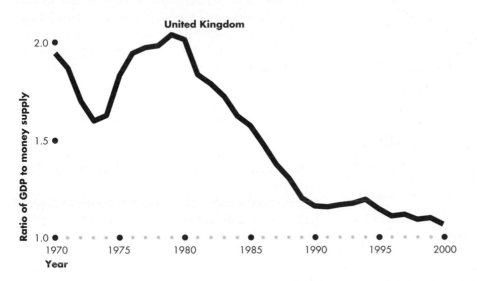

The velocity of circulation has declined steadily because the cash substitutes that have resulted from financial innovation are new types of deposit that are part of the money supply.

Sources: *Bank of England*

---

financial innovation. The flatenning out of the M4 velocity in the 1990s is a signal that the pace of deregulation and financial innovation may have come to an end.

The **equation of exchange** states that the quantity of money (*M*) multiplied by the velocity of circulation (*V*) equals GDP, or:

$$MV = PY$$

Given the definition of the velocity of circulation, this equation is always true – it is true by definition. With *M* equal to £475 billion and *V* equal to 2, *MV* is equal to £950 billion, the value of nominal GDP.

The equation of exchange becomes the quantity theory of money by making two assumptions:

1 The velocity of circulation is not influenced by the quantity of money.

2 Potential real GDP is not influenced by the quantity of money.

If these two assumptions are true, the equation of exchange tells us that in the long run, a given percentage change in the quantity of money brings

about an equal percentage change in the price level. You can see why by solving the equation of exchange for the price level. Dividing both sides of the equation by real GDP (*Y*) gives:

$$P = (V/Y)M$$

In the long run, real GDP (*Y*) equals potential GDP, so if potential GDP and velocity are not influenced by the quantity of money, the relationship between the change in the price level (ΔP) and the change in the quantity of money (ΔM) is:

$$\Delta P = (V/Y)\,\Delta M$$

Divide this equation by the previous one ($P = (V/Y)M$) to give:

$$\Delta P/P = \Delta M/M$$

($\Delta P/P$) is the percentage increase in the price level and ($\Delta M/M$) is the percentage increase in the quantity of money. So this equation is the quantity theory of money. In the long run, the percentage increase in the price level equals the percentage increase in the quantity of money.

The Quantity Theory and the *AS–AD* Model

The quantity theory of money can be interpreted in terms of the *AS–AD* model. The aggregate demand curve is a relationship between the quantity of real GDP demanded (*Y*) and the price level (*P*), other things remaining constant. We can obtain such a relationship from the equation of exchange:

$$MV = PY$$

Dividing both sides of this equation by real GDP (*Y*) gives:

$$P = MV/Y$$

This equation may be interpreted as describing an aggregate demand curve. In Chapter 22 (pp. 469–473) you saw that the aggregate demand curve slopes downward – as the price level increases the quantity of real GDP demanded decreases. The above equation also shows such a relationship between the price level and the quantity of real GDP demanded. For a given quantity of money (*M*) and a given velocity of circulation (*V*), the higher the price level (*P*), the smaller is the quantity of real GDP demanded (*Y*).

In general, when the quantity of money changes, the velocity of circulation might also change. But the quantity theory asserts that velocity is not influenced by the quantity of money. If this assumption is correct, an increase in the quantity of money increases aggregate demand and shifts the aggregate demand curve upward by the same amount as the percentage change in the quantity of money.

The quantity theory of money also asserts that real GDP, which in the long run equals potential GDP, is not influenced by the quantity of money. This assertion is true in the *AS–AD* model. Figure 25.5 shows the quantity theory result in the *AS–AD* model. Initially the economy is at full employment on the long-run aggregate supply curve *LAS* and at the intersection of the aggregate demand curve *AD*$_1$ and the short-run aggregate supply curve *SAS*$_1$. A 10 per cent increase in the quantity of money shifts the aggregate demand curve from *AD*$_1$ to *AD*$_2$. This shift, measured by the vertical distance between the two demand curves, is 10 per cent. In the long run, wages rise (also

by 10 per cent) and shift the *SAS* curve leftward to *SAS*$_2$. A new full-employment (long-run) equilibrium occurs at the intersection of *AD*$_2$ and *SAS*$_2$. Real GDP remains at potential GDP of £825 billion and the price level rises to 127. The new price level is about 10 per cent higher than the initial one (127 – 115 = 12, which is 10.4 per cent of 115).

So the *AS–AD* model predicts the same outcome as the quantity theory of money. The *AS–AD* model also predicts a less precise relationship between the quantity of money and the price level in the short run than in the long run. For example, Figure 25.4 shows that starting out with unemployment, an increase in the quantity of money increases real GDP. In this case, a 10 per cent increase in the money supply increases the price level from 110 to 115 – a 4.5 per cent increase. That is, the price level changes by a smaller percentage than the percentage change in quantity of money.

How good a theory is the quantity theory of money? Let's answer this question by looking at the relationship between money and the price level, both historically and internationally.

Historical Evidence on the Quantity Theory of Money

The percentage increase in the price level is the inflation rate, and the percentage increase in the quantity of money is the money supply growth rate. So the quantity theory predictions can be cast in terms of money growth and inflation. The quantity theory predicts that at a given level of potential GDP and in the long run, the inflation rate will equal the money growth rate. But over time, potential GDP expands. Taking this expansion into account, the quantity theory predicts that in the long run, the inflation rate will equal the money growth rate minus the growth rate of potential GDP.

We can test the quantity theory of money by looking at the historical relationship between money growth and inflation in the United Kingdom. Figure 25.7 shows this relationship for the years between 1963 and 2000. The inflation rate is the percentage change in the GDP deflator and growth in the broad money supply – M4. The chart shows year-to-year changes in money and the price level. These changes show the relationship between money growth and inflation. If the quantity theory is a reasonable guide to reality, there should be a strong correlation between inflation and money growth.

Figure 25.7

Money Growth and Inflation in the United Kingdom: 1964–2000

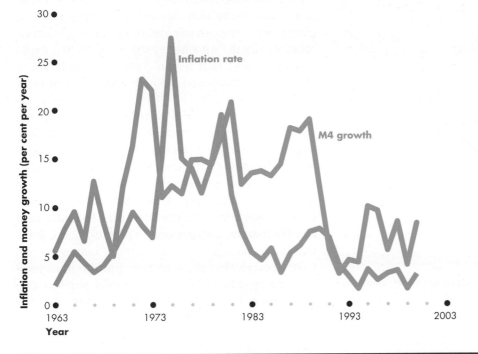

Year-to-year fluctuations in money growth and inflation are loosely correlated. The growth of M4 and inflation appeared to have a strong correlation in the 1960s and 1970s but that correlation has weakened in the 1980s and restored in the 1990s.

Source: *Bank of England*.

The data are broadly consistent with the quantity theory. The money growth rate and the inflation rate are correlated but the relationship is not precise. In the 1960s and 1970s, M4 growth preceded changes in inflation. In the 1980s, the relationship between M4 growth and inflation appears to have broken down. In the 1990s, the association between the rate of growth of M4 and inflation has strengthened. The reason why the correlation between M4 and inflation in the 1980s was weaker is because of the deregulation and financial innovation during that period.

International Evidence on the Quantity Theory of Money

Another way to test the quantity theory of money is to look at the cross-country relationship between money growth and inflation. Figure 25.8 shows this relationship for 60 countries during the 1980s. By looking at a decade average, we again are smoothing out the short-run effects of money growth and focusing on the long-run effects. There is in these data an unmistakable tendency for high money growth to be associated with high inflation.

Correlation, Causation and Other Influences

Both the historical evidence for the United Kingdom and the international data tell us that in the long run, money growth and inflation are correlated. But the correlation between money growth and inflation does not tell us that money growth causes inflation. Money growth might cause inflation; inflation might cause money growth; or some third variable might simultaneously cause inflation and money growth.

According to the quantity theory and according to the *AS–AD* model, causation runs from money growth to inflation. But neither theory denies the possibility that at different times and places, causation might run in the other direction, or that some third factor might be the root cause of both rapid money growth and inflation. One possible third factor is a large and persistent government budget deficit that gets financed by newly created money.

But some occasions give us an opportunity to test our assumptions about causation. One of these is the Second World War and the years immediately following it. Rapid money growth during the war

Figure 25.8

Money Growth and Inflation in the World Economy

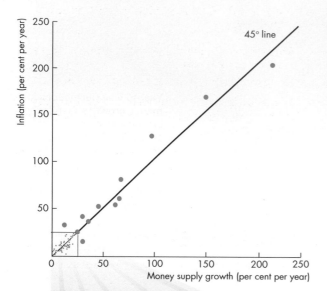

(a) All countries

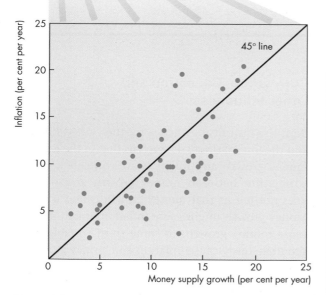

(b) Low-inflation countries

Inflation and money growth in 60 countries (in part a) and low-inflation countries (in part b) show that money growth is one influence, though not the only influence, on inflation.

Source: Federal Reserve Bank of St Louis, *Review*, May/June 1988, p. 15.

years accompanied by price controls almost certainly caused inflation to rise in the immediate post-war period. The inflationary consequences of the money growth were delayed by the controls but not removed. It is inconceivable that this was an example of reverse causation – of post-war inflation causing wartime money growth. Another is the early 1970s. Rapid money growth that began during the early 1970s almost certainly caused the high and persistent inflation of the mid-1970s.

The combination of historical and international correlations between money growth and inflation, and independent evidence about the direction of causation, leads to the conclusion that the quantity theory is correct in the long run. It explains the long-term fundamental source of inflation. But the quantity theory is not correct in the short run. To understand the short-term fluctuations in inflation, the joint effects of a change in the quantity of money on real GDP, the velocity of circulation and the price level must be explained. The *AS–AD* model provides this explanation. It also points to the possibility of other factors that influence both aggregate supply and aggregate demand influencing the inflation rate independently of the money growth rate.

Review Quiz

◆ Why has the velocity of circulation declined in the UK?
◆ What are the short-run and long-run effects on the price level and GDP of an increase in the quantity of money?
◆ What is the long-run impact on the price level of an increase in the quantity of money, when real GDP equals potential GDP?
◆ What is the historical and international evidence on the relationship between money growth and inflation?

In the next chapter, we're going to study the role of the central bank and monetary policy. We'll see how the central bank's actions can change the quantity of money and influence interest rates, which in turn influence aggregate demand. Then, in Chapter 28, we'll return to the problem of inflation and explore more deeply its causes, its consequences and ways of keeping it under control.

Summary

Key Points

What is Money? (pp. 545–550)

- Money is the means of payment and it has three functions. It is a medium of exchange, a unit of account and a store of value.

- The main measure of money in the United Kingdom today is M4, which is currency held by the public and all bank and building society sight and time deposits.

Financial Intermediaries (pp. 550–553)

- The main financial intermediaries whose liabilities are money are commercial banks and building societies.

- These institutions take in deposits, hold cash and liquid assets as reserves so that they can meet their depositors' demands and use the rest either to buy securities or to make loans.

- Financial intermediaries provide four main economic services. They create liquidity, minimize the cost of obtaining funds, minimize the cost of monitoring borrowers and pool risks.

Financial Regulation, Deregulation and Innovation (pp. 553–555)

- Financial intermediaries face two types of regulation: deposit insurance and balance sheet rules.

- The most important balance sheet regulations are: capital requirements and reserve requirements.

- The three main influences on financial innovation are: the economic environment, technology and regulation.

How Banks Create Money (pp. 555–558)

- Banks create money by making loans.

- The total quantity of deposits that can be supported by a given amount of reserves (the deposit multiplier) is equal to 1 divided by the desired reserve ratio.

Money, Real GDP and the Price Level (pp. 558–564)

- An increase in the quantity of money increases aggregate demand and, in the short run, increases both the price level and real GDP.

- In the long run an increase in the quantity of money increases the price level and leaves real GDP unchanged.

- Like the *AS–AD* model, the quantity theory of money predicts no long-run relationship between money and real GDP.

Key Figures

Key Terms

Problems

•1 Which of the following items are money?

   a Bank of England notes in the commercial bank's cash machines.

   b Your Visa card.

   c The coins inside public phones.

   d Pound coins in your wallet.

   e The cheque you have just written to pay for your rent.

   f The student loan you took out in September to pay for your school fees.

2 Which of the following items are money? Which are deposit money?

   a Demand deposits at the Bank of England.

   b British Telecom shares held by individuals.

   c The £5 commemorative crown for the Queen's Jubilee.

   d UK government securities.

•3 Sara withdraws £1,000 from her savings account at her building society, keeps £50 in cash, and deposits the balance in her demand deposit account at her commercial bank. What is the immediate change in M1 and M2+?

4 Monica takes €10,000 from her demand deposit account at her commercial bank and puts the funds into her building society savings account. What is the immediate change in M1 and M2+?

•5 The banks in Zap have:

Reserves	£250 million
Loans	£1,000 million
Deposits	£2,000 million
Total assets	£2,500 million

   a Construct the banks' balance sheet. If you are missing any assets, call them 'other assets'; if you are missing any liabilities, call them 'other liabilities'.

   b Calculate the banks' reserve ratio.

   c If banks hold no excess reserves, calculate the deposit multiplier.

6 The banks in Zip have:

Reserves	£125 million
Loans	£1,875 million
Deposits	£2,000 million
Total assets	£2,100 million

   a Construct the banks' balance sheet. If you are missing any assets, call them 'other assets'; if you are missing any liabilities, call them 'other liabilities'.

   b Calculate the banks' reserve ratio.

   c If banks hold no excess reserves, calculate the deposit multiplier.

•7 The spreadsheet figure provides information about the demand for money in Minland. Column A is the interest rate, R. Columns B, C, and D show the quantity of money demanded at three different levels of real GDP: Y_0 is €10 billion, Y_1 is €20 billion, and Y_2 is €30 billion. The quantity of money supplied by the Minland central bank is €3.0 billion. Initially, real GDP is €20 billion. What happens in Minland if the interest rate:

	A	B	C	D
1	R	Y_0	Y_1	Y_2
2	7	1.0	1.5	2.0
3	6	1.5	2.0	2.5
4	5	2.0	2.5	3.0
5	4	2.5	3.0	3.5
6	3	3.0	3.5	4.0
7	2	3.5	4.0	4.5
8	1	4.0	4.5	5.0

   a Exceeds 4 per cent a year?

   b Is less than 4 per cent a year?

   c Equals 4 per cent a year?

8 In problem 7, Minland experiences a severe recession. Real GDP falls to €10 billion. The Minland central bank takes no action to change the quantity of money.

   a What happens in Minland if the interest rate is 4 per cent a year?

   b What is the equilibrium interest rate?

   c Compared with the situation in problem 7, does the interest rate in Minland rise or fall? Why?

•9 In problem 7, Minland experiences a severe business cycle. Real GDP rises to €30 billion and then falls to €10 billion. The Minland central bank takes no actions to change the quantity of money. What happens to the interest rate in Minland during the:

   a Expansion phase of the cycle?

   b Recession phase of the cycle?

10 In problem 7, a financial innovation changes the demand for money. People plan to hold €0.5 billion less than the numbers in the spreadsheet.

   a What happens to the interest rate if the Minland central bank takes no action?

b What happens to the interest rate if the Minland central bank decreases the quantity of money by €0.5 billion? Explain.

•**11** The figure shows the demand for real money in Upland.

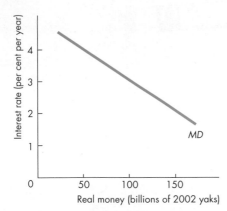

a Draw the supply of money curve if the interest rate is 3 per cent a year.

b If the Upland central bank wants to lower the interest rate by 1 percentage point, by how much must it change the quantity of real money?

12 In problem 11, a new smart card replaces currency and the demand for money changes.

Also, the new smart card causes business to boom and real GDP increases.

a Use the figure for problem 11 and draw a new demand for money curve that is consistent with the events just described.

b If the Upland central bank wants to prevent the interest rate from changing, what must it do to the supply of money?

•**13** In problem 9, when Minland experiences a severe business cycle, what happens to autonomous consumption expenditure, investment, the exchange rate, and net exports during the:

a Expansion phase of the cycle?

b Recession phase of the cycle?

14 In problem 10, when Minland experiences a financial innovation that changes the demand for money:

a What happens to autonomous consumption expenditure, investment, the exchange rate, and net exports if the Minland central bank takes no actions?

b What happens to autonomous consumption expenditure, investment, the exchange rate, and net exports if the Minland central bank decreases the quantity of money by €0.5 billion? Explain.

Critical Thinking

1 Study Reading Between the Lines on pp. 568–569 and then answer the following questions:

a What is dinero B and can it be distinguished from dinero A?

b What has happened to the measured velocity of circulation of money in Spain? How will this measure change if we could identify the size of the black economy.

c How will people try to get rid of their holdings of 'dinero B' before the changeover to euros?

d What is your prediction as to what will happen to the price level, real GDP and the size of the black economy in Spain, in the short run and the long run?

2 Rapid inflation in Brazil caused the cruzeiro, the currency of Brazil, to lose its ability to function as money. People were unwilling to accept it because it lost value too fast. Which of the following commodities do you think would be most likely to take the place of the cruzeiro and act as money in the Brazilian economy?

a Tractor parts.

b Packs of cigarettes.

c Loaves of bread.

d Impressionist paintings.

e Baseball trading cards.

3 Use the link on the Parkin, Powell and Matthews website to visit Mark Bernkopf's Central Banking Resource Center. Read the short article on Electronic Cash and also read 'The End of Cash' by James Gleick (first published in the *New York Times Magazine*, 16 June 1996). Then answer the following questions:

a What is e-cash?

b Mark Bernkopf asks: 'Will "e-cash" enable private currencies to overturn the ability of governments to make monetary policy?' Will it? Why or why not?

c When you buy an item on the Internet and pay by using a form of e-cash, are you using money? Explain why or why not.

d In your opinion, is the concern about e-cash a real concern or hype?

 http://www.econ100.com

The Quantity of Money

THE FINANCIAL TIMES, 20 APRIL 2001

FT

Spending spree in Spain heralds end of 'black peseta'

Leslie Crawford

The launch of euro notes and coins next January is posing an awkward problem for many Spaniards; what to do with all the pesetas they have stuffed in mattresses to avoid paying tax on undeclared earnings.

Economists estimate there are 4,000bn–10,000bn black pesetas (£15bn–£37bn) = equivalent to 4–10 per cent of gross domestic product.

Black money, which Spaniards call 'dinero B', pays for cards, travel, wages in construction and agricultural sectors, and goods and services for which official invoices are not required. It is the grease that oils Spain's small and medium-sized companies, which have perfected the art of double accounting: one book for the tax man and a second one kept under lock and key.

The laundering of dinero B has spawned an industry of its own. For the affluent there are financial boutiques, headed by soft-spoken lawyers with weighty surnames, impeccable credentials and murky contacts, who are specialists in transforming dinero B into dinero A or into dollars, sterling or Swiss francs.

Most Spaniards cannot pay for such services and so risk drawing the attention of tax authorities when they try to exchange their black pesetas for euros in the first quarter of next year. The peseta ceases to be legal tender on 1 March 2002, although it will remain exchangeable at banks.

The Bank of Spain, fearing a liquidity crunch, is bending over backwards to make matters easy for anyone with black pesetas. From 1 January Spaniards will be able to exchange lump sums of up to Pta2.5m for euros without having to identify themselves or explain the provenance of the money. Cheques worth up to Pta500,000 will also require no identification.

But holders of dinero B remain suspicious, and have turned to other ways of getting value from their soon-to-expire currency. Their favourite solution has been real estate, fuelling the hottest housing boom since the late 1980s.

House prices have on average increased by 27 per cent in the past two years and by 55 per cent in affluent regions such as the Balearics. The price rise has invigorated the construction sector, another mainstay of the black economy, which built more than half a million homes last year.

But these statistics underestimate the amount of black money that is being funnelled into real estate. To avoid capital gains tax and hefty stamp duties, buyers and sellers agree on an artificially low 'official' price. Dinero B makes up the difference.

Home improvements and building renovations, which are tax deductible, are another favourite method of laundering dinero B.

Economists believe most Spaniards have by now figured out what to do with their dinero B. There is broad public support for the conversion to the euro, particularly as a result of the low interest rates and financial stability that have accompanied Spain's inclusion in Europe's economic and monetary union.

In any event it is unlikely dinero B will disappear. Tax dodging habits do not change with a change in currency. The only difference will be that, come January, dinero B will be denominated in euros.

The Essence of the Story

- Euro notes and coin will go into circulation on 1 January 2002.

- There are 4,000–10,000 billion pesetas, equivalent to 4 to 10 per cent of Spain's GDP, that are held by people engaged in the black economy.

- Black money, which is called dinero B, pays for cars, travel, and wages in the construction and agricultural sectors.

- The changeover from pesetas to euros has caused a problem for all those holding 'dinero B' as to how to convert their black currency without attracting the attention of the authorities.

- The Bank of Spain is making things easy by allowing people to exchange large sums of up to 2.5 million pesetas for euros without having to identify themselves.

Economic Analysis

■ The amount of currency being held by people who have obtained it from transactions in unrecorded economic activity is a stock. The size of the black economy in Spain is not measured with certainty and is a flow (go back to Chapter 20 if you need to revise the concepts of stock and flow).

■ Currency is usually used in black economy transactions rather than bank deposits because in principle bank deposits can be traced by the authorities but cash is anonymous.

■ Figure 1 shows the velocity of circulation in Spain measured by GDP divided by the stock of currency. The velocity of circulation has risen from 9.0 in 1995 to 10.125 in 2000. The rise in the velocity is an indication that people are economizing on the use of cash. But velocity would be even higher if we could measure the size of the black economy.

■ The dilemma for the holders of 'dinero B' is that they want to get rid of their holdings without attracting attention to themselves. The favourite solution is to convert their 'dinero B' monetary wealth into another form of wealth – namely real estate.

■ The increase in demand for houses has added to the house price and construction sector boom already fuelled by the low interest rates from Spain joining the EMU.

■ Figure 2 shows the short-run effect of an increase in demand as people try to get rid of their 'dinero B' before pesetas get converted to euros. The AD schedule shifts out to AD_1. Real GDP and the price level increases. In the long run because real GDP is greater than potential GDP, the SAS curve will shift to the left and the price level will increase further but real GDP will return to potential GDP.

■ Figure 3 shows inflation and the growth of real GDP in Spain relative to the rest of the EU (Spanish figure minus EU figure). Since 1995, Spain has had higher real GDP growth and higher inflation than the rest of the EU.

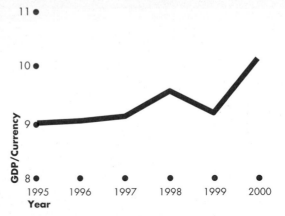

Figure 1 Velocity of circulation

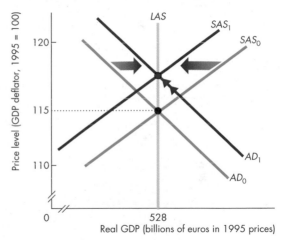

Figure 2 AS–AD

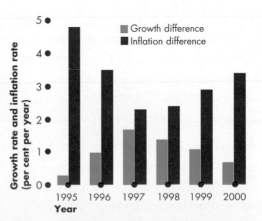

Figure 3 Growth and inflation differences between Spain and EU

Money and Inflation

Inflation is always and everywhere a monetary phenomenon.

Milton Friedman, The Counter-Revolution in Monetary Theory

The Economist: Milton Friedman

Milton Friedman was born into a poor immigrant family in New York City in 1912. He was an undergraduate at Rutgers and graduate student at Columbia University during the Great Depression. Today, Professor Friedman is a Senior Fellow at the Hoover Institution at Stanford University. But his reputation was built between 1946 and 1983, when he was a leading member of the 'Chicago School', which developed an approach to economics at the University of Chicago based on the views that free markets allocate resources efficiently and that stable and low money supply growth delivers macroeconomic stability.

Friedman has advanced our understanding of the forces that determine aggregate demand and clarified the effects of the quantity of money. For this work, he was awarded the 1977 Nobel Prize for Economic Science (much overdue in the opinion of his many admirers).

By reasoning from basic economic principles, Friedman predicted that persistent demand stimulation would *not* increase output but *would* cause inflation. When output growth slowed and inflation broke out in the 1970s, Friedman seemed like a prophet and, for a time, his policy prescription, known as 'monetarism', was embraced around the world.

The Issues and Ideas

The combination of history and economics has taught us a lot about the causes of inflation. Severe inflation – hyperinflation – arises from a breakdown of the normal fiscal policy processes at times of war or political upheaval. Tax revenues fall short of government spending, and newly printed money fills the gap between them. As inflation increases, the quantity of money needed to make payments increases, and a shortage of money can even result. So the rate of money growth increases yet further, and prices rise yet faster. Eventually, the monetary system collapses. Such was the experience of Germany during the 1920s and Brazil during the 1990s.

In earlier times, when commodities were used as money, inflation resulted from the discovery of new sources of money. The most recent occurrence of this type of inflation was at the end of the nineteenth century when gold, then used as money, was discovered in Australia, the Klondike and South Africa.

In modern times, inflation has resulted from increases in the money supply that has accommodated increases in costs. The most dramatic of such inflations occurred during the 1970s when central banks around the world accommodated oil price increases.

To avoid inflation, money supply growth must be held in check. But at times of severe cost pressure, central banks feel a strong tug in the direction of avoiding recession and accommodating the cost pressure.

Yet some countries have avoided inflation more effectively than others. One source of success is central bank independence. Traditionally, in low-inflation countries such as Germany, the central bank decides how much money to create and at what level to set interest rates and does not take instructions from the government. In former high-inflation countries, such as Italy, the central bank takes direct orders from the government about interest rates and money supply growth. The architects of a new monetary system for the European Union have noticed this connection between central bank independence and inflation, and they have modelled the European Central Bank on Germany's Bundesbank.

Then . . .

When inflation is especially rapid, as it was in Germany in 1923, money becomes almost worthless. In Germany at that time, bank notes were more valuable as fire kindling than as money, and the sight of people burning Reichmarks was a common one. To avoid having to hold money for too long, wages were paid and spent twice a day. Banks took deposits and made loans, but at interest rates that compensated both depositors and the bank for the falling value of money – interest rates that could exceed 100 per cent a month. The price of a dinner might double during the course of an evening, making lingering over coffee a very expensive pastime.

. . . And Now

In 1994, Brazil had a computer-age hyperinflation, an inflation rate that was close to 50 per cent a month. Banks installed ATMs on almost every street corner and refilled them several times an hour. Brazilians tried to avoid holding currency. As soon as they were paid, they went shopping and bought enough food to get them through to the next payday. Some shoppers filled as many as six carts on a single monthly trip to the supermarket. Also, instead of using currency, Brazilians used credit cards whenever possible. But they paid their card balances off quickly because the interest rate on unpaid balances was

50 per cent a month. Only at such a high interest rate did it pay banks to lend to cardholders, because banks themselves were paying interest rates of 40 per cent a month to induce customers to keep their money in the bank.

CHAPTER 26

The Central Bank and Monetary Policy

After studying this chapter you will be able to:

◆ Describe the role of the Bank of England

◆ Describe the tools used by the Bank of England to conduct its monetary policy

◆ Explain what an open market operation is and how it works

◆ Explain how an open market operation changes the money supply

◆ Explain how a central bank controls the money supply

◆ Explain what determines the demand for money

◆ Explain how the Bank of England influences interest rates

◆ Explain how interest rates influence the economy

The Old Lady and the New Kid

Many young economists working in financial institutions in London or Frankfurt use a great deal of ingenuity in trying to predict the monthly money supply figures ahead of their publication. Why did they do this? The reason is that by predicting the money supply figures ahead of the Central Bank they were hoping to predict the movement of interest rates and the reaction of the financial markets so that they could take speculative positions on behalf of their institutions. ◆ During November 2001, interest rates were reduced in unison by the US Federal Reserve, the European Central Bank and the Bank of England. Many economic analysts working in the City of London and Frankfurt warned of a rapidly slowing world economy and expected interest rates to be cut. During most of 2000 the European Central Bank and the Bank of England continuously raised interest rates. But since the beginning of 2001 both central banks have been cutting interest rates. ◆ Why do interest rates move up and down in this yo-yo fashion? What determines interest rates? Is there some reason for their up-and-down behaviour or is it purely random? You suspect that there is some reason. You may read in the newspapers that the central bank supports an interest rate rise because money supply growth is too high. Then, some months later, you may read that the central bank supports an interest rate cut because output growth is expected to fall. How does the central bank change interest rates? How do interest rates influence the economy? And how do interest rates keep inflation in check? In Reading Between the Lines (pp. 600–601) you will examine the monetary policy of the European Central Bank and their objective of low inflation.

◆ ◆ ◆ ◆ In this chapter you will learn about the central bank and monetary policy. You will learn how the Bank of England, the European Central Bank and other central banks influence interest rates and how interest rates influence the economy. You'll discover that interest rates depend, in part, on the amount of money in existence. You will also discover how the central bank influences the quantity of money to influence interest rates as it attempts to smooth the business cycle and keep inflation in check.

A New Central Bank

The **Bank of England**, affectionately known as the 'Old Lady of Threadneedle Street', is the central bank of the United Kingdom and one of the oldest central banks in existence. The **European Central Bank** (ECB) in Frankfurt is one of the youngest. A **central bank** is a bankers' bank and a public authority charged with regulating and controlling a nation's monetary and financial institutions and markets. As the bankers' bank, the central bank provides banking services to the commercial banks. But a central bank is not a citizens' bank. That is, it does not provide general banking services for businesses and individual citizens.

The central bank conducts the nation's **monetary policy**, which means that it adjusts the quantity of money in circulation. In the case of the ECB, it conducts the monetary policy for the countries that belong to the eurozone. The ECB and the Bank of England's goal in its conduct of monetary policy is to keep inflation within a specified target range but its other objectives are to moderate the business cycle, and manage and sometimes defend the exchange rate. Complete success in the pursuit of these goals is impossible, and typically a central bank's more modest goal is to improve the performance of the economy and to get closer to the goals than a 'hands off' approach would achieve. Whether the central bank succeeds in improving economic performance is a matter on which there is a variety of opinion.

If the United Kingdom joins the European Monetary Union (EMU), the powers the Bank of England currently exercises over monetary policy will be handed over to the European Central Bank. The ECB, through its Governing Council which consists of ECB officials and the Governors of the participating countries of the EMU meet regularly to set the rate of interest for the countries in the EMU. For the time being the UK remains outside the EMU which allows the Bank of England to decide monetary policy for the UK.

Our aim in this chapter is to learn about the tools available to the central bank in its conduct of monetary policy and the effects of its actions on the economy.

The Bank of England

The Bank of England was formally recognized as the central bank of the United Kingdom in the 1946 Bank of England Act. It had been established in 1694 by an act of Parliament following a loan of £1.2 million by a syndicate of wealthy individuals to the government of King William and Queen Mary. The creation of the Bank formalized the process whereby the syndicate lent to the government in return for the right to issue bank notes. Between 1688 and 1815, the United Kingdom was involved in seven wars and several small conflicts which needed funding. The growing dependence on the Bank of England for raising funds in times of crisis created the role of the government's bank. In April 1997, the government made the Bank of England operationally independent in the determination of monetary policy.

The ECB was established on 1 June 1998. The principal function of the ECB is the guardian of price stability in the eurozone. The ECB is the 'new kid on the block' as far as central banks go. But it has the credibility and expertise that built the reputation of the central banks of the countries that belong to the eurozone. The highest decision making body in the ECB is the Governing Council which is made up of the Executive Board and the Governors of the central banks of the eurozone.

The functions of the Bank of England as a central bank have developed over the three centuries since its creation. Today these functions can be summarized as:

◆ Banker to the government.

◆ Bankers' bank.

◆ Lender of last resort.

◆ Regulator of banks.

◆ Manager of monetary policy.

The ECB has only one function, which is the manager of monetary policy. The other four functions are devolved to the national central banks of each country. Let us briefly examine each of these functions.

Banker to the Government

The banker to the government means that the government's own deposits – called public deposits – are held at the Bank of England. These are the accounts of the revenue raising agencies such as the Inland Revenue and HM Customs and Excise, and the spending departments such as the Ministry of Defence. A business that needs to pay tax will pay a cheque to the Inland Revenue, which will eventually be deposited at the Bank of England. If the Ministry of Defence has to pay for a new fighting ship, it will issue a cheque based on its account at the Bank. Acting as the government's bank also means that the

Bank handles the government's borrowing needs. There are two ways in which the government can borrow: directly from the Bank of England in the form of a loan or by selling bonds. Direct lending amounts to the same thing as printing money. The alternative is to manage the government's borrowing by selling government bonds to the public. The function of selling government debt gives the Bank a pivotal role in the conduct of monetary policy.

Banker's Bank

The commercial banks keep a certain amount of money as deposits at the Bank of England. This is a convenient means by which banks can settle debts they have with each other by simply transferring funds between accounts at the Bank. The Bank is also the sole effective issuer of bank notes. If the general public increase their demand for notes, this will result in a decrease in the amount of notes kept by the banks. The banks will replenish their stock of notes by cashing their deposits at the Bank of England. The Bank of England in turn will issue bank notes as it has an effective monopoly. Even though the Scottish banks issue their own bank notes they must be backed fully by Bank of England notes.

Lender of Last Resort

The Bank of England acts as the lender of last resort to the banking system. It operates on two levels. On a day-to-day basis, when the commercial banks run short of cash, it is the Bank of England that restores the cash levels of the banks. The Bank of England also acts as lender of last resort to any individual bank or group of banks that are experiencing liquidity problems. The aim of the Bank is to ensure the smooth working of the financial system.

Regulator of Banks

As the Bank ultimately guarantees the stability of the banking and financial system, it also faces the problem of moral hazard (see Chapter 25, p. 553). Some economists argue that banks may be tempted to act imprudently if they think that the central bank is always there to provide liquidity in a crisis. To guard against this possibility, the central bank also undertakes the prudential regulation of commercial banks. In the UK, regulation is based on the supervision of individual banks by the Financial Services Authority.

There are two levels at which a central bank can monitor and regulate commercial banks. At one level,

it licenses the entry and establishment of a bank. The central bank must be convinced that a new commercial bank is a fit and proper organization to conduct the business of banking, and any breach of the set criteria will result in loss of authorization to act as a bank. At the second level, the central bank or an independent agent monitors the liquidity and capital adequacy of the commercial bank. We examined such regulations in Chapter 25.

Manager of Monetary Policy

The Bank of England is operationally independent in the conduct of monetary policy. This means that it is no longer the agent of the government but determines monetary policy based on a set of objectives decided by the Chancellor of the Exchequer. The primary objective of the Bank of England is to maintain inflation between $1\frac{1}{2}$ and $2\frac{1}{2}$ per cent but it is also concerned with output growth because that also influences inflation. The primary goal of the ECB is to keep inflation in the eurozone below 2 per cent a year.

The main channel by which the central bank conducts monetary policy is through the setting of the rate of interest at which it deals with the commercial banks.

The Bank's Financial Structure

For accounting purposes, the Bank of England is separated into two departments: the Issue department and the Banking department. The Issue department is treated as part of the government, whereas the Banking department is a public corporation. The separation is largely historical and is not particularly important from an analytical viewpoint. The Issue department is the bank note issuing arm of the Bank of England and the Banking department takes deposits from the commercial banks. Also, the Issue department has as its liabilities the notes in circulation including the notes held by the Banking department. Table 26.1 shows the consolidated balance sheet of the Bank of England. It is arrived at by adding the assets and liabilities of the two departments and subtracting the assets of the one department that are liabilities of the other.

The largest liability of the Bank of England is notes in circulation. The reason these are entered as a liability is because when Bank of England notes were in principle convertible into coin or gold, the note represented a liability which could be redeemed on demand. Up until 1931, it was possible in principle to

Table 26.1 Balance sheet of the Bank of England, 15 August 2001

Assets (billions of pounds)		Liabilities (billions of pounds)	
Government securities	15.3	Notes in circulation	28.2
Other securities	14.7	Public deposits	0.4
Advances and other accounts	6.2	Bankers' deposits	1.8
Premises, equipment and other	3.4	Reserves and other accounts	9.2
Total	**39.6**	**Total**	**39.6**

Source: *Financial Statistics* October 2001, National Statistics.

redeem Bank of England notes for gold. Since 1931, the note issue has been backed by securities, most of which are government securities as seen on the asset side of the balance sheet. Bank notes are non-convertible, which means that they cannot be converted into anything. But the tradition of being able to convert Bank of England notes remains even though the reality is different. If you look at a £10 note it says on it *I promise to pay the bearer on demand the sum of Ten pounds*. This only means that the Bank of England is willing to accept one £10 note for another. While notes are the liability of the Bank of England, coin is issued by the Royal Mint and is therefore not a liability.

The other important liability of the Bank of England is the commercial banks' deposits it holds. These are the deposits that the commercial banks keep at the Bank of England to act as a means of clearing interbank debt. At the end of the working day, if the National Westminster Bank has a deficit with Barclays Bank, funds can be transferred from the National Westminster account to the Barclays account held at the Bank of England. The banks' deposits at the Bank of England include a mandatory 0.35 per cent of the eligible deposits at commercial banks. Eligible deposits are defined as sterling deposits of up to two years' maturity.

Public deposits are the deposits of individual government departments. The final item on the liability side of the balance sheet are accounts held by foreign central banks such as the German Bundesbank or the US Federal Reserve.

The asset side of the balance sheet shows that the Bank of England holds government securities, such as Treasury bills and government bonds and lending to the government. Other securities that are held by the Issue department include commercial bills issued by businesses.

The two largest items on the liabilities side of the Bank's balance sheet make up most of the monetary base. The **monetary base** is also known as **M0**. In theory, a central bank can control the supply of the monetary base, and through it control the total money supply and interest rates. However, traditionally the Bank of England has not attempted to control the supply of M0. As we shall see the main instrument of control is the rate of interest.

The Central Bank's Policy Tools

We have seen that the Bank of England has many responsibilities, but we'll examine its most important one – regulating the amount of money. How does any central bank control the money supply? It uses three main policy tools to achieve its objectives:

1 Required reserve ratios.

2 Discount rate.

3 Open market operations.

Required Reserve Ratios

As a rule central banks require that commercial banks have minimum reserve requirements in the form of cash or liquidity holdings as a percentage of deposits. This minimum percentage is known as a *required reserve ratio*. The practice of minimum required reserve ratios varies from central bank to central bank. Most central banks determine a required reserve ratio for each type of deposit. The ECB has set a minimum reserve ratio of 2 per cent for all commercial banks in the countries of the European Monetary Union.

By increasing required reserve ratios, the central bank can create a shortage of reserves for the banking system and decrease bank lending. A decrease in lending decreases the money supply by a process similar to that described in Chapter 25. We'll look at this process later in this chapter.

Although changes in required reserve ratios can be used to influence the money supply, a central bank rarely uses this policy tool. That is, the central bank does not often *change* required reserve ratios as an active tool to *change* the money supply. In the United Kingdom, the last time the Bank of England used this method was in the mid-1970s. The current requirement for United Kingdom banks is to keep 0.35 per cent of their eligible deposits with the Bank of England. The commercial banks keep a little extra at the Bank of England to cover interbank transactions. These extra deposits are called *operational deposits*.

Discount Rate

The **discount rate** is the interest rate at which the central bank stands ready to lend reserves to commercial banks. A rise in the discount rate makes it more costly for banks to borrow reserves from the central bank and encourages them to cut their lending, which reduces the money supply. A fall in the discount rate makes it less costly for banks to borrow reserves from the central bank and stimulates bank lending, which increases the money supply.

Open Market Operations

An **open market operation** is the purchase or sale of government securities – Treasury bills and bonds – by the central bank in the open market. The term 'open market' refers to commercial banks and the general public but not the government. Thus when the Bank of England conducts an open market operation, it does a transaction with a bank or some other business but it does not transact with the government.

Open market operations influence the money supply. We'll study the details of this influence in the next section. Briefly, when the central bank sells government securities it receives payment with bank deposits and bank reserves, which creates tighter monetary and credit conditions. With lower reserves, the banks cut their lending, and the money supply decreases. When the central bank buys government securities, it pays for them with bank deposits and bank reserves, which creates looser monetary and credit conditions. With extra reserves, the banks increase their lending, and the money supply increases.

Accountability and Control of the Central Bank

In some countries central banks decide monetary policy and in other countries the central bank is virtually an arm of government policy. Since May 1997, the Bank of England conducts monetary policy independently of the government. Monetary policy is set by a committee of experts known as the Monetary Policy Committee. The Monetary Policy Committee is made up of the Governor, the two Deputy Governor and six other members including two academic economists. The Committee meets monthly to set the discount rate. The decision to raise, lower, or keep interest rates the same is made by a vote. The minutes of the monthly meeting are published so that everyone can see the level of agreement between the members and how they voted. The purpose of publishing the minutes is to introduce a sense of openness to the deliberations. In contrast, the governing council of the ECB do not publish their minutes. The argument for secrecy is that the governors of individual country central banks would be free of political pressure if their voting behaviour was not publicly known.

Central banks all over the world face some kind of political pressure at some time. The political constraints will depend on the legal relationship between the government and the central bank, and the history and traditions that have governed this relationship. The relationship can range from total dependence to one of total independence.

Dependence versus Independence for the Central Bank

A dependent central bank acts entirely as the agent of the government and carries out monetary policy dictated by it. The argument for dependence is that monetary policy is a political issue and therefore central banks must follow the dictates of their political masters. While, some central banks are not independent in the sense of having to follow the policy dictated by the government, it does not mean that it has no power. Few democratic governments will be willing to run the risk of the governor of the central bank resigning because of a disagreement with the government. Therefore the notion of dependence is one of degree. A low degree of dependence means a high degree of independence and vice versa.

However, economists have argued that higher inflation is usually associated with countries that have central banks with low degrees of independence. The reason for this is that governments are inclined to conduct relaxed monetary policies at election times. The evidence appears to confirm that countries with central banks that have high degrees of independence are associated with lower inflation than the average, while countries with central banks that have low degrees of independence are associated with higher inflation than the average.

The European Central Bank is an independent central bank modelled on the existing Bundesbank. All countries that belong to the EMU have independent central banks and countries that hope to join the EMU at a later stage are expected to give independence to their respective central banks.

Review Quiz

◆ What are the functions of a country's central bank and how does it differ from the functions of the European Central Bank?
◆ What are policy tools available to the central bank to conduct a nation's monetary policy?
◆ How does the decision making process differ between the Bank of England Monetary Policy Committee and the ECB's Governing Council?
◆ How does the the Central Bank regulate the quantity of money?
◆ What are the arguments for an independent central bank?

Next, we're going to study how the central bank influences the quantity of money.

Controlling the Money Supply

The Bank of England constantly monitors and adjusts the quantity of money in the economy. To change the quantity of money, the central bank conducts an open market operation. When the central bank *buys* securities in an open market operation, the monetary base *increases*, banks *increase* their lending and the quantity of money *increases*. When the central bank *sells* securities in an open market operation, the monetary base *decreases*, banks *decrease* their lending and the quantity of money *decreases*.

Let's study these changes in the quantity of money, beginning with the effects of open market operations on the monetary base.

How an Open Market Operation Works

When the Bank of England conducts an open market operation, the reserves of the banking system, a component of the monetary base, change. To see why this outcome occurs, we'll trace the effects of an open market operation both when the central bank *buys* securities and when it *sells* securities.

The Bank Buys Securities

Suppose the Bank of England buys £100 million of government securities in the open market. There are two cases to consider: when the central bank buys from a commercial bank and when it buys from the public (a person or business that is not a commercial bank). The outcome is essentially the same in either case, but you need to be convinced of this fact so we'll study the two cases, starting with the simplest case in which the central bank buys from a commercial bank.

Buys from Commercial Bank

When the Bank of England buys £100 million of securities from Barclays bank, two things happen:

1 Barclays has £100 million fewer securities and the Bank of England has £100 million more securities.

2 The Bank of England pays for the securities by crediting Barclays deposit account at the Bank of England by £100 million.

Figure 26.1(a) shows the effects of these actions on the balance sheets of the Bank of England and Barclays. Ownership of the securities passes from Barclays to the Bank of England, so Barclays' assets decrease by £100 million and the Bank of England's assets increase by £100 million – shown by the blue arrow running from Barclays to the Bank of England. The Bank of England pays for the securities by crediting Barclays' deposit account – its reserves – at the Bank by £100 million – shown by the green arrow running from the Bank to Barclays. This action increases the monetary base and increases the reserves of the banking system.

The Bank of England's assets increase by £100 million and its liabilities also increase by £100 million. Barclays' total assets remain constant but their composition changes. Its deposits at the Bank of England increase by £100 million and its holdings of government securities decrease by £100 million. So the bank has additional reserves, which it can use to make loans.

We've just seen that when the Bank of England buys government securities from a bank, the bank's reserves increase. But what happens if the Bank of England buys government securities from the public – say from Goldman Sachs International, a financial services company?

Buys from Public

When the Bank of England buys £100 million of securities from Goldman Sachs, three things happen:

Figure 26.1

The Bank of England Buys Securities in the Open Market

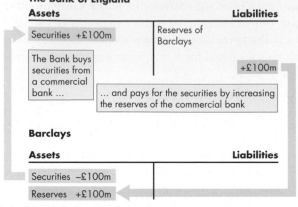

(a) The Bank buys securities from a commercial bank

The Bank of England

Assets	Liabilities
Securities +£100m	Reserves of Barclays
	+£100m

The Bank buys securities from a commercial bank ...

... and pays for the securities by increasing the reserves of the commercial bank

Barclays

Assets	Liabilities
Securities −£100m	
Reserves +£100m	

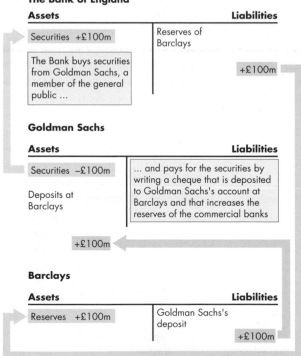

(b) The Bank buys securities from the public

The Bank of England

Assets	Liabilities
Securities +£100m	Reserves of Barclays
	+£100m

The Bank buys securities from Goldman Sachs, a member of the general public ...

Goldman Sachs

Assets	Liabilities
Securities −£100m	
Deposits at Barclays	
+£100m	

... and pays for the securities by writing a cheque that is deposited to Goldman Sachs's account at Barclays and that increases the reserves of the commercial banks

Barclays

Assets	Liabilities
Reserves +£100m	Goldman Sachs's deposit
	+£100m

When the Bank of England buys securities in the open market, bank reserves increase. If the Bank of England buys from a commercial bank (part a), bank reserves increase when the Bank of England pays the bank for the securities. If the Bank buys from the public (part b), bank deposits and bank reserves increase when the seller of the securities deposits the Bank's cheque and the commercial bank collects payment from the Bank of England.

1 Goldman Sachs has £100 million fewer securities and the Bank of England has £100 million more securities.

2 The Bank of England pays for the securities with a cheque for £100 million drawn on itself, which Goldman Sachs deposits in its account at Barclays.

3 Barclays collects payment of this cheque from the Bank of England, and £100 million is deposited in Barclays' deposit account at the Bank of England.

Figure 26.1(b) shows the effects of these actions on the balance sheets of the Bank, Goldman Sachs and Barclays. Ownership of the securities passes from Goldman Sachs to the Bank, so Goldman Sachs's assets decrease by £100 million and the Bank's assets increase by £100 million – shown by the blue arrow running from Goldman Sachs to the Bank. The Bank pays for the securities with a cheque payable to Goldman Sachs. This payment increases Goldman Sachs's deposit at Barclays by £100 million and it also increases Barclays' reserves by £100 million – shown by the green arrow running from the Bank to Barclays and the red arrow running from Barclays to Goldman Sachs. Just as when the Bank of England buys from a bank, this action increases the monetary base and increases the reserves of the banking system.

Again, the Bank of England's assets increase by £100 million and its liabilities also increase by £100 million. Goldman Sachs has the same total assets as before, but their composition has changed. It now has more money and fewer securities. Barclays' total assets increase and so do its liabilities. Its deposits at the Bank of England – its reserves – increase by £100 million and its deposit liability to Goldman Sachs increases by £100 million. Because its reserves have increased by the same amount as its deposits, the bank has excess reserves, which it can use to make loans.

We've now studied what happens when the Bank of England buys government securities from either a bank or the public. If the Bank *sells* securities, all the stages that you have studied are reversed. Reserves decrease, and the commercial banks are short of reserves.

The effects of an open market operation on the balance sheets of the Bank of England and the commercial banks that we have just described represent only the beginning of the story. With an increase in their reserves, the commercial banks are able to make more loans, which increases the quantity of money. Conversely, with a decrease in reserves, the commercial banks must cut loans, which decreases the quantity of money.

We learned how loans create deposits in Chapter 25. Here, we build on that basic idea but instead of studying the link between bank reserves and deposits, we examine the related broader link between the quantity of money and the monetary base.

Monetary Base and Bank Reserves

The *monetary base* is the sum of notes and coins, and bankers' deposits at the Bank. It is known as M0 and is used by the Bank of England Monetary Policy Committee as one of the indicators of monetary conditions in the economy. The monetary base is held either by banks as *reserves* or outside the banks as currency in circulation. When the monetary base increases, both bank reserves and currency in circulation increase. Only the increase in bank reserves can be used by banks to make loans and create additional money. An increase in currency held outside the banks is called a **currency drain**. A currency drain reduces the amount of additional money that can be created from a given increase in the monetary base.

The **money multiplier** is the amount by which a change in the monetary base is multiplied to determine the resulting change in the quantity of money. It is related to but differs from the deposit multiplier that we studied in Chapter 25. The *deposit multiplier* is the amount by which a change in bank reserves is multiplied to determine the change in bank deposits.

Let's now look at the money multiplier.

The Multiplier Effect of an Open Market Operation

Let's work out the multiplier effect of an open market operation in which the Bank buys securities from the banks. In this case, although the open market operation increases the banks' reserves, it has no immediate effect on the quantity of money. The banks are holding more reserves and fewer securities and they have excess reserves. When the banks have excess reserves, the sequence of events shown in Figure 26.2 takes place. These events are:

Figure 26.2

A Round in the Multiplier Process Following an Open Market Operation

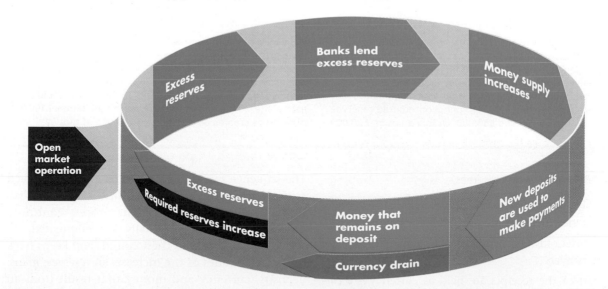

An open market purchase of government securities increases bank reserves and creates excess reserves. Banks lend the excess reserves and new loans are used to make payments. Households and firms receiving payments keep some of the receipts in the form of currency – a currency drain – and place the rest on deposit in banks. The increase in bank deposits increases banks' reserves, but also increases banks' desired reserves. Desired reserves increase by less than actual reserves, so the banks still have some excess reserves, although less than before. The process repeats until excess reserves have been eliminated. There are two components to the increase in the quantity of money: the currency drain and the increase in deposits.

Figure 26.3

The Multiplier Effect of an Open Market Operation

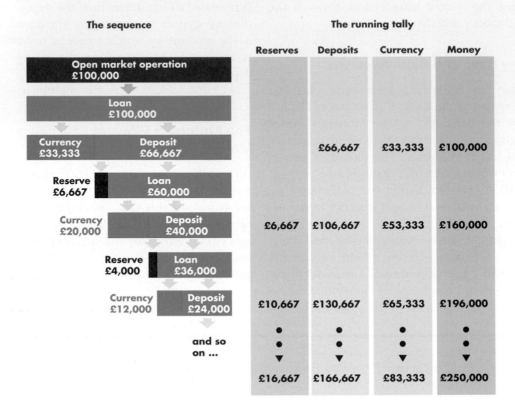

When the Bank provides the banks with £100,000 of additional reserves in an open market operation, the banks lend those reserves. Of the amount lent, £33,333 (33.33 per cent) leaves the banks in a currency drain and £66,667 remains on deposit. With additional deposits, desired reserves increase by £6,667 (10 per cent required reserves ratio) and the banks lend £60,000. Of this amount, £20,000 leaves the banks in a currency drain and £40,000 remains on deposit. The process keeps repeating until the banks have created enough deposits to eliminate their excess reserves. The running tally tells us the amounts of reserves, deposits, currency drain and money created at each stage. At the end of the process, an additional £100,000 of reserves creates an additional £250,000 of money.

- ◆ Banks lend excess reserves.

- ◆ Deposits are created equal in value to the new loans.

- ◆ The new deposits are used to make payments.

- ◆ Households and firms receive payments from the borrowers.

- ◆ Part of the receipts are held as currency – a *currency drain*.

- ◆ Part of the receipts remain as deposits in banks.

- ◆ Desired reserves increase (by a fraction – the desired reserve ratio – of the increase in deposits).

- ◆ Excess reserves decrease, but remain positive.

- ◆ Banks lend the excess reserves and the process repeats itself.

The sequence repeats in a series of rounds, but each round begins with a smaller quantity of excess reserves than did the previous one. The process continues until excess reserves have finally been eliminated.

Figure 26.3 illustrates these rounds and keeps track of the magnitudes of the increases in reserves, loans, deposits, currency and money that result from an open market operation of £100,000. In this figure, the *currency drain* is 33.33 per cent and the *desired reserve ratio* is 10 per cent.

The Bank buys £100,000 of securities from the banks. The banks' reserves increase by this amount but deposits do not change. The banks have excess reserves of £100,000, and they lend those reserves. When the banks lend £100,000 of excess reserves,

Figure 26.4

The Cumulative Effects of an Open Market Operation

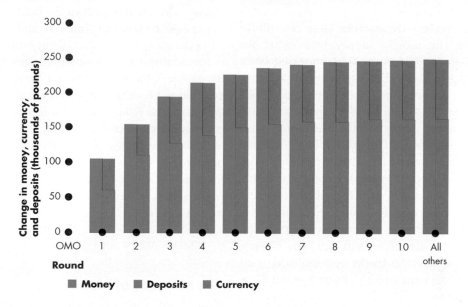

An open market operation (OMO) in which the Bank buys £100,000 government securities from the commercial banks has no immediate effect on the money supply but creates excess reserves in the banking system. When loans are made with these reserves, bank deposits and currency holdings increase. Each time new loans are made, part of the loan drains out from the banks and is held as

currency, and part of the loan stays in the banking system in the form of additional deposits and additional reserves. The commercial banks continue to increase their lending until excess reserves have been eliminated. The magnitude of the ultimate increase in the money supply is determined by the money multiplier.

£66,667 remains in the banks as deposits and £33,333 drains off and is held outside the banks as currency. The quantity of money has now increased by £100,000 – the increase in deposits plus the increase in currency holdings.

The increased bank deposits of £66,667 generate an increase in desired reserves of 10 per cent of that amount, which is £6,667. Actual reserves have increased by the same amount as the increase in deposits – £66,667. So the banks now have excess reserves of £60,000. At this stage we have gone around the circle shown in Figure 26.3 once. The process we've just described repeats but begins with excess reserves of £60,000. Figure 26.3 shows the next two rounds. At the end of the process, the quantity of money has increased by £250,000.

Figure 26.4 illustrates the accumulated increase in the quantity of money and in its components: bank deposits and currency. When the open market opera-

tion takes place (labelled OMO in the figure), there is no initial change in either the quantity of money or its components. Then, after the first round of bank lending, the quantity of money increases by £100,000 – the size of the open market operation. In successive rounds, the quantity of money and its components continue to increase but by successively smaller amounts until, after 10 rounds, the quantities of currency and deposits and their sum, the quantity of money, have almost reached the values to which they are ultimately heading.

Review Quiz

◆ What happens when the Bank of England buys securities in the open market?
◆ What happens when the Bank of England sells securities in the open market?

United Kingdom Money Supply

Let us briefly review the factors that contribute to changes in the money supply from what we have learned so far. We know that increased bank lending raises the money supply. The sale of government bonds, an open market operation, decreases the money supply. An increase in monetary base decreases the money supply through the money multiplier. We also know that in principle the money supply can be increased by reducing the reserve ratio, although this method of monetary control is rarely used by central banks. Let us bring all these factors together to set out a complete statement of the determinants of the change in the money supply. The ingredients for this statement will need the balance sheets of the commercial banks and building societies, the financing requirement of government fiscal policy, **M0** and **M4**.

We can think of the consolidated balance sheet of banks and building societies as the assets that are made up of loans (advances) to the private sector and cash reserves including bankers' deposits at the Bank of England. We are ignoring all the other types of assets such as Treasury bills, commercial bills and other securities. Let's call the level of loans issued L and cash reserves R. The largest liabilities of the banks and building societies are their deposits. These are the sight deposits and time deposits of the commercial banks, the share accounts of the building societies and certificates of deposits. The other liabilities of the commercial banks are the capital of their shareholders. These are the shares of banks held by people and are called non-deposit liabilities, calling the total level of deposits D and non-deposit liabilities E, we can write the balance sheet statement *assets = liabilities* as:

$$L + R = D + E$$

The Financing of Fiscal Policy

In Chapter 24, pp. 516–532, we examined the role of fiscal policy in the macroeconomy. The government deficit, which is government sector spending less revenues, is referred to as the *Public Sector Net Cash Requirement* (PSNCR). It is called the PSNCR because the deficit has to be financed by borrowing cash. The three ways the government finances its deficit are:

borrowing from the public by selling bonds, borrowing from abroad by selling bonds to foreigners and borrowing from the Bank of England, issuing base money. The sale of bonds to the public is the addition to the existing stock of bonds (B) and is denoted as ΔB – the *change in bonds*. The sale of bonds to foreigners is the addition to the existing stock of bonds held by people outside the United Kingdom (F) and is denoted as ΔF – the *change in the stock of bonds held by foreigners*. The issue of base money is the addition to the existing stock of base money (M0) and is denoted as $\Delta M0$ – the *change in* M0. Therefore the PSBR can be stated as follows. The government deficit can be financed by selling bonds to the public, selling bonds to foreigners or issuing base money or any combination of all three.

$$PSNCR = \Delta M0 + \Delta B + \Delta F$$

The Measure of Money

We examined the official measure of money in the United Kingdom in Chapter 25, pp. 548–549. We can state M0 as the sum of currency in circulation with the public, and cash reserves of the banks and building societies including bankers' deposits at the Bank of England (R). Let us denote the amount of currency in circulation as C. The definition of M4 is currency in circulation with the public plus all bank and building society deposits and share accounts including certificates of deposits. These two statements are:

$$M0 = C + R$$
$$M4 = C + D$$

The Change in the Money Supply

We can use the above four equations to arrive at a statement about the factors that determine the money supply in the United Kingdom. We can begin by eliminating currency from the two equations for M0 and M4. This is done by equating $C = M0 - R$ and $C = M4 - D$. This gives us an expression for M4 as: $M4 = M0 - R + D$. We can now eliminate D from this expression by using the equation describing the bank and building society balance sheet. Now the equation becomes: $M4 = M0 - R + L + R - E$. Notice that reserves get cancelled out and we arrive at a shorter expression: $M4 = M0 + L - E$. Before we proceed any further, we note that the expression for M4 can also be stated in terms of changes. That is, the change in M4 is the

Table 26.2 M4 Counterparts

Year	PSNCR	Purchases of public sector debt by UK private sector $-\Delta B$	External and foreign currency counterparts $-\Delta F$	Sterling lending to the UK private sector ΔA	Net non-deposit sterling liabilities ΔE	Change in money stock $\Delta M4$
1993	42,503	−30,195	3,478	22,636	−41,766	23,843
1994	39,342	−22,949	−6,235	31,605	−15,021	25,292
1995	35,446	−21,860	−6,553	57,743	−8,336	56,116
1996	24,778	−19,241	7,032	41,591	−12,213	59,395
1997	11,851	−16,121	22,429	68,311	−6,187	80,287
1998	−6,395	1,517	8,957	63,929	−7,905	60,095
1999	−1,740	−1,254	−40,220	78,087	−2,224	32,588
2000	−36,962	13,231	10,706	111,229	−30,821	67,386

Source: National Statistics, *Financial Statistics, October 2001*, London. Numbers do not add up to ∆M4 because of rounding.

change in M0 and the change in bank and building society loans and advances less the change in non-deposit liabilities:

$$\Delta M4 = \Delta M0 + \Delta L - \Delta E$$

We can now eliminate ∆M0 from this expression by using the statement describing the financing of the government deficit – the PSNCR. From the expression for the PSNCR we have: ∆M0 = PSNCR − ∆B − ∆F. Substituting this into the expression for ∆M4 above we arrive at our final statement:

$$\Delta M4 = PSNCR - \Delta B - \Delta F + \Delta L - \Delta E$$

The expression for the *change in* M4 describes what is known as the M4 *counterparts*. This expression states that the money supply increases as a result of the government deficit – the PSNCR and increases in bank and building society lending. The money supply decreases if the government, through the Bank of England, increases its sales of government bonds and increases if it decreases its sales of government bonds – an open market operation. The money supply will increase if the government reduces its borrowing from foreigners, and the money supply will decrease if it increases its borrowing from abroad. Table 26.2 shows how the counterparts to M4 have evolved in recent years. The columns in Table 26.2 correspond to each of the counterparts of M4. You can see that in recent years the government deficit has been contributing to the increase in the money supply, but that this increase has been largely offset by borrowing

from the UK public – that is, the non-bank private sector. The penultimate column is the change in non-deposit liabilities, which is the increase in banks' share capital. The shareholders capital is also a liability of the bank, but it is a non-deposit liability. The major contributor to the increase in the money supply has been the increase in bank and building society lending.

Review Quiz

◆ What are the components that make up the M4 counterparts in the United Kingdom?
◆ Which of the counterparts have the largest influences on the change in the money supply?

The central bank's objective in conducting open market operations, or taking other actions that influence the quantity of money in circulation are not simply to affect the money supply for its own sake. An important objective is to influence the course of the economy – especially the level of output, employment and prices – by influencing aggregate demand. But the central bank's influence on aggregate demand is indirect. Its immediate objective is to move interest rates up or down. To work out the effects of the central bank's actions on interest rates, we need to work out how and why interest rates change when the quantity of money changes. We'll discover the answer to these questions by first studying the demand for money.

The Demand for Money

The amount of money we *receive* each week in payment for our labour is income – a flow. The amount of money that we hold in our wallets or in a sight deposit account at our local bank is an inventory – a stock. There is no limit to how much income – or flow – we would like to receive each week. But there is a limit to how big a stock of money each of us would like to hold, on the average.

The Influences on Money Holding

The quantity of money that people choose to hold depends on four main factors. They are:

1   The price level.
2   The interest rate.
3   Real GDP.
4   Financial innovation.

Let's look at each of them.

The Price Level

The quantity of money measured in current pounds is called the quantity of *nominal money*. The quantity of nominal money demanded is proportional to the price level, other things remaining the same. That is, if the price level (GDP deflator) increases by 10 per cent, people will want to hold 10 per cent more nominal money than before, other things remaining the same. What matters is not the number of pounds that you hold but their buying power. If you hold £20 to buy your weekly groceries and beer at the Students' Union, you will increase your money holding to £22 pounds if the prices of groceries and beer – and your student grant – increase by 10 per cent.

The quantity of money measured in constant pounds (for example, in 1995 pounds) is called *real money*. Real money is equal to nominal money divided by the price level. The quantity of real money demanded is independent of the price level. In the above example, you held £20, on the average, at the original price level. When the price level increased by 10 per cent, you increased your average cash holding by 10 per cent, keeping your *real* cash holding constant. Your £22 pounds at the new price level is the same quantity of *real money* as your £20 pounds at the original price level.

The Interest Rate

A fundamental principle of economics is that as the opportunity cost of something increases, people try to find substitutes for it. Money is no exception. The higher the opportunity cost of holding money, other things remaining the same, the lower is the quantity of real money demanded. But what is the opportunity cost of holding money? It is the interest rate. But which interest rate? Bank and building society deposits of a certain type earn interest. So money, if held as a time deposit, earns interest. Do we mean the interest rate on bank and building society deposits? Surely a rise in the bank and building society deposit rate makes money more attractive and a rise in this rate will increase the demand for money not lower it? The interest rate we mean is the interest paid on a financial asset that is a close substitute for money. To see why, recall that the opportunity cost of any activity is the value of the best alternative forgone. The alternative to holding money is holding an interest-earning financial asset such as a savings bond or Treasury bill. By holding money instead, you forgo the additional interest that you otherwise would have received. This forgone additional interest is the opportunity cost of holding money.

Money loses value because of inflation. Why isn't the inflation rate part of the cost of holding money? It is, other things remaining the same, the higher the expected inflation rate, the higher are interest rates and the higher, therefore, is the opportunity cost of holding money.

Real GDP

The quantity of money that households and firms plan to hold depends on the amount they are spending, and the quantity of money demanded in the economy as a whole depends on aggregate expenditure – real GDP.

Again, suppose that you hold an average of £20 to finance your weekly purchases of goods. Now imagine that the prices of these goods and of all other goods remain constant but that your income increases. As a consequence, you now spend more and you also keep a larger amount of money on hand to finance your higher volume of expenditure.

Financial Innovation

Financial innovations have altered the quantity of money held by people. Specifically these are the introduction of:

Figure 26.5 ◆
The Demand for Money

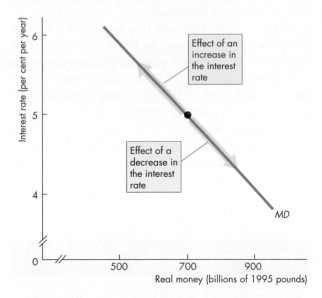

The demand for money curve, *MD*, shows that the lower the interest rate, the larger is the quantity of money that people plan to hold. The demand curve for money slopes downward because the interest rate is the opportunity cost of holding money. The higher the interest rate, the larger is the interest forgone on holding another asset. A change in the interest rate leads to a movement along the demand curve.

Figure 26.6 ◆
Changes in the Demand for Money

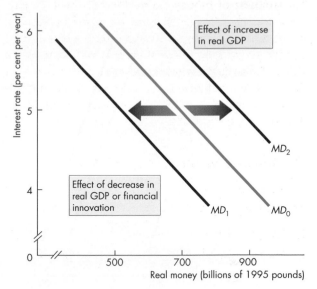

A decrease in real GDP decreases the demand for money and shifts the demand curve leftward from MD_0 to MD_1. An increase in real GDP increases the demand for money and shifts the demand curve rightward from MD_0 to MD_2. Financial innovation can either increase or decrease the demand for money depending on the specific innovation.

1   Interest-bearing sight deposits.
2   Automatic transfers between sight and time deposits.
3   Automatic teller machines.
4   Credit cards.
5   Bank debit cards.

These innovations have occurred because of the development of computing power that has lowered the cost of calculations and record keeping.

We can summarize the effects of the influences on money holding by using the demand for money curve.

The Demand for Money Curve

The *demand for money* is the relationship between the quantity of real money demanded and the interest rate, holding constant all other influences on the amount of money that people wish to hold. Figure 26.5 shows

a demand for money curve, *MD*. When the interest rate rises, everything else remaining the same, the opportunity cost of holding money rises and the quantity of money demanded decreases – there is a movement along the demand for money curve. Similarly, when the interest rate falls, the opportunity cost of holding money falls and the quantity of money demanded increases – there is a downward movement along the demand for money curve.

Shifts in the Demand Curve for Real Money

Figure 26.6 shows the effects of factors that change the demand for money. A decrease in real GDP decreases the demand for money and shifts the demand curve leftward from MD_0 to MD_1. An increase in real GDP has the opposite effect. It increases the demand for money and shifts the demand curve rightward from MD_0 to MD_2. The influence of financial innovation on the demand for money curve is

Figure 26.7

The Demand for Money in the United Kingdom

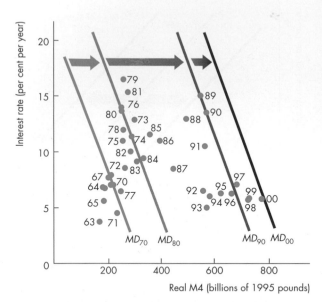

Real M4 (billions of 1995 pounds)

The figure shows the demand for real M4 – the quantity of M4 graphed against the interest rate. The demand for M4 has increased – its demand curve has shifted rightward – because financial innovation developed new types of deposit that are part of M4.

Source: Bank of England.

more complicated. It might increase the demand for some types of deposit and decrease the demand for others – and decrease the demand for currency. We'll look at its effects by studying the demand for money in the United Kingdom.

The Demand for Money in the United Kingdom

Figure 26.7 shows the relationship between the interest rate and the quantity of real money demanded in the United Kingdom since 1963. Each dot shows the interest rate and the amount of real money held in a given year.

During the 1960s and 1970s, the demand for M4 increased and the demand curve shifted rightward. During the 1980s – a period of strong financial innovation and deregulation – the demand for M4 increased and the demand curve shifted further to the right. During the recession of the 1990s, the demand for M4 fell briefly but in the following recovery the demand for M4 increased and the demand curve continued to shift rightward.

Why did these shifts in the demand for money occur? Firstly, the increase in real income caused an increase in the demand for money at every given rate of interest, but secondly, financial innovation also played a part. The evolution of new financial products has lead to a steady decrease in the demand for bank deposits. In addition, the abolition of certain types of control on the commercial banks' ability to take deposits meant that more and more businesses and financial institutions began to deposit their money with banks, causing the demand for M4 to shift rightward.

Review Quiz

◆ What are the main influences on the quantity of real money that people and businesses plan to hold?
◆ What does the demand for money curve show?
◆ How does an increase in the interest rate change the quantity of money demanded and how would you use the demand for money curve to show the effects?
◆ How does an increase in real GDP change the demand for money and how would you use the demand for money curve to show the effects?
◆ How has financial innovation altered the demand for M4?

We now know what determines the demand for money. And we've seen that a key factor is the interest rate – the opportunity cost of holding money. But what determines the interest rate? Let's find out.

Interest Rate Determination

An interest rate is the percentage yield on a financial asset such as a *bond* or a *share*. The higher the price of a financial asset, other things being equal, the lower is the interest rate. An example will make things clearer. Suppose the government sells a bond to the public that promises to pay £10 a year. A bond is a promise to make a sequence of future payments. There are many different possible sequences but the most simple one, for our purposes, is the case of a bond called a perpetuity. A *perpetuity* is a bond that promises to pay a certain fixed amount of money each year forever – in our example £10. The fixed pound payment is called the *coupon*. If the price of the bond is £100, the interest rate is 10 per cent per year – £10 is 10 per cent of £100. If the price of the bond is £50, the interest rate is 20 per cent – £10 is 20 per cent of £50. And if the bond costs £200, the interest rate is 5 per cent – which gives £10 return on a £200 bond holding.

There is an inverse relationship between the price of a bond and the interest rate earned on the bond. People divide their wealth between money and bonds as well as other interest yielding assets. The amount they hold as money will depend on the interest rate earned on bonds.

Money Market Equilibrium

The interest rate is determined at each point in time by equilibrium in the markets for financial assets. The quantity of money supplied is determined by the actions of the banking system and the Bank of England. On any given day, the supply of M4 money is a fixed quantity. The *real* quantity of money supplied is equal to the nominal quantity supplied divided by the price level. At a given moment in time, there is a particular price level and so the quantity of real money supplied is also a fixed amount. The supply curve of real money is shown in Figure 26.8 as the vertical line labelled *MS*. The quantity of real money supplied is £700 billion.

The demand for real money depends on the level of real GDP and on the interest rate. When the quantity of money supplied equals the quantity of money demanded, the money market is in equilibrium. Figure 26.8 illustrates equilibrium in the money market. Equilibrium is achieved by changes in the interest rate. If the interest rate is too high, people demand a smaller quantity of money than the quantity supplied. They are holding too much money. In this situation, they try to get rid of money by buying bonds. As they do so, the price of bonds rises and the interest rate falls. Conversely, if the interest rate is too low, people demand a larger quantity of money than the quantity supplied. They are holding too little money. In this situation, they try to get more money by selling bonds. As they do so, the price of bonds falls and the interest rate rises. Only when the interest rate is at the level at which people are holding the

Figure 26.8
Money Market Equilibrium

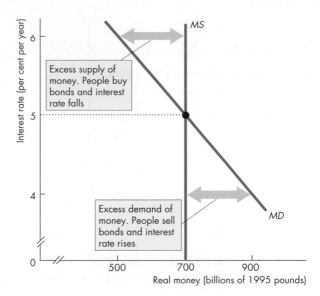

Money market equilibrium occurs when the interest rate has adjusted to make the quantity of money demanded equal to the quantity supplied. Here, equilibrium occurs at an interest rate of 5 per cent. At interest rates above 5 per cent, the quantity of money demanded is less than the quantity supplied, so people sell bonds and the interest rate falls. At interest rates below 5 per cent, the quantity of real money demanded exceeds the quantity supplied, so people buy bonds and the interest rate rises. Only at 5 per cent is the quantity of real money in existence willingly held.

quantity of money supplied do they willingly hold the money and take no actions to change the interest rate.

Changing the Interest Rate

Suppose that the economy is overheating and the central bank fears that inflation is about to rise. It decides to take action to decrease aggregate demand and spending. To do so, it wants to raise interest rates and discourage borrowing and expenditure on goods and services. What does the central bank do?

The central bank sells securities in the open market. As it does so, it mops up bank reserves and induces the banks to cut their lending. The banks make a smaller quantity of new loans each day until the stock of loans outstanding has fallen to a level consistent with the new lower level of reserves. The money supply decreases.

Figure 26.9

Interest Rate Changes

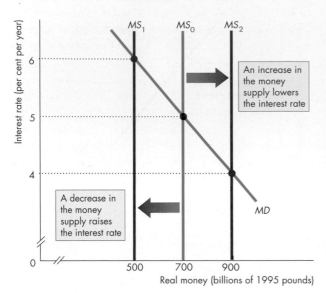

An open market sale of securities shifts the money supply curve leftward to MS_1 and the interest rate rises to 6 per cent. An open market purchase of securities shifts the money supply curve rightward to MS_2 and the interest rate falls to 4 per cent.

Suppose that the central bank undertakes open market operations on a sufficiently large scale to decrease the money supply from £700 billion to £500 billion. As a consequence, the supply curve of real money shifts leftward, as shown in Figure 26.9, from MS_0 to MS_1.

The demand for money is shown by MD. This curve tells us the quantity of money that households and firms plan to hold at each interest rate. With an interest rate of 5 per cent, and with £500 billion of money in the economy, firms and households are now holding less money than they wish to hold. They attempt to increase their money holding by selling financial assets. As they do so, the prices of bonds and stocks fall and the interest rate rises. When the interest rate has increased to 6 per cent, people are willing to hold the smaller £500 billion stock of money that the Bank and the banks have created.

Conversely, suppose that the economy is slowing and the central bank fears recession. It decides to take action to stimulate spending and increases the money supply. In this case, the Bank buys securities.

As it does so, it increases bank reserves and induces the banks to increase their lending. The banks make new loans until the stock of loans outstanding has increased to a level consistent with the new higher level of reserves. Suppose that the Bank undertakes an open market sale of securities on a scale big enough to increase the real money supply to £900 billion. Now the supply of money curve shifts rightward, as shown in Figure 26.9, from MS_0 to MS_2. With more money available, people attempt to get rid of money by buying interest-earning assets. As they do so, asset prices rise and interest rates fall. Equilibrium occurs when the interest rate has fallen to 4 per cent, at which point the new higher money stock of £900 billion is willingly held.

Review Quiz

◆ What is a bond and what is the relationship between the price of a bond and the interest rate?
◆ How is the short-term rate of interest determined?
◆ What happens to the interest rate if the quantity of money increases or decreases?

You've now seen how the interest rate is determined and how the actions of the Bank of England can influence the interest rate. We are now going to examine the influence of the interest rate on expenditure plans.

The Interest Rate and Expenditure Plans

You've seen that the interest rate affects the quantity of money that people plan to hold. The interest rate also influences people's spending decisions. The reason is the same in both cases. The interest rate is an opportunity cost. But the interest rate that is relevant for the money holding decision is not quite the same as the interest rate that is relevant for a spending decision. Let's find out why.

Nominal Interest and Real Interest

We distinguish between two interest rates: the **nominal interest rate** and the **real interest rate**. The nominal interest rate is the percentage return on an asset such as a bond expressed in terms of money. It is the interest rate that is quoted in everyday transactions and news reports. The real interest rate is the percentage return on an asset expressed in terms of what money will buy. It is the nominal interest rate adjusted for inflation and is approximately equal to the nominal interest rate minus the inflation rate.[1]

Here, we'll use the approximate formula. Suppose that the nominal interest rate is 10 per cent a year and the inflation rate is 4 per cent a year. The real interest rate is 6 per cent a year – 10 per cent minus 4 per cent.

To see why the real interest rate is 6 per cent, think about the following example. Jackie lends Joe £1,000 for one year. At the end of the year, Joe repays Jackie the £1,000 plus interest. At 10 per cent a year, the interest is £100, so Jackie receives £1,100 from Joe.

Because of inflation, the money that Joe uses to repay Jackie is worth less than the money that Jackie originally loaned to Joe. At an inflation rate of 4 per cent a year, Jackie needs an extra £40 a year to compensate her for the fall in the value of money. So when Joe repays the loan, Jackie needs £1,040 to buy the same items that she could have bought for £1,000 when she made the loan. Because Joe pays Jackie £1,100, the interest that she *really* earns is £60, which is 6 per cent of the £1,000 that she lent to Joe.

Interest Rate and Opportunity Cost

Now that you understand the distinction between the nominal interest rate and the real interest rate, let's think about the effects of interest rates on decisions.

The interest rate influences decisions because it is an opportunity cost. *The nominal interest rate is the opportunity cost of holding money.* And it is the nominal interest rate that is determined by the demand for real money and the supply of real money in the money market. To see why the nominal interest rate is the opportunity cost of holding money, think about the *real* interest rate on money compared with the real interest rate on other financial assets. Money loses value at the inflation rate. So the real interest rate on money equals *minus* the inflation rate. The real interest rate on other financial assets equals the nominal interest rate minus the inflation rate. So the difference between the real interest rate on money and the real interest rate on other financial assets is the nominal interest rate. By holding money rather than some other financial asset, we incur a *real* opportunity cost equal to the nominal interest rate.

The real interest rate is the opportunity cost of spending. Spending more today means spending less in the future. But spending one additional dollar today means cutting future spending by more than a dollar. And the real amount by which future spending must be cut is determined by the *real* interest rate.

A change in the real interest rate changes the opportunity cost of two components of aggregate expenditure:

1 Consumption expenditure.

2 Investment.

Consumption Expenditure

Other things remaining the same, the lower the real interest rate, the greater is the amount of consumption expenditure and the smaller is the amount of saving.

You can see why the real interest rate influences consumption expenditure and saving by thinking about the effect of the interest rate on a student loan. If the real interest rate on a student loan fell to 1 per cent a year, students would be happy to take larger loans and spend more. But if the real interest rate on a student loan jumped to 20 per cent a year, students would cut their expenditure, buying cheaper food and finding lower-rent accommodation for example, to pay off their loans as quickly as possible.

The effect of the real interest rate on consumption expenditure is probably not large. And it is certainly not as powerful as the effect of disposable income that we studied in Chapter 23 (pp. 486–490). You can think of the real interest rate as influencing *autonomous consumption expenditure*. The lower the real interest rate, the greater is autonomous consumption expenditure.

Investment

Other things remaining the same, the lower the real interest rate, the greater is the amount of investment.

The funds used to finance investment might be borrowed, or they might be the financial resources of

---

[1] The exact calculation allows for the change in the purchasing power of the interest as well as the amount of the loan. To calculate the *exact* real interest rate, use the formula: *real interest rate = nominal interest rate – inflation rate* divided by (1 + *inflation rate*/100). If the nominal interest rate is 10 per cent and the inflation rate is 4 per cent, the real interest rate is $(10 - 4)\sqrt{(1 + 0.04)} = 5.77$ per cent. The lower the inflation rate, the better is the approximation.

the firm's owners (the firm's retained earnings). But regardless of the source of the funds, the opportunity cost of the funds is the real interest rate. The real interest paid on borrowed funds is an obvious cost. The real interest rate is also the cost of using retained earnings because these funds could be loaned to another firm. The real interest rate foregone is the opportunity cost of using retained earnings to finance an investment project.

To decide whether to invest in new capital, firms compare the real interest rate with the expected profit rate from the investment. For example, suppose that Ford(UK) expects to earn 20 per cent a year from a new car assembly plant. It is profitable for Ford(UK) to invest in this new plant as long as the real interest rate is less than 20 per cent a year. That is, at a real interest rate below 20 per cent a year, Ford(UK) will build this assembly line, and at a real interest rate in excess of 20 per cent a year, it will not. Some projects are profitable at a high real interest rate, but other projects are profitable only at a low real interest rate. So the higher the real interest rate, the smaller is the number of projects that are worth undertaking and the smaller is the amount of investment.

The interest rate has another effect on expenditure plans. It changes net exports. Let's find out why.

Net Exports and the Interest Rate

Net exports change when the interest rate changes because, other things remaining the same, a change in the interest rate changes the exchange rate.

Net Exports and the Exchange Rate
Let's first see why the exchange rate influences exports and imports. When a Briton buys a Dell PC that is shipped from the USA, the price of the PC equals the US dollar price converted into sterling. If the PC price is US$2,000, and if the exchange rate is 1.60 $s per £, the PC price in the UK is £1,250. If the pound sterling rises to 1.65 $s per £, the PC price in the UK falls to £1,212.12. When the price of a US PC falls, the UK imports more PCs.

Similarly, when a US retailer buys a consignment of Burberry raincoats from London, the price of the consignment of 100 raincoats equals the UK sterling price converted into US dollars. If the price of a Burberry is £100 each, the consignment is £10,000 and if the exchange rate is 1.60 $s per £, the price in the United States is $16,000 for the consignment. If the pound sterling rises to 1.65 $s per £, the price of the consign-

ment in the United States *rises* to $16,500. When the price of a British rainwear rises, Americans buy fewer of them and Britain's exports decrease.

So when the pound sterling rises, imports increase, exports decrease, and net exports decrease. Similarly, when the pound sterling falls, imports decrease, exports increase, and net exports increase.

The Interest Rate and the Exchange Rate
When the interest rate in the UK rises, and other things remain the same, the pound sterling exchange rate rises. The reason is that more people move funds into the UK to take advantage of the higher interest rate. But when money flows into the UK, the demand for pounds increases, so the pound sterling exchange rate (the price) rises. And when the interest rate in the UK falls, and other things remain the same, the pound sterling exchange rate falls.

Because the interest rate influences the exchange rate, it also influences net exports. A rise in the interest rate decreases net exports and a fall in the interest rate increases net exports, other things remaining the same.

Money, Interest and Expenditure

Figure 26.10 illustrates the effects of money and the interest rate on expenditure plans. In part (a), the demand for money is MD and the supply of money is MS_0. Part (b) shows the relationships between the real interest rate and expenditure plans.

The CD curve shows the relationship between autonomous consumption expenditure and the real interest rate, other things remaining the same.

The curve labelled $CD + ID$ shows the influence of the real interest rate on the sum of autonomous consumption expenditure and investment. And the IE curve in Figure 26.10(b) shows the relationship between all the components of aggregate expenditure and the real interest rate.

We'll assume that the inflation rate is zero so that the nominal interest rate (on the y-axis of part a) equals the real interest rate (on the y-axis of part b). So, when the interest rate is 5 per cent a year, interest-sensitive expenditure is £125 billion.

If the quantity of real money increases to £900 billion, the supply of money curve shifts rightward to MS_1 and the interest rate falls to 3 per cent a year. Interest-sensitive expenditure increases to £137.5 billion. If the quantity of real money decreases to £500 billion, the supply of money curve shifts leftward to

Figure 26.10

Money, Interest and Expenditure

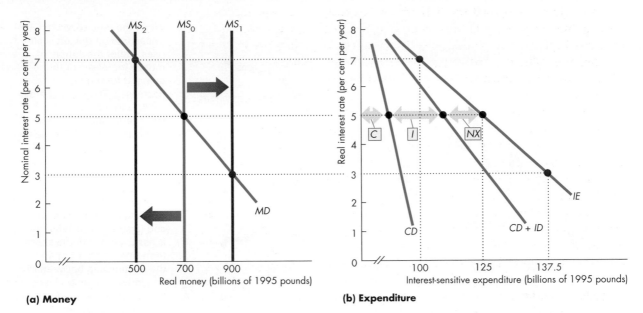

(a) Money

(b) Expenditure

In part (a), when the money supply increases from MS_0 to MS_1, the interest rate falls from 5 per cent a year to 3 per cent a year and when the money supply decreases from MS_0 to MS_2, the interest rate rises from 5 per cent a year to 7 per cent a year. In part (b), when the real interest rate is 5 per cent a year, interest-sensitive expenditure is

£125 billion a year. Other things remaining the same, when the interest rate falls to 3 per cent a year, expenditure increases to £137.5 billion a year and when the interest rate rises to 7 per cent a year, expenditure decreases to £100 billion a year.

MS_2 and the interest rate rises to 7 per cent a year. Interest-sensitive expenditure decreases to £100 billion.

You've now seen how the quantity of money influences the interest rate and how the interest rate influences expenditure plans. Next we will see how the Bank of England has used monetary policy to influence the course of the economy. Then, in the next chapter, we will see how fiscal policy and monetary policy interact to influence the course of the economy.

Review Quiz

◆ What is the real interest rate and how does it differ from the nominal interest rate?
◆ Which interest rate influences the quantity of money that people plan to hold and why?
◆ Which interest rate influences expenditure decisions and why?
◆ How does the interest rate influence net exports?

Monetary Policy

You have now learned a great deal about how a central bank and the Bank of England in particular can take monetary policy actions and the effects of those actions on short-term interest rates. But you are possibly thinking: all this sounds nice in theory, but does it really happen? Does the Bank of England actually do the things we've learned about in this chapter? Indeed, it does happen, and sometimes with dramatic effect. To see the Bank in action, we'll look at the policy it has conducted since the United Kingdom left the Exchange Rate Mechanism of the European Monetary System.

The Bank of England in Action

You've seen that the immediate effect of the Bank's actions is a change in the short-term interest rate. But does the short-term interest rate rise and fall in response to changes in the quantity of money, like

Figure 26.11

Money and Interest Rates

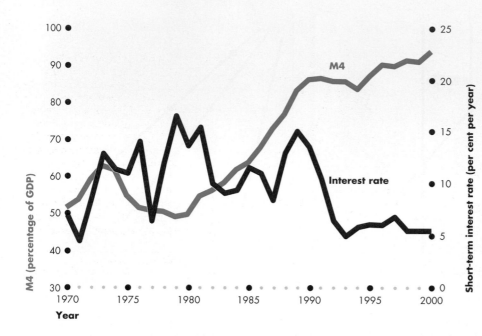

When the ratio of M4 to GDP (measured on the left scale) rises, either the supply of money increases or the demand for money decreases. The result, before 1985, is that a fall in the short-term rate of interest (measured on the right scale) is matched by a rise in M4 relative to GDP. Similarly, when the ratio of M4 to GDP falls, either the supply of money decreases or the demand for money increases and (again before 1985) this is associated with the short-term rate rising. After 1985, the relationship between M4 and interest rates broke down because of deregulation and financial innovation.

Source: Bank of England.

the theory we've just studied predicts? Mostly, but not quite always, it does. Figure 26.11 illustrates this connection. It shows the Treasury bill rate at the end of the year and M4 expressed as a percentage of GDP. The reason for expressing M4 as a percentage of GDP is that we can see both the supply side and demand side effects on interest rates in a single measure. Interest rates rise if the quantity of money decreases. Interest rates also rise if the demand for money increases. But the demand for money increases if GDP increases. So the ratio of M4 to GDP rises either if the supply of money increases (M4 increases) or if the demand for money decreases (GDP decreases).

You can see by studying Figure 26.11 that between 1973 and 1980, the rise in the interest rate is matched by a decrease in the ratio of M4 to GDP. Lower interest rates between 1982 and 1987 were matched by an increase in the ratio of M4 to GDP. An increase in the supply of money relative to the demand for money brought a fall in the interest rate in the 1980s. And a decrease in the supply of money relative to the demand for money brought a rise in the interest rate between 1979 and 1981.

You can also see in Figure 26.11 that after 1985, the former relationship between money and interest rates broke down and a longer lag emerged between changes in the rate of interest and subsequent changes in the M4 to GDP ratio. When the interest rate rose in 1988, the M4 to GDP ratio did not fall but its rate of increase began to decrease a year later. The reason the demand for M4 continued to rise is that as interest rates rose so did the interest rate on time deposits, and people continued to demand M4 deposits. It was only when the differential between the time deposit rate and the rate of interest on government securities widened that the increase in M4 relative to GDP began to decline.

You've now seen that we can explain short-term interest rate fluctuations as arising from fluctuations in the supply of money relative to the demand for money. But this relationship doesn't tell us whether actions by the Bank or fluctuations in GDP brought the fluctuations in the M4 to GDP ratio. Do the Bank's own actions move interest rates around? Let's answer this question by looking at two episodes in the life of the Bank.

Figure 26.12

Monetary Policy and the Interest Rate

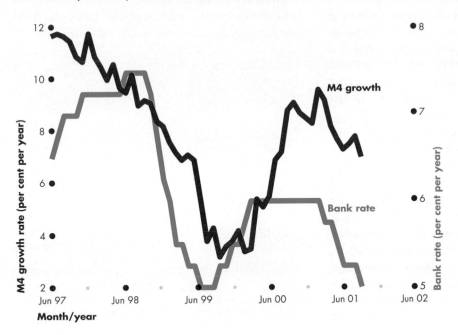

The Bank of England alters interest rates by creating a change in the supply of money relative to the demand for money. If the supply of money is growing too fast, the Bank of England engineers a rise in the rate of interest by creating a decrease in the supply of money relative to demand. Once the rate of growth of money has declined and the threat of inflation reduced, the rate of interest is lowered.

Source: Bank of England.

The Bank in Action 1997–2001

Figure 26.12 shows the rate of growth of M4 and the Bank's base rate of interest between June 1997 and August 2001. At the beginning of the period the Bank had been made operationally independent with the task of bringing inflation under control and keeping it within the narrow bands of 2.5–1.5 per cent. If the long-run rate of growth of the economy is about 2.5 per cent and inflation is to remain between 2.5 and 1.5 per cent, then long-run nominal GDP must grow at between 4 and 5 per cent (inflation plus the rate of growth of *real* GDP). If the money supply is growing at above the rate of growth of long-run GDP, then the ratio of M4 to GDP will be rising. The Bank will have to raise interest rates to reduce the rate of growth of money and lower it once money supply growth has fallen and inflation is under control. In June 1996, money supply growth was 11.7 per cent per year. Such a rate of growth of money if left unchecked will eventually create higher inflation. Figure 26.12 shows that interest rates were raised from 6.5 per cent in June 1996 to 7.5 per cent in June 1997 and held there for several months. By September, the rate of growth of

the money supply had fallen to 9.2 per cent. As the economy slowed and the rate of growth of money continued to fall, interest rates were lowered so as not to allow the rate of growth of money to fall too fast. By August 1999, the rate of growth of money had fallen to 5.4 per cent and the base rate was lowered to 5 per cent. During 2000 the rate of interest was raised to 6 per cent as money growth began to increase once again. Interest rates were lowered during 2001 as money growth declined and the economy began to show signs of slowing.

Profiting by Predicting the Bank of England

The Bank of England influences interest rates by its open market operations and as lender of last resort to loans to discount houses. By increasing the money supply, the Bank can lower interest rates; by lowering the money supply, the Bank can increase interest rates. Sometimes such actions are taken to offset other influences and keep interest rates steady. At other times the Bank moves interest rates up or down. The higher the interest rate, the lower is the price of a bond; the lower the interest rate, the higher is the price of a bond. Thus predicting interest rates is the same as predicting bond prices. Predicting that interest rates are going to fall is the same as predicting that bond prices are going to rise – a good time to buy bonds. Predicting that interest rates are going to rise is the same as predicting that bond prices are going to fall – a good time to sell bonds.

Because the Bank is the major player whose actions influence interest rates and bond prices, predicting what the Bank will do is profitable and a good deal of effort goes into this activity. But people who anticipate that the Bank is about to ease monetary policy and increase the money supply buy bonds straight away, pushing their prices upward and pushing interest rates downward, *before* the Bank acts. Similarly, people who anticipate that the Bank is about to tighten monetary policy and decrease the money supply sell bonds straight away, pushing their prices downward and pushing interest rates upward, before the Bank acts. In other words, bond prices and interest rates change as soon as the Bank's actions are foreseen. By the time the Bank actually takes its actions, if those actions are correctly foreseen, they have no effect. The effects occur in anticipation of the Bank's actions. Only changes in the money supply that are not foreseen change the interest rate at the time that those changes occur.

The Ripple Effects of Monetary Policy

You've now seen that the Bank's actions do indeed change interest rates and seek to influence the course of the economy. These monetary policy measures work by changing aggregate demand. When the Bank slows money growth and pushes interest rates up, it decreases aggregate demand, which slows both real GDP growth and inflation. When the Bank speeds up money growth and lowers interest rates, it increases aggregate demand, which speeds up real GDP growth and inflation. The mechanism through which aggregate demand changes involves several channels. Higher interest rates bring a decrease in consumption expenditure and investment. Higher interest rates bring an appreciation in the exchange rate that makes UK exports more expensive and imports less costly. So net exports decrease. Tighter bank credit brings fewer loans, which reinforces the effects of higher interest rates on consumption

expenditure and investment. What we have just described is sometimes referred to as the transmission mechanism of monetary policy.

Schematically, the effects of the Bank's actions ripple through the economy in the following way:

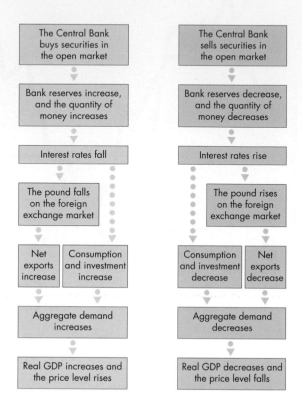

Interest Rates and the Business Cycle

You've seen the connection between the Bank's actions and interest rates in Figure 26.12. What about the ripple effects that we've just described? Do they really occur? Do changes in interest rates ultimately influence the real GDP growth rate? Yes they do. You can see these effects in Figure 26.13. The blue line shows the short-term interest rate minus the long-term interest rate. The short-term interest rate is influenced by the Bank in the way that you've studied earlier in this chapter. The long-term interest rate is determined by saving and investment plans and by long-term inflation expectations. The red line in Figure 26.13 is the real GDP growth rate *one year later*. You can see that when short-term interest rates rise or long-term interest rates fall the real GDP growth rate slows down in the following year. Long-term interest rates fluctuate less than short-term rates, so when short-term rates rise above long-term rates, it is because the Bank has pushed short-term rates

Figure 26.13

Interest Rates and Real GDP Growth

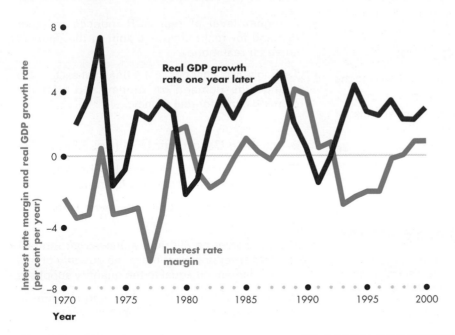

When the Bank increases short-term interest rates, the short-term rate rises above the long-term rate and later real GDP growth slows down. Similarly, when the Bank decreases short-term interest rates, the short-term rate falls below the long-term rate and later real GDP growth speeds up.

Source: National Statistics.

upward. And when short-term rates fall below long-term rates, it is because the Bank has pushed short-term rates downward. So when the Bank stimulates aggregate demand the GDP growth rate speeds up, and when the Bank lowers aggregate demand, the real GDP growth rate slows down. The inflation rate also increases and decreases in sympathy with these fluctuations in real GDP growth.

In this chapter, we've studied the determination of interest rates and discovered how the Bank can influence interest rates by open market operations that change the quantity of money. We've also seen how interest rates influence expenditure plans, which in turn influence aggregate demand. In the next chapter, we're going to explore how fiscal and monetary policy interact to influence the course of the economy.

Review Quiz

◆ Describe the channels by which monetary policy ripples through the economy and explain why each channel operates.
◆ Do interest rates fluctuate in response to the Bank of England's actions?
◆ How do the Bank of England's actions influence real GDP and how long does it take for real GDP to respond to the Bank's policy actions?
◆ How do the Bank's actions on interest rate influence inflation and the exchange rate?

Summary

Key Points

A New Central Bank (pp. 573–577)

- The Bank of England is the central bank of the United Kingdom.
- The European Central Bank is the central bank for the countries in the EMU.
- The central bank influences the economy by setting the base lending rate at which it is willing to lend to the banking system – and by open market operations.

Controlling the Money Supply (pp. 577–581)

- By buying government securities in the market (an open market purchase), the central bank is able to increase the reserves available to banks.
- As a result, there is an expansion of bank lending and the quantity of money increases.
- By selling government securities, the central bank is able to decrease the reserves of banks and other financial institutions, thereby curtailing loans and decreasing the quantity of money.

United Kingdom Money Supply (pp. 582–583)

- The process of the money supply in the United Kingdom is best understood by the method of counterparts.
- The M4 counterpart describes the different influences on the money supply.
- The change in the money supply is influenced by the government budget deficit, by the sale or purchase of government bonds, and by the increase in bank and building society lending.

The Demand for Money (pp. 584–586)

- The quantity of money demanded is the amount of money that people plan to hold.
- The quantity of nominal money demanded is proportional to the price level, and the quantity of real money demanded depends on the interest rate and real GDP.
- A higher interest rate induces a smaller quantity of real money demanded – a movement along the demand curve for real money.

- A higher level of real GDP induces a larger demand for real money – a shift in the demand curve for real money.
- Technological changes in the financial sector also change the demand for money and shift the demand curve for real money.

Interest Rate Determination (pp. 586–588)

- There is an inverse relationship between the interest rate and the price of a financial asset.
- The higher the interest rate, the lower is the price of a financial asset.
- Money market equilibrium achieves an interest rate and asset price that make the quantity of real money demanded equal to the quantity supplied.
- Changes in interest rates achieve equilibrium in the markets for money and financial assets.
- There is an inverse relationship between the interest rate and the price of a financial asset.
- The higher the interest rate, the lower is the price of a financial asset.
- Money market equilibrium achieves an interest rate and asset price that make the quantity of real money available willingly held. If the quantity of real money is increased by the actions of the central bank, the interest rate falls and the prices of financial assets rise.

The Interest Rate and Expenditure Plans (pp. 588–591)

- The real interest rate approximately equals the nominal interest rate minus the inflation rate.
- The nominal interest rate is the opportunity cost of holding money.
- The real interest rate is the opportunity cost of consumption expenditure and investment.
- A fall in the interest rate increases interest sensitive expenditure.
- A fall in the interest rate leads to a fall in the pound sterling exchange rate and an improvement in net trade.
- A rise in the interest rate leads to a rise in the pound sterling exchange rate and a fall in net trade.

Monetary Policy (pp. 591–595)

- The Bank of England directly controls the discount rate, but all short-term rates fluctuate together.

- The fluctuations in short-term interest rates are usually mirrored by fluctuations in the ratio of M4 to GDP.

- Before the 1980s, rises and falls in the interest rate were matched by decreases or increases in the ratio of M4 to GDP.

- After 1980, the relationship between M4 and interest rates broke down because of financial innovation and deregulation of the banking market.

- People attempt to profit by predicting the actions of the central bank.

- To the extent that they can predict the central bank, interest rates and the prices of financial assets move in anticipation of the central bank's actions rather than in response to them.

- When the central bank lowers interest rates, it increases aggregate demand, which speeds real GDP growth and inflation.

- When the central bank raises interest rates, it decreases aggregate demand, which slows real GDP growth and inflation.

Key Figures

Key Terms

Problems

°1 You are given the following information about the economy of Nocoin: the banks have deposits of €300 billion. Their reserves are €15 billion, two-thirds of which is in deposits with the central bank. There are €30 billion notes outside the banks. There are no coins!

a Calculate the monetary base.

b Calculate the quantity of money.

c Calculate the banks' reserve ratio.

d Calculate the currency drain as a percentage of the quantity of money.

2 You are given the following information about the economy of Freezone: the people and businesses in Freezone have bank deposits of €500 billion and hold €100 billion in notes and coin. The banks hold deposits at the Freezone central bank of €50 billion and they keep €5 billion in notes and coin in their vaults and ATM machines.

a Calculate the monetary base.

b Calculate the quantity of money.

c Calculate the banks' reserve ratio.

d Calculate the currency drain as a percentage of the quantity of money.

°3 In problem 1, suppose that the Bank of Nocoin, the central bank, undertakes an open market purchase of securities of €1 billion. What happens to the money supply? Explain why the change in the money supply is not equal to the change in the monetary base.

4 In problem 2, suppose that the Freezone central bank undertakes an open market sale of securities of €1 billion. What happens to the money supply? Explain why the change in the money supply is not equal to the change in the monetary base.

•5 The figure shows the economy of Freezone. The aggregate demand curve is *AD* and the short-run aggregate supply curve is *SAS*$_A$. Potential GDP is €300 billion.

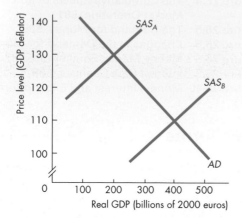

a What is the price level and real GDP in Freezone?

b Does Freezone have an unemployment problem or an inflation problem? Why?

c What do you predict will happen in Freezone if the central bank takes no monetary policy actions?

d What monetary policy action would you advise the central bank to take and what do you predict the effect of that action will be?

6 In Freezone, shown in the figure, the aggregate demand curve is still *AD* and potential GDP is €300 billion but the short-run aggregate supply curve is *SAS*$_B$.

a What is the price level and real GDP?

b Does Freezone have an unemployment problem or an inflation problem? Why?

c What do you predict will happen in Freezone if the central bank takes no monetary policy actions?

d What monetary policy action would you advise the central bank to take and what do you predict the effect of that action will be?

•7 Suppose that in Freezone, shown in the figure above, the short-run aggregate supply curve is *SAS*$_B$ and potential GDP increases to €350 billion.

a What happens in Freezone if the central bank buys securities on the open market?

b What happens in Freezone if the central bank sells securities on the open market?

c Do you recommend that the central bank buy securities or sell securities? Why?

8 Suppose that in Freezone, shown in the figure above, the short-run aggregate supply curve is *SAS*$_A$ and a drought decreases potential GDP to €250 billion.

a What happens in Freezone if the central bank buys securities on the open market?

b What happens in Freezone if the central bank sells securities on the open market?

c Do you recommend that the central bank buy securities or sell securities? Why?

•9 For a given real GDP, the demand for money in Minland (shown in the figure) fluctuates between *MD*$_B$ and *MD*$_C$ and on the average is *MD*$_A$. If the Bank of Minland (the central bank) fixes the quantity of money at €150 billion,

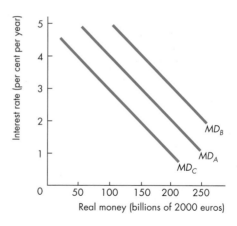

a What is the interest rate in Minland on the average?

b What is the range of interest rate in Minland?

c What do you expect to happen to aggregate demand, real GDP, and the price level, when the demand for money changes but the quantity of money remains fixed?

10 In Minland, shown in the figure, the central bank pegs the interest rate at 3 per cent a year.

a How does the Bank of Minland prevent the interest rate from rising when the demand for money increases to *MD*$_B$?

b How does the Bank of Minland prevent the interest rate from falling when the demand for money decreases to *MD*$_C$?

c Suppose that potential GDP decreases in Minland. Do you think that the Bank of Minland will maintain the 3 per cent a year interest rate target? If not, do you think the Bank will try to raise the interest rate or lower it? What actions would the Bank have to take to change the interest rate?

d If inflation breaks out in Minland, do you think that the Bank of Minland will maintain its interest rate target?

Critical Thinking

1 Study Reading Between the Lines on pp. 600–601 and then answer the following questions:

a Why is inflation falling in the eurozone economy?

b Why has the fall in inflation in the German states raised hopes that the ECB will lower interest rates?

c What is the likely impact of lowering interest rates on the eurozone economy?

2 Use the links on the Parkin, Powell and Matthews website to link on the Bank of England website. Find the latest data on M0, M4 and the base interest rate as well as the latest minutes of the Monetary Policy Committee (MPC). Then answer the following questions.

a Is the Bank trying to slow economic growth or speed it up? How can you tell which?

b What has the MPC decided about interest rates in the past month?

c Skim the latest minutes of the MPC and see if you can discover which way interest rates will move at the next meeting by the voting behaviour of its members.

d In light of the Bank's recent actions, what ripple effects do you expect over the coming months?

e What do you think the effects of the Bank's recent actions will be on bond prices and stock prices?

Monetary Policy in the Eurozone

THE FINANCIAL TIMES, 24 OCTOBER 2001

Inflation fall fuels talk of rate cut by ECB

Tony Major

Inflation data from three German states yesterday showed consumer prices edging lower in October, reinforcing expectations that the European Central Bank will cut interest rates again soon.

In North Rhine-Westphalia, inflation slowed to an annual rate of 1.9 per cent in October from 2 per cent in September; in Bavaria it slowed from 2.1 per cent to 2 per cent; and in Baden-Würtemberg it was steady at 2.3 per cent.

German inflation has fallen rapidly since its peak of 3.5 per cent in May because of slowing economic growth, an appreciation of the euro and lower oil prices. It stood at 2.1 per cent in September and is expected to fall to 2 per cent this month.

Economists said declining German inflation would increase the ECB's confidence that euro-zone inflation, which eased to 2.5 per cent in September, will fall below its 2 per cent price stability ceiling early next year.

Any improvement in the medium-term inflation outlook would also provide the bank, whose prime focus is maintaining price stability, with the scope it needs to cut rates again soon.

The ECB last cut its key refinancing rate to 3.75 per cent on September 17 in a coordinated move with the US Federal Reserve aimed at bolstering faltering economic confidence in the wake of the terrorist attacks.

Most analysts expect the bank to cut rates by 25 basis points at one of its next two meetings – either tomorrow or on November 8 – especially after last week's big fall in the Ifo business climate index.

But Deutsche Bank economists said the ECB was likely to wait until November 8 before deciding, in order to gather more data on the state of the US and eurozone economies.

The Essence of the Story

- Inflation in three German states has fallen raising hopes that inflation in Germany will fall below the ECB's target rate of inflation.

- Germany is the largest economy in the eurozone. A fall in inflation in Germany could reduce measured inflation in the eurozone towards its target ceiling of 2 per cent.

- The improvement to the medium-term outlook for inflation means that the ECB could safely reduce its rate of interest further.

- The last time the ECB lowered interest rates was in a coordinated action with the US Federal Reserve following the terrorist attacks of 11 September 2001.

- Other indicators show that the eurozone economies are slowing in concert with the world economy.

Economic Analysis

- A slowdown in aggregate demand in Germany means that inflation has begun to fall in a number of states.

- Germany is the largest economy in the eurozone. A slowdown in the German economy means that the eurozone economy will slow down and eurozone inflation will fall towards the ECB stability ceiling of 2 per cent.

- Figure 1 shows that the eurozone measured by real GDP growth has slowed down markedly in the first half of 2001.

- Figure 2 shows that eurozone inflation has fallen from May to September 2001 and the ECB has reduced the rate of interest in stages to 3.75 per cent in September.

- The weakening of economic confidence is shown in Figure 3 as a moderate rightward shift in aggregate demand from AD_{00} to AD_{01} along the short-run aggregate supply curve, raising the price level from 110 to 113. But the increase in actual GDP is less than potential GDP as shown by the gap between actual GDP in 2001 and LAS_{01} maintaining a recessionary gap.

- A lowering of the interest rate by the ECB will increase the money supply and push aggregate demand further to the right to narrow the recessionary gap.

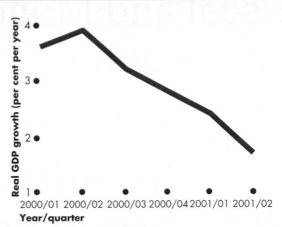

Figure 1 Eurozone growth

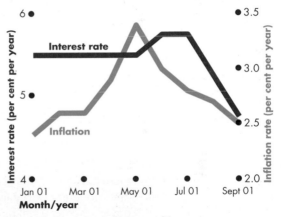

Figure 2 Eurozone inflation and interest rate

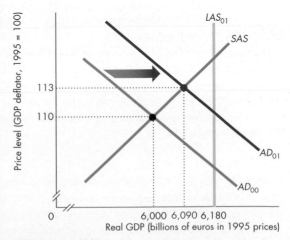

Figure 3 *AS–AD*

CHAPTER 27

Fiscal and Monetary Interactions

After studying this chapter, you will be able to:

◆ Explain how fiscal and monetary policy interact to influence interest rates and aggregate demand

◆ Explain the relative effectiveness of fiscal policy and monetary policy

◆ Describe the Keynesian–monetarist controversy about policy and explain how the controversy was settled

◆ Explain how the mix of fiscal and monetary policies influences the composition of aggregate expenditure

◆ Explain how fiscal and monetary policy influence real GDP and the price level

Harmonic policy

In March 2001, Gordon Brown, the Chancellor of the Exchequer in his budget speech to Parliament, announced significant new spending commitments and tax cuts of £5.3 billion. A few miles to the east, the Bank of England pulls the monetary policy levers that influence interest rates and the exchange rate for the UK. How does the government's fiscal policy interact with the Bank of England's monetary policy to influence interest rates, the exchange rate, and real GDP? ◆ Sometimes, fiscal policy and monetary policy are in harmony with each other. At other times, they come into conflict. Do fiscal and monetary policies need to be coordinated? Are they equivalent to each other? ◆ If a recession is looming on the horizon, is an interest rate cut by the Bank of England just as good as a tax cut by Parliament? Or is one of these actions likely to have more desirable effects than the other? ◆ If the economy is overheating, is an interest rate hike by the Bank of England just as good as a tax increase by Parliament? Or again, is one of these actions likely to have more desirable effects than the other? ◆ When the government has a large budget deficit, must interest rates rise? Can the Bank of England simply give the government some newly created money so that it can increase spending without putting stress on capital markets and raising interest rates?

◆ ◆ ◆ ◆ We are going to answer these questions in this chapter. You already know a lot about the effects of fiscal policy and monetary policy. And you know that their ultimate effects work through their influences on both aggregate demand and aggregate supply. This chapter gives you a deeper understanding of the aggregate demand side of the economy and how the combined actions of the government and the Bank of England affect aggregate demand.

Macroeconomic Equilibrium

Our goal in this chapter is to learn how changes in government expenditure and changes in the quantity of money interact to change real GDP, the price level, and the interest rate. But before we study the effects of *changes* in these policy variables, we must describe the state of the economy with a given level of government expenditure and a given quantity of money.

The Basic Idea

Aggregate demand and short-run aggregate supply determine real GDP and the price level. And the demand for and supply of real money determine the interest rate. But aggregate demand and the money market are linked together.

Other things remaining the same, the greater the level of aggregate demand the higher are real GDP and the price level. A higher real GDP means a greater demand for money; a higher price level means a smaller supply of real money; so a greater level of aggregate demand means a higher interest rate.

And aggregate demand depends on the interest rate. The reason is that consumption expenditure, investment and net exports are influenced by the interest rate (see Chapter 26, pp. 588–595). So, other things remaining the same, the lower the interest rate, the greater is aggregate demand.

Only one level of aggregate demand and one interest rate are consistent with each other in macroeconomic equilibrium. Figure 27.1 describes this unique equilibrium.

AD–AS Equilibrium

In Figure 27.1(a) the intersection of the aggregate demand curve, *AD*, and the short-run aggregate supply curve, *SAS*, determines real GDP at £825 billion and the price level at 115.

The equilibrium amounts of consumption expenditure, investment, government expenditures and net exports lie behind the *AD* curve. But some components of these expenditures are influenced by the interest rate. And the interest rate, in turn, is determined by equilibrium in the money market. Assume that interest-sensitive expenditures total £125 billion, government expenditure is £100 billion, and the rest of real GDP totals £600 billion.

Money Market Equilibrium and Interest-sensitive Expenditure

In Figure 27.1(b) the intersection of the demand for money curve, *MD*, and the supply of money curve, *MS*, determines the interest rate at 5 per cent a year.

The position of the *MD* curve depends on the level of real GDP. Suppose that the demand for money curve shown in the figure describes the demand for money when real GDP is £825 billion, which is equilibrium real GDP in Figure 27.1(a).

The position of the *MS* curve depends on the quantity of nominal money and the price level. Suppose that the supply of money curve shown in the figure describes the supply of real money when the price level is 115, which is the equilibrium price level in Figure 27.1(a).

In Figure 27.1(c), the *IE* curve determines the level of interest-sensitive expenditure at the equilibrium interest rate of 5 per cent a year. Interest-sensitive expenditure is £125 billion, which is the level of this expenditure that lies behind the aggregate demand curve *AD* in Figure 27.1(a).

Check the Equilibrium

The *AD–AS* equilibrium in Figure 27.1(a), the money market equilibrium in Figure 27.1(b), and interest-sensitive expenditure in Figure 27.1(c) are consistent with each other. And there is no other equilibrium.

To check this claim, assume that aggregate demand is less than *AD* in Figure 27.1(a) so that real GDP is less than £825 billion. If this assumption is correct, the demand for money curve lies to the left of *MD* in Figure 27.1(b) and the equilibrium interest rate is less than 5 per cent a year. With an interest rate less than 5 per cent a year, interest-sensitive expenditure exceeds the £125 billion in Figure 27.1(c). If interest-sensitive expenditure exceeds £125 billion, the *AD* curve lies to the right of the one shown in Figure 27.1(a) and equilibrium real GDP exceeds £825 billion. Thus if we assume a real GDP of less than £825 billion, equilibrium real GDP is greater than £825 billion. There is an inconsistency. The assumed equilibrium real GDP is too small.

Now assume that aggregate demand is greater than *AD* in Figure 27.1(a) so that real GDP exceeds £825 billion. If this assumption is correct, the demand for money curve lies to the right of *MD* in Figure 27.1(b) and the equilibrium interest rate exceeds 5 per cent a year. With an interest rate above 5 per cent a year,

Figure 27.1

Equilibrium Real GDP, Price Level, Interest Rate and Expenditure

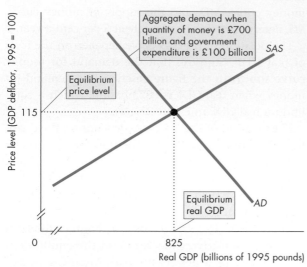

(a) Aggregate supply and aggregate demand

In part (a), the intersection of the aggregate demand curve, *AD*, and the short-run aggregate supply curve, *SAS*, determines real GDP at £825 billion and the price level at 115. Behind the *AD* curve, interest-sensitive expenditure is £125 billion, government expenditure is £100 billion and the rest of real GDP is £600 billion. In part (b), when real GDP is £825 billion, the demand for money is *MD* and when the price level is 115, the supply of (real) money is *MS*. The intersection of the demand for money curve, *MD*, and the supply of money curve, *MS*, determines the interest rate at 5 per cent a year. In part (c), on the *IE* curve, interest-sensitive expenditure is £125 billion at the equilibrium interest rate of 5 per cent a year.

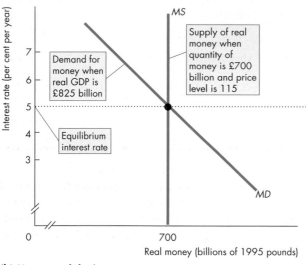

(b) Money and the interest rate

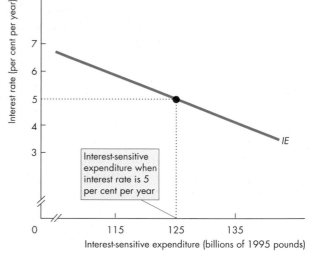

(c) Expenditure and the interest rate

interest-sensitive expenditure is less than the £100 billion in Figure 27.1(c), in which case the *AD* curve must lie to the left of the one shown in Figure 27.1(a) and equilibrium real GDP must be smaller than £825 billion. Thus if we assume that real GDP exceeds £825 billion, equilibrium real GDP is less than £825 billion. There is another inconsistency. The assumed equilibrium real GDP is too large.

Only one level of aggregate demand delivers the same money market equilibrium and *AD–AS* equilib-

rium. In this example, it is the aggregate demand curve *AD* in Figure 27.1(a). Assuming this level of aggregate demand implies this level of aggregate demand. Assuming a lower level of aggregate demand implies a higher level. And assuming a higher level of aggregate demand implies a lower level.

Now that you understand how aggregate demand and the interest rate are simultaneously determined, let's study the effects of a change in government expenditures.

Fiscal Policy in the Short Run

Real GDP growth is slowing, and the Chancellor is concerned that a recession is likely. So the government decides to head off the recession by using fiscal policy to stimulate aggregate demand. A fiscal policy that increases aggregate demand is called an *expansionary fiscal policy*.

The effects of an expansionary fiscal policy are similar to those of throwing a pebble into a pond. There's an initial splash followed by a series of ripples that become ever smaller. The initial splash is the 'first round effect' of the fiscal policy action. The ripples are the 'second round effects'. You've already met the first round effects in Chapter 24, pp. 522–531, so here is a refresher.

First Round Effects of Fiscal Policy

The economy starts out in the position shown in Figure 27.1. Real GDP is £825 billion, the price level is 115, the interest rate is 5 per cent a year, and interest-sensitive expenditure is £100 billion. The government now increases its expenditures on goods and services by £50 billion.

Figure 27.2 shows the first round effects of this action. The increase in government expenditures has a multiplier effect because it induces an increase in consumption expenditure. (You can refresh you memory about the government expenditures multiplier on pp. 522–531.) Let's assume that the multiplier is 4, so a £50 billion increase in government expenditure increases aggregate demand at a given price level by £200 billion. The aggregate demand curve shifts rightward from AD_0 to AD_1. At a price level of 115, the quantity of real GDP demanded increases from £825 billion to £1,025 billion.

Real GDP now starts to increase and the price level starts to rise. These are the first round effects of expansionary fiscal policy.

Second Round Effects of Fiscal Policy

Through the second round, real GDP increases and the price level rises until a new macroeconomic equilibrium is reached. But to find that equilibrium and to describe the changes that result from the initial increase in government expenditures, we must keep track of further changes in the money market and in expenditure plans.

Figure 27.2

First Round Effects of an Expansionary Fiscal Policy

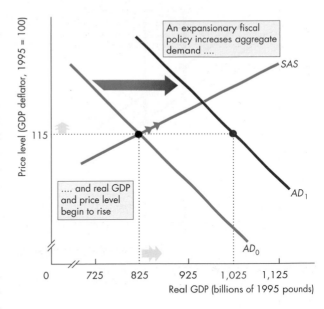

Initially, the aggregate demand curve is AD_0, real GDP is £825 billion and the price level is 115. A £50 billion increase in government expenditures on goods and services has a multiplier effect and increases aggregate demand by £200 billion. The aggregate demand curve shifts rightward to AD_1. Real GDP begins to increase and the price level begins to rise. These are the first round effects of an expansionary fiscal policy.

It is easier to keep track of the second round effects if we split them into two parts, one that results from the increasing real GDP and the other that results from the rising price level. We follow these effects in Figure 27.3.

First, the increasing real GDP increases the demand for money. In Figure 27.3(a), the demand for money curve shifts rightward. Eventually, it shifts to MD_1 and the interest rate rises to 6 per cent a year. At this interest rate, interest-sensitive expenditure decreases to £112.5 billion in Figure 27.3(b). The decrease in planned expenditure decreases aggregate demand and the aggregate demand curve shifts leftward to AD_2 in Figure 27.3(c).

Second, with a given quantity of nominal money, the rising price level decreases the quantity of real money. In Figure 27.3(a), the money supply curve shifts leftward to MS_1. The decrease in the quantity of real money raises the interest rate further to 7 per cent

Figure 27.3

Second Round Effects of an Expansionary Fiscal Policy

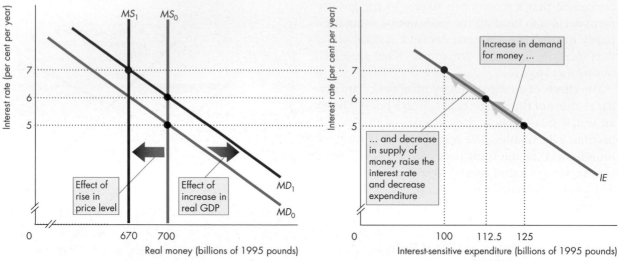

(a) Money and the interest rate

(b) Expenditure and the interest rate

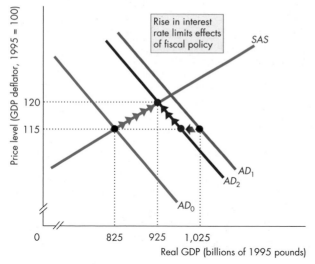

(c) Aggregate supply and aggregate demand

Initially, (part a) the demand curve for money is MD_0, the supply of real money is MS and the interest rate is 5 per cent a year. With an interest rate of 5 per cent a year, interest-sensitive expenditure is £125 billion on the curve IE (part b). With the increased level of government expenditures, the aggregate demand curve is AD_1 (part c). Real GDP is increasing, and the price level is rising. The increasing real GDP increases the demand for money and the demand for money curve shifts rightward to MD_1. The higher interest rate decreases interest-sensitive expenditure, which decreases aggregate demand to AD_2. The rising price level brings a movement along the new AD curve. It does so because it decreases the supply of real money to MS_1, which in turn raises the interest rate further and decreases expenditure. The new equilibrium occurs when real GDP has increased to £925 billion and the price level has risen to 120.

a year. In Figure 27.3(b), the higher interest rate decreases interest-sensitive expenditure to £100 billion. Because this decrease in spending plans is induced by a rise in the price level, it decreases the quantity of real GDP demanded and is shown as a movement along the aggregate demand curve AD_2 in Figure 27.3(c).

During this second round process, real GDP is increasing and the price level is rising in a gradual movement up along the short-run aggregate supply

curve as indicated by the arrows. In the new equilibrium, real GDP is £925 billion, the price level is 120, the interest rate is 7 per cent a year, and interest-sensitive expenditure is £100 billion.

Just as the initial equilibrium in Figure 27.1 was consistent, so the new equilibrium is consistent. The AD–AS equilibrium in Figure 27.3(a), the money market equilibrium in Figure 27.3(b), and interest-sensitive expenditure in Figure 27.3(c) are all consistent with each other. And there is no other equilibrium.

Figure 27.4

How the Economy Adjusts to an Expansionary Fiscal Policy

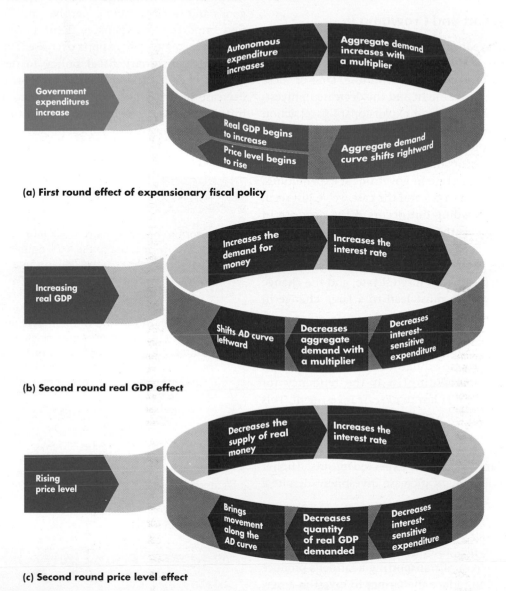

(a) First round effect of expansionary fiscal policy

(b) Second round real GDP effect

(c) Second round price level effect

Figure 27.4 summarizes the first round and the two parts of the second round adjustments as the economy responds to an expansionary fiscal action.

Other Fiscal Policies

A change in government expenditures is only one possible fiscal policy action. Others are a change in transfer payments, such as an increase in unemployment compensation or an increase in social benefits

and a change in taxes. All fiscal policy actions work by changing expenditure. But the magnitude of the initial change in expenditure differs for different fiscal actions. For example, changes in taxes and transfer payments change expenditure by smaller amounts than a change in government expenditures on goods and services. But fiscal policy actions that change autonomous expenditure by a given amount and in a given direction have similar effects on equilibrium real GDP, the price level, and the interest rate regardless of the initial fiscal action. Let's take a closer look at the effect of the rise in the interest rate.

Crowding Out and Crowding In

Because an expansionary fiscal policy increases the interest rate, it decreases all the interest-sensitive components of aggregate expenditure. One of these components is investment and the decrease in investment that results from an expansionary fiscal action is called crowding out.

Crowding out may be partial or complete. Partial crowding out occurs when the decrease in investment is less than the increase in government expenditures. This is the normal case – and the case we've just seen.

Complete crowding out occurs if the decrease in investment equals the initial increase in government expenditures. For complete crowding out to occur, a small change in the demand for real money must lead to a large change in the interest rate, and the change in the interest rate must lead to a large change in investment.

But another potential influence of government expenditures on investment works in the opposite direction to the crowding-out effect and is called 'crowding in'. **Crowding in** is the tendency for expansionary fiscal policy to *increase* investment. This effect works in three ways.

First, in a recession, an expansionary fiscal policy might create expectations of a more speedy recovery and bring an increase in expected profits. Higher expected profits might increase investment despite a higher interest rate.

Second, government expenditures might be productive and lead to more profitable business opportunities. For example, a new government built highway might cut the cost of transporting a farmer's produce to a market and induce the farmer to invest in a new fleet of refrigerated trucks.

Third, if an expansionary fiscal policy takes the form of a cut in taxes on business profits, firms' after-tax profits increase and investment might increase.

The Exchange Rate and International Crowding Out

We've seen that an expansionary fiscal policy leads to higher interest rates. But a change in interest rates also affects the exchange rate. Higher interest rates make the dollar rise in value against other currencies. With interest rates higher in the UK than in the rest of the world, funds flow into Britain and people around the world demand more pounds sterling. As the pound rises in value, foreigners find UK-produced goods and services more expensive and UK residents find imports less expensive. Exports decrease and imports increase – net exports decrease. The tendency for an expansionary fiscal policy to decrease net exports is called **international crowding out**. The decrease in net exports offsets, to some degree, the initial increase in aggregate expenditure brought about by an expansionary fiscal policy.

Review Quiz

◆ Describe macroeconomic equilibrium. What conditions are met in such an equilibrium? What are the links between aggregate demand, the money market, and investment?
◆ What is an expansionary fiscal policy and what are its first round effects? What is happening at the end of the first round?
◆ What are the second round effects of an expansionary fiscal policy action? Describe the forces at work and the changes that occur in the interest rate, investment, real GDP, and the price level.
◆ What are crowding out and crowding in? How do they influence the outcome of a fiscal policy action?
◆ How does an expansionary fiscal policy affect the exchange rate? What happens to imports and exports?

Monetary Policy in the Short Run

To study the effects of an expansionary monetary policy, we look at the first round effects and the second round effects, just as we did for fiscal policy. Figure 27.5 describes the economy, which is initially in the situation that we studied in Figure 27.1. The quantity of money is £700 billion, the interest rate is 5 per cent a year, interest-sensitive expenditure is £125 billion, real GDP is £825 billion and the price level is 115.

The Bank of England now increases the money supply so that the quantity of money increases to £1,265 billion. With a price level of 115, the quantity of real money increases to £1,100 billion. Figure 27.5(a)

Figure 27.5

First Round Effects of an Expansionary Monetary Policy

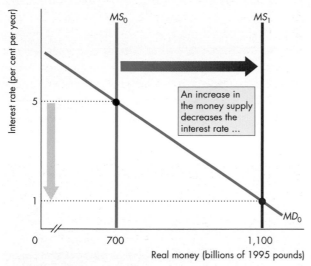

(a) Change in money supply

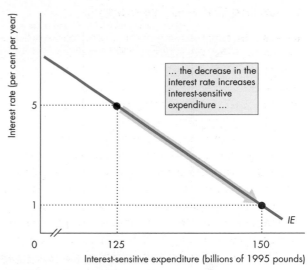

(b) Change in expenditure

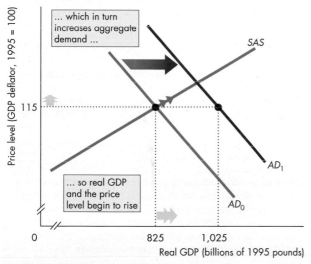

(c) Change in aggregate demand

Initially, the demand curve for real money is MD_0, the real money supply is MS_0, and the interest rate is 5 per cent a year (part a). With an interest rate of 5 per cent a year, interest-sensitive expenditure is £125 billion on the IE curve (part b). The aggregate demand curve is AD_0 and equilibrium real GDP £825 billion and the price level is 115 (part c). An increase in the quantity of money shifts the money supply curve rightward to MS_1 (part a). The increased money supply lowers the interest rate to 1 per cent a year and interest-sensitive expenditure increases to £150 billion (part b). The increase in expenditure increases aggregate demand to AD_1 (in part c). Real GDP begins to increase and the price level begins to rise.

shows the immediate effect. The real money supply curve shifts rightward from MS_0 to MS_1, and the interest rate falls from 5 per cent to 1 per cent a year. The lower interest rate increases interest-sensitive expenditure to £150 billion (part c). The increase in interest-sensitive expenditure increases aggregate demand and shifts the AD curve rightward from AD_0 to AD_1 (part c). The increase in aggregate demand sets off

a multiplier process in which real GDP and the price level begin to increase towards their equilibrium levels.

These are the first round effects of an expansionary monetary policy. An increase in the money supply lowers the interest rate and increases aggregate demand. Real GDP and the price level begin to increase.

Let's now look at the second round effects.

Figure 27.6

Second Round Effects of an Expansionary Monetary Policy

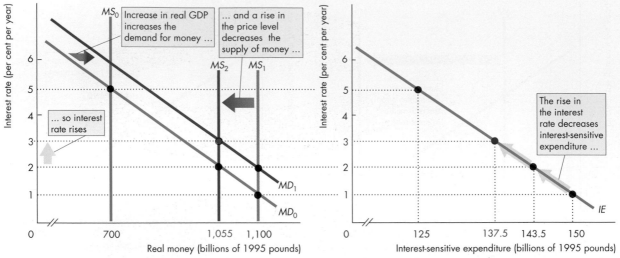

(a) Money and the interest rate

(b) Decrease in expenditure

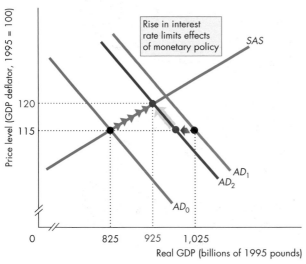

(c) Aggregate demand and aggregate supply

At the start of the second round, the demand curve for money is still MD_0 (part a), the supply of real money is MS_1, and the interest rate is 1 per cent a year. With an interest rate of 1 per cent a year, interest-sensitive expenditure is £150 billion on the curve IE (part b). With the increased quantity of money and expenditure level, the aggregate demand curve is AD_1 (part c). Real GDP is increasing and the price level is rising. The increasing real GDP increases the demand for money and the demand for money curve shifts rightward to MD_1. The higher interest rate decreases interest-sensitive expenditure, which decreases aggregate demand to AD_2. The rising price level brings a movement along the new AD curve. It does so because it decreases the supply of real money to MS_2, which in turn raises the interest rate further and decreases expenditure. The new equilibrium occurs when real GDP has increased to £925 billion and the price level has risen to 120.

Second Round Effects

The increasing real GDP and rising price level set off the second round, which Figure 27.6(b) illustrates. And as in the case of fiscal policy, it is best to break the second round into two parts: the consequence of increasing real GDP and the consequence of the rising price level.

The increasing real GDP increases the demand for money from MD_0 to MD_1 in Figure 27.6(a). The increased demand for money raises the interest rate

to 2 per cent a year. The higher interest rate brings a decrease in interest-sensitive expenditure from £150 billion to £143.5 billion in Figure 27.6(b). And the lower level of expenditure decreases aggregate demand and shifts the aggregate demand curve leftward to AD_2 in Figure 27.6(c).

The rising price level brings a movement along the new aggregate demand curve in Figure 27.6(c). This movement occurs because the rising price level decreases the real money supply. As the price level rises, the real money supply decreases to £1,055

Figure 27.7

How the Economy Adjusts to an Expansionary Monetary Policy

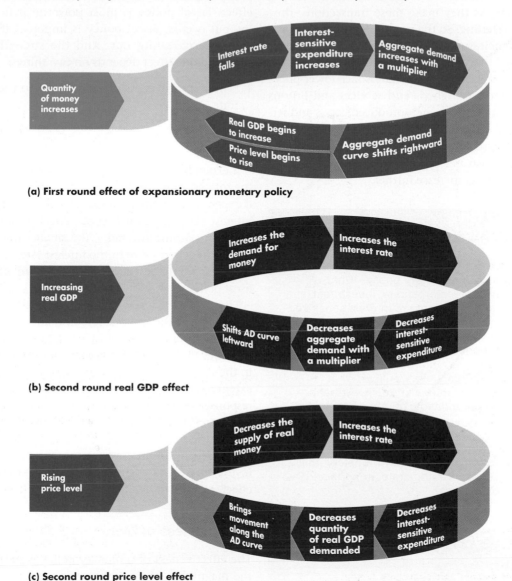

(a) First round effect of expansionary monetary policy

(b) Second round real GDP effect

(c) Second round price level effect

billion and the money supply curve shifts leftward to MS_2 (part a). The interest rate rises further to 3 per cent a year. And interest-sensitive expenditure decreases to £137.5 billion (part b).

In the new short-run equilibrium, real GDP has increased to £925 billion, and the price level has risen to 120, where aggregate demand curve AD_2 intersects the short-run aggregate supply curve SAS.

The demand for money is MD_1, the supply of (real) money is MS_2, and the interest rate is 3 per cent a year in part (a). With an interest rate of 3 per cent

a year, interest-sensitive expenditure is £137.5 billion (part b).

The new equilibrium is the only consistent one and is like that of Figure 27.1. Figure 27.7 summarizes the adjustments that occur to bring the economy to this new equilibrium.

Money and the Exchange Rate

An increase in the money supply lowers the interest rate. If the interest rate falls but does not fall in the rest of the EU, the United States and Japan, international investors buy the now higher-yielding foreign assets and sell the relatively lower-yielding British assets. As they make these transactions, they sell pounds sterling. So the pound depreciates against other currencies. (This mechanism is explained in greater detail in Chapter 34, pp. 792–800.)

With a cheaper pound, foreigners face lower prices for British produced goods and services and Britons face higher prices for foreign-produced goods and services. Foreigners increase their imports from the UK, and Britons decrease their imports from the rest of the world. British net exports increase and real GDP and the price level increase further.

Review Quiz

◆ What are the first round effects of an expansionary monetary policy? What happens to the interest rate, investment and other components of interest-sensitive expenditure, aggregate demand, the demand for money, real GDP, and the price level in the first round?

◆ What are the second round effects of an expansionary monetary policy? What happens to the interest rate, investment and other components of interest-sensitive expenditure, aggregate demand, the demand for money, real GDP, and the price level in the second round?

◆ How does an expansionary monetary policy influence the exchange rate, imports and exports?

Relative Effectiveness of Policies

We've seen that aggregate demand and real GDP are influenced by both fiscal and monetary policy. But which policy is the more potent? This question was once at the centre of a controversy among macroeconomists. Later in this section we'll look at that controversy and see how it was settled. But we begin by discovering what determines the effectiveness of fiscal policy.

Effectiveness of Fiscal Policy

The effectiveness of fiscal policy is measured by the magnitude of the increase in aggregate demand that results from a given increase in government expenditures (or decrease in taxes). The effectiveness of fiscal policy depends on the strength of the crowding-out effect. Fiscal policy is most powerful if no crowding out occurs. Fiscal policy is impotent if there is complete crowding out. And the strength of the crowding-out effect depends on two things:

1 The responsiveness of expenditure to the interest rate.

2 The responsiveness of the quantity of money demanded to the interest rate.

If expenditure is not very responsive to a change in the interest rate, the crowding-out effect is small. But if expenditure is highly responsive to a change in the interest rate, the crowding-out effect is large. Other things remaining the same, the smaller the responsiveness of expenditure to the interest rate, the smaller is the crowding-out effect and the more effective is fiscal policy.

The responsiveness of the quantity of money demanded to the interest rate also affects the size of the crowding-out effect. An increase in real GDP increases the demand for money and with no change in the supply of money, the interest rate rises. But the extent to which the interest rate rises depends on the responsiveness of the quantity of money demanded to the interest rate. Other things remaining the same, the greater the responsiveness of the quantity of money demanded to the interest rate, the smaller is the rise in the interest rate, the smaller is the crowding-out effect, and the more effective is fiscal policy.

Effectiveness of Monetary Policy

The effectiveness of monetary policy is measured by the magnitude of the increase in aggregate demand that results from a given increase in the money supply. The effectiveness of monetary policy depends on the same two factors that influence the effectiveness of fiscal policy:

1 The responsiveness of the quantity of money demanded to the interest rate.

2 The responsiveness of expenditure to the interest rate.

The starting point for monetary policy is a change in the quantity of money that changes the interest rate. A given change in the quantity of money might bring a small change or a large change in the interest rate. Other things being the same, the larger the initial change in the interest rate, the more effective is monetary policy. And the initial change in the interest rate is greater, the less responsive is the quantity of money demanded to the interest rate.

But effectiveness of monetary policy also depends on how much expenditure changes. If expenditure is not very responsive to a change in the interest rate, monetary actions do not have much effect on expenditure. But if expenditure is highly responsive to a change in the interest rate, monetary actions have a large effect on aggregate expenditure. The greater the responsiveness of expenditure to the interest rate, the more effective is monetary policy.

The effectiveness of fiscal policy and monetary policy that you've just studied were once controversial. During the 1950s and 1960s, this issue lay at the heart of what was called the Keynesian–monetarist controversy. Let's look at the dispute and see how it was resolved.

The Keynesian–Monetarist Controversy

The Keynesian–monetarist controversy was an ongoing dispute in macroeconomics between two broad groups of economists. A **Keynesian** is a macroeconomist whose views about the functioning of the economy are based on the theories of John Maynard Keynes, published in Keynes's *The General Theory of Employment, Interest and Money*. Keynesians regard the economy as being inherently unstable and as requiring active government intervention to achieve stability. Traditionally they assigned a low degree of importance to monetary policy and a high degree of importance to fiscal policy. Modern Keynesians assign a high degree of importance to both types of policy. A **monetarist** is a macroeconomist whose views about the functioning of the economy are based on theories most forcefully set forth by Milton Friedman (see pp. 570–571). Monetarists regard the economy as being inherently stable and as requiring no active government intervention. Monetarists believe that most macroeconomic fluctuations are caused by fluctuations in the quantity of money. Traditionally they assigned a low degree of importance to fiscal policy. But modern monetarists, like modern Keynesians, assign a high degree of importance to both types of policy.

The nature of the Keynesian–monetarist debate has changed over the years. During the 1950s and 1960s, it was a debate about the relative effectiveness of fiscal policy and monetary policy in changing aggregate demand. We can see the essence of that debate by making three points of view distinct:

1 Extreme Keynesianism.

2 Extreme monetarism.

3 Intermediate position.

Extreme Keynesianism

The extreme Keynesian hypothesis is that a change in the money supply has no effect on aggregate demand, and a change in government expenditures on goods and services or in taxes has a large effect on aggregate demand. The two circumstances in which a change in the money supply has no effect on aggregate demand are:

1 Expenditure demand is completely insensitive to the interest rate.

2 The demand for real money is highly sensitive to the interest rate.

If expenditure is completely insensitive to the interest rate (if the *IE* curve is vertical), a change in the money supply changes interest rates, but those changes do not affect aggregate planned expenditure. Monetary policy is impotent.

If the demand for real money is highly sensitive to the interest rate (if the *MD* curve is horizontal), people are willing to hold any amount of money at a given interest rate – a situation called a *liquidity trap*. With a liquidity trap, a change in the money supply affects only the amount of money held. It does not affect interest rates. With an unchanged interest rate, expenditure remains constant. Monetary policy is impotent. Some people believe that Japan was in a liquidity trap during the late 1990s.

Extreme Monetarism

The extreme monetarist hypothesis is that a change in government expenditures on goods and services or in taxes has no effect on aggregate demand and that a change in the money supply has a large effect on aggregate demand. Two circumstances give rise to these predictions:

1 Expenditure is highly sensitive to the interest rate.

2 The demand for real money is completely insensitive to the interest rate.

If an increase in government expenditures on goods and services induces an increase in interest rates that is sufficiently large to reduce expenditure by the same amount as the initial increase in government expenditures, then fiscal policy has no effect on aggregate demand. This outcome is complete crowding out. For this result to occur, either the demand for real money must be insensitive to the interest rate – a fixed amount of money is held regardless of the interest rate – or expenditure must be highly sensitive to the interest rate – any amount of expenditure will be undertaken at a given interest rate.

The Intermediate Position

The intermediate position is that both fiscal and monetary policy affect aggregate demand. Crowding out is not complete, so fiscal policy does have an effect. There is no liquidity trap and expenditure responds to interest rates, so monetary policy does indeed affect aggregate demand. This position is the one that now appears to be correct and is the one that we've spent most of this chapter exploring. Let's see how economists came to this conclusion.

Sorting Out the Competing Claims

The dispute between monetarists, Keynesians and those taking an intermediate position was essentially a disagreement about the magnitudes of two economic parameters:

1. The responsiveness of expenditure to the interest rate.

2. The responsiveness of the demand for real money to the interest rate.

If expenditure is highly sensitive to the interest rate or the demand for real money is barely sensitive to the interest rate, then monetary policy is powerful and fiscal policy relatively ineffective. In this case, the world looks similar to the claims of extreme monetarists. If expenditure is very insensitive to the interest rate, or the demand for real money is highly sensitive, then fiscal policy is powerful and monetary policy is relatively ineffective. In this case, the world looks similar to the claims of the extreme Keynesians.

By using statistical methods to study the demand for real money and expenditure and by using data from a wide variety of historical and national experiences, economists were able to settle this dispute. Neither extreme position turned out to be supported by the evidence and the intermediate position won. The demand curve for real money slopes downward.

And expenditure *is* interest sensitive. Neither demand curve is vertical nor horizontal, so the extreme Keynesian and extreme monetarist hypotheses are rejected.

Interest Rate and Exchange Rate Effectiveness

Although fiscal policy and monetary policy are alternative ways of changing aggregate demand, they have opposing effects on the interest rate and the exchange rate. A fiscal policy action that increases aggregate demand raises the interest rate and increases the exchange rate. A monetary policy action that increases aggregate demand lowers the interest rate and decreases the exchange rate. Because of these opposing effects on interest rates and the exchange rate, if the two policies are combined to increase aggregate demand, their separate effects on the interest rate and the exchange rate can be minimized.

Review Quiz

◆ What two macroeconomic parameters influence the relative effectiveness of fiscal policy and monetary policy?
◆ Under what circumstances is the Keynesian view correct and under what circumstances is the monetarist view correct?
◆ How can fiscal policy and monetary policy be combined to increase aggregate demand yet at the same time keep the interest rate constant?

We're now going to look at expansionary fiscal and monetary policy at full employment.

Policy Actions at Full Employment

An expansionary fiscal policy or monetary policy can bring the economy to full employment. But it is often difficult to determine whether the economy is below full employment. So an expansionary fiscal policy or monetary policy might be undertaken when the economy is at full employment. What happens then? Let's answer this question starting with an expansionary fiscal policy.

Expansionary Fiscal Policy at Full Employment

Suppose the economy is at full employment and the government increases expenditure. All the effects that we worked out earlier in this chapter occur. Except that these effects determine only a *short-run equilibrium*. That is, the first round and second round effects of policy both occur in the short run. There is a third round, which is the long-run adjustment.

Starting out at full employment, an expansionary fiscal policy will create an above full-employment equilibrium in which there is an *inflationary gap*. The money wage rate begins to rise, short-run aggregate supply decreases, and a long-run adjustment occurs in which real GDP decreases to potential GDP and the price level rises.

Figure 27.8 illustrates the combined first and second round short-run effects and the third round long-run adjustment.

In Figure 27.8, potential GDP is £825 billion. Real GDP equals potential GDP on aggregate demand curve AD_0 and short-run aggregate supply curve SAS_0. An expansionary fiscal action increases aggregate demand. The combined first round and second round effect increases aggregate demand to AD_1. Real GDP increases to £925 billion and the price level rises to 120. There is an inflationary gap of £100 billion.

With the economy at above full-employment, a shortage of labour puts upward pressure on the money wage rate, which now begins to rise. And a third round of adjustment begins. The rising money wage rate decreases short-run aggregate supply and the *SAS* curve starts moving leftward towards SAS_1.

As the short-run aggregate supply decreases, real GDP decreases and the price level rises. This process continues until the inflationary gap has been eliminated at full employment. At the long-run equilibrium is a real GDP of £825, which is potential GDP, and a price level of 135.

Crowding Out at Full Employment

You've just seen that when government expenditures increase at full employment, the long-run change in real GDP is zero. The entire effect of the increase in aggregate demand is to increase the price level. This outcome implies that at full employment, an increase in government expenditures either *completely crowds out investment*, or *creates an international (net exports) deficit*, or results in a combination of the two.

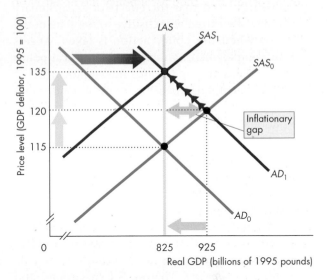

Figure 27.8

Fiscal Policy at Full Employment

The long-run aggregate supply curve is *LAS* and initially the aggregate demand curve is AD_0 and the short-run aggregate supply curve is SAS_0. Real GDP is £825 billion and the GDP deflator is 115. Fiscal and monetary policy changes shift the aggregate demand curve to AD_1. At the new short-run equilibrium, real GDP is £925 billion and the GDP deflator is 120. Because real GDP exceeds potential GDP, the money wage rate begins to rise and the short-run aggregate supply curve begins to shift leftward to SAS_1. At the new long-run equilibrium, the GDP deflator is 135 and real GDP is back at its original level.

The easiest way to see why is to recall that aggregate expenditure, which equals consumption expenditure, C, plus investment, I, plus government expenditures, G, plus net exports, NX, equals real GDP. That is:

$$Y = C + I + G + NX$$

Comparing the initial situation with the outcome, real GDP has not changed. So consumption, which depends on income (GDP), has not changed. With no change in Y and C, the sum $I + G + NX$ is constant between the two situations.

But government expenditures have increased, so either investment or net exports must have decreased. If net exports have not changed, investment has decreased by the full amount of the increase in government expenditures. If investment has not changed, net exports have decreased by an amount equal to the increase in government expenditures. A decrease in net exports is an increase in our international deficit.

You've now seen that the effects of expansionary fiscal policy are extremely sensitive to the state of the economy when the policy action is taken. At less than full employment, an expansionary fiscal policy can move the economy towards full employment. At full employment, an expansionary fiscal policy raises the price level, crowds out investment and creates an international deficit.

Expansionary Monetary Policy at Full Employment

Now suppose the economy is at full employment and the Bank of England increases the money supply. Again, all the effects that we worked out earlier in this chapter occur. But again, these effects determine only a *short-run equilibrium*. That is, the first round and second round effects of monetary policy both occur in the short run. And again, there is a third round, which is the long-run adjustment.

Starting out at full employment, an expansionary monetary policy will create an above full-employment equilibrium in which there is an *inflationary gap*. The money wage rate begins to rise, short-run aggregate supply decreases, and a long-run adjustment occurs in which real GDP decreases to potential GDP and the price level rises.

Figure 27.8, which illustrates the effects of an expansionary fiscal policy at full employment also illustrates the effects of an expansionary monetary policy at full employment.

In the short run, an expansionary monetary policy increases real GDP and the price level. But in the long run, it increases only the price level and leaves real GDP unchanged at potential GDP.

Long-run Neutrality

In the long run, a change in the quantity of money changes only the price level and leaves real GDP unchanged. The independence of real GDP from the quantity of money is an example of the long-run neutrality of money.

But **long-run neutrality** applies not only to real GDP but also to all real variables. The so-called long-run neutrality proposition is that in the long run, a change in the quantity of money changes the price level and leaves all real variables unchanged.

You can see this outcome in the case of real GDP in Figure 27.8. Because a change in the quantity of money leaves real GDP unchanged, it also leaves consumption expenditure unchanged. With no change in real GDP, the demand for money does not change. The price level rises by the same percentage as the increase in the quantity of money, so the supply of real money does not change. With no change in the demand for money and no change in the supply of real money, the interest rate does not change. And with no change in the interest rate, expenditure remains the same. Finally, with no change in real GDP, consumption expenditure, investment, and government expenditures, net exports are unchanged.

Review Quiz

♦ Contrast the short-run effects of an expansionary fiscal policy on real GDP and the price level with its long-run effects when the policy action occurs at full employment.
♦ Contrast the short-run effects of an expansionary monetary policy on real GDP and the price level with its long-run effects when the policy action occurs at full employment.
♦ Explain crowding out at full employment.
♦ Explain the long-run neutrality of money.

Policy Coordination and Conflict

So far, we've studied fiscal policy and monetary policy in isolation from each other. We are now going to consider what happens if the two branches of policy are coordinated and if they come into conflict.

Policy coordination occurs when the government and the Bank of England work together to achieve a common set of goals. **Policy conflict** occurs when the government and the Bank of England pursue different goals and the actions of one make it harder (perhaps impossible) for the other to achieve its goals.

Policy Coordination

The basis for policy coordination is the fact that either fiscal policy or monetary policy can be used to increase aggregate demand. Starting from a position of *unemployment equilibrium*, an increase in aggregate demand increases real GDP and decreases unemployment. If the size of the policy action is well judged, it can restore full employment. Similarly, starting from a position of *above full-employment equilibrium*, a decrease in aggregate demand decreases real GDP and can, if the size of the policy action is well judged, eliminate an *inflationary gap*. Because either a fiscal policy or a monetary policy action can achieve these objectives, the two policies can (in principle) be combined to also achieve the same outcome.

If either or both policies can restore full employment and eliminate inflation, why does it matter which policy is used? It matters because the two policies have different side effects – different effects on other variables about which people care. These side effects work through the influence of policy on two key variables:

1   The interest rate.
2   The exchange rate.

Interest Rate Effects

An expansionary fiscal policy *raises* the interest rate while an expansionary monetary policy *lowers* the interest rate. When the interest rate changes, investment changes, so an expansionary fiscal policy lowers investment (crowding out) while an expansionary monetary policy increases investment. So if an expansionary fiscal policy increases aggregate demand, consumption expenditure increases and investment decreases. But if an expansionary monetary policy increases aggregate demand, consumption expenditure and investment increase.

By coordinating fiscal policy and monetary policy and increasing aggregate demand with an appropriate combination of the two, it is possible to increase real GDP and lower unemployment with either no change in the interest rate, or with any desired change in the interest rate. A big dose of fiscal expansion and a small dose of monetary expansion raises the interest rate and lowers investment while a small dose of fiscal expansion and a big dose of monetary expansion lowers the interest rate.

The interest rate affects our long-term growth prospects because the growth rate of potential GDP depends on the level of investment. The connection between investment, capital and growth is explained in Chapter 30, pp. 684–685.

Exchange Rate Effects

An expansionary fiscal policy raises not only the interest rate but also the exchange rate. In contrast, an expansionary monetary policy *lowers* the exchange rate. When the exchange rate changes, net exports change. An expansionary fiscal policy lowers net exports (international crowding out) while an expansionary monetary policy increases net exports. So if full employment is restored by expansionary policy, net exports decrease with fiscal expansion and increase with monetary expansion.

Policy Conflict

Policy conflicts are not planned. But they sometimes happen. When they arise, it is usually because of a divergence of the political priorities of the government and the objectives of the Bank of England.

The government pays a lot of attention to employment and production over a short time horizon. It looks for policies that make its re-election chances high. The Bank of England pays a lot of attention to price level stability and has a long time horizon. It doesn't have an election to worry about.

So a situation might arise in which the government wants the Bank to pursue an expansionary monetary policy but the Bank wants to keep its foot on the monetary brake. The government says that an increase in the money supply is essential to lower interest rates and the exchange rate and to boost investment and exports. The Bank says that the problem is with fiscal policy. Spending is too high and revenues too low. With fiscal policy too expansionary, interest rates and the exchange rate are high and they cannot be lowered permanently by monetary policy. To lower interest rates and give investment and exports a boost, fiscal policy must become contractionary. Only then can an expansionary monetary policy be pursued. Such a conflict between the governments of the eurozone economies and the ECB is discussed in Reading Between the Lines, pp. 630–631.

A further potential conflict between the government and the Bank of England concerns the financing of the government deficit. A government deficit can be financed either by borrowing from the general public or by borrowing from the Bank. If the government borrows from the general public, it must pay interest on its debt. If it borrows from the Bank, it pays interest to the Bank. But the government owns the Bank, so the interest comes back to the government. Financing a deficit by selling debt to the central bank costs the government no interest. So the temptation to sell debt to the central bank is strong.

But when the Bank of England buys government debt, it pays for the debt with newly created monetary base. The money supply increases. And such finance leads to inflation. In many countries, for example in Eastern Europe, Latin America and Africa, government deficits are financed by the central bank.

In the UK, they are not. Indeed, the independence of the Bank of England and of the central banks in the EU ensures that such a possibility cannot happen. However, the policy conflict that arises because of a difference between the objectives of an independent central bank and an electorally dependant government is a real issue that has been addressed in the 'Growth and Stability Pact' for countries in the eurozone.

Growth and Stability Pact

Membership of the EMU imposes certain fiscal constraints on individual countries. In 1997 the European Council resolved by treaty to ensure that the national budgetary policies of countries in the EMU will support the ECB's monetary policy of a target rate of inflation of less than 2 per cent a year.

The Stability Pact states that member countries of the eurozone will aim to have a balanced fiscal budget. Countries that have a budget deficit in excess of 3 per cent of GDP will be fined up to 0.5 per cent of GDP. However, if exceptional circumstances occur such as a natural disaster or severe recession then the fines are not applicable. The exceptional circumstance is if real GDP falls by more than 2 per cent in a year but if the fall is between 0.75 per cent and 2 per cent the fine would be subject to the approval of the European Council.

The provisions of the 'pact' appear draconian in its measures but there are good arguments as to why fiscal policy may need to be constrained in the EMU. This is because one country's policy could have negative externalities on the other countries in the EMU.

If one country in the EMU conducts an expansionary fiscal policy, this will increase aggregate demand and increase the demand for money in that country and in the whole of the eurozone. The increase in the demand for money will raise the rate of interest. The rise in the rate of interest will lead to an appreciation of the euro exchange rate against the dollar and reduce eurozone exports (see Chapter 34, pp. 765–800). Particularly badly hit would be countries in the eurozone that are not following an expansionary fiscal

policy but will face a fall in demand for their exports outside the eurozone.

Furthermore, the rise in the rate of interest will reduce interest sensitive expenditure in the eurozone countries and together with the fall in export demand the counries that do not follow an expansionary fiscal policy will face a fall in aggregate demand. So the country that follows an expansionary fiscal policy would gain at the expense of those that do not.

The expansionary fiscal policy poses another potential conflict between the fiscal authorities of the countries in the EMU and the ECB. The budget deficit will increase the debt of the country conducting the expansionary fiscal policy. But the higher rate of interest caused by the increased borrowing will lead to larger interest payments for all the countries in the eurozone which in turn will add to their deficit and debt (see Chapter 24, pp. 520–521).

Countries that are hurt by the higher rate of interest will attempt to pressure the ECB to increase the money supply and cut the rate of interest. You can see from Reading Between the Lines (pp. 630–631) that the stability pact can interfere with the automatic fiscal policy that occurs as the economy goes into a downturn. A country that has a structural budget deficit will have little room to engage in automatic fiscal policy if the economy moves into a recession.

Review Quiz

◆ What are the main things that can be achieved by coordinating fiscal policy and monetary policy?
◆ What are the main sources of conflict in policy between the Bank of England and the government?
◆ Explain what happens if the government pursues an expansionary fiscal policy while the Bank of England pursues a contractionary monetary policy.
◆ Explain how inflation can be avoided despite a government building up a large budget deficit.

You have now studied the interaction of fiscal policy and monetary policy. Reading Between the Lines on pages 630–631 takes another look at the way these two sets of policies interact by studying the monetary policy actions of the ECB and the fiscal policies of the big economies in the eurozone in 2001. You've seen that these policies are alternative ways of changing aggregate demand and real GDP. But they have different effects on interest rates and the exchange rate. You've seen what determines the relative effectiveness of fiscal and monetary policies and how the mix of these policies can influence the composition of aggregate expenditure. But you've also seen that the ultimate effects of these policies on real GDP and the price level depend not only on the behaviour of aggregate demand but also on aggregate supply and the state of the labour market.

Summary

Key Points

Macroeconomic Equilibrium (pp. 603–604)

- Equilibrium real GDP, the price level and the interest rate are determined simultaneously by equilibrium in the money market and equality of aggregate demand and aggregate supply.

Fiscal Policy in the Short Run (pp. 605–608)

- The first round effects of an expansionary fiscal policy are an increase in aggregate demand, increasing real GDP, and a rising price level.

- The second round effects are an increasing demand for money and a decreasing supply of (real) money that limit the increase in real GDP and the rise in the price level.

- Interest-sensitive expenditure, which includes investment and net exports, decreases.

Monetary Policy in the Short Run (pp. 608–612)

- The first round effects of an expansionary monetary policy are a fall in the interest rate, an increase in aggregate demand, an increasing real GDP and a rising price level.

- The second round effects are an increasing demand for money and a decreasing supply of (real) money that limit the increase in real GDP and the rise in the price level.

- Interest-sensitive expenditure, which includes investment and net exports, increases.

Relative Effectiveness of Policies (pp. 612–614)

- The relative effectiveness of fiscal and monetary policy depends on the interest-sensitivity of expenditure and the demand for money.

- The extreme Keynesian position is that only fiscal policy affects aggregate demand. The extreme monetarist position is that only monetary policy affects aggregate demand. Neither extreme is correct.

- The mix of fiscal and monetary policy influences the composition of aggregate demand.

Policy Actions at Full Employment (pp. 614–616)

- An expansionary fiscal policy at full employment increases real GDP and the price level in the short run but increases only the price level in the long run. Complete crowding of investment occurs or the international deficit increases.

- An expansionary monetary policy at full employment increases real GDP and the price level in the short run but increases only the price level in the long run. Money is neutral – has no real effects – in the long run.

Policy Coordination and Conflict (pp. 616–619)

- Policy coordination can make changes in the interest rate and the exchange rate small.

- Policy conflict can avoid inflation in the face of a government deficit.

Key Figures ◆

Key Terms

Problems

●1 In the economy described in Figure 27.1, suppose the government decreases its expenditures on goods and services by £100 billion.

   a Work out the first round effects.

   b Explain how real GDP and the interest rate change.

   c Explain the second round effects that take the economy to a new equilibrium.

2 In the economy described in Figure 27.1, suppose the government increases its expenditures on goods and services by £25 billion.

   a Work out the first round effects.

   b Explain how real GDP and the interest rate change.

   c Explain the second round effects that take the economy to a new equilibrium.

   d Compare the equilibrium in this case with the one described in the chapter on pp. 605–606. In which case does the interest rate change by most? Why?

●3 In the economy described in Figure 27.1, suppose the Central Bank decreases the money supply by £450 billion.

   a Work out the first round effects.

   b Explain how real GDP and the interest rate change.

   c Explain the second round effects that take the economy to a new equilibrium.

4 In the economy described in Figure 27.1, suppose the Central Bank increases the money supply by £250 billion.

   a Work out the first round effects.

   b Explain how real GDP and the interest rate change.

   c Explain the second round effects that take the economy to a new equilibrium.

   d Compare the equilibrium in this case with the one described in the chapter on pp. 608–611. In which case does real GDP change by most? In which case does the interest rate change by most? Why?

●5 The economies of two countries, Alpha and Beta, are identical in every way except the following: in Alpha, a change in the interest rate of 1 percentage point (for example, from 5 per cent to 6 per cent) results in a €1 billion change in the quantity of real money demanded. In Beta, a change in the interest rate of 1 percentage point results in a €0.1 billion change in the quantity of real money demanded.

   a In which economy does an increase in government expenditures on goods and services have a larger effect on real GDP?

   b In which economy is the crowding-out effect weaker?

   c In which economy does a change in the money supply have a larger effect on equilibrium real GDP?

   d Which economy, if either, is closer to the Keynesian extreme and which is closer to the monetarist extreme?

6 The economies of two countries, Gamma and Delta, are identical in every way except the following: in Gamma, a change in the interest rate of 1 percentage point (for example, from 5 per cent to 6 per cent) results in a €0.1 billion change in interest-sensitive expenditure. In Delta, change in the interest rate of 1 percentage point results in a €10 billion change in interest-sensitive expenditure.

   a In which economy does an increase in government expenditures on goods and services have a larger effect on real GDP?

   b In which economy is the crowding-out effect weaker?

c In which economy does a change in the money supply have a larger effect on equilibrium real GDP?

d Which economy, if either, is closer to the Keynesian extreme and which is closer to the monetarist extreme?

°**7** The economy is in a recession and the government wants to increase aggregate demand, stimulate exports, and increase investment. It has three policy options: increase government expenditures on goods and services, decrease taxes, and increase the money supply.

a Explain the mechanisms at work under each alternative policy.

b What is the effect of each policy on the composition of aggregate demand?

c What are the short-run effects of each policy on real GDP and the price level?

d Which policy would you recommend that the government adopt? Why?

8 The economy has an inflationary gap and the government wants to decrease aggregate demand, cut exports, and decrease investment. It has three policy options: decrease government expenditures on goods and services, increase taxes, and decrease the money supply.

a Explain the mechanisms at work under each alternative policy.

b What is the effect of each policy on the composition of aggregate demand?

c What are the short-run effects of each policy on real GDP and the price level?

d Which policy would you recommend that the government adopt? Why?

°**9** The economy is at full employment, but the government is disappointed with the growth rate of real GDP. It wants to increase real GDP growth by stimulating investment. At the same time, it wants to avoid an increase in the price level.

a Suggest a combination of fiscal and monetary policies that will achieve the government's objective.

b Which policy would you recommend that the government adopt?

c Explain the mechanisms at work under your recommended policy.

d What is the effect of your recommended policy on the composition of aggregate demand?

e What are the short-run and long-run effects of your recommended policy on real GDP and the price level?

10 The economy is at full employment, and the government is worried that the growth rate of real GDP is too high because it is depleting the country's natural resources. The government wants to lower real GDP growth by lowering investment. At the same time it wants to avoid a fall in the price level.

a Suggest a combination of fiscal and monetary policies that will achieve the government's objective.

b Which policy would you recommend that the government adopt?

c Explain the mechanisms at work under your recommended policy.

d What is the effect of your recommended policy on the composition of aggregate demand?

e What are the short-run and long-run effects of your recommended policy on real GDP and the price level?

Critical Thinking

1 Study Reading Between the Lines on pp. 630–631 and then answer the following questions:

   a Why has the budget deficit of Germany increased above the minister of finance's expectation?

   b In the absence of the EMU and the stability pact, what would be the effect of a fiscal expansion on real GDP, the rate of interest and the exchange rate in Germany?

   c If Germany did not belong to the EMU, what would be the effect of an expansionary monetary policy by the Bundesbank on real GDP, the price level, interest rates, investment, the exchange rate and net exports?

   d If Germany did not belong to the EMU what policy mix of fiscal and monetary action would you recommend to deal with the slow-down in the economy?

   e Since Germany is in the EMU, what policy would you expect the ECB to conduct to generate growth without inflation?

2 Use the link on the Parkin, Powell and Matthews website to visit the website of Office of National Statistics and look at the current economic conditions. On the basis of the current state of the UK economy, and in the light of what you now know about fiscal and monetary policy interaction, what do you predict would happen to real GDP and the price level:

   a If the Bank of England conducted an expansionary monetary policy?

   b If the Bank of England conducted a contractionary monetary policy?

   c If the government conducted an expansionary fiscal policy?

   d If the government conducted a contractionary fiscal policy?

   e If the Bank of England conducted an expansionary monetary policy and the government conducted a contractionary fiscal policy?

   f If the Bank of England conducted a contractionary monetary policy and the government conducted an expansionary fiscal policy?

Appendix to Chapter 27
The *IS–LM* Model of Aggregate Demand

Equilibrium Expenditure and Real GDP

Aggregate planned expenditure depends on real GDP because consumption increases as real GDP increases. Aggregate planned expenditure also depends on the interest rate because the higher the interest rate, the lower is planned investment. These two influences on aggregate planned expenditure give rise to the *IS* curve.

The *IS* Curve

The *IS* curve shows combinations of real GDP and the interest rate at which aggregate expenditure is at its equilibrium level – aggregate planned expenditure equals real GDP.

Figure A27.1 shows how the *IS* curve is derived. Part (a) is similar to Figure 23.5. The 45° line shows all the points at which aggregate planned expenditure equals real GDP. Curves AE_a AE_b, and AE_c, are aggregate planned expenditure curves. Curve AE_a represents aggregate planned expenditure when the interest rate is 6 per cent (row *a* of the table). Curve AE_b shows aggregate planned expenditure when the interest rate is 5 per cent (row *b*) and AE_c shows aggregate planned expenditure when the interest rate is 4 per cent (row *c*).

There is just one expenditure equilibrium on each of these aggregate planned expenditure curves. On curve AE_a, the expenditure equilibrium is at point *a*, where real GDP is £625 billion. The expenditure equilibrium on AE_b, occurs at point *b*, where real GDP is £825 billion. The expenditure equilibrium on AE_c, occurs at point *c*, where real GDP is £1,025 billion.

Figure A27.1(b) shows each expenditure equilibrium again but highlights the relationship between the interest rate and real GDP at the expenditure equilibrium. Its horizontal axis, like Figure A27.1(a), measures real GDP. Its vertical axis measures the interest rate. Point *a* in part (b) illustrates the expend-

iture equilibrium at point *a* in part (a) of the figure (or in row *a* of the table). It tells us that if the interest rate is 6 per cent, the expenditure equilibrium occurs at a real GDP of £625 billion. Points *b* and *c* in the figure illustrate the expenditure equilibrium at points *b* and *c* of part (a). The continuous line through these points is the *IS* curve.

Some relationships show 'cause' and 'effect'. For example, the consumption function in Chapter 23, pp. 487–493, tells us the level of consumption (effect) at a particular level of income. The investment demand curve tells us the level of investment (effect) at a particular interest rate (cause). The *IS* curve is *not* a 'cause and effect' relationship. It can be read in two ways. It tells us that if the interest rate is 5 per cent, then aggregate planned expenditure equals real GDP only if real GDP is £825 billion. It also tells us that if real GDP is £825 billion, then the interest rate at which aggregate planned expenditure equals real GDP is 5 per cent.

The *IS* curve shows combinations of the interest rate and real GDP at which aggregate expenditure is at its equilibrium level. To determine the interest rate and real GDP, we need an additional relationship between those two variables. That second relationship between interest rates and real GDP comes from equilibrium in the money market.

Money Market Equilibrium

We have seen that the quantity of money demanded depends on the price level, real GDP and the interest rate. The quantity of money demanded is proportional to the price level. If the price level doubles, so does the quantity of money demanded. Real money is the ratio of the quantity of money to the price level. The quantity of real money demanded increases as real GDP increases and decreases as the interest rate increases.

The supply of money is determined by the actions of the Bank of England, the commercial banks and

Figure A27.1

Aggregate Planned Expenditure, Flow Equilibrium and the *IS* Curve

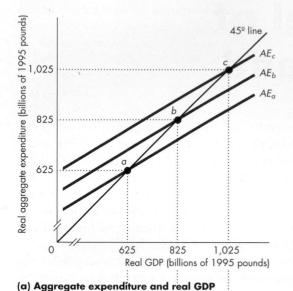

(a) Aggregate expenditure and real GDP

The table shows aggregate planned expenditure – the sum of autonomous expenditure and induced expenditure – that occurs at different combinations of the interest rate and real GDP. For example, if the interest rate is 6 per cent and real GDP is £1,025 billion, aggregate planned expenditure is £925 billion (top right-hand number). Flow equilibrium (equality of aggregate planned expenditure and real GDP) is shown by the green squares. Each of rows *a*, *b* and *c* represents an aggregate expenditure schedule, plotted as the aggregate expenditure curves AE_a, AE_b and AE_c, respectively, in part (a). Expenditure equilibrium positions are shown in part (a), where these *AE* curves intersect the 45° line and are marked *a*, *b* and *c*. Part (b) shows these same equilibrium positions but highlights the combinations of the interest rate and the real GDP at which they occur. The line connecting those points is the *IS* curve.

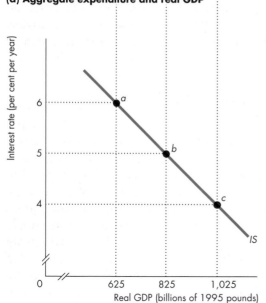

(b) The *IS* curve

Interest rate (per cent per year)	Autonomous expenditure (billions of 1995 pounds)	Aggregate planned expenditure (billions of 1995 pounds)		
a	6	155	625	775	925
b	5	205	675	825	975
c	4	255	725	875	1,025

Induced expenditure	470	620	770
Real GDP (billions of 1995 pounds)	625	825	1,025

other financial intermediaries. Given those commercial actions, and given the price level, there is a given quantity of real money in existence. Money market equilibrium occurs when the quantity of real money supplied is equal to the quantity demanded. Equilibrium in the money market is a stock equilibrium. Figure A27.2 contains a numerical example that enables us to study money market equilibrium.

Suppose that the quantity of money supplied is £805 billion. Suppose also that the GDP deflator is 115 so that the quantity of real money supplied is £700 billion (805 divided by 1.15 = 700. The real money supply is shown in the bottom part of the table. Money market equilibrium occurs when the quantity of real money demanded equals the quantity supplied. The table tells us about the demand for real money. Each row tells us how much real money is demanded at a given interest rate as real GDP varies and each column tells us how much is demanded at a given real GDP as the interest rate varies. For example, at an interest rate of 6 per cent and real GDP at £625 billion, the quantity of real money demanded is £600 billion. Alternatively, at an interest rate of 5 per cent and real GDP of £825 billion, the quantity of real money demanded is £700 billion. The rest of the numbers in the table are read in a similar way.

Money market equilibrium occurs when the quantity of real money demanded equals the quantity supplied, £700 billion in this example. The green squares in the table indicate positions of money market equilibrium – combinations of interest rate and real GDP at which the quantity of money demanded is equal to the quantity supplied. For example, look at column *d*. Real GDP is £625 billion, and the quantity of real money demanded is £700 billion (equal to the quantity supplied) when the interest rate is 4 per cent. Thus at real GDP of £625 billion and an interest rate of 4 per cent, the money market is in equilibrium. At the other two green squares the interest rate is such that the quantity of real money demanded is £700 billion when real GDP is £825 billion and £1025 billion respectively. That is, the green squares show combinations of the interest rate and real GDP at which the money market is in equilibrium.

The *LM* Curve

The *LM* curve shows the combinations of real GDP and the interest rate at which the quantity of real money demanded equals the quantity of real money supplied. Figure A27.2 derives the *LM* curve. Part (a) shows the demand and supply curves for real money. The quantity supplied is fixed at £700 billion, so the supply curve *MS* is vertical. Each of the columns of the table labelled *d*, *e* and *f* is a demand schedule for real money – a schedule that tells us how the quantity of real money demanded rises as the interest rate falls. There is a different schedule for each level of real GDP. These three demand schedules for real money are graphed as demand curves for real money in part (a) of the figure as MD_d, MD_e and MD_f. For example, when real GDP is £625 billion, the demand curve for real money is and MD_d. Money market equilibrium occurs at the intersection of the supply curve and the demand curves for real money at points *d*, *e* and *f* in part (a).

Figure A27.2(b) shows each money market equilibrium again but highlights the relationship between the interest rate and real GDP at which an equilibrium occurs. Points *d*, *e* and *f* in part (b) illustrate the money market equilibrium represented by the green squares in the table and by those similarly labelled points in part (a). The continuous line through these points is the *LM* curve. The *LM* curve shows the interest rate and real GDP at which money market equilibrium occurs when the real money supply is £700 billion.

Like the *IS* curve, the *LM* curve does not have a 'cause and effect' interpretation. The *LM* curve illustrated in Figure A27.2(b) tells us that if the quantity of real money supplied is £700 billion and real GDP is £625 billion, then for money market equilibrium the interest rate is 4 per cent. It also tells us that if the quantity of real money supplied is £700 billion and the interest is 4 per cent, then for money market equilibrium real GDP is £625 billion. That is, the *LM* curve shows combinations of the interest rate and real GDP at which there is money market equilibrium.

We now have two relationships between the interest rate and real GDP. The *IS* curve and the *LM* curve. Together, and at a given price level, these two relationships determine the interest rate or real GDP. They also enable us to derive the *aggregate demand curve*. Let's see how.

Equilibrium and the Aggregate Demand Curve

Equilibrium real GDP and the interest rate are shown in Figure A27.3, which brings together the *IS* curve and the *LM* curve. This equilibrium is at the point of intersection of the *IS* curve and *LM* curve. Point *b* on the *IS* curve is a point of expenditure equilibrium. The interest rate and real GDP are such that aggregate real expenditure equals real GDP. Point *e* on the *LM* curve is a point of money market equilibrium. The interest rate and real GDP are such that the quantity of real money demanded equals the quantity of real money supplied. At this intersection point, there is both flow equilibrium in the goods market and stock equilibrium in the money market. The equilibrium interest rate is 5 per cent and real GDP is £825 billion.

At all other points, there is no expenditure equilibrium or the money market is not in equilibrium or both. At a point such as *a*, the economy is on its *IS* curve but off its *LM* curve. With real GDP at £625 billion and the interest rate at 6 per cent, the interest rate is too high or real GDP is too low for money market equilibrium. Interest rates adjust quickly and would fall to 4 per cent to bring about money market equilibrium putting the economy at point *d*, a point on the *LM* curve. But point *d* is off the *IS* curve. At

Figure A27.2

The Money Market, Stock Equilibrium and the *LM* Curve

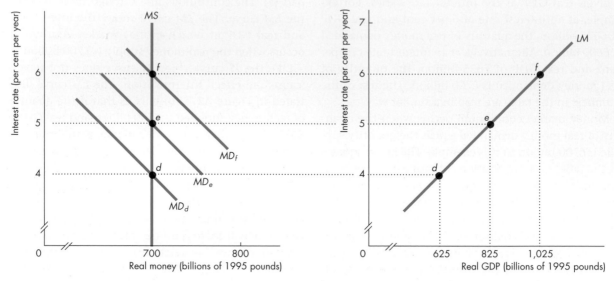

(a) Money market equilibrium

(b) The *LM* curve

The table shows the quantity of real money demanded at different combinations of the interest rate and real GDP. For example, if the interest rate is 6 per cent and real GDP is £625 billion, the quantity of real money demanded is £600 billion (top-left number). Stock equilibrium – equality between the quantity of real money demanded and supplied – is shown by the green squares. Each of the columns *d*, *e* and *f* represents a demand schedule for real money, plotted as the demand curves for real money MD_d, MD_e and MD_f, respectively, in part (a). Money market equilibrium positions are shown in part (a), where these *MD* curves intersect the supply curve of real money *MS* and are marked *d*, *e* and *f*. Part (b) shows these same equilibrium positions but highlights the combinations of the interest rate and real GDP at which they occur. The line connecting those points is the *LM* curve.

Interest rate (per cent per year)	Quantity of real money demanded (billions of 1995 pounds)		
6	600	650	700
5	650	700	750
4	700	750	800
Real GDP	625	825	1,025

Real money supply (billions of 1995 pounds)	700	700	700
	d	*e*	*f*

point *d*, with the interest rate at 4 per cent and real GDP at £625 billion, aggregate planned expenditure exceeds real GDP. By checking back to the table in Figure A27.1, you can see that aggregate planned expenditure is £725 billion, which exceeds real GDP of £625 billion. With aggregate planned expenditure larger than real GDP, real GDP will increase. But as real GDP increases, so does the demand for real money and so does the interest rate. Real GDP and the interest rate would rise, and continue to do so, until the point of intersection of the *IS* and *LM* curves is reached.

The account that we have just given of what *would* happen if the economy was at a point like *a* or *d* tells us that the economy cannot be at such points. The forces that operate in such situations would be so strong that they would always push the economy to the intersection of the *IS* and *LM* curves.

The Effects of a Change in Price Level on the *LM* Curve

The price level enters the *IS–LM* model to determine the quantity of real money supplied. The Bank of

Figure A27.3

IS–LM Equilibrium

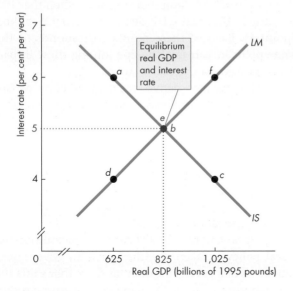

All points on the *IS* curve are points where aggregate planned expenditure equals real GDP. All points on the *LM* curve are points at which the quantity of real money demanded equals the quantity of real money supplied. The intersection of the *IS* curve on the *LM* curve determines the equilibrium interest rate and real GDP – 5 per cent and £825 billion. At this interest rate and real GDP, there is flow equilibrium in the goods market and stock equilibrium in the money market.

Figure A27.4

Deriving the Aggregate Demand Curve

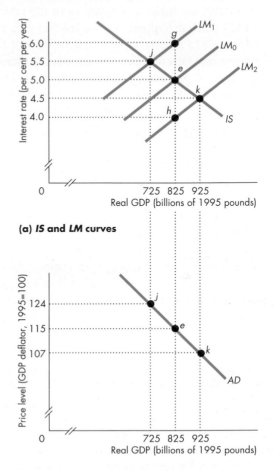

(a) *IS* and *LM* curves

(b) Aggregate demand curve

England determines the money supply as a certain number of current pounds. The higher the price level, the lower is the real value of those pounds. Because the price level affects the quantity of real money supplied, it also affects the *LM* curve. Let's see how.

Begin by asking what happens if the price level, instead of being 115, is 124 – 7.8 per cent higher. The money supply is £805 billion. With a GDP deflator of 124, the real money supply is £649.2 billion. (The real money supply is £805 billion divided by 1.24, which equals £649.2 billion.) For money market equilibrium we can see in the table of Figure A27.2 what happens to the interest rate at a real GDP of £825 billion. With a GDP deflator of 124, the interest rate rises to 6 per cent in order to decrease the quantity of real money demanded to £650 billion – equal to the real money supply. Thus with a GDP deflator of 124, an interest rate of 6 per cent and real GDP of £825 billion become a point on the *LM* curve – point *g* in Figure A27.4(a).

In part (a), if the GDP deflator is 115, the *LM* curve is LM_0. If the GDP deflator increases to 124, the *LM* curve shifts to the left to LM_1. A lower real money supply requires a higher interest rate at each level of real GDP for money market equilibrium. For example, if real GDP is £825 billion, the interest rate has to increase from 5 per cent to 6 per cent (point *g*). If the price level falls, the real money supply increases and the *LM* curve shifts to the right to LM_2. If real GDP is £825 billion, the interest rate falls to 4 per cent (point *h*) to maintain money market equilibrium. When the GDP deflator is 115, the *IS* and *LM* curves intersect at point *e* – real GDP of £825 billion. This equilibrium is shown in part (b) at point *e* on aggregate demand curve *AD*. This point tells us that when the GDP deflator is 115, the quantity of real GDP demanded is £825 billion. If the GDP deflator is 124, the *LM* curve is LM_1 and real GDP is £725 billion. A second point on the aggregate demand curve is found at *j*. If the GDP deflator is 107, the *LM* curve is LM_2 and real GDP is £925 billion. Another point on the aggregate demand curve is generated at point *k*. Joining points *j*, *e* and *k* gives the aggregate demand curve.

Next, suppose that the GDP deflator is lower than the original case – 107 instead of 115. Now the real money supply becomes £752.3 billion. Again for money market equilibrium we can see in the table of Figure A27.2 what happens to the interest rate at a real GDP of £825 billion. With a GDP deflator of 107, the interest rate falls to 4 per cent in order to increase the quantity of real money demanded. Thus with a GDP deflator of 107, an interest rate of 4 per cent and real GDP of £825 billion become a point on the LM curve – point h in Figure A27.4(a).

The LM Curve Shift

The example that we have worked through tells us that there is a different LM curve for each price level. Figure A27.4(a) illustrates the LM curves for the three different price levels we have considered. The initial LM curve has the GDP deflator equal to 115. This curve has been relabelled as LM_0 in Figure A27.4(a). When the GDP deflator is 124 and real GDP is £825 billion, the interest rate that achieves equilibrium in the money market is 6 per cent. This equilibrium is shown as point g on curve LM_1 in Figure A27.4(a). The entire LM curve shifts left to LM_1 in order to pass through point g. When the GDP deflator is 107 and real GDP is £825 billion, the interest rate that achieves equilibrium in the money market is 4 per cent. This equilibrium is shown as point h on the curve LM_2 in Figure A27.4(a). Again, the entire LM curve shifts right to LM_2 in order to pass through point h.

Now that we have worked out the effects of a change in the price level on the position of the LM curve, we can derive the aggregate demand curve.

The Aggregate Demand Curve Derived

Figure A27.4 shows the derivation. Part (a) shows the IS curve and the three LM curves associated with the three different price levels (GDP deflators of 107, 115 and 124). When the GDP deflator is 115, the LM curve is LM_0. Equilibrium is at point e where real GDP is £825 billion and the equilibrium interest rate is 5 per cent. If the GDP deflator is 124, the LM curve is LM_1. Equilibrium is at point j where real GDP is £725 billion and the interest rate is 5.5 per cent. If the GDP deflator is 107, the LM curve is LM_2. Equilibrium is at point k where real GDP is £925 billion and the interest rate is 4.5 per cent. At each price level there is a different equilibrium real GDP and interest rate.

Part (b) traces the aggregate demand curve. The price level is measured on the vertical axis of part (b) and real GDP on the horizontal axis. When the GDP deflator is 115, equilibrium real GDP is £825 billion (point e). When the GDP deflator is 124 equilibrium real GDP is £725 billion (point j). And when the GDP deflator is 107, real GDP demanded is £925 billion (point k). Each of these points corresponds to the same point in part (a). The line joining these in part (b) is the aggregate demand curve.

Now that we have derived the demand curve we can work out the effects of fiscal and monetary policy.

Fiscal and Monetary Policy

Figure A27.5(a) and (b) illustrates the effects of a change in fiscal and monetary policy. Parts (a) and (b) illustrate the normal cases and parts (c) and (d) illustrate the special cases.

In part (a) and (b), the LM curve is upward sloping. Fiscal policy is taken as either a rise in government purchases or a cut in autonomous taxes that shifts the IS curve from IS_0 to IS_1. A change in government purchases or in taxes shifts the IS curve and the aggregate demand curve. An expansionary fiscal policy shifts the IS curve up to the right and the aggregate demand curve up to the right. A contractionary fiscal policy shifts the IS curve and the aggregate demand curve down to the left. When the IS curve shifts because of an expansionary fiscal policy, the interest rate rises and so does real GDP. But the increase in real GDP is less than the magnitude of the shift in the IS curve. The reason is that the rise in the rate of interest leads to a decrease in investment which partially offsets the effect of the increase in expenditure caused by the expansionary fiscal policy. This is what is meant by partial 'crowding out'. Figure A27.5(a) shows the effect of fiscal policy on the rate of interest and real GDP.

Monetary policy is taken as an increase in the money supply. We saw earlier in this appendix that when the LM curve shifts because of a change in the price level, equilibrium GDP changes and there is a movement along the aggregate demand curve. But a change in the money supply also shifts the LM curve. An increase in the money supply shifts the LM curve down to the right and the aggregate demand curve up to the right. A decrease in the money supply shifts the LM curve up to the left and the aggregate demand curve down to the left. The magnitude of the shift in the aggregate demand curve caused by a shift in the LM curve will be due to two factors – the size of the shift of the LM curve and the slope of the IS curve.

Figure A27.5

Fiscal Policy and Monetary Policy (Normal Case)

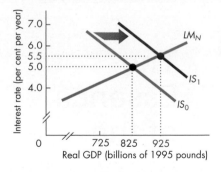

(a) Fiscal policy: normal case

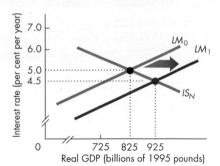

(b) Monetary policy: normal case

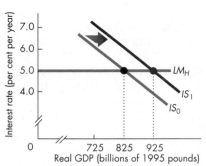

(c) Fiscal policy: maximum effect on GDP

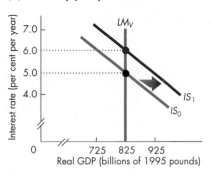

(d) Fiscal policy: no effect on GDP

An increase in government purchases or an autonomous tax cut shifts the *IS* curve to the right. The effects of fiscal policy on real GDP and the interest rate depend on the slope of the *LM* curve. In the normal case (part a), interest rates and real GDP rise. An increase in the money supply shifts the *LM* curve to the right. The effect of the monetary action on interest rates and real GDP depends on the slope of the *IS* curve. In the normal case (part b), interest rates fall and real GDP rises. The lower interest rates stimulate investment. If there is a 'liquidity trap', the *LM* curve is horizontal (part c), fiscal policy has the maximum effect on GDP, but monetary policy has no effect. If the demand for money is insensitive to the rate of interest, the *LM* curve is vertical (part d), fiscal policy has no effect on GDP. But monetary policy will shift the *LM* curve and will have minimum effect.

Figure 27.5(b) illustrates the effect of an expansionary monetary policy. The *LM* curve shifts from LM_0 to LM_1. You can see that the result of this is a lower interest rate and higher real GDP. The rise in real GDP occurs because the lower interest rate induced by the expansionary monetary policy creates extra investment and increases aggregate demand.

Parts (c) and (d) illustrate the two extreme cases which can be considered as extreme Keynesian and extreme monetarist. The extreme Keynesian case is when the *LM* curve is horizontal (LM_H). The *LM* curve is horizontal only if there is a 'liquidity trap' – a situation when people are willing to hold any quantity of money at a specific rate of interest. This situation may describe what has been happening in Japan in 1997–2000. When the *IS* curve shifts to the right, real GDP increases by the same amount as the shift to the right of the *IS* curve. The reason is that the rate of interest does not rise and there is no partial 'crowding out'.

The extreme monetarist case is when the *LM* curve is vertical (LM_V). In this case, although the *IS* curve

shifts to the right as in the extreme Keynesian case, the higher interest rate reduces investment by exactly the same as the increase in initial expenditure resulting from the expansionary fiscal policy. There is full 'crowding out'. Full 'crowding out' occurs if the demand for money is completely insensitive to the interest rate. Notice that the extreme monetarist case shows that fiscal policy is completely ineffective and the extreme Keynesian case shows that fiscal policy is fully effective.

In contrast you can see that in the extreme Keynesian case monetary policy is ineffective. This is because any increase in the money supply is willingly held because the demand for money is perfectly elastic at the specific interest rate. So an increase in the money supply will not result in a lowering of the rate of interest and investment will therefore remain unchanged. In the extreme monetarist case, an increase in the money supply causes a shift to the right of LM_V. You can try this yourself and see that the result is a lower rate of interest and higher real GDP.

Fiscal and Monetary Policy in Action

THE FINANCIAL TIMES, 19 OCTOBER 2001

Europe's Tight Corner

Tony Barber

Vanishing economic growth, rising budget deficits, higher unemployment and a central bank accused of mismanaging monetary policy: it is a formidable mix that confronts European government leaders as they gather today in the Belgian city of Ghent.

The latest bad news comes from Berlin, where Hans Eichel, finance minister sharply reduced his forecasts for German economic growth to 0.75 per cent this year and 1–1.5 per cent next year.

But Mr Eichel's insistence that his government will not adopt an emergency spending programme underlines the complexity of the debate about how to revive the eurozone economy – a debate often caricatured as a struggle between governments eager to spend more and pressing for lower interest rates, and a European Central Bank wedded to an anti-inflationary strategy that risks tipping the region into recession.

For eurozone governments, one burning question is how to use fiscal policy to promote recovery without triggering deficits so large that they undermine a common commitment to budgetary discipline. For the ECB, there is the dual challenge of defending its legally enshrined status as an institution free from political pressure, and winning public confidence in its ability to manage an economic crisis. Last, for the governments of Germany and France, which face elections next year, the pressure is growing every day to show voters that policymakers are taking quick and effective action to protect jobs and incomes.

But finding the right balance between fiscal stimulus and monetary easing is a challenge to which European policymakers have not yet found an answer.

In the eurozone, six countries – Belgium, Finland, Ireland, Luxembourg, the Netherlands and Spain – are forecast to have budgets in balance or in surplus this year. But they account for only 23 per cent of the region's economic output. The other six – Austria, France, Germany, Greece, Italy and Portugal – will all run deficits. Most important, three of the largest deficits are expected in France, Germany and Italy, which account for 70 per cent of output. These three governments have limited room to pursue fiscal expansion, if they are to respect an EU stability and growth pact. This sets a medium-term goal of budget balance and says that, in normal times, deficits must not exceed 3 per cent of gross domestic product.

Even without an emergency fiscal stimulus, the German deficit could hit 2.3 per cent of GDP this year and 2.3 per cent next year, according to Goldman Sachs, the investment bank. For France it forecasts 1.5 and 2.1 per cent and for Italy 1.6 and 1.1 per cent.

Every eurozone government is desperate to restore growth but none wants to break ranks and breach the stability pact. This explains why leaders such as Mr Schröder and Laurent Fabius, France's finance minister, insist that the ECB is better placed to boost the eurozone's recovery by cutting interest rates.

The Essence of the Story

- Slow economic growth in the eurozone economies during 2001 has reduced government revenues and increased their budget deficits.

- The problem is particularly acute in Germany where the Finance Minister, Hans Eichel, had expected real GDP growth to be 2 per cent, and a budget deficit of 1.5 per cent. His latest prediction is that growth would fall to 0.75 per cent and the budget deficit could rise to 2.3 per cent.

- The Stability Pact of the eurozone countries puts a ceiling on the budget deficit of 3 per cent of GDP. Three of the largest economies, Germany, France and Italy already have large deficits leaving little room for expansionary fiscal policy.

- Mounting political pressure on the governments to do something about the economic slowdown has focused attention on the ECB to relax monetary policy.

- The ECB is caught between public pressure to relax monetary policy and lower interest rates and the need to maintain its independence and freedom from political pressure.

Economic Analysis

- The independence of the ECB means that monetary policy is independent of fiscal policy and set to achieve a specified inflation target. Fiscal policy is set by the governments of each country in the eurozone.

- Inflation in the eurozone is above the 2 per cent ceiling and therefore the ECB has been slow in reducing interest rates in response to falling aggregate demand.

- Figure 1 shows a recessionary gap opening up in Germany. Aggregate demand is shown by AD_{01} which intersects the short-run aggregate supply curve SAS_{01} at a level of GDP that is less than potential GDP.

- Expansionary fiscal policy or expansionary monetary policy will shift the aggregate demand curve to the right and help close the recessionary gap.

- Figure 2 shows the same position as Figure 1 but using the IS–LM model of the appendix to Chapter 27. IS_{01} is the IS curve for Germany in 2001 and the LM curve is LM_{01}. A fiscal expansion will shift the IS curve to the right which will increase GDP and the rate of interest. An expansionary monetary policy will shift the LM curve to the right, increasing GDP and lowering the rate of interest. Either policy will help to close the recessionary gap.

- The problem is that an expansionary fiscal policy will push the German budget deficit over the 3 per cent ceiling set by the Stability Pact. No government wants to be the first to break the pact and monetary policy is dictated by the independent ECB.

- Figure 3 shows the forecast budget deficit for Germany, France and Italy as a percentage of GDP for 2001 and 2002. Germany is the largest economy in the eurozone and its expected budget deficit leaves it little room for a fiscal expansion.

- The constraint on fiscal policy means that Germany has to depend on the ECB to conduct an expansionary monetary policy. The constraint on the ECB is that an expansionary monetary policy will raise the price level and keep inflation above the target rate of 2 per cent.

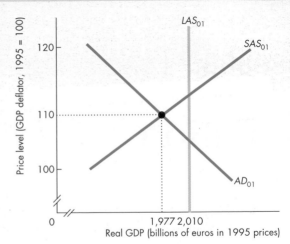

Figure 1 AS–AD

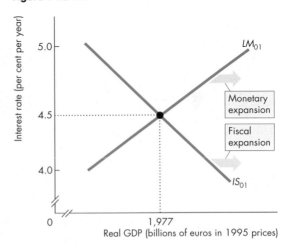

Figure 2 IS–LM

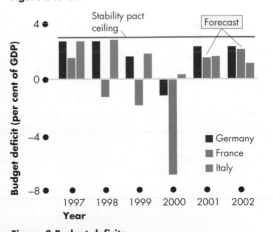

Figure 3 Budget deficits

- The ECB will want to see inflation falling before it relaxes monetary policy and allows interest rates to fall. In Figure 1 the ECB will want to see wage costs declining which will shift the short-run aggregate supply curve to the right before it relaxes monetary policy which will shift the AD curve right. This would enable a non-inflationary increase in growth.

CHAPTER 28

Inflation

After studying this chapter you will be able to:

◆ Distinguish between inflation and a one-time rise in the price level

◆ Explain the different ways in which inflation can be generated

◆ Describe how people try to forecast inflation

◆ Explain the short-run and long-run relationships between inflation and unemployment

◆ Explain the short-run and long-run relationships between inflation and interest rates

◆ Describe the political origins of inflation

From Rome to Russia

At the end of the third century AD, during the dying days of the Roman empire, Emperor Diocletian struggled to contain a rampant inflation. Prices increased at a rate of more than 300 per cent a year. At the end of the twentieth century, during the years of transition from a central planning system to a market economy, President Boris Yeltsin struggled to contain an even more severe inflation in Russia. At its peak, in the winter of 1993–94, prices increased in Russia at a rate of close to 1,000 per cent a year. But the most rapid inflations in today's world are in Latin America and Africa. For example, in 1994, Brazil's inflation hit 40 per cent *per month* and the tiny African country of Zaire had an inflation rate of 75 per cent *per month*. What causes rapid inflation? ◆ In comparison with the cases just described, the United Kingdom has had remarkable price stability. Nevertheless, during the 1970s, the UK price level trebled – an inflation of more than 200 per cent over the decade. Today, along with the other rich industrial countries, the United Kingdom has a low inflation rate of about 2.5 per cent a year. Why do some countries have a low inflation rate? And why did a more serious inflation break out in the United Kingdom during the 1970s? ◆ Most of life's big economic decisions – whether to buy or rent a house, whether to save more for retirement, whether to buy stocks or keep more money in the bank – turn on what is going to happen to inflation. Will inflation increase so our savings buy less? Will inflation decrease so our debts are harder to repay? To make good decisions, we need good forecasts of inflation, not just for next year but for many years into the future. How do people try to forecast inflation? And how do expectations of inflation influence the economy? ◆ As the inflation rate rises and falls, the unemployment rate and interest rates also fluctuate. What are the links between inflation and the economy that make unemployment and interest rates fluctuate when inflation fluctuates? In Reading Between the Lines (pp. 654–655) you will see why the ECB is reluctant to ease monetary policy. Inflation is above the target ceiling set by the ECB but also unemployment is higher than the natural rate in the eurozone.

◆ ◆ ◆ ◆ In this chapter you will learn about the forces that generate inflation, the effects of inflation and the way that people try to forecast inflation. You will pull together several of the threads you have been following through your study of macroeconomics. In particular, you will use the *AS–AD* model of Chapter 22 and the analysis of the money market of Chapter 26 and put them to work in understanding the process of inflation. But first, let's recall what inflation is and how its rate is measured.

Inflation and the Price Level

Inflation is a process in which the *price level is rising* and *money is losing value*. Inflation is not a serious problem today but it was in the 1970s and even towards the end of the 1980s.

If the price level rises persistently, then people need more and more money to make transactions. It is the price *level* and therefore the *value of money* that is changing, not the price of some particular commodity. For example, if the price of oil rises but prices of computers fall so that the price level (an average of prices) is constant, there is no inflation.

A one-off jump in the price level is not inflation. Inflation is an ongoing *process*, not a one-shot affair. Figure 28.1 illustrates this distinction. The red line shows the price level rising continuously. That is inflation. The blue line shows a one-off rise in the price level. This is not inflation.

To measure the inflation *rate*, we calculate the annual percentage change in the price level. Call this year's price level P_1 and last year's price level P_0. Then:

$$\text{Inflation rate} = \frac{P_1 - P_0}{P_0} \times 100$$

For example, if this year's price level is 126 and last year's price level was 120, the inflation rate is 5 per cent per year. That is:

$$\text{Inflation rate} = \frac{126 - 120}{120} \times 100$$

$$= 5 \text{ per cent per year}$$

This equation shows the connection between the *inflation rate* and the *price level*. For a given price level last year, the higher the price level in the current year, the higher is the inflation rate. If the price level is *rising*, the inflation rate is *positive*. If the price level rises at a *faster* rate, the inflation rate *increases*. Also, the higher the price level, the lower is the value of money and the higher the inflation rate.

Inflation can result from an increase in aggregate demand, a decrease in aggregate supply, or both. To study the forces that generate inflation, we distinguish two types of impulse that can get inflation started. These impulses are called:

1 Demand-pull.

2 Cost-push.

We'll first study a demand-pull inflation.

Figure 28.1

Inflation Versus a One-time Rise in the Price Level

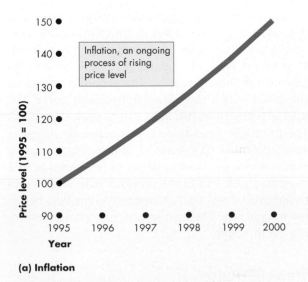

(a) Inflation

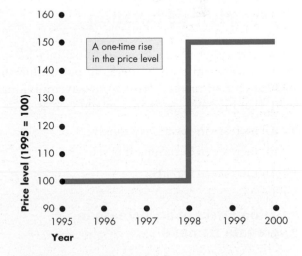

(b) One-time rise in price level

An economy experiences inflation when the price level rises persistently, as shown in part (a). An economy experiences a one-time rise in the price level if some disturbance increases the price level but does not set off an ongoing process of a rising price level, as shown in part (b).

Figure 28.2

A Demand-pull Rise in the Price Level

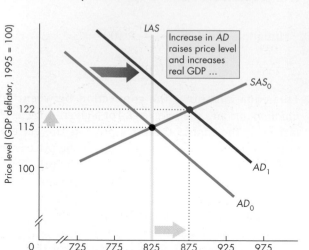

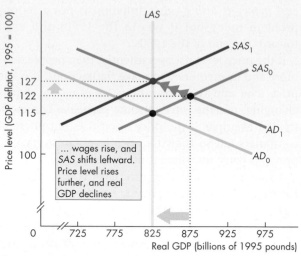

(a) Initial effect

(b) Wages adjust

In part (a), the aggregate demand curve is AD_0, the short-run aggregate supply curve is SAS_0 and the long-run aggregate supply curve is LAS. The price level is 115 and real GDP is £825 billion, its long-run level. Aggregate demand increases to AD_1 (because the Bank increases the money supply or the government increases its purchases of goods and services). The new equilibrium occurs where

AD_1 intersects SAS_0. The economy experiences inflation (the price level rises to 122) and real GDP increases to £875 billion. In part (b), starting from above full employment, wages begin to rise and the short-run aggregate supply curve shifts leftward towards SAS_1. The price level rises further, and real GDP returns to its long-run level.

Demand-pull Inflation

An inflation that results from an initial increase in aggregate demand is called **demand-pull inflation**. Such an inflation may arise from any individual factor that increases aggregate demand such as:

◆ An increase in the money supply.

◆ An increase in government purchases.

◆ An increase in exports.

Inflation Effect of an Increase in Aggregate Demand

Suppose that last year the price level was 115, real GDP was £825 billion and long-run real GDP was also £825 billion – shown in Figure 28.2(a). The aggregate demand curve is AD_0, the short-run aggregate supply curve is SAS_0, and the long-run aggregate supply curve is LAS.

In the current year, aggregate demand increases to AD_1. Such a situation arises if, for example, the government increases its purchases of goods and services or the Bank of England (the Bank) loosens its grip on the money supply. The economy moves to the point where the aggregate demand curve AD_1 intersects the short-run aggregate supply curve SAS_0. The price level rises to 122, and real GDP increases above potential GDP to £875 billion. The economy experiences 6 per cent inflation (a price level of 122 compared with 115 in the previous year) and a rapid expansion of real GDP. Unemployment falls below the natural rate. The next step in the unfolding story is a rise in wages.

Wage Response

Real GDP cannot remain above potential GDP for ever. With unemployment below its natural rate, there is a shortage of labour. Wages begin to increase, and the short-run aggregate supply curve starts to shift leftward. Prices rise further, and real GDP begins to fall. With no further change in aggregate demand – the aggregate demand curve remains at AD_1 – this process comes to an end when the short-run aggregate demand curve has moved to SAS_1 in Figure 28.2(b). At this time, the price level has increased to 127 and real GDP has returned to potential GDP of £825 billion, the level from which it started.

A Demand-pull Inflation Process

The process we've just studied eventually ends when, for a given increase in aggregate demand, wages have adjusted enough to restore the real wage rate to its full-employment level. We've studied a one-time rise in the price level like that described in Figure 28.1. For inflation to proceed, aggregate demand must persistently increase.

The only way in which aggregate demand can persistently increase is if the quantity of money persistently increases. The quantity of money persistently increases. Suppose the government has a large budget deficit that it finances by creating more and more money each year. In this situation, aggregate demand increases year after year. The aggregate demand curve keeps shifting rightward and puts continual upward pressure on the price level. The economy now experiences demand-pull inflation.

Figure 28.3 illustrates the process of demand-pull inflation. The starting point is the same as that shown in Figure 28.2. The aggregate demand curve is AD_0, the short-run aggregate supply curve is SAS_0, and the long-run aggregate supply curve is *LAS*. Real GDP is £825 billion and the price level is 115. Aggregate demand increases, shifting the aggregate demand curve to AD_1. Real GDP increases to £875 billion, and the price level rises to 122. The economy is at an above full-employment equilibrium. There is a shortage of labour and the wage rate rises, shifting the short-run aggregate supply curve to SAS_1. The price level rises to 127, and real GDP returns to its long-run level.

But the money supply increases again and aggregate demand continues to increase. The aggregate demand curve shifts rightward to AD_2. The price level rises further to 135 and real GDP again exceeds potential GDP at £875 billion. Yet again, the wage rate rises and decreases short-run aggregate supply. The SAS curve shifts to SAS_2 and the price level rises further to 140. As the money supply continues to grow, aggregate demand increases and the

Figure 28.3

A Demand-pull Inflation Spiral

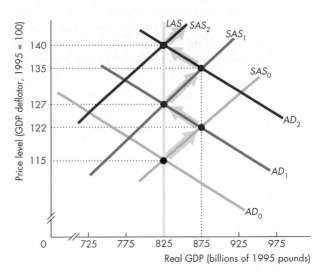

Each time the money supply increases, aggregate demand increases and the aggregate demand curve shifts rightward from AD_0 to AD_1 to AD_2, and so on. Each time real GDP goes above potential GDP and unemployment goes below the natural rate, the money wage rate rises and the short-run aggregate supply curve shifts leftward from SAS_0 to SAS_1 to SAS_2, and so on. As aggregate demand continues to increase, the price level rises from 115 through 122, 127, 135 to 140, and so on. There is a perpetual demand-pull inflation. Real GDP fluctuates between £825 billion and £875 billion.

price level rises in an ongoing demand-pull inflation process.

The process you have just studied generates inflation – an ongoing process of a rising price level.

Demand-pull Inflation in Kalamazoo

You may better understand the inflation process that we've just described by considering what is going on in an individual part of the economy, such as a Kalamazoo lemonade bottling plant. Initially, when aggregate demand increases, the demand for lemonade increases and the price of lemonade rises. Faced with a higher price, the lemonade plant works overtime and increases production. Conditions are good for workers in Kalamazoo, and the lemonade factory finds it hard to hang on to its best people. To do so it has to offer higher wages. As wages increase, so do the costs of the lemonade factory.

What happens next depends on what happens to aggregate demand. If aggregate demand remains constant (as in Figure 28.2(b)), the firm's costs are increasing, but the price of lemonade is not increasing as quickly as its costs. Production is scaled back. Eventually, wages and costs increase by the same percentage as the price of lemonade. In real terms, the lemonade factory is in the same situation as it initially was – before the increase in aggregate demand. The bottling plant produces the same amount of lemonade and employs the same amount of labour as before the increase in demand.

But if aggregate demand continues to increase, so does the demand for lemonade, and the price of lemonade rises at the same rate as wages. The lemonade factory continues to operate above full employment, and there is a persistent shortage of labour. Prices and wages chase each other upward in an unending spiral.

Demand-pull Inflation in the United Kingdom

A demand-pull inflation like the one you've just studied occurred in the United Kingdom during the 1970s. In 1972–73 the government expanded the economy to reduce the level of unemployment that had been growing steadily since the late 1960s. As a consequence, the aggregate demand curve shifted rightward, the price level increased quickly and real GDP moved above its long-run or full-employment level. The money wage rate then started to rise more quickly and the short-run aggregate supply curve shifted leftward. The Bank responded with a further increase in the money supply growth rate and a demand-pull inflation spiral unfolded.

Review Quiz

◆ How does demand-pull inflation begin? What are the initial effects of demand-pull inflation on real GDP and the price level?
◆ When real GDP moves above potential GDP, what happens to the money wage rate and short-run aggregate supply? How do real GDP and the price level respond?
◆ What must happen to create a price-wage inflation spiral?

Next, let's see how shocks to aggregate supply can create a cost-push inflation.

Cost-push Inflation

An inflation that results from an initial increase in costs is called **cost-push inflation**. The two main sources of increases in costs are:

1 An increase in money wage rates.
2 An increase in the money prices of raw materials.

At a given price level, the higher the cost of production, the smaller is the amount that firms are willing to produce. So if money wage rates rise or if the prices of raw materials (for example oil) rise, firms decrease their supply of goods and services. Aggregate supply decreases and the short-run aggregate supply curve shifts leftward.[1] Let's trace the effects of such a decrease in short-run aggregate supply on the price level and real GDP.

Initial Effect of a Decrease in Aggregate Supply

Suppose that last year the price level was 115 and real GDP was £825 billion. Long-run real GDP was also £825 billion. This situation is shown in Figure 28.4. The aggregate demand curve was AD_0, the short-run aggregate supply curve was SAS_0 and the long-run aggregate supply curve was LAS. In the current year, a sharp increase in world oil prices decreases short-run aggregate supply. The short-run aggregate supply curve shifts leftward to SAS_1. The price level rises to 122, and real GDP decreases to £775 billion. The combination of a rise in the price level and a fall in real GDP is called **stagflation**.

The events we've just studied have created a one-shot change in the price level, like that in Figure 28.1. A supply shock on its own cannot cause inflation. Something more must happen. And it often does as you will now see.

Aggregate Demand Response

When real GDP falls the unemployment rate rises above the natural rate. In such a situation, there is usually an outcry of concern and a call for action to

---

[1] Some cost-push forces, such as an increase in the price of oil accompanied by a decrease in the availability of oil, can also decrease long-run aggregate supply. We'll ignore such effects here and examine cost-push factors that change only short-run aggregate supply.

Figure 28.4 ◆

A Cost-push Rise in the Price Level

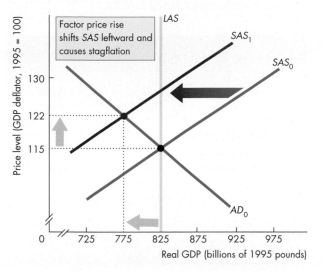

Initially, the aggregate demand curve is AD_0, the short-run aggregate supply curve is SAS_0 and the long-run aggregate supply curve is LAS. A decrease in aggregate supply (for example, resulting from an increase in the world price of oil) shifts the short-run aggregate supply curve to SAS_1. The economy moves to the point where the short-run aggregate supply curve SAS_1 intersects the aggregate demand curve AD_0. The price level rises to 122, and real GDP decreases to £775 billion. The economy experiences inflation and a contraction of real GDP – *stagflation*.

Figure 28.5

Aggregate Demand Response to Cost-push

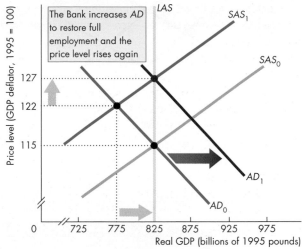

Following a cost–push increase in the price level, real GDP is below potential GDP and unemployment is above the natural rate. If the Bank responds by increasing aggregate demand to restore full employment, the aggregate demand curve shifts rightward to AD_1. The economy returns to full employment, but at the expense of higher inflation. The price level rises to 127.

restore full employment. Suppose the Bank increases the money supply. Aggregate demand increases. In Figure 28.5, the aggregate demand curve shifts rightward to AD_1. The increase in aggregate demand has restored full employment. But the price level rises to 127, a 10 per cent rise over the original price level.

A Cost-push Inflation Process

Suppose now that the oil producers, who see the prices of everything that they buy with the dollars they receive increase by 10 per cent, decide to increase the price of oil again. Figure 28.6 continues the story. The short-run aggregate supply curve now shifts to SAS_2, and another bout of stagflation ensues. The price level rises further to 135, and real GDP falls to £775 billion. Unemployment increases above its natural rate. If the Bank responds yet again with an increase in the money supply, aggregate demand increases and the aggregate demand curve shifts to

AD_2. The price level rises even higher – to 140 – and full employment is again restored. A cost-push inflation spiral results. But if the Bank does not respond, the economy remains below full employment.

You can see that the central bank has a dilemma. If it increases the money supply to restore full employment, it invites another oil price hike that will cause yet a further increase in the money supply. Inflation will rage along at a rate decided by the oil exporting countries. If the Bank keeps the lid on money supply growth, the economy operates with a high level of unemployment.

Cost-push Inflation in Kalamazoo

What is going on in the Kalamazoo lemonade bottling plant when the economy is experiencing cost-push inflation? When the oil price increases, so do the costs of bottling lemonade. These higher costs decrease the supply of lemonade, increasing its price and decreasing the quantity produced. The lemonade plant lays off some workers. This situation will persist

Figure 28.6

A Cost-push Inflation Spiral

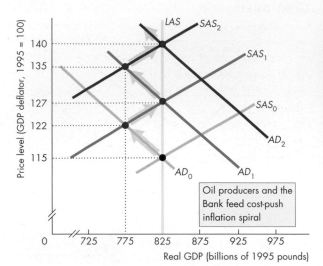

When a cost increase (for example, an increase in the world oil price) decreases short-run aggregate supply from SAS_0 to SAS_1, the price level rises to 122 and real GDP decreases to £775 billion. The central bank responds with an increase in the money supply that shifts the aggregate demand curve from AD_0 to AD_1. The price level rises again to 127 and real GDP returns to £825 billion. A further cost increase occurs, which shifts the short-run aggregate supply curve again, this time to SAS_2. Stagflation is repeated and the price level now rises to 135. The central bank responds again and the cost-push inflation spiral continues.

until either the Bank increases aggregate demand or the price of oil falls. If the Bank increases aggregate demand, as it did in the mid-1970s, the demand for lemonade increases and so does its price. The higher price of lemonade brings higher profits and the bottling plant increases its production. The lemonade factory re-hires the laid-off workers.

Cost-push Inflation in the United Kingdom

A cost-push inflation like the one you've just studied occurred in the United Kingdom during the 1970s. It began in 1974 when OPEC raised the price of oil four-fold. The higher oil price decreased aggregate supply, which caused the price level to rise more quickly and real GDP to shrink. The Bank then faced a dilemma. Would it increase the quantity of money and accommodate the cost-push forces, or would it keep aggregate demand growth in check by limiting money

growth? Money wages began to grow as fast as prices as the unions fought to maintain real wages. The Bank repeatedly allowed the money supply to grow fast and inflation proceeded rapidly.

Review Quiz

◆ How does cost-push inflation begin? What are its initial effects on real GDP and the price level?
◆ What is *stagflation* and why does cost-push inflation cause stagflation?
◆ What must the central bank do to convert a one-time rise in the price level into a freewheeling cost-push inflation?

Effects of Inflation

Regardless of whether inflation is demand-pull or cost-push, the failure to *anticipate* it correctly results in unintended consequences. These unintended consequences impose costs on firms and workers. Let's examine these costs.

Unanticipated Inflation in the Labour Market

Unanticipated inflation has two main consequences for the operation of the labour market. They are:

1 Redistribution of income.

2 Departure from full employment.

Redistribution of Income

Unanticipated inflation redistributes income between employers and workers. Sometimes employers gain at the expense of workers and sometimes they lose. If an unexpected increase in aggregate demand increases the inflation rate, then wages will not have been set high enough. Profits will be higher than expected and wages will buy fewer goods than expected. In this case, employers gain at the expense of workers. But if aggregate demand is expected to increase rapidly and it fails to do so, workers gain at the expense of employers. Anticipating a high inflation rate, wages are set too high and profits are squeezed. Redistributions between employers and workers create an incentive for both firms and workers to try to forecast inflation correctly.

Departures from Full Employment

Redistribution brings gains to some and losses to others. But departures from full employment impose costs on everyone. To see why, let's return to the lemonade bottling plant in Kalamazoo. If the bottling plant and its workers do not anticipate inflation, but inflation occurs, the money wage rate does not rise to keep up with inflation. The real wage rate falls and the firm tries to hire more labour and increase production. But because the real wage rate has fallen, the firm has difficulty in attracting the labour it wants to employ. It pays overtime rates to its existing workforce and because it runs its plant at a faster pace, it incurs higher plant maintenance and parts replacement costs. Also, because the real wage rate has fallen, workers begin to quit the bottling plant to find jobs that pay a real wage rate closer to that prevailing before the outbreak of inflation. This labour turnover imposes additional costs on the firm. So even though its production increases, the firm incurs additional costs and its profit does not increase. The workers incur additional costs of job search and those who remain at the bottling plant end up feeling cheated. They've worked overtime to produce the extra output and, when they come to spend their wages, they discover that prices have increased, so their wages buy a smaller quantity of goods and services than expected.

If the bottling plant and its workers anticipate a high inflation rate that does not occur, they increase the money wage rate by too much and the real wage rate rises. At the higher real wage rate, the firm lays off some workers and the unemployment rate increases. Those workers who keep their jobs gain, but those who become unemployed lose. The bottling plant also loses because its output and profits fall.

Unanticipated Inflation in the Capital Market

Unanticipated inflation has two consequences for the operation of the capital market. They are:

1 Redistribution of income.
2 Scarcity or abundance of finance.

Redistribution of Income

Unanticipated inflation redistributes income between borrowers and lenders. Sometimes borrowers gain at the expense of lenders; sometimes they lose. When inflation is unexpected, interest rates are not set high enough to compensate lenders for the falling value of money. In this case, borrowers gain and lenders lose. If inflation is expected and does not occur, interest rates will have been set too high. Then borrowers lose and lenders gain. This unintended redistribution of income between borrowers and lenders provides incentives for both parties to try and forecast inflation correctly.

Scarcity or Abundance of Finance

When inflation is *higher* than expected, real interest rates are lower than expected. Borrowers wish that they had borrowed more and lenders wish that they had lent less. Both groups would have made different lending and borrowing decision if they had correctly forecasted inflation. When inflation is *lower* than expected, the real interest is higher than expected. Borrowers wish that they had borrowed less and lenders wish that they had lent more.

So unanticipated inflation imposes costs regardless of whether the inflation turns out to be higher or lower than anticipated. The presence of these costs gives everyone an incentive to forecast inflation correctly. Let's see how people go about this task.

Forecasting Inflation

People devote considerable resources to forecasting inflation. Some people specialize in economic forecasting and make a living from it. Other people buy the services of these specialists. The specialist forecasters are economists who work for public and private macroeconomic forecasting agencies and for banks, insurance companies, trade unions and large corporations. The returns these specialists make depend on the quality of their forecasts, so they have a strong incentive to forecast as accurately as possible. The most accurate forecast possible is one that is correct on the average and that has the minimum possible range of error.

Specialist forecasters use statistical models of the economy that are based on (but more detailed than) the aggregate supply–aggregate demand model that you are studying in this book. In the United Kingdom, there are publicly available forecasts of the economy produced by a range of institutions such as the National Institute of Economic and Social Research, Liverpool Macroeconomic Group and Oxford Economic Forecasting. Short-term forecasts are produced by HM Treasury, but City of London financial institutions also produce forecasts of the economy for their clients and there are several private forecasting agencies such as Lombard Street Research Ltd and the ITEM Group.

Forecasts that use all the relevant information available are usually the most accurate. If some information is available that can lead to a better forecast, it will be used. We call a forecast based on all the available relevant information a **rational expectation**. A rational expectation has two features:

1   It is correct on the average.

2   The range of the forecast error is as small as possible.

A forecast that is correct *on the average* is not always correct. Suppose you forecast the outcome of tossing a coin 10 times. You predict there will be 5 heads and 5 tails. On the average (repeating the experiment of coin tossing many times) you are correct. But often you will get 6 heads and 4 tails. So a rational expectation is not always the correct forecast but it is the best that anyone can do.

You've seen the effects of inflation when people fail to anticipate it. You've also seen why it pays to try and anticipate inflation. Let's now see what happens if inflation is correctly anticipated.

Anticipated Inflation

In the demand-pull and cost-push inflations that we studied earlier in this chapter, money wages are sticky. When aggregate demand increases, either to set off a demand-pull inflation or to accommodate a cost-push inflation, the money wage does not change immediately. But if people correctly anticipate increases in aggregate demand, they will adjust money wage rates so as to keep up with anticipated inflation.

In this case, inflation proceeds with real GDP equal to potential GDP and unemployment equal to the natural rate. Figure 28.7 explains why. Suppose that last year the price level was 115 and real GDP was £825 billion, which is also potential GDP. The aggregate demand curve was AD_0, the aggregate supply curve was SAS_0 and the long-run aggregate supply curve was LAS.

Suppose that potential GDP does not change so the LAS curve does not shift. Also suppose that aggregate demand is expected to increase and that the expected aggregate demand curve for this year is AD_1. In anticipation of the increase in aggregate demand, money wage rates rise and the short-run aggregate supply curve shifts leftward. If the money wage rate rises by

Figure 28.7
Anticipated Inflation

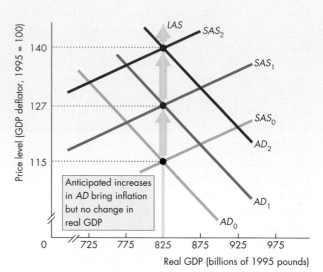

The actual and expected long-run aggregate supply curve (*LAS*) is at a real GDP of £825 billion. Last year, aggregate demand was AD_0 and the short-run aggregate supply curve was SAS_0. The actual price level was the same as the expected price level – 115. This year, aggregate demand is expected to rise to AD_1. The rational expectation of the price level changes from 115 to 122. As a result, the short-run aggregate supply curve shifts up to SAS_1. If aggregate demand actually increases as expected, the actual aggregate demand curve AD_1 is the same as the expected aggregate demand curve. Equilibrium occurs at a real GDP of £825 billion and an actual price level of 127. The inflation is correctly anticipated. Next year the process continues with aggregate demand increasing as expected to AD_2 and wages rising to shift the short-run aggregate supply curve to SAS_2. Again, real GDP remains at £825 billion and the price level rises, as anticipated, to 140.

the same percentage as the rise in the price level, the short-run aggregate supply for next year is SAS_1.

If aggregate demand turns out to be the same as expected, the actual aggregate demand curve is AD_1. The intersection point of AD_1 and SAS_1 determines the actual price level – where the price level is 127. Between last year and this year, the price level increased from 115 to 127 and the economy experienced an inflation rate of just over 10 per cent, the same as the inflation rate that was anticipated. If this anticipated inflation is ongoing, in the following year aggregate demand increases further (as anticipated) and aggregate demand shifts to AD_2. Again the money wage rises to reflect anticipated inflation, and the short-run aggregate supply curve shifts to SAS_2. The price level rises by a further 10 per cent to 140.

What caused the inflation? The immediate answer is that because people expected inflation, they increased wages and increased prices. But the expectation was correct. Aggregate demand was expected to increase and it did increase. Because aggregate demand was *expected* to increase from AD_0 to AD_1, the short-run aggregate supply curve shifted upward from SAS_0 to SAS_1. Because aggregate demand actually did increase by the amount that was expected, the actual aggregate demand curve shifted from AD_0 to AD_1. The combination of the anticipated and actual shifts of the aggregate demand curve rightward produced an increase in the price level that was anticipated.

Only if aggregate demand growth is correctly forecasted does the economy follow the course described in Figure 28.7. If the expected growth rate of aggregate demand is different from its actual growth rate, the expected aggregate demand curve shifts by an amount different from the actual aggregate demand curve. The inflation rate departs from its expected level and, to some extent, there is unanticipated inflation.

Unanticipated Inflation

When aggregate demand increases by more than expected, there is some unanticipated inflation that looks just like demand-pull inflation that you examined earlier. Some inflation is expected and the money wage rate is set to reflect that expectation. The *SAS* curve intersects the *LAS* curve at the expected price level. Aggregate demand then increases, but by more than expected. The *AD* curve intersects the *SAS* curve at a level of real GDP that exceeds potential GDP. The money wage rate adjusts, aggregate demand increases again and the demand-pull spiral unwinds. So demand-pull inflation can be interpreted as being an unanticipated inflation in which aggregate demand increases by *more* than was expected.

When aggregate demand increases by less than expected, there is unanticipated inflation that looks like cost-push inflation. Again, some inflation is expected and based on this expectation, the money wage rate rises and the *SAS* curve shifts leftward. Aggregate demand then increases, but by *less* than expected. The *AD* curve intersects the *SAS* curve at a level of real GDP below potential GDP. Aggregate demand increases to restore full employment. But if the increase in aggregate demand is less than

expected wages again rise and short-run aggregate supply again decreases and a cost-push spiral unwinds. So cost-push inflation can be interpreted as being an unanticipated inflation in which aggregate demand increases by *less* than was expected.

We've seen that only when inflation is unanticipated does real GDP depart from potential GDP. When inflation is anticipated, real GDP remains at potential GDP. Does this mean that an anticipated inflation has no costs?

The Costs of Anticipated Inflation

An anticipated inflation at a moderate rate – 2 or 3 per cent a year – probably has a small cost. But an anticipated inflation at a rapid rate is extremely costly. The costs can be summarized under four broad headings:

1 'Shoeleather costs'.
2 Efficiency costs.
3 Decrease in potential GDP.
4 Economic growth costs.

'Shoeleather Costs'

The so-called 'shoeleather costs' of inflation are costs that arise from an increase in the velocity of circulation of money and an increase in the amount of running around that people do to try to avoid incurring losses from the falling value of money.

When money loses value at a rapid anticipated rate, it does not function well as a medium of exchange and people try to avoid holding money. They spend their incomes as soon as they receive them, and firms pay out incomes – wages and dividends – as soon as they receive revenue from their sales. The velocity of circulation increases. During the 1920s, when inflation in Germany reached *hyperinflation* levels (rates in excess of 50 per cent a month), wages were paid and spent twice in a single day!

The 'shoeleather costs' have been estimated to be between 1 and 2 per cent of GDP for a 10 per cent inflation. For a rapid inflation they are much higher.

Efficiency Costs

At high anticipated inflation rates, people seek alternatives to money as a means of payment and use tokens and commodities or even barter, all of which are less efficient than money as a means of payment. For example, during the 1980s when inflation in Israel reached 1,000 per cent a year, the US dollar started to replace the increasingly worthless shekel. As a result, people had to keep track of the exchange rate between the shekel and the dollar hour by hour and engage in many additional and costly transactions in the foreign exchange market.

A Decrease in Potential GDP

Because anticipated inflation increases transactions costs, it diverts resources from producing goods and services and it decreases potential GDP. In terms of the aggregate supply–aggregate demand model, a rapid anticipated inflation decreases potential GDP and shifts the *LAS* curve leftward. The faster the anticipated inflation rate, the further leftward the *LAS* curve shifts. By how much does potential GDP fall?

Economic Growth Costs

The most serious cost of an anticipated inflation is a fall in the long-term growth rate of GDP. This cost has three sources. The first comes from the way inflation interacts with the tax system. Anticipated inflation swells the money returns on investments, but it does not change the real returns. However, money returns are taxed, so effective tax rates rise. With lower after-tax returns, businesses have less incentive to invest in new capital. A decrease in investment cuts the rate of real GDP growth. This effect becomes serious at even modest inflation rates. Let's consider an example.

Suppose the real interest rate is 4 per cent a year and the tax rate is 50 per cent. With no inflation, the nominal interest is also 4 per cent a year and 50 per cent of this rate is taxable. The real *after-tax* interest rate is 2 per cent a year (50 per cent of 4 per cent). Now suppose the inflation rate is 4 per cent a year so that the nominal rate is 8 per cent a year. The *after-tax* nominal rate is 4 per cent (50 per cent of 8 per cent). Now subtract the 4 per cent inflation rate from this amount and you see that the *after-tax real interest* rate is zero! The true tax rate on interest income is 100 per cent. If the inflation rate was greater than 4 per cent in this example, the true tax rate would exceed 100 per cent and the after-tax real interest rate would be negative.

With a low or possibly even negative after-tax real interest rate, the incentive to save is weakened and the saving rate falls. With a fall in saving, the pace of capital accumulation slows and so does the long-term growth rate of real GDP.

The second economic growth cost arises because instead of concentrating on the activities at which

they have a comparative advantage, people find it more profitable to search for ways of avoiding the losses that inflation inflicts. As a result, inventive talent that might otherwise work on productive innovations works on finding ways of profiting from or avoiding losses from the inflation.

The third source of a fall in the economic growth rate arises because when the inflation rate is high, there is increased uncertainty about the long-term inflation rate. Will inflation remain high for a long time or will price stability be restored? This increased uncertainty makes long-term planning difficult and gives people a shorter-term focus. Investment falls and so the growth rate slows.

Efficiency costs and economic growth costs are estimated to be much higher than the shoeleather and other costs and range between 5 per cent and 7 per cent of GDP for a 10 per cent inflation. The productivity growth slowdown of the 1970s can be attributed partly to the inflation outburst at that time.

There are many examples of rapid anticipated inflations around the world, especially in Argentina, Bolivia and Brazil, in Russia and other East European countries, and in some of the African countries where the costs of anticipated inflation are much greater than the modest numbers given here.

Review Quiz

◆ What is a *rational expectation*? Are people who form rational expectations ever wrong?
◆ Why do people forecast inflation and what information do they use to do so?
◆ How does anticipated inflation occur?
◆ What are the effects of a rapid anticipated inflation? Does anticipated inflation bring an increase in real GDP?

We've seen that an increase in aggregate demand growth that is not fully anticipated increases both the price level and real GDP growth. It also decreases unemployment. Similarly, a decrease in aggregate demand that is not fully anticipated slows down both inflation and real GDP growth. It also increases unemployment. Do these relationships imply a trade-off between inflation and unemployment? That is, does low unemployment always bring inflation and low inflation bring high unemployment? Let's explore this question next.

Inflation and Unemployment: The Phillips Curve

The aggregate supply–aggregate demand model that we have used to obtain these results gives predictions about the level of real GDP and the price level. Given these predictions, we can work out how unemployment and inflation have changed. But the aggregate supply–aggregate demand model does not place inflation and unemployment at the centre of the stage.

Another way of studying inflation and unemployment uses a relationship called the Phillips curve. The Phillips curve approach uses the same basic ideas as the *AS–AD* model, but it focuses directly on inflation and unemployment. The Phillips curve is so named because it was popularized by a New Zealand economist, A.W. Phillips, when he was working at the London School of Economics in the 1950s. A **Phillips curve** is a curve showing the relationship between inflation and unemployment. There are two time-frames for Phillips curves:

1 The short-run Phillips curve.
2 The long-run Phillips curve.

The Short-run Phillips Curve

The **short-run Phillips curve** is a curve showing the relationship between inflation and unemployment, holding constant:

1 The expected inflation rate.
2 The natural unemployment rate.

Figure 28.8 shows a short-run Phillips curve, *SRPC*. Suppose that the expected inflation rate is 10 per cent a year and the natural unemployment rate is 6 per cent, point *a* in the figure. A short-run Phillips curve passes through this point. If inflation rises above its expected rate, the unemployment rate falls below its natural rate. This joint movement in the inflation rate and the unemployment rate is illustrated as a movement up the short-run Phillips curve from point *a* to point *b* in the figure. Similarly, if inflation falls below its expected rate, unemployment rises above the natural rate. In this case, there is movement down the short-run Phillips curve from point *a* to point *c*.

This negative relationship between inflation and unemployment along the short-run Phillips curve is explained by the aggregate supply–aggregate demand model. Figure 28.9 explains the connection between

Figure 28.8

A Short-run Phillips Curve

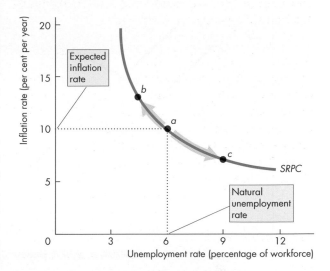

The short-run Phillips curve *SRPC* shows the relationship between inflation and unemployment at a given expected inflation rate and given natural unemployment rate. With an expected inflation rate of 10 per cent a year and a natural unemployment rate of 6 per cent, the short-run Phillips curve passes through point *a*. An unanticipated increase in aggregate demand lowers unemployment and increases inflation – a movement up the short-run Phillips curve. An unanticipated decrease in aggregate demand increases unemployment and lowers inflation – a movement down the short-run Phillips curve.

the two approaches. Suppose that, initially, inflation is anticipated to be 10 per cent a year and unemployment is at its natural rate.

In Figure 28.9 the aggregate demand curve is AD_0, the short-run aggregate supply curve is SAS_0, and the long-run aggregate supply curve is *LAS*. Real GDP is £825 billion and the price level is 115. Money growth increases aggregate demand and the aggregate demand curve shifts rightward to AD_1, and anticipating this increase in aggregate demand, the money wage rate rises, which shifts the short-run aggregate supply curve to SAS_1. The price level rises from 115 to 127 and the inflation rate is an anticipated 10 per cent a year. We can describe the economy as being at point *a* in Figure 28.9. It is also at point *a* on the short-run Phillips curve in Figure 28.8.

Now suppose that instead of increasing as expected to AD_1, aggregate demand increases to AD_2. The price level now rises to 130, a 13 per cent inflation rate and real GDP rises above potential GDP. We can now

Figure 28.9

AS–AD and the Short-run Curve

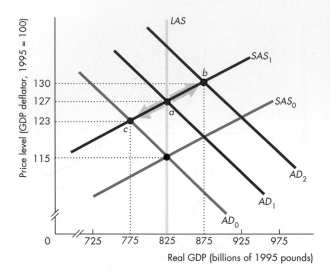

Figure 28.10

Short-run and Long-run Phillips Curves

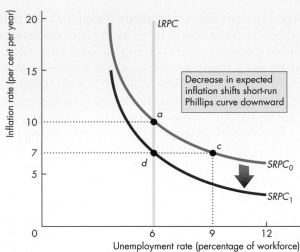

If aggregate demand is expected to increase and shift the aggregate demand curve from AD_0 to AD_1, then the money wage rate rises by an amount that shifts the short-run aggregate supply curve from SAS_0 to SAS_1. The price level rises to 127, a 10 per cent rise, and the economy is at point *a* in this figure and at point *a* on the short-run Phillips curve in Figure 28.8. If with the same expectations, aggregate demand increases and shifts the aggregate demand curve from AD_0 to AD_2, the price level rises to 130, a 13 per cent rise, and the economy is at point *b* in this figure and at point *b* on the short-run Phillips curve in Figure 28.8. If with the same expectations, aggregate demand does not change, the price level rises to 123, a 7 per cent rise, and the economy is at point *c* in this figure and at point *c* on the short-run Phillips curve in Figure 28.8.

The long-run Phillips curve is *LRPC*, a vertical line at the natural unemployment rate. A fall in inflation expectations shifts the short-run Phillips curve downward by the amount of the fall in the expected inflation rate. In this figure, when the expected inflation rate falls from 10 per cent a year to 7 per cent a year, the short-run Phillips curve shifts downward from $SRPC_0$ to $SRPC_1$. The new short-run Phillips curve intersects the long-run Phillips curve at the new expected inflation rate – point *d*. With the original expected inflation rate (of 10 per cent), an inflation rate of 7 per cent a year would occur at an unemployment rate of 9 per cent, at point *c*.

describe the economy as being at point *b* in Figure 28.9 or at point *b* on the short-run Phillips curve in Figure 28.8.

Finally, suppose that instead of increasing as expected to AD_1, aggregate demand remains constant at AD_0. The price level now rises to 123, a 7 per cent inflation rate, and real GDP falls below potential GDP. We can now describe the economy as being at point *c* in Figure 28.9 or at point *c* on the short-run Phillips curve in Figure 28.8.

The Long-run Phillips Curve

The **long-run Phillips curve** is a curve that shows the relationship between inflation and unemployment,

when the actual inflation rate equals the expected inflation rate. The long-run Phillips curve is vertical at the natural unemployment rate. It is shown in Figure 28.10 as the vertical line *LRPC*. The long-run Phillips curve tells us that any anticipated inflation rate is possible at the natural unemployment rate. This proposition is the same as the one you discovered in the *AS–AD* model. When inflation is anticipated, real GDP remains at potential GDP. Real GDP being at potential GDP is equivalent to unemployment being at the natural rate.

If the expected inflation rate is 10 per cent a year, the short-run Phillips curve is $SRPC_0$. If the expected inflation rate falls to 7 per cent a year, the short-run Phillips curve shifts downward to $SRPC_1$. The distance by which the short-run Phillips curve shifts downward when the expected inflation rate falls is equal to the change in the expected inflation rate.

To see why the short-run Phillips curve shifts when the expected inflation rate changes let's do a thought experiment. The economy is at full employment and a fully anticipated inflation is 10 per cent a year. The Bank now begins a permanent attack on inflation by slowing money supply growth. Aggregate demand growth slows down and the inflation rate falls to 7 per cent a year. At first, this decrease in inflation is unanticipated, so wages continue to rise at their original rate, shifting the short-run aggregate supply curve leftward at the same pace as before. Real GDP falls and unemployment increases. In Figure 28.10, the economy moves from point a to point c on the short-run Phillips curve $SRPC_0$.

If the actual inflation rate remains steady at 7 per cent a year, eventually this rate will come to be expected. As this happens, wage growth slows down and the short-run aggregate supply curve shifts leftward less quickly. Eventually it shifts leftward at the same pace at which the aggregate demand curve is shifting rightward. The actual inflation rate equals the expected inflation rate and full employment is restored. Unemployment is back at its natural rate. In Figure 28.10, the short-run Phillips curve has shifted from $SRPC_0$ to $SRPC_1$ and the economy is at point d.

Changes in expected inflation cause shifts in the Phillips curve. Another important source of shifts in the Phillips curve is a change in the natural rate of unemployment.

Changes in the Natural Unemployment Rate

The natural unemployment rate changes for many reasons that are explained in Chapter 29 (pp. 640–673). A change in the natural unemployment rate shifts both the short-run and the long-run Phillips curves. Such shifts are illustrated in Figure 28.11. If the natural unemployment rate increases from 6 per cent to 9 per cent, the long-run Phillips curve shifts from $LRPC_0$ to $LRPC_1$, and if expected inflation is constant at 10 per cent a year, the short-run Phillips curve shifts from $SRPC_0$ to $SRPC_1$. Because the expected inflation rate is constant, the short-run Phillips curve $SRPC_1$ intersects the long-run curve $LRPC_1$ (point e) at the same inflation rate at which the short-run Phillips curve $SRPC_0$ intersects the long-run curve $LRPC_0$ (point a).

Figure 28.11

A Change in the Natural Unemployment Rate

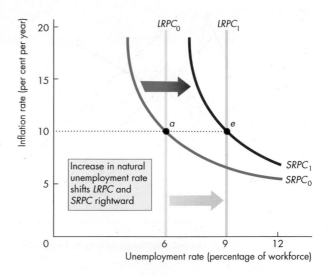

A change in the natural unemployment rate shifts both the short-run and long-run Phillips curves. Here the natural unemployment rate increases from 6 per cent to 9 per cent, and the two Phillips curves shift rightward to $SRPC_1$ and $LRPC_1$. The new long-run Phillips curve intersects the new short-run Phillips curve at the expected inflation rate – point e.

The Phillips Curve in the United Kingdom

Figure 28.12(a) a scatter diagram between inflation and unemployment in the United Kingdom. Each dot in the figure represents the combination of inflation and unemployment for a particular year. We certainly cannot see a Phillips curve similar to that shown in Figure 28.8. But we can interpret the data in terms of a shifting short-run Phillips curve as in Figure 28.12(b).

Three short-run Phillips curves appear in the figure. The short-run Phillips curve of the 1960s is $SRPC_0$. At that time, the expected inflation rate was 2 per cent a year and the natural unemployment rate was also 2 per cent.

The short-run Phillips curve of the mid-1970s to mid-1980s is $SRPC_1$. The second period has a natural unemployment rate higher than that of the 1960s, and an expected inflation rate that is much higher. The short-run Phillips curve of the 1990s is $SRPC_2$. During the 1980s and 1990s the natural rate of unemployment fell and expected inflation declined.

Figure 28.12

Phillips Curves in the United Kingdom

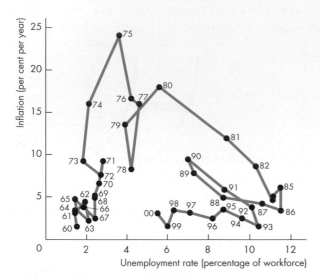

(a) Time sequence

(b) Three Phillips curves

In part (a) each dot represents the combination of inflation and unemployment for a particular year in the United Kingdom. There is no clear relationship between the two variables. Part (b) interprets the data in terms of a shifting short-run Phillips curve. The short-run Phillips curve of the 1960s when the expected inflation rate was 2 per cent a year, and the natural unemployment rate was also 2 per cent, is $SRPC_0$. The short-run Phillips curve of the mid-1970s to mid-1980s $SRPC_1$. This period has a higher natural unemployment rate and a higher expected inflation rate.

The oil price shock increased both the natural unemployment rate and the expected inflation rate in the 1970s. By the early 1980s, the effect of the oil shock and domestic supply factors had increased the natural rate of unemployment to over 10 per cent. The 1990s short-run Phillips curve is $SRPC_2$. The monetary policy and supply side reforms of the Thatcher government during the 1980s caused the natural rate of unemployment to decline to 6 per cent and the expected rate of inflation to fall to 3 per cent by 2000 as shown by $SRPC_2$.

Review Quiz

◆ How would you illustrate an unanticipated change in the inflation rate by using the Phillips curve?

◆ What are the effects of an unanticipated increase in the inflation rate on the unemployment rate?

◆ If the expected inflation rate increased by 10 percentage points, how would the short-run Phillips curve change and how would the long-run Phillips curve change?

◆ If the natural unemployment rate increases, what happens to the short-run Phillips curve? What happens to the long-run Phillips curve? What happens to the expected inflation rate?

◆ Can you identify a short-run Phillips curve for the UK? Has the UK short-run Phillips curve remained stable?

◆ Does the UK have a stable long-run Phillips curve?

So far, we've studied the effects of inflation on real GDP, real wages, employment and unemployment. But inflation lowers the value of money and changes the real value of the amounts borrowed and repaid. As a result, interest rates are influenced by inflation. Let's see how.

Interest Rates and Inflation

Today, good risk companies can borrow at interest rates of less than 6 per cent a year. Companies in Russia pay interest of 60 per cent, and those in Turkey pay 75 per cent a year. While companies in the UK never had to pay interest rates as high as that, they have been much higher in the 1980s. In the early 1980s, borrowing interest rates were around 15 per cent a year. Why do interest rates fluctuate so much across countries and across time? (The **real interest rate** is the *nominal* interest rate minus the inflation rate.) Fluctuations in the real interest rate are caused by fluctuations in saving supply and investment demand. But another part of the answer – a major part – is that the inflation rate was low during the 1960s and high during the early 1980s. With changes in the inflation rate, nominal interest rates change to make borrowers pay and to compensate lenders for the fall in the value of money. Let's see how inflation affects borrowers and lenders.

The Effects of Inflation on Borrowers and Lenders

The *nominal* interest rate is the price paid by a borrower to compensate a lender only for the amount loaned. The *real* interest rate is the price paid by a borrower to compensate a lender for the amount loaned and for the fall in the value of money that results from inflation. The forces of demand and supply determine an equilibrium real interest rate that does not depend on the inflation rate. These same forces also determine an equilibrium nominal interest rate that *does* depend on the inflation rate and that equals the equilibrium *real* interest rate plus the expected inflation rate.

To see why these outcomes occur, imagine there is no inflation and that the nominal interest rate is 4 per cent a year. The real interest rate is also 4 per cent a year. The amount that businesses and people want to borrow equals the amount that businesses and people want to lend at this real interest rate. British Petroleum (BP) is willing to pay an interest rate of 4 per cent a year to get the funds it needs to pay for its global investment in new oil exploration sites. Sue, and thousands of people like her, are willing to lend BP the amount it needs for its exploration work if they can get a *real* return of 4 per cent a year. (Sue wants to buy a new car and she plans a consumption and saving strategy to achieve this objective.)

Now suppose inflation breaks out at a steady 6 per cent a year. All prices and values, including oil exploration profits and car prices, rise by 6 per cent a year. If BP was willing to pay a 4 per cent interest rate when there was no inflation, it is now willing to pay 10 per

cent interest. The reason is that its profits are rising by 6 per cent a year, owing to the 6 per cent inflation, so it is *really* paying only 4 per cent. Similarly, if Sue was willing to lend at a 4 per cent interest rate when there was no inflation, she is now willing to lend only if she gets 10 per cent interest. The price of the car Sue is planning to buy is rising by 6 per cent a year, owing to the 6 per cent inflation, so she is *really* getting only a 4 per cent interest rate.

Because borrowers are willing to pay the higher rate and lenders are willing to lend only if they receive the higher rate, when inflation is anticipated the *nominal interest rate* increases by an amount equal to the expected inflation rate. The *real interest rate* remains constant. The real interest rate might change because the supply of saving or investment demand has changed for some other reason. But a change in the expected inflation rate alone does not change the real interest rate.

Do the effects of inflation on interest rates that we have just described actually happen? Let's look at the UK experience.

Inflation and Interest Rates in the United Kingdom

Figure 28.13 shows the relationship between inflation and nominal interest rates between 1960 and 2000. The relationship between inflation and nominal interest rates in the United Kingdom is illustrated in Figure 28.13. The interest rate measured on the vertical axis is that paid by the Treasury on 3-month bills. Each point on the graph represents a year in recent UK macroeconomic history between 1960 and 2000. The blue line shows the relationship between the nominal interest rate and the inflation rate if the real interest rate is constant at 3 per cent a year, its actual average value in this period. As you can see, there is a clear relationship between the inflation rate and the interest rate, but it is not exact. When the red dot lies above the blue line, the real interest rate exceeds 3 per cent. When the red dot lies below the blue line, the real interest rate is less than 3 per cent.

During the 1960s, both inflation and nominal interest rates were low. In the early 1970s, inflation began to increase, but it was not expected to increase much and certainly not to persist. As a result, nominal interest rates did not rise much at that time. By the mid-1970s, there was a burst of unexpectedly high inflation. Interest rates increased somewhat but not by nearly as much as the inflation rate. During the late 1970s and early 1980s, inflation of between

Figure 28.13

Inflation and the Interest Rate

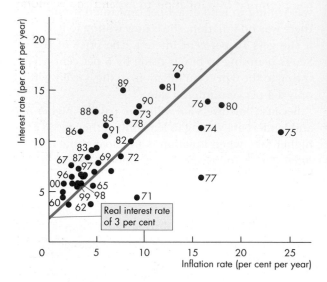

Other things remaining the same, the higher the expected inflation rate, the higher is the nominal interest rate. A graph showing the relationship between interest rates and the actual inflation rate reveals that the influence of inflation on interest rates is a powerful one. Here, the interest rate is that paid by banks on 3-month loans between each other. Each point represents a year in UK macroeconomic history between 1960 and 2000.

Source: National Statistics.

15 and 20 per cent a year came to be expected as an ongoing and highly persistent phenomenon. As a result, nominal interest rates increased to around 12–14 per cent a year. Then in 1982, the inflation rate fell – at first unexpectedly. Interest rates began to fall but not nearly as quickly as the inflation rate. Short-term interest rates fell more quickly than long-term interest rates because, at that time, it was expected that inflation would be lower in the short term but not so low in the longer term.

The relationship between inflation and interest rates is even more dramatically illustrated by international experience. For example, in recent years Chile has experienced an inflation rate of around 30 per cent with nominal interest rates of about 40 per cent. Brazil has experienced inflation rates and nominal interest rates of 30 per cent a *month*. At the other extreme, such countries as Japan and Belgium have low inflation and low nominal interest rates.

The Politics of Inflation

We noted at the beginning of this chapter that inflation has plagued nations over many centuries, from the Roman empire to modern Russia. (There are examples of inflation from even earlier times going back to the earliest civilizations.) What are the deeper sources of inflation that are common to all these vastly different societies? The answer lies in the political situation. There are two main political sources of inflation. They are:

1 Inflation tax.
2 Poor reputation and weak credibility.

Inflation Tax

Inflation is not a tax in the usual sense. Governments don't pass inflation tax laws like income tax and sales tax laws. But inflation works just like a tax. One way in which a government can finance its expenditure is by selling bonds to the central bank. If the government sells bonds to the central bank, those bonds are paid for with new money – with an increase in the monetary base. When the government finances its expenditure in this way, the quantity of money increases. So the government gets revenues from inflation just as if it had increased taxes. And the holders of money pay this tax to the government. They do so because the real value of their money holdings decreases at a rate equal to the inflation rate.

Inflation is not used as a major source of tax revenue in the United Kingdom or in any developed economy. But in some countries it is. The closing years of the Roman empire and the transition years to a market economy in Russia and Eastern Europe are examples. In the case of the Roman empire, the empire had grown beyond its capacity to administer the collection of taxes on a scale sufficient to cover the expenditures of the government. In the case of Russia, the traditional source of government revenue was from state-owned enterprises. In the transition to a market economy, government revenue from these enterprises dried up but expenditure commitments did not decline in line with this loss of revenue. In both cases, the inflation was used to finance expenditures.

As a general rule, the inflation tax is used when conventional revenue sources are insufficient to cover expenditures and the larger the revenue shortfall, the larger is the inflation tax and the inflation rate.

Poor Reputation and Weak Credibility

One objective of fiscal and monetary policy is to stabilize aggregate demand and keep the economy close to full employment. If demand increases too quickly, the economy overheats and inflation increases. If demand increases too slowly, recession occurs and inflation declines.

One of the problems with conducting a low inflation policy is that people who need to forecast inflation and interest rates may have a different expectation of inflation from the central bank. The government, through the central bank, may conduct a policy that decreases the rate of growth of money and reduces inflation. Short-term rates of interest may decline because inflation in the short term may be lower, but long-term rates may not decline because people expect long-term inflation to remain high. This can occur if people anticipate that the policy of low monetary growth now will be reversed at some point in the future. While current inflation may be low, bond holders may anticipate higher inflation in the future and decide to sell some bonds, thus reducing the price of bonds and raising the long-term rate of interest. Why would people have such an expectation? The reason is that they do not believe that the central bank, and through it the government, will stick to its plans of keeping control of inflation. They may believe that once people adjust their expectations of inflation and anticipate low inflation, the government may be tempted to increase the money supply growth and increase aggregate demand by more than expected. In other words, people do not think that the policy has *credibility*. One reason people do not trust the government is that it may not have a *reputation* for trustworthiness. Too often governments have said one thing and done another.

A policy is credible if the cost to the government of following it is viewed as less than not following it. There is always an incentive for a government that has promised low inflation to expand the economy by increasing the growth rate of money and to temporarily reduce unemployment – particularly before an election year. The benefits of lower unemployment will be reaped immediately, but the costs of higher inflation and unemployment will be felt in the future. A government may avoid the temptation to expand demand after reducing inflation only if it values its reputation.

Some economists argue that independence for the central bank improves the credibility of a low inflation policy; others suggest that credibility is obtained by joining an exchange rate agreement such as the European Monetary System or the European Monetary Union. A good reputation for consistent macroeconomic policy can only be earned over a period of time. The German central bank, the Bundesbank, has a good reputation for low inflation. Reading Between the Lines on pp. 654–655 examines the anti-inflation policy of the European Central Bank in its aim to sustain the stock of credibility inherited by the Bundesbank.

Review Quiz

◆ What is an inflation tax and when is it used as a source of government revenue?
◆ Why does a government find it hard to obtain a low inflation reputation?
◆ When is a low inflation policy credible?

You have now completed your study of inflation and the aggregate demand side of the economy. Our next task in the following chapters is to focus more deeply on the supply side, long-term trends and the business cycle. Then, with a good understanding of both the long-term trends and the business cycle fluctuations, we'll study in Chapter 32 the policy challenges that make it difficult to achieve rapid growth and avoid excessive unemployment and inflation.

Summary

Key Points

Inflation and the Price Level (pp. 633–634)

- Inflation is a process of persistently rising prices and falling value of money.

- The price level rises when the inflation rate is positive and falls when the inflation rate is negative.

Demand-pull Inflation (pp. 634–636)

- Demand-pull inflation arises from increasing aggregate demand.

- The main factor that increases aggregate demand is an increase in the money supply or an increase in government spending.

Cost-push Inflation (pp. 636–638)

- Cost-push inflation can result from any factor that decreases aggregate supply, but the main factors are increasing wage rates and increasing prices of key raw materials.

Effects of Inflation (pp. 638–642)

- Inflation is costly when it is unanticipated because it redistributes income and wealth and creates inefficiencies in the economy.

- People try to anticipate inflation to avoid its costs. Forecasts of inflation based on all the available information are called rational expectations.

- When changes in aggregate demand are correctly anticipated, inflation is anticipated, and, if its rate is moderate, it does not affect real GDP, real wages, or employment. But a rapid anticipated inflation decreases potential GDP.

Inflation and Unemployment: The Phillips Curve (pp. 643–646)

- The short-run Phillips curve shows the trade-off between inflation and unemployment, holding constant the expected inflation rate and the natural unemployment rate.

- The long-run Phillips curve which is vertical, shows that when the actual inflation rate equals the expected inflation rate, the unemployment rate equals the natural unemployment rate.

- Unexpected changes in the inflation rate bring movements along the short-run Phillips curve.

- Changes in expected inflation shift the short-run Phillips curve.

- Changes in the natural unemployment rate shift both the short-run and long-run Phillips curves.

Interest Rates and Inflation (pp. 646–648)

- The higher the expected inflation rate, the higher is the nominal interest rate.

- As the anticipated inflation rate rises, borrowers willingly pay a higher interest rate and lenders successfully demand a higher interest rate.

- The nominal interest rate adjusts to equal the real interest rate plus the expected inflation rate.

The Politics of Inflation (pp. 648–649)

- The government can print or create new base money, so inflation is another source of revenue – it is a tax – and its rate increases when the government has financial needs that exceed the income taxes and other taxes it is able to collect.

- This source of revenue explains the extremely high inflation rates that sometimes occur and that today are present in many developing countries.

- Inflation breeds mistrust of the intentions of the government. People do not trust a government with a poor reputation when it conducts policy with the aim of reducing inflation.

Key Figures ◈

Key Terms

Cost-push inflation, **636**
Demand-pull inflation, **634**
Inflation, **633**
Long-run Phillips curve, **644**

Problems

•1 The figure shows an economy's long-run aggregate supply curve, *LAS*, three aggregate demand curves AD_0, AD_1, and AD_2, and three short-run aggregate supply curves SAS_0, SAS_1, and SAS_2. The economy starts out on the curves AD_0 and SAS_0. Some events then occur that generate a demand-pull inflation.

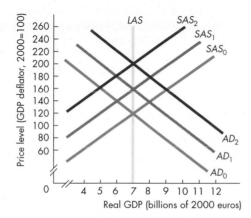

  a List the events that might cause demand-pull inflation.

  b Using the figure, describe the initial effects of demand-pull inflation.

  c Using the figure, describe what happens as a demand-pull inflation spiral unwinds.

2 In the economy described in problem 1, some events then occur that generate a cost-push inflation.

  a List the events that might cause cost-push inflation.

  b Using the figure, describe the initial effects of cost-push inflation.

  c Using the figure, describe what happens as a cost-push inflation spiral unwinds.

•3 Quantecon is a country in which the quantity theory of money operates. The country has a constant population, capital stock, and techno-logy. In year 1, real GDP was €400 million, the price level was 200, and the velocity of circulation of money was 20. In year 2, the quantity of money was 20 per cent higher than in year 1.

  a What was the quantity of money in year 1?

  b What was the quantity of money in year 2?

  c What was the price level in year 2?

  d What was the level of real GDP in year 2?

  e What was the velocity of circulation in year 2?

4 In Quantecon, described in problem 3, in year 3, the quantity of money falls to one-fifth of its year 2 level.

  a What is the quantity of money in year 3?

  b What is the price level in year 3?

  c What is the level of real GDP in year 3?

  d What is the velocity of circulation in year 3?

  e If it takes more than one year for the full quantity theory effect to occur, what do you predict happens in Quantecon in year 3 to real GDP? Why?

•5 In the economy described in problem 1, some events then occur that generate a perfectly anticipated inflation.

  a List the events that might cause a perfectly anticipated inflation.

  b Using the figure, describe the initial effects of anticipated inflation.

  c Using the figure, describe what happens as anticipated inflation proceeds.

6 In the economy described in problem 1, suppose that people anticipate deflation (a falling price level) but aggregate demand turns out to not change.

  a What happens to the short-run and long-run aggregate supply curves? (Draw some new curves if you need to.)

  b Using the figure, describe the initial effects of anticipated deflation.

c Using the figure, describe what happens as it becomes obvious to everyone that the anticipated deflation is not going to occur.

●7 An economy with a natural unemployment rate of 4 per cent and an expected inflation rate of 6 per cent a year has the following inflation and unemployment history:

Year	Inflation rate (per cent per year)	Unemployment rate (per cent)
1999	10	2
2000	8	3
2001	6	4
2002	4	5
2003	2	6

a Draw a diagram of the economy's short-run and long-run Phillips curves.

b If the actual inflation rate rises from 6 per cent a year to 8 per cent a year, what is the change in the unemployment rate? Explain why it occurs.

8 For the economy described in problem 7, the natural unemployment rate rises to 5 per cent and the expected inflation rate falls to 5 per cent a year. Draw the new short-run and long-run Phillips curves in a diagram.

●9 An economy has an unemployment rate of 4 per cent and an inflation rate of 5 per cent a year at point a in the figure. Some events then occur that move the economy to point d.

a Describe the events that could move the economy from point a to point d.

b Draw in the diagram the economy's short-run and long-run Phillips curves when the economy is at point a.

c Draw in the diagram the economy's short-run and long-run Phillips curves when the economy is at point d.

10 In the economy described in problem 9, some events occur that move the economy from point b to point c.

a Describe the events that could move the economy from point b to point c.

b Draw in the diagram the economy's short-run and long-run Phillips curves when the economy is at point b.

c Draw in the diagram the economy's short-run and long-run Phillips curves when the economy is at point c.

Critical Thinking

1 Study Reading Between the Lines on pp. 654–655 and then answer the following questions.

   a Why did the ECB fail to lower the rate of interest in the eurozone?

   b Explain why the fall in the rate of inflation in the eurozone had not been greater?

   c Why might inflation expectations in the eurozone be slow to adjust downwards?

   d What would you expect to happen to inflation and unemployment in the eurozone once inflation expectations adjust?

2 Use the link on the Parkin, Powell and Matthews website to obtain the latest data on inflation, unemployment, and money growth in Japan, UK, USA and Canada. Then:

   a Interpret the data for each country in terms of shifting Phillips curves.

   b Which country do you think has the lowest expected inflation rate? Why?

Inflation Control in the Eurozone

THE FINANCIAL TIMES, 3 AUGUST 2001

Inflation is key to ECB thinking

Tony Barber

By deciding not to cut interest rates yesterday, the European Central Bank has shown that it regards the fire of inflation as a bigger threat than the fog of sluggish economic growth.

Sceptics suspect the bank's diagnosis of the dangers facing the eurozone is wrong. The manufacturing sector is virtually in recession, unemployment is going up in Germany and France, and business confidence is falling, they point out.

Only yesterday, the European Commission said its survey of economic sentiment in the eurozone had fallen for the seventh straight month in July.

Whereas other central banks have reacted to the global slowdown with a substantial relaxation of monetary policy, the ECB has made one rate cut this year – a modest trim of 0.25 percentage points in May that reduced its main rate to 4.5 per cent.

The ECB's reluctance to take more aggressive action reflects the seriousness with which it takes its primary responsibility – the preservation of price stability in the eurozone.

It underlies the ECB's view that monetary conditions in the eurozone, including the euro's external exchange rate, have not been choking economic growth. By historical standards, the ECB says, real interest rates have been low since the euro's launch in 1999.

'Many experts are trying to apply pressure on the ECB to disregard its inflation target and instead act to increase economic growth in the eurozone,' Otmar Issing the ECB's chief economist wrote last month.

'But such monetary policy measures cannot cure the European Union's illness. The key to sustainable growth in the euro area is, in other words, a broad programme of structural reform. The monetary policy objectives that the ECB is aiming for cannot substitute for such reforms.'

The ECB defines price stability as annual inflation of no more than 2 per cent in the medium term. Measured by this yardstick, the bank ought to be performing better.

For a bank perceived as the successor to the rigidly anti-inflationary Bundesbank, this is not good enough. Annual inflation hit 3.4 per cent in May and though it fell to 3 per cent in June, will probably average 2.7 per cent this year.

Many private sector economists do not think inflation will fall below the 2 per cent target ceiling until the second quarter of 2002. Wim Duisenberg, the ECB president, suggested last month that even this goal might be difficult to reach without keeping interest rates at their current level for some time to come.

The Essence of the Story

- The European Central Bank at its monthly meeting decided not to cut the rate of interest for the eurozone economies.

- By not cutting interest rates, the ECB is signalling that it fears the dangers of inflation more than a slowdown in growth.

- Sceptics think that the ECB have the wrong priorities. The threat of low growth and rising unemployment is stronger than inflation.

- While other central banks have cut interest rates in reaction to the global slowdown, the ECB has stuck to its policy of not loosening monetary policy.

- The ECB's chief economist Otmar Issing said that monetary policy cannot be used to promote high growth. Sustainable growth in the euro area can only be created following a programme of structural reform.

Economic Analysis

- One of the reasons the ECB has not cut interest rates is because, although inflation has fallen in the eurozone it still remains above the target ceiling of 2 per cent a year. Figure 1 shows the path of inflation in the eurozone.

- A low inflation policy has still as yet not delivered low inflation expectations. The situation can be described by Figure 2 which shows unemployment higher than the natural rate but inflation is still above the target ceiling of 2 per cent as shown by point *a*.

- Expectations of inflation have not fallen because the ECB is still developing an anti-inflation reputation. Its credibility remains weak because it has not delivered inflation below the ceiling and it continues to face pressure from governments to relax monetary conditions as growth slows down.

- Figure 3 shows what would happen if there was a fall in expected inflation. The short-run Phillips curve falls from $SRPC_0$ to $SRPC_1$. Inflation falls and unemployment moves towards the natural rate given by *LRPC*.

- However, monetary policy would not produce a sustainable reduction in unemployment below the natural rate. The only way the natural rate can be reduced is through supply-side policy.

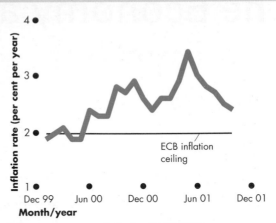

Figure 1 Eurozone inflation 2000–2001

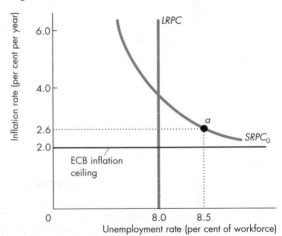

Figure 2 Eurozone inflation and unemployment

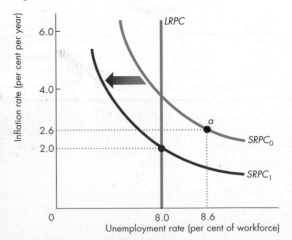

Figure 3 Eurozone Phillips curve

CHAPTER 29

The Economy at Full Employment

After studying this chapter you will be able to:

◆ Describe the relationship between the quantity of labour employed and real GDP

◆ Explain what determines the demand for labour and the supply of labour

◆ Explain how labour market equilibrium determines employment, the real wage rate, and potential GDP

◆ Explain the influences on employment, the real wage rate and potential GDP of an increase in the population, an increase in capital and an advance in technology

◆ Explain what determines unemployment when the economy is at full employment

Production and Jobs

At the height of the Second World War, real GDP in the United Kingdom was 25 per cent higher than four years earlier. This was an unprecedented annual growth of 6 per cent a year – more than double what is currently considered to be the growth in potential real GDP. How could production increase so rapidly in such a short space of time? ◆ Over longer periods, we gradually become more productive and our incomes grow. On the average, each hour that we worked in 2000 earned us 70 per cent more than it did in 1970. Despite setbacks during the past few years, the economies of Japan and China have expanded more rapidly than ours and incomes in these countries have grown more quickly than ours. What makes production and incomes grow over the years? ◆ What are the forces that determine employment, wage rates and real GDP when our economy is at full employment? ◆ Our population grows every year. What effect does population size have on employment, wage rates, and potential GDP? ◆ We also hear about the need to invest more and about the importance of education, and about the need to support science and technology. How do capital accumulation, education and advances in technology influence employment, wage rates and potential GDP? In Reading Between the Lines we examine the European Commission's analysis of the EU labour market and the policy implications of skills training and reform. ◆ We have already seen (Chapter 21, pp. 452–457) that when we talk about full employment, we don't mean there is *no* unemployment. So what determines the amount of unemployment when the economy is at full employment?

◆ ◆ ◆ ◆ In this chapter, we study the economy at full employment. We'll study the relationship between production and employment and learn about the forces that determine the quantity of employment. We'll also discover how changes in population, capital and technology influence employment and incomes. And we'll learn about the forces that create unemployment when the economy is at full employment.

Real GDP and Employment

To produce more output, we must use more inputs. We can increase real GDP by employing more labour, increasing the quantity of capital, or developing technologies that are more productive. In the short term, the quantity of capital and the state of technology are fixed. So to increase real GDP in the short term, we must increase the quantity of labour employed. Let's look at the relationship between real GDP and the quantity of labour employed.

Production Possibilities

When you studied the limits to production in Chapter 2, (see pp. 22–23) you learned about the production possibility frontier, which is the boundary between those combinations of goods and services that can be produced and those that cannot. We can think about the production possibility frontier for any pair of goods or services when we hold the quantities of all other goods and services constant. Let's think about the production possibility frontier between two special items – real GDP and the quantity of leisure time.

Real GDP is a measure of the final goods and services produced in the economy in a given time period (see Chapter 20, pp. 425–432). We measure real GDP as a number of 1995 pounds but the measure is a *real* one. Real GDP is not a quantity of pounds sterling. It is a quantity of goods and services. Think of it as a number of big shopping carts filled with goods and services. Each cart contains some of each of the different goods and services produced, and one cartload of items costs £10 billion. To say that real GDP is £800 billion means that real GDP is 80 big shopping carts of goods and services.

The quantity of leisure time is the number of hours we spend not working. It is the time we spend doing sports, seeing movies, and hanging out with friends. Leisure time is a special type of good or service.

Each hour that we spent pursuing fun could have been an hour that we spent at work. So when the quantity of leisure time increases by one hour, the quantity of labour employed decreases by one hour. If we spent all our time having fun rather than working, we would not produce anything. Real GDP would be zero. The more leisure time we forgo to work, the greater is the quantity of labour employed and the greater is real GDP.

The relationship between leisure time and real GDP is a **production possibility frontier**. Figure 29.1(a) shows an example of this frontier. Here, an economy has 150 billion hours of leisure time available. If people use all these hours to pursue leisure, no labour is employed and real GDP is zero. As people forgo leisure and work more, real GDP increases. If people took 100 billion hours in leisure and spent 50 billion hours working, real GDP would be £825 billion at point *a*. If people spent all the available hours working, real GDP would be £1,200 billion.

The bowed out *PPF* displays increasing opportunity cost. In this case, the opportunity cost of a given amount of real GDP is the amount of leisure time forgone to produce the real GDP. The additional hours of leisure forgone to produce a given additional amount of real GDP increases as real GDP increases. The reason is that we use the most productive labour first and, as we use more labour, we use increasingly less productive labour.

The Production Function

We have already been introduced to the concept of the **production function** in Chapter 22 (see pp. 463–467). The production function is the relationship between real GDP and the quantity of labour employed when all other influences on production remain the same. The production function shows how real GDP varies as the quantity of labour employed varies, other things remaining the same.

Because one more hour of labour employed means one less hour of leisure, the production function is like a mirror image of the leisure time-real GDP *PPF*. Figure 29.1(b) shows the production function for the economy whose *PPF* is shown in Figure 29.1(a). You can see that when the quantity of labour employed is zero, real GDP is also zero. And as the quantity of labour employed increases, so does real GDP. When 50 billion labour hours are employed, real GDP is £825 billion (at point *a*).

A decrease in leisure hours and the corresponding increases in the quantity of labour employed and real GDP bring a movement along the production possibility frontier and along the production function. The arrows along the *PPF* and production function in Figure 29.1 show these movements. Such movements occurred when employment and real GDP surged during the first four years of the Second World War. But the increase in real GDP during the Second World War changed for an additional reason. Labour became more productive. Let's study the influences on the productivity of labour.

Figure 29.1

Production Possibilities and the Production Function

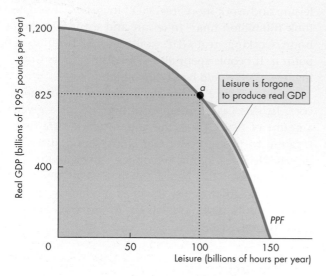

(a) Production possibility frontier

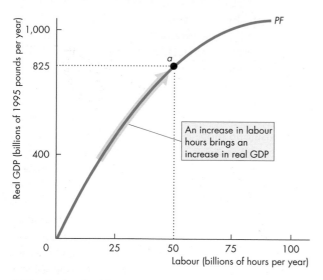

(b) Production function

On the production possibility frontier in part (a), if we enjoy 150 billion hours of leisure, we produce no real GDP. If we forgo 50 billion hours of leisure time and spend only 100 billion hours of leisure, we produce a real GDP of £825 billion, at point *a*. The production function in part (b) is like a mirror image of the *PPF*. At point *a* on the production function, we use 50 billion hours of labour to produce £800 billion of real GDP.

Changes in Productivity

When we talk about **productivity**, we usually mean the labour productivity. Labour productivity is real GDP per hour of labour. Three factors influence labour productivity:

1 Physical capital.

2 Human capital.

3 Technology.

Physical Capital

A farm worker equipped with only a stick and primitive tools can cultivate almost no land and grow barely enough food to feed a single family. One equipped with a steel plough pulled by an animal can cultivate more land and produce enough food to feed a small village. One equipped with high-yield seeds, a modern tractor, plough, and harvester can cultivate thousands of acres and produce enough food to feed hundreds of people.

By using physical capital on our farms and in our factories, shops, and offices, we enormously increase labour productivity. And the more physical capital we use, the greater is our labour productivity, other things remaining the same.

Human Capital

An economy's human capital is the knowledge and skill that people have obtained from education and on-the-job training.

The average university graduate has a greater amount of human capital than the average school leaver possesses. Consequently, the university graduate is able to perform some tasks that are beyond the ability of the school leaver. The university graduate is more productive. For the nation as a whole, the greater the amount of schooling completed by its citizens, the greater is its real GDP, other things remaining the same.

Regardless of how much schooling a person has completed, on the first day at work, not much production is accomplished. Learning about the new work environment consumes the newly hired worker. But as time passes and experience accumulates, the worker becomes more productive. We call this activity of 'on-the-job training' or 'learning-by-doing'.

Learning-by-doing can bring incredible increases in labour productivity. The more experienced the workforce, the greater is its labour productivity, and, other things remaining the same, the greater is real GDP.

The Second World War provides a carefully documented example of the importance of this source of increase in labour productivity. In the shipyards of the USA that produced transport vessels called *Liberty ships*, labour productivity increased by an astonishing 30 per cent purely as a result of learning-by-doing.

Technology

A student equipped with a pen can complete a readable page of writing in perhaps 10 minutes. This same task takes 5 minutes with a typewriter and 2 minutes with a computer. Travelling on foot from London to Edinburgh might take a fit person 10 days. In a train, the trip takes less than 5 hours but by air the trip is 1 hour. These are examples of the enormous impact of technology on productivity. Imagine the profound effect of these advances in technology on the productivity of a business executive who works in London and Edinburgh!

Shift in the Production Function

Any influence on production that increases the productivity of a given quantity of labour shifts the production function upward (and shifts the *PPF* outward). Real GDP increases at each level of labour hours. In Figure 29.2(a), the production function is initially PF_0. Then an increase in physical capital and human capital and an advance in technology occurs. The production function shifts upward to PF_1.

At each quantity of labour employed, real GDP is greater on the new production function than it was on the original one. For example, at 50 billion hours, real GDP increases from £825 billion (point *a*) to £1,050 billion (point *b*).

Figure 29.2(b) shows how the UK production function has shifted upward between 1980 and 2000. Along PF_{00}, labour productivity is 60 per cent greater than on PF_{80}. Labour productivity in the UK increased by about 4.8 per cent a year in the two decades to 2000.

Figure 29.2

An Increase in Labour Productivity

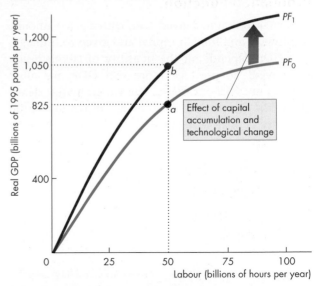

(a) An increase in labour productivity

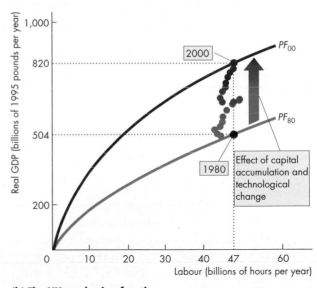

(b) The UK production function

The production function is initially PF_0 and 50 billion labour hours produces a real GDP of £825 billion (point *a*). An increase in capital or an advance in technology that increases labour productivity shifts the production function upward to PF_1 and 50 billion labour hours can now produce a real GDP of £1,050 billion (point *b*). UK real GDP (part b) has increased because labour has become more productive and the quantity of labour employed has increased.

Source: National Statistics, and author calculations.

The Labour Market and Aggregate Supply

You've seen that in a given year, with a given amount of physical and human capital and given technology, real GDP depends on the quantity of labour hours employed. To produce more real GDP, we must employ more labour hours. The labour market determines the quantity of labour hours employed and the quantity of real GDP supplied. We'll learn how by studying:

◆ The demand for labour.

◆ The supply of labour.

◆ Labour market equilibrium.

◆ Aggregate supply.

The Demand for Labour

The quantity of labour demanded is the labour hours hired by all the firms in the economy. The demand for labour is the relationship between the quantity of labour demanded and the real wage rate when all other influences on firms' hiring plans remain the same. The real wage rate is the quantity of goods and services that an hour of labour earns. In contrast, the money wage rate is the number of pounds that an hour of labour earns. A real wage rate is equal to a money wage rate divided by the price of a good. We reviewed measures of the real wage rate in Chapter 21 pp. 450–451.

The *real* wage rate influences the quantity of labour demanded because what matters to firms is not the amount of pounds they pay (money wage) but how much output they must sell to earn those pounds.

We can represent the demand for labour as either a demand schedule or a demand curve. The table in Figure 29.3 shows part of a demand for labour schedule. It tells us the quantity of labour demanded at three different real wage rates. For example, if the real wage rate falls from £8.5 an hour to £8 an hour, the quantity of labour demanded increases from 50 billion hours a year to 55 billion hours a year. (You can find these numbers in rows *a* and *b* of the table.)

The **labour demand curve** is *LD*. Points *a*, *b*, and *c* on the curve correspond to rows *a*, *b*, and *c* of the demand schedule. The labour demand curve shows the quantity of labour that firms plan to hire at each

Figure 29.3

The Demand for Labour

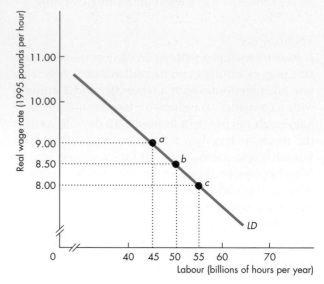

	Real wage rate (1995 pounds per hour)	Quantity of labour demanded (billions of hours per year)
a	9.00	45
b	8.50	50
c	8.00	55

The labour demand curve, *LD*, shows the aggregate hours of labour that firms plan to hire at each real wage rate. The table shows part of a demand for labour schedule. Points *a*, *b*, and *c* on the demand for labour curve correspond to the rows of the table. The lower the real wage rate, the greater is the quantity of labour demanded.

possible real wage rate. The lower the real wage rate, the greater is the quantity of labour that firms plan to hire. That is, the labour demand curve slopes downward. The reason the quantity of labour demanded depends on the *real* wage rate is that firms care only about the amount they pay for labour relative to the amount they get for their output. If money wages and prices change in the same proportion, the quantity of labour that firms plan to hire is unaffected.

Why does the quantity of labour demanded *increase* as the real wage rate *decreases*? That is, why does the demand for labour curve slope downward? To answer these questions, we must first return to the production function and learn about the marginal product of labour.

The Marginal Product of Labour

The marginal product of labour is the additional real GDP produced by an additional hour of labour when all other influences on production remain the same. We calculate the marginal product of labour as the change in real GDP divided by the change in the quantity of labour employed. Figure 29.4(a) shows some marginal product calculations and Figure 29.4(b) shows the marginal product curve.

In Figure 29.4(a), when the quantity of labour employed increases from 35 billion hours to 45 billion hours, an increase of 10 billion hours, real GDP increases from £680 billion to £775 billion, an increase of £95 billion. The marginal product of labour equals the increase in real GDP (£95 billion) divided by the increase in the quantity of labour employed (10 billion hours), which is £9.50 an hour. When the quantity of labour employed increases from 45 billion hours to 55 billion hours, an increase of 10 billion hours, real GDP increases from £775 billion to £860 billion, an increase of £85 billion. The marginal product of labour equals the increase in real GDP (£85 billion) divided by the increase in the quantity of labour employed (10 billion hours), which is £8.50 an hour.

In Figure 29.4(b), as the quantity of labour employed increases, the marginal product of labour diminishes. Between 35 billion and 45 billion (at 40 billion), marginal product is £9.50 an hour. And between 45 billion and 55 billion (at 50 billion), marginal product is £8.50 an hour.

Diminishing Marginal Product

The marginal product of labour diminishes as the quantity of labour employed increases because all the labour, both the old and the new, works with the same fixed amount of physical capital and given technology. As more labour hours are hired, the physical capital is worked more intensively, and more breakdowns and bottlenecks arise. Eventually, as more labour hours are hired, workers get in each other's way and output increases barely at all.

The diminishing marginal product of labour limits the demand for labour.

Figure 29.4

The Marginal Product and the Demand for Labour

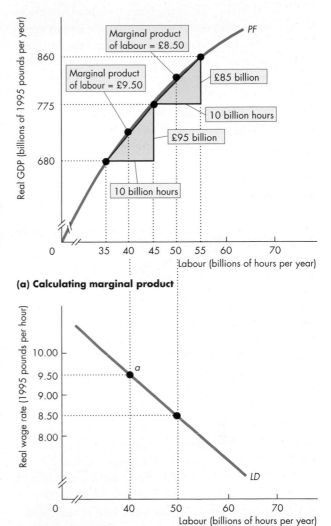

(a) Calculating marginal product

(b) The marginal product curve

An increase in labour from 35 billion to 45 billion hours increases real GDP by £95 billion. The marginal product of labour is £9.50 an hour. An increase in labour from 45 billion to 55 billion hours increases real GDP by £85 billion. The marginal product of labour is £8.50 an hour. At point *a* on the *MP* curve the marginal product of labour is £9.50 an hour at 40 billion hours (midpoint between 35 billion and 45 billion). The *MP* curve is the demand for labour curve.

Diminishing Marginal Product and the Demand for Labour

Firms are in business to maximize profits. Each hour of labour that a firm hires increases output and adds to costs. Initially, an extra hour of labour produces more output than the real wage that the labour costs. Marginal product exceeds the real wage rate. But each additional hour of labour produces less additional output than the previous hour – the marginal product of labour diminishes.

As a firm hires more labour, eventually the extra output from an extra hour of labour is exactly what that hour of labour costs. At this point, marginal product equals the real wage rate. Hire one less hour and marginal product exceeds the real wage rate. Hire one more hour and the real wage rate exceeds the marginal product. In either case, profit is less.

Because marginal product diminishes as the quantity of labour employed increases, the lower the real wage rate, the greater is the quantity of labour that a firm can profitably hire. The marginal product curve is the same as the demand for labour curve.

You might gain a clearer understanding of the demand for labour by looking at an example.

The Demand for Labour in a Ketchup Factory

Suppose that when a ketchup factory employs one additional hour of labour, output increases by 11 bottles. Marginal product is 11 bottles an hour. If the money wage rate is £5.50 an hour and if ketchup sells for 50p a bottle, the real wage rate is 11 bottles an hour. (We calculate the real wage rate as the money wage rate of £5.50 an hour divided by a price of 50p a bottle, which equals a real wage rate of 11 bottles an hour.) Because marginal product diminishes, we know that if the firm did not hire this hour of labour, marginal product would exceed 11 bottles. Because the firm can hire the hour of labour for a real wage rate of 11 bottles, it pays it to do so.

If the price of ketchup remains at 50p a bottle, and the money wage rate falls to £5.00 an hour, the real wage rate falls to 10 bottles an hour, and the firm increases the quantity of labour demanded.

Similarly, if the money wage rate remains at £5.50 an hour and the price of ketchup rises to 55p a bottle, the real wage rate falls to 10 bottles an hour, and the firm increases the quantity of labour demanded.

When the firm pays a real wage rate equal to the marginal product of labour, it is maximizing profit.

Changes in the Demand for Labour

When the marginal product of labour changes, the demand for labour changes and the demand curve for labour shifts. You've seen that an increase in capital (both physical and human) and an advance in technology that increase productivity shift the production function upward. These same forces increase the demand for labour and shift the demand for labour curve rightward.

The Supply of Labour

The quantity of labour supplied is the number of labour hours that all the households in the economy plan to work. The supply of labour is the relationship between the quantity of labour supplied and the real wage rate when all other influences on work plans remain the same.

We can represent the supply of labour as either a supply schedule or a supply curve. The table in Figure 29.5 shows a supply of labour schedule. It tells us the quantity of labour supplied at three different real wage rates. For example, if the real wage rate rises from £7.50 an hour (row *a*) to £8.50 an hour (row *b*), the quantity of labour supplied increases from 45 billion hours a year to 50 billion hours a year. The curve *LS* is a **labour supply curve**. Points *a*, *b*, and *c* on the curve correspond to rows *a*, *b*, and *c* of the supply schedule.

The *real* wage rate influences the quantity of labour supplied because what matters to people is not the number of dollars they earn (the money wage rate) but what those dollars will buy.

The quantity of labour supplied increases as the real wage rate increases for two reasons:

1 Hours per person increase.

2 Economic activity rate increases.

Hours Per Person

In choosing how many hours to work, a household considers the opportunity cost of not working. This opportunity cost is the real wage rate. The higher the real wage rate, the greater is the opportunity cost of taking leisure and not working. And as the opportunity cost of taking leisure rises, other things remaining the same, the more the household chooses to work.

Figure 29.5

The Supply of Labour

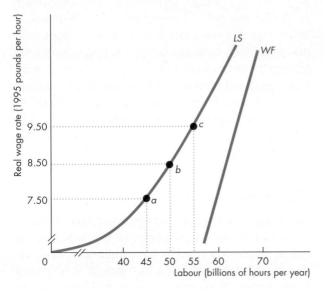

	Real wage rate (1995 pounds per hour)	Quantity of labour supplied (billions of hours per year)
a	7.50	45
b	8.50	50
c	9.50	55

The table shows part of a supply of labour schedule. Points a, b, and c on the supply of labour curve correspond to the rows of the table. The higher the real wage rate, the greater is the quantity of labour supplied.

The labour supply curve, LS, shows the aggregate hours that households plan to work at each wage rate. The WF curve shows the potential hours available if everyone of working age who wants to work at a particular wage rate is employed. The gap between the LS curve and the WF curve defines the natural rate of unemployment. The slope of the WF curve is steeper than the LS curve because as the real wage rises the gap between the LS and WF curves narrows.

But other things don't remain the same. The higher the real wage rate, the greater is the household's income. And the higher the household's income, the more it wants to consume. One item that it wants to consume more of is leisure.

So a rise in the real wage rate has two opposing effects. By increasing the opportunity cost of leisure, it makes the household want to consume less leisure

and to work more. And by increasing the household's income, it makes the household want to consume more leisure and to work fewer hours. For most households, the opportunity cost effect is stronger than the income effect. So the higher the real wage rate, the greater is the amount of work that the household chooses to do.

Economic Activity Rate

Some people have productive opportunities outside the labour force. These people choose to work only if the real wage rate exceeds the value of these other productive activities. For example, a parent might spend time caring for her or his child. The alternative is day care. The parent will choose to work only if he or she can earn enough per hour to pay the cost of child care and have enough left to make the work effort worthwhile. The higher the real wage rate, the more likely it is that a parent will choose to work and so the greater is the labour force participation rate.

The **workforce curve** shows the potential quantity of labour available for employment at a particular real wage rate. The potential quantity of labour is made up of the actual supply of available labour and labour hours expended in job search and in long-term structural unemployment. The gap between the labour supply curve and the workforce curve is the natural rate of unemployment. The workforce curve is steeper than the labour supply curve because as real wages rise, the amount of labour hours expended in job search declines and even those who are in long-term structural unemployment will be willing to take on any kind of work.

Labour Market Equilibrium and Potential GDP

The forces of supply and demand operate in labour markets just as they do in the markets for goods and services. The price of labour is the real wage rate. A rise in the real wage rate eliminates a shortage of labour by decreasing the quantity demanded and increasing the quantity supplied. A fall in the real wage rate eliminates a surplus of labour by increasing the quantity demanded and decreasing the quantity supplied. If there is neither a shortage nor a surplus, the labour market is in equilibrium.

In macroeconomics, we study the economy-wide labour market to determine the total quantity of labour employed and the average real wage rate.

Figure 29.6

The Labour Market and Potential GDP

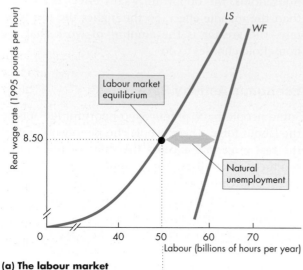

(a) The labour market

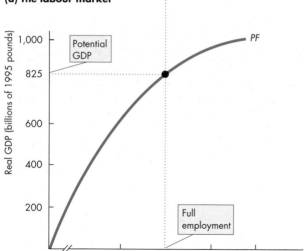

(b) Potential GDP

Labour market equilibrium occurs (in part *a*) when the quantity of labour demanded equals the quantity of labour supplied. The equilibrium real wage rate is £8.50 an hour, and equilibrium employment, full employment, is 50 billion hours a year. Part (b) shows how potential GDP is determined. It is the quantity of real GDP determined by the production function and the full-employment quantity of labour.

Labour Market Equilibrium

Labour demand and labour supply interact to determine the equilibrium level of employment, unemployment and the real wage rate. In Figure 29.6(a), at an average real wage rate below £8.50 an hour based on 1995 prices, there is a labour shortage. People find jobs easily, but businesses are short of labour. But this situation doesn't last for ever. Because there is a shortage of labour, the real wage rate rises towards the equilibrium wage rate of £8.50 an hour.

At wage rates above £8.50 an hour, there is a labour surplus. People have a hard time finding jobs and businesses can easily hire all the labour they want. Unemployment will be a mixture of the labour surplus created by the excess supply of labour and the natural rate shown by the gap between the labour supply curve and the workforce curve. In this situation, the real wage rate falls towards the equilibrium wage rate. The equilibrium level of employment is 50 billion hours a year. This equilibrium is **full-employment equilibrium** and the actual unemployment rate coincides with the **natural rate**.

Potential GDP

You've seen that the quantity of real GDP depends on the quantity of labour employed. The production function tells us how much real GDP a given amount of employment can produce. At the labour market equilibrium, employment is at its full-employment level. And the quantity of real GDP produced by the full-employment quantity of labour is potential GDP.

Figure 29.6(b) shows potential GDP. The equilibrium level of employment in Figure 29.6(a) is 50 billion hours. The production function in Figure 29.6(b) tells us that 50 billion hours of labour can produce a real GDP of £825 billion. This amount is **potential GDP**.

Aggregate Supply

The long-run aggregate supply curve is the relationship between the quantity of real GDP supplied and the price level when real GDP equals potential GDP. Figure 29.7 shows this relationship as the vertical *LAS* curve. Along the long-run aggregate supply curve, as the price level changes, the money wage rate also changes to keep the real wage rate at the full-employment equilibrium level in Figure 29.6(a). With

Figure 29.7

The Aggregate Supply Curves

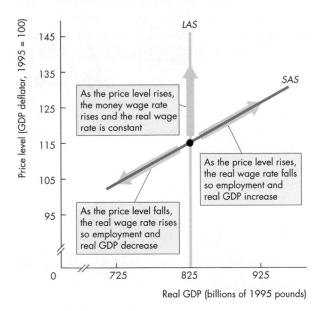

A rise in the price level accompanied by a rise in the money wage rate that keeps the real wage rate at its full-employment equilibrium level keeps the quantity of real GDP supplied at potential GDP – a movement along the long-run aggregate supply curve. A rise in the price level with no change in the money wage rate lowers the real wage rate and increases employment and the quantity of real GDP supplied – a movement along the short-run aggregate supply curve.

no change in the real wage rate and no change in employment, real GDP remains at potential GDP.

The short-run aggregate supply curve is the relationship between the quantity of real GDP supplied and the price level when the money wage rate and potential GDP remain constant. Figure 29.7 shows a short-run aggregate supply curve as the upward-sloping *SAS* curve. Along the short-run aggregate supply curve, as the price level rises, the money wage rate remains fixed so the real wage rate *falls*. In Figure 29.6, when the real wage rate falls, the quantity of labour demanded increases and real GDP increases.

When the economy is on its short-run aggregate supply curve above potential GDP, the real wage rate is below the full-employment equilibrium level. And when the economy is on the short-run aggregate supply curve below potential GDP, the real wage rate is above the full-employment equilibrium level. In

both cases, the quantity of labour employed, which is chosen by firms, differs from the quantity that households would supply if they could choose their work hours.

Production is efficient in the sense that firms operate on their production functions. But the allocation of time is inefficient. In an above full-employment equilibrium, people do more work and produce more real GDP than they would if they could choose their work hours. And in below full-employment equilibrium, people do less work and produce less real GDP than they would if they could choose their work hours.

When the real wage rate departs from its full-employment equilibrium level, the resulting shortage or surplus of labour brings market forces into play that move the real wage rate and quantity of labour employed back towards their full-employment levels.

Review Quiz

◆ Why does a rise in the real wage rate bring a decrease in the quantity of labour demanded, other things remaining the same?

◆ Why does a rise in the real wage rate bring an increase in the quantity of labour supplied, other things remaining the same?

◆ What happens in the labour market if the real wage rate is above or below the full-employment level?

◆ How is potential GDP determined?

◆ What is the relationship between full-employment equilibrium in the labour market, the natural rate of unemployment and long-run aggregate supply?

◆ What is the relationship between the labour market and short-run aggregate supply?

Next, we study changes in potential GDP

Changes in Potential GDP

Real GDP will increase if:

1 The economy recovers from recession.

2 Potential GDP increases.

Recovery from recession means the economy moves along the real GDP–leisure *PPF* from a point at which real GDP is less than potential GDP. Equivalently, the economy moves along the short-run aggregate supply curve. Economists have a lot to say about such a move, and Chapters 22–28 explain this type of short-term change in real GDP.

Increasing potential GDP means expanding production possibilities. We're going to study such an expansion in the rest of this chapter and in Chapter 30. We begin this process here by examining two influences on potential GDP:

1 An increase in population.
2 An increase in labour productivity.

An Increase in Population

As the population increases and additional people reach working age, the supply of labour increases. With more labour available, and with capital and technology remaining the same, production possibilities expand. But does the expansion of production possibilities mean that potential GDP increases? And does it mean that potential GDP *per person* increases?

The answers to these questions have intrigued economists for many years. And they cause heated political debate today. In China, for example, families are under enormous pressure to limit the number of children they have. In other countries, an example of which is France, the government encourages large families. We can study the effects of an increase in population by using the model of the full-employment economy in Figure 29.8.

In Figure 29.8(a), the demand for labour is LD and initially the supply of labour is LS_0. At full employment, the real wage rate is £8.50 an hour and employment is 50 billion hours a year. In Figure 29.8(b), the production function (PF) shows that with 50 billion hours of labour employed, potential GDP is £825 billion. We're now going to work out what happens when the population increases.

An increase in the working-age population increases the supply of labour. In Figure 29.8, the labour supply curve and the workforce curve shifts rightward to LS_1 and WF_1 – both curves shift to the left by an equivalent amount. At a real wage rate of £8.50 an hour, there is now a surplus of labour. So the real wage rate falls. In this example, it falls until it reaches £8.00 an hour. At £8.00 an hour, the quantity of labour demanded equals the quantity of labour supplied. Equilibrium employment increases to 55 billion hours a year.

Figure 29.8

An Increase in Population

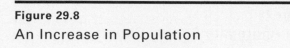
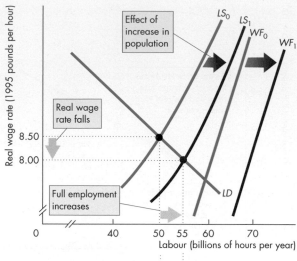

(a) The labour market

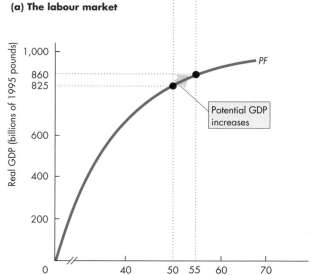

(b) Potential GDP

An increase in population increases the supply of labour and shifts the LS curve rightward (in part a). The WF curve moves to the right by an equivalent amount because the potential labour supply has also increased. The real wage rate falls and the quantity of labour employed at full employment increases. In part (b), the increase in full-employment equilibrium employment increases potential GDP. Because the marginal product of labour diminishes, the increased population produces a greater potential GDP but a smaller potential GDP per hour of work.

Figure 29.8(b) shows the effect of the increase in equilibrium employment on real GDP. As the full-employment quantity of labour increases from 50 billion hours to 55 billion hours, potential GDP increases from £825 billion to £860 billion.

So at full employment, an increase in population increases employment, increases potential GDP, and lowers the real wage rate.

An increase in population also decreases potential GDP per hour of work. You can see this decrease by dividing potential GDP by total labour hours. Initially, with potential GDP at £825 billion and labour hours at 50 billion, potential GDP per hour of work was £16.50. With the increase in population, potential GDP is £860 billion and labour hours are 55 billion. Potential GDP per hour of work is £15.64. Diminishing returns is the source of the decrease in potential GDP per hour of work.

You've seen that an increase in population increases potential GDP and decreases potential GDP per work hour. Some people challenge this conclusion and argue that people are the ultimate economic resource. They claim that a larger population brings forth a greater amount of scientific discovery and technological advance. Consequently, these people argue that an increase in population never takes place in isolation. It is always accompanied by an increase in labour productivity. Let's now look at the effects of this influence on potential GDP. For example, if the real interest rate on your student loan was 12 per cent, you would probably cut your consumption expenditure (buy cheaper food, find cheaper accommodation) and borrow a smaller amount. Similarly, with a 12 per cent real interest rate, lenders try to cut back on current consumption in order to increase their lending and profit from the high real interest rate. But if the real interest rate on your student loan was 1 per cent a year, you might increase your consumption and borrow a larger amount.

An Increase in Labour Productivity

We've seen that three factors increase labour productivity:

1 An increase in physical capital.

2 An increase in human capital.

3 An advance in technology.

The quantity of physical capital increases over time because of saving and investment. Human capital increases because of education and on-the-job training and experience. And technology advances because of research and development efforts. We study the way all these forces interact to determine the growth rate of potential GDP in Chapter 30.

Here, we study the *effects* of an increase in physical capital, or an increase in human capital, or an advance in technology on the labour market and potential GDP. We'll see how the real wage rate, employment, and potential GDP change when any of these three influences on labour productivity changes.

An Increase in Physical Capital

If the quantity of physical capital increases, labour productivity increases. With labour being more productive, the economy's production possibilities expand. How does such an expansion of production possibilities change the equilibrium real wage rate, employment and potential GDP?

The additional capital increases the real GDP that each quantity of labour can produce. It also increases the marginal product of labour and so increases the demand for labour. Some physical capital replaces some types of labour. So the demand for those types of labour decreases when capital increases. But an increase in physical capital creates a demand for those types of labour that build, sell and maintain the additional capital. The increases in demand for labour are always larger than the decreases in demand and the economy-wide demand for labour increases.

With an increase in the economy-wide demand for labour, the real wage rate rises and the quantity of labour supplied increases. Equilibrium employment increases.

Potential GDP now increases for two reasons. First, a given level of employment produces more real GDP. Second, equilibrium employment increases.

An Increase in Human Capital

If the quantity of human capital increases, labour productivity increases. Again, with labour being more productive, the economy's production possibilities expand. And this expansion of production possibilities changes the equilibrium real wage rate, employment and potential GDP in a similar manner to the effects of a change in physical capital.

Figure 29.9

An Increase in Labour Productivity

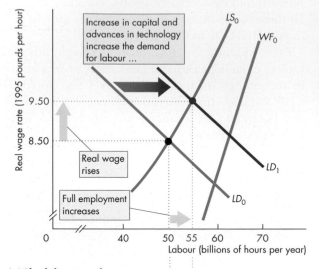

(a) The labour market

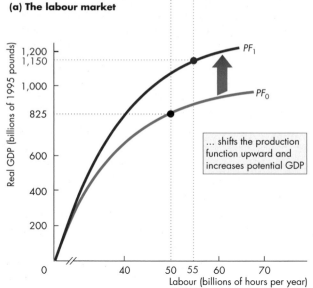

(b) Potential GDP

An increase in labour productivity shifts the demand for labour curve rightward from LD_0 to LD_1 (part a) and the production function upward from PF_0 to PF_1 (part b). The real wage rate rises from £8.50 to £9.50 an hour, full employment increases from 50 billion to 55 billion hours, and the natural rate of unemployment declines. Potential GDP increases from £825 billion to £1,150 billion. Potential GDP increases because labour becomes more productive and full employment increases

An Advance in Technology

As technology advances, labour productivity increases. And exactly as in the case of an increase in capital, the economy's production possibilities expand. Again, just as in the case of an increase in capital, the new technology increases the real GDP that each quantity of labour can produce and increases the marginal product of labour and the demand for labour.

With an increase in the demand for labour, the real wage rate rises, the quantity of labour supplied increases, and equilibrium employment increases. And again, potential GDP increases because a given level of employment produces more real GDP and because equilibrium employment increases.

Illustrating the Effects of an Increase in Labour Productivity

Figure 29.9 shows the effects of an increase in labour productivity that results from an increase in capital or an advance in technology. In part (a), the demand for labour initially is LD_0 and the supply of labour is LS. The real wage rate is £8.50 an hour, and full employment is 50 billion hours a year.

In part (b), the production function initially is PF_0. With 50 billion hours of labour employed, potential GDP is £825 billion.

Now an increase in capital or an advance in technology increases the productivity of labour. In Figure 29.9(a), the demand for labour increases and the demand curve shifts rightward to LD_1. In Figure 29.9(b), the productivity of labour increases, and the production function shifts upward to PF_1.

In Figure 29.9(a), at the original real wage rate of £8.50 an hour, there is now a shortage of labour. So the real wage rate rises. In this example, it keeps rising until it reaches £9.50 an hour. At £9.50 an hour, the quantity of labour demanded equals the quantity of labour supplied and full-employment increases to 55 billion hours a year. Because more people are encouraged to take work at the higher wage rate, less time is spent in job search and even those who are in the workforce but are structurally unemployed will take work, the gap between the LS curve and WF curve narrows. At the new equilibrium, the natural rate of unemployment is lower.

Figure 29.9(b) shows the effects of the increase in full-employment combined with the new production function on potential GDP. As employment increases

Figure 29.10

Explaining the Trends in Employment and Real Wage Rates

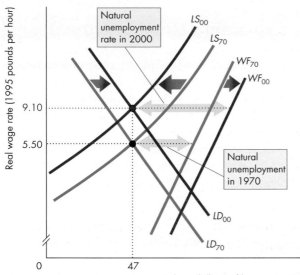

In 1970, the labour demand curve was LD_{70} and the labour supply curve was LS_{70}. The equilibrium real wage rate was £5.50 an hour in 1995 prices, and 47 billion hours of labour were employed. Over the years, labour became more and more productive. The demand curve shifted rightward to LD_{00}. At the same time, an increase in the working-age population increased the potential supply of labour, and the workforce curve shifted rightward to WF_{00}. An increase in union militancy and restrictive practices led to a leftward shift of the LS curve to LS_{98}. As a result the quantity of labour employed remained the same, the average real wage rose and unemployment increased.

The Trends in Employment and Wage Rates

We can use the model of labour demand and labour supply to understand the long-term trends in aggregate hours and real wage rates. We saw in Chapter 21, Figure 21.4, p. 450 that aggregate hours in 2000 were much the same as in 1970. We saw in Figure 21.5 that the real wage rate increased. The average real wage rate for the entire economy, including the value of pay supplements, increased from £5.50 an hour in 1970 to about £9.00 an hour in 2000. We also saw in Figure 21.2 that the unemployment rate increased from 2.4 per cent in 1970 to 5.3 per cent in 2000.

Figure 29.10 shows how these changes came about. In 1970, the labour demand curve was LD_{70} and the labour supply curve was LS_{70}. The equilibrium real wage rate was £5.50 an hour, and 47 billion hours of labour were employed.

Throughout the period since the Second World War, labour has become more and more productive. The reason is that capital per worker has increased and technology has advanced. We'll explore the reasons for this increased labour productivity in Chapter 30. But regardless of the reasons, the effect of an increase in labour productivity is an increase in the demand for labour. If an hour of labour can produce more output, firms are willing to pay a higher wage rate to hire that hour of labour. This would be shown by a rightward shift in the labour demand curve, resulting in a rise in the real wage and an increase in the quantity of labour employed. This increase in demand is shown by a rightward shift in the labour demand curve from LD_{70} to LD_{00}.

At the same time the population grew and so did the working-age population. With a larger working-age population, the supply of labour available for work increased. This increase is shown by the rightward shift in the workforce curve from WF_{70} to WF_{00}. Normally, we would expect the supply of labour to shift in the same direction; however, labour supply decreased, and the labour supply curve shifted leftwards from LS_{70} to LS_{00}, resulting in roughly the same amount of labour hours being hired in 2000 as in 1970. How could this be? There are a number of microeconomic reasons behind the leftward shift in aggregate labour supply. During the 1970s there was an increase in trade union militancy aimed at increasing the cost of labour and protecting the interest of those employed (known as *insiders* – see Explaining

from 50 billion hours to 55 billion hours, potential GDP increases from £825 billion to £1,150 billion.

Potential GDP per hour of work also increases. You can see this increase by dividing potential GDP by total labour hours. Initially, with potential GDP at £825 billion and labour hours at 50 billion, potential GDP per hour of work was £16.50. With the increase in labour productivity, potential GDP is £1,150 billion and labour hours are 55 billion, so potential GDP per hour of work is £20.90.

We've just studied the effects of a change in population and an increase in labour productivity separately. In reality, these changes occur together. We can see the combined effects by examining an episode in the life of the UK economy.

Unemployment, pp. 670–673). At the same time, taxes on income increased, reducing incentives to work, creating a substitution for leisure. Also unemployment benefits were raised, increasing *frictional unemployment* – see Chapter 21, p. 455. This resulted in the leftward shift of the labour supply curve.

During the 1980s, trade union reform, tax cuts and other supply-side policies by the government were aimed at making the labour market more flexible. This had the effect of relieving the pressures caused by structural change in the economy which resulted in more jobs but not more hours worked. The jobs that were destroyed in the 1980s were mostly in manufacturing and in the low-skill sectors. These jobs were replaced by high skilled jobs in high-tech industries and in services and also part-time jobs, mostly in services and assembly related work.

Technological change and international competition during the 1980s and 90s, brought a decrease in the demand for labour in manufacturing. The same technological change and international competition that destroyed jobs in manufacturing created jobs in services and also high-tech areas. There was an increase in demand for labour in these growing sectors. Those who lost their jobs in manufacturing had to look for work in services. So while the demand curve for labour in manufacturing shifted left, the supply curve for labour in the service sector shifted to the right. The overall effect was to shift the aggregate supply of labour leftwards.

Thus the quantity of labour employed remained the same, the average real wage rate increased, and unemployment increased. But also the natural rate of unemployment increased.

Review Quiz

♦ When the population increases but nothing else changes, why does real GDP per hour of work decrease?

♦ How does an increase in capital change the real wage rate, full employment and potential GDP?

♦ How do advances in technology change the real wage rate, full employment and potential GDP?

♦ If, as some people suggest, capital accumulation and technological change always accompany an increase in population, is it possible for potential GDP per hour of work to decrease?

♦ How does an increase in trade union militancy and restrictive practice increase the natural rate of unemployment?

We've now studied the main trends in employment and wage rates, and we have seen how the demand and supply model can help us to understand these trends. Our next task is to explain unemployment.

Explaining Unemployment

We've described *how* people become unemployed – they are job losers, job leavers, or workforce entrants and re-entrants. And we have classified unemployment – it can be frictional, structural and cyclical. But this description and classification do not *explain* unemployment. Why is there always some unemployment and why does its rate fluctuate? Unemployment is always present for three reasons:

1 Job search.
2 Job rationing.
3 Sticky wages.

Job Search

Job search is the activity of people looking for acceptable vacant jobs. The labour market is in a constant state of change. Jobs are destroyed and created as businesses fail and new businesses start up and as new technologies and new markets evolve. In the process, people lose jobs. Other people enter or re-enter the labour market. Yet other people leave their jobs to look for better ones and others retire. This constant churning in the labour market means that there are always some people looking for jobs – the unemployed. Job search even takes place when the quantity of labour demanded equals the quantity supplied. In this situation, some people have not yet found a job and some jobs have not yet been filled.

Job search explains frictional, structural and cyclical unemployment. All three types of unemployment occur because job losers, job leavers and workforce entrants and re-entrants don't know about all the jobs available to them so they must take time to *search* for an acceptable one. This search takes time, and the average amount of time varies. When there is a small amount of structural change and when the economy is close to a business cycle peak, search times are low and the unemployment rate is low. But when structural change is rapid and when the economy is in a recession, search times increase and the unemployment rate increases.

Although job search is cyclical, it also changes more slowly and brings changes in the natural rate of unemployment. The main sources of these slower changes are:

◆ Demographic change.

◆ Unemployment benefit.

◆ Technological change.

◆ Hysteresis.

Demographic Change

An increase in the proportion of the working-age population brings an increase in the entry rate into the workforce and an increase in the unemployment rate. This is described by a rightward shift in the *WF* curve in Figure 29.10. A bulge in the birth rate occurred in the late 1940s and early 1950s, following the Second World War. This bulge increased the proportion of new entrants into the workforce during the 1970s and brought an increase in the unemployment rate. Another demographic trend is an increase in the number of households with two working adults. If unemployment hits one person with income coming in from the other, job search can take longer, increasing frictional unemployment.

Unemployment Benefit

The length of time that an unemployed person spends searching for a job depends, in part, on the opportunity cost of job search. With no income during a period of unemployment, an unemployed person faces a high opportunity cost of job search. In this situation, search is likely to be short and an unattractive job is likely to be accepted as a better alternative to continuing a costly search process. With generous unemployment benefits, the opportunity cost of job search is low. In this situation, search is likely to be prolonged. An unemployed worker will hold out for the ideal job.

The opportunity cost of job search has fallen over the years as unemployment benefits have increased. In 1966, unemployment benefit included a flat-rate component and an earnings-related component. As a result of these changes, the natural rate of unemployment was on an upward trend during the 1970s. In 1982, earnings-related benefit was abolished in the United Kingdom and during the 1990s the conditions for the receipt of benefit were tightened. During the 1980s and 1990s estimates of the natural rate decreased.

Technological Change

Labour market flows and unemployment are influenced by the pace and direction of technological change. Sometimes technological change brings a *structural slump*, in which some industries die and regions suffer and other industries are born and regions flourish. When these events occur, labour turnover is high – the flows between employment and unemployment and the pool of unemployed people increases. The decline of traditional heavy industries such as shipbuilding, steel and coal and the rapid expansion of industries in the electronics and car components sectors are examples of the effects of technological change and sources of the increase in unemployment during the 1970s and early 1980s. While these changes were taking place, the natural rate of unemployment increased. Supply-side policies that increased job market flexibility in the 1980s resulted in the labour market being able to adjust more rapidly to technological shocks.

Hysteresis

The unemployment rate fluctuates around the natural rate of unemployment. But it is possible that the natural rate itself depends on the path of the actual unemployment rate. So where the unemployment rate ends up depends on where it has been. Such a process is called **hysteresis**.

If hysteresis is present, then an increase in the unemployment rate brings an increase in the natural rate. A possible source of hysteresis is that the human capital of unemployed workers depreciates, and people who experience long bouts of unemployment usually find it difficult to get new jobs as good as the ones they have lost. An increase in the number of long-term unemployed workers means an increase in the amount of human capital lost and possibly a permanent increase in the natural rate of unemployment. The hysteresis theory is controversial and has not yet been thoroughly tested, but it is also consistent with the view that the long-term unemployed are willing to remain on state benefits indefinitely.

Job search unemployment is present even when the quantity of labour demanded equals the quantity supplied. The other possible explanations of unemployment are based on the view that the quantity of labour demanded does not always equal the quantity supplied.

Job Rationing

Job rationing is the practice of paying employed people a wage that creates an excess supply of labour and a shortage of jobs. Three reasons why jobs might be rationed are:

1   Efficiency wages.

2   Insider interest.

3   The minimum wage.

Efficiency Wages

A firm can increase its labour productivity by paying wages above the competitive wage rate. The higher wage attracts a higher quality of labour, encourages greater work effort, and cuts down on the firm's labour turnover rate and recruiting costs. But the higher wage also adds to the firm's costs. So a firm offers a wage rate that balances productivity gains and additional costs. The wage rate that maximizes profit is called the **efficiency wage**.

The efficiency wage will be higher than the competitive equilibrium wage. If it was lower than the competitive wage, competition for labour would bid the wage up. With an efficiency wage above the competitive wage, some labour is unemployed and employed workers have an incentive to perform well to avoid being fired.

The payment of efficiency wages is another reason the natural rate of unemployment is not zero.

Insider Interest

Why don't firms cut their wage costs by offering jobs to unemployed workers for a lower wage rate than that paid to existing workers? One explanation, called **insider–outsider theory**, is that to be productive, new workers – outsiders – must receive on-the-job training from existing workers – insiders. If insiders provide such training to outsiders who are paid a lower wage, the insiders' bargaining position is weakened. So insiders will not train outsiders unless outsiders receive the same rate of pay as insiders.

When bargaining for a pay deal, unions represent only the interests of insiders so the wage agreed exceeds the competitive wage and there are always outsiders unable to find work. Thus the pursuit of rational self-interest by insiders is another reason the natural rate of unemployment is positive. The weakening of trade union power through legislation may have reduced the insiders' bargaining position.

The Minimum Wage

A minimum wage is legislated by the government at a level higher than the one the market would determine. As a result, the quantity of labour supplied exceeds the quantity demanded and jobs are rationed. The minimum wage for the UK is £3.60 an hour for workers aged 22 and over. A lower minimum wage of £3.20 exists for those on training programmes, and a lower wage of £3 for 18–21 year-olds. It is estimated that the minimum wage will only affect 4.3 per cent of employees in London, but 11.6 per cent of employees in the north-east. It will also affect nearly one-third of employees in the hotel and restaurant business and a quarter of security guards and cleaners.

Minimum wages exist in a number of EU countries. The 'Social Chapter' of the Treaty of European Union gives the EU commission and the European Court powers in enforcing the minimum wage. While a minimum wage will be expected to result in job rationing, there are arguments in favour of such a policy. One argument is that if firms are forced to pay a minimum wage, they will have to use labour more efficiently and improve productivity. The improvement in productivity will result in very small effects on job rationing and therefore unemployment. One study that was published to coincide with the introduction of the minimum wage in the UK on 1 April 1999, predicted that only 80,000 jobs over 2–3 years would be lost as a result, of which half would be in the wholesaling, hotel and catering sectors.

Job rationing is a possible reason for a high natural rate of unemployment. It is a source of persistent and possibly high frictional unemployment. The distinction between unemployment that arises from job search and that which arises from job rationing can be illustrated by musical chairs. If there are equal numbers of chairs (jobs) and players (people who want jobs), when the music stops, everyone finds a chair. If there are more players than chairs, when the music stops, some players can't find a chair. The chairs are rationed. The minimum wage has contributed to higher unemployment for the young and unskilled.

Job rationing is a source of long-term frictional unemployment. The final explanation of unemployment is one reason why unemployment is cyclical.

Sticky Wages

Wages don't change as often as prices do. So if the demand for labour decreases, the real wage rate

Figure 29.11

Sticky Wages and Unemployment

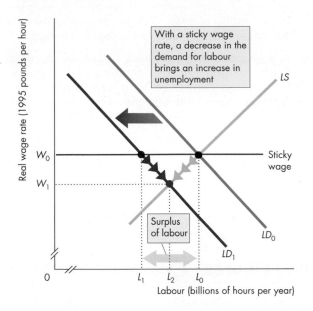

With a sticky wage rate, a decrease in the demand for labour brings an increase in unemployment

When the demand for labour is LD_0 and the supply of labour is LS, employment is L_0 billion hours and the real wage rate is W_0 an hour. The demand for labour decreases and the demand curve shifts leftward to LD_1 but the real wage rate is sticky at W_0 an hour. Employment decreases and there is a surplus of $L_0 - L_1$ billion hours. Eventually, the real wage rate falls to W_1 an hour and the quantity of labour employed increases to L_2 billion hours.

begins to move towards its new equilibrium, but it takes some time to get there. During this process of gradual wage adjustment, there is a surplus of labour and unemployment is temporarily high.

Figure 29.11 illustrates this type of unemployment. Initially, the demand for labour is LD_0 and the supply

of labour is LS. The equilibrium level of employment is L_0 billion hours and the real wage rate is W_0 an hour. The demand for labour then decreases and the demand curve shifts leftward to LD_1. But the real wage rate is temporarily sticky at W_0 an hour. At this real wage rate and in the new conditions, firms are willing to hire only L_1 billion hours of labour. So there is a surplus of $L_0 - L_1$ billion hours and extra unemployment is created.

Eventually, as prices and wages change, the real wage rate falls to its equilibrium level. In this example, when the real wage rate has fallen to W_1 an hour, the quantity of labour demanded equals the quantity supplied and the surplus of labour vanishes. The only unemployment that remains is the natural rate of unemployment consistent with the new equilibrium.

Review Quiz

◆ Why does the economy experience unemployment at full employment?
◆ Why does the natural rate of unemployment fluctuate?
◆ What is job rationing and why does it occur?
◆ How does an efficiency wage influence the real wage rate, employment and unemployment?
◆ How does the minimum wage create unemployment?

In this chapter, you've seen how the economy operates at full employment. Reading Between the Lines, pp. 678–679 looks at labour markets in the EU.

Summary

Key Points

Real GDP and Employment
(pp. 657–659)

- The production function is the relationship between real GDP and the quantity of labour employed when all other influences on production remain the same.

- The factors that influence labour productivity are *physical capital, human capital* and *technology*.

- Any influence on production that increases the productivity of a given quantity of labour shifts the production function upward.

The Labour Market and Aggregate Supply (pp. 660–665)

- The demand for labour is the relationship between the quantity of labour demanded and the real wage rate when all other influences on firms' hiring plans remain the same.

- The supply of labour is the relationship between the quantity of labour supplied and the real wage rate when all other influences on work plans remain the same.

- Labour demand and labour supply interact to determine the equilibrium level of employment, unemployment and the real wage rate.

- The quantity of real GDP produced by the full-employment quantity of labour is potential GDP.

Changes in Potential GDP (pp. 665–669)

- An increase in potential GDP comes from an increase in population, or an increase in labour productivity, or both.

- An increase in population increases potential GDP and decreases potential GDP per work hour.

- An increase in labour productivity, increases potential GDP and increases potential GDP per hour of work.

The Trends in Employment and Wage Rates (pp. 669–670)

- Throughout the period since the Second World War, labour has become more and more productive. The reason is that capital per worker has increased and technology has advanced.

- During the 1970s there was an increase in trade union militancy aimed at increasing the cost of labour and protecting the interests of those employed.

- During the 1980s, trade union reform, tax cuts and other supply-side policies by the government were aimed at making the labour market more flexible.

Explaining Unemployment (pp. 670–673)

- Unemployment arises from *job search*, *job rationing* and *sticky wages*.

- The amount of job search unemployment fluctuates with the business cycle, but it also changes for other reasons, which bring changes in the natural rate of unemployment. These other reasons are *demographic change*, *changes to unemployment benefit entitlement* and *technological change*.

- A high unemployment rate brings an increase in the natural rate of unemployment because the human capital of long-term unemployed workers depreciates and they find it hard to get new jobs.

- Job rationing, which can arise from efficiency wages, insider interest and the minimum wage, can be the source of long-term frictional unemployment.

- Sticky wages – the gradual adjustment of wage rates – can bring cyclical unemployment.

Key Figures ◆

Key Terms

Problems

•1 Robinson Crusoe lives on a desert island on the equator. He has 12 hours of daylight every day to allocate between leisure and work. The table shows seven alternative combinations of leisure and real GDP in the economy of Crusoe:

Possibility	Leisure (hours per day)	Real GDP (€ per day)
a	12	0
b	10	10
c	8	18
d	6	24
e	4	28
f	2	30
g	0	30

a Make a graph of Crusoe's *PPF* for leisure and real GDP.

b Make a table and a graph of Crusoe's production function.

c Find Crusoe's marginal product of labour at different quantities of labour.

2 The people of Nautica have 100 hours every day to allocate between leisure and work. The table shows the opportunity cost of real GDP in terms of leisure time forgone in the economy of Nautica:

Possibility	Leisure (hours per day)	Opportunity cost of leisure (€ of real GDP per hour)
a	0	0
b	20	5
c	40	10
d	60	15
e	80	20
f	100	25

a Make a table and a graph of Nautica's *PPF* for leisure and real GDP.

b Make a table and a graph of Nautica's production function.

c Find Nautica's marginal product of labour at different quantities of labour.

•3 Use the information provided in problem 1 about the economy of Crusoe. Also, use the information that Crusoe must earn €4.50 an hour. If he earns less than this amount, he does not have enough food on which to live. He has no interest

in earning more than €4.50 an hour. At a real wage rate of €4.50 an hour he is willing to work any number of hours between zero and the total available to him.

a Make a table that shows Crusoe's demand for labour schedule and draw Crusoe's demand for labour curve.

b Make a table that shows Crusoe's supply of labour schedule and draw Crusoe's supply of labour curve.

c What is the full-employment equilibrium real wage rate and quantity of labour in Crusoe's economy?

d Find Crusoe's potential GDP.

4 Use the information provided in problem 2 about the economy of Nautica. Also, use the information that the people of Nautica are willing to work 20 hours a day for a real wage rate of €10 an hour. And for each €0.50 an hour *increase* in the real wage, they are willing to work an *additional* hour a day.

a Make a table that shows Nautica's demand for labour schedule and draw Nautica's demand for labour curve.

b Make a table that shows Nautica's supply of labour schedule and draw Nautica's supply of labour curve.

c Find the full-employment equilibrium real wage rate and quantity of labour in Nautica's economy.

d Find Nautica's potential GDP.

•5 Crusoe, whose economy is described in problems 1 and 3, gets a bright idea. He diverts a stream and increases his food production by 50 per cent. That is, each hour that he works produces 50 per cent more real GDP than before.

a Make a table that shows Crusoe's new production function and new demand for labour schedule.

b Find the new full-employment equilibrium real wage rate and quantity of labour in Crusoe's economy.

c Find Crusoe's new potential GDP.

d Explain and interpret the results you have obtained in parts (a), (b), and (c).

6 Nautica's economy, described in problems 2 and 4, experiences a surge in its population.

The supply of labour increases and 50 per cent more hours are supplied at each real wage rate.

a Make a table that shows Nautica's new supply of labour schedule.

b Find the new full-employment equilibrium real wage rate and quantity of labour in Nautica's economy.

c Find Nautica's new potential GDP.

d Explain and interpret the results you have obtained in parts (a), (b), and (c).

°7 The figure describes the labour market in Cocoa Island. In addition (not shown in the figure) a survey tells us that when Cocoa Island is at full employment, people spend 1,000 hours a day in job search.

a Find the full-employment equilibrium real wage rate and quantity of labour employed.

b Find potential GDP in Cocoa Island. [Hint: the demand for labour curve tells you the *marginal* product of labour. How do we calculate the marginal product of labour?]

c Calculate the natural rate of unemployment in Cocoa Island.

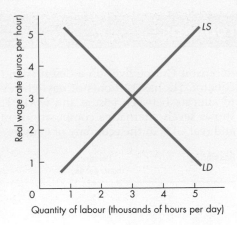

8 In problem 7, the government of Cocoa Island introduces a minimum wage of €4 an hour.

a Find the new equilibrium real wage rate and quantity of labour employed.

b What now is potential GDP in Cocoa Island?

c Calculate the new natural rate of unemployment in Cocoa Island.

d How much of the unemployment results from the minimum wage?

Critical Thinking

1 Study Reading Between the Lines on pp. 678–679 and then answer the following questions:

   a What would be the effect of a policy of skills development on employment, real wages, unemployment and potential GDP, in the EU?

   b What would be the effect of a policy of tax incentives on employment, real wages, unemployment and potential GDP that make it worthwhile for an unemployed person to take on low paid work?

   c Account for the improvement in labour productivity in the UK. What effect is this likely to have had on employment and real wages in the UK? Do you agree with the European Commission that the UK needs to improve the basic skills of its workers? What evidence do you have to support your answer?

2 Use the link on the Parkin, Powell and Matthews website to obtain information about the economy of Russia during the 1990s. Try to figure out what has happened to the production possibility frontier and production function and to the demand for labour and supply of labour in Russia during the 1990s. Tell a story about the Russian economy during these years using only the concepts and tools that you have learned about in this chapter.

3 Visit the Parkin, Powell and Matthews website and use the links provided there to obtain information about the economy of China during the 1990s. Try to figure out what has happened to the production possibility frontier and production function and to the demand for labour and supply of labour in China during the 1990s. Tell a story about the Chinese economy during these years using only the concepts and tools that you have learned about in this chapter.

4 You are working as an Economic Assistant in the Treasury and must write a memo for the Chancellor that provides a checklist of policy initiatives that will increase potential GDP. Be as imaginative as possible but justify each of your suggestions with reference to the concepts and tools that you have learned about in this chapter.

Labour Markets in the EU

THE FINANCIAL TIMES, 30 NOVEMBER 2001

Brussels in call to free more labour markets

Daniel Dombey

The European Commission yesterday scolded the big continental economies for not doing more to free up their labour markets, but also warned the UK could lack the skills and training needed to improve productivity in the longer term.

In a report on employment in each of the European Union 15 member states, Brussels said that more had to be done to live up to past promises on jobs and competitiveness.

Overall, the Commission said the EU had made 'marked progress' in the field, thanks to labour market reforms since 1997, as well as economic growth and budget discipline.

But it warned that the EU was 'lagging behind' its target of full employment by 2010 – by which it means an employment rate of 70 per cent for the population as a whole and 60 per cent for women.

According to its figures, dating from the end of last year, the proportion of people at work was 63 per cent overall and 54 per cent for women. Since then many countries have seen unemployment begin to rise again.

Commission officials said that, by virtue of its size, Germany was the key to achieving the targets, but the country needed to do more in improving training and tax incentives to bring more people into work. Even last year, when the economy grew at its fastest for a decade, employment fell in parts of eastern Germany.

Brussels also noted 'significant structural problems' in France, arguing that plans to extend the country's 35-hour week to smaller companies next year should be closely monitored. The concern is that 'smaller, less stable' companies will see their costs go up – with adverse effects on employment.

Other concerns are Spanish unemployment of 14.1 per cent, still much higher than the EU average of 8.1 per cent, and unemployment rates of 20 per cent in some southern parts of Italy.

By contrast, the Commission hailed Britain as one of four member states that had already met its definition of full employment, partly because of flexible working practices. But Brussels noted there were 'low levels of basic skills in the workforce' and called for a greater policy role for unions and employers groups.

The Essence of the Story

- Labour market reforms since 1997 have improved competitiveness in Europe's labour markets.

- But Europe is slow in reaching its target of full employment (70 per cent employment rate) by 2010.

- The employment-to-population ratio is 63 per cent overall, 54 per cent for women.

- Unemployment has begun to rise in Europe and it is noted that Germany and France continue to have structural problems.

- The UK satisfies the definition of full employment but is criticized for poor basic skills training.

Economic Analysis

- Unemployment in the large economies in continental Europe remains uncomfortably high and employment is still a long way from the full-employment target.

- Figure 1 shows that unemployment remains a pressing problem in the large EU economies of Germany, France and Italy.

- The European commission says that labour market reforms, training and tax incentives are needed to increase employment.

- Labour market reforms and tax incentives to take up low paid work will have the effect of shifting the *LS* curve in Figure 2 to the right from LS_0 to LS_1, increasing employment and reducing the natural rate of unemployment.

- An improvement in basic skills will increase the human capital of the labour force which will increase labour productivity. This will shift the *LD* curve to the right from LD_0 to LD_1.

- It is claimed that while unemployment in the UK is low, poor skills have meant that productivity has also remained low. Figure 3 shows that the productivity gap with the USA has improved only a little since 1995 but it has improved considerably with its partners in the EU.

- Figure 3 shows that UK labour productivity, measured as GDP per hour worked, has improved relative to the EU. So part of the reduction in unemployment in the UK is due to an improvement in labour productivity.

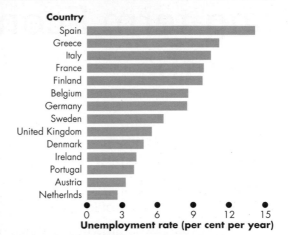

Figure 1 Unemployment in 2000

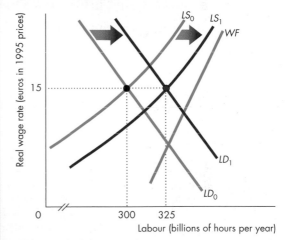

Figure 2 The labour market

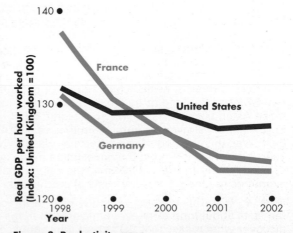

Figure 3 Productivity gaps

CHAPTER 30

Long-term Economic Growth

After studying this chapter you will be able to:

◆ Describe the long-term growth trends in the United Kingdom and other countries and regions

◆ Identify the main sources of long-term real GDP growth

◆ Explain the productivity growth slowdown during the 1970s and recovery in the 1980s

◆ Explain the rapid economic growth rates that have been achieved in East Asia

◆ Explain the theories of economic growth

◆ Describe the policies that might be used to speed up economic growth

Economic Miracles

Real GDP per person in the United Kingdom has more than doubled between 1960 and 2000. If you stay in a university residence, the chances are that it was built during the 1960s and equipped with two power points, one for a desk lamp and one for a bedside lamp. Today, with the help of a multi-plug (or two), your room bulges with a television and VCR, CD player, electric kettle and computer – the list goes on – which were not contemplated in the 1960s when the residence was built. What has brought about this growth in productivity and incomes? ◆ Although our economy expands, its growth is uneven. In some periods, such as the 1960s, growth is rapid. In other periods, such as the 1970s and early 1980s, growth slows down. What makes our long-term growth rate vary? What can be done to prevent growth from slowing down? And what can be done to speed up economic growth? ◆ We can see even greater extremes of economic growth if we look at modern Asia. On the banks of the Li River in southern China, Songman Yang breeds cormorants, amazing birds that he trains to fish and to deliver their catch to a basket on his simple bamboo raft. Songman's work, the capital equipment and technology he uses, and the income he earns are similar to those of his ancestors going back some 2,000 years. Yet all around Songman, in China's bustling towns and cities, people are participating in an economic miracle. They are creating businesses, investing in new technologies, developing both local and global markets, and experiencing income growth of more than 6 per cent a year. Similar rapid economic growth is taking place in other economies in Asia such as Hong Kong, South Korea, Singapore and Taiwan. In all these countries, real GDP has doubled *three times* – an eightfold increase – between 1960 and 1999. Why have incomes in these Asian economies grown so rapidly? What makes an economic miracle? In recent years growth in East Asia has slowed. In some countries real GDP has fallen as a result of the financial crisis in the Far East. Was this the end of the miracle or was it a temporary fall back that will be reversed in the coming years? It has been argued that investment in the new information technologies explains the rapid growth of productivity in the USA during the second half of 1990s. Reading Between the Lines (pp. 700–701) examines the 'new economy' view of productivity in the USA, in the light of recent revisions to the data.

◆ ◆ ◆ ◆ In this chapter we study long-term economic growth. We begin by looking more closely at the facts about long-term economic growth in the United Kingdom and other parts of the world. We then discover what makes real GDP grow, why some countries grow faster than others and why the long-term growth rate sometimes slows down. We'll also look at ways of achieving faster economic growth.

Long-term Growth Trends

The long-term growth trends that we study in this chapter are the trends in *potential GDP*. But potential GDP growth has two components, population growth and growth in potential GDP per person. It is the growth of potential GDP per person that brings rising living standards. And it is changes in the growth of potential GDP per person that are the main causes for concern about economic growth. Let's look at the growth of real GDP per person.

Growth in the UK Economy

Figure 30.1 shows real GDP per person in the United Kingdom for the 145 years from 1855 to 2000. The average growth rate over this entire period is 1.3 per cent a year. But the long-term growth rate has varied. For example, the long-term growth rate slowed during the 1970s to 1.8 per cent a year, down from 2.4 per cent a year during the 1960s. But growth picked up again in the 1980s and 1990s to 2.4 per cent a year.

You can see the recent productivity growth slow-down in a longer perspective in Figure 30.1, and you can see that it is not unique. The interwar period and the early years of the 1900s had even slower growth than we have today.

In the middle of the graph are two extraordinary events: the two recessions of the interwar period and the Second World War in the 1940s. The recession in the interwar period and the bulge during the war obscure changes in the long-term growth trend that might have occurred within these years. But between 1919 and 1953, averaging out the depression and the war, the long-term growth rate was 1.2 per cent a year.

A major goal of this chapter is to explain why our economy grows and why the long-term growth rate varies. A related goal is to explain variations in the economic growth rate across countries. Let's look at some facts about these variations.

Real GDP Growth in the World Economy

Figure 30.2 shows real GDP growth in the largest economies in the world since 1960. The data shown in this figure are from the Penn World Tables and are measured in a common currency (1985 US dollars). Part (a) looks at the richest countries. The United

---

Figure 30.1

A Hundred and Forty-five Years of Economic Growth in the United Kingdom

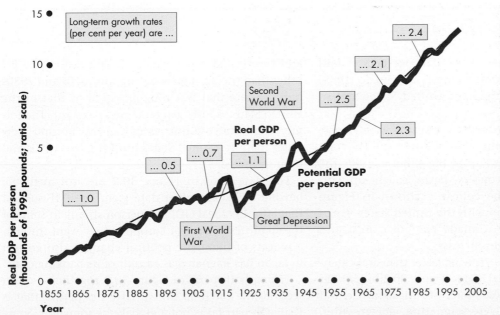

During the 145 years from 1855 to 2000, long-run real GDP per person in the United Kingdom grew by 1.3 per cent a year, on the average. The growth rate was above average during the 1950s, 1960s, 1980s and 1990s. It was below average in the 1900s, the interwar period and 1973–1979.

Source: Charles Feinstein, *National Income Expenditure and Output of the United Kingdom 1855–1965*, Cambridge, Cambridge University Press, 1972; National Statistics.

Figure 30.2

Economic Growth Around the World: Catch-up or Not?

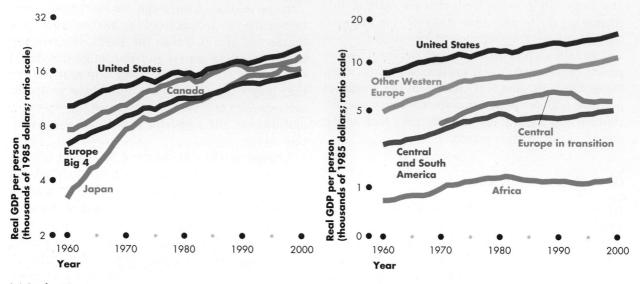

(a) Catch up?

(b) No catch up?

Real GDP per person has grown throughout the world economy. Among the rich industrial countries (part a), real GDP growth has been faster in low-income countries and income levels have converged. The most spectacular growth was in Japan during the 1960s. But Canada and the big four West European countries (the United Kingdom, France,

Germany and Italy) have got closer to the United States income level.

Among a wider range of countries (part b), there is less sign of convergence. The gaps between the income levels of the United States, West European countries, Central and Eastern Europe, Central and South America, and Africa have remained remarkably constant.

Sources: Robert Summers and Alan Heston, http://datacentre.chass.utoronto.ca/ 'The Penn World Table (Mark 5): An Expanded Set of International Comparisons, 1950–1988', *Quarterly Journal of Economics*, May 1991, 327–368.

States has the highest real GDP per person and Canada has the second highest. But up to 1989, Canada grew faster than the United States and so was catching up.

Until 1985, the third richest countries were France, Germany, Italy and the United Kingdom. They are shown in the figure as Europe Big 4. But in 1985, the fastest growing rich country, Japan, caught up with Europe Big 4. All the countries shown in Figure 30.2(a) are catching up with the United States. Japan has caught up most, Canada has got closest and Europe Big 4 has caught up least.

Not all countries are growing faster than and catching up with the United States. Figure 30.2(b) looks at some of these. The economies of Africa and Central and South America were stagnating, not growing, during the 1980s. As a result, the gap between them

and the United States widened. The rest of the EU other than the Big 4 grew during the 1970s and 1980s but at a rate that was roughly equal to that of the United States. So the gap remained constant. The former communist countries of Central Europe grew faster than the United States until the late 1980s and then stagnated.

The data used in Figure 30.2 are not available beyond 1992. But other data from the IMF suggest that after 1992 real GDP per person shrank in some of the countries of Central Europe as they went through a process of traumatic political change. Also growth in Japan has stagnated as a result of its banking crisis.

Taking both parts of Figure 30.2 together, we can see that the catch-up in real GDP per person that is visible in part (a) is not a global phenomenon. Some rich countries are catching up with the United States

Figure 30.3

Catch-up in Asia

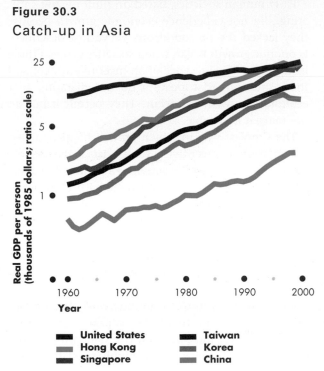

The clearest examples of catch-up have occurred in five economies in Asia. Starting out in 1960 with incomes as little as one-tenth of that in the United States, four Asian economies (Hong Kong, South Korea, Singapore and Taiwan) have substantially narrowed the gap on the United States. In 1996 from being a very poor developing country in 1960, China has caught up with the income level that Hong Kong had in 1960 and is growing at a rate that is enabling it to continue catching up with the United States.

Source: Robert Summers and Alan Heston, http://datacentre.chass.utoronto.ca/ to update The Penn World Table (Mark 5): An Expanded Set of International Comparisons, 1950–1988, *Quarterly Journal of Economics*, May 1991, 327–368.

United Kingdom's and 6 per cent of the United States's, but by 1998 it was 18 per cent of the United Kingdom's and 13 per cent of the United States's.

The four small Asian countries shown in Figure 30.3 are like fast trains running on the same track at similar speeds and with a roughly constant gap between them. Hong Kong is the lead train and runs about 12 years in front of Korea, which is the last train. Real GDP per person in Korea was similar to that of Hong Kong in 1978. In the 30 years between 1960 and 1990 Hong Kong transformed itself from a poor developing country into one of the world's richest countries.

The countries of East Asia have been badly affected by the financial crisis that broke out in 1997. Growth in the fastest growing economies has slowed and in 1997 output fell in a number of countries. It is difficult to predict how long the growth slowdown will last and when the countries of East Asia will revert to the fast pace of growth witnessed during the past decade. But as Figure 30.3 shows, their long-term growth has been spectacular.

Review Quiz

◆ What is the average rate of economic growth in the UK over the past one hundred and forty five years? In which periods was growth the most rapid and in which was it the slowest?

◆ Describe the gaps between the levels of real GDP per person in the EU Big 4 and other countries. For which countries are the gaps narrowing?

◆ Compare the growth rates and levels of real GDP per person in Hong Kong, Singapore, Taiwan, Korea, China, and the EU Big 4.

but the gaps between the United States and many poor countries are not closing.

There is another group of countries that in 1960 had low levels of real GDP per person and that are catching up with the United States and the other Western economies in a dramatic way. These are the economies of Hong Kong, South Korea, Singapore and Taiwan. Figure 30.3 shows how these economies are catching up with the United States. The figure also shows Asia's giant economy, China which is also catching up, but from a long way behind. In 1960 China's real GDP per person was 8 per cent of the

We've described some facts about economic growth in the developed economies and around the world. Our next task is to study the causes of economic growth. Economic growth is a complex process and its causes are difficult to discover. We'll study the causes of economic growth in three stages. First, we'll describe the sources of growth. Second, we'll study 'growth accounting', which is an attempt to measure the quantitative importance of the sources of growth. Third, we'll study the theories of economic growth that explain how the sources of growth interact to determine the growth rate.

The Sources of Economic Growth

Most human societies have lived for centuries and even thousands of years, with no economic growth. The key reason is that they have lacked some fundamental social institutions and arrangements that are essential preconditions for economic growth. Let's see what these preconditions are.

Preconditions for Economic Growth

The most basic precondition for economic growth is an appropriate *incentive* system. Three institutions are crucial to the creation of incentives. They are:

1 Markets.

2 Property rights.

3 Monetary exchange.

Markets enable buyers and sellers to get information and to do business with each other, and market prices send signals to buyers and sellers that create *incentives* to increase or decrease the quantities demanded and supplied. Markets enable people to specialize and trade and to save and invest. But to work well, markets need property rights and monetary exchange.

Property rights are the social arrangements that govern the ownership, use and disposal of factors of production and goods and services. They include the right to physical property (land, buildings and capital equipment), to financial property (claims by one person against another) and to intellectual property (such as inventions). Clearly established and enforced property rights give people an assurance that the income they earn and their savings will not be confiscated by a capricious government.

Monetary exchange facilitates transactions of all kinds, including the orderly transfer of private property from one person to another. Property rights and monetary exchange create incentives for people to specialize and trade, to save and invest, and to discover new technologies.

There is no unique political system that is necessary to deliver the preconditions for economic growth. Liberal democracy, founded on the fundamental principle of the rule of law, is the system that does the best job. It provides a solid base on which property rights can be established and enforced. But authoritarian political systems have sometimes provided an environment in which economic growth has occurred.

Early human societies, based on hunting and gathering, did not experience economic growth because they lacked the preconditions we've just described. Economic growth began when societies evolved these institutions. The presence of an incentive system and the institutions that create it do not guarantee that economic growth will occur. They permit it but do not make it inevitable.

The simplest way in which growth happens when the appropriate incentive system exists is that people begin to specialize in the activities at which they have a comparative advantage and trade with each other. You saw in Chapter 2, pp. 29–32, how everyone can gain from such activity. By specializing and trading, everyone can acquire goods and services at the lowest possible cost. Equivalently, everyone can obtain a greater volume of goods and services from their labour.

As an economy moves from one with little specialization to one that is highly specialized, it grows. Real GDP per person increases and the standard of living rises. But once the economy is highly specialized, this source of economic growth runs its course.

For growth to continue, people must face incentives that encourage them to pursue three activities that generate ongoing economic growth. These activities are:

1 Saving and investment in new capital.

2 Investment in human capital.

3 Discovery of new technologies.

These three sources of growth, which interact with each other, are the primary sources of the extraordinary growth in productivity during the past 200 years. Let's look at each in turn.

Saving and Investment in New Capital

Saving and investment in new capital increase the amount of capital per worker and increase human productivity. Human productivity took the most dramatic upturn when the amount of capital per worker increased during the Industrial Revolution. Production processes that use hand tools can create beautiful objects, but production methods that use large amounts of capital per worker, such as car plant assembly lines, are much more productive.

The accumulation of capital on farms, in textiles factories, in iron foundries and steel mills, in coal mines, on building sites, in chemical plants, in car plants, in banks and insurance companies, and in retail stores, have added incredibly to the productivity of our economy. From your knowledge of life 100 years ago try to imagine how productive you would be in such circumstances compared with your productivity today.

Investment in Human Capital

Human capital is fundamental to the growth process. The basic human skills of reading, writing and mathematics as well as knowledge of physical forces and chemical and biological processes are the foundation of all technological change.

But much human capital, which is extremely productive, is much more humble. It takes the form of millions of individuals learning and repetitively doing simple production tasks and becoming remarkably more productive in the task. One carefully studied example illustrates this kind of human capital. Between 1941 and 1944 (during the Second World War), US shipyards produced some 2,500 units of a cargo ship, called the Liberty Ship, to a standardized design. In 1941, it took 1.2 million person hours to build a ship. By 1942, it took 600,000, and by 1943, it took only 500,000. Thousands of workers and managers learned from experience and accumulated human capital that more than doubled their productivity in two years.

Discovery of New Technologies

People are many times more productive today than they were 100 years ago, not because we have more steam engines per person and more horse-drawn carriages per person, but because we have engines and transport equipment that use technologies unknown 100 years ago, which are more productive than those old technologies were. Technological change makes an enormous contribution to our increased productivity. It arises from formal research and development programmes and from informal trial and error, and it involves discovering ways of getting more out of our resources.

To reap the benefits of technological change, capital must increase. Some of the most powerful and far-reaching fundamental technologies are embodied in human capital – for example, language, writing and mathematics. But most technologies are embodied in physical capital. For example, to reap the benefits of the internal combustion engine, millions of horse-drawn carriages and horses had to be replaced by cars; and, more recently, to reap the benefits of computerized word processing, millions of typewriters had to be replaced by PCs.

Review Quiz

◆ How do markets, property rights, and monetary exchange facilitate economic growth? What are the economic activities that they make possible that lead to economic growth?
◆ What are the roles of saving and investment in new capital, the growth of human capital, and the discovery of new technologies in economic growth?
◆ Provide some examples of how human capital has created new technologies that are embodied in both human and physical capital.

We've described the sources of economic growth. Let's now see how we can begin to quantify their contributions by studying growth accounting.

Growth Accounting

Real GDP grows because the quantities of labour and capital grow and because technology advances. The purpose of **growth accounting** is to calculate how much real GDP growth has resulted from growth of labour and capital and how much is attributable to technological change.

The first task of growth accounting is to define productivity. **Productivity** is real GDP per hour of work. It is calculated by dividing real GDP by aggregate labour hours. (Chapter 20, pp. 429–432, explains how real GDP is measured and Chapter 21, pp. 450–451, explains how aggregate hours are measured.) We are interested in productivity because it determines how much income an hour of labour can earn. Figure 30.4 shows productivity for the period 1960–2000. In the 1960s productivity growth was 4.2 per cent a year. Between 1973 and 1979 it fell to 0.8 per cent per year. Productivity growth picked up again in the 1980s to 2.1 per cent and again to 2.5 per cent in the 1990s.

The second (and main) task of growth accounting is to explain the fluctuations in productivity. Growth accounting answers this question by dividing the growth in productivity into two components and then measuring the contribution of each. The components are:

Figure 30.4

Real GDP per Hour of Work

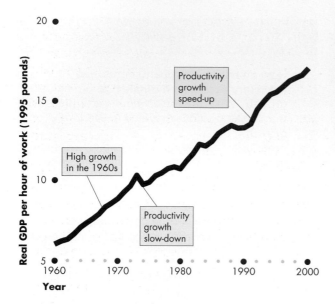

Real GDP divided by aggregate hours equals real GDP per hour of work, which is a broad measure of productivity. During the 1960s, the productivity growth rate was high. It slowed during the 1970s and speeded up again during the 1990s.

Sources: ONS, Labour Force Survey; R.C.O. Matthews, C.H. Feinstein and J.C. Odling-Smee, *British Economic Growth 1856–1953*, 1982, Oxford, Clarendon Press.

Figure 30.5

How Productivity Grows

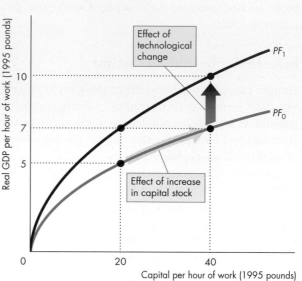

Productivity can be measured by real GDP per hour of work. Productivity can grow for two reasons: (1) capital per hour of work increases, and (2) technological advances occur. The productivity function, *PF*, shows the effects of an increase in capital per hour of work on productivity. Here, when capital per hour of work increases from £20 to £40, real GDP per hour of work increases from £5 to £7 along the productivity curve PF_0. Technological advance shifts the productivity curve upward. Here, an advance in technology shifts the productivity curve from PF_0 to PF_1. With this technological advance, real GDP per hour of work increases from £7 to £10 when there is £40 of capital per hour of work.

1 Growth in capital per hour of work.

2 Technological change.

The technological change includes everything that contributes to productivity growth. In particular, it includes human capital. Human capital growth and technological change are intimately interrelated. Technology advances because knowledge improves and knowledge is part of human capital.

The analytical engine of growth accounting is a relationship called the productivity function. Let's learn about this relationship and see how it is used.

The Productivity Function

The **productivity function** is the relationship that shows how real GDP per hour of work changes as the amount of capital per hour of work changes with no change in technology. Figure 30.5 illustrates the productivity function. Capital per hour of work is

measured on the *x*-axis and real GDP per hour of work is measured on the *y*-axis. The figure shows two productivity functions as the curves labelled PF_0 and PF_1.

An increase in the amount of capital per hour of work results in an increase in real GDP per hour of work, which is shown by a movement along a productivity function. For example, on the curve labelled PF_0, when capital per hour of work is £20, real GDP per hour of work is £5. As capital per hour of work increases to £40, real GDP per hour of work increases to £7.

Technological change increases the amount of GDP per hour of work that can be produced by a given amount of capital per hour of work. It is shown by an upward shift of the productivity function. For example, if capital per hour of work is £20 and a technological change increases real GDP per hour of work from £5 to £7, the productivity function shifts upward from PF_0 to PF_1 in Figure 30.5. Similarly, if capital per hour of work is £40, the same technological change increases real GDP per hour of work from £7 to £10 and shifts the productivity function upward from PF_0 to PF_1.

To calculate the contributions of capital growth and technological change to productivity growth, we need to know the shape and slope of the productivity function. The shape of the productivity function reflects a fundamental economic law – the law of diminishing returns. The **law of diminishing returns** states that as the quantity of one input increases with the quantities of all other inputs remaining the same, output increases but by ever smaller increments. You examined this phenomenon in Chapter 10, p. 200. For example, two typists working with one computer type fewer than twice as many pages per day as one typist working with one computer.

Applied to capital, the law of diminishing returns states that if a given number of hours of work use more capital (with the same technology), the additional output that results from the additional capital gets smaller as the amount of capital increases. One typist working with two computers types fewer than twice as many pages per day as one typist working with one computer. More generally, one hour of work working with £40 of capital produces less than twice the output of one hour of work working with £20 of capital. But how much less? The answer is given by the 'one-third rule'.

The One-third Rule

On the average, across all types of work, a 1 per cent increase in capital per hour of work, with no change in technology, brings a *one-third of 1 per cent* increase in output per hour of work. In the aggregate a 1 per cent increase in capital per hour of work, with no change in technology, brings a *one-third of 1 per cent* increase in real GDP per hour of work.

This one-third rule, which was first discovered by Robert Solow of the Massachusetts Institute of Technology (MIT), can be used to calculate the contributions of an increase in capital per hour of work and technological change to the growth of real GDP. Let's do such a calculation. Suppose that capital per hour of work grows by 3 per cent a year and real GDP grows by 2.5 per cent a year. The one-third rule tells us that capital growth has contributed one-third of 3 per cent, which is 1 per cent. The rest of the 2.5 per cent growth of real GDP comes from technological change. That is, technological change has contributed 1.5 per cent, which is the 2.5 per cent growth of real

GDP minus the estimated 1 per cent contribution of capital growth.

Why the One-third Rule

Why is the one-third rule used to separate contributions of capital growth and technological change to productivity growth? How do we know that one-third is the correct proportion? The answer is that we don't know for sure, but there is one strong piece of evidence pointing to one-third being the correct proportion. This evidence is the share of real GDP received by capital and labour.

A fundamental principle of economics is that factors of production receive incomes in proportion to their contributions to production. On the average, capital receives one-third of real GDP and labour receives two-thirds. (In 1997, for example, UK GDP was £677 billion and capital income was £250 billion,[1] nearly one-third of GDP.) If the factors of production are rewarded in proportion to their contributions, then a 1 per cent increase in capital brings a one-third of 1 per cent increase in real GDP. The one-third rule is based on historical experience. It is an average and not a hard and precise fixed number.

Accounting for the Productivity Growth Slowdown and Speed-up

We can use the productivity function and the one-third rule to study the reasons for the slowdown and subsequent speed-up of productivity growth in the United Kingdom. Figure 30.6 shows you what has been happening.

1950 to 1973

In 1950 capital per hour of work (measured in 1995 prices) was £13.70. Real GDP per hour of work was £5.50 at the point marked 50 on PF_0 in Figure 30.6. Over the next 23 years capital per hour grew at about 2.2 per cent a year to £22.69 and GDP per hour increased at about 2.8 per cent a year to £10.32. With no change in technology, the economy would have moved to point a at £6.70 (one-third of the percentage increase in capital per hour) on PF_0. But rapid technological change increased productivity and shifted the productivity function upward from PF_0 to PF_1. And the economy moved to the point marked 73.

---

[1] In current accounting practices, £250 is an overestimate as it includes the income from self-employment, which cannot easily be separated into labour and capital income.

Figure 30.6

Growth Accounting and the Productivity Growth Slowdown

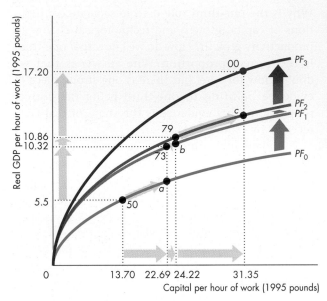

Between 1950 and 1973, which was a period of rapid growth in potential GDP, capital per hour of work increased from £13.70 to £22.69, and technological progress shifted the productivity function upward from PF_0 to PF_1. Between 1973 and 1979, when potential GDP grew slowly, capital per hour of work increased from £22.69 to £24.22 but the productivity function shifted slightly to PF_2. The technological change that occurred was absorbed by the negative effects of oil price shocks, change in the composition of output and X-inefficiency. Between 1979 and 2000, capital per hour of work increased from £24.22 to £31.35, and technological progress shifted the productivity function upward from PF_2 to PF_3. Although the growth in potential GDP was not as rapid as in the 1960s, the productivity growth rate did increase.

Sources: Figures derived from R.C.O. Matthews, C.H. Feinstein and J.C. Odling-Smee, *British Economic Growth 1856–1953*, 1982, Oxford, Clarendon Press; and A. Maddison, *Dynamic Forces in Capitalist Development*, 1991, Oxford, Oxford University Press; ONS, and the author's calculations.

1973 to 1979

The story continues between 1973 and 1979 when capital per hour of work increased from £22.69 in 1973 to £24.22 in 1979. This is an increase of 6.7 per cent. Real GDP per hour of work increased by 54 pence to £10.86, from £10.32 in 1973, which is a 5.2 per cent increase. This increase is slightly more than two-thirds of 6.7 per cent, so technological

change made a less significant contribution to real GDP growth during this period and the productivity function barely shifted from PF_1 to PF_2.

The reason for the productivity growth slowdown has now been isolated. It was not the result of slower growth in capital per hour of work. Rather it occurred because the contribution of technological change to real GDP growth dried up.

1979 to 2000

Between 1979 and 2000 technological change shifted the productivity function upward from PF_2 to PF_3. While real GDP per hour increased from £10.86 in 1979 to £17.20 in 2000 – a 58.4 per cent increase. Capital per hour of work increased from £24.22 to £31.35 – a 29.4 per cent increase in total. Using the one-third rule, the increase in capital per hour of work generated an extra real GDP per hour of work of roughly 19 per cent. Technological change contributed the remaining 39 per cent – roughly 1.6 per cent per year. Thus technological change resumed its contribution to productivity growth but at a slower pace than during the 1960s.

Technological Change During the Productivity Growth Slowdown

Technological change itself did not stop. On the contrary, there was a lot of it. But the technological change that occurred did not increase productivity. Instead, it offset negative shocks to productivity. We'll look at these negative factors below. We've seen that during the productivity growth slowdown of the 1970s, the contribution of technological change dried up. But why? Three factors have been identified as being responsible. They are:

1. Energy price shocks.
2. Changes in the composition of output.
3. X-inefficiency.

Energy Price Shocks

The price of oil quadrupled during 1973–74 and quickly on the tail of this increase, the prices of coal and natural gas – substitutes for oil – also increased dramatically. Energy prices increased sharply again in 1979–80.

The immediate effect of higher energy prices was an increase in the rate at which fuel-intensive cars, aircraft and heating systems were scrapped. But this effect shows up in Figure 30.6 as a leftward movement along the productivity function as capital per hour of work decreased. A longer drawn out effect was the development of new energy-saving technologies. Research and development efforts concentrated on developing new types of automobile and aircraft engines, heating furnaces and industrial processes that used fuel more sparingly than their predecessors. As a result, despite a huge amount of technological change and investment in new technologies, productivity did not increase. The new technologies produced a given amount of real GDP with a much smaller amount of fuel, but not with a smaller amount of capital per hour of work. So the productivity function did not shift upward.

Changes in the Composition of Output

During the 1950s and 1960s, a lot of our growth came from a movement of resources out of the farm sector into the small business sector. Farm productivity grows less quickly than small business productivity, so as resources move, average productivity grows quickly. During the 1970s and 1980s, the main movement of resources was out of manufacturing into services. Productivity growth in services is less than in manufacturing, so average productivity growth slowed. In the growth accounting exercise, this type of change shows up as a slowdown in aggregate productivity growth.

X-inefficiency

During the 1970s, trade union membership as a proportion of the employed labour force increased from 45 per cent to 59 per cent. The growth in union membership brought with it an increase in restrictive practices, overmanning and an increase in strikes. The period of the 1970s is characterized as one of X-inefficiency that contributed to the increasing productivity gap between the United Kingdom and other developed economies.

Review Quiz

◆ Explain the *one-third* rule and explain how the rule is used in growth accounting to isolate the contributions of capital growth and technological change to productivity growth.
◆ Explain how growth accounting can be used to provide information about the factors that contributed to the productivity growth slowdown.

Growth Theory

We've seen that real GDP grows when aggregate hours of work grow, when the quantity of capital per hour of work grows and when improvements in technology (including additions to human capital) bring increases in productivity. But what is the *cause* of economic growth and what is the *effect*?

The causes of economic growth are hard to unravel because so many factors interact with each other. Population growth might create pressures on land use which result in advances in plant biology which increase crop yields, and advances in architecture and building technology which increase building heights. Here, population growth causes technological change, which in turn causes saving and investment, which in turn brings economic growth. Alternatively, a surplus of saving might lower interest rates and bring an increase in the pace of investment in human capital and physical capital which speed up the growth rate. Here, saving and investment have caused economic growth. A lucky break might bring an unlooked for and unexpected technological advance which increases the productivity of labour and capital and causes a burst of saving and investment and rapid economic growth. Each of these possible sources of growth can operate. We must also examine the reasons why a country's long-term growth rate sometimes speeds up and sometimes slows.

We are going to look at three main theories of economic growth. All three contain some fundamental insights into the process of economic growth. But none gives a firm and sure answer to the basic question: what causes growth and makes growth rates vary? The three theories are:

1 Classical growth theory.
2 Neoclassical growth theory.
3 New growth theory.

Classical Growth Theory

Classical growth theory is a theory of economic growth based on the view that population growth is determined by the level of income per person. This theory was suggested by Adam Smith, Thomas Robert Malthus and David Ricardo, the leading economists of the late eighteenth century and early nineteenth century (see Economics in History, pp. 702–703).

Figure 30.7

Classical Growth Theory

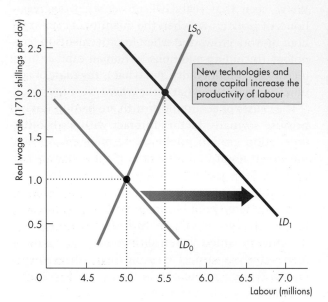

(a) Initial effect

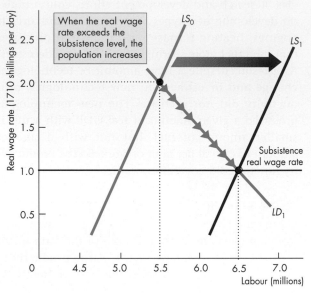

(b) Long-term effect

In classical growth theory, economic growth is temporary and the real wage rate keeps returning to the subsistence level. Initially, in part (a), the demand for labour is LD_0 and the supply of labour is LS_0. There are 5 million people employed and they earn 1 shilling a day. An advance in technology and an increase in capital increases the productivity of labour and the demand for labour increases to LD_1. The real wage rate rises to 2 shillings and the quantity of labour supplied increases to 5.5 million.

The real wage rate is now above the subsistence real wage, which in this example is 1 shilling a day. The population begins to increase. With an increase in population, the supply of labour increases and the labour supply curve shifts rightward to LS_1. As it does so, the real wage rate falls and the quantity of labour employed increases. The population stops growing when the real wage rate is back at the subsistence level.

To understand classical growth theory let's transport ourselves back to the world of 1710. Many of the 5.3 million people who lived in England at this time worked on farms or on their own land and performed their tasks using simple tools and animal power. They earned about 1 shilling and 4 pence for working a 10-hour day. Then advances in farming technology brought new types of ploughs and seeds that increased farm productivity. As farm productivity increased, farm production rose and some farm workers moved from the land to the cities, where they got work producing and selling the expanding range of farm equipment. Incomes rose and the people seemed to be prospering. But would the prosperity last? Classical growth theory says it would not.

Figure 30.7 illustrates classical growth theory and

explains why it reaches a pessimistic conclusion. Before growth begins, the economy is in the situation shown in part (a). The labour demand curve is LD_0 and the labour supply curve is LS_0. There is equilibrium in the labour market: the quantity of labour demanded equals the quantity supplied at a real wage rate of 1 shilling a day and 5 million people are employed. (We will use constant 1710 prices in this example to keep it in its historical context.)

Advances in technology – in both agriculture and industry – lead to investment in new capital and labour becomes more productive. More and more businesses start up and try to hire the now more productive labour. So the demand for labour increases and the labour demand curve shifts rightward to LD_1. With this greater demand for labour, the real wage rate rises from 1 shilling a day to 2 shillings a day and this higher wage rate causes an increase in the quantity of labour supplied (a movement along the labour supply curve). In the new situation, 5.5 million people are employed.

At this stage, economic growth has occurred and everyone has benefited from it. Real GDP has increased and real wages have also increased. But the classical economists believed that this new situation could not last and would be disturbed because it would induce an increase in the population.

Classical Theory of Population Growth

The classical theory of population growth is based on the idea of a **subsistence real wage rate**. The subsistence real wage rate is the minimum real wage rate needed to maintain life. By its definition, if the actual real wage rate is less than the subsistence real wage rate, some people cannot survive and the population decreases. But in the classical theory, whenever the real wage rate exceeds the subsistence real wage rate, the population grows. This assumption, combined with the diminishing marginal product of labour, has a dismal implication – one that resulted in economics being called the *dismal science*. This implication is that no matter how much investment and technological change occurs, real wage rates are always pushed towards the subsistence level.

Figure 30.7(b) shows this process. Here, the subsistence real wage rate is (by assumption) 1 shilling a day. The actual real wage rate, at the intersection of LS_0 and LD_1, is 2 shillings a day. Because the actual real wage rate exceeds the subsistence real wage rate, the population grows and the labour supply increases. The labour supply curve shifts rightward to LS_1. As it does so, the real wage rate falls and the quantity of labour increases. Eventually, in the absence of further technological change, the economy comes to rest at the subsistence real wage rate of 1 shilling a day and 6.5 million people are employed.

The economy has grown, real GDP is higher and a larger population is earning the subsistence wage rate. But the benefits of economic growth have gone to the suppliers of capital and the entrepreneurs who have put the new technology to work.

The Modern Theory of Population Growth

When the classical economists were developing their ideas about population growth, a population explo-

sion was under way. In the United Kingdom and other West European countries, advances in medicine and hygiene had lowered the death rate but the birth rate remained high. For several decades, population growth was extremely rapid. But eventually the birth rate fell and while the population continued to increase, its rate of increase was moderate.

The population growth rate is influenced by economic factors. For example, the birth rate has fallen as women's wage rates have increased and job opportunities have expanded. Also the death rate has fallen as greater investment has been made in advances in medicine. But despite the influence of economic factors, to a good approximation, the rate of population growth is independent of the rate of economic growth. To the extent that there is a connection, as incomes increase, the population growth rate eventually decreases. This inverse relation between real income growth and the population growth rate is contrary to the assumption of the classical economists and it invalidates their conclusions.

Neoclassical Growth Theory

Neoclassical growth theory is the proposition that real GDP per person grows because technological change induces savings and investment. Technological change is the fundamental cause of growth. This theory was suggested during the 1950s by Robert Solow of MIT. In the neoclassical theory, the rate of technological change influences the rate of economic growth. But economic growth does not influence the rate of technological change. Rather, technological change is determined by chance. When we are lucky, we have rapid technological change, and when bad luck strikes, the pace of technological advance slows down. But there is nothing we can do to influence its pace.

At the heart of the neoclassical growth theory is the stock of capital and the *productivity function* – the relationship between capital per unit of labour and output per unit of labour. For simplicity, the theory assumes that people work a fixed number of hours and that everyone works. So labour equals population. The faster the capital stock per person grows, the faster real GDP and income per person grow. But what determines the growth rate of the capital stock per person? The answer is the demand for and supply of capital per person.

Figure 30.8

Neoclassical Growth Theory

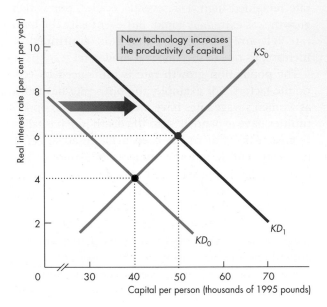

(a) Initial effect

(b) Long-term effect

In neoclassical growth theory, economic growth results from technological change. In the absence of technological change, real GDP per person converges to a constant level. Initially, in part (a), the demand for capital is KD_0 and the supply of capital is KS_0. The capital stock is £40,000 per person and the real interest rate is 4 per cent a year. An advance in technology increases the productivity of capital and the demand for capital increases to KD_1. The real interest rate rises to 6 per cent a year and the quantity of capital supplied increases to £50,000.

The real interest rate is now above the rate of time preference, which in this example is 4 per cent a year (part b). Saving is positive and the supply of capital increases. The capital supply curve shifts rightward to KS_1. As it does so, the real interest rate falls and the quantity of capital per person increases. The quantity of capital per person stops growing when the real interest rate is back at the rate of time preference.

The Demand for and Supply of Capital per Person

Figure 30.8 illustrates the neoclassical growth theory by showing how the demand for and supply of capital determine the capital stock and its growth rate. In this figure, we measure the capital stock per person on the x-axis and the real interest rate on the y-axis. The demand for capital and the supply of capital are determined by investment and saving decisions. Briefly, the lower the real interest rate, the larger is the number of capital projects that are profitable and the greater is the demand for capital. On the other hand, in the short run, the lower the interest rate, the less strong is the incentive to save, rather than consume, and the smaller is the supply of capital.

In Figure 30.8, the demand for capital is shown by

the downward-sloping KD_0 curve in part (a). Along this curve, as the real interest rate falls, other things remaining the same, the quantity of capital demanded increases. The supply of capital is shown by the upward-sloping KS_0 curve. Along this curve, as the real interest rate falls, other things remaining the same, the quantity of capital supplied decreases.

The real interest rate adjusts to achieve an equilibrium in which the quantity of capital demanded equals the quantity supplied. In Figure 30.8, the economy is in equilibrium at a real interest rate of 4 per cent a year and with a capital stock of £40,000 per person, shown in part (a). In the absence of technological change, capital per person converges to its equilibrium level. As a result, real GDP per person converges to a constant level and there is no economic growth.

Figure 30.9

New Growth Theory

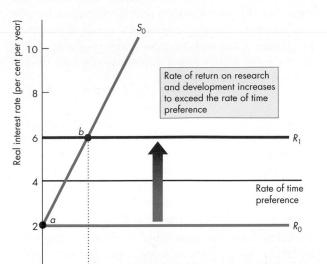

(a) Growth begins

(b) Knowledge capital grows

In new growth theory, economic growth results from *endogenous* technological change. The returns to knowledge capital do not diminish and growth proceeds indefinitely. Initially, in part (a), the rate of return on knowledge capital is R_0 and the supply of knowledge capital is S_0. The stock of knowledge capital is zero. The development of the scientific method and the creation of research and development organizations increases the rate of return on knowledge capital to R_1. The real interest rate rises to 6 per cent a year and the quantity of knowledge capital supplied increases to £100 billion.

The real interest rate is now above the rate of time preference, which in this example is 4 per cent a year. Saving is positive and the supply of knowledge capital increases. The knowledge capital supply curve shifts rightward successively to S_1, S_2, S_3, and so on. As it does so, the economy grows but the real interest rate does not fall because there are no diminishing returns to knowledge capital. Growth continues as long as the rate of return on knowledge capital exceeds the rate of time preference.

But with technological change, real GDP per person grows. Figure 30.9 illustrates this growth process. A technological advance increases the productivity of capital and the demand for capital increases. The capital demand curve shifts rightward to KD_1. The greater demand for capital raises the real interest rate to 6 per cent a year and the higher real interest rate causes an increase in saving. The quantity of capital supplied increases to £50,000 per person.

The economy has experienced a period of economic growth. Because the capital stock per person has increased, output per person has increased. Also, labour has become more productive and the demand for labour has increased, bringing an increase in real wages and employment. But economic growth continues beyond the point shown in Figure 30.9(a). To understand why, we need to look at the neoclassical theory of saving.

Neoclassical Theory of Saving

The neoclassical theory of saving is based on the idea called a constant rate of time preference. The **rate of time preference** is the target real interest rate that savers want to achieve. If the real interest rate exceeds the rate of time preference, saving is positive and the supply of capital increases. If the real interest rate is less than the rate of time preference, saving is negative and the supply of capital decreases. If the real interest rate equals the rate of time preference, people are happy with the amount of wealth they have accumulated and saving is zero.

Figure 30.8(b) illustrates the consequences of a constant rate of time preference. Here, the rate of time preference is 4 per cent a year. So when the real interest rate rises to 6 per cent a year, saving is positive and the supply of capital increases. The capital supply curve shifts rightward towards KS_1. As the supply of capital increases, the real interest rate falls and the quantity of capital demanded increases. Eventually, the economy reaches the point at which the real interest rate has fallen to equal the rate of time preference. At this point, saving is zero and the supply of capital is constant.

Throughout the process just described, real GDP per person has been increasing. The capital stock per person and real wage rates have also been increasing. The economy has experienced long-term growth.

Ongoing advances in technology are constantly increasing the demand for capital and raising the real interest rate above the rate of time preference. The process we've just examined repeats indefinitely to create an ongoing process of long-term economic growth.

Problems with Neoclassical Growth Theory

Neoclassical growth theory tells us how capital accumulation and saving interact to determine the economy's growth rate. But the growth rate itself depends on the *exogenous* rate of technological change. We need to go one step further and determine the rate of technological change.

Because all economies have access to the same technologies, and because capital is free to roam the world seeking the highest available rate of return, neoclassical growth theory predicts that growth rates and income levels per person will converge. While there is some sign of convergence among the rich countries (shown in Figure 30.2a), convergence does not appear to be present for all countries (as we saw in Figure 30.2b).

New growth theory attempts to overcome these two shortcomings of neoclassical growth theory.

New Growth Theory

New growth theory is a theory of economic growth based on the idea that technological change results from the choices that people make. (New growth theory is sometimes called *endogenous growth theory*.) New growth theory starts with two facts about market economies:

1 Discoveries result from choices and actions.

2 Discoveries bring profits, and competition destroys profit.

Discoveries and Choices

When someone discovers a new product or technique, they think of themselves as being lucky. They are right. But the pace at which new discoveries are made – at which technology advances – is not determined by chance. It depends on how many people are looking for a new way of doing something and how intensively they are looking.

Discoveries and Profits

The spur to seeking new and better ways of producing is profit. The forces of competition are constantly squeezing profits, so to make a profit greater than the average, a person must constantly seek out either lower-cost methods of production or new and better products for which people are willing to pay a higher price. Inventors can maintain a profit for several years by taking out a patent or a copyright. But eventually, a new discovery is copied and profits disappear.

Two further facts play a key role in the new growth theory:

1 Discoveries can be used by many people at the same time.

2 Physical activities can be replicated.

Discoveries Used by All

Once a profitable new discovery has been made, it is difficult to prevent others from copying it. But also, unlike inputs such as labour and capital, it can be used by everyone who knows about it without reducing its availability to others. This means that as the benefits of a new discovery are dispersed through the economy, resources are made available free to those who reap the benefit but didn't pay the price of making the discovery. But there is more.

Replicating Activities

Replicas can be made of many (perhaps most) production activities. For example, there might be two, three or 53 identical firms making fibre optic cable using an identical assembly line and production technique. This means that the economy as a whole does not experience diminishing returns. (Each firm experiences diminishing returns but the economy does not.)

These features of the economy can be summarized in the neat idea that knowledge – the stock of productive ideas that has been accumulated as a result of research and development efforts – is a special kind of capital that can be used by all and whose marginal product does not diminish. The implication of this simple and appealing idea is shown in Figure 30.9, which illustrates new growth theory. In this figure, we measure the knowledge capital stock on the x-axis and the real interest rate on the y-axis.

The supply of knowledge capital is shown by the upward-sloping S_0 curve. Along this curve, as the real interest rate rises, other things remaining the same, the quantity of saving and of resources devoted to accumulating knowledge capital increases.

Because the marginal product of knowledge capital does not diminish, the demand for knowledge capital does not slope downward like the demand curve for other types of capital. If knowledge capital yields a higher return than the rate of time preference, the quantity of knowledge capital demanded is unlimited. And if knowledge capital yields a lower return than the rate of time preference, then the demand for knowledge capital is zero.

Initially, before growth begins, the marginal product of knowledge capital is 2 per cent a year, shown by the horizontal line, R_0 in Figure 30.9(a). At this rate of return, and given the supply of knowledge capital curve, the economy is in equilibrium at a real interest rate of 2 per cent a year and has no knowledge capital. The economy is stuck at point a.

The invention of such basic tools as language and writing (the two most basic pieces of knowledge capital), and later the development of the scientific method and the establishment of communities of scientists, inventors and research institutions. The rate of return line shifted upward to R_1. The initial effect of this increase in the return on knowledge capital was to increase the real interest rate to 6 per cent a year and to cause an increase in the quantity of knowledge capital supplied (to £100 billion in the figure). The economy moved to point b.

The economy has experienced a period of economic growth. Because the stock of knowledge capital has increased, real GDP has increased. But economic growth continues and it continues indefinitely. The reason is that the real interest rate now exceeds the rate of time preference. So saving is positive and the supply of capital (which includes knowledge capital) increases.

Figure 30.9(b) illustrates the process. The rate of time preference is 4 per cent a year and the rate of return on knowledge capital is 6 per cent a year. With positive saving, the supply curve shifts rightward and continues to do so indefinitely. The speed with which

the saving supply curve shifts rightward depends on the extent to which the real interest rate exceeds the rate of time preference. The higher the marginal productivity of knowledge capital, the higher is the real interest rate and the faster the saving curve shifts rightward, so the faster the economy grows.

Unlike the neoclassical theory, with its diminishing marginal productivity of capital, which eventually lowers the real interest rate to the rate of time preference, there is no such mechanism at work in the new growth theory. Real GDP per person increases and does so indefinitely as long as people can undertake research and development that yields a higher return than the rate of time preference.

New growth theory sees the economy as a kind of perpetual motion mechanism. Economic growth is driven by our insatiable wants that lead us to pursue profit and innovate. The result of this process is new and better products. But new and better products result in firms going out of business and new firms starting up. In this process, jobs are destroyed and created. The outcome is more consumption, new and better jobs, and more leisure. All this adds up to a higher standard of living. But our insatiable wants are still there: profits, innovation, new products and higher living standards.

The economy's growth rate depends on people's ability to innovate, the rate of return to innovation and the rate of time preference, which influences the rate of saving.

Review Quiz

- What are the factors that contribute to economic growth?
- What is the central idea of classical growth theory that leads to the dismal outcome?
- Explain the mechanism at work in the classical growth theory and describe the role played by diminishing returns.
- What, according to the neoclassical growth theory, is the fundamental cause of economic growth?
- What is the key proposition of the new growth theory that makes growth persist? Is the proposition believable? Is the conclusion believable?

Your final task in this chapter is to examine the policy actions that might be taken to speed up the growth rate.

Achieving Faster Growth

To achieve faster economic growth, we must either increase the growth rate of capital per hour of work or increase the pace of technological advance (which includes improving human capital).

The main suggestions for achieving faster economic growth are:

◆ Stimulate saving.

◆ Stimulate research and development.

◆ Target high-technology industries.

◆ Encourage international trade.

◆ Improve the quality of education and training.

Stimulate Saving

Saving finances investment, which brings capital accumulation and economic growth. So stimulating saving can also stimulate economic growth. Up until recent years, China, Hong Kong, Japan, South Korea, Singapore and Taiwan have experienced the highest growth rates. They also have the highest saving rates. Some countries of Africa have the lowest growth rates. They also have the lowest saving rates. The saving rates in the European Union and the other rich countries are modest.

The most obvious way in which saving could be increased is by providing tax incentives. Some incentives already exist, but more radical measures are possible. For example, instead of taxing incomes (which means taxing both consumption and saving), we could tax only consumption. Such a tax would encourage additional saving and probably increase the economy's growth rate.

Stimulate Research and Development

Patents protect inventors and provide incomes that give incentives to research and development. But everyone can use the fruits of *basic* research and development efforts. For example, VisiCalc invented the basic idea of the spreadsheet, but it did not take long for Lotus Corporation to use this idea to develop the famous 1–2–3, and for Microsoft Corporation to bring out a Lotus 1–2–3 lookalike, Excel. Because basic inventions can be copied, the inventor's profit is limited. For this reason, the free market allocates too few resources to basic research.

This situation is one in which government subsidies might help. By using public funds to finance basic research and development that bring social benefits, it might be possible to encourage an efficient level of research. But the solution is not foolproof. The main problem is that some mechanism must be designed for allocating the public funds. The universities and research councils are the main channels through which public funds in the United Kingdom are used to finance research.

Target High-technology Industries

It is argued by some people that by providing public funds to high-technology firms and industries, a country can become the first to exploit a new techology and can earn above average profits for a period while others are busy catching up. But this strategy can be risky and can just as likely to use resources inefficiently as to speed up growth.

Encourage International Trade

Free international trade stimulates growth by extracting all the available gains from specialization and exchange. It is no accident that the fastest growing countries today are those with the fastest growing international trade – both exports and imports.

Improve the Quality of Education and Training

Education and training, like basic research, brings benefits to people other than those who have received the education. By its nature, education is a good the value of which is fully appreciated only after receiving it. Like basic research the free market underprovides education and training. By funding basic education and training in skills such as language, mathematics, science and technology, the government can contribute to a nation's growth potential.

In this chapter, we've studied the sources of economic growth, learned how we can measure the contributions of hours, capital and technological change, and we've studied the theories of economic growth. Finally, we've seen some policy actions that might speed up growth rates. Economic growth is the single most decisive factor in influencing a country's living standard, but it is not the only one. Another is the extent to which the country fully employs its scarce resources, especially its labour. In recent years, unemployment has become a severe problem for many countries. In the next chapter we study the fluctuations of real GDP, employment and unemployment around their long-term trends.

Summary

Key Points

Long-term Growth Trends (pp. 681–683)

- Between 1855 and 2000, real GDP per person in the United Kingdom grew at an average rate of 1.3 per cent a year.
- Catch-up in real GDP per person occurs sometimes but it is not a global phenomenon. The United States is still the richest country. Some rich countries are catching up with the United States, but the gaps between the United States and many poor countries are not closing.
- Hong Kong, South Korea, Singapore, Taiwan and China are catching up the fastest but their catch-up has been interrupted by the Asian crisis of 1997.

The Sources of Economic Growth (pp. 684–685)

- Economic growth occurs when an *incentive* system, which is created by markets, property rights and monetary exchange, encourages saving and investment in new capital, the growth of human capital and the discovery of new technologies.
- Saving and investment in new capital, human capital accumulation and technological advances interact to increase production and raise living standards and they are the main sources of economic growth.

Growth Accounting (pp. 685–689)

- Growth accounting measures the contributions of capital accumulation and technological change to productivity growth.
- The analytical engine of growth accounting is the productivity function, which is the relationship between real GDP per hour of work and capital per hour of work, holding technology constant.
- The contributions of capital growth and technological change to productivity growth are estimated by using the *one-third rule* – a 1 per cent increase in capital per hour of work brings a one-third of 1 per cent increase in real GDP per hour of work.
- Growth accounting isolates the reason for the productivity growth slowdown of the 1970s. Technological change made hardly any contribution to real GDP growth.

Growth Theory (pp. 689–695)

- The three main theories of economic growth are the classical theory, the neoclassical theory and the new growth theory.

- The classical theory is that the population grows whenever incomes rise above the *subsistence* level and declines whenever incomes fall below the subsistence level. This assumption, combined with the diminishing marginal product of labour, implies that incomes are always pushed towards the subsistence level.
- The neoclassical growth theory is that the long-term growth rate is determined by the rate of technological change, which in turn is determined by chance.
- New growth theory is that the growth rate depends on the costs and benefits of developing new technologies.

Achieving Faster Growth (p. 696)

- To achieve faster economic growth, we must increase the growth of capital per hour of work or increase the pace of technological advance.
- It might be possible to achieve faster growth by stimulating saving, subsidizing research and development, targeting (and possibly subsidizing) high-technology industries, encouraging more international trade and encouraging more education and training.

Key Figures ◆

Key Terms

Problems

•1 The following information has been discovered about the economy of Longland: The economy's productivity function is:

Capital per hour of work (1995 pounds per hour)	Real GDP per hour of work (1995 pounds per hour)
10	3.80
20	5.70
30	7.13
40	8.31
50	9.35
60	10.29
70	11.14
80	11.94

Does this economy conform to the one-third rule? If so, explain why. If not, explain why not and explain what rule, if any, it does conform to. Explain how you would do the growth accounting for this economy.

2 The following information has been discovered about the economy of Flatland: the economy's productivity function is:

Capital per hour of work (1995 pounds per hour)	Real GDP per hour of work (1995 pounds per hour)
10	3.00
20	3.75
30	4.22
40	4.57
50	4.86
60	5.10
70	5.31
80	5.50

Does this economy conform to the one-third rule? If so, explain why. If not, explain why not and explain what rule, if any, it does conform to. Explain how you would do the growth accounting for this economy.

•3 In Longland, described in problem 1, capital per hour of work in 1999 was £40 and real GDP per hour of work was £8.31. In 2001, capital per hour of work had increased to £50 and real GDP per hour of work had increased to £10.29 an hour.

a Does Longland experience diminishing returns? Explain why or why not.

b Use growth accounting to find the contribution of the change in capital between 1999 and 2001 to the growth of productivity in Longland.

c Use growth accounting to find the contribution of technological change between 1999 and 2001 to the growth of productivity in Longland.

4 In Flatland, described in problem 2, capital per hour of work in 1999 was £30 and real GDP per hour of work was £4.22. In 2001, capital per hour of work had increased to £60 and real GDP per hour of work had increased to £6.37 an hour.

a Does Flatland experience diminishing returns? Explain why or why not.

b Use growth accounting to find the contribution of the change in capital between 1999 and 2001 to the growth of productivity in Flatland.

c Use growth accounting to find the contribution of technological change between 1999 and 2001 to the growth of productivity in Flatland.

•5 The following information has been discovered about the economy of Cape Despair. The subsistence real wage rate is £7 an hour. Whenever the real wage rate rises above this level the population grows, and when the real wage rate falls below this level the population decreases. With its current population, the demand and supply schedules for labour in Cape Despair are:

Real wage rate (1995 pounds per hour)	Quantity of labour demanded (billions of hours per year)	Quantity of labour supplied (billions of hours per year)
3	8	4
5	7	5
7	6	6
9	5	7
11	4	8
13	3	9
15	2	10
17	1	11

Initially, the labour force of Cape Despair is constant, and the real wage is at its subsistence level. Then a technological advance increases the amount that firms are willing to pay for labour by £2 at each level of employment.

a What is the initial level of employment and real wage rate in Cape Despair?

b What happens to the real wage rate immediately following the technological advance?

c What happens to the population growth rate following the technological advance?

d What is the employment level when Cape Despair returns to a long-run equilibrium?

6 Martha's Island is an economy that behaves according to the neoclassical growth model. The economy is in long-run equilibrium and is described in the following table.

Real interest rate (percent per year)	Quantity of capital demanded (billions of dollars)	Quantity of capital (billions of dollars)
1	9	7
2	8	7
3	7	7
4	6	7
5	5	7
6	4	7
7	3	7
8	2	7

a What is the initial real interest rate on Martha's Island?

b What is the target rate?

A technological advance increases the demand for capital £2 billion at each real interest rate.

c What is the real interest rate immediately following the technological advance?

d What is the real interest rate and quantity of capital when Martha's Island returns to a long-run equilibrium?

•7 Romeria is a country that behaves according to the predictions of new growth theory. The target rate is 3 per cent a year. A technological advance increases the demand for capital and raises the real interest rate to 5 per cent a year. Describe the events that happen in Romeria and contrast them with the events in Martha's Island in problem 6.

8 Suppose that in Romeria, which is described in problem 7, technological advance slows and the real interest rate falls to 3 per cent a year. Describe what happens in Romeria.

Critical Thinking

1 After studying Reading Between the Lines on pp. 700–701, answer the following questions:

a What is the 'new economy' argument for the productivity miracle of the USA in the 1990s?

b Real GDP in 2000 was $9,224 billion in 1996 prices. What is the real value of the downward revision in GDP growth in 2000?

c Assuming that potential GDP is $9,224 billion, what would potential GDP be in 2010 if the growth of potential GDP was 4 per cent a year? Now work it out for 3 per cent a year.

2 Visit the Penn World Table website (linked from the Parkin, Powell and Matthews website) and obtain data on real GDP per person for the United States, China, South Africa and Mexico since 1960.

a Draw a graph of the data.

b Which country has the lowest real GDP per person and which has the highest?

c Which country has experienced the fastest growth rate since 1960 and which the slowest?

d Explain why the growth rates in these four countries are ranked in the order you have discovered?

e Return to the Penn World Table website and obtain data for any four other countries that interest you. Describe and explain the patterns that you find for these countries.

Productivity and Growth

THE FINANCIAL TIMES, 3 AUGUST 2001 **FT**

A miracle revised

Gerard Baker

Last week, the Commerce Department published its annual revisions to previous estimates of national income and output.

Most strikingly, the government's statisticians lopped sizeable chunks off their earlier estimates of the economy's overall growth in the past three years, reducing the US's estimated annual output by $90 bn (£63 bn) – 1 per cent of total output – last year. The data also included a sharp downward revision to estimates of corporate profits over the past three years.

Neither set of changes was large enough to undermine seriously most economists' faith in what is now the conventional US economic history of the late 1990s – that a surge of investment in new technologies fostered an improvement in the economy's underlying growth potential. But the new figures suggest that earlier estimates of the scale of that change were seriously over-optimistic.

Instead of expanding at a rate of 5 per cent in 2000 – the fastest annual rate of growth in a decade – output grew by 4.1 per cent. Growth estimates for the previous two years were also revised down, although by much smaller amounts.

The overall growth trend for the years 1997–2000 thus changes noticeably. Instead of three years from 1997 to 1999 of steady growth of 4 per cent, followed by a leap to 5 per cent in 2000, there was more or less steady expansion at around 4 per cent throughout the four-year period.

This statistical revision not only reduces the economy's average growth rate in the four-year period – generally regarded as the 'miracle years' of new economy-induced accelerated productivity – from 4.5 to 4.1 per cent. It also lowers plausible estimates of the sustainable rate of US growth.

The new figures suggest that it was the 4 per cent rate of expansion over the past four years that proved unsustainable and resulted in the fall-out of the last year. This indicates that the sustainable rate of growth is probably no more than 3.5 per cent. It would still be an improvement on the average annual rate of around 2.6 per cent for most of the previous 25 years but not as dramatic as some new economy proponents have claimed.

Looking at aggregate rates of growth is a crude way of measuring potential output growth. More reliable are the productivity figures and the different picture formed by the new data is evident here too. Since labour productivity is output divided by hours worked, if output falls, productivity will also fall.

The effect would be to bring output-per-hour growth in 2000 back into line with the trend of the previous three years – a little over 2.5 per cent per year.

The new estimates point out an improvement rather than a transformation in US economic performance in the past few years. Productivity growth increased from its 25 year trend of 1.3 per cent per year to perhaps double that but no faster.

The Essence of the Story

- The US Commerce Department has published revised figures for real GDP and corporate profits.

- The revised figures show that growth in the US in the four years to 2000 was less than originally thought.

- The new figures still show that the growth of potential output was higher than historic trends.

- The revisions have not altered the conventional view that investment in new technology has increased productivity and the growth of potential output.

Economic Analysis

- The Chairman of the Federal Reserve, Alan Greenspan, among others, has long held the view that productivity in the 1990s has been boosted by investment in information technology.

- Investment in IT increases the capital stock, which brings higher productivity. Business investment in the USA has grown from under 9 per cent of GDP in 1990 to over 15 per cent in 2000.

- The proponents of the 'new economy' view argue that the increase in the amount of IT capital per worker have accounted for two-fifths of the total increase in productivity growth since 1995.

- The technological effect of more investment in IT is shown in Figure 1 as an improvement in technological change. In Figure 1, the effect of technological change is to shift the productivity function up from PF_0 to PF_1.

- The recent revisions to the data has shown a reduced rate of growth of GDP for 1998–2000. Figure 2 shows that real GDP instead of expanding at the phenomenal rate of 5 per cent a year, output has grown by 4.1 per cent in 2000.

- Figure 3 shows the old productivity growth figures and the revised figures. The recent figures suggest that the annual average rate of growth of productivity has been revised down to 2.5 per cent in the five years to 2000. But this is still well above the 1.5 per cent recorded in the first half of the 1990s.

- The recent productivity gains have been exaggerated by the surge in business investment in IT which has gone into reverse. The revisions to corporate profits have shown that profit expectations have been over exuberant.

- Realistic profit expectations have resulted in a sharp fall in share prices and a fall in business investment suggesting that underlying productivity after taking out the cyclical effect is around 2 to 2.25 per cent.

- Adding 0.7 per cent for the rate of growth of population produces a growth of potential output in the order of 3 per cent rather than the 4 per cent the 'new economy' supporters have been saying, which still leaves room for an IT based explanation of the improvement in productivity growth.

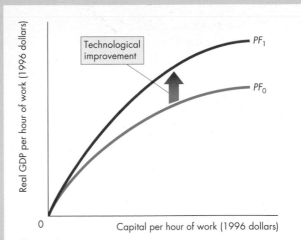

Figure 1

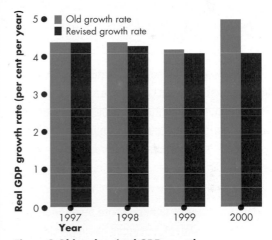

Figure 2 Old and revised GDP growth

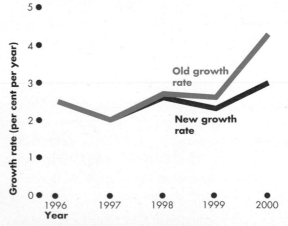

Figure 3 Non-farm business productivity

Economic Growth

Economic progress, in capitalist society, means turmoil.

Joseph Schumpeter, Capitalism, Socialism and Democracy

The Economist: Joseph Schumpeter

Joseph Schumpeter, the son of a textile factory owner, was born in Austria in 1883. He moved from Austria to Germany during the tumultuous 1920s when those two countries experienced hyperinflation and in 1932, in the depths of the Great Depression, he came to the United States and became a professor of economics at Harvard University.

This creative economic thinker wrote on economic growth and development, business cycles, political systems and economic biography. He was a person of strong opinions who expressed them strongly and delighted in verbal battles.

Schumpeter has become the unwitting founder of modern growth theory. He saw the development and diffusion of new technologies by profit-seeking entrepreneurs as the source of economic progress. But he saw economic progress as a process of creative destruction – the creation of new profit opportunities and the destruction of currently profitable businesses. For Schumpeter, economic growth and the business cycle were a single phenomenon.

When Schumpeter died in 1950, he had achieved his self-expressed life's ambition: he was regarded as the world's greatest economist.

The Issues and Ideas

Technological change, capital accumulation and population growth all interact to produce economic growth. But what is cause and what is effect, and can we expect productivity and income per person to keep growing?

The classical economists of the eighteenth and nineteenth centuries believed that technological advances and capital accumulation were the engines of growth. But they also believed that no matter how successful people were at inventing more productive technologies and investing in new capital, they were destined to live at the subsistence level. These economists based their conclusion on the belief that productivity growth causes population growth, which in turn causes productivity to decline. These classical economists believed that whenever economic growth raises incomes above the subsistence level, the population will increase. And they went on to reason that the increase in population brings diminishing returns that lower productivity. As a result, incomes must always return to the subsistence level. Only when incomes are at the subsistence level is population growth held in check.

A new approach, called neoclassical growth theory, was developed by Robert Solow of MIT during the 1950s. Solow, who was one of Schumpeter's students, received the Nobel Prize for Economic Science for this work.

Solow challenged the conclusions of the classical economists. But the new theories of economic growth developed during the 1980s and 1990s went further. They stand the classical belief on its head. Today's theory of population growth is that rising income slows the population growth rate because it increases the opportunity cost of having children and lowers the opportunity cost of investing in children and equipping them with more human capital, which makes them more productive. Productivity and income grow because technology advances and the scope for further productivity growth, which is stimulated by the search for profit, is practically unlimited.

Then . . .

In 1830, a strong and experienced farm worker could harvest three acres of wheat in a day. The only capital employed was a scythe to cut the wheat, which had been used since Roman times, and a cradle on which the stalks were laid, which had been invented by Flemish farmers in the fifteenth century. With newly developed horse-drawn ploughs, harrows and planters, farmers could plant more wheat

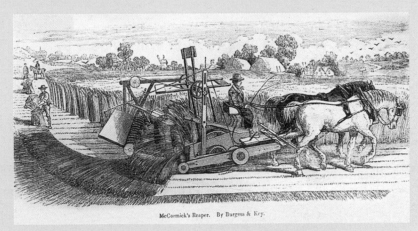

McCormick's Reaper. By Burgess & Key.

than they could harvest. But despite big efforts, no one had been able to make a machine that could replicate the swing of a scythe. Then in 1831, 22-year-old Cyrus McCormick built a machine that worked. It scared the horse that pulled it, but it did in a matter of hours what three men could accomplish in a day. Technological change has increased productivity on farms and brought economic growth. Do the facts about productivity growth mean that the classical economists, who believed that diminishing returns would push us relentlessly back to a subsistence living standard, were wrong?

. . . And Now

Today's technologies are expanding our horizons beyond the confines of our planet and are expanding our minds. Geosynchronous satellites bring us global television, voice and data communication, and more accurate weather forecasts, which incidentally increase agricultural productivity. In the foreseeable future, we might have superconductors that revolutionize the use of electric power, virtual reality theme parks and training facilities, pollution-free hydrogen cars, wristwatch telephones, and optical computers that we can talk to. With these new technologies, our ability to create yet more dazzling technologies increases. Technological change begets technological change in an (apparently) unending process and makes us ever more productive and brings ever higher incomes.

CHAPTER 31

The Business Cycle

After studying this chapter you will be able to:

◆ Distinguish between different theories of the business cycle

◆ Explain the Keynesian and monetarist theories of the business cycle

◆ Explain the new classical and new Keynesian theories of the business cycle

◆ Explain real business cycle theory

◆ Describe the origins and mechanisms at work during a recent recession and expansion

◆ Describe the origins and mechanisms at work during the Great Depression

Must What Goes Up Always Come Down?

The period between the two world wars was a time of mixed fortunes for many of the people in the United Kingdom who survived the horrors of the First World War (1914–18). The end of the war saw a severe recession; returning soldiers were demobbed and the economy was thrown back into peacetime production. After a shaky start, the economic machine was slowly getting back to work. Then, almost without warning, in October 1929, came the Wall Street crash. Share prices in the United States fell by 30 per cent and a wave of deflation was sent around the whole world. By 1933, real GDP in the United States had fallen by 30 per cent and unemployment had increased to 25 per cent of the workforce. This major downturn in the world's largest economy had severe effects on the economies of Europe. In Germany unemployment rose to 5.6 million or 30 per cent of the workforce in 1932 and in the United Kingdom it reached nearly 16 per cent. In 1931 the United Kingdom left the gold standard and joined the rest of the world in the Great Depression. ◆ By the standard of the interwar years, recent recessions have been mild. But recessions have not gone away. Our economy has experienced five recessions since the Second World War ended in 1945. In 1974, real GDP decreased by 1.7 per cent; in 1980, it decreased by 2.1 per cent; in 1981 it decreased again in a back-to-back recession by 1.2 per cent, and most recently, in 1991–92, it decreased by 2.6 per cent over the two years. Between these recessions, expansions took real GDP to new heights. Since the 1990s recession, real GDP has recovered. In 1994, GDP grew by 4.4 per cent, and by the end of 2000 it stood some 25 per cent higher than at the bottom of the recession. What causes a repeating sequence of recessions and expansions in our economy? Will we have another recession in the early years of the new millennium? There is a strong likelihood that 2001–2002 will see a recession in the western economies but there may be a severe recession in Argentina if the banking system collapses. Reading Between the Lines (pp. 728–729) looks at the Argentine economic crisis and discusses the similarities with the causes of the Great Depression in the USA in 1929.

◆ ◆ ◆ ◆ In this chapter we are going to explore these questions. You will see how all the strands of macroeconomics that you've been following come together and weave a complete picture of the forces and mechanisms that generate economic growth and fluctuations in production, employment and unemployment, and inflation. You will draw on your study of the labour market, consumption, saving and investment, economic growth, aggregate supply and aggregate demand, expenditure multipliers and the money market.

Cycle Patterns, Impulses and Mechanisms

We'll begin by summarizing the key business cycle facts that we want to understand and then examine the complex patterns it makes. The business cycle is an irregular and non-repeating up-and-down movement of business activity that takes place around a generally rising trend and that shows great diversity. Figure 31.1 shows some of this diversity by comparing business cycles since the turn of the century. You can see that there are basically nine business cycle turning points we can identify since 1990. On the average, recessions have lasted about two years and real GDP has fallen from peak to trough by nearly 10 per cent. Expansions have, on the average, lasted for just over six years and real GDP has risen from trough to peak at an average of nearly 10 per cent. But these averages mask huge variations from one cycle to another. Each cycle has a different story to tell. The onset of the First World War near the beginning of the century led to a boom followed by a sharp slump at the end of the war. The interwar period witnessed two cycles with a severe recession occurring in the 1930s, earning it the title of the 'Hungry Thirties'.

The next big expansion occurred during the Second World War. But there have been five cycles since the Second World War with major expansions occurring during the 1960s and 1980s.

You can see by examining Figure 31.1 that although the average of peak to trough decline and trough to peak boom is almost the same, most of the downturns are not as severe as the upturns. This is because the post-First World War recession was so severe that it pulled the average down. If we exclude the years up to 1918, the average trough to peak is 10.4 per cent and the average peak to trough is 8.8 per cent. Another interesting observation is the *amplitude* – the slump–boom–slump movement of the business cycle. You can see that the slump–boom–slump cycle was greater before the Second World War than after. Also the *frequency* of the cycle was greater before the Second World War than after. The 1960s heralded a long expansion period which looks unusual compared with other expansion phases of the cycle. There is no correlation between the length of an expansion and the length of the preceding recession.

With this enormous diversity of experience, there is no simple explanation of the business cycle. Also there is no (currently available) way of forecasting when the next turning point will come. But there is a

Figure 31.1

Some Business Cycle Patterns

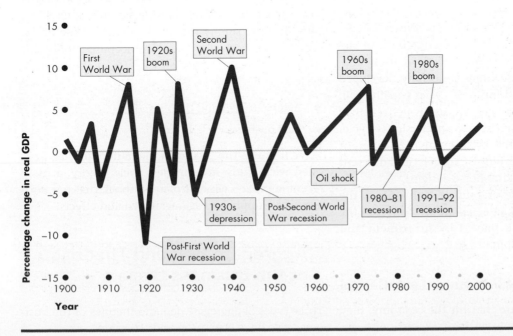

There have been nine business cycle turning points since the turn of the century. Recessions have lasted on average two years. Real GDP has fallen from peak to trough by nearly 9 per cent. Expansions have, on the average, lasted for about six years and real GDP has risen from trough to peak at an average of 10 per cent.

body of theory about the business cycle that helps us to understand its causes. A good place to begin studying this theory is to distinguish the possible ways in which cycles can be created.

Cycle Impulses and Mechanisms

The business cycle can occur either because the economy is hit by a succession of impulses that alternate between the up-and-down directions or because the economy has a built-in cycle mechanism that causes it to move up and down regardless of how it is hit. Some analogies might help you to see the distinction between cycle impulses and cycle mechanisms. In a tennis match, the ball cycles from one side of the court to the other and back again in a way that is determined entirely by the impulses that hit the ball. The tide is a cycle that is determined purely by a mechanism and has no impulses. The rotation of the earth and the gravitational pull of the moon interact to bring the ebb and flow of the tide with no outside forces intervening. A child's rocking horse is an example of a cycle mechanism that needs an external force to create the cycle. If the horse is pushed, it rocks to-and-fro in a cycle. The cycle will eventually die out unless the horse is pushed again, and each time the horse is pushed the cycle temporarily becomes more severe.

The economy seems to be a bit like all three of these examples. It can be hit like a tennis ball by shocks that send it in one direction or another; it can cycle indefinitely like the ebb and flow of the tide; and it can cycle like a rocking horse in swings that get milder until another shock sets off a new burst of bigger swings. But no one is sure which of these analogies is correct because there is no fully developed theory that explains all business cycles equally well. While none of the analogies we use is perfect, they all contain some insights into the business cycle. Different theories of the cycle emphasize different outside forces (different tennis racquets) and different cycle mechanisms (rocking horse designs).

Although there are several different theories of the business cycle, they all agree about one aspect of the cycle: the central role played by investment and the accumulation of capital.

The Central Role of Investment and Capital

Whatever the shocks are that hit the economy, they hit one crucial variable: investment. Recessions begin when investment in new capital slows down and they turn into expansions when investment speeds up. Investment and capital also create a cycle propagation mechanism. They interact like the spinning earth and the moon to create an ongoing cycle.

In an expansion investment proceeds at a rapid rate and the capital stock grows quickly. Capital per hour of labour grows and labour becomes more productive. But the *law of diminishing returns* begins to operate and this brings a fall in the rate of return on capital as the gain in productivity from the additional units of capital declines. With a lower rate of return, the incentive to invest weakens and investment eventually falls. When it falls by a large amount, recession begins. If in a recession investment proceeds at a modest rate, the capital stock grows slowly and diminishing returns work in reverse.

The *AS–AD* Model

Investment and capital are just part of the business cycle mechanism. To study the broader business mechanism, we need a broader framework. That framework is the *AS–AD* model. All the theories of the business cycle can be described in terms of the *AS–AD* model of Chapter 22. Theories differ in what they identify as the impulse and the propagation mechanism. But all theories can be thought of as making assumptions about the factors that make either aggregate supply or aggregate demand fluctuate and assumptions about their interaction with each other to create a business cycle. Business cycle impulses can hit either the supply side or the demand side of the economy or both. But there are no pure supply-side theories. We can classify all theories of the business cycle as:

◆ Aggregate demand theories, or

◆ Real business cycle theory.

We'll study the aggregate demand theories first. Then we'll study real business cycle theory, a more recent approach which isolates a shock that has both aggregate supply and aggregate demand effects.

Aggregate Demand Theories of the Business Cycle

Three types of aggregate demand theories of the business cycle have been proposed. They are:

1   Keynesian theory.

2   Monetarist theory.

3   Rational expectations theory.

Keynesian Theory of the Cycle

The **Keynesian theory of the business cycle** regards volatile expectations as the main source of economic fluctuations. This theory is distilled from Keynes' *The General Theory of Employment, Interest and Money*. We'll explore the Keynesian theory by looking at its main impulse and the mechanism that converts this impulse into a real GDP cycle.

Keynesian Impulse

The *impulse* in the Keynesian theory of the business cycle is expected future sales and profits. A change in expected future sales and profits changes the demand for new capital and changes the level of investment.

Keynes had an interesting and sophisticated view about *how* expectations of sales and profits are determined. He reasoned that these expectations would be volatile because most of the events that shape the future are unknown and impossible to forecast. So, he reasoned, news or even rumours about future tax rate changes, interest rate changes, advances in technology, global economic and political events, or any of thousands of other relevant factors that influence sales and profits, change expectations in ways that can't be quantified but that have large effects.

To emphasize the volatility and diversity of sources of changes in expected sales and profits, one of Keynes' followers, Joan Robinson, described these expectations as *animal spirits*. In using this term, Keynesians are not saying that expectations are irrational. Rather, they mean that because future sales and profits are impossible to forecast, it is rational to take a view about them based on rumours, guesses, intuition and instinct. Further, it might be rational to *change* one's view of the future, perhaps radically, in the light of scraps of new information.

Keynesian Cycle Mechanism

In the Keynesian theory, once a change in animal spirits has changed investment, a cycle mechanism begins to operate that has two key elements. First, the initial change in investment has a multiplier effect. The change in investment changes *aggregate* expenditure, real GDP and disposable income. The change in

disposable income changes consumption expenditure and aggregate demand changes by a multiple of the initial change in investment. (This mechanism is described in detail in Chapter 23.) The aggregate demand curve shifts rightward in an expansion and leftward in a recession.

The second element of the Keynesian cycle mechanism is the response of real GDP to a change in aggregate demand. The short-run aggregate supply curve is horizontal (or nearly so). With a horizontal *SAS* curve, swings in aggregate demand translate into swings in real GDP with no changes in the price level. But the short-run aggregate supply curve depends on the money wage rate. If the money wage rate is fixed (sticky), the *SAS* curve does not move. And if the money wage rate changes, the *SAS* curve shifts. In the Keynesian theory, the response of the money wage rate to changes in aggregate demand are *asymmetric*.

On the downside, when aggregate demand decreases and unemployment rises, the money wage rate does not change. It is completely rigid in the down direction. With a decrease in aggregate demand and no change in the money wage rate, the economy gets stuck in an unemployment equilibrium. There are no natural forces operating to restore full employment. The economy remains in that situation until animal spirits are lifted and investment increases again.

On the upside, when aggregate demand increases and unemployment falls below the natural rate, the money wage rate rises quickly. It is completely flexible in the up direction. Above full employment, the horizontal *SAS* curve plays no role and only the vertical *LAS* curve is relevant. With an increase in aggregate demand and an accompanying rise in the money wage rate, the price level rises quickly to eliminate the shortages and bring the economy back to full employment. The economy remains in that situation until animal spirits fall and investment and aggregate demand decrease.

Figures 31.2 and 31.3 illustrate the Keynesian theory of the business cycle by using the aggregate demand–aggregate supply model. In Figure 31.2, the economy is initially at full employment (point *a*) on the long-run aggregate supply curve, *LAS*, the aggregate demand curve, AD_0, and the short-run aggregate supply curve, SAS_0. A fall in animal spirits decreases investment, and aggregate demand decreases. The aggregate demand curve shifts leftward to AD_1. Real GDP falls to £725 billion and the economy moves to point *b*. Unemployment has increased and there is a surplus of labour, but the money wage rate does not fall and

Figure 31.2

A Keynesian Recession

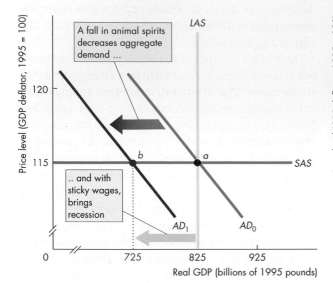

The economy is operating at point *a* at the intersection of the aggregate demand curve, AD_0, the short-run aggregate supply curve, SAS_0, and the long-run aggregate supply curve, *LAS*. A Keynesian recession begins when a fall in animal spirits causes investment demand to decrease. Aggregate demand decreases and the *AD* curve shifts leftward to AD_1. With sticky money wages and sticky price level, real GDP falls to £725 billion and the economy moves to point *b*.

Figure 31.3

A Keynesian Expansion

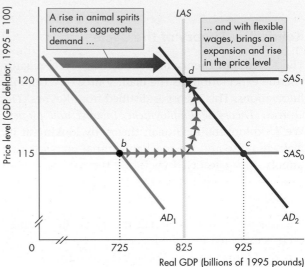

Starting at point *b*, a Keynesian expansion begins when a rise in animal spirits causes investment demand to increase. Aggregate demand increases and the *AD* curve shifts rightward to AD_2. With sticky money wages, real GDP increases to £825 billion. But the economy does not go all the way to point *c*. When full employment is reached, the money wage rate rises and the *SAS* curve shifts toward SAS_1. The price level rises as the economy heads towards point *d*.

the economy remains at point *b* until some force moves it away.

That force is shown in Figure 31.3. Here, starting out at point *b*, a rise in animal spirits increases aggregate demand and shifts the *AD* curve to AD_2. The multiplier process comes in to play and real GDP begins to increase. An expansion is under way. As long as real GDP remains below potential GDP (£825 billion in this example), the money wage rate and the price level remain constant. But real GDP never gets to point *c*, the point of intersection of SAS_0 and AD_2. The reason is that once real GDP exceeds potential GDP and unemployment falls below the natural rate, the money wage rate begins to rise and the *SAS* curve starts to shift upward towards SAS_1. As the money wage rate rises, the price level also rises and real GDP growth slows down. The economy follows a path like the one shown by the arrows connecting

point *b*, the initial equilibrium, with point *d*, the final equilibrium.

The Keynesian business cycle is mainly like a tennis match. It is caused by outside forces – animal spirits – that change direction and set off a process that ends at an equilibrium that must be hit again by the outside forces to disturb it.

Monetarist Theory

The **monetarist theory of the business cycle** regards fluctuations in the money stock as the main source of economic fluctuations. This theory is distilled from the writings of Milton Friedman and several other economists. We'll explore the monetarist theory as we did the Keynesian theory, by looking first at its main impulse and second at the mechanism that creates a cycle in real GDP.

Monetarist Impulse

The *impulse* in the monetarist theory of the business cycle is the *growth rate of the quantity of money*. A speedup in money growth brings expansion, and a slowdown in money growth brings recession. The source of the change in the growth rate of quantity of money is the monetary policy actions of the Bank of England.

Monetarist Cycle Mechanism

In the monetarist theory, once the Bank has changed the money growth rate, a cycle mechanism begins to operate which, like the Keynesian mechanism, first affects aggregate demand. When the money growth rate increases, the quantity of real money in the economy increases. Interest rates fall and real money balances increase. The foreign exchange rate also falls – the pound loses value on the foreign exchange market. These initial financial market effects begin to spill over into other markets. Investment demand and exports increase, and consumers spend more on durable goods. These initial changes in expenditure have a multiplier effect, just as investment has in the Keynesian theory. Through these mechanisms, a speedup in money growth shifts the aggregate demand curve rightward and brings an expansion. Similarly, a slowdown in money growth shifts the aggregate demand curve leftward and brings a recession.

The second element of the monetarist cycle mechanism is the response of aggregate supply to a change in aggregate demand. The short-run aggregate supply curve is upward-sloping. With an upward-sloping *SAS* curve, swings in aggregate demand translate into swings in both real GDP and the price level. But monetarists think that real GDP deviations from full employment are temporary in both directions.

In monetarist theory, the money wage rate is only *temporarily sticky*. When aggregate demand decreases and unemployment rises, the money wage rate eventually begins to fall. As the money wage rate falls, so does the price level and after a period of adjustment, full employment is restored. When aggregate demand increases and unemployment falls below the natural rate, the money wage rate begins to rise. As the money wage rate rises so does the price level, and after a period of adjustment, real GDP returns to potential GDP and the unemployment rate returns to the natural rate.

Figure 31.4 illustrates the monetarist theory. In part (a), the economy is initially at full employment

(point *a*) on the long-run aggregate supply curve, *LAS*, the aggregate demand curve, AD_0, and the short-run aggregate supply curve, SAS_0. A slowdown in the money growth rate decreases aggregate demand and the aggregate demand curve shifts leftward to AD_1. Real GDP falls to £775 billion and the economy moves to point *b*. Unemployment increases, and there is a surplus of labour. The money wage rate begins to fall. As the money wage rate falls, the short-run aggregate supply curve shifts from SAS_0 to SAS_1. The price level falls and real GDP begins to expand as the economy moves to point *c*, its new full-employment equilibrium, and GDP is back at its full-employment level.

Figure 31.4(b) shows the effects of the opposite initial money shock – a speedup in money growth. Here, starting out at point *c*, a rise in the money growth rate increases aggregate demand and shifts the *AD* curve to AD_2. Both real GDP and the price level rise as the economy moves to point *d*, the point of intersection of SAS_1 and AD_2. With real GDP above potential GDP and unemployment below the natural rate, the money wage rate begins to rise and the *SAS* curve starts to shift leftward towards SAS_2. As the money wage rate rises, the price level also rises and real GDP decreases. The economy moves from point *d* to point *e*, its new full-employment equilibrium.

The monetarist business cycle is like a rocking horse. It needs an outside force to get it going but once going, it rocks to-and-fro (but just once). It doesn't matter how the economy is hit. If it is hit with a money growth slowdown, the economy cycles with a recession followed by recovery. If it is hit by a money growth speedup, the economy cycles with a recovery followed by recession.

Rational Expectations Theories

A **rational expectation** is a forecast that is based on all the available relevant information. Rational expectations theories of the business cycle are theories based on the view that money wages are determined by a rational expectation of the price level. Two distinctly different rational expectations theories of the cycle have been proposed. A **new classical theory of the business cycle** regards *unanticipated* fluctuations in aggregate demand as the main source of economic fluctuations. This theory is based on the work of Robert E. Lucas Jr. A different **new Keynesian theory of the business cycle** regards *both anticipated and unanticipated* fluctuations in aggregate demand as

Figure 31.4

A Monetarist Business Cycle

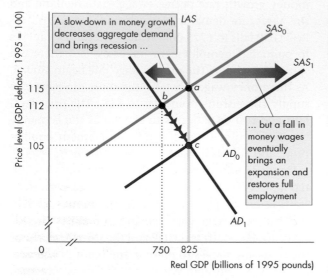

(a) Recession

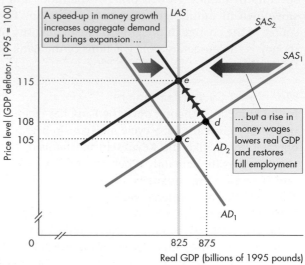

(b) Expansion

A monetarist recession begins when a slowdown in money growth decreases aggregate demand. The *AD* curve shifts leftward from AD_0 to AD_1 (part a). With sticky money wages, real GDP decreases to £775 billion and the price level falls to 112 as the economy moves from point *a* to point *b*. With a surplus of labour, the money wage rate falls and the *SAS* curve shifts rightward to SAS_1. The price level falls further, and real GDP returns to potential GDP at point *c*.

Starting at point *c* (part b), a monetarist expansion begins when an increase in money growth increases aggregate demand and shifts the *AD* curve rightward to AD_2. With sticky money wages, real GDP rises to £875 billion, the price level rises to 108, and the economy moves to point *d*. With a shortage of labour, the money wage rate rises and the *SAS* curve shifts towards SAS_2. The price level rises and real GDP decreases to potential GDP as the economy heads towards point *e*.

---

sources of economic fluctuations. We'll explore these theories as we did the Keynesian and monetarist theories, by looking first at the main impulse and second at the cycle mechanism.

Rational Expectations Impulse

The *impulse* that distinguishes the rational expectations theories from the other aggregate demand theories of the business cycle is the *unanticipated change in aggregate demand*. A larger than anticipated increase in aggregate demand brings an expansion and a smaller than anticipated increase in aggregate demand brings a recession. Any factor that influences aggregate demand – for example, fiscal policy, monetary policy, or developments in the world economy that influence exports – whose change is not anticipated, can bring a change in real GDP.

Rational Expectations Cycle Mechanisms

To describe the rational expectations cycle mechanisms, we'll deal first with the new classical version. When aggregate demand decreases, if the money wage rate doesn't change, real GDP and the price level both decrease. The fall in the price level increases the *real* wage rate, and employment decreases and unemployment rises. In the new classical theory, the events you've just reviewed occur only if the decrease in aggregate demand is not anticipated. If the decrease in aggregate demand *is* anticipated, both firms and workers will agree to a lower money wage rate. By doing so, they can prevent the real wage from rising and avoid a rise in the unemployment rate.

Similarly, if firms and workers anticipate an increase in aggregate demand, they expect the price level to rise and will agree to a higher money wage rate. By doing so, they can prevent the real wage from falling and avoid a fall in the unemployment rate below the natural rate.

Only fluctuations in aggregate demand that are unanticipated and not taken into account in wage contracts bring changes in real GDP. *Anticipated* changes in aggregate demand change the price level, but they leave real GDP and unemployment unchanged and do not create a business cycle.

New Keynesian economists, like new classical economists, think that money wages are influenced by rational expectations of the price level. But new Keynesians emphasize the long-term nature of most wage contracts. They say that *today's* money wages are influenced by *yesterday's* rational expectations. These expectations, which were formed in the past, are based on old information that might now be known to be incorrect. After they have made a long-term wage agreement, both firms and workers might anticipate a change in aggregate demand, which they expect will change the price level. But because they are locked into their agreement, they are unable to change money wages. So money wages are sticky in the new Keynesian theory and with sticky money wages, even an *anticipated* change in aggregate demand changes real GDP.

New classical economists say that long-term contracts are renegotiated when conditions change to make them outdated. So they do not regard long-term contracts as an obstacle to money wage flexibility, provided both parties to an agreement recognize the changed conditions. If both firms and workers expect the price level to change, they will change the agreed money wage rate to reflect that shared expectation. In this situation, anticipated changes in aggregate demand change the money wage rate and the price level and leave real GDP unchanged.

The distinctive feature of both versions of the rational expectations theory of the business cycle is the role of unanticipated changes in aggregate demand, and Figure 31.5 illustrates its effect on real GDP and the price level. Potential GDP is £825 billion and the long-run aggregate supply curve is LAS. Aggregate demand is expected to be EAD. Given potential GDP and EAD, the money wage rate is set at the level that is expected to bring full employment. At this money wage rate, the short-run aggregate supply curve is SAS. Imagine that, initially, aggregate demand equals expected aggregate demand, so there is full employment. Real GDP is £825 billion and the price level

is 115. Then, unexpectedly, aggregate demand turns out to be less than expected and the aggregate demand curve shifts leftward to AD_0 (in Figure 31.5(a)). Many different aggregate demand shocks, such as a slowdown in the money growth rate or a collapse of exports, could have caused this shock. A recession begins. Real GDP falls to £775 billion and the price level falls to 112. The economy moves to point *b*. Unemployment increases and there is surplus of labour. But aggregate demand is expected to be at EAD so the money wage rate doesn't change and the short-run aggregate supply curve remains at SAS.

The recession ends when aggregate demand increases again to its expected level. A larger shock that takes aggregate demand to a level that exceeds EAD brings an expansion. In Figure 31.5(b), the aggregate demand curve shifts rightward to AD_1. Such an increase in aggregate demand might be caused by a speedup in the money growth rate or an export boom. Real GDP now increases to £875 billion and the price level rises to 118. The economy moves to point *c*. Unemployment is now below the natural rate. But aggregate demand is expected to be at EAD so the money wage rate doesn't change and the short-run aggregate supply curve remains at SAS.

Fluctuations in aggregate demand between AD_0 and AD_1 around expected aggregate demand EAD bring fluctuations in real GDP and the price level between points *b* and *c*.

The two versions of the rational expectations theory differ in their predictions about the effects of a change in expected aggregate demand. The new classical theory predicts that as soon as expected aggregate demand changes, the money wage rate also changes so the SAS curve shifts. The new Keynesian theory predicts that the money wage rate changes gradually when new contracts are made so that the SAS curve moves slowly. This difference between the two theories is crucial for policy. According to the new classical theory, anticipated policy actions change only the price level and have no effect on real GDP and unemployment. The reason is that when policy is expected to change, the money wage rate changes so the SAS curve shifts and offsets the effects of the policy action on real GDP. In contrast, in the new Keynesian theory, because money wages change only when new contracts are made, even anticipated policy actions change real GDP and can be used in an attempt to stabilize the cycle.

Like the monetarist business cycle, these rational expectations cycles are similar to rocking horses.

Figure 31.5

A Rational Expectations Business Cycle

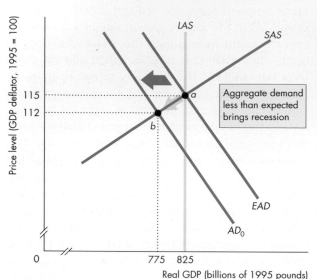

(a) Recession

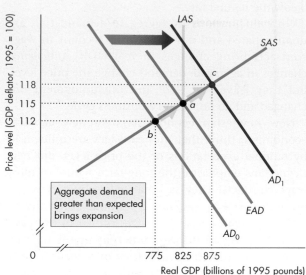

(b) Expansion

The economy is expected to be at point *a* at the intersection of the *expected* aggregate demand curve, *EAD*, the short-run aggregate supply curve, *SAS*, and the long-run aggregate supply curve, *LAS*. A rational expectations recession begins when an unanticipated decrease in aggregate demand shifts the *AD* curve leftward to AD_0. With money wage rates based on the expectation that aggregate demand will be *EAD*, real GDP decreases to £775 billion and the price level falls to 112 as the economy moves to point *b*. As long as aggregate demand is

expected to be *EAD* there is no change in the money wage rate.

A rational expectations expansion begins when an unanticipated increase in aggregate demand shifts the *AD* curve rightward from AD_0 to AD_1. With money wage rates based on the expectation that aggregate demand will be *EAD*, real GDP increases to £875 billion and the price level rises to 118 as the economy moves to point *c*. Again, as long as aggregate demand is *expected* to be *EAD*, there is no change in the money wage rate.

They need an outside force to get going, but once going the economy rocks around its full-employment point. The new classical horse rocks faster and comes to rest more quickly than the new Keynesian horse.

AD–AS General Theory

All the theories of the business cycle that we've considered can be viewed as particular cases of a more general *AD–AS* theory. In this more general theory, the impulses of both the Keynesian and monetarist theories can change aggregate demand. A multiplier effect makes aggregate demand change by more than any initial change in one of the components of expenditure. The money wage rate can be viewed as responding to changes in the rational expectation of

the future price level. Even if the money wage is flexible, it will change only to the extent that price level expectations change. As a result, the money wage will adjust gradually.

Although in all three types of business cycle theory that we've considered the cycle is caused by fluctuations in aggregate demand, the possibility that an occasional aggregate supply shock might occur is not ruled out. A recession could occur because aggregate supply falls. For example, a widespread drought that cuts agricultural production could cause a recession in an economy that has a large agricultural sector. But these demand theories of the cycle regard supply shocks as rare rather than normal events. Aggregate demand fluctuations are the normal ongoing sources of fluctuations.

Review Quiz

◆ What according to Keynesian theory is the main business cycle impulse?

◆ What according to Keynesian theory are the main business cycle mechanisms? Describe the roles of *animal spirits*, the multiplier, and a sticky money wage rate in this theory.

◆ What according to monetarist theory is the main business cycle impulse?

◆ What according to monetarist theory are the business cycle mechanisms? Describe the roles of the central bank and the money supply in this theory.

◆ What according to new classical theory and new Keynesian theory causes the business cycle? What are the roles of rational expectations and unanticipated fluctuations in aggregate demand in these theories?

◆ What are the differences between the new classical theory and the new Keynesian theory concerning the money wage rate over the business cycle?

A new theory of the business cycle challenges the mainstream and traditional demand theories that you've just studied. It is called the real business cycle theory. Let's take a look at this new theory.

Real Business Cycle Theory

The newest theory of the business cycle, known as **real business cycle theory** (or RBC theory), regards random fluctuations in productivity as the main source of economic fluctuations. These productivity fluctuations are assumed to result mainly from fluctuations in the pace of technological change, but they might also have other sources such as international disturbances, climate fluctuations, or natural disasters. The origins of real business cycle theory can be traced to the rational expectations revolution set off by Robert E. Lucas Jr, but the first demonstration of the power of this theory was given by Edward Prescott and Finn Kydland, and by John Long and Charles Plosser. Today, real business cycle theory is part of a broad research agenda called *dynamic general equilibrium*, and hundreds of young macroeconomists do research on this topic.

Like our study of the demand theories, we'll explore the RBC theory by looking first at its impulse and second at the mechanism that converts that impulse into a cycle in real GDP.

The RBC Impulse

The *impulse* in the RBC theory is the *growth rate of productivity that results from technological change*. RBC theorists think this impulse is generated mainly by the process of research and development that leads to the creation and use of new technologies. Sometimes technological progress is rapid and productivity grows quickly; and at other times, progress is slow and productivity grows moderately. Occasionally, technological change is so far reaching that it makes a large amount of existing capital, especially human capital, obsolete. It also, initially, destroys jobs and shuts down businesses. These initial effects of far-reaching technological change *decrease* productivity and can create recession. Other supply shocks, such as the world oil embargo of the mid-1970s, can temporarily decrease productivity.

To isolate the RBC theory impulse – the growth rate of productivity that results from technological change – economists use the tool of growth accounting, which is explained in Chapter 30, pp. 685–689.

Figure 31.6 shows the RBC impulse for the United Kingdom from 1971 to 1998. This figure also shows that fluctuations in productivity growth are correlated with GDP fluctuations. This RBC productivity variable is a catch-all variable. Economists are not sure what it actually measures or what causes it to fluctuate.

The RBC Mechanism

The mechanism that creates the business cycle according to the RBC theory is more complex and intricate than the demand theory mechanisms. Two immediate effects follow from a change in productivity that get an expansion or a contraction going:

1 Investment demand changes.

2 Demand for labour changes.

We'll study these effects and their consequences during a recession. In an expansion, they work in the opposite direction to what is described here.

A wave of technological change makes some existing capital obsolete and temporarily lowers productivity. Firms expect the future profit rate to fall and see their labour productivity falling. With lower profit

Figure 31.6

The Real Business Cycle Impulse

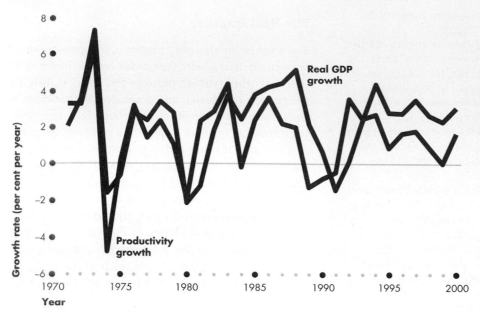

The real business cycle is caused by changes in technology that bring fluctuations in productivity. The fluctuations in productivity shown here are calculated by using growth accounting (the one-third rule) to remove the contribution of capital accumulation to productivity growth. Productivity fluctuations are correlated with real GDP fluctuations. Economists are not sure what the productivity variable actually measures or what causes it to fluctuate.

Sources: National Statistics; and the authors' calculations.

expectations, they cut back their purchases of new capital, and with lower labour productivity they plan to lay off some workers. So the initial effect of a decrease in productivity is a decrease in investment demand and a decrease in the demand for labour.

Figure 31.7 illustrates these two initial effects of a decrease in productivity. Part (a) shows investment demand, *ID*, and saving supply, *SS* (in RBC theory investment demand and savings supply depend on the real interest rate). Initially, investment demand is ID_0, and the equilibrium level of investment and saving is £100 billion at a real interest rate of 6 per cent a year. A decrease in productivity lowers the expected profit rate and decreases investment demand. The *ID* curve shifts leftward to ID_1. The real interest rate falls to 4 per cent a year, and investment and saving decrease to £70 billion.

Part (b) shows the demand for labour, *LD*, and the supply of labour, *LS*. Initially, the demand for labour is LD_0, and the equilibrium level of employment is 50 billion hours a year at a real wage rate of £8.50 an hour. The decrease in productivity decreases the demand for labour and the *LD* curve shifts leftward to LD_1.

Before we can determine the new level of employment and the real wage rate, we need to take a ripple effect into account – the key ripple effect in RBC theory.

The Key Decision: When to Work?

According to the RBC theory, people decide *when* to work by doing a cost–benefit calculation. They compare the return from working in the current period with the *expected* return from working in a later period. You make such a comparison every day at college. Suppose your goal in this course is to get a first. To achieve this goal, you work pretty hard most of the time. But during the few days before the midterm and final exams, you work especially hard. Why? Because you think the return from studying close to the exam is greater than the return from studying when the exam is a long time away. So during the term you hang around the Students' Union bar, go to parties, play squash and enjoy other leisure pursuits, but at exam time you work every evening and weekend.

Real business cycle theory says that workers behave like you. They work fewer hours, and sometimes zero

Figure 31.7

Factor Markets in a Real Business Cycle

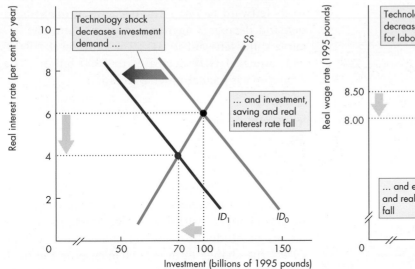

(a) Investment, saving, and interest rate

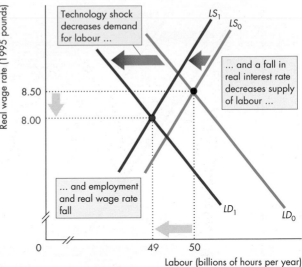

(b) Labour and wage rate

Saving supply is *SS* (part a) and, initially, investment demand is *ID*$_0$. The real interest rate is 6 per cent a year and saving and investment are £100 billion. In the labour market (part b), the demand for labour is *LD*$_0$ and the supply of labour is *LS*$_0$. The real wage rate is £8.50 an hour and employment is 50 billion hours. A technological change decreases productivity, and both investment demand and the demand for labour decrease. The two demand curves

shift leftward to *ID*$_1$ and *LD*$_1$. In part (a), the real interest rate falls to 4 per cent a year, and investment and saving fall. In part (b), the fall in the real interest rate decreases the supply of labour (the when-to-work decision) and the supply curve shifts leftward to *LS*$_1$. Employment decreases to 49 billion hours and the real wage rate falls to £8.00 an hour. A recession is under way.

hours, when the real wage rate is temporarily low and they work more hours when the real wage rate is temporarily high. But to compare properly the current wage rate with the expected future wage rate, workers must use the real interest rate. If the real interest rate is 6 per cent a year, a real wage rate of £1 an hour earned this week will become £1.06 a year from now. If the real wage rate is expected to be £1.05 an hour next year, today's wage of £1 looks good. By working longer hours now and shorter hours a year from now, a person can get a 1 per cent higher real wage. But suppose the real interest rate is 4 per cent a year. In this case, £1 earned now is worth £1.04 next year. Working fewer hours now and more next year is the way to get a 1 per cent higher real wage.

So the when-to-work decision depends on the real interest rate. The lower the real interest rate, other

things remaining the same, the smaller is the supply of labour. Many economists think this *intertemporal substitution effect* to be of negligible size. RBC theorists say the effect is large, and it is the key element in the RBC mechanism.

You've seen in Figure 31.7(a) that the decrease in investment demand lowers the real interest rate. This fall in the real interest rate lowers the return to current work and decreases the supply of labour. In Figure 31.7(b), the labour supply curve shifts leftward to *LS*$_1$. The effect of a productivity shock on demand is larger than the effect of the fall in the real interest rate on the supply of labour. That is, the *LD* curve shifts farther leftward than does the *LS* curve. As a result, the real wage rate falls to £8 an hour and employment falls to 49 billion hours. A recession has begun and is intensifying.

Figure 31.8

AD–AS in a Real Business Cycle

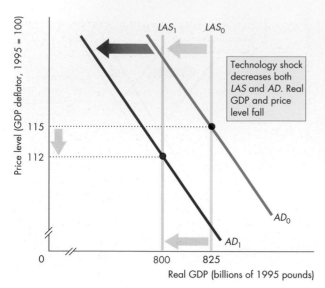

Technology shock decreases both LAS and AD. Real GDP and price level fall

Initially, the aggregate demand curve is AD_0 and the long-run aggregate supply curve is LAS_0. Real GDP is £825 billion (which equals potential GDP) and the price level is 115. There is no *SAS* curve in the real business cycle theory because the money wage rate is flexible. The technological change described in Figure 31.6 decreases potential GDP and the *LAS* curve shifts leftward to LAS_1. The decrease in investment demand decreases aggregate demand, and the *AD* curve shifts leftward to AD_1. Real GDP decreases to £800 billion and the price level falls to 112. The economy goes into recession.

Real GDP and the Price Level

The next part of the RBC story traces the consequences of the changes you've just seen for real GDP and the price level. With a decrease in employment, aggregate supply decreases; and with a decrease in investment demand, aggregate demand decreases. Figure 31.8 illustrates these effects, using the *AD–AS* framework. Initially, the aggregate demand curve is AD_0 and the long-run aggregate supply curve is LAS_0. The price level is 115 and real GDP is £825 billion. There is no short-run aggregate supply curve in this figure because in the RBC theory, the *SAS* curve has no meaning. The labour market moves relentlessly toward its equilibrium, and the money wage rate adjusts freely (either upward or downward) to ensure that the real wage rate keeps the quantity of labour demanded equal to the quantity supplied. In the RBC theory, unemployment is always at the natural rate,

and the natural rate fluctuates over the business cycle because the amount of job search fluctuates.

The decrease in employment lowers total production, and aggregate supply decreases. The *LAS* curve shifts leftward to LAS_1. The decrease in investment demand decreases aggregate demand, and the *AD* curve shifts leftward to AD_1. The price level falls to 112, and real GDP decreases to £800 billion. The economy has gone through a recession.

What Happened to Money?

The name *real* business cycle theory is no accident. It reflects the central prediction of the theory: that the business cycle is caused by real things and not by nominal or monetary things. If the quantity of money changes, aggregate demand changes. But with no real change – with no change in the use of the factors of production and no change in potential GDP – the change in money changes only the price level. In real business cycle theory, this outcome occurs because the aggregate supply curve is the *LAS* curve, which pins real GDP down at potential GDP, so that when the *AD* curve changes only the price level changes.

Cycles and Growth

The shock that drives the business cycle of the RBC theory is the same as the force that generates economic growth: technological change. On the average, as technology advances, productivity grows. But it grows at an uneven pace. You saw this fact when you studied growth accounting in Chapter 30. There, we focused on slow-changing trends in productivity growth. Real business cycle theory uses the same idea but says there are frequent shocks to productivity that are mostly positive but that are occasionally negative.

Criticisms of RBC Theory

RBC theory is controversial, and when economists discuss it they often generate more heat than light. Its detractors claim that its basic assumptions are just too incredible. Money wages *are* sticky, they claim, so to assume otherwise is at odds with a clear fact. Intertemporal substitution is too weak, they say, to account for large fluctuations in labour supply and employment with small changes in the real wage rate.

But what really kills the RBC story, say most economists, is an implausible impulse. Technology shocks are not capable of creating the swings in productivity that growth accounting reveals. These shocks are caused by something, they concede, but they are as likely to be caused by *changes in aggregate demand* as by technology. If they are caused by demand fluctuations, then the traditional demand theories are needed to explain these shocks. Fluctuations in productivity do not cause the cycle but are caused by it!

Building on this theme, the critics point out that the so-called productivity fluctuations that growth accounting measures are correlated with changes in the growth rate of money and other indicators of changes in aggregate demand.

Defence of RBC Theory

The defenders of RBC theory claim that the theory works. It explains the macroeconomic facts about the business cycle and is consistent with the facts about economic growth. In effect, a single theory explains *both growth and cycles*. The growth accounting exercise that explains slowly changing trends also explains the more frequent business cycle swings. Its defenders also claim that RBC theory is consistent with a wide range of *microeconomic* evidence about labour supply decisions, labour demand and investment demand decisions, and information on the distribution of income between labour and capital.

RBC theorists acknowledge that money and the business cycle are correlated. That is, rapid money growth and expansion go together, and slow money growth and recession go together. But, they argue, causation does not run from money to real GDP as the traditional aggregate demand theories state. Instead, they view causation as running from real GDP to money – so-called reverse causation. In a recession, the initial fall in investment demand that lowers the interest rate decreases the demand for bank loans and lowers the profitability of banking. So banks increase their reserves and decrease their loans. The quantity of bank deposits and hence the quantity of money decreases. This reverse causation is responsible for the correlation between money growth and real GDP according to real business cycle theory.

Its defenders also argue that the RBC view is significant because it at least raises the possibility that the business cycle is efficient. The business cycle does not signal an economy that is misbehaving; it is business as usual. If this view is correct, it means that policy to smooth the cycle is misguided. Smoothing the troughs can be done only by taking out the peaks. But peaks are bursts of investment to take advantage of

new technologies in a timely way. So smoothing the business cycle means delaying the benefits of new technologies.

Review Quiz

◆ What, according to real business cycle theory causes the business cycle? What is the role of fluctuations in the rate of technological change?

◆ How, according to real business cycle theory does a fall in productivity growth influence investment demand, the real interest rate, the demand for labour, the supply of labour, employment, and the real wage rate?

◆ How, according to real business cycle theory does a fall in productivity growth influence long-run aggregate supply, aggregate demand, real GDP, and the price level?

You've now reviewed the main theories of the business cycle. Your next task is to examine some actual business cycles. In pursuing this task, we will focus on the recession phase of the cycle. We'll do this mainly because it is the recessions that cause most trouble. We begin by looking at the 1991–92 recession.

The 1991–92 Recession

In the theories of the business cycle that you've studied, recessions can be triggered by a variety of forces, some on the aggregate demand side and some on the aggregate supply side. Let's identify the shocks that triggered the most recent recession in the United Kingdom – the 1991–92 recession.

The Origins of the 1991–92 Recession

Two forces were at work in United Kingdom during 1990 that appear to have contributed to the recession and subsequent sluggish growth. They were:

1 Monetary policy.

2 A slowdown in the world economy.

Monetary Policy

Three factors made monetary policy deflationary during 1990. First, the United Kingdom joined the Exchange Rate Mechanism (ERM) of the European

Monetary System (EMS). Second, the Bank of England slowed the growth rate of the money supply. Third, German reunification put upward pressure on interest rates which, through the ERM, were transmitted quickly to the United Kingdom.

Inflation had reached a peak of 10 per cent by the time the United Kingdom was taken into the ERM in October 1990. Keen to restore its anti-inflation credentials, the government decided that the best way to restore low inflation was through the discipline of the ERM. The ERM is a pegged exchange rate system with a central rate and a wide or narrow band of fluctuations with other currencies in the system. The central rate was set at DM2.95 to the £1 with a band of ±6 per cent around its central rate.

When the United Kingdom entered the ERM, inflation was above that of the EU average. With the exchange rate fixed around a band of ±6 per cent this meant that UK goods became increasingly expensive in European markets. The high real interest rates that were needed to take the economy into the ERM and the loss of competitiveness had a strong negative influence on aggregate demand. The economy went into recession. Currency speculators anticipated that the UK economy could not carry on at the existing central rate of DM2.95 and expected a devaluation, causing a continuous downward pressure on the pound.

Bank of England Response

To convince currency speculators that the government did not intend to devalue, the Bank of England kept interest rates higher than in the rest of Europe. However, the more the Bank resisted currency speculators by keeping interest rates high, the wider was the belief that the economy could not continue in recession with high real interest rates and that a devaluation must occur.[1] This is like a game of 'chicken' between two cars, except that it is between the Bank and speculators. Like a game of chicken, someone has to give way and be the chicken. In September 1992 the government of the United Kingdom became the chicken and left the ERM.

The extent to which the Bank slowed the economy can be seen from the slowdown in the growth rate of the money supply between 1990(q1) and 1992(q2)

---

[1] This process is known as the 'Walters critique' after Professor Sir Alan Walters, who suggested that the ERM would create such destabilizing forces, see p. 800.

Figure 31.9

Money Supply Growth: 1990(1)–1992(4)

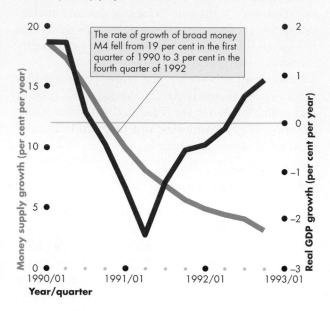

The entry of the United Kingdom into the ERM meant that the Bank of England had to pursue a tight monetary policy. The money supply growth rate began to slow during 1989. It slowed even further during 1990. Tight monetary policy contributed to the fall in real GDP.

Source: Bank of England and National Statistics.

shown in Figure 31.9. The growth rate of the broad definition of money, M4, slowed from 19 per cent in the first quarter of 1990 to 3 per cent in the fourth quarter of 1992. Figure 31.9 also shows the decline in real GDP during the same period.

German Reunification

In November 1989 the Berlin Wall came down, and in October 1990 East Germany was reunited with West Germany. The cost of the reunification was enormous. Fiscal transfers to the eastern states pushed the government budget into deficit. From being a net lender in the world capital market, the new Germany began its life as a net borrower. The German central bank, the Bundesbank, raised interest rates to forestall the inflationary implications of the unification. As the Deutschmark was the anchor currency for the ERM, the rise in German interest rates meant that the rest of the members of the ERM had to

Figure 31.10

The 1991–1992 Recession

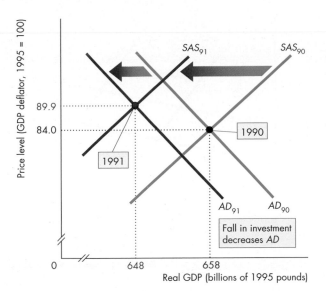

At the end of 1990, the economy was on its aggregate demand curve, AD_{90}, and its short-run aggregate supply curve, SAS_{90}, with real GDP at £658 billion and a GDP deflator of 84. The combination of a decrease in both aggregate supply and aggregate demand put the economy into recession. Real GDP decreased to £648 billion and the price level increased to 89.9.

Figure 31.11

The Labour Market in the 1990s

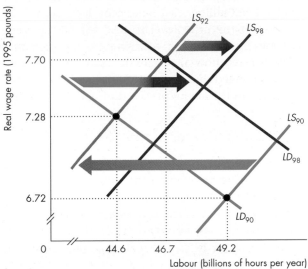

In 1990, the demand for labour was LD_{90} and the supply of labour was LS_{90}. If the quantity of labour supplied equalled the quantity of labour demanded, the real wage was £6.72 an hour and employment was 49.2 billion of hours. Money wages continued to rise because people did not anticipate the fall in inflation in 1991 and 1992, and LS shifted leftward to LS_{92}. Real wages increased to £7.70 and employment fell to 46.7 billion hours. In the rest of the 1990s, money wages grew less than inflation, LS shifted rightward to LS_{98}, and as real wages fell employment increased.

raise their interest rates if they were to remain within the specified bands of their respective central rates.

A Slowdown in Economic Expansion in the World Economy

After its longest ever period of peacetime expansion, US real GDP growth began to slow in 1989 and 1990 and the United States went into recession in mid-1990. The slowdown of the US economy brought slower growth in demand for the rest of the world's exports and resulted in lower export volumes and a decline in world economic activity.

Let's see how the events we've just described influenced the UK economy in 1990.

Aggregate Demand and Aggregate Supply in the 1991–92 Recession

Figure 31.10 describes the effects of the various events that triggered the recession of 1991–92. The aggregate demand curve was AD_{90} and the short-run aggregate

supply curve was SAS_{90}. Real GDP was £658 billion and the price level was 84.

The 1991–92 recession was caused by a decrease in both aggregate demand and aggregate supply. Aggregate demand decreased, initially, because of the high real interest rate, the overvalued exchange rate and the slowdown in the growth rate of the quantity of money. These factors were soon reinforced by the slowdown in the world economy that brought a decline in the growth of exports. The combination of these factors triggered a massive decline in investment. The resulting decrease in aggregate demand is shown by the shift of the aggregate demand curve leftward to AD_{91}. Aggregate supply decreased because money wages continued to increase throughout 1990 at a rate similar to that in 1989. This decrease in aggregate supply is shown in Figure 31.11 as the shift in the short-run aggregate supply curve leftward to SAS_{91}.

(The figure does not show the long-run aggregate supply curve.)

The combined effect of the decreases in aggregate supply and aggregate demand was a decrease in real GDP to £648 billion – a 1.5 per cent decrease, and an increase in the price level to 89.9 – a 6.8 per cent increase.

You've seen how aggregate demand and aggregate supply changed during the 1991–92 recession. What happened in the labour market during this recession?

The Labour Market in the 1990s

The unemployment rate increased persistently from the beginning of 1990 to the end of 1993. Figure 31.11 shows two other facts about the labour market during this period – facts about employment and the real wage rate. As employment decreased through 1990, 1991 and 1992, the real wage rate increased. Later, during the recovery in mid-1993, employment increased and the real wage rate decreased. These movements in employment and the real wage rate suggest that the forces of supply and demand do not operate smoothly in the labour market. Money wages continued to rise because people did not anticipate the slowdown in inflation. When inflation did slow down, the real wage rate increased and the quantity of labour demanded decreased. The loss of employment meant that when inflation fell money wages fell faster. The recovery in mid-1993 also led to a rise in labour demand in the rest of the 1990s to 1998.

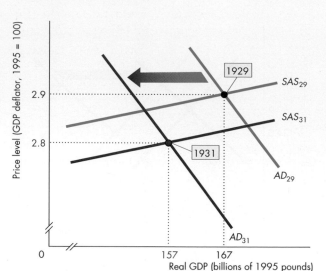

Figure 31.12

The Great Depression

In 1929, real GDP was £167 billion and the GDP deflator was 2.9 – at the intersection of AD_{29} and SAS_{29}. Increased pessimism from a fall in world trade resulted in a drop in investment, resulting in a decrease in aggregate demand to AD_{31}. To some degree, this decrease was reflected in the labour market and wages fell, so the short-run aggregate supply curve shifted to SAS_{31}. Real GDP and the price level fell. By 1931, real GDP had fallen to £157 billion (94 per cent of its 1929 level) and the GDP deflator had fallen to 2.8 (97 per cent of its 1929 level).

Review Quiz

◆ What were the factors that contributed to the 1991–92 recession?
◆ What role was played by external factors and what role was played by domestic policy.
◆ What mechanisms translated the shocks into a recession?

You've now seen what caused the 1991–92 recession. Let's look next at the greatest of recessions – the Great Depression.

The Great Depression

The late 1920s were years of economic revival in some parts of the UK economy. While the traditional industries like coal and shipbuilding stagnated, others like motor manufacturing were booming. New firms were created, and the capital stock of the nation expanded. At the beginning of 1929, UK real GDP nearly equalled potential GDP. But as that eventful year unfolded, increasing signs of economic weakness began to appear. The most dramatic events occurred in October when the US stock market collapsed, losing more than one-third of its value in two weeks. The four years that followed were years of monstrous economic depression all over the world.

Figure 31.12 shows the dimensions of the Great Depression. On the eve of the Great Depression in 1929, the economy was on aggregate demand curve AD_{29} and short-run aggregate supply curve SAS_{29}. Real GDP was £167 billion (1995 pounds) and the GDP deflator was 2.9 (1995 = 100).

In 1931, there was a widespread expectation that the price level would fall, and the money wage rate fell. With a lower money wage rate, the short-run aggregate supply curve shifted from SAS_{29} to SAS_{31}. But increased pessimism and lower trade decreased investment, and aggregate demand decreased to AD_{31}. In 1931, real GDP fell to £157 billion and the price level fell by 2.8.

Although the Great Depression brought enormous hardship, the distribution of that hardship was uneven. At its worst point, 16 per cent of the workforce had no jobs at all. Although there was unemployment benefit and other forms of poor relief, there was a considerable level of poverty for those on the dole. But the wallets of those who kept their jobs barely noticed the Great Depression. It is true that wages fell. But at the same time, the price level fell by more, so real wages actually rose. Thus those who had jobs were paid a wage rate that had an increasing buying power during the Great Depression.

You can begin to appreciate the magnitude of the Great Depression if you compare it with the 1991–92 recession. In 1991, real GDP fell by 1.5 per cent. In comparison, in 1931, it fell by 5.3 per cent.

Why the Great Depression Happened

The late 1920s were years of economic recovery in the world economy, but they were also years of increasing uncertainty. The main source of increased uncertainty was international. The world economy was going through tumultuous times. The patterns of world trade were changing as the United Kingdom began its period of relative economic decline and new economic powers such as Japan began to emerge. International currency fluctuations and the introduction of restrictive trade policies by many countries (see Chapter 33) further increased the uncertainty faced by firms. There was also domestic uncertainty arising from the restrictive monetary and fiscal policy followed by the government to ensure that the pound remained on the gold standard. Because prices in the United States fell, prices in the United Kingdom had to fall to maintain an exchange rate of $4.86 per pound sterling, and remain on the gold standard. This meant that the recovery in the United Kingdom was good but not booming as in the United States.

This environment of uncertainty was fuelled by the slowdown in the world economy following the stock market crash of 1929. It was this slowdown in the world economy which led to a drop in exports, which led to a fall in income, consumer spending and investment, which led to the initial leftward shift of the aggregate demand curve from AD_{29} to AD_{31} in Figure 31.12.

Output fell for two years after 1929, but what stopped the Great Depression in the United Kingdom developing into the disaster that hit the United States was the fact that the United Kingdom left the gold standard. Leaving the gold standard meant that the pound was no longer convertible into gold, and interest rates that were kept high to make the pound attractive relative to the price of gold in US dollars could now be lower. Indeed, interest rates fell dramatically in the 1930s. Money was cheap, and lower interest rates fuelled a consumer revival and a housebuilding boom.

What really distinguishes the Great Depression was not what happened in the United Kingdom but what happened to the world's largest economy – the United States. Between 1929 and 1933 in the United States real GDP fell by nearly 30 per cent. But economists, even to this day, have not reached an agreement on how to explain those events. One view, argued by Peter Temin,[2] is that spending continued to fall for a wide variety of reasons – including a continuation of increasing pessimism and uncertainty. According to Temin's view, the continued contraction resulted from a collapse of expenditure that was independent of the decrease in the quantity of money. The investment demand curve shifted leftward. Milton Friedman and Anna J. Schwartz have argued that the continuation of the contraction was almost exclusively the result of the subsequent worsening of financial and monetary conditions.[3] According to Friedman and Schwartz, it was a severe cut in the money supply that lowered aggregate demand, prolonging the contraction and deepening the depression.

Although there is disagreement about the causes of the contraction phase of the Great Depression in the United States, the disagreement is not about the elements at work but the degree of importance attached to each. Everyone agrees that increased pessimism and uncertainty lowered investment demand, and everyone agrees that there was a massive contraction of the real money supply. Temin and his supporters assign primary importance to the fall in autonomous

---

[2] Peter Temin, *Did Monetary Forces Cause the Great Depression?* 1976 (New York, W.W. Norton).

[3] This explanation was developed by Milton Friedman and Anna J. Schwartz in *A Monetary History of the United States 1867–1960*, 1963 (Princeton, Princeton University Press), Chapter 7.

expenditure and secondary importance to the fall in the money supply. Friedman and Schwartz and their supporters assign primary responsibility to the money supply and regard the other factors as being of limited importance.

Let's look at the contraction of aggregate demand a bit more closely. Between 1930 and 1933, the nominal money supply in the United States decreased by 20 per cent. This decrease in the money supply was not directly induced by the Federal Reserve's actions. The *monetary base* (currency in circulation and bank reserves) hardly fell at all. But the bank deposits component of the money supply suffered an enormous collapse. It did so primarily because a large number of banks failed. Before the Great Depression, fuelled by increasing share prices and booming business conditions, bank loans expanded. But after the stock market crash and the downturn, many borrowers found themselves in hard economic times. They could not pay the interest on their loans, and they could not meet the agreed repayment schedules. Banks had deposits that exceeded the realistic value of the loans that they had made. When depositors withdrew funds from the banks, the banks lost reserves and many of them simply couldn't meet their depositors' demands to be repaid.

Bank failures feed on themselves and create additional failures. Seeing banks fail, people become anxious to protect themselves and so take their money out of the banks. This happened in the United States in 1930. The quantity of notes and coins in circulation increased and the volume of bank deposits declined. But the very action of people who took money out of the bank to protect their wealth accentuated the process of banking failure. Banks were increasingly short of cash and unable to meet their obligations.

Monetary contraction also occurred in the United Kingdom, although on a less serious scale than in the United States. The broad money supply fell in 1931 by 1 per cent and did not decline in any other year, in contrast to the whopping 20 per cent in the United States. Also, the United Kingdom had no serious problems with bank failure in contrast to the United States. This was because lower interest rates meant that money was cheap and also banks always had access to the Bank of England. Another reason was the development of branch banking in the United Kingdom, which meant that if a particular sector that was concentrated in a geographical region was to collapse, the commercial bank would not go down with

it. The main bank office in London could shore up any loss-making branches in a region.

What role did the stock market crash of 1929 play in producing the Great Depression in the United States? It certainly created an atmosphere of fear and panic, and probably contributed to the overall air of uncertainty that dampened investment spending. It also reduced the wealth of shareholders, encouraging them to cut their consumption spending. But the direct effect of the stock market crash on consumption, although a contributory factor to the Great Depression, was not the major source of the drop in aggregate demand. It was the collapse in investment arising from increased uncertainty that brought the 1930 decline in aggregate demand.

The stock market crash was, however, a predictor of severe recession. It reflected the expectations of shareholders concerning future profit prospects. As those expectations became pessimistic, people sold their shares. There were more sellers than buyers and the prices of shares were bid lower and lower. That is, the behaviour of the stock market was a consequence of expectations about future profitability and those expectations were lowered as a result of increased uncertainty.

Can It Happen Again?

Because we have an incomplete understanding of the causes of the Great Depression, we are not able to predict such an event or to be sure that it cannot occur again. The stock market crash of 1987 did not translate into a world slowdown or a contraction anything like that of 1929. But there are some significant differences between the economy of the 1990s and that of the 1930s that make a severe depression much less likely today than it was 60 years ago. The most significant features of the economy that make severe depression less likely today are:

◆ Bank deposit protection.

◆ The Bank of England's role as lender of last resort.

◆ Taxes and government spending.

◆ Multi-income families.

Let's examine these in turn.

Bank Deposit Protection

The Bank of England deposit protection scheme covers 90 per cent of the first £20,000 per depositor of the banks that come under the scheme. So small depositors are virtually fully covered. With some form of deposit insurance, depositors have little to lose if a bank fails and so have no incentive to cause a panic by withdrawing their deposits, and thereby precipitating a bank crisis.

Although bank failure was not a severe problem in the United Kingdom during the Great Depression, it clearly was an important factor in intensifying the depression in the United States. And the severity of the US recession certainly had an impact on the United Kingdom and the rest of the world. World trade fell dramatically from 1930 to 1933 with the fall in aggregate demand in the United States.

Lender of Last Resort

The Bank of England is the lender of last resort in the UK economy and the individual central banks in the European Monetary Union continue to act as the lender of last resort for their country banks. If a single bank is short of reserves, it can borrow reserves from other banks. If the entire banking system is short of reserves, banks in the UK can borrow from the Bank of England. By making reserves available (at a suitable interest rate), the Bank of England is able to make the quantity of reserves in the banking system respond flexibly to the demand for those reserves. Bank failure can be prevented, or at least contained, to cases where bad management practices are the source of the problem. Widespread failures of the type that occurred in the Great Depression can be prevented.

Taxes and Government Spending

The government sector was a much smaller part of the economy in 1929 than it has become today. On the eve of that earlier recession, government purchases of goods and services were less than 25 per cent of GDP. Today, government purchases exceed 40 per cent of GDP. Government transfer payments were about 6 per cent of GDP in 1929. Today, they are 18 per cent of GDP.

A higher level of government purchases of goods and services means that when recession hits, a large component of aggregate demand does not decline. But government transfer payments are the most sensitive economic stabilizer. When the economy goes into recession and depression, more people qualify for unemployment insurance and social assistance. As a consequence, although disposable income decreases, the extent of the decrease is moderated by the existence of such programmes. Consumption expenditure, in turn, does not decline by as much as

it would in the absence of such government programmes. The limited decline in consumption spending further limits the overall decrease in aggregate expenditure, thereby limiting the magnitude of an economic downturn.

Multi-income Families

At the time of the Great Depression, families with more than one wage earner were much less common than they are today. The workforce participation rate in 1929 was around 45 per cent. Today, it is 75 per cent. Thus even if the unemployment rate increased to around 20 per cent today, 60 per cent of the adult population would actually have jobs. During the Great Depression, only 40 per cent of the adult population had work. Multi-income families have greater security than single-income families. The chance of both (or all) income earners in a family losing their jobs simultaneously is much lower than the chance of a single earner losing work. With greater family income security, family consumption is likely to be less sensitive to fluctuations in family income that are seen as temporary. Thus when aggregate income falls, it does not induce an equivalent cut in consumption. For example, during the 1980–81 recession real GDP fell but personal consumption expenditure did not.

For the four reasons we have just reviewed, it appears the economy has better shock-absorbing characteristics today than it had in the 1920s and 1930s. Even if there is a collapse of confidence leading to a decrease in investment, the recession mechanism that is now in place will not translate that initial shock into the large and prolonged decrease in real GDP and increase in unemployment that occurred more than 60 years ago.

Because the economy is now more immune to severe recession than it was in the 1930s, even a stock market crash of the magnitude that occurred in 1987 had barely noticeable effects on spending. A crash of a similar magnitude in 1929 resulted in the collapse of investment and consumer durable purchases in the United Kingdom. In the period following the 1987 stock market crash, investment and spending on durable goods continued to grow.

None of this is to say that there might not be a deep recession or even a Great Depression in the next few years (or beyond). But it would take a very severe shock to trigger one. Reading Between the Lines (pp. 728–729) looks at a potential banking collapse in Argentina that could turn into a severe contraction in the money supply as in the case of the USA in 1929.

We have now completed our study of the business cycle. Economic analysts use theories of the business cycle to forecast recessions and booms. We have discovered that these issues pose huge policy challenges. How can we speed up the rate of economic growth while at the same time keeping inflation low and avoiding big swings of the business cycle? Our task in the next chapter is to study these macroeconomic policy challenges.

Summary

Key Points

Cycle Patterns, Impulses and Mechanisms (pp. 705–706)

- Since the turn of the century, there have been nine business cycle turning points.

- Recessions have on the average lasted about two years, while expansions have lasted on the average about six years.

- The Great Depression was the most severe contraction of real GDP.

- Postwar recessions have been milder than prewar recessions.

Aggregate Demand Theories of the Business Cycle (pp. 706–713)

- Aggregate demand theories of the cycle are based on the aggregate supply–aggregate demand model.

- Keynesian theory is based on volatile expectations about future sales and profits.

- Monetarist theory regards fluctuations in the money stock as the main source of economic fluctuations.

- Rational expectations theories identify unanticipated fluctuations in aggregate demand as the main source of economic fluctuations.

Real Business Cycle Theory (pp. 713–717)

- In real business cycle (RBC) theory, economic fluctuations are caused by fluctuations in the influence of technological change on productivity growth.

- A temporary slowdown in the pace of technological change decreases investment demand and both the demand for labour and the supply of labour.

The 1991–92 Recession (pp. 717–720)

- Three forces contributed to the weak performance of the UK economy in the early 1990s: the ERM, the reunification of Germany and a slowdown in economic expansion in the world economy.

The Great Depression (pp. 720–724)

- The Great Depression started with increased uncertainty and pessimism that brought a fall in investment and spending.

- Increased uncertainty and pessimism also brought on the stock market crash. The crash added to the pessimistic outlook and further spending cuts occurred.

- In the United States, banks failed and the money supply decreased, resulting in a continued decrease in aggregate demand. The chaos in the United States influenced economic activity throughout the world.

- A repeat of such a depression is much less likely today. The central bank's willingness to act as lender of last resort and the introduction of the deposit protection scheme both reduce the risk of bank failure and financial collapse.

- Higher taxes and government spending have given the economy greater resistance against depression, and an increased workforce participation rate provides a greater measure of security, especially for families with more than one wage earner.

Key Figures ◈

Key Terms

Problems

Use the figure for all the problems.

●**1** The figure shows the economy of Virtual Reality. When the economy is in a long-run equilibrium, it is at points *b*, *f* and *j*. When a recession occurs in Virtual Reality, the economy moves away from these points to one of the three other points identified in each part of the figure.

   a If the Keynesian theory is the correct explanation for the recession, to which points does the economy move?

   b If the monetarist theory is the correct explanation for the recession, to which points does the economy move?

   c If the new classical rational expectations theory is the correct explanation for the recession, to which points does the economy move?

   d If the new Keynesian rational expectations theory is the correct explanation for the recession, to which points does the economy move?

   e If real business cycle theory is the correct explanation for the recession, to which points does the economy move?

2 The figure shows the economy of Vital Signs. When the economy is in a long-run equilibrium, it is at points *a*, *e* and *i*. When an expansion occurs in Vital Signs, the economy moves away from these points to one of the three other points identified in each part of the figure.

   a If the Keynesian theory is the correct explanation for the recession, to which points does the economy move?

   b If the monetarist theory is the correct explanation for the recession, to which points does the economy move?

   c If the new classical rational expectations theory is the correct explanation for the recession, to which points does the economy move?

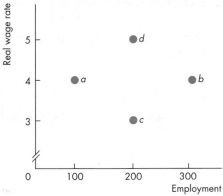

(a) Labour market

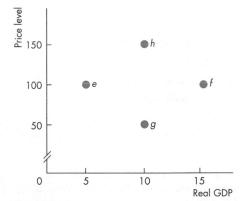

(b) AS-AD

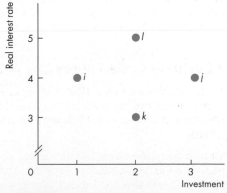

(c) Investment

d If the new Keynesian rational expectations theory is the correct explanation for the recession, to which points does the economy move?

e If real business cycle theory is the correct explanation for the recession, to which points does the economy move?

●**3** Suppose that when the recession occurs in Virtual Reality, the economy moves to *d*, *g* and *k*. Which theory of the business cycle, if any, explains this outcome?

4 Suppose that when the expansion occurs in Vital Signs, the economy moves to *d*, *h* and *l*. Which theory of the business cycle, if any, explains this outcome?

●**5** Suppose that when the recession occurs in Virtual Reality, the economy moves to *c*, *g* and *k*. Which theory of the business cycle, if any, explains this outcome?

6 Suppose that when the expansion occurs in Vital Signs, the economy moves to *c*, *h* and *l*. Which theory of the business cycle, if any, explains this outcome?

●**7** Suppose that when the recession occurs in Virtual Reality, the economy moves to *d*, *h* and *k*. Which theory of the business cycle, if any, explains this outcome?

8 Suppose that when the expansion occurs in Vital Signs, the economy moves to *d*, *g* and *l*.

Which theory of the business cycle, if any, explains this outcome?

●**9** Suppose that when the recession occurs in Virtual Reality, the economy moves to *c*, *h* and *k*. Which theory of the business cycle, if any, explains this outcome?

10 Suppose that when the expansion occurs in Vital Signs, the economy moves to *c*, *g* and *l*. Which theory of the business cycle, if any, explains this outcome?

●**11** Suppose that when the recession occurs in Virtual Reality, the economy moves to *d*, *g* and *l*. Which theory of the business cycle, if any, explains this outcome?

12 Suppose that when the expansion occurs in Vital Signs, the economy moves to *c*, *h* and *k*. Which theory of the business cycle, if any, explains this outcome?

●**13** Suppose that when the recession occurs in Virtual Reality, the economy moves to *c*, *g* and *l*. Which theory of the business cycle, if any, explains this outcome?

14 Suppose that when the expansion occurs in Vital Signs, the economy moves to *d*, *h* and *k*. Which theory of the business cycle, if any, explains this outcome?

Critical Thinking

1 Study Reading Between the Lines on pp. 728–729 and then answer the following questions:

  a What is the reason for the banking crisis in Argentina? Why do people want to withdraw their dollar deposits from the banks?

  b Why is there an expectation that the Argentine government will default on its debt?

  c Why have interest rates on Argentine government bonds risen so sharply?

  d What is the likely effect of the rise in interest rates on aggregate demand?

  e What are the dangers to the Argentine economy of a banking collapse? What solution would you recommend for the government to ride this crisis?

2 Use the links on the Parkin, Powell and Matthews website to obtain information about the current state of the US economy. Then:

  a List all of the features of the US economy during the current year that you think are consistent with a pessimistic outlook for the next two years.

  b List all of the features of the US economy during the current year that you think are consistent with an optimistic outlook for the next two years.

  c Describe how you think the US economy is going to evolve over the next year or two. Explain your predictions, drawing on the pessimistic and optimistic factors that you listed in parts (a) and (b) and on your knowledge of macroeconomic theory.

The Argentine Depression – 1929 Repeated?

THE FINANCIAL TIMES, 1ST DECEMBER 2001

Argentina appeals for calm as bank withdrawals rise

Thomas Catán

Domingo Cavallo, Argentina's economy minister, yesterday appealed for calm as nervous Argentines began to step up their withdrawals from banks.

Interbank interest rates soared above 500 per cent as banks faced difficulties meeting increased withdrawals. Talk that the government would be forced to impose capital controls next week to prevent a collapse of the banking system further spurred jitters among Argentines.

'Deposits are being withdrawn and there are expectations of a devaluation, and that is terrible,' Mr Cavallo said in a televised press conference. Mr Cavallo blamed 'irresponsible people talking about devaluation' for the fresh wave of worries engulfing the Argentine economy. 'People's savings are safe,' Mr Cavallo insisted.

The government has moved to restructure much of its $95 bn in bonds at lower interest rates. Yesterday Mr Cavallo said that more than $40 bn in bonds had been tendered to the local tranche of the debt exchange designed to reduce the government's interest payments.

Despite the beneficial effects from the swap, the country's bonds fell to new lows yesterday, with the interest premium on Argentina's borrowing rising above 34 percentage points. The country's stock market also fell to a 10-year low, and peso futures rose sharply as investors bet the country would be forced to abandon its 10-year peg to the dollar.

For over a year, investors have feared that Argentina would be forced to default on its $155 bn public sector debt as a three-year recession showed no signs of abating. Cut off from credit, the country has so far stayed afloat by pressuring banks and pension funds to buy government debt.

Since June, banks have lost around 15 per cent of deposits, as crisis-wary Argentines withdrew their savings. In recent days, that process appeared to accelerate, sparking fears that the country's debt crisis was now moving into a full-blown banking crisis.

Yesterday, Fernando de la Rua, Argentina's president, insisted that the government would not devalue its currency. However, analysts are increasingly concerned about the erosion of the country's foreign currency reserves, which back the country's peg with the dollar.

The Essence of the Story

- Bank deposits in Argentina are being withdrawn by customers nervous that they would be unable to get their money if the government imposed controls on withdrawals.

- The Argentine peso is one-to-one convertible with the US dollar. Argentine depositors are withdrawing their funds from the bank because there is wide-spread expectation that the peso will be devalued against the dollar.

- The government in Argentina has maintained a high level of expenditure and accumulated a high level of debt.

- For three years Argentina has suffered recession and government revenues have been insufficient to pay the interest on the accumulated debt.

- The fear of a major debt default by the Argentine government has sent government bond interest rates up to 33 per cent.

- Much of government debt is held by pension funds, domestic banks and domestic branches of foreign banks.

Economic Analysis

- A history of high inflation (sometimes higher than 2000 per cent a year) and poor monetary management has left the Argentine authorities with low anti-inflation credibility (look ahead to Chapter 32 on Inflation policy). The lack of monetary credibility has persuaded the Argentine government to adopt a currency board system linked to the US dollar.

- A currency board system is one where the central bank allows the peso to be fully convertible to the dollar, and allows dollars to be used in transactions alongside the peso. For the currency board system to work, the central bank must hold as many dollars in reserves as the total of pesos in circulation.

- The banks create dollar deposits by making dollar loans using the deposit multiplier (see Chapter 25). In November 2001, the dollar deposits of banks were $49 billion and peso deposits were $21 billion.

- A long recession has reduced the government's revenues and its ability to pay the interest on its dollar denominated debt. Figure 1 shows that both real GDP and the price level has fallen in the three years to 2001.

- The technical insolvency of the government has led to a fall in demand for Argentine government bonds and a rise in the rate of interest (Chapter 26 explains why the rate of interest and the price of the bond is inversely related). Figure 2 shows how much the rate of interest has risen in 2001.

- The rise in the rate of interest has increased the cost of borrowing and reduced aggregate demand, increasing the recessionary gap as shown in Figure 3. The AD curve would shift to the left from AD_{01} to AD_{02}. The widespread belief that the government will default and devalue the peso against the dollar has people rushing to get their dollar deposits from the banks.

- But if people try to withdraw all their dollar deposits from the banks, the banks could fail and there could be a massive contraction in the money supply as occurred in the USA in 1929. In which case the shift of the AD curve in Figure 3 would be much greater.

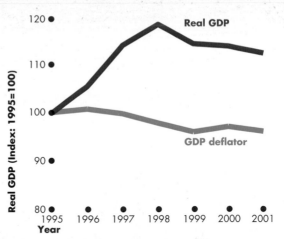

Figure 1 **Real GDP and GDP deflator**

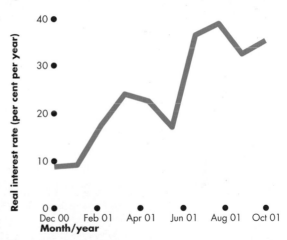

Figure 2 **Interest rate**

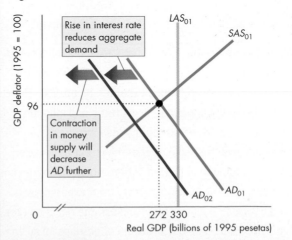

Figure 3 **AS–AD**

Business Cycles

. . . in the great booms and depressions, . . . the two big bad actors are debt disturbances and price level disturbances.

Irving Fisher, The Debt Deflation Theory of Depressions, Econometrica, 1933

The Economist: Irving Fisher

Irving Fisher (1867–1947) is the greatest American-born economist. The son of a Congregational minister who died as Irving was finishing high school, he paid his way through Yale and earned enough money to support his mother and younger brother by tutoring his fellow students.

Irving Fisher came to economics by way of mathematics. He was Yale's first PhD candidate in pure economics, but was a student in the mathematics department!

The contributions that Fisher made to economics cover the entire subject. He is best known for his work on the quantity theory of money (Chapter 25, pp. 560–564) and the relation between interest rates and inflation (Chapter 28, pp. 647–648). But he also wrote on the business cycle. He believed that the Great Depression was caused because the fall in the price level increased the real burden of debts. He wrote from experience: he had borrowed heavily to buy stocks in the rising market of the late 1920s and lost a fortune of perhaps 10 million dollars in the crash of 1929.

The Issues and Ideas

Economic activity has fluctuated between boom and bust for as long as we've had records. And understanding the sources of economic fluctuations has turned out to be difficult. One reason is that there are no simple patterns. Every new episode of the business cycle is different from its predecessor in some way. Some cycles are long and some short, some are mild and some severe, some begin in Europe and some abroad. We never know with any certainty when the next turning point (down or up) is coming or what will cause it. A second reason is that the apparent waste of resources during a recession or depression seems to contradict the very foundation of economics: resources are limited and people have unlimited wants – there is scarcity. A satisfactory theory of the business cycle must explain why scarce resources don't *always* get fully employed.

One theory is that recessions result from insufficient aggregate demand. The solution is to increase government spending, cut taxes and cut interest rates. But demand stimulation must not be overdone. Countries that stimulate aggregate demand too much, such as Brazil, find their economic growth rates sagging, unemployment rising and inflation accelerating.

Today's new theory, real business cycle theory, predicts that fluctuations in aggregate demand have no effect on output and employment and change only the price level and inflation rate. But this theory ignores the real effects of financial collapse of the type that occurred in the 1930s. If banks fail on a large scale and people lose their wealth, other firms also begin to fail and jobs are destroyed. Unemployed people cut their spending, and output falls further. Demand stimulation may not be called for, but action to ensure that sound banks survive certainly is.

While economists are trying to understand the sources of the business cycle, the government and the Bank of England are doing the best they can to moderate the cycle. In the years since the Second World War, there appears to have been some success. Although the business cycle has not disappeared, it has become much less severe.

Then . . .

What happens to the economy when people lose confidence in banks? They withdraw their funds. These withdrawals feed on themselves, creating a snowball of withdrawals and, eventually, panic. Short of funds with which to repay depositors, banks call in loans and previously sound businesses are faced with financial distress. They close down and lay off workers. And recession deepens and turns into depression. Bank failures and the resulting decline in the nation's supply of money and credit were a significant factor in deepening and prolonging the Great Depression. But they taught us the importance of stable financial institutions and gave rise to the establishment of a bank deposit protection scheme to prevent such financial collapse.

. . . And Now

How can a building designed as a shop have no better use than to be boarded up and left empty? Not enough aggregate demand, say the Keynesians. Not so, say the real business cycle theorists. Technological change has reduced the building's current productivity as a shop to zero. But its expected future productivity is sufficiently high that it is not efficient to refit the building for some other purpose.

All unemployment, whether of buildings or people, can be explained in a similar way. For example, how can it be that during a recession, a person trained as a shop assistant is without work? Not enough aggregate demand is one answer. Another is that the current productivity of shop assistants is low, but their expected future productivity is sufficiently high that it does not pay an unemployed assistant to retrain for a job that is currently available.

CHAPTER 32

Macroeconomic Policy Challenges

After studying this chapter you will be able to:

◆ Describe the goals of macroeconomic policy

◆ Describe the main features of recent fiscal and monetary policy in the European Union and the eurozone

◆ Explain how fiscal policy and monetary policy influence long-term economic growth

◆ Evaluate fixed-rule and feedback-rule policies to stabilize the business cycle

◆ Explain how fiscal policy influences the natural unemployment rate

◆ Evaluate fixed-rule and feedback-rule policies to contain inflation

◆ Explain why lowering inflation usually brings recession

What Can Policy Do?

The UK economy has been doing well since the last recession in 1991–92. Real GDP growth has been higher than historic trends, inflation has fallen to less than 2 per cent, and unemployment has fallen consistently. The United Kingdom was not alone in achieving a respectable macroeconomic performance over this period. The USA has had a phenomenal growth performance, but also low inflation and falling unemployment. In 2000 the UK grew by 3.1 per cent, and the EU grew by 3.4 per cent, but the USA grew by 4.1 per cent. At the other end of the spectrum, Japan grew by only 1.5 per cent in 2000 ◆ But now there are clouds, even in the USA's economic sky. The world economy had grown so fast in 2000, no one believed that it could be sustained. Over investment in IT had seen a fall in profits and everyone was expecting a rapid cooling down of the US and world economies. Then came the terrorist attacks of 11 September 2001 and the world was hit by further uncertainty as aggregate spending in the US slowed even further and the world slid closer to recession. With Japan already showing signs of falling growth, the danger for the UK is the possibility of the economy sliding into another recession. ◆ The new dangers to the world econnomy raises questions about macroeconomic policy. How do fiscal and monetary policy influence the economy? What can policy do to improve macroeconomic performance? Can the government use its fiscal policy to speed up long-term growth, keep inflation in check and maintain a low unemployment rate? Can the central bank use its monetary policy to achieve any of these ends? Are some policy goals better achieved by fiscal policy and some by monetary policy? And what specific policy actions do the best job? Are some ways of conducting policy better than others? In Reading Between the Lines, pp. 754–755, we examine the problems of the Japanese economy and the policy options available to the Bank of Japan to encourage spending and increase aggregate demand.

◆ ◆ ◆ ◆ In this chapter we're going to study the challenges of using policy to influence the economy and achieve the highest sustainable long-term growth rate and low unemployment while avoiding high inflation. At the end of the chapter, you will have a clearer and deeper understanding of the macroeconomic policy problems facing the United Kingdom and other EU countries today and of the debates that surround us concerning those problems.

Policy Goals

The goals of macroeconomic policy are to:

◆ Achieve the highest sustainable rate of long-term real GDP growth.

◆ Smooth out avoidable business cycle fluctuations.

◆ Maintain low unemployment.

◆ Maintain low inflation.

Long-term Real GDP Growth

We examined growth briefly in Chapter 30 (Figure 30.1, p. 681). Rapid sustained real GDP growth can make a profound contribution to economic well-being. With a growth rate of 2.5 per cent a year, it takes 28 years for production to double. With a growth rate of 5 per cent a year, production doubles in just over 14 years. The limits to *sustainable* growth are determined by the availability of natural resources, by environmental considerations, and by the willingness of people to save and invest in new capital and new technologies rather than consume everything they produce.

How fast can the economy grow over the long term? Between 1987 and 2000, through one complete business cycle, potential GDP grew at a rate of 2.3 per cent a year. Because the UK population grows at about 0.5 per cent a year, a real GDP growth rate of 2.3 per cent a year translates into a growth rate of real GDP per person of 1.8 per cent a year, which means that output per person doubles every 39 years. So increasing the long-term growth rate is of critical importance.

The Business Cycle

Potential GDP probably does not grow at a constant rate. Fluctuations in the pace of technological advance and in the pace of investment in new capital bring fluctuations in potential GDP. So some fluctuations in real GDP represent fluctuations in potential GDP. But when real GDP grows less quickly than potential GDP, output is lost, and when real GDP grows more quickly than potential GDP, bottlenecks arise that create inefficiencies and inflationary pressures. Keeping real GDP growth steady and equal to long-run aggregate supply growth avoids these problems.

It is not known how smooth real GDP can be made. Real business cycle theory regards all the fluctuations in real GDP as arising from fluctuations in potential GDP. The aggregate demand theories of the business cycle regard most of the fluctuations in real GDP as being avoidable deviations from potential GDP.

Unemployment

When real GDP growth slows, unemployment increases and rises above the natural rate of unemployment. The higher the unemployment rate, the longer is the time taken by unemployed people to find jobs. Productive labour is wasted and there is a slowdown in the accumulation of human capital. If high unemployment persists, serious psychological and social problems arise for the unemployed workers and their families.

When real GDP growth speeds up, unemployment decreases and falls below the natural rate of unemployment. The lower the unemployment rate, the harder it becomes for expanding industries to get the labour they need to keep growing. If extremely low unemployment persists, serious bottlenecks and production dislocations occur, sucking in imports and creating inflationary pressure.

Keeping unemployment at the natural rate avoids both of these problems. But just what is the natural rate of unemployment? Assessments vary. The actual average unemployment rate over the most recent business cycle – 1987 to 2000 – was 8.2 per cent. Most economists would put the natural rate at about 5–6 per cent. But real business cycle theorists believe the natural rate fluctuates and equals the actual unemployment rate.

If the natural unemployment rate becomes high, then a goal of policy is to lower the natural rate itself. This goal is independent of smoothing the business cycle.

Inflation

When inflation fluctuates unpredictably, money becomes less useful as a measuring rod for conducting transactions. Borrowers and lenders and employers and workers must take on extra risks. Keeping the inflation rate steady and predictable avoids these problems.

Keeping inflation steady also helps keep the value of the pound abroad steady. Other things remaining the same, if the inflation rate goes up by 1 percentage point, the pound loses 1 per cent of its value against the currencies of other countries. Large and unpredictable fluctuations in the foreign exchange rate – the value of the pound against other currencies – make international trade and international borrowing and lending less profitable and limit the gains from international specialization and exchange. Keeping inflation low and predictable helps avoid such fluctuations in the exchange rate and enables international transactions to be undertaken at minimum risk and on the desired scale.

What is the most desirable inflation rate? Some economists say that the *rate* of inflation doesn't matter much as long as the rate is *predictable*. So, say these economists, any predictable inflation rate will serve well as a target for policy. But most economists believe that price stability, which they translate at an inflation rate of between 0 and 2 per cent, is desirable. The reason zero is not the target is that some price increases are due to quality improvements – a measurement bias in the price index – so a positive average *measured* inflation rate is equivalent to price stability. It has been suggested that a good definition of price stability is a situation in which no one considers inflation to be a factor in the decisions they make.

Three Core Policy Indicators: Unemployment, Inflation and Growth

Although macroeconomic policy pursues the four goals we've just considered, the goals are not independent. Three of these goals – increasing real GDP growth, smoothing the business cycle and maintaining low unemployment – are interlinked and they lie at the core of economic policy in Europe. The level of unemployment tells us about the state of the business cycle and the structural problems of the economy. The goal of reducing the number of long-term unemployed people – a particularly pressing problem in the European Union – is linked to the goal of high and sustainable long-term growth. If unemployment falls below the natural rate, then growth may be too rapid. If unemployment rises above the natural rate, then growth may be too slow. So monitoring unemployment at its natural rate is equivalent to avoiding business fluctuations and keeping real GDP growing steadily at its maximum sustainable rate.

Policy performance, judged by the three core policy targets – inflation, unemployment and growth – is shown in Figure 32.1. In Figure 32.1(a), the blue dot is the coordinate of inflation and unemployment for each of the European Union countries in 2000. You can see that all the countries in the EU except for

Figure 32.1

Macroeconomic Performance: EU Inflation and Unemployment, 2000

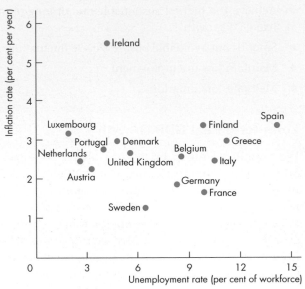

(a) Inflation and unemployment, 2000

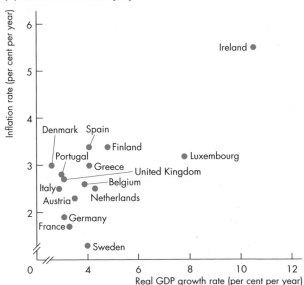

(b) Inflation and real GDP growth, 2000

Unemployment reduction, low inflation and high growth are important objectives of the EU states. Part (a) shows that most countries in the EU have low inflation but there is considerable variation in unemployment. Spain and Greece have the highest unemployment in the EU. Ireland had the highest inflation in 2000. Part (b) shows that there has been considerable convergence in growth. The core countries of Italy, Germany and France have low inflation but lower than average growth.

Source: European Commission.

Ireland have converged to a low rate of inflation. But unemployment remains a huge problem for some countries. Unemployment has fallen in Austria, Denmark, Sweden, Portugal, Netherlands, Ireland and the UK, but remains stubbornly high in Spain, Greece and Finland and in the core area of the EU – Germany, France and Italy. Figure 32.1(b) shows the coordinates of inflation and real GDP growth in 2000. The figure shows that there has been stronger convergence in growth (except for Ireland) in 2000. One of the stated objectives of the European Commission is to raise the sustainable rate of growth of GDP in the European Union to 3 per cent a year, to aid the process of unemployment reduction, and to carry out microeconomic reforms to reduce the natural rate of unemployment.

Review Quiz

◆ What are the objectives of macroeconomic stabilization policy?
◆ Can stabilization policy keep the unemployment rate below the natural rate.
◆ Why are GDP growth, inflation and unemployment the three core policy indicators.

We've examined the policy goals. Let's now look at the policy tools and the way they have been used.

Policy Tools and Performance

The tools used to try to achieve macroeconomic performance objectives are fiscal policy and monetary policy. **Fiscal policy**, which is described in Chapter 24 (pp. 516–533), is the use of the government budget to achieve macroeconomic objectives. The detailed fiscal policy tools are tax rates and government purchases of goods and services. **Monetary policy**, which is described in Chapter 26 (pp. 572–594), is the adjustment of the quantity of money in circulation and interest rates by the central bank to achieve macroeconomic objectives. How fiscal and monetary policy is used together is examined in Chapter 27 (pp. 602–618). How have the tools actually been used in the European Union and the European Central Bank? Let's answer this question by summarizing the main directions of fiscal and monetary policy in recent years.

Recent Fiscal Policy in the European Union

Figure 32.2 gives a broad summary of fiscal policy since 1999 for the countries of the European Union. One of the conditions of entry to EMU was that budget deficits be reduced. Figure 32.2 shows general government spending as a percentage of GDP in part (a) and the general government deficit as a percentage of GDP in part (b). Fiscal policy has been tightened considerably in most countries. But the high average level of unemployment in the EU for 2000 – 8.4 per cent made it difficult for the member states to tighten fiscal policy. Automatic fiscal policy rises when unemployment increases. But discretionary fiscal policy was tight. Most governments reduced government spending as a proportion of GDP between 1999 and 2000. The movement of the budget deficit also supported a general fiscal tightening. All the countries reduced their budget deficits or increased their surplus. Economists of the Keynesian school argue that the general fiscal tightening in Europe has made it difficult to reduce the additional unemployment caused by the recession of 1990–92. But, countries in the EMU have agreed to a Stability Pact that aims to keep the budget deficit within a maximum ceiling. The purpose of the stability pact is to coordinate eurozone-wide fiscal policy to have a low budget deficit which would allow the European Central Bank to conduct monetary policy with low interest rates. The low interest rate is expected to produce a favourable growth in private investment.

The Stability Pact has hindered governments from using fiscal policy to stabilize the economy according to Keynesian theory.

Let's now look at monetary policy.

Recent Monetary Policy by the ECB

Since 1 January 1999, the monetary policy of the countries that comprise the single currency area of the eurozone has been conducted by the European Central Bank (ECB) in Frankfurt. The objective of the ECB is to maintain price stability and to support the Commission's objective of non-inflationary growth.

The task of monetary policy has been to keep a lid on inflationary pressure, defined as an inflation rate of below 2 per cent a year. In this task, the ECB monitors the rate of growth of broad money (M3) and adjusts the rate of interest upwards if the money supply and other monetary indicators show that the eurozone economy as a whole is expanding above

Figure 32.2

The Fiscal Policy Record

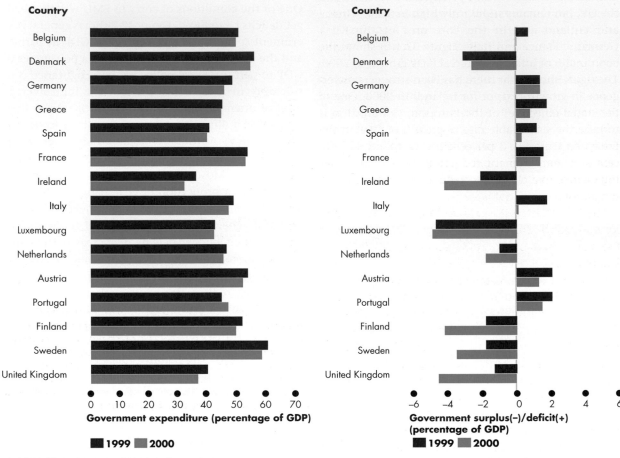

(a) General government expenditure of EU member states 1999 and 2000

(b) General government budget deficit of EU member states, 1999 and 2000

Fiscal policy is summarized here by the performance of general government spending (part a) and the deficit (part b) between 1999 and 2000 for the EU member states. The general trend was for a tightening in fiscal policy. All countries except Portugal reduced government expenditure. All countries in the EU reduced their budget deficit as a proportion of GDP or increased their surplus.

Source: *European Commission.*

potential output, and adjusting interest rates downward if the reverse was expected. However, there has been concern as to whether one monetary policy can suit so many different countries in the EMU. In 2000, real GDP growth in Ireland was 10.5 per cent. At the other extreme Denmark's real GDP growth was 2.6 per cent. On inflation, Ireland had the highest with an inflation of 5.5 per cent in 2000 and Sweden had the lowest with inflation of 1.3 per cent.

In 2000 the ECB raised interest rates and tightened monetary policy. The growth of the money supply in the eurozone was brought under control but inflation in the eurozone crept up above the 2 per cent ceiling set by the ECB. While this was good news for the fast growing economies of the periphery like Ireland, Finland, Spain and Greece, it created deflationary pressure in the core countries of Germany, France and Italy.

Evidence of a strong slowing down in the world economy and the eurozone economy emerged during 2001. There was strong pressure from the governments of the larger countries for monetary policy to be eased, the money supply to be increased and interest rates to be lowered. The ECB was caught between a number of conflicting objectives. To appear to give in to political pressure would undermine its credibility as an independent central bank but a slowing down in the eurozone economy means that aggregate demand will grow less than potential output and inflation will fall as a consequence. Yet inflation in the eurozone had not fallen below the ceiling of 2 per cent and the longer it remained above it, the greater the chance that the ECB would lose its low inflation reputation as a central bank.

The ECB resisted the calls to loosen monetary policy and reduce the rate of interest until the middle of the year. The money supply increased but inflation still remained above 2 per cent. In August the ECB cut the rate of interest further as inflation began to fall with the slowdown in the eurozone economy. In coordination with the Federal Reserve in the USA, the ECB cut the rate of interest again in September 2001 following the terrorist attack in New York. Inflation had fallen again and the money supply was increased again. Figure 32.3 shows the monetary policy record of the ECB with the EU rate of inflation.

The independence of the ECB with the specific objective of price stability has raised concerns that monetary policy can no longer be coordinated with fiscal policy. The policy of the ECB in aiming for price stability has reduced the ability of the individual countries in the eurozone to conduct stabilization policies.

Figure 32.3

The Monetary Policy Record of the ECB, 2000–2001

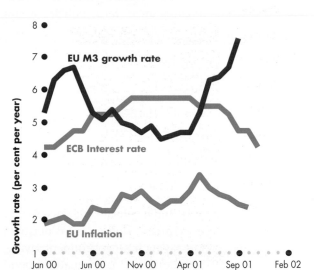

The monetary policy record is summarized here by the growth rate of M3, the ECB lending rate of interest, and the rate of inflation which the ECB is given the task of keeping below 2 per cent a year. In 2000 the ECB raised interest rates up to 5.75 per cent from 4.25 per cent. The rate of growth of money declined during 2000. The rate of interest was lowered during 2001 as the eurozone economy slowed down and particularly after September 11.

Sources: ECB.

You've now studied the goals of policy and seen the broad trends in fiscal and monetary policy in recent years in the European Union and the ECB. Let's now study the ways in which policy might be better used to achieve its goals. We'll begin by looking at long-term growth policy.

Long-term Growth Policy

The sources of the long-term growth of potential GDP, which are explained in Chapter 30 (pp. 684–685), are the accumulation of physical and human capital and the advance of technology. Here, we probe more deeply into the problem of boosting the long-term growth rate.

The factors that determine long-term growth result from millions of individual decisions; the role of government in influencing growth is limited. The

European Commission believes that any role that governments can play should be coordinated with other members of the European Union. Policy can influence the private decisions on which long-term growth depends in three areas. Such policies would increase:

1 National saving.

2 Investment in human capital.

3 Investment in new technologies.

National Saving Policies

National saving within the EU countries equals private saving plus government saving. Figure 32.4 shows the scale of national saving within the European Union since 1960 and its private and government components. The government component is obtained by subtracting private saving from government saving. From 1960 to 1975, national saving fluctuated around an average of 25 per cent of GDP. There then began a steady slide that saw national saving fall to 21 per cent in 1975 and fluctuate between 21 and 19 per cent of GDP between 1982 and 1992. Private saving has remained remarkably stable over a long period. It actually increased a little as a percentage of GDP between 1960 and 1979, when it peaked at 22 per cent of GDP, but over the whole period it has remained between 20 and 22 per cent of EU GDP. Government saving became increasingly negative during the 1980s and 1990s but ended the decade with positive saving to satisfy the conditions of entry into the EMU.

EU investment, one of the engines of growth, is not limited by saving in the European Union. The reason is that foreign saving can be harnessed to finance EU investment. But the European Union is a mature economy with the demographic problem of an ageing population. It needs to have sufficient saving to lend to the developing world and the emerging economies to meet the consumption needs of its population. Boosting the EU saving rate can help to bring faster real GDP growth for two reasons. First, the European Union represents a significant proportion of the world economy, so an increase in EU saving would increase world saving and bring lower real interest rates around the world. With lower real interest rates, investment would be boosted everywhere. The EU economy and the world economy could grow faster. Second, with more domestic saving, there might be an increase in investment in domestic high-risk, high-return new technologies that could boost long-term EU growth.

Figure 32.4

National Savings Rates in the European Union: 1960–2000

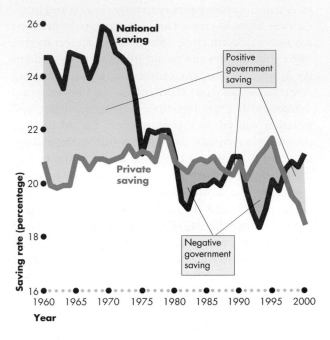

The EU gross saving rate peaked in 1970 at 25.8 per cent of EU GDP. Gross saving has fallen since that year and government saving has been the highest contributor to the fall. Private savings have remained remarkably constant since 1960, ranging between 19 and 22 per cent but has fallen in the last years of the 1990s. Government saving became positive in the last years of the 1990s in an effort to meet the strict fiscal criteria for joining the EMU.

Source: European Commission.

How can national saving be increased? The two points of attack are:

1 Increasing government saving.

2 Increasing private saving.

Increasing Government Saving

Government saving was negative during most of the 1980s, and has been an average of –1.3 per cent of GDP during the 1990s. The decline in the national savings of the EU economy is due to the public sector deficits in many European countries. Increasing government saving means eliminating the public sector deficit of the EU countries. They are one and the same action. Achieving a substantial cut in the deficit is part of the Stability Pact the eurozone countries have accepted by Treaty as a condition of the EMU. The reduction in the deficit in the EMU countries has been difficult and was achieved by privatization of some previous government-provided functions and cuts in sensitive areas such as welfare spending.

Increasing Private Saving

Private saving in the European Union as a whole has remained remarkably stable over the four decades since 1960. The only way that government actions can boost private saving is by increasing the after-tax rate of return on saving.

The most effective way of stimulating private saving is to cut taxes on interest income. But such a tax cut would be costly and could only be financed either by a further decrease in government expenditures or by increases in taxes on labour incomes or in Value Added Tax (VAT). This would be difficult politically and cannot be carried out at the EU level on existing political arrangements. So governments are limited to making minor changes to the taxation of interest income, which will have negligible effects on the saving rate.

Private Saving and Inflation

Inflation erodes the value of saving, and uncertainty about future inflation is bad for saving. One further policy, therefore, that increases the saving rate is a monetary policy that preserves stable prices and minimizes uncertainty about the future value of money. Chapter 28, pp. 638–641, spells out the broader connection between inflation and real GDP and explains why low inflation may bring greater output and faster growth.

Human Capital Policies

The accumulation of human capital plays a crucial role in economic growth and two areas are relevant: schooling and on-the-job experience. Economic research shows that schooling and training pay. That is, on the average, the greater the number of years a person remains at school or in training, the higher are that person's earnings. Schooling and higher education training in Europe are fairly good by international standards. The UK government has made it a policy issue to increase the number of university places to allow one-third of all school leavers to enter higher education.

If education and on-the-job training yield higher earnings, why does the government or the European Commission need a policy towards investment in human capital? Why can't people simply be left to get on with making their own decisions about how much human capital to acquire? The answer is that the *social* returns to human capital possibly exceed the *private* returns. The extra productivity that comes from the interactions of well-educated and experienced people exceeds what each individual can achieve alone. So left to ourselves we would probably accumulate too little human capital.

Economic research has also shown that on-the-job training pays. This type of training can be formal, such as a school at work, or informal, such as learning-by-doing. The scope for government involvement in these areas is limited, but it can set an example as an employer and it can encourage best-practice training programmes for workers.

Investment in New Technologies

As Chapter 30 explains, investment in new technologies is special for two reasons. First, it appears not to run into the problem of diminishing returns that plague all other factors of production. Second, the benefits of new technologies spill over to influence all parts of the economy, not just the firms undertaking the investment. For these reasons, a particularly promising way of boosting growth is to stimulate investment in the research and development efforts that create new technologies.

Governments can fund and provide tax incentives for research and development activities. Through the various research councils, the universities and research institutes, the governments of the European Union already fund a large amount of basic research. The European Commission estimates that about 2 per cent of EU GDP, 2.8 per cent of US GDP and 3 per cent of Japanese GDP is spent on research and technological development (RTD).

Review Quiz

- ◆ Why do long-term growth policies focus on increasing saving and increasing investment in human capital and new technologies?
- ◆ What policies can the governments in the EU take to increase the national saving rate of the EU economies?
- ◆ What action can the EU governments take to increase the rate of investment in human capital?
- ◆ What actions can the EU governments take to increase investment in new technologies?

We've seen how government might use fiscal and the central bank use monetary policy to influence long-term growth. How can the business cycle and unemployment be influenced? Let's now address this question.

Business Cycle and Unemployment Policies

Many different fiscal and monetary policies can be pursued to stabilize the business cycle and prevent swings in real GDP growth and the inflation rate. But all these polices fall into three broad categories:

1 Fixed-rule policies.

2 Feedback-rule policies.

3 Discretionary policies.

Fixed-rule Policies

A **fixed-rule policy** specifies an action to be pursued independently of the state of the economy. An everyday example of a fixed rule is a stop sign. It says 'stop regardless of the state of the road ahead – even if no other vehicle is trying to use the road'. Several fixed-rule policies have been proposed for the economy. One, proposed by Milton Friedman, is to keep the quantity of money growing at a constant rate year in and year out, regardless of the state of the economy, to make the *average* inflation rate zero. Another fixed-rule policy is to balance the government budget. Fixed rules are rarely followed in practice, but they have some merits in principle; later in this chapter we'll study the way they would work if they were pursued.

Feedback-rule Policies

A **feedback-rule policy** specifies how policy actions respond to changes in the state of the economy. A give way sign is an everyday feedback rule. It says 'stop if another vehicle is attempting to use the road ahead but otherwise, proceed'. A macroeconomic feedback-rule policy is one that changes the money supply, or interest rates, or even tax rates, in response to the state of the economy. Some feedback rules guide the actions of policy-makers. For example, the Monetary Policy Committee of the Bank of England uses a feedback rule that raises interest rates when inflation is above its target. Other feedback-rule

policies are automatic. For example, the automatic rise in taxes during an expansion and the automatic fall in taxes during a recession are feedback-rule policies.

Discretionary Policies

A **discretionary policy** responds to the state of the economy in a possibly unique way that uses all the information available, including perceived lessons from past 'mistakes'. An everyday discretionary policy occurs at an unmarked junction. Each driver uses discretion in deciding whether to stop and how slowly to approach the junction. Most macroeconomic policy actions have an element of discretion because every situation is to some degree unique. For example, before the Bank of England was made independent, between 1994 and 1995, interest rates were raised three times but by half percentage points in each case to forestall an expansion in the economy. The then Chancellor, Kenneth Clarke, used discretion based on lessons learned from earlier expansions. The granting of independence to the Bank of England was in part to remove government discretion. But despite the fact that all policy actions have an element of discretion, they can be regarded as modifications to a basic feedback-rule policy. Discretionary policy is sophisticated feedback policy, where the rules gradually evolve to reflect new knowledge about the way the economy works.

We'll study the effects of business cycle policy by comparing the performance of real GDP and the price level with a fixed rule and a feedback rule. Because the business cycle can result from demand shocks or supply shocks, we need to consider these two cases. We'll begin by studying demand shocks.

Stabilizing Aggregate Demand Shocks

We'll study an economy that starts out at full employment and has no inflation. Figure 32.5 illustrates this situation. The economy is on aggregate demand curve AD_0 and short-run aggregate supply curve *SAS*. These curves intersect at a point on the long-run aggregate supply curve, *LAS*. The GDP deflator is 115 and real GDP is £825 billion. Now suppose that there is an unexpected and temporary fall in aggregate demand. Let's see what happens.

Perhaps investment falls because of a wave of pessimism about the future, or perhaps exports fall because of a recession in the rest of the world. Regardless of the

Figure 32.5

A Decrease in Aggregate Demand

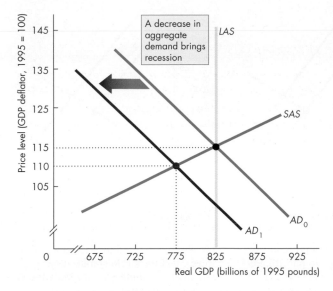

The economy starts out at full employment on aggregate demand curve AD_0 and short-run aggregate supply curve *SAS*, with the two curves intersecting on the long-run aggregate supply curve *LAS*. Real GDP is £825 billion and the GDP deflator is 115. A fall in aggregate demand (owing to pessimism about future profits, for example) unexpectedly shifts the aggregate demand curve to AD_1. Real GDP falls to £775 billion, and the GDP deflator falls to 110. The economy is in a recession.

origin of the fall in aggregate demand, the aggregate demand curve shifts leftward, to AD_1 in the figure. The aggregate demand curve AD_1 intersects the short-run aggregate supply curve *SAS* at a GDP deflator of 110 and a real GDP of £775 billion. The economy is in a depressed state. Real GDP is below its long-run level and unemployment is above its natural rate.

Assume that the fall in aggregate demand from AD_0 to AD_1 is temporary. As confidence in the future improves, firms' investment picks up, or as economic recovery proceeds in the rest of the world, exports gradually rise. As a result, the aggregate demand curve gradually returns to AD_0, but it takes some time to do so.

We are going to work out how the economy responds under two alternative monetary policies during the period in which aggregate demand gradually increases to its original level: a fixed rule and a feedback rule.

Fixed Rule: Monetarism

The fixed rule that we'll study here is one in which the levels of government purchases of goods and services, taxes and the deficit remain constant and the money supply remains constant. Neither fiscal policy nor monetary policy responds to the depressed economy. This is the rule advocated by *monetarists*.

The response of the economy under this fixed-rule policy is shown in Figure 32.6(a). When aggregate demand falls to AD_1, no policy measures are taken to bring the economy back to full employment. But the fall in aggregate demand is only *temporary*. As aggregate demand returns to its original level, the aggregate demand curve shifts rightward gradually back to AD_0. As it does so, real GDP and the GDP deflator gradually increase. The GDP deflator gradually returns to 115 and real GDP to its long-run level of £825 billion, as shown in Figure 32.6(a). Throughout this process, the economy experiences more rapid growth than usual but beginning from a state of excess capacity. Unemployment remains high until the aggregate demand curve has returned to AD_0.

Figure 32.6(b) illustrates the response of the economy under a fixed rule when the decrease in aggregate demand to AD_1 is *permanent*. Gradually, with unemployment above the natural rate, the money wage rate falls and the short-run aggregate supply curve shifts rightward to SAS_1. As it does so, real GDP gradually increases and the GDP deflator falls. Real GDP gradually returns to potential GDP of £825 billion and the GDP deflator falls to 100, as shown in Figure 32.6(b). Again, throughout the adjustment, real GDP is less than potential GDP and unemployment exceeds the natural rate.

Let's contrast this adjustment with what occurs under a feedback-rule policy.

Feedback Rule: Keynesian Activism

The feedback rule that we'll study is one in which government purchases of goods and services increase, taxes decrease, the deficit increases and the money supply increases when real GDP falls below its long-run level. In other words, both fiscal and monetary policy become expansionary when real GDP falls below long-run real GDP. When real GDP rises above its long-run level, both policies operate in reverse, becoming contractionary. This rule is advocated by *Keynesian activists*.

The response of the economy under this feedback rule policy is shown in Figure 32.6(c). When aggregate demand falls to AD_1, the expansionary fiscal and

Figure 32.6

Two Stabilization Policies: Aggregate Demand Shock

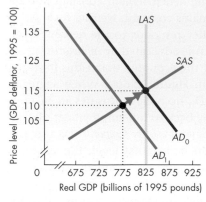

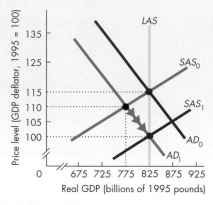

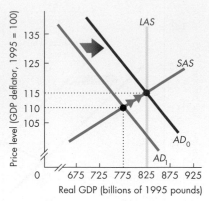

(a) Fixed rule: temporary demand shock **(b) Fixed rule: permanent demand shock** **(c) Feedback rule**

The economy is in a depressed state with a GDP deflator of 110 and real GDP of £775 billion. The short-run aggregate supply curve is *SAS*. If the depressed state of the economy is temporary, fixed-rule stabilization policy (part a) leaves aggregate demand initially at AD_1, so the GDP deflator remains at 110 and real GDP at £775 billion. As other influences on aggregate demand gradually increase, the aggregate demand curve shifts back to AD_0. As it does, real GDP gradually rises back to £825 billion and the GDP deflator increases to 115. When the decrease in demand is permanent, the money wage rate falls and the short-run

aggregate supply curve shifts rightward to SAS_1, shown in part (b). Part (c) shows a feedback-rule stabilization policy. Expansionary fiscal and monetary policy increase aggregate demand and shift the aggregate demand curve from AD_1 to AD_0. Real GDP returns to £825 billion and the GDP deflator returns to 115. Fiscal and monetary policy becomes contractionary as the other influences on aggregate demand increase its level. As a result, the aggregate demand curve is kept steady at AD_0, real GDP remains at £825 billion and the deflator remains at 115.

monetary policy increases aggregate demand, which shifts the aggregate demand curve immediately to AD_0. As other influences begin to increase aggregate demand, fiscal and monetary policy become contractionary and hold the aggregate demand curve steady at AD_0. Real GDP is held steady at £825 billion and the GDP deflator remains at 115.

The Two Rules Compared

Under a fixed-rule policy, the economy goes into a recession and stays there for as long as it takes for aggregate demand to increase again under its own steam. Only gradually does the recession come to an end and the aggregate demand curve return to its original position.

Under a feedback-rule policy, the economy is pulled out of its recession by the policy action. Once back at its long-run level, real GDP is held there by a gradual, policy-induced decrease in aggregate demand that exactly offsets the increase in aggregate demand coming from private spending decisions.

The price level and real GDP fall and rise by exactly the same amounts under the two policies, but real GDP stays below capacity GDP for longer with a fixed rule than it does with a feedback rule.

So Feedback Rules are Better?

Isn't it obvious that a feedback rule is better than a fixed rule? Can't the government and the central bank use feedback rules to keep the economy close to full employment with a stable price level? Of course, unforecasted events – such as a collapse in business confidence – will hit the economy from time to time. But by responding with a change in tax rates, spending, interest rates and money supply, can't the government and the central bank minimize the damage from such a shock? It appears to be so from our analysis.

Despite the apparent superiority of a feedback rule, many economists remain convinced that a fixed rule stabilizes aggregate demand more effectively than a feedback rule. These economists argue that fixed rules are better than feedback rules because:

◆ Full-employment real GDP is not known.

◆ Policy lags are longer than the forecast horizon.

◆ Feedback-rule policies are less predictable than fixed-rule policies.

Let's look at these arguments.

Knowledge of Full-employment Real GDP

To decide whether a feedback policy needs to stimulate aggregate demand or retard it, it is necessary to determine whether real GDP is currently above or below its full-employment level. But full-employment real GDP is not known with certainty. It depends on a large number of factors, one of which is the level of employment when unemployment is at its natural rate. But there is uncertainty and disagreement about how the labour market works, so we can only estimate the natural rate of unemployment. As a result, there is uncertainty about the *direction* in which a feedback policy should be pushing the level of aggregate demand.

Policy Lags and the Forecast Horizon

The effects of policy actions taken today are spread out over the following two years or even more. But no one is able to forecast that far ahead. The forecast horizon of the policy-makers is less than one year. Furthermore, it is not possible to predict the precise timing and magnitude of the effects of policy itself. Thus feedback policies that react to today's economy may be inappropriate for the state of the economy at that uncertain future date when the policy's effects are felt.

For example, suppose that today the economy is in a recession and prices are falling. The ECB reacts with an increase in the money supply growth rate. When the central bank puts on the monetary accelerator, the first reaction is a fall in interest rates. Some time later, lower interest rates produce an increase in investment and the purchases of consumer durable goods. Some time still later, this rise in expenditure increases income which in turn induces higher consumption expenditure. Later still, the higher expenditure increases the demand for labour and eventually wages and prices rise. The sectors in which the spending increases occur vary and so does the impact on employment. It can take from nine months to two years for an initial action by the central bank to cause a change in real GDP, employment and the inflation rate.

By the time the central bank's actions are having their maximum effect, the economy has moved on to

a new situation. Perhaps a world economic slowdown has added a new negative effect on aggregate demand that is offsetting the government's expansionary actions. Or perhaps a boost in business confidence has increased aggregate demand yet further, adding to the government's own expansionary policy. Whatever the situation, the central bank can only take the appropriate actions today if it can forecast those future shocks to aggregate demand.

Thus to smooth the fluctuations in aggregate demand, the central bank needs to take actions today, based on a forecast of what will be happening over a period stretching two or more years into the future. It is no use taking actions a year from today to influence the situation that then prevails. It will be too late.

If the central bank economics team is good at economic forecasting and bases its policy actions on its forecasts, then it can deliver the type of aggregate demand-smoothing performance that we assumed in the model economy we studied earlier in this chapter. But if the central bank takes policy actions that are based on today's economy rather than on the forecasted economy a year into the future, then those actions will often be inappropriate ones.

When unemployment is high and the central bank puts its foot on the accelerator, it speeds the economy back to full employment. But the central bank cannot see far enough ahead to know when to ease off the accelerator and gently tap the brake, holding the economy at its full-employment point. Usually it keeps its foot on the accelerator for too long and, after the central bank has taken its foot off the accelerator pedal, the economy races through the full-employment point and starts to experience shortages and inflationary pressures. Eventually, when inflation increases and unemployment falls below its natural rate, the central bank steps on the brake, pushing the economy back below full employment.

The central bank's own reaction to the current state of the economy has become one of the major sources of fluctuations in aggregate demand and the major factor that people have to forecast in order to make their own economic choices.

The problems for fiscal policy feedback rules are similar to those for monetary policy, but they are more severe because of the lags in the implementation of fiscal policy. The government can take actions fairly quickly. But before a fiscal policy action can be taken, the entire legislative process must be completed. Thus even before a fiscal policy action is implemented, the economy may have moved on to a new situation that calls for a different feedback from the one that is in the legislative pipeline.

Predictability of Policies

To make decisions about long-term contracts for employment (wage contracts) and for borrowing and lending, people have to anticipate the future course of prices – the future inflation rate. To forecast the inflation rate, it is necessary to forecast aggregate demand. And to forecast aggregate demand, it is necessary to forecast the policy actions of the government and the central bank.

If the government and the central bank stick to rock-steady, fixed rules for tax rates, spending programmes, and money supply growth, then policy itself cannot be a contributor to unexpected fluctuations in aggregate demand.

In contrast, when a feedback rule is being pursued there is more scope for the policy actions to be unpredictable. The main reason is that feedback rules are not written down for all to see. Rather, they have to be inferred from the behaviour of the government and the central bank. The deliberations of the Central Bank Monetary Policy Committee are published and the decision to change or keep interest the same is explained in the minutes. This means that over time it will be possible to predict the central bank's action by knowing what factors guided its policy in the past.

Thus with a feedback policy it is necessary to predict the variables to which the government and central bank react and the extent to which they react. Consequently, a feedback rule for fiscal and monetary policy can create more unpredictable fluctuations in aggregate demand than a fixed rule.

Economists disagree about whether these bigger fluctuations offset the potential stabilizing influence of the predictable changes the government and the central bank make. No agreed measurements have been made to settle this dispute. Nevertheless, the unpredictability of the government in its pursuit of feedback policies is an important fact of economic life, and the government does not always go out of its way to make its reactions clear. This is one of the reasons for taking monetary policy out of the hands of the government.

To the extent that the government's actions are discretionary and unpredictable, they lead to unpredictable fluctuations in aggregate demand. These fluctuations, in turn, produce fluctuations in real GDP, employment and unemployment.

It is difficult for the government to pursue a predictable feedback stabilization policy. Such policies are formulated in terms of spending programmes and tax laws announced at the time of the Budget. Because these programmes and tax laws are the outcome of a political process of negotiation between the Treasury and the spending departments of government, there can be no effective way in which a predictable feedback fiscal policy can be adhered to.

We reviewed three reasons why feedback policies may not be more effective than fixed rules in controlling aggregate demand. But there is a fourth reason why fixed rules are preferred by some economists: not all shocks to the economy are on the demand side. Advocates of feedback rules believe that most fluctuations do come from aggregate demand. Advocates of fixed rules believe that aggregate supply fluctuations are the dominant ones. Let's now see how aggregate supply fluctuations affect the economy under a fixed rule and a feedback rule. We will also see why those economists who believe that aggregate supply fluctuations are the dominant ones also favour a fixed rather than a feedback rule.

Stabilizing Aggregate Supply Shocks

Real business cycle (RBC) theorists believe that fluctuations in real GDP (and in employment and unemployment) are caused not by fluctuations in aggregate demand but by fluctuations in productivity growth. According to RBC theory, there is no useful distinction between long-run aggregate supply and short-run aggregate supply. Because wages are flexible, the labour market is always in equilibrium and unemployment is always at its natural rate. The vertical long-run aggregate supply curve is also the short-run aggregate supply curve. Fluctuations occur because of shifts in the long-run aggregate supply curve. Normally, the long-run aggregate supply curve shifts to the right – the economy expands. But the pace at which the long-run aggregate supply curve shifts to the right varies. Also, on occasion, the long-run aggregate supply curve shifts leftward, bringing a decrease in aggregate supply and a fall in real GDP.

Economic policy that influences the aggregate demand curve has no effect on real GDP. But it does affect the price level. If a feedback policy is used to increase aggregate demand every time real GDP falls, and if the RBC theory is correct, the feedback policy will make price level fluctuations more severe than they otherwise would be. To see why, consider Figure 32.7.

Imagine that the economy starts out on aggregate demand curve AD_0 and long-run aggregate supply

Figure 32.7

Responding to a Productivity Growth Slowdown

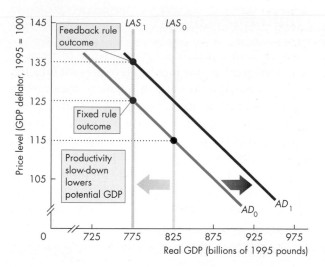

A productivity slowdown shifts the long-run aggregate supply curve from LAS_0 to LAS_1. Real GDP falls to £775 billion and the GDP deflator rises to 125. With a fixed rule, there is no change in the money supply, taxes or government spending, aggregate demand stays at AD_0, and that is the end of the matter. With a feedback rule, the central bank increases the money supply and/or the government cuts taxes or increases spending, intending to increase real GDP. Aggregate demand moves to AD_1, but the long-run result is an increase in the price level – the GDP deflator rises to 135 – with no change in real GDP.

curve LAS_0 at a GDP deflator of 115 and with real GDP equal to £825 billion. Now suppose that the long-run aggregate supply curve shifts to LAS_1. An actual decrease in long-run aggregate supply can occur as a result of a severe drought or other natural catastrophe, or perhaps as the result of a disruption of international trade such as the OPEC embargo of the 1970s.

Fixed Rule

With a fixed rule, the fall in the long-run aggregate supply has no effect on the central bank or the government and no effect on aggregate demand. The aggregate demand curve remains AD_0. Real GDP falls to £775 billion and the GDP deflator increases to 125.

Feedback Rule

Now suppose that the central bank and the government use feedback rules. In particular, suppose that

when real GDP falls, the central bank increases the money supply and Parliament approves a tax cut to increase aggregate demand. In this example, the money supply increases and the tax cut shifts the aggregate demand curve to AD_1. The policy goal is to bring real GDP back to £825 billion. But the long-run aggregate supply curve has shifted so long-run real GDP has decreased to £775 billion. The increase in aggregate demand cannot cause an increase in output if the economy does not have the capacity to produce that output. So real GDP stays at £775 billion but the price level rises still further – the GDP deflator goes to 135. You can see that in this case the attempt to stabilize real GDP using a feedback policy has no effect on real GDP, but it generates a substantial price level increase.

We've now seen some of the shortcomings of using feedback rules for stabilization policy. Some economists believe that these shortcomings are serious and would like to see simple fixed rules. A popular view among some economists is to have an exchange rate rule, as in the ERM. Others, regarding the potential advantages of feedback rules as greater than their costs, advocate the continued use of such policies but with an important modification that we'll now look at.

Nominal GDP Targeting

Attempting to keep the growth rate of nominal GDP steady is called **nominal GDP targeting**. This policy target was first proposed by a leading Keynesian activist economist, the late James Tobin of Yale University. It is a policy that recognizes the strengths of a fixed rule but that regards the monetarist fixed rule as inappropriate. Instead, nominal GDP targeting uses feedback rules for fiscal and monetary policy to hit a fixed nominal GDP growth target.

Nominal GDP growth equals the real GDP growth rate plus the inflation rate. When nominal GDP grows quickly, it is usually because the inflation rate is high. When nominal GDP grows slowly, it is usually because real GDP growth is negative – the economy is in recession. Thus if nominal GDP growth is held steady, excessive inflation and deep recession might be avoided.

Nominal GDP targeting uses feedback rules. Expansionary fiscal and/or monetary actions increase aggregate demand when nominal GDP is below target and contractionary fiscal and/or monetary actions decrease aggregate demand when nominal GDP is above target. The main problem with nominal GDP targeting is that there are long and variable time lags between the identification of a need to change aggregate demand and the effects of the policy actions taken.

Natural-rate Policies

All the business cycle stabilization policies we've considered have been directed at smoothing the cycle and keeping unemployment close to the natural rate. It is also possible to pursue policies directed towards lowering the natural rate of unemployment. But there are no simple costless ways of lowering the natural rate of unemployment.

The main policy tools that influence the natural rate of unemployment are supply-side factors dealing with tax rates, employers' additional costs of hiring labour, unemployment benefits, union regulation and minimum wages. But to use these tools the government faces tough trade-offs. To lower the natural rate of unemployment, the government could lower the tax rate on income or employers' social security contributions, or lower unemployment benefits or even shorten the period for which benefits are paid. These policy actions might create hardships and have costs that exceed the cost of a high natural rate of unemployment.

Some economists have argued that the supply-side policies of the 1980s in the UK had the effect of reducing the natural rate of unemployment. Taxes on income were reduced, trade union activity was regulated, employers' social security contributions were reduced and the eligibility for unemployment benefits was reduced. The outcome of all these policies has been to make the labour market more flexible and labour less costly to employ.

Review Quiz

◆ What is a fixed-rule fiscal policy and a fixed-rule monetary policy?

◆ Can you provide two examples of fixed rules in everyday life (other than those in the text)?

◆ What is a feedback fiscal policy and a feedback monetary policy?

◆ When might a feedback policy be used? Can you provide two examples of feedback rules in everyday life (other than those in the text)?

◆ Why do some economists say that feedback rules do not necessarily deliver a better macroeconomic performance than fixed rules? Do you agree or disagree with them? Why?

We've studied growth policy and business cycle and unemployment policy. Let's now study inflation policy.

Inflation Policy

There are two inflation policy problems. In times of price level stability, the problem is to prevent inflation from breaking out. In times of inflation, the problem is to reduce its rate and restore price stability. Avoiding demand inflation is just the opposite of avoiding demand-driven recession. So keeping aggregate demand steady is an anti-inflation policy as well as an anti-recession policy. But avoiding cost-push inflation raises some special issues that we need to consider. So we will look at two issues for inflation policy:

1 Avoiding cost-push inflation.

2 Slowing inflation.

Avoiding Cost-push Inflation

Cost-push inflation is inflation that has its origins in cost increases. In 1973–74, the world oil price exploded. Cost shocks such as these become inflationary if they are accommodated by an increase in the quantity of money. Such an increase in the quantity of money can occur if a monetary policy feedback rule is used. A fixed-rule policy for the money stock makes cost-push inflation impossible. Let's see why.

Figure 32.8 shows the economy at full employment. Aggregate demand is AD_0, short-run aggregate supply is SAS_0 and long-run aggregate supply is LAS. Real GDP is £825 billion and the GDP deflator is 115. Now suppose that OPEC tries to gain a temporary advantage by increasing the price of oil. The short-run aggregate supply curve shifts leftward from SAS_0 to SAS_1.

Monetarist Fixed Rule

Figure 32.8(a) shows what happens if a fixed rule for monetary policy is followed and the government follows a fixed rule for fiscal policy. Suppose that the fixed rule is for zero money growth and no change in taxes or government purchases of goods and services. With these fixed rules, the government pays no attention to the fact that there has been an increase in the price of oil. No policy actions are taken. The short-run aggregate supply curve has shifted to SAS_1 but the aggregate demand curve remains at AD_0. The GDP

Figure 32.8

Responding to an OPEC Oil Price Increase

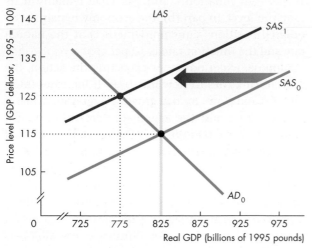

(a) Fixed rule

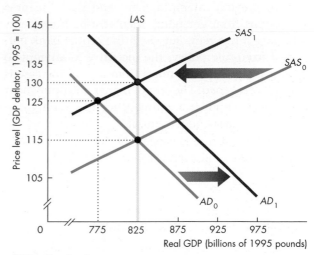

(b) Feedback rule

The economy starts out on AD_0 and SAS_0, with a GDP deflator of 115 and real GDP of £825 billion. OPEC forces up the price of oil and the short-run aggregate supply curve shifts to SAS_1. Real GDP decreases to £775 billion and the GDP deflator increases to 125. With a fixed money supply rule (part a), the central bank makes no change to aggregate demand. The economy stays depressed until

the price of oil falls again, and the economy returns to its original position. With a feedback rule (part b), the central bank injects additional money and aggregate demand increases to AD_1. Real GDP returns to £825 billion (full employment) but the GDP deflator increases to 130. The economy is set for another round of cost-push inflation.

deflator rises to 125, and real GDP falls to £775 billion. The economy has experienced *stagflation*. Unless the price of oil falls, the economy will remain depressed. But eventually, the low level of real GDP and low sales will probably bring a fall in the price of oil. When this happens, the short-run aggregate supply curve will shift back to SAS_0. The GDP deflator will fall to 115 and real GDP will increase to £825 billion.

Keynesian Feedback Rule

Figure 32.8(b) shows what happens if the central bank and the government operate a feedback rule. The starting point is the same as before – the economy is on SAS_0 and AD_0 with a GDP deflator of 115 and real GDP of £825 billion. OPEC raises the price of oil and the short-run aggregate supply curve shifts to SAS_1. Real GDP falls to £775 billion and the price level rises to 125.

A monetary feedback rule is followed. That rule is to increase the quantity of money when real GDP is below potential GDP. With potential GDP perceived

to be £825 billion and with actual real GDP at £775 billion, the central bank pumps money into the economy. Aggregate demand increases and the aggregate demand curve shifts rightward to AD_1. The price level rises to 130 and real GDP returns to £825 billion. The economy moves back to full employment but at a higher price level.

What if the government and central bank reacted in a different way? Let's run through the example again. OPEC engineers a new rise in the price of oil which decreases aggregate supply, and the short-run aggregate supply curve shifts leftward once more. The central bank, realizing this danger, does *not* respond to the OPEC price increase. Instead, it holds firm and even slows down the growth of aggregate demand to dampen further the inflationary consequences of OPEC's actions.

Incentives to Push Up Costs

You can see that there are no checks on the incentives to push up costs if the government accommodates price rises. If some groups see a temporary gain from pushing up the price at which they are selling their resources, and if the central bank always accommodates to prevent unemployment and slack business conditions from emerging, then cost-push elements will have a free rein. But when the central bank pursues a fixed-rule policy, the incentive to attempt to steal a temporary advantage from a price increase is severely weakened. The cost of higher unemployment and lower output is a consequence that each group will have to face and recognize.

Thus a fixed rule is capable of delivering a steady inflation rate (and even zero inflation), while a feedback rule, in the face of cost-push pressures, leaves the inflation rate free to rise and fall at the whim of whichever group believes a temporary advantage to be available from pushing up its price.

Slowing Inflation

So far, we've concentrated on *avoiding* inflation. But often the problem is not to avoid inflation but to tame it. How can inflation, once it has set in, be cured? We'll look at two cases:

1   A surprise inflation reduction.
2   A credible, announced inflation reduction.

A Surprise Inflation Reduction

We'll use two equivalent approaches to study the problem of lowering inflation: the aggregate supply–aggregate demand model and the Phillips curve. The *AS–AD* model tells us about real GDP and the price level, while the Phillips curve, which is explained in Chapter 28, pp. 643–645, lets us keep track of inflation and unemployment.

Figure 32.9 illustrates the economy at full employment with inflation raging at 10 per cent a year. In part (a), the economy is on aggregate demand curve, AD_0, and short-run aggregate supply curve, SAS_0. Real GDP is £825 billion and, at a moment in time, the GDP deflator is 115. With real GDP equal to potential GDP on the *LAS* curve, there is full employment. Equivalently, in part (b), the economy is on its long-run Phillips curve, *LRPC*, and short-run Phillips curve, $SRPC_0$. The inflation rate of 10 per cent a year is anticipated so unemployment is at its natural rate.

Next year, aggregate demand is *expected* to increase and the aggregate demand curve in Figure 32.9(a) is expected to shift rightward to AD_1. Expecting this increase in aggregate demand, wages increase to shift the short-run aggregate supply curve to SAS_1. If expectations are fulfilled, the GDP deflator rises to 126.5 – a 10 per cent inflation – and real GDP remains at its long-run level. In part (b), the economy remains at its original position – unemployment is at the natural rate and the inflation rate is 10 per cent a year.

Suppose, when no one is expecting the action, the central bank tries to slow inflation. It increases interest rates and slows money growth. Aggregate demand growth slows and the aggregate demand curve (in part a) shifts to AD_2. With no change in the expected inflation rate, wages rise by the same amount as before and the short-run aggregate supply curve shifts left to SAS_1. Real GDP decreases to £775 billion and the GDP deflator rises 124.2 – an inflation rate of 8 per cent a year. In Figure 32.9(b), there is a movement along the short-run Phillips curve $SRPC_0$ as unemployment rises to 9 per cent and inflation falls to 8 per cent a year. The policy has succeeded in slowing inflation, but at the cost of recession. Real GDP is below potential GDP and unemployment is above its natural rate.

A Credible Announced Inflation Reduction

Suppose that instead of simply slowing down the growth of aggregate demand, the government announces its intention ahead of its action in a credible and convincing way, so that its announcement is believed. The lower level of aggregate demand is expected so wages increase at a pace consistent with the lower level of aggregate demand. The short-run aggregate supply curve (in Figure 32.9a) shifts leftward but only to SAS_2. Aggregate demand increases by the amount expected and the aggregate demand curve shifts to AD_2. The GDP deflator rises to 120.75 – an inflation rate of 5 per cent a year – and real GDP remains at its full-employment level.

In Figure 32.9(b), the lower expected inflation rate shifts the short-run Phillips curve downward to $SRPC_1$, and inflation falls to 5 per cent a year while unemployment remains at its natural rate.

Inflation Reduction in Practice

When the UK government slowed down inflation in 1980, the economy paid a high price. The government's monetary policy action was unexpected. As a result, it occurred in the face of wages that had been

Figure 32.9

Lowering Inflation

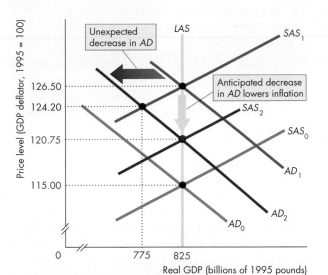

(a) Aggregate demand and aggregate supply

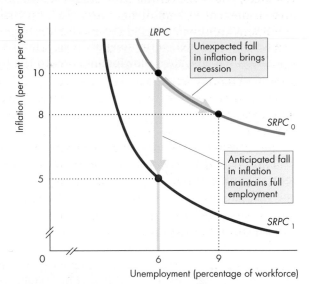

(b) Phillips curves

Initially, aggregate demand is AD_0 and short-run aggregate supply is SAS_0. Real GDP is £825 billion (its full-employment level on the long-run aggregate supply curve, *LAS*). Inflation is proceeding at 10 per cent a year. If it continues to do so, the aggregate demand curve shifts to AD_1 and the short-run aggregate supply curve shifts to SAS_1. The GDP deflator rises to 126.5. This same situation is shown in part (b) with the economy on the short-run Phillips curve $SRPC_0$.

With an unexpected slowdown in aggregate demand growth, the aggregate demand curve (part a) shifts to AD_2,

real GDP falls to £775 billion and inflation slows to 8 per cent (a GDP deflator of 124.2). In part (b), unemployment rises to 9 per cent as the economy slides down $SRPC_0$.

If a credible, announced slowdown in aggregate demand growth occurs, the short-run aggregate supply curve (part a) shifts to SAS_2, the short-run Phillips curve (part b) shifts to $SRPC_1$, inflation slows to 5 per cent, real GDP remains at £825 billion and unemployment remains at its natural rate of 6 per cent.

set at too high a level to be consistent with the growth of aggregate demand that the government subsequently allowed. The consequence was recession – a decrease in real GDP and a rise in unemployment. Couldn't the government have lowered inflation without causing recession by telling people far enough ahead of time that it did indeed plan to slow down the growth rate of aggregate demand?

The answer appears to be no. The main reason is that people form their expectation of the government's action (as they form expectations about anyone's actions) on the basis of actual behaviour, not on the basis of stated intentions. How many times have you told yourself that it is your firm intention to reduce weight, or to keep within a budget and put a

few pounds away for a rainy day, only to discover that, despite your best intentions, your old habits win out in the end?

Forming expectations about the government's behaviour is no different except, of course, it is more complex than forecasting your own behaviour. To form expectations of the government's actions, people look at its past *actions*, not its stated intentions. On the basis of such observations they try to work out what the government's policy is, to forecast its future actions, and to forecast the effects of those actions on aggregate demand and inflation. When Mrs Thatcher came to power in June 1979, the forecast for her policy was to do the same as all previous governments had done – that is, to say one thing and do another. In other words, the Thatcher government had no reputation for an anti-inflation policy. Its credibility was low.

Over a period of time, the government won credibility for its anti-inflation policies by earning a reputation for being tough with monetary policy. But this reputation was lost after allowing inflation to rise by the end of the 1980s.

An Independent Central Bank

Recent research on central bank performance has strengthened the view that a more independent central bank can deliver a lower average inflation rate without creating either a higher unemployment rate or lower real GDP growth rate. The Treaty on European Union – the Maastricht Treaty – provides for independence for all national central banks that wish to join the EMU. The independent ECB is assigned the task of maintaining price stability (inflation below 2 per cent a year) and takes a growth rate of M3 for the Euro area of 4.5 per cent a year as its reference value for price stability over the medium term. The Bank of England do not admit to a monetary target but target inflation directly. The independence of central banks is now part of conventional economic policy thinking. The central banks of the EU, Switzerland, Japan and New Zealand are fully independent. Other central banks that have explicit inflation targets are: Canada, Australia and Sweden.

> ## Review Quiz
>
> ◆ Why does a fixed rule provide more effective protection against a cost-push inflation than a feedback rule?
> ◆ Why does a recession usually result as inflation is being tamed?
> ◆ How does establishing a reputation of being an inflation fighter improve the ability of the central bank to maintain low inflation and to lower the cost of fighting inflation?

You've examined the main issues of macroeconomic policy. You've looked at the goals of policy and the fiscal and monetary policies pursued. You've examined policies for achieving faster long-term real GDP growth and you've seen how fixed and feedback rules operate to stabilize the business cycle and contain inflation. You've also seen why lowering inflation is usually accompanied by recession and higher unemployment. You have now completed your study of macroeconomics and of the problems and challenges of improving macroeconomic performance. In this study, your main focus has been the UK and EU economies. Occasionally, we have taken into account linkages between the United Kingdom and the rest of the world. In Chapter 33, we turn our attention to the international economy.

Summary

Key Points

Policy Goals (pp. 733–735)

● The goals of macroeconomic policy are to achieve the highest sustainable rate of long-term real GDP growth, smooth out avoidable business fluctuations, and maintain low unemployment and low inflation.

Policy Tools and Performance (pp. 735–737)

● The macroeconomic policy tools are fiscal policy and monetary policy.

● Fiscal and monetary policy within the EMU is dictated by the targets and stability pact set by the Maastricht Treaty.

Long-term Growth Policy (pp. 737–740)

● The sources of the long-term growth of potential GDP are the accumulation of physical and human capital and the advance of technology.

● Policies to increase the long-term growth rate focus on increasing saving and investment in human capital and new technologies.

- The EU national saving rate has been on a generally falling path since 1970.

- To increase the saving rate, government saving, which was negative in much of the 1980s, must be increased and incentives for private saving must be strengthened.

- Human capital investment might be increased with improved education and by improving on-the-job training programmes.

- Investment in new technologies can be encouraged by tax incentives and EU sponsored research programmes.

Business Cycle and Unemployment Policies (pp. 740–746)

- In the face of an aggregate demand shock, a fixed-rule policy takes no action to counter the shock. It permits aggregate demand to fluctuate as a result of all the independent forces that influence it.

- A feedback-rule policy adjusts taxes, government purchases, or the money supply to offset the effects of other influences on aggregate demand. An ideal feedback rule keeps the economy at full employment, with stable prices.

- Some economists argue that feedback rules make the economy less stable because they require greater knowledge of the state of the economy than we have, they operate with time lags that extend beyond the forecast horizon, and they introduce unpredictability about policy reactions.

- By using feedback policies aimed at keeping nominal GDP growth steady – nominal GDP targeting – it is possible that the extremes of inflation and recession might be avoided.

Inflation Policy (pp. 746–750)

- A fixed rule minimizes the threat of cost-push inflation.

- A feedback rule validates cost-push inflation and leaves the price level and inflation rate free to move to wherever they are pushed.

- Inflation can be tamed, and at little or no cost in terms of lost output or excessive unemployment, by slowing the growth of aggregate demand in a credible and predictable way. But usually, when inflation is slowed down, a recession occurs.

- Published inflation targets aid the process of building up a good inflation reputation.

Key Figures ◆

Key Terms

Problems

°1 A productivity growth slowdown has occurred. Explain its possible origins and describe a policy package that is designed to speed up growth again.

2 A nation is experiencing a falling saving rate. Explain its possible origins and describe a policy package that is designed to increase the saving rate?

°3 The economy shown in the figure is initially on aggregate demand curve AD_0 and short-run aggregate supply curve SAS. Then aggregate demand decreases and the aggregate demand curve shifts leftward to AD_1.

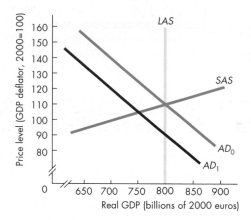

a What is the initial equilibrium real GDP and price level?

b If the decrease in aggregate demand is temporary and the government follows a fixed-rule fiscal policy, what happens to real GDP and the price level? Trace the immediate effects and the adjustment as aggregate demand returns to its original level.

c If the decrease in aggregate demand is temporary and the government follows a feedback-rule fiscal policy, what happens to real GDP and the price level? Trace the immediate effects and the adjustment as aggregate demand returns to its original level.

d If the decrease in aggregate demand is permanent and the government follows a fixed-rule fiscal policy, what happens to real GDP and the price level?

e If the decrease in aggregate demand is permanent and the government follows a feedback-rule fiscal policy, what happens to real GDP and the price level?

4 The economy shown in the figure is initially on aggregate demand curve AD and short-run aggregate supply curve SAS_0. Then sort-run aggregate supply decreases and the short-run aggregate supply curve shifts leftward to SAS_1.

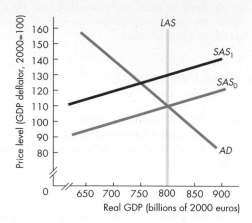

a What is the initial equilibrium real GDP and price level?

b What type of event could have caused the decrease in short-run aggregate supply?

c If the government follows a fixed-rule monetary policy, what happens to real GDP and the price level? Trace the immediate effects and the adjustment as short-run aggregate supply returns to its original level.

d If the government follows a feedback-rule monetary policy, what happens to real GDP and the price level? Trace the immediate effects and the adjustment as aggregate demand and short-run aggregate supply respond to the policy action.

°5 The economy is experiencing 10 per cent inflation and 7 per cent unemployment. Real GDP growth has sagged to 1 per cent a year. The stock market has crashed.

a Explain how the economy might have gotten into its current state.

b Set out policies for the Bank of England and the government to pursue that will lower inflation, lower unemployment, and speed real GDP growth.

c Explain how and why your proposed policies will work.

6 The inflation rate has fallen to 1 per cent a year but the unemployment rate is stubborn and has not fallen much. Real GDP is growing at more than 3 per cent a year. The stock market is at a record high.

   a Explain how the economy might have gotten into its current state.

   b Set out policies for the Bank of England and the government to pursue that will keep inflation low, lower unemployment, and maintain a high real GDP growth rate.

   c Explain how and why your proposed policies will work.

•7 When the economies of Indonesia, Korea, Thailand, Malaysia, and the Philippines entered into recession in 1997, the International Monetary Fund (IMF) made loans but only on condition that the recipients of the loans increased interest rates, raised taxes, and cut government expenditures.

   a Would you describe the IMF prescription as a feedback-rule policy or a fixed-rule policy?

   b What do you predict the effects of the IMF policies would be?

   c Do you have any criticisms of the IMF policies? What would you have required these countries to do? Why?

8 As the UK economy continued to expand and its stock market soared to new record levels during 1998, the Bank of England cut interest rates.

   a Would you describe the Bank of England's actions as a feedback-rule policy or a fixed-rule policy?

   b What do you predict the effects of the Bank of England's policies would be?

   c Do you have any criticisms of the Bank of England's policies? What monetary policy would you have pursued? Why?

Critical Thinking

1 Study Reading Between the Lines on pp. 754–755 and then answer the following questions.

   a Why are falling prices a problem in Japan?

   b Why has aggregate demand been weak in Japan?

   c What is the danger to the world economy of a weak Japanese economy?

   d What policy can the BoJ and the Japanese government conduct to increase aggregate demand?

   e What other policy options are available to the Bank of Japan and how effective do you think they will be?

Stabilization Policy Dilemma

THE FINANCIAL TIMES, 7 DECEMBER 2001

Tokyo 'needs to loosen monetary policy'

Gillian Tett

Japan faces a serious deflation problem that it must address using policy tools such as looser monetary policy, Kenneth Dam, deputy US Treasury secretary warned yesterday.

He said in Tokyo: 'There is an increasing deflation problem in Japan. It is not a runaway problem but it is time to do something about it'.

The Bank of Japan (BoJ) has already cut interest rates to virtually zero, and thus exhausted conventional monetary policy tools. However, some economists are urging the bank to consider unconventional measures such as the purchase of Japanese government bonds or foreign bonds.

A senior US official, for example, recently suggested that Washington would not oppose purchases of foreign bonds. The idea has already been discreetly floated by Kunio Okina, head of the BoJ's research department. In addition Toshio Miki, a member of the bank's policy board, yesterday called for a debate about the idea.

However, the bank has been reluctant to take these steps. This is partly because some senior officials, such as Masaru Hayami, bank governor, argue that the deflation in Japan partly reflects a flood of cheap imports – and thus cannot be cured by domestic monetary policy measures alone.

However, Mr Dam yesterday disputed the idea that price falls were due to imports or restructuring. 'Deflation is a monetary phenomena which has to be addressed with monetary means. I think that expansion of the money supply by whatever means is what the Treasury economists [think needs to happen].' Consumer prices are falling at about 1 per cent a year, while broader price measures point to declines of almost 2 per cent a year.

The Essence of the Story

- The Deputy US Treasury said Japan is in the middle of a deflation crisis and it needs to loosen monetary policy.

- The Bank of Japan has cut interest rates to almost zero.

- Some economists are urging unconventional methods of pumping money into the system.

- Some senior Bank of Japan officials are resisting this arguing that the falling prices are due to cheap imports and not due to monetary policy.

Economic Analysis

■ Japan has had a serious deflation problem for a number of years. Figure 1 shows real GDP growth and inflation between 1995 and 2001. For over two years prices have been falling and there has been little growth in real GDP.

■ Falling asset prices have destroyed the wealth of consumers who in turn have reduced consumption expenditure and increased saving to rebuild their wealth. Falling consumer spending has been translated into falling aggregate demand. Bank failures and collapsing commercial companies have created an atmosphere of economic uncertainty, reducing planned investment and worsening falling aggregate demand.

■ The Bank of Japan has inceased the money supply to the point that interest rates have reached nearly zero. Figure 2 shows that the growth of the money supply has been strong during the period of deflation.

■ But the increase in the money supply needs to increase faster to encourage spending and reverse the trend of falling asset prices and falling goods prices.

■ The Bank of Japan is being urged to consider novel ways of expanding the money supply. One such method is for the BoJ to buy Japanese government and foreign government bonds. To buy foreign bonds, the BoJ will have to sell yen and buy foreign currency in which to buy the foreign bonds. This will have the effect of depreciating the yen and encouraging exports and the foreign component of aggregate demand.

■ Buying more Japanese government bonds will only result in exchanging yen for bonds from the holders of government bonds. This will not necessarily encourage more spending. The Japanese government will have to issue more bonds than they need to fund their spending which can be bought by the bank. This will put money in the hands of the government who will be able to spend or disburse the funds as they see fit.

■ The increase in aggregate demand that comes from pumping more money into the economy will shift the aggregate demand curve in Figure 3 up to the right, reversing the fall in real GDP and raising the price level.

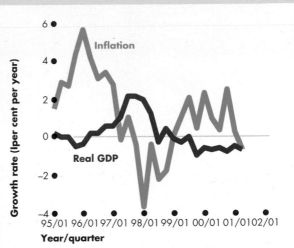

Figure 1 Japan real GDP growth and inflation 1995–2001

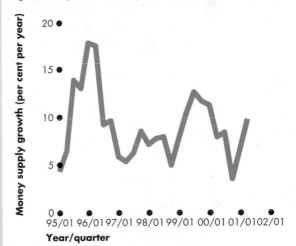

Figure 2 Japan's money supply growth

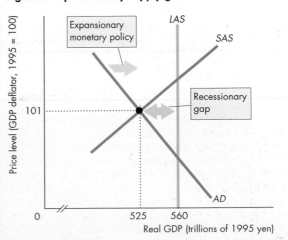

Figure 3 *AS–AD*

Part 7

The Global Economy and the Euro

Talking with **Lord Terry Burns**

Lord Burns, 57, took up the position of Chairman of Abbey National plc on 1st February, 2002. He is also Chairman of Glas Cymru Ltd (Welsh Water) and a non-executive director of Pearson Group plc and British Land plc.

Terence Burns graduated with a BA in economics from the University of Manchester before joining the London Business School in 1965. His career there began with a research post and he rose to become Professor of Economics in 1979. In 1980, he was appointed Chief Economic Advisor to the Treasury and Head of the Government Economic Service and in 1991, he became Permanent Secretary to the Treasury, a post he held until 1998.

More recently, Lord Burns has been a non-executive director of Legal & General Group plc (1999–2001), and Chairman of the National Lottery Commission (2000–2001). He is also a Member of the House of Lords Economic Affairs Select Committee.

Lord Burns was made a Life Peer when he stepped down from the Treasury in 1998. He holds honorary doctorates and professorships from five British universities. His current professional roles include President of the Society of Business Economists, Fellow of the London Business School, Companion of the Institute of Management, Governor of the National Institute of Economic and Social Research and Vice-President of the Royal Economic Society. He was a Visiting Fellow of Nuffield College, Oxford, from 1989–1997.

How did you get into economics?

I went to Manchester University to study Politics and Modern History. Economics was one of the first-year courses for this degree. I enjoyed it immensely and at the end of the first year my tutor suggested that I should transfer to an Economics degree.

In my final year Jim Ball (now Sir James Ball) was my tutor and taught me macro-economics and quantitative economics. After graduating, he offered me a post as his research assistant at the London Business School, which he was joining as Professor of Economics.

Shortly after joining him at the London Business School in 1965 we started work constructing an econometric model of the UK economy. Within 15 months or so we began using it to make forecasts and offer policy advice in the columns of the *Sunday Times*. In 1977 Jim Ball obtained a grant from the Social Science Research Council to fund an Econometric Forecasting Unit, which enabled us to develop this work.

Who are the economists that have inspired you?

Jim Ball had been a student of Lawrence Klein in Oxford in the 1950s when they had worked on an early econometric model of the UK economy. Lawrence Klein remained an inspiration throughout the years I was involved in econometric research. The early versions of these models were of course heavily influenced by the work of John Maynard Keynes. During the 1970s the emphasis was very much on the origins of the high inflation experienced in those years and the possible policy solutions. The work of Milton Friedman and Harry Johnson were very important in trying to incorporate the influences of monetary policy into the models we were using.

What was your role as Professional Economist in Government?

Towards the end of 1979 I was offered the post of Chief Economic Adviser to the Treasury. The post also carried the responsibility of being Head of the Government Economic Service.

My main policy responsibilities were in relation to macro-economics. The first big challenge was to help in setting up and developing the government's medium term financial strategy. The main task was to design monetary and fiscal policy with the aim of reducing the high rate of inflation and provide a stable economic background for the operation of other policies.

The most difficult ongoing policy problem was in dealing with the big variations in the sterling exchange rate, both in terms of its impact on the economy and how it should influence the operation of policy. Sterling was regularly either too strong or too weak in the perceptions of ministers and they struggled with the policy consequences. The most dramatic aspect of this was dealing with the difficulties of remaining in the ERM in 1992 against a background of recession in the UK and high interest rates in Germany, the anchor currency of the ERM at the time.

There were also some interesting micro problems in regard to the design of tax policy and the government's heavy privatisation programme.

How do you use your economics in business today?

Most issues in business are influenced by the behaviour of the macro-economy and financial services are even more heavily affected because of the influence of interest rates. So I still monitor the behaviour of the macro-economy both in the UK and elsewhere and seek to understand the factors influencing the policy choices of the authorities.

But business is not only about macro-economics. The discipline of micro-economics remains equally important in understanding and evaluating the strategic choices affecting companies. I still find the discipline of applying demand and supply analysis very helpful with most problems, although that simple description usually disguises the complexities of applying it in specific situations. I also still get a great deal of mileage from the application of simple modelling skills in trying to understand situations with complicated relationships between different aspects of the problem. This often applies in situations where it is important to understand the incentives and likely behaviour of the competition.

What do you think are the most pressing macro-economic problems today?

Most advanced industrial countries have dealt with the problem of inflation through a process of determined monetary policy over many years. A lot of attention has also been given to the appropriate institutional arrangements to provide the right incentives to maintain low and stable inflation. One challenge is to keep this relevant and to adapt it to changing conditions. Institutional arrangements can easily become stale if not continuously refreshed. The European countries who are members of the Euro-zone have the additional task of applying this to a group of economies which are different in some important respects.

We have seen in the case of Japan the huge difficulties of turning round an economy that seems to be locked into recession and deflation. For those of us who have spent most of our professional lives dealing with the challenge of high inflation it seems very puzzling to see the opposite problem. But the interaction of weak demand with the balance sheet problems of companies and financial institutions opens up a series of acute conceptual and practical dilemmas.

There are some important differences between countries in terms of the success in getting unemployment down. One unresolved question for some economies is judging the contribution of macro policy as opposed to micro or supply side policy in reducing unemployment. Similarly, understanding variations in productivity growth remains a puzzle for most economies. Economics still has some way to go in identifying the main drivers for productivity growth and the policy responses that will make the biggest difference.

For the UK the biggest macro problem facing the policy makers is the decision on whether or not to become a member of the Euro-zone. Having lived in Whitehall during the debates of whether or not to join (and then leave) the ERM I can appreciate all too easily the problems of both economics and politics this decision is likely to generate.

What advice would you give a student of economics?

The importance of studying both macro and micro economics; to be familiar with the relevant quantitative techniques that apply to any problem; to be able to set out your approach to a problem clearly and succinctly in words as well as numbers; and to recognise that there are often many other aspects of a problem in addition to the economics.

CHAPTER 33

Trading with the World

After studying this chapter you will be able to:

◆ Describe the trends and patterns in international trade

◆ Explain comparative advantage and why all countries can gain from international trade

◆ Explain how economies of scale and diversity of taste lead to gains from international trade

◆ Explain why trade restrictions reduce the volume of imports and exports and reduce our consumption possibilities

◆ Explain the arguments used to justify trade restrictions and show how they are flawed

◆ Explain why we have trade restrictions

Silk Routes and Containers

Since ancient times, people have striven to expand their trading as far as technology allowed. Marco Polo opened up the silk route between Europe and China in the thirteenth century. Today, container ships laden with cars and machines and Boeing 747s stuffed with farm-fresh foods ply sea and air routes, carrying billions of pounds worth of goods. Why do people go to such great lengths to trade with those in other countries? ◆ Low-wage Mexico has entered into a free trade agreement with high-wage Canada and the United States – the North American Free Trade Agreement or NAFTA. Within the European Union it has been estimated by the US Bureau of Labor Statistics that a German manufacturing worker is paid twice that of an equivalent British one, but a worker in Hong Kong costs one-third of his or her British equivalent. How can any country compete with another that pays its workers a fraction of European wages? Are there any industries in which Europe has an advantage? After the Second World War, a process of trade liberalization brought about a gradual reduction of tariffs. What are the effects of tariffs on international trade? Why don't we have completely unrestricted international trade? In Reading Between the Lines, pp. 780–781, we will examine the case made by the steel producing industry in the US for restricting imports of steel.

◆ ◆ ◆ ◆ In this chapter we're going to learn about international trade. We'll discover how *all* nations can gain by specializing in producing the goods and services in which they have a comparative advantage and trading with other countries. We'll discover that all countries can compete, no matter how high their wages. We'll also explain why, despite the fact that international trade brings benefits to all, countries restrict trade.

Patterns and Trends in International Trade

The goods and services that we buy from people in other countries are called **imports**. The goods and services that we sell to people in other countries are called **exports**. What are the most important things that we import and export? Most people would probably guess that a relatively rich country such as the United Kingdom imports raw materials and exports manufactured goods. While that is one feature of UK international trade, it is not its most important feature. The vast bulk of our merchandise exports *and* imports are manufactured goods. We sell foreigners Land Rovers, aircraft, machines and scientific equipment, and we buy televisions, video recorders, blue jeans and T-shirts from them. Also, we are a major exporter of primary materials, particularly North Sea oil, and we export chemical goods. We import and export a huge volume of services. Let's look at the international trade of the United Kingdom in a recent year.

UK International Trade

The **balance of trade** is the value of exports minus the value of imports. If the balance is positive, then the value of exports exceeds the value of imports and the United Kingdom is a **net exporter**. But if the balance is negative, the value of imports exceeds the value of exports and the United Kingdom is a **net importer**.

Trade in Goods

About 75 per cent of UK international trade is trade in goods and 25 per cent is trade in services. Of the categories of goods traded, by far the most important is manufactured goods. The total value of exports of manufactured goods is less than the total value of imports – the United Kingdom is a net importer of manufactured goods. The United Kingdom is also a net importer of primary materials and of agricultural products. It is a net exporter of chemical goods and services. Figure 33.1 highlights some of the major items of UK imports and exports of goods. The largest items of both imports and exports are machinery and transport equipment (including motor vehicles). Our imports of machinery and transport equipment (shown by the red bars) are greater than the value of exports of these items (shown by the blue bars).

Trade in Services

A quarter of UK international trade is not of goods but of services. You may be wondering how a country can 'export' and 'import' services. Let's look at some examples.

Suppose that you decided to take a holiday in Spain, travelling there from Manchester on Iberian Airways. What you buy from Iberian Airways is not a

Figure 33.1

UK Exports and Imports: 2000

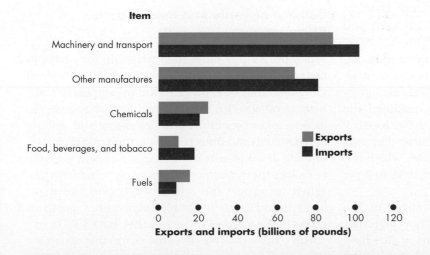

We export large quantities of capital goods such as machinery and transport equipment. We also export large quantities of manufactured goods and cars. But we import even larger quantities of some of these items. We also export and import fuel.

Source: National Statistics.

good but a transport service. Although the concept may sound odd at first, in economic terms you are importing that service from Spain. The money you spend in Spain on hotel bills, restaurant meals and other things is also classified as the import of services. Similarly, the holiday taken by a Spanish student in the United Kingdom counts as an export of services to Spain.

When we import TV sets from South Korea, the owner of the ship that carries these TV sets might be Greek and the company that insures the cargo might be with Lloyds in London. The payment that we make for the transport to the Greek company is a payment for the import of services, and the payment the Greek shipowner makes to the London insurance company is a payment for the export of a service. Similarly, when a UK shipping company transports Scotch whisky to Tokyo, the transport cost is an export of a service to Japan.

Geographical Patterns

The United Kingdom has trading links with almost every part of the world. Figure 33.2 shows the scale of these links in 2000. Our trade with the rest of the European Union is the largest. North America, which includes the United States, Canada and Mexico, takes a significant share of UK trade at 18 per cent of exports and 16 per cent of imports. We have a trade deficit with all regions except the oil exporting countries.

Trends in Trade

International trade has always been an important part of our economic life. In 1960, we exported 14 per cent of GDP and imported 15 per cent of GDP. In 2000 exports from the UK were 33 per cent and imports were 38 per cent of GDP.

On the export side, all the major commodity categories have shared in the increased volume of international trade. Mechanical and electrical machinery and semi-manufactured goods have remained the largest components of exports and have roughly maintained their share in total exports. The one major change has been the export of fuel, which has increased from 4 per cent of exports in 1963 to 7 per cent in 2000.

But there have been dramatic changes in the composition of imports. Food and raw materials imports have declined steadily, imports of fuel have decreased as North Sea oil came on stream in the

Figure 33.2

The Geographical Pattern of UK International Trade: 2000

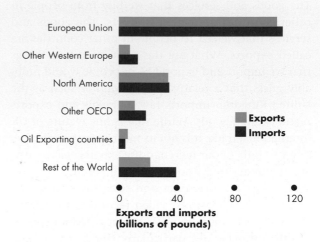

Exports and imports
(billions of pounds)

In 2000, our largest trading partner was the rest of the European Union. Within the Union our largest trading partner was Germany. Traditionally our largest trading partner was the United States, but in recent years our trade with Germany has overtaken our trade with the United States.

Source: ONS.

1970s and imports of machinery of all kinds and semi-manufactured goods have increased dramatically, from 33 per cent of imports in 1963 to 80 per cent in 2000. In 2000, the balance of trade (goods and services) was a deficit of £17.9 billion.

Balance of Trade and International Borrowing

When people buy more than they sell, they have to finance the difference by borrowing. When they sell more than they buy, they can use the surplus to make loans to others. This simple principle that governs the income and expenditure and borrowing and lending of individuals and firms is also a feature of our balance of trade. If we import more than we export, we have to finance the difference by borrowing from foreigners. When we export more than we import, we make loans to foreigners to enable them to buy goods in excess of the value of the goods they have sold to us.

This chapter does *not* cover the factors that determine the *balance* of trade and the scale of international borrowing and lending that finance that balance. Our goal is to understand the factors that influence the *volume* and *directions* of international trade rather than its balance. The keys to understanding these factors are the concepts of opportunity cost and comparative advantage.

Opportunity Cost and Comparative Advantage

Let's apply the lessons that we learned in Chapter 2, pp. 29–32, about the gains from trade to the trade between countries. We'll begin by recalling how we can use the production possibility frontier to measure opportunity cost.

Opportunity Cost in Farmland

Farmland (a fictitious country) can produce grain and cars at any point inside or along the production possibility frontier shown in Figure 33.3. (We're holding constant the output of all the other goods that Farmland produces.) The Farmers (the people of Farmland) are consuming all the grain and cars that they produce and they are operating at point *a* in the figure. That is, Farmland is producing and consuming 15 billion kilograms of grain and 8 million cars each year. What is the opportunity cost of a car in Farmland?

We can answer this question by calculating the slope of the production possibility frontier (*PPF*) at point *a*. The magnitude of the slope of the *PPF* measures the opportunity cost of one good in terms of the other. To measure the slope of the frontier at point *a*, place a straight line tangential to the frontier at point *a* and calculate the slope of that straight line. Recall that the formula for the slope of a line is the change in the value of the variable measured on the *y*-axis divided by the change in the value of the variable measured on the *x*-axis as we move along the line. Here, the variable measured on the *y*-axis is billions of kilograms of grain and the variable measured on the *x*-axis is millions of cars. So the slope is the change in the number of kilograms of grain divided by the change in the number of cars. As you can see from the red triangle at point *a* in the figure, if the number of cars produced increases by 2 million, grain production decreases by 18 billion kilograms. Therefore the magnitude of the slope is 18 billion divided by 2 million, which equals 9,000. To get one more car, the

Figure 33.3
Opportunity Cost in Farmland

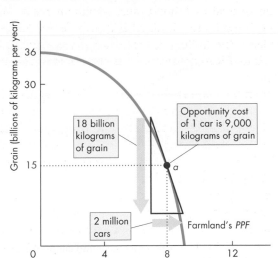

Farmland produces and consumes 15 billion kilograms of grain and 8 million cars a year. That is, it produces and consumes at point *a* on its production possibility frontier. Opportunity cost is equal to the magnitude of the slope of the production possibility frontier. The red triangle tells us that at point *a*, 18 billion kilograms of grain must be forgone to get 2 million cars. That is, at point *a*, 2 million cars cost 18 billion kilograms of grain. Equivalently, 1 car costs 9,000 kilograms of grain or 9,000 kilograms of grain cost 1 car.

people of Farmland must give up 9,000 kilograms of grain. Thus the opportunity cost of 1 car is 9,000 kilograms of grain. Equivalently, 9,000 kilograms of grain cost 1 car. For the people of Farmland, these opportunity costs are the prices they face. The price of a car is 9,000 kilograms of grain and the price of 9,000 kilograms of grain is 1 car.

Opportunity Cost in Mobilia

Now consider the production possibility frontier in Mobilia (another fictitious country and the only other country in our model world). Figure 33.4 illustrates its *PPF*. Like the Farmers, the Mobilians (the people in Mobilia) consume all the grain and cars that they produce. Mobilia consumes 18 billion kilograms of grain a year and 4 million cars, at point *a'*.

At point *a'*, the magnitude of the slope of Mobilia's *PPF* is 6 billion kilograms of grain divided by 6 million

Figure 33.4

◆

Opportunity Cost in Mobilia

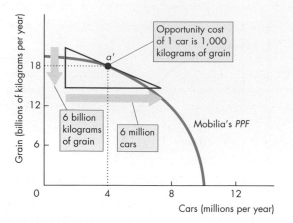

Mobilia produces and consumes 18 billion kilograms of grain and 4 million cars a year. That is, it produces and consumes at point *a'* on its production possibility frontier. Opportunity cost is equal to the magnitude of the slope of the production possibility frontier. The red triangle tells us that at point *a'*, 6 billion kilograms of grain must be forgone to get 6 million cars. That is, at point *a'*, 6 million cars cost 6 billion kilograms of grain. Equivalently, 1 car costs 1,000 kilograms of grain or 1,000 kilograms of grain cost 1 car.

cars, which equals 1,000 kilograms of grain per car. To get one more car, the people of Mobilia must give up 1,000 kilograms of grain. Thus the opportunity cost of 1 car is 1,000 kilograms of grain, or, equivalently, the opportunity cost of 1,000 kilograms of grain is 1 car. These are the prices faced in Mobilia.

Comparative Advantage

Cars are cheaper in Mobilia than in Farmland. One car costs 9,000 kilograms of grain in Farmland but only 1,000 kilograms of grain in Mobilia. But grain is cheaper in Farmland than in Mobilia – 9,000 kilograms of grain costs only 1 car in Farmland while that same amount of grain costs 9 cars in Mobilia.

Mobilia has a comparative advantage in car production. Farmland has a comparative advantage in grain production. A country has a **comparative advantage** in producing a good if it can produce that good at a lower opportunity cost than any other country. Let's see how opportunity cost differences and comparative advantage generate gains from international trade.

Gains from Trade

If Mobilia bought grain for what it costs Farmland to produce it, then Mobilia could buy 9,000 kilograms of grain for 1 car. That is much lower than the cost of growing grain in Mobilia, for there it costs 9 cars to produce 9,000 kilograms of grain. If the Mobilians can buy grain at the low Farmland price, they will reap some gains.

If the Farmers can buy cars for what it costs Mobilia to produce them, they will be able to obtain a car for 1,000 kilograms of grain. Because it costs 9,000 kilograms of grain to produce a car in Farmland, the Farmers would gain from such an opportunity.

In this situation, it makes sense for Mobilia to buy their grain from Farmers and for Farmers to buy their cars from Mobilia. Let's see how such profitable international trade comes about.

Reaping the Gains from Trade

We've seen that the Farmers would like to buy their cars from the Mobilians and that the Mobilians would like to buy their grain from the Farmers. Let's see how the two groups do business with each other, concentrating attention on the international market for cars.

Figure 33.5 illustrates such a market. The quantity of cars *traded internationally* is measured on the *x*-axis. On the *y*-axis we measure the price of a car. This price is expressed as the number of kilograms of grain that a car costs – the opportunity cost of a car. If no international trade takes place, the price of a car in Farmland is 9,000 kilograms of grain, indicated by point *a* in the figure. Again, if no trade takes place, the price of a car in Mobilia is 1,000 kilograms of grain, indicated by point *a'* in the figure. The no-trade points *a* and *a'* in Figure 33.5 correspond to the points identified by those same letters in Figures 33.3 and 33.4. The lower the price of a car (in terms of grain), the greater is the quantity of cars that the Farmers are willing to import from the Mobilians. This fact is illustrated in the downward-sloping curve, which shows Farmland's import demand for cars.

The Mobilians respond in the opposite direction. The higher the price of cars (in terms of kilograms of grain), the greater is the quantity of cars that Mobilia are willing to export to Farmers. This fact is reflected in Mobilia's export supply of cars – the upward-sloping line in Figure 33.5.

Figure 33.5

International Trade in Cars

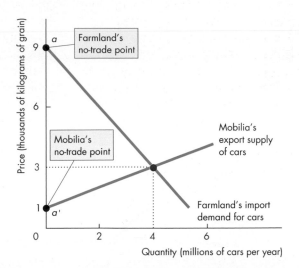

As the price of a car decreases, the quantity of imports demanded by Farmland increases – Farmland's import demand curve for cars is downward-sloping. As the price of a car increases, the quantity of cars supplied by Mobilia for export increases – Mobilia's export supply curve of cars is upward-sloping. Without international trade, the price of a car is 9,000 kilograms of grain in Farmland (point *a*) and 1,000 kilograms of grain in Mobilia (point *a'*). With free international trade, the price of a car is determined where the export supply curve intersects the import demand curve – a price of 3,000 kilograms of grain. At that price, 4 million cars a year are imported by Farmland and exported by Mobilia. The value of grain exported by Farmland and imported by Mobilia is 12 billion kilograms a year, the quantity required to pay for the cars imported.

The international market in cars determines the equilibrium price and quantity traded. This equilibrium occurs where the import demand curve intersects the export supply curve. In this case, the equilibrium price of a car is 3,000 kilograms of grain. Four million cars a year are exported by Mobilia and imported by Farmland. Notice that the price at which cars are traded is lower than the initial price in Farmland but higher than the initial price in Mobilia.

Balanced Trade

The number of cars exported by Mobilia – 4 million a year – is exactly equal to the number of cars imported by Farmland. How does Farmland pay for its cars? By exporting grain. How much grain does Farmland

export? You can find the answer by noticing that for 1 car Farmland has to pay 3,000 kilograms of grain. Hence for 4 million cars it has to pay 12 billion kilograms of grain. Thus Farmland's exports of grain are 12 billion kilograms a year. Mobilia imports this same quantity of grain.

Mobilia is exchanging 4 million cars for 12 billion kilograms of grain each year and Farmland is doing the opposite, exchanging 12 billion kilograms of grain for 4 million cars. Trade is balanced between these two countries. The value received from exports equals the value paid out for imports.

Changes in Production and Consumption

We've seen that international trade makes it possible for Farmers to buy cars at a lower price than they can produce them for themselves. Equivalently, Farmers can sell their grain for a higher price. International trade also enables Mobilia to sell their cars for a higher price. Equivalently, Mobilia can buy grain for a lower price. Thus everybody gains. How is it possible for *everyone* to gain? What are the changes in production and consumption that accompany these gains?

An economy that does not trade with other economies has identical production and consumption possibilities. Without trade, the economy can only consume what it produces. But with international trade an economy can consume different quantities of goods from those that it produces. The production possibility frontier describes the limit of what a country can produce, but it does not describe the limits to what it can consume. Figure 33.6 will help you to see the distinction between production possibilities and consumption possibilities when a country trades with other countries.

First, notice that the figure has two parts, part (a) for Farmland and part (b) for Mobilia. The production possibility frontiers that you saw in Figures 33.3 and 33.4 are reproduced here. The slopes of the two black lines in the figure represent the opportunity costs in the two countries when there is no international trade. Farmland produces and consumes at point *a* and Mobilia produces and consumes at *a'*. Cars cost 9,000 kilograms of grain in Farmland and 1,000 kilograms of grain in Mobilia.

Consumption Possibilities

The red line in each part of Figure 33.6 shows the country's consumption possibilities with international trade. These two red lines have the same slope

Figure 33.6

Expanding Consumption Possibilities

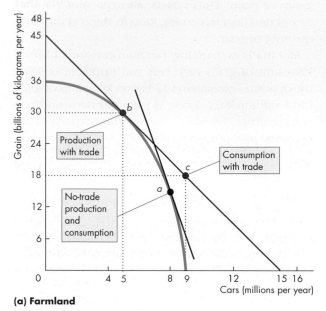

(a) Farmland

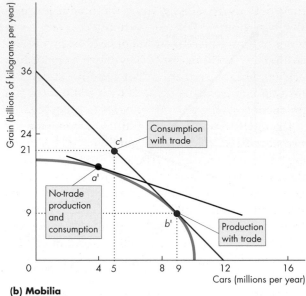

(b) Mobilia

With no international trade, the Farmers produce and consume at point *a* and the opportunity cost of a car is 9,000 kilograms of grain (the slope of the black line in part a). Also, with no international trade, the Mobilians produce and consume at point *a′* and the opportunity cost of 1,000 kilograms of grain is 1 car (the slope of the black line in part b).

Goods can be exchanged internationally at a price of 3,000 kilograms of grain for 1 car along the red line in each part of the figure. In part (a), Farmland decreases its

production of cars and increases its production of grain, moving from *a* to *b*. It exports grain and imports cars, and it consumes at point *c*. The Farmers have more of both cars and grain than they would if they produced all their own consumption goods – at point *a*. In part (b), Mobilia increases car production and decreases grain production, moving from *a′* to *b′*. Mobilia exports cars and imports grain, and it consumes at point *c′*. The Movers have more of both cars and grain than they would if they produced all their own consumption goods – at point *a′*.

and the magnitude of that slope is the opportunity cost of a car in terms of grain on the world market – 3,000 kilograms per car. The *slope* of the consumption possibilities line is common to both countries because its magnitude equals the *world* price. But the position of a country's consumption possibilities line depends on the country's production possibilities. A country cannot produce outside its production possibility curve so its consumption possibility curve touches its production possibility curve. Thus Farmland could choose to consume at point *b* with no international trade or, with international trade, at any point on its red consumption possibilities line.

Free Trade Equilibrium

With international trade, the producers of cars in Mobilia can get a higher price for their output. As a

result, they increase the quantity of car production. At the same time, grain producers in Mobilia are getting a lower price for their grain and so they reduce production. Producers in Mobilia adjust their output by moving along their production possibility frontier until the opportunity cost in Mobilia equals the world price (the opportunity cost in the world market). This situation arises when Mobilia is producing at point *b′* in Figure 33.6(b).

But the Mobilians do not consume at point *b′*. That is, they do not increase their consumption of cars and decrease their consumption of grain. Instead, they sell some of their car production to Farmland in exchange for some of Farmland's grain. They trade internationally. But to see how that works out, we first need to check in with Farmland to see what's happening there.

In Farmland, producers of cars now get a lower price and producers of grain get a higher price. As a consequence, producers in Farmland decrease car production and increase grain production. They adjust their outputs by moving along the production possibility frontier until the opportunity cost of a car in terms of grain equals the world price (the opportunity cost on the world market). They move to point *b* in part (a). But the Farmers do not consume at point *b*. Instead, they exchange some of their additional grain production for the now cheaper cars from Mobilia.

The figure shows us the quantities consumed in the two countries. We saw in Figure 33.5 that Mobilia exports 4 million cars a year and Farmland imports those cars. We also saw that Farmland exports 12 billion kilograms of grain a year and Mobilia imports that grain. Thus Farmland's consumption of grain is 12 billion kilograms a year less than it produces and its consumption of cars is 4 million a year more than it produces. Farmland consumes at point *c* in Figure 33.6(a).

Similarly, we know that Mobilia consumes 12 billion kilograms of grain more than it produces and 4 million cars fewer than it produces. Thus Mobilia consumes at *c'* in Figure 33.6(b).

Calculating the Gains from Trade

You can now literally see the gains from trade in Figure 33.6. Without trade, Farmers produce and consume at *a* (part a) – a point on Farmland's production possibility frontier. With international trade, Farmers consume at point *c* in part (a) – a point *outside* the production possibility frontier. At point *c*, Farmers are consuming 3 billion kilograms of grain a year and 1 million cars a year more than before. These increases in consumption of both cars and grain, beyond the limits of the production possibility frontier, are the gains from international trade.

Mobilians also gain. Without trade, they consume at point *a'* in part (b) – a point on Mobilia's production possibility frontier. With international trade, they consume at point *c'* – a point outside the production possibility frontier. With international trade, Mobilia consumes 3 billion kilograms of grain a year and 1 million cars a year more than without trade. These are the gains from international trade for Mobilia.

Gains for All

In popular discussions about international trade, we hear about the need for a 'level playing field' and other measures to protect people from foreign competition. International trade seems like a type of contest in which there are winners and losers. But the trade between the Farmers and the Mobilia that you've just studied does not create winners and losers. Everyone wins.

Sellers add the net demand of foreigners to their domestic demand, and so their market expands. Buyers are faced with domestic supply plus net foreign supply and so have a larger total supply available to them.

Review Quiz

♦ In what circumstances can countries gain from international trade?
♦ What determines the goods and services that a country will export? What determines the goods and services that a country will import?
♦ What is a comparative advantage and what role does it play in determining the amount and type of international trade that occurs?
♦ How can it be that all countries gain from international trade and that there are no losers?

Gains from Trade in Reality

The gains from trade that we have just studied between Farmland and Mobilia in grain and cars occur in a model economy – in a world economy that we have imagined. But these same phenomena occur every day in the real global economy.

Comparative Advantage in the Global Economy

We buy cars made in Japan and Europe, shirts and fashion goods from the people of Sri Lanka, TV sets and video recorders from South Korea and Taiwan. In exchange we sell chemicals, pharmaceuticals and financial services to those countries. We make some kinds of machines, and Europeans and Japanese make other kinds, and we exchange one type of manufactured good for another.

These are all examples of international trade generated by comparative advantage, just like the international trade between Farmland and Mobilia in our model economy. All international trade arises from comparative advantage, even when it is trade in similar goods such as tools and machines. At first, it seems puzzling that countries exchange manufactured goods. Why doesn't each developed country produce all the manufactured goods its citizens want to buy? Let's look a bit more closely at this question.

Trade in Similar Goods

Why does it make sense for the United Kingdom to produce cars for export and at the same time to import large quantities of them from Japan, Germany, Italy and Sweden? Wouldn't it make more sense to produce all the cars that we buy here in the United Kingdom? After all, we have access to the best technology available for producing cars. Car workers in the United Kingdom are surely as productive as their fellow workers in Germany and Japan. Capital equipment, production lines, robots and so on used in the manufacture of cars are as available to UK car producers as they are to any others. This line of reasoning leaves a puzzle concerning the sources of international exchange of similar commodities produced by similar people using similar equipment. Why does it happen? Why does the United Kingdom have a comparative advantage in some types of cars and Japan and Europe in others?

Diversity of Taste and Economies of Scale

The first part of the answer to the puzzle is that people have a tremendous diversity of taste. Let's stick with the example of cars. Some people prefer sports cars, some prefer estates, some prefer hatchbacks and some prefer the urban jeep look. In addition to size and type of car, there are many other ways in which cars vary. Some have low fuel consumption, some have high performance, some are spacious and comfortable, some have a large boot, some have four-wheel drive, some have front-wheel drive, some have manual gears, some are durable, some are flashy, some have a radiator grill that looks like a Greek temple, others look like a wedge. People's preferences across these many variables differ. The tremendous diversity in tastes for cars means that people would be dissatisfied if they were forced to consume from a limited range of standardized cars. People value variety and are willing to pay for it in the marketplace.

The second part of the answer to the puzzle is *economies of scale* – the tendency for the average cost of production to be lower, the larger is the scale of production. In such situations, larger and larger production runs lead to ever lower average production

costs. Many manufactured goods, including cars, experience economies of scale. For example, if a car producer makes only a few hundred (or perhaps a few thousand) cars of a particular type and design, the producer must use production techniques that are much more labour-intensive and much less automated than those employed to make hundreds of thousands of cars in a particular model. With low production runs and labour-intensive production techniques, costs are high. With very large production runs and automated assembly lines, production costs are much lower. But to obtain lower costs, the automated assembly lines have to produce a large number of cars.

It is the combination of diversity of taste and economies of scale that produces comparative advantages and generates such a large amount of international trade in similar commodities. With international trade, each manufacturer of cars has the whole world market to serve. Each producer can specialize in a limited range of products and then sell its output to the world market. This arrangement enables large production runs on the most popular cars and feasible production runs even on the most customized cars demanded by only a handful of people in each country.

The situation in the market for cars is also present in many other industries, especially those producing specialized equipment and parts. For example, the United Kingdom exports machines but imports machine tools, and it exports mainframe computers but imports PCs. Thus international exchange of similar but slightly differentiated manufactured products is a highly profitable activity.

Let's see what happens when governments restrict international trade. We'll see that free trade brings the greatest possible benefits. We'll also see why, in spite of the benefits of free trade, governments sometimes restrict trade.

Trade Restrictions

Governments restrict international trade in order to protect domestic industries from foreign competition. The restriction of international trade is called **protectionism**. There are two main protectionist methods employed by governments:

1 Tariffs.
2 Non-tariff barriers.

A **tariff** is a tax that is imposed by the importing country when an imported good crosses its international boundary. A **non-tariff barrier** is any action other than a tariff that restricts international trade. Examples of non-tariff barriers are quantitative restrictions and licensing regulations which limit imports. We'll consider non-tariff barriers in more detail below. First, let's look at tariffs.

The History of Tariffs

UK tariffs today are modest compared with their historical levels. Total customs duties on imports as a percentage of imports was about 1 per cent in 2000. Countries in the European Union have no tariffs on trade with each other. It was not always like this. In the 1930s many countries including the United Kingdom and the United States hid behind tariff barriers, but these barriers were slowly dismantled after the Second World War.

The reduction in tariffs since the Second World War followed the establishment of the **General Agreement on Tariffs and Trade** (GATT). Since its formation, the GATT has organized several rounds of negotiations that have resulted in tariff reductions. One of these, the Kennedy Round that began in the early 1960s, resulted in large tariff cuts starting in 1967. Another, the Tokyo Round, resulted in further tariff cuts in 1979. The most recent, the Uruguay Round, which started in 1986 and was completed in 1994, was the most ambitious and comprehensive of the rounds and led to the creation of a new **World Trade Organization** (WTO). Membership of the WTO brings greater obligations on countries to observe the GATT rules.

In other parts of the world, trade barriers have virtually been eliminated. The *Single European Market* (SEM) in the European Union has created the largest unified tariff-free market in the world. The SEM programme has simplified border formalities for the movement of trade; capital and labour have complete freedom of movement within the European Union, other forms of protection such as non-tariff barriers are to be eliminated; and public procurement is to be made open to all EU firms. In the longer term, the SEM programme provides for all indirect taxes within the European Union to be harmonized so that no individual country can tax a good differently from another country in the Union. In 1994, discussions among the Asia-Pacific Economic group (APEC) led to an agreement in principle to work towards a free-trade area that embraces China, all the economies of East Asia and the South Pacific, and the United Kingdom and Canada. These countries include the fastest growing economies and hold the promise of heralding a global free-trade area. But the Asia crisis of 1997 and other problems with China make it unlikely that free trade will come to APEC in the near term.

The effort to achieve freer trade underlines the fact that trade in some goods is still subject to extremely high tariffs. In the European Union, buyers of agricultural products face prices that are on average 40 per cent above world prices as part of the **Common Agricultural Policy** (CAP). The CAP is a price support programme for farmers in the European Union and acts as a tariff on non-EU agricultural products. The meat, cheese and sugar that you consume cost significantly more because of protection than they would with free international trade. Figure 33.7 shows the average protective tariff the CAP imposes on world

Figure 33.7

Average Implied Tariffs on EU Agricultural Products 1979–2000

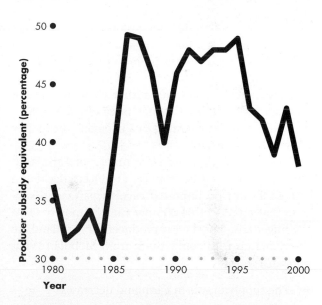

The OECD estimates the average percentage subsidy paid to EU farmers that would give them the same additional income as the actual CAP intervention price, which artificially holds agricultural prices above world prices. The graph is an estimate of the percentage by which EU prices are raised above world prices.

Sources: OECD, *Agricultural Policies in OECD Countries, Monitoring and Outlook*, 2001.

agricultural goods. The implied average tariff varies because the world price of agricultural goods varies from year to year.

The temptation for governments to impose tariffs is a strong one. They do, of course, provide revenue to the government, but this is not particularly large compared with other sources. Their most important attribute is that they enable the government to satisfy special interest groups in import-competing industries. But, as we'll see, free international trade brings enormous benefits that are reduced when tariffs are imposed. Let's see how.

How Tariffs Work

To analyse how tariffs work, let's return to the example of trade between Farmland and Mobilia. Figure 33.8 shows the international market for cars in which these two countries are the only traders. The volume of trade and the price of a car are determined at the point of intersection of Mobilia's export supply curve of cars and Farmland's import demand curve for cars.

In Figure 33.8, these two countries are trading cars and grain in exactly the same way that we analysed before in Figure 33.5. Mobilia exports cars and Farmland exports grain. The volume of car imports into Farmland is 4 million a year and the world market price of a car is 3,000 kilograms of grain. To make the example more concrete and real, Figure 33.8 expresses prices in pounds rather than in units of grain and is based on a money price of grain of £1 a kilogram. With grain costing £1 a kilogram, the money price of a car is £3,000.

Now suppose that the government of Farmland, perhaps under pressure from car producers, decides to impose a tariff on imported cars. In particular, suppose that a tariff of £4,000 per car is imposed. (This is a huge tariff, but the car producers of Farmland are pretty fed up with competition from Mobilia.) What happens?

◆ The supply of cars in Farmland decreases.

◆ The price of a car in Farmland rises.

◆ The quantity of cars imported by Farmland decreases.

◆ The government of Farmland collects the tariff revenue.

◆ Resource use is inefficient.

◆ The value of exports changes by the same amount as the value of imports and trade remains balanced.

Figure 33.8
The Effects of a Tariff

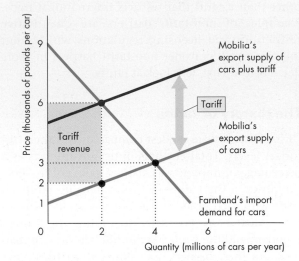

Farmland imposes a tariff on car imports from Mobilia. The tariff increases the price that Farmers have to pay for cars. It shifts the supply curve of cars in Farmland upward. The distance between the original supply curve and the new one is the amount of the tariff, £4,000 per car. The price of cars in Farmland increases and the quantity of cars imported decreases. The government of Farmland collects a tariff revenue of £4,000 per car – total of £8 billion on the 2 million cars imported. Farmland's exports of grain decrease because Mobilia now has a lower income from its exports of cars.

Change in the Supply of Cars
Cars are no longer going to be available at the Mobilia export supply price. The tariff of £4,000 must be added to that price – the amount paid to the government of Farmland on each car imported. So the supply curve in Farmland shifts upward by the amount of the tariff as shown in Figure 33.8. The new supply curve becomes that labelled 'Mobilia's export supply of cars plus tariff'. The vertical distance between Mobilia's export supply curve and the new supply curve is the tariff imposed by the government of Farmland – £4,000 a car.

Rise in Price of Cars
A new equilibrium occurs where the new supply curve intersects Farmland's import demand curve for cars. That equilibrium is at a price of £6,000 a car up from £3,000 with free trade.

Fall in Imports

Car imports fall from 4 million to 2 million cars a year. At the higher price of £6,000 a car, domestic car producers increase their production. Domestic grain production decreases as resources are moved into the expanding car industry.

Tariff Revenue

Total expenditure on imported cars by the Farmers is £6,000 a car multiplied by the 2 million cars imported (£12 billion). But not all of that money goes to Mobilia. They receive £2,000 a car or £4 billion for the 2 million cars. The difference – £4,000 a car or a total of £8 billion for the 2 million cars – is collected by the government of Farmland as tariff revenue.

Inefficiency

The people of Farmland are willing to pay £6,000 for the marginal car imported. Obviously, the government of Farmland is happy with this situation. It is now collecting £8 billion that it didn't have before. But the opportunity cost of that car is £2,000. So there is a gain from trading an extra car. In fact, there are gains – willingness to pay exceeds opportunity cost – all the way up to 4 million cars a year. Only when 4 million cars are being traded is the maximum price that a Farmer is willing to pay equal to the minimum price that is acceptable to a Mobilian. Thus restricting international trade reduces the gains from international trade.

Trade remains balanced

With free trade, Farmland was paying £3,000 a car and buying 4 million cars a year from Mobilia. Thus the total amount paid to Mobilia for imports was £12 billion a year. With a tariff, Farmland's imports have been cut to 2 million cars a year and the price paid to Mobilia has also been cut to only £2,000 a car. Thus the total amount paid to Mobilia for imports has been cut to £4 billion a year. Doesn't this fact mean that Farmland is now importing less than it is exporting and has a balance of trade surplus?

It does not! The price of cars in Mobilia has fallen from £3,000 to £2,000 a car. But the price of grain remains at £1 a kilogram. So the relative price of cars has fallen and the relative price of grain has increased. With free trade, Mobilia could buy 3,000 kilograms of grain for 1 car. Now they can buy only 2,000 kilograms for 1 car. With a higher relative price

of grain, the quantity demanded by Mobilia decreases and Mobilia imports less grain. But because Mobilia imports less grain, Farmland exports less grain. In fact, Farmland's grain industry suffers from two sources. First, there is a decrease in the quantity of grain sold to Mobilia. Second, there is increased competition for inputs from the now expanded car industry. Thus the tariff leads to a contraction in the scale of the grain industry in Farmland.

It seems paradoxical at first that a country imposing a tariff on cars would hurt its own export industry, lowering its exports of grain. It may help to think of it this way: Mobilians buy grain with the money they make from exporting cars to Farmland. If they export fewer cars, they cannot afford to buy as much grain. In fact, in the absence of any international borrowing and lending, Mobilia has to cut its imports of grain by exactly the same amount as the loss in revenue from its export of cars. Grain imports into Mobilia will be cut back to a value of £4 billion, the amount that can be paid for by the new lower revenue from Mobilia's car exports. Thus trade is still balanced in this post-tariff situation. Although the tariff has cut imports, it has also cut exports, and the cut in the value of exports is exactly equal to the cut in the value of imports. The tariff, therefore, has no effect on the *balance* of trade – it reduces the *volume* of trade.

The result that we have just derived is perhaps one of the most misunderstood aspects of international economics. On countless occasions, politicians and others have called for tariffs in order to remove a balance of trade deficit or have argued that lowering tariffs would produce a balance of trade deficit. They reach this conclusion by failing to work out all the implications of a tariff.

Let's now turn our attention to the other range of protectionist weapons – non-tariff barriers.

Non-tariff Barriers

There are two important forms of non-tariff barriers:

1   Quotas.
2   Voluntary export restraints.

A **quota** is a quantitative restriction on the import of a particular good. It specifies the maximum amount of the good that may be imported in a given period of time. A **voluntary export restraint** is an agreement between two governments in which the government of the exporting country agrees to restrain the volume of its own exports. Voluntary export restraints are often called VERs.

Non-tariff barriers have become important features of international trading arrangements in the period since the Second World War, and there is general agreement that non-tariff barriers are now a more severe impediment to international trade than tariffs.

Quotas are especially important in the textile industries, where there exists an international agreement called the Multi-Fibre Arrangement, which establishes quotas on a wide range of textile products. Agriculture is also subject to extensive quotas. Voluntary export restraints are particularly important in regulating the international trade in cars between Japan and the United States.

How Quotas and VERs Work

To see how a quota works, suppose that Farmland imposes a quota on car imports that restricts imports to not more than 2 million cars a year. Figure 33.9 shows the effects of this action. The quota is shown by the vertical red line at 2 million cars a year. Because it is illegal to import more than that number of cars, car importers buy only that quantity from Mobilia producers. They pay £2,000 a car to the Mobilia producers. But what do they sell their cars for? The answer is £6,000 each. Because the import supply of cars is restricted to 2 million cars a year, people with cars for sale will be able to get £6,000 each for them. The quantity of cars imported equals the quantity determined by the quota.

The value of imports – the amount paid to Mobilia – declines to £4 billion, exactly the same as in the case of the tariff. Thus with lower incomes from car exports and with a higher relative price of grain, Mobilia cut their imports of grain in exactly the same way as they did under a tariff.

The key difference between a quota and a tariff lies in who gets the profit represented by the difference between the import supply price and the domestic selling price. In the case of a tariff, that difference goes to the government of the importing country. In the case of a quota, that difference goes to the person who has the right to import under the import-quota regulations.

A voluntary export restraint is like a quota arrangement where quotas are allocated to each exporting country. The effects of voluntary export restraints are similar to those of quotas but differ from them

Figure 33.9
The Effects of a Quota

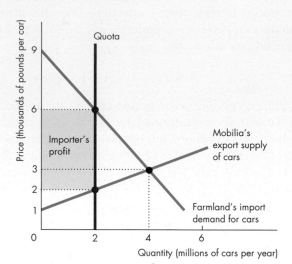

Farmland imposes a quota of 2 million cars a year on car imports from Mobilia. That quantity appears as the vertical line labelled 'Quota'. Because the quantity of cars supplied by Mobilia is restricted to 2 million, the price at which those cars will be traded increases to £6,000. Importing cars is profitable because Mobilia is willing to supply cars at £2,000 each. There is competition for import quotas – rent seeking.

in that the gap between the domestic price and the export price is captured not by domestic importers but by the foreign exporter. The government of the exporting country has to establish procedures for allocating the restricted volume of exports among its producers.

'Invisible' Non-tariff Barriers

In addition to quotas and VERs, there are thousands of non-tariff barriers that are virtually impossible to detect – that are almost invisible. They arise from domestic laws that are not (necessarily) aimed at restricting foreign competition but have that effect. For example, for a long time German purity laws on brewing meant that beer brewed in other countries of Europe that did not meet the specifications set out by the ancient laws could not be sold as beer in Germany. This apparently harmless law effectively restricted competition from foreign beer makers. In 1990 German citizens were allowed access to foreign beer.

Let's now look at some commonly heard arguments for restricting international trade.

The Case Against Protection

For as long as countries and international trade have existed, people have debated whether a country is better off with free international trade or with protection from foreign competition. The debate continues, but for most economists a verdict has been delivered and it is the one you have just explored. Free trade is the arrangement most conducive to prosperity, and protection creates more problems than it solves. We've seen the most powerful case for free trade in the example of how Farmland and Mobilia both benefit from their comparative advantage. But there is a broader range of issues in the free-trade versus protection debate. Let's review these issues.

Three arguments for restricting international trade are:

1 National security.

2 Infant Industry.

3 Dumping.

Let's examine each in turn.

National Security

The national security argument for protection is that a country is better off if it protects its strategic industries – industries that produce defence equipment and armaments, and the industries on which the defence industries rely for their raw materials such as coal and steel and other intermediate inputs. This argument does not stand up to close scrutiny.

First, it is an argument for international isolation, for in time of war, there is no industry that does not contribute to national defence. Second, even if the case is made for maintaining or increasing the output of a strategic industry, there is always a more efficient way of doing so than by protecting the industry from international competition. A direct subsidy to the firms in a strategic industry, financed out of taxes on all sectors of the economy, would keep the industry operating at the scale judged appropriate and free international trade would keep the prices faced by consumers at their world market levels.

Infant Industry

The second argument that is used to justify protection is the **infant-industry argument** – the proposition that protection is necessary to enable an infant industry to grow into a mature industry that can compete in world markets. The argument is based on the idea of *dynamic comparative advantage* which can arise from *learning-by-doing* (see Chapter 2, p. 32).

There is no doubt that learning-by-doing is a powerful engine of productivity growth and that comparative advantage evolves and changes because of on-the-job experience. But these facts do not justify protection.

First, the infant-industry argument is valid only if the benefits of learning-by-doing not only accrue to the owners and workers of the firms in the infant industry but also spill over to other industries and parts of the economy. For example, there are huge productivity gains from learning-by-doing in the manufacture of aircraft. But almost all of these gains benefit the shareholders and workers of BAe, Westland and other aircraft producers. Because the people making the decisions, bearing the risk and doing the work are the ones who benefit, they take the dynamic gains into account when they decide on the scale of their activities. In this case, almost no benefits spill over to other parts of the economy, so there is no need for government assistance to achieve an efficient outcome.

Second, even if the case is made for protecting an infant industry, it is more efficient to do so by a direct subsidy to the firms in the infant industry, with the subsidy financed out of taxes.

Dumping

Dumping occurs when a foreign firm sells its exports at a lower price than its cost of production. Dumping might be used by a firm that wants to gain a global monopoly. In this case, the firm sells at a price below its cost in order to drive domestic firms out of business. When the domestic firms have gone, the foreign firm takes advantage of its monopoly position and charges a higher price for its product. Dumping is usually regarded as a justification for temporary – countervailing – tariffs.

But there are powerful reasons to resist the dumping argument for protection. First, it is virtually impossible to detect dumping because it is hard to determine a firm's costs. As a result, the test for dumping is whether a firm's export price is below its domestic price. But this test is a weak one because it can be rational for a firm to charge a low price in markets in which the quantity demanded is highly sensitive to price and a higher price in markets in which demand is less price-sensitive.

Second, there are virtually no goods that are natural global monopolies. So even if all the domestic firms did get driven out of business in some industry, it would always be possible to find several and usually many alternative foreign sources of supply and to buy at prices determined in competitive markets.

Third, if a good or service was a truly global natural monopoly, the best way of dealing with it would be by regulation, just as in the case of domestic monopolies. Such regulation would require international cooperation.

The three arguments for protection we've just examined have an element of credibility. The counter-arguments are in general stronger so these arguments do not make the case for protection. But they are not the only arguments that you might encounter. The many other arguments commonly heard are quite simply wrong. They are fatally flawed. The most common of them are that protection:

◆ Saves jobs.
◆ Allows us to compete with cheap foreign labour.
◆ Brings diversity and stability.
◆ Penalizes lax environmental standards.
◆ Safeguards national culture.
◆ Prevents rich countries from exploiting developing countries.

Saves Jobs

The argument is that when we buy shoes from Brazil or shirts from Taiwan, workers in Lancashire lose their jobs. With no earnings and poor prospects, these workers become a drain on the welfare state and they spend less, causing a ripple effect of further job losses. The proposed solution to this problem is to ban imports of cheap foreign goods and protect jobs at home. The proposal is flawed for the following reasons.

First, free trade does cost some jobs, but it also creates other jobs. It brings about a global rationalization of labour and allocates labour resources to their highest-value activities. Because of international trade in textiles, tens of thousands of workers in the United Kingdom have lost jobs because textile mills and other factories have closed. But tens of thousands of workers in other countries have got jobs because textile mills have opened there. And tens of thousands of workers in the United Kingdom have got better-paying jobs than textile workers because other industries have expanded and created more jobs than have been destroyed.

Second, imports create jobs. They create jobs for retailers which sell imported goods and for firms which service these goods. They also create jobs by creating incomes in the rest of the world, some of which are spent on UK-made goods and services.

Although protection does not save jobs, it changes the mix of jobs. But it does so at inordinate cost. For example, in the United States jobs in the textile industry are protected by quotas imposed under an international agreement called the Multi-Fibre Arrangement. It has been estimated that because of the quotas, 72,000 jobs existed in textiles in the United States that would otherwise have disappeared. But each textile job saved cost more than $300,000 a year in added clothing costs!

Allows us to Compete with Cheap Foreign Labour

The late Sir James Goldsmith, multimillionaire and Euro MP, argued that if Europe does not build protective tariffs against cheap imports from the newly industrializing economies of East Asia, there will be a loss of jobs that will threaten the way of life in Europe. The loss of jobs will occur as firms relocate in the Far East to take advantage of cheap labour. Let's see what's wrong with this view.

The labour cost of a unit of output equals the wage rate divided by labour productivity. For example, if a

UK production assembly worker earns $30 an hour and produces 10 units of output an hour, the average labour cost of a unit of output is $3. (We will use dollars to measure the outputs of workers from different countries.) If a Chinese production assembly worker earns $3 an hour and produces 1 unit of output an hour, the average labour cost of a unit of output is $3. Other things remaining the same, the higher a worker's productivity, the higher is the worker's wage rate. High-wage workers have high productivity. Low-wage workers have low productivity.

Although high-wage UK workers are more productive, on the average, than low-wage Chinese workers, there are differences across industries. UK labour is relatively more productive at some activities than others. For example, the productivity of UK workers in producing chemical products, luxury cars and high-quality engineering is relatively higher than in the production of metals and some standardized machine parts. The activities in which UK workers are relatively more productive than their Chinese counterparts are those in which the United Kingdom has a *comparative advantage*. By engaging in free trade, increasing our production and exports of the goods at which we have a comparative advantage and decreasing our production and imports of the goods at which our trading partners have a comparative advantage, we can make ourselves and the citizens of other countries better off.

Brings Diversity and Stability

A diversified investment portfolio is less risky than one that has all its eggs in one basket. The same is true for an economy's production. A diversified economy fluctuates less than an economy that produces only one or two goods.

But big, rich, diversified economies like the United States, Japan and the European Union do not have this type of stability problem. Even a country like Saudi Arabia, which produces almost only one good (oil), can benefit from specializing in the activity at which it has a comparative advantage and then investing in a wide range of other countries to bring greater stability to its income and consumption.

Penalizes Lax Environmental Standards

A new argument for protection that was used extensively in the Uruguay Round of the GATT negotiations is that many poorer countries, such as Mexico, do not have the same environmental policies we have and, because they are willing to pollute and we are not, we cannot compete with them without tariffs. So if they want free trade with the richer and 'greener' countries, they must clean up their environments to our standards.

The environment argument for trade restrictions is weak. First, it is not true that all poorer countries have significantly lower environmental protection standards than the United Kingdom has. Many poor countries, and the former communist countries of Eastern Europe, do have a bad record on the environment. But some countries, one of which is Mexico, have strict laws and they enforce them. Second, a poor country cannot afford to be as concerned about its environment as a rich country can. The best hope for a better environment in Mexico and in other developing countries is rapid income growth through free trade. As their incomes grow, developing countries such as Mexico will have the *means* to match their desires to improve their environment.

Safeguards National Culture

A national culture argument for protection is one that is frequently heard in Europe. The expressed fear is that free trade in books, magazines, film and television programmes means the erosion of local culture and the domination of US culture. The argument continues, that it is necessary to protect domestic culture industries to ensure the survival of national cultural identity. This is an argument that is often used in connection with the European film industry.

Protection of these industries usually takes the form of non-tarrif barriers. For example, local content regulations on radio and television broadcasting and in magazines is often required.

The cultural identity argument for protection has no merit, and it is one more example of rent seeking (see Chapter 12, pp. 249–250). Writers, publishers and broadcasters want to limit foreign competition so that they can earn larger economic profits. There is no actual danger to national culture. In fact, many of the creators of so-called American cultural products are not Americans, but the talented citizens of other countries, ensuring the survival of their national culture in Hollywood! Also, if national culture is in danger, there is no surer way of helping it on its way down than by impoverishing the nation whose culture it is. Protection is an effective way of doing just that.

Prevents Rich Countries from Exploiting Developing Countries

Another new argument for protection is that international trade must be restricted to prevent the people of the rich industrial world from exploiting the poorer people of the developing countries, forcing them to work for slave wages.

Wage rates in some developing countries are, indeed, very low. But by trading with developing countries, we increase the demand for the goods that these countries produce, and, more significantly, we increase the demand for their labour. When the demand for labour in developing countries increases, the wage rate also increases. So, far from exploiting people in developing countries, trade improves their opportunities and increases their incomes.

We have reviewed the arguments commonly heard in favour of protection and the counter-arguments against them. There is one counter-argument to protection that is general and quite overwhelming. Protection invites retaliation and can trigger a trade war. The best example of a trade war occurred during the Great Depression of the 1930s when the Smoot-Hawley Tariff was introduced in the United States. Country after country retaliated with its own tariff and in a short time, world trade had almost disappeared. The costs to all countries were large and led to a renewed international resolve to avoid such self-defeating moves in future. They also led to the creation of the GATT and are the impetus behind NAFTA, APEC and the European Union.

Review Quiz

◆ Is there any merit to the view that we should restrict international trade to achieve national security goals, to stimulate the growth of new industries, or to restrain foreign monopoly?
◆ Is there any merit to the view that we should restrict international trade to save jobs, compensate for low foreign wages, make the economy more diversified, compensate for costly environmental policies, protect national culture, or protect developing countries from being exploited?
◆ Is there any merit to the view that we should restrict international trade for any reason? What is the main argument against trade restrictions?

Why is International Trade Restricted?

Why, despite all the arguments against protection, is trade restricted? There are two key reasons:

1 Tariff revenue.
2 Rent seeking.

Tariff Revenue

Government revenue is costly to collect. In the developed economies, income taxes, VAT, and excise taxes are the major sources of revenue. A tariff plays a very small role if at all. But governments in developing countries have a difficult time in collecting taxes from their citizens. Much economic activity takes place in the informal sector, with few financial records. So only a small amount of revenue is collected from income taxes and indirect taxes from these countries. The one area in which economic transactions are well recorded and audited is in international trade. So this activity is an attractive base for tax collection in these countries and is used more extensively than in the developed countries.

Rent Seeking

The major reason why international trade is restricted is because of rent seeking. Free trade increases consumption possibilities *on the average* but not everyone shares in the gain and some people even lose. Free trade brings benefits to some and costs to others, with total benefits exceeding total costs. The uneven distribution of costs and benefits is the principal impediment to achieving more liberal international trade.

Returning to our example of international trade in cars and grain between Farmland and Mobilia, the benefits from free trade accrue to all the producers of grain and those producers of cars who would not have to bear the costs of adjusting to a smaller car industry. These costs are transition costs, not permanent costs. The costs of moving to free trade are borne by those car producers and their employees who have to become grain producers. The number of people who gain will, in general, be enormous compared with the number who lose. The gain per person will, therefore, be rather small. The loss per person to those who bear the loss will be large. Because the loss that falls on those who bear it is large, it will pay those people to incur considerable expense in order to lobby against free trade. On the other hand, it will not pay those who gain to organize to achieve free trade. The gain from trade for any one individual is too small for that individual to spend much time or money on a political organization to achieve free trade. The loss from free trade will be seen as being so great by those bearing that loss that they *will* find it profitable to join a political organization to prevent free trade. Each group is optimizing – weighing benefits against costs and choosing the best action for themselves. The anti-free trade group will, therefore, undertake a larger quantity of political lobbying than the pro-free trade group.

Compensating Losers

If, in total, the gains from free international trade exceed the losses, why don't those who gain compensate those who lose so that everyone is in favour of free trade? To some degree, such compensation does take place.

The losers from freer or marginal improvements in international trade are compensated indirectly through the normal unemployment benefit payments. But only limited attempts are made to compensate those who lose from total free international trade. The main reason full compensation is not attempted is that the costs of identifying all the losers and estimating the value of their losses would be enormous. Also, it would never be clear whether or not a person who has fallen on hard times is suffering because of free trade or for other reasons, perhaps reasons largely under the control of the individual. Furthermore, some people who look like losers at one point in time may, in fact, end up gaining. The young steel worker in South Wales who loses his job and becomes a computer assembly worker resents the loss of work and the need to move. But a year or two later, looking back on events, he counts himself fortunate. He's made a move that has increased his income and given him greater job security.

It is because we do not, in general, compensate the losers from free international trade that protectionism is such a popular and permanent feature of our national economic and political life.

Political Outcome

The political outcome that emerges from this activity is one in which a modest amount of restriction on international trade occurs and is maintained. Politicians react to constituencies pressing for protection and find it necessary, in order to get re-elected, to support legislative programmes that protect those constituencies. The producers of protected goods are far more vocal and much more sensitive swing-voters than the consumers of such goods. The political outcome, therefore, often leans in the direction of maintaining protection.

Review Quiz

◆ What are the two main reasons for imposing tariffs on imports?
◆ What type of country benefits most from the revenue from tariffs? Do countries in the EU need to use tariffs to raise revenue for the government?
◆ If trade restrictions are costly, why do we use them? Why don't the people who gain from trade organize a political force that is strong enough to ensure their interests are protected?

You've now seen how free international trade enables all countries to gain from increased specialization and exchange. By producing goods at which we have a comparative advantage and exchanging some of our own production for that of others, we expand our consumption possibilities. Placing impediments on that exchange when it crosses national borders restricts the extent to which we can gain from specialization and exchange. Reading Between the Lines on pp. 780–781 examines a specific case of a proposed trade restriction on streel imports that will be challenged by the EU by taking it to the WTO for a judgement. The restriction means that steel users in the US will pay a higher price than they would in its absence. By opening our country up to free international trade, the market for the things which we sell expands and the relative price rises. The market for the things that we buy also expands and the relative price falls. All countries gain from free international trade. As a consequence of price adjustments, and in the absence of international borrowing and lending, the value of imports adjusts to equal the value of exports.

In the next chapter, we're going to study the ways in which international trade is financed, and also learn why international borrowing and lending, which permit unbalanced international trade, arise. We'll discover the forces that determine the balance of payments and the value of the pound in terms of foreign currency.

Summary

Key Points

Patterns and Trends in International Trade (pp. 759–761)

- Large flows of trade take place between rich and poor countries.

- Resource-rich countries exchange natural resources for manufactured goods, and resource-poor countries import resources in exchange for their own manufactured goods. However, by far the biggest volume of trade is in manufactured goods exchanged among the rich industrialized countries.

- Finished manufactured goods constitute the largest group of export items by the United Kingdom.

- Trade in services has grown in recent years.

- Total trade has also grown over the years.

Opportunity Cost and Comparative Advantage (pp. 761–762)

- When opportunity costs differ among countries, the country with the lowest opportunity cost of producing a good is said to have a comparative advantage in that good.

- Comparative advantage is the source of the gains from international trade.

- A country can have an absolute advantage, but not a comparative advantage, in the production of all goods.

- Every country has a comparative advantage in something.

Gains from Trade (pp. 762–765)

- Trading allows consumption to exceed production. By specializing in producing the good in which it has a comparative advantage and then trading some of that good for imports, a country can consume at points outside its production possibility frontier.

- Each country can consume at such a point.

- In the absence of international borrowing and lending, trade is balanced as prices adjust to reflect the international supply and demand for goods.

- The world price balances the production and consumption plans of the trading parties.

- At the equilibrium price, trade is balanced.

Gains from Trade in Reality (pp. 765–766)

- Comparative advantage explains the enormous volume and diversity of international trade that takes place in the world.

- Much trade, however, takes the form of exchanging similar goods for each other – one type of car for another. Such trade arises because of economies of scale in the face of diversified tastes.

Trade Restrictions (pp. 766–771)

- A country can restrict international trade by imposing tariffs or non-tariff barriers – quotas and voluntary export restraints.

- All trade restrictions raise the domestic price of imported goods, lower the volume of imports and reduce the total value of imports.

- They also reduce the total value of exports by the same amount as the reduction in the value of imports.

The Case Against Protection (pp. 771–774)

- Three arguments for trade restrictions – the national security argument, the infant-industry argument and the dumping argument – are weak.

- Other arguments for protection – that it saves jobs, is necessary because foreign labour is cheap, makes the economy diversified and stable, protects national culture, and is needed to offset the costs of environmental policies that poorer countries do not incur – are fatally flawed.

Why is International Trade Restricted? (pp. 774–775)

- Trade is often restricted because, although it increases consumption possibilities *on the average*, a small number of losers bear a large loss per person and a large number of gainers enjoy a small gain per person.

- Those who lose from free trade undertake a larger quantity of political lobbying than those who gain from it.

Key Figures ◈

Key Terms

Problems

•1 The table provides information about Virtual Reality's production possibilities.

TV sets (per day)		Computers (per day)
0	and	36
10	and	35
20	and	33
30	and	30
40	and	26
50	and	21
60	and	15
70	and	8
80	and	0

a Calculate Virtual Reality's opportunity cost of a TV set when it produces 10 sets a day.

b Calculate Virtual Reality's opportunity cost of a TV set when it produces 40 sets a day.

c Calculate Virtual Reality's opportunity cost of a TV set when it produces 70 sets a day.

d Using the answers to parts (a), (b), and (c), graph the relationship between the opportunity cost of a TV set and the quantity of TV sets produced in Virtual Reality.

2 The table provides information about Vital Signs' production possibilities.

TV sets (per day)		Computers (per day)
0	and	18.0
10	and	17.5
20	and	16.5
30	and	15.0
40	and	13.0
50	and	10.5
60	and	7.5
70	and	4.0
80	and	0

a Calculate Vital Signs' opportunity cost of a TV set when it produces 10 sets a day.

b Calculate Vital Signs' opportunity cost of a TV set when it produces 40 sets a day.

c Calculate Vital Signs' opportunity cost of a TV set when it produces 70 sets a day.

d Using the answers to parts (a), (b), and (c), sketch the relationship between the opportunity cost of a TV set and the quantity of TV sets produced in Vital Signs.

•3 Suppose that with no international trade, Virtual Reality in problem 1 produces and consumes 10 TV sets a day and Vital Signs produces and consumes 60 TV sets a day. Now suppose that the two countries begin to trade with each other.

a Which country exports TV sets?

b What adjustments are made to the amount of each good produced by each country?

c What adjustments are made to the amount of each good produced by each country?

d What can you say about the terms of trade (the price of a TV set expressed as computers per TV set) under free trade?

4 Suppose that with no international trade, Virtual Reality in problem 1 produces and consumes

50 TV sets a day and Vital Signs produces and consumes 20 TV sets a day. Now suppose that the two countries begin to trade with each other.

a Which country exports TV sets?

b What adjustments are made to the amount of each good produced by each country?

c What adjustments are made to the amount of each good consumed by each country?

d What can you say about the terms of trade (the price of a TV set expressed as computers per TV set) under free trade?

•5 Compare the total quantities of each good produced in problems 1 and 2 with the total quantities of each good produced in problems 3 and 4.

a Does free trade increase or decrease the total quantities of TV sets and computers produced in both cases? Why or why not?

b What happens to the price of a TV set in Virtual Reality in the two cases? Why does it rise in one case and fall in the other?

c What happens to the price of a computer in Vital Signs in the two cases? Why does it rise in one case and fall in the other?

6 Compare the international trade in problem 3 with that in problem 4.

a Why does Virtual Reality export TV sets in one of the cases and import them in the other case?

b Do the TV producers or the computer producers gain in each case?

c Do consumers gain in each case?

•7 The figure depicts the international market for soybeans.

a If the two countries did not engage in international trade, what would be the prices of soybeans in the two countries?

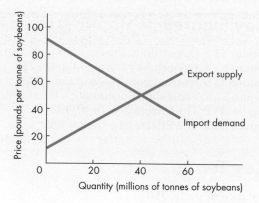

b What are the terms of trade if there is free trade between these countries?

c What quantities of soybeans are exported and imported?

d What is the balance of trade?

8 If the soybean importing country in problem 7 imposes a tariff of £2 per tonne, what are the terms of trade and what quantity of soybeans gets traded internationally? What is the price of soybeans in the importing country? Calculate the tariff revenue.

•9 If the soybean importing country in problem 7 imposes a quota of 300 million tonnes on imports of soybeans,

a What is the price of soybeans in the importing country?

b What is the revenue from the quota?

c Who gets this revenue?

10 If the soybean exporting country in problem 7 imposes a VER of 300 million tonnes on its exports of soybeans,

a What are the terms of trade now?

b What is the revenue of soybean growers in the exporting country?

c Which country gains from the VER?

Critical Thinking

1 Study Reading Between the Lines on pp. 780–781 and then answer the following questions.

   a What is the argument for limiting steel imports into the US?

   b What will be the effect of the restriction on the US steel consuming industry? What will be the effect on the EU?

   c Is the argument to limit steel imports correct in your opinion?

   d Should the EU impose trade restrictions on US exports to Europe in a tit-for-tat gesture?

   e What are the potential dangers from a trade war between the US and the EU?

Steelmakers Battle About Trade

WALL STREET JOURNAL EUROPE, 24 OCTOBER 2001

European Steelmakers are Set to Fight U.S. Trade Proposal

Robert Guy Matthews and Geoff Winestock

European steelmakers are preparing for battle after a US government agency cleared the way for George Bush to raise major trade barriers to billions of dollars of steel imports.

The International Trade Commission, which hears claims of unfair trade competition in the US, ruled that the domestic US steel industry has been 'seriously injured' by foreign steelmakers flooding the country since 1998 with cheap imports that have sent steel prices to near 20-year lows.

The six-member commission found that 12 product lines, representing 79 per cent of all the steel produced in the US, have sustained serious injury because of foreign imports. The products include key lines such as hot-rolled, cold-rolled and steel slabs, which are components in autos, heavy machinery and shipping containers.

The panel will disclose details of penalties on foreign steel producers on December 19, which could include high tariffs, quotas and other barriers to entry. The measures will then go to President Bush, who has until February 19 to approve the commission's recommendations. The president is likely to do so.

The commission was ordered by Mr Bush in June to investigate whether domestic steel companies were financially injured by the actions of foreign steel companies after domestic steelmakers and their powerful representatives in the US Congress complained of unfair trade.

The US decision however drew an immediate threat from the European Commission to challenge, in the World Trade Organization, any protectionist measures. European Trade Commissioner Pascal Lamy said that steel imports hadn't caused injury to the US steel industry. He said that the problems in the US steel sector were confined to integrated steelmakers that had failed to restructure over the past decade.

'We disagree with the ITC's findings. If the US decides to close its market as a result of this investigation it should be in no doubt that we will take this matter up in the WTO,' he said. 'Shifting responsibility for the problems facing the US steel industry onto the rest of the world by imposing protectionist measures will only make matters worse.'

The decision threatens about $2.5 billion to $3 billion (2.8 billion euros to 3.36 billion euros) of EU steel exports to the US, or 60 per cent of the total, and EU officials say it could also destabilize the entire world market for steel, shifting about nine millions tons of steel from the US to the EU.

But the US steel lobby is pressing for a big increase in protectionist barriers. 'The objective of this remedy is to give the industry breathing time to return to profitability,' said Thomas J. Usher, chairman and chief executive of USX-US Steel Group, the largest US Steelmaker. Leo Gerard, president of the United Steelworkers of America, said he wants to see the stiffest penalties allowable against the foreign steelmakers: 'We want strong quotas and substantial tariffs for as long as we can get them.'

Steel-consuming industries, such as appliance and heavy-equipment makers, said that if President Bush approves trade curbs, they would have to pay higher prices, which would be passed on to consumers. Mr Bush has paid an unusual amount of attention to the domestic steel industry, launching an unprecedented move earlier this year to push all of the world's steelmakers to voluntarily limit steel production and pump up world prices.

The Essence of the Story

- The EU is threatening the USA to launch a complaint with the WTO over its potential imposition of import restrictions on steel.

- This follows the publication of the USITC (US International Trade Commission) investigation which ruled that the US steel producers are losing out due to 'unfair' and 'illegal' imports.

- According to the USITC, cheap steel from foreign government supported industries have been dumping steel on the US market driving prices down to a 20 year low.

- The EU, which is a major exporter of steel to the US, say that the US steel sector has failed to restructure in the past ten years. This is another way of saying that the US steel industry needs to contract.

- The steel-consuming industries said that if trade curbs were brought in, they would have to pay higher prices which will be passed on to consumers.

Economic Analysis

- The article says that the USITC claims that unfair competition from cheap imports has resulted in substantial losses to the domestic steel industry.

- Calls for protection seem unjustified. The US steel mills supply more than two-thirds of domestic steel consumption.

- Figure 1 shows the effect of import restrictions on the price of steel. The free trade price is P_0. A tariff or quota raises the domestic price to P_2 and reduces the price paid to the supplier to P_1. The gap is the rent accrued to the importer.

- As a result of the increased price, consumers and the steel using sector such as transport equipment, industrial machinery and construction will have to pay more for their inputs. Estimates of the cost of quantitative restrictions on steel in the 1980s cost the US economy $6.8 billion a year.

- The EU fears that in addition to the direct effects of trade barriers on EU exporters, trade restrictions would divert substantial quantities of of the world's steel onto the EU market. In Figure 2, the export supply curve facing the EU shifts right from S_0 to S_1, the price falls to P_1 and the quantity consumed rises to Q_1.

- Market analysts point to substantial global over-capacity and fragmentation in the US steel industry. Figure 3 shows that the decline in US steel jobs is unrelated to imports. During the period of import restrictions in the 1980s, imports declined, but so did employment in the steel sector.

- This exercise demonstrates the power of the political lobby for rent seeking by the US steelmakers. Employment in steelmaking in the US is less than two hundred thousand whereas there are 8 million employees in the steel using industries.

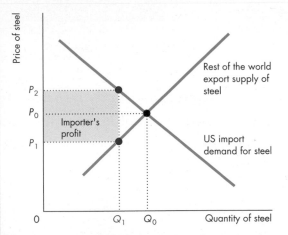

Figure 1 The US market

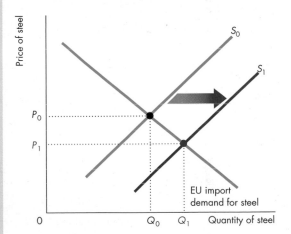

Figure 2 The EU market

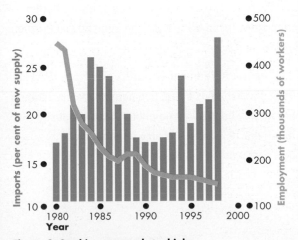

Figure 3 Steel imports and steel jobs

Understanding the Gains from International Trade

Under a system of perfectly free commerce, each country naturally devotes its capital and labour to such employments as are most beneficial to each.

David Ricardo, The Principles of Political Economy and Taxation, 1817

The Economist: David Ricardo

David Ricardo (1772–1832) was a highly successful 27-year-old stockbroker when he stumbled on a copy of Adam Smith's *The Wealth of Nations* (see p. 40) on a weekend visit to the country. He was immediately hooked and went on to become the most celebrated economist of his age and one of the all-time great economists. One of his many contributions was to develop the principle of comparative advantage, the foundation on which the modern theory of international trade is built. The example he used to illustrate this principle was the trade between England and Portugal in cloth and wine.

The General Agreement on Tariffs and Trade (GATT) was established as a reaction against the devastation wrought by beggar-my-neighbour tariffs imposed during the 1930s. But it is also a triumph for the logic first worked out by Smith and Ricardo.

The Issues and Ideas

Until the mid-eighteenth century, it was generally believed that the purpose of international trade was to keep exports greater than imports and to pile up gold. If gold was accumulated, it was believed, the nation would prosper; and if gold was lost through an international deficit, the nation would be drained of money and impoverished. These beliefs are called *mercantilism*, and the *mercantilists* were pamphleteers who advocated with missionary fervour the pursuit of an international surplus. If exports did not exceed imports, the mercantilists wanted imports restricted.

In the 1740s, David Hume explained that as the quantity of money (gold) changes, so does the price level, and the nation's *real* wealth is unaffected. In the 1770s, Adam Smith argued that import restrictions would lower the gains from specialization and make a nation poorer, and 30 years later, David Ricardo proved the law of comparative advantage and demonstrated the superiority of free trade. Mercantilism was intellectually bankrupt but remained politically powerful.

Gradually, through the nineteenth century, the mercantilist influence waned and North America and Western Europe prospered in an environment of increasingly free international trade. But despite remarkable advances in economic understanding, mercantilism never quite died. It had a brief and devastating revival in the 1920s and 1930s when tariff hikes brought about the collapse of international trade and accentuated the Great Depression. It subsided again after the Second World War with the establishment of the General Agreement on Tariffs and Trade (GATT).

But mercantilism lingers on. The often expressed view that the United States should restrict Japanese imports and reduce its deficit with Japan and fears that the NAFTA will bring economic ruin to the United States are modern manifestations of mercantilism. It would be interesting to have David Hume, Adam Smith and David Ricardo commenting on these views. But we know what they would say – the same things that they said to the eighteenth century mercantilists. And they would still be right today.

Then . . .

In the eighteenth century, when mercantilists and economists were debating the pros and cons of free international exchange, the available transportation technology limited the gains from international trade. Sailing ships with tiny cargo holds took nearly a month to cross the Atlantic Ocean. But the potential gains were large, and so was the incentive to cut shipping costs. By the 1850s, the clipper ship had been developed, cutting the journey from Boston to Liverpool to only $12\frac{1}{4}$ days. Half a century later, 10,000-ton steamships were sailing between America and England in just four days. As sailing times and costs declined, so the gains from international trade increased and the volume of trade expanded.

. . . And Now

The container ship has revolutionized international trade and contributed to its continued expansion. Today, most goods cross the oceans in containers – metal boxes – packed into and piled on top of ships like the one shown here. Container technology has cut the cost of ocean shipping by economizing on handling and by making cargoes harder to steal, lowering insurance costs. It is unlikely that there would be much international trade in goods such as television sets and VCRs without this technology. High-value and perishable cargoes such as flowers and fresh foods, as well as urgent courier packages, travel by air. Every day, dozens of cargo-laden 747s fly between all major European cities and destinations across the Atlantic and Pacific Oceans.

CHAPTER 34

International Finance

After studying this chapter you will be able to:

◆ Explain how international trade is financed

◆ Describe a country's balance of payments accounts

◆ Explain what determines the amount of international borrowing and lending

◆ Explain how the foreign exchange value of the pound is determined

◆ Explain why the foreign exchange value of the pound fluctuates

◆ Understand the implications of European Monetary Union and the place of the euro in the global economy

The Yen, the Dollar and the Euro

The yen (¥), the euro (€), and the dollar ($) are the world's three big currencies. The yen (the currency of Japan) and the dollar (the currency of the United States) have been around for a long time. The euro is new. It was launched on 1 January 1999 as the fledgling currency of 11 members of the European Union, and it will not be used for ordinary transactions until 2002. But it is already an international currency. Most of the world's international trade and finance is conducted using these three currencies. ◆ Currencies fluctuate in value. In 1971, one pound sterling was enough to buy 8.5 Deutschmarks, and 2.44 US dollars. In December 2001, that same pound bought only DM3.13 and $1.43. But the slide in the value of the pound from DM8.5 to DM3.13 or from $2.44 to $1.43 was not a smooth one. At some times the pound rose in value against all currencies, as it did, for example, in 1980. In 1999, the pound rose against the euro – the new currency of the European Monetary Union (EMU). But at other times the pound's slide was precipitous, as in September 1992 when the pound left the Exchange Rate Mechanism (ERM). What makes the pound fluctuate in value against other currencies? Why have the fluctuations been particularly extreme, as in the 1980s and in 1992? Is there anything we can do to stabilize the value of the pound? Can an exchange rate agreement help to stabilize the pound? The pound has also fallen against the Yen over this same period but recently the pound has strengthened against the Yen. In Reading Between the Lines, pp. 808–809, we examine the circumstances that has led to the weakening of the Yen against the dollar and the pound. ◆ In 1986, the United Kingdom owned £721.2 billion in assets abroad and foreigners owned £622.9 billion of assets in the United Kingdom. Foreign assets exceeded foreigners' assets in the United Kingdom so that net foreign assets – the difference between what people in the United Kingdom hold of foreign assets and what foreigners hold of UK assets – were £98.3 billion. In 2000 the balance had tipped the other way. Net foreign assets were – £118 billion. What caused this turnaround? Part of the reason is that the United Kingdom is a good place to invest and foreign companies have been buying UK firms or setting up companies. Think of BMW's acquisition of Rover, Nestlés purchase of Rowntree, or the Hongkong & Shanghai Bank's purchase of Midland Bank. Why have foreigners been buying more businesses in the United Kingdom than British people have been buying abroad?

◆ ◆ ◆ ◆ International economics has always been an important issue for an economy such as the United Kingdom. In this chapter we're going to study the questions that we've just raised. We're going to discover why the United Kingdom has become such an attractive target for foreign investors; why the value of the pound fluctuates against the values of other currencies; and why interest rates vary from country to country.

Financing International Trade

When Currys, an electrical goods retail chain, imports Sony CD players, it does not pay for them with pounds – it uses Japanese yen. When Harrods imports Armani suits, it pays for them with Italian lire. And when a Japanese retail company buys a consignment of Scotch malt whisky, it uses pounds sterling. Whenever we buy things from another country, we use the currency of that country in order to make the transaction. It doesn't make any difference what the item being traded is; it might be a consumer good or a capital good, a building, or even a firm.

We're going to study the markets in which money – in different types of currencies – is bought and sold. But first we're going to look at the scale of international trading and borrowing and lending and at the way in which we keep our records of these transactions. Such records are called the balance of payments accounts.

Balance of Payments Accounts

A country's **balance of payments accounts** record its international trading and its borrowing and lending. There are three balance of payments accounts:

1. Current account.
2. Capital and financial account.
3. Change in reserve assets.

The **current account** records the receipts from the sale of goods and services to foreigners, the payments for goods and services bought from foreigners, and gifts and other transfers (such as foreign aid payments) received from and paid to foreigners. By far the largest items in the current account are the receipts from the sale of goods and services to foreigners (the value of exports) and the payments made for goods and services bought from foreigners (the value of imports). Net income is the earnings from foreign financial assets such as bonds and shares, and net earnings of UK workers abroad and foreign workers in the UK. Net transfers – gifts to foreigners minus gifts from foreigners – are relatively small items. The **capital and financial account** records all the international borrowing and lending transactions. Whereas the earnings from investments abroad are recorded in the current account, the financial account balance records the actual investments abroad and foreigners' investments in the UK. It is the difference between

the amount that a country lends to and borrows from the rest of the world. The **change in reserve assets** shows the net increase or decrease in a country's holdings of foreign currency reserves that comes about from the official financing of the difference between the current account and the capital and financial accounts. In practice, the change in reserve assets is an item in the capital and financial accounts. It is itemized separately here so that you can see how the financing of the gap between current and capital and financial accounts adds to or subtracts from reserve assets.

Table 34.1 shows the UK balance of payments accounts in 2000. Items in the current account and financial account that provide foreign currency to the United Kingdom have a plus sign and items that cost the United Kingdom foreign currency have a minus sign. The table shows that in 2000, UK imports of goods exceeded UK exports of goods and the net trade in goods had a deficit of £30.4 billion. But exports of services exceeded imports so that net trade in services was in surplus by £14.7 billion. How do we pay for imports that exceed the value of our exports? That is, how do we pay for our current account deficit? We pay by borrowing from abroad. The financial account tells us by how much. We borrowed £532.6 billion but made loans of £502.2 billion. Thus our identified net foreign borrowing was £32.4 billion.

Table 34.1 UK Balance of Payments Accounts in 2000

Current account	(billions of pounds)
Net trade in goods	−30.4
Net trade in services	+14.7
Net income	+6.1
Net transfers	−8.8
Current account balance	−18.4
Capital and financial account	
Capital account	+2.0
Foreign investment in the UK	+532.6
UK investment abroad	−502.2
Capital account balance	32.4
Balancing Item	−10
Change in reserves assets	
Decrease (+) in official UK reserves	−4.0

Source: UK Balance of Payments: The Pink Book, 2001, ONS, London.

Figure 34.1

The Balance of Payments: 1987–2000

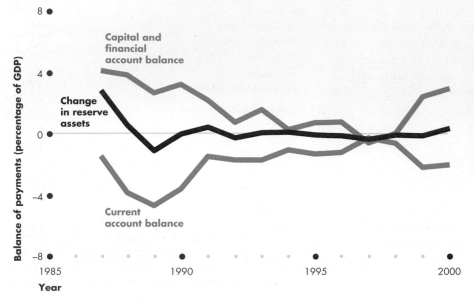

The balance of payments show a continuous current account deficit during the late 1980s and 1990s. The capital and financial account balance mirrors the current account balance. When the current account balance is negative, the capital and financial account balance is positive – we borrow from the rest of the world. Fluctuations in the change in reserve assets are usually small compared with fluctuations in the current account balance and the capital and financial account balance.

Source: National Statistics.

A statistical discrepancy arises known as the balancing item. This discrepancy represents a combination of capital and current account transactions such as unidentified borrowing from abroad, illegal international trade – for example, the import of illegal drugs – and transactions not reported in order to evade tariffs or taxes. In 2000 this was £10 billion.

In theory our net borrowing from abroad minus our current account deficit represents the balance that is financed from official UK reserves. Official UK reserves are the government's holdings of foreign currency. In 2000, those reserves increased by £4 billion.

The numbers in Table 34.1 give a snapshot of the balance of payments accounts in 2000. Figure 34.1 puts that snapshot into perspective by showing the balance of payments between 1987 and 1997. Because the economy grows and the price level rises, changes in the sterling value of the balance of payments do not convey much information. To remove the influences of growth and inflation, Figure 34.1 shows the balance of payments as a percentage of nominal GDP.

As you can see, the current account balance is almost a mirror image of the capital and financial account balance. The change in reserve assets is small compared with the balances on these other two accounts. A large current account deficit (and capital and financial account surplus) occurred during the late 1980s, but declined after 1990.

You will perhaps obtain a better understanding of the balance of payments accounts and the way in which they are linked together if you consider the income and expenditure, borrowing and lending, and the bank account of an individual.

Individual Analogy

An individual's current account records the income from supplying the services of factors of production and the expenditure on goods and services. Consider, for example, Joanne. She earned an income in 1995 of £25,000. Joanne has £10,000 worth of investments that earned her an income of £1,000. Joanne's current account shows an income of £26,000. Joanne spent £18,000 buying goods and services for consumption. She also bought a new house, which cost her £60,000. So Joanne's total expenditure was £78,000. The difference between her expenditure and income is £52,000 (£78,000 minus £26,000). This amount is Joanne's current account deficit.

To pay for expenditure of £52,000 in excess of her income, Joanne has either to use the money that she has in the bank or to take out a loan. In fact Joanne took a mortgage of £50,000 to help buy her house.

This mortgage was the only borrowing that Joanne did, so her capital and financial account surplus was £50,000. With a current account deficit of £52,000 and a capital and financial account surplus of £50,000, Joanne is still £2,000 short. She got that £2,000 from her own bank account. Her cash holdings decreased by £2,000.

Joanne's income from her work and investments is analogous to a country's income from its exports. Her purchases of goods and services, including her purchase of a house, are analogous to a country's imports. Joanne's mortgage – borrowing from someone else – is analogous to a country's foreign borrowing. The change in her own bank account is analogous to the change in the country's reserve assets.

Borrowers and Lenders, Debtors and Creditors

A country that is borrowing more from the rest of the world than it is lending to it is called a **net borrower**. Similarly, a **net lender** is a country that is lending more to the rest of the world than it is borrowing from it. A net borrower might be going deeper into debt or might simply be reducing its net assets held in the rest of the world. The total stock of foreign investment determines whether a country is a debtor or a creditor. A **debtor nation** is a country that during its entire history has borrowed more from the rest of the world than it has lent to it. It has a stock of outstanding debt to the rest of the world that exceeds the stock of its own claims on the rest of the world. The United Kingdom is currently a debtor nation, but for a long time it was a creditor. A **creditor nation** is a country that has invested more in the rest of the world than other countries have invested in it. The largest creditor nation today is Japan.

At the heart of the distinction between a net borrower/net lender and a debtor/creditor nation is the distinction between flows and stocks, which you have encountered many times in your study of macroeconomics. Borrowing and lending are flows – amounts borrowed or lent per unit of time. Debts are stocks – amounts owed at a point in time. The flow of borrowing and lending changes the stock of debt. But the outstanding stock of debt depends mainly on past flows of borrowing and lending, not on the current period's flows. The current period's flows determine the *change* in the stock of debt outstanding.

During the 1960s and the 1970s, the United Kingdom would periodically swing from surplus to deficit on its current account. When it was in current account surplus it had a deficit on its capital account. On the whole the United Kingdom was a net lender to the rest of the world. It was not until the late 1980s that it became a significant net borrower.

Most countries are net borrowers. But a small number of countries, which includes oil-rich Saudi Arabia and Japan, are huge net lenders.

The United Kingdom today is a small net debtor. There are many countries that are debtor nations. The United States is one. But the largest debtor nations are the capital-hungry developing countries. The international debt of these countries grew from less than a third to more than a half of their gross domestic product during the 1980s and created what was called the 'Third World debt crisis'.

Does it matter if a country is a net borrower rather than a net lender? The answer to this question depends mainly on what the net borrower is doing with the borrowed money. If borrowing is financing investment that in turn is generating economic growth and higher income, borrowing is not a problem. If the borrowed money is being used to finance consumption, then higher interest payments are being incurred and, as a consequence, consumption will eventually have to be reduced. In this case, the more the borrowing and the longer it goes on, the greater is the reduction in consumption that will eventually be necessary. We'll see below whether the United Kingdom has been borrowing for investment or for consumption.

Current Account Balance

What determines the current account balance and the scale of a country's net foreign borrowing or lending?

To answer this question, we need to recall and use some of the things that we learned about the national income accounts. Table 34.2 will refresh your memory and summarize the necessary calculations for you. Part (a) lists the national income variables that are needed, with their symbols. Their values in the United Kingdom in 2000 are also shown.

Part (b) presents two key national income equations. First, equation (1) reminds us that GDP, Y, equals aggregate expenditure, which is the sum of consumption expenditure, C, investment, I, government purchases of goods and services, G, and net exports (exports, X, minus imports, M). Equation (2) reminds us that aggregate income is used in three different

Table 34.2   The Current Account Balance, Net Foreign Borrowing and the Financing of Investment ◆

	Symbols and equations	UK in 2000 (billions of pounds)
(a) VARIABLES		
Gross domestic product (GDP)	Y	934.9
Consumption expenditure	C	612.2
Investment	I	167.8
Government purchases of goods and services	G	173.9
Exports of goods and services	X	254.2
Imports of goods and services	M	273.2
Saving	S	124.5
Taxes, net of transfer payments	T	198.2
(b) DOMESTIC INCOME AND EXPENDITURE		
Aggregate expenditure	(1) $Y = C + I + G + X - M$	
Uses of income	(2) $Y = C + S + T$	
Subtracting (1) from (2)	(3) $0 = I - S + G - T + X - M$	
(c) SURPLUSES AND DEFICITS		
Current account	(4) $X - M = (T - G) + (S - I)$ $= 24.3 - 43.3 = -19.0$	
Government budget	(5) $T - G = 198.2 - 173.9 = 24.3$	
Private sector	(6) $S - I = 124.5 - 167.8 = -43.3$	
(d) FINANCING INVESTMENT		
Investment is financed by the sum of:		
private saving,	$S = 124.5$	
net government saving and	$T - G = 24.3$	
net foreign saving	$M - X = 19.0$	
That is:	(7) $I = S + (T - G) + (M - X)$ $= 167.8$	

Source: National Statistics.

ways. It can be consumed, saved or paid to the government in the form of taxes (net of transfer payments). Equation (1) tells us how our expenditure generates our income. Equation (2) tells us how we dispose of that income.

Part (c) of the table takes you into some new territory. It examines surpluses and deficits. We'll look at three surpluses/deficits – those of the current account, the government's budget and the private sector. To get at these surpluses and deficits, first subtract equation (2) from equation (1) in Table 34.2. The result is equation (3). By rearranging equation (3), we obtain a relationship for the current account – exports minus imports – that appears as equation (4) in the table.

The current account, in equation (4), is made up of two components. The first is taxes minus government spending and the second is saving minus investment. These items are the surpluses/deficits of the government and private sectors. Taxes (net of transfer payments) minus government purchases of goods and services is the budget surplus or deficit. If that number is positive, the government's budget is a surplus and if the number is negative, it is a deficit. The **private sector surplus or deficit** is the difference between saving and investment. If saving exceeds investment, the private sector has a surplus to lend to other sectors. If investment exceeds saving, the private sector has a deficit that has to be financed by borrowing from other sectors. As you can see from our calculations, the current account deficit is equal to the sum of the other two deficits – the government's budget deficit and the private sector surplus. In the UK in 2000, the private sector had a deficit of £43.3 billion and the government sector had a surplus of £24.3 billion. The government sector surplus minus the private sector surplus equals the current account deficit of £19 billion.

Part (d) of Table 34.2 shows you how investment is financed. To increase investment, either private saving, the government surplus, or the current account deficit, must increase.

The calculations that we've just performed are really nothing more than bookkeeping. We've manipulated the national income accounts and discovered that the current account deficit is just the sum of the deficits of the government and private sectors. But these calculations do reveal a fundamental fact: our international balance of payments can change only if either our government budget balance changes or our private sector financial balance changes.

We've seen that our international deficit is equal to the sum of the government deficit and the private sector surplus. Is the private sector surplus equal to the government's budget deficit so that the external account deficit is zero? Does an increase in the government budget deficit bring an increase in the current account deficit?

You can see the answer to this question by looking at Figure 34.2. In this figure, the general government sector budget balance is plotted alongside the current account balance and the private sector balance. To remove the effects of growth and inflation, all three balances are measured as percentages of nominal GDP. The private sector balance tends to mirror the government deficit. The private sector surplus began

Figure 34.2

Sector Balances

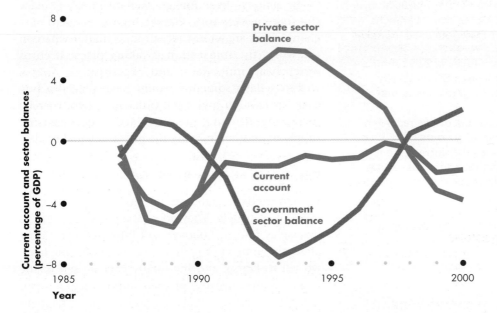

During the 1990s the private sector surplus increased as consumption fell and savings rose during the recession, but the government sector was in deficit while the current account was also in deficit. In the late 1990s, the government sector was in surplus but the private sector was in strong deficit as consumer spending boomed.

Source: National Statistics.

to increase in the mid-1990s and the increasing government sector deficit meant that the current account was in deficit during this period. In the late 1990s, the government sector moved into surplus, but now the private sector was in a strong deficit so that the current acccount remained in deficit. The private sector surplus or deficit is saving minus investment. If saving exceeds investment, a private sector surplus is lent to other sectors. If investment exceeds saving, borrowing from other sectors finances a private sector deficit.

Is the UK Borrowing for Consumption or Investment?

We noted above that whether international borrowing is a problem or not depends on what that borrowing is used for. Since 1987, the United Kingdom has borrowed nearly £11 billion a year, on the average. Over these same years, the government sector has had an average deficit of £14 billion a year, and the private sector has had an average surplus (saving minus investment has been positive) of £3 billion a year. So private sector saving has been more than sufficient to pay for investment in plant and equipment. Does

the fact that foreign borrowing has financed a government deficit mean that we are borrowing to consume?

Our foreign borrowing probably has been financing public consumption to some degree. But not all government purchases are consumption purchases. Over 10 per cent of government purchases are of investment goods. But there is no sure way to divide government purchases into a consumption component and an investment component. Some items, such as the expenditure on improved roads and bridges, are clearly investment. But what about expenditure on education and health care? Are these expenditures consumption or investment? A case can be made that they are investment – investment in human capital – and that they earn a rate of return at least equal to the interest rate that we pay on our foreign debt.

However, most of the foreign investment in the United Kingdom is in the private sector and is undertaken in the pursuit of the highest available profit. Foreigners diversify their lending to spread their risk. We do the same. Some of our saving is used to finance investment in firms in the United Kingdom, some is lent to the government and some is used to finance investment in other countries.

Review Quiz

◆ When a British wine merchant makes an order for a consignment of wine from a French vineyard, which currency gets used to make the transaction?

◆ When a German manufacturer buys semi-manufactured parts from a South Welsh factory, which currency gets used to make the transaction?

◆ What types of transactions do we record in the balance of payments account?

◆ What transactions does the current account record? What transactions does the capital and financial account record? What does the change in reserves record?

◆ How are the current account deficit, the government sector deficit, and the private sector surplus related?

Sterling in the Global Market

When we buy foreign goods or invest in another country, we have to obtain some of that country's currency to make the transaction. When foreigners buy UK-produced goods or invest in the United Kingdom, they have to obtain sterling. We get foreign currency and foreigners get pounds sterling in the foreign exchange market. The **foreign exchange market** is the market in which the currency of one country is exchanged for the currency of another. The foreign exchange market is made up of thousands of people: importers and exporters, banks and specialists in the buying and selling of foreign exchange called foreign exchange brokers. The foreign exchange market opens on Monday morning in Hong Kong. As the day advances, markets open in Singapore, Tokyo, Bahrain, Frankfurt, London, New York, Chicago and San Francisco. As the West Coast markets in the United States close, Hong Kong is only an hour away from opening for the next day of business. The sun barely sets on the foreign exchange market. Dealers around the world are continually in contact by telephone and on any given day, billions of dollars, yen, euros and pounds change hands. The price at which one currency exchanges for another is called a **foreign exchange rate**. For example, on 6 December 2001, one pound sterling bought 1.596 euros, 176.1 Japanese yen, and 1.42 US dollars. The exchange rate between the US dollar and the pound sterling was £0.70 per $1, and the rate between euros and the pound was £0.63 per euro. Exchange rates can be expressed either way.

The actions of the foreign exchange brokers make the foreign exchange market highly efficient. Exchange rates are almost identical no matter where in the world the transaction is taking place. If euros were cheap in London and expensive in Tokyo, within a flash someone would have placed a buy order in London and a sell order in Tokyo, thereby increasing demand in one place and increasing supply in another, moving the prices to equality.

Foreign Exchange Systems

Foreign exchange rates are of critical importance for millions of people. They affect the costs of things as diverse as foreign holidays and imported cars. They affect the number of pounds that we get for the lamb we sell to France and the luxury cars we sell to the United States. Because of their importance, governments pay a great deal of attention to what is happening in the foreign exchange market and, more than that, take actions designed to achieve what they regard as desirable movements in exchange rates. In deciding how to act in the foreign exchange market, a government must choose among three alternative strategies that give rise to three foreign exchange systems. They are:

1 Fixed exchange rate.

2 Flexible exchange rate.

3 Managed exchange rate.

A **fixed exchange rate** is a system in which the value of a country's currency is pegged by the country's central bank. Under a fixed exchange rate system the Bank of England would declare the pound sterling to be worth a certain number of units of some other currency and would take actions on the foreign exchange market to try to maintain the pound's declared value. Below we'll study what those foreign exchange market actions would be.

A **flexible exchange rate** is a system in which the value of a country's currency is determined by market forces in the absence of central bank intervention. Under a flexible exchange rate, the Bank of England would take no actions on the foreign exchange market.

A **managed exchange rate** is a system in which the value of a country's currency is not fixed at some pre-announced level but is influenced by central bank intervention in the foreign exchange market. This intervention is in the form of using the official reserves to buy or sell the currency to stabilize its value.

Like many currencies the pound has experienced all three exchange rate systems at some time in its history. So before we learn how the foreign exchange market operates in these three systems, let's look at the recent history of the foreign exchange market.

Recent Exchange Rate History

At the end of the Second World War, the major countries of the world set up the International Monetary Fund (IMF). The **International Monetary Fund** is an international organization that monitors balance of payments and exchange rate activities. The IMF is based in Washington, DC. It came into being as a result of negotiations between the United States and the United Kingdom during the Second World War. In July 1944, at Bretton Woods, New Hampshire, 44 countries signed the Articles of Agreement of the IMF. At the centre of these agreements was the establishment of a worldwide system of fixed exchange rates among currencies. The anchor for this fixed exchange rate system was gold. One ounce of gold was defined to be worth 35 US dollars. All other currencies were pegged to the US dollar at a fixed exchange rate. For example, the pound sterling was set to be worth $4.80 and the Japanese yen was set at 360 yen per dollar. The rules of the Bretton Woods system allowed for countries to alter the exchange rates subject to agreement. The pound was devalued in September 1949 and November 1967, to $2.80 and $2.40 respectively. Although the fixed exchange rate system established in 1944 served the world well during the 1950s and early 1960s, it came under increasing strain in the late 1960s and, by 1971, the order had almost collapsed. In the period since 1971, the world has operated with different countries adopting a variety of flexible and managed exchange rate arrangements as well as fixed exchange rates. Some currencies have increased in value, and others have declined. The pound sterling and the US dollar are among the currencies that have declined, while the Japanese yen is the currency that has had the most spectacular increase in value. In 1972, the pound's link with the dollar was broken and the pound began to float. At times between 1972 and 1990, the Bank of England intervened to influence the value of the pound, but there were also times when it was allowed to float freely.

Figure 34.3 shows what happened to the exchange rate between 1975 and 1998. The blue line shows the

Figure 34.3

Exchange Rates

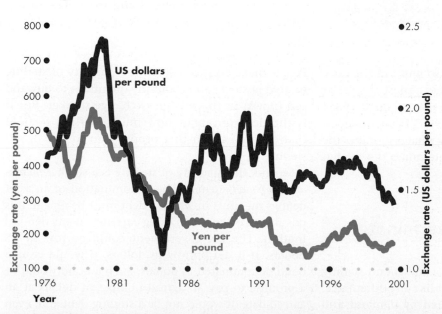

The exchange rate is the price at which two currencies can be traded. The yen–sterling exchange rate, expressed as yen per pound, shows that the pound has fallen in value – depreciated – against the yen. The dollar exchange rate is expressed as US dollars per pound. The pound depreciated against the US dollar between 1980 and 1985 and appreciated against the dollar between 1985 and 1990, and fluctuated around 1.60–1.40 since then.

Source: Bank of England.

value of the pound against the Japanese yen. The value of the pound has fallen against the yen – the pound has depreciated. **Currency depreciation** is the fall in the value of one currency in terms of another currency. For example, in December 1975, the pound was worth yen 617.8 and in June 2001 it was worth yen 171.4. So the pound has depreciated by 72 per cent ((617.8 − 171.4) ÷ 171.4 × 100) of its 1975 value.

Although the pound has depreciated in terms of the yen, it has not depreciated at the same rate against all other currencies. The red line of Figure 34.3 shows the value of the pound against the US dollar. As you can see, the value of the pound depreciated strongly against the US dollar from 1980 to 1985; and after 1985 it appreciated against the dollar and stabilized around $1.55 but continued to depreciate against the yen until 1996 when it began to appreciate. In the 1990s the pound fluctuated in value against the dollar and the yen.

Review Quiz

♦ Describe the three possible foreign exchange market systems.
♦ In which periods after the Second World War did the world economy experience each of the foreign exchange market systems?
♦ What has been the long term trend in the value of the pound? What has happened to the pound in recent years?

Why did the pound fluctuate so much in the early 1980s? Why did it climb in value against the dollar during 1980 and then decline sharply until 1985? Why did it appreciate again in 1986? To answer questions like these, we need to know what determines the foreign exchange rate. What determines the foreign currency value of the pound?

Exchange Rate Determination

The exchange rate is the price of the pound sterling in terms of other currencies. Just like any other price, the exchange rate is determined by demand and supply – the demand for pounds and the supply of pounds. But what exactly do we mean by the demand for and supply of pounds? And what is the quantity of sterling?

The quantity of sterling demanded in the foreign exchange market is the amount that people would buy on a given day at a particular exchange rate (price) if they found a willing seller. The quantity of sterling supplied in the foreign exchange market is the amount that people would sell on a given day at a particular exchange rate (price) if they found a willing buyer. What determines the quantities of sterling demanded and supplied in the foreign exchange market?

To answer this question, we need to think about the alternative to demanding and supplying pounds sterling. For a demander of sterling, the alternative is to hang on to foreign currency. For a supplier, the alternative is to hang on to sterling. The decision to buy or sell is also the decision to hold sterling or foreign currency.

To understand the forces that determine demand and supply in the foreign exchange market, we need to study people's decisions about the quantities of pounds sterling and foreign currencies to hold. Let's see what we mean by the quantity of sterling held.

The Quantity of Pounds

The **quantity of sterling assets** (which we'll call the quantity of pounds sterling) is the *net stock* of financial assets denominated in pounds sterling held outside the Bank of England and the public sector. Three things about the quantity of sterling need to be emphasized.

First, the quantity of sterling is a *stock*, not a *flow*. People make decisions about the quantity of sterling to hold (a stock) and about the quantities to buy and sell (flows) in the foreign exchange market. But it is the decision about how much sterling to hold that determines whether people plan to buy or sell sterling.

Second, the quantity of sterling is a stock *denominated in pounds sterling*. The denomination of an asset defines the units in which a debt must be repaid. It is possible to make a loan using currency of any denomination. The UK government could borrow in US dollars. If it did borrow in dollars, it would issue a bond denominated in dollars. Such a bond would be a promise to pay an agreed number of dollars at an agreed date. It would not be a sterling debt and, even though issued by the government, it would not be part of the supply of sterling. Many governments actually do issue bonds in currencies other than their own. The Canadian government, for example, issues bonds denominated in US dollars.

Third, the supply of sterling is a *net* supply – the quantity of assets *minus* the quantity of liabilities. This means that the quantity of sterling supplied does not include sterling assets created by private households, firms, financial institutions, or foreigners. The reason is that when a private debt is created, there is both an asset (for the holder) and a liability (for the issuer), so the *net* financial asset is zero. For example, if Pat loans Matt £1,000, then Pat's asset of £1,000 cancels out Matt's £1,000 liability. The quantity of sterling includes only the sterling liabilities of the government *plus* those of the Bank of England. This quantity is equal to the government debt held outside the Bank of England, plus the sterling liabilities of the Bank of England – the monetary base. In the United Kingdom, the monetary base is also known as M0. We first came across the monetary base in Chapter 26, p. 579. The quantity of pounds sterling is:

$$\text{Quantity of pounds sterling} = \text{Government debt held outside the Bank of England} + \text{Monetary base}$$

We've seen what sterling assets are. Let's now study the demand for and the supply of these assets and see what makes the demand and supply change.

The Demand for Sterling Assets

The law of demand applies to sterling assets just as it does to anything else that people value. The quantity of sterling demanded increases when the price of sterling in terms of foreign currency falls and decreases when the price of sterling in terms of foreign currency rises. Suppose, for example, that the pound is trading at €1.55. If the pound rises to €1.65, with everything else remaining the same, the quantity of sterling demanded decreases and if the pound falls to €1.45, with everything else remaining the same, the quantity of sterling demanded increases. There are two separate reasons why the law of demand applies to sterling:

1 Transactions effect.

2 Expected capital gains effect.

Transactions Effect

A transactions cost is incurred whenever a foreign currency is converted into pounds. This transactions cost can be avoided by holding a stock of sterling. With such a stock, it is not necessary to convert foreign currency into sterling on the foreign exchange market each time a sterling payment must be made. The larger the value of sterling payments, the larger is the inventory of stock that people hold. But the value of sterling payments depends on the exchange rate. The lower the value of the pound, with everything else remaining the same, the larger is the demand for UK exports and the lower is UK demand for imports. Hence the lower the value of the pound, the larger is the value of sterling payments and the greater is the demand for sterling. Foreigners demand more pounds to buy UK exports and we demand fewer units of foreign currency and more pounds as we switch from importing to buying UK-produced goods.

Expected Capital Gains Effect

Suppose you think the pound will be worth $1.50 by the end of the month. If today, it is trading at $1.55 per pound, and if your prediction about the future value of the pound is correct, you can make a quick capital gain. Suppose you buy £1,000-worth of dollars today. You get $1,550 for your £1,000. If the exchange rate at the end of the month is $1.5 per pound, as you predict it will be, you can sell your $1,550 for £1,033.33 (1,550 ÷ 1.5 = 1,033.33). (If your bank charges you £8 in fees, you've made a profit of £25.33 on these transactions.) If you are pretty confident about your prediction, you will not hold sterling during the current month. You will hold dollars instead.

If today the pound is trading not at $1.55 but at $1.45 per pound, and if your prediction about the future value of the pound – $1.50 – is correct, you will incur a capital loss if you undertake the transactions we've just looked at. If you buy £1,000-worth of dollars today, you now get only $1,450 for your £1,000. If the exchange rate at the end of the month is $1.50 per pound, as you predict it will be, you will sell your $1,450 for £966.67 (1,450 ÷ 1.5 = 966.67). (If your bank charges you £8 in fees, you've incurred a loss of £41.33 on these transactions.) You will hang on to your pounds during the current month. You will *not* hold dollars instead.

For a given expected future value of the pound, the lower the current value of sterling, the greater is the expected capital gain from holding sterling and the greater is the quantity of sterling demanded.

Figure 34.4

The Demand for Sterling Assets

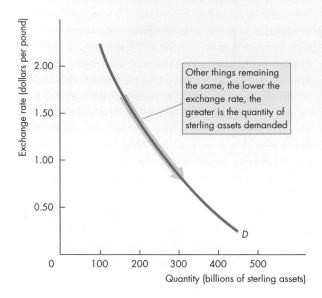

Other things remaining the same, the lower the exchange rate, the greater is the quantity of sterling assets demanded

The quantity of sterling assets that people demand, other things remaining the same, depends on the exchange rate. The lower the exchange rate (the smaller the amount of foreign currency per pound sterling), the larger is the quantity of sterling assets demanded. The increased quantity demanded arises from an increase in the volume of sterling trade (foreigners buy more UK goods and we buy fewer foreign goods) and an increase in the expected appreciation (or decrease in the expected depreciation) of sterling assets.

Figure 34.4 shows the relationship between the foreign currency price of the pound sterling in terms of US dollars and the quantity of sterling assets demanded – the demand curve for sterling assets. When the foreign exchange rate changes, other things remaining the same, there is a movement along the demand curve.

Changes in the Demand for Sterling Assets

Any other influence on the quantity of sterling assets that people want to hold results in a shift in the demand curve. Demand either increases or decreases. These other influences are:

◆ UK GDP.
◆ The expected future value of the pound.
◆ The UK interest rate differential.

UK GDP

You've seen that a transactions cost can be avoided by holding a stock of sterling and that the larger the value of sterling payments, the larger is the stock of sterling that people hold. A major influence on the value of sterling payments is UK GDP. An increase in UK GDP brings an increase in the value of sterling payments, which increases the demand for sterling. When the demand for sterling increases, the demand curve for sterling shifts rightward.

The Expected Future Value of Sterling

You've seen that for a given expected future value of the pound, the lower the current value of the pound, the greater is the expected capital gain from holding pounds and the greater is the quantity of sterling demanded. But what happens if the expected future value of the pound changes while the current exchange rate is unchanged?

You can answer this question by returning to the capital gain example. Suppose the pound is trading at $1.55 and you think it is going to fall to $1.50 by the end of the month. You are confident in your view and you buy $1,550 with your £1,000. At the end of the month, the dollar falls to $1.50 as you predicted it would. You now sell your $1,550 and buy pounds. At $1.5 per pound, you collect £1,025.33 after paying bank charges. You have made a capital gain. In this circumstance, you hold dollars rather than pounds during this month. But suppose the pound is trading at $1.55 and you think it is going to rise to $1.60 by the end of the month. If in this situation you do the transactions we've just considered, you will incur a capital loss. Your £1,000 still buys $1,550 but, when you sell these dollars at the end of the month at $1.60 per pound, you collect only £960.75 after deduction of £8 for bank charges. In this circumstance, you hold pounds rather than dollars during this month.

The lower the expected future value of the pound, other things remaining the same, the smaller is the demand for sterling (and the greater is the demand for other currencies). Similarly, the higher the expected future value of the pound, other things remaining the same, the greater is the demand for sterling (and the smaller is the demand for other currencies).

The UK Interest Rate Differential

People and businesses buy financial assets to make a return that has two components: a capital gain and an interest rate. You've just seen how the expected capital gain is determined by the current exchange

Table 34.3 The Demand for Sterling Assets

The law of demand

The quantity of sterling assets demanded

Increases if:	*Decreases if:*
◆ The foreign exchange rate falls	◆ The foreign exchange rate rises

Changes in demand

The demand for sterling assets

Increases if:	*Decreases if:*
◆ UK GDP increases	◆ UK GDP decreases
◆ The expected future value of the pound sterling rises	◆ The expected future value of the pound sterling falls
◆ The UK interest rate differential increases	◆ The UK interest rate differential decreases

rate and the expected future exchange rate. Let's now look at the interest component of the return on financial assets.

People can hold sterling assets or foreign currency assets. To choose the currencies in which to hold their wealth, people look at the interest rate on sterling assets and compare it with the interest rate on a foreign currency asset. The interest rate on a sterling asset minus the interest rate on a foreign currency asset is called the UK interest rate differential. If the interest rate on sterling assets increases and the interest rate on a foreign currency asset remains constant, the **UK interest rate differential** increases. The larger the UK interest rate differential, the greater is the demand for sterling assets.

Table 34.3 summarizes the above discussion of the influences on the demand for sterling.

The Supply of Sterling Assets

Remember that the *flows* of pounds and other currencies through the foreign exchange market are determined by decisions about *stocks*. A decrease in the demand for sterling brings a flow of pounds sterling on to the foreign exchange market. But this flow of sterling on to the market is *not* what we mean when we talk about the *supply of sterling*. The supply of sterling is the quantity of sterling assets available for people to hold.

The quantity of sterling supplied is determined by the actions of the Bank of England. We've seen that the quantity of sterling is equal to government debt plus the monetary base. Of these two items, the monetary base is by far the smallest. But it plays a crucial role in determining the supply of sterling. The behaviour of the monetary base depends crucially on the foreign exchange rate system.

In a fixed exchange rate system, the supply curve of sterling assets is horizontal at the chosen exchange rate. The Bank of England stands ready to supply whatever quantity of sterling assets is demanded in exchange for foreign currency assets at the fixed exchange rate. In a managed exchange rate system, the Bank of England wants to smooth fluctuations in the exchange rate, and the supply curve of sterling assets is upward-sloping. The higher the foreign exchange rate, the larger is the quantity of sterling assets supplied by the Bank of England in exchange for foreign currency assets. In a flexible exchange rate system, a fixed quantity of sterling assets is supplied, regardless of their price. As a consequence, in a flexible exchange rate system, the supply curve of sterling assets is vertical.

Changes in the Supply of Sterling Assets

There are two ways in which the quantity of sterling supplied can change:

1 The government has a budget deficit or surplus.

2 The Bank of England buys or sells foreign currency assets.

The government influences the quantity of sterling assets supplied through its budget. If the government has a budget deficit, it borrows by issuing bonds, which are denominated in pounds sterling. The sale of new government bonds to finance a deficit increases the supply of sterling assets. Similarly, if the government has a budget surplus, it buys back previously issued bonds and the supply of sterling assets decreases.

The Bank of England influences the quantity of sterling supplied through its transactions in the foreign exchange market. If the Bank buys foreign currency, it increases the quantity of sterling assets supplied. If the Bank sells foreign currency, it decreases the quantity of sterling assets supplied.

An open market operation in which the Bank buys or sells government securities changes the monetary base but it does not change the quantity of sterling assets supplied. It changes the composition of sterling assets supplied. For example, if the Bank buys government bonds, the quantity of sterling denominated bonds decreases and the monetary base increases. But

Table 34.4 The Supply of Sterling Assets

Supply

Fixed exchange rate system

The supply curve of sterling assets is horizontal at the fixed exchange rate.

Managed exchange rate

In order to smooth fluctuations in the price of the pound sterling, the quantity of sterling assets supplied by the Bank of England increases if the foreign currency price of the pound rises and decreases if the foreign currency price of the pound falls. The supply curve of sterling assets is upward-sloping.

Flexible exchange rate

The supply curve of sterling assets is vertical.

Changes in supply

The supply of sterling assets

Increases if:	*Decreases if:*
◆ The UK government has a deficit	◆ The UK government has a surplus
◆ The Bank of England buys foreign currency	◆ The Bank of England sells foreign currency

the increase in the monetary base equals the decrease in sterling bonds so the total quantity of sterling assets remains unchanged.

Table 34.4 summarizes the above discussion of the influences on the supply of sterling assets.

The Market for Sterling

Let's now bring the demand and supply sides of the market for sterling assets together and determine the exchange rate. Figure 34.5 shows how the exchange rate is determined in the three systems for fixed, flexible and managed exchange rates. The demand side of the market is the same in the three cases but the supply side differs. First, let's look at a fixed exchange rate system such as that from the end of the Second World War to 1971.

Fixed Exchange Rate

This case is illustrated in Figure 34.5(a). The supply curve of sterling is horizontal at the fixed exchange rate of $1.50 per pound. If the demand curve is D_0, the quantity of sterling assets is Q_0. An increase in demand to D_1 results in an increase in the quantity of sterling assets from Q_0 to Q_1 but no change in the exchange rate.

Flexible Exchange Rate

Next look at Figure 34.5(b), which shows what happens in a flexible exchange rate system. In this case, the quantity of sterling assets supplied is fixed at Q_0, so the supply curve of sterling assets is vertical. If the demand curve for sterling is D_0, the exchange rate is $1.50 per pound. If the demand for sterling increases from D_0 to D_1, the exchange rate increases to $1.60 per pound.

Managed Exchange Rate

Finally, consider a managed exchange rate system, which appears in Figure 34.5(c). Here, the supply curve is upward-sloping. When the demand curve is D_0, the exchange rate is $1.50 per pound. If demand increases to D_1, the dollar value of the pound rises but only to $1.55 per pound. Compared with the flexible exchange rate case, the same increase in demand results in a smaller increase in the exchange rate when it is managed. The reason for this is that the quantity supplied increases in the managed exchange rate case.

Exchange Rate System and Official Reserves

The behaviour of the official financing balance (change in reserves) depends on the foreign exchange rate system. The official financing account of the balance of payments records the change in the country's official holdings (by the government and the Bank of England) of foreign currency. In a fixed exchange rate system (as shown in Figure 34.5(a)), every time the demand for sterling assets changes, the Bank must change the quantity of sterling assets supplied to match it. When the Bank has to increase the quantity of sterling assets supplied, it does so by offering sterling assets in exchange for foreign currency assets. In this case, the official holdings of foreign exchange reserves increase. If the demand for sterling assets decreases, the Bank must decrease the quantity of sterling assets supplied. To decrease the quantity of sterling supplied, the Bank buys pounds and pays for them with its foreign exchange reserves. In this case, official foreign exchange reserves decrease. Thus with a fixed exchange rate, fluctuations in the demand for sterling assets result in fluctuations in official reserves.

In a flexible exchange rate system, there is no central bank intervention in the foreign exchange market. Regardless of what happens to the demand for sterling, no action is taken to change the quantity of sterling supplied. Therefore there are no changes in

Figure 34.5

Three Exchange Rate Systems

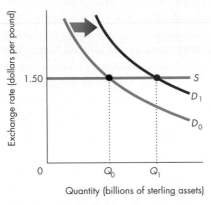

(a) Fixed exchange rate

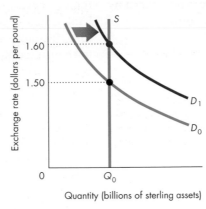

(b) Flexible exchange rate

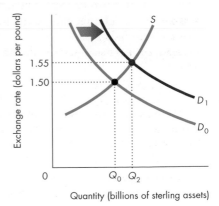

(c) Managed exchange rate

In a fixed exchange rate system (part a), the Bank of England stands ready to supply sterling assets or to take sterling assets off the market (supplying foreign currency in exchange) at a fixed exchange rate. The supply curve for sterling assets is horizontal. Fluctuations in demand lead to fluctuations in the quantity of sterling assets outstanding and to fluctuations in the nation's official holdings of foreign exchange. If demand increases from D_0 to D_1, the quantity of sterling assets increases from Q_0 to Q_1 and the exchange rate does not change. In a flexible exchange rate system (part b), the quantity of sterling assets is fixed so that the supply curve is vertical. An increase in the demand for sterling assets from D_0 to D_1 results only in an increase in the value of the pound – the exchange rate rises from $1.50 to $1.60. The quantity of sterling assets remains constant at Q_0. In a managed exchange rate system (part c), the Bank of England has an upward-sloping supply curve of sterling assets, so that if demand increases from D_0 to D_1, the pound sterling appreciates but the quantity of sterling assets supplied also increases – from Q_0 to Q_2. The increase in the quantity of sterling assets supplied moderates the rise in the value of the pound sterling but does not completely prevent it as in the case of fixed exchange rates.

the country's official reserves. In this case, the official financing balance is zero and there is no change in official foreign currency reserves.

With a managed exchange rate, official holdings of foreign exchange are adjusted to meet fluctuations in demand but in a less extreme manner than in a fixed exchange rate system. As a consequence, fluctuations in the official financing balance are smaller in a managed floating system than in a fixed exchange rate system.

The Exchange Rate in the Long Run

We have seen how changes in the expected future exchange rate can influence the demand for sterling assets. If the exchange rate regime is floating or managed, we know that an expectation that the future exchange rate will rise results in a rightward shift of the demand for sterling assets and an appreciation of the exchange rate. So an expectation of a rise in the future exchange rate will result in a rise in the current exchange rate if the exchange rate is not fixed. But

we have not said why the future exchange rate is expected to be different from the current exchange rate. However, before we discuss this we need to understand two important arguments.

First, we must recognize that the argument that the current exchange rate is influenced by the expected exchange rate in one month's time means that in turn the exchange rate in one month's time is influenced by the expectation of the exchange rate in two months' time. This argument can be extended to any future value of the exchange rate.

Second, we can appeal to rational expectations (we looked at this in Chapter 31, p. 709). The expected exchange rate in one month's time will, on the average, be the actual exchange rate in one month's time. So the current exchange rate will depend partly on the expected exchange rate in one month's time. The expected future exchange rate will, on the average, be correct, and the expected future exchange rate will depend partly on the expected exchange rate further in the future. We can extend this argument to the point where the current exchange rate will depend partly on the expected exchange rate somewhere in the distant future. Another way of looking at it is that the current exchange rate is influenced by the expected exchange rate in the long-run.

Purchasing Power Parity

Purchasing power parity (PPP) is a condition that holds when the prices of goods in different countries are equalized once adjustment is made for the exchange rate. For example, suppose the price of Levi jeans in the UK is £20. Suppose the same pair of jeans costs $30 in the United States, and the exchange rate is $1.50 per pound. Then we have PPP in Levi jeans. This means that the jeans can be bought for the same price in both countries once we take into account the exchange rate (£20 = $30 ÷ 1.50).

PPP is a condition that results from the application of *the law of one price* and *arbitrage* in international trade. The law of one price simply states that two identical goods must sell for the same price. How do we know that the law of one price holds? Imagine what would happen if it did not. Suppose for some reason that Doc Marten boots can be bought for £5 less in Glasgow than in London. An enterprising person could buy Doc Marten boots in Glasgow and sell them at a higher price in London. The process of buying or selling something to exploit a price differential to make a riskless profit is known as arbitrage. What would be the effect of this arbitrage process on Doc Marten boots? The retailers of Doc Martens in Glasgow will face a run down of their stocks and will have to order more from the suppliers. The suppliers will face additional costs of diverting resources to meet the extra demand in Glasgow and will demand a higher price. In the meantime, shoe retailers in London will find that they are building up stocks as they will no longer be selling the same volume as in the past. In an attempt to move the stock they will lower the prices of Doc Martens in London. The result will be that the prices of Doc Martens in Glasgow and London will converge until it will no longer be profitable to ship the boots from one area to another. This occurs when the prices are the same. In reality small differences will exist to allow for the costs of transportation.

International Arbitrage

The same process of arbitrage can be applied to trade across countries. Let's go back to the example of the Levi jeans. Suppose Levis are selling for £30 in the United Kingdom and $30 in the United States and the exchange rate is $1.50 per pound. It will pay to import Levis into the United Kingdom from the United States and to sell them for a profit. In the long run, this process will cause prices of Levis to change in the United Kingdom and in the United States. But imagine what happens when we apply this logic to many goods, not just Levis. Identical goods in the United States will be selling at a lower price than in the United Kingdom after allowing for the exchange rate. Firms in the United Kingdom will import more US goods and pay for them in dollars. At the same time, UK exporters will export fewer goods to the United States. The demand for dollar assets will rise and the demand for sterling assets will fall. Hence the price of sterling in terms of the dollar will decline. To go back to our example of the Levi jeans, PPP in Levis will be restored when the exchange rate falls to $1 per pound (£30 = $30 ÷ $1 per pound). In other words, we can state that the price of goods in the United Kingdom measured in sterling $P(£)$ is equal to the price of goods in the United States measured in dollars $P($)$ divided by the exchange rate (S – dollars per pound):

$$P(£) = \frac{P(£)}{S}$$

We can rearrange this equation to arrive at an expression for the exchange rate in the long run:

$$S = \frac{P($)}{P(£)}$$

We now have a theory that explains what determines the exchange rate in the long run. The exchange rate will adjust so as to bring about PPP in the long run. So if the price of goods in the UK were higher than in the United States, the exchange rate with the dollar would decline in the long run. In reality there are many difficulties with the theory of PPP. There are difficulties in constructing comparable price indices between countries. The theory of PPP holds only for identical goods, but not all goods are identical – Levi jeans are an exception, not the rule. Similarly, not all goods are traded. Some goods are sold only in the United Kingdom and there is no international competition or arbitrage process that brings about a PPP in them. These goods are known as *non-traded goods*. A haircut is an often used as an example of a non-traded good. It is not possible to

Figure 34.6

Why the Exchange Rate is so Volatile

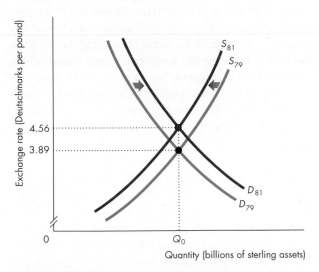

(a) 1979 to 1981

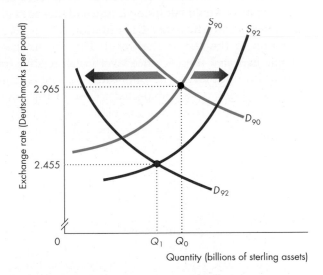

(b) 1990 to 1992

The exchange rate is volatile because shifts in the demand and supply curves for sterling assets are not independent of each other. Between 1979 and 1981 (part a), the DM–sterling exchange rate appreciated from 3.89 to 4.56. The supply curve of sterling assets shifted leftward and higher interest rates and expectations of a rise in the exchange rate induced an increase in demand for sterling assets, shifting the demand curve rightward. The result was a large appreciation of the pound. The rise in the price of

oil also added to the expectation of a rise in the value of the pound sterling. Between October 1990 and October 1992 (in part b), the quantity of sterling assets increased and the supply curve of sterling shifted rightward. As the pound started to fall in value, further falls were expected so the demand for pounds sterling decreased and the demand curve shifted leftward. The result was a steep fall in the exchange rate, from DM2.965 in October 1990 to DM2.455 in October 1992.

---

buy a cheap haircut in Spain and sell it at a profit in Sweden. Transport costs, taxes and tariffs are other factors that also reduce the convergence to PPP. However, the evidence that PPP holds on a long-run basis is strong.

Why is the Exchange Rate So Volatile?

There have been times during the 1970s, the early 1980s and early 1990s when the pound has moved dramatically. On some of these occasions sterling has depreciated spectacularly, but on other occasions it has appreciated strongly.

The main reason the exchange rate fluctuates so remarkably is that fluctuations in supply and demand are not always independent of each other. Sometimes a change in supply will trigger a change in demand that reinforces the effect of the change in supply. Let's see how these effects work by looking at two

episodes, one in which sterling rose in value and one in which it fell.

An Appreciating Pound: 1979–81

Between 1979 and 1981, the value of sterling against the Deutschmark (the German currency before the adoption of the euro) appreciated by over 17 per cent. Figure 34.6(a) explains why this happened. In 1979, the demand and supply curves were those labelled D_{79} and S_{79}. The Deutschmark rate was 3.89 – where the supply and demand curves intersect. The period between 1980 and 1981 was one of severe recession. This recession was brought about in part by the tight monetary policy pursued by the new conservative government. The Bank of England raised interest rates sharply in November 1979, cutting back the supply of sterling assets. The direct effect was a shift in the supply curve from S_{79} to S_{81} – a decrease in the supply of sterling. But higher UK interest rates induced an increase in the demand for sterling assets. Furthermore, the tight monetary policy created expectations that inflation would fall in the future and that the fall in inflation would make UK inflation lower than inflation in the rest of the world. This means that people expected the UK price level to fall relative to the world price level. The implication of PPP is that the exchange rate was expected to rise in the long run. We know from our discussion of exchange rate expectations that the implication of an expected appreciation of the exchange rate in the long run is an expectation of a rise in the exchange rate in the near future, which causes the demand for sterling assets to rise even further. As a result the demand curve shifted from D_{79} to D_{81}. These two shifts reinforced each other, increasing the exchange rate to 4.56. But there were other factors that also contributed to the rise in the exchange rate. The oil shock of 1979 meant that UK exports of North Sea oil would result in higher dollar receipts, and a stronger current account added to the expectation of a rise in the value of sterling.

A Depreciating Pound: 1990–1992

There was a spectacular depreciation of the pound in terms of the Deutschmark from DM2.965 in October 1990 to DM2.455 in October 1992 – a fall of over 17 per cent. This fall came about in the following way. First, in October 1990, the United Kingdom was taken into the Exchange Rate Mechanism (ERM) of the European Monetary System (EMS) at a central parity of DM2.95. The ERM is like a fixed exchange rate system but with a band around the central parity in which the value of the currency is allowed to fluctuate. The United Kingdom entered the ERM with a band of ±6 per cent around the central parity of DM2.95. The demand and supply curves were those labelled D_{90} and S_{90} in Figure 34.6(b). The supply curve is shaped in this elongated reverse 'S' because it is meant to show the upper and lower bounds at which the Bank of England will support the currency around its central parity. The Deutschmark price of the pound – the price at which these two curves intersect – was DM2.965 per pound. In retrospect this was an unsustainable rate of exchange given the large current account deficit in 1989–90. To keep sterling at its central parity, the Bank had to raise interest rates and tighten monetary policy. The economy moved sharply into recession, raising expectations that interest rates would have to fall. The expectation of lower interest rates fuelled expectations of lower exchange rates in the future, causing the demand for sterling assets to fall and pushing the exchange rate to the bottom of the band. A large government budget deficit increased the supply of sterling assets and the supply of sterling assets curve shifted rightward from S_{90} to S_{92}. Because the expected future value of the pound fell, the demand for sterling assets decreased from D_{90} to D_{92}. The result of this combined increase in supply and decrease in demand was a dramatic fall in the value of the pound to DM2.455 on 16 September 1992.

Review Quiz

◆ How is the exchange rate determined?
◆ How does the Bank of England operate a fixed exchange rate system?
◆ How do changes in the expected future exchange rate influence the actual exchange rate in the flexible exchange rate system?
◆ What is purchasing power parity and how does it influence exchange rate expectations?
◆ How can the Bank of England influence the foreign exchange market?

Before completing this chapter let's look at one of the momentous events that marks a turning point in the international financial economy – the creation of the European Monetary Union and the birth of a new currency, the euro. The creation of a new currency for Europe – the euro, is the realization of the dream of stronger economic and political union, and challenges the dominance of the US dollar as an international currency.

The European Monetary Union

On 1 January 1999 some 11 countries of the European Union formed a monetary union (eurozone) whereby the value of the currency of each participating economy was irrevocably fixed against the euro. On the 1 January 2001, Greece joined the EMU. Table 34.5 shows the exchange rates for the 12 participating countries.

Monetary policy for the 12 countries would be conducted by the European Central Bank. The amendment to the Treaty of Rome in 1991 at Maastricht in

Table 34.5 Determination of the Euro Conversion Rates

Country	Currency unit	Units per euro
Belgium	franc	40.3399
Germany	deutschmark	1.95583
Spain	peseta	166.386
France	franc	6.55957
Ireland	pound	0.787564
Italy	lira	1936.27
Luxembourg	franc	40.3399
Netherland	guilder	2.20371
Austria	schilling	13.7603
Portugal	escudo	200.482
Finland	markka	5.94573
Greece	drachma	340.750

Source: ECB

the Netherlands laid the foundations for Economic and Monetary Union in Europe (**EMU**). It is argued that a single currency is the natural outcome of closer economic integration and the development of the *Single European Market*.

The Economic Benefits of the Euro

There are good arguments in favour of a single currency. Since the purpose of a single European market is to remove all barriers to trade and to promote competition, a single currency has the advantage of ensuring that all prices in the European Union will be denominated in a common unit and the process of arbitrage will enforce the law of one price, just like our example of the Doc Marten boots in Glasgow and London. Countries will not be able to exploit a competitive advantage by artificially lowering the price of their exports through devaluation.

Other arguments are that a single currency will remove foreign exchange transactions costs – the costs associated with exchanging pesetas for francs at a bank or travel agent, such as commission charges or the margin between buy and sell exchange rates we see posted in banks and currency exchanges. The removal of these costs will benefit the consumer, who will know that a eurofranc in France will buy the same as a euromark in Germany. A single currency will also remove foreign exchange risk associated with exports and imports. For example, Alpine Gardens, an Austrian garden company, has ordered a consignment of garden gnomes to be supplied by a UK company, Britannia Gnomes Ltd, in three months' time. The contract and the price are set today, but payment will take place in three months' time. Alpine Gardens has to pay £50,000 in three months' time. To protect itself against an adverse change in the exchange rate, it pays a small premium to insure against an exchange rate change.[1]

It is also argued that the reduction in exchange rate risk could improve trade between EU countries. Cacharel, the French clothing designer can source its material from Rome or from Paris. On a strict exchange rate comparison, the Italian product is cheaper. However, in the past the exchange rate between the French franc and Italian lira has been subject to considerable volatility. Cacharel is unsure that they want to be tied into a contract with the Italian supplier if the price in francs would fluctuate with the exchange rate. They source the material from the more expensive French supplier because they are guaranteed a price but they have to charge their customers the higher price. A single currency would eliminate the exchange rate risk. Cacharel can source their material from Rome, pay a lower price and pass the benefits of the lower price on to their customers. The lower price increases the demand for Cacharel clothing which in turn increases the orders from Rome.

The removal of exchange risk will mean that many large companies would be able to reduce their administration and treasury management costs. They would also no longer need to diversify their operations across boundaries but consolidate them on one location. This will cause a significant redistribution of wealth and jobs in eurozone.

The total benefit of the removal of transactions costs associated with currency exchange has been estimated as 0.3–0.4 per cent of EU GDP a year.[2] For a country with an advanced banking system as in the UK, the EU Commission estimates that the benefits would be 0.1 per cent of GDP a year.

[1] Alpine Gardens buys sterling in the forward market, paying a commission to the foreign currency operator which ensures the delivery of £50,000 in three months' time at an exchange rate specified today irrespective of what the exchange rate will be in three months' time.
[2] Commission of the European Communities, 'One Market, One Money: An Evaluation of the Potential Benefits and Costs of Forming an Economic and Monetary Union', 1990, *European Economy*, 44, Brussels.

The Economic Costs of the Euro

While the arguments in favour of a single currency are largely microeconomic, the arguments against are largely macroeconomic. There is the criticism of the 'one size fits all' approach to monetary policy. The main cost of EMU is the loss of an independent monetary policy and the adoption of strict fiscal controls in acccordance with the stability pact. But how important is the loss of an independent monetary policy and what difference will the stability pact make? It depends on the frequency of the shocks that hit one country that do not hit other eurozone countries. For example, suppose Italy were in recession but the other countries in eurozone were either at full employment or above full employment. Under a flexible exchange rate system, the Italian central bank would expand the money supply and lower the rate of interest. The lower rate of interest would increase interest sensitive expenditure and increase aggregate demand as we saw in Chapter 27 (p. 603). The lower rate of interest will also reduce the demand for Italian assets and the value of the lira would fall. As the exchange rate falls Italian goods become cheaper and exports to the rest of eurozone would increase, increasing aggregate demand.

But under the single currency, monetary policy is run by the European Central Bank. If the rest of eurozone were at full employment or above full employment, the ECB would want to tighten monetary policy and raise the rate of interest. It would not be possible for the interest rate in Italy to be lowered, and the exchange rate cannot be devalued. This leaves fiscal policy as the only policy option available to the Italian government. In principle, expansionary fiscal policy can be used to increase aggregate demand. But the stability pact places limits on the use of fiscal policy and except under exceptional circumstances, countries that already have a high budget deficit may not be allowed to expand government spending or cut taxes sufficiently to increase aggregate demand.

So how could the economy recover? The Delors Report[3] states that an EMU will consist not only of a common market with free mobility of capital and labour, but also of a common competition policy and a common regional policy. A common regional policy

___

[3] Committee for the Study of Economic and Monetary Union, 'Report on Economic and Monetary Union in the European Community', 1989, Luxembourg.

implies that fiscal transfers can be made to Italy from the other countries of the European Union. However, before fiscal transfers can be made from some countries in the eurozone to others, there has to be a political consensus on the part of the donor countries and the receiver countries, which in turn can only occur if there is a political union. This is perhaps the greatest objection to EMU for some people. A single currency implies a political union. A loss of monetary sovereignty implies a loss of political sovereignty.

The Euro Record

When the euro came into being on 1 January 1999, many people expected it to appreciate against the pound sterling and the US dollar. The reason people thought this would happen was because financial institutions like pension funds would want to buy euros so that they could purchase assets in the eurozone. For a few days the euro did appreciate but very soon after the value of the euro began to fall. Figure 34.7 shows the path of the euro since January 1999.

The decline in the value of the euro has puzzled many economists. Some have tried to explain it as the result of the strength of the dollar. The long period of growth in the USA during the 1990s has increased the demand for dollar assets relative to assets from other countries. While this is true in the case of the euro–dollar exchange rate, it cannot explain the fall in the value of the euro against all other curencies. As Figure 34.7 shows, the euro has fallen in value against the pound as well as the dollar.

An alternative argument is that prior to the general circulation of the euro, a large proportion of Deutschmarks was in circulation outside Germany, principally in East and South Eastern Europe. The Bundesbank estimate that one-third of the stock of DMs or about €46 billion was in circulation outside Germany and used to finance Eastern Europe's large black economy. Because the DM ceased to exist on 1 January 2002, when the euro came into circulation in the eurozone, the holders of these 'black DMs' switched into US dollars, Swiss francs and pounds sterling. The demand for DMs fall and since the DM is the dominant currency in the euro, the sale of DMs pushed the value of the euro down against the dollar and the pound. If this argument is true, we can expect the euro to rise now that it has come into general circulation and replaces the DM as the main medium of exchange in Europe's black economy. Figure 34.8 shows that the sale of DM assets before

Figure 34.7

The Movement of the Euro against the US dollar and the pound sterling

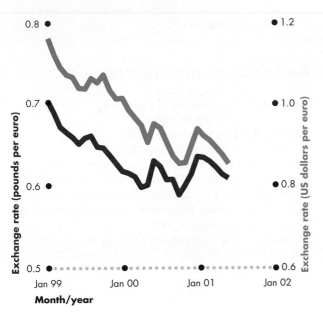

Month/year

Since the euro came into existence 1 January 1999, it has been falling in value against the US dollar and the pound sterling. Part of the decline is due to the strength of the US economy which has increased the demand for US dollar assets but this does not explain the decline in the value of the euro against the pound sterling.

Source: ECB.

the euro came into general circulation reduced the demand for euro assets, resulting in a fall in the equilibrium value of the euro.

Figure 34.8

The Fall in the Demand for Euro Assets

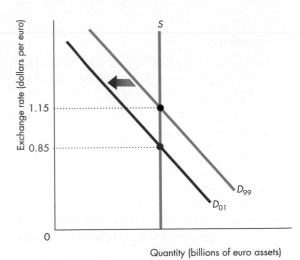

Quantity (billions of euro assets)

The Deutschmark is a euro asset. The sale of Deutschmarks is represented as a fall in the demand for euro assets. The demand for euro assets falls from D_{99} to D_{01}. The equilibrium value of the euro falls from 1.15 dollars per euro to 0.85 dollars per euro.

We have discovered what determines a country's current account balance, and the value of its currency. We have used what we have learned to examine the volatility of the pound exchange rate in 1979–81 and the collapse of the ERM. Finally we have looked at the record of the euro and used what we have learned to explain the fall in its value since it came into existence.

Summary

Key Points

Financing International Trade (pp. 785–790)

- International trade, borrowing and lending are financed using foreign currency.

- A country's international transactions are recorded in its balance of payments accounts.

- The current account records receipts and expenditures connected with the sale and purchase of goods and services, as well as investment income and net transfers to and from the rest of the world; the capital and financial account records international borrowing and lending transactions.

Sterling in the Global Market (pp. 790–792)

- Foreign currency is obtained in exchange for domestic currency in the foreign exchange market.

- The exchange rate can be fixed, flexible or managed. A fixed exchange rate is one that is pegged by a central bank.

- A flexible exchange rate is one that adjusts freely with no central bank intervention in the foreign exchange market.

- A managed exchange rate is one in which the central bank smooths out fluctuations but does not peg the rate at a fixed value.

Exchange Rate Determination
(pp. 792–800)

- The exchange rate is determined by the demand for and supply of sterling assets. The quantity of sterling assets demanded, a stock, is greater the lower the exchange rate. A change in the exchange rate brings a movement along the demand curve for sterling.

- Changes in UK GDP, the expected future exchange rate and the UK interest rate differential change the demand for sterling and bring a shift in the demand curve.

- The supply of sterling assets depends on the exchange rate system.

- In a fixed exchange rate system, the supply curve is horizontal; in a flexible exchange rate system, the supply curve is vertical; in a managed exchange rate system, the supply curve is upward-sloping. The position of the supply curve depends on the government's budget and the Bank of England's monetary policy.

- The larger the budget deficit or the greater the purchases of foreign currency by the Bank of England, the greater is the supply of sterling.

The European Monetary Union
(pp. 800–803)

- The EMU came into being on 1 January 1999 with 11 countries of the EU joining the first wave of the currency union.

- The arguments in favour of a single currency are mostly microeconomic.

- The arguments against are mostly macroeconomic and political.

- The decline in the value of the euro could be caused by the sale of DMs held in Eastern and Southern Europe, before the euro comes into general circulation.

Key Figures and Tables

Key Terms

Problems

1 Silecon, whose currency is the grain, conducted the following transactions in 1999:

Item	Billions of grains
Imports of goods and services	350
Exports of goods and services	500
Borrowing from the rest of the world	60
Lending to the rest of the world	200
Increase in official holdings of foreign currency	10

a Set out the three balance of payments accounts for Silecon.

b Does the Silecon central bank intervene in the foreign exchange market?

2 Spin, whose currency is the wheel, conducted the following transactions in 1999:

Item	Billions of wheels
Imports of goods and services	50
Exports of goods and services	60
Borrowing from the rest of the would	2
Lending to the rest of the world	12
Increase in official holdings of foreign currency	0

a Set out the three balance of payments accounts for Spin.

b Does the Spin central bank intervene in the foreign exchange market?

3 The figure below shows the flows of income and expenditure in Dreamland in 2000. The amounts are in millions of euros. GDP in Dreamland is €60 million.

a Calculate Dreamland's net exports.

b Calculate saving in Dreamland.

c How is Dreamland's investment financed?

4 The figure below shows the flows of income and expenditure in Dreamland in 2001. The amounts are in millions of euros. Dreamland's GDP has increased to €65 million but all the other items whose values are provided in the figure remain the same as they were in 2000.

a Calculate Dreamland's net exports in 2001.

b Calculate saving in Dreamland in 2001.

c How is Dreamland's investment financed?

5 The following tables tell you about Ecflex, whose currency is the band.

Item	Billions of bands
GDP	100
Consumption expenditure	60
Government expenditures on goods and services	24
Investment	22
Exports of goods and services	20
Government budget deficit	4

Calculate the following for Ecflex:

a Imports of goods and services

b Current account balance

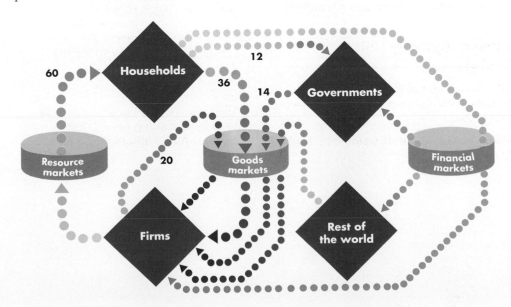

c   Capital account balance

d   Net taxes

e   Private sector surplus

6   The following table tells you about Ecfix, whose currency is the rock:

Item	Billions of rocks
GDP	200
Consumption expenditure	120
Government expenditures on goods and services	50
Investment	50
Exports of goods and services	40
Saving	45

Calculate the following for Ecfix:

a   Imports of goods and services

b   Current account balance

c   Capital account balance

d   Net taxes

e   Private sector surplus

f   Government deficit or surplus

•7 A country's currency appreciates, and its official holdings of foreign currency increase. What can you say about:

a   Intervention in the foreign exchange market by the country's central bank?

b   The possible central bank sources of the currency appreciation?

c   The possible private actions behind the appreciation?

•8 A country's currency depreciates, and its official holdings of foreign currency decrease. What can you say about:

a   Intervention in the foreign exchange market by the country's central bank?

b   The possible sources of the depreciation?

c   The possible private actions behind depreciation?

Critical Thinking

1 Study Reading Between the Lines on pp. 808–809 and then answer the following questions.

   a What events in the foreign exchange market does the news article describe?

   b What are the reasons for the weakening of the yen?

   c What other explanations does the article give for the fall in the value of the yen?

   d How can the Bank of Japan influence the value of the yen?

2 Use the link on the Parkin, Powell and Matthews website to get recent data on the exchange rate of the US dollar against the pound sterling and the Japanese yen. Then:

   a Use the demand and supply model of the foreign exchange market to explain the changes (or absence of changes) in the exchange rates.

   b What specific events might have changed exchange rate expectations?

   c What forces might have prevented the exchange rates from changing?

   d What information would you need to be able to determine whether central bank intervention has prevented either exchange rate from changing by as much as it otherwise would have?

A Weaker Yen?

THE FINANCIAL TIMES, 26 NOVEMBER 2001

Yen mystery unravelled

Krishna Guha

One of the enduring mysteries of Japan's economic crisis is the obstinate strength of the yen.

For the past six months – as Japan's trade surplus has shrunk and its economic prospects have gone from bad to worse – the currency has held its ground against the dollar. Now at last it appears to be weakening.

There are several reasons for this. First, the narrowing of the interest rate differential between the US and Japan, which had helped to support the yen, appears to be coming to an end as the Federal Reserve approaches the turn of the interest rate cycle.

At the start of the year the interest rate gap between the US and Japan was 6.5 percentage points. It is now 2 percentage points. But investors believe the US will bounce back.

Japan, meanwhile, appears to be sinking deeper into a spiral of recession and deflation, which could turn into depression.

Even if a US recovery prevents Japan from going into a tailspin, it might not pull it out of stagnation.

With diverging economic prospects come diverging capital flows. Goldman Sachs on Friday reduced its recommended weighting in Japanese equities, saying: 'We are increasingly downbeat about Japan's growth prospects.'

Meanwhile, there is continuing disappointment on trade. Last month Japan's trade surplus shrank 33 per cent year-on-year to ¥463bn – the tenth consecutive month of seasonally adjusted decline.

A study by the Nomura Research Institute suggests more than half the decline is cyclical. It and some other economists believe the surplus should now stabilise.

But a structural shift is taking place. The decline in imports has still not caught up with the fall in exports.

Then there is the possibility of US-sanctioned currency intervention to drive down the yen and break Japan's deflationary trap.

The government, which would have to authorise intervention, is hoping instead for a gentle market-led depreciation that would be less likely to provoke trade friction and competitive devaluation in Asia.

The Bank of Japan is unenthusiastic. It wants to keep up the pressure for structural reform.

The Essence of the Story

- The value of the yen has held up despite a worsening economic crisis in Japan and a shrinking trade surplus.

- In recent months there have been signs of a weakening in the value of the yen.

- The article provides a number of explanations for the yen's weakening.

- The article says that the US may want intervention by the Bank of Japan to drive the yen down further.

- The Bank of Japan prefers structural reform of imports to enable the trade deficit to decline and bring the yen down by market forces.

Economic Analysis

■ The value of the yen has remained resilient even though the Japanese economy has weakened and the trade surplus has shrunk.

■ However, signs of a weakening of the yen have emerged. Figure 1 shows that the US dollar per yen has fallen in the later months of 2001. The exchange rate is expressed as US cents per yen.

■ One of the reasons for this is that the fall in the gap between the US interest rate and the Japanese rate of interest has come to an end. The market expects the Federal Reserve to raise interest rates as soon as there is a sign that the recession in the US is over.

■ Figure 2 shows the interest rate differential between the US and Japan has narrowed. The expectation is that the interest differential will widen in the near future.

■ Investment banks like Goldman Sachs have recommended that Japanese assets be reduced in international portfolios. The expected decline in Japan's GDP growth will reduce the demand for yen assets.

■ Figure 3 shows that the demand for yen assets has fallen from D_{jan} to D_{nov}. The exchange rate has declined from 0.85 to 0.8 cents per yen.

■ The US government would like the Bank of Japan to sell yen and buy dollars in the foreign exchange market to drive the value of the yen down further.

■ The Bank of Japan would prefer imports to rise by reforming Japan's restrictive distribution system that makes it difficult for foreign companies to break into the market. If imports rise, it is hoped that the decline in the trade surplus will lead to a natural decline in the exchange rate by increasing the demand for dollars by Japanese importers.

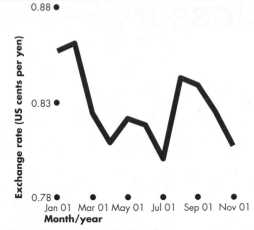

Figure 1 Japanese exchange rate

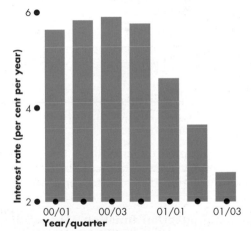

Figure 2 US–Japan interest rate differential

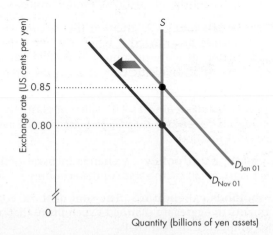

Figure 3 Foreign exchange market

Glossary

Above full-employment equilibrium A situation in which macroeconomic equilibrium occurs at a level of real GDP above long-run real GDP.

Absolute advantage A person has an absolute advantage in the production of two goods if by using the same quantities of inputs, that person can produce more of both goods than another person. A country has an absolute advantage if its output per unit of inputs of all goods is larger than that of another country.

Aggregate demand The relationship between the aggregate quantity of goods and services demanded (real GDP demanded) and the price level (the GDP deflator).

Aggregate hours The total number of hours worked by all the people employed, both full-time and part-time, during a year.

Aggregate planned expenditure The expenditure that economic agents (households, firms, governments and foreigners) plan to undertake in given circumstances.

Aggregate production function The relationship that shows how the maximum real GDP attainable varies as quantities of factors of production vary.

Allocative efficiency A situation that occurs when no resources are wasted – when no one can be made better off without someone else being made worse off. Allocative efficiency is also called Pareto efficiency.

Arc elasticity of demand The value of elasticity of demand between two points calculated by the average price method.

Automatic fiscal policy A change in fiscal policy that is triggered by the state of the economy.

Autonomous expenditure The sum of those components of aggregate planned expenditure that are not influenced by real GDP.

Average cost pricing rule A rule that sets price equal to average total cost.

Average fixed cost Total fixed cost per unit of output – total fixed cost divided by output.

Average product The average productivity of a factor of production – total product divided by the quantity of the factor employed.

Average revenue The revenue per unit of output sold – total revenue divided by the quantity sold. Average revenue also equals price.

Average total cost Total cost per unit of output.

Average variable cost Total variable cost per unit of output.

Balance of payments accounts A country's record of international trading, borrowing and lending.

Balance of trade The value of exports minus the value of imports.

Balanced budget A government budget in which tax revenues and expenditures are equal.

Balanced budget multiplier The amount by which a simultaneous and equal change in goverment purchases and taxes is multiplied to determine the change in equilibrium expenditure.

Bank A private firm licensed by the Bank of England under the Banking Act of 1987 to take deposits and make loans and operate in the United Kingdom.

Bank of England The central bank of the United Kingdom.

Barriers to entry Legal or natural impediments protecting a firm from competition from potential new entrants.

Barter The direct exchange of one good or service for other goods and services.

Below full-employment equilibrium A macroeconomic equilibrium in which potential GDP exceeds real GDP.

Bilateral monopoly A situation in which there is a single seller (a monopoly) and a single buyer (a monopsony).

Big Trade-off The conflict between efficiency and equity.

Black market An illegal trading arrangement in which buyers and sellers do business at a price higher than the legally imposed price ceiling.

Bond A legally enforceable debt obligation to pay specified amounts of money at specified future dates.

Bond market A market in which the bonds of corporations and governments are traded.

Budget deficit A government's budget balance that is negative – expenditures exceed tax revenues.

Budget line The limits to a household's consumption choices.

Budget surplus A government's budget balance that is positive – tax revenues exceed expenditures.

Building society A financial intermediary that traditionally obtained its funds from savings deposits (sometimes called share accounts) and that made long-term mortgage loans to home buyers.

Business cycle The periodic but irregular up-and-down movement in economic activity, measured by fluctuations in real GDP and other macroeconomic variables.

Capacity output The output at which average total cost is at a minimum.

Capital The equipment, buildings, tools and manufactured goods that are used in the production of goods and services.

Capital and financial account A record of a country's international borrowing and lending transactions.

Capital accumulation The growth of capital resources.

Capital stock The stock of plant, equipment, buildings (including residential housing) and unsold finished goods.

Capture theory A theory of regulation that states that the regulations are supplied to satisfy the demand of producers to maximize producer surplus – to maximize economic profit.

Cartel A group of firms that has entered into a collusive agreement to restrict output so as to increase prices and profits.

Central bank A public authority charged with regulating and controlling a country's monetary policy and financial institutions and markets.

Central plan A detailed economic blueprint that sets out *what* will be produced, *how*, *when* and *where* it will be produced, and *who* will get what is produced, and that establishes a set of sanctions and rewards designed to ensure that the plan is fulfilled as fully as possible.

Ceteris paribus Other things being equal – all other relevant things remaining the same.

Change in demand A change in buyers' plans that occurs when some influence on those plans other than the price of the good changes. It is illustrated by a shift of the demand curve.

Change in supply A change in sellers' plans that occurs when some influence on those plans other than the price of the good changes. It is illustrated by a shift of the supply curve.

Change in the quantity demanded A change in buyers' plans that occurs when the price of a good changes but all other influences on buyers' plans remain unchanged. It is illustrated by a movement along the demand curve.

Change in the quantity supplied A change in sellers' plans that occurs when the price of a good changes but all other influences on sellers' plans remain unchanged. It is illustrated by a movement along the supply curve.

Choice at the margin When a choice is made by considering the effect of small changes in amount or the effect of changes a little at a time.

Classical growth theory A theory of economic growth based on the view that population growth is determined by the level of income per person.

Coase theorem The proposition that if property rights exist and transactions costs are low, private transactions are efficient – equivalently, there are no externalities.

Collective bargaining A process of negotiation between representatives of employers and unions.

Collusive agreement An agreement between two (or more) producers to restrict output so as to increase prices and profits.

Command system A system in which some people give orders and others obey them.

Commodity money A physical commodity that is valued in its own right and is also used as a means of payment.

Common Agricultural Policy (CAP) The agricultural policy implemented by the European Union in member countries.

Company A firm owned by two or more shareholders.

Comparative advantage A person or country has a comparative advantage in an activity if that person or country can perform the activity at a lower opportunity cost than anyone else or any other country.

Competition A situation where individuals and firms are forced into a contest for the command of scarce resources because of scarcity.

Complement A good that is used in conjunction with another good.

Constant returns to scale Technological conditions under which a given percentage increase in all the firm's inputs results in the firm's output increasing by the same percentage.

Consumer efficiency A situation that occurs when consumers cannot make themselves better off by reallocating their budgets.

Consumer equilibrium A situation in which a consumer has allocated his or her income in the way that maximizes his or her utility.

Consumer surplus The value that the consumer places on a good minus the price paid for it.

Consumption demand The relationship between consumption expenditure and the real interest rate, other things remaining the same.

Consumption expenditure The total payment made by households for consumption goods and services.

Consumption function The relationship between consumption expenditure and disposable income, other things remaining the same.

Contestable market A market structure in which there is one firm (or a small number of firms) and because of freedom of entry and exit, the firm (or firms) faces competition from potential entrants and so operates like a perfectly competitive firm.

Contractionary fiscal policy A decrease in government expenditures or an increase in tax revenues.

Convertible paper money A paper claim to a commodity (such as gold) that circulates as a means of payment.

Cooperative equilibrium The outcome of a game in which players agree to collude to make and share monopoly profit.

Copyright A government-sanctioned exclusive right granted to the inventor of a good, service, or productive process to produce, use, and sell the invention for a given number of years.

Corporation A large-scale firm owned by shareholders whose liability is legally limited to the value of their initial investment.

Cost-push inflation Inflation that results from an initial increase in costs.

Creditor nation A country that has invested more in the rest of the world than other countries have invested in it.

Cross elasticity of demand The responsiveness of the demand for a good to the price of a substitute or complement, other things remaining the same. It is calculated as the percentage change in the quantity demanded of the good divided by the percentage change in the price of the substitute or complement.

Cross-section graph A graph that shows the values of an economic variable for different groups in a population at a point in time.

Crowding out The tendency for an increase in government purchases of goods and services to bring a decrease in investment.

Currency The notes and coins that we use today.

Currency depreciation The fall in the value of one currency in terms of another currency.

Currency drain An increase in currency held outside banks.

Current account A record of receipts from the sale of goods and services to foreigners, the payments for goods and services bought from foreigners, the interest income received from and paid to foreigners, and gifts and other transfers (such as foreign aid payments) received from and paid to foreigners.

Cyclical deficit A budget deficit that is present only because real GDP is less than potential GDP and taxes are temporarily low and transfer payments are temporarily high.

Cyclical unemployment The unemployment arising from the slowdown in the pace of economic expansion.

Cyclically adjusted deficit The budget deficit that would occur if the economy were at full employment.

Deadweight loss A measure of allocative inefficiency. It is equal to the loss in total surplus (consumer surplus plus producer surplus) that results from producing less than the efficient level of output.

Debtor nation A country that during its entire history has borrowed more from the rest of the world than it has lent to it.

Decentralized planning An economic system that combines state ownership of capital and land with incentives based on a mixture of market prices and laws and regulations.

Decreasing returns to scale Technological conditions under which a given percentage increase in all the firm's inputs results in the firm's output increasing by a smaller percentage.

Deflation Falling aggregate demand, falling prices and falling output.

Demand The relationship between the quantity of a good that consumers plan to buy and the price of the good, with all other influences on buyers' plans remaining the same. It is described by a demand schedule and illustrated by a demand curve.

Demand curve A curve that shows the relationship between the quantity demanded of a good and its price, all other influences on consumers' planned purchases remaining the same.

Demand-pull inflation Inflation that results from an initial increase in aggregate demand.

Deposit money Deposits at banks and other financial institutions; an accounting entry in an electronic database in the banks' and other financial institutions' computers.

Deposit multiplier The amount by which an increase in bank reserves is multiplied to calculate the increase in bank deposits.

Depreciation The decrease in the value of capital stock or the value of a durable input that results from wear and tear and the passage of time.

Deregulation The removal of regulatory rules to restrict or control economic activity in price setting, product standards, trading standards and the conditions under which firms can enter an industry.

Derived demand Demand for an item not for its own sake but for use in the production of goods and services.

Desired reserve ratio Ratio of reserves to deposits that banks consider as prudent to hold in order to meet withdrawals and to carry on their business.

Diminishing marginal rate of substitution The general tendency for the marginal rate of substitution of one good for another to diminish as a consumer increases consumption of the first good.

Diminishing marginal returns The tendency for the marginal product of a variable factor eventually to diminish as additional units of the variable factor are employed.

Diminishing marginal utility The marginal utility that a consumer gets from a good decreases as more of the good is consumed.

Direct relationship A relationship between two variables that move in the same direction.

Discount rate The interest rate at which the central bank stands ready to lend reserves to commercial banks.

Discounting The conversion of a future amount of money to its present value.

Discouraged workers People who do not have jobs and would like to work but have stopped seeking work.

Discretionary fiscal policy A policy action that is initiated by the Chancellor of the Exchequer.

Discretionary policy A policy that responds to the state of the economy in a possibly unique way that uses all the information available, including perceived lessons from past 'mistakes'.

Discrimination Occurs in the labour market when employment decisions are taken on the basis of ethnic origin or gender rather than ability.

Diseconomies of scale Technological conditions under which long-run average cost increases as output increases.

Dominant strategy equilibrium The outcome of a game in which there is a single best strategy (a dominant strategy) for each player, regardless of the strategy of the other players.

Dumping The sale of a good in a foreign market for a lower price than in the domestic market or for a lower price than its cost of production.

Duopoly A market structure in which two producers of a good or service compete.

Dynamic comparative advantage A comparative advantage that a person or country possesses as a result of having specialized in a particular activity and then, as a result of learning-by-doing, becoming the producer with the lowest opportunity cost.

Economic activity rate The state of the labour market is indicated by this, the employment-to-population ratio and the unemployment rate.

Economic depreciation The decrease in the market price of a piece of capital over a given period.

Economic efficiency A situation that occurs when the cost of producing a given output is as low as possible.

Economic growth The expansion of production possibilities that results from capital accumulation and technological change.

Economic information Data on prices, quantities and qualities of goods and services and factors of production.

Economic model A description of some aspect of the economic world that includes only those features of the world that are needed for the purpose at hand.

Economic profit A firm's total revenue minus its opportunity cost.

Economic rent The income received by the owner of a factor of production in excess of the amount required to induce that owner to offer the factor for use.

Economic stability The absence of wide fluctuations in the economic growth rate, the level of employment and average prices.

Economic theory A generalization that summarizes what we think we understand about the economic choices that people make and the performance of industries and entire economies.

Economics The study of the choices people make to cope with scarcity.

Economies of scale Technological conditions under which long-run average cost decreases as output increases.

Economies of scope Decreases in average total cost made possible by increasing the range of goods produced.

Economy A mechanism that allocates scarce resources among competing uses.

Efficiency A point in production where it is not possible to produce more of one good without producing less of some other good.

Efficiency wage The wage rate that maximizes profit.

Efficient/Efficient Allocation/Efficient choice Choice which leads to the production of the most highly valued goods and services and the efficient use of resources.

Efficient market A market in which the actual price embodies all currently available relevant information.

Elastic Where a small percentage change in price results in a proportionately larger change in the quantity demanded.

Elasticity of supply The responsiveness of the quantity supplied of a good to a change in its price, other things remaining the same.

Emission charges Any form of pollution control that uses the market to create incentives for producers to cut pollution emissions.

Emission standards Pollution control in the form of regulations limiting the quantity of pollution emissions.

Employment-to-population ratio The percentage of people of working age who have jobs.

Entrants People who enter the workforce.

Entrepreneurship A special type of human resource that organizes the other three factors of production – labour, land and capital – and makes business decisions, innovates and bears business risk.

Environment capital Includes elements of land which are lost forever when used in the production process as well as the degree of biodiversity among species and the ability of the environment to absorb waste from production.

Equal pay for equal worth Where employees are paid the same wage for different jobs considered to be of comparable worth.

Equation of exchange An equation that states that the quantity of money multiplied by the velocity of circulation equals GDP.

Equilibrium expenditure The level of aggregate planned expenditure that equals real GDP.

Equilibrium price The price at which the quantity demanded equals the quantity supplied.

Equilibrium quantity The quantity bought and sold at the equilibrium price.

Equity In economics, equity has two meanings: economic justice or fairness and the owner's stake in a business.

Equity withdrawal Borrowing by owner-occupiers from the mortgage issuer against the value of their home without actually moving house.

European Currency Unit (ECU) A composite currency unit made up of the currencies of the member countries of the European Union.

European Monetary System (EMS) The system by which members of the European Union cooperate on monetary matters to achieve exchange rate stability.

European Monetary Union (EMU) A currency union of all participating member countries of the European Union, where a single currency, the euro, will replace individual country currencies.

Eurozone Countries in the European Monetary System.

Excess reserves A bank's actual reserves minus its required reserves.

Exchange efficiency A situation in which a good or service is exchanged at a price that equals both the marginal social benefit and the marginal social cost of the good or service.

Exchange Rate Mechanism (ERM) A system of pegged exchange rates among participating currencies. It is a parity grid system where each currency has a set of bilateral central parities and a band by which it is allowed to float.

Excise tax A tax on the sale of a good or service. The tax is paid when the good or service is bought.

Exhaustible natural resources Natural resources that can be used only once and that cannot be replaced once they have been used.

Expansion A business cycle phase in which there is a speedup in the pace of economic activity.

Expansionary fiscal policy An increase in government expenditure or a decrease in tax revenues.

Expenditure The price of good multiplied by the quantity of the good that is bought.

Exports The goods and services that we sell to people in other countries.

External benefits Benefits that accrue to members of the society other than the buyer of the good.

External costs Costs that are borne by members of society other than the producer of the good.

External diseconomies Factors outside the control of a firm that raise the firm's costs as the industry produces a larger output.

External economies Factors beyond the control of a firm that lower the firm's costs as the industry produces a larger output.

Externality A cost or a benefit arising from an economic activity that affects people other than those who decide the scale of the activity.

Factors of production The economy's productive resources – land, labour, capital and entrepreneurial ability.

Feedback-rule policy A rule that specifies how policy actions respond to changes in the state of the economy.

Fiat money An intrinsically worthless (or almost worthless) commodity that serves the functions of money.

Financial capital The supply of funds by households to firms for the purchase of capital, either directly through share ownership or indirectly through the financial and banking system.

Financial innovation The development of new financial products – new ways of borrowing and lending.

Financial intermediary An institution that receives deposits and makes loans.

Firm An institution that hires factors of production and that organizes those factors to produce and sell goods and services.

Fiscal policy The government's attempt to influence the economy by varying its purchases of goods and services and taxes to smooth the fluctuations in aggregate expenditure; use of the government budget to achieve macroeconomic objectives such as full employment, sustained long-term economic growth and price level stability.

Five-firm concentration ratio The percentage of the value of sales accounted for by the largest five firms in one industry.

Fixed cost The cost of a fixed input; a cost that is independent of the output level.

Fixed exchange rate A system in which the value of a country's currency is pegged by the country's central bank.

Fixed-rule policy A rule that specifies an action to be pursued independently of the state of the economy.

Flexible exchange rate A system in which the value of a country's currency is determined by market forces in the absence of central bank intervention.

Flow A quantity per unit of time.

Foreign exchange market The market in which the currency of one country is exchanged for the currency of another.

Foreign exchange rate The price at which one currency exchanges for another.

Free rider A person who consumes a good without paying for it.

Frictional unemployment Unemployment arising from normal labour turnover – new entrants are constantly coming into the labour market, and firms are constantly laying off workers and hiring new workers.

Full employment A situation which occurs when the unemployment rate equals the natural rate of unemployment – when all unemployment is frictional and structural and there is no cyclical unemployment.

Full employment equilibrium Macroeconomic equilibrium in which real GDP equals potential GDP.

Futures market An organized market operated on a futures exchange in which large-scale contracts for the future delivery of goods can be exchanged.

Fundamental economic problem How to use limited resources to produce and consume the most highly valued goods and services.

Game theory A method of analysing strategic behaviour.

GDP deflator A price index that measures the average level of the prices of all goods and services that make up GDP.

General Agreement on Tariffs and Trade An international agreement that limits government intervention to restrict international trade.

Gold standard A monetary system with fractionally backed convertible paper in which a currency could be converted into gold at a guaranteed value on demand.

Goods and services All the things that people are willing to pay for.

Government budget Finances the activities of the government.

Government debt The total amount of borrowing that the government has undertaken and the total amount that it owes to households, firms and foreigners.

Government purchases Goods and services bought by the government.

Government purchases multiplier The amount by which a change in government purchases of goods and services is multiplied to determine the change in equilibrium expenditure that it generates.

Great Depression A decade (1929–39) of high unemployment and stagnant production throughout the world economy.

Green tax A form of pollution control where a tax equal to the marginal external cost of pollution is charged on output.

Gresham's Law The tendency for bad (debased) money to drive good (not debased) money out of circulation.

Gross domestic product (GDP) The value of all final goods and services produced in the economy in a year.

Gross investment The amount spent on replacing depreciated capital and on net additions to the capital stock.

Growth accounting A method of calculating how much real GDP growth has resulted from growth of labour and capital and how much is attributable to technological change.

Hotelling Principle The proposition that the market for the stock of a natural resource is in equilibrium when the price of the resource is expected to rise at a rate equal to the interest rate on similarly risky assets.

Human capital The skill and knowledge of people, arising from their education and on-the-job training.

Hysteresis The idea that the natural rate of unemployment depends on the path of the actual unemployment rate; where the unemployment rate ends up depends on where it has been.

Implicit rental rate The rent that a firm pays to itself for the use of the assets that it owns.

Import function The relationship between imports and real GDP.

Imports The goods and services that we buy from people in other countries.

Incentive An inducement to take a particular action.

Incentive system A method of organizing production that uses a market-like system within a firm.

Income The amount of money that people earn.

Income effect The change in consumption that results from a change in the consumer's income, other things remaining the same.

Income elasticity of demand The responsiveness of demand to a change in income, other things remaining the same. It is calculated as the percentage change in the quantity demanded divided by the percentage change in income.

Increasing marginal returns The tendency for the marginal product of a variable factor initially to increase as additional units of the variable factor are employed.

Increasing returns to scale Technological conditions under which a given percentage increase in all the firm's inputs results in the firm's output increasing by a larger percentage.

Indifference curve A line that shows combinations of goods among which a consumer is indifferent.

Individual demand The relationship between the quantity of a good or service demanded by a single individual and the price of a good or service.

Induced expenditure The part of aggregate planned expenditure on UK-produced goods and services that varies as real GDP varies.

Induced taxes Taxes that vary as real GDP varies.

Industrial union A group of workers who have a variety of skills and job types but who work for the same firm or industry.

Inelastic Where a small percentage change in price results in a proportionately smaller change in the quantity demanded.

Infant-industry argument The proposition that protection is necessary to enable an infant industry to grow into a mature industry that can compete in world markets.

Inferior good A good for which demand decreases as income increases.

Inflation An upward movement in the average level of prices; a process in which the price level is rising and money is losing value.

Inflationary gap Actual real GDP minus potential GDP when actual real GDP exceeds potential GDP.

Information cost The cost of acquiring information on prices, quantities and qualities of goods and services and factors of production – the opportunity cost of economic information.

Insider–outsider theory A theory of job rationing that says that to be productive, new workers – outsiders – must receive on-the-job training from existing workers – insiders.

Intellectual property rights Property rights for discoveries owned by the creators of knowledge.

Interest rate The amount received by a lender and paid by a borrower expressed as a percentage of the amount of the loan.

Intermediate goods and services Goods and services that are used as inputs into the production process of another good or service.

International Monetary Fund (IMF) An international organization that monitors balance of payments and exchange rate activities.

International substitution effect The substitution of domestic goods and services for foreign goods and services or of foreign goods and services for domestic goods and services.

Intertemporal substitution effect The substitution of goods and services now for goods and services later or of goods and services later for goods and services now.

Inverse relationship A relationship between variables that move in opposite directions.

Investment The purchase of new plant, equipment and buildings and additions to stock.

Investment demand The relationship between the level of planned investment and the real interest rate, all other influences on investment remaining the same.

Isocost line A line showing all possible combinations of two inputs that can be bought for a given total cost.

Isocost map A map of all possible isocost lines, holding the price of inputs constant.

Isoquant A curve showing the possible combinations of two inputs required to produce a given quantity of output.

Isoquant map A map of all possible isoquants.

Job leavers People who voluntarily quit their jobs.

Job losers People who are laid off, either permanently or temporarily, from their jobs.

Job rationing The practice of paying employed people a wage that creates an excess supply of labour and a shortage of jobs, and increases the natural rate of unemployment.

Job search The activity of people looking for acceptable vacant jobs.

Keynesian theory of the business cycle A theory that regards volatile expectations as the main source of economic fluctuations.

Labour The time and effort that people allocate to producing goods and services.

Labour demand curve A curve that shows the quantity of labour that firms plan to hire at each possible real wage rate.

Labour supply curve A curve that shows the quantity of labour that households plan to supply at each possible real wage rate.

Land All the natural resources used to produce goods and services.

Law of diminishing returns A law stating that as the quantity of one input increases with the quantities of all other inputs remaining the same, output increases but by ever smaller increments.

Learning-by-doing People become more productive in an activity (learn) just by repeatedly producing a particular good or service (doing).

Least-cost technique The combination of inputs to produce a given output that minimizes total cost.

Legal monopoly A market structure in which there is one firm and entry is restricted by the granting of a public franchise, licence, patent or copyright, or the firm has acquired ownership of a significant portion of a key resource.

Limit pricing The practice of charging a price below the monopoly profit-maximizing price and producing a quantity greater than that at which marginal revenue equals marginal cost so as to deter entry.

Limited information and uncertainty A form of market failure caused when the assumption of full information and full knowledge of all future outcomes fails to hold.

Limited resources The land, labour, capital and entrepreneurship used to produce goods and services.

Linear relationship A relationship between two variables that is illustrated by a straight line.

Liquidity The property of being instantly convertible into a means of payment with little loss in value.

Long run A period of time in which a firm can vary the quantities of all its inputs.

Long-run aggregate supply curve The relationship between the aggregate quantity of final goods and services (GDP) supplied and the price level (GDP deflator), other things remaining the same and there is full employment.

Long-run average cost curve The relationship between the lowest attainable average total cost and output when all inputs are varied.

Long-run industry supply curve The industry supply curve after all possible production adjustments have taken place.

Long-run Phillips curve A curve that shows the relationship between inflation and unemployment when the actual inflation rate equals the expected inflation rate.

Long-term unemployed People who have remained unemployed for over 12 months.

Lorenz curve A curve that plots the cumulative percentage of income against the cumulative percentage of population.

Lump-sum tax multiplier The amount by which a change in lump-sum taxes is multiplied to determine the change in equilibrium expenditure that it generates.

Lump-sum taxes Taxes that are fixed by the government and do not vary with real GDP.

M0 Consists of currency held by the public, the banks, the building societies and banks' deposits at the Bank of England. See also Monetary base.

M4 Currency held by the public and all bank and building society sight and time deposits.

Macroeconomic long run A period that is sufficiently long for the prices of all the factors of production to have adjusted to any disturbance.

Macroeconomic short run A period during which the prices of goods and services change in response to changes in demand and supply but the prices of factors of production do not change.

Macroeconomics The study of the national economy and the global economy, the way that economic aggregates grow and fluctuate, and the effects of government actions on them.

Managed exchange rate A system in which the value of a country's currency is not fixed at some pre- announced level but is influenced by central bank intervention in the foreign exchange market.

Marginal benefit The extra benefit received from a small increase in the consumption of a good or service. It is calculated as the increase in total benefit divided by the increase in consumption.

Marginal cost The change in total cost that results from a unit increase in output. It is calculated as the increase in total cost divided by the increase in output.

Marginal cost pricing rule A rule that sets the price of a good or service equal to the marginal cost of producing it.

Marginal product The extra output produced as a result of a small increase in the variable factor. It is calculated as the increase in total product divided by the increase in the variable factor employed, when the quantities of all other factors are constant.

Marginal propensity to consume The fraction of the last pound of disposable income that is spent on consumption goods and services.

Marginal propensity to import The fraction of the last pound of real GDP spent on imports.

Marginal propensity to save The fraction of the last pound of disposable income that is saved.

Marginal rate of substitution The slope of an isoquant showing how much one input must increase for a given decrease in another input to keep output constant. (The rate at which a person will give up one good or service in order to get more of another good or service and at the same time remain indifferent.)

Marginal revenue The extra total revenue received from selling one additional unit of the good or service. It is calculated as the change in total revenue divided by the change in quantity sold.

Marginal revenue product The extra total revenue received from employing one more unit of a factor of production while the quantity of all other factors remains the same. It is calculated as the increase in total revenue divided by the increase in the quantity of the factor.

Marginal social benefit The marginal benefit received by the producer of a good (marginal private benefit) plus the marginal benefit received by other members of society (external benefit).

Marginal social cost The marginal cost incurred by the producer of a good (marginal private cost) plus the marginal cost imposed on other members of society (external cost).

Marginal utility The change in total utility resulting from a one-unit increase in the quantity of a good consumed.

Marginal utility per pound spent The marginal utility obtained from the last unit of a good consumed divided by the price of the good.

Market Any arrangement that enables buyers and sellers to get information and to do business with each other.

Market activity People undertake market activity when they buy goods and services in goods (or services) markets or sell the services of the factors of production that they own in factor markets.

Market demand The total demand for a good or service by everyone in the population. It is illustrated by the market demand curve.

Market failure The failure of an unregulated market to achieve an efficient allocation of resources.

Market power The ability to influence market price by influencing market quantity.

Marketable permits A permit to emit up to a given level of pollution which can be bought and sold in a market.

Maximize total utility A major assumption of marginal utility theory which implies that individuals choose as if they made the marginal utility per pound spent on each good equal.

Means of payment A method of settling a debt.

Median voter theorem The proposition that political parties will pursue policies that appeal most to the median voter.

Merger The combining of the assets of two firms to form a single, new firm.

Microeconomics The study of the decisions of people and businesses, the interactions of those decisions in markets, and the effects of government regulation and taxes on the prices and quantities of goods and services.

Minimum efficient scale The smallest level of output at which long run average cost is at its lowest level.

Minimum wage law A price floor regulation that prohibits labour services being paid at less than a specified wage rate.

Monetarist theory of the business cycle A theory that regards fluctuations in the money stock as the main source of economic fluctuations.

Monetary base The sum of the notes and coins in circulation and banks' deposits at the Central Bank. See also M0.

Monetary policy The government's attempt to achieve macroeconomic objectives by adjusting the quantity of money in circulation and interest rates.

Money Any commodity or token that is generally acceptable as a means of payment for goods and services.

Money multiplier The amount by which a change in the monetary base is multiplied to determine the resulting change in the quantity of money.

Monopolistic competition A market structure in which a large number of firms compete with each other by making similar but slightly different products.

Monopoly An industry that produces a good or service for which no close substitute exists and in which there is one supplier that is protected from competition by a barrier preventing the entry of new firms.

Monopoly control law A law that defines and regulates practices which lead to the monopoly structure and monopoly power in industry.

Monopoly power The ability to exercise the power of a monopoly to raise price by restricting output.

Monopsony A market structure in which there is just a single buyer.

Moral hazard A situation in which one of the parties to an agreement has an incentive, after the agreement is made, to act in a manner that brings additional benefits to himself or herself at the expense of the other party.

Multiplier The change in equilibrium real GDP divided by the change in autonomous expenditure.

Nash equilibrium The outcome of a game that occurs when player A takes the best possible action given the action of player B, and player B takes the best possible action given the action of player A.

National saving Private saving plus government saving; also equals GDP minus consumption expenditure minus government purchases.

Natural monopoly A monopoly that occurs when one firm can supply the entire market at a lower price than two or more firms can.

Natural rate of unemployment The unemployment rate when the economy is at full employment.

Natural resources The non-produced factors of production, which can be exhaustible or non-exhaustible.

Negative income tax A redistribution scheme that gives every family a *guaranteed annual income* and decreases the family's benefit at a specified *benefit-loss rate* as its market income increases.

Negative relationship A relationship between variables that move in opposite directions.

Neo-classical growth theory A theory of economic growth that explains how saving, investment and economic growth respond to population growth and technological change.

Net borrower A country that is borrowing more from the rest of the world than it is lending to it.

Net exporter A country whose value of exports exceeds its value of imports – its balance of trade is positive.

Net exports The expenditure by foreigners on UK-produced goods minus the expenditure by UK residents on foreign-produced goods – exports minus imports.

Net importer A country whose value of imports exceeds its value of exports – its balance of trade is negative.

Net investment Net additions to the capital stock – gross investment minus depreciation.

Net lender A country that is lending more to the rest of the world than it is borrowing from it.

Net present value The present value of the future flow of marginal revenue product generated by capital minus the cost of the capital.

Net taxes Taxes paid to governments minus transfer payments received from governments.

New classical theory of the business cycle A rational expectations theory of the business cycle that regards unanticipated fluctuations in aggregate demand as the main source of economic fluctuations.

New growth theory A theory of economic growth based on the idea that technological change results from the choices that people make in the pursuit of ever greater profit.

New Keynesian theory of the business cycle A rational expectations theory of the business cycle that regards unanticipated fluctuations in aggregate demand as the main source of economic fluctuations.

Nominal GDP targeting An attempt to keep the growth rate of nominal GDP steady.

Nominal interest rate The interest rate actually paid and received in the marketplace.

Non-excludable A property of market failure in the form of public goods where non-payers cannot be excluded from receiving the benefits of the public good or service.

Non-exhaustible natural resources Natural resources that can be used repeatedly without depleting what is available for future use.

Non-market activity Leisure and non-market production activities, including education and training, shopping, cooking and other activities in the home.

Non-rival A property of market failure in the form of public goods where one person's consumption of the good or service does not affect the consumption possibilities of anyone else.

Non-tariff barrier An action other than a tariff that restricts international trade.

Normal good A good for which demand increases as income increases.

Normal profit The expected return for supplying entrepreneurial ability.

Oligopoly A market structure in which a small number of producers compete with each other.

Open market operation The purchase or sale of government securities by the Bank of England designed to influence the money supply.

Opportunity cost The opportunity cost of an action is the best forgone alternative.

Pareto efficiency Another term for allocative efficiency where the market could not reallocate resources through trade, production or consumption to make at least one person better off without making anybody else worse off.

Patent A government-sanctioned exclusive right granted to the inventor of a good, service, or productive process to produce, use and sell the invention for a given number of years.

Payment system The generally accepted method of payment for trade in an economy.

Payoff matrix A table that shows the payoffs for every possible action by each player for every possible action by each other player.

Perfect competition A market structure in which there are many firms; each firm sells an identical product; there are many buyers; there are no restrictions on entry into the industry; firms in the industry have no advantage over potential new entrants; and firms and buyers are completely informed about the price of each firm's product.

Perfectly elastic Demand with an infinite price elasticity; the quantity demanded is infinitely responsive to a change in price.

Perfectly inelastic Demand with a price elasticity of zero; the quantity demanded remains constant when the price changes.

Phillips curve A curve that shows a relationship between inflation and unemployment.

Political equilibrium A situation in which the choices of voters, politicians and bureaucrats are all compatible and in which no one group can improve its position by making a different choice.

Poor definition of property rights A form of market failure where the legal rights to property are not clearly defined.

Positive relationship A relationship between two variables that move in the same direction.

Potential GDP A situation in which all the economy's labour, capital, land and entrepreneurial ability are fully employed.

Poverty A state in which a family's income is too low to be able to buy the quantities of food, shelter and clothing that are deemed necessary.

Preferences A person's likes and dislikes for goods and services which are described by the economist's measure of utility.

Present value The amount of money that, if invested today, will grow to be as large as a given future amount when the interest that it will earn is taken into account.

Price ceiling A regulation that makes it illegal to charge a price higher than a specified level.

Price discrimination The practice of charging some customers a lower price than others for an identical good or of charging an individual customer a lower price per unit on a large purchase than on a small one, even though the cost of servicing all customers is the same.

Price effect The change in consumption that results from a change in the price of a good or service, other things remaining the same.

Price elasticity of demand The responsiveness of the quantity demanded of a good to a change in the price of a good or service, other things remaining the same.

Price floor Regulation that makes setting or paying a price below a specified level illegal.

Price level The average level of prices as measured by a price index.

Price taker A firm that cannot influence the price of the good or service it produces.

Principal–agent problem A form of market failure arising in a contractual relationship when one party, the principal, cannot fully monitor the activities of the other party, the agent.

Private information Information that is available to one person but is too costly for anyone else to obtain.

Private sector surplus or deficit The difference between saving and investment.

Privatization The process of selling a public company or public sector assets to private shareholders.

Producer efficiency A situation in which it is not possible to produce more of one good without producing less of some other good.

Producer surplus The price a producer gets for a good or service minus the opportunity cost of producing it.

Product differentiation Making a good or service slightly different from that of a competing firm.

Production efficiency The level of production when no more of one good can be produced without producing less of some other good.

Production function The relationship that shows how the maximum output attainable varies as quantities of all inputs vary.

Production possibility frontier The boundary between those combinations of goods and services that can be produced and those that cannot.

Productivity The amount of output produced per unit of inputs used to produce it.

Productivity function A relationship that shows how real GDP per hour of labour changes as the amount of capital per hour of labour changes with no change in technology.

Productivity growth slowdown A slowdown in the growth rate of output per person.

Progressive income tax A tax on income at a marginal rate that increases with the level of income.

Property rights Social arrangements that govern the ownership, use and disposal of factors of production and goods and services.

Proportional income tax A tax on income that remains at a constant rate, regardless of the level of income.

Protectionism The restriction of international trade.

Public choice theory A theory predicting the behaviour of the government sector of the economy as the outcome of the individual choices made by voters, politicians and bureaucrats interacting in a political marketplace.

Public good A good or service that can be consumed simultaneously by everyone and from which no one can be excluded.

Public interest theory A theory of regulation that states that regulations are supplied to satisfy the demand of consumers and producers to maximize total surplus – that is, to attain allocative efficiency.

Public ownership Ownership of corporations by government rather than private shareholders.

Public Sector Borrowing Requirement (PSBR) The budget deficit of the government and public corporations.

Public Sector Debt Repayment (PSDR) The budget surplus of the government and public corporations.

Quantity demanded The amount of a good or service that consumers plan to buy during a given time period at a particular price.

Quantity of sterling assets The net stock of financial assets denominated in pounds sterling held outside the Bank of England and the government.

Quantity supplied The amount of a good or service that producers plan to sell during a given time period at a particular price.

Quantity theory of money The proposition that in the long run, an increase in the quantity of money brings an equal percentage increase in the price level.

Quota A restriction on the quantity of a good that a firm is permitted to produce or that a country is permitted to import.

Rate of return regulation A regulation that determines a regulated price by setting the price at a level that enables the regulated firm to earn a specified target percentage return on its capital.

Rate of time preference The target real interest rate that savers want to achieve.

Rational expectation A forecast based on all available relevant information.

Rational ignorance The decision not to acquire information because the cost of doing so exceeds the expected benefit.

Real business cycle theory A theory that regards random fluctuations in productivity that result from technological change as the main source of economic fluctuations.

Real exchange rate An index number that gives the opportunity cost of foreign-produced goods and services in terms of UK-produced goods and services.

Real GDP per person Real GDP divided by the population.

Real gross domestic product (real GDP) The output of final goods and services valued at prices prevailing in the base period.

Real income The quantity of a good that a consumer's income will buy. It is the consumer's income expressed in units of a good and is calculated as income divided by the price of the good.

Real interest rate The interest rate paid by a borrower and received by a lender after taking into account the change in the value of money resulting from inflation; the nominal interest rate minus the inflation rate.

Real money A measure of money based on the quantity of goods and services it will buy.

Real money balances effect The change in real GDP demanded as a result of a change in the quality of real money.

Real price A relative price where the money price of a good is divided by the price of a representative basket of goods.

Real wage rate The wage rate per hour expressed in constant pounds.

Recession A downturn in the level of economic activity in which real GDP falls in two successive quarters.

Recessionary gap Potential GDP minus actual real GDP when actual real GDP is less than potential GDP.

Re-entrants People who re-enter the workforce.

Regressive income tax A tax on income at a marginal rate that decreases with the level of income.

Regulation Rules enforced by a government agency to restrict or control economic activity in price setting, product standards, trading standards and the conditions under which firms can enter an industry.

Relative price The ratio of the price of one good or service to the price of another good or service. A relative price is an opportunity cost.

Rent ceiling A regulation that makes it illegal to charge a rent higher than a specified level.

Rent seeking The activity of searching out or creating a monopoly from which an economic profit can be made.

Required reserve ratio The ratio of reserves to deposits that banks are required, by regulation, to hold.

Reservation price The highest price that a buyer is willing to pay for a good.

Reservation wage The lowest wage rate for which a person will supply labour to the market. Below that wage, the person will not supply labour.

Reserve ratio The fraction of a bank's total deposits that are held in reserves.

Reserves Cash in a bank's vault plus the bank's deposits at the Bank of England.

Restrictive practice An agreement between two firms not to compete in some respect such as price, output levels or quality.

Retail Prices Index (RPI) An index of the prices of a basket of goods purchased by a typical UK family.

Returns to scale The increase in output that results when a firm increases all its inputs by the same percentage.

Risk A situation in which more than one outcome might occur and the probability of each possible outcome can be estimated.

Saving Income minus consumption. Saving is measured in the national income accounts as disposable income (income less taxes) minus consumption expenditure.

Saving function The relationship between saving and disposable income, other things remaining the same.

Saving supply The relationship between saving and the real interest rate, other things remaining the same.

Savings bank A financial intermediary owned by its depositors that accepts deposits and makes loans, mostly for consumer mortgages.

Scarcity The universal state in which wants exceed resources.

Scatter diagram A diagram that plots the value of one economic variable against the value of another.

Search activity The time spent in looking for someone with whom to do business.

Shares Long-term assets issued by firms which can be traded in stock markets.

Short run The short run in microeconomics has two meanings. For the firm, it is the period of time in which the quantity of at least one of its inputs is fixed and the quantities of the other inputs can be varied. The fixed input is usually capital – that is, the firm has a given plant size. For the industry, the short run is the period of time in which each firm has a given plant size and the number of firms in the industry is fixed.

Short-run aggregate supply curve A curve showing the relationship between the quantity of real GDP supplied and the price level, other things remaining the same.

Short-run industry supply curve A curve that shows how the quantity supplied by the industry varies as the market price varies when the plant size of each firm and the number of firms in the industry remain the same.

Short-run macroeconomic equilibrium A situation that occurs when the quantity of real GDP demanded equals the short-run quantity of real GDP supplied at the point of intersection of the *AD* curve and the *SAS* curve.

Short-run Phillips curve A curve showing the relationship between inflation and unemployment, when the expected inflation rate and the natural rate of unemployment remain the same.

Shutdown point The price and output level at which the firm just covers its total variable cost. In the short run, the firm is indifferent between producing the profit-maximizing output and shutting down temporarily. If it produces, it makes a loss equal to its total fixed cost.

Single price monopoly A monopolist that must sell each unit of output for the same price to all its customers.

Slope The change in the value of the variable measured on the y-axis divided by the change in the value of the variable measured on the x-axis.

Socialism   An economic system with state ownership of capital and land and incentives based on laws and regulations.

Stagflation   The combination of a rise in the price level and a fall in real GDP.

Stock   A quantity measured at a point in time.

Stock market   A market in which the shares of corporations are traded.

Strategies   All the possible actions of each player in a game.

Structural deficit   A budget that is in deficit even though real GDP equals potential GDP; expenditures are high relative to tax revenues over the entire business cycle.

Structural unemployment   The unemployment that arises when there is a decline in the number of jobs available in a particular region or industry.

Subsidy   A payment made by the government to producers that depends on the level of output.

Subsistence real wage rate   The minimum real wage rate needed to maintain life.

Substitute   A good that can be used in place of another good.

Substitution effect   The effect of a change in price of one good or service on a consumer's consumption of goods and services when the consumer remains indifferent between the original and the new consumption bundles – that is, the consumer remains on the same indifference curve.

Sunk cost   The past economic depreciation of a firm's capital (buildings, plant and equipment).

Supply   The relationship between the quantity of a good that producers plan to sell and the price of the good, with all other influences on sellers' plans remaining the same. It is described by a supply schedule and illustrated by a supply curve.

Supply curve   A curve that shows the relationship between the quantity supplied and the price of a good, all other influences on producers' planned sales remaining the same.

Symmetry Principle   The principle that states that people in similar situations should be treated equally.

Takeover   The purchase of the stock of one firm by another firm.

Tariff   A tax on an import by the government of the importing country.

Technological efficiency   A situation that occurs when it is not possible to increase output without increasing inputs.

Technological progress   The development of new and better ways of producing goods and services and the development of new goods.

Technology   Any method of combining inputs to produce goods and services.

Total cost   The sum of the costs of all the inputs a firm uses in production.

Total fixed cost   The total cost of the fixed inputs.

Total product   The total output produced by a firm in a given period of time.

Total revenue   The value of a firm's sales. It is calculated as the price of the good multiplied by the quantity sold.

Total surplus   The sum of consumer surplus and producer surplus.

Total utility   The total benefit or satisfaction that a person gets from the consumption of goods and services.

Total variable cost   The total cost of the variable inputs.

Trade-off   A constraint that entails giving up one thing to get something else.

Trade union   A group of workers organized principally for the purpose of increasing wages and improving conditions.

Trade-weighted index   The value of a basket of currencies in which the weight placed on each currency is related to its importance in UK international trade.

Transactions costs   The costs incurred in searching for someone with whom to do business, in reaching an agreement about the price and other aspects of the exchange, and in ensuring that the terms of the agreement are fulfilled.

Transfer earnings   The income that an owner of a factor of production requires to induce the owner to supply the factor.

Trend   A general direction (rising or falling) in which a variable is moving over the long term.

UK interest rate differential   The interest rate on a UK sterling asset minus the interest rate on a foreign currency asset.

Uncertainty   A situation in which more than one event might occur but it is not known which will occur.

Unemployed A person who does not have a job but is available for work, willing to work and has made some effort to find work within the previous four weeks.

Unemployment rate The number of people unemployed expressed as a percentage of the workforce.

Unit elastic demand Demand with a price elasticity of 1; the percentage change in the quantity demanded equals the percentage change in price.

Utilitarianism The principle that states that we should try to achieve the greatest happiness for the greatest number.

Utility The benefit or satisfaction that a person gets from the consumption of a good or service.

Utility of wealth The amount of utility that a person attaches to a given amount of wealth.

Utility maximization The attainment of the greatest possible utility.

Value The maximum amount that a person is willing to pay for a good.

Value added The value of a firm's output minus the value of the intermediate goods bought from other firms.

Value of production The value of goods and services produced in an economy.

Variable cost A cost that varies with the output level. It is the cost of a variable input.

Velocity of circulation The average number of times a pound is used annually to buy the goods and services that make up GDP.

Voluntary exchange Any transaction undertaken voluntarily.

Voluntary export restraint (VER) A self-imposed restriction by an exporting country on the volume of its exports of a particular good.

Wealth The value of all the things that people own.

Welfare state capitalism An economic system that combines the private ownership of capital and land with state interventions in markets that modify the price signals to which people respond.

Workforce curve This shows the potential quantity of labour available for employment at a particular real wage rate.

Workforce The sum of employed and unemployed people.

Working-age population The total number of people aged 16 and over who are not in jail, hospital, or some other form of institutional care.

Index

Entries and page numbers in **bold** refer to key terms; those in *italics* refer to figures.